Communication Yearbook I

Communication Yearbook I

Edited by
Brent D. Ruben

An Annual Review
Published by the
International Communication Association

Transaction Books
New Brunswick, New Jersey

Library of Congress Catalog Number: 76–45943.
ISBN: 0–87855–206–5.
Printed in the United States of America.

CONTENTS

COMMUNICATION YEARBOOK 1

EDITOR

Brent D. Ruben, *Rutgers University*

CONTRIBUTING EDITORS

David K. Berlo, *Center of Communication Analysis*

James Campbell, *University of Alabama*

James W. Carey, *University of Iowa*

Frank E.X. Dance, *University of Denver*

David Davidson, *Rutgers University*

Brenda Dervin, *University of Washington*

Kenneth D. Frandsen, *Pennsylvania State University*

George Gerbner, *University of Pennsylvania*

Bradley S. Greenberg, *Michigan State University*

Randall P. Harrison, *University of California*

Todd Hunt, *Rutgers University*

Mark Knapp, *Purdue University*

Klaus Krippendorff, *University of Pennsylvania*

Nan Lin, *State University of New York-Albany*

Nathan Maccoby, *Stanford University*

Gerald R. Miller, *Michigan State University*

Kaarle T. Nordenstreng, *University of Tampere*

Edwin B. Parker, *Stanford University*

Everett M. Rogers, *Stanford University*

Andrew H. Ruszkowski, *Saint Paul University*

Alfred G. Smith, *University of Texas*

Jay Weston, *Carleton University*

John Wiemann, *Rutgers University*

Osmo A. Wiio, *Helsinki Research Institute for Business Economics*

THE INTERNATIONAL COMMUNICATION ASSOCIATION

Communication Yearbook is an annual review. The series is sponsored by the International Communication Association, one of the several major scholarly organizations in the communication field. It is composed of 2,500 communication scholars, teachers, and practitioners.

Throughout its 27-year history, the Association has been particularly important to those in the field of communication who have sought a forum where the behavioral science perspective was predominant. The International Communication Association has also been attractive to a number of individuals from a variety of disciplines who hold communication to be central to work within their primary fields of endeavor. The Association has been an important stimulant to the infusion of behavioral concepts in communication study and teaching, and has played a significant role in defining a broadened set of boundaries for the discipline as a whole.

The International Communication Association is composed of eight subdivisions: information systems, interpersonal communication, mass communication, organizational communication, intercultural communication, political communication, instructional communication, and health communication.

In addition to *Communication Yearbook,* the Association publishes *Human Communication Research,* the *ICA Newsletter, ICA Directory* and is affiliated with the *Journal of Communication.* Several divisions also publish newsletters and occasional papers.

PREFACE

A project such as the *Communication Yearbook* series is not initiated and seen through to tangibility without substantial contributions from a great many persons. Unfortunately, it is impossible to appropriately acknowledge, by name, each of those individuals whose interest and input have been important in the development of the series and *Communication Yearbook 1*. Still, some of the many persons whose guidance and concern have been so valuable can be mentioned.

First, appreciation is expressed to present and former members of the International Communication Association Executive Committee. From the beginning, the concept of the *Yearbook* was actively supported by Dick Budd; Bob Kibler, Mark Knapp, and Bob Cox furthered this concern. Each assisted in numerous ways throughout the project's nearly two-year history. Other members of the Board of Directors of the International Communication Association during 1975–1976 and 1976–1977 provided encouragement and continuity.

Throughout the maturation of the *Communication Yearbook* series, and the preparation of *Communication Yearbook 1*, the contributing editors have been consistent sources of enthusiasm and guidance. Their confidence in the *Yearbook* concept and their willingness to give freely of their expertise and time to provide editorial guidance, to evaluate and review "Overview" manuscripts, and to referee papers entered into "Top 3" competition, deserves very special recognition. My thanks and appreciation to Dave Berlo, Jim Campbell, Jim Carey, Frank Dance, David Davidson, Brenda Dervin, Ken Frandsen, George Gerbner, Brad Greenberg, Randy Harrison, Todd Hunt, Mark Knapp, Klaus Krippendorff, Nan Lin, Nate Maccoby, Gerry Miller, Kaarle Nordenstreng, Ed Parker, Ev Rogers, Andrew Ruszkowski, Fred Smith, Jay Weston, John Wiemann, and Osmo Wiio.

In addition to their other responsibilities as contributing editors, Fred Smith, Nan Lin, and Dave Berlo graciously responded to my invitation to prepare "Review and Commentary" papers on selected topics for publication in *Communication Yearbook 1*. Joe Cappella also kindly contributed an invited piece, and Kaarle Nordenstreng provided a paper for that same section of the *Yearbook*, which *Diogenes* consented to be included in a specially edited form.

To the authors of "Overviews" included in *Communication Yearbook 1*—Klaus Krippendorff, Chuck Berger, Jim Anderson, Gary Richetto, Tulsi Saral, Dan Nimmo, Mike Scott, Bud Wheeless, and Dan Costello—I also want to extend special thanks. Developing integrated summaries of years of research and theory to conform to a set of standards for which no models exist—within a time-frame of five to six months—is obviously no small chore. Each acted upon evaluation and reviews from contributing editors and myself with constructiveness, speed, and conscientiousness. The resulting "Overviews" add a crucial dimension to the contents of this *Yearbook*, and provide some strong models for future *Yearbook* "Overview" authors.

Several other persons were helpful in providing assessments and suggestions to "Overview" authors and I want to thank the following special reviewers: Chuck Atkin, Louie Bender, Dick Budd, Gerry Goldhaber, Bill Richards, Bill Todd, and Lee Thayer. The effort of Lee Brown, who provided the major editing on "A History of the International Communication Association" included in the Appendix of this volume, is also appreciated.

Preparation of nearly 2,000 manuscript pages, subsequent proofreading, and index preparation, compressed into a period of several months is not a trivial task, and neither is it one which is possible without the concerted efforts of a number of persons. Initially, in this regard, I should thank the divisional chairpersons of the International Communication Association, and the contributors of "Selected Studies" within each, for their care in preparation and submission of manuscripts and art work.

Crucial editorial assistance has been provided by a number of persons at Rutgers, including Kathi Teichman, Jo Ann Zsilavetz, Ellen Diamond, Gina Geslewitz, Larry Askling, Bruce Kalter, and Jayne Ghuzzi. Transaction, Inc. personnel have also been very helpful, and particular recognition is due Alex Fundock, Scott Bramson, and Irving Louis Horowitz.

The preparation of the index for a volume such as this is a massive undertaking, and I am thankful to David Davidson for providing leadership in this endeavor, and to Larry and Jan Askling for their industrious and thoughtful contributions.

Most particularly, I would like to thank Todd Hunt, a colleague at Rutgers, whose unselfish contributions to editorial supervision have been critical and much appreciated throughout the entire manuscript preparation and production process.

Though my involvement with the *Yearbook* series has on most days been a labor of love, it has none the less been a *labor*; I want to thank Rutgers College and my colleagues in the Department of Human Communication for their encouragement and their understanding and acceptance of the major commitment of my time and energy which this project has necessitated.

Lastly, I want to thank my wife, Jann for her help with *Yearbook* correspondence, and the rest of my family for putting up with the late nights and long weekends which I've spent working in my basement office during the past 18 months. Perhaps the most lucid and succinct commentary was provided by my daughter Robbi, who enjoys telling friends and acquaintances that Marc—our 20-month-old-son—"thinks Daddy lives in the basement."

April 1977

B.R.
New Brunswick, N.J.

Communication Yearbook I

OVERVIEW

OVERVIEW

BRENT D. RUBEN
Rutgers University

The nature of any academic discipline is defined by its extant literature and by the systems which have evolved for the exchange of scientific information among its members. Scientific knowledge or scientific information is, thus, the currency of a discipline. It is the coinage which is created, borrowed, exchanged, cherished, and utilized by scholars and researchers linked to one another through formal and information communication networks.

PHASES IN DISCIPLINARY EVOLUTION

Research by Price (1963) suggests that the literature of a discipline passes through a series of stages that might be presumed to be reflective of the field's intellectual evolution (Kuhn, 1970; Barnes, 1974). During the initial phase, absolute increases in the amount of scientific information are small, although the rate of growth doubles at regular intervals. Subsequently, in a third phase, rate of growth declines, but the annual increments remain relatively constant. In a fourth and final stage, both rate of increase and absolute increments decline toward zero (Crane, 1972, p. 2).

Communication at present seems quite clearly in the major growth stage. The past several years have seen the initiation of a number of new academic journals, and the publications devoted to the advanced study of communication processes, structures, and functions have also increased dramatically in number. During this same period, several established speech, rhetoric, and journalism journals have indicated increasing concern with communication, and in several instances names of these publications have been changed to reflect a new focus. Rapid increases in the number of communication textbooks of all varieties have also been noticeable.

It is perhaps inevitable that differentiation, specialization, and segmentation accompany disciplinary growth. Greater numbers of scholars, pursuing a progressively widening array of topics, in more numerous and variegated scholarly and professional associations and divisions, leads to increasing intradisciplinary specialization and segmentation of both the literature of a field and the patterns by which scientific information is exchanged. This diversification can result in fragmented communities of scholars, pursuing their work in intellectual isolation from one another, ignorant of the generic characteristics of the parent discipline. Commenting on this general tendency, and the problems which occur as a result, Bertalanffy (1956) has argued that:

> Science is characterized by its ever-increasing specialization, necessitated by the enormous amount of data, the complexity of techniques and of theoretical structures within every field. This . . . has led to a breakdown of science as an integrated realm: The physicist, the biologist, the psychologist and the social scientist are, so to speak, encapsulated in a private universe, and it is difficult to get word from one cocoon to the other. (p. 1)

The pattern Bertalanffy describes seems to pertain also to individual disciplines and divisional substrates therein. Such a perspective suggests that disciplinary growth is essentially a two-edged sword. On the one hand, it is growth that makes possible the differentiation of focus and precision of method necessary for advancing the outer edges of a field. At the same time, however, growth progressively increases both the need for and the difficulty of integration.

THE EVOLUTION OF COMMUNICATION

There is growing evidence that this is currently the situation in communication. At a stage in the evolution of the field where diversification of topic and refinement of methodology are unparalleled, the need for overview, synthesis, and integration—for identifying what it is that is common and generic to the field—seems especially great. The need is probably most obvious to those who encounter the field with a detached perspective. Commenting on communication research and theory as reflected at a national conference, a European communication scholar (Stubbs, 1975) notes:

> I approached the [communication] . . . convention primarily as a sociologist by training and experience, and found that a good deal of the communication research reported seemed to be being done within the traditional paradigms and parameters of social science disciplines. To approach this work "as sociology," or "as political science" seems in some ways inappropriate, and as in any event I have no expertise in social psychology, social anthropology, or political science. To give just one example, my ability to judge a paper on "The Effects of Inadmissable Testimony on Information Processing and Decision-making in Jury Trails" in any other than its broad methodological and theoretical approach would be negligible. And yet I was not helped to any great extent by this convention to approach it with more specific or refined sets of criteria. The rather disjointed and partial view that I have, then, of the American communications scene could in part be a function of any own disciplinary training, and consequent inability to perceive a commonality (other than at a very forced level) between papers as apparently diverse as "Strategies to Elicit Self-disclosure in Mixed Sex Dyads," "Agenda-Setting for the Media: Determinants of Senatorial News Coverage," and "Bilingualism and Cognition." . . . I was hoping that at some point in the convention, these areas of common concern, method, use of models, etc. would be explored.

Despite differences in perspective one might attribute solely to contrasting traditions of European and American communication research (Nordenstreng, 1977), and the peculiar limitations of the professional convention as a medium for the exchange of scientific information (Ruben & Andriate, 1975), the central theme of these observations seems to underscore the sentiments of a growing number of communication researchers and theoreticians. This concern is cited by a variety of authors in this and other works. Among the contributors to this volume who note the importance of increased theoretical integration are Budd, Smith, Lin, Cappella, Berger, and Richetto. There is, it seems, an increasing need for meta-theoretical study of communication, for clarification of existing and alternative paradigms, for refinement of theoretical taxonomies, and for review, integration, analysis, and commentary.

THE COMMUNICATION YEARBOOK SERIES

There are a number of publications devoted primarily, if not exclusively, to the publication of specialized studies in communication. There are few, if any, whose primary function is overview and synthesis. It is the pursuit of these generic goals which inspired the development of the *Communication Yearbook* series. These same objectives have guided in the selection and subsequent activities of contributing editors, in the development of format for the series, in the determination of content, and in all phases of editorial decision making for *Communication Yearbook 1*.

Yearbook Format

To achieve this goal, the *Yearbook* series consists of: (1) disciplinary reviews and commentaries, (2) overviews of subdivisions within the field, (3) current research selected to represent the interest areas within the field, and (4) topic, concept, and author.

Reviews and Commentaries

A primary means of fostering integration are the *Review and Commentary* papers, solicited on generic topics selected by the editor, with input from contributing editors. The aim of these articles is to provide substantive input of generic relevance to scholars and researchers in all subdivisions of the field. In *Communication Yearbook 1, Reviews and Commentaries* focus on *Communication as Process, Perspectives on a Discipline, Communication Effects, Communication Taxonomies, Research Methodology in Communication,* and *European Communication Theory.*

Overviews

A second means of facilitating synthesis are annual Overviews. Prepared by International Communication Association divisional chairpersons, or their designates, Overviews examine trends in theory and research in various substantive domains within the field. In *Communication Yearbook 1, Overviews* were written to provide an historical, as well as theoretical, taxonomy of each area. Appropriate contributing editors refereed, evaluated, and critiqued drafts of each *Overview*. The versions published here reflect those suggestions, criticisms, and reactions.

Selected Papers

Communication Yearbook also provides a forum for the presentation of edited versions of outstanding current research, competitively selected for presentation at the annual conference of the International Communication Association.

Many academic associations have published all or selected studies authored for presentation at annual meetings. The American Psychological Association, among others, has systematically studied the results of publication of preconference papers (APA, 1963a, 1963b, 1965a, 1965b, 1969a, 1969b). Findings suggest that the availability of papers in published form prior to a conference favorably influences participation at sessions (Johns Hopkins University, 1967b, 1976e), increases correspondence between authors and readers, renders informal exchanges during the conference more substantive, and provides for the infusion of scholarly work into the literature of the field 12-15 months earlier than would be possible through journal or book publication (Garvey & Griffith, 1966; APA, 1969a). The tangible nature of such publications also leads to acquisition by libraries, abstraction by the various services, and increased efficiency in locating, utilizing, and citing such work by scholars from outside, as well as within, the field (Garvey & Griffith, 1966).

In *Communication Yearbook 1* competitively selected studies are included which represent general communication, as well as information systems, interpersonal communication, mass communication, organizational communication, political communication, intercultural communication, and health communication.

Index

The index for Communication has also been designed to facilitate intradisciplinary continuity and integration. Each work appearing in the volume has been indexed on *author, topic, concept,* and *methodology* dimensions. The intent is to provide easy access to persons or ideas of interest that may be cited in *Reviews and Commentaries, Overviews,* or *Selected Studies* from various subdivisions within the field.

Organization of the Communication Yearbook

The volume is organized in the following manner: Section One consists of disciplinary-wide *Reviews and Commentaries* followed by *Selected Studies* representative of general communication. For each of the sections, the first piece included is the *Theory and Research Overview* followed by three *Selected Studies* which exemplify research in the area. Included in the *Appendix* is a specially edited history of the International Communication Association followed by the *Index*.

REFERENCES

American Psychological Association. Convention attendants and their use of the convention as a source of scientific information. *Reports of the American Psychological Association's project on scientific information exchange in psychology, Vol. 1.*, Washington, D.C.: APA, 1963a.

American Psychological Association. Convention participants and the dissemination of information at scientific meetings. *Reports of the American Psychological Association's project on scientific information exchange in psychology, Vol. 1.* Washington, D.C.: APA, 1963b.

American Psychological Association. The discovery and dissemination of scientific information among psychologists in two research environments. *Reports of the American Psychological Association's project on scientific information exchange in psychology, Vol. 2.* Washington, D.C.: APA, 1965a.

American Psychological Association. Theoretical and methodological considerations in undertaking innovations in scientific information exchange. *Reports of the American Psychological Association's project on scientific information exchange in psychology, Vol. 2.* Washington, D.C.: APA, 1965b.

American Psychological Association. Information exchange at the American Psychological Association annual convention and the functions of the convention proceedings in such exchange. *Reports of the American Psychological Association's project on scientific information exchange in psychology, Vol. 3.* Washington, D.C.: APA, 1969a.

American Psychological Association. Innovation in scientific communication in psychology. *Reports of the American Psychological Association's project on scientific information exchange in psychology, Vol. 3.* Washington, D.C.: APA, 1969b.

BARNES, B. *Scientific knowledge and sociological theory,* London: Routledge & Kegan Paul, 1974.

BERGER, C. Interpersonal communication theory and research: An overview. In B.D. Ruben (Ed.), *Communication yearbook I,* New Brunswick, N.J.: Transaction-International Communication Association, 1977.

BERTALANFFY, L. von, General system theory, *General Systems,* 1956, 1, 1-10.

BUDD, R.W. Perspectives on a discipline: Review and commentary. In B.D. Ruben (Ed.), *Communication yearbook I,* New Brunswick, N.J.: Transaction-International Communication Association, 1977.

CAPPELLA, J.N. Research methodology in communication: Review and commentary. In B.D. Ruben (Ed.), *Communication yearbook I.* New Brunswick, N.J.: Transaction-International Communication Association, 1977.

CRANE, D. Information needs and uses. In C.A. Cuadra, (Ed.), *Annual review of information science and technology. Vol. 6.* Chicago: Encyclopedia Britannica, 1971.

CRANE, D. *Invisible colleges: Diffusion of knowledge in scientific communities.* Chicago: University of Chicago Press, 1972.

GARVEY, W.D., & GRIFFITH, B.C. Studies of social innovations in scientific communication in psychology. *American Psychologist,* 1966, 21, 1026-1036.

Johns Hopkins University. A comparison of the dissemination of scientific and technical information, informal interaction, and the impact of information associated with two meetings of the American Institute of Aeronautics and Astronautics. *Report 1.* Baltimore, Maryland: Center for Research in Scientific Communication, 1967a.

Johns Hopkins University. A study of scientific information exchange at the 96th Annual Meeting of the American Institute of Mining, Metallurgical, and Petroleum Engineers, *Report 2.* Baltimore, Maryland: Center for Research in Scientific Communication, August 1967b.

Johns Hopkins University. The dissemination of scientific information, informal interaction and the impact of information received from two meetings of the Optical Society of America, *Report 3.* Baltimore, Maryland: 1967c.

Johns Hopkins University. Scientific information-exchange behavior at the 1966 Annual Meeting of the American Sociological Association, *Report 4.* Baltimore, Maryland: Center for Research in Scientific Communication, 1967d.

Johns Hopkins University. The dissemination of scientific information, informal interaction, and the impact of information associated with the 48th Annual Meeting of the American Geophysical Union, *Report 5.* Baltimore, Maryland: Center for Research in Scientific Communication, 1967e.

Johns Hopkins University. A comparison of the dissemination of scientific information, informal interaction, and the impact of information received from two meetings of the American Meteorological Society, *Report 6.* Baltimore, Maryland: Center for Research for Scientific Communication, 1967f.

Johns Hopkins University. A study of scientific information exchange at the 63rd Annual Meeting of the Association of American Geographers, *Report 7.* Baltimore, Maryland: Center for Research in Scientific Communication, 1967g.

KUHN, T.S. *The structure of scientific revolutions.* Second Edition. Chicago: University of Chicago Press, 1970.

LIN, N. Communication effects: Review and commentary. In B.D. Ruben (Ed.), *Communication yearbook I,* New Brunswick, N.J.: Transaction-International Communication Association, 1977.

LINGWOOD, D.A. Interpersonal communication, research productivity, and invisible colleges. Unpublished doctoral dissertation, Stanford University, 1969.

NELSON, C.E., & POLLOCK, D.K. (Eds.) *Communication among scientists and engineers.* Lexington, Mass.: Heath, 1970.

NORDENSTRENG, K. European Communication Theory: Review and commentary. In B.D. Ruben (Ed.) *Communication yearbook I*, New Brunswick, N.J.: Transaction-International Communication Association, 1977.

PRICE, D.J. De S. *Little science, big science,* New York: Columbia University Press, 1963.

PRICE, D.J. de S. Networks of scientific papers, *Science*, 1965, 149, 510-515.

RICHETTO, G. Organizational communication theory and research: An overview. In B.D. Ruben (Ed.), *Communication yearbook I*. New Brunswick, N.J.: Transaction-International Communication Association, 1977.

RUBEN, B.D., & ANDRIATE, G.S. The academic convention: Notes toward an evaluative framework. Paper presented at the annual meeting International Communication Association, Chicago, 1975.

SMITH, A.G. Communication taxonomies: Review and commentary. In B.D. Ruben (Ed.), *Communication yearbook I*, New Brunswick, N.J.: Transaction-International Communication Association, 1977.

STUBBS, C. *Communication Studies Bulletin*. Sunderland, England: Department of History and Communication, Sunderland Polytechnic, 1975.

COMMUNICATION
Reviews and Commentaries
Selected Studies

COMMUNICATION AS PROCESS:
REVIEW AND COMMENTARY

DAVID K. BERLO
Center for Communication Analysis

For more than two decades, communication scholars have talked about communication as *process*. Yet, little of their research has been consistent with their philosophical discussion. *Process* has been used in at least four senses: (1) as mystery, (2) as complex organization, (3) as change over time, and (4) as an activity—processing. When we recognize that communication is a make-believe process, not natural, not subject to *laws of nature* except indirectly, we can begin to attack problems of hierarchical and probablistic definitions of major concepts, attempting to meet Whitehead's criterion that the "what of being is the how of becoming." Organization can be viewed as the change in relationships, relationships can be viewed as the basic unit of communication analysis, and both information and control can be defined in probabilistic and relativistic terms, leading to such propositions as the more information one has, the less control one has.

Reviewing the impact of the concept of *process* on communication research, David H. Smith (1972) suggested that "we have come to expect that from time to time some one of us will take pen in hand to lament the absence of process research." He supported earlier comments by other communication scholars that there is no relationship between our liturgical commitment to *communication as process* and the causal deterministic frame in which most of our research has been conducted.

Smith agreed with Samuel Becker's evaluation (1967) that research in recent years has not made "the slightest difference in our lives." Smith added that the comment still was true in 1972, and argued that "a review of our whole concept of science and the phenomena on which our inquiry is focused" is needed.

One might quarrel with the severity of the criticism by Becker, Smith, and others. We have begun to move away from the hypodermic metaphor of communication as something a source sticks in a receiver, and moved toward concentrating on relationships other than the relationship of causally dependent change. More recent emphasis on how people process the information in messages and media (e.g., Ward et al., 1977) and the emphasis reported by Richetto (1977) in this volume on the data being gathered on information and communi-

cation relationships in complex social organizations lead me to the impression that we *are* concerned with our traditional behavioristic views of science.

Still, though one might disagree with the harshness of the indictment, it appears that the weight of the evidence supports Smith's critical comments. For our present purposes, there is little value in choosing sides or counting noses. The reader can make a personal judgment after reading the survey articles and the competitive research papers that comprise the bulk of this volume. Many will suggest that we indeed have not reviewed our concept of the phenomena on which our inquiry is focused or, when we have (e.g., Clarke, 1973), we have not made such a review operative in our conduct of research.

When asked by the editor to comment on "process revisited" for reasons I assumed associated with "squatter's rights" (Berlo, 1960), I reviewed Dr. Smith's (1972) article. I take no issue with his major premise, and will not repeat his argument. Instead, I commend his article to the reader, have taken the liberty of incorporating it as a preface to my comments, and will try to state some of the propositions on which alterations in our approach to communication research as *process* might be based.

In particular, I will report on my own struggle for the past several years to code the poetry of

Whitehead into practical suggestions for the conduct of inquiry. How are we to make sense of Whitehead's (1929) statement that "the *how* an actual entity *becomes* constitutes *what* that entity *is*?" Can we . . . should we . . . try to escape from the traditional view of *nature* and *reality* that distinguishes clearly between *substance* and *flux*, and equates process with *flux*? Can we make sense of the statement that there is nothing but flux, that the only permanence is change, and that freedom and restraint are not antagonistic, but definitionally interdependent? Is it useful to assume that questions of the order *Where am I?* and *Who am I?* are not as adequately answered by naming a place and attributes, as they are by suggesting a conceptual intersection based on the relationship between where *you were and where you will be, who you were and who you will be?* These are the *process* questions.

Professor Smith (1972) was kind in referring to my earlier writing on process as a landmark of clarity and brevity in describing the nature of Whitehead's thinking, as applied to communication. At the same time, he suggested that the "irony" of my work was that I didn't practice what I preached; i.e., that I moved from a processual discussion to "a model of communication (S-M-C-R) which is essentially linear in form."

Smith's criticism is well-taken. It could be argued that S-M-C-R was not intended as a "model" of communication, that it met none of the tests of theoretic modelling, and that it was developed as an audio-visual aid to stimulate recall of the components of a communication relationship; however, the defense costs exceed the benefits. The fact of the matter is that, like many of my colleagues, I simply did not understand the underlying assumptions and theoretic consequences of what I believed, and had not grasped the limited fertility of the research tradition in which I had been trained. I did not recognize that the assumptions underlying linear causal determinism may account for the major proportion of communication events, but not account for the portion that makes a significant difference in our lives.

PROCESS CONCEPTS

We have used the term *process* in at least four different ways. As we review those approaches, the

eclectic base for how we might move closer to Whitehead's view may become apparent.

Ah, Sweet Mystery of Process

Much of the effort of communication academicians between the middle 1940s and the late 1960s was devoted to political and intellectual legitimization of communication as a focus of teaching and research. On being asked to specify the locus and boundaries of the field, many of us would respond that "all behavior is communication." We may or may not have recognized that the purpose of definition is to delimit. In either case, we did recognize that criticism for our avoidance of that purpose could be obviated if we imbedded our political aggrandizement and theoretic fuzziness in a mystique. *Process* served nicely as such a mystical context.

If asked to provide operationalizations and constitutive definitions for our terms, we could respond by stating that communication is not definable: it is a *process*. After all, we might argue, any description is *static,* and communication is *dynamic.* As I recollect, I was at first pleased though later dismayed to hear self and colleagues respond to the question *"What do you teach at an AID Communication Seminar?"* by saying that such a seminar could not be described, it had to be experienced. After all, communication is a process, without beginning or end, or boundaries.

Such responses in a digital code frequently were accompanied by the analogic effort to talk with one's hands, waving them in nonsystematic ways to simulate *process.*

Fortunately for our intellectual future, the referent of *process-as-mystery* has diminished as our acceptance within the academy has risen. Process-as-mystery was not an intellectual position that could be translated into scholarly activity. It was a rhetorical tool, and one which violated the canon of *elocutio.*

Process as Complex Organization

Process-as-mystery assumes that everything is relative, or at least related . . . and that any one thing is related in an infinite number of ways to everything else . . . in noncodable ways.

As we attempted to defend the imperative of "look, mom, no hands," some of us tried to reduce the assumption of uniqueness to a more operational statement that some things are related in several ways to several other things. Given that, the study of those complex relationships might be the way to study process. Organization is nothing but a set of relationships. Therefore, if we can isolate and quantify multivariable relationships, *process* is complex organization—of an individual or group of individuals.

Those who have focused on *process* as organizational complexity have used relationships as the unit of analysis—multiple relationships and multivariate analysis of relationships. They have focused on *control* as the removal of uncertainty from the Cartesian product of possible relationships. The concept of control as uncertainty removal does not involve causal relationships. The traditional basis for the deductive process we refer to as explanation. Rather, an organization is under control to the extent that the uncertainty within that organization is removed. If the product-moment correlation, r, is the measure of the amount of relationship, r^2 is the measure of control—control as variance accounted for. Explanation is not separated from description-prediction.

Control as uncertainty removal makes no implications as to the source of control—the "cause" of predictability. Measures of relationship can not be inferred to be evidence of cause and effect. Within an organizational paradigm, an organization can be totally under control—no uncertainty remaining—without positing any thesis as to a *controller*. Relationships control. The amount of relationship can be measured, and the contribution of a relationship to the control of the organization can be measured as a *relative* variable. R^2 is the proportion of the total possible uncertainty that has been removed.

Process-as-organizational complexity implements the principle of relativity in at least two ways: (1) individual behavior, in isolation, is not the unit of analysis; *relationships* are; (2) the "amount" of control accounted for by a relationship is not measured absolutely, but in the context of the amount of variability possible within the total organization—

r^2 is a relative covariance—it is relative to the amount of variability in either component of the relationship. Correlational analysis does not treat individual behavioral events as separate and additive; however, it does, usually, treat relationships themselves as separate and additive. At a higher level of analytic complexity, it treats sets of relationships—factors—as separate and additive.

Factor analytic methodology introduces a minimal hierarchical analysis. At the lowest level, there are dyadic relationships, and at higher levels there are related relationships—factors. Factors themselves can be factored, introducing another level in the hierarchy. Sophisticated correlational methodology assumes that behavior is *hierarchical*, not *linear*.

Correlational methodology implies nothing about the source of control within the relationship; however, most co-relational scholars do impose external control over the *nature* of the relationship. To state it differently, r-methodology imposes researcher-control, theory-control. The research approaches the subject with an a priori view as to how that subject—whether individual or group—*is* organized. Given the theory, data are gathered on researcher-developed variables, and analysis is performed to determine how the variables are related across subjects. The nature of organization is restricted to the theory. If the theory makes sense, useful data are gathered. If not, nothing of value is learned.

An alternative is to approach the data without theory, and to ask how an individual or group organizes itself, according to its own theory. This approach presumes that the *subject* is the client, not the theory. The consequences may not lead to generalizable theory, however, the approach guarantees that something of value, the structure of the organization at any given point in time, will be described.

Given the oft-stated liturgy of the communication scholar that the individual is important, one might assume that individual-oriented research would prevail. Just the opposite, of course, is true. Though correlational and factor analytic measures are equally applicable to *theory-oriented* and *client-oriented research*, only William Stephenson (1953, 1976) and his relatively few cohorts, through

Q-methodology, have worked to help individuals and organizations understand how they organize themselves, relate their own experience and beliefs and environments. Using different methodology, Milton Rokeach (1968) is another who has concentrated on how an individual systematizes his own beliefs into hierarchical structure.

The credentials of other accomplishments and the lucidity of their work have prohibited the rejection of the kind of client-based research engaged in by heretics like Stephenson and Rokeach and a few others; however, at theory-based church meetings, they are assigned a special pew. For those of us who share their view that the person being studied should be the client of the research, recent emphasis on network analysis and other hypothesis-free data-gathering methods is reassuring as a predictor of future emphasis.

Those who have focused on process-as-organizational complexity, have on occasion looked at changes in relationships over time. They have considered, for example, a comparison of *r-structures* or, for Stephenson, a much greater emphasis on a comparison of *Q-structures* over time. For the most part, however, co-relational analysts have been "one-shot" data gatherers, attempting to describe the nature of organization at one point in time. The emphasis has been on description of *substance,* not *flux, permanence,* not *change.*

Process as Effect: Measuring Change Over Time

Those of us who have viewed *process* as the organization of relationships, have treated communication as a social science, with social relationships as the primary focus—leadership is a relationship, mental disturbance is a relationship, etc. Behavior is defined *relationally,* control is viewed as uncertainty removal, organization is hierarchical. There is varying emphasis on theory and considerable emphasis on describing the state of relationships at a given point in time, with or without predictive intent.

Meanwhile, others of us have viewed communication as a behavioral science, with individual units of behavior, measured absolutely, as the primary focus—leadership is a set of traits, mental distur-

bance an illness, etc. Behaviorists fit closely the more traditional Newtonian view of *process* as *chance,* as *flux.* Behaviorists are less interested in a variety of kinds of relationships, and focus particularly on a given relationship: change over time, attributable to a causal relationship.

The behaviorist shares the belief with the social scientist that relationships can be isolated and added; however, we (for I have been one) took the concept of independence and additivity one step further. For the behaviorist, the basic unit of analysis is an individual *behavioral act*—a response. If we can find those causal forces which produce the response, we can explain as well as predict the behavior—we can deduce the theoretic prediction. Causal forces can be summed, and are best explored in experiments of minimal complexity. For example, until fairly recently, a behavioral research dictum was that any experiment that contains two experimental (causal) variables has one experimental variable too many.

As we aged in our experiencing of communication behavior, we have been forced to discard the belief in single-variable experiments, recognizing that communication behavior is more complex than a simple additive model can account for. However, even though sophisticated analytic procedures such as complex analysis of variance permit us to separate out the effects of conjunctive relationships, our discomfort in talking about interactions remains. Few behaviorists are proud to interpret fourth-order interactions, and few are comfortable with the assumptions underlying the appropriate statistical test. Such hierarchical analysis is possible within behaviorism, but the analytic tools are restricted, and the behaviorist's value for reductionism is inhibiting.

The discomfort is in part attributable to the behaviorist's primary assumption that events are more serial than hierarchical. Things happen, in serial order and adjacencies such as stimulus-response which permit causal relationships.

For the organizational researcher, control usually refers to reduction in systemic uncertainty, with or without causal attribution. For the behaviorist, *control=cause.* Thinking within the frame of linear equations, functional relationships, the behaviorist manipulates some variable or variables ("independent''), and measures others (''dependent''), and does a variety of things to others (''control'') so that they will not obscure a possible causal relationship between the independent and dependent variables.

Behavior—response—is a *natural* phenomenon; responses consist of matter and energy. Statements of relationship are made by man; behavior is natural. Given that, the behaviorist assumes that behavior is subject to the *rules of nature,* the *principles of natural force,* the *laws of thermodynamics,* the *law of cause and effect. Description*—the reporting of an experiment—is basic. It is not, however, the focus of the behaviorist's interest. Rather, inductive generalization (based on a rigorous theory of inference) and deductive implications . . . (based on hypothetico-deductive rigor) are the goals. *Prediction* and *control* (causal explanation) are the objective, *theory* is the focus.

The only kind of relationship of interest to the behaviorist is a relationship of causal dependency. *Interdependency* is restricted to reciprocal dependency. In studying communication within a behavioristic frame, concepts such as *accountability* and *responsibility* are easy to articulate. For every effect, there is a *cause,* and the *cause* is ''responsible'' for the *effect. Cause controls—cause =control.* Therefore, whenever there is evidence of *control,* there is corresponding attribution of a *controller.*

The behaviorist is not disinterested in uncertainty reduction, and has statistical tools to compute it. The tools, however, are used infrequently in that the strength of a relationship is not as central as is the detection of relationship. The accuracy of prediction at any given point is the focus, not the amount of predictability over time. For the behaviorist, life is a series of ''now's'' and ''then's,'' and the concept of ''in the long run,'' a probabilistic hierarchical concept, is restricted to his theory of Error in the making of inductive inferences.

The concept of *effect* is relative to time. Evidence supportive of a cause-effect relationship requires observation at at least two points in time, before the intervention of the potentially causal variable and after the intervention. The measure of discrepancy is the dependent variable being measured, the change in value of that variable over time is the unit of analysis. If the discrepancy exceeds chance by some predetermined amount, the assertion of relationship is confirmed. If the assertion also is deducible from other propositions, the relationship is *theoretic,* and the causal nature of the relationship has been explained.

The behavioral theorist operates under the assumption that nature is deterministic, that given a ''perfect'' theory, all behavior is predictable. His choice of terms is consistent with this assumption: Any behavior that can be attributed to a causal agent is called an ''effect'' and all remaining behavior that can not be attributed is grouped into a category called ''error.'' The elimination of error is the test of theory, and the optimal level of uncertainty posited is zero.

The behaviorist focuses on a particular kind of change over time—convergence of response. Through his statistical tools would permit him to study social convergence (increase or decrease) as related to communication events, they seldom have been so used. Rather, the emphasis is on a given type of convergence—compliance with an a priori criterion of ''correct'' response. Again, the bias is revealed in the choice of terms. Responses systematically different from those predicted often are labelled as ''side effects'' and individuals who do not behave as predicted are labelled as ''deviant cases.''

Given his interest in compliant convergence, the behaviorist who studies communication has emphasized compliant processes, instruction, and persuasion. That emphasis has elicited support from those who seek instructional and persuasive success in the communication market-place—the instructor, the salesman, the media operator, and special-interest sources who profit from achieving convergent compliance on the part of others. Such emphasis on the ''productive'' uses of communication also helps us understand why others who are more interested in social maintenance and human and organizational development, and the more humanistic communication processes, have been less enthusiastic about the behavioristic view of the reward they would receive for the behaviorist's efforts.

The Process Game: Organization vs. Change

There is no intellectual necessity for an adversarial relationship between those who have viewed communication as an organizing process and those who have viewed it as a change process. Indeed, some of us, more of us recently, are becoming eclectic in choosing tools to fit the problem. For the most part, though, change and organization have been adversarial positions in the research "game" of communication. For most of the game, behaviorism has been winning.

For at least two decades after World War II, the causal determinists in communication enjoyed the status of scholarly princes. I recall my own research strategy training at Illinois in the mid 1950s. On arrival, all graduate students were enrolled in the same course. After a few weeks, we took our first examination. Those of us who did well remained in the class, and began our training as experimentalists. Those who did not do well were assigned to another section, and began to learn correlational procedures. Never did we meet together again, and the only belief we shared was the common agreement that the experimentalists were superior beings.

Why this stratification in academic social status? Communication researchers were emerging from the ghetto of trade-school education, and straining for the intellectual respect of their academic colleagues. For all of this century, maximal respect outside the artistic fields has been accorded to the scientist, and the physical scientist has presided over the hierarchy.

As we observed the attributes of physical scientists, we inferred three propositional bases for their intellectual and social success:

1. *Data* should be restricted to that which is directly observable, by multiple observers.
2. *Theory* is more important than correlative data, and "sciences" can be ranked by their relative dependence on theory and data.
3. The physicist is correct in his view of *nature* as deterministic, *external, fixed, processual* only in a Newtonian sense.

Given the acceptability of those propositions, we concluded that the best intellectual strategy for leaving the ghetto and contributing to knowledge as well as personal success was to: (1) reject introspective information, either from our subjects or ourselves,

(2) concentrate on theory construction, and (3) accept the behaviorist's view of nature. After all, the behaviorist had preceeded us out of the ghetto of speculative philosophy and was beginning to enjoy the plaudits of both the academy and the outside world.

That has been the dominant liturgy. Yet, even among some of its most able practitioners, there has been a disquieting and rising belief that we're not making much progress intellectually under that control system. What's the problem?

First, we didn't pay enough attention to our own formulations of the diffusion-adoption process. If we chart the time-curve for the acceptance of causal determinism within the scientific community, communication scholars would be categorized as late adopters, possibly even laggards. As Smith (1972) points out, the innovators and early adopters in the natural and biological sciences were moving away from linear determinism just as the "soft" sciences were accepting it as part of our puberty rites. As the natural sciences moved toward a concept of nature as *indeterminate, relativistic* and *probabilistic,* the behavioral and, to a lesser extent, the social sciences were occupying the vacated positions.

Second, our interests in communication are changing. As long as we focus on questions of induced compliance, and the corresponding emphasis on communication as productive change (*instruction* and *persuasion*), cause as control seems feasible. As we have turned to less "do it to others" processes (reporting, negotiating, counseling, planning, imagining, playing), S-R theories or even S-O-R theories simply can not account for the data. Many of the titles for the competitive papers in this volume demonstrate this change in interest. We are turning more to cognitive information processing, creating and maintaining social relationships of an enduring and satisfying nature, processes facilitating self and organizational development, and procedures for monitoring and depicting complex information-communication systems. Given those interests, we can't afford to ignore the wealth of data in the introspective reports of both subject and researcher.

Third, as we have begun to internalize such propositions as *meanings are in people, everything is relative,* and *reality is a construct*, we have begun to realize that the reality we construct does not have to correspond to the reality we experience. Reality is not a given. It is a set of rules. Man can participate in making the rules, and cause-and-effect is only one game among several. Given the inherent pessimism about the human condition incorporated in behavioristic theology, many of us have turned to a search for a new theory of theory. The fact shouldn't be ignored that the most distinguished of the causal determinists published a later work with the thesis that man is beyond freedom and dignity. If we are free to make the rules, at least in part, as to how we will play the "life game," some of us would like to change the behavioristic rules as we play the game of "communication inquiry" as well.

I suggest that the score is changing in the organization vs. change as process game. At the moment, the behaviorists are losing. I don't suggest that that change will benefit our attempts at communication inquiry. On the contrary. Whichever side is winning, the game is not Whiteheadian. It violates his basic "rule" that the distinction between *organization* and *change* must itself be eliminated.

If we are tying to implement the view that the only *substance* is *flux*, that *the what of being is the how of becoming*, that *organization is change in relationship*, we need a new game, new rules, new guidelines for inquiry. An examination of a fourth way in which some of us have come to use *process* should precede our attempt to formulate at least a few new rules.

PROCESS AS ACTIVITY: COMMUNICATORS PROCESS

While drafting my earlier work on the communication process, I was intrigued by Kenneth Boulding's characterization of *The Image* (1956). Building on Lippmann's much earlier notion of the concept of stereotypes as pictures in our head (1922), Boulding tried to organize those pictures, to systematize the role of expectations and beliefs through which we imagined—constructed—the reality we were or might be experiencing. Boulding focused on *organization* as such, as Rokeach (1968) continued to do. Neither placed much attention on *flux*, on *movement*—although Rokeach's theory of social

comparison moved in that direction. Their seminal thinking, however, provided a base for later work.

Given my behaviorist indoctrination, I found no way to incorporate Boulding and Rokeach into my own thinking. However, I could not dismiss their point of view and "filed it" for future speculation. Even that level of approach-avoidance conflict was overwhelmed when I read the report of Miller, Gallanter, and Pribram (1960), published shortly after my own, and representing an attempt to continue Boulding's work.

Miller et al. followed Boulding to the Palo Alto Center. Their work, *Plans and the Structure of Behavior*, combined Boulding's interdisciplinary way of conceptualizing with their own rigorous background in psychology. Their major thesis is that the basic unit of behavior should not be defined as *response*, but as *processing*. Stated within our terms of discourse, they argued that *behavior is an organizing process—flux is substance*.

Recognizing, as we all must, that experiencing is ordered in a time-sequence, they rejected the accompanying behavioristic assumption that the same time-sequence is the way in which we must conceive of and analyze behavior. Rather than endorsing the S-R view that processing merely is responding, and that processing experience consists of linkages in a sequence of paired events, such as stimulus-response, response-consequence, they accepted the view that processing behavior is hierarchical, that the basic behavioral act involves more than pairing—it involves comparing.

For Miller et al., the basic behavioral act is labelled as TOTE for *Test-Operate-Test-Exit*. They separate an individual's operational level of behavior—what he can do, what he can perceive— from his control or test level (the criteria of want, the test for success). The basic act of behavior can be described as beginning with a test—a criterion for success, the basis for operational instruction. Given the criteria—an instructional program— operations are begun. The operation level has two components: (1) performing a behavior and (2) perceiving the consequences of that behavior.

The third component of their basic behavioral act is the comparison between the original test and the state of affairs that exists after the operational component has been performed. It is that comparison process, the second test in TOTE, that they refer to as *feedback*.

For the behaviorist, feedback is the consequence of response, the sequal which can serve as a stimulus. For Miller et al. that consequence is incorporated as only part of feedback. *Feedback* is the comparison and decision process on which a decision is based as to whether to repeat the operations (if the criterion was not adequately achieved) or to cease operating—the *exit* instruction in *test-operate-test-exit*.

The thinking of Miller et al. is important to our discussion in at least three ways. For one thing, it focuses on the individual as an active participant in any relationship between his perceptual and his glandular-muscular behavior. At first thought, it might appear that it merely has specified that O in S-O-R formulations. It is, however, more than that. Within S-O-R theory, the O is merely intervening, another step in serial linkage. It is a covert act, at the same conceptual level as overt stimuli and responses. For TOTE, it is an organizing process. It stipulates that man does more than respond—he proposes and disposes. At least he can, depending on his coding and comparing rules or processing rules.

Second, through the component of comparison, Miller et al. posit a hierarchical structure, implying at least two things: (1) complex behavior is *hierarchical*, not *serially sequential*; and (2) the notion of *structure* and the notion of *flux* are fused—*movement* is defined as *organization*.

Third, their work and later work place a central emphasis on the *rules*—the rules of coding behavior and the rules for making comparisons. The rules of processing become a central variable and variability in those rules is a significant aspect of understanding communication activity.

The disavowal of traditional views of serial sequence was further supported by a provocative book by Powers (1973), in which he argues most convincingly that one of the main bases for glandular-muscular behavior is the control of perceptual behavior. Stated more simply, one of the bases for response is the preparation to receive a stimulus.

For those of us interested in communication processes, for example, Powers makes it easier to conceive of the nonlinearity of a communication

relationship. For example, a listening "response" may precede the onset of a "stimulus" to which one will attend. Listening can be thought of as preceeding speaking, planning for consumption may precede actual consumption of information, feedback can be anticipatory. In short, the "natural" events involved in communication occur in a natural time sequence. The communication events, however, need not be viewed either as time-ordered or serially sequential. It depends on the rules under which we're playing.

Schroder, Driver, and Streufert (1967) were among the first to examine some of those rule options in human information processing. In recent years, as reflected by several of the papers in this volume, that work has intensified. Within the context of system and systems theory, both human and machine information processing are being studied and used as models for our conceptions of *process*. It is ironic to note that our increased understanding of information-technology and the possibilities of heuristic information machines have contributed to our tentative willingness to restore man to an active role in processing his own experience. Weizenbaum (1976) and others are increasingly concerned with some of those analogues and the advantages and dangers they represent.

It seems poetically justifiable that our earlier attempts to use the mechanistic aspects of power-technology as a model for man are being displaced by our present attempts to use the heuristic aspects of information-technology as a model for restoring self-controlled humaneness and dignity. In many ways, our view of technology determines our view of humans.

TOWARD COMMUNICATION AS PROCESS

Each of the three intellectual approaches to communication as process (*complex organization, change over time,* and *activity*) have contributed to our understanding of human communication. Each has been taken by scholars of insight and ability. It has been my experience that theoretic conflict between scholars of ability usually implies some merit on all sides, and that an attempt to choose sides results in a loss of perceptiveness. Rather, we can try to develop an approach which incorporates some of the merits in each.

Behaviorism has contributed a rigor of observation, a demand for articulate operationalization and a rigorous language in which to talk about inductive inference. The latter, although used primarily as a theory of error in induction, can be shown to have theoretic utility as well. Behaviorism also has placed fundamental importance on the notion of time sampling—frequent time-monitoring of the system.

Complex organizational research has emphasized the importance of selecting relationships, not discrete events, as a basic unit of analysis. It has demonstrated the necessity for a study of complex sets of relationships in our attempts to gain insight into complex communication activity, and it has given us at least some insight into both the importance of and methodology for study of hierarchical relationships. Probably most importantly, it has emphasized an analytic procedure which can be adopted as a theoretic notion: control does not imply cause and effect, but simply the reduction of uncertainty. It is expressed as a measure—relative to the total amount of uncertainty that could be in the system if there were no control elements.

Information processing—*process* as activity—has emphasized the central importance of hierarchical structure even in the definitions of our basic concepts. Such definitions as TOTE begin at least to blunt the traditional distinction between *substance* and *flux*. Processing research focuses on the *processor*, and suggests the crucial import of understanding the rules under which that processor is playing, and the changes in outcome that occur as those rules are varied. That emphasis also gives credence to the view long held by Stephenson and others that our orientation should be toward describing what the individual does, within the structure he provides, rather than within the context of researcher-imposed theoretic structure.

As we continue to explore optimal ways of conceptualizing communication relationships and activities, those contributions from earlier approaches can guide us to some fundamental assumptions about the nature of communication as process. As a tentative guide to that exploration, let me suggest at least a few such assumptions that have helped in my

current efforts to articulate a processual view of human communication (Berlo, 1977).

Communication is Make-believe, but Make-believe is Real

Communication activity is rooted in natural events; i.e., all symbols for which users have significance are imbedded in units of matter and energy which constitute the sensory messages we exchange. Message events are natural events; however, the communicative significance is not natural. It is symbolic.

Symbolic activity is based on shared meanings and shared rules. Within the taxonomy of semiotics, there are three kinds of rules: rules of reference (*semantics*), rules of internal symbolic relationships (*syntactics*), and rules linking semantic and syntactic rules to user meaning (*pragmatics*).

Those rules are made by users, primarily human users, not by nature. We choose whether to accept the rules, and to believe or disbelieve assertions we make under those rules. That is the basis for saying that communication is made and believed—*make-believe*. A symbolic relationship is a social relationship. It is imbedded in natural phenomena, but not a natural relationship. *Information* is pattern, as perceived and signified, not natural substance. Communication relies on social agreement, not on natural substance.

What is the referent of "social" in the statement that communication is a social relationship? Not any requirement that two or more people be directly involved. In fact, much of the definitional apparatus of many concepts of communication (e.g., *the requirement of two people, the awareness of one another, social intent*, etc.) could better be treated as variables, not part of the definition.

Communication is *social* in that it occurs through social coding, subject to a history and future of shared agreement as to the coding rules. Those rules are made and believed, *make-believe*; however, *make-believe* is real, social reality is as "real" as is natural reality. In fact, many would argue that physical reality is itself a set of propositions, made and believed.

Communication Relationships Are Not Subject to Natural Law

Traditionally, we have assumed that natural games are played by nature's rules—the *Why?– Because game*. Contemporary views of natural reality question that assumption; however, when we analyze communication, the point is moot. Communication is not a natural process; therefore, it is not necessarily subject to any laws of nature, except for those that control the matter-energy units in which communication is imbedded. What are some of the implications of the thesis that *make-believe* is not subject to the *Law of Cause and Effect, the Laws of Thermodynamics*, etc.?

Cause≠control. To talk about a communication system coming under control is not necessarily to imply that the control is attributable to a *controller*—that the relationship involves one communicator doing something to another—causing or even controlling the behavior of the other. Relationships control. Some may be causal, but they need not be. To be under control is to be predictable under a set of expectations which lead to a set of predictions. Control is measurable as the reduction of uncertainty in a system over time. Causality is only one source of that reduction.

Interdependence is not restricted to mutual dependency. In the natural and causally deterministic game of *Why?–Because,* all relationships are dependency relationships. The mathematics of linear functions serve as a model and as a language for expressing relationships. Interdependency is nothing but mutual dependency, expressed by the regression coefficients of one variable on the other.

In a communication relationship, interdependency may be based on mutual dependency; however, the assumption that cause does not equal control implies that interdependency may be a joint dependency on the relationship itself, expressed less restrictively in Bayesian terms than in regression terms. Communication may be controlled by *make-believe* law, not just natural law. We can choose among options as to how we want to be interdependent, bringing ourselves under control.

Communication need not be a directional relationship. Messages are natural events, subject to the same laws of movement and transformation and time-sequencing as other forms of merchandise. Our most popular "models" of communication, including S→M→C→R, are neither models nor about communication. They are descriptions of the movement of natural merchandise, whether based on the electronic signal transmission of a telephone circuit or the conditioning learning base for hypodermic insertion of persuasive statements.

An information-communication relationship may be directional as we conceive it, or it may not. If we look on the "source" as intentional and initiatory and the "receiver" as passive and a receptive container—e.g., if the message is stimulus and the effect is response—the relationship is directional. On the other hand, if the relationship is one in which both users approach the engagement with expectations, plans, and anticipations, the uncertainty reduction attributable to the contact may better be understood in terms of how both parties use and approach a message-event than in terms of how one person uses the contact to direct the other.

"Natural" languages are not optimal to discuss communication. What we call "natural" languages (e.g., English, Russian, etc.) are structured on a Newtonian concept of process, on a causally determined construct of nature, on the basic distinction between *substance* and *flux*. In English, for example, the simplest assertive sentence is comprised of the juxtaposition of an actor and an action, of a subject (substance, the causal force) and a predicate (the flux or movement). The assertive sentence links *substance* and *flux* by asserting a relationship. The relationship may be directed toward another, the object, either directly or indirectly, or it may simply express a nontransitive but deterministic relationship. Interestingly, it is only in the passive voice, usually evaluated pejoratively by professionals, that the directionality and causally deterministic aspects of a relationship can be avoided. The *Why?–Because game* is the basis for the rules of syntactical structure of so-called "natural" languages.

A language based on the *Nature of Newton* is ill-equipped to report on the *Nature of Whitehead*. It is difficult and often implies fuzziness in thinking to talk processually in a scholastic and deterministic code, a language that posits *being* as separable from *activity, organization* as distinct from *change*. A respectable defense of those who used process as "mystery" is that they are trying to express concepts that can't be expressed in English; e.g., how can one say "the only permanence is change" or "flux is substance" in a code that imposes a strict (except for gerunds) separateness between the two concepts being joined?

Many of our young are searching for optional codes to express the *make-believe* reality in which they function. A most serious problem for journalists who use print is the difficulty in trying to report *make-believe* events (e.g., communication) in the "natural" language of cause and effect. Certainly, in speculating about communication itself, we need "artificial" codes which are closer in syntactic structure to the reality about which we are inquiring. We need *make-believe* languages to process process. The concept of "is-ness" itself poses problems transcending those long identified by students of general semantics. Dating assertions provides warning of their relativity to time and place; however, the more basic problem of hierarchical relativity remains.

Shared rules (not shared meanings) is where the action is. As we learned that communication is not a process of transferring meanings, but rather a process in which meanings are elicited, we learned to concentrate on the importance of shared meanings—shared internal states and shared understanding of self and other.

Many of us accepted a theological premise that communication is good and that more of it is better, because it increases commonality. Such a premise is not defensible as an inductive generalization. Communication sometimes increases understanding through shared meanings, and sometimes not. As our overlap in meanings and the experiences on which they are based decreases, reliance on shared meaning as a basis for symbolic interaction increases in risk. Some would argue that our major communication problem today is learning how to communicate with people we'll never understand (i.e., share meanings with) very well.

We can communicate with minimal reliance on meaning. Learning to do that is a major objective for the journalist. It is called *reporting*—an increasingly important communication process in a *make-believe* world. Trying to "tell it like it is" requires minimization of meaning, and focus on following the rules of reporting: semiotic rules of reference and syntax. As we focus more on the structure of the communication user, we also will focus on processing rules, not just the idiosyncratic rules of a particular user or the biochemical natural base for processing, but on the learnable rules of processing which will facilitate other communication processes such as planning and imagining. If we concentrate on processes of imposed compliance through manipulation of meanings, shared meaning probably is the optimal focus; however, as we move to processes of jointly accepted control relationships, the rules of relationship are where the action is. We make those rules, and there are options to be exercised.

A focus on *rules* provides another benefit to the communication scholar who wants the field to make a distinctive contribution to social understanding. As we concentrate on meaning alteration, our focus is on individual behavior. Our lack of distinctive scholarly contributions under such a focus suggests that communication behavior is not that different from other kinds of behavior.

As we concentrate on rules of semiotic, processing, and relationships, our focus is on communication as a social "game," in the sense that it involves players, outcomes, and rules and regulations of play. The rules define the game, and changes in the rules change the game. Just as the economist or the political scientist attempts to gain insight into his game, the communication scientist can articulate how we play various "talk games," and how the outcomes vary with the players and the rules and regulations of the relationship.

MATHEMATICAL MODELS: *MAKE-BELIEVE GAMES*

To talk about communication as a *make-believe game,* we need a make-believe language. Fortunately, mathematicians are make-believe linguists and have constructed a large number of make-believe games. Mathematics, of course, is *totally make-believe,* with no semantic rules that tie symbols to natural referents. Mathematics is a syntactic game in which adherence to the rules of relationship within the context of the game's underlying assumptions determines which of the statements we make can be believed and which can't.

Mathematical games are recognized by all as a potentially useful conceptual base for talking about natural events, if the natural scientist can specify semantic rules which tie the mathematical symbols to natural events. When those analogues can be specified and the underlying assumptions of the mathematics game can be accepted in the *Nature* game, we have a model.

For those of us studying communication as *make-believe,* modelling on mathematical games is more than useful, it is crucial, in that the underlying assumptions of our so-called "natural" languages can not be accepted in the communication game. As we review our inventory of mathematical games and make new games, the criteria for utility of any given game include: (1) can we accept the underlying assumptions, (2) can we develop the semantic rules, the epistemic correlations, (3) is it a processual game, and (4) is it a probabilistic rather than a deterministic game?

Statistical Inference: A Whiteheadian Game

Of course, there is no "right" mathematical language on which to model communication. Different communication games require different analogues. Within the context of speculating on how to cope with uncertainty in a *make-believe* world, it is useful to talk in the language of *sets* and *relations.* And, based on that approach to the process of inductive generalization, it is useful to talk in the language of statistical inference, not as a model of error as used by behaviorists, but as a theoretic model of communication as an informational process.

Sets and relations. If relationships are to be our unit of analysis, and symbolic behavior is to be conceived as hierarchical (e.g., TOTE), the language of *sets* and *relations* would seem to hold potential value. The formation of a *set* is the creation of a hierarchy. When we collect a number of

events and name the collectivity, we have established two levels. As we understand the notion of *levels,* we can dispose of the traditional question as to whether the whole is greater than the sum of its parts. That is a linear question, and the answer is "no." The whole is different from its parts in that it is at a different level in the hierarchical structure. As we form *sets* of *sets,* the number of levels is increased.

The language of sets and relations also provides a clear operational statement of what is referred to by the term *relationship,* as well as a measure of the strength of a relationship. For example. Given two sets, *A* and *B,* there is a relationship between an element of *A* and a corresponding (i.e., related) element of *B* if and only if the probability of occurrence of the element in one set is altered, given the occurrence of the element in the other set. To state it differently, the elements are related if the freedom to vary of one or both is restricted. Relationships are restrictions of freedom—freedom to vary.

Relationships, of course, may be of various kinds: e.g., *dependent, symmetric, transitive, reflexive.* The language of sets and relations also provides a vocabulary for talking about kinds of relationships. It also provides a rigorous operational statement of the strength of a relationship: i.e., the more restricted the freedom to vary, the stronger the relationship. A total relationship, maximally strong, exists if and only if there is no freedom to vary—total restriction of freedom.

Probability sets: Variability in what is expected. The language of sets and relations also is useful as a base for talking about variability within a given set as to what is going to happen both in the long run and at any given point in time. That base is generated by forming a special kind of set, usually referred to as a *probability set* or an *expectation set.* All students of statistical inference are familiar with probability sets or distributions in that they are the prerequisite for application of a rigorous inferential test of the acceptability of hypotheses.

To generate a probability set, we specify all of the events that we believe are possible, within a given context (such as outcomes of a political contest, things a friend might say or do, happenings in the stock market, etc.). For each event, we estimate—

on whatever criteria we choose—how frequently each event will occur, *relative* to the occurrence of the others. We estimate relative frequencies—the probability of occurrence of each alternative event *in the long run*. That set of alternatives with attached probabilities is the referent of the term expectation. *Expectations* as a concept is at the hierarchical level of "in the long run."

On the basis of our expectations, with the acceptance of the underlying assumption that the universe is orderly—events that happen most frequently in the long run are more likely to happen at any point in time—we can make a prediction as to what will happen at any given point in time, any "now." "Prediction" as a concept is at the hierarchical level of "now" or "then." The prediction is our measure of the central tendency of our expectations—the mean of the expectation set.

We also can make a statement as to how uncertain we are about our expectations in the long run. That is based on our measure of the variability within our expectations, such as the standard deviation of the expectation set. That is a measure of the long run uncertainty within our expectations.

Statistical inference: An information process. The scientist interested in statistical inference makes use of the concepts of *expectation, prediction,* and *long-run uncertainty*. He also uses another concept, a *report* of what did happen at any given point in time. That's *information*—a report of what happened. "Information" as a concept is, like prediction, at the hierarchical level of "now" or "then."

In the typical inferential statistical test, the discrepancy is calculated between what was predicted and what was observed. That discrepancy is standardized, relative to the amount of uncertainty anticipated on the basis of the long-run uncertainty within the expectation. To put the test in its most familiar form, it is the *Critical Ratio: o-e/s.e.* If this relative discrepancy exceeds some predetermined amount, the expectation set is altered to take the information into account. If the information is consistent with the expectation, the confidence in that expectation—*theory*—is increased or maintained. The inferential process is a continuous process, without beginning or end, dynamic in the relationship between information and expectation, hierar-

chical in the "long run" context for interpreting the "now," and probablistic in its language.

INFORMATION AND CONTROL: LINKING BEING AND BECOMING

My assignment in these remarks was not extended to a brief and elementary articulation of the scientific process of hypothesis testing through statistical inferential processes. The interesting point, however, to someone like me who taught statistical inference for nearly 20 years, is that we didn't recognize the fact that the language of statistical inference can serve as a model for human information-communication processes. Scientific inquiry is an information-seeking, expectation-developing, and information processing activity. As such, it is a rational process, with clear processing rules. If human activity meets the assumptions underlying those rules—and occurs within those rules—the concepts and relationships of statistical inference are useful.

Information: Relative Uncertainty Reduction in the Now

In studying communication, *information* is a basic concept. Communication processes are subsets of information processes in that they consist of symbolic informational activity.

Information can be defined as assertions as to the state of affairs at a given *now,* a report on what happened, an element in a set of statements that "tell it like it is." Information can be operationalized in natural terms—in units of matter and energy, such as pieces, pounds, inches, broadcast time, etc. Those are absolute measures of information as a natural event, and assume that information is *in* the message or user.

Information can be viewed within the context of *make-believe*, information processes, and defined relatively—probabilistically. Actually, the definition is the same—assertions as to what happened in a given "now." However, the question of measuring the amount of information changes. The *amount of information* can be operationalized as the amount of uncertainty reduced at any given point in time and space, for any given user. *Information* is a *now* concept, and relative to the amount of uncertainty existing prior to the report.

Using subjective probability estimates for any given individual, we can generate *expectation sets*. To take a simple example, suppose we believe that only three things can occur within a grouping of events: *a, b,* and *c*. In the long run, we believe that *a* will occur 60% of the time, *b* will occur 30%, and *c* will occur 10%. Those are our subjective probability estimates. Given those expectations, suppose we receive a report that *b* occurred. How much information is involved?

If we measure absolutely, we could say "one piece"—one assertive relationship. Measuring relatively and probabilistically, we could operationalize the amount of information as: 100% *expectation of occurrence*. Within that context, the amount of information in an assertion is equal to the unlikelihood of its occurrence in the long run, under our expectations. There are alternative coding systems that could be used; however, this one is adequate for our purposes. Accordingly, then, the information value of *a* is .40 (1.00 − .60); of *b*, .70 (1.00 − .30); of *c* .90 (1.00 − .10). The rarer the event, the more the information, within the context of expectations.

Under the assumption that the most probable occurrence in the long run is the most likely occurrence at any given point in time, we would predict, before receiving the report, that *a* would occur. We would be right 60% of the time, in the long run, if our expectations are accurate. We could standardize our information scores by using the discrepancy between what was predicted and what was observed. To do so, however, would imply that no information is involved if we obtain what we predicted. That does not take into account the inherent variability within the expectation. Given variance, there is some information even if we obtain exactly what we predicted, for, after all, we expected to be wrong 40% of the time when we made that prediction.

Information scores can be recorded to take that into account, under certain assumptions, if we compute the mean of the expectation set, and measure information value as the discrepancy between the *probability of what was observed* and the *mean probability in the long run*. That measure (*o-e*)

standardizes our information scores across distributions of varying expectations. In this case, the mean of the expectation set is .54. Using that as the *expected value*, the amount of information obtained from *a, b,* and *c* would be .06, .24, and .44. Again, different coding systems are available; however, all should meet the criteria of expressing the amount of information in probabilistic terms, relative to: (1) long-run expectations, (2) the best prediction, (3) the best expectation—the mean, and (4) the best estimate of the amount of uncertainty in the expectation set itself. The measure relates the *now* and the *long run*.

To take the inherent unpredictability of the expectation set into account, we need to standardize our information measures once more. The Critical Ratio, under appropriate assumptions, serves as a descriptive measure of the amount of information, using the standard deviation of the expectation set as our estimate of expected unpredictability. The information measure is:

$$z_I = \frac{O_I - E_I}{SD_I}$$

When z_I is distributed as z, the measure also provides an operational reference for such terms as "ritual," "news," and "information overload." For example, if z is "significantly" small, the result is *ritual*. If it is significantly large, the consequence is *news*. And, if it is sufficiently large to inhibit further relating by the individual of the "now" to the long-run expectation, the result is *information overload*. Of course, in all three cases, we have to take levels of information into account.

As a "rational" model of information processing, the measure also lets us assess the rationality of the user by comparing subjective estimates of *ritual, news,* and *overload* with the computed measure. This dynamic and on-going relationship between *organization* (the *expectation set*) and *change* (variability in the information amount received), at least approximates the Whiteheadian notion of *process*. It also leads to an operationalization of amount of control, and to an interesting statement as to the relationship between *information* and *control*.

CONTROL: RELATIVE CERTAINTY IN THE LONG RUN

Information is a "now" concept, referring to the unlikelihood of expectation of occurrence of an event at any given point in time. *Control* is a "long run" concept, referring to the ongoing stability, certainty, or predictability of the system. An expectation system is under control to the extent that the expectations lead to predictions that minimize the amount of surprise (i.e., information) obtained for a given report.

Control also can be expressed relatively. First, we need a measure of minimal control, maximal uncertainty. An expectation set is maximally uncertain when no prediction can be derived from it that is better than any other prediction (i.e., a random distribution of expectations). Given a random distribution, the amount of uncertainty is determined solely by the number of alternatives that are expected. As alternatives rise, uncertainty rises and control and predictability are reduced.

To standardize our measure of minimal control, we need to eliminate the number of alternatives as a variable. To do that, we can operationalize *maximal uncertainty* as "all the uncertainty" (100% of the uncertainty), computed on the basis of the number of alternatives in the expectation set.

Maximal Uncertainty

Given any *expectation set*, even a random one, some predictive accuracy is possible. For example, if there are two alternatives in the set—a random set—each will occur 50% of the time, in the long run. If we select either alternative, and predict it every time, we will be right 50% of the time. If there are three alternatives, we'll be right 33% of the time; ten alternatives; 10% of the time, etc. If *control* equals *predictability* in the long run, the amount of control of a random expectation set is: 1/N, where N is the number of alternatives. If we create a *make-believe* concept of total uncertainty—100% of the uncertainty—then:

$$\text{Max Unc.} = 1.00 - \frac{1}{N}, \text{ where N} =$$

number of alternatives.

In our *a,b,c* example, assuming that all three events are equally likely to occur, the maximal uncertainty within the *expectation set* is:

$$\text{Max. Unc.} = 1.00 - \frac{1}{3}, \text{ or } 66.67\%$$

On the basis of whatever relationships we can assume—for relationship control—we can compute the *expected "actual uncertainty"* of the set. In our simple example, the only relationship we have is our expectation as to the relative frequencies of occurrence: 60%, 30%, and 10%. Under this expectation, we would always predict *a*, the most probable alternative. We would be correct in our predictions, in the long run, 60% of the time. We would be incorrect 40% of the time—that is the actual uncertainty would be 40%.

Relative Uncertainty and Control

Given our measure of *maximal* uncertainty and our measure of *actual* uncertainty, we can standardize our uncertainty measures across *expectation sets* by expressing it as *relative uncertainty*:

$$\text{Rel. Unc.} = \frac{\text{Actual Uncertainty}}{\text{Maximal Uncertainty}}$$

In our example:

$$\text{Rel. Unc.} = \frac{.40}{.67}, \text{ or } \text{R.U.} = 60\%$$

Stated in words, the measure says that, of all the *uncertainty* that could exist in an *expectation* with three alternatives, 60% of it remains after we take into account the distribution of our *expectations*. Given that:

Control = 100% − R.U., or, in our
example 40%

Again to state it in words, we have brought our *predictability* under *control* by 40%; i.e., given our *expectations*, we have reduced *maximal uncertainty* by 60%. *Control* is calculated as the proportion of *maximal uncertainty* which has been removed in the long run.

INFORMATION AND CONTROL: AN INTERESTING RELATIONSHIP

The amount of information is the amount of surprise obtained from a report in the now. Information always reduces uncertainty in the now. The amount of uncertainty that was to be reduced is the amount of information: the less likely an event, under our expectation, the more information.

Control is the amount of surprise which has been removed from the reports within an expectation context in the "long run." To the extent that reports are predictable, control is established. To the extent that reports are not predictable, control is minimized.

It often is assumed by some that *information* and *control* are positively and directly related, under the assumption that information reduces uncertainty and that the reduction in uncertainty is control. The assumption apparently is a corollary of the traditional belief that "knowledge is power."

It would seem that the confusion between *make-believe reality* and *natural reality* is reflected in the statement that "knowledge is power"; however, if we substitute the statement that "knowledge is control," there is no problem with the proposition. To equate *information* with *knowledge*, however, is to fail to distinguish between the *now* and the *long run*, and to ignore the long-run consequences of information. In the now, information always reduces uncertainty; however, in the long run, information may reduce, increase, or leave unaltered the predictive capacity of our expectations. To the extent that the reports we receive increase the number of alternatives within our expectation sets, or *homogenize*—reduce the polarity among—the probabilities of those alternatives, information increases long-run uncertainty.

Under our operationalization of *information*, increasing the number of options we must take into account, reporting on options we thought had small or no probability of occurrence, and homogenizing the probabilities of occurrence are the criteria for "high information value." Therefore, over time, the more information we receive, other things being equal, the less control we perceive ourselves to have. At the extreme, if we are told that everything is possible and equally likely—that there are no relationships among occurrences—information leads to maximal uncertainty (zero control).

Knowledge can be viewed as information for which there are accompanying reports of relation-ships through which we can incorporate the short-term information into long-run expectations in ways that use those relationships to maintain or increase the predictability of the system. Relationships control. Without maintaining and increasing the control system, the consumption of information reduces control. Total freedom—no relationships, no control restrictions—indeed becomes just another word for nothing left to lose. The consumption of uncontrolled information is injurious to our health.

IS WHITEHEAD ALL THERE IS?

It has been my intent to suggest a few of the ways in which we might approach definitions of our terms and construction of our assertions which posit a continuing hierarchical, probabilistic, *being-becoming* relationship. If we view communication users as active copers, with *expectation sets, value sets* (instructional programs), *behavioral repertoires* (motor-glandular and perceptual activities), *comparison programs*, and *coding programs*, we can begin to think of communication as a *make-believe*, nondirectional, noncausal interactive process between *the now* of symbolic experience and *the long run* (past and future) of hierarchical expectations. The expectations I have are dependent on where I've been and where I anticipate I'm going. The information obtained from symbolic experience depends on planning and expectations about that information. Each is definitionally interdependent on the other—each influencing and influenced by the other and each inherently indeterminate and probabilistic. *Structure* at any point in time is defined within the context of a set of points in time, not a series. That structure—organization—is the temporal intersection of past and future experience. That is what I believe Whitehead was suggesting.

The Whiteheadian notion of *process* can be incorporated into our view of communication—our theory of theory—our conceptual and analytical approach to the study of communication games, and the rules by which they are played. Must it be?

No. We can conceive of communication in a variety of ways. Behavioristic concepts of sequential influence do indeed explain a great amount of behavior. Single-point descriptions of structure provide insight into *flow*. Better descriptions of processing provides insight into the *rules* we use and could use. Even the poetry of process-as-mystery facilitates our thinking as to alternative ways of thinking. There is no right way to insight.

Should the Whiteheadian notion of process be incorporated? That's a matter for individual judgment. In my own thinking, sometimes yes, sometimes no. Yet, if we are to gain insight into that distinctively human intervention that is derived from developing rules by which to play the life-game, I think it represents the highest cost-benefit decision.

REFERENCES

BECKER, S.L. Approaches to inquiry in communication. Paper presented to the Speech Association of America convention. Los Angeles, December 1967.

BERLO, D.K. *The process of communication.* New York: Holt, Rinehart and Winston, 1960.

BERLO, D.K. *Information and communication.* New York: Holt, Rinehart and Winston, 1977.

BOULDING, K.E. *The image.* Ann Arbor, Michigan: The University of Michigan Press, 1956.

CLARKE, P. *New models for communication research.* Beverly Hills, California: Sage, 1973.

LIPPMANN, W. *Public opinion.* New York: Harcourt, Brace, 1922.

MILLER, G.A., GALANTER, E., & PRIBRAM, C.H. *Plans and the structure of behavior.* New York: Holt, Rinehart and Winston, 1960.

POWERS, W.T. *Behavior: the control of perception.* Chicago: Aldine, 1973.

RICHETTO, G. Organizational Communication Theory and Research: An Overview. In B.D. Ruben (Ed.), *Communication yearbook I.* New Brunswick, N.J.: Transaction-International Communication Association, 1977.

ROKEACH, M. *Beliefs, attitudes, and values.* San Francisco: Jossey-Bass, 1968.

SCHRODER, H.M., DRIVER, M.J., & STREUFERT, S. *Human information processing.* New York: Holt, Rinehart, and Winston, 1967.

SMITH, D.H. Communication research and the idea of process. *Speech Monographs*, 1972, 39, 3.

STEPHENSON, W. *The study of behavior.* Chicago and London: University of Chicago Press, 1953.

STEPHENSON, W. *Newton's fifth rule: An exposition of Q pro ro theologica pro re scientia.* Unpublished, 1976.

WARD, S., WACKMAN, D., & WARTELLA, D. *How children learn to buy.* Beverly Hills, California: Sage, 1977.

WEIZENBAUM, J. *Computer power and human reason.* San Francisco: W.H. Freeman, 1976.

WHITEHEAD, A.N. *Process and reality.* New York: Macmillan, 1929.

PERSPECTIVES ON A DISCIPLINE:
REVIEW AND COMMENTARY

RICHARD W. BUDD
Rutgers University

The history of the study of human communication indicates both a narrowing definition of the phenomenon and the emergence of a more fragmented and less coordinated pattern of research pursuits. There is a growing confusion between communication scholarship and methodological ingenuity. Among the consequences have been a turning away from the empirical world as a source of researchable hypotheses and a means of validating research findings; conflicting but equally "proven" theories of communication; conduct of research in areas where researchers possess little first-hand knowledge; and redundant application of already devised instruments. A major shortcoming of the heavy emphasis of empirical research is its unwitting exclusion of other methods of inquiry and its failure to thus far provide a useful creative synthesis. A new ethnic of communication study is called for, involving broadened training for graduate students, wider recognition of and forum for alternative methods of study, and the undertaking of framework building by those in the field who possess both the status and experience to do so.

I have, for a considerable time, been badgered by a relatively simple paradox in our field, one which ultimately served as the impetus for this paper.[1] On the one hand we claim that communication, by its nature, is supradisciplinary. On the other, we stand subservient to methods of inquiry developed by others. And, because of our preoccupation with methodological elegance and failure to develop our own comprehensive theory, we depend upon the syntheses of other disciplines to provide our more generic frameworks of communication and human behavior. At the same time, seemingly unsensitized to this state of affairs, we ask why our field often seems to lack an identity of its own, and why we must face the continuing inquisitions of university colleagues and practitioners aimed at requiring us to justify our existence. Some of these onslaughts, as we know, have been successful—others are likely to be.

The emerging question of concern is, what is the overarching framework upon which our field is built? I am in agreement with Mark Knapp (1976) that the divisional structure of the International Communication Association provides little help in addressing the question. The now eight divisions of the association are more products of historical accident and concurrent research interests, than they are representative of any thoughtfully developed taxonomy of the discipline. Perhaps an answer is that the phenomenon of communication is so ubiquitous, and transcends so many disciplinary boundaries, that any sort of comprehensive framework or theory defies development. But as an Association, we collectively represent those scholars who boldly moved to stake out the domain of human communication as our own. It is therefore incumbent upon us—indeed it is our only justification for existence as a discipline—to provide a full synthesis from which we can begin to derive a comprehensive theory of human communication. But in a much deeper sense, it may be that the difficulty we encounter in addressing this fundamental question, and in defending our discipline to others, arises now because we have been and remain reluctant to ask ourselves these same hard questions. Nor have we appeared very responsive to permitting an appropriate forum for divergent points of view.

Strangely enough, we know mostly what we are not. We are not traditional speech, we are not clas-

sical rhetoric, we are not "nuts and bolts" journalism, or at least we do not wish to be identified with
those fields. That simple fact alone, however, may
be symptomatic of a larger issue. At any rate, we
have decided—if not by design, at least by a kind of
proactive default—that we do not wish to be known
by our works as a "soft" science. It is, I think, fair
to say that we have in recent years moved quite
rapidly toward the embracement of empirical science as our major means of studying communication phenomena. In many circles within the field,
that embracement has become a permanent bond
which precludes other methodologies and approaches of scholarship. The problem is not so
much the research effort *per se,* as it is the consequences to our field of the exclusivity of that effort.
It is, of course, a problem when it blinds us and our
students to other legitimate forms of analysis. It is,
of course, a problem when "the ability to prove you
are right and to deduce conclusions from premises,
is felt to be more important than the ability to
impose new kinds of order on experience, and to
generate novel and meaningful points of view"
(Adelson, 1966). If indeed this is the case, then we
labor under a misguided understanding of science
and the scientific method. As Kuhn (1970) has
noted, a paradigm—and it seems clear that empirical research procedures are emerging as our guiding
paradigm—can insulate a community from socially
important issues and problems because they are not
reducible to the terms of currently popular tools of
research.

GENESIS OF THE PROBLEM

But my argument is running out ahead of my
documentation. There are a number of deterrents
impeding the development of our understanding of
human communication, not the least of which is our
own conceptualization of what it is we are about. If
at some generic level we can agree that *communication* is the process of naming relationships between
man and environment and consequent behavior
(*intrapersonal communication*), and between *man
and man* and consequent behavior (*interpersonal
communication*), then we must agree that we are
subject to both the processes and consequences of

that phenomenon (Budd, 1974; Budd & Ruben,
1977). Altogether too briefly, our own epistemic
community (some overlapping aspects of our field
and our Association) has threaded itself together
through a mutually created and maintained set of
symbolic realities, matured into some institutional
form, out of which has grown a solidification of
structure and a resistance to renewal, which maintains its stability through appropriate socialization
of its young. Campbell and Mickelson (1975) might
be tempted to identify this as the description of a
decaying system. Whatever, it will be my intent, at
some abstract level—and employing the insights of
other social and behavioral scientists—to play
through these concepts in viewing our field.

My primary concern is the failure of our field thus
far to develop a comprehensive theory of communication. The main thrust of the paper concerns the
extent to which our preoccupation with strict research protocols has contributed to that failure, and
some suggestions for evolving a new ethic of communication scholarship.

Interestingly enough, we were perhaps closer to
being able to develop a broader and more general
view of communication at the beginnings of our
disciplinary history than we likely are now. In point
of fact, one of the first major works in our field,
Walter Lippmann's *Public Opinion* (1922), perhaps
yet remains the unsurpassed grand theory of human
communication. Other contributors to this broader
empirical view were Lasswell (1948), Schramm
(1955), Berlo (1960), Klapper (1960), among others. A review of our recent literature, however,
indicates both a narrowing definition of communication and the emergence of a more fragmented and
uncoordinated pattern of study and research. And
while we have increased considerably the volume of
output of research studies, we have likely lost some
of our more global impact. Only a cursory review of
citation indices bears out the fact that we are citing
works of scholars in other disciplines to a much
greater extent than scholars outside our field seem
to find our works useful. The second revelation is
the marked increase with which we cite and recite
the works of a central core of researchers in our own
field. One could be more comfortable with the latter
statistic if the range of citations were broader. At the
least, it does provide an important benchmark for

gauging the extent of the institutionalization of our field. At the outside, it might well mean we have not cast our conceptual nets either wide enough or deep enough.

What is perhaps more important is to attempt to understand the reasons for this dramatic shift in both the form and scope of communication study. There are a number of factors which have contributed to the change, but what perhaps accounts for most of the variance in the convergence and narrowing of our field of study has been the introduction and rise to popularity of empiricism. Quantative research has become the arbiter of our theory, the primary source of our credibility, and the ideal of our advanced graduate students and our young professionals. It has been perceived as our discipline's path to respectability in the academic community. But it has not come without cost. Our apparent appetite for legitimization through research protocol and the consequences of its inherent problem-orientation have to some extent had an attenuating effect upon the conceptual base of our discipline.

EMPIRICAL SCIENCE IN AN EMPIRICAL WORLD

Blumer (1969) has provided an extensive and well thought through critique of the impact of empirical research procedures on the social sciences in general. His commentary is so relevant to present concerns that an attempt will be made to summarize his views by making application of them to our own field. Blumer asserts that empirical science assumes an *empirical world* available for study and observation. That *empirical world*, he maintains, must be both the *point of departure* and the *point of return* for the empirical scientist. It must serve as the ultimate testing ground for any assertion made about it. The belief that the empirical world exists in a fixed state—and whose description is the sole domain of empirical science—can and has been a formidable barrier to avenues of new inquiry and discovery. The history of science has demonstrated that the reality of the empirical world is, Blumer contends, in the "here and now," and is continually reordered by new conceptualizations. As elementary as that statement might appear on its face,

much of the current research in the behavioral sciences, by implication, seems not to reflect that fundamental notion.

It is, for example, an empirical fact that we are, as humans, unique entities, and have evolved out of a set of uniquely different communication experiences. By the same reasoning, the nexus of conditions, experiences, and responses surrounding any human interaction grow from and add to that uniqueness, and are not likely to be reproducible in a laboratory setting. Nor are they likely to be reinstituted in all or any of their time-space-sequence patterns in any future relationship. It therefore follows that not all aspects of human communication are productively amenable to reduction to scientific research procedures, as we have come to know them, nor are all aspects of human communication generalizable to any meaningful predictive model.

It is for these reasons that Blumer adamantly contends that "methodology" must be conceived of as the totality of those processes and principles underlying the entire scientific study of the empirical world, as well as all aspects of the scientific act. This declaration provides the context for his counterpoint that today, *methodology* is regarded by the social scientist as synonymous with *advanced quantitative procedures* rather than as the *cornerstone of scientific inquiry*. In this same context, I, and perhaps many others, never fully understood the implication of Malcolm MacLeans' habitual modification of the word *science*, wherein he always said: "by that I mean the broad view of science." As an empiricist, he clearly understood the necessity for a researcher to "wallow in the source of his data."

Blumer (1969) claims much of present-day methodology is inadequate and misguided, concerned with such preoccupations as:

> the devising and use of sophisticated research techniques, usually of an advanced statistical character; the construction of logical and mathematical models all too frequently guided by criterion of elegance; the elaboration of formal schemes on how to construct concepts and theories; valiant application of imported schemes, such as input-output analysis, systems analysis, and stochastic analysis; studious conformity to the canons of research design; and the promotion of particular procedures as *the* method of scientific research. (p. 27)

I think one can share in Blumer's concern if what he is implying is that we in communication lack any sort of world view. I think we can legitimately question whether or not such a world view is likely to emerge from what appears to be a rising wave of scientism to which Blumer refers. It is certainly debatable whether or not a comprehensive theory of human communication can be fashioned by looking at such limited parts of the process—particularly in the eclectic manner reflected in our brief history—regardless of the elegance and precision of the techniques we use. And if indeed we have canonized the protocols of research to the point where they—rather than the substantive problems of our field—form our guiding paradigm, the likelihood of ever assembling enough pieces to fashion even the most abstract picture of the phenomenon, appears very slim indeed.

FRAGMENTATION AND RELEVANCY

Granted science begins with the perception of a problem; what today often passes for problem-naming is often little more than what Kuhn (1970) calls puzzle-solving. While puzzle-solving is an intriguing and seductive activity, and one in which the existence of a solution is assured, it may do little in the long run to lead us to a more comprehensive understanding of human communication. One might be very hard pressed if he were asked to provide some explanation and overview of our recent research accomplishments. From the contents of our own Association journals during the past six years, we have reported findings on *self-disclosure, communication apprehension, empathy, persuasion, communication competence, attitudes and attitude formation, turn-taking, fear arousal, cognitive dissonance, source credibility, diffusion, violence and aggression, self-esteem, homophily-heterophily, dogmatism, meaning, co-orientation, deception, selective exposure/perception, nonverbal, small groups,* and others. Our array of methods for attacking these concepts—which frequently occupy more article space than discussion of the concept itself—included *semantic differentials, multivariate analysis, stochastic modeling, causal modeling, Markov analysis, regression and multiple regression, Q-analysis, path analysis, multi-dimensional scaling, ANOVA, factor analysis,* and *content analysis,* among others.

The problem here is not so much whether such research ought to be undertaken as it is the development of methodology and the pursuit of concepts independent of the operational characteristics of the empirical world to which they apply. We have too frequently come to confuse communication scholarship with methodological ingenuity. And we cannot with much conviction argue that we have carefully extracted our hypotheses regarding these concepts from a comprehensive, synthesized overview of human communication, where none exists. We leave ourselves open to charges that the communication problems and concepts we research have become incidental to the selection of an intricate, clever, and elegant research design. We run the risk of being branded a nomadic band of research opportunists who, with our enviable array of research designs and procedures, belong to a disciplinary-free epistemic community of puzzle-solvers. But as Blumer (1969) so aptly reminds us:

> Reality exists in the empirical world and not in the methods used to study that world; it is to be discovered in the examination of that world and not in the analysis or elaboration of the methods used to study that world. (p. 27)

We have discussed among ourselves on more than a few occasions how our research findings often seem to violate the evidence of our own senses and intuition. We have more than once encountered the fact that theory which we have evolved in the laboratory seems not to obtain in social settings in which we also have been observers. But in spite of such exceptions, we continue to write and talk as if adherence to strict protocols of research were tantamount to achieving results valid for the empirical world. Blumer would caution us that "to select (usually arbitrarily) some one form of empirical reference and to assume the operationalized study of this one form catches the full empirical coverage of the concept is of course begging the question" (1969, p. 31).

Nisbet (1976), referring to this same issue, notes that the literature of the social sciences reveals the inability of researchers to distinguish between the *logic of discovery* and the *logic of demonstration*. He writes, "The second is properly subject to rules and prescriptions; the first isn't" (1976, p. 5). Of greater concern, writes Nisbet, is the assertion in current literature on methodology and theory construction that discovery will somehow automatically ensue from strict application of the rules of demonstration. "Only intellectual drouth [drought] and barrenness can result from that misconception," he observes (1976, p. 5).

Both Blumer and Nisbet agree that modern social science, rather than looking at the empirical world first, resorts to use of *a priori* theoretical schemes and sets of unverified concepts. Blumer in particular calls any finding of empirical research "unverified" until its operation has been examined and analyzed in the empirical world to see whether one's image and interpretations for it have actually been borne out. This failure to either derive hypotheses from or carry our findings back to the empirical world, Blumer maintains, is the greatest deficiency of empirical science. It is this reliance upon *a priori* theory that he brands *canonization of the protocols of research procedures*. If he were to apply his criticism to the field of human communication, he would offer the following as evidence from our literature:

1. Conflicting hypotheses regarding the nature of some aspect of human communication, each of which has been easily validated by the data and research presented by its proponents.
2. Key conceptual notions which have not yet been adequately linked to empirical referents in the empirical world, so that one could say with confidence which does and does not represent an instance of the concept.
3. Research being conducted in areas where the researcher has little or no knowledge of intimacy with the social life being studied.
4. The redundant application of already devised instruments to divergent groups and in multiple settings.
5. The design of research studies and the application of advanced statistical techniques without concomitantly reporting the findings of a prior exhaustive study of the empirical world to determine the appropriateness of the use of such instruments.

VALIDITY AND EMPIRICAL CONGRUENCE

There has been, I believe, considerable evidence in our field that we are more and more tending in the direction of placing matters of research protocol above the significance of the problem under study. With increasing frequency, critiques of research papers presented at our academic conferences focus more upon the subtleties of research procedures and less and less upon the substance of the communication problems being studied. As Blumer (1969) observes:

A diligent effort, apart from the research study one undertakes, to see if the empirical area under study corresponds in fact to one's underlying images of it, is a rarity. Similarly, a careful independent examination of the empirical area to see if the problem one is posing represents meaningfully what is going on in that empirical area is scarcely done. Similarly, an independent careful examination of the empirical area to see if what one constructs as data are genuinely meaningful data in that empirical area is almost unheard of. Similarly, a careful identification of what one's concepts are supposed to refer to, and then an independent examination of the empirical area to see if its content sustains, rejects, or qualifies the concept, are far from being working practices. (p. 32)

Further evidence might be drawn from an earlier observation regarding the seeming convergence of our divisional interests, not because of overlap of the substantive areas they represent, but because of the increasing preoccupation with research methodology both in paper presentation and response.

Before finishing a summary of Blumers commentary, it is worth noting that he does strike upon more than a few responsive chords. In what little conceptual framework we have developed to date, there seems to be some agreement regarding the relationship between communication and behavior—humans are likely to act on the basis of how they understand their world. Lippmann (1922) called the notion "pictures in our heads." Given that communication researchers are now moving into worlds in which they themselves have rarely participated (medicine, law, race relations, psychiatry, etc.), they will necessarily be limited to a reasonably simple understanding of those empirical worlds. But as researchers, they will form a picture of that world and its participants anyway. What remains, however, is that those pictures in our heads will form the basis for our theories about that empirical world. And since we rarely choose the route of "wallowing in the source of our data," those pictures must to some degree be based upon pre-existing images (Lippmann called them *stereotypes*). However one wishes to characterize them, these less than complete theories still serve to form the bases of our hypotheses.

Issues such as these deserve raising, for they speak to the quality and credibility of our research and subsequent findings, and, ultimately, to whatever emerging framework of communication our pursuit of such research will bring us—not to mention how our findings translate into prescriptions for the empirical world.

This latter concern is exemplified in an oft-quoted Lippmann (1922) observation. It was his contention that inserted between man and his environment is what he called a "psuedo-environment":

> To that psuedo-environment his behavior is a response. But because it *is* behavior, the consequences, if they are acts, operate not in the psuedo-environment where the behavior is stimulated, but in the real environment where action eventuates. (1922, p. 15)

There is another kind of "stereotype" that can and does, albeit unwittingly, influence the nature of our research activity. The pictures one develops about his or her own discipline regarding what that discipline will sanction, both in terms of acceptable topics of study and current research methodologies, plays a major role in what gets researched and what doesn't. At the same time, there is no device built into the research protocol to test whether or not the researcher's concepts of problems, data, assumed relationships, and interpretations in fact are borne out in the empirical world. It is for these reasons, claims Blumer, that simply replicating a study will not always substantiate its validity, and why he urges repeatedly that empirical findings must be validated in the empirical world.

TOWARD A NEW ETHIC OF COMMUNICATION STUDY

It would seem to be time for our field to indulge in some self-study, to be willing to expend at least a portion of the effort devoted to our farflung research interests on studying our own discipline, and to develop, as it were, a predictive model that will help fashion our future. Nisbet (1976) makes the following observation in his new little volume:

> The great harm of the present concentration of method, including theory construction, is that it persuades students that a small idea abundantly verified is worth more than a large idea still insusceptable to textbook techniques of verification. (p. 17)

The point of Nisbet's essay is that what is lacking in the social sciences today is a respect for the methodology of art. This is not to suggest that our sciences be replaced by art, but that there now exists a major imbalance between the two in favor of empirical science. Further, he contends that the critical intuitive leaps forward which contribute significantly to the development of a more comprehensive framework of a discipline, are more likely to come from the creativeness of art than the specifics of science. In a similar vein, Kuhn (1970) observes that scientific revolutions which bring significant intellectual progress have most always been brought about by a reconceptualization of the basic phenomenon rather than from generalizations of specific hypotheses.

But there are, it would seem, a number of conditions existent in our field which augur against the notion that we are poised on the brink of such conceptual breakthrough.

The major reason revolves around our programs of graduate education, the primary means through which we socialize our young. What has developed here is a reasonably tight tautology which, unfortunately, has come to serve as our guiding philosophy of education. It goes, since the coinage of the realm is increasingly based upon proficiency in empirical research, we would do our students a disservice not to steep them the mechanizations of research procedures. Our students, in turn, ultimately become full members of the epistemic community, and through their work, the arbiters of our future. Why this is problematical is that in the process of becoming skilled methodologians, there seems to be a concommitant underdevelopment of the processes of creative synthesis. About our educational approach, MacLean (1966) wrote, "But I do think that much more than we seem to be doing now, we must stretch our students' intellects, hone their skills of intuitive judgment and synthesis, and stimulate their creative thinking" (p. 5).

There are some additional complexities involved here. If we find any credence in the positions of Blumer, Nisbet, and Kuhn, it is unlikely that any sort of comprehensive theory will emerge from scientism, because it precludes the broad sweep necessary to synthesize that framework. Kuhn (1970) further points out that "Almost always the men who achieve these fundamental inventions of new paradigms have been either very young or very new to the field whose paradigm they change" (p. 90). The implication of that statement is that such major breakthroughs are achieved by persons not caught up in the realities of an epistemic community, and as Kuhn further notes, many of these important discoveries have derived from "error." Error is the seed from which creativity grows. But if our educational system is constrained to service as a reproductive and not a regenerative process, where then is error permitted to creep in?

If creative thinking in communication science has indeed been reduced to the process of formulating hypotheses which are amenable to testing through empirical research protocols, then clearly the road to stardom in our discipline requires little more than mastery of mathematics and statistics. This perhaps explains why so many novices to the discipline seem to rapidly gain notoriety among their peers; they are perhaps not, at the same time, those young people Kuhn looks toward to dramatically reshape a discipline.

While we must acknowledge the limiting effect upon creativity that many of the central figures of our field have unwittingly exercised, we must also believe that such influence could be made an equally enabling one. There are most certainly those in our field today with both the capacity and the status to take on the job of creative synthesis, who could take some rather well-grounded intuitive

leaps toward building a more comprehensive framework for the discipline. Such an effort, however, quite clearly involves the risk of introducing a foreign currency on the market, without some prior assurance that its value is equal to or greater than the prevailing coinage of the realm.

We can teach our students to more critically question our theories and methods, and permit them the freedom to do so employing tools other than our own sanctioned theories and methods. We can proceed at less of a breakneck pace in the mass production of articles and papers and books, and in the tradition of Gene Webb (1966) provide more time for training in observation and thoughtful study of empirical world phenomena. We show an unhealthy disrespect for the empirical world, and our ignorance of it and its operations perhaps explains why our research has had such little impact upon its directions. We perhaps need to review and revise our criteria for what constitutes research and scholarship, and leave behind our frequent and fruitless argument that "pure" science needs no mission or pragmatic referent.

In short, we need a new ethic of science, one that places at its fore a commitment to scientific inquiry in the fullest sense of that concept, coupled with a deep and abiding dedication to the field. We need an ethic that not only rewards the glamorous pursuit of concepts through elegant research design and hypothesis testing, but makes also worthwhile the often slower and more difficult process of empirical world observation, analysis, and verification of results generated from empirical research. We need an ethic in which the pursuit of our goal to better understand human communication is open to all sorts of inquiry demonstrated to be in that interest.

In preparing for this presentation, I wrestled for some time with the question of whether to write about what would probably be expected, or write about that which it seemed must be talked about. I opted to take the latter, which proved the more difficult path. I have done so with some trepidation and considerable concern about being misunderstood; I am concerned that the substance of the presentation might be viewed as an "anti" position, rather than one which urges counterbalance and extends an invitation to both broaden and enrich the dialogue in our field. Most of what was said here has been suggested before by other scholars in other disciplines, with seemingly little impact. But in the context of this *Communication Yearbook*, it seemed that the position advanced here ought to be represented, with the hope that its fate might be better served than has been the case elsewhere.

NOTE

1. This article is the text of Budd's Presidential Address to the annual meeting of the International Communication Association, West Berlin, June 1977.

REFERENCES

ADELSON, M. Educational needs and innovational means. Santa Monica: Systems Development Corporation, 1966.

BERLO, D.K. *The process of communication*. New York: Holt, Rinehart and Winston, 1960.

BLUMER, H. *Symbolic interactionism*. Englewood Cliffs: Prentice-Hall, 1969.

BUDD, R.W. Human communication: A framework for the behavioral sciences. *Proceedings of the American Society of Information Science*, 1974.

BUDD, R.W., & RUBEN, B.D. *Mass communication and mass communication institutions: Dialogue and alternatives*. Rochelle Park, N.J.: Hayden, 1977.

CAMPBELL, J.H., & MICKELSON, J.S. Organic communication systems: speculations on the study, birth, life, and death of communication systems. In B.D. Ruben and J.Y. Kim (Eds.), *General systems and human communication*. Rochelle Park, N.J.: Hayden, 1975, 222-236.

KLAPPER, J.T. *The effects of mass communication*. New York: Free Press, 1960.

KNAPP, M.L. Whats wrong with elitism? Unpublished presidential address, International Communication Association, 1976.

KUHN, T.S. *The structure of scientific revolutions*. Chicago: University of Chicago Press, 1970.

LASSWELL, H.D. The structure and function of communication in society. In B. Lyman (Ed.), *The communication of ideas*. Institute for Religion and Ideas, 1948.

LIPPMANN, W. *Public opinion*. New York: Macmillan, 1922.

MacLEAN, M.S. JR. A process concept of communication education. Unpublished manuscript, University of Iowa School of Journalism, 1966.

NISBET, R. *Sociology as an art form*. London: Oxford University Press, 1976.

SCHRAMM, W. (Ed.) *The process and effects of mass communication*. Urbana: University of Illinois Press, 1955.

THAYER, L. On theory-building in communication: IV. Some observations and speculations. Unpublished manuscript, International Communication Association, 1968.

WEAVER, C. A history of the International Communication Association. In B.D. Ruben (Ed.), Communication yearbook. New Brunswick, N.J.: Transaction-International Communication Association, 1977.

WEBB, E.J., CAMPBELL, D.T., SCHWARTZ, R.D., & SECHREST, L. *Unobtrusive measures: Non-reactive research in the social sciences*. Chicago: Rand McNally, 1966.

RESEARCH METHODOLOGY IN COMMUNICATION: REVIEW AND COMMENTARY

JOSEPH N. CAPPELLA
University of Wisconsin–Madison

While most reviews of methodology and research in communication have not failed to recognize the importance of theory to guide research, such calls for "more theory" are useless and even misleading unless pragmatic direction can be offered to guide theory construction efforts. Formal modeling techniques are suggested as one set of logics useful to aid the construction of small theories. Since there are good reasons to view research methods as the servant of theory, then research design, measurement, and analysis should be treated within the perspective of the model or theory which makes it relevant. Accordingly several recent and continuing trends in theoretical approaches to communication are isolated and the more obvious methodological implications of each explored.

> *To paraphrase an old saying: Beware of the man of one method or one instrument either experimental or theoretical. He tends to become method oriented rather than problem oriented. The method oriented man is shackled; the problem oriented man is at least reaching freely toward what is most important.*
>
> —*Platt, 1964, p. 351*

Essays like this one should be read with a skeptical eye and with some a priori inoculation against persuasion. While the title suggests that what is being offered is a "review," and a "commentary," both commentary and review are strongly influenced by one's personal *gods* and *devils*. We, each of us, are tainted by the original sin of our research socialization and bombarded daily with the bad example of our mentors, heroes, and colleagues.

This essay will revolve around *god* and *devil* terms (as its predecessors have done). The satirical religious tone of my remarks is meant to portray the ideological and personal character of a review of this sort. Just as religions change to the demands of their social and historical contexts, so too must modes of inquiry. *Devil* terms, here, will in certain instances be the *god* terms of other reviewers of research methodology in other eras. The goal will be to promote those perspectives which are functional in the current historical and social milieu of research in human communication.

Toward this end, this essay will consider a four-stage genesis of the research act: (1) the reasons for undertaking a particular study, (2) issues relevant to the design of a given study, (3) issues surrounding the type of data gathered, and (4) procedures involved in the analysis of data.

THE SUPPORTING STRUCTURE OF THE RESEARCH ACT: *THE MORE THEORY DEVIL*

In almost every review of research in communication written in the last 15 years, the author has called for more, bigger, better, and brighter theories to undergird the particular act of research (Thayer, 1963; Miller, 1964; Clevenger, 1967; Clevenger, 1969; Smith, 1969; Nebergall, 1969; O'Keefe, 1975; McDermott, 1975). In fact, the 1968 New Orleans Conference on Research and Instructional Development adopted the explicit recommendation that developments in theory be encouraged:

> Recommendation 28: The conferees encourage speech-communication scholars to undertake a program of formally defining the outlines of speech-communication theories. (Kibler & Barker, 1969, p. 34)

Miller (1964), Clevenger (1969) and his critics

Nebergall (1969) and Smith (1969) unanimously assert that the quality, interpretability, impact, and systematization of knowledge accumulated through quantitative research would improve if that research were carried on within the confines of theory development. It is probably impossible to find a theme in contemporary communication research which is as acceptable to the spectrum of research practitioners as this one. Even when the researcher's own work falls squarely at the center of the "dust-bowl" empiricist category, that researcher usually believes (sometimes rightly) that his or her work is done in the interests of advancing theory. It would seem that the call for more theory is a call in vain unless there are explicit methods and strategies to guide the construction and not merely the post hoc evaluation of theory. Such methods and strategies are available under the headings of modeling techniques.

Although "More Theory" has been labeled as one of the *devil-terms* of communication research, there are several powerful arguments which favor it. First, there is the increasing recognition on the part of philosophers (Polanyi, 1964; Hanson, 1971) and scholars in communication (O'Keefe, 1975) that no observation, let alone research hypothesis, is free of the implicit theory carried by the observer to the situation. If observation was theory-free, then the aim of research could merely be the blind recording of as many positive facts as the energy of practitioners would permit. Observation of course does have a decision base; it is guided by hunch, hypothesis, and theory (Polanyi, 1964, p. 138). Since observation is implicitly guided by presupposition, the call for "more theory" can be seen as a call to make explicit those presuppositions before observation. O'Keefe (1975) notes that without a theory-based observation "the cumulativity of scientific knowledge at the level of data-sentences . . . is questioned" (p. 175). Without theory, there can be no cumulation of knowledge.

Second, there are an infinity of potential hypotheses which can be studied and investigated. No one would claim that the individual researcher makes capricious or random choices as to which relationships to investigate. Once again, the researcher has some hunches, perhaps an implicit theory, as to which relationships are expected to exhibit some regularity. The researcher commits him or herself to

hypotheses which are intellectually, aesthetically, or rationally compelling (Polanyi, 1964). The call for theory can be seen as a call to explicate these hunches and the compelling implicit forces which motivate the research undertaking.

Third, as research interests turn to more complex patterns of relationships among variables, statistical procedures of data reduction alone cannot reveal unique patterns of relationship. For example, with just five variables there are over a thousand different causal patterns (even ignoring reciprocal causation) which are possible (Blalock, 1964). Heise (1969) shows that several possible causal orderings of a set of variables can reproduce, equally well, an observed correlation matrix. Mulaik (1972) citing an article by Jones (1960) reports that factor analysis, aimed at reproducing the structure of a known chemical compound from observed data, failed to produce a structure even remotely related to the known structure. Birnbaum (1973) presents a counter example in which the blind use of correlation as an index of fit was successful (correlations greater than .95) in fitting an incorrect model to his artificial data. There is no methodology which can specify a unique pattern of relationships from data alone. What is required is an a priori specification of pattern and, hence, the calls for *more theory*.

Of course, there are many other reasons for recommending more theory and philosophers of science, historians of science, bad-mannered critics, and arrogant colleagues are armed to the teeth with this weaponry; theories are systematic, parsimonious, abstract, efficient, explanatory, heuristic, suggestive, and so on. But please do not misunderstand the flipancy of these remarks. The reasons behind the call for "more theory" are intellectually, philosophically, scientifically, and pragmatically sound. Such calls place before researchers goals toward which to aspire. Yet "more theory" is *a devil-term* of research. It is not inherently Mephistophelian but only subtly, indirectly, and perhaps unconsciously a bane to researchers and perhaps a bane to theorists as well. Samuel Becker (1967) made the point in strong terms:

> This preaching about the importance of deriving hypotheses from theory tends to have one of two unfortunate effects on our students. Either they become frustrated upon discovering that it cannot be

done or they are forced into slovenly thinking habits. (p. 71)

Nagel's (1961) classic reference *The Structure of Science* asserts that theories generally are a set of systematically connected relationships, usually relating unobservable to observable phenomena, and of greater generality and explanatory power than isolated laws. But more impressive and more formidable, the components of a theory in Nagel's eyes, consist in "an abstract set of postulates which implicitly define the basic terms of a theory, a model or interpretation of the postulates, and rules of correspondence for terms in the postulates or in the theorems derived from them" (p. 106). Diesing (1972) sets even more explicitly unattainable goals for the would-be theorist[1]: "A [theory] is not affected by any of its interpretations, but can be understood and studied in abstraction from all of them; one can work with a [theory] . . . without referring to anything empirical" (p. 31).

The conduct of theoretically grounded research is of the utmost importance. But in answer to questions asking "How is good theory to be devised?" we have turned to the philosophers and historians of science who have more to tell us about the post hoc evaluation of existing theory (an important set of evaluations indeed) than about strategies, gimmicks, and tools for the construction of theories. Tools in the form of modeling techniques are available to guide the generation of models and theories.

While the work of Nagel, Hanson, Polyani, Ziman, Kuhn, Oppenheim, Feyerabend, Popper, Hemple, Schutz, and many others provides a necessary perspective on an enterprise as complex and value-laden as communication inquiry, study of their writings has the uncanny knack of forging excellent critics and not original theorists.

By the standards for theory which Nagel and Diesing have put forward, few social scientific theories would survive scrutiny. Shannon & Weaver's (1963) work in information theory, Chomsky's (1957, 1965) work in formal theories of language competence, and Collins and Quillian's (1972) work in semantic networks, are examples. Each is formal, abstract, relevant to a general substantive question and yet permits manipulation of content independent of the substantive aspects of the theory. One hopes and strives for theoretical breakthroughs and developments of this magnitude, but we should neither expect them as the daily output of researchers and theorists nor hope to achieve the goal by calling upon others to attain them. To call for theory is to call for intuition, creativity, hard work and logical thinking of a magnitude comparable to that of Chomsky or Shannon or Weaver. One does not call for these values, one exhibits them. The call for theory is not misplaced, but the goals that such calls set for researchers and theorists are so elevated as to stymie and forestall action rather than encourage it. More limited goals, while upholding certain of the advantages of abstract theory, can direct and guide research based upon methods and procedures which are well-developed and which can be taught. Modeling techniques can fulfill these goals.

Models and Theories

The distinction between *model* and *theory* has never been particularly clear. For the purposes of this discussion take *theory* to be that definition provided by Nagel above. A *model*, like a theory, consists of a set of formally stated relationships among concepts but, in contrast to a theory, a model

is intrinsically about something in the real world, and one cannot make any changes in the [model] without referring to the real world to see whether the change is allowable. (Diesing, 1972, p. 31)[2]

Of course, models are usually the precursors to theories since it is "quite difficult to state fully and with precision the abstract postulates, freed of all interpretations, that are embedded in a theory" (Nagel, 1961, p. 107). As the model has the interpretations of multiple situations attached to it, the generalized relationships which are common across the situations become more divorced from their particularized interpretations and, hence, more theoretical. Models, then, focus upon more limited problems than theories, perhaps studying even a single, particular system rather than an entire class of systems. For example, one might model mutual influence processes in two-person informal discussions rather than attitude change in general. Ashby (1963) has noted that any attempt to construct a machine which represents some reality will fall short and be but a *homomorph* or partial representation of that reality. Knowledge gained in this way can be both partial and accurate (Ashby, 1963, p. 104). To require modeling efforts to remain close to specific substantive concerns does not necessarily trivialize them nor introduce fundamental inaccuracies.

But a focus upon more particularized substantive considerations is only a part of the advantage of what Diesing (1972) calls formal models. Formal models are distinguished from *descriptive, explicative,* and *purely pragmatic* models (Hawes, 1975; Kaplan, 1964) on the grounds that they employ a pre-existing logic or calculus of operations whose implications have already been worked through. Meehan (1968) offers a succinct description of the general characteristics of formal models (which he calls systems):

> A system consists of a set of variables . . . and a set of rules that define interactions among those variables . . . any change in the value of one of the variables in the set can be accounted for *completely* in terms of changes in the values of the other variables. The entailment of the system . . . can be any outcome of the interaction of the variables. (p. 50)

The emphasis of Meehan's general discussion is clear: the formal model (or system) generates expectations from variables, rules of association, and the calculus of entailments. The complete set of entailments constitutes the deductions of the model which must be interpreted in terms of available evidence.

The mathematical theory of *Markov Chains* would be such a calculus (Hewes, 1975; Coleman, 1964; Kemeny & Snell, 1960). Verbal models have great difficulty in specifying a clear and complete set of postulates which unambiguously distinguish the status of definitions, tautologies, and substantive propositions (Diesing, 1972). In relying on a preexistent calculus, formal models can more readily work through the dynamics and implications of the postulates, can determine the directions of movement of the system, and can foresee the changes necessary to alter those movements (Diesing, 1972). Thus, it is expected that the use of formal modeling procedures would produce results which are not immediately obvious based upon the specified relationships alone,[3] and would clarify the implications which do and do not follow from existing postulates, definitions, and relationships (see, for example, Harris [1976] for some startling examples).

Most importantly though, the call for a new *god* in formal modeling efforts is a call for "small theories" based upon techniques which are available and are being employed throughout the various social sciences. This call attempts to set forth approachable goals and suggests that the techniques necessary for achieving those goals are teachable and are being taught, are usable and are being used. These techniques fall into four major categories: (1) verbal logics, (2) pictorial logics, (3) mathematical logics, and (4) algorithmic logics.

Verbal Logics

Verbal logic is closer to ordinary syllogistic reasoning than any of the four types. Its simplest and least interesting form as a formal logic was first discussed by Zetterberg (1963). More recently, Bailey (1970) reacted to Costner and Leik's (1964) criticisms of this formal deductive process by distinguishing *synthetic deductive* from *explanatory deductive* systems. The former employs postulates which are empirically tested and testable. The latter relies on the theorems deduced from the untested explanatory postulates for its validation. Berger and Calabrese (1975) showed that explanatory deductive approaches to the formal modeling of acquaintance formation processes could be used advantageously.

Pictorial Logics

Pictorial logics are derived from the recent emphasis in sociology on path analysis (Duncan, 1975). While path analysis has primarily been used as a set of parameter estimation procedures, its pictorial format can be profitably mined to yield insights into the logical consistency of the model behind the path diagram *before* it is tested.[4] The first significant attempt to use path diagrams as a formal modeling technique can be attributed to Blalock (1969). In addition, work by Fisher and Ando (1969), Land (1975), Bonacich and Bailey (1971), and Heise (1976) has focused on the value of path analysis in exploring the logical character of models before exploring their empirical validity. While path models have been tested in the published literature in communication (Salteil & Woelfel, 1975; Fink and Noell, 1975; Florence, 1975; no published work has used path diagrams to explore a model's dynamics, stability, and likely direct and indirect effects).

Mathematical Logics

Mathematical logics are considerably more general, more powerful, more diverse, and more difficult to learn than either pictorial or verbal logics. The payoff may be greater, although the investment will certainly be dear. There are two general subclasses of mathematical logics: *dynamic* and *nondynamic*. *Nondynamic mathematical* logics include *graph theory, group theory*, and certain *algebras*. *Dynamic logics* can be further subdivided into *stochastic processes (Markov chains, Markov processes, Poisson processes,* etc.) and *deterministic processes (linear* and *nonlinear systems)*. Graph theory (Harary, Norman, & Cartwright, 1965) has been employed in the study of communication networks (Flament, 1963; White, Boorman, & Breiger, 1976), sociometric structure (Davis, 1970; Hallinan, 1974), and balance theory approaches to attitude change (Feather, 1971). Group theory has seen limited application, although Boorman & White (1976) used its properties to reduce the complex structure of communication networks with multiple relations to simpler ones. None of the published work from the field of communication has yet employed these techniques.

On the other hand, dynamic mathematical models have had a longer and richer history in the social sciences than their non-dynamic counterparts. Ashby's (1963) *Introduction to Cybernetics* provides the best introduction to the mathematics of stochastic and deterministic linear systems with Coleman (1964) and Fararo (1973) offering more extended discussions. Substantive applications of these techniques are extensive. Reviews by Abelson (1967) and by Rapoport (1963) are general enough to show what has been done and what can be done with mathematical logics. Work within the communication field has recently shown an unexpected maturity in the use of dynamic models. In the small group area, work by Scheidel and Crowell (1964), Hawes and Foley (1973), and Ellis and Fisher (1975) has focused on the conditional probabilities that communicative actions will follow other communicative actions. Group structure and its evolution may be studied using stochastic sequences. With only small modification these efforts can take fuller advantage of the power of stochastic processes. Hewes (in press) has modeled the attitude-behavior relationship using stochastic modelling techniques. On the deterministic side Hunter, Levine, and Sayres (1976) have modeled hierarchical attitude change and successfully explained many common results such as the *sleeper effect* without appealing to extramodel fudge factors. Capella (1976) has modeled two-person mutual influence processes under different assumptions about interaction style showing how style can control outcome under certain conditions. The use of mathematical techniques, while requiring some sophistication in application, are growing both outside and within the field.

Algorithmic Logics

Finally algorithmic logics are primarily associated with computer simulation approaches. When mathematical logics fail as useful formats for modeling certain substantive areas either because of excessive complexity or because there can be no in-principle solutions to the matchmatical postulates, then simulation becomes the most likely alternative. While there has been much work employing simulation strategies (see Abelson [1968], for a review) in sociology (McPhee, 1963; Abelson & Bernstein, 1961), in social psychology (Abelson, 1973), and, most interestingly, in linguistics and artificial intelligence (Winograd, 1972; Woods, 1970, 1973), the strategy has been almost totally ignored within the communication field (see Lashbrook and Sullivan [1973], for an exception).

While algorithmic logics have the same advantages as all formal models, they have the added benefit of permitting a more realistic degree of complexity than mathematical logics and offering logics not available in mathematical systems (e.g., flexible list and symbol manipulation as found in the LISP language). By the same token, the complexity of simulations makes them difficult to validate, difficult to alter when unacceptable outcomes result, and difficult to completely analyze, since the set of initial conditions and parameter values may be extremely large. Nonetheless, the excitement generated by Winograd's (1972) simulation[5] of a natural language processor highlights the potential of this modeling technique over the other types.

Each of these four techniques above can—depending upon the particular substantive problem—meet the call for increased efforts at formal modeling. In the past, social scientists have not hesitated to require years of training in the complexities of various statistical and measurement procedures, and yet have avoided training researchers in the various logics for modeling. If statistical techniques are only the servants of model and theory anyway, then to bypass logical systems which may aid in the development of models and theory is an illogical inversion of the research enterprise. The skeptical reader may rightly argue that the call for increased training in formal modeling techniques will not guarantee more research in the service of theoretical aims. While training in formal modeling is certainly not sufficient to the modeling goals, there is no question that such training is a necessary condition.

THE PERVASIVE "LAW OF THE HAMMER" IN COMMUNICATION RESEARCH

Thus far the role modeling efforts should play in providing context for the research enterprise has been emphasized. In giving primacy to the more abstract concerns of theory and modeling method, the reader might be left with the inaccurate impression that the "details" of research—design, measurement, and data analysis—are in a healthier state than theoretical activities. In fact, as Bochner (1974) points out, reviewers of the small group literature both within and outside the field of communication are unanimous in condemning the absence of theory and theory-directed research, and consistently maintain that methodological ques-

tions and shortcomings are inconsequential contributors to the problems and inadequacies of small group communication.

After reviewing eight studies on small group processes, Bochner concluded that they "do not substantiate the claims that small group research is methodologically rigorous and sophisticated" (p. 178). As Bochner rightfully notes the point is not that theory must have precedence over research—or research over theory—but that a systematic emphasis on one or the other can lead to deleterious effects on both.

Certainly recent criticisms of research efforts within the field (Cronkhite & Liska, 1976; Chase & Tucker, 1975; Katzer & Stodt, 1973) more generally support the notions Bochner derived from a limited review of the small group research. Beyond our own disciplinary boundaries, Fishbein and Ajzen's (1975) reanalysis of the attitude-behavior problem depends in significant ways on purely methodological considerations. Jacob's (1975) summary of research on family interaction patterns points out so many methodological inadequacies as to render significant portions of this data base unuseable.

The design and analysis choices that most researchers make in the conduct of their studies can be summarized in a well-known social scientific law, the "law of the hammer." When the researcher (like the young child) is given a new tool, be it factor analysis, or ethnomethodology, or path analysis he or she finds that every research question needs to be "factor analyzed," or "ethnomethodologized," or "path analyzed." While these statements need not be proved to be the avid journal reader, the statistics and authoritative opinions are nonetheless surprising in their unanimity.

The *Journal of Personality and Social Psychology* published 56 percent experimental studies in 1961 and 87 percent experimental in 1974 (Helmrich, 1975). The preeminence of *ANOVA* statistics with experimental design goes without saying. Certainly the "hammer" for American social psychologists is the *orthogonal design* along with its *ANOVA* counterpart. Helmrich (1975) points out that this emphasis is only slightly less true of the journals in social psychology (e.g., *The Journal of Applied Social Psychology*). Sociologists seem no less immune to the law of the hammer. In his 1975 presidential address to the American Sociological Association, Lewis Coser roundly and bitterly criticized his colleagues for permitting methodological developments to dictate problem orientations. Both extremes of the methodological spectrum come under fire: path analysts and ethnomethodologists (stranger bedfellows would be difficult to find). Coser concludes: "In both cases . . . preoccupation with method largely has led to neglect of significance and substance" (p. 698). While research in communication tends to be more eclectic and, hence, less susceptible to methodological monism, there can be little doubt that the same social and psychological forces driving other social scientists toward methodological fetishes also drive various enclaves and cliques within our own discipline toward increasingly fervent devotion to a given methodological stance.

The upshot of all this preaching about the domination of methods in social scientific inquiry is of course to insist upon a 180 degree shift. As Bierstedt (1974) puts it, we can no longer permit the methodological tail to wag the substantive dog. Rather, prominence must first be given to substantive concerns, which will in turn determine the most appropriate methodological tools. To the extent that methodology is determined by substantive theories and models, then the review of research methodologies in communication must be carried out within the confines of the prevailing theories and models which currently capture the imaginations of communication researchers.

CURRENT PERSPECTIVES ON THE COMMUNICATION PROCESS

To adequately assess the methodological armamentarium of researchers necessitates knowing the theories and models which these methodologies must validate or falsify. Certainly no set of theories or models currently grasps the research imagination of even a plurality of the disciples of human communication. There is no paradigm or even battle of paradigms; and this is as it should be for a field whose oldest scholars are still in their prime. Yet, it is difficult to miss the developing consensus, the controversial viewpoint, and

the general *god terms* of which paradigms are made. Considered here are, first, a view of potential constituents of theory and, second, the methodological implications which these potential constituents will demand of research design, measurement, and analysis.

In 1961, Johnson and Klare (1961) reviewed the models of communication research which dominated the previous decade. The models of this era were closely allied with and dominated by Shannon and Weaver's views of communication. Each tended to focus upon one-way information flows—except Westley and Maclean (1955)—and to be constituted of the basic five elements *Who?, Says what?, To whom?, In what channel?* and *With what effects?* which Lasswell (1948) made famous. With these models as mind sets and an historical interest in the art of persuasion, it is little wonder that so much of the research in communication has been oriented toward the influence of passive audiences. By the same token, research methods in the context of these questions can be relatively straight forward.

It is not difficult to imagine the impact that Berlo's (1960) initial introduction of *process* into communication flows had upon the prevailing one-way conceptions. *Process* has remained a prominent *god-term* of the field from Berlo's introduction until now (Miller, 1966; Krippendorff, 1970; Clevenger & Matthews, 1971; Smith, 1972; Hewes, 1975). But the term has different meanings. For some (Clevenger & Matthews, 1971; Hewes, 1975; Krippendorff, 1970) *process* suggests the time-dependent and sequential character of communicative interchanges. For Smith (1972) and Berlo (1960), on the other hand, process entails viewing events and relationships as ever-changing, without beginnings, ends, or any fixed sequence of events, and with all factors affecting one another (Berlo, 1960; Smith, 1972). Each of these views has profound methodological implications on the design of research and the types of statistical analyses required.

One of the descendants of the *god of process* is the interaction sequence. If indeed communication is processual (according to the Berlo and Smith views), then, in informal interaction, sequences of communicative acts should occur over time and these acts should mutually influence one another. Recognition of the importance of interaction sequences can be found in the research of Scheidel and Crowell, (1964), Stech (1970, 1975), Gouran and Baird (1972), Ellis and Fisher (1975), and Hawes and Foley (1973), among others. Discussions of the issue at a more theoretical level by Krippendorff (1970), Fisher and Hawes (1971), and Hawes (1973) have maintained: (1) that certain data sets—aggregational data—cannot provide information on elementary communication processes; (2) that interaction sequences be embedded in systems models; (3) that the contiguous pair of acts, the interact, be the fundamental unit of analysis; and (4) that sequences of observable interactions form the basis of an individual's phenomenal reality. The methodology which thorough analysis of interaction sequences requires is only beginning to be recognized (Hewes, 1975; Hewes & Evans-Hewes, 1975).

Behind the concept of *process* that Berlo, Smith, and to a certain extent, Miller have offered lies the fundamental presumption that communication phenomena are incredibly complex and, at heart, indeterminate. Smith (1972) makes quite clear that his view of process would require dismissal of the determinism of a Newtonian mechanics and the causality of a behavioristic psychology. Two recent trends within the field can be seen as substantive reactions to the presumed indeterminacy and complexity of communication phenomenon. They are the *rules perspective* (Cushman & Whiting, 1972; Mischel, 1969) and *situationism* (Delia et al., 1975; Pervin, 1976).

The rules perspective has a rich history in linguistics (Chomsky, 1957; 1965) and in the philosophy of language (Austin, 1962; Searle, 1969). However, in a pivotal article, Toulmin (1969) argued that *rules* rather than *laws* undergird social processes, especially those involving language. The chief difference centered on the violability of rules by actors (and the concomitant sanctions which might be incurred) versus the inviolate character of law governed processes. Toulmin's arguments served as the cornerstone for Cushman and Whiting's views as well as the views of Harré and Secord (1972). To say that various offspring of the rules perspective have infatuated communication researchers and

other social scientists would be an understatement. In the area of language and communication competence work by Sanders (1973), Nofsinger (1975, 1976) and Frentz and Farrell (1976) mark significant substantive contributions. In interpersonal and small group processes, Cushman and Craig (1976) and Pearce (1976) have offered general perspectives centering around *rules*. Outside the boundaries of our own literature, anthropologists and sociologists (Labov, 1972; Sacks, Schegloff, & Jefferson, 1974; Garfinkel, 1972), and philosophers of language (Grice, 1968; Searle, 1969) have all significantly forwarded research in the rules perspective. If the rules perspective is to develop and flourish, certain methodological alterations at the level of design, measurement, and analysis will need to occur. These will be considered subsequently.

One of the complexities that the process orientation promises has been realized in a recent rash of work on situational factors in language, (Rommetveit, 1974; Carswell & Rommetveit, 1971), small groups (Bochner, 1974; Hackman & Morris, 1975), attitude change (Delia et al., 1975; Siebold, 1975; McDermott, 1974; Cappella & Folger, 1976), and personality (Mischel, 1968; Endler & Magnusson, 1976a; Endler & Magnusson, 1976b; Hewes et al., 1976; Hewes et al., 1977). Situational factors seem to act as catalysts or attentuators so that relationships hypothesized and validated in one context are modified or perhaps reversed in other contexts. Thus complexities are introduced in the form of situational contingencies. For example, personality traits can no longer be expected to predict communication behaviors (R^2 less than .10) unless situational factors are accounted for. Methodologically, the simple expedient of controlling the situation (that is, using a single situation) will not do. If the generalizability of results from one context to other contexts is continually challenged, then the common expedient of control must be replaced. However, simple manipulation of *situation A* versus *situation B* without some theoretical basis for choice of situations, can only add to knowledge of the question *Do situations make a difference?* and not to the question *How do situations make a difference?* This latter question requires a typology, category scheme, or continuum which can order situations, such as tasks in small group research, and permit systematic study of *how*.

This section has aimed at providing a broad overview of prevailing perspectives on communication which are likely to have impact upon developing communication models and theories. The purpose is not to outline and direct modeling efforts but is rather to assess methodological tools in terms of their ability to realize the goals of substantive perspectives. With an eye turned to the trends outlined in this section, let us turn specifically to the question of methodology in the categories of research design, measurement, and analysis.

DESIGN, MEASUREMENT, AND ANALYSIS IMPLICATIONS OF THEORY TRENDS

"Communication phenomena must be conceived as time-dependent processes"

If the time-dependent character of communication processes is to be upheld, then the common use of one-shot experimental, nonexperimental, and survey designs and their concomitant data analysis procedures cannot be expected to provide *process* data (in the sense suggested by Krippendorff, 1970). In an excellent introduction to the design of time series studies, Glass, Willson, and Gottman (1975) criticize experimental designs in the Fisherian tradition. These designs were constructed to deal with crop yields under various conditions. The planting and harvesting seasons not only have definite beginnings and ends but rates and patterns of growth and failure are essentially inconsequential to questions of crop yield. Such is not the case with most social and behavioral processes, as both Berlo (1960) and Smith (1972) are quick to point out. Points of origination and termination are difficult to determine, and gross, cumulative effects are seldom of interest apart from the pattern of effects in which they are embedded.

To circumvent these problems, Glass et al. suggest the time-series design. Time series designs necessitate multiple observation of the units under study. Embedded in the sequence of observations would be one or more experimenter-induced interventions (the planned time-series experiment) or measurements on other naturally occurring poten-

tial causal factors (concomitant variation replicated over time), or the occurrance of consciously induced social changes (*study of the effects of social reforms*). Time series studies have the advantage over one-shot designs for analyzing process because: (1) time-series base line can be established from the multiple observations before the intervention and (2) the type of effect (Glass et al., 1975, p. 44) can be determined from the multiple observations after the intervention. In place of an arbitrary beginning and end point in one-shot experiments, the time-series experiment bounds interventions with *pre-* and *post-* baselines. Not only are simple between-treatment differences sought, but the form of the intervention effect is sought in the decay pattern of the post-intervention observations. One-shot experimental and nonexperimental studies would not necessarily be replaced but their format would be changed significantly from what we now know.

Whereas the overall context of experimental and nonexperimental research remains intact in their time-series counterparts so that many of the prior skills transfer, there are some definitive changes which accompany time-series designs. First, studies are simply more difficult to carry out logistically when multiple observations and, perhaps, multiple interventions are required. For example, subject mortality and subject fatigue become more significant considerations (Crider, Willits, & Bealer, 1973).

Second, test re-test sensitization may significantly affect a time-series baseline when a series of observations is obtained. The degree of such sensitization depends, of course, upon the type of data being gathered. When the type of data to be studied is shrouded from the subject's conscious control (for example, sound-silence patterns in informal conversations, nonobvious content coding across time in group studies, physiological responses to media programming, and so on), then limitations on the number of observations due to test sensitization is not appreciable. However, when measures are not easily masked from subject's control, recall, and constructive memory (for example, attitudinal responses, perceptions of the other, satisfaction and attraction, and so on), then other precautions are necessary. For example, an *independent* measurement-sensitization study might be undertaken to determine how much sensitization various tests are introducing (Wiley & Wiley, 1970, 1974). If sensitization is great, then the number of observation times may need to be reduced or other less desirable designs (Caporaso & Ross, 1973) using comparable groups at different stages of development may be required.

Third, since time-series designs often generate a great deal of data about a single observational unit (for example, Jaffee & Feldstein, 1970), inferences to individual units—rather than groups of units—as is more common in the analysis of variance, become possible. Since variance explained can be computed in N-of-one time-series studies, under certain conditions (Hewes and Evans-Hewes, 1975), we can then ask if explaining 50 percent of the variance in an individual's behavior is more or less inspiring than explaining the same variance in the behavior of a group of individuals. There is no obvious statistical answer to this question.

Fourth, the set of observations cannot be made at the whim of the observer since the timing of observations can significantly alter the substantive conclusions drawn (see for example the controversy between Hayes, Meltzer, & Wolf, 1970 and Jaffe & Feldstein, 1970). Arundale (1976) has written a thoughtful paper on this issue in the area of sound and silence patterns which raises many of the relevant issues for any time-series study. Pelz and Law (1970) simulated a two-variable time-series study under different degrees of violation of the correct time lags. Even small deviations from the correct time lags produced remarkably inaccurate inferences for positive and negative feedback situations.

Fifth, the conduct of time-series studies often involves fitting the predictions of some particular class of time-series models, such as Markov Chains, to the observed data. "Good" results in this case become finding no difference between the predictions of the model and the observed results.[6] Thus the time-series researcher is faced with advocating a null hypothesis with all of the attendant biases against its acceptance (Greenwald, 1975)[7] Advocating the *null* should not be difficult in this setting as long as the researcher has guarded against charges of low power (Cohen, 1969, especially Chapter 7; Katzer & Sodt, 1973; Chase & Tucker,

1975) which generally indicate that the probability of accepting the *null*, when it is false, is high.

Finally, and most importantly, data analysis procedures in time-series studies require techniques currently uncommon in most of the social sciences and certainly in communication studies. To summarize the substance of these procedures is not possible here. The reader is asked to consult Glass, Willson, and Gottman (1975) for time-series in experimental settings, Hewes (1975) for an introduction to Markov Chains, and Coleman (1964) and Fararo (1973) for other cases of stochastic models, and Hibbs (1974) for the analysis of deterministic time-series. The most significant juncture separating time-series studies from one-shot studies, at the level of analysis, is dependence among observations rather than the expected independence of observations. One-shot studies employing ANOVA or regression-type analysis assume that errors are independent of one another and recautions are taken at the design stage to insure this independence. Time-series studies, on the other hand, not only permit dependence among observations, but in fact actively recognize the natural dependence among consequent and subsequent social acts, and seek to handle that dependence at the statistical level rather than designing it away at the inception of a study. The procedures for handling dependence in observations are multiple, but one common technique is known to attitude change researchers. In obtaining pre- and postmeasures of attitudes, a dependence is introduced which must be removed. Taking different scores accomplishes this independence.[8] With multiple observations the differencing procedures are often much fancier but the principle remains.

If, then, one wishes to conduct research which meets the call for communication as a time-dependent process, the enterprise cannot merely adapt the prevailing tools of the field to the task. Other tools, which are neither inherently more powerful, more flexible, more elegant, or more persuasive, but simply more appropriate, need to be applied.

"Communication must be studied as an ever-changing, unbounded, unsequenced, and totally interdependent process"

This view of process espoused by Berlo (1960)

and Smith (1972) has one simple methodological implication. No methodologies exist (or are likely to exist) which can meet the demands of such a conception. Every methodological tool, whether one as quantitative as path analysis (Duncan, 1975) or one as qualitative as participant observation (Diesing, 1972), carries a set of assumptions or restrictions which limit its applicability. The restrictions inevitably require simplifications of the reality to be studied and inquired about. The conception of *process* cited above offers no substantive simplifications, only the agnostic's maze-without-end. The most extreme interpretation of this *process view* would have us conceive of communication as essentially structureless in any scientific sense.[9]

It is likely that such an interpretation, despite the language, was not intended by Berlo or Smith. Rather, the attempt was to represent the extent of the complexity of communication processes. Few would disagree with this assessment, even mechanists like Ashby (1963). But even accepting the insistence on complexity does not permit the methodological license which Smith (1972) suggests:

> Correlational designs become desirable as a means of suggesting relationships. Factor analysis becomes particularly useful for the development of patterns and categories. Research without hypotheses becomes sensible. (p. 179)

Such a view implicitly accepts the maxim that more complex research methodology alone can generate structure from data. Helmreich (1975) has recently implied a similar conclusion.

No maxim could be more misleading or detrimental to the scientific study of communication. Complex structures will never simply be revealed by employing complex data reduction techniques. Coser (1975), Duncan (1975), and Heise (1969) have argued this point with respect to path analysis. Mulaik (1972) and Jones (1960) have made the argument with respect to factor analysis, and Einhorn (1972) has raised the interpretation issue with respect to more complex correlational analysis. The implication is *not* that exploratory analyses are anathema, nor that data snooping cannot reveal potentially interesting relationships. Rather, data-snooping carried out in response to the motive of curiosity must be clearly separated from data-snooping carried out as a response to a driving theoretical concern—*process*. The methodological implications of such a concern, as described by Smith, are incompatible with current knowledge about what is required to squeeze meaningful, consistent, and coherent results from complex data reduction procedures.

The concern with process as complexity does not grant rights to whimsical searches, hoping categories and structures will magically appear. Quite the contrary. Because there are frequently many possible structures which could satisfy a given set of observations, complexity requires even greater attention to potential a priori structures and relationships.

"Communication processes must be studied as interaction sequences"

There are at least two important aspects of this position which determine its methodological implications. First, an interest in sequential interaction requires gathering data over a time period, but does not require the analysis of these data as if they were time-series data. For example, the distribution of acts summarized over all time periods may be the object of analysis, or the structure of a single total-time transition matrix may be analyzed. The studies on interaction sequences referenced earlier by Hewes and Foley (1973), and Scheidel and Crowell (1964) fall into this category. Data is gathered over time but is aggregated for the purposes of structural rather than time-series analyses. Such approaches have many of logistic difficulties of gathering sequential data, but draw upon little of the analytical power of time-series models. On the other hand, a few studies, Hewes and Evans-Hewes (1975), Scheidel (1974), and Cappella (1976), have employed time series designs to analyze the patterns of interaction over time. While these studies represent only small efforts[10] at treating the complex issues in the sequencing of communicative acts, the trend is an important one because it links process concerns with interaction sequences.

Second, interaction sequences may be studied for the patterning of the acts themselves or for the inferences to individual or dyadic characteristics which the act patterns represent. A good deal of recent work by Mark (1971), Ericson and Rogers (1973), Folger and Puck (1976), Rogers and Farace (1975), and Millar and Rogers (1976) has been concerned with coding message exchange patterns and making inferences to control aspects of relationships (Watzlawick, Beavin, & Jackson, 1967). Whenever researchers seek to make extrapolations from objectively coded interaction patterns to phenomenological variables such as relational satisfaction, attraction, personality perceptions, and so on, the question arises as to whether the inferences drawn by the researcher are at all related to the implicit inferences drawn by the participants (Hawes, 1973; Grossberg & O'Keefe, 1975; Hawes 1975). This is a validity question and two ingenious methods of handling this matter have been recently employed.

Hawes (1975) reports that he was successful in using a stimulated recall procedure to have subjects generate their own category system from observation of their own interaction. The advantages of such a procedure are significant when a strong link between interaction sequences and the perceptions of the participants is specified as in the research on relational control. On the other hand Hawes' techniques add significantly to the already burdensome effort required in coding interaction. In addition, the experimenter must exhibit considerable care in order that subtle influences over the structure of coding system are not generated by the researcher or by persuasive participants over the long periods of contact which are obviously required.

A somewhat more risky but more efficient procedure for validating content categories was employed by Sarah Puck in a portion of her dissertation research. Statements were first coded as bids for dominance or submission and affection or hostility using the Folger and Puck (1976) scheme. A set of statements which filled out the Folger and Puck categories were selected, paired, and given to subjects to rate on the degree of similarity and dissimilarity the statements implied about the relationships between conversants. A multidimensional scaling procedure revealed that the raters' perceptions of the example questions largely agreed with the positioning of the questions in the two-dimensional space predicted a priori by the coding scheme. Of special importance is that the MDS procedure is not

as susceptible to labeling biases found in factoring procedures, because similarities between paired comparisons rather than content-specific ratings constitute the data base. While the validation could have failed (and, hence, was riskier than Hawes' procedures), its success bodes well for the inferences drawn from the resulting various Folger and Puck categories.

To the extend that the study of interaction sequences is unconcerned with inferences to interaction outcomes, then the validation of coding schemes in terms of the perceptions of the participants is not a significant matter. However, such inferences should be the goal of researchers in small group and interpersonal processes, and, hence, the validation of interaction categories an important concern.

"Communication must be studied as a system of constitutive and regulative rules"

There is no generally accepted view of how rules should be studied and developed either within or outside the field. However, the current modes of study of rules can be classified as either *descriptive* or *generative* analyses of either *constitutive* or *regulative* rules. *Descriptive analyses* are just that, descriptions, (1) of what an act counts as, means, or is interpreted as in certain social contexts—constitutive—such as a ritual insult (Labov, 1972); or (2) of how an act governs the acts which follow it— regulative—such as getting the floor (Nofsinger, 1975). *Generative analyses* are less *descriptive* and more *explanatory*. They search for the social and individual generative mechanisms (Cushman & Pearce, 1977) which make possible the various constitutive and regulative rule *systems*. The ultimate exemplar of generative rules systems remains Chomsky's generative grammar, a regulative rule system. Duncan (1973) has attempted to formalize the regulation of turns in informal conversation, and Grice (1968) the interpretation of apparent nonsequiturs in conversation.

While it is difficult to speculate about the methodological implications of a perspective as much in flux as the rules area, two indications are clear. First, partly because of the research socialization of many communication scholars, the number and variety of descriptive studies (Donahue & Laufersweiler, 1976; Philipsen, 1976) will grow. The design of these studies is at odds with the prevailing experimental and nonexperimental designs, and will probably take two different methodological directions which can be termed the anthropological case study and the linguistic case study. In an anthropological case study one or more groups is observed at length within its own cultural or social setting. The goal of such observational studies is to develop *constitutive* and *regulative* *rules* particular to the cultural or social grouping under study and to compare rules among various cultural and social units. Labov and Philipsen's work exemplify this approach. Contrary to the statements of some ethnomethodologists (Mehan & Wood, 1975, p. 3), the observational study is a principled method of research (Diesing, 1972, Chapters 10, 11, and 13) with a rich history in both anthropology and clinical psychology. It should not be forced outside the boundaries of scientific inquiry simply because it fails to carry the trappings of mathematics associated with the harder sciences. On the other hand, neither should the observational study be adopted simply for reasons of inadequate experimental and nonexperimental research training. Rather its adoption must be prompted by theoretical and substantive concerns which find prevailing designs inadequate to the task. The linguistic case study is distinguished from the anthropological in that a small class of linguistic examples is analyzed to determine the principles which undergird the set. Searle (1969) has done this with *promising*, and Nofsinger (1976) with indirect answers. Contrary to the anthropological case study, in which claims are carefully qualified by the cultural and social setting, the linguistic case study seeks to make large claims from a small set of observations. The principles behind such analyses are fundamentally at odds with sampling and inference procedures of normal experimental techniques. It seems clear that: (1) case study designs are in wide use in other areas to study phenomena which could be unequivocally classified as communication rules, and (2) there is some advantage in pursuing the same question with multiple methodologies (where feasible) so that substantive conclusions are not determined by the artifacts of a single dominant

methodology. Constitutive and regulative rules will be studied using linguistic and anthropological case studies. The principles behind such methods must be explicated with the same clarity as the principles behind experimental designs so that the biases introduced by these methods may be understood and expected a priori.

The second general indication in the study of rules is that the formalization of sequencing rules, such as for speaking turns, can benefit from the logical calculus of stochastic models. In a working paper, Hewes (1976b) has explored some of the relationships between stochastic models and rules which regulate social interaction sequences. Stochastic models, of course, imply time-series observations and the time-series experiments discussed earlier. However, as Hewes is careful to point out, most rules theories offer a prominent place to the individual's subjective choice and stochastic models provide no obvious mechanism for incorporating decision-making operations in initiating certain rule sequences. Thus, stochastic processes seem an obvious candidate for modeling and testing rules as regularities (e.g., Duncan, 1973) but are a less obvious candidate for treating *rules* as *actions* involving *choice*.

CONCLUSION

To review research methodology in communication comprehensively would produce a small library. To review it briefly could produce a triviality. Volume II of *The Handbook of Social Psychology*, several articles in *The Annual Review of Psychology*, and the *Sociological Methodology* series are suited to the details of training researchers. No matter how well-trained the researcher, however, two patterns tend to emerge: (1) researchers are little trained in the methods of model construction and (2) researchers obey the "law of the hammer." This essay has tried to argue that model building techniques are as significant a tool in the researcher's repertoire as any statistical techniques. Further, it has been suggested that research methods must be geared to and subservient to the theoretical perspective which they hope to validate or invalidate. The "law of the hammer" will simply not do.

NOTES

1. Diesing (1972) makes no strict distinction between *theory* and *model* and, in fact, advises his readers to substitute "*model* for *theory* and *theory* for *model* in the following pages" (p. 31) if the reader prefers. I have done so to make the discussion coherent.
2. See footnote 1.
3. Ordinary *syllogistic reasoning* usually offers little information that is not already available in the premises. The deductions are often trivial in terms of generating new insights.
4. The *potential* power of pictorial logics should not be missed. Systems science (see for example Caswell, Koenig, Resh, and Ross, 1974) in general, and linear systems theory, in particular (Wiberg, 1971, Chapter 2), have rather completely developed pictorial representations for complex systems.
5. *Cognitive Psychology Monographs* for the first time in its history devoted an entire issue to reporting Winograd's (1972) work.
6. This is especially true of *stochastic models* which employ frequency data but less true of time series models in the regression and path analysis traditions (see Hibbs, 1974, for a review). These latter models are generally concerned first with estimating parameters and then with *chi-squared measures* of fit when there is overidentifying information (Wiley, 1973).
7. The *null hypothesis* in this case is not one which maintains there is no relationship between variables, but rather one maintaining that there is a strong relationship between *observed* and *expected*. It happens that the significance testing procedure has the same form in these different cases.
8. This technique does not undergird all *time-series methods*, but is especially common when the data are *nonstationary*. For example *Markov Chain* models require transition probabilities to be constant over time units (i.e., stationary) so that certain simplicities can be achieved.
9. It does not matter if the scientific sense is that of Newtonian and LaPlacian mechanism or a quantum relativistic "mechanism of indeterminacy" in which the extent of indeterminacy is specified.
10. More significant programs of research outside the field can be found in the work of Jaffee and Feldstein (1970), Mayhew and Levinger (1976), and Mayhew, Gray, and Mayhew (1971).

REFERENCES

ABELSON, R.P. The structure of belief systems. In R.C. Schank and R.M. Colby (Eds.), *Computer models of thought and language*. San Francisco: Freeman, 1973.

ABELSON, R.P. Simulation of social behavior. In G. Lindzey and E. Aronson (Eds.), *The handbook of social psychology*, Vol. 2. Second Edition. Reading, Mass.: Addison-Wesley, 1968.

ABELSON, R.P. The structure of belief systems. In R.C. Schank and R.M. Colby (Eds.), *Computer models of thought and language*. San Francisco: Freeman, 1973.

ABELSON, R.P., & BERNSTEIN, A. A computer simulation of community referendum controversies. *Public Opinion Quarterly*, 1961, 27, 93-122.

ARUNDALE, R. Sampling intervals and the study of change over time in communication. Paper presented at the annual meeting of the International Communication Association, Portland, 1976.

ASHBY, W.R. *An introduction to cybernetics*. New York: Science Editions (Wiley), 1963.

AUSTIN, J.L. *How to do things with words*. Cambridge, Mass.: Harvard University Press, 1962.

BAILEY, K.D. Evaluating axiomatic theories. In E.F. Borgatta and G.W. Bohrnstedt (Eds.), *Sociological methodology 1970*. San Francisco: Jossey-Bass, 1970.

BECKER, S. Developing the empirical scholar. *Western Speech*, 1967, 31, 70-76.

BERGER, C.R., & CALABRESE, R.J. Some explorations in initial interaction and beyond: Toward a developmental theory of interpersonal communication. *Human Communication Research*, 1975, 1, 99-112.

BERLO, D. *The process of communication*. New York: Holt, Rinehart, & Winston, 1960.

BIERSTEDT, R. *Power and progress*. New York: McGraw-Hill, 1974.

BIRNBAUM, M.H. The devil rides again: Correlation as an index of fit. *Psychological Bulletin*, 1973, 79, 239-242.

BLALOCK, H.M. *Causal inferences in nonexperimental research*. New York: Norton, 1964.

BLALOCK, H.M. *Theory construction: From verbal to mathematical formulations*. Englewood Cliffs: Prentice-Hall, 1969.

BONACICH, P., & BAILEY, K.D. Key variables. In H.L. Costner (Ed.), *Sociological methodology 1971*. San Francisco: Jossey-Bass, 1971.

BOORMAN, S.A., & WHITE, H.C. Social structure from multiple networks. II. Role structures. *American Journal of Sociology*, 1976, 81, 1384-1446.

BOCHNER, A.P. Task and instrumentation variables as factors jeopardizing the validity of published group communication research, 1970-71. *Speech Monographs*, 1974, 41, 169-178.

CAPORASO, J.A., & ROOS, L.L. *Quasi-experimental approaches: Testing theory and evaluating relationships*. Evanston, Ill.: Northwestern University Press, 1973.

CAPPELLA, J.N. Modeling interpersonal communication systems as a pair of machines coupled through feedback. In G.R. Miller (Ed.), *Explorations in interpersonal communication*. Beverly Hills: Sage, 1976.

CAPPELLA, J.N., & FOLGER, J.R. An information processing explanation of the attitude-behavior inconsistency. In D.P. Cushman (Ed.), *Explorations in the message, attitude, behavior relationship*. Ann Arbor: Brown, in press.

CARSWELL, E.A., & ROMMETVEIT, R. *Social contexts of messages*. New York: Academic Press, 1971.

CASWELL, H., KOENIG, H.E., RESH, J.A., & ROSS, Q.E. An introduction to systems science for ecologists. Unpublished manuscript, Department of engineering, Michigan State University, East Lansing, 1974.

CHASE, L.J., & TUCKER, R.K. A power analytic examination of contemporary communication research. *Speech Monographs*, 1975, 42, 29-41.

CHOMSKY, N. *Syntactic structures*. The Hague: Mouton, 1957.

CHOMSKY, N. *Aspects of the theory of syntax*. Cambridge, Mass.: MIT Press, 1965.

CLEVENGER, T. Research methodologies in speech-communication. In R.J. Kibler and L.L. Barker (Eds.),

Conceptual frontiers in speech-communication. New York: Speech Communication Association, 1969.

CLEVENGER, T. Developing the empirical scholar: A devil's advocate view. *Western Speech*, 1967, 31, 77-84.

CLEVENGER, T., & MATTHEWS, J. *The speech-communication process.* Glenview, Ill.: Scott Foresman, 1971.

COHEN, J. *Statistical power analysis for the behavioral sciences.* New York: Academic Press, 1969.

COLEMAN, J.S. *Introduction to mathematical sociology.* New York: Free Press, 1964.

COLLINS, A.M., & QUILLIAN, M.R. How to make a language user. In E. Tulving and W. Donaldson (Eds.), *Organization of memory.* New York: Academic Press, 1972.

COSER, L.A. Presidential address: Two methods in search of a substance. *American Sociological Review*, 1975, 40, 691-700.

COSTNER, H.L., & LEIK, R.K. Deductions from axiomatic theory. *American Sociological Review*, 1964, 29, 819-835.

CRIDER, D.M., WILLITS, F.K., & BEALER, R.C. Panel studies: Some practical problems. *Sociological Methods and Research*, 1973, 2, 3-20.

CRONKHITE, G., & LISKA, J. A critique of factor analytic approaches to the study of credibility. *Communication Monographs*, 1976, 43, 91-107.

CUSHMAN, D.P., & WHITING, G.C. An approach to communication theory: Toward consensus on rules. *Journal of Communication*, 1972, 22, 220-241.

CUSHMAN, D.P., & CRAIG, R. Communication systems: Interpersonal implications. In G.R. Miller (Ed.), *Explorations in interpersonal communication.* Beverly Hills: Sage, 1976.

CUSHMAN, D.P., & PEARCE, W.B. Generality and necessity in three types of theory about human communication with special attention to rules theory. In B.D. Ruben (Ed.), *Communication yearbook 1.* New Brunswick, N.J.: Transaction-International Communication Association, 1977.

Testing two graph theoretic models of 742 sociomatrices. *American Sociological Review*, 1970, 35, 843-851.

DELIA, J.G., CROCKETT, W.H., PRESS, A.N., & O'KEEFE, D.J. The dependency of interpersonal evaluations on context-relevant beliefs about the other. *Speech Monographs*, 1975, 42, 10-19.

DIESING, P. *Patterns of discovery in the social sciences.* Chicago: Aldine-Atherton, 1972.

DONOHUE, W.A., & LAUFERSWEILER, C. A system of rules governing topicality: Expanding the interact system model. Paper presented at the annual meeting of the International Communication Association, Portland, 1976.

DUNCAN, O.D. *Introduction to structural equation models.* New York: Academic Press, 1975.

DUNCAN, S. On the structure of speaker-auditor interaction during speaker turns. *Language in society*, 1973, 2, 161-180.

EINHORN, H. Alchemy in the behavioral sciences. *Public Opinion Quarterly*, 1972, 36, 367-378.

EKEHAMMER, B. Interactionism in personality from a historical perspective. *Psychological Bulletin,* 1974, 81, 1026-1048.

ELLIS, D.G., & FISHER, B.A. Phases of conflict in small group development: A Markov analysis. *Human Communication Research*, 1975, 1, 195-212.

ENDLER, N.S., & MAGNUSSON, D. Toward an interactional psychology of personality. *Psychological Bulletin*, 1976a, 83, 956-974.

ENDLER, N.S., & MAGNUSSON, D. *Interactional psychology and personality.* New York: Wiley, 1976b.

ERICSON, P.M., & ROGERS, L.E. New procedures for analyzing relational communication. *Family Process*, 1973, 12, 245-267.

FARARO, T.J. *Mathematical sociology.* New York: Wiley, 1973.

FEATHER, N.T. Organization and discrepancy in cognitive structures. *Psychological Review*, 1971, 78, 355-379.

FINK, E.L., & NOELL, J.J. Interpersonal communication following the Wallace shooting. *Human Communication Research*, 1975, 1, 159-167.

FISHBEIN, M., & AJZEN, I. *Beliefs, attitudes, intentions, and behaviors.* Reading, Mass.: Addison-Wesley, 1975.

FISHER, B.A., & HAWES. L.C. An interact system model: Generating a grounded theory of small groups. *Quarterly Journal of Speech*, 1971, 57, 444-453.

FISHER, F.M., & ANDO, A. Two theorems on *ceteris paribus* in the analysis of dynamic systems. In H.M. Blalock (Ed.), *Causal models in the social sciences.* Chicago: Aldine-Atherton, 1969.

FLAMENT, C. *Applications of graph theory to group structure.* Englewood Cliffs: Prentice-Hall, 1963.

FLORENCE, B.T. An empirical test of the relationship of evidence to belief systems and attitude change. *Human Communication Research*, 1975, 1, 145-158.

FOLGER, J.R., & PUCK, S. Coding relational communication: A question approach. Paper presented at the annual meeting of the International Communication Association, Portland, 1976.

FRENTZ, T., & FARRELL, T. Language-action: A paradigm for communication. *Quarterly Journal of Speech*, 1976, 62, in press.

GARFINKEL, H. Studies of the routine grounds of everyday activities. In D. Sudnow (Ed.), *Studies in social interaction.* New York: Free Press, 1972, 1-30.

GLASS, G.V., WILLSON, V.L., & GOTTMAN, J.M. *Design and analysis of time-series experiments.* Boulder: Colorado University Press, 1975.

GOURAN, D.S., & BAIRD, J.E. An analysis of distributional and sequential structure in problem-solving and informal group discussions. *Speech Monographs*, 1972, 39, 16-22.

GREENWALD, A.G. Consequences of prejudice against the null hypothesis. *Psychological Bulletin*, 1975, 82, 1-20.

GRICE, H.P. The logic of conversation. Part II. Unpublished manuscript, 1968.

GROSSBERG, L., & O'KEEFE, D.J. Presuppositions, conceptual foundations and communication theory: On Hawes approach to communication. *Quarterly Journal of Speech*, 1975, 61, 195-208.

HACKMAN, J.R., & MORRIS, C.G. Group tasks, group interaction process, and group performance effectiveness: A review and proposed integration. In L. Berkowitz (Ed.), *Advances in experimental social psychology*, Vol. 8. New York: Academic Press, 1975.

HALLINAN, M. *The structure of positive sentiment.* Amsterdam: Elsevier, 1974.

HANSON, N.R. *Observation and explanation: A guide to the philosophy of science.* New York: Harper & Row, 1971.

HARARY, F., NORMAN, R.Z., & CARTWRIGHT, D.

Structural models. New York: Wiley, 1965.

HARRÉ, R., & SECORD, P.F. *The explanation of social behavior.* Oxford: Blackwell, 1972.

HARRIS, R.J. The uncertain connection between verbal theories and research hypotheses in social psychology. *Journal of Experimental Social Psychology*, 1976, 12, 210-219.

HAWES, L.C. Elements of a model for communication processes. *Quarterly Journal of Speech*, 1973, 59, 11-21.

HAWES, L.C. A response to Grossberg and O'Keefe: Building a human science of communication. *Quarterly Journal of Speech*, 1975, 61, 209-219.

HAWES, L.C., & FOLEY, J.M. A Markov analysis of interview communication. *Speech Monographs*, 1973, 40, 208-219.

HAWES, L.C. *Pragmatics of analoguing.* Reading, Mass.: Addison-Wesley, 1975.

HAYES, D.P., MELTZER, L., & WOLF, G. Substantive conclusions are dependent upon techniques of measurement. *Behavioral Science*, 1970, 15, 265-268.

HEISE, D.R. Problems in path analysis and causal inference. In E.F. Borgatta (Ed.), *Sociological Methodology 1969.* San Francisco: Jossey-Bass, 1968, 38-73.

HEISE, D.R. *Causal analysis.* New York: Wiley, 1976.

HELMRICH, R. Applied social psychology: The unfilled promise. *Personality and Social Psychology Bulletin*, 1975, 1, 548-560.

HEWES, D.E. Finite stochastic modeling of communication processes. *Human Communication Research*, 1975, 1, 271-283.

HEWES, D.E. Rules of social interaction and stochastic models: An integration. Unpublished mimeo, Department of Communication Arts, University of Wisconsin, Madison, 1976b.

HEWES, D.E., & EVANS-HEWES, D. Toward a process model of social interaction. Paper presented at the annual meeting of the International Communication Association, Chicago, 1975.

HEWES, D.E. An axiomatized stochastic process theory of the relationships among messages, mediating variables, and behaviors. In D.P. Cushman (Ed.), *Explorations in the message, attitude, behavior relationship.* Ann Arbor: Brown, in press.

HEWES, D.E., HAIGHT, L., SZALAY, S.M., & EVANS, D.E. On predicting none of the people none of the time: A test of two alternative relationships between personality and communicative choice. Paper presented at the annual meeting of the International Communication Association, Berlin, 1977.

HEWES, D.E., HAIGHT, L., & SZALAY, S.M. The utility and cross-situational consistency of measures of verbal output: An exploratory study. Paper presented at the annual meeting of the International Communication Association, Portland, 1976.

HIBBS, D.A. Problems of statistical estimation and causal inference in time-series regression models. In H.L. Costner (Ed.), *Sociological methodology 1973-74.* San Francisco: Jossey-Bass, 1974.

HUNTER, J., LEVINE, R., & SAYRES, S.E. Attitude change in hierarchical structures. *Human Communication Research*, 3, 1976, in press.

JACOB, T. Family interaction in disturbed and normal families: A methodological and substantive review. *Psychological Bulletin*, 1975, 82, 33-65.

JAFFEE, J., & FELDSTEIN, S. *Rhythms of dialogue.* New York: Academic Press, 1970.

JOHNSON, F.C., & KLARE, G.R. General models of communication research: A survey of the developments of a decade. *Journal of Communication*, 1961, 11, 13-26.

JONES, M.B. Molar correlational analysis. *Monograph series #4*, 1960, U.S. School of Aviation Medicine, Pensacola, Fla.

KAPLAN, A. *The conduct of inquiry.* San Francisco: Chandler, 1964.

KATZER, J., & SODT, J. An analysis of the use of statistical testing in communication research. *Journal of Communication*, 1973, 23, 251-265.

KEMENY, J.G., & SNELL, J.L. *Finite Markov chains.* New York: Van Nostrand, 1960.

KRIPPENDORFF, K. On generating data in communication research. *Journal of Communication*, 1970, 20, 241-269.

LABOV, W. Rules for ritual insults. In D. Sudnow (Ed.), *Studies in Social interaction.* New York: Free Press, 1972.

LAND, K.C. Comparative statics in sociology: Including a mathematical theory of growth and differentiation in organizations. In H.M. Blalock et al. (Eds.), *Quantitative Sociology.* New York: Academic Press, 1975.

LASHBROOK, W., & SULLIVAN, J. Apathetic and neutral audiences: More on simulation and validation. *Speech Monographs*, 1973, 40, 317-321.

LASSWELL, H.D. The structure and function of communication in society. In L. Bryson (Ed.), *The communication of ideas.* New York: Harper & Row, 1948.

MARK, R.A. Coding communication at the relationship level. *Journal of Communication*, 1971, 21, 221-232.

MAYHEW, B.H., & LEVINGER, R.L. On the emergence of oligarchy in human interaction. *American Journal of Sociology,* 1976, 81, 1017-1049.

MAYHEW, B.H., GRAY, L.N., & MAYHEW, M.L. Behavior of interaction systems. *General Systems*, 1971, 16, 13-29.

McDERMOTT, V. The development of a functional message variable: The locus of control. Paper presented at the annual meeting of the Speech Communication Association, Chicago, 1974.

McDERMOTT, V. Literature on classical theory construction. *Human Communication Research*, 1975, 1, 83-103.

McPHEE, W.N. *Formal theories of mass behavior.* New York: MacMillan, 1963.

MEEHAN, E. *Explanations in the social sciences: A system paradigm.* Homewood, Ill.: Dorsey Press, 1968.

MEHAN, H., & WOOD, H. *The reality of ethnomethodology.* New York: Wiley, 1975.

MILLAR, F.E., & ROGERS, L.E. A relational approach to interpersonal communication. In G.R. Miller (Ed.), *Explorations in interpersonal communication.* Beverly Hills: Sage, 1976.

MILLER, G.R. Theory in quantitative speech research. *Western Speech*, 1964, 28, 15-22.

MILLER, G.R. *Speech communication: A behavioral approach.* Indianapolis: Bobbs-Merrill, 1966.

MISCHEL, T. Scientific and philosophical psychology. In T. Mischel (Ed.), *Human action.* New York: Academic Press, 1969.

MISCHEL, W. *Personality and assessment.* New York: Wiley, 1968.

MULAIK, S.A. *The foundations of factor analysis.* New York: McGraw-Hill, 1972.

NAGEL, E. *The structure of science.* London: Routledge, 1961.

NEBERGALL, R.E. A response to "Research methodologies in speech-communication." In R.J. Kibler and L.L. Barker (Eds.), *Conceptual Frontiers in speech-communication.* New York: Speech Communication Association, 1969.

NOFSINGER, R. The demand ticket: A conversational device for getting the floor. *Speech Monographs*, 1975, 42, 1-9.

NOFSINGER, R. Answering questions indirectly. *Human Communication Research*, 1976, 2, 172-181.

O'KEEFE, D.J. Logical empiricism and the study of human communication. *Speech Monographs*, 1975, 42, 169-183.

PEARCE, W.B. The coordinated management of meaning. In G.R. Miller (Ed.), *Explorations in interpersonal communication.* Beverly Hills: Sage, 1976.

PELZ, D.C., & LEW, R.A. Heise's causal model applied. In E.F. Borgatta (Ed.), *Sociological methodology 1970.* San Francisco: Jossey-Bass, 1970.

PERVIN, L.A. A free-response description approach to the analysis of person-situation interaction. *Journal of Personality and Social Psychology*, 1976, 34, 465-474.

PHILIPSEN, G. Places for speaking in teamsterville. *Quarterly Journal of Speech*, 1976, 62, 15-25.

PLATT, H. Strong inference. *Science*, 1964, 146, 347-353.

POLANYI, M. *Personal knowledge.* New York: Harper & Row, 1964.

RAPOPORT, A. Mathematical models of social interaction. In R.D. Luce, R.R. Bush, and E. Galanter (Eds.), *Handbook of mathematical psychology*, Vol. 2, New York: Wiley, 1963.

ROGERS, L.E., & FARACE, R.V. Analysis of relational communication in dyads: New measurement procedures. *Human Communication Research*, 1975, 1, 222-239.

ROMMETVEIT, R. *On message structure.* London: Wiley, 1974.

SACKS, H., SCHEGLOFF, E.A., & JEFFERSON, G. A simplest systematics for the organization of turn-taking for conversation. *Language*, 1974, 50, 696-735.

SALTIEL, J., & WOELFEL, J. Inertia in cognitive processes: The role of accumulated information in attitude change. *Human Communication Research*, 1975, 1, 333-344.

SANDERS, R.E. The question of a paradigm for the study of speech-using behavior. *Quarterly Journal of Speech*, 1973, 59, 1-10.

SCHEIDEL, T.M. A systems analysis of two-person conversations. Unpublished paper presented to the Doctoral Honors Seminar on Systems Theory in Communication, University of Utah, Salt Lake City, 1974.

SCHEIDEL, T.M., & CROWELL, L. Idea development in small discussion groups. *Quarterly Journal of Speech*, 1964, 50, 140-45.

SEARLE, J.R. *Speech acts.* Cambridge: University Press, 1969.

SEIBOLD, D.R. Communication research and the attitude-verbal report-overt behavior relationship: A critique and theoretical formulation. *Human Communication Research*,

1975, 2, 1-32.

SHANNON, C.E., & WEAVER, W. *The mathematical theory of communication.* Urbana, Ill.: U. of Illinois Press, 1963.

SMITH, R.G. A response to "Research methodologies in speech-communication." In R.J. Kibler and L.L. Barker (Eds.), *Conceptual frontiers in speech-communication.* New York: Speech Communication Association, 1969.

SMITH, D.H. Communication research and the idea of process. *Speech Monographs*, 1972, 39, 174-182.

STECH, E.L. Sequential structure in human social communication. *Human Communication Research*, 1975, 1, 168-179.

STECH, E.L. An analysis of interaction structure in the discussion of a ranking task. *Speech Monographs*, 1970, 37, 249-256.

THAYER, L.O. On theory-building in communication: Some conceptual problems. *Journal of Communication*, 1963, 13, 217-235.

TOULMIN, S. Concepts and the explanation of human behavior. In T. Mischel (Ed.), *Human action.* New York: Academic Press, 1969.

WATZLAWICK, P., BEAVIN, J.H., & JACKSON, D.D. *The pragmatics of human communication.* New York: Norton: 1967.

WESTLEY, B.H. & MacLEAN, M. A conceptual model for communication research. *Audio-Visual Communication Review*, 1955, 3, 3-12.

WHITE, H.C., BOORMAN, S.A., & BREIGER, R.L. Social structure from multiple networks. I. Block models of roles and networks. *American Journal of Sociology*, 1976, 81, 730-780.

WIBERG, D.M. *State space and linear systems.* New York: McGraw-Hill (Schaum's Outline Series), 1971.

WILEY, D.E. The identification problem for structural equation models with unmeasured variables. In A.S. Goldberger and O.D. Duncan (Eds.), *Structural equation models in the social sciences.* New York: Seminar Press, 1973.

WILEY, J.A., & WILEY, M.G. A note on correlated errors in repeated measurements. *Sociological Methods and Research*, 1974, 3, 172-188.

WILEY, D.E., & WILEY, J.A. The estimation of measurement error in panel data. *American Sociological Review*, 1970, 35, 112-117.

WINOGRAD, T. *Understanding natural language.* New York: Academic Press, 1972.

WOODS, W. Transition network grammars for natural language analysis. *Communications of the ACM*, 1970, 13, 591-606.

WOODS, W. An experimental parsing system for transition network grammars. In R. Rustin (Ed.), *Natural language processing.* New York: Algorithmics Press, 1973.

ZETTERBERG, H.L. *On theory and verification in sociology.* Third edition. New York: Bedminster Press, 1963.

COMMUNICATION EFFECTS: REVIEW AND COMMENTARY

NAN LIN
State University of New York at Albany

Three theoretical perspectives have been used by researchers to examine the various aspects of communication effects: The directive perspective, which explores the manipulation and control of communication components; the selective perspective, which studies the patterns of communication utilized by participants; and the interactive perspective, which focuses on the interplay of directive and selective contributions. It is suggested that the interactive perspective is most useful in the development of a theoretical paradigm. A theoretical framework and a series of propositions are then discussed within this perspective, and research evidence is cited. This framework, incorporating major concepts such as *encounter, exchange, influence,* and *control and adaptation,* shows promise of a middle-range theory for the study of communication effects.

The essay consists of two major parts. In the first section, the discussion focuses on the various theoretical perspectives dominant and visible in current research. A comparison of the perspectives leads to an attempt, in the second section, to integrate empirical and conceptual developments within a single theoretical framework.

THE THEORETICAL PERSPECTIVES

The recent trends in the area of communication research are encouraging. Diversification of both research areas and research strategies have occurred. In terms of research areas, the "traditional" schools of persuasion, mass media, and diffusion are complimented by efforts in the application of information theory concepts and orientations in the study of the processes of information transfer, the integration of nonverbal and verbal codes in the analysis of human interactions, the critical analysis of the control mechanisms in mediated human communication situations, and so forth.

Likewise, research strategies are expanding. The sampling frames have expanded from the use of captive and available groups to representative and longitudinal data points. Testing procedures have advanced from paired-variable significance tests to multivariate analyses in which communication variables are used as both exogenous (independent) and endogenous (dependent) variables. Serious attempts are being made to construct testable theoretical structures with deducible hypotheses.

However, diversifications in research areas and strategies do not imply a scientific revolution in the Kuhnian (1962) sense. The task of working toward a new paradigm must begin with an understanding of current paradigms. There are distinctive theoretical perspectives in the study of communication effects. These perspectives serve as guides in the formulation of research problems, the selection and construction of research instruments and designs, and the analysis and reporting of data. Presented here is the beginning of an analysis of the perspectives which are so often implicit in contemporary research. By fleshing out these perspectives and the assumptions they embody it should then become possible to identify a theoretical framework which will provide a fruitful integration of theory and research. Three theoretical perspectives which seem dominant as guides for research are described. By pointing out the major assumptions involved, the potential consequences in the type of data generated, and conclusions implied, one perspective emerges as particularly useful for theoretical and research integration.

The Directive Perspective

One dominant theoretical perspective in the study of communication effects takes the view that communication variables (the source, the channel, the message, etc.) have or should have psychological and/or behavioral influence on the receivers. In other words, this perspective makes the important assumption or postulation that a communication situation is directive in that the effects on participants depend, to a great extent, on the manipulations and controls of the source, the message, the channel, and the like. One immediate deduction of this assumption is, therefore, that it is crucial to examine the control and manipulation of the communication variables by the "directive participants." The classical examples of research enterprises using the *directive perspective* include persuasion and attitude change (McGuire, 1973), diffusion of innovations (Rogers & Shoemaker, 1971), political communication (Chaffee, 1975), and some areas of mass communication such as television effects on children (Comstock, 1975).

Research efforts reflective of this orientation have taken into account the importance of the receiver's social and cognitive systems. However, the major thrust clearly is to determine the best "directive" mix for achieving the best result—to mold and change the receiving participants toward the image or pattern of influence as intended by the directive participants.

A recent extension of this perspective is the concern with the manipulation and control of media content and organization. For example, the agenda-setting approach focuses on the ability or the extent to which media content set issues and agenda (McCombs & Shaw, 1972, 1976; McLeod, Becker, & Byrnes, 1974; Donohue, Tichenor, & Olien, 1972; Fuchs & Lyle; Tichenor, Rodenkirchen, Olien & Donohue, 1973; Siune & Borre, 1975; Cochran, 1975; Rutkus, 1976). Other efforts have been made to examine the representation of certain demographic and social characteristics such as sex and race in the media (Dohrmann, 1975; Busby, 1950; Culley & Bennett, 1976) and the dominance of foreign materials in the media of certain countries (Guback, 1974; Schiller, 1974; Varis, 1974). While no explicit association is made,

the prominence and visibility of the topics—for example, about 34% of the *Journal of Communication* article space since 1974 has been devoted to pieces addressing this concern—and the usually critical nature of the discussion, makes clear the assumption that the media play an influential role in the audience's perception, attitudes and/or behavior. In other words, the directive perspective, whereby it is assumed that the participants consuming the content of the media are affected by the information manipulated and controlled by certain interest groups, is accepted as the model for conceptualizing the effects of mass media.

The directive perspective, therefore, is *source-oriented*. It critically examines: (1) the motivational and behavioral patterns of the directive individuals (such as the city editor of a newspaper) and the directive organization (such as a corporation or a government) on the formulating and structuring of the communication content presented to an audience; and (2) the subsequent evidence that the audience becomes receptive (informatively, attitudinally, or behaviorally) to the explicitly or implicitly packaged messages.

The Selective Perspective

The other dominant perspective in studies of communication effects reflects the assumption that the participant is active and selective in his use of communication content for the fulfillment of his perceived purposes or needs. A cogent statement arguing the concept of the obstinate audience was made years ago by Bauer (1964), and the *play theory* of communication (Stephenson, 1967; Streicher & Bonney, 1974) emphasizes the selective nature of interaction between the users of mass media and its content.

The *selective perspective*, then, makes use of the assumption that the receiving participants in the communication situation dictate, to a large extent, the content to which they wish to be exposed, for purposes and uses defined by themselves. Research efforts along this perspective include studies of the decision-making process (Edelstein, 1973), and the information-seeking process (Atkins, 1973; Donohew & Tipton, 1973). A recent extension of this perspective is the gratification research (Blumler &

McQuail, 1969; McLeod & Becker, 1974; Katz, Blumler, & Gurevitch, 1974) which focuses on the selective process of communication content for personal gratifications and uses.

The selective perspective, while *receiver-oriented*, does not ignore the fact that the choice of communication content and media is limited by the manipulation and control exercised by certain gatekeeping participants and organizations. Nevertheless, the major focus and emphasis is on the active and selective participation of the audience in the communication situation.

The Two Orientations

The two perspectives mentioned above, of course, are not unique in the discipline of communication. Coexistence of perspectives has appeared in a number of other social science disciplines. For example, sociologists have long provided the structural versus cultural perspectives of explanation for social behaviors. In *structural perspective*, explanations of human behavior are provided in terms of roles and positions within the social structure. On the other hand, the *cultural perspective* explains human behavior by considering the acts and interactions of individual actors. The parallel can also be found in psychology, where the stimulus vs. response perspectives have been topics of debate. In the *stimulus (stimulation) perspective*, the strategic manipulation of stimuli provides the focus of analysis. In the *response perspective*, the selective response for the purpose of reinforcing predispositions is the main concern. In economic and marketing research, the conflicting perspectives can be identified as the *supply perspective* and the *demand perspective*. The *supply perspective* focuses on the marketing characteristics of consumption induction of a product, while the demand perspective identifies the needs and desires of consumers and their selection patterns. In political science, political campaigns have been analyzed also from two perspectives. The "selling" of a political candidate can be analyzed either in terms of features of the candidate and his campaign strategies, or relative to the attitudes and opinions of the electorate.

However, the identification of the two perspectives should not be stretched so far as to suggest that these are polarized categories in a zero-sum game situation. Many researchers have utilized both perspectives in different research environments, and most of us do not see the two orientations as an either-or proposition. Nevertheless, it is important to flesh out the postures and assumptions of these perspectives in the assessment and integration of research discussions and reports.

The Interactive Perspective

It should become apparent that a third, and probably more fruitful, perspective in the study of communication effects lies in the intersecting of the directive and selective perspectives. That is, effects of communication may occur and, therefore, must be assessed when and only when the directive and selective processes overlap.

The cognitive and balance theories in social psychology represent the early development of this perspective. One recent extension and elaboration of this perspective in interpersonal communication research is the concerted research activities in the area of co-orientational analysis (Chaffee, 1972; Pearce & Stamm, 1973, 1974). Miller (1975) in his effort to clarify the conceptualization of interpersonal communication, has focused on the predictive nature of communication actions and reactions between participants in the communication situation. It was suggested that interpersonal communication occurs when there is a substantial probability of success for the participants to predict the responses of one another.

From the information theory point of view, the intersect of the two interacting information components is considered as the transmitted information (Lin, 1973), or the portion of the information successfully transferred from one participant to another. The transmitted information, relative to the total amount of information involved in the particular communication situation, thus represents the extent of effective communication between the source and the receiver. Other portions of information brought to bear in the communication situation may represent the *directive* and *selective* efforts which, as far as the information transmission is concerned, have failed.

Other interactive concepts have appeared in the research literature. *Homophily-heterophily*, for example—gauging the degree to which characteristics of the communication participants are similar or different—has been proposed and demonstrated to be linked to certain types of communication effectiveness (Homans, 1950; Lazarsfeld & Merton, 1964; Laumann, 1973).

At the mass communication level, the joint effects of media characteristics, receiver characteristics, and environment are well documented (Rogers & Shoemaker, 1971; Lin & Burt, 1975). Its utility in the analysis of television effects is demonstrated in the violence profile project conducted by Gerbner, Gross, and others (1976).

The converging picture is that the extent of communication success, at both interpersonal and mass level, depends on the extent to which the *directive* process employed by one participant (e.g., a source) and the *selective* process of another (e.g., a receiver) intersect. In a situation where participants all serve both as sources and receivers, communication effects depend on the extent of the overlap between the directive and selective processes by each participant and those of another.

The importance of the above discussion goes beyond the identification of the three perspectives, all of which have had long historical roots. Rather, it lies in the fact that as far as studies of communication effects are concerned, the directive perspective and the selective perspective make contributions only when the interactive perspective is taken into account. The evidence that the mass media in a social system are controlled and manipulated by certain interest groups gains significance *only* if it has been demonstrated that the content in the mass media, as manipulated and controlled by the interest groups, is assimilated and used by the audience.

Similarly, the demonstration that a user assimilates communication content to gratify his needs would be incomplete, as far as communication effects are concerned, if the extent to which the content has been manipulated and controlled by certain interest groups is not examined.

Provided in the following is an attempt to apply the interactive perspective to integrate recent research findings. The attempt shall begin with a discussion on some convergent trends in recent in-

tegrative conceptual efforts.

THE THEORETICAL INTEGRATION

Recent efforts in the attempts to integrate research findings show an evolution toward several distinct views about communication effects.

Process Orientation

There has been an evolution toward a process view of communication effects, as opposed to a structural perspective.

Traditionally, researchers were component-oriented, viewing the communication situation as a structure consisting of certain components (e.g., the source, the channel, the message, the receiver, and the socio-psychological environment). Communication effects, therefore, tended to be viewed in terms of the impact one component had on another. This view has gradually been substituted and supplemented by interest in viewing the communication situation as an ongoing process. Studies in the phases of conflict (Ellis & Fisher, 1975), the sequential structure of interaction (Mabry, 1975; Donohew & Tipton, 1973), initiation and turn-taking in conversations (Wolf, 1974; Wiemann & Knapp, 1975), and signal stopping techniques (Carter, Ruggles, Jackson, & Heffner, 1973) are some recent examples of research interest in the *processes* of communication.

Relational Orientation

There has also been a shift from an individual view toward a relational view. The importance of relational concepts has been advocated for some time (Coleman, 1959), however, the use of traditional units of analysis—individual and aggregated characteristics—continued to dominate research designs. The shift to more relational concepts has been significant. Concepts such as *homophily* and *co-orientation* take into account positions and roles of different participants in the communication situation, and the recent methodological advances in *network analysis* (Lin, 1976; Coleman, 1964; Richards, 1971; Bonacich, 1972; Alba, 1973; Roistacher, 1974; Burt & Lin, 1977) provide the necessary technical impetus for the relationship analysis. Discussions taking place in interpersonal communication (Miller, 1975), in which the predictability of actions and reactions occupy the central focus, provide another piece of evidence of the movement toward a relational view.

Cumulative Stimulus-Response Orientation

A third shift is from a short-term stimulus-response view of communication effects toward a long-term cumulative stimulus-response view. Partly resulting from disappointment with research findings about short-term stimulus-response effects, and partly due to theoretical interest in the cumulative effects, there is a thrust toward identifying and demonstrating cumulative effects of communication. For example, it has been argued and supported empirically that cumulative information can change an attitude (Woelfel, Woelfel, Gillham, & McPhail, 1974; Saltiel & Woelfel, 1975; Barnett, Serota, & Taylor, 1976), that repeated advertisings result in behavior change (Rothschild & Ray, 1974), and that the effect of information gain is additive (Salomon, 1976).

Configurational Orientation

Finally, one sees increasing use of a configurational view of the codes and symbols used in communication situation, as compared to the traditional emphasis on verbal codes alone. The upsurge of interest in nonverbal behavior in the 1960s (for a summary, see Lin, 1973, Chapter 30; Weitz, 1974) is finally coming to fruition in the 1970s with the integration of both verbal and nonverbal codes in the analysis of communication relations (Buck, 1976; Keiser, 1976; Argyle & Cook, 1976). The configurational approach also witnesses the studies of properties of *doing* communication, such as sequential structure (Mabry, 1975), grammar (Nofsinger, 1976), signal stopping (Carter et al., 1973) and turn-taking (Wiemann & Knapp, 1975).

Discussion

These shifts toward a *processal, relational, cumulative,* and *configurational* approach to the

study of human communication, and especially communication effects, are paralleled, not coincidentally, by a *processal, relational, cumulative,* and *configurational* approach to the development of a communication paradigm.

The suggestion that such an approach be used in the guidance and synthesis of communication research is almost as ancient as the emergence of the discipline itself. Cartwright (1949), for example, pointed out that the "principles of mass persuasion" involved the creation of three structures—the cognitive, the motivational, and the behavioral structures. The *cognitive* structure focused on the aspects of selectivity and acceptance; the *motivational* structure on the aspects of the perceived goal-orientations and competition with other courses of action toward the same goal. The *behavioral* structure concerned aspects of the mapping of control over the cognitive and motivational structures of behavior regarding the specificity of a path of action within a time frame.

In the 1970s, there has been a convergence of similar theory and research approaches from a variety of disciplinary foci. McGuire (1973), representative of the social psychological tradition, has shown a shift in his continuous monitoring of research on persuasion and attitude change from a component view (source, message, channels, receiver, and destination) to a "behavioral steps" orientation in which *presentation, attention, comprehension, yielding, retention,* and *overt behavior* were singled out for analysis. Schramm (1971), representative of the mass communication research tradition, has repeatedly pointed to various objectives of communication: *knowledge, socialization, entertainment,* and *consensus.*

Cognitive, affective, and *conative* aspects of communication have been used in the framework presented by Fischer (1975) in a discussion of communication effects in primitive systems, and Ray (1973) in an analysis of marketing communication (1973). And, Dance and Larson (1976) differentiated the *linking, mentation,* and *regulatory* functions of interpersonal communication.

What distinguishes these proposals is that their authors all view communication as a process. Thus, the terms used to study the effects of communication reflect the processal, relational, cumulative,

FIGURE 1
Phases of Human Communication (Lin, 1973, p. 15)

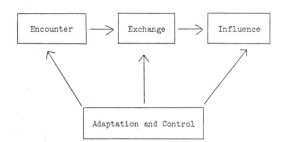

and configurational characteristics. Thus, comparison of these recently suggested analytical views with the interactive perspective discussed in the previous section suggests that they are highly compatible.

AN INTEGRATIVE PARADIGM

In the following, these perspectives are utilized in an effort to integrate research conducted on communication effects in the last few years. The conceptual framework to be used singles out four phases of communication: (1) *encounter*, (2) *exchange*, (3) *influence*, and (4) *adaptation* and *control* (Lin, 1973). These phases overlap, of course, but each has its distinctive characteristics, structure, and process. The mapping of these phases is depicted in Figure 1.

Encounter, the initial phase of human communication, is the process by which a specific piece of information and the receiving participants are linked through a particular medium. Encounter can be analyzed in terms of: (1) the extent to which information structure of codes is transmitted successfully to the receiver's cognitive boundary—the information system; and (2) the nature of the networks through which encounter becomes probable—the network system.

The *information system* examines the information source's encoding process, the availability and capacity of channels utilized to transmit and receive the information, the noise contained in the channels, and the receiver's decoding process.

The *network system* concerns the processal and structural properties by which information is re-

layed through spatial, mass media, and interpersonal channels.

Exchange, defined as the flow of shared meaning, represents the effort on the part of the communication participants to maintain shared meaning through a set of symbols. The study of exchange includes topics such as: (1) how meaning is developed, (2) what forms and modalities exchange of meanings may take, and (3) functions and consequences of exchange.

Influence is defined as the change (discrepancy) between: (1) a participant's behavior or attitudinal pattern toward an object or situation before his participation, either voluntary or involuntary, in encounter and/or exchange; and (2) his behavioral or attitudinal pattern after such encounter and/or exchange. Until a firm theoretical and empirical grasp is made for the relationship between attitude and behavior, it is advisable to trace the cumulated knowledge regarding the two concepts separately, as well as jointly. It is further emphasized that, from the communication point of view, only influence related to communication processes is of interest. The topics of interest include: (1) the mechanisms with which encounter and/or exchange is transferred into influence, (2) the properties and types of influence, and (3) the consequences of influence for all participants involved in the communication situation.

Finally, the effectiveness over time of *encounter*, *exchange*, or *influence* depends, to a large extent, on *control*, the process by which the fidelity of information flow, the efficiency of message flow, and induced changes are achieved or maintained. Thus, *control* can be regarded as the organizational phase of human communication. Control utilizes two mechanisms: (1) the feedback mechanism and (2) the dissemination mechanism. The feedback mechanism, also called the cybernetic element of human communication, focuses on negative feedback which informs the directive (source) participant of the extent to which the transmission has failed.

The dissemination mechanism provides a communication participant with the means to arrest the failing aspect of the transmission as informed by the feedback mechanism. The dissemination mechanism can be regarded as the enforced transmission in which the transmission intent of the participant is relatively strong, the delineation of the receiver system is relatively complete, and the manipulation and maintenance of transmission are deliberately carried out by the source.

Adaptation represents the control aspect from the receiving participant's point of view. The receiver can also utilize the feedback mechanism and the dissemination mechanism to achieve and maintain the fidelity of information flow, the efficiency of message flow, and induced changes optimal to the receiver system.

Thus, the encounter phase is the cognitive process of overlapping presentation (from a source) and attention (of a receiver). The exchange phase represents the semantic process of comprehension and interpretation. The influence phase monitors the psychological and/or behavioral changes resulting from encounter and/or exchanges. Control and adaptation complete the cybernetic requirement of the communication system.

This conceptual framework seems to fulfill the requirements for a general theory of human communication, and for the examination of communication effects, in particular. It presents a processal view as a sequence of phases. While any particular communication situation may involve a different sequence or segmentation of the phases, the basic processal components are described.

The terms selected for use in the framework (*encounter*, *exchange*, *influence*, *control*, and *adaptation*) are all relational concepts; each concept is a construct indicating the participation of multiple-actors coupled for a particular communication situation. The framework allows a cumulative view of the communication process; each phase, while having its identifiable properties and indicators, is antecedent or consequent to another phase. Thus, the cumulative effects of antecedent phases on consequent phases—as well as the structural equilibrium as reflected in the linkages from control and adaptation to encounter, exchange and influence—may be depicted.

The following, then, is an attempt to integrate recent research efforts into the conceptual framework. It is intended to provide for the development of a theoretical structure of communication effects as propositions are constructed from the

matching of concepts and variables and to encourage the identification of areas for research and theoretical modification.

ENCOUNTER

The initial effect of communication is the transmission of codes in encounters. The encounter can be examined as a process involving two clusters of causal factors: (1) the communication environment of the participants, and (2) the triggering events on the outcomes of encounter.

The Communication Environment

For an *encounter* to occur, predictability begins with the *communication environment* in which the potential participants (some of which may be non-human) operate. For example, to understand an encounter between a child and a television commercial or program, one must examine a series of communication environment questions. For example, for the communication environment of the child, is there a television set available to the child? What is his usual pattern of TV use? What other activities compete with his TV watching? How much do his parents and other members in the family compete and constrain his use of television? What social networks does he participate in? What are the primary needs and interests at this particular time of his development and life cycles (Ward & Wackman, 1973)? Similarly, the communication environment of the particular television commercial or program must be examined. Who produces it? Why is it adopted and used by the particular network or station at the particular time? What characteristics of the product or the roles are portrayed? How is the information structured (Watt & Krull, 1974)? Thus, the communication environment can be considered as the predispositional structure within which encounter is initiated. Recent research efforts in the description and analysis of the communication environment of both the media (and its content) and individuals are quite consistent in finding its causal role in the encounter.

Demographic and developmental characteristics. The communication environment consists

FIGURE 2
Clusters of Causal Factors for Encounter
(Between Two Coupled Participants*)

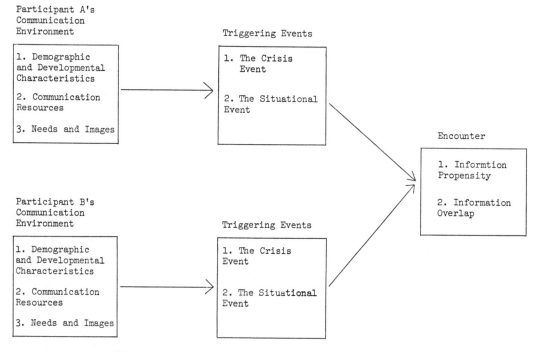

Participant A's
Communication
Environment

Triggering Events

1. Demographic
and Developmental
Characteristics

2. Communication
Resources

3. Needs and Images

1. The Crisis
Event

2. The Situational
Event

Encounter

1. Informtion
Propensity

2. Information
Overlap

Participant B's
Communication
Environment

Triggering Events

1. Demographic
and Developmental
Characteristics

2. Communication
Resources

3. Needs and Images

1. The Crisis
Event

2. The Situational
Event

*One may be a non-human medium.

of several important components. One component concerns the demographic and developmental characteristics of the participants. That socioeconomic characteristics predict communication behaviors is no surprise, for such characteristics increase the likelihood of access to certain communication media and networks. For example, there has been a relationship between higher socio-economic status and the use of mass media and channels of communication external or cosmopolitan to a person's immediate social environment. Furthermore it has been demonstrated that persons of higher social status, while not necessarily having a more interactive interpersonal network (in terms of number of friends and frequency of interactions), do have a more heterogenous interpersonal communication network. In other words, a person of higher socioeconomic status tends to know others with a more heterogenous background than a person of lower socioeconomic status. Thus, Shotland (1970)

found that in a university community, the administrators were more effective in identifying a target person on campus in a small world exercise than the faculty who, in turn, were more effective than the students. Similarly, in a small world study of urban communication networks, Lin and Dayton (1976) found that the higher social status (occupational prestige) an intermediary had, the more likely the task of forwarding a packet to the target.

In other words, socioeconomic status does not necessarily have a positive relationship with the frequency of interpersonal contacts or the size of the interpersonal network (for example, number of friends), but it is positively related to the heterogeneity of the interpersonal network. A more heterogenous network enables one to be more efficient in a searching or seeking behavior.

Similarly, cognitive development defines the communication environment. As recent studies (Ward & Wackmann, 1973; Wartella & Ettema,

1974; Collins, 1975) showed, children at different ages differed in their ability to understand television commercial messages. These differences in cognitive ability affected their differential attention and perception of the messages. Such differentiation should extend into adult and later life stages, although evidence to substantiate this view has not yet been gathered.

Behavioral utility. A second component of the communication environment is the behavioral utility of communication resources. If the socioeconomic and developmental characteristics generate and define the *availability* of communication resources (interpersonal network and mass media), then the actual extent of *utilization* of the communication resources provides a dynamic view of a person's active participation in the communication environment. There is evidence that gregariousness is highly related to the extent of use of communication resources through interpersonal, mass, and institutional channels (Katz & Lazarsfeld, 1955; Dervin & Greenberg, 1973). Whether there are factors other than personality contributing to the active use of communication resources remains to be studied. But, it is clear that the use of communication resources is contingent upon the availability of such resources. Thus, the socioeconomic and developmental characteristics and personality factors may jointly determine the extent of use of the communication resources.

Needs and images. A third component of the communication environment concerns the needs and images of the participant. A *need* may be defined as the propensity toward reducing the discrepancy between what one possesses or is oriented toward and what one may possess or be oriented toward. Atkins (1973), in a discussion of instrumental utilities of information seeking, suggested that the needs for information derive from an evaluation of one's adaptation requirements, including cognitive, affective, and behavioral orientations. The states of these orientations at a given time provide the imageries of self and the external world necessary for defining potential needs. However, we must expand the needs to include orientations which are not necessarily adaptive in nature. An important orientation,

for example, concerns the management of leisure. Stephenson's *play theory* (1967) has pointed out the important need for entertaining stimuli in one's life. In general, needs arise from imageries of self and the external world constructed from life orientations and life management schedules at a given time. They, in turn, provide impetus for the gathering of information.

The Triggering Events

These components of communication environment set the stage for *encounter*. The occurrence of an encounter, however, requires *triggering events*. The triggering events make possible the linkage of a person with a specified set of communication environment characteristics and another communication participant with its own communication environment. At least two ideal—extreme—types of *triggering events* can develop for a potential participant: (1) a *crisis event* and (2) a *situational event*.[1] A *crisis event* occurs when uncertainty arises from an evaluated inconsistency or discrepancy between one's current cognitive or affective structure and the cognitive or affective expectation or prediction one wishes to achieve and make relative to a stimulus in its communication environment. The stimulus can either come from internal restructuring or external events. There are two types of crises: (1) The *integrative crisis:* a crisis demanding the resolution of a discrepancy or inconsistency with integrative functions, such as status-conferral; and (2) the *disruptive crisis.* In this case crisis demands resolution of a discrepancy or inconsistency with disruptive functions, such as with cognitive dissonance. Such inconsistency or discrepancy constitutes a trigger for information gathering and uncertainty reduction. The resulting encounter represents the *active* information seeking effort on the part of the participant as described extensively in the literature (Atkins, 1973; Donohew, 1973; Coulthard & Ashby, 1975; Wright, 1975).

Another much less obvious triggering event is *situational exposure.* It is a "chancy" happening, in the sense that no inconsistency or discrepancy activates the effort. Rather, the encounter is afforded by the presence of an occasion for information exposure. In other words, this type of encounter is triggered by the routinized interaction between the participant and his communication environment. For example, a habitual watcher of daily televised evening news may encounter information although there is no cognitive crisis present. Similarly, a child may learn from television without involvement (Krugman, 1965).

These two types of triggering events differ not only in terms of the extent of effort involved in the seeking out of the encounter on the part of the participant, but also in the eventual structure, process, and consequences of encounter. For example, encounter resulting from a cognitive crisis tends to be asymmetric in the relationships among participants. The encounter occurs in a structure which defines certain expected roles and information discrepancies. A patient's encounter with a physician probably represents an ideal type of the asymmetric structure of encounter following a cognitive (and other) crisis (Coulthard & Asby, 1975). On the other hand, a *situational exposure* is not contingent upon a cognitive crisis and, therefore, tends to be symmetric in the enounter relations.

Further, the crisis-based encounter tends to be less reciprocal or interactive in process than the situation-based encounter. The transmission of information in the crisis-based encounter tends to be one-way, even when the situation allows for reciprocal or interactive transmission, such as in the interpersonal encounter.

Finally, the two types of encounter have different consequences. The information transmitted in each crisis-based encounter is assessed relative to the inconsistency or discrepancy at hand. Future and further encounters are planned according to the extent to which each encounter has reduced or minimized the inconsistency or discrepancy. The information transmitted in each situation-based encounter is assessed, on the other hand, relative to the existing information repertoire in the participant's life orientation and management system. Future and further encounters are pursued in accordance with the extent to which the particular encounter has created a cognitive crisis or the information is useful in his communication environment. Thus, the crisis-based encounter has a more specific evaluative criterion, and, therefore, serves as a more predictive factor in future, similar encounters.

The evaluative criteria for the situation-based encounter, on the other hand, are more general and diffused and, therefore, serve as a less predictive factor in future, similar encounters.

Consider, further, the case where one of the participants is a nonhuman medium, such as a newspaper or a television set. The presentation and structure of information it conveys is also specified and contingent upon and organized around its communication environment and a set of triggering events. Such a structure reveals itself in terms of agenda, issues, formats of presentation. Studies since White's classic case study of newspaper editor's gatekeeping activities have attempted to document the communication environment of the particular medium. Questions have been raised as to who controls the medium, (Donohue, Tichenor, & Olien, 1972; Pearce, 1976) and who controls the issues and formats of presentations (Breen, 1975; Siune & Borre, 1975; Cardona, 1975). Also examined is the resulting evidence of such an environment. Topics such as agenda and issue setting, (McLeod, Becker, & Byrnes, 1974) and content patterns (Fuchs & Lyle, 1972), are also treated.

There are two additional types of triggering events for the communication medium. One type concerns a *perceived crisis situation* (an airplane hijacking, a political assassination, a substantial change of stock market prices, etc.) in which the occurrence is relatively infrequent and reduction of the uncertainty information is perceived to be relatively significant. The second type of triggering event is of the *situational exposure type*. Included in this type are the regular reporting and exposure of "human interest" stories, classified ads, sports pages, television and radio program listings, and the regular TV programs. Information uncertainty is also present. The uncertainty of occurrence of the event itself, however, is relatively low.

The Outcomes of Encounter

These triggering events activate an encounter. Thus, the amount and extensiveness of information transmission in an encounter can be predicted from the compatibility of the triggering events of the participants involved. A simple typology is provided in Figure 3. Two variables can be identified in

FIGURE 3
A Typology of Encounter by Types of Triggering Events

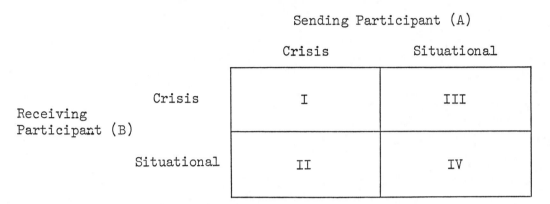

		Sending Participant (A)	
		Crisis	Situational
Receiving Participant (B)	Crisis	I	III
	Situational	II	IV

the encounter: (1) *the information propensity* and (2) the *information overlap*. The information propensity is defined as the amount of information capability brought into the encounter. It is postulated that the *crisis event* induces a relatively greater information propensity than the situational event for a participant. In other words, the crisis event predisposes a participant to a greater degree of information transfer than the situational event does. A second variable, the information overlap, is defined as the extent to which information transfer is successful. If the information system brought to bear in an encounter is represented by a circle, then the information propensity can be represented by the relative size of the circle, and the information overlap by the area where the encountering information systems converge. The outcome of an encounter can then be predicted as follows:

1. When both the participants are confronted with a *crisis event*, the *information propensity* for both parties is great, and the *information overlap* is extensive (Type I in Figure 3).

2. When a receiving participant (B) perceives a *situational event*, while the sending participant (A) perceives a *crisis event*, the *information propensity* for Participant B is small, but the *information overlap* for the Participant B is substantial (Type II in Figure 3).

3. When the receiving participant (B) perceives a *crisis event*, while the sending participant (A) perceives a *situational event*, the receiving participant's *information propensity* is substantial,

FIGURE 4
Outcomes of Information Transfer (Propensity and Overlap) for the Typology in Figure 3.

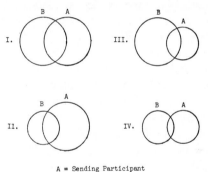

A = Sending Participant

B = Receiving Participant

but the *information overlap* for the participant (B) is small (Type III in Figure 3).

4. Finally, when both the participants perceive a *situational event*, the *information propensity* and *overlap* are both relatively small for the receiving participant (B) (Type IV in Figure 3).

These predictions are illustrated in Figure 4.

In the encounter between an individual (or a group) and a medium, the roles of sending and receiving are specified as a constant. Thus, the effects are analyzed in terms of the outcomes for the individual or group, In an interpersonal encounter, the outcomes can then be predicted for each participant, where each would alternately assume the sending or receiving role as a specific information transfer in the encounter dictates.

The effect of the encounter not only concerns

FIGURE 5
The Process of Exchange

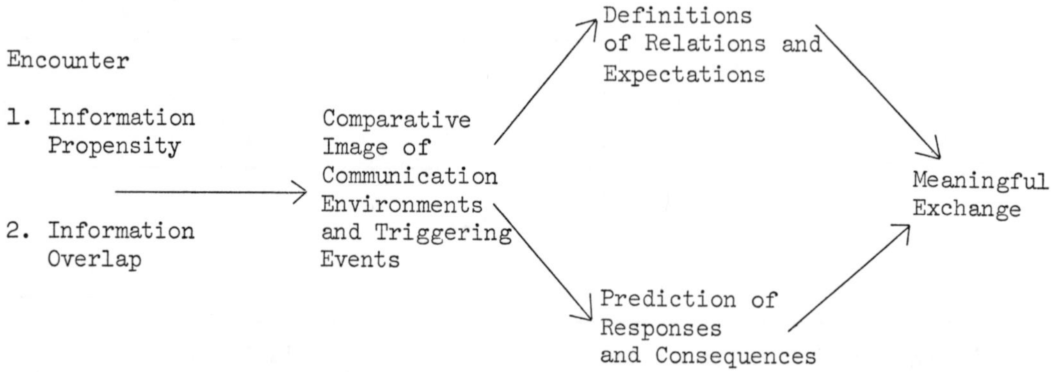

Encounter

1. Information
   Propensity

2. Information
   Overlap

Comparative
Image of
Communication
Environments
and Triggering
Events

Definitions
of Relations and
Expectations

Prediction of
Responses
and Consequences

Meaningful
Exchange

the particular information gain during the *encounter,* but also involves the accumulation of information which, in turn, increases the tendency for *exchanges* and the development of affection. Much research literature in the past has attempted to account for the "marginal" information gain. But, it must be argued that the information gain is cumulative in nature. Therefore, a participant who possesses a greater amount of information going into an encounter situation is also more likely to gain additional information (Salomon, 1976). Further, the participant with the greater amount of information gain over time is likely to demonstrate a greater tendency for the development of affection (for example, attitude change). The anticipated benefit of cumulative information gain should affect the optimal matching of participants in encounters. Thus, *it can be hypothesized that there is a correspondence between information propensity and information overlap in encounters. Empirically, Types I and IV in Figure 3 should have significantly greater numbers of observations than Types II and III.*

EXCHANGE

One direct consequence of accumulated information and repeated *encounters* with similar participants is the development of shared meaning and identification in *exchanges* (Berger & Calabrese, 1975).

The *communication environment* and the *triggering events* persist in their influence on the development of shared meaning. In fact, evidence suggests that the participants' image of the communication environments contributes to the initial development of a meaningful exchange. This image activates two important processes: (1) the construction of definitions of relations and expectations, and (2) the prediction of potential responses in exchanges. With the presence and functioning of these two processes, meaningful exchange may then occur. A processal view of the exchange appears in Figure 5.

The acquisition of information in encounters leads to the formulation of a cognitive map or image of the communication environment (the demographic and developmental characteristics, the communication resources, and the needs and images) of the other participants. This image is further compared with the participant's own communication environment. The assessment of the extent of perceived similarities of the characteristics of the participant's communication environments, in turn, leads to the formation of expectations of agreement or disagreement, as discussed by Stamm, Chaffee, Pearce, and others (Pearce & Stamm, 1973; Stamm & Pearce, 1974; Chaffee, 1973; Buchli & Pearce, 1974).

With the expected relations, agreement, and predictions, the participants enter into an *exchange* situation in which messages with certain shared meanings are transferred. The outcome or success of the exchange can, therefore, be predicted from the extent to which the images of the other's communication environment, the expected relations, agreement, and predictions are accurate. For example, it has been found that expected relations affect the degree of disclosure (Pearce, Wright, Sharp, & Slama, 1974; Gilbert & Horenstein, 1975) and deception (Knapp, Hart, & Dennis, 1974).

In an effort to achieve high degrees of accuracy, participants attempt to transfer messages not only through verbal codes, but, when the situation permits, also extensively through nonverbal codes. Recent concerted research efforts on the codification and meaningfulness of nonverbal codes have begun to accumulate knowledge about the complexity and importance of the structuring and use of nonverbal codes in exchanges (Keiser & Altman, 1976; Buck, 1976).

Exchange also utilizes a variety of mechanisms to construct, maintain, and achieve a more efficient and accurate transfer of meanings. For example, it has been shown that signal-stopping techniques (Carter et al., 1973), turn-taking (Wiemann & Knapp, 1975), and other mechanisms are used in exchange.

Exchange between an individual and a medium is infrequent. Letters to the editor, readers' corner, and the like are relatively ineffective. As Miller (1975) suggested, the interpersonal exchange is more effective because of the greater predictability of responses among participants. Within the technical development of interactive media devices, the ineffectiveness of mass media in *exchange* may decrease.

Nevertheless, it is doubtful that mass media, in the foreseeable future, can achieve the same level of interactive ability and predictability as human participants. Thus, the current proposition that interpersonal exchange is most effective in the transmission and maintenance of meanings shall probably remain valid for a long time to come.

Exchange is such a rich communication phenomenon that our present knowledge about its structure and process is limited. However, with a developing theoretical structure (as suggested in Figure 5), and the continuous and systematic gathering of data, especially in the areas of nonverbal codes and exchange mechanisms, there is potential for increasing *exchange* effects research in the near future.

INFLUENCE

Probably the most visible communication effects, as evidenced in the research literature, concern changes observed in the participant's attitude or behavior. The flow of the information in *encounters* and shared meanings in *exchanges* transmit the desires and wishes of the participants. The process by which participants evaluate these desires and wishes relative to their own attitudes and behaviors has been analyzed from a number of theoretical perspectives, the most dominant of which are the cognitive theories, as discussed by Heider, Newcombs, Osgood, Festinger, and others; the *social judgment theories,* as advanced by Sherif and Sherif, and others; and the participant's interactions with the components of the communication situation such as the source, the channel, etc., as examined by Hovland and numerous social psychologists. Thus, the evaluation of the incoming information and meanings is made relative to at least three reference systems. The first reference set is the cognitive structure of the participant; the second reference set his relationships with the specific communication situation; and the third his relations with his social environment.

The evaluation of the information and meanings relative to cognitive structure seems to follow two stages, as indicated in research evidence. The consistency theories suggest that, initially, an evaluation is made as to *whether* the incoming information and meanings are congruent with the participant's own cognitive images. When there is a perceived incongruity, then a further evaluation is made *as to what extent* these stimuli differ from one's images. The theories of social judgment inform us that the shorter such perceived difference, the more likely the person would be to change his cognitive image. However, such changes are likely to take place only when a number of alternatives (e.g., discontinuity of exchange, blocking off or distortion of incoming information and meanings, and termination of behavioral commitments) are not available.

Evaluation of the information and meanings is also made relative to the specific communication component operating the transmission. Each communication component, such as a source, channel, or message, has an attached value for its availability and utility to the participant's needs and images. Thus, changes attitudinally may more likely take place when the component is more "credible" and/or useful to the participant.

These evaluations relative to one's cognitive structure and valence attached to the specific communication situation may promote the formation or change of an attitude. They, however, do not necessarily activate the behavioral commitment of the participants. Behavioral commitment usually occurs only after the acquired information and meanings have undergone the "reality tests."

The reality tests serve two purposes: *reinforcement* and *instrumentation*. *Reinforcement* is the process through which the participant ascertains the degree to which a proposed course of action is consistent with the normative expectations of his social environment. It is important to note that the participant is involved in a multifaceted environment; therefore, alternative reference groups may be consulted relative to the proposed action. However, there is also a rank order of significance attached to the various reference groups relative to the specific attitude or action at hand. For example, it has been found that interpersonal influence, especially exerted from members of primary groups—rather than mass media—tends to be the more effective determinant of channel and sources of voting intentions (Robinson, 1976). It is hypothesized that the reinforcement from one's social environment accounts for a large portion of such influence.

Instrumentation, on the other hand, is the process by which symbols, and instructions necessary for the implementation of the action, are acquired. Instrumentation provides the specific details as to how the participant may go about expressing or implementing an action. It has been found in general that mass media, as well as interpersonal channels, are effective in providing instrumental information.

The relative importance of *interpersonal exchange* in providing *reinforcement*—and the equal importance of the interpersonal sources and mass media in providing *instrumentation*—can be derived from the role which predictability of re-

sponses plays in the reality tests. Reinforcement characteristically requires interactions in which responses and potential responses from one's reference groups, relative to the action one is contemplating, are essential. Thus, the participant must play both the roles of a sender and a receiver, as a participant in exchanges.

Instrumentation, on the other hand, is more asymmetric in nature. The participant contemplating an action primarily plays the role of a receiver in terms of the specific information and clarification of meanings necessary to carrying out the action. Further encounters or exchanges in which such information and clarification are acquired may be sufficient.

Traditionally, interpersonal sources were identified as the major channels for providing reinforcement. More recently, it has been found that the local media should be differentiated from other personal media in this regard. Local media (e.g., teachers, police, church leaders) provide reinforcement, at least in the rural areas (Lin & Burt, 1975).

Both reinforcement and instrumentation are essential in inducing the implementation of behavioral change. Take the example of family planning. It is important to provide both the reinforcement and instrumentation for the participant to adopt a practice promoted by a source. It is equally important for the participant to seek reinforcement and instrumentation. The lack of inadequacy of any of these communication activities may bring about a failure of change. The process of *influence* is depicted in Figure 6.

This theoretical framework may account for several intriguing issues confronting social scientists interested in social change. The observed discrepancy of attitude and behavior, for example, may be attributed to the absence of social and environmental reinforcement exerted upon the participant to express certain attitudes. Similarly, the extensive failure of family planning campaigns in less developed areas points to the gap between the existence of *reinforcement* (in many cultures women are unfavorable to a small family size, and to family planning as a concept) and the absence of *instrumentation* (what methods of family planning are available, where to obtain the necessary supplies,

FIGURE 6
The Process of Influence

```
Encounter
          ↘
           Evaluation relative ─────────────→ Further encounter/exchange ──────────────→ Influence
           to:                                for

           A.  The Cognitive structure        A. Reinforcement                    A.  Psychological
                                                                                      commitment
           B.  The relations to the           B. Instrumentation
               specific communication                                             B.  Behavioral
                                                                                      commitment
           C.  The social environment
          ↗
Exchange
```

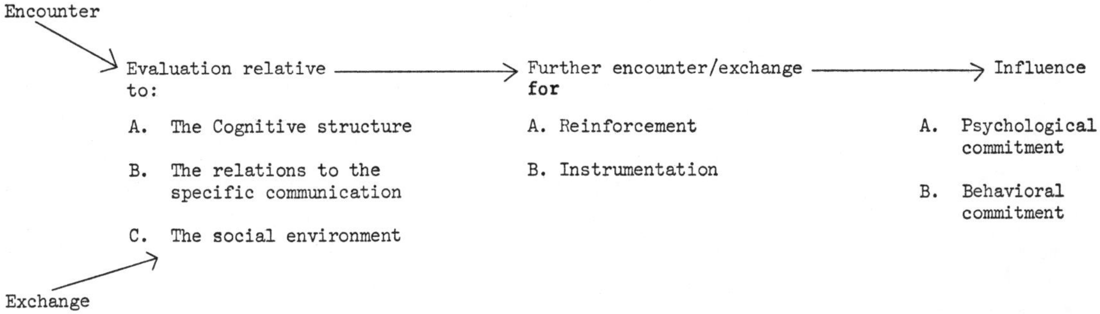

how is a method appropriately applied; what effects and remedies should be anticipated, etc.).

The well-known *two-step flow hypothesis* was built on the awareness that primary and secondary reference groups provide the necessary reinforcement for intended behavioral change. It has failed, however, to take into account the instrumental contributions of the mass media and the reinforcement provided by impersonal and local media (Lin & Burt, 1975) in the implementation of behavioral change.

One concept playing an important role in the process of influence is the decision-making process. The decision process should help identify and resolve the dynamic use of evaluation and exchange activities in the movement from attitudinal formation to behavioral commitment. Unfortunately, not enough research attention has been given to this process. Edelstein's probing analysis of the decision-making process (1973) demonstrates the usefulness of an open-ended approach toward a description and understanding of the process. The concept of the decision period (the relative length of time between initial encounter and psychological commitment relative to a change-oriented communication)—as a potential contributing factor in the explanatory model of influence (especially behavioral change)—has also been suggested (Lin, 1971). More effort is needed in this important area of research.

CONTROL AND ADAPTATION

Communication effects proceed beyond the in-

fluence phase where much of current research attention focuses and terminates. As evidence of influence become available to the participants, the effects of this influence on one's communication and social environment is evaluated. The mechanism of feedback is used to make further adjustments of one's communication activities.

From a sending participant's point of view, *control* is exercised to minimize any discrepancy between the expected effect and the actual effect on the receiving participant. *Gatekeeping* in both form and substance allows further agenda-setting (and unsetting), and image projection.

Manipulation of presence-absence, intensity, extensity, redundancy, and value associations are exercised in the formation and structure of information, meanings, and influence for further transmission.

The receiving participant, on the other hand, exercises *adaptation* to maintain and improve his or her position in the communication and social environment. The assumed attitudinal and behavioral posture is further assessed in terms of one's further *encounters* and *exchanges* in which alternative attitudinal and behavioral patterns become plausible and are considered.

The adopted attitude and behavior shall remain in force as long as control is continuously exercised and the perceived benefit/cost ratio remains high to the receiving participant in his continuous assessment of the attitude and/or behavior relative to his or her communication environment and alternative attitudes and behaviors.

FIGURE 7
Overview of the Process and Effects of Human Communication

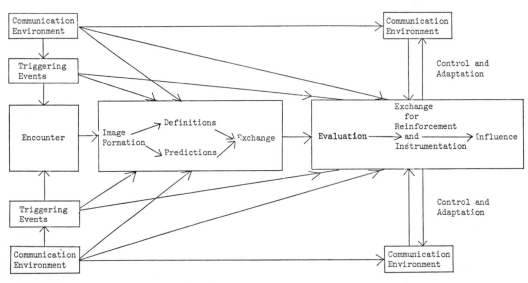

Participant B

The utility of the systems approach to study control and adaptation has been pointed out frequently in the communication literature (Ruben & Kim, 1975), yet research utilizing such a framework remains scarce. With recent methodological developments necessary to analyze the often nonrecursive, and overidentified, causal processes incorporating theoretical (unobserved) concepts (Joreskog, 1973, 1976), we should witness a surge of such research activities in the near future.

The overall theoretical framework incorporating all phases of communication is shown in Figure 7.

SUMMARY

This paper began with a brief review of the theoretical perspectives utilized in the study of human communication and, in particular, the study of communication effects. By contrasting the *directive* and *selective* perspectives, the divergence and convergence of research interests were pointed out. While each of these perspectives expresses the focus of a given research topic and effort, the *interactive perspective* must be the dominant and ultimate orientation within which theoretical integration is carried out.

Such an integration was attempted in the next section, in which a series of phases of human com-

munication were elaborated, and available empirical support provided. *Encounter, exchange, influence* and *control/adaptation* are dynamic concepts involving relations, processes, and outcomes. As a whole, they represent the dominant terms in a potentially useful theoretical structure of human communication, as depicted simplistically in Figure 7.

Theoretical gaps remain unfilled, and empirical confirmations and modifications need to be carried out. Nevertheless, the theoretical framework and some derived propositions suggested in this paper integrate a large portion of theory and research, and show logical consistency within the *interactive perspective*. Perhaps, the potential for a middle-range theory of communication and its effects is within our grasp.

NOTE

1. The terms are relative, rather than dichotomous. In research, a simple variable may be constructed to tap the extent that a *triggering event* conforms to one ideal type or the other. For illustrative purposes, the ideal types constitute the focal points for discussion in this paper.

REFERENCES

ALBA, R.D. A Graph-theoretical definition of a sociometric clique. *Journal of Mathematical Sociology,* 1973, 3, 113-126.

ARGYLE, M., & COOK, M. *Gaze and mutual gaze.* N.Y.: Cambridge University Press, 1976.

ATKIN, C. Instrumental utilities and information seeking. In P. Clarke (Ed.), *New models for mass communication research.* Beverly Hills, California: Sage, 1973, 205-242.

BARNETT, G.A., SEROTA, K.B., & TAYLOR, J.A. Campaign communication and attitude change. *Human Communication Research,* 1976, 2, 227-244.

BAUER, R. The obstinate audience. *The American Psychologist,* 1964, 19, 319-328.

BERGER, C.R., & CALABRESE, R.J. Some explorations in initial interaction and beyond: Toward a developmental theory of interpersonal communication. *Human Communication Research,* 1975, 1, 99-112.

BLUMLER, J.G., & McQUAIL, D. *Television in politics.* Chicago: University of Chicago Press, 1969.

BONACICH, P. Factoring and weighting approaches to status scores and clique identification. *Journal of Mathematical Sociology,* 1972, 2, 113-120.

BREEN, M.P. Severing the American connection. *Journal of Communication,* 1975, 25, 183-186.

BUCHLI, V., & PEARCE, W.B. Listening behavior in coorientational states. *Journal of Communication,* 1974, 24, 62-70.

BUCK, R. A test of nonverbal receiving ability: Preliminary studies. *Human Communication Research,* 1976, 2, 162-171.

BURT, R.S., & LIN, N. Network time series from archival records. In D. Heise (ed.), *Sociological Methodology 1977.* San Francisco: Jossey-Bass, 1977.

BUSBY, L.J. Sex-role research on the mass media. *Journal of Communication,* 1975, 25, 107-131.

CARDONA, E. de. Multinational television. *Journal of Communication,* 1975, 25, 122-127.

CARTER, R.F., RUGGELS, W.L., JACKSON, K.M., & HEFFNER, M.B. Application of signaled stopping technique to communication research. In P. Clarke (Ed.), *New models for mass communication research.* Beverly Hills, California: Sage, 1973, 15-43.

CARTWRIGHT, D. Some principles of mass persuasion: Selected findings of research on the sale of U.S. war bonds. *Human Relations,* 1949, 2, 253-267.

CHAFFEE, S.H. The interpersonal context of mass communication. In F. Gerald Kline and P.J. Tichenor (Eds.), *Current perspectives in mass communication research.* Beverly Hills, California: Sage, 1972, 95-120.

CHAFFEE, S.H. (Ed.) *Political communication: Issues and strategies for research.* Beverly Hills, California: Sage, 1975.

COCHRAN, T.C. Media as business: A brief history. *Journal of Communication,* 1975, 25, 155-165.

COLEMAN, J.S. Relational analysis: The study of social organizations with survey methods. *Human Organization,* 1959, 17, 28-36.

COLEMAN, J.S. *Introduction to mathematical sociology.* N.Y.: Free Press, Chapter 14, 1964.

COLLINS, W.A. The developing child as viewer. *Journal of Communication,* 1975, 25, 35-44.

COMSTOCK, G. The effects of television on children and adolescents: The evidence so far. *Journal of Communication,* 1975, 25, 25-34.

COULTHARD, M., & ASHBY, M. Talking with the doctor, 1. *Journal of Communication,* 1975, 25, 140-147.

CULLEY, J.D., & BENNETT, R. Selling women, selling blacks. *Journal of Communication,* 1976, 26, 160-174.

DANCE, E.X., & LARSON, C.E. *The functions of human communication.* N.Y.: Holt, Rinehart and Winston, 1976.

DERVIN, B., & GREENBERG, B.S. The communication environment of the urban poor. In F.G. Kline and P.J. Tichenor (Eds.), *Current perspectives in mass communication research.* Beverly Hills, California: Sage, 1973, 195-233.

DOHRMANN, R. A gender profile of children's educational TV. *Journal of Communication,* 1975, 25, 56-65.

DONOHEW, L., & TIPTON, L. A conceptual model of information seeking, avoiding, and processing. In P. Clarke (Ed.), *New models for mass communication research.* Beverly Hills, California: Sage, 1973, 243-268.

DONOHUE, G.A., TICHENOR, P.J., & OLIEN, C.N. Gatekeeping: Mass media systems and information control. In F.G. Kline and P.J. Tichenor (Eds.), *Current perspectives in mass communication research.* Beverly Hills, California: Sage, 1972, 41-69.

EDELSTEIN, A.S. Decision-making and mass communication: A conceptual and methodological approach to public opinion. In P. Clarke (Ed.), *New models for mass communication research.* Beverly Hills, California: Sage, 1973, 81-118.

ELLIS, D.G., & FISHER, B.A. Phases of conflict in small group development: A Markov analysis. *Human Communication Research,* 1975, 1, 195-212.

FISCHER, J.L. Communication in primitive systems. In I. de Sola Pool, W. Schramm et al. (Eds.), *Handbook of Communication.* Chicago: Rand McNally, 1975, 313-336.

FUCHS, D.A., & LYLE, J. Mass media portrayal—Sex and violence. In F.G. Kline and P.J. Tichenor (Eds.), *Current perspectives in mass communication research.* Beverly Hills, California: Sage, 1972, 235-264.

GERBNER, G., & GROSS, L.P. Living with television: The violence profile. *Journal of Communication,* 1976, 26, 172-199.

GILBERT, S.J., & HORENSTEIN, D. The communication of self-disclosure: Level versus valence. *Human Communication Research,* 1975, 1, 316-322.

GUBACK, T.H. Film as international business. *Journal of Communication,* 24, 1974, 90-101.

HOMANS, G. *The Human Group.* N.Y.: Harcourt, Brace and World, 1950.

JORESKOG, K.G. A general method for estimating a linear structural equation system. In A.S. Goldberger and O.D. Duncan (Eds.), *Structural equation models in the social sciences.* N.Y.: Seminar Press, 1973.

JORESKOG, K.G. Structural equation models in the social sciences: Specification, estimation and testing. Sweden: Uppsala University, Statistics Department, 1976.

KATZ, E., BLUMLER, J.G., & GUREVITCH, M. Utilization of mass communication by the individual. In J.G. Blumler and E. Katz (Eds.), *The uses of mass communications.* Beverly Hills, California: Sage, 1974, 19-32.

KATZ, E., & LAZARSFELD, P.F. *Interpersonal Influence.* N.Y.: Free Press, 1955.

KEISER, G.J., & ALTMAN, I. Relationship of nonverbal behavior to the social penetration process. *Human Communication Research,* 1976, 2, 147-161.

KNAPP, M.L., HART, R.P., & DENNIS, H.S. An exploration of deception as a communication construct. *Human Communication Research,* 1974, 1, 15-29.

KRUGMAN, H.E. The impact of television advertising: Learning without involvement. *Public Opinion Quarterly,* 1965, 29, 349-356.

KUHN, T.S. The structure of scientific revolutions. Chicago: University of Chicago Press, 1962.

LAUMANN, E.O. *Bonds of Pluralism.* N.Y.: Wiley, 1973.

LAZARSFELD, P.F., & MERTON, R.K. Friendship as social process: A substantive and methodological analysis. In M. Berger and others (Eds.), *Freedom and control in modern society.* N.Y.: Octogon, 1964.

LIN, N. Information flow, Influence flow, and the decision-making process. *Journalism Quarterly,* 1971, 48, 33-40.

LIN, N. *The Study of Human Communication.* Indianapolis: Bobbs-Merrill, 1973.

LIN, N. *Foundations of social research.* N.Y.: McGraw-Hill, 1976.

LIN, N., & BURT, R.S. Differential roles of information channels in the process of innovation diffusion. *Social Forces,* 1975, 54, 256-274.

LIN, N., & DAYTON, P.W. The uses of social status and social resources in the urban network. Paper presented at the annual meeting of the American Sociological Association, New York, August 1976.

MABRY, E.A. Sequential structure of interaction in encounter groups. *Human Communication Research,* 1975, 1, 302-307.

McCOMBS, M., & SHAW, D. The agenda-setting function of mass media. *Public Opinion Quarterly* 1972, 36, 176-187.

McCOMBS, M.E., & SHAW, D.L. Structuring the "unseen environment." *Journal of Communication,* 1976, 26, 18-28.

McGUIRE, W.J. *Persuasion, resistance, and attitude change.* In I. de Sola Pool, W. Schramm et al. (Eds.), *Handbook of Communication.* Chicago: Rand McNally, 1973, 216-252.

McLEOD, J.M., & BECKER, L.B. Testing the validity of gratification measures through political effects analysis. In J.G. Blumler, and E. Katz (Eds.), *The uses of mass communication.* Beverly Hills, California: Sage, 1974, 137-164.

McLEOD, J.M., BECKER, L.B., & BYRNES, J.E. Another look at the agenda-setting function of the press. *Communication Research,* 1974, 1, 131-166.

MILLER, G.R. Interpersonal communication: A conceptual perspective. *Communication,* 1975, 2, 93-105.

NOFSINGER, R.E. On answering questions indirectly: Some rules in the grammar of doing conversation. *Human Communication Research,* 1976, 2, 172-181.

PEARCE, A. The TV networks. *Journal of Communication,* 1976, 26, 54-59.

PEARCE, W.B., & STAMM, K.R. Coorientational states and interpersonal communication. In P. Clarke (Ed.), *New models for mass communication research.* Beverly Hills, California: Sage, 1973, 177-203.

PEARCE, W.B., WRIGHT, P.H., SHARP, S.M., & SLAMA, K.M. Affection and reciprocity in self-disclosing communication. *Human Communication Research,* 1974, 1, 5-14.

RAY, M.L. Marketing communication and the hierarchy-of-effects. In P. Clarke (Ed.), *New models for mass communication research.* Beverly Hills, California: Sage, 1973, 147-176.

RICHARDS, W.D. A conceptually based method for the analysis of communication networks in large complex organizations. Paper presented at the meeting of the International Communication Association, 1971.

ROBINSON, J.P. Interpersonal influence in election campaigns: Two step-flow hypotheses. *Public Opinion Quarterly,* 1976, 40, 304-319.

ROGERS, E.M., & SHOEMAKER, F.F. *Communication of Innovations.* N.Y.: Free Press, 1971.

ROISTACHER, R.C. A review of mathematical methods in sociometry. *Sociological methods and research,* 1974, 2, 123-171.

ROTHSCHILD, M.L., & RAY, M.L. Involvement and political advertising effect. *Communication Research,* 1974, 1, 264-263.

RUBEN, B.D., & KIM, J.Y., (Eds.), *General systems theory and human communication.* Rochelle Park, N.J.: Hayden, 1975.

RUTKUS, D.S. Presidential television. *Journal of Communication,* 1976, 26, 73-78.

SALOMON, G. Cognitive skill learning across cultures. *Journal of Communication,* 1976, 26, 138-144.

SALTIEL, J., & WOELFEL, J. Inertia in cognitive processes: The role of accumulated information in attitude change. *Human Communication Research,* 1975, 1, 333-344.

SCHILLER, H.I. Freedom from the "free flow." *Journal of Communication,* 1974, 24, 110-117.

SCHRAMM, W. Nature of communication between humans. In W. Schramm and D.F. Roberts (Eds.), *The process and effects of mass communication.* Urbana, Ill.: University of Illinois, 1971, 3-53.

SHORTLAND, R.L. The communication patterns and the structure of social relationships at a large university. Unpublished Ph.D. dissertation, Michigan State University, 1970.

SIUNE, K., & BORRE, O. Setting the agenda for a Danish election. *Journal of Communication,* 1975, 25, 65-73.

STAMM, K.R., & PEARCE, W.B. Message locus and message content: Two studies in communication behavior and coorientational relations. *Communication Research,* 1974, 1, 184-203.

STEPHENSON, W. *The play theory of mass communication.* Chicago: University of Chicago Press, 1967.

STREICHER, L.H., & BONNEY, N.L. Children talk about television. *Journal of Communication,* 1974, 24, 54-61.

TICHENOR, P.J., RODENKIRCHEN, J.M., OLIEN, C.N., & DONOHUE, G.A. Community issues, conflicts, and public affairs knowledge. In P. Clarke (Ed.), *New models for mass communication research.* Beverly Hills, California: Sage, 1973, 54-79.

VARIS, T. Global traffic in television. *Journal of Communication,* 1974, 24, 102-109.

WARD, S., & WACKMAN, D.B. Children's information processing of television advertising. In P. Clarke (Ed.), *New models for mass communication research.* Beverly Hills, California: Sage, 1973, 119-146.

WARTELLA, E., & ETTEMA, J.S. A cognitive developmental study of children's attention to television commercials. *Communication Research,* 1974, 1, 69-88.

WATT, J.H., & KRULL, R. An information theory measure for television programming. *Communication Research,* 1974, 1, 44-68.

WEITZ, S. (Ed.). *Nonverbal Communication.* N.Y.: Oxford University Press, 1974.

WIEMANN, J.M., & KNAPP, M.L. Turn-taking in conversations. *Journal of Communication,* 1975, 25, 75-92.

WOELFEL, J., WOELFEL, J., GILLHAM, J., & McPHAIL, T. Political radicalization as a communication process. *Communication Research,* 1974, 1, 243-263.

WOLF, G. Some conversational conditions and processes of brief encounters. *Communication Research,* 1974, 1, 167-183.

WRIGHT, W.R. Mass media as sources of medical information. *Journal of Communication,* 1975, 25, 171-173.

EUROPEAN COMMUNICATIONS THEORY:
REVIEW AND COMMENTARY

KAARLE NORDENSTRENG
Tampere University—Finland

Communication study in Europe has traditionally centered on the media of communication and was typically approach from traditional disciplinary perspectives such as history and law. More recently, European mass communication research has expanded in focus. Considered in addition to the media, their messages, and the psychological dynamics of reception, are the social and material living conditions of the people. In such a perspective emphasis is upon both *subjective* and *objective* informational needs. Additional trends in communication research in Europe—and elsewhere—include a tendency toward the use of more holistic frameworks and increasing concern with mass communication policy, as well as emphasis on *processes* and *contexts*.

Communications research and theory has its origins in the development of the media of communication, particularly mass media. In the beginning, starting around the turn of the century, studies of mass communication were occasional exercises, carried out from the traditional bases of history, law, etc. But as the social importance of mass communication increased with mass-circulated commercial press, and particularly after the introduction of radio broadcasting in the twenties, social communications research began to grow and take shape. First, it was usually associated with particular media, like the German *Zeitungswissenschaft*—newspaper science—or American radio research. The latter was strongly stimulated by the market needs of rapidly expanding commercial broadcasting. Audience research at the same time served as the main force to develop general public opinion surveys (Schiller, 1974). Gradually, however, media-bound approaches were replaced by a more general view of mass media. In German scholarship this development led, between the wars, to the emergence of *Publizistik*—science of public communication—while the concept of communication research broke through in the American arena towards the end of the forties.

During the three decades that have passed since the last war, mass communication research in Europe has constantly increased. This growth, however, is nothing like the boom which has taken place in the United States. In fact, compared with the rise of social sciences in general, and sociology in particular, the field of mass communication research has become an especially popular area of study in only a few countries, one of which is Finland.

The European mass communication research area is not a very abundant source of intellectual development. Usually there are only one or two significant bases of communication research in a country. Despite this quantitative limitation, qualitatively, European communication research provides a most varied spectrum of activities, approaches, and traditions. They extend from routine audience research carried out for the press and broadcasting organizations to experimental studies of media effects, content analyses of media output, and various kinds of journalism research. And besides this sort of research activity, which more or less duplicates American patterns, there is much research which might be characterized as uniquely European. Semiotic and structuralist schools in France and Italy, studies of contemporary culture in Great Britain, and Marxist orientations in Eastern Europe—and increasingly also in the West (particularly in the Federal Republic of Germany—are examples of these emerging traditions.

Given this variety, a fair and balanced reporting of the whole European arena—especially if Europe is considered to include the socialist countries—is therefore impossible in the space provided here. What will be provided, instead, is an overview of current trends in the more basic theoretical orientations in which European communications research is being executed. The review will be limited to the Western part of Europe, because the socialist countries would deserve a completely separate treatment.

The Scope of Research

It is typical of current European communication research to expand the focus beyond the media, their messages, and the psychological reception process of the messages. Included also are the social and material living conditions of the people. In listing factors that determine the reception of adult education programs, one must recognize, for example, "however good the timing policy, however dominant the channel, however close to real-life experiences the programs may be, however easy the language, and however much promotional information and even organizational mobilization may be exercised, nothing helps if a person is seriously deprived in his objective and physical surroundings, and consequently, if he is psychologically so apathetic and alienated that the total motivation for improvement and change in his socioeconomic situation is missing" (Nordenstreng, 1973).

Manifestations of this way of thinking are the Scandinavian projects started in the early seventies. In Finland, similar research projects focus on citizens' informational needs, and in Sweden they focus on information gaps in society. Both were initiated and are mainly being carried out within the broadcasting organizations, which is an indication of the social and informational commitment of these mass communication institutions.

The points of departure of the Swedish project are stated by the researchers as follows:

> Marked differences among social groups with respect to access to and utilization of essential information constitute a problem in our society. ("Essential" information is tentatively defined as information that enables the individual to survey and understand the society he lives in, and allows him actively to influence the conditions of his daily life.) These differences are primarily functions of factors outside the control of mass media, factors such as the structure of society, the social and economic status of various groups and individuals, their personal capabilities, etc. Even so, the roles and potential roles of mass media should not be considered a priori to lack significance. Depending on how they are controlled and utilized—in terms of policy, on planning and production levels—the media may doubtless contribute either to the broadening or to the closing of information gaps. (Sveriges Radio Bulletin, 1973)

The Finnish project on citizens' informational needs shares these concerns, and stresses the socioeconomically determined mechanisms which accumulate material and mental wealth and lead to informational activity on the one hand, and material and mental poverty accompanied by informational passivity on the other. In analyzing the mechanism of social inequality, the project committee pointed out the functions of segregation in society: Minimization of contacts between the privileged and underprivileged reduces the informational and social fields of operation of both groups, leaving the privileged to enjoy their benefits with good conscience, and the underprivileged to remain satisfied with their lot. It was also noted that social studies and official statistics had, until recent years, largely supported these same overall tendencies.

Empirical results of a nationwide survey carried out for this project further verified the presence of this vicious circle: Those who were already well informed were most open to new knowledge and most capable of finding relevant knowledge, whereas the ill-informed—the socioeconomically underpriviledged—were passive and unable to tell where to find relevant knowledge. Furthermore, the latter group did not regard information and knowledge as particularly important.

SUBJECTIVE AND OBJECTIVE INFORMATION NEEDS

An essential theoretical distinction applied in the project is between *subjective* and *objective* informational needs. It was not deemed sufficient to carry out an opinion survey and register subjectively perceived informational needs and wishes alone. It was thought necessary, additionally, to construct an all-round picture of the respondent's objective living conditions and his possibilities for social action.

The aim was to see an individual's subjective assessment of his informational needs and behavior as an integral part of his total living conditions and social environment. Expressed in these terms, it is evident that informational needs are least satisfied among the underprivileged sections of the population, and that the greatest difference between the subjective and objective levels of informational need is to be found among those who are unable to accumulate material and informational wealth in society. The "haves" do not objectively have many informational needs unsatisfied, and yet they subjectively have more informational hunger than the "have-nots," whose objective informational needs are burning.

Besides social segregation, the socioeconomic system is seen to employ various mechanisms which tend to keep the level of subjective informational needs low. One central concept in this connection is the *(bourgeois) hegemony*, which may be understood as a filter extending to the personal world-view of an individual, and biasing or blocking his process of perceiving reality. The de facto function of the bulk of mass media is taken to be an overall support of this hegemony. By means of a long-term indoctrination of certain implicit values and a fragmentation of message supply, the media are thought to inhibit an individual's effort to construct a holistic view of objective reality.

The Finnish project—as well as the corresponding Swedish one—might well be classified as an exercise in political science, or in general sociology, rather than as communication research. The general problem is to study the actual and potential conditions for social equality and participatory democracy, and there is a tendency to avoid a narrow communicologist's point of view, taking instead a broad perspective which integrates a wide range of socioeconomic (objective) factors that interplay with (subjective) communication phenomena. In this context, media of mass communication are studied as a dependent, rather than independent, variable.

It may be said that such an approach is no innovation in the tradition of communication research. However, a close look will reveal that the theoretical framework used in these studies usually differs from those applied in earlier research into the same problems. The social factors employed go far beyond the primary group considerations which dominated earlier receiver studies. Now it is the economic structure of society—the total system—that is taken as the point of departure, instead of some more or less loosely defined groups within a society.

In fact, having once left the media-bound perspective, and focusing more broadly on mass communication, the field may be advancing to still another stage. The evolution seems to be from a still narrow approach centered around the media (as separated from society) to a wider approach with the media viewed as simply one of the integral parts of the overall ideological machinery in society. And it is usually understood that this machinery—which is seen as an integrated function of all social and cultural institutions with potential effects on peoples' consciousness—has a hegemonistic character.

The concept of "mass consciousness," introduced along with the traditional concept of *public opinion,* is seen not only as a sum or average of a number of individual pieces of consciousness (a phenomenon at the micro level), but also as a social phenomenon (at the macro level), relatively independent of individuals. One might even say that the field, after only recently gaining an identity, has now started to move from mass communication research towards a general social science, i.e., political economy of society on the one hand, and an overall study of culture on the other.

AN APPARENT DILEMMA

At this point, one might observe a dilemma in the theoretical orientation that has been described. In one sense, it is the material living conditions of people and the socioeconomic structures that are seen as vital in describing and explaining communication phenomena. At the same time, there seems to be a strong emphasis on the ideological and manipulative process taking place at the level of mass consciousness and contemporary culture. Serious questions may be raised concerning the philosophical origins of these levels and their methodological compatibility.

And, indeed, a vivid debate is currently taking place in Europe about the relative importance of material and ideological factors in communications theory. Not surprisingly, this debate is occurring in the context of the social sciences in general.

As is well known, the Western orientation in sociology has largely avoided a materialistic, structural concept of society, and has instead constructed a model of society based largely on individual and group interaction, with communication processes as the critical factor. Such an orientation has facilitated, among other things, a conceptual confusion of power relations with the relations of communication. The result is a tendency to conceive of objective power antagonisms as simply linguistic complications. It is not difficult to note how such a notion of society is politically useful in the context of capitalist economy, where disturbances in industrial relations may be explained by notions like "semantic noise," and pressures towards industrial democracy are met by measures to "facilitate the flow of information."

This approach in social sciences has increasingly been opposed by a strictly materialistic approach—inspired by the classics of Marxism and Leninism—which introduces materialistic socioeconomic structures, in addition to interaction processes and related phenomena of (mass) consciousness. This perspective also claims that these socioeconomic factors must be taken as primary dimensions in explaining individual and social behavior. The socioeconomic structures are seen as composed of the material arrangements of production in society, with the nature of ownership and production systems, and the relationship of production to the corresponding social and economic institutions, determining relations between individuals. The nature of these structures is materialistic, although in practice they may operate mostly by means of symbolic (and, in that sense, immaterial) communication.

Consequently, the rise of modern communication research—advocating a societal approach, and equipped with new concepts of nonmaterial social communication processes—present a dilemma. Paradoxically, many of those who thought they had advanced a broad approach to mass communication as a social process and to mass media as social institutions, are often finding themselves among the traditional "ideologizers" of social phenomena. In fact, the same criticism is being directed towards some of the most outstanding representatives of the current leftist schools in France and Germany, such as Louis Althusser and Jurgen Habermas. And, as is typical of social scientific debates in Europe, criticism and counter-criticism are coupled with statements of political positions in which many of those communication researchers who consider themselves "progressive"—and who certainly, by North American standards, would be classified "leftists" if not "ultra-marxists"— have been labeled by the critics as "right-wing deviants."

This debate, as hot and bitter as it may be to those concerned, will certainly prove to be a very useful medicine for the field—not only for communications research, but for the study of social and cultural phenomena in general. First of all, it serves as a guarantee that the field does not fall back into the era of narrow communicology, but continues to be socially oriented. Secondly, such a scientific debate will eliminate what might be called a "petit-bourgeois reform" of the field, i.e., a superficial reorientation without questioning the fundamental theoretical conceptions. Examples of the "half-way approach" are studies of the economic structure of media industries and critical appraisals of media contents which are not accompanied by a comprehensive theory of socioeconomic processes. Thirdly, the debate compels research in this traditionally quite eclectic field to undertake an explicit analysis of its basic theoretical and philosophical propositions. And, finally, the debate on the nature of communication and communication research is welcome because it seems to further the tendency in several traditional social and even humanistic sciences to "discover" the concept of communication, and to recapitulate their own theories in terms of human communication.

Naturally there is nothing wrong with attempts of the traditional fields to incorporate concepts and findings of communications research and information theory in their theoretical frameworks. But in Western tradition there is a potential risk of communication becoming another magic phenomenon which could easily occupy a dominant position in many fields of art and sciences, from literature to economics. This development could mask and obscure—rather than clarify and advance—the state of the art in these fields. A German participant in the debate on the nature of communication and its research, Karl Held (1973), has directed the following bitter words to modern communication researchers who are overlooking material elements in the process, and to those outsiders who have become so fascinated by the concept of communication that is understood as *the* element of human nature: "The general tendency to explain everything . . . [as] communication . . . it not science but *ideology*. As not a single one of the objects of communication research is essentially composed of communication, communication becomes a fetish which not only explains nothing, but even largely disturbs" (p. 184; emphasis added).

FUTURE DIRECTIONS

As to the future, it is becoming clear that these developments and debates are certainly not isolated from the general trends in social and humanistic sciences, nor from the changing patterns of the overall sociopolitico-economic system. There are some universal tendencies in the field of mass communication research occurring more or less everywhere in the Western, capitalist world, as well as in current European thinking.

The global trends in the field of mass communication research can be summarized in terms of two interrelated tendencies on change: (1) a tendency towards a more holistic framework and (2) a tendency towards policy orientation. The holistic approach, for its part, may be seen to imply two subaspects: (a) a stressing of the *process approach* covering, simultaneously, various stages of communication process; and (b) a stressing of the *contextual approach,* tying the particular communication phenomena into wider sociopolitico-economic settings.

It is not difficult to trace in these tendencies a rebellion against the positivist-behaviorist tradition. In terms of the philosophy of science, it is exactly this shift from positivism towards antipositivism that may be seen as crucial in the present reorientation of communication research—as well as in the Western social sciences in general.

In the present context, it is particularly important to note the implications of positivism for policy considerations. The crucial notion of positivism—called in philosophical debate the "Humean guillotine"—argues that one cannot obtain from "how things are" an inference of "how they should be." Goals of social activity are understood as something voluntary and subjective; value-bound choices are placed by definition outside the scope of objective knowledge. Consequently, *research* and *politics* are sharply separated from each other, suggesting a relativity of values. Anti-positivism, for its part, claims that a study of the objective laws of social processes, in their widest sense, can be derived from social goals grounded on objective facts. It is a contention that these social goals—"how things should be"—can be inferred, at least to a great extent, from the laws followed by goal-directed social processes, once the latter have been discovered. Consequently, research and politics cannot and should not be sharply separated.

At this point one might ask why such a reorientation in the social sciences in general—and mass communication research in particular—has begun to take place. What are the cultural and social determinants behind this movement? In the present analysis only one overall factor will be singled out.

In industrialized societies, efforts at ideological control over the mass consciousness have become increasingly difficult. Since traditional methods for ideological control have proved inadequate, more effective means to touch the minds of the masses are being sought. This may be one reason so much is said today of "comprehension of messages," "audience passivity," etc. These kinds of new perspectives into the mass communication process (including the activists of "citizen participation") seem a must for the maintenance of social order.

In the social sciences there seems to be an objective need for social forces to turn the positivistic tradition into a more holistic approach. It is no longer sufficient to contribute to theories of manipulation with piecemeal studies and conceptualizations which by-pass many significant features of social development.

Systematic policies and long-range planning are another vital response. A need for policies and planning in the communication field derives not only from motives of ideological control, but also from a general tendency towards more coherent socioeconomic processes. All these pressures have the positivist tendency to define policy-related goals and objectives as "nonscientific." Western social sciences, including communications research, have moved closer to the Marxist concept of social science.

CONCLUSION

The philosophical and political situation is far from a simple one. In terms of the present analysis, the new approach in communication research, as well as boosting interest in communication policies, can be seen to reflect the same basic tendency of having the mechanism of the prevailing social order brought up-to-date, and thus supporting the basic tendencies of the status quo. Accordingly, a "progressive" communication researcher finds himself in a paradoxical situation: no matter what he subjectively might advocate, his services are largely channeled in the given socioeconomic context for the benefit of the existing social order. However, this certainly is not a deterministic process, and there always remains a certain range of movement within the scientific tradition, as well as in social development in general.

REFERENCES

HELD, K. Kommunikationsforschung—Wissenchaft oder ideologie? Materialien zur Kritik einer neuen Wissenschaft. Munich: Carl Verlag, 1973.

NORDENSTRENG, K. Definition of the audience and how to increase it. *Adult Education by Television*. Geneva: European Broadcasting Union, 1973, 31-38.

NORDENSTRENG, K. From mass media to mass consciousness. In G. Gerbner (Ed.), Current trends in mass communications. Netherlands: Mouton, 1977.

POOL, I. de S. The rise of communications policy research. *Journal of Communication*, 1974, 31-42.

SCHILLER, H.I. Waiting for orders—Some current trends in mass communications research in the United States. *Gazette*, 1974, 11-21.

Sveriges Radio Bulletin (Swedish Broadcasting Corporation). Audience and Program Research Bulletin No. 3, 1973.

UNESCO. Proposals for an international programme of communication research (COM/MD/20, 1971).

UNESCO. Meeting of experts on communication policies and planning (COM/MD/24, 1972).

THE TAXONOMY OF COMMUNICATION

ALFRED G. SMITH
University of Texas

The communication taxonomies we live by are represented by curricula, tables of contents, and the line items of budgets. Many of these are political products. Communication means different things at different times to different people, even to the same person. Therefore the communication taxonomy changes, is relative rather than absolute, and is probabilistic. Its categories are fuzzy sets, and generally multimodal. Computers can manage this complexity. Beyond a taxonomy, the field of communication rests on a philosophy and choices of priorities.

Unless our view of communication is somehow systemic, our work in communication will be chaotic. Individual studies, courses, and operations can be adequate without a comprehensive framework, but the output of the total field will be an unholy mess. Unless we view communication through some sturdy principles that are profound and sweeping, flexible yet well ordered, the field will be just a grabbag of odds and ends. Work assignments will be at cross purposes. Investments of resources will be non compos. A slapdash notion of the field can cripple our thinking about communication.

Basically, botanists tell us, bananas, corn, and orchids belong together in one group, while oaks, sunflowers, and peas belong together in another group. These groups, and the algae, mosses, ferns, and all the rest, form the botanical taxonomic system. This taxonomy sorts and arranges all observations of plant life into a single comprehensive model.

Taxonomies give some order to the chaos of life. They provide a framework for explaining what we see and guide our search for further meaning. The ancient Greek taxonomy of *earth, air, fire,* and *water* was such a classification for the whole cosmos. The Chinese hit the bedrock of binary coding with *yin* and *yang*. Man needs some form or structure, some grammar or model, to make some sense out of his world.

Taxonomy in communication, unlike taxonomy in botany, is not based on evolutionary and genetic relations. There are other relations, however, and we can even choose which ones we will take to be basic. Our choices do need to be consistent if the taxonomy is to organize the field reasonably and fruitfully.

In communication textbooks there are chapters on feedback, semantics, entropy, and informal channels. A communication association has divisions of information systems, interpersonal communication, mass communication, organizational communication, and four or five more. In a school of communication there are departments of advertising, journalism, radio-television-film, and speech. These divisions, departments, and other codifications may form a taxonomy of communication.

It is clear, however, that these various codifications are not uniform or in step with one another. Does the department of speech coincide with the division on interpersonal communication and do these two coincide with the chapter on informal channels? Does advertising coincide with mass communication and do these two coincide with the chapter on feedback? In communication there is little correspondence among the organization of a department, the divisions of an association, and the table of contents of a textbook. It is as if algae, mosses, and ferns were not related to one another in the same way in a botany course as in the parks department.

The schools, texts, and the field of communication as a whole are recently formed conglomerates of previously separate enterprises. Each of these conglomerates is different. Their different parts came from very different philosophical points of departure. Rhetoricians in speech generally had academic orientations for humanistic scholarship, while electronic journalists were oriented to work in the media. Moreover, each of the previously separate enterprises was itself a conglomerate whose range of varied pursuits was wider than its coherence was binding. Such conglomerates of the miscellaneous within bigger conglomerates of the heterogeneous can make the field as a whole irreducible to any taxonomic order.

Naturally, this paper will not present the final solution. It will, however, outline how to cope with the problem. The ways and means will be developed to the taxonomy of communication, the approach rather than the outcome. It is not an easy or a simple approach.

My main concern is with the taxonomy we live by. That often differs from the elegant and smart taxonomies to be found in print (Blake & Haroldson, 1975; Kibler & Barker, 1969; Dance & Larson, 1976). I will first consider some of the pitfalls in the approach of the workaday world. Then we will do a little experiment to establish a basic sense of the problem. Next, the general idea of *communication* has to be considered, and also further characteristics of taxonomy as usable in communication. Here we also need to consider how we can approach the ambiguity of communicational categories, and use computers in developing the taxonomy of communication. The paper will conclude by considering basic choices.

REGRETTABLE TAXONOMIES

All taxonomies are not created equal. There are defective ones that corrupt our understanding and foul our work. These regrettable taxonomies are only good as bad examples. They point out the pitfalls to be avoided in our own methods and standards. Regrettably they are like the Indian snake oils the quacks used for bilking the gilpins: a little licorice and turpentine and a lot of water. Those snake oils did not kill anybody, but they did keep people away from the bona fide medicine they needed.

Some of these taxonomies are superficial. They class the bats with the birds. Some are merely lists of labels, and some lists are too long while others are too short. Some are diagrams of un-operationalized abstractions. One type of taxonomy warrants special consideration.

Most taxonomies of communication are political. They are drawn up by men of action to meet the here and now problems of governance. The graduate committee of the communication school has to choose a set of courses for next year. The committee members face a mongrel miscellany of offerings including information theory, print journalism, film criticism, deaf education, and rhetoric. The claims of the various courses are bounced back and forth at the meeting. Self interests jocky for position. The stakes are high. The adrenalin flows. The graduate curriculum, like most taxonomies, is not a product of pure reason and scientific objectivity.

Elsewhere the editor has to select and arrange a set of writings, and meet scores of diverse demands. What topics shall be included and excluded, and how shall they be arranged? In another building, the department chairman is drafting a budget for the next biennium. He tries to dovetail many warring requests and keep them within an overall budget he can fight for. Curricula, tables of contents, and the line items of budgets are taxonomies that come into the world pushed and pulled by managers, zealots, researchers, clods, and fortune seekers. The resulting domains and classifications are at best a gerrymandered balance of power.

"We'll put news broadcasters under journalism, but broadcasters generally will go under radio and television, except when they employ speech. That's good enough. There's no ideal answer anyway." The rough and ready sorting of topics cuts through all complexities. Even so, these quick and dirty solutions are shortsighted and superficial. They meet immediate and apparent demands at the expense of broader and deeper needs.

Rough and ready was not the way chemists mapped out the *acids, bases,* and *salts,* the *proteins, fats,* and *carbohydrates,* and the *hypo-, ortho-, per-,* and *pyro-* of their taxonomic system. Nor did Linnaeus rely on the politically quick and dirty in developing his biological system. In the field of communication, regrettably, taxonomy is primarily political. Self interests push and pull to make the decisions that subdivide the field. Thereby journalism may include public relations but not advertising, which is over in marketing. Thereby the department of radio, television, and film gives the courses in performance, except for those in the oral interpretation of literature which are taught in the speech department, and both these sets of performance courses scrupulously stay out of the jurisdiction of the drama department, which is far out on the other side of the campus. This leaves us out in limbo somewhere between casuistry and absurdity.

Both scholars and administrators need taxonomies, yet their needs are different. The one can do with the rough and ready, the other cannot. The one leaves problems to argument, the other to research. All things considered, it is far better for administrators to base their decisions on the findings of scholars than for scholars to base their work on the taxonomic decisions of administrators. Communication scholarship and operations are group enterprises that require consensus. We need to fix the beliefs of the group through free thinking and discussion. This should, of course, be founded on objective inquiry. That promotes the long range advantage and mutual interests of teachers, workers, administrators, researchers, students, and the field as a whole.

A TAXONOMIC EXPERIMENT

In our work, in industries, colleges, associations, foundations, journals, and books, we are so involved in one or another map of the field that we do not see any map objectively and critically. We regard communication wholly through our own departmental structure, or through the items on our own agenda. These are blinders that protect our sense of place and direction. We seldom go beyond our immediate concerns and ask whether our map is adequate and reliable for the field as a whole. Yet we need at least to know what a good map should be.

The first requirements for an objective taxonomy of communication are that it be *abstract, ambiguous, constrained*, and *complex*. To support this initial contention let us conduct a small experiment in two parts. In the first part let us present to a number of people 30 cards with one of the following words printed on each card:

1. *french toast*	16. *wheatgerm*
2. *rice*	17. *french pastry*
3. *muffin*	18. *cup cake*
4. *cheese cake*	19. *waffle*
5. *danish pastry*	20. *bread*
6. *cookie*	21. *brownie*
7. *fruit cake*	22. *cornbread*
8. *graham cracker*	23. *popcorn ball*
9. *roll*	24. *ginger snap*
10. *cornflakes*	25. *tortilla*
11. *donut*	26. *oatmeal*
12. *cream puff*	27. *dumpling*
13. *chocolate eclair*	28. *toast*
14. *pancake*	29. *biscuit*
15. *pretzel*	30. *rye*

We ask each person to arrange the cards in any order that will show the relations of the items to one another. After they have completed their arrangement, we can also give each person five more cards: *bread stick, popover, corn starch pudding, spaghetti,* and *grits.* How readily can each of these cards be placed in one of the piles already formed? We can also ask whether any cards were missing, or whether any cards do not belong.

Some people will sort all these cards by the shape, texture, or color of what each card represents. This turns the experiment into a kind of *Hanfmann-Kasanin test.* Some people may arrange the cards in the order of what they like best. Others may group the cards by meals: breakfast, lunch, and dinner. Still others may arrange them by ingredients: wheat, corn, rice, oats, and rye. Literal people may arrange them alphabetically.

The different arrangements are not equally appropriate for different uses. An arrangement by individual personal preferences is not adequate for a national information storage and retrieval system. A classification by shape, texture, and color is less important for dietetics than a classification based on ingredients. An alphabetical order hides the relations among the objects and only lines up the spellings of their names in English. Such a nominal relation is informative only for the most mechanical storage and retrieval. An index is not a taxonomy.

For the second part of the experiment let us turn these 30 cards over. On this side the cards have the following on them:

1. *censorship*	16. *feedback*
2. *sensitivity*	17. *symbol*
3. *copyright*	18. *information*
4. *socialization*	19. *message*
5. *network*	20. *receiver*
6. *cybernetics*	21. *rumor*
7. *computer*	22. *libel*
8. *gatekeeper*	23. *telecommunications*
9. *education*	24. *channel*
10. *style*	25. *propaganda*
11. *television*	26. *poll*
12. *language*	27. *noise*
13. *newspaper*	28. *library*
14. *public relations*	29. *advertising*
15. *nonverbal*	30. *editorial*

Again we ask people to arrange the cards in any order that will show the relations of the items to one another.

The words on this side of the cards are more abstract. The baked goods terms could have been more abstract: time, temperature, and specific gravity, instead of cornflakes and toast; the communication words could have been more concrete: television set rather than television, and classroom rather than education. Fundamentally, however, the difference between the two sides illustrates the first feature of a taxonomy of communication: it is a *codification* of concepts.

The communication terms are also more ambiguous, more semantically noisy. It is more difficult to describe a *style* or a *message* than a *pancake* or a *brownie*. It is more difficult to distinguish *messages* from *censorship* than *creampuffs* from *pretzels*. Far from being a fault or deficiency, ambiguity is an important asset of communicational terms. It keeps codifications from being rigid and keeps the taxonomy flexible and usable. If a taxonomy in the behavioral sciences is to be successful, it generally has to be ambiguous (Smith, 1964).

There are also more constraints on the ways communicational terms can be arranged. A cookbook can arrange baked goods alphabetically, or by ingredients, or by meal, or by breads, cookies, pastries, and cakes. A taxonomy of communication cannot choose from so many alternate arrangements. The abstractions of communication cannot be sorted by shape, texture, and color, nor

by personal preference. There are choices but they are more limited and constrained.

The communication taxonomy is also more complex and tight knit. The paradigm for a cookbook need have no more rhyme or reason than mere alphabetization, but a taxonomy of communication should show how the parts of communicational processes fit together. That requires more than the one dimensional, linear ordering the alphabet allows. It requires at least two dimensions as in Mendeleev's periodic table of chemical elements, or three dimensions as in the codifications of molecular biology. Communication is a complex and varied process. Taxonomies reduce variety and complexity to some understandable order. Therefore the taxonomy of communication has to be complex. It either matches the field and obeys the law of requisite variety, or it fails as a taxonomy.

Most taxonomies are not sufficiently *abstract, ambiguous, constrained,* and *complex.* Therefore they can't pay off when they are brought to account. Question: *What is the place of computer science and library science in communication?* Question: *Is speech a subdivision of English, and English a subdivision of linguistics?* The taxonomies we have are not broad and complex enough to answer these questions. Question: *Can't we just divide the field into face to face communication and print and electronic media?* That is not abstract enough, particularly as it becomes more clear that media are not the prime independent variables in communication. *Channel capacity, noise,* and *elasticity of demand* are the kind of variables that are much more basic. Question: *By what criteria are some communication studies academic while others professional?* Existing taxonomies do not have enough constraints to answer questions of criteria. Our taxonomic experiment presents some of the first requirements of an objective map of the field.

THE GENERAL IDEA OF COMMUNICATION

Of making many definitions of communication there is no end. But we are not alone. Philosophers have been making their living for twenty five hundred years trying to define philosophy. Lawyers do this with law (Smith, 1969), and historians still ask, *What is history?* If there are ten professors in any field anywhere who are sure what their field is about, who agree with each other, and who can define it for me, then their field probably has rigor mortis.

A taxonomy of communication requires some general idea of communication: not rigid definitions, but some overall dimensions. Some consensus is more likely there than on the field's actual content. For this approach to communication let me propose four features of its outlines: *Change, dissonance, expansion,* and *surprises.*

Change

The first feature is *change.* The field was quite different 25 years ago. The "academic" committees of the National Society for the Study of Communication were (Nichols, 1951; Weaver, 1977):

—Primary and Secondary School Programs
—College Communication Programs
—General Methodologies
—Basic Research and Evaluation
—Mass Media
—Propaganda
—Communication in Industry
—Intercultural Relations
—Military Service and Civilian Morale
—Communication in Government
—Communication in the Family
—Reading Comprehension
—Listening Comprehension
—Communication Centers

This taxonomy emphasized the practice of communication, particularly the teaching of the practice in reading and listening in schools and colleges. It also had a "how-to" emphasis on communicating in industry, government, family, and the military. The National Society for the Study of Communication of 1950 attached less importance to the media; journalists, broadcasters, and film makers were in separate organizations. In 1950, interpersonal communication has not yet been drawn together out of communication in the family, industry, and interculturally. Theory did not amount to much at all. The list of this and this and this committee did not add up to a system.

The field has also changed since 1965. In that

year the *Journal of Communication* established an index or catalog system for Current Developments in Communication Research (Borden, 1965). This taxonomy consisted of six dimensions of research:

—General - Specific
—Verbal - Nonverbal
—Human, animal, mechanical
—Empirical, normative, experimental, theoretical
—Language, semantics, perception, thought, learning effect
—Physiological, neurological, psychological

This was much less applied than in 1950, and had an almost exclusive emphasis on interpersonal communication. There was practically no emphasis on the *media, government,* or *industry.* It was much more empirical. There was some theory, but it was either empirically based and of very narrow scope, or it was general and sidestepped the findings of research.

History speaks to us in many voices, and I have presented only two. They illustrate that the general idea of communication changes. More voices would not change this thesis. This kind of change implies that the system is open rather than closed. It implies that a taxonomy of communication cannot be rigid and must be permeable. Our enlightened and modern categories of 1977 will look as primeval in the year 2000 as the categories of 1950 and 1965 look to us now.

Dissonance

The second feature of the general idea of communication is *dissonance.* Ten years ago the dominant theme in communication research was symbolic interaction. Communication was not simply a sending and receiving of messages, but also involved *interpretation.* Human interaction was mediated by symbols. The symbolic interactionists studied the development and expression of such interpretations. In 1950, investigators had talked about *conditioning* and *effectiveness;* in 1966 they spoke of *symbols* and *meaning.* Although there were general agreements among communication scholars, there were also differences. For example, Gerald Miller (1966) defined the field of communication as "those behavioral situations in which a source transmits a message to a receiver(s) with conscious intend to affect the latter's behaviors." George Gerbner (1966) maintained, however, that "communication is social interaction through *symbols and message systems*. The production and perception of message systems cultivating stable structures of generalized images—rather than any tactic calculated to result in 'desirable' (or any other) response—is at the heart of the communications transaction."

From our perspective today we see substantial agreements between Miller and Gerbner 10 years ago. They also disagreed, specifically on whether *intention to affect* is an essential ingredient in the general concept of *communication*. At any one time there is substantial dissonance in the idea of *communication*. Such discord and tension does not disappear in time, but the principles and principals change. Tomorrow the debate may be between two dedicated cyberneticists instead of symbolic interactionists, and the issue may be efficiency rather than affect. Communication means different things at different times, and at any one time it means different things to different people, or even to one person.

Expansion

The third feature is *expansion*. Communication is a conglomerate. Some of its investigators started in journalism, others in film, still others in anthropology. Some were concerned with *gatekeepers,* others with *audience response,* and still others with *intercultural communication*. To deal with each concern adequately, its scope had to be expanded. *Intercultural communication* had to include the press and film; *audience response* had to consider intercultural variables.

This expansion continues. We see the reaching out to computer science and library science, to economics and management. I doubt, however, that there is a manifest destiny toward some communicational colossus. Bigness becomes awkward and clumsy, and leads to self-destruction. Library science, economics, and all the other fields are also expansive. Expansion into other fields does not mean becoming a colossus and dominating them.

More and more it means simply a cooperative information exchange.

The continuing expansion of the field implies that its categories and classifications have to be compatible with those of other fields. If communication expands to consider libraries as another print medium, but librarianship is expanding into person to person communication, the cooperative interchange between them will fizzle in dissonance. It is the same in marketing, medicine, and every other field. More and more we need cooperation in developing categories. No field is an island anymore.

Surprises

The fourth feature of the general idea of communication is *surprises*. The general idea of the field can take some unexpected turns. Mathematics used to be a study of numbers. Then we learned that numbers rested on a deeper and broader foundation of set theory. A whole new conception of mathematics was born. Today communication may be a *study of senders and receivers*. This is rapidly becoming the more generalized *study of inputs and outputs of systems*. These systems can be whole communities or industries. One day further on we may consider the field to be the *study of equilibria* among such systems, and after that it may become the even more abstract study of *entropy and redundancy, chaos and order*. Communication could end up as pure variety engineering. This would be quite surprising to those now studying communication as persuasive copy writing, small group interaction, or library automation. The field will change and expand not only at its fringes and extremities but at its very core.

THE CHARACTERISTICS OF TAXONOMY

Taxonomies are needed arrangements of similarities into testable models that improve our understanding. Taxonomies of communication are information transducers that have a number of special features.

A geological taxonomy is a classification of rocks: *igneous, sedimentary,* and *metamorphic*. A kinship taxonomy is a classification of relatives: *uncles, cousins, grandmothers, brothers,* and *step-daughters.* Different cultures group different things together in different ways (Tyler, 1969), but taxonomies themselves are universal. When I speak of this thing here as a table, or as wood, or as the tip of my finger, I use taxonomic categories.

If we did not group things together we would have to talk about individual things. That would be so fitful and disconnected, all we could ever say would be entropic gibberish. Without taxonomy there is no meaning.

On the surface a taxonomy is an arrangement of similarities. People and pythons are grouped together when we observe they both have backbones. When we observe that one lays eggs and the other bears its young alive they are put into separate groups. We further arrange these similarities and differences into an evolutionary tree of vertebrates, and mammals and reptiles.

More profoundly than an arrangement of similarities, a taxonomy is a simulation. Ruben (1974) has identified five structural elements in simulations of human communication: *roles, interactions, rules, goals,* and *criteria.* These are also elements of taxonomies. *Roles* are assumed *identities*; taxonomic classifications are roles, as when people and pythons assume the same identities, *vertebrates.* The interaction among *roles* or classifications is the branching of the vertebrate tree into *mammals* and *reptiles,* or the rows and columns of halogens and alkali-metals in a periodic arrangement of the elements. The *rules* govern the interactions, while the *goals* and *criteria* set the parameters of the taxonomy qua simulation.

A model or simulation can give information about components we could not get in other ways. A taxonomy in biology reveals the roles of backbones and eggs. A taxonomy of communication reveals the relative importance in communication curricula of make-up and layout, of phonetics, and of managerial grids. A taxonomy is a plan of action. An aeronautical engineer makes a model of an airframe not just to display it by hanging it on a string over his bed. The model is made to be tested in a wind tunnel, then to be modified and tested again. Similarly, a taxonomy is not just a reasonable or pleasing arrangement but a verifiable and revisable model. It is a simulation brought to trial by working to improve our understanding.

Taxonomies, therefore, are dynamic rather than static. They are instruments that change. They are part of the endless *process* of communication (Berlo, 1960). As time-binders, however, they also need to be stable, for change can dissolve similarities back into a meaningless entropy. The amount of change and of stability presents one of the first problems in developing any taxonomy. Another problem is how broad a taxonomy should be: broad enough to include all observations, but if it is so broad that one taxonomy includes everything in the world, it may become untestable and probably unusable. Still another problem is how predictive rather than descriptive should it be? And can it have any discontinuities or emergences, or should it be a solid plenum (Lovejoy, 1936)?

A taxonomy of communication has special characteristics. It is still a *transducer of information*, a *black box* with *inputs* and *outputs*. It takes in *raw data* and puts out *classified data*. It converts *information* into *meaning*. It is also *relative* rather than *absolute*. There is more than one way to simulate and organize the field. Human communication varies and is ambiguous and can be represented in different ways. I believe a taxonomy of communication had best be a general system in which we can know the whole without knowing each part. It may also be probabilistic. The communication taxonomy need not be a determinate machine. We may not be wholly sure what kind of output it will produce from the input.

FUZZY SETS

No two things are the same. But some things have to be somewhat similar or we couldn't know anything. If each thing were unique everything would be an unintelligible chaos.

Is an editorial a form of propaganda? They are not quite the same, but neither are they totally different. *Is advertising a form of education?* Well maybe somewhat, but not completely. *Does communication include transportation?* Perhaps a little bit. *Does communication include sending letters back and forth?* Yes, most of the time.

On the one hand A is never B. An airedale is not a kangaroo, and your airedale is not my airedale. On the other hand we need to classify in order to reduce the variety in the world so we can cope with the world. Classifications are storage and retrieval units for our experiences. These units are *time-binders,* and they are dynamite: both useful and dangerous. They may lead us to false expectations.

Every classification or set of things is ambiguous. It has many characteristics and at different times and for different purposes we select different features for emphasis (Smith, 1964). We can best deal with ambiguities of this sort in a taxonomy by availing ourselves of the branch of mathematics known as *fuzzy set theory* (Kaufmann, 1975; Zadeh, 1965).

There are *sets* or groups of things that have clearly defined memberships. The coins in my pocket are such a discrete group. Something is either a member of that set or it is not. The coins in your pocket are not in my set. We can add these discrete sets, divide them, and do other things to them.

Most of the categories in a taxonomy of communication are not like that. *Is advertising a form of education?* These are fuzzy sets and they have degrees of membership. The boundaries of each set are not clear and distinct and they are permeable. The sets of advertising and education overlap to a degree, perhaps in more than one place. The degree of membership is measurable to a degree.

Incidentally, I believe that fuzzy sets themselves are fuzzy, that there are degrees of membership in the set of *fuzzy sets:* slicks, fuzzy, kinky, and out of sight. A few categories in communication are slick such as *bits.* Most categories are fuzzy such as *gatekeepers* and *polls;* some are kinky such as *channels* and *styles;* and some are way out there such as *meaning* and *function.*

We can add fuzzy sets, divide them, and subject them to other algorithms developed specifically for them. Naturally, these additions and multiplications are quite different from first grade arithmetic. One major theorem of fuzzy algorithms particularly suggestive for the taxonomy of communication is that the intersection of two convex sets is itself a convex set. A *convex set* can be represented by a *bell shaped curve;* one kind of *non-convex set* can be represented by a *bimodal curve.* If information theory is a convex set, it may trail off at one end into semantics and at the other into electronics. If

readership studies are another convex set, they may trail off into *content analysis* in one direction and into *graphics* in the other. A combination of information theory and readership studies would then produce another convex set.

I suspect, however, that most sets in communication are not convex nor even bimodal, but *multimodal.* Perceptions of figure and ground can be bimodal, but personality profiles and community attitudes are multimodal. *Journalism* and *radio-television-film* are *multimodal,* and when we add them together the result is indeed complex.

In the physical and biological sciences some taxonomies can have discrete sets. This is either fluorine or not; this is either a wrinkled pea or not. In *communication* we need to appreciate how fuzzy our human systems are. We have to have more fuzzy thinking. That is not sloppy or casual. It is a rigorous and demanding discipline.

THE COMPUTER DESIGN OF TAXONOMIES

All these criteria may make it seem impossible to arrange a taxonomy. As we think of communication more *abstractly, broadly, deeply, complexly,* and even *fuzzily,* the field may seem too complex. Has the new taxonomy become some monstrous behemoth? The specifications may seem beyond the capacity of any human taxonomist to follow, or of any user to understand.

But this is the age of the computer. We can handle complexity. We can take a great jumble like the *donut* and *cream puff* cards, and those other cards about *networks, languages,* and *editorials,* and arrange them in some order. It is like the jumble of pieces in a jig saw puzzle. Even if there are a million pieces, they can be fit together. As a matter of fact, computer programs have been developed for doing jigsaw puzzles.

There are also computer programs that reconstruct the history of the horse, and of man. These simulations are biological taxonomies. There is in fact a whole methodology of designing taxonomies by computer (Jardine & Sibson, 1971; Sokol & Sneath, 1963). Numerical taxonomy has been widely used in such fields as entomology and bacteriology. We too can lift our taxonomy out of the stone age into the era of electronic communication.

The old taxonomies were monothetic, based on one characteristic at a time. Animals were classified by *number of legs*. Birds and people were *bipeds*. Then a second characteristic could be introduced: *feathers*. Computer generated taxonomies are polythetic, based on aggregates of characteristics, all at the same time. These characteristics are basic observations. A cupcake or a computer has *height, width, depth, weight, color,* and *shape*. If we do not have an already established taxonomic category like *cupcake* or *computer* we can make a *cluster analysis* of our observations and create categories.

We do this all the time in communication studies. The semantic differential is a taxonomy of meaning produced by factor analysis (Osgood, Suci, & Tannenbaum, 1957). The categorizations in content analysis are computer generated taxonomies (Gerbner, Holsti, Krippendorff, Paisley, & Stone, 1969; Budd, Thorpe, & Donohew, 1967). Taxonomies of executive positions, of human performance, and other social classifications have been devised by factor analyses of questionnaire responses (Hemphill, 1960; Tornow & Pinto, 1976). Even these taxonomies do not have the requisite complexity and flexibility to be more than middling models for communication. But their method is good.

The computer analysis and sorting of human communication call for operationalizations. First we have to operationalize our observations. We cannot simply jump to the conclusion that political speeches belong under speech or under journalism. We first need to specify each characteristic of these speeches. Then we have to operationalize our principles of sorting. The computer program is the instructions for sorting the speeches with other kinds of communicational events. The result could be that political interviews belong with speeches but last year's magazine piece by the candidate belongs with background instead.

It is most unlikely to be a total belonging. It is rather a matter of degree, a matter of overlapping fuzzy sets. Computers manage matters of degree with ease. They can also manage the fuzzy algorithms of the field of communication. This includes weighting the various characteristics differentially, calculating the coefficient of each vector in the taxonomy. In determining man's place in nature, his broad toenails are less important than the surface area of his cortex. In communication we could find that game theory, decision theory, and operations research form one group while information theory and cybernetics form another group. The most important difference—the vector with the largest coefficient—could be that one group uses algebraic equations and the other uses differential equations.

We need to write our specifications for a taxonomy of communication as a computer program. Then we need to put all our concepts and facts about communication into the computer. In all, we need to do for *communication,* itself and as a whole, what we do for *meaning, content,* and other classifications.

AIMS AND PRIORITIES

Finally, the field of communication needs more than a taxonomy of topics, more than a classification of different kinds of communication. It needs a theory and philosophy to give it purpose and direction. The field still needs to develop these aims and priorities. Current announcements on goals are made in brochures from communication schools, associations, organizations, and publishers. They generally say, "Our aim is to provide a broad basis for achievement in the study and practice of communication." These goals are so general the field can neither fail nor succeed in meeting them. They don't point anywhere.

Without overall meaningful conceptions and goals there will be suboptimization. That is the principal problem in classifying and arranging any set of operations. The sales department of Widget Inc. brings in millions in orders, but the production department cannot keep up with them. Sales is suboptimizing and can make Widgets flunk out. We need to specify in detail all our concerns and aims, and arrange them by hard priorities.

This means choices. Which concept or aim is most important, and which next? The field can have both a disciplinary orientation and a sense of mission. There will be a big difference, however, if we give the disciplinary orientation a higher priority, or if that priority goes to the sense of mission. The field can promote skills and sensitivities, emphasizing group dynamics and the use of film as social tools. It can also stress basic research, empirical data, and theoretical models. We need to identify each alternative in detail. Then we can work to achieve consensus on relative priorities (Smith, 1950). If we try to do everything, however, we will probably end doing nothing.

The basic idea of *communication* is like any other idea. Take the idea, for example, of what an intellectual is. There are many theories and philosophies. John Dewey thought intellectuals were escapists and played a too esthetic role. Eric Hoffer held they were parasites, always hanging on to those who hold the reins of power. Karl Mannheim held that intellectuals transcend the class society. These differences in conception were not simple differences in observation. They were differences in philosophy. Whatever intellectuals may be—if anything—is perhaps less important than what we say they are. We decide rather than observe, and when we have made this overall decision we can go on to arrange programs. Are communication studies an activist or escapist enterprise? Are they patrician or plebian? Input, output, or interface? We have to choose if we are to have a theory and philosophy. Then we can go on to taxonomizing, objectively and systematically.

REFERENCES

BERLO, D.K. *The process of communication*. New York: Holt, Rinehart and Winston, 1960.

BLAKE, R.H., & HAROLDSON, E.O. *A Taxonomy of Concepts in Communication*. New York: Hastings House, 1975.

BORDEN, G.A. Current developments in communication research. *Journal of Communication*, 1965, 15, 47-53.

BUDD, R.W., THORPE, R.K., & DONOHEW, L. *Content analysis of communications*. New York: Macmillan, 1967.

DANCE, F.E.X., & LARSON, C.E. *Functions of human communication*. New York: Holt, Rinehart and Winston, 1976.

GERBNER, G. On defining communication: Still another view, *Journal of Communication*, 1966; 16, 99-103.

GERBNER, G., HOLSTI, O.R., KRIPPENDORFF, K., PAISLEY, W.J., & STONE, P.J. (Eds.), *The analysis of communication content*. New York: Wiley, 1969.

HEMPHILL, J.K. *Dimensions of executive positions*. Columbus: Ohio State University Bureau of Business Research, 1960.

JARDINE, N., & SIBSON, R. *Mathematical taxonomy*. New York: Wiley, 1971.

KAUFMANN, A. *Introduction to the theory of fuzzy subsets*. Vol. 1. New York: Academic Press, 1975.

KIBLER, R.J., & BARKER, L.L. (Eds.) *Conceptual Frontiers in Speech-Communication*. New York: Speech Association of America, 1969.

LOVEJOY, O.A. *The great chain of being*. Cambridge: Harvard University Press, 1936.

MILLER, G.R. On defining communication: Another stab, *Journal of Communication*, 1966, 16, 88-98.

NICHOLS, R.G. Development and growth of NSSC, *Journal of Communication*, 1951, 1, 2-3.

OSGOOD, C.E., SUCI, G.J., & TANNENBAUM, P.H., *The measurement of meaning*. Urbana: University of Illinois Press, 1957.

RUBEN, B.D. The what and why of gaming: A taxonomy of experiential learning systems. In J.E. Moriarty (Ed.), *Simulation and gaming. Proceedings of the annual symposium of the National Gaming Council and the annual conference of the International Simulation and Gaming Association*, Gaithersburg, Md., National Bureau of Standards, Publication 395, Washington, 1974.

SMITH, A.G. Can philosophy be taught? *Journal of Higher Education*, 1950, 21, 318-321.

SMITH, A.G. The dionysian innovation, *American Anthropologist*, 1964, 66, 251-265.

SMITH, A.G. Communication in law, *Jurimetrics Journal*, 1969, 10, 20-23.

TORNOW, W.W., & PINTO, P.R. The development of a managerial job taxonomy, *Journal of Applied Psychology*, 1976, 61, 410-418.

TYLER, S.A. (Ed.) *Cognitive anthropology*. New York: Holt, Rinehart and Winston, 1969.

WEAVER, C. A history of the International Communication Association. In B.D. Ruben (Ed.), *Communication yearbook*. New Brunswick, N.J.: Transaction-International Communication Association, 1977.

ZADEH, L.A. Fuzzy sets, *Information and Control*, 1965, 8, 338-353.

CONSTRUCTS FOR A THEORY OF
HUMAN COMMUNICATION

GEORGE A. BORDEN
University of Delaware

This paper presents a humanistic systems approach to understanding the human communication process. Drawing on the work of the three schools of psychology represented by Freud, Skinner, and Rogers, it assimilates some of the ideas of Kelly, Piaget, Rokeach, Bem, and Berne with systems theory to develop basic theoretical constructs that may be used to explain and investigate human communication processes. Each construct and assumption is a point for analysis of communication events, diagnosis of problems, and generation of solutions. The theory assumes an ideal system allowing evaluations of real events to be made against an idealized standard.

There are as many definitions of human communication as there are humans who have thought about it. Each has his or her own idiosyncratic way of putting the pieces of the human communication process together. To be sure, the definitions have changed somewhat over the years, but these changes are due more to the perspective of the scholar than to basic differences in the conceptualization of the human communication process.

Aristotle, though writing things that can now be construed to show he was aware of the total communication process, focused upon the *message*—the speech—what we today call the *signal* (Borden, 1971); that part of the communication process that passes from one person to another or from one to many. This concern only recently gave way to its technological counterpart, the *channels*, with their signals (Weaver, 1949). This was later humanized to some extent by Berlo (1960), but with the technological revolution, even the basic humanistic elements suggested by Weaver (Borden & Stone, 1976) were forgotten.

Essentially, to communicate has meant to affect another's mind through symbolic processes. *To communicate effectively has been to affect another's mind through symbolic processes in such a way as to produce the desired behavior from that person.* Both of these are Machiavellian, stimulus-response definitions of communication. A more humanistic definition is the sharing of meaning through symbolic processes (Myers & Myers,

1973). When the concept of *sharing* is included, it introduces the humanistic idea of *interdependence* and *two-way, give and take,* communication. Then the above definition may be rewritten as: *To communicate is to share meaning in such a way that mutual understanding, growth, and progress are facilitated.* This definition assumes the involvement of both parties and their commitment to mutual understanding.

The former definitions are linear, emphasizing the phases or nodes through which the process passes. The latter are systemic, emphasizing the basic elements which interact in the process of human communication. It is with the latter definition that we are concerned, for we have obtained from the former about all we can until we find the neurological unit of memory. Even the latter definition has been limited by our concerns with mechanistic principles, for it is hard to shake loose from the concepts of the closed system. However, if we open up the system, we may find that new areas of research will become apparent and new epistomologies will emerge.

This paper will present the variables for a humanistic systems approach to an explanation of the human communication process. It will be impossible to go into too much detail, but it is hoped that sufficient information can be given to lead those who are interested into vigorous speculations on research and new solutions to old problems.

ON SYSTEMS

By a system is meant "an ongoing process of a set of elements, each of which is functionally and operationally united with the others in the achievement of an objective" (Beckett, 1971, p 27). Thus, we are not as much concerned with its *organizational denotations* as its *process denotations*. Second, there seems no way that a human being can be thought of as "being in" or being a closed system. Some situations are closer to the closed end of the continuum than others, but there always seems to be a need for an open systems approach. Third, the system is a self-regulating (cybernetic) system. Thus we have three basic assumptions: The human communication system must be *open, cybernetic,* and in *process*. Each assumption or construct is a point at which a real-life human communication system may be analyzed, investigated, and/or evaluated, and where therapy may be found useful. This will be true throughout the paper, for this principle forms the basis for the theory's usefulness in communication research, teaching, and therapy.

The elements of a system may themselves be systems, and thus, we can talk about a *hierarchy* of systems (Borden, Gregg, & Grove, 1969). The elements have subparts, attributes, or characteristics which they share, and it is this process of sharing that defines the functional and operational aspects of the system. Every system functions for a purpose or objective, and it is that operation for which the cybernetic is set. For every system there is a boundary by which it is defined, and an environment in which it functions. Finally, we cannot talk about the parts of a system without the systems assumption—i.e., that a higher level of organization exists and is composed of these parts—and to analyze a system, one must necessarily talk about its parts.

While the foregoing summary is, obviously, abbreviated, it will suffice for initial purposes here. There are a number of texts that explain systems theory, and the usage of these terms will become clearer as we proceed. The basic ingredients of a system are two or more basic components (or elements), having attributes or characteristics which they share for a specific purpose, within an environment, which necessitates a set of boundaries by which the system is constrained (Buckley, 1968; Emery, 1969; Heimstra & Ellingstad, 1972; Ruben & Kim, 1975).

THE BASIC COMPONENTS

The basic element (component, part, subsystem) of the human communication system is the *person*—not the individual of Freud (1943) or Erikson (1968) and psychoanalysts, nor the organism of Skinner (1971, 1974) and the behaviorists, but the *person,* in all the fullness of Rogers (1961, 1967), Maslow (1962, 1971), Kelly (1963), and Piaget (Furth, 1969). The person is born an active being, seeking information and desiring communication (Trevarthen, 1976). The basic assumption is that, being an active system, the person is always in process, even though this process may become imperceptable through the conditioning effects of society (Greene & Lepper, 1974). We are speaking here of cognitive processes, for in spite of some behaviorists' attempts to deny it, we are cognitive beings.

In his review of Piaget, Hans Furth (1969) points out that a person is a biological structure, and that "a biological structure implies functioning; it requires no source of motivation external to itself in order to function." He further states that "Piaget likens the internal scheme to a starving animal looking for food which the scheme finds in its interaction with the environment; the scheme assimilates the environmental stuff that provides the necessary food for its function" (p. 45).

As we move through the various stages of understanding both ourselves and others, where we are, in a cognitive sense, after we experience an event depends on where we were, cognitively, before we experienced the event. Thus, our cognitive growth may be said to be psychologically determined. It can also be assumed that the cognitive system is a *cybernetic system*, using *internal* and *external feedback* to regulate its activity and structure its growth processes (Borden, 1971).

Thus we begin with the person whose cognitive growth is psychologically determined. This means that each person is unique, and it is this uniqueness that is our most valuable attribute. This is an idealized system. If it were not, we would not be able to use it to analyze and investigate the human communication process. Each assumption and variable gives us a chance to compare what we see with what we might predict.

The assumption that a person is a cognitive system says more than that he or she is in process. It also says that the person is active, not passive, a creator of stimuli, not only a respondor to it, acting on the environment, not just receiving stimuli from it. As an active, ongoing system, we can both respond to and create stimuli, whichever is appropriate to us. As active systems, we may seek information as well as process that which naturally comes to us; we may instigate communication as well as respond to it. Thus, we may have goals for which we strive that have no external reward or internal ulterior motive. They may be purely cognitive goals, and fulfillment comes upon completion of and participation in the cognitive processes of creating, discovering, and learning for their own sake. Granted, in our present society these activities are soon conditioned out of most of us, but from the humanistic point of view, we have the potential to find fulfillment in ourselves, in the realization of our mental images, and in the completion of our cognitive structures.

Another aspect of humanness, as seen from the humanistic viewpoint, is that we may become aware of ourselves and our embeddedness in society. The awareness of self is a highly controversial concept. It is a basic tenet of humanistic psychology, and as a factor in human communication theory it helps us to understand some of the facets of the process. *Awareness of self* helps us realize that in any communication situation we have choices as to how we are to behave. A conditioned organism has no choice but those established by its environment. One who knows oneself and is aware of one's involvement with society can determine why he or she behaves as he or she does. We can determine our intentions and act on the dictates of our humanistic conscience. We can be aware of the repercussions of our behavior on ourselves and our society, and we can choose what behavior we will exhibit.

Other factors result from the assumption of *choice*. Given the ability to choose our own behavior, we may then become internally, but rationally, controlled. We are not driven by unknown urges nor pulled by environmental reinforcement unless we allow it. The degree to which we are not in control of our actions becomes an important variable in the communication process and in our awareness of our own communicative behavior, as well as in understanding the behavior of others. Further, it places the responsibility of this behavior squarely on the person, and it focuses the attention of the communicator and the researcher there, as well. In doing this, it helps us understand each other as persons and not as objects pulled by the environment or driven by unseen internal urges. Humans are seen as autonomous beings able to make choices and to take responsibility for their subsequent behaviors (Borden, 1976).

Thus, we see the person as the basic element in a communication system. A person who is *cognitive, in process, active, unique, having choices* (and so being aware of, and responsible for, his or her communicative behavior), and being *autonomous* but aware of his or her social embeddedness.

Attributes

It is not yet clear what all the attributes and characteristics are that persons share in developing a communication system, but the sharing of attributes by the elements of a system is one of the necessary aspects of a system. It seems that there are both physical and psychological attributes that persons might share, but that the sharing is always symbolic (cognitive). We may share our bodies, and in this sharing there is perhaps a dimension of nonsymbolic behavior. But if we attach any meaning to it at all, it immediately becomes symbolic (cognitive). Strictly speaking, physical contact may be nonsymbolic behavior, depending on the situation, but it may also have symbolic connotations in a personal relationship.

The parts (persons) of a communication system, then, share their attributes through symbolic processes, natural language being the most obvious. Research (Borden & Puhl, 1973) indicates that there are 10 dimensions of human compatibility (areas of sharing) that are important to long-term male-female relationships (communication systems). They are given in Table 1 in the order of their

TABLE 1
Dimensions of Compatibility

1. Personal	Degree to which one is able, comfortable, and/or needs to reveal oneself to another, e.g., talk about fears, weaknesses, desires, feelings.	6. Domestic	Degree to which one is able to cope with, be comfortable with, and/or needs a specific type of "home" environment, e.g., children, structure, tidiness.
2. Emotional	Degree to which one is able, comfortable, and/or needs to be in control or is controlled by one's emotions, e.g., ability to laugh, cry, feel, empathize.	7. Physical	Degree to which another fits one's ideal image in terms of physical attractiveness, personal hygiene, physical behavior, e.g., body language, dress, comeliness.
3. Cognitive	Level of abstraction on which one is able, comfortable, and/or needs to communicate, e.g., accepts the "way things are" or asks "why."	8. Social	Degree to which one is able, comfortable, and/or needs to partake of social activities, e.g., parties, public entertainment, outings.
4. Sexual	Degree to which one is able, comfortable, and/or needs to partake of human sexual behavior, e.g., kissing, petting, intercourse, deviations.	9. Environmental	Degree of desire, acceptance and/or need for a specific environment in which to live, e.g., city, country, suburban, geographical location.
5. Intensity	Degree to which one is able to cope with, is comfortable with, and/or needs a certain level of personal drive or motivation, e.g., psychological, physical, professional.	10. Spiritual	Degree to which one is able to cope with, be comfortable with and/or needs some form of supernatural phenomena in one's lifestyle, e.g., religion, mysticism, humanism.

importance, as seen by college students. Thus, we know something about the attributes persons feel must be shared. But in what terms can we discuss these sharings, and are there measurable units one can find to analyze and/or investigate them?

Sharing

Although there is a great deal of work needed in this area, it seems the basic unit of sharing is the *stroke*. A stroke is defined as "a unit of recognition" (Berne, 1972, p. 448). Berne (1964) elaborates on this definition in his earlier work:

> Stroking may be used as a general term for intimate physical contact; in practice it may take various forms. Some people literally stroke an infant; others hug or pat it, while some people pinch it playfully or flip it with a fingertip. These all have their analogues in conversations, so that it seems one might predict how an individual would handle a baby by listening to him talk. By an extension of meaning, "stroking" may be employed colloquially to denote any act implying recognition of another's presence. Hence a stroke may be used as the fundamental unit of social action. An exchange of strokes constitutes a transaction, which is the unit of social intercourse. (p. 15)

Berne's definition of a stroke, and his explanation of it, gives us a basic unit for the process of sharing. His concept of *transaction* is also important, in that it is the *exchange of strokes*, and this gives us a way of evaluating a communication system. Is there a one-for-one exchange? Are there differently valued strokes? ("You're always bringing me candy and flowers, but you never say you love me.") Obviously, there are, at least to different people, and one of the major concerns in human relationships (communication systems) is to find out what strokes are positive or negative and what their relative values are. Whether we are playing games or being genuine, we still need to know the values the other person places on our strokes.

Another very important problem area is the magnitude of behavior constituting a *stroke*. It may be as little as a glance, eye contact, or as much as a week's vacation in Berlin. In any case it is psychological, symbolic, and personal, and it will be very difficult to operationalize and measure. But that's how it should be. If human communication can be objectified, it becomes dehumanized, and we have obliterated what we set out to investigate. We then

FIGURE 1
Intensity of Involvement Scale

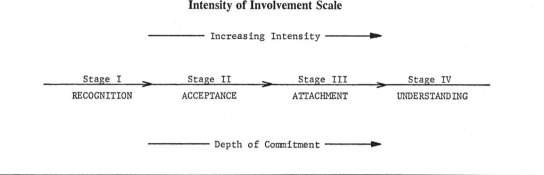

end up talking about make-believe truths. In using the *stroke* as our *unit of sharing*, we force the evaluator to return to the human element, and to be able to substantiate his or her evaluation on a personal basis.

Purpose

Every system exists for a *purpose* and is initiated by one or more of its parts. The environment is never the initiator of a system. For example, two people may be locked in a cell, but they *choose* to communicate—to form a system. In the development of a human communication system, the *purpose*, *function*, or *product*, is a *relationship*. The development of a relationship proceeds in rather uniform stages, though the time it takes to pass from the initial stage to a full relationship may vary greatly.

Recognition. We may use the concept of *intensity of involvement* to indicate how a relationship develops (see Figure 1). The first stage, *recognition*, occurs may times each day. We pass someone on the street, our eyes meet, we nod or say hello; we have recognized that person as another living being. This does not differ much from the interaction we might have with a dog or some other animal. We have this type of interaction almost continuously in our social lifestyle. It is most noticeable when it is absent. If we do not recognize another living being as such—by pretending he or she is not there—we are communicating the fact that we do not want any part of even the beginning of a relationship.

Acceptance. It goes without saying that we must recognize another person as a living being before we can accept that person as a human being. At the acceptance stage, the involvement becomes a little more intense. Two people may never go further than recognition, but if they have recognized each other, they are now able to do something about it. *Acceptance* means that you are willing to get acquainted. The need to get acquainted is quite different for each person, and it is based on many different kinds of likes and dislikes. Physical attraction has been propagated as the major variable in bringing about this stage in a relationship, but since we are sharing very little at this stage, this type of beginning is pretty much an ego trip.

As the acceptance stage develops, we must find more and more of ourselves and our experiences that we can and are willing to share with others. *Mutual sharing*, or, should we say, *equal sharing* (since sharing demands mutuality), increases the involvement we feel in the relationship. We may first only share (communicate) on an *environmental dimension* (e.g., where are you from, where do you live, or where are you going?). We may then move to the *social dimension* and talk about activities and people we know, and get friendly enough to say something about the attractiveness of the other person, the *physical dimension*. In all of these phases we are accumulating knowledge about the other person, and they are doing the same with us. This leads to the stage of a relationship we call *attachment*.

Attachment. During the acceptance period we are

also picking up information about the other's *domesticity* and *intensity*. These dimensions appear to be very crucial in the move into the *attachment* stage of relationships. The structure you exhibit in your life, and the intensity with which you pursue it, may make all the difference in the world as to whether a relationship develops or not.

As we pass from the *acceptance* to the *attachment* stage of a relationship, our communication becomes much more involved with meaningful experiences—with those events in which we have a more personal commitment. We become more involved with each other and more committed to that involvement. The attachment stage may last for some time, and as we become more committed to the relationship, we may explore each other's feelings about sex, probe each other's minds to see how we think, experience each other's emotions to see how strong they are, and dig into each other's lives to see how open we care to be. We are now in the *understanding* stage of a relationship, and the depth of our commitment to this relationship depends very much on what we find out about each other in this stage.

Understanding. We do not usually make a firm commitment to a long-term relationship until we have investigated each other's feelings or behaviors on each of these dimensions. Once we have, we can make a decision on whether we want to commit to this relationship or not. A frightening possibility (too often a reality) is that we may move into *understanding* and back into *attachment* without ever knowing it. In that case we find out just enough about the other person to satisfy our immediate desires and generalize this knowledge to make the person fit our ideal. We may wake up sometime and wonder how we got hooked into a relationship. We can then, almost always, look back and see where and when we stopped *sharing*. Even when both parties consciously make a decision to commit to each other, they may find that the very fact that they have reached this level of their relationship seems to engender a lack of communication (Borden, 1976).

Why is this? What happens to communication when relationships become old? Sharing meaning is a key to this phenomenon. We did not define communication as the sharing of meaning because that

is what happens, but while that is what should happen through communication, it may not. It takes energy and effort to maintain a relationship. That is why we insist that the system is an open system. It requires that there be an input of energy. Once this stops, the system rapidly disintegrates.

Environment

For every system there is an *environment*—a context in which communication takes place. The relevant variables in this context can be subsumed under three dimensions. Communicative behavior at any given instance occurs as the result of the interaction of the variables contained in these three dimensions. Since the basic element in this system is a person who has physical and psychological attributes, it seems imperative that the environment in which the communication system takes place must also have physical and psychological aspects. Thus, the three dimensions of the communication context are: (1) the *internally perceived variables*, somewhat similar to Eugene White's (1975) urgencies, but more appropriately called *choice variables*; (2) the *externally perceived variables*, modified somewhat from the rhetorical situation of old; and (3) our *nonconscious ideologies*, perhaps a new dimension for us to consider.

In defining these variables, we must keep in mind the factors we have ascribed to the person, for these play an important role in the determination of the environment. *Choice variables* are defined as those factors that proceed actions. These differ widely from *exigencies* (Bitzer, 1970) in that they are internally perceived rather than externally perceived variables. They may best be categorized by the extent to which they are do-able and the extent to which they require investment in the communicative event. Since we are looking at the person as an active agent, we can ask what choices he has in the behavior he is about to display or has been displaying in any given communication event.

George Kelly's (1963) *personal construct theory* is particularly valuable here, especially the idea that "a person's processes are psychologically channelized by the ways in which he anticipates events" (p. 46). Thus, the choice behavior in any communicative event is forward looking, concerned with the future. This is primarily true because the person is reaching out, setting up anticipations of events, and making choices based on these anticipations. The degree to which we invest ourselves in the event will make a great deal of difference in what we feel the "do-ables" are. The *choice dimension* contains all the internal, psychological or physical, pressures we feel in any communication event and may be focused primarily on the future and our self image.

The immediately perceivable external aspects of the communication event are the situational variables of the context of human communication. That is, they are all the external aspects of the communication event (psychological and physical variables) that affect the choices we make in our communicative behavior (for example, the weather, our deadlines, the time, the place, the tension you perceive in the other person, and his or her sex, age and status). All of these have a profound effect on what we feel we can do and say in a given encounter.

If one goes back to the rhetorical situation, the exigencies fit in here quite well. The situational variables are all those external forces and contingencies which stimulate behavior. One can subsume practically all the work done on the human communication process in the behaviorists' school under this heading, for they are concerned with the perceived external stimuli that impinge on the communication process. Surely they affect behavior, but one can always deviate from the path which external stimuli would seem to dictate.

The cultural aspect of the context within which human communication takes place is concerned with the attitudinal frame of reference we develop throughout our lifetime (Rokeach, 1960, 1968, 1973). That is, it takes into consideration all of the beliefs, fears, desires, and expectations we have developed as a result of our exposure to the culture in which we live. Most of our attitudinal frame of reference is nonconscious; that is, we are not consciously aware of these feelings. Daryl Bem (1970) calls them nonconscious ideologies:

> As we noted earlier, only a very unparochial and intellectual fish is aware that his environment is wet. After all, what else could it be? Such is the nature of a nonconscious ideology.
>
> A society's ability to inculcate this kind of ideology

into its citizens is the most subtle and most profound form of social influence. It is also the most difficult kind of social influence to challenge because it remains invisible. Even those who consider themselves sufficiently radical or intellectual to have rejected the basic premises of a particular societal ideology often find their belief systems unexpectedly cluttered with its remnants. (p. 89)

Male supremacy is a very good example of a nonconscious ideology. We usually are not aware of it, but most men (and women) will say, "How else should it be?"

How do these nonconscious ideologies develop? It is a basic tenet of humanistic psychology that a person grows through many complex stages of cognitive development. We don't have to be motivated to do this because, once it is turned on—when we are born—it is a continuing process, unless we are conditioned out of it by a behavioristic world (Greene & Lepper, 1974). Through our own innate pattern recognition, assimilation, accommodation, and memory processes (Furth, 1969), we construct a mental (cognitive) model of reality. Thus, we carry around in our heads a model or view of reality that is developed from all the experiences we have had with the outside world in conjunction with the internal focus we apply to them. What's more, the pursuit of this cognitive structure must come from within:

> In our present undertaking the psychological initiative always remains a property of the person—never the property of anything else. What is more, neither past nor future events are themselves ever regarded as basic determinants of the course of human action—not even the events of childhood. But one's way of anticipating them, whether in the short range or in the long view—this is the basic theme in the human process of living. Moreover, it is that events are anticipated, not merely that man gravitates toward more and more comfortably organic states. Confirmation and disconfirmation of one's predictions are accorded greater psychological significance than rewards, punishments, or the drive reduction that reinforcements produce . . .
>
> Thus we envision the nature of life in its outreach for the future, and not in its perpetuation of its prior conditions or in its incessant reverberation of past events. (Kelly, 1970, p. 10-11)

Those events which are meaningful to us shape our expectations about future events. Essentially, our attitudinal frame of reference is a structure against which we can make predictions about future events. Thus, the human mind approaches each situation with an assumption about what the event will be like. It then compares its perception of the event with its anticipation, to see if they agree. If they don't, then it has to do something about the dissonance that occurs. A closed mind may alter its perception of the event, or even reject the perception altogether, while an open mind would be more apt to accept its failure to anticipate correctly and revise its anticipation of future events. This is the core activity for a growing mind. The more mature a person is, the more consistent the agreement between anticipation and perception will be. With a little thought, it should be clear that one must be involved in an event before it can have much meaning. To be involved means that we are actively seeking congruence between our anticipations and perceptions by consciously updating our internal structure to enable it to make more precise anticipations of communicative events.

George Kelly (1970) gives some particularly useful insights into this process:

> It begins to be clear that the succession we call experience is based on the constructions we place on what goes on. If those constructions are never altered, all that happens during a man's years is a sequence of parallel events having no psychological impact on his life. But if he invests himself—the most intimate event of all—in the enterprise, the outcome, to the extent that it differs from his expectation or enlarges upon it, dislodges the man's construction of himself. In recognizing the inconsistency between his anticipation and the outcome, he concedes a discrepancy between what he was and what he is. A succession of such investments and dislodgements constitutes the human experience. . . .
>
> The unit of experience is, therefore, a cycle embracing five phases: anticipation, investment, encounter, confirmation or disconfirmation, and constructive revision . . .
>
> Stated simply, the amount of a man's experience is not measured by the number of events with which he collides, but by the investments he has made in his anticipations and the revisions of his constructions that have followed upon his facing up to consequences. (p. 18-19)

Thus our nonconscious ideologies, the cultural dimension of our environment, are built up throughout our lifetime and are dependent on both the experiences we have had and the way we have construed these experiences (Borden, 1976).

These three dimensions (*internal perceptions, external perceptions,* and *nonconscious ideologies*) constitute the environment in which communication systems are formed and in which they function. True to the systems definition of environment, the parts of the communication system may interact with these aspects of the environment and may even effect them somewhat, but they are never a part of the system, for they only influence our symbolic processes.

Boundaries

The final aspect of a humanistic system is the boundary of the system. Where does the system stop and the environment begin? Of course it must also have physical and psychological aspects, and one would expect it to fit into the above three dimensions of the environment. The boundaries on the *cultural dimension* are the cultural norms. If a part of the system tries to step over this boundary, it is immediately in danger of being stricken from the system. Thus, these norms put definite constraints on the system and its development. On the *situational dimension*, the boundaries that constrain the system are time, space, and artifacts. Any of these can determine the limits of a communication system. On the *choice of behavior dimension*, the boundaries are our physical energy and our degree of self-actualization, i.e., the degree to which we are aware of our self and our human potential and are able to constructively assert our individuality. All of these boundaries constrain any communication system.

SUMMARY

These are the basic ingredients of a humanistic systems approach to the human communication process. To reiterate: the basic element is the *person*, the subparts consist of *physical* and *psychological attributes*; the basic function is to relate, and this is done through the *sharing* of subparts in symbolic processes; the basic unit of *sharing* is the *stroke*; all communication goes on within a context made up of *choice of behavior, situational* and *cultural* variables; and the communication system has *boundaries* which constrain it on each of these dimensions.

REFERENCES

BECKETT, J.A. *Management dynamics: The new synthesis.* New York: McGraw-Hill, 1971.

BEM, D. *Beliefs, attitudes, and human affairs.* Monterey, Calif.: Brooks/Cole, 1970.

BERLO, D.K. *The process of communication.* New York: Holt, Rinehart and Winston, 1960.

BERNE, E. *Games people play.* New York: Grove, 1964.

BERNE, E. *What do you say after you say hello?* New York: Grove, 1972.

BITZER, L.F. The rhetorical situation. *Philosophy and Rhetoric*, 1968, 1, 1-14.

BORDEN, G.A., GREGG, R., & GROVE, T. *Speech behavior and human interaction.* Englewood Cliffs, N.J.: Prentice-Hall, 1969.

BORDEN, G.A. *An introduction to human-communication theory.* Dubuque, Iowa: Brown, 1971.

BORDEN, G.A., & PUHL, C.A. Observations of the effects of population norms on the members of the population. *The Pennsylvania Speech Communication Annual*, July 1973, 71-77.

BORDEN, G.A., & STONE, J.D. *Human communication: The process of relating.* Menlo Park, Calif.: Cummings, 1976.

BUCKLEY, W. (Ed.) *Modern systems research for the behavioral scientist.* Chicago: Aldine, 1968.

EMERY, F.E. (Ed.) *Systems thinking.* London: Penguin, 1969.

ERICKSON, E.H. *Identity: Youth and crisis.* New York: Norton, 1968.

FREUD, S. *A general introduction to psychoanalysis.* Translated by Joan Riviere. Garden City, N.Y.: Doubleday, 1943.

FURTH, H.G. *Piaget and knowledge.* Englewood Cliffs, N.J.: Prentice-Hall, 1969.

GREENE, D., & LEPPER, M.R. How to turn play into work. *Psychology Today.* September 1974, 49-54.

HEIMSTRA, N.W., & ELLINGSTAD, V.G. *Human behavior: A systems approach.* Monterey, Calif.: Brooks/Cole, 1972.

KELLY, G.A. *A theory of personality.* New York: Norton, 1963.

KELLY, G.A. A brief introduction to personal construct theory. In D. Bannister (Ed.), *Perspectives in personal construct theory.* London: Academic Press, 1970.

MASLOW, A.H. *Toward a psychology of being.* New York: Van Nostrand-Reinhold, 1962.

MASLOW, A.H. *The further reaches of human nature.* New York: Viking, 1971.

MYERS, G.E., & MYERS, M.T. *The dynamics of human communication.* New York: McGraw-Hill, 1973.

ROGERS, C.R. *On becoming a person.* Boston: Houghton Mifflin, 1961.

ROGERS, C.R., & STEVENS, B. *Person to person: The problem of being human.* Lafayette, Calif.: Real People Press, 1967.

ROKEACH, M. *The open and closed mind.* New York: Basic Books, 1960.

ROKEACH, M. *Beliefs, attitudes, and values.* San Francisco: Jossey-Bass, 1968.

ROKEACH, M. *The nature of human values.* New York: The Free Press, 1973.

RUBEN, B.D., & KIM, J.Y. *General systems theory and human communication.* Rochelle Park, N.J.: Hayden, 1975.

SKINNER, B.F. *Beyond freedom and dignity.* New York: Knopf, 1971.

SKINNER, B.F. *About behaviorism.* New York: Knopf, 1974.

TREVARTHEN, C. Babies can communicate at birth. *The National Observer.* July 24, 1976, 20.

WEAVER, W. The mathematics of communication. *Scientific American.* 1949, July, 11-15.

WHITE, E. *A Pou Sto.* Chapter one of unpublished manuscript; Penn State.

CONCEPTUALIZING INTERCULTURAL COMMUNICATION

HUBER W. ELLINGSWORTH
University of Hawaii

Intercultural communication has been a growing academic area since 1960. An examination of the premises undergirding these developments may be appropriate to planning for future teaching, research, and theory in the area. A survey of literature suggests the following propositions: (1) that intercultural communication is an unique phenomenon deserving of treatment as a special class of communication; (2) that differences function as barriers; (3) that anyone is potentially an intercultural communicator; (4) that culture learning is useful for predicting individual behavior; and (5) that nationality designates culture.

Analysis and restatement of these propositions can lead to the conclusion that all (or no) communication is intercultural, that cultural differences are not necessarily either barriers or facilitators, that as cultural difference increases, the number of potential participants declines, and vice versa, that knowledge of a culture is not necessarily useful in predicting individual behavior, and that nationality is not of itself a reliable synonym for culture.

The implication of this view would be to deemphasize the focus on *intercultural communication per se*, in courses, publications, research designs and organizations, and alternatively, to enrich the study of communication through increased attention to cultural variability as a dimension of all human interaction.

The excitement and adventure of contacting "exotic" or "barbaric" peoples of other lands has been reported throughout human history, whoever the sojourners and whatever their motives. This sense of the bizarre and romantic seems as much a part of the twentieth century as it was in the ages of exploration and conquest. For several years the author has used a projective exercise for opening discussion on the subject of intercultural contact: "In a moment I will say a two-word phrase. Please respond by generating a visual image. No synonyms or definitions, please. The phrase is 'intercultural communication.' " The verbal reports of the images are solicited by asking respondents questions about who was participating, the setting, and the nature of the activity they imaged. In general, the responses have clustered reliably. The perceived location usually is a very large room, possibly a palace or ballroom; the participants are racially different; they are standing and often sipping tea; some are dressed in robes or other non-Western garb; they are talking in English or sometimes in French and are discussing international relations or

world peace. In an alternate version, a Western agricultural agent or Peace Corps volunteer is standing in an open field beside a "native" of some kind, demonstrating a farming technique. These brave images probably reveal as much about the imaginers as about the nature of intercultural contact. Out of such speculation, much experience, and some scholarship has grown a burgeoning academic enterprise.

"Intercultural communication" is a phrase employed by a variety of academicians, and it is casually used in the general-circulation press. As an interested observer and occasional contributor in this area, the author undertook an investigation of its current state of development. In a preliminary step, he searched for the originator of the phrase or its first appearances in scholarly print. The results were inconclusive.[1] After about 1960, however, the tempo of use accelerates rapidly, with a number of variations and combinations, including "culture and communication," "cross-cultural communications," "cross-national communication," "international communication," "intercultural inter-

change," "interracial communication," "intercommunication," "interethnic communication,"
"interculturation," and "male-female communication." Clearly the most venerable is "international
communication," which has been prevalent since
the 1930s. Often these terms have been casually
interchanged; attempts have also been made to assign denotative meanings which refer to particular
aspects of encounter which occur between culturally, politically, or ethnically different individuals or
to the passage of messages across national boundaries. At least a minimal orthodoxy appears to be
growing out of this effort.[2] Apparently it is well-
intended, but not always functional.[3]

Acknowledging that cultural difference makes a
difference in communication has now become so
generally accepted by the academic community that
few texts, anthologies or trade books in the areas of
speech, communication, mass media, international
relations, sociology, or public relations are complete without some attention to the matter. Institutionalization of this idea has proceeded in the
instructional and professional realms, with both
undergraduate and graduate courses being offered
by a growing number of institutions, extended in
some cases to specialized degree programs. Professional organizations have shared in this development.[4]

No one could seriously dispute the importance
and salutary effects of affirming that cultural differences can have a profound effect on the degree of
satisfaction and the outcomes of communication.
What this paper proposes is that it is time to make a
critical examination of how the field has evolved
and how its future development might be planned.
The hazard of the present situation lies in our being
caught up by the romantic appeal of the concept and
its bandwagon effect, so that we fail to scrutinize
the logical premises upon which the concept rests,
and thus proceed to develop our training, teaching,
research, and theory on a base that is less productive
and defensible than it could be.

The author has examined a variety of text and
trade books, conference papers, research studies,
and annotated bibliographies in an attempt to discern some general propositions on which the
present concept appears to be grounded. Based
upon this review, it may tentatively be concluded

that there are at least five major propositions which
underlie current thinking on the matter, and that
each of them is deserving of scrutiny and possible
restatement.

PROPOSITIONS EXTRAPOLATED FROM THE LITERATURE

1. Intercultural Communication (in its various
   stylistic forms) is a unique dimension of communication which requires special labeling, attention, methodology, and instruction.
2. Cultural differences between communicators
   function as boundaries or barriers which must be
   overcome if understanding and satisfaction are to
   be achieved.
3. Any given member of a cultural group is a potential interactor with any member of another cultural group.
4. Learning about a cultural pattern is an important
   means of reducing uncertainty about the behavior of a member of that culture.
5. Culture is primarily a phenomenon of region or
   nationality; national identity predicts culture.

Discussion of Propositions

*Proposition I. Intercultural communication is a
unique dimension of communication which requires
special labeling, attention, methodology, and instruction.*

Adding *intercultural* to *communication* signals
that there is a special class, or kind, of communication distinguished by the phenomenon of cultural
difference between participants. The phrase logically requires another class, *intracultural communication,* where cultural differences are minimal
or absent, and implies the necessity of dividing all
human communication into one of the two classes.
Yet treating this complex phenomenon as a
dichotomous (rather than continuous) variable requires us to imagine one set of communication
events which is culture-free and another which is
bound to the cultures represented.

One can fantasize, if not observe, a situation free
of cultural disparity, in which the only variability is
generated by personality differences. Such an event
might be a conversation between identical 10-

year-old male twins who have been reared in the same house by the same parents and subjected to the same experience. Their talk may represent intracultural communication in its purest obtainable form. At the other extreme would be a fantasy in which a person who had never traveled outside his home county in the United States is parachuted into a central valley of New Guinea so remote that the inhabitants believe they are the only people in the world. Almost certainly, any attempts at symbolic interaction between the tribe and the newcomer would be characterized by virtually complete dissimilarity in views about what constitutes human existence.

But these two cases, if they occurred at all, would make up a minute portion of total human interaction. To return to the twins, if we specify that one is a male and one a female, we have introduced cultural variability, because boys and girls in most societies are subjected to differing cultural nurture, which by age ten will have generated somewhat different vocabularies, tool skills, role perceptions, food preferences, ideas of dress and adornment, attitudes toward sex, recreational patterns, and other classic dimensions of culture. To dismiss these differences as having minimal importance and being "subcultural" is not to accomplish much by way of definition, because then a reliable way of determining the threshholds among "intracultural," "subcultural," and "intercultural" must be produced. This would require sufficient precision to classify reliably the interactions of a cattle rancher from Montana and another from Saskachewan, two French engineers of different ethnic backgrounds, or two Mexicans, one a farm laborer and one a jet-setter.

This should lead, in turn, to the realization that the term *culture*, like *communication*, is plagued with denotative ambiguity and diversity of meaning. *Culture* is often used to designate a large general area of human activity and of scholarly concern, rather than an operational concept. Cultural anthropologists, perhaps the most catholic of that group of scholars, have generated definitions such as "A historically-derived system of explicit and implicit designs for living, which tends to be shared by all or specially designated members of a group" (Kluckhohn & Kelly, 1945). Such definitions are

boundary-setting, but reveal little of the interior. Another alternative is to use definitions from more specialized anthropologists who have sought to explore a segment of the broad concept of culture. Such specialists include ethno-biologists, ethno-linguists, "national-character" anthropologists, archeologists, physical anthropologists, paleopathologists, and some geographers. The communication scholar, seldom a well-grounded anthropologist of any persuasion, is likely to find himself pragmatically deriving definitions and concepts from a number of general and special viewpoints in anthropological science, without a clear picture of their compatibility or usefulness in dealing with the phenomena he wishes to study. Of course, a parallel problem lies in the definition of *communication*, as most scholars will testify.

Thus, *intercultural communication* is probably an imprecise, nonoperational label for all but the most contrived cases of human interaction. For all the rest, some cultural variability between participants will be present, but its amount is not a reliable predictor of the ease or difficulty of communication. Dealing with cultural variability probably does require special strategies, but determining what differences make a difference—and under what conditions of interaction—will require the gathering and assimilation of much more anecdotal and empirical data. The quest for the marker that separates *intra-* from *inter-*, as well as more subtle cues to the transitional stages marking subcultures, is probably a pointless search. The amount of cultural difference in a situation is theoretically free to vary from "none" to "complete." Rejecting the dichotomy and accepting the continuum deals with only some of the conceptual problems.

There are two alternate and pre-emptive ways of rephrasing the widely-asserted Proposition I, upon which the present development of the concept rests. Both directly refute the assertion of intercultural communication as a unique phenomenon. One is "*All communication is intercultural.*"[5] The other is "*No communication is intercultural.*" These are alternate forms of the same statement. Both point to the same conclusion—that cultural variability is a universal element of the communication experience. Except as a public relations strategy, the term *intercultural communication* should be used spar-

ingly by scholars, and then most properly as a post
hoc description of encounters where cultural differences became manifest, were recognized, and were
successfully compensated for. As an a priori prediction of what will be the dominant aspect of an
encounter, it must be advanced very tentatively, if
at all.

*Proposition II. Cultural differences between
communicators function as boundaries or barriers
which must be overcome if understanding and satisfaction are to be achieved.*

There is a recurrent theme in present literature
that difference and difficulty tend to parallel one
another. Probably no one would deny that communication is easier when cultural difference is
minimal. Whether the converse is true is a researchable question. Almost anyone with extracultural
experience can testify that difficulty of communication does not arbitrarily vary directly with amount
of cultural difference. Many such persons could
describe highly satisfying encounters with individuals of quite different backgrounds, perhaps because the manifest differences gave them warning
that almost nothing could be taken for granted.
Conversely, there are ample illustrations of how
a single, culturally-rooted difference, as in beliefs
about religion or sex, became so crucial that the
communicative effort collapsed. As previously
noted, the more manifest the difference, the more
warning is available to a participant that compensa-
tion is called for. Hidden or minimal differences
may create a false sense of ease or congruity.

A virtually unexamined dimension of this proposition concerns the effects of purpose on the interaction. If the situation is casual or recreational, the
prevailing mood may be tolerant and perhaps didactic, with interchange about dress, customs, or food
in the respective cultures. Differences here are
facilitative, except as fluency in the shared language may intervene. In a task-oriented interchange, difference in concepts of time, space, values, and specialized terminology may function initially as barriers proportionate to difference. If the
task is urgent and affects mutual welfare, the level
of accommodation and cooperation may be high,
despite the reality of the cultural dissimilarity.

Still another little-examined dimension is the de-

termination of territoriality, or of whose rules are
being applied. The effect of cultural differences is
often partially waived by this determination. When
a person travels to another area to conduct business,
the normal expectation is that he will accommodate
himself to the cultural rules of the host. If his hosts
expect that he will conform and he is unable or
unwilling to do so, then the barriers may damage or
destroy the interaction. If for reasons of politeness
or status difference, the host strives to conform to
the visitor's cultural pattern, the barrier effect may
be reduced, though at some cost to the host.

Proposition II might appropriately be modified to
*"Cultural differences signify the need for accom-
modation in communication, but they are not arbitrarily either barriers or facilitators."*

*Proposition III. Any given member of a culture is a
potential interactor with any member of another
culture.*

In the abstract, this is an appealing idea. Proponents point to technologies like jet planes, cables,
and communication satellites as means of moving
people, voices, images, and writing easily around
the "global village," with the promise of greater
things to come. But any number of factors, singly
and interactively, greatly reduce the likelihood of
contact between two randomly-selected individuals
of different cultural backgrounds, whether they re-
side in the same or in different countries. Among
these factors are the existence of purposes for interacting, financial access to the means of generating face-to-face or interposed communication, political and social freedom to interact, a shared spoken language or a shared literacy, differences in
ease of surface transportation, uneven distribution
of telephones world-wide, national postal services
which are capable, by some estimates, of delivering
a letter to less than ten percent of the world's population, physical and atmospheric effects on radio
signals. If we realistically dismiss the finite, but
incomprehensible, possibility of random contact
between any two of the world's four billion-plus
people, the tasks of developing research, theory,
and instruction about "intercultural" interaction
becomes somewhat less impossible. A strategy
question arises at this point: whether to begin at the
minimum-difference or the maximum-difference

end of the cultural interaction scale. Interest to date has been focused on the latter, more exotic end, and this emphasis is likely to continue.[6] In some respects, it may be easier to deal with, because the actors and situations are more easily identifiable. When we find an individual with a purpose for contacting persons of another cultural set, mutual agreement to proceed, the financial and physical means of making the contact, (by either face-to-face or interposed means), a shared spoken and/or written language, and mutual political and social freedom to interact, we have discovered the necessary and sufficient conditions for an *intercultural* encounter. Since these conditions will not exist randomly in any two populations, *intercultural* communicators will almost certainly be drawn from elite or sub-elite social classes in their respective societies.[7] The actors are probably brought together by shared backgrounds in business and industry, intergovernmental relations and diplomacy, art, scholarly pursuits, or specialization in such matters as health, education, agriculture, labor, military operations, transportation, meteorology, mass communications, or the like. Given these conditions, candidates for maximum-difference *intercultural* encounters make up a minute percentage of the members of any given society. Based on these assumptions, Proposition III would say *"Training, research and theory in intercultural communication should reflect the probability that the population of participants is relatively small and identifiable."*

Proposition IV. Learning about a cultural pattern is an important means of reducing uncertainty about the behavior of a member of that culture.

Hall's influential *Silent Language* (1959) makes an appealing case for the learning of generalizations or stereotypes about cultures in order to increase understanding of how and why people behave as they do. His memorable examples of Persian appointments, Latin proximity, and Pueblo time-sense have come to stand for expectations that Persians will not predictably keep appointments, that Latins will insist on standing close while conversing, and that Pueblo Indians are not prompt. As post hoc explanations of how things turned out, these generalizations are socially reinforcing. As predictors of individual behavior (which Hall does

not claim) they may range from highly accurate to badly misleading. If we did accept the premise that everyone is a potential interactor with everyone else, then such culture learning would be somewhat functional. To the extent that the generalizations are accurate, they will probably predict with some accuracy the behavior of monocultural individuals. But if the necessary and sufficient conditions stated in the discussion of Proposition III are accepted and the population of potential interactors is perceived accordingly, the predictive power and accuracy of any within-culture generalization is greatly diminished. A candidate for intercultural contact as specified is not monocultural. As a result of education, involvement with foreigners, use of foreign mass media, and possibly of foreign travel, such a person is aware of the varieties of human experience and probably has a culturally-mixed repertoire of responses at his disposal, to be tried out as he perceives them to be appropriate. This repertoire can give rise to unexpectedly reliable Persians, remote Latins, and prompt Pueblos.

John Useem and associates (1963) were among the first proponents of the "third culture" model, which they used to describe the cultural milieu of scholars and technicians from India who had been exposed to Western technological culture and had then returned home to function as agents of change. Such persons were perceived as representing a transitional orientation between Indians and Westerners. The third-culture idea appears to have great potential for the development of research and theory in intercultural contact, but it has received minimal attention from researchers and theorists of the subject. The coming together of two persons with a somewhat cosmopolite view represents three sets of cultural resources. Let "A" stand for those of a person from one culture, "B" for those of a representative from the other, and "X" for the indeterminate cosmopolite dimension. This latter element denotes each person's past contact with other-culture individuals and/or a cognitive store of information and attitudes about such contacts.[8] Of course, it is logically possible that A and B would have studied the cultural stereotypes of the other and would negotiate a straightforward tradeoff involving, say, coffee for tea in exchange for sitting further apart, but this is unlikely. The more probable resolution is for A and B to move laterally—on a tentative, trial-and-error basis—into X, the synthetic third-culture orientation, which will unconsciously include elements of A and B. It may also involve invented or previously-learned behaviors not a part of either culture. The most manifest of these accommodations is likely to be language, in cases where a shared first language is not available. One unplanned residue of past British world influence, augmented by more recent U.S. involvement in world affairs, has been to make English (which is second only to Chinese as a first language worldwide) the primary medium of international contact. The chosen language for the "X" interaction is more likely than not to be English. This is true whether the participants are from Canada and South Africa or from Afghanistan and Japan. The distribution of the English "world" language within subelites of most nations means that an unparalleled amount of direct converse has become possible in the past few decades. The use of this "international" language reinforces the third-culture ambiance. Another pressure toward lateral synthesis of culture pertains to the purposes of intercultural contact. Very many of these purposes relate to technological or "developmental" matters generated by the more industrialized societies of the Northern hemisphere. This is often true whether one of the participants is a northerner from Europe, North America, Northeast Asia, Israel, or the Soviet Union, or whether both are from one of the less-technologically-oriented countries of the southern hemisphere. Technology embodies a synthetic supraculture which transcends or displaces many traditional elements of social relationships, diet, politics, religion, art, dress, craftsmanship, etc., and consequently generates its own communication genre. Much of the interaction of culturally-different persons involving matters affected by technology is expectably carried out in the requisite third-culture orientation. Given prior assumptions about potential candidates for intercultural contact, Proposition IV can be rephrased to

"Culture learning is a useful background for intercultural contact: it may not predict behavior for a given situation, which is likely to occur in a synthetic third culture ambiance."

Proposition V. Culture is primarily a phenomenon of region or nationality.

This view is especially appealing to many northern-hemisphere social scientists, because of their experience with relatively homogeneous social-political-economic nation-systems. Concomitant assumptions are that persons within a national boundary are more culturally alike than different and that collectively they have more in common with one another than with persons of other nationalities. Such a common-sense view is reinforced by any map showing the "vertical" political boundaries which delineate nations. For the student of intercultural contact, perhaps already burdened with the belief that in culture he is examining a definable and discrete phenomenon, the "nation-equals-culture" idea is a potential source of additional error.

In his statement entitled "Is Latin America a Myth?" John T. McNelly (Deutschmann, Ellingsworth, & McNelly, 1968) points out defects in the convenient generalization called Latin America, as well as the assumed homogeneity of many countries in that region. As evidence he cites the presence of language groups, racial stocks, crop groups, climate groups, rural-urban contrasts, religious adaptations, and various distinct heritages of Hispanic colonialism scattered across the land mass. Thus, realistic cultural maps of Latin America might largely ignore political boundaries and define more precise cultural homogeneity among noncontiguous portions of the continent, such as intact Indian populations of Guatemala, Bolivia, and Brazil, heavy industry workers of Mexico, Brazil, and Uruguay, potato farmers of the Andean slopes, and the aristocracies of Peru, Mexico, and El Salvador.

This challenge to the assumption of cultural identity based on national identity strongly suggests that the investigator of intercultural contact should cautiously examine the easy parallels between *nation* and *culture*. He may find much greater viability in a "horizontal" analysis based on common occupation, socio-economic class, or ethnicity—independent of citizenship—in his quest for cultural variables that make a difference in communication.

Generalization V might profitably be rephrased to *"Nationality is one major dimension of cultural identity: it is not by itself a reliable indicator of the cultural behaviors of its citizens."*

SUMMARY

An informal summary of these arguments generates the view that cultural difference is a universal property of communicative interaction and this difference should be regarded as a continuous variable, not as the basis for a unique class of communication. Differences signal the need for accommodation, but do not necessarily specify the a priori degree of difficulty they present. When differences are apparently large, the population of potential interactors is probably small and identifiable. When the difference is small, the population of potential interactors will be large. The need for study of minimum-difference interaction may be less appealing, but it is no less important. Culture learning is a helpful background, so long as it is utilized to understand individual behavior, rather than to predict it. Subelites from manifestly different cultures will probably utilize a synthetic third culture as they interact. Because cultural plurality is a characteristic of many nation-states, the prediction of cultural identity from national citizenship should be approached with caution.

Implications

If communication scholars were to accept this statement as a point of view, or to reach similar conclusions from a different set of inductions, what would be some of the likely effects on teaching, research, and professional association in communication? We might expect the honorable retirement of the term "intercultural communication" in its various forms from course titles, publications, research designs, and organizations, at least in any specific or technical sense. The disappearance of the term should not and probably would not signal any decline of interest in the study of cultural difference as a dimension of communication. If our preoccupation with intercultural contact as a unique phenomenon could be abated, we could generate an enriched approach to the study of all human communication. The insights and values of the past two exploratory decades in this area are so important that, henceforth, no instruction in spoken or written communication could be regarded as sound without full attention to cultural identity as a characteristic of sources and receivers.

Research designs in communication would be complete only if they included the means of examining demographic and sociocultural characteristics as potential sources of variance and also of investigating the interaction of these differences with communicative purposes.[9] The ultimate goal of such research would be the generation of middle-range theories with the power to predict process and outcomes where cultural variability is found. This would represent the ultimate convergence of intercultural and intracultural communication study.

NOTES

1. Among the first users of the terms in professional literature were Hall and Whyte (1960). Few would disagree that Hall (1959) played a central role in calling the attention of communication scholars to the interrelationship of culture and communication. Berlo (1960) cites the "social-cultural context" of source and receiver in the SMCR model but makes no reference to interactions which should be labeled as intercultural. In the "Author and Key-Work Index" of the *Journal of Communication*, 1951-68, the terms appear only once, in a 1968 citation about using motion pictures.
2. Compare the generally-similar terms and definitions in Harms (1973); Prosser (1973); Rich (1974).
3. A recent ERIC annotated bibliography of 67 books and articles announces that an "international-intercultural" dichotomy will be used to distinguish between official and unofficial contact. The compiler acknowledges that this distinction is "somewhat arbitrary" and it is not actually employed in the report. See Casmir (1973).
4. Three organizations reflect their concern with international and intercultural matters through their structure. The International Communication Association has "Intercultural Communication" as the fifth of its seven major divisions. The Association for Education in Journalism has an "International Communications Division." The Speech Communication Association has established a "Commission on International and Intercultural Communication."
5. On this subject, Smith (in Larson & Dance, 1970, p. 166) asserts, "My first idea is that all communication is intercultural. Not just some communication. At the very least, all communication is between subcultures."
6. Concentration on maximum-difference interaction will be detrimental to the viewpoint being developed here if we do not concurrently move ahead on research and theory about the more subtle aspects of difference and the difference they make. If we define sex as a genesis of male and female

acculturation within a society, what will be the differences and similarity in vocabulary, nonverbal styles, attitudes and value structures attributable to sex-group membership? What is the range of these differences? What apparent effects will they have under what conditions? The same questions are appropriate for age, racial, ethnic, occupational, and social class interactions within a society. Because the markers are less dramatic and the potential actors less easy to specify, the investigation will be more difficult, but no less important.

7. There are special cases in which not all of the participants can be comfortably described as subelites. These include tourism, foreign military service, and Peace Corps activity, where the sojourners possess some degree of elitism, while their potential contacts may or may not.

8. For example, see "Change Agents as Receivers of Mass Communication," Deutschmann, Ellingsworth, & McNelly (1968) Ch. V, for a report of what a group of subelites say they learned about life in other countries from foreign mass media.

9. Edward T. Hall's "Map of Culture" (1959, pp. 174-175) is a comprehensive model of the cultural matrix.

REFERENCES

BERLO, D.K. *The process of communication.* New York: Holt, Rinehart & Winston, 1960.

CASMIR, F. Bibliography on international, inter-cultural communication. New York: ERIC Clearinghouse on Reading and Communication Skills, August, 1973.

DEUTSCHMANN, P.J., ELLINGSWORTH, H.W., & McNELLY, J.T. *Communication and social change in Latin America.* New York: Praeger, 1968, 15-17.

HALL, E.T. *The silent language.* New York: Doubleday, 1959.

HALL, E.T., & WHITE, W.F. Intercultural communication: A guide to men of action. *Human Organization,* 1960, 19.

HARMS, L.S. *Intercultural communication.* New York: Harper and Row, 1973.

KLUCKHOHN, C., & KELLY, W. The concept of culture. In R. Linton (Ed.), *The science of man in the world crisis.* New York: Columbia University Press, 1945.

LARSON, C.E., & DANCE, F. E. (Eds.) *Perspectives on communication.* Shorewood, Wisconsin: Helix Press, 1970.

PROSSER, M.H. (Ed.) *Intercommunication among nations and people.* New York: Harper and Row, 1973.

RICH, A.L. *Interracial communication.* New York: Harper and Row, 1974.

USEEM, J. et al. Men in the middle of the third culture. *Human Organization,* 1963, 22, 169-179.

THE URBAN COMMUNICATION NETWORK AND SOCIAL STRATIFICATION: A "SMALL WORLD" EXPERIMENT[1]

NAN LIN
State University of
New York–Albany

PAUL DAYTON
New York State Department
of Health

PETER GREENWALD
New York State Department of Health

A *small world* experiment, using four targets, and controlling information regarding the identification of the target's race and occupation in the packet, was conducted in a tri-city area in the Northeast. The data showed that the packets had difficulty crossing from white participants to the black network in order to reach the black targets. Within the racially defined network, communication flow is more effective downward in the status hierarchy, from males to females rather than from females to males, and from persons with higher occupational status toward targets of relatively low occupational status, rather than from persons with moderate or low occupational status.

Further, there is a positive relationship between social status and the ability to manipulate one's social resources. The higher a person's social status, the more able that person is to search the status hierarchy for communication purposes. Also, the higher a person's social status is, the less willing a person will be to manipulate his social resources for communication downward.

One of the interesting problem areas of research in social structure and communication concerns the effects of social stratification on the flow of communication. The general questions raised are whether or not people can communicate effectively with persons in the same or different socioeconomic strata and, if so, to what extent. In other words, do certain social stratification variables enhance or deter the flow of communication?

To answer such questions, a series of conceptual and methodological issues must be examined. Conceptually, one must ask, what are the theoretical relationships between social stratification and communication flow? Past research suggests that communication becomes more effective among participants of homogeneous characteristics and less effective among participants of heterogeneous characteristics (Lazarsfeld & Merton, 1954; Rogers & Bhowmik, 1970). Also, persons in the higher social class strata have more contacts in different strata than those in the lower strata (Shotland, 1970). However, while these discussions provide information about dyadic communication, they do not cover extended interpersonal networks. For example, there is little information assessing the ability or willingness of a person to communicate indirectly with another person in the same or in a different social stratum, regardless of how social strata are defined. Further, past research tends to consider only undifferentiated social status variables (e.g., sex, race, socio-economic status). Conceptual advancement must be made in order to determine how each status affects communication effectiveness.

Methodologically, one faces the problem of mapping the communication network by tracing the flow of communication as it involves participants with various socioeconomic characteristics. The mapping of communication relations in a restricted system poses little methodological problems, for sociometric data can be gathered and subjected to various structural analyses (Roistacher, 1974; Lin, 1975; Lin, 1976). However, when the mapping takes place in a large-scale system, such as an urban area, the sociometric data are impractical to gather and analyze. Until the time arrives when computer capacities and the level of research funding permit the gathering and analysis of the sociometric data, an alternative mapping strategy must be used.

One such strategy is the *small world technique*, in

which chains of communication are mapped by tracing the forwarding processes involved in the delivery of a packet to a described *target* person. In this technique, a target is selected and described (name, address, age, sex, occupation, etc.) in a packet which is then sent to a starter. The starter is asked to send the packet either directly to the target—if the target is an acquaintance of the starter—or to a friend who may know the target, or a friend of the target. By keeping track of the persons who send and receive the packets until the packet either successfully reaches the target or terminates, it becomes possible to gather data on the intermediaries, as well as the starters, and to map the flow of communication and the characteristics of participants.

Regarding the conceptual issue at hand, what seems to be valuable about the *small world technique* is the possibility of its being used to map communication flow, identify the socioeconomic characteristics of the participants, and thereby examine the relationships between social stratification and communication flows. For example, Korte & Milgram (1970) found that participants immediately preceding the targets tended to have higher social status than the targets. They also found that when the starter group was predominantly white, a white target had a greater likelihood of being reached than a black target.

Similarly, Milgram (1967) and Beck and Cadamagnani (1968) found that participants tended to send packets to persons of similar sex. Travers & Milgram (1967) found that selection of the next link was differentiated in terms of acquaintance and friendship, residence of the target, and the occupation of the target.

The *small world technique,* then, allows detection of communication networks available to each participant to accomplish a social identification task (i.e. to reach a target of certain socioeconomic characteristics). It has been shown that to maximize chances of success in reaching the target, participants do discriminate in their selection of the next person in the chains. This selection process, as well as the likelihood of success, are governed by the socioeconomic characteristics of the participants and the targets, and the effectiveness of the matching of characteristics of the next link and the target.

These characteristics include the sex, race, social status and occupational status of the participants and the target.

This paper reports part of a study utilizing the *small world technique* to examine the relationship between social stratification and communication flow as defined in the target-searching task.

CHARACTERISTICS OF THE STUDY

This study differs from previous *small world* investigations in several important respects. First and most importantly, the *small world technique* was employed as a means to examine the relationship between social stratification and communication. To do so, it was decided to confine the study to a single urbanized area. By restricting both the starters and the targets to the same urbanized community, it was hoped that the major portion of the forwarding activities would take place within that area; consequently, the mapping would approximate the communication networks within and across certain socioeconomic strata. The study site selected was a tri-city area in the Northeast, classified as an urbanized area by the U.S. Census Bureau.

Furthermore, control and manipulation of the target characteristics, and of the packet information describing the targets, was exercised. Contrasting with other *small world* studies, this study utilized both male and female, white and black targets. The four targets were selected and matched in terms of their length of residence in the community, age, marital status, education, occupational status, and social involvement (participation in religious and civic activities). However, the targets were manipulated on the variables of sex and race; namely, the four targets were white-male, black-male, white-female, and black-female. The selection of sex and race in the target characteristics was used to ascertain the effect these major ascribed characteristics might have on the communication flow. All four targets resided in one of the three cities in the tri-city area.

For each target, information in the packets regarding his/her race and occupation was permutated: (1) race and occupation of the target both given, (2) race but not occupation of the target

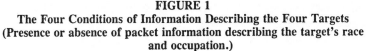

FIGURE 1
The Four Conditions of Information Describing the Four Targets
(Presence or absence of packet information describing the target's race
and occupation.)

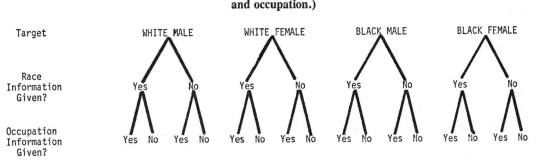

given, (3) occupation, but not race of the target given, and (4) neither race nor occupation of the target given. These variations resulted in the 16 packet types presented in Figure 1.

We believe this is the first empirical *small world* study in which the target descriptions were experimentally controlled and manipulated for the purpose of investigating the effect of social stratification on the communication flow.

METHODOLOGY AND DATA

A random sample of the households in the largest city of the tri-city area was drawn from the city directory, and a letter of solicitation to participants in the study was sent to each household. Accompanying each letter was a business reply postcard for indicating whether the head of the household, spouse, or both, would be willing to participate as starters in the study. The final list of starter households included the first 300 voluntary households whose returned postcards reached us. Thus, it was not our intention to select a starter group representative of the city households—to do so would require not only prohibitive costs, but also involuntary participation. Analysis showed that the voluntary participants were of slightly higher social status than the population in the area, with the ethnic minorities slightly under-represented. This trend is consistent with earlier findings of relationships between social class and voluntary participation in a *small world* study (Beck & Cadamagnani, 1968).

Past research indicated that the success rate

(number of packets reaching the target over the number of packets initiated) should be about 25 to 30 percent. Given 300 volunteers, we anticipated that about 60 percent would actually participate (start), or about 180 volunteers would forward the packets. If each volunteer were to send one packet, the anticipated number of successful packets would be between 50 to 60 packets (180x.30). Since there were 16 packet types involved, the anticipated number of successful packets for each type would have been reduced to 3 or 4 packets, much too small a number to administer any meaningful comparative analysis. Thus, it was decided that each volunteer would receive two packets describing two different targets. The 300 volunteers received 600 packets; each packet type was delivered to 37 or 38 volunteers. If we achieved the normal success rates, we should anticipate at least 6 successes for each packet type.

This decision to send two packets to each volunteer raised a number of conceptual and methodological issues. First, would this cause the volunteer to forward both packets indiscriminately? An examination of the forwarding behavior of starters showed that this was not the case. Only 13 (5%) of the actual starters sent both packets to the same next person, and in each case the next person was in some way closer to the target (same race, same sex, same city, etc.).

A second possible bias in sending two packets to each volunteer concerns data analysis. Since the starters initiated two packets, would the mapped communication chain for each packet be completely independent? Again, the fact that most (95%) of the packets were sent by the starters to different persons suggested discriminate effort and selection of next links by the starters. If there were any bias, it would result in less differentiation among the packet types, and it would increase the probability of failing to reject the null hypothesis that social stratification, as represented by packet types, will have no effect on the communication flow. Thus, there would be an increased likelihood of committing a Type II error—failing to reject the null hypothesis when it is false. This possible error would be against the confirmation of the theoretical hypothesis, forcing a more conservative estimate of the relationship under test.

The packet sent to each volunteer identified the sponsoring university and department on the cover. Attached to the inside of the cover page were 10 stamps and blank address labels to use in forwarding the packet. The next page consisted of a roster of the names and addresses (city and state) of those who have previously forwarded the packet. A description of the project preceded the description of the target. Described characteristics of the target included: name, address, marital status, number of children, first name of spouse, religion and church affiliation, social and professional organizational affiliations, and education (school and year). Depending on the packet type, race and/or occupation (including name and location of employer) was or was not provided. The next three pages gave the detailed procedure for participation. On the inside-back-cover page were stapled 10 business reply postcards. Each sender was requested to detach a postcard, fill it out and send it to the investigator. The postcard contained a brief questionnaire requesting information about the sender and the person he was sending it to (next link). For the sender, the information included name, address, education of self and spouse, occupation of self and spouse, age, sex, race, number of years residing in the community, number of affiliated clubs and organizations, and number of persons known on a first name basis (best guess). For the next link, information requested included name, address, occupation, age, sex, race, date when the sender last saw the intended receiver, nature of relationship between the sender and the receiver, and reasons for selecting the receiver.

As soon as each postcard was received, information was entered into a computer file for both the sender and receiver; each sender was identified as an observation. A week after each observation was entered into the file, a search was made to ascertain whether the intended receiver had returned the postcard—whether the intended receiver had been entered as an observation. If not, a follow-up note was sent to the intended receiver, reminding him of the packet which was forwarded to him and requesting his participation.

In the event the participant needed additional stamps, address labels, postcards or had any questions regarding the study, he or she was asked to contact the investigator by phone.

In the end, only 3 chains exceeded 10 links, requiring additional materials, and few persons called for clarification of the procedure.

Of 596 packets sent to the 298 volunteers, 375 packets were forwarded. Of the 375 packets initiated, 112 packets successfully reached the targets within four and a half months (about 140 days), when the field work was terminated. The result was a completion rate of 30 percent, slightly higher than response rates reported in previous *small world* studies.

MEASUREMENTS OF VARIABLES

While most of the measurements of the variables were straight-forward and usual, several need clarification. Occupational status was indexed by the *Siegel's prestige scale* (1971). The scale ranged from the low teens to the high 80s, with higher scale scores indicating higher occupational prestige.

Furthermore, a relative occupational status was constructed for each participant relative to the target described in his or her packet. This index contained three values: higher, equal, and lower. To construct the index, the standard deviation of the volunteers' occupational statuses was computed. It was found the standard deviation was between 13 and 14. Given the occupational statuses for the four targets as 40 for the white-male, 35 for the black-male, 52 for the white-female, and 42 for the black-female, a

TABLE 1
Construction of Values for the Relative Occupational Status Index*

	Occupational Prestige of Targets			
Participants Relative Occupational Status	White Male (Prestige = 40)	White Female (Prestige = 52)	Black Male (Prestige = 35)	Black Female (Prestige = 42)
Greater	47	59	42	49
Equal	33-47	45-59	28-42	35-49
Lower	33	45	28	35

*Values of the Siegel Scale (1971)

participant was assigned a relatively *equal* occupational status for a given target when his or her occupational status was within ±7 of the occupational status of the target. A relatively greater or lower occupational status was assigned to a participant when his or her occupational status was more than 7 points higher or lower than the target's. The assignment of values of the relative occupational status for each participant and each target is presented in Table 1.

In cases where a participant had no regular occupation, but the spouse was employed, the occupational status of the spouse was used to compute the relative occupational status for the participant. This decision was made in order not to exclude a large number of female participants from the data analysis. Also, it was felt that the social communication network of a nonworking participant, particularly an occupation-related network, is to a substantial extent affected by the wage-earning spouse.

It must be pointed out that while an effort was made to find targets with homogeneous characteristics, the effort was not entirely successful. As shown in Table 1, the white-female target had a much higher occupational status than did the other three targets.

DATA ANALYSIS AND FINDINGS

For the purpose of this report, the analysis focused on two major issues: (1) what affected the likelihood of a packet being forwarded and (2) what affected the likelihood of a packet successfully reaching a target? These two issues shall be discussed only in terms of the social status characteristics of the target, as defined by the packet types, and the social status characteristics of the participants.

To simplify discussions, several definitions must be introduced. The volunteers were divided into two categories: *starters* and *nonstarters*. A starter was a volunteer who forwarded the packet to another person; a nonstarter did not. The packets which did not leave the volunteers are called *dead chains*, and the packets which were forwarded are called the *live chains*. Live chains were then categorized into either *successful chains*, which reached the targets within the experimental period, or *unsuccessful chains,* which did not.

In this report, the discussion shall be restricted to analyzing the likelihood of a packet becoming a live chain and the likelihood of a packet becoming a successful chain. These analyses were conducted in terms of the social status characteristics of the

TABLE 2
Likelihood of Becoming a Live Chain by Target Race, Target Race
Identification, and Volunteer's Sex

	Percent of Packets Started					
	White Targets		Black Targets		Row Total	
Volunteer's Sex	Race Given	Race Not Given	Race Given	Race Not Given	Race Given	Race Not Given
Male	69 (62/90)*	64 (60/94)	55 (48/88)	66 (58/88)	62	65
Female	71 (37/52)	72 (31/43)	66 (33/50)	63 (32/51)	69	67
Column Total	70$\checkmark$	66	59$\checkmark$	65	64	66

* The numbers in the parentheses are the number of packets started over all packets in that catetory.

$\checkmark$ Percentage difference test, p < .05

TABLE 3
Percent of Chains Started by Target Race, Target Sex,
and Volunteer's Sex

	Percent of Packets Started					
	White Targets		Black Targets		Row Total	
Volunteer's Sex	Male	Female	Male	Female	Male	Female
Male	60$\checkmark$[4] (55/92)*	73$\checkmark$[4] (67/92)	58 (52/89)	63 (55/88)	59$\checkmark$[5]	68$\checkmark$[5]
Female	70 (33/47)	73 (35/48)	61 (30/49)	67 (35/52)	66	70
Column Total	63$\checkmark$[1]	73$\checkmark$[1]	59$\checkmark$[2]	74$\checkmark$[2]	61$\checkmark$[3]	69$\checkmark$[3]

* The numbers in parenthesis are the number of packets started over the number of all packets in the catetory.

[1],[2],[3],[4],[5]$\checkmark$ Percentage comparison test, p < .05

TABLE 4
Likelihood of Becoming a Live Chain by Relative Occupational Status
Between Volunteer and Target and Target's Occupation Identified or
Not Identified by Volunteer's Sex

Volunteer's Sex	Percent of Packets Started						Row Total	
	Occupational Status of the Starter Relative to the Target							
	Higher		Equal		Lower			
	Occupation Given	Occupation Not Given	Occupation Given	Occupation Not Given	Occupation Given	Occupation Not Given	Occ. Given	Occ. Not Given
Male	72√[7] (61/85)*	78√[5] (69/88)	53√[7] (20/38)	50 (20/40)	65 (17/26)	52√[5] (12/23)	66	67
Female	75 (27/36)	88√[4] (28/32)	59 (16/27)	69 (20/29)	67 (8/12)	63√[4] (10/16)	68	75
	73√[3]	81√[1] √[2]	55√[3]	58√[1]	66	56√[2]	67	70

* In parenthesis, number of packets started over number of all packets in the category.

[1,2,3,4,5,6,7]√ Percentage comparison tests, $p < .05$

starters, subsequent participants, and nonstarters as they related to the appropriate packet types defined in Figure 1.

Likelihood of Becoming a Live Chain

The likelihood of a packet becoming a live chain shall be analyzed in terms of the starters' and nonstarters' sex, race, and their relative occupational status as they interacted with the packet and target types.

Because so few nonwhite starters and nonstarters were involved (3% [6] of the starters were nonwhite; and 11% [13] of the nonstarters, were nonwhite), the comparison shall deal only with white starters and nonstarters.

Presented in Table 2 is an estimate of the likelihood of a chain becoming a live chain in terms of the race of the target and the packet type, where the race of the target was either identified or not identified. First, the target race affected the participation rates of the volunteers, while race identification in the packet by itself did not (see column totals). When the interaction between the target race and the race identification variable was examined, race identification improved the initiation of the chain toward white targets by the white male volunteers. On the other hand, race identification may have dampened the likelihood of initiating a live chain toward the black targets by the white male volunteers.

The next variables examined were the target sex and the volunteers' sex, as they affected the likelihood of a packet becoming a live chain. As shown in Table 3, females were more likely to start than were male volunteers (the second rows), and packets were slightly more likely to be started toward male targets (the column total). Analysis of the interaction between the volunteers' sex, the target race, and the target sex indicates that a female volunteer was about equally likely to start a packet toward either a male or female target, for both white and black targets. On the other hand, a male volunteer was more likely to start a packet toward a white female target, than toward a white male target.

Finally, we examined what effect knowing or not knowing the target's occupation and the volunteer's relative occupational status would have on the likelihood of a volunteer starting the chain. In Table 4, it is shown that the likelihood of starting a live chain was related to the relative occupational status of the volunteer to the target: The higher the relative status, the more likely the packet would be started (the column totals). Identification of the targets' occupation, by itself, did not affect the likelihood of a packet being started (the row totals). However, given the relative occupational status of the volunteers, identification of the target occupation had a differential effect on the likelihood of starting. When the volunteer's occupational status was lower than the target's, identification of the target's occupation increased the likelihood of the packet being started. On the other hand, when the volunteer's occupational status was higher than the target's, identification of the target's occupation had a slight tendency to dampen the interest in starting the packet. The major difference was between the higher and lower status groups when the occupation of the target was not given.

If one considers the starting of a chain towards an identified stranger as a behavioral indication of willingness on the part of the starter to communicate indirectly with that stranger, then the assumption can be made that the starter has at least tentative confidence in his or her communication network extending to such a stranger. The data show that the social status characteristics of potential starters and targets are crucial factors in making such a commitment. For instance, racial identification of the stranger either helps such commitment, as in the case of homogeneous racial identity, or hinders it, as in the case of heterogenous identity. It suggests, at the minimum, that the racial boundary constitutes a perceived barrier in communication relay.

Depending on the sex of the potential starter, sex identification of the stranger also has an effect on such commitment. While it has minimal effect on the female potential starters, the male potential starter is more likely to start if the stranger is identified as a female. Many explanations can be offered as to why such a different pattern emerges. However, the data also show that the potential starter is much more likely to start if he or she is of higher occupational status, in general, than the stranger. In combination, if sex and occupational status are two indicators of social status, then the data suggest that willingness to establish communication indirectly and confidence in reaching a stranger, through one's extended communication network, increases as a person perceives his or her own status to be superior (male over female and higher occupational status) to the stranger's. Such a relationship holds, however, only intraracially. The racial factor seems to have the opposite effect: Crossing the racial line decreases a person's willingness to attempt communication, and confidence in one's communication network extending to that stranger decreases.

Thus, the data suggest that, at least in American urban communities, the perceived communication network is constrained somewhat by the racial boundary. Within each racial group, communication is affected by the social class of the participants. Persons with perceived higher social status seem to have greater confidence in reaching others with lower status. But, willingness or desire to extend the communication network to someone with higher status is also strong, as indicated by the fact that more volunteers with lower occupational status started the packets when the occupation of the target was identified than when it was not.

However, does confidence in one's communication network extending downward, and willingness or desire to reach upward, make any difference in the actual success of reaching the target? This constitutes the next topic for discussion, the likelihood of a live chain becoming successful in reaching the target.

Likelihood of Becoming a Successful Chain

To examine the likelihood of becoming a successful chain, all live chains were included. Further, data were analyzed at each link of the chains. A *link* is defined as an intermediary between a starter and a terminal person (a person from whom the packet was not forwarded). By comparing the characteristics of the participants serving as starters and links, as well as the packet types, one may gain insights into the specific relationship between each social status variable and actual communication effectiveness. Data are presented for the first six links. By the sixth link, the probability of chains staying alive or becoming a successful chain was reduced to 12 percent, and comparisons involving the small numbers of participants would be unreliable.

FIGURE 2
Percent of Successful Chains by Race of Target, by Race Identification, by Sex of Participants, by Position in Chain
(Numbers in parentheses are frequency counts for those points when fewer than 10 observations occurred)

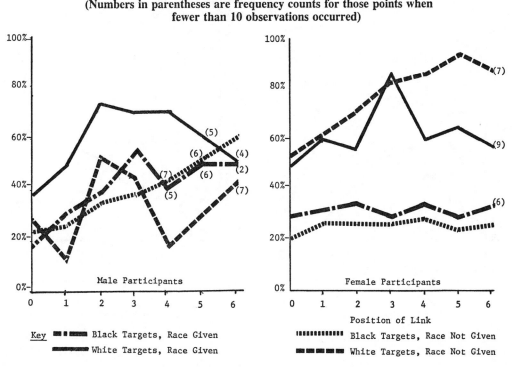

Figure 2 (A and B) examines the likelihood of success in terms of target race and identification of target race in the packet. Data are presented separately for the male participants and the female participants. First, we examined the interactive effects of target race, and race identification in the packet, among male participants, on the likelihood of the packet reaching the target. As can be seen in Figure 2-A, identification of the race of the target, had no effect on the likelihood of a chain reaching a black target. But, identification of the race of a white target consistently increased the likelihood of success. In fact, a white-target packet without race identification had as low a likelihood of success, as a black-target packet.

On the other hand, among the female participants, (Figure 2B), race of the target, rather than the identification of the target race, affected the likelihood of success.

In general, chains involving female participants were more likely to succeed than those involving male participants. Among male participants, the likelihood of success increased for packets directed toward white targets when the race of the target was given. Among female participants, the likelihood of success increased for the packets toward white targets, regardless of whether the race of the target was given or not.

In other words, the male participants, much more than the female participants, were sensitive to the identification of the racial status of the target.

The analysis now turns to the effects on the likelihood of success of the target's sex and participant's sex. Figure 3 (A and B) presents the analysis separately for packets directed toward the white target and the black targets.

First, the likelihood was much greater that a packet would reach a white target than a black target. Also, for white targets, the packet was more likely to succeed in reaching a female target than a male target, regardless of the sex of the participant (see Figure 3A). For black targets, a packet from a

FIGURE 3
Percent of Successful Chains by Race of Target, by Sex of Participants at Each Link in the Chains
(Numbers in parentheses are frequency counts for those points where fewer than 10 observations occurred)

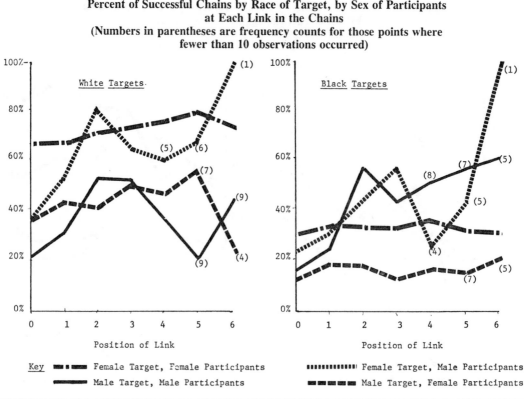

female participant toward a male target was less likely to succeed than others (see Figure 3B).

Again, the male participants seemed more sensitive to the white targets, while the female participants were consistent toward both the white and black targets.

Finally, the effect on likelihood of success of the relative occupational status of the starter to the target was examined. As can be seen in Figure 4 (A-C), contrary to the pattern between the relative occupational status and the likelihood of a packet becoming a live chain (see Table 4), the packets involving a higher status participant did not show a greater likelihood of reaching the target, as compared to those involving the equal and lower status participants. Further, identification of the target's occupation did not have any effect on the likelihood of a packet reaching a target. However, the small numbers of participants in the *equal* and *lower* occupational status groups renders the comparison unreliable.

To further examine the potential effect of the identification of the target's occupation on the likelihood of success, the mean occupational status was computed in terms of the sex of the participants (male vs. female), identification of the target's occupation (given vs. not given), and type of chains (successful vs. unsuccessful). As shown in Figure 5, there was a consistent, though slight, pattern between higher occupational status of the participant and successful chains, regardless of identification of the target's occupation and the sex of the participant.

The data suggest, then, that the effective strategy in the search task is one where a participant is relatively high on the occupational status hierarchy, so that a panoramic view of the structure below enhances the search for, and identification of, a target relatively low in the status hierarchy (cf. Lin & Dayton, 1977).

In summary, the likelihood of a packet successfully reaching the target increases (1) when the

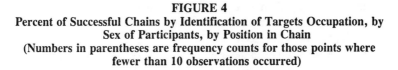

FIGURE 4
Percent of Successful Chains by Identification of Targets Occupation, by
Sex of Participants, by Position in Chain
(Numbers in parentheses are frequency counts for those points where
fewer than 10 observations occurred)

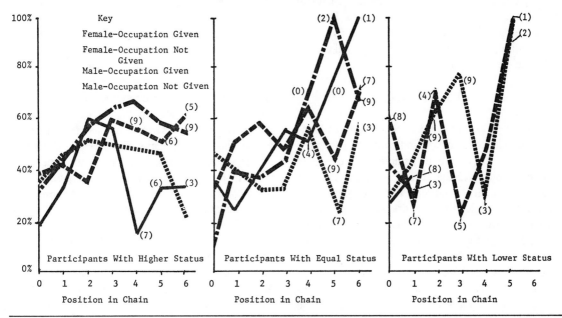

FIGURE 5
Mean Occupational Status by Type of Chain (Successful or
Unsuccessful), by Identification of the Target Occupation (Given or
Not Given), by Sex of the Participants

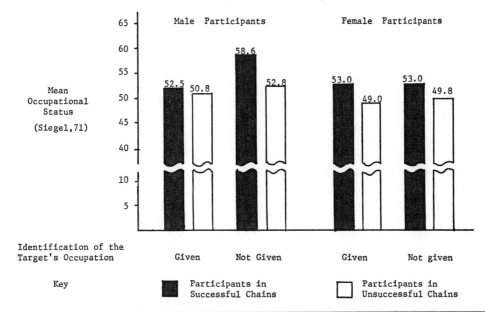

target is white rather than black, (2) when the target is female rather than male, (3) when the participant is female rather than male, (4) when the race of the target is given, in the case of a white target for male participants, and (5) when the occupational status of the participant is relatively high. Further, the male participants seem much more sensitive to the identification of the target's statuses and use the information differentially.

DISCUSSION

If the likelihood to start a packet toward an identified stranger is taken as an indication of a person's willingness and desire to establish an extended communication with that stranger, and a measure of the starter's own estimation of the probability of his or her communication network reaching such a stranger, then the data show that such assessments are affected by the race, sex, and the relative occupational status of the target. If the ability and desire of one's communication network participants to establish such a link with the stranger is examined, the data again show that it is affected by the race, sex, and the relative occupational status of the target. Specifically, the data show the following patterns:

1. Communication flows mainly within racial groups. Crossing the racial boundary is less likely to be attempted and less likely to be effective.
2. Communication flow is affected by the relative social status between participants, even though they are remotely linked. There is a tendency for persons with higher social status to show confidence in their communication network extending downward, such as from males toward females, and from persons with higher occupational status toward those with lower status. Further, the actual likelihood of reaching the stranger in a lower social stratum remains strong (e.g., from male or female participant toward a female target rather than a male target, from a participant with relatively higher status toward a target of lower status).

What theoretical explanation can be offered to account for these patterns of relationships? In the following section, one such explanation is attempted.

TOWARD A THEORY OF SOCIAL STRATIFICATION AND COMMUNICATION

Social stratification influences both the structure and process of communication. The major stratifying factors in American urban society—racial identification, sex differences, and occupation—all show their effects on communication. The racial identification sets not only the perceived boundary of communication networks, but also the effectiveness of the communication flow. One's perception of his or her extended communication network tends to be delineated by the racial boundary of one's own social identification. Furthermore, that communication flow which does cross racial boundaries is ineffective.

Within the racially identified communication structure, perceived confidence in the ability of one's communication network to flow downward—and to reach a stranger with lower social status—is stronger than when one's network has to reach upward toward a stranger with higher social status. This pattern is reflected both in terms of sex (more confidence from males to females) and relative occupational status (more confidence from persons of higher status to persons of lower status), in the extended relaying of communication.

Such confidence is justified in the actual likelihood of success in reaching a stranger. That is, the female stranger is more likely to be reached than the male stranger in communication relays initiated either by a male or female, and a participant with a relatively higher occupational status is more likely than one with a relatively low occupational status to ultimately reach the target.

SUMMARY

Thus, in the American cultural context, in the urban setting, and within the racially defined communication structure, communication flow is more effective downward in the status hierarchy.

Further, there seems to be an association between social status and the willingness and ability to manipulate one's social resources for communication purposes (Lin & Dayton, 1976; Vaughn & Lin, 1976). The higher a person's social status is, the more able that person is to search the status hierarchy for communication purposes. For example, manipulation of the information regarding the target's race and occupation particularly affected the communication strategy of the male participants. Race identification of a white target enabled white male participants to successfully search for the target.

The higher a person's social status, the less willing that person will be to manipulate his social resources for communication downward. For example, when the *(relatively low)* occupational status of the target is not given to the male participant, he tends to search upward, increasing the likelihood of eventual success. However, when such information was provided, the male participant, realizing the status gap, changed the communication strategy by not searching upward. As a result there was less manipulation of one's social resources but the likelihood of finding the target was decreased.

What has been found here regarding the relationships between social statuses and communication flow has potentially important implications for a theory linking social stratification and communication. Additional evidence is needed to verify the relationships proposed here. For example, it would be interesting to construct a situation where black starters are used toward white targets, which the reported study did not examine, again controlling for packet information regarding the various statuses of the target.

Also, it would be interesting to examine the effect of identification or lack of identification of the target's sex in the packet. It should be possible to manipulate this variable by simply providing the initials of the target, rather than the full name as given in the packets, and adding or dropping the sex information in the packet as required.

CONCLUSION

In the nonorganizational context of communication research, we too often emphasize the association of communication, in terms of behavioral change, and homophilous characteristics of participants. A paradigm is needed to specify the associations of communication, in terms of task performance and communication relay, and differential social statuses of the participants. The reported study represents a small step toward that direction.

NOTE

1. Supported in part by Grant No. 12707 from the National Cancer Institute. We thank Linda Armour, Charles Kennedy, Nora Searing, and Jean Streck for their participation in data collection.

REFERENCES

BECK, M., & CADAMAGNANI, P. The extent of intra- and extra-social group contact in American society, unpublished manuscript, John Carroll University, May, 1968.

KORTE, C., & MILGRAM, S. Acquaintance networks between racial groups: Application of the small world method, *Journal of Personality and Social Psychology*, 1970, 15-2, 101-108.

LAZARSFELD, P.F., & MERTON, R.K. Friendship as a social process: A substantive and methodological analysis, in M. Berger, et al. (Eds.), *Freedom and control in modern society*, N.Y.: Van Nostrand, 1954, 18-66.

LIN, N. Analysis of communication relations in G.J. Hanneman and W.J. McEwen (Eds.), *Communication and behavior*, N.Y.: Addison-Wesley, 1975, 237-252.

LIN, N. Foundations of social research. N.Y.: McGraw-Hill. Chapter 17, 1976, 329-349.

LIN, N., & DAYTON, P.W. The uses of social status and social resources in the urban network, paper presented at the annual meetings of the American Sociological Association, August 1976, New York.

MILGRAM, S. The small world problem, *Psychology Today*, May, 61-67, 1967.

ROGERS, E.D., & BHOWMIK, D.K. Homophily-heterophily: Relational concepts for communication research, *Public Opinion Quarterly*, 34, 1970. Winter, 523-538.

ROISTACHER, R.C. A review of mathematical methods in sociometry, *Sociological Methods and Research*, 3-2, November, 1974, 123-171.

SHOTLAND, R.L. The communication patterns and the structure of social relationships at a large university, unpublished Ph.D. dissertation, Michigan State University, 1970.

SIEGEL, P.M. Prestige in the American occupational structure, unpublished Ph.D. dissertation, University of Chicago, 1971.

TRAVERS, J., & MILGRAM, S. An experimental study of the small world problem, *Sociometry*, 1969, 32-4, December, 425-443.

VAUGHN, J.C., & LIN, N. Social resources and occupational mobility, paper presented at the annual meetings of the American Sociological Association, August 1976, New York.

REFLEXIVITY IN HUMAN COMMUNICATION[1]

KLAUS MERTEN
University of Bielefeld

Communication research, though an established interdisciplinary field, is hampered by a set of difficulties which are based in the object of interest itself and can be named in particular as profanity, transitoriness, inevitableness, universality, and causality. From a systems theory point of view, an alternative approach is outlined, which strives to alleviate these difficulties. Communication is thereby defined as the smallest social system which fullfils the criterion of reflexivity in the temporal, social, and objective dimension, and which generates all higher social systems. This assumption is examined on three levels of communication: animal communication, human communication and mass communication. It is shown that these levels build a hierarchic and reflexive superstructure. Modern world communication is defined and analyzed as the correlation of three social systems—organized, abstract, and real communications systems. It is suggested further, from an epistemological point of view, that the state of communication theory demands reflexive theory.

"'Communication' is a catchword of our times, 'communication problems' an apparent national pastime," lamented Lee Thayer (1970, p. 37). Even when this lament is fairly justified, it is now, as before, startling, since communication is a basic social process, or, as Charles Horton Cooley (1909, p. 61) has put it, "the mechanism through which human relations exist and develop." What are the reasons that the most basic of all social phenomena has received only poor attention, and the progress in communication research is up to now hampered by a set of different difficulties?

In the following, some of these difficulties are explored. Keeping these difficulties in view a system approach to communication which is based not on causality, but on reflexivity is suggested. The applicability of this approach is illustrated by the analysis of three types of communication— nonverbal communication, verbal communication, and mass communication.

SOME DIFFICULTIES IN COMMUNICATION RESEARCH

There seem to be barriers to progress in communication research which are inherent in the phenomenon of communication itself. These can be termed: *profanity, transitoriness, inevitableness, universality,* and *noncausality.*

Profanity

The first difficulty of communications research is the *profanity* of communication. Communication is a most profane process—economical to get under- way and easy to keep going. The practitioners of communication show us how to deal effectively with communication; they show, also, how one can succumb to the fallacy that what is easy to handle is also easily explicated. The worldwide scientific dif- fusion of the so-called *Lasswell formula* (Lasswell, 1948, p. 37) is a famous example of this fallacy.[2]

Transitory

Second, communcation is *transitory*. The com- munication scientist cannot watch the object of his interest like the physicist, describing it by a set of well-defined dimensions and measuring it precise in inches, kilograms, or ergs. Communication does not fossilize, and therefore up to now it has been impossible to give an interpersonal description of

FIGURE 1
Communication and Understanding in Circular Relations

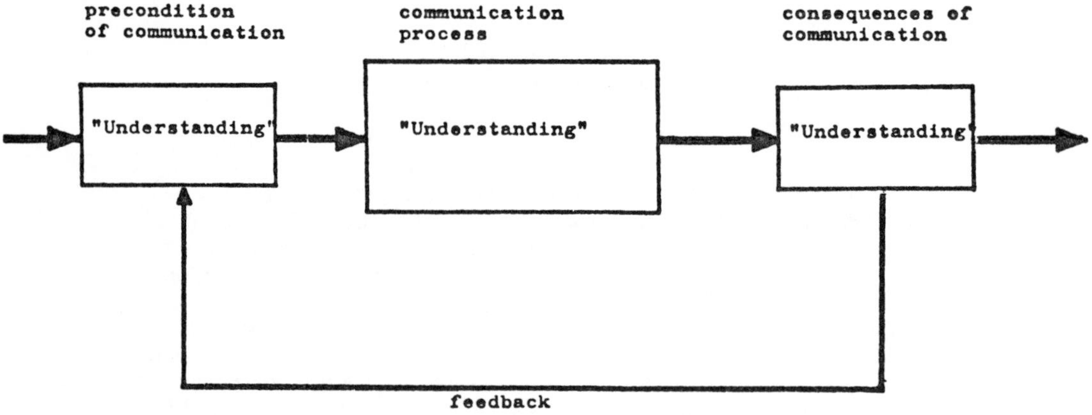

precondition   communication   consequences of
of communication   process   communication

"Understanding"   "Understanding"   "Understanding"

feedback

communication; such an interpersonal description could only duplicate and therefore perpetuate the difficulties, since it again requires communication.[3]

Inevitable

Third, communication is *inevitable*. Since "one cannot not communicate" (Watzlawick, Beavin, & Jackson, 1967, p. 51) there is no exception to communication. But function and structure of complex phenomena, particularly if they are transitory as communication is, are analyzable in the best and often in the only way by the rule of exception. Since there are few exceptions, there are few chances for fruitful insight too.[4]

Universal

Fourth, communication is *universal*. It is this universality that creates a barrier to communication research. As Thayer (1967, p. *v*.) notes:

A phenomen ubiquitous as communication, a phenomenon which transcendents so many traditional boundaries, is destined to languish. Welcome everywhere as an issue; but homeless, belonging to everyone but no one, an illegitimate handmaiden of so many disciplines, communication languishes in its own amorphousness. Its universality is its illegitimacy.

It is perhaps commonplace to indicate that communication research is, appropriately, interdiscipli-

nary. In such efforts, one may suffer the loss of much time and a good deal of motivation because of the divergent points of departure members of various disciplines claim. Paradoxically, communication about communication presents great communication difficulties.

Causality

Fifth, communication is a process not sufficiently analyzable in terms of *causality*. We are accustomed to describe the communication process in classificatory terms (like communicator, recipient, content)—but is this "actually" a description of communication? If we regard communication as a dynamic process, we cannot describe it in static, causality oriented terms. Communication does not begin at the communicator and end at the recipient; it is, rather, a relation between and within them which has a very specific and complicated structure. There are many problems in communication research which show strikingly that a causal explanation fails because it generates paradoxes. Take for example the term *understanding*. Some academic people say that understanding is a precondition of communication and prove this by the fact of language (Meier, 1962, p. 8); others argue, that understanding is the consequence or the effect of communication (Lasswell, 1948, p. 83). Still others see *understanding* and *communication* as identical terms. This paradox can be solved only by introducing circular, not causal, explanations (Figure 1). Or take some process of public opinion, during a voting campaign: To win the voters, what can a party do? Should it start a great campaign to win the undecided voters, or should the party stop all activities to win the voters, avoiding an underdog effect? On the descriptive level, causal assumptions lead to static classifications and categories which lack fruitfulness for the analysis of problems of this sort. On the empirical level, there are communication effects which cannot be explicated by simple yes-no decisions. The concept of causality does not help very much in the analysis of communication.

Looking at the communication process not as a *profane,* dealing with a *complex* and not a simple communication reality, facing the problem of *universality* and of *noncausality,* one must search for a more adequate analytic concept.

The following outline suggests some steps towards a new, alternative approach.

REFLEXIVITY AS CRITERION FOR COMMUNICATION

To avoid the named difficulties, one must look for dynamic, noncausal concepts. Modern systems theory, especially the functional-structural systems theory of Niklas Luhmann (1970, 1972, 1975) provides a sound basis for an alternative approach to communication.

The main assumption of the functional-structural systems theory is that all social systems develop a difference in complexity between themselves and their environment and reduce the complexity of their environment by selective strategies. Powerful selection requires, at specific points of all systems, the installation of reflexive processes and mechanisms (Luhmann, 1970, p. 92).

Examining even the smallest social systems, one detects communication processes (Luhmann, 1972). A careful analysis of communication processes with reference to the functional-structural systems theory shows that communication processes possess a specific structure, which involves the property of a reflexivity in *social, objective,* and *temporal* dimension. These properties account at the same time for the catalyzing or genetic effect of all communication processes.

Social Reflexivity

Reflexivity in the *social* dimension suggests that the presence of two or more persons, and the possibility for reciprocal observation, forces the reflexivity of perception: A perceives that B perceives, and B perceives him *simultaneously.* A acts on B's actions, and the same holds for B. Both input and output, perception and action, are interlocked, permitting the perception of action. The function of reflexivity in the social dimension lies in the connection of psychic systems by generating a social system. In terms of selectivity, social reflexivity allows double contingent selection and makes the genesis of a social system both possible and inevitable (Luhmann, 1972, p. 53). The effects of this *social reflexivity* are often striking, as Laing (1966), McLeod (1973), and Scheff (1973) have shown.

Objective Reflexivity

Reflexivity in the *objective* dimension means that it is possible (and necessary) to make statements about statements. The function of this type of reflexivity lies in the regulation of the system. In terms of selectivity, *objective reflexivity* allows the selection of statements. First, there is selectivity by perception, second by translating the perception (or the stored perception) into a statement, and third and most relevant for communication, a selection by making a statement about a statement. In communication, this type of reflexivity is to be found in the relation of information and comment, or in the relation of information and opinions about the information. Watzlawick et al. (1967, p. 51) termed this the relation of information and command:

> The report aspect of a message conveys information and is, therefore, synonymous in human communication with the content of the message. It may be about anything that is communicable regardless of whether the particular information is true or false, valid, invalid, or undecideable. The command aspect, on the other hand, refers to what sort of message it is to be taken as . . .

Bertrand Russell named the reflexivity in the objective dimension by the prefix *meta.* All *metacommunication,* as described here, is a case of reflexivity in the objective dimension.

Time Reflexivity

Reflexivity in the *time* dimension means that communication over time further structures communication. The function of this type of reflexivity, which is widely known as *feedback,* lies in the catalysis of social structure. In terms of selectivity, the range of possible states of a system over time is reduced by the acting states of that system. Krippendorff (1971, p. 171) had this type of reflexivity in mind when he said "any communication process, once initiated and maintained, leads to the genesis of structure—whether or not such structure is anticipated or deemed desirable." Watzlawick et al. (1967, p. 131) call this the "limiting effect of communication" and describe it by the hypothesis that "in a communication sequence, every exchange of messages narrows down the number of possible next moves." It is clear, also, that there is a direct analogy to the second law of thermodynamics. In communication research, this reflexivity has also been recognized in processes of group-formation, or in acquaintance processes (Newcomb, 1961; Mehrabian, 1974). Luhmann (1976, p. 145) defines social communication as "a nontemporal extension of time."

The joint presence of these three types of *reflexivity,* then, generates results like consensus, understanding, and sympathy, which are directly identifiable as communication effects. Thus, one can define communication as the *smallest social system which fulfills the criterion of reflexivity in three dimensions* (Merten, 1976b).

AN APPLICATION

At this point, many questions rise. For example, in which specific relations do these reflexivities operate? Are they interchangeable, and are there priorities and ranks between them? These questions are also problems for development of a general system theory and are yet unsolved. The following provides an application of reflexivity concept at three levels of communication.

Level I: Nonverbal Communication

The term nonverbal communication is somewhat

misleading, for it is used as an opposite to verbal communication or interaction. Under this heading we shall discuss briefly some results of animal communication. One can thereby gain important insights into the process of nonverbal communication.

At the animal level, there is indeed no verbal communication, and this lack is seen as the crucial difference between animal and man. But on the other hand it is quite clear that there is a type of communication between animals on a signal level.

One can show (Smith, 1969, p. 145; Altmann, 1967, p. 331) that higher, developed animals use not simply signals, but a combination of signals and meta-signals. The signals provide some information, and the meta-signals allow an interpretation of the information and/or a regulation of the communication process. These meta-signals are called *modifiers* or *address* and have metacommunicational functions: "Those components of a message that serve to direct it may be referred to as the address of the message. Note that the addresses are, themselves, messages. They are communication about communication, that is metacommunication" (Altmann, 1967, p. 331). Since the view expressed by Altmann has strong support from others (Marler, 1961; Marler, 1967; Marler & Tamura, 1969; Thorpe, 1972) it seems to offer strong support for the hypothesis that all communication systems (or processes) demand reflexivity in the objective dimension.

Bateson (1968, 1956; p. 625) has shown, further, that the "play" between animals involves meta-signals. And Hinde (1973, p. 301) shows that play and learning are opposite sides of the same coin. Typically, the use of meta-signals implies a certain level of development and is most sophisticated in the communication of the higher apes. This leads to the assumption that the genesis of a verbal language presumes a reflexivity of signals to build symbols, and this again means reflexivity, or, as Krippendorff (1969, p. 110) has put it: "communication about communication presupposes communication."

A second type of reflexivity in the social dimension on the animal level deserves further discussion. Higher developed species of animals use alarm-cries, by which one member of a troop may warn all

FIGURE 2
A Human Communication Model

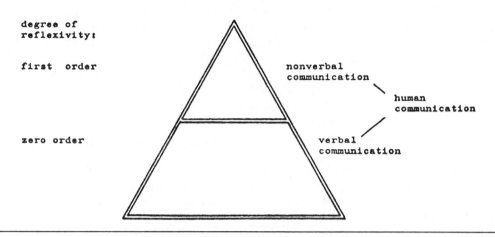

other members. Once an alarm-cry is uttered, all members of the troop within reach turn their heads to the direction of that cry. These animals not only perceive the same danger, they also perceive that the others perceive. The function of attention, then, lies here in the establishment of a momentary perceptual consensus or collective sensation, and provides the basis for the hierarchic structure of animal societies—by means of communication, or, more specifically, by reflexivity in the social dimension. Hierarchic structured troops in apes and other animals show concentric circles of attention around the leader or overlord of the troop (Ito, 1970). As Chance (1967, p. 509) says: "Attention has a binding quality. If this is so for an understanding of the interindividual bond and of social organization, it is the amount of attention that is of paramount importance." Members low in the hierarchy of a troop must direct part of their attention to maintaining a certain physical and symbolic distance. Through communication hierarchy is guaranteed. Continuous fighting among the members of an animal society is not necessary, but hierarchy is maintained through symbolic means. This is a further proof for the thesis that communication—as the smallest social system—generates, over time, social structures, which in turn generate more efficient communication.

Level II: Human Communication

Human communication implies verbal and non-

verbal communication. Processes of human communication or human interaction have, therefore, a double structure, and it is useful to look at the relation of the verbal and nonverbal channels. In an evolutionary view, the verbal channel has supplanted the nonverbal channel, for it allows a far higher selectivity and precision. But the nonverbal channel has not been relegated to an inferior role. Because the verbal channel is more elaborated, but works much more slowly, and the nonverbal channel is not elaborated, but works much more quickly, both channels are complementary, and in a very specific way: The nonverbal channel takes the function of a meta-channel (Mehrabian, 1971; Knapp, 1972, p. 20), whose function is the regulation of the process by commenting on the verbal messages (Ekman & Friesen, 1969). These operations must be performed through the nonverbal channel, for the function of the meta-communication lies in more powerful selectivity, requiring a rigid and quick selective mechanism.

A model of human communication (Figure 2) embraces both verbal and nonverbal communication. The two are hierarchically related: The nonverbal channel represents the quality of reflexivity (in the *objective* dimension) in the first order, whereas the verbal channel is basic and can be spoken of, therefore, as zero order reflexivity.

This framework suggests that in human communication it is not sufficient to describe the verbal actions of some persons, as developed in the interaction process analysis by Bales (1950); rather it is of great importance to observe the nonverbal channels simultaneously, for these channels provide the interpretation, and therefore refer to the possible effects of verbal communication. The pioneering studies by Hall (1959) and Birdwhistell (1970) initiated not only for nonverbal communication, but also for human communication processes as a whole, a new area of important insight.

Since the nonverbal channel in human communication is in most cases the visual channel, the possibility of reciprocal viewing is of utmost relevance for the human communcation process. Visual signals not only allow the regulation of the process (Duncan, 1969, p. 124), but they permit also contradictions between verbal and nonverbal content. Interestingly, the nonverbal channel enjoys the highest credibility because of the few possibilities of manipulation. Ekman and Friesen (1969) call this *nonverbal leakage*.

When communication is to be defined by a threefold reflexivity in three dimensions, this criterion must also be found in more complex human communication processes, such as *rumor*. The motive to disseminate information is dependant upon the credibility and/or relevance of that information. While it is at once clear that relevance reaches the commenting dimension, i.e. a form of reflexivity in the *objective* dimension, the other dimensions are not so easy to identify. But when one asks a person from whom he heard a particular story, one is very often told that it was not an acquaintance (this could be too easily falsified) but an "acquaintance of an acquaintance" (Merten, 1976c) who told the story. By referring to the acquaintance, credibility of the message is built up. When one refers to "friends of friends," the whole world may consist of friends (Boissevain, 1974). By referring to the acquaintance of an acquaintance, the necessary social principle of connection is met, i.e. reflexivity, in the *social* dimension. Other types of this reflexivity include the imagination or expectation of something that others know or do. Here we touch once more the logical extensions of reflexivity, for not only the knowing of something, but also the not-knowing of something (what others know or don't know) creates a strong collective motive, which F. Allport

called *pluralistic ignorance* (O'Gorman, 1975).

Reflexivity in the temporal dimension can be detected if one follows the process over time. It is a very common fact for rumor or diffusion researchers that the spread of a rumor is dependent upon previous dissemination, for the rate of knowers respective of not-knowers varies with the rumor. Genesis and spread of a rumor can therefore be explicated in terms of reflexivity, and described as a transitory social system.

Level III: Mass Communication

The crucial point for the term *communication* is the term *mass communication*. It is clear that mass communication is abstracted from the presence and the reciprocal perceiving of the involved persons, and therefore cannot fulfill the criterion of reflexivity of perceiving in the social dimension. For the same reason, mass communication can't be interaction, nor *para-social interaction* (Horton & Wohl, 1956).

A more rigorous analysis of the mass communication situation shows at first that there are similarities to the alarm-cry situation at the animal-level: The mass-communication situation involves the attention of many people to the same stimulus, too. The recipients of mass communication may not see the communicator, nor one another, but they know that there is a communicator and other recipients. Accordingly, every recipient knows what the other recipients know, and perhaps he knows that they know what he knows. Reflexivity in the *social* dimension in mass communication is generated by a reflexivity of knowing, and thus has a communicative structure.

Reflexivity in the *objective* dimension occurs because, in the course of societal evolution, content (themes), and evaluation of content (opinion), have become differentiated. In modern societies we refer to the institutionalization of these opinions as *public opinion*.[5] Therefore, one knows not only what others know, but one has opinions about the knowledge of others, and knowledge about the opinions of others, and finally, opinions about the opinions of others. In mass communication, therefore, we have in the social dimension not a simple reflexivity by perception or action, but a more complicated reflexivity of knowledge and opinions, which is in

FIGURE 3
Reflexive Relation Between Information
and Opinion

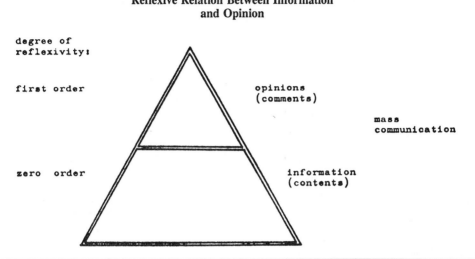

itself reflexive in the *objective* dimension. One can speak of mass communication, therefore, as *reflected reflexivity*.

Like the relation between verbal and nonverbal communication, there is the same reflexive relation between information and opinions in mass communication (Figure 3). Reflexivity in the time dimension in mass communication is given by the fact that, by publication of some content, questions arise as to opinions. Repeated publication of themes or continuous reporting of an affair stimulates opinions, which in turn generate their own publicity, so that opinions may or may not cumulate over time. The crucial point seems to be the actuality of a theme. If the stimulated opinions about the theme are strong enough, they can generate, by their own publicity, further publicity.

But the analysis of *mass communication* as *communication* isn't complete if we neglect informal *human communication*. Historically, one can show again that the evolution of mass communication has not made the human communication channel superfluous. As in the case of verbal and nonverbal communication, the less effective verbal channel takes a new function in relation to the media channel, for the human communication allows communication about mediated communication. One could integrate the relation between *nonverbal communication* (NC) and *verbal communication*

(VC) on the one side, and *verbal communication* (VC) and *mediated communication* (MC) as a proportional equation:

$$NC: VC = VC : MC$$

This creates a further communication hierarchy as portrayed in Figure 4.

It is not surprising, then, that the informal, human communication now has a strategic position, because it allows the *ex post* evaluation of all mediated content. Whole volumes of important books, great debates in TV, or a press report can be devaluated by an *ex post* informal statement like "what nonsense," uttered by an influential person.

A HIERARCHY

The modern world communication system consists of all modalities and shows, therefore, a three-level hierarchy as indicated in Figure 5. The content or information of the media, is basic and therefore can be considered to have zero-order reflexivity (in the *objective* dimension). At the first order level we find, on the one hand, *opinions* and on the other all *human communication*, insofar as it evaluates media content. At the level of second order reflexivity we find, on the one hand the *nonverbal communication*. An example would be if some persons receive, simultaneously, some media content and

FIGURE 4
Nonverbal, Verbal and Mediated Communication

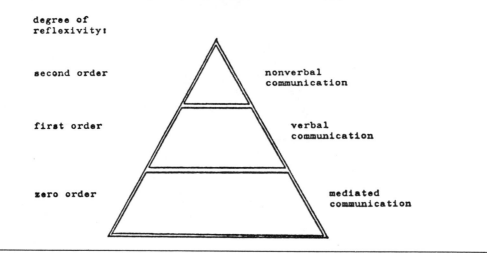

FIGURE 5
World Communication System

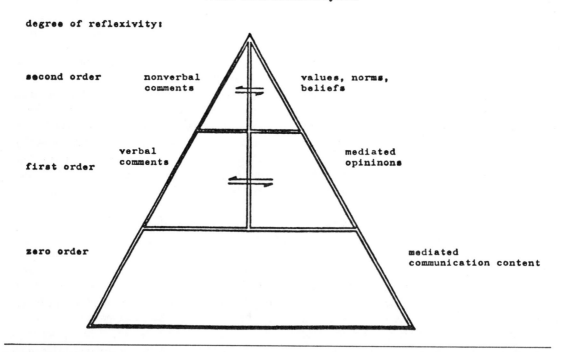

one person says, "What a nice show," but comments simultaneously by nonverbal signs that he feels great boredom. One could find a corresponding relation by the reflexivity of opinions, which reach therefore a normative level. Corresponding- ly, the nonverbal cues belong in a specific manner to this normative level. For example, the behavior of a person, his dress, and the manner in which he presents himself are very much normatively sanctioned, and are at the same moment nonverbal cues of strategic relevance for other persons, for example for status, dominance, etc.

World Communication

Correspondingly, one can describe *world communication* as a process of threefold selection, consisting of three intercorrelated social systems.

First, the editorial staff of a medium can be seen as an organized social system (Ruehl, 1969) which collects, selects, and distributes mediated information and opinions. The selective function of this system is widely known, and the *gatekeepers*, have received considerable attention (Snider, 1967). From the view of the recipient, the *gatekeeper* is the communicator.

Second, there is a communication system which is not dependent on the presence of its members. We may term such a unit an *abstract communication system*. It constitutes itself by the reflexivity of knowing and of thinking what others know or think, what opinions others may have, etc. In comparison with the concrete *human communication system*, it is more flexible, because it can be abstracted from the presence of others and requires only the imagination that one knows something, shares some opinion, etc. for its existence. There is, thus, a second selection of the presumed or represented knowledge and/or opinions. But this sytem is dependent on continuous support, which is given by the communicator of the so-called mass communication: He becomes the visible or audible focus of the anonymous "others," and thereby wins his influence. Abstract communication is, therefore, mainly a diffuse relation between all recipients, and requires a point of intersection—the communicator.

Finally, we will consider the *real communication system,* consisting of real interactions between present persons. It may be characterized as strategical, since its selection occurs last, and therefore has the strongest effect. It is not surprising that persons who occupy a position which enables them to evaluate some content in the presence of others have received substantial attention in communication research, and are named (Lazarsfeld, 1944, p. 151) *opinion-leaders*. Their influence, then, lies not in their presumable higher access to media content, as earlier studies supposed, but in the possibility to articulate opinions which succeed. In terms of reflexibity (Merten, 1976d) the content of the media is filtered by a hierarchic-structured web of influentials (*opinion-leaders*), so that the content is in a specific way evaluated. A hierarchy of people structures content and imposes, thereby, a superstructure for evaluation of all communication. Analytically, opinion-leaders mediate intersections between a vertical influence hierarchy and a horizontal content hierarchy.

EPISTEMOLOGICAL CONSIDERATIONS

The foregoing has presented an outline of an alternative approach to communication theory, based on a systems perspective. Its main characterization is that it stresses the *selectivity* of all communication, especially the possibilities to strengthen it by reflexivity. In this way, communication can be defined as the basic social system with threefold *reflexivity* in *objective, social* and *temporal* dimensions. *World communication* is described and analyzed as interrelation of three communication systems (*organized, abstract,* and *real*).

It seems appropriate to reconsider the term *communication*. It has been suggested that the term can be replaced by a specification of types and combinations of *reflexivity,* which is the criterion for all communication. Such a change presents a number of difficulties, but it provides on the other hand, on this abstract level, the possibility of relating communication processes to higher social processes and phenomena.

Second, there are further implications for theory-building in general. For example, in the discussion of mass communication, it was necessary to describe some structures in terms of *reflected reflexivity* or *meta-reflexivity* or *hierarchy of reflexivity.* These three theoretical terms represent some type of reflexive structure, not on the reality level (where the phenomena themselves are), but on the modelling level. That is, the property of reflexivity, which is used to describe certain phenomena, returns in the description of the phenomena—at least in the case of communication. Therefore, to describe or to analyze communication, one needs some sort of theory, which is reflexive itself.

This consideration may have further consequences: If communication is indeed the smallest social system and generates all higher social systems, all social theory must be self-referential. This problem is not a new one. The *theory of dialectic materialism* has tried to handle it. And the rise of cybernetics and systems theory has brought it up again: The necessary devaluation of causality will go side by side with the search for a suitable, more valued logic (Günther, 1962) with self-referencing terms, or with the measurement of systems complexity, etc. Watzlawick et al. (1967) have already suggested that these problems are essentially within the domain of communication theory:

> Systems with feedback distinguish themselves not only by a quantitatively higher degree of complexity; they are also qualitatively different from anything that falls into the domain of classical mechanics. Their study requires new conceptual frames; their logic and epistemology are discontinuous from some traditional tenets of scientific analysis, such as the "isolate one variable" approach or the Laplacean belief that the complete knowledge of all facts at a given time will enable one to predict all future states. (p. 32)

The attempt to analyze one considerable problem leads to many additional problems. The fact—that it is the common process of communication—which joins these problems is worthy of reflection.

NOTES

1. This paper was selected as one of the outstanding reports prepared for the annual meeting of the International Communication Association, Berlin, 1977.
2. There are good reasons to suspect that the worldwide diffusion of the Lasswell-formula is less the result of its heuristic value, and more of its simplicity. I have tried to explicate some of these reasons elsewhere (Merten, 1974).
3. That is the problem all the techniques of social research have to face. The methods for collecting data about social reality—mainly inquiry, observation, experiment and content analysis—require the initiation of some sort of communication process, which itself filters the reality in a specific manner.
4. Exceptions from communication are rare; but when they are given in a situation, they provide excellent materials for analysis. For example, Ruesch (1957) and Watzlawick, Beavin, and Jackson (1967) detected important structures of communication by the fact of disturbed communication. And Berelson (1949) demonstrated by the New York press-strike in 1945, in a very convincing manner, functions of the press for the people.
5. Public opinion gets its influence by another reflexive structure—it results in beliefs, what the others believe. In this sense wrote Riezler (1944, p. 412) "the power of public

opinion over Me and You is the power not of what people are really thinking but of what I and You assume they think." And questionnaires for the investigation of public opinion ask therefore not only the opinion from the respondent. They also wish to know what the respondent thinks what the others think (Noelle-Neumann, 1971, p. 215).

REFERENCES

ALTMANN, S.A. (Ed.) *Social communication among primates*. Chicago: University of Chicago Press, 1967.

BALES, R.F. *Interaction process analysis*. Cambridge: Cambridge University Press, 1950.

BATESON, G. The message "this is play." In B. Schaffner (Ed.), *Group processes*. Transactions of the second conference on group processes. New York: Josiah Macy Jr. Foundation, 1956, 145-242.

BATESON, G. Redundancy and coding. In T.A. Sebeok (Ed.), *Animal communication*. Techniques of study and results of research. Bloomington/London: Indiana University Press, 1968.

BIRDWHISTELL, R.L. *Kinesics and context*. Essays on body motion communication. Philadelphia: University of Pennsylvania Press, 1970.

BOISSEVAIN, J. *Friends of friends*. Networks, Manipulators and Coalitions. Oxford: Basil Blackwell 1974.

CHANCE, M.R. Attention structure as the basis of primate rank orders. *Man*, 1967, 2, 503-518.

COOLEY, C.H. *Social organization*. A study of the larger mind. New York: Scribner, 1909.

DUNCAN, S. Noverbal communication. *Psychological Bulletin*, 1969, 72, 118-137.

EKMAN, P., & FRIESEN, W.V. Non-verbal leakage and clues to deception. *Psychiatry*, 1969, 32, 88-106.

GÜNTHER, G. Cybernetic ontology and transjunctional operations. In M.C. Yovits, G.T. Jacobi, and G.D. Goldstein (Eds.), *Self-organizing system*. Rochelle Park, N.J.: Hayden/Spartan, 1962, 313-392.

HALL, E.T. *The silent language*. Garden City: Doubleday, 1959.

HINDE, R.A., & STEVENSON-HINDE, J. (Eds.), *Constraints on learning*. London/New York: Academic Press, 1973.

HORTON, O., & WOHL, R.R. Mass communication and para-social interaction. *Psychiatry*, 1956, 19, 215-229.

ITO, Y. Groups and family bonds in animals in relation to their habitat. In L.R. Aronson, E. Tabach, D.S. Lehrman, and J.S. Rosenblatt (Eds.), *Development and evolution of behavior*. Essays in memory of T.C. Schneirla. San Francisco: Freeman, 1970, 389-415.

KNAPP, M.L. *Nonverbal communication in human interaction*. New York: Holt, 1972.

KRIPPENDORFF, K. Values, modes and domains of inquiry into communication. *Journal of Communication*, 1969, 19, 105-133.

KRIPPENDORFF, K. Communication and the genesis of structure. *General Systems*, 1971, 16, 171-185.

LAING, R.D., PHILLIPSON, H., & LEE, R.L. *Interpersonal perception*. A Theory and a method of research. London/New York: Tavistock, 1966.

LASSWELL, H. The structure and function of communication in society. In L. Bryson (Ed.), *They Communication of*

Ideals. New York: Harper, 1948, 37-52.

LAZARSFELD, P.F., BERELSON, B., & GAUDET. H. *The people's choice.* How the voter makes up his mind in a presidential campaign. New York: Columbia Press, 1944.

LUHMANN, N. *Soziologische aufklärung I.* Köln, Westdeutscher Verlag, 1970.

LUHMANN, N. Einfache sozialsysteme. *Zeitschrift für soziologie,* 1972, 1, 51-65.

LUHMANN, N. *Soziologische aufklärung II.* Opladen: Westdeutscher Verlag, 1975.

LUHMANN, N. The future cannot begin: Temporal structures in modern society. *Social Research,* 1976, 43, 130-152.

MARLER, P. The logical analysis of animal communication. *Journal of Theoretical Biology,* 1961, 1, 295-317.

MARLER, P. Animal communication signals. *Science,* 1967, 157, 769-774.

MARLER, P., & TAMURA, M. Culturally transmitted patterns of vocal behavior in sparrows. In B. Zajonc (Ed.), *Animal social behavior.* New York: Wiley, 1969, 220-224.

McLEOD, J.M., & CHAFFEE, S.H. Interpersonal approaches to communication research. *American Behavioral Scientist,* 1973, 16, 469-499.

MEHRABIAN, A. *Silent messages.* Belmont: Wadsworth, 1971.

MEHRABIAN, A., & KSIONZKY, S. *A theory of affiliation.* London: Saxon House, 1974.

MEIER, R.L. *A communications theory of urban growth.* Cambridge: M.I.T. Press, 1962.

MERTEN, K. Vom Nutzen der Lasswellformel, oder Ideologie in der kommunikationsforschung. *Rundfunk und Fernsehen,* 1974, 22, 143-165.

MERTEN, K. *Kommunikation: Eine begriffs und prozeβanalyse zu einem sozialwissenschaftlichen grundbegriff.* Wiesbaden: Westdeutscher Verlag, 1976a.

MERTEN, K. Reflexivität als grundbegriff der kommunikationsforschung. *Publizistik,* 1976b, 21, 171-179.

MERTEN, K. *The cut off hand.* A case-study on the diffusion of rumors. Unpublished Manuscript, Faculty of Sociology, University of Bielefeld, 1976c.

MERTEN, K. Kommunikation und "two-step-flow of communication." *Rundfunk und Fernsehen,* 1976d, 24 (in press).

NEWCOMB, T. *The acquaintance process.* New York: Holt, Rinehart & Winston, 1961.

NOELLE-NEUMANN, E., & SCHULZ, W. (Eds.) *Publizistik,* Frankfurt: Fischer, 1971.

O'GORMAN, H.J. Pluralistic ignorance and white estimates of white support for racial segregation. *Public Opinion Quarterly,* 1975, 39, 313-330.

RIEZLER, K. What is public opinion? *Social Research,* 1944, 11, 397-427.

RUEHL, M. *Die zeitungsredaktion als organisiertes soziales System.* Bielefeld: Bertelsmann, 1969.

RUESCH, J. *Disturbed communication.* New York: Norton, 1957.

SCHEFF, T.J. Intersubjectivity and emotion. *American Behavioral Scientist,* 1973, 16, 501-511.

SMITH, W.J. Messages of vertebrate communication. *Science,* 1969, 165, 145-150.

SNIDER, P. Mr. Gates revisited. A 1966 Version. *Journalism Quarterly,* 1967, 44, 419-427.

THAYER, L. *Communication: Theory and research.* Springfield: Thomas, 1967.

THAYER, L. On theory-building in communication: Some persistent obstacles. In J. Akin, A. Goldberg, and Myers (Eds.), *Language Behavior.* The Hague/Paris: Mouton, 1970, 34-42.

THORPE, W.H. The Comparison of vocal communication in animals and men. In R.A. Hinde (Ed.), *Non-verbal communication.* Cambridge: Cambridge University Press, 1972, 27-47.

WATZLAWICK, P., BEAVIN, J.H., & JACKSON, D.D. *Pragmatics of human communication.* New York: Norton, 1967.

LAZARSFELD AND ADORNO IN THE UNITED STATES:
A CASE STUDY IN THEORETICAL ORIENTATIONS

WAYNE M. TOWERS
University of Oklahoma

During the years 1938 to 1941, two European scholars of differing viewpoints—Paul Lazarsfeld and Theodor Adorno—worked for the Office of Radio Research in the United States of America. The inability of these two scholars to reconcile their fundamental theoretical differences precluded their ability to work together. Lazarsfeld's essentially quantitative orientation toward theory-building and Adorno's essentially philosophical (critical) orientation toward theory-building, and details concerning the nature of these fundamental theoretical differences, are examined. The paper recapitulates Lazarsfeld's often reproduced statements on quantitative theory-building and, taking advantage of translations only recently available to U.S. scholars, provides a summary of much of Adorno's thought on the philosophical (critical) orientation toward theory-building. The disagreement between Lazarsfeld and Adorno is seen not as a scholarly squabble, but as a fundamental theoretical dispute about the nature of the world.

A classic problem in intercultural communication is the activity of value orientations in fostering or precluding communicative exchanges among members of varying cultural groups. Often this problem is couched in terms of mechanical innovations among technologically less advanced nations, or it is expressed in terms of a comparison of known cultural variables. Another way to approach this problem is to study the exchange of information among cultural elites, to discover what concepts were able to make the intercultural transition, and why. One situation where such a study of intercultural exchange was feasible occurred during the years 1938-1941 when two renowned European scholars—Paul Lazarsfeld and Theodor Adorno—were both in residence at the Office of Radio Research in the United States of America.

By examining the intellectual and theoretical backgrounds of these two scholars, this study proposes to isolate some of the major cultural orientations which permitted Paul Lazarsfeld to transfer his work successfully to America, and which precluded Theodor Adorno from making a similar transition. The basic thrust of this paper will be to show that Lazarsfeld was able to make the transition from his European background to the American situation because his orientation was congenial to entry into his new environment. This paper will also show that Adorno's orientations were different from Lazarsfeld's mode of thought, and that these differences virtually precluded Adorno's transition because of American inhospitality to those differences. Ultimately, this paper will show that the primary reason for Lazarsfeld's ability, and Adorno's inability, to make the transition resulted from the theoretical orientations of the two men—Lazarsfeld's orientation being adaptable to and congenial with his new cultural milieu, and Adorno's orientation being both less adaptable and less congenial. The implication to be drawn from such a conclusion is that intercultural communication hinges not only on the receptivity of cultures to particular modes of thought, but also on the ability of advocates of particular modes of thought to match their ideas with their new environment.

HISTORICAL BACKGROUND:
PAUL LAZARSFELD

Of the two scholars, Paul Lazarsfeld is the better known to most American scholars. Lazarsfeld's advocacy of social research institutes and of quantitative methodology for studying social concepts (Lazarsfeld, 1969) has earned him a place of note in

American scholarship. Indeed, Lazarsfeld's work has become so ingrained in American scholarship that students in the field are often surprised to learn that Lazarsfeld was not born in the United States. He emigrated there from Austria in 1933 (Lazarsfeld, 1969).

In Europe, Lazarsfeld had been a student at a time when the continental social sciences were primarily speculative and philosophical in their orientations (Lazarsfeld, 1969); indeed Lazarsfeld seems to have drifted into an empirical orientation. While a student, Lazarsfeld became active in the Student Socialist Movement, and this activity, combined with his studies in psychology, led him to wonder why Student Socialist propaganda was not successful—and to consider how psychological studies could explain this lack of success (Lazarsfeld, 1969). This interest led to a belief in explicating ideas by finding out "how things are done," (Lazarsfeld, 1969), and resulted in a doctorate in applied mathematics (Lazarsfeld, 1969), an area that not only included the methods of statistics, but also involved collecting quantitative data on social phenomena (Schad, 1972).

Around 1927, Lazarsfeld set up a division of social psychology in the Psychological Institute of the University of Vienna. This division allowed Lazarsfeld to pursue his interests and to work on paid contracts, from which he was able to draw a modest, but adequate salary (Lazarsfeld, 1969). One of the clients of Lazarsfeld's division was the Frankfurt *Institute für Sozialforschung* (Institute for Social Research), with which Theodor Adorno would later be affiliated. Lazarsfeld contracted to do a part of the field work for the Institute's massive study on authority and the family (Lazarsfeld, 1969). This contract assured Lazarsfeld's familiarity with the Frankfurt Institute's personnel and with their theoretical orientations before Lazarsfeld and Adorno made contact in the United States.

Lazarsfeld came to the United States in 1933 on a traveling fellowship to meet with American scholars. In 1934, a shift in the Austrian political situation forced Lazarsfeld to remain in the United States; he was given a year's extension on his fellowship. By 1935, Lazarsfeld had decided to remain in America, and, with the help of Columbia University sociologist Robert Lynd, Lazarsfeld

began work with the National Youth Administration, whose New Jersey headquarters were at the University of Newark. By the next year, Lazarsfeld was director of a research center at the University of Newark, which was patterned after the research center he had left behind in Vienna. In 1937, a Rockefeller Foundation Grant to Princeton University, for studying the effect of radio on American society, resulted in Lazarsfeld becoming director of the Office of Radio Research. Two years later, in 1939, the Office of Radio Research was moved to Columbia University in New York City. In 1940, Lazarsfeld had become an associate professor in Columbia's sociology department and, by 1945, Columbia had incorporated the Office of Radio Research—renamed the Bureau of Applied Social Research—into the university structure (Lazarsfeld, 1969). He remained at Columbia until his death in 1976.

Lazarsfeld's work through this period was, by and large, empirical. From an early interest in using statistical analysis to describe entire choice processes, Lazarsfeld began to look for manageable ways to study social phenomena. His view was that studies of relatively trivial acts, such as the buying of soap, could lead to findings at a higher level of generalization, if only they were properly interpreted and integrated. By going beyond simple description, data could be used to generate insights of a higher order through the integration of constructs (Lazarsfeld, 1969). Lazarsfeld's point of view enjoyed a particularly congenial reception when he emigrated to America: a group of younger psychologists—Rensis Likert, then an assistant professor at New York University, among them—began advocating Lazarsfeld's approach of integrating unstructured interviews with statistical data. A small group of commercial market researchers—especially Percival White, an early textbook writer on marketing research—became interested in Lazarsfeld's work and drew him into the fledgling American Marketing Association (Lazarsfeld, 1969). From the early Austrian phase, where relative penury had forced him to apply diverse techniques to relatively small samples, Lazarsfeld found himself turned about and facing the problem of relatively large samples where little was known about each respondent. He reacted by becoming concerned with multivariate analysis (Lazarsfeld, 1969), and embarked on an empirically based career of data analysis in the United States.

HISTORICAL BACKGROUND: THEODOR ADORNO

While Lazarsfeld had been able to make the transition to the American scholarly situation, Theodor Adorno simply was not able.

> By nature and personal history, I was unsuited for adjustment in intellectual matters. Fully as I recognize that individuality can only develop through processes of adjustment and socialization, I still consider it the obligation and at the same time the proof of mature individuality to transcend mere adjustment . . . (Adorno, 1969, p. 338)

Theodor Adorno's intellectual preparation featured the curious intertwining of two often segregated disciplines: philosophy and music. After writing a doctorate in philosophy on Husserl's phenomenology in 1924 (Jay, 1973), Adorno left the University of Frankfurt in 1925 to study music under Alban Berg, the atonal composer, in Vienna. Adorno remained in Vienna for three years, 1925 through 1928, studying under Berg and enjoying the company of a circle that had grown up around Arnold Schönberg, another modernist composer (Jay, 1973). With the dissolution of the Schönberg circle in 1928, Adorno returned to Frankfurt and resumed his career in philosophy, eventually acquiring an academic position by writing a study of Kierkegaard's aesthetics in 1931 (Jay, 1973).

During the 1930s, Adorno began to study and to write about the sociology of music, especially American jazz (Jay, 1973). During this period, Adorono began a gradual drift toward the Frankfurt *Institut für Sozialforschung* (Institute for Social Research), largely on the strength of his friendship with the Institute's director, Max Horkheimer, whom Adorno had known since 1922 when both had been students at the University of Frankfurt (Jay, 1973). Under Horkheimer's direction, the *Institut für Sozialforschung* had achieved two distinguishing characteristics: financial stability and an intellectual point of view. The financial stability resulted from the discreet management of the Insti-

tute's endowment so that its members were not dependent on outside sources for financial assistance (Jay, 1973). The intellectual point of view came from the coalescing of an intellectual circle around Horkheimer, and featured an interest in the integration of philosophy and social analysis (Jay, 1973). This integration, with its stress on Hegelian dialectics and Marxian social conceptions, became known as *critical theory*, and its practitioners became identified as members of the Frankfurt School (Jay, 1973).

Before Adorno could completely join the Frankfurt School, however, the rise of National Socialism in Germany forced many of the Institute's members to emigrate, first to Switzerland and eventually to the United States (Jay, 1973). Adorno remained in Germany until 1938, when, through the good offices of Max Horkheimer, Adorno was offered a job in Paul Lazarsfeld's Office of Radio Research (Jay, 1973).

Adorno spent almost three stormy years at the Office of Radio Research (1938-1941) before he left for Los Angeles to join Horkheimer and a host of German emigres who had gathered there (Jay, 1973). Horkheimer seems to have been the only person ever able to collaborate closely with him (Jay, 1973). Adorno had been particularly uncomfortable at the Office of Radio Research. His philosophical training had shaped his mind strongly in a speculative direction: He felt that it was his job to interpret phenomena as a philosophical endeavor, and that it was not his job to classify data in an attempt to turn them into facts (Adorno, 1969). The straightforward quantitative orientation of Lazarsfeld's Office of Radio Research was simply not acceptable to a person of Adorno's philosophical and speculative bent.

From 1941 to 1944, Adorno and Horkheimer substantially completed a philosophical collaboration called the *Dialectic of Enlightenment (Dialektik der Aufklarüng)*—subsequently published in 1947 (Jay, 1973)—which spelled out many of the assumptions of their earlier works (Hughes, 1975). Completion of this work was delayed because of both Horkheimer's and Adorno's involvement in a grant from the American Jewish Committee which led to a series of researches called *Studies in Prejudice* (Jay, 1973). From 1944 to 1949, Adorno

worked on an aspect of that project involving attitudes toward authority and feeling of anti-
Semitism: the result was the 1950 publication of
The Authoritarian Personality, the single aspect of
Adorno's efforts that has enjoyed widespread recognition among scholars in the United States (Jay,
1973). However, Adorno was not destined to bask
in that recognition; in 1949, he returned to Germany, where he resided until his death in 1969
(Dialectical Methodology, 1970; Jay, 1973).

HISTORICAL BACKGROUND:
LAZARSFELD'S VIEW, 1938-1941

Despite the pressures toward quantitative analysis in American scholarship, Lazarsfeld was not
utterly committed to empiricism alone. In the early
years of the Office of Radio Research, he had hoped
to establish links between American and European
research approaches—especially in terms of combining quantitative and humanistic studies—and of
adding the historical dimension to quantitative research (Lazarsfeld, 1969). Since Lazarsfeld knew
and admired Adorno's work on the sociology of
music, and since Lazarsfeld felt indebted to Horkheimer and his colleagues for their support of the
Newark research center, he decided to accept the
challenge of persuading Adorno to test philosophical ideas with an empiricist's approach (Lazarsfeld,
1969).

Lazarsfeld was not as persuasive as he had
hoped. Adorno's conceptualizations proved in-
tractable when the time came to translate them into
typologies, which would then be used to formulate
questionnaires (Lazarsfeld, 1969). Adorno felt his
ideas about listening to radio music simply did not
lend themselves to translation into quantitatively
testable hypotheses (Lazarsfeld, 1969; Jay, 1973).
Relations between the two men became strained
and, during the Summer of 1939, Lazarsfeld wrote
a memorandum to Adorno praising the brilliance of
his working habits, but chiding him for his arro-
gance toward work on the project (Jay, 1973). During the Fall of 1939, the Rockefeller Foundation
reviewed the budget of the Office of Radio Research and withdrew funding for Adorno's part of
the project (Jay, 1973). Some 30 years later,
Lazarsfeld ruefully reflected on his association with

Adorno and wondered how a group of scholars who
coalesced at the University of California (Berkeley)
in the late 1940s were able to take Adorno's ideas on
response to authority and to turn them into the
quantitative scales of *The Authoritarian Personality*
(Lazarsfeld, 1969).

HISTORICAL BACKGROUND:
ADORNO'S VIEW, 1938-1941

Adorno's view of the difficulties at the Office of
Radio Research was somewhat different from
Lazarsfeld's. Noting that the purpose of the Office
of Radio Research was to collect data that would
benefit planning departments in the mass media
field (both business and government), Adorno, accustomed to a more independent and reflective approach to scholarship, was astonished at the practical orientation that surrounded him (Adorno,
1969). Since the Rockefeller Foundation grant had
limited study to the American commercial radio
system, and since Adorno felt it would be ungra-
cious to question the economic bases of a culture
with which he was only beginning to familiarize
himself, Adorno felt obliged to soft pedal his preference for *critical theory*, and to work within the
American framework (Adorno, 1969).

Despite his good intentions, however, Adorno
quickly developed a hesitancy concerning the concept of methodology. In Europe, the term *method*
implied questions on the limits and validity of
knowledge. In the United States, *method* had come
to signify practical techniques (Adorno, 1969).
Adorno (1969) was expected to provide information
(data) about the interrelationship of society and
music:

> When I was confronted with the demand to "meas-
> ure culture," I reflected that culture might be pre-
> cisely that condition that excludes a mentality capable
> of measuring it. In general, I resisted the indiscrimi-
> nate application of the principle "science in mea-
> surement," which was little criticized even in the
> social sciences . . . The task of translating my reflec-
> tions into research terms was equivalent to squaring
> the circle . . . (Adorno, 1969, p. 347).

He was able to overcome his reservations in
California not through any theoretical shiftings, but
because of the research group with which he
worked. The group was united by the American

spirit of teamwork and by a common orientation favorable to Freudian theory (Adorno, 1969). Most important to Adorno, the group was interested not only in measurement per se, but also in the development of methods (in both the European and American meanings) which would permit measurement in areas which had not lent themselves to measurement before (Adorno, 1969). Where the Office of Radio Research had sought to build theory out of its data collection (Lazarsfeld's concept of using data to generate insights and constructs), the California group sought to use insights to shape their data gathering the Frankfurt Institute's general orientation of not compromising theoretical constructs because of practical difficulties in transforming the ideas into empirical form (Schad, 1972). Adorno simply found the latter approach more congenial to his point-of-view.

Reflecting on his experiences at the Office of Radio Research some 30 years later, Adorno did not see his difficulties with Lazarsfeld in terms of the problem of translating speculatively-based insights into empirical terms. Rather, Adorno saw the difficulties in terms of the distinctive orientations of American and European scholars. Adorno saw American scholars as fundamentally technicians who could neither relate the twin concept of pure intellectual endeavor and objectivity, nor separate the concept of intellect from the particular person who bore a particular intellect (Adorno, 1969). Chiding American empirical thinking as an "apotheosis of the average" (Adorno, 1969), he felt that it was incumbent on the European scholar in America to raise the fundamental and difficult question of whether or not qualitative differences also mattered in the day-to-day world (Adorno, 1969). As far as Adorno was concerned, he was better able to work with the California group because their orientation had been theory-based, while Lazarsfeld's orientation was more data-based. From Adorno's point of view, his differences with Lazarsfeld had been a question of theory against technique.

THEORETICAL PERSPECTIVES: LAZARSFELD'S VIEW

To deny a theoretical orientation to Lazarsfeld,

however, is somewhat unfair. Lazarsfeld was well aware of the limitations of working within the existing environment of American commercial radio, and he articulated that awareness in terms of the conservatism of the American broadcasting system. Lazarsfeld noted that because American broadcasting was essentially commercial, it needed to attract large audiences. To attract these audiences, commercial American broadcasting did not attempt to deviate too sharply from what its audience found acceptable. American broadcasters knew all too well that American listeners tended to tune in only those programs with which they agreed (Lazarsfeld, 1942). Lazarsfeld noted a further conservative element in American broadcasting through the balancing forces of big business and government in the control of broadcasting (Lazarsfeld, 1942). Under the American regulatory scheme, broadcasting is owned by private businessmen (usually representing complex corporate structures known as big business), and is regulated by the national government. Conceptually at least, big business and big government represent countervailing forces, both of which represent large numbers of the nation's people. The emphasis on numbers, especially large numbers, in American thought on broadcasting is not difficult to understand.

As an empiricist, Lazarsfeld was at home in the American numerological orientation. He was able to concentrate on his concept of using the American love of numbers as data to generate the integrating constructs he felt would lead to the development of theory. The study of complex social phenomena, as Lazarsfeld saw it, involved four basic steps: "an initial imagery of the concept, the specification of dimensions, the selection of observable indicators, and the combination of indicators into indices" (Lazarsfeld, 1959, p. 109). Of the four steps outlined, the first three steps are especially germane to this discussion. Adorno and his colleagues of the Frankfurt Institute did not devote a great deal of attention to the construction of indices; rather, they questioned whether the first three steps of Lazarsfeld's approach were possible at all. Given that the first three steps may not have been possible, discussion of a fourth step based on the first three steps would have been simply a moot question. Lazarsfeld's first three steps of theory building are important, however, because they serve to illuminate the theoretical aspects of his thought that differentiated him from Adorno's point of view.

The first step in Lazarsfeld's concept of theory development was developing a preliminary imagery of the concept to be studied. He noted that everyday language was vague and often ambiguous. To be of use in a scientific context, Lazarsfeld felt that this colloquial manner of speaking and thinking needed to go through a process of purification and clarification (Lazarsfeld & Rosenberg, 1955). By developing a preliminary imagery, the vague concepts of colloquialisms could be identified and organized into tentative, but testable, constructs. In short, the first step in Lazarsfeld's scholarly approach was to seek out the denotative aspects of the phenomena under study.

Lazarsfeld never expected that the complexities of social thought would fit neatly into denotative categories—he was still aware that thought and words used to embody those thoughts carry with them the additional burden of a connotative structure. But he was less concerned with the connotative than with the denotative aspects of social thought. Lazarsfeld was willing to sacrifice connotation in the interest of making the denotative aspects "more precise and more amenable to verification and proof" (Lazarsfeld & Rosenberg, 1955, p. 2). Lazarsfeld's second step was to specify dimensions so that the adequacy and the limitations of concepts could be judged.

The third step in Lazarsfeld's approach was to select sets of indicators that would reflect the conceptualizations of the first two steps. Aware of the limits of the first two steps—the favoring of denotation over connotation, and the attendant sacrifice of the absolute in favor of the adequate—Lazarsfeld (1959) noted that this third step involved movement from the world of social thought to the world of social reality, and that it brought with it all of the difficulties involved in the first two steps.

> No science deals with its objects of study in their full concreteness. It selects certain of their properties and attempts to establish relations among them. The findings of such laws is the ultimate goal of all scientific inquiries. But in the social sciences the singling out of relevant properties is in itself a major problem. No standard terminology has yet been developed for this task. (p. 108)

For Lazarsfeld, the selection of indicators was a transitional step. They were selected for their usefulness, with an eye toward refining them for future use. The indicators were not in themselves concepts; rather they were bits and pieces that could gradually be built into a larger mosaic of knowledge. Lazarsfeld's concern was with relative, not absolute, truth.

The result of this approach, as Lazarsfeld saw it, was neither simple description nor abstract theory. Lazarsfeld was most concerned with finding the "underlying regularities" in the social situation, and then generalizing these regularities over as wide an area as was practicable (Lazarsfeld, 1964, p. 529). He felt that generalizable theory would come not from the actual indicators that he had chosen, but instead from the forms underlying the indicators, which would eventually lead to theoretical development (Lazarsfeld, 1967). In short, Lazarsfeld believed that the integration of discrete data would eventually reveal the underlying regularities of the social context.

Because of this fragmentary approach to assumed underlying regularities, Lazarsfeld was able to assimilate at least a part of the Frankfurt Institute's *critical theory* into his own viewpoint. He looked at the Frankfurt Institute's critical posture not as a competing theory, but as a complementary function. He saw *critical theory* functioning in the analysis of the social context, in the same way that criticism functioned in literature and in the arts. This critical function, in Lazarsfeld's view, was not so much to disapprove of a particular piece of work as it was to analyze the work's structure. This analysis would then expose the assumptions and foundations of the particular work (Lazarsfeld & Rosenberg, 1955), and could then be used to determine whether the work had met the test of adequacy and relative truth.

Since Lazarsfeld was confident in his approach to the social context—indeed his widespread success in the United States could not help but bolster that confidence—he was able to accept the idea of a critical approach questioning his ideas and assumptions. As Lazarsfeld envisioned such an approach, it involved the scrutiny of specific studies in terms of the procedures used, the assumptions involved, and the explanations produced (Lazarsfeld &

Rosenberg, 1955). In short, criticism was viewed as the analytical examination of analytic studies.

When Adorno and his colleagues at the Frankfurt Institute bypassed such analytical criticism and instead engaged in far more unspecific and freewheeling criticism, Lazarsfeld chided them for following "a bent of mind rather than a system of organized principles" (Lazarsfeld & Rosenberg, 1955) and provided his own vision of the analytic critic:

> He tells other scholars what they have done, or might do, rather than what they should do. He tells them what order of finding has emerged from their research, not what kind of result is or is not preferable. (p. 4)

From Lazarsfeld's viewpoint, the critic also dealt with the material of empirical inquiry. While the empirical scholar dealt directly with the data and the theory that emerged from that data, the critic dealt with how the empirical scholar had explained the theory that had emerged from the data (Lazarsfeld & Rosenberg, 1955). In Lazarsfeld's view, the function of the critic was to deal with how the empiricist had handled his or her data, and not with the question of whether or not the handling of data could actually lead to theory. In short, Lazarsfeld's concept of criticism was analytical criticism of empirical approaches to theory, not philosophical speculation about whether or not empirical approaches could even be used to develop theory. Yet the question of whether or not empiricism could yield theory was the conceptual point at which Adorno and his colleagues found their greatest divergence from Lazarsfeld's viewpoint.

THEORETICAL PERSPECTIVES: ADORNO'S VIEW

Adorno and his colleagues viewed the empirical, cumulative approach to theory, which Lazarsfeld advocated, as too limited in scope to generate sound theory, and they criticized the approach advocated by Lazarsfeld under the rubric of "positivism" (Jay, 1973). Drawing on two main themes of the empiricist (or positivist) approach—the belief that the social whole was made up of individuals, and the search for invariant rules underneath the social surface—Adorno and his colleagues were able to

develop and internalize a critique of the empiricist approach (Dialectical Methodology, 1970).

Individuals and the Social Whole

The assumption that the social whole was composed of the activities of individuals, Adorno was reluctant to accept. He pointed out that the ability to start from individual reactions and to proceed to an understanding of the social structure and the social essence was an unproven assumption, and not simply a routine truism (Adorno, 1969). According to Adorno, implicit in the assumption of moving from individuals to the social structure was a definite conception of the nature of society. By beginning from individual data and working toward conceptualizations of the social structure, empiricists were offering a theory that *society* was an abstraction derived from data (Adorno, 1969). This descriptive theory implied that society was a summing up of individual attributes and that it had its existence only as a collection of behaviors. Adorno pointed out an alternative possibility: by starting from a theory of society as a fundamental process that controlled the particular details of its manifestations, the term society became a reality, not an abstraction, and the particular manifestations of society reflected, rather than constituted, the theory (Adorno, 1969). In short, rather than advocating the building of theory from evidence, Adorno was arguing for the seeking of evidence based on theory.

To support the approach of seeking evidence based on theory, Adorno cited sociologist Robert Merton's insight that "virtually all findings can be explained theoretically once they are in hand, but not conversely" (Adorno, 1969, p. 364). If an approach started out with a wide range of theories, only some of those theories would eventually gain support from the findings. Since theory could always explain results, Adorno advocated the widespread development of theory rather than the widespread development of findings (Adorno, 1969). This preference for theory over findings meant that Adorno had committed himself to a global, theoretical approach rather than to a narrow, empirical one. The result of this orientation gave Adorno's work an open-ended, unfinished quality (Jay, 1973).

Criticism of Invariant Structures

Since Adorno dealt in theory and not data, he was concerned with the expansion of thought on the social structure, and this concern expressed itself in the criticism of existing theories of the social structure. Rather than committing himself to the generation of a comprehensive theory of society, Adorno instead chose to build on existing theories. His starting point was to analyze existing theories in terms of their strengths and weaknesses (Jay, 1973). The point of these critiques was to develop a more comprehensive understanding of society—not necessarily a total understanding, but a realistic understanding based on the limits of the theories and the theory-builders.

From Adorno's point of view, a theoretical weakness that afflicted many of his contemporaries, and which provided his second major objection to the empiricist viewpoint, was the assumption of invariant rules underlying society. The concept of underlying structures was amenable to Adorno and his colleagues. They had accepted a distinction between a world of appearances open to the human senses and an intelligible world underneath the appearances that was open to the rational processes of the human mind (Dialectical Methodology, 1970, 270). However, he felt that empiricism was trying to project from the world of appearances to the underlying intelligible world, while a more fruitful approach would emphasize the intelligible world, and deal only in appearances when they reflected the intelligible world (Dialectical Methodology, 1970).

The difference between inferring from the world of appearances to the intelligible world and inferring from the intelligible world to the world of appearances was more than directional. This distinction was developed by Max Horkheimer (1947) who argued that study in the world of appearances dealt only in surface phenomena, and as such could grasp reality only as a world of facts. This perception of the world as facts precluded penetration to the underlying "phenomena of experience" (Horkheimer, 1947, 39), and deprived concepts of their full meaning in the historical process of society (Horkheimer, 1947, 165). The world of appearances provided only a surface understanding of phenomena; total understanding would explore the relationships among meanings that lay hidden within and beyond the appearances (Horkheimer, 1947). What Horkheimer was advocating was not the simple re-experiencing of the past in a historian's mind. He rejected the idea that a historian who was the product of one society could experience the life of another society, especially since no reason existed to believe that the totality of the previous society had survived (Jay, 1973). Instead, Horkheimer was advocating an awareness of the shades of meaning that had built up around theoretical concepts (Horkheimer, 1947). He argued that a history of meaning lay beneath any given term, and that simply using that term did not necessarily call up all of its meanings. The term belonged to the world of appearances, its meanings to the intelligible world. Empiricism dealt only in the terminology of *theory*, not in the constructs that would build theory. The intelligible world related to those terms was neglected and ignored. Empirical study had deprived itself of the important concept of *context*.

Context and the World of Appearance

The concept of *context* was important to Horkheimer (and, by extension, to Adorno) because it helped minimize two of the fallacies attendant upon dealing exclusively in the world of appearance—man as the model for—or the explanation of society, and abstract principles as the causes of concrete reality.

By looking only at appearances, the scholarly mind could be misled into thinking that man could make his present or could have made his past. Horkheimer pointed out, however, that there was insufficient evidence (if any at all) to indicate that the present or the past had been made consciously by man (Jay, 1973). Further, Horkheimer (1947) argued, looking to man as an explanation of society was a futile gesture. No reason existed to believe that either society or the world in which that society existed had been made in the image of man. By Horkheimer's reasoning, theories that used man as a model or as a simple explanation of society were the result of a fallacious confusion of man with the society, or with the world in which he lived—a confusion of man as a part of the world of appearance with man as a part of the intelligible world.

The second fallacy, which Horkheimer perceived as arising from the confusion of mistaking the world of appearances for the intelligible world, was the perception of abstract qualities as the primary and essential qualities of the intelligible world. Horkheimer (1947) again pointed out that insufficient evidence existed to demonstrate that abstract qualities should be considered primary or essential in discussions of the structure or essence of society. By restricting itself to the discussion of appearances, empirical thought was forced to resort to an appeal to an underlying abstract reality to explain how interrelations in the world of appearance did or did not work. This appeal to an underlying abstract reality meant that empiricism was restricted to the concept of society as an abstraction—a position that Adorno (1969) did not find necessarily tenable. Adorno thought that the question of whether society was a reality or an abstraction was still unresolved, and that any theoretical approach like empiricism which restricted itself to an abstract model of society (through its overemphasis on the world of appearance) had put too great an emphasis on the generation of society from primary, abstract principles.

To protect theory from the fallacies that resulted from an emphasis on the world of appearance, Adorno and his colleagues emphasized *contingent* and *particular* explanations, and de-emphasized appeals to universal and abstract explanations (Jay, 1972; Hughes, 1975). Rather than seek *general* explanations of *particular* phenomena, Adorno and his colleagues sought *particular* explanations for *particular* phenomena. The result of this emphasis on particularity was a virulent insistence on treating the social whole as a totality in which contradictions were bound to exist (Jay, 1972).

Totality

In Adorno's vision of the world, totality was not the interlocking of invariant structures that the empiricist approach supposed. Rather, specific societal phenomena represented complex social interactions which could be understood not through reduction and simplification, but through awareness of the totality of the phenomena involved (Jay, 1972). Empiricist approaches were thought to operate as if some sort of organized intelligence were at work beneath the surface of social complexity (Horkheimer, 1947). Adorno's approach, on the other hand, was to seek out the complexities and inconsistencies of the social fabric—even to the point of flatly contradicting empirical conclusions with theoretical work (Jay, 1972).

Adorno's theoretical approach could contradict empirical work because of the tenet advanced by Horkheimer (and supported by Adorno) that insights generated by a theoretical approach could not be verified or falsified in terms of the existing social order. The insights could not be checked against the present order because they implied the possibility of a different social order (Jay, 1973). The historical component of the work of Adorno and Horkheimer was not the rigid march of general principles, it was an examination of present situations in the light of historical possibilities (Jay, 1973). This historical component, according to Adorno and Horkheimer, meant that as the reality of the social situation changed, the theoretical constructions used to explain the situation must also change to reflect the changing situation (Jay, 1973). Instead of the absolute principles that the empiricists wished to identify, Adorno and his colleagues sought changing principles to explain a changing world. While Lazarsfeld was seeking the invariant rules of a regular world, Adorno was studying the varying relations of a world that was not necessarily regular.

This concept of an irregular world enabled Adorno and Horkheimer to reject the need for general and internally-consistent principles governing the world around them (Jay, 1973). Only when society was ordered according to rules would it be possible to explain and to predict in terms of strict regularity (Jay, 1973). A premature emphasis on unified and coherent principles would only serve to obscure the work that was needed to produce a truly theoretical approach to society (Jay, 1972). To thinkers of Adorno's persuasion, such premature reconciliations in an attempt to generate invariant rules would result in either *fetishization* or *reification*.

Fetishization and Reification

In Adorno's line of thought, *fetishization* was the overemphasis of one facet of the social whole (Jay, 1972). By isolating theoretical terms from their historical context, empiricist approaches were isolating aspects of a conceptual whole and using those isolates as abbreviations for the contextual whole. The result of such isolation was inference about large movements based on only a tiny part of that movement. By singling out a part as representative of the whole, empiricists were elevating a single aspect to a totality—they were inferring an intelligible whole from a few appearances.

Reification, on the other hand, was an attempt to transform individual phenomena into abstract principles (Jay, 1973, 53, 177-178). Since empiricism attempted to infer from the world of appearances to the intelligible world, empiricism ran the grave danger of attempting to transform individual phenomena from the world of appearance into abstract principles in the intelligible world. Since Adorno had already rejected the concept of abstract principles as formulating principles, and since Adorno did not believe that inference could necessarily move from appearance to intelligibility, the danger of empiricism transforming appearance into principles was particularly unattractive.

For Adorno, the way to avoid the twin difficulties of *fetishization* and *reification* was to make judgements on the basis of theory, not data (Adorno, Frenkel-Brunswik, Levinson, & Sanford, 1950). The theorist was called upon to go beyond the givens of his or her particular experience (Jay, 1973), and was urged to depart from architectural systems where abstraction and coherency were the dominant values. Instead they were encouraged to develop theory through subjective, private reflection, where insight would replace oversight (Jay, 1973). This private reflection was to be an attempt to "grasp the whole as it was embodied in concrete particulars" (Jay, 1973, 82), rather than to build a whole out of concrete particulars. Theory was to be built not by *identity* but by *analogy*· (Jay, 1973)—even if it meant combining "highly abstract statements with seemingly trivial observations" (Jay, 1973). Such analogical and associative thinking often forced Adorno to operate in a state of

suspended judgement (Jay, 1973), but such thinking did permit another key concept in Adorno's thinking to emerge: "a down-to-earth insistence that 'things' took priority over one's perception of them" (Hughes, 1975, 144).

Verstand and Vernunft

Adorno was very careful to distinguish between *phenomena*, on the one hand, and a *person's perception of those phenomena* on the other. He believed that phenomena neither existed totally outside an individual's consciousness, nor did they exist totally as a creation of the individual's consciousness (Jay, 1973). By implication, he believed that phenomena existed as an interaction of consciousness and reality.

With the positing of phenomena as the interaction of consciousness and reality, Adorno rejected the idea that *reality* was an objective process of nature, dutifully recorded by the conscious, and that human consciousness was able to impose its order—and thereby control—on a meaningless world (Jay, 1969). Adorno's interaction concept also allowed him to reject the idea that reality was constituted completely outside the conscious, and that reality was constituted completely inside consciousness (Jay, 1969). In short, because of the concept of the interaction between consciousness and reality, Adorno was able to argue that *insight* resided not in consciousness nor in reality, but instead in a "force-field" between the two (Jay, 1969, 64). This meant that to understand reality, the scholar needed to understand consciousness; and, conversely, to understand consciousness, the scholar needed to understand reality. The problem remained of how to discriminate between the two.

As discussed earlier, Adorno had split reality into the world of appearance and the intelligible world. The world of appearance dealt with sense data and was often mistaken (especially by empiricists) for the intelligible world. The intelligible world, on the other hand, partook of both sensory data and of any ordering beyond immediate sensory appearance. To reflect understanding of both these levels of reality within the conscious, Horkheimer (and implicitly Adorno) adopted the distinguishing terms of *Verstand* and *Vernunft*. *Verstand* was used to designate a lower faculty of the mind. It structured the world in a commonsensical way (Jay, 1973), and was therefore suited for involvement in the world of appearances. *Vernunft*, on the other hand, was a higher faculty. It went beyond appearance to the deeper insights within and beyond appearance (Jay, 1973). It was suited for exploration of the intelligible world.

This distinction between *Verstand* and *Vernunft* also provided the key to differentiating between *consciousness* and *reality*. *Verstand*, with its base level comprehension of reality, implied the perceptions of the unreflective conscious—the internalization of the world of appearance without the insights of the intelligible world. At such a level of comprehension, individual consciousness would be dominant over reality because it would retain the *appearance of reality* without partaking of the *intelligibility of reality*.

On the other hand, *Vernunft*, which was the repository of insights into intelligible reality, implied the perceptions of a reflective conscious—the acceptance of the intelligible world with both its insights and its grounding in and beyond the world of appearances. At this upper level of comprehension, reality would be dominant over individual perceptions of reality because intelligibility would override the limitations of simple appearance. In short, the distinction between consciousness and reality could be based on whether theory was derived from *Verstand*—commonsense organization of the *world of appearance*—or on *Vernunft*—rational insights from the *intelligible world*. In the former, individual *consciousness* could be assumed to be the dominant force; in the latter, the *context of reality* could be assumed to be dominant. As a scholar, Adorno could not help but to prefer the insightful *Vernunft* to the mundane *Verstand*.

Adorno's Conflict

So when Lazarsfeld called upon Adorno to translate his earlier work on the sociology of music into empirical terms, Adorno was not simply being asked to transform his thoughts into empirical terms through a simple mechanical process. Instead, Adorno was being called upon to choose between individuals and the social whole, findings and

theory, invariant rules and a changing world, appearance and intelligibility, fetishization/reification and totality, individual consciousness and reality, and (ultimately) *Verstand* and *Vernunft*. Given that Adorno was an advocate of a philosophical approach which questioned and rejected the conceptual underpinnings of an empirical approach he had been requested to attempt, small wonder that Adorno was unable to comply and that he regarded his assignment (despite his host's good intentions) as a stressful situation.

THEORETICAL PERSPECTIVES: TWO CONTRASTING THEORIES

The major theoretical differences between Lazarsfeld and Adorno that emerged from the previous discussions fall along two major dimensions: (1) differing pictures of the world, and (2) differing analytical approaches.

Different Worlds

Lazarsfeld was committed to the concept of a world of underlying, invariant rules (usually abstract). By a careful cumulative study of the surrounding world, Lazarsfeld believed that the underlying regularities could be detected, identified, and eventually analyzed. Adorno, however, was skeptical of the concept of a world of invariant rules. Opting instead for a world of contingent and changing relations, Adorno posited a world of fluctuations which might or might not have detectable rules, but which certainly did not necessarily operate in terms of some underlying rationality. Instead of a regular world of abstract rules, Adorno assumed an irregular world of fluctuating relations.

Different Approaches

The second difference between Lazarsfeld and Adorno was in terms of conceptualization of approach. Each believed he was working in the area of *Vernunft* (and its associated intelligible world), and each believed the other to be working in the area of *Verstand* (and its associated world of appearance). Because of Lazarsfeld's conception of a regular world of invariant rules, he was able to believe that a denotative, cumulative approach was the most effective way to understanding the intelligible world—the way to *Vernunft*. From Lazarsfeld's point of view, Adorno would lapse into *Verstand* because of Adorno's rabid insistence on accounting for *all* of the concrete particulars in a given phenomenon. This insistence (in terms of Lazarsfeld's view of the world) meant that Adorno was emphasizing a few minor aberrations at the expense of the general principles that were involved. Such an emphasis would mean that Adorno would be guilty of unjustifiably inferring larger implications from a small part of the phenomenon studied *(fetishization),* and of claiming to have detected invariant rules from only a few aberrations that appeared in the phenomenon *(reification).*

Adorno, on the other hand, did not share Lazarsfeld's belief in a regular world of underlying rules. Instead, Adorno believed in an irregular world of changing relations. Consequently, Adorno favored a connotative, exploratory approach over Lazarsfeld's denotative, cumulative approach as the most effective way to gain *Vernunft* about the intelligible world. This connotative, exploratory approach would preserve the context of a changing world and permit the consciousness to rise above the world of appearances (the dominion of *Verstand*), and to partake instead in the intelligible world. To Adorno, the changing world was too complex to yield itself to the sparse contexts of the empirical approach. Consequently, Adorno's exploratory approach would see Lazarsfeld's cumulative approach as bogged down in the *Verstand* of the world of appearances. To Adorno, Lazarsfeld's approach was an attempt to carve out chunks of the totality and to use those chunks as abbreviations for the totality *(fetishization).* Further, Lazarsfeld's approach was also an attempt to take individual reports from the world of appearance, and to project those reports into general rules for understanding the changing totality *(reification).*

Differences

What Lazarsfeld had perceived as Adorno's inability to translate theoretical ideas into empirical questions, and what Adorno had seen as the intractability of his theoretical ideas of translation into empirical questions, was not a simple matter of differences in technique. Rather, it was a situation of fundamental conceptual and theoretical disagreement.

When Lazarsfeld called for a critical approach, he was seeking a fellow believer in an invariant world to refine the implications of that belief. When Adorno was called upon to be a critic, he acted as a doubter of the invariant world, and he questioned the implications of belief in that kind of world. In such a situation, full-fledged cooperation was difficult, if not impossible.

CONCLUSION

From the previous material, the theoretical differences between Lazarsfeld and Adorno can be seen in terms of three levels: (1) personal background, (2) differing perceptions of each other's backgrounds, and (3) fundamental theoretical and philosophical discrepancies.

The first level involved the scholars' background. Lazarsfeld's mode of thinking was empirical and practically oriented. This point of view enabled him to adapt to the numerical orientations of the United States and to flourish. In contrast, Adorno, whose personal background pointed his mode of thinking more toward speculation and intellectual orientation, was unable to adapt his manner of thinking to the prevailing climate of opinion in the United States. Consequently, the orientations of Adorno and his colleagues returned to Germany when he did, to flourish in the speculative atmosphere of German social thought (Katona, 1953-54), leaving only traces in American social thought.

The second level involved Lazarsfeld's and Adorno's differing perceptions of the other's point of view. Lazarsfeld perceived Adorno's difficulties in terms of the latter's inability to transfer theoretical ideas to an empiricist framework. Adorno, however, perceived his difficulty in developing an empiricist framework in terms of the inability of empiricist thought to make the transfer to theory. The gist of this conflict was that each person perceived the other as unable to make the appropriate transition from empiricism to theory (or vice versa).

The third, and most important, level of the difference between the two scholars involved the fundamentally different conception of the world that both men brought to their work. Lazarsfeld viewed his work as the study of a regular world, under which lay invariant rules for explaining how that world worked. Adorno, on the other hand, viewed his work as the study of an irregular world, under which and within which lay varying interrelations which could be used to explain how that world worked. Where Lazarsfeld expected a world that played by the rules, Adorno expected a world that could deceive him with its shiftings.

On all three dimensions, the two scholars' viewpoints were so discrepant that, from their perspectives, reconciliation was not possible. In this irreconcilable conflict situation, the dominant values of society in which the two men were located took over. Lazarsfeld's views flourished in America, while Adorno's views, except among a few scholars like the historian Martin Jay, have not enjoyed widespread success. In intercultural terms, Lazarsfeld found the dominant value orientations in America congenial, and he adapted. Adorno found American value orientations disagreeable, and he refused adaptation. What seemed to be a simple technical disagreement was actually a fundamental philosophical dispute—a dispute that was not carried out because the two scholars were focused on the elaborations, and not the causes, of their differences.

The task that remains is not to choose between two different scholars, but to examine both theories to see if they yield conceptualizations that assist in understanding both our world and ourselves. Lazarsfeld and Adorno have provided an example of the sheer difficulty of communication when philosophical and cultural values intervene. More importantly, they have also provided a starting point from which both empirical studies and critical studies can depart from traditions of self-aggrandizement and begin to question both the implications of their origins and their findings. The conflict between empirical theory and critical theory is not technical, nor is it superficial—it is a fundamental philosophical dispute revolving around the scholar's conception of the world. Any reconciliation of Lazarsfeld's and Adorno's views are not in their pasts, but in our futures.

REFERENCES

ADORNO, T.W. "Sociology and psychology" (I.N. Wohlfarth, trans.). *New Left Review*, 1967, 46, 67-80.

ADORNO, T.W. "Scientific experiences of a European scholar in America" (D. Fleming, trans.). In D. Fleming and B. Bailyn (Eds.), *The intellectual migration: Europe and America, 1930-1960*. Cambridge, Massachusetts: The Belknap Press of Harvard University Press, 1969.

ADORNO, T.W., FRENKEL-BRUNSWIL, E., LEVINSON, D.J., & SANFORD, R.N. *The Authoritarian Personality*. New York: Harper and Row, 1950.

Dialectical Methodology. *The Times Literary Supplement*, 1970, 3550, 269-272.

HORKHEIMER, M. *Eclipse of reason*. New York: Oxford University Press, 1947.

HUGHES, H.S. *The sea change: The migration of social thought, 1930-1965*. New York: Harper and Row, 1975.

JAY, M. The permanent exile of Theodor W. Adorno. *Midstream*, 1969, 15, 62-69.

JAY, M. The Frankfurt School in Exile. *Perspectives in American history*, 1972, 6, 339-385.

JAY, M. *The dialectical imagination: A History of the Frankfurt School and the Institute of Social Research 1923-1950*. Boston: Little, Brown and Company, 1973.

KATONA, G. Survey research in Germany. *Public Opinion Quarterly*, 1953-54, 17, 471-480.

LAZARSFELD, P.F. The Effects of Radio on Public Opinion. In D. Waples (Ed.), *Print, radio, and film in a democracy*. Chicago: The University of Chicago Press, 1942.

LAZARSFELD, P.F. & ROSENBERG, M. (Eds.), *The Language of Social Research: A Reader in the Methodology of Social Research*. Glencoe, Illinois: Free Press, 1955.

LAZARSFELD, P.F. Evidence and inference in social research. In D. Lerner (Ed.), *Evidence and inference*. Glencoe, Illinois: Free Press, 1959.

LAZARSFELD, P.F. A note on empirical social research and interdisciplinary relationships. *International Social Science Journal*, 1964, 16, 529-533.

LAZARSFELD, P.F. Some recent trends in United States methodology and general sociology. In *Contemporary sociology in Western Europe and in America*. First International Congress of Social Sciences of the Luigi Sturzo Institute, Rome, Italy, September 5-10, 1967.

LAZARSFELD, P.F. An episode in the history of social research: A memoir. In D. Fleming and B. Bailyn (Eds.), *The intellectual migration: Europe and America, 1930-1960*. Cambridge, Massachusetts: The Belknap Press of Harvard University Press, 1969.

SCHAD, S.P. *Empirical social research in Weimar-Germany*. The Hague, Netherlands: Mouton, 1972.

INFORMATION SYSTEMS

Theory and Research: An Overview
Selected Studies

INFORMATION SYSTEMS
THEORY AND RESEARCH: AN OVERVIEW

KLAUS KRIPPENDORFF
University of Pennsylvania–Philadelphia

Communication in its present conception reflects three fundamental revolutions in human understanding of social reality and is now transcended by another revolution, still in progress. This fourth revolution provides the background of this paper.

The first revolution occurred in ancient Greece, and had the disassociation of language and reality as its impetus. A result was the introduction of a variety of concepts such as *sign, symbol, meaning, rhetoric*, and *logic*, all of which may be summarized in the notion of *message*. A *message* stands for something other than itself.

The second revolution was prompted by technological intrusions in the process of message exchange—printing in particular—through which attention shifted from the *form* and *content* of a message to the capabilities of a particular mode of production and media of dissemination—the *channel*. A *channel* facilitates, and yet imposes limits on, the ability to transmit messages.

The social consequences of media technologies were at the base of the third revolution. The result was a view of communication reflecting the recognition that media uses develop new forms of dependencies between individuals as senders and receivers. Although there can be no doubt that the *process* of communication is as old as mankind, it evolved only slowly until technology entered this process, fostered rapid social change, and created problems. The culmination of these led to the notion of *communication*. *Communication* transcends the notion of *message* and *channel*, and acquires social significance because of the relations it connotes between individuals, and between institutions, including machines.

The fourth revolution referred to above is identified with the term *cybernetics*, and with *the systems approach*. It has emerged in response to certain recognizable inadequacies of the communication paradigm. While far from being completed, it aims at putting communication into a larger context of society.

Among the inadequacies of the communication paradigm elaborated elsewhere and apparent in the remainder of this paper are: the inability to accommodate the concepts of *process* (Krippendorff 1970, 1975a; Ruben & Kim, 1973; Fisher, 1975), *mutual causation*, (Maruyama, 1963, 1969; Watzlawick, Beavin, & Jackson, 1967) *nonlinear relations* (Thayer, 1968a), *complex interdependencies* (Krippendorff, 1976), *hierarchical conceptualization* (Thayer, 1968b; Simon, 1969; Ruben, 1975a), functional necessity (Deutsch, 1963; Churchman, 1968; Miller, 1965; Thayer, 1968b; Thayer, 1968b; Ruben 1972, 1975a; Campbell & Mickelson, 1975).

CYBERNETICS AND SYSTEMS THEORY

Both cybernetics and systems theory are concerned with wholes that are composed of many related parts. Neither focuses on a particular materiality. What then distinguishes the two? Part of the distinction lies in the intellectual histories of their main contributors. Cybernetics is concerned with communication and control processes in man, machines, and society and is associated with Wiener (1954, 1961), Ashby (1956, 1960), McCulloch, (1943, 1956) and Shannon (Shannon & Weaver, 1949). Since World War II, the study of *cybernetics* has generated many concepts, including theories of communication and information processing, theories of purposive behavior and control, and theories of adaptation and self-organization. The importance of mathematical, model building, and simulation approaches to understanding reality have been established, as a consequence.

Perhaps because of its preference for formal theory and mathematical techniques of analysis, cybernetics has grown particularly strong in the "harder" natural sciences, where it contributed to the development of communication technology, artificial intelligence, and information processing systems. In the "softer" social sciences it has primarily introduced and sharpened major concepts, including *information, communication, feedback,* and *purpose.*

Systems theory, which is associated with Bertalanffy (1968), Rapoport (1966), and Boulding (1956), developed a decade or two before World War II and primarily in the area of biology. It gave the *Gestalt* concept of an organism—according to which the whole is more than the sum of its parts—a more formal representation. And it had the unification of the sciences as an aim (Kuhn, 1963; Grinker, 1968; Laszlo, 1969).

For a mathematically-oriented systems theorist, a *system* consists of a set of states that are chained in time by a transformation. The states take account of the relations between the parts of the system, so that changes over time imply changes in the relations among the system's parts. It is thereby recognized that the properties of a system as a *whole* are not deducible from the properties of its *parts.* Much of systems theory therefore focuses attention on how systems are organized. Explanations by systems theorists typically follow the formula:

Property of the Whole = F (Properties of Parts + Organization)

And as the wholes are composed of more and more similar parts (the cells of an organism, the individual members of a society, etc.), the properties of the parts become less and less important, and organizational characteristics move to the foreground of systems theoretical explanations.

One form of organization that has a prominent place in systems theory is *hierarchy.* Any system may be viewed as a part of a super system. At the same time, it is composed of several subsystems. Each is viewed from a separate level of analysis. Koestler (1967) coined the word *wholon* to designate a unit of analysis that is both a part of a whole and the whole for its parts. Thus, Gerard (1957), J.G. Miller (1955), and many others distinguish such levels of analysis as the cell, the organ, the individual, the small group, the institution, and the

society.

Objects of concern are often too complex to be classified in terms of a set of states and transformations. Systems theorists then accept what Rapoport (1970) called a "soft"—as opposed to the above mentioned "hard"—definition of system. Such a definition can be viewed as a generalization of the notion of an organism. Indeed, one seems to be able to describe all living organisms in terms of three fundamental characteristics which can be used to identify and to study similar objects as systems: (1) a system has a *structure*—it consists of interrelated parts . . . this is true for living things, complex machines and a languages alike; (2) material systems that maintain some steady state have a *function*—they behave towards an environment, move relative to other systems, and consume matter and energy; and (3) systems have a history in the course of which they undergo slow evolutionary changes—grow, develop, or evolve. Gerard (1957) called these characteristics *being, acting,* and *becoming.* He showed that, because different sciences tend to specialize in one or another such characteristics at the exclusion of others, they can achieve only a partial understanding of their objects of analysis.

Another orientation also stems from biology: The parts of a system are often viewed as *integrated* into a whole so that they *serve a common or overriding purpose.* This conception is fundamental to engineering, conforms to much theorizing in medicine, and suits the concept of management (Ackoff & Emery, 1972; Churchman, 1968). While a malfunctioning of the human body may become quite easily identifiable, at least in extreme situations, as when a cancer has been localized, the extension of such a notion to social organizations is not nearly as obvious and clear. Revolutionary transformations of society always start with small deviations from norms, grow and verify themselves often only after they have taken over the whole. Contrary to the view of social systems of Merton (1949) and Parsons (1957), functions and dysfunctions are not unambiguously distinguished from one another in social organizations. Individuals in natural social settings can easily be rearranged or organize themselves to constitute new social structures. Thus, the biological analogy—with its notion of wholeness-with-purpose—might be inappropriate for the analysis of social phenomena.

For a cybernetician, the parts of a system are likely to be viewed as dynamically changing, and the relations among them then become processes of communication—variations in structure that are transmitted across space and time. Explanations by cyberneticians tend to utilize a formula similar to the following:

Behavior of the Whole = F (Behavior of Parts
                              + Networks of Communication)

Again, in large and complex systems it is the flow of information through communication networks that occupies a central position in cybernetic explanations. For example, electronic computers consist of a very large number of basically identical and behaviorally primitive elements. None alone yield clues as to what the whole might be doing. However, the causal network that links these components into large functional units, which is what a computer program specifies and controls, helps the cybernetician explain how the whole system behaves and evolves. Thus, *intelligence, adaptation,* and *growth* become a correlate of networks of communication and of the self-modification characteristics inherent in these networks.

Cyberneticians have found circular flows of information not only the most challenging and difficult features of large systems, but also the most revealing ones. The architects of complex machinery, and the rational managers of large organizations, are keenly aware of their own dependence on communication. To be successful in coping with an environment about which knowledge is incomplete, information about the effects of one's actions must be fed back to correct further controlling actions. Such a circular flow "feeds on itself" in such a way that the behavior of the larger whole containing such a flow converges toward a prescribed goal (Vickers, 1959). Systems that are so designed are *purposive* by prescription.

While circular flows of information have been shown to be a prerequisite for achieving prescribed goals, it is also possible to turn cybernetic feedback theory around and predict or infer from a given communication network how the whole will behave, regardless of possible intentions. Systems that embody circular flows either converge towards, or maintain, some state of affairs, or result in a runaway that tends to break old forms and create new ones. These processes may exist quite independent of their adequate recognition by participants and are often unrelated to whether their results are desirable. All systems containing processes of circular communication may be viewed as *purposive* by *inference*, and the understanding of such systems is facilitated by using cybernetics predictively. Note that cybernetics neither assumes that systems are organized hierarchically nor that the form of an organization derives its meaning from common or overall purposes. It is not necessary to assume that, among the many components which might be involved in a feedback loop, one must be designated *controller*, others as *receptors* and *affectors*, etc. All components may be merely viewed as connected through circular communication.

Another aspect of cybernetics is the epistemological approach taken in the study of information, communication networks, and complex systems. This can be stated in conjunction with the notion that *information* implies a choice of one message from a larger repertoire of possible messages, with the realization of constraint on conceivable alternatives.

Ashby (1958) once distinguished two approaches to the study of systems. The one associated with systems theory, as developed by Bertalanffy (1968), essentially studies existing systems, one at a time. After sampling a sufficient number, it ventures generalizations in the form of principles which underly all of the systems. The approach associated primarily with cybernetics favors the study of all conceivable systems, existing or not, so that those observed become a subset of those actually studied. This approach, chiefly associated with axiomatics, provides a novel context for searching for answers to "why?" questions. Given a communication network, as observed, a cybernetician does not take this fact as is. Instead, by considering all or at least a large number of possible communication networks, he asks *why* many of the alternatives failed to develop (Bateson, 1967).

A Comparison

The difference between cybernetics and systems theory, then, reflects their different historical origins. Also, systems theory emphasizes properties of *wholes* and *parts, relationships* and *hierarchies*, while cybernetics focuses attention on *behavior, processes,* and *circular communication* (Klir, 1970). Systems theory is generalization primarily from biological organisms, while cybernetics seeks to study all possible systems involving communication, regardless of whether they exist or could be designed in fact. Much of systems theory carries the burden of assuming that systems are inherently *purposeful* and are organized accordingly.

In Ashby's (1956) work, it is apparent that the two ways of looking at complex systems are distinct, but not incompatible. At least in principle, it is possible to deduce the trajectory of a whole system's behavior from a knowledge of the dynamic relations that may exist among its parts, and vice versa, provided that the system is known in sufficient detail. It is only when systems become very large that each approach makes different simplifying assumptions. A systems theory of very large objects is likely to emphasize overall systems properties, including organizational forms, the integration of components into the whole, and common purposes—usually at the expense of how the parts interact—while the cybernetics of very large systems is likely to focus on how some portions of such systems communicatively influence others and ultimately themselves—perhaps at the expense of recognizing global systems properties. A systems theory is likely to assume purposes to be inherent in existing organizational forms and easily supports normative judgements. Cybernetics, at least in the domain of social organization, attempts to infer overall purposes and modifications of organizational structures from ongoing processes of communication.

Both cybernetics and systems theory have lead scholars of communication to a study of the larger context of systems within which communication is qualitatively, and sometimes even quantitatively, identifiable.

NONSYSTEMS APPROACHES[2]

To appreciate what distinguishes systems approaches from others, let me give a few examples of research strategies that are either excluded from systems considerations or regarded as of less interest.

The first example is found in attempts *to isolate a single and often unique event* and to describe it from various different perspectives. This is the approach of those historians who contribute to knowledge by searching out the many ways a particular historical event may be interpreted or by elaborating on one such interpretation so as to gain maximum possible depth. While judgments regarding whether an interpretion makes sense is presumably cognitively linked to the interpretations of other, possibly similar, historical events, each such contribution to knowledge then stands relatively isolated. In choosing this example, I do not wish to imply that historians refuse to describe successions of states and evolutionary processes as a consequence of the interaction between the components of a system. I merely argue that a confinement to the study of isolated events—however many dimensions may be considered in each case, and in whichever discipline this strategy is adopted—will not aid the understanding of how such events are related to other events, how they come about, and to what they will lead in the future.

A second example is found in attempts to single out for attention one or more observed variables and to try to understand their variations in terms of their dependencies on another set of observed variables. This is the approach common to much of traditional sociological research, with its conceptual distinction between "dependent" and "interdependent" variables and in much of psychological research involving experimental designs with its synonymous distinction between "criterion" and "predictor" variables. While this methodology clearly recognizes many variables, and possibly many relations holding between them, by preconceiving the direction of the possible explanations, causal or otherwise, interaction and mutual causal dependencies can hardly be discovered, and the kind of system properties which underlie the observed behavior are likely to be missed. A corollary to this is the attempt in much experimental work to hold constant as many variables as possible and to vary only one at a time. This is a method which reduces the complexity of an object of study by forcing possible complex interactions out of existence.

A third example for what a systems approach would exclude or regard as of less interest is found in attempts to reduce an obviously complex organism by analysis into certain individually comprehensible units without regard to the relationships among them. This has been clearly observed by Ashby (1958) who writes:

> . . . for two hundred years [science] has tried primarily to find, within the organism, whatever is *simple*. Thus, from the whole complexity of spinal action, Sherrington isolated the stretch reflex, a small portion of the whole, simple within itself and capable of being studied in functional isolation. From the whole complexity of digestion, the biochemist distinguished the action of pepsin or protein, which could be studied in isolation. And avoiding the whole complexity of cerebral action, Pavlov investigated the salivary conditioned reflex as an essentially simple function, only a fragment of the whole, that could be studied in isolation. The same strategy—of looking for the simple part—has been used incessantly in physics and chemistry. Their triumphs have been chiefly those of identifying the *units* out of which the complex structures are made.

Thus, we know more about the nerve fibers of which the brain is made than about the properties of the mind. We have more and clearer conceptions for dealing with human individuals than for social organizations of which they are a part and through which they derive their significance. We have mastered the design, production, and control of cars, but we fail to understand the car complex which involves many industries, the network of public roads, and the masses of drivers.

Books on system engineering and management are full of illustrations for how the systemic consequences of an improvement can lead to fantastic failures, the current ecological problems caused by excessive industrialization being a case in point. These examples all boil down to the fact that whenever many component parts are interacting with each other to form a larger whole, the complexity that does emerge can be handled neither by in depth understanding of isolated events, nor by selectively controlling the variation of a few "independent"

variables, nor by functionally isolating its constituent parts. Such strategies would presumably be avoided by systems approaches.

Consider three more negative examples of systems approachs from the field of communication research. Lasswell's conception of communication research may serve as a starting point. Lasswell (1960) argues:

> A convenient way to describe an act of communication is to answer the following questions:
> Who
> Says What
> In Which Channel
> To Whom
> With What Effect?

The scientific study of the process of communication tends to concentrate upon one or another of these questions. Scholars who study the "who," the communicator, look into the factors that initiate and guide the act of communication. We call this subdivision of the field of research *control analysis*. Specialists who focus upon the "says what" engage in content analysis. Those who look primarily at the radio, press, film, and other channels of communication are doing *media analysis*. When the principal concern is with the person reached by the media, we speak of *audience analysis*. If the question is the impact upon audiences, the problem is *effect analysis*. Whether such distinctions are useful depends entirely upon the degree of refinement which is regarded as appropriate to a given scientific and managerial objective. Often it is simpler to combine audience and effect analysis, for instance, than to keep them apart. On the other hand, we may want to concentrate on the analysis of content, and for this purpose subdivide the field into the study of purport and style, the first referring to the message, and the second to the arrangement of the elements of which the message is composed.

This strategy proposes not only a particular unitization of the process—in terms of sender, message, channel, receiver and effects—but it also suggests that an understanding of the process is obtainable by studying each unit *separately*. From the point of view of systems theory, there is nothing wrong either with a particular unitization or with studying these units independently of each other. The terms refer to units on different levels of analysis (sender and receiver are the parts of a system, the channel is a binary relation between them, the effects are presumably measured on the receiver, etc.), and that is not objectionable. However, if the notion of communication process does have some wholistic qualities—some supra-individual properties, as many communication researchers would contend—then a research strategy which observes each unit separately could not possibly gain insights into the very properties of communication processes. It would at best discover certain primitive correlates of the process without coming to grips with what in fact accounts for it.

A second negative example comes from the same school of thought. It is an attempt by Lerner (1960) to compare communication systems (his term) across different societies. Instead of describing the systems either in terms of transformations, states, relations between any of their component parts or in terms of their wholistic properties, he is satisfied merely with giving names to certain units:

Units	Media Systems
Channel	Media (Broadcast)
Audience	Mass (Heterogeneous)
Source	Professional (Skill)
Content	(Descriptive)

Oral Systems

Oral (Point to Point)
Primary (Homogeneous)
Hierarchical (Status)
(Prescriptive)

This is neither to say that such comparisons would not provide interesting insights, nor is it intended to claim that communication technologies could not constitute or be constituent parts of large systems. But the way such "systems" are described does not lend itself to any study of their properties. What is described here are a few aspects or dimensions of some "system" that is vaguely conceptualized and lies outside the researcher, to be discovered in the real world. The data that are gathered in such cases do not lend themselves to an analysis of the objects as systems. Rather, they are at best real correlates of systems properties, and are thus far removed from the systems under consideration.

A third example, also taken from Lasswell (1960) comes a bit closer to a systems approach. It is possible, Lasswell argues, to take acts of communication as the units of analysis—thereby rendering the constituent components as less important—and to study the functions of these acts within the

context of a society. Just as particular organs of an organism are assigned several roles or are specialized to perform certain tasks, so can acts of communication be assigned certain responsibilities. This interpretation comes closer to a systems approach, because at least an attempt is made to relate various units of analysis—here acts of communication involving senders and receivers—and certain other social activities with each other. However it differs from a systems approach because these relations are specified not in terms of interactions from which some behavior may be concluded, not in terms of transformations which would specify how some events imply others, etc. These relations have primarily *cognitive significance*. They render the existence of each unit meaningful to the observer, or to the participant of the social process, by the assumption of a shared purpose. Lasswell takes for granted, for example, that something like "rationality in society" is a value toward which communication is to be employed. He assumes that communication is to serve "the maintenance of cultural heritage" and "the correlation of the various units of society with each other." He thereby ignores the possibility that communication may also heighten emotionality, selectively destroy such heritage, or contribute to conflicts, all of which may well be socially creative.

It is not the issue here to question the ideological underpinnings of Lasswell's conceptual frames of reference. Rather, the example is chosen to demonstrate that this form of integrating the units of analysis is merely cognitive and derived from some purpose superimposed upon the whole. The explanation, while subjectively highly meaningful, has neither formal logical implications nor predictive value.

Institutional Barriers

There are two institutional barriers to the development of a systems approach in communication. Both are rooted in the fact that the concept of communication as a relation *between* individuals is *mediated* by the exchange of symbols and messages, and therefore has *no obvious materiality as referent,* whereas the objects of most traditional academic disciplines, like physics, biology, psychology, and engineering, are materially definable. To fit traditional disciplinary delineations and institutional categories, the concept of communication is then often stripped of much of its explanatory power, by reducing it either to a medium or to an explanatory variable.

The former is manifest by focussing attention on those features of the communication process that have clear material forms—the *channel*. Such an approach equates *communication* with *technology* and results in such categorical distinctions as between telephone communication, electronic mass communication, newsprint, and business communications. From an engineering perspective, questions of efficiency are raised and in the context of traditional journalism and the social sciences, questions regarding the possible effects of such technology become predominant. Characteristic of this institutional barrier is the view of communication as *thing-like*.

The latter adaptation of the concept is actually even more alien to a systems approach. It reduces the process of communication to an explanatory variable—as a different kind of stimulus to which responses are to be assessed. This is evident in much of audience research in sociology and public opinion research, and in socialization studies in which exposure to information is considered merely as contributory to the understanding of such things as attitude formation and social stratification. The binary character of a communication relationship is thereby reduced in ordinality to unitary relation, a property, and an independent variable which is of no interest in itself, except when it is found to correlate with some phenomenon within the empirical domain of a traditional discipline. Such a conception of communication inhibits the growth of theory and comprehension of the processes involved.

SYSTEMS APPROACHES

Systems approaches to communication stem primarily from advances made in cybernetics and systems theory, and are manifest in what might be said to be attempts to contextualize communication. To see the binary and somewhat static concept of communication in the larger context of society is certainly not new. Efforts in this direction reflect the feeling that the narrow concept of communication is inadequate as the sole source of explanation, and that it is unproductive as an object of study in and of itself. However, a systems approach proceeds differently and offers a conceptual methodology in which the traditional concept of communication may become absorbed and transcended. The following focusses on a few ways in which cybernetics and systems theory accommodate the concept of communication.

Modes of Inquiry

One of the innovations of the systems approach, particularly owing to cybernetics, is its axiomatic base. As mentioned, Ashby saw cybernetics as the discipline concerned with all conceivable systems. "Cybernetics stands to the real machine—electronic, mechanical, neutral, or economic—much as geometry stands to a real object in our terrestrial space" (Ashby, 1956). Ashby's view is thereby tied to *axiomatics* (which is concerned with purely *mathematical-logical systems* and rules of deduction, and provides a formal-symbolic apparatus in terms of which existing phenomena may be described and contrasted. Bertalanffy's general systems approach is tied to the traditional aims of science, which is concerned with understanding and predicting reality from data obtained by a remote observer. Unfortunately, the latter mode of inquiry is often confused with the more practical concern for application. Kotarbinski (1965) called this mode of inquiry *praxiology*.

The praxiologist is intimately involved in—if not part of—the object of his interest. The scientist observes from the outside, while the mathematician needs no observation at all. The distinction is reflected in the *language used to describe the objects of concern* respectively as participatory and that of an interested party, and as removed and free of expressions of preference, and in purely formal syntax. The distinction is more pronounced regarding the *criteria* each mode employs for accepting or rejecting knowledge about its respective objects (see Table 1), and the problems toward which each is sensitive: loss or failure, disconfirmation and inconsistency, respectively (Krippendorff, 1969).

TABLE 1
Modes of Inquiry and Concepts of Systems,
Communication, and Information

Mode of Inquiry	Axiomatic	Scientific	Praxiological
Criteria for Accepting Knowledge as Valid	consistency	consistency predictivity	consistency predictivity utility
Dynamic Systems	A set of logical expressions (state descriptions consisting of several symbols) and transformations (imposing an ordering, trajectories, etc.) defined on them so that some expressions imply others including in time.	A set of parts together with the network of communication that ties them into a larger whole. Something exhibiting structure, function, and evolution.	An arrangement of parts that are organized to achieve given objectives as a whole. A complex instrument, a living organism.
Communication	Inability to decompose without loss the transformations of a system so that the trajectories of the whole is the mere aggregate of the trajectories of its parts. logical conditions, dependencies, implications forward in time.	Inability to predict or understand one part of a system without reference to prior behavior of another part of that system. A constraint imposed forward in time and across the parts of a system. Transmission of structure, information flow.	The process of manipulating a portion of the real world towards desired ends. Prescriptive control.
Information	logical constraint on the organization of symbols into expressions always preventing some symbols from co-occuring with others. Logical conditions, dependencies, implications without references to time. A co-occurence grammar	Constraint on the organization of events, symbols, or messages into larger wholes always either resulting from choice among alternatives or imposing a constraint on a set of alternatives. What (and how much) a message is about or what it implies about phenomena other than itself.	Patterns of events, symbols, or messages which are chosen from a larger set to have and indeed do have the effect of constraining, instructing, or changing the receiver towards desired ends. A successful treatment plan, program, or instruction.

These modes of inquiry are distinguished here not only because of their epistemological implications for research, but also because they lead to different conceptionalizations of *system, communication,* and *information,* which are presented in Table 1.

Without an extensive discussion, Table 1 indicates some of the conceptual differences between scholars who couple evidence about communication with the observation of intended effects (*praxiological mode*), and those who equate communication with any effect across individuals, anticipated or not, desirable or not (*scientific mode*). The table also highlights obvious differences between knowledge about systems that are designed and/or used for specific purposes, such as management and/or information systems (*praxiological mode*), those that are naturally grown and whose inherent purposes may well become the subject of an investigation (*scientific mode*), and purely formal symbol systems which are the object of study in mathematics and logic (*axiomatic mode*). While the latter may aid the mapping of reality, the mathematician is not particularly concerned with realism as a criterion for validity.

Knowledge provided by the systems approach is not tied exclusively to any one mode of inquiry. Each has its own set of criteria for validity, and each conceptualizes problems and proposes solutions differently.

Variety, Choice, and Information

Perhaps the most elementary contextualization stems from advances in information theory (Shannon & Weaver, 1949; Bar Hillel, 1952). *Information* is equated with the making of choices. Accordingly, a sender who is forced to transmit some prescribed message without the option of modification cannot communicate anything he may wish to convey, whereas, someone who is able to select a message from a larger repertoire of possible messages may. A message conveys *information* to the extent it is, in fact, and is perceived as the *product of choices.* Indeed many misunderstandings arise not from physical distortions of a message carrier, such as acoustical noise in telephone connections, but from differences in the perception of the sizes of repertoires from which a transmitted message is

FIGURE 1
Information as Constraint on Alternatives

presumed to be chosen. Also, a sender may attempt to convince the receiver that he had little choice but to say what he did, given his convictions and the circumstances of the interaction. The meaning of a message that the receiver then infers is quite different from that of the same message, with concurrent evidence that the sender has exhausted a large number of alternatives, weighing their possible effects.

This interpersonal example may distract from the generality of the notion. Crucial is that this contextualization relieves information of its previously almost *thing-like* denotation, and ties it instead to the *making of choices.* Information is manifest in the constraint imposed on the set of alternatives. And, without references to this context of possible alternatives, the meaning, purpose, function, and even form of any object is considered indeterminable.

Constraints on combinatorial possibilities are also a condition of structure. The equation of information with patterned events that are invariant throughout transmission (Deutsch, 1963), and definitions of communication as the transmission of structure between systems that are differentiated in time and in space (Krippendorff, 1969), are consistent with this contextualization.

This contextualization extends to the very notion of cybernetics as a discipline concerned with communication and control in all systems, existing and imaginable. A cybernetician is interested in the development, growth, and evolution of one, rather than the possibly large variety, of conceivable systems excluded by choices made.

Besides the elaborate calculus to which this notion of information has given birth (Shannon & Weaver, 1949; McGill, 1954; Garner, 1962; Ashby, 1969; Krippendorff, 1975c), variety and choice, fundamental to the systems approach to communication, also impinge on such fundamental issues as freedom, uncertainty, rationality, and intelligence.

Process, Homeostasis, and Morphogenesis

Most textbooks on communication theory and research, starting with Berlo's (1960), refer to communication as a *process*. But formal theory and research undertaken rarely consider communication that way. For example, the use of the experimental paradigm to establish whether a change in attitude is the result of the presence, absence, or kind of message received, clearly involves the measurement of some change, and *communication* is reduced to a cause, independent variable, or a stimulus. Similarly, when an attempt is made to establish which variables account for successful influence, such as in propaganda studies or in evaluations of psychological treatment, one could argue that it is the sender-receiver relationship that is subject of prediction here, but the process aspect is entirely omitted from such considerations. From a systems perspective, data generated under these conditions neither provide insights into the web of interconnections nor into the complex dynamics that are so characteristic of the fabric of social organization and society (Krippendorff, 1970).

The notion of *process* connotes a continuity of change, a somewhat orderly transformation of a system's states. A systems perspective favors consideration of many states and their succession over a longer time span, not a single transition from one kind of attitude to another, nor random alteration of some system's state. Processes have neither a beginning nor an end (except for the practical limitations of their observability).

The process of communication requires, in addi-

tion, that the changes in the states of some part of the system be neither state-determined nor solely a function of time, but dependent on changes in some other part of that system. The simplest (in the sense of being deterministic and defined in continuous variables) example of a formal system with n parts is the system of differential equations:

$$\frac{dx_1}{dt} = a_1 + b_{11}x_1 + b_{12}x_2 + \ldots + b_{1n}x_n$$

$$\frac{dx_2}{dt} = a_2 + b_{21}x_2 + b_{22}x_2 + \ldots + b_{2n}x_n$$

$$\frac{dx_n}{dt} = a_n + b_{n1}x_2 + b_{n2}x_2 + \ldots + b_{nn}x_n$$

Here, nonzero coefficients b_{ji} account for communication form i to j and the analysis of communication within such a system reduces to the problem of measuring this effect.

More general, and yet totally consistent with the above, is the equation of communication with the observer's inability to predict or understand the behavior of one part of a system without reference to another. This inability might also be experienced in terms of a constraint (in the sense of limiting the freedom of movement), imposed forward in time and across different parts of a system, or in terms of the transmission of structure or patterns across parts of a system that differ in space and in time (see Table 1). Such notions provide the basis of formal tests applicable to data, without presupposing such notions as "mind," "intentionally," or the "symbolic characteristics" of messages.

Processes, whether they involve communication or not, make a system either converge toward a smaller set of states—where behavior either oscillates or remains constant—or move it onward, perhaps with accellerating speed, to new states, until the system changes structurally, breaks into pieces, or finds a new trajectory. These are the two fundamental behavioral consequences for dynamic systems as wholes. An example of the former is the engine of a car which, under conditions of constant energy supply and workload, will come to rest at a calculable number of revolutions. An example of the latter is an arms race between two nations.

Notwithstanding the good intentions of either party, their policies may just be such as to lead to an accelerating arms development and production, until a war is inevitable, whereupon both parties change their behavior. Systems that converge toward a dynamic or stable equilibrium and stay there despite disturbances from the environment are said to be *homeostatic systems,* while systems that "run away" in the sense described above are termed *morphogenetic systems*—at least for the period in which they exhibit this behavior. Most living biological organisms attempt to hold a variety of variables constant, and are thus, basically homeostatic. Bertalanffy termed the capacity of such systems to use different ways to reach the same final condition *equifinality.* While many aspects of social organizations are *homeostatic* too, they usually contain morphogenetic features, as well. Morphogenesis is the motor of innovation, of structural change, and, in particular, of the self-modification of communication networks.

If one now looks at the communication pattern underlying such behavior, one finds that some form of circular flow of information within the system is a necessary prerequisite for either result. Homeostasis is achieved when the parts of a system that are connected through this circular flow are such that an increase in some variable is met by compensatory actions, so that the joint effect is *deviation reducing.* Morphogenesis is achieved when the parts stimulate each other by responding to a deviation with more deviation, so that the joint effect is *deviation amplifying.* Because of the fundamental role of circular information flows, cybernetics has regarded communication that feeds on itself as its basic unit for analyzing control processes.

Communication patterns underlying a system's behavior can offer more powerful explanations than the mere description of and extrapolation from observed behavioral sequences, for they shed light on the possible behaviors (observed or not) a system is capable of. Communication patterns, where they can be described as processes linking the parts of a system, hold the key to structural-functional accounts of dynamic systems (Churchman, 1968). And, assuming these patterns are fixed, they can be used to predict the behavior of organizations in changing environments.

Algorithms and Information Processing

An *algorithm* is a stepwise instruction that specifies a process which transforms data. For example, a good computer program contains all instructions needed for the computer to do its job, from reading data to printing transforms. It is an algorithm that is also representative of the process to be executed, and may thus be regarded as a *theory of that process.* In computer programing, writing a program precedes the computation, whereas in communication research, the behavior of a social system precedes the formulation of a theory to account for it. But the relation between program and computation, and between a system theory and social behavior, are the same. If a systems theory is basically consistent and complete and formulated as a procedure, it can be used to simulate the process it purportedly represents.

Analogies between the human brain and electronic computers, mediated through the notion of algorithm, have yielded a systems paradigm for analysis, experimentation and theorizing that has become known as *information processing.* It rests on the proposition that much of human cognitive behavior is fed not by quantities of matter and energy, but by *information* in the sense discussed above. Wheras the stimulus-response paradigm postulates mere associative links between incoming stimuli and internally triggered responses—and leaves the individual little if any freedom—the information processing approach considers cognition as a computational process that involves possibly large quantities of information stemming from past experiences, including fictional accounts, future projections, values, and purposes. It considers information to be organized hierarchically. Processes by which this information is transformed are regarded as recursive, so that the emission of information need not reflect any input at all.

From the point of view of this paradigm, the human individual is viewed as an information processor, paralleling the action of a cell on a social organization. Social organizations develop procedures for handling information internally: sorting, coding, selective transmission, storing, deciding on and executing instructions to its executive organs, consulting social memories—explicitly, in the form

FIGURE 2
An Information Processing Model of Man

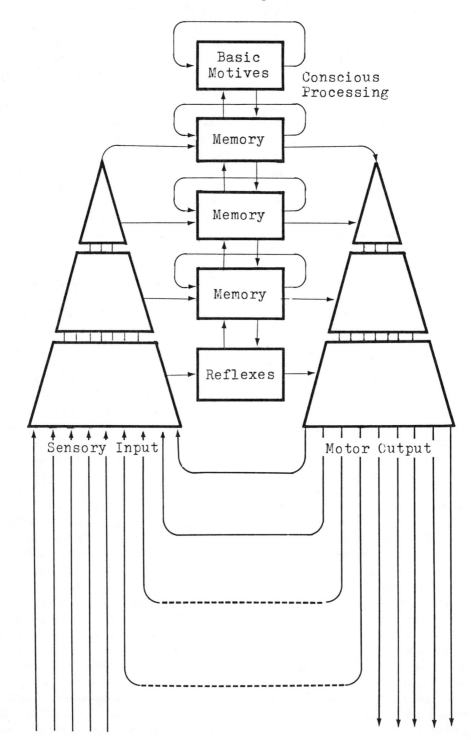

of libraries and files, and implicitly in the form of net attitudes, etc. (Krippendorff, 1975b). Despite the great differences in complexity, capacity and accessability, information processors share several components which can in turn be used in the analysis of existing systems. Figure 2 depicts such a schematic of man as an information processor.

On the incoming side, there are the receptor organs which passively survey or actively monitor portions of an organization's environment. As information is passed on to the interior, it is successively coded into a language internal to the organization and selectively reduced in quantity. This process, which is typical of all system boundaries, is sometimes called selective and reductive coding or filtering. The memory of an organization is not conceived of as a single mammoth filing system. There may be central memories, but memories may also be distributed over the parts of a complex organization. There are short-term, low-capacity memories and long-term, large-capacity memories. Information stored in them is not instantly available when needed. Rather, it must be searched for and retrieved before it can be utilized, using the communication network that links these memories. Information in memory is also subject to natural decay when not used. To maintain such information, it must be revived and upgraded by suitable procedures. In almost all living social organizations, one finds a variety of autonomous transformations that are applied on the contents of a memory, regardless of information input. Some simplify through organization. Others remove or isolate inconsistencies that may emerge, all of which induce interactions among items of information stored. A memory may thus have a life of its own and may be as important to the behavior of an organization as the information from the environment introduced into memory (Boulding, 1956). Incoming information is always mapped into the context of stored information and becomes subject to the time and quantitative constraints of search, retrieval, and processing. On the motor side, we find the inverse of a filtering process in which a small amount of instruction is routinely detailed to govern the organization's actions which impinge on its environment and ultimately modify the information it receives in return.

The information processing approach has found major support in early applications of information theory to estimate quantitative limits on an organization's ability to handle information (Miller, 1960, 1962) and to develop strategies to cope with information overload problems (Miller, 1964; Platt & Miller 1969) and resultant communication stress (Meier, 1972). It has also stimulated inquiries into perception as coding processes (Miller, 1956), and behavior as a communication process (Campbell, 1958), and is the foundation of research relating the structure of cognition to the individual's environment (Schroder, Driver, & Streufert, 1967). Recent inquiries also focus on the structure of individual memories: *spatial, algebraic, network,* and *lexicographic list structure conceptions of information storage.*

Networks and Organization

Traditionally, communication researchers have sought to explain the binary communication relation between individuals in terms of extraneous or noncommunication, variables. The idea is expressed most clearly by Westley and MacLean (1957) who depict a large number of variables in a sender's environment affecting what is in fact transmitted to a receiver, and a large number of variables in the receivers environment—which may include the sender—affecting how a message will be interpreted upon receipt. Much research has been devoted to study how these "independent variables" affect "who says what to whom and with what effects" as a "dependent variable." The list of predictor variables—*personality variables, situational variables, message variables, perception variables*—increases steadily. However, even the attempt to describe the receiver statistically—as in mass media audience and marketing research—or the view of the sender not as an individual but as an institution, has not changed the basic paradigm of communication as a binary, unsymmetrical, and often static relation that needs to be explained in terms of a possibly large number of contextual variables.

Perhaps the first extension of the communication paradigm to networks could be seen in the so called *two-step flow model of communication* (Katz, 1957), which admits that a mass media audience is neither homogeneous and passive, nor directly accessable by the media. Rather, the audience consists of a group of highly attentive opinion leaders who relay information from the media through interpersonal channels to the larger public (indirect audience). While these opinion leaders tend to possess certain personality characteristics—being cosmopolitan in orientation—their role is largely explained in their ability to establish interaction between two kinds of communication networks: electronic and interpersonal. Here, then, one communication process (and its effects) are explained in terms of other communication processes (and their effects), which are joined by a class of individuals into one large communication network.

It is now realized that much of what a contemporary individual knows about the world comes to him in the form of vicarious experiences, in the form of messages from other sources and, most importantly, through networks of communication not necessarily under his control. Networks have an influence of their own by selectively blocking or distorting particular message contents and correcting the transmission errors of others, by routing messages to particular modes which individuals occupy, by assigning priorities to the transmission and handling of messages, by modifications that occur in response to disturbances and new situations. Indeed, what an individual is, and how he understands himself relative to his environment, is in significant ways determined not by the variables impinging upon him, but by the *node* he occupies in particular communication *nets*.

Communication networks are also the backbone of any social organization. Formal structure, as depicted in a hierarchical organization chart, is rarely observed in fact. It is polluted by informal communication patterns and other goal-oriented information flows. The study of communication networks presents an approach to large social systems in operation, just as it has made major contributions in neurology, semantic nets, transportation, planning, telecommunication, and other areas.

Kleinrock (1964) explains that a communication network consists essentially of the following:

1. *Nodes:* Communication centers that receive, store, process and emit messages.

2. *Links:* Communication channels between modes that may be one-way or two-way, require time, and process certain transmission characteristics (noise, redundancy, equivocation, etc.).
3. *Network:* A finite collection of pairs of nodes connected to each other by links.
4. *Messages:* Carriers of information that are specified by their origin, origination time, length, priority class and destination.
5. *Routing procedures:* Decision rules which are exercised when a message is passed from one node to another.

These create a *traffic matrix* of the number of messages sent between any two *nodes* that allows one to compute a variety of characteristics which are of interest to different people: the user, the individual occupying a *node*, the designer or manager of a *network*.

The *user* might be interested in: (1) the time involved for a message to reach its distinction or for the answer to be returned to him; (2) the costs involved in using the net for messages of a certain length, priority class or destination; and (3) the capacity of the network.

The *individual* at a node might be interested in: (1) the routing procedures applicable; (2) the way priorities are assigned and recognized; (3) the storage capacities available at the node; (4) the volume of messages to be processed; and (5) costs and benefits and satisfaction derived from occupying the *node*.

The manager or designer of a *net* might be concerned with all of the above plus: (1) the channel capacities of each link; (2) the topological structures of the nets in which cliques, isolates, liasons bottlenecks, redundancy, etc. may be identified; and (3) the total cost of maintenance, operation and change of the network.

Inquiries into communication networks have taken quite different turns, depending on the richness of available data. At least since the early fifties, several investigators (Jacobson & Seashore, 1951) used sociometric questions to query subjects about their communication with others, and thereby opened the door to the application of sociometric methods of analysis networks, chiefly in the identification of cliques, isolates, and liaison persons in

FIGURE 3
Typical Networks

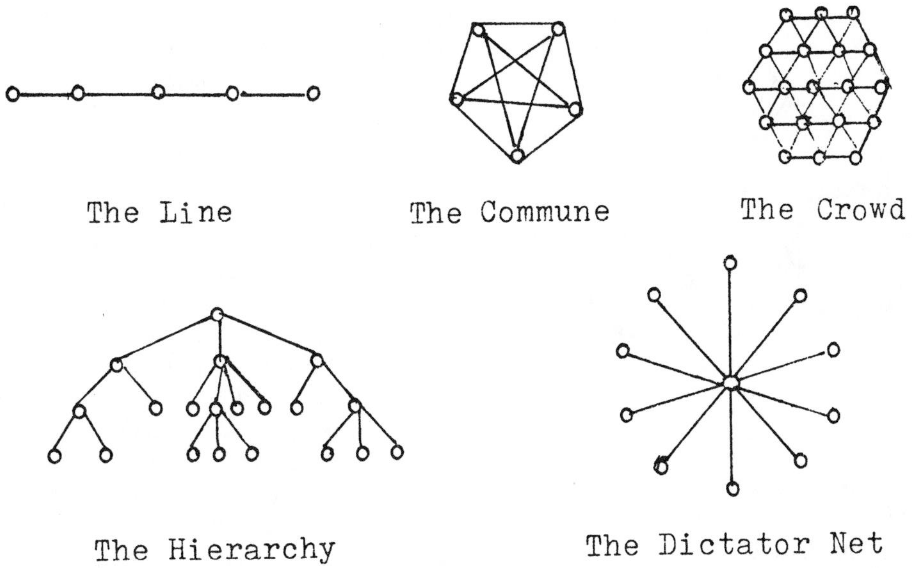

The Line

The Commune

The Crowd

The Hierarchy

The Dictator Net

social organizations. Suspecting the significance of communication pattern in small human groups, Bavelas (1950), Leavitt (1951), Shaw (1954, 1964), and many others conducted a variety of experiments with small groups which differed in task assignment and network topology. And to correlate network variables with individual performance and satisfaction measures, nodes were characterized by a variety of indices, such as centrality. Unfortunately, the number of individuals involved in such experiments never went much beyond five. However, one of the chief findings has been that the topology of communication networks does have a profound effect on the behavior of the group as a whole, that individual work satisfaction depends on the position of the *node* within a *net*, and that while individuals in more central positions are likely to achieve leadership status, such individuals are also subject to increasing pressures and information overload. Kleinrock (1964), on the other hand, was much less concerned with the individuals involved rather than with the dynamic properties of the network as a whole. He simulated information flows within such networks to establish theoretical propositions regarding *delay times, que lengths*, and

bottlenecks for various network topologies and channel characteristics. Network analysis methods applicable to communication within large social organizations have been developed and applied primarily at Michigan State University (Monge & Lindzey, 1973; Richards, 1975).

The most important advancement offered by the notion of communication networks, and by recent progress in analyzing such networks, is that communication is seen as a constituent part of a larger system of interactive links which provide mutual sources of explanation. Dependent and independent variables then become interchangeable. Extraneous variations are not discarded, but they are merely replaced by the informationally richer structural concept of *information flow* that, in fact, constitutes many of these variables. Some typical networks are illustrated in Figure 3.

Systems Decomposition and Analysis

Decomposition refers to a process of breaking up a system into a network of separately describable parts. *Composition* refers to a process of building up a system from known parts. Systems approaches

FIGURE 4
Communication Within and Across Subsystems

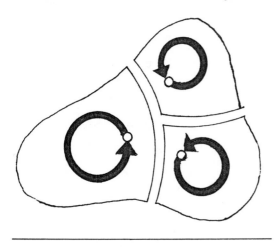

---

consider the processes of *decomposition* and processes of *composition* to be the inverse of one another. What confounds the distinction somewhat is the fact that decomposition is more common to scientific inquiries into systems, whereas composition is the basis for practical systems development and design.

In the above, the notion of decomposition was already implied by equating *communication* with the inability to understand or to predict the behavior of one part of a system without reference to another. Accordingly, when communication is evident, separate descriptions of the parts' behavior do not *add up to* how these parts behave in conjunction. There is a difference between what these parts do in isolation and what they do together, so that something would be lost if one were to describe a system by its parts alone. The idea of *decomposition* is given quantitative expressions in information theory where the *information transmitted, T,* between *parts A, B, C, . . .* is the difference between the *entropies, H,* they exhibit when observed without reference to others and the *entropy* of all parts together:

$$T(A{:}B{:}C...) = H(A) + H(B)$$
$$+ H(C) + ... - H(ABC...)$$

Depending on which data are analyzed, this difference can be given many names including: *structure, organization, interdependence,* and, of course, *communication* (Ashby, 1956).

Decomposition in this sense probably is the most important analytical concept of the systems approach. It transcends two heretofore antithetical scientific traditions, Atomism and Gestaltism, with the concept of communication as the synthetical bridge. *Atomism* postulates that all knowledge is reducable to the knowledge of parts, of parts of parts, etc., down to the smallest elements— atoms. Understanding the parts means understanding the whole. *Gestaltism* postulates the opposite, that a whole must be comprehended as a whole. Any attempt to disect it—to analyze it into separate parts—will make the whole unrecognizeable, and destroy its "essence." In reference to the above equation of information theory, if the difference is zero, then communication, and/or structure, is absent, the whole can be regarded as made up of separately describable parts, and atomism is justified. The difference thus expresses the degree to which interconnections are to be taken seriously, or how much is actually lost if parts are taken as separately describable.

The most obvious task of communication research into large systems is to segment a whole system, composed of many interrelated parts, into subsystems so that communication between them is relatively weak but communication within them is relatively strong, as depicted in Figure 4.

Another task, typical of both interpersonal and organizational communication research, is to decompose the rich flow of information between systems into relatively independent channels, each of which has its own properties, and across which dependencies are negligible or more easily accountable for than within, as suggested in Figure 5.

Decomposition is also the basis for the development of grammar—the segmentation of a flow of messages into units (words, sentences, movements, gestures) plus their interdependencies (configurations, syntax, and semantics).

The development of methods for decomposition and analysis is still in its infancy. As such, it is also not restricted to communication research. An interesting application in an entirely different domain is the attempt to develop methods for decomposing a complex architectual problem into subproblems so as to make the interconnections between these subproblems transparent (Alexander, 1964). The method attempts to bridge the gap between a purely aggregated approach to architecture and one that capitulates in the face of overwhelming problem complexity.

Logical Typing, Epistemic Constraints, and Systems Hierarchies

The tools of another important aspect of systems approaches to communication are found in Bateson (1942, 1972) and Ruesch and Bateson's (1951) work which applies cybernetics to certain problems in psychiatry and interpersonal communication. The results, summarized by Watzlawick, Beavin and Jackson (1967) focus on the simultaneous typing of symbolic communication processes. "For instance, the messages 'It is important to release the clutch gradually and smoothly' and 'Just let the clutch go; it'll ruin the transmission in no time' have approximately the same information content (report aspect), but they obviously define very different relationships" (command aspect), Watzlawick et al. 1967, p. 52). Interpersonal messages convey meanings on at least two logically distinct levels simultaneously: What is said, or the content, the message, and how the speaker sees himself related to the listener. In information processing terms, it is the latter that specifies how the former is to be interpreted. To distinguish communication from communication about communication, the latter is called *meta-communication*.

This work points to several general characteristics of social systems, and especially to the systemic nature of knowledge and symbolic communication in society.

First, information exchanged among individuals consists not only of information about events outside the communication situation but also of *meta-information* about the interpersonal relationships, *meta-meta-information* about the situation in which they meet and in the context of which the interpersonal relationship is significant, *meta-meta-meta-information* about the social organization in which the situation arises . . . up to the highest level epistemic constraints imposed by the ideological paradigms of a society to which all levels are subservient.

FIGURE 5
Independent Channels

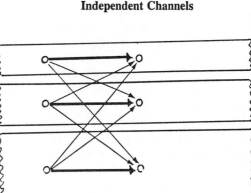

Time

Second, at any point in time, individuals may be aware of only very few logical levels involved (consider where the infinite regression starts to become incomprehensible: *I know you; I know you know me; I know you know I know you; I know you know I know you know me . . .*). Logically higher levels in the double sense of being on the meta-level and involving more arguments, more individuals, and so on, are taken for granted and are often fixed and shared during ongoing communication processes. However, implicit compliance with higher level understandings must be reaffirmed continuously, and it is carried by the medium of communication as well. When Shannon computed language to be 50% redundant, this may well stem from the systemic constraints that social knowledge imposes.

Thirdly, while the process of translating individually held knowledge into interactions and social communication is not fully understood, it is probably analogous to the way plans (computer programs) are related to the behavior (transformation of data) they control (Miller, Galanter, & Pribram, 1960).

These epistemic constraints would seem to function by linking individuals into larger operating structures without the physical wiring common to almost all mechanical and electrical systems. They are the aim of socialization and the basis for social control. Messages in transition carry these constraints and can provide the data for their analysis. Kuhn's (1970) *paradigm* is just one example of describing information processing behavior—here scientific inquiry—as controlled by a system of epistemological assumptions that their users are barely, if at all, aware of. *Ideological superstructure* is the Marxian term for describing analogous phenomena. *Paradigmatology* is Maruyama's (1974) term to denote the systematic study of patterns of knowledge in relation to cross-disciplinary, cross-professional, and cross-cultural communication. What Watzlawick et al. (1967) have initiated is the development of a variety of analytical concepts for the epistemic analysis of *communication as system-creating constraints* across individuals.

The recognition of such epistemic constraints—hierarchies of plans that are omni-present in each communication—is nothing but an informational way of analyzing the role of communication at different levels of organization. Rooted in biology, level differentiations have been mentioned above (Boulding, 1956; Gerard, 1957; Miller, 1965). Attempts to integrate knowledge across different levels are found in Lawson (1975), the relation between biological and linguistic organization; Schroder, Driver, and Streufert (1967), the relation between cognitive structure and the structure of individuals' environment; Kuhn (1963), the relation between human individuals and social organization; and, specifically related to communication, Fisher (1975), the relation between communication among individuals and social systems; Ruben (1975), the relation between intrapersonal, interpersonal, and mass communication; and others. From a systems perspective, the key to such notions is the concept of a wholon as unit of analysis (Koestler, 1967), referred to previously, which conceives a *system* as both embedded in a suprasystem of which it is a part, and through which it is constrained, and composed of constituent subsystems that have their own identity, but are subject to constraints through their (multiple) membership (on different levels of a systems hierarchy).

Systems Technology, Functionalism, and Design

Systems approaches are also often considered a tool, particularly in systems engineering, management, and other disciplines that pursue primarily practical ends. In such disciplines, systems theory becomes a methodology for decision making in the planning, implementation, and maintenance of complex technologies involving human operators.

Communication technology, which ranges from transportation networks—the telephone system and the mass media—to the most complex information processing installations is a particularly fruitful object of this kind of systems thinking because it is—unlike traditional power engineering—a *linking technology.* It mediates between different individuals (without necessarily bringing them close to each other on a human level), coordinates their activities (without necessary directing them towards common goals), and knits them into larger operating wholes they themselves rarely understand.

Three systems approaches to communication technology can be distinguished: *technological determinism, functionalism,* and *systems design.* These share the same conception of systems methodology, but may be said to make quite different assumptions regarding practical pursuits. Whether these assumptions are valid depends on a particular technology—its state of development, its social significance, its comprehendability to a planner-designer—and the means available to control or synthesize it.

Technological determinism essentially assumes that communication technology has developmental laws and a life of its own and should be studied as a semi-autonomous organism. Many convincing facts speak in favor of technological determinism. Communication technology has a structure in the sense of literally wiring large numbers of components into complex wholes. Consider, for example, the telephone system with its numerous stations near its boundaries, complex switching, routing and connecting devices, and huge social institutions set up to support that structure. It has a function in the sense that it exhibits a behavior vis-a-vis its environment of customers, and satisfies their needs just as much as the customers satisfy the needs of the system. And it evolves and grows by linking more and more customers into fewer and bigger institutions, by extending its control over competing networks, suppliers, and material resources, and by creating new services. While everyone draws satisfaction from the ideological belief that "it is, after all, people who decide to have telephones installed," nobody has ever advocated abolishing a technology. The evolution of communication technology (as an organism) is based on the fact that it *has created its own needs*, and this seems true not only for the telephone but also for the mass media (radio, television, and the recording industry), and the growing number of data services and computer installations. Other than investigations of the growth and decline of communication technology (Campbell & Mickelson, 1975; Miller, 1965), the assumption of technological determinism restricts studies of the social context of these technologies to how individual users adapt to their development and growth, and the effects they have—individually and collectively—on an essentially passive society.

Functionalism is predicated on the assumption that individual or collective actions—all ongoing social processes, including technology—fulfill (or ought to fulfill) some vital function of society as a whole. In contrast to dysfunctions and nonfunctions, "*functions* are those observed consequences which make for the adaptation or adjustment of a given system" (Merton, 1949). There is no agreement as to what the primary functions or the functional prerequisites of society are. Parson's adaptation, goal attainment, pattern maintenance and integration functions (Parsons & Smelser, 1957) is only one proposal. It is taken for granted, however, that while certain functions are indispensable for the persistence of a society, the mechanisms fulfilling these functions are somewhat variable.

While the claims that society is organized directively are doubtful in their implied generality, where it can be maintained, functionalism provides the logical basis for two approaches to systems analysis.

The first consists of the large class of performance optimization techniques that stem principally from operations research and are aimed at improving the efficiency of operation of communication technology. The use of these techniques require clear criteria (consistent with the assumed directionality of society) and leave the principal structure unaltered.

The second stems from the notion of the *substitutability of mechanisms* that fulfill the same function. So, one can argue that literacy emerged because of its greater efficiency over the exclusive reliance on the spoken word. And, one can study the extent to which telecommunication systems (computer networking, teleconferencing, automated offices) substitute for transportation networks (Hannemann, 1974) or one can evaluate alternative technologies regarding their capabilities to serve a *given* function.

Both functionalist approaches share the rationalist assumption that the directionality of society from which evaluative criteria are derivable is known and the conservative assumption that change or substitution occurs within given structures only. Functionalism is therefore intrinsically committed to maintaining the status quo, has the effect of inducing slow incremental changes, and is unable to recognize or control morphogenesis (structural change).

Systems design, at least in its modern version (Beer, 1959, 1966; Churchman, 1968; Ackoff & Emery, 1972), recognizes that social systems may be much too large, both in number of components and in complexity of structure, to be assembled according to a plan that is worked out in advance. Designers of a defense system, of a welfare system, even of a computer network, just do not possess the information-processing capacity for specifying all details necessary for the whole to work (Ashby, 1972). In addition, such systems are often part of a turbulent environment (Emery & Trist, 1969) that cannot become fully known, making it thus impossible to anticipate all contingencies with which the system may have to cope in the future.

System design usually starts out by recognizing a continued social need, such as the need of a community for access to a particular kind of information—for example, about its own members and activities—or the need for communication among independent research and development organizations. A prerequisite of communication systems design is, therefore, an understanding not only of the present information need, but also what creates this need and how it is modified—its internal dynamic. While a functionalist perspective would suggest that such problems be solved by evaluating available technology which may satisfy those needs most efficiently (e.g., closed circuit or cable television for the community and a central information retrieval network for the R & D organizations), a systems design perspective would suggest the need to install (1) the nucleus of an organization embedded into a fertile environment, with (2) sufficient resources to choose among alternatives, with (3) sufficient communication with (and barriers against disturbances from) its stake-holders, i.e., individuals and social organizations whose need may be satisfied and whose behavior may be constraint as a consequence, and (4) an incentive structure that rewards the organization as it approaches its given ideals and thereby directs its growth. Finally, when the organization has overcome its ''critical mass'' (5) the contact with the designer is severed and the organization is left to grow (or die) by itself.

Systems design, as outlined here, avoids the trap of functionalism by taking the functions or needs not as indispensable or given but as modifiable, not as the ultimate authorian ruler but as co-evolving in interaction between learning individuals and growing socio-technical organizational structures. It therefore does not work toward the structural status quo (making existing mechanisms merely more efficient), but instead introduces an element of uncertainty into social development that we experience anyway.

INFORMATION SYSTEMS RESEARCH

In line with the views and perspectives of this overview, research underway within the Information Systems Division of the International Communication Association has turned from a focus on computers and communication technologies to a broader systems approach for the study of human communication.

In Monge's (1975) words:

> Systems theory provides a theoretical structure for organizing knowledge about human communication. The knowledge structure it generates would be organized around—at least in part—the following concepts: information, the symbolic patterning of matter and/or energy; networks, the channels through which information flows and the limitations imposed upon message processing by channel characteristics; memory, the storage, manipulation and retrieval of information; boundary processes, the interface between communication systems at the same or different levels and the

seeking, avoiding, and filtering of information; control, feedback processes and the use of information to manipulate and influence other systems or subsystems or components within the communication system. Furthermore, each of these elements would be viewed as a part of the communication process whenever it might occur and whatever level it might occur on. For example, knowledge about communication networks would be generated which would be applicable to neural processing, small group processes, organizational networks, and networks which exist in the larger society. Additionally, since the knowledge is to be organized to represent an ongoing dynamic system, the emphasis would be placed upon discovering both morphostatic and morphogenetic characteristics, i.e., its homeostatic and its evolutionary dimensions.

The result is a focus on two kinds of systems: (1) large systems whose components are linked through communication, mediated by sociotechnological organizations or by more conventional communication media—whether the components of the system consist of individuals, machines or social institutions; and (2) systems whose components are signs, symbols, and all varieties of information-bearing elements that are linked with each other through relations of reference, co-occurance, or semantic association. The first kind of system poses major problems of description and analysis of the dynamics of large communication networks. The second kind of system poses problems of understanding *meaning*, information storage, and information processing.

Within the framework of these broad sets of questions, research in the Information Systems Division has been concentrated on systems methodology, systems conceptions in communication research, the study of large and small social networks, research in information processing, and information economics.

SUMMARY

Systems approach expands the study of communication complexity by overcoming the traditional *sender-receiver* concept of message exchange focusing attention on communication *process, networks, mutual causality,* and *hierarchy.* Further, the approach de-emphasizes the traditional single-valued conceptions of *symbols, referents,* and *content* by stressing the knowledge structures in the context of which messages obtain specific meanings.

NOTES

1. A version of this chapter will appear in the forthcoming book *Viestinnan Virtauksia (The Flows of Communication)* by Eija Erholm and Leif Aberg (Eds.). Helsinki: Otava Oy.
2. Portions of *Nonsystems Approaches* section are reprinted from Krippendorff (1975a) pp. 148-152.

REFERENCES

ACKOFF, R.L., & EMERY, F.E. *On purposeful systems.* London: Travistock, 1972.

ALEXANDER, C. *Notes on the synthesis of form.* Cambridge, Mass.: Harvard University Press, 1964.

ASHBY, W.R. General system theory as a new discipline, *General Systems*, 3:1-6, 1958.

ASHBY, W.R. General theory as a new discipline, General Systems, 3:1-6, 1958.

ASHBY, W.R. *Design for a brain*, 2nd ed. London: Chapman & Hall, 1960.

ASHBY, W.R. Two tables of identities governing information flows within large systems. *American Society of Cybernetics Communications*, 1969, 1, 3-8.

ASHBY, W. R. Setting goals in cybernetics systems. In H.W. Robinson and D.E. Knight (Eds.), *Cybernetics, artificial intelligence, and ecology.* New York: Spartan, 1972.

BAR HILLEL, Y. Semantic information and its measures. In H. von Forester (Ed.), *Transactions of the tenth conference on cybernetics.* New York: Josiah Macy Jr. Foundation, 1952.

BERTALANFFY, L. von. *General system theory.* New York: Braziller, 1968.

BOULDING, K.E. *The image.* Ann Arbor: University of Michigan Press, 1956.

BOULDING, K.E. *Beyond economics.* Ann Arbor: University of Michigan Press, 1968.

BUCKLEY, W. (Ed.) *Modern Systems Research for the Behavioral Scientist.* Chicago: Aldine, 1968.

BATESON, G. Social planning and the concept of "deutero-learning" in relation to the democratic way of life. In *Science, philosophy and religion, second symposium.* New York: Harper, 1942.

BATESON, G. Cybernetic explanation. *American Behavioral Scientist*, 1967, 10, 8, 29-32.

BATESON, G. *Steps towards an ecology of mind.* New York: Ballantine, 1972.

BAVELAS, A. Communication patterns in task-oriented groups. *Journal of the Acoustical Society of America*, 1950, 22, 727-730.

BEER, S. *Cybernetics and management.* London: English University Press, 1959.

BEER, S. *Decision and control.* New York: Wiley, 1966.

BERLO, D.K. *The process of communication.* New York: Holt, Rinehart, and Winston, 1960.

CAMPBELL, D.T. Systematic error on the part of human links in communication systems. *Information and control.* 1, 334-369, 1958.

CAMPBELL, J.H., & MICKELSON, J.S. Organic communication systems: Speculations on the study, birth, life and death of communication systems. In B.D. Ruben and J.Y. Kim (Eds.), *General systems theory and human communication.* Rochelle Park, N.J.: Hayden, 1975.

CHURCHMAN, C.W. *The systems approach.* New York: Delacorte, 1968.

DEMERATH, N.J., & PETERSON, R.A. (Eds.) *System, change, and conflict.* New York: Free Press, 1967.

DEUTSCH, K.W. *The nerves of government.* New York: Free Press, 1963.

EMERY, F.E., & TRIST, E.L. The causal texture of organizational environments: In F.E. Emery, (Ed.), *Systems thinking.* Harmondsworth, England: Penguin, 1969.

FISHER, B.A. Communication study in system perspective: In B.D. Ruben and J.M. Kim (Eds.), *General systems theory and human communication.* Rochelle Park, N.J.: Hayden, 1975.

GARNER, W.R. *Uncertainty and structure as psychological concepts.* New York: Wiley, 1962.

GERARD, R.W. *Units and concepts in biology. Science*, 1957, 125, 429-433.

GRINKER, R.R. *Toward a unified theory of behavior.* New York: Basic Books, 1956.

HANNEMAN, G.J. Communication substitutes for transportation: The Movement of information versus the movement of people. Unpublished Manuscript. Los Angeles, Calif.: University of Southern California, 1974.

HANNEMAN, G.J., & McEWEN, W.J. (Eds.) *Communication and behavior.* Reading, Mass.: Addison Wesley, 1975.

JACOBSON, E., & SEASHORE, S. Communication patterns in complex organizations. *Journal of social issues*, 1951, 7, 28-40.

KATZ, D., & KAHN, R.L. *The social psychology of organizations.* New York: Wiley, 1966.

KATZ, E. The two-step flow of communication: An up-to-date report on an hypothesis. *Public Opinion Quarterly*, 1957, 21, 61-78.

KLEINRODE, L. *Communication nets.* New York: Doren, 1964.

KLIR, G.J. On the relation between cybernetics and general systems theory: In J. Rose (Ed.), *Progress of cybernetics,* Vol. I. New York: Gordon and Breach, 1970.

KOESTLER, A. *The ghost in the machine.* New York: MacMillan, 1967.

KOTARBINSKI, T. *Praxiology.* New York: Pergamon, 1965.

KRIPPENDORFF, K. Values, modes and domains of inquiry into communication. *Journal of Communication*, 1969, 19, 105-133.

KRIPPENDORFF, K. On generating data in communication research. *Journal of Communication*, 1970, 20, 241-269.

KRIPPENDORFF, K. The systems approach in communication. In B.D. Ruben and J.Y. Kim (Eds.), *General systems theory and human communication.* Rochelle Park, N.J.: Hayden, 1975a.

KRIPPENDORFF, K. Some principles of information storage and retrieval in society. General Systems, 1975b, 20, 15-35.

KRIPPENDORFF, K. Information Theory. In G.J. Hanneman and McEwen, W.J. (Eds.), *Communication and behavior.* Reading, Mass.: Addison-Wesley, 1975c.

KRIPPENDORFF, K. A spectral analysis of relations. Unpublished manuscript. Philadelphia: University of Pennsylvania, 1976.

KUHN, A. *The study of society: A unified approach*. Homewood, Ill.: Irwin, 1963.

KUHN, T.S. *The structure of scientific revolutions* (2nd ed.). Chicago: University of Chicago Press, 1970.

LASSWELL, H.D. The structure and function of communication in society. In W. Schramm, (Ed.), *Mass communications*. Urbana: University of Illinois Press, 1960.

LASZLO, E. *System, structure, and experience*. New York: Gordon and Breach, 1969.

LAWSON, C.A. Biological organization. In B.D. Ruben and J.Y. Kim, (Eds.), *General systems theory and human communication*. Rochelle Park, N.J. Hayden, 1975.

LEAVITT, H.J. Some effects of certain communication patterns or group performance. *Journal of Abnormal and Social Psychology*, 1951, 46, 38-50.

LERNER, D. Communication systems and social systems. In W. Schramm, (Ed.), *Mass communications*. Urbana: University of Illinois Press, 1960.

MARUYAMA, M. The second cybernetics: Deviation-amplifying mutual causal processes. *American Scientist*, 1963, 51, 164-179.

MARUYAMA, M. Morphogenesis and morphostasis. *Methodos: Language and Cybernetics*, 1969, 12, 48.

MARUYAMA, M. Paradigmatology and its application to cross-disciplinary, cross-professional, and cross-cultural communication. *Cybernetica*, 1974, 2, 136-156; 4, 237-281.

McCULLOCH, W.A., & PITTS, W. A logical calculus of the ideas immanent in nervous activity. *Bulletin of Mathematical Biophysics*, 1945, 5, 115-133.

McCULLOCH, W.A. *Embodiments of mind*. Cambridge, Mass: MIT Press, 1956.

McGILL, W.J. Multivariate information transmission. *Psychometrica*, 1954, 19, 97-116.

MEIER, R.L. Communication stress. Unpublished Manuscript. Berkeley: University of California, 1972.

MERTON, R.K. *Social theory and social structure*. Glencoe, Ill.: Free Press, 1949.

MILLER, G.A. The magical number seven, plus or minus two: Some limits on our capacity for processing information. *Psychological Review*, 1956, 63, 2, 81-97.

MILLER. G.A., GALANTER, E., & PRIBRAM, K.H. *Plans and the structure of behavior*. New York: Holt, 1960.

MILLER, J.G. Information input overload and psychopathology. *American Journal of Psychiatry*, 1960, 116, 695-704.

MILLER, J.G. Information input overloads. In M.C. Yovitz, G.T. Jacobi and G.D. Goldstein (Eds.), *Self-organizing systems* 1962. Washington, D.C.: Spartan Books, 1962.

MILLER, J.G. Adjusting to overloads of information: In D.M. Rioch and E.A. Weinstein (Eds.), *Disorders of communication*. Baltimore: Williams and Wilkins, 1964.

MILLER, J.G. Living systems: Basic concepts; structure and process; Cross-level hypotheses. *Behavioral Science*, 1965, 10, 337-411.

MONGE, P.R., & LINDSEY, G. Communication patterns in large organizations. Unpublished Manuscript. San Jose, Calif.: San Jose State University, 1973.

MONGE, P.R. Alternative theoretical bases for the study of human communication: The systems perspective. Unpublished Manuscript. San Jose, Calif.: San Jose State University, 1975.

PARSONS, T. *The social system*. New York: Free Press, 1957.

PARSONS, T. & SMELSER, N.J. *Economy and society*. New York: Free Press, 1959.

PIAGET, J. *Structuralism*. New York: Harper & Row, 1968.

PLATT, J., & MILLER, J.G. Handling information overload. *Ekistics*, 1969, 28, 169, 295-296.

POWERS, W.T. *Behavior: The control of perception*. Chicago: Aldine, 1973.

RAPOPORT, A. Mathematical aspects of general systems theory. *General Systems*, 1966, 11, 3-11.

RAPOPORT, A. Modern systems theory: An outlook for coping with change. *General Systems*, 1970, 15, 15-25.

RICHARDS, W.D. *A manual for network analysis* (Using the *negopy* network analysis program) Unpublished manuscript. Stanford, Calif.: Stanford University, 1975.

RUBEN, B.D. General system theory: An approach to human communication. In R.W. Budd and B.D. Ruben (Eds.), *Approaches to Human Communication*. Rochelle Park, N.J.: Sparten-Hayden, 1972.

RUBEN, B.D., & KIM, J.Y. Human communication and systems theory: Provocations. Paper presented at the annual meeting of the Northeast Division of the Society for General Systems Research. New York: City University of New York, 1973.

RUBEN, B.D. Intrapersonal, interpersonal, and mass communication processes in individual and multi-person systems. In B.D. Ruben and J.Y. Kim (Eds.). *General systems theory and human communication*. Rochelle Park, N.J.: Hayden. 1975a.

RUBEN, B.D., & KIM, J.Y. (Eds.) *General systems theory and human communication*. Rochelle Park, N.J.: Hayden, 1975b.

RUESCH, J., & BATESON, G. *Communication: The social matrix of psychiatry*. New York: Norton, 1951.

ROGERS, L.E., & FARACE, R.V. Analysis of relational communication in dyads: New measurement procedures. *Human Communication Research*, 1975, 1, 222-239.

SCHRODER, H.M., DRIVER, M.J., & STREUFERT, S. *Human information processing*. New York: Holt, Rinehart and Winston, 1967.

SHANNON, C.E., & WEAVER, W. *The mathematical theory of communication*. Urbana: University of Illinois Press, 1949.

SHAW, M.E. Some effects of unequal distribution of information upon group performance in various communication nets. *Journal of Abnormal and Social Psychology*, 1954, 49, 547-553.

SHAW, M.E. Communication networks. In L. Berkowitz, (Ed.), *Advances in experimental psychology*. New York: Academic Press, 1964.

SIMON, H.A. *The sciences of the artificial*. Cambridge, Mass.: MIT Press, 1969.

SMITH, A.G. (Ed.) *Communication and culture*. New York: Holt, Rinehart & Winston, 1966.

THAYER, L. *Communication and communication systems*. Homewood, Ill.: Irwin, 1968a.

THAYER, L. Communication: *Sine qua non* of the behavioral sciences. In Arm, D.L. (Ed.), *Vistas in science*. Albuquerque: University of New Mexico Press, 1968b.

VICKERS, C. *Value systems and social process*. New York: Basic Books, 1959.

WATZLAWICK, P., BEAVIN, J., & JACKSON, D.D. *Pragmatics of human communication*. New York: Norton, 1967.

WESTLEY, B.H., & MacLEAN, M.S. JR. A conceptual model for communication research. *Journalism Quarterly*, 1957, 34, 31-38.

WIENER, N. *The human use of human beings*. Garden City, N.Y.: Doubleday, 1954.

WIENER, N. *Cybernetics*. Cambridge: MIT Press, 1961.

YOUNG, O.R. A survey of general systems theory. *General Systems*, 1964, 9, 61-80.

GENERALITY AND NECESSITY IN THREE TYPES OF HUMAN COMMUNICATION THEORY — SPECIAL ATTENTION TO RULES THEORY[1]

D. P. CUSHMAN
Michigan State University

W. BARNETT PEARCE
University of Massachusetts

A review of the philosophy of science literature suggests that any viable theory must meet the criteria of *generality,* that is, that the regularities described are pervasive within a definable domain rather than idiosyncratic, and of *necessity,* that is, that the theoretic statements specify relationships which obtain because of the operation of some definable force rather than occur capriciously. Three types of theories which have been applied to communication—those based on laws, systems, and rules—are analyzed by these criteria. All three are shown to be acceptably general, but to differ significantly in the manner in which they achieve necessity. Laws theories assume *nomic* necessity; systems theories assume *logical* necessity; and rules theories assume the necessity of *practical force*. The theoretic and epistemic requirements of rules theories are discussed, citing the use of "generative mechanisms" as the basis for generality and a measurement procedure for assessing practical force. The practical syllogism is suggested as the model for explanation, with several logics required depending on the amount of practical force in particular situations.

Revolutions occur periodically in the development of scientific theories which reveal new perspectives for inquiry, transform the meaning and measurement of terms, and permutate the procedures for developing rigorous and fruitful theories. Three such revolutions have given rise to the laws, systems, and rules perspectives for constructing human communication theories. While each of these perspectives generates different questions for inquiry, employs alternative principles of explanation, prediction, and control, and advocates diverse criteria of proof, the perspectives hold in common the requirement that all acceptable theories *must employ premises which are both general and necessary*. Regardless of context, content or structure, a set of propositions does not constitute a theory unless it refers to phenomena which are general, rather than particular, and unless it describes relations which are necessary, rather than accidental.

However, the way each perspective meets the criteria of generality and necessity differs substantially, depending largely on its respective assumptions about the nature of the relevant subject-matter and about the nature of knowledge. While no theory of human communication achieves—or is likely to achieve—absolute generality and necessity, it is highly instructive to compare the various perspectives in terms of the manner and extent to which they approximate these ends.

Of the three perspectives, rules theory is, in its present form, the most recently developed, least adequately articulated, least tied to commonly accepted standards of structure, and least buttressed by a set of powerful research procedures. For some time now, we have been trying to develop rules theories (Cushman & Whiting, 1972; Pearce, 1973; Cushman & Florence, 1974; Pearce, 1976a; Cushman & Craig, 1976). This paper attempts to extend the criteria of generality and necessity to the rules perspective, in order to establish criteria for the rigorous development of rules theories. More specifically it will be the purpose of this essay to: (1) provide an explication of the concepts of generality and necessity; (2) explore the application of these two criteria to the laws, systems, and rules perspective; and (3) provide a programmatic approach which researchers within the rules perspective might take in meeting these criteria.

GENERALITY AND NECESSITY

To be accepted as a theory, a set of propositions must refer to a *sufficiently general* category of relationships. While it is easy to identify propositions which are too specific, such as a description of one rock's motion after falling off a table, and those which are general enough, such as a description of the properties of falling bodies, it is difficult to specify what "sufficiently" means. To some extent, the metaphysical and epistemic assumptions of a theorist, as well as the specification of the subject-matter to which the theory applies, determine how general is enough. Two tests of generality are suggested by Achinstein (1971, pp. 25-38): the first, *syntactical* generality, refers to the form of the propositions in the theory. The theory is general, to the extent that the propositions are expressible as sentences in which the universal *all* or *none* is followed by a subject, copula and object. If the propositions have to be qualified, the theory is shown to be less than absolutely general. The second, *domain* generality refers to the range of phenomena covered by the theory, and can be assessed by examining the extent to which the propositions are limited by initial conditions: "All A's are B's" under conditions 1, 2, 3 . . . etc. The degree of generality is restricted by the number and type of initial conditions which must be met for the relationships in the theory to hold. Taken collectively, syntactical and domain tests define the level of generality at which a given theory is cast.

The second defining characteristic of a theory is necessity. The phenomena accounted for by a theory must possess some knowable characteristic which makes the occurrence of regularities expected and interpretable. But the "knowable characteristic" varies widely in theories of different phenomena, which make different epistemic and metaphysical assumptions. Three types of necessity may be identified, each of which has a different type of force.

Nomic necessity depends on locating a causal relationship between two classes of objects. This type of necessity carries deterministic force, and can be felt in the difference between the mere generalization "All A's are B's" and the necessary statement "All A's have to be B's." The former

asserts that it happens to be the case that all A's are also B's; the latter claims that it is necessary, nature being as it is, that all A's will be B's. Nomic necessity represents the element of must or inevitability. The force of *nomic necessity* rests on the power of a set of observable, antecedent conditions to yield deterministically observable consequences regardless of time or space (Rescher, 1973).

Logical necessity depends on definitional force, and applies to systems of relationships defined as internally consistent. If, for example, the mathematical relations among all possible pairs of six elements have been defined, and a calculus exists such that any change in any of the elements has a necessary and specifiable effect on all of the others, then that system of elements has logical necessity. The power of logical necessity depends on the observer's commitment to maintain the logic of the system as defined. The force of *logical necessity* rests on the power of a set of conceivable propositions to entail a conceivable conclusion, given the rules of consistency yielded by a logical calculus (Deutsher, 1976).

Practical necessity depends on the type and amount of normative force an actor feels to perform (or not perform) a given activity in a specified way. Normative forces exert pressure on actors to select certain goals, and the appropriate means for achieving the specified goal. Normative pressures may be exerted on an actor by a culture, an organization, a group, or by the actor's own set of values. The force of *practical necessity* rests on the power of an actor to respond to normative pressures in selecting goals, and the means for achieving them (Von Wright, 1971).

THE APPLICATION OF GENERALITY AND NECESSITY TO THE LAWS, SYSTEMS, AND RULES PERSPECTIVES

While the syntactical and domain tests of generality function in a common manner for evaluating theories constructed in the laws, systems, or rules perspectives, the concept of necessity varies in accordance with the epistemological and metaphysical assumptions of a given perspective. In accordance with their epistomological and metaphysical assumptions, the laws perspective is based on nomic necessity, systems on logical necessity and rules on practical necessity.

The Laws Perspective

A theory of human communication, according to this perspective, takes the form of a set of (1) universal propositions and (2) initial conditions, "All A's are B's under conditions 1, 2, 3, etc. . . . ." Each proposition in the set is a general statement with nomic force.

The distinguishing metaphysical assumption of this perspective is that there is an underlying deterministic order "behind" observed regularities, which can be accounted for by causal or class-inclusion relations. The appropriate epistemic procedure is to discover the existence of the laws, to verify their existence, and to demonstrate that particular instances are subsumed under sets of related laws. Since the laws are thought to exist independently of the process of observation, the *context of discovery* is considered relatively unimportant, while the *context of verification* is subjected to meticulous scrutiny, and rigorous procedures are required.

Benign neglect of discovery procedures and equivocation in the use of the term "law" — it denotes both propositions and the facts which those propositions describe — mask conceptual diversity within the laws approach. There are at least two conceptualizations of the relationship between law-propositions and law-facts. The *logical positivists'* position views law-propositions simply as the articulation of regularities in nature (Hemple, 1965). The phenomena described by a law are to be logically independent, and the relationship among them is to be based on observed occurrences. The proposition "All A's are B's" contains the implicit statements that it is possible to observe both A's and B's, they have been observed, and every A that has been observed was also a B.

The second conceptualization of the laws perspective, *natural necessity,* views laws as descriptions of the effects of "powerful particulars" (Madden & Harre, 1973). In this view, entities exist which have powers to act in describable ways. Such descriptions constitute a set of law-propositions, or theory, about the entity. Explanation, prediction, and control are achieved by demonstrating that a given "generative mechanism," by its nature, has the power to create certain regularities. For example, a magnet may be viewed as a generative mechanism which has the power to create certain regularities in the space around it. The properties of a magnetic field can be "marked" by bringing the magnet close to a pile of iron filings. The pattern of iron filings "marks" the regularities created by the power of the generative mechanism. These regularities flow from the nature of the mechanism, the nature of a magnet. This procedure generates laws which take the form "All A's are B's, by virtue of the power of a generative mechanism, A."

Although both concepts of laws are adequately general to create theory, neither is absolutely general. Positivistic laws are limited in domain to the relationships and initial conditions of previously observed events, with the syntactical qualifier "All A's which have been observed so far . . ." Natural necessity laws are limited to the domain in which a generative mechanism exerts its power, presuming that no two generative mechanisms with competing powers occupy the same domain. Further, the natural necessity position is caught in a conceptual regress involving the "nature" of the generative mechanism which has specified "powers" (Harre, 1973), making a specification of domain problematic.

Both laws approaches assert nomic necessity, based on the assumption that a network of deterministic relations exists among variables. Although there continue to be attempts to develop a laws theory of human communication (Woelfel, 1972), the number of staunch advocates of this approach has been steadily declining. Social scientists have simply been unable to discover laws which have generality and necessity comparable to those in the natural sciences.

The Systems Perspective

A theory of human communication according to this perspective is composed of: (1) a set of elements, (2) a set of propositions expressing the relationship between all the elements; and (3) a calculus for manipulating or drawing implications from the system. The set of relationships among the elements must meet certain initial conditions to qualify as a system. They must consist of a collation of elements which has the properties of nonsummativity, wholeness, and equifinality. The relationships among the components take the form of a set of propositions which are general statements with logical force. Traditionally, one of three sets of logics or calculi are viewed as governing a system. First, we may assume that it operates as a *state-determined system* such that one can deduce almost exactly the next state of the system from the last state of the system. Second, we may assume that it operates as a *Markov System,* such that one can say that if the system is in a certain state now, it will go to one of several possible states next, and determine the relative probability of it going to each of these other states. Third, we may assume that it operates as a *self-organizing system,* where the system alters its nature from moment to moment, so that a matrix which is correct for describing its behavior at one moment is inadequate at the next (Moray, 1963).

The systems perspective is based on the metaphysical assumption that the nature of an entity changes as a function of the system of which it is a part. Specifically, systems theorists feel that single relationships are poor objects of study. The theorist must account for the logical system of which that relationship is a part. Opinions differ among systems theorists regarding the ontological status of systems logics. One group views such logics as existing in nature and possessing nomic necessity, while the other group views them as the arbitrary constructions of man and evaluate their logical force in terms of utility. In the first group are the General Systems theorists who argue that the systems approach provides a speculative philosophy (Bertalanffy, 1959). This group argues that the investigation of systems will reveal regularities of organization which can serve as interdisciplinary laws capable of unifying the diverse areas of human knowledge. This viewpoint was articulated by Ludwig von Bertalanffy when he called for:

> . . . a hypothetic deductive system of those principles which follow from the definition of system and by the introduction of more or less special conditions. In this sense, systems theory is *a priori* and independent of its interpretation in terms of empirical phenomena, but is applicable to all empirical realms concerned with sys-

tems. Its position is similar to that, for example, of probability theory, which is in itself a formal mathematical doctrine but which can be applied, by way of empirical interpretation of its terms, to different fields, from games to thermodynamics, to biological and medical experimentation, to genetics, to life insurance statistics. And so on. (1959)

The search for a general systems theory has proceeded along two complementary paths: (1) the attempt to identify general phenomena which are common to many different disciplines and to model such phenomena, and (2) the attempt to model basic units of behavior in different fields and develop a hierarchy among the various systems based on differences in complexity of organization. The epistemic program of the general systems theorists is comparable to that of the laws theorists (Boulding, 1956).

In the second group are the somewhat less ambitious efforts by systems modelers utilizing logic, mathematics, statistics, and computer modeling techniques to investigate the organization and behavior of various conceptual systems' (Meehan, 1968). Systems modelers balk at the assumption that systems possess ontological validity, arguing instead that systems are created by an observer, and serve as useful models for reality. They do research by exploring the effects of simulations within the system or by determining the goodness of fit—isomorphism—between the model and the "real world." System modeling leads to an epistemic program of analoging, or proposing and testing models for conceivable rather than merely observable systems.

The generality of systems theories can be variously assessed. Many general systems theorists claim considerable generality in their insistence that the structure of reality is systemic. A somewhat more qualified claim is made by those who assert that systemic properties (wholeness, equifinality, etc.) are common to a wide range of phenomena. A very limited claim is made by those who envision systems simply as constructs modeling particular groups of phenomena. The latter claim seems so specific as to jeopardize the status of theory; the first has substantial problems in developing adequate empirical support.

The structure of systems theory entails logical necessity. The description of a system comprises a definitional statement of the relations among its components, and with the relations defined and a known logical operator, a change somewhere in the system will have calculable effects throughout. For those specific effects not to occur is logically impossible. If those effects are not paralleled in a set of phenomena which the system purportedly represents, it could be concluded that the system was a poor model or the definition of the system should be changed, but once a system is defined, even complex behaviors of the system follow by the force of tautology.

Systems theory provides a rigorous and flexible method of discovery and verification in science, yet has produced relatively little significant research or theory-construction in communication. The low productiveness of this approach may be attributed to the vagueness of the concept of a system (Tashdjin, 1974, said that "system is just a 'synonym for relatedness' ") and to the limitation of necessity in systems theory to logical, rather than some form of empirically-relevant force (Meehan, 1968). The heuristic and explanatory value of systems concepts has repeatedly been demonstrated (Watzlawick, Beavin, & Jackson, 1967; Hague, 1974), but there are more staunch advocates of the systems perspective than producers of theory or research.

The Rules Perspective

The development of a rules theory has been impeded by the ambiguity of the concept "rule," and by the need to devise appropriate methods of research and theory construction, at least some of which may differ from conventional practice. As a result, the rules perspective is the least "paradigmatic" (Kuhn, 1970) of the three major perspectives, and the presentation of it here is fully as much a construction and extension, as it is a summary.

A theory of human communication, according to this perspective, takes the form of a practical syllogism. An individual, or group, A intends to bring about C; A considers that in order to bring about C he must do B; and therefore A sets himself to do B (Von Wright, 1971). There is considerable disagreement among rules theorists as to whether the practical syllogism is governed by nomic, logical, or practical necessity. Recent research on communication behaviors between the genes involved in controlling biological traits attributes nomic necessity to the force of normative rules (Rensberger, 1976). The epistemic program for generating a theory of genetic rules was outlined in our discussion of the laws perspective. In linguistics, research by Chomsky and his associates on the communicative behavior involved in a generative grammar attributes logical necessity to the force of normative rules (Sanders & Martin, 1975). The epistemic program for generating such a theory of grammatical rules was discussed in our consideration of the systems perspective. Finally, research on communication between individuals involved in coordinated behaviors, aimed at achieving some goal, attributes practical necessity to the force of normative rules (Cushman, 1976; Pearce, 1976b).

The viability of a rules theory, based on practical necessity, depends on a series of metaphysical assumptions. First, it is assumed that human behavior can be divided into two classes of activity: those which are stimulus-response activities and governed by nomic necessity, and those which are purposive and choice-oriented responses and governed by practical necessity. The former behaviors are habitual and may be termed *movements,* while the latter are evaluative and may be termed *actions.* Rules theorists argue that there exists a realm of human action in which persons have some degree of choice among alternatives, critique their performance, exercise self-monitoring capacities, and act in response to practical or normative forces (Toulmin, 1969; Von Wright, 1971). Unlike the positivists, for example, rules theorists assume that the same explanatory structure cannot be applied to all forms of phenomena, committing them to both metaphysical and epistemic pluralism (Pearce, 1976).

Second, rules theorists argue that there exist two classes of human actions—those which require communication for the individual to choose among alternatives, critique his performance, and exercise his self-monitoring capacity in response to practical force, and those which do not require communication. The former are termed *coordination situations* and function to regulate consensus among individuals in regard to a common task, while the latter are termed *information processing situations* and function to regulate human perception and thought in regard to some task (Lewis, 1974). Communication rules theorists thus argue that: (1) there exists a class of human action which involves conjoint, combined, and associated behavior; (2) the transfer of symbolic information facilitates such behavior; (3) the transfer of symbolic information requires the interaction of sources, messages, and receivers guided and governed by communication rules; and (4) the communication rules form general and specific patterns which provide the basis for the explanation, prediction, and control of communication behavior (Cushman & Whiting, 1972). The *function* of human communication in this context is to regulate consensus in order to coordinate human behavior. The *structure* of human communication is the code and network rules involved in regulating consensus. The *process* of human communication is the adaptation of the rules involved in regulating consensus to the task at hand (Cushman & Craig, 1976).

Third, rules theorists in a coordination framework argue that the basic unit of analysis for communication research is a standardized usage (Cappella, 1972). More specifically they suggest:

> . . . that there exist systems of rule governed symbol meaning associations which are relatively persistent because the participants engaged in some task have found the system particularly useful for coordinating their activities in regard to that task. (Cushman & Whiting, 1972)

Such a system of code and network rules is termed a standardized usage. For example, General Motors has such a standardized usage for the production of cars. Each employee is socialized into a common system of code and network rule sequences so that individuals can coordinate their behavior to produce cars. Within such a system of communication rule sequences, there will exist individual sequences of communication behaviors which are termed *episodes*. Episodes consist of communicators' interpretation of the actual sequence of messages they jointly produce (Pearce, 1976b). These episodes are aimed at facilitating coordination in regard to some task and carry differential practical force, depending on their contribution to the coordination process. Such episodic sequences of communication behavior are the basis for theories of communication behaviors in a rules context. They will take the form of a practical syllogism which contains some degree of practical force. For example, if you work for General Motors and assemble cars, there is a specific sequence of communication rules, or episodes, involved in ordering automobile parts, which you are obligated to follow if you want the parts. The explanatory model is this: A intends to bring about C; A knows that if he is to get C he must undertake communication sequence B; A sets himself to do B.

The epistemic program consistent with these assumptions involves locating the task which is the generative mechanism for a standardized usage, describing the episodic sequences which constitute the standardized usage, and assessing their generality and practical force. Such an approach assumes the existence of an underlying normative order "behind" the observed regularities of human action which is modeled by the practical syllogism. Traditionally normative sequences of rules exert one of four types of practical force: obligation, prohibition, permission, or normative indifference (Von Wright, 1968).

Although the concept of a rules theory of communication as a coordination situation, modeled by the practical syllogism and grounded in practical necessity, is adequately general to create theory, it is not absolutely general. Communication theory is restricted to the subclass of human behavior termed action. It is further limited to the subclass of action involving coordination. Even within this set, adequate theory can only be developed regarding those relationships which are obligatory, prohibited, or permitted by some set of communication rules.

While the number of studies undertaken which claim to fall within a rules perspective has been increasing, most remain atheoretical. Two reasons exist for the atheoretic nature of most rules research. First, the concept rule can be used in a variety of ways (causal, logical, practical), and only recently have we become aware of the theoretic implications of its many meanings. This awareness has led researchers to begin to untangle its many theoretic usages (Toulmin, 1974). Second, in many cases the investigation of rules, within a practical necessity framework, required the modification or development of new methods of theory construction (Von Wright, 1971). Both of these problems have only recently been resolved in such a manner as to allow programatic research to develop.

Summary

In concluding our rather extended analysis of the laws, systems, and rules perspective, it will be useful to restate in its most general form the thrust of our analysis. We have argued that the defining characteristic of all research which is to have scientific theoretical significance is the establishment of propositions which are both general and necessary. We have suggested two criteria of generality, a *syntactical criterion of universal class-inclusion* (e.g., "All A's are B's") and a *domain criterion of limiting conditions* which allows the researcher to preserve syntactical generality (e.g., "All A's are B's under conditions 1, 2, 3, etc."). We have argued that while the criterial of generality apply equally well to our three theoretic perspectives, this is not the case with the necessity criterion. The concept of necessity varies with the types of epistemological and metaphysical assumptions a researcher is willing to make. Three types of necessity were discussed and tied to the fundamental assumptions of their respective theoretical perspectives. Necessity is achieved by researchers in the laws perspective by locating causal relationships with nomic necessity, in the systems perspective by locating systems calculi which have logical necessity, and in the rules perspective by locating tasks which generate standardized usages and episodes with practical necessity.

A PROGRAMATIC APPROACH FOR DEVELOPING RULES THEORIES

If research which is to have theoretic import in the rules perspective must locate tasks which generate standardized usages and episodic sequences with practical force, then a programatic approach for developing rules theories must be guided by the answers to several rather specific questions. First, what types of tasks generate standardized usages? Second, how can one locate and measure the generality and necessity of episodic sequences? Third, what form will rules theories take in order to indicate different levels of generality and types of necessity?

We begin by asking what types of tasks generate standardized usages, because it is a task which requires coordination through communication, and which gives generality and necessity to a given communication sequence. A given communication episode takes on quite different levels of generality and types of practical necessity when employed in the same manner for different tasks. For example, when one employs a communication episode to express his or her preference for president, it takes on quite different levels of generality and necessity when one's task is casting a ballot for president, talking with one's family, or answering questions in a political poll. The first instance would have the force of an obligatory sequence, the second a permissable sequence, and the last would have no practical necessity at all. This suggests that, unless we begin by locating the task which acts as the generative mechanism for a standardized usage and episodic sequence, we will be unable to determine a given communication sequence's theoretic value, its generality, and necessity. Any task that requires the coordination of individual behaviors through communication is a potential source of communication regularities for a rules theory.

Second, we need to consider how we might locate and measure standardized usages and episodic structures, and determine how they manifest generality and practical force. When a coordination task has been located, it can be turned into a communication variable by quantifying the number of points at which communication is required, prohibited, or permitted in order to coordinate human activity. Tasks can then be quantified as more or less difficult, depending on the number of points of coordination required to complete a task. Each point where coordination is required is a potential source of obligatory episodic sequences.

An important feature of the epistemic program of the rules theorist is that rules sequences are measured from the actor's, not the theorist's, point of view (Fisher, 1974; Pearce, 1976b). One method for measuring the generality and normative force of rules sequences has been developed by Jackson (1975) in his research on normative power. Jackson taps two dimensions in his attempt to measure normative power. The first dimension he terms *crystalization,* and it refers to the *perceived commonality of expectations* held by others for an actor to perform a given sequence of behavior in a given situation. The greater the commonality of perceived expectations, the greater the crystalization. The greater the diversity of expectations, the less likely a given sequence will be performed. The second dimension he terms *intensity,* and it refers to the *perceived consequences* which will follow from performing or not performing a given sequence of behavior. If we view crystalization as a measure of generality, and intensity as a measure of practical force, then we can examine episodic sequences which are obligatory, prohibited, permissible, and normatively neutral, and characterize their generality accordingly. Their generality will range from high—a common set of expectations regarding an episodic sequence as obligatory, prohibitive, permissible or neutral—to low—a diverse set of expectations regarding an episodic sequence. The practical force of such sequences will range from high—a significant set of consequences which will ensue from an obligatory, prohibitive, permissible or neutral sequence—to low, where the consequences of performing the action sequence are meaningless. Jackson's measurement system allows us to turn the generality and necessity of episodic sequences into measurable variables with theoretic import.

Finally, we must discuss the various structures which rules theories will take, given differential levels of generality and practical necessity. Let us begin our inquiry by applying our previous analysis to the modal structure for rules theories, the practical syllogism.

> A intends to bring about C.
> A considers that in order to bring about C he must do B.
> Therefore A sets himself to do B.

The major premise indicates the goal, the minor premise the episodic sequence's contribution to achieving the goal, and the conclusion specifies that the action is triggered. The practical force of the syllogism rests on the strength of intention or the consequences which follow from achieving the goal. The generality of the syllogism is tied to the commonality of expectations regarding the major and minor premises.

The simplest type of coordination situation is one in which an episodic sequence of behavior involving two persons is necessary and sufficient to yield the desired goal.

> A intends to bring about C.
> A knows that *in order to bring about* C he must engage in episode B.
> A engages in episode B.

A's belief, which is expressed in the minor premise, is based on his knowledge of and assumption that the relevant other person shares a set of rules in regard to a given task.

A second type of coordination situation is one in which an episodic sequence of behavior involving two persons is necessary, but not sufficient, to yield the desired goal.

> A intends to bring about C.
> A knows that *without* episode B, C will not occur.
> A engaged in episode B.

A's belief which is expressed in the minor premise, depends on both the value of C for A, and the degree of probability he associates with the other necessary conditions being performed.

A third type of coordination situation is one in which an episodic sequence of behaviors involving two persons involves multiple sufficient conditions.

> A intends to bring about C.
> A knows that C will occur if he and the other person engage in episodes B, or C, or D . . .
> A believes the other person will do B.
> A engages in episode B.

The amount of practical force in this context depends on the value of X for A, and on the strength of his belief that the other person will do B.

Each of these syllogisms may carry the generality and practical force of obligation, prohibition, and permission.

CONCLUSION

Our task has been to indicate those procedures which *must* be followed if research is to have theoretic import in a rules perspective. We have argued that such research must locate tasks which require coordination, because such tasks serve as the generative mechanisms for communication rules which take the form of standardized usages and episodic sequences. Next, a researcher must define and measure the generality and necessity of the standardized usage and its various episodic sequences. Finally, we outlined three forms which the practical syllogism may take in modeling the generality and necessity of episodic sequences. Each of these is a necessary condition for rules research to have theoretic import. Collectively they represent the sufficient condition for such an outcome.

In conclusion, using generality and necessity as the criteria for any viable theory, we have examined laws, systems, and rules approaches to theory. Because it is least paradigmatic, we have been most closely concerned with rules theory.

The following conclusions seem warranted. None of these approaches achieves absolute generality or necessity, but all of them have the potential for achieving adequate generality and demonstrating some form of necessity. The metaphysical and epistemic assumptions of each approach importantly affect the manner in which each theory achieves generality and necessity. Specifically, each stipulates a different domain of relevant phenomena, and each employs a different type of necessity.

On the basis of these characteristics, the choice of which approach is the most useful for understanding a particular phenomenon, such as human communication, hinges on assumptive rather than formal grounds. To the extent that communication is best described by the assumptions of rules theory, then theorists must utilize the form required by those assumptions, even though it may be less elegant than a laws or systems theory. This paper has focused only on the formal characteristics of theories and has shown that a rules theory is viable, given its potential for achieving generality and necessity comparable to laws and systems theories.

NOTE

1. This paper was selected as one of the outstanding reports prepared for the annual meeting of the International Communication Association, Berlin, 1977.

REFERENCES

ACHINSTEIN, P. *Concepts of science*. Baltimore: Johns Hopkins Press, 1968.

ACHINSTEIN, P. *Laws and explanation*, Oxford: University Press, 1971.

BERTALANFFY, L. V. Problems of general systems theory. *Human Biology*, 1952, 205.

BOULDING K. General systems theory—Skeleton of science. *General Systems Yearbook 1*, 1956, 11-18.

CAPPELLA, J. N. The functional prerequisites of intentional communication systems. *Philosophy and Rhetoric*, 1972, 231-274.

CUSHMAN, D. P., & WHITING, G. C. An approach to communication theory: Towards consensus on rules. *Journal of Communication*, 1972, 22, 217-238.

CUSHMAN, D. P., & FLORENCE, B. T. The development of interpersonal communication theory. *Today's Speech*, 1974, 22, 11-15.

CUSHMAN, D. P., & CRAIG, R. T. Communication system: Interpersonal implications. In G. Miller (Ed.), *Explorations in Interpersonal Communication*, Beverly Hills: Russell Sage, 1976.

DEUTSHER, M. Conceptual connection and causal relations. *Australasian Journal of Philosophy*, 1976, 54, 3-13.

FISHER, J. Knowledge of rules. *Review of Metaphysics*, 1974, 28, 237-260.

HAGE, J. *Communication and organization control*. New York: John Wiley, 1974.

HARRE, R. Surrogates for necessity. *Mind*, 1973, 42, 358-381.

HARRE, R., & MADDEN, E. Natural powers and powerful natures. *Philosophy*, 1973, 209-230.

HARRE, R., & MADDEN E. H. *Causal powers*. Rowland and Littlefield, 1975.

HEMPEL, C. G. *Aspects of scientific explanation and other essays in the philosophy of science*. New York: The Free Press, 1965. Also see R. Ackermann, Deductive scientific explanation. *Philosophy of Science*, 32, 1965.

KUHN, A. The logic of social systems. San Francisco: Jossey-Bass, 1974.

KUHN, T. S. *The structure of scientific revolutions*. Chicago: University of Chicago Press, 1962.

LEWIS, D. K. *Convention: A philosophical study*. Cambridge, Mass.: Harvard University Press, 1974.

MEEHAN, E. J. *Explanation in social science: A systems paradigm*. Dorsey, 1968.

MORAY, N. Cybernetics. *Twentieth Century Encyclopedia of Catholocism*, New York: Hawthorn, 1963.

PEARCE, W. B. Consensual rules in interpersonal communication: A reply to Cushman and Whiting. *Journal of Communication*, 1973, 23, 160-168.

PEARCE, W. B. The coordinated management of meaning: A rules-based theory of interpersonal communication. In G. Miller (Ed.), *Explorations in Interpersonal Communication*, Beverly Hills, Calif.: Sage, 1976(a).

PEARCE, W. B. *An overview of communication and interpersonal relationships*. Palo Alto: Science Research Association, 1976(b).

PEARCE, W. B., & ROSSITER, C. *Communicating interpersonally*. Indianapolis: Bobbs Merrill, 1975.

RENSBERGER, B. Team at M.I.T., Construct a fully functioning gene, *New York Times*, Aug. 29, 1976, 45.

RESCHER, N. *Conceptual idealism*. Oxford: Basil and Blackwell, 1973.

SANDERS, R., & MARTIN, L. Grammatical rules and explanations of behavior. *Inquiry*, 1975, 18, 75-76.

TASCHDJAN, E. The entropy of complex dynamic systems.

Behavioral Science, 1974, 19, 93-99.

TOULMIN, S. Concepts and the explanation of human behavior. In Theodore Mischel (Ed.), *Human Action,* New York: Academic, 1969, 71-104.

TOULMIN, S. Rules and their relevance for understanding. In Theodore Mischel, (Ed.) *Understanding other persons,* Oxford: University Press, 1974, 185-216.

Von WRIGHT, G. H. Practical inference. *Philosophical Review,* 1963, 22, 159-179.

Von WRIGHT, G. H. The logic of practical discourse. In Raymond Klibinsk (Ed.), *Contemporary philosophy,* New York, 1968, 141-167.

Von WRIGHT, G. H. *Explanation and understanding.* Ithaca, N.Y.: Cornell University Press, 1971.

WATZLAWICK, P., BEAVIN, J., & JACKSON, D. *The pragmatics of human communication,* New York: Norton, 1967.

WOELFEL, J. *A theory of force aggregation in attitude formation and attitude change.* Unpublished manuscript, Department of Communication, Michigan State University, 1972.

THE VALIDATION OF MATHEMATICAL INDICES OF COMMUNICATION STRUCTURE[1]

JANE A. EDWARDS and PETER R. MONGE
San Jose State University

Considering their widespread use and importance in mathematical sociology, mathematical psychology, social anthropology, and organizational communication, amazingly little research attention has been paid to the systematic validation of mathematical indices of social structure. The validation strategies in use remain largely implicit, and generally fail to acknowledge the multidimensionality of structure. This research proposes a new method, designed to avoid these shortcomings, and reports the results of its use in evaluating a set of 11 indices having potential utility in measuring communication structure. Recommendations regarding the use of these indices for particular research purposes are provided, along with suggestions for future research.

The interdependence of theory and observation or measurement practices has often been noted (Woelfel, 1974). By influencing the way the world is perceived, observation or measurement practices obviously influence theory. In turn, theory—even inchoate or implicit theory—dictates what it is considered important to observe or measure.

Because of this interdependence, self-consciousness regarding measurement practices seems essential if sound theoretical statements are to be made. The vast number of pages devoted to social science measurement issues indicates this self-consciousness is generally widespread. However, there are still some specialized subfields in which such scrutiny has been severely lacking. A case in point is *socio-network analysis*, an interdisciplinary research area of which communication *network analysis* is a subtype. Before stating the problem more precisely, several definitions are needed.

BASIC CONCEPTS

A *socio-network*—or, more briefly, *network*—may be defined as the set of relationships of a particular type, such as *communication, friendship, power,* or *kinship,* existing among a group of individuals. In *network analysis*, these relationships may be identified using several distinctly different methods (Davis, 1953; Edwards & Monge, 1976;

Farace, Monge, & Russell, in press). However, the most common methods seem to use the reports of the network members themselves regarding those people with whom they share relationships of the type under study.

These relationships may be coded dichotomously, as being either present or absent, or they may be more precisely quantified in terms of their frequency, intensity, etc. In any case, for networks with more than three members, many different configurations of the relationships comprising a network are theoretically possible. The particular topological configuration which does exist is called that network's *structure*.

Structures are assumed to vary along many different theoretical continua, such as *connectiveness*, called *dimensions*. Since networks are composed of discrete, overt, countable, quantifiable entities—namely, the individual relationships existing between pairs of network members—the dimensions of structure are overtly describable. The mathematical formulae used as operational definitions of structural dimensions are here termed *indices*, and called *metrics* by Richards (1974) and others. An example of one such index is network *density* (Niemeijer, 1973)—termed *connectedness* or *connectiveness* by other writers. It is computed as the percentage of theoretically possible relationships within a group which actually exist.

An index is here considered a *valid* measure of a

particular dimension if its values *systematically* reflect variations in that dimension, either consistently increasing or consistently decreasing with increases in that dimension, that is, if it bears a monotonic relationship with the dimension under study.

Some dimensions—termed *theoretically distinct*—are assumed capable of varying largely independently of one another, and of entering into functional relationships with different nonstructural variables. In this case, an index which covaries closely with (i.e., is a *valid* measure of) variations in one structural dimension may correlate poorly with variations in the other. This implies that index validity can be judged only with respect to a *specific* dimension of structure and not relative to an undifferentiated concept of *structure*. That is, even the validation procedure must recognize the multidimensional nature of social structure.

METHODS OF VALIDATION

Mathematical indices for measuring social structure have been used widely in fields as diverse as social anthropology, mathematical sociology, mathematical psychology, administrative science, and, of course, organizational communication. Yet, to date, amazingly little attention has been paid to their formal validation relative to the dimensions of structure they are employed to measure. The validation strategies seen in the structural literature are largely implicit, and none of them has adequately appreciated the multidimensionality of structure.

Authors subscribing to a *construct* validation strategy have advocated selecting indices on the basis of correlations between those indices and measures of nonstructural variables which are believed to be related to an undifferentiated structural variable. Such an approach may be adequate for strictly pragmatic purposes, such as the selection of a structural index to serve as an indication of work group satisfaction. Its failure to enumerate specific dimensions of structure, however, makes this method seem uniquely unsuited for the more theoretical purpose of elucidating the relationships among structural and nonstructural variables. Additional disadvantages of the method include: (1)

the inherent circularity of all construct validation approaches (Dubin, 1969; James, 1973); (2) the assumption that the subject population used in the validation study is essentially the same as all future populations on which the index is to be used (since correlations between structural and nonstructural variables may change from subject population to subject population); (3) the still embryonic state of theory and the consequent possibility of error in choosing an appropriate nonstructural variable; and (4) the possibility that the operational definition chosen for the nonstructural variable might introduce substantial measurement error and spuriously deflate the correlation coefficient for the structure-to-nonstructure relationship.

Researchers who have used previous *face* or *content* validation approaches have demonstrated a similar disregard for the multidimensionality of structure. While some have assessed index sensitivity to a dimension it is desired to measure—that is, sensitivity to a *target dimension*—most have neglected the equally important question of the degree to which an index's values may at the same time be affected by variations in *nontarget dimensions*. Three different methods of face validation are found in the literature.

In the first face validation method—termed *dimensional specification* by Coleman (1964)—the researcher simply examines the index's computational formula and subjectively judges whether it "makes sense." In addition to this method's subjectivity, the difficulty in conceptualizing simultaneous variations along several dimensions (as would be required by a multidimensional approach) renders this method virtually useless to the validation problem posed here.

In the second method of face validation, the researcher actually *computes* the index for those hypothetical networks which manifest extremely high or low values of the target dimension. While this method is more objective than the previous one, its disregard for the multidimensionality of structure is seen in its assumption that the correlation between an index's values and the amount of a particular structural dimension will not change substantially, regardless of what values are assumed by other, nontarget, dimensions.

Presently, the most rigorous form of face validation in the structural literature is Sabidussi's (1966) method, termed here *mathematical axiomatic deduction*. In using this method, the researcher formally enumerates the mathematical properties a true measure of a particular target dimension would have to possess, and then evaluates indices believed to measure that dimension according to these criterial properties. While this method is rigorous as previously applied, it too has focused primarily on the sensitivity of an index to only one dimension—in this case, *centrality*. This method is potentially expandable to the multidimensional case, but the complexity of axiomatic systems for even one structural dimension make it, too, seem inadequate to resolve the validation problem posed here.

Yet the need for systematic validation is unmistakable. In the absence of adequate validation data, researchers run the risks of both suboptimal use of data and potentially misleading results. Unhappily, examples of each of these may already be found in the literature (Edwards & Monge, 1975). The present paper describes a new type of face validation and reports the results of using it to evaluate 11 indices of communication structure.

METHOD

Related to Nosanchuk's (1963) method of comparing clique-identification procedures, the method used here in some ways resembles Bridgman's (1922) *dimensional analysis*. However, it is called *multidimensional analysis*—not to be confused with *multidimensional scaling*—to emphasize that, unlike previous methods, it evaluates indices with reference to *several* dimensions rather than to only one.

The method involves the construction of sets of imaginary networks to serve as empirical standards. Its application here proceeded in four stages: (1) identification of dimensions which previous researchers have considered it important to measure; (2) construction of sets of networks differing incrementally along these dimensions; (3) selection of indices from among the dimensional categories; and (4) evaluation of each index's val ty with respect to each dimension.

Identification of Dimensions

The literature lacks an explicit list of theoretically distinct dimensions which researchers agree *upon as* important to measure. Yet researchers obviously have theoretical dimensions in mind when they design and use indices. Consequently, a good source of these dimensions would seem to be the careful scrutiny of the indices themselves.

An examination of the most common indices of social structure—static structure only—in social anthropology, mathematical sociology, mathematical psychology, and organizational communication was undertaken to identify recurring measurement intentions of researchers in these disciplines.[2] These indices were found easily classifiable with reference to two dimensions (each having two sub-dimensions): *magnitude* (with subdimensions of *size* and *volume*), and *disparity* (with *concentration* and *diameter*).

The *magnitude* dimension focuses primarily on the number of group members (i.e., network *size*) and the number of relationships among them (network *volume*), and has little concern with the distribution of those relationships within the network. In contrast, the *disparity* dimension focuses on the *distribution* of relationships in terms of either their *concentration*—the degree to which the relationships are concentrated upon one or a few individuals rather than distributed equally to all members—or the network's *diameter*, that is, the length of the shortest chain linking the two most "distant" individuals in the network. As in mathematical topology (Flament, 1963; Harary, Norman, & Cartwright, 1965), the *distance* between two network members is measured as the least number of intermediary network members one would need to contact to pass a message between them.

The reason they are listed as two dimensions with two sub-dimensions each, rather than as four separate dimensions, is that *size* and *volume* (and, likewise, *concentration* and *diameter*) do not seem "theoretically distinct" enough to warrant status as separate dimensions. Future empirical research may reveal important differences between the functional relationships involving *size* and *volume* (and likewise for *concentration* and *diameter*). However, lacking empirical evidence of this kind, it seems

FIGURE 1
Beginning and Intermediate Networks for Each of Nine Families

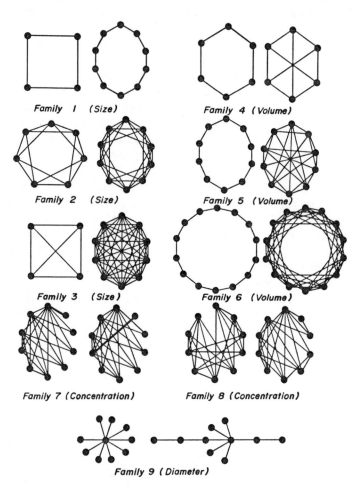

Family 1 (Size)

Family 4 (Volume)

Family 2 (Size)

Family 5 (Volume)

Family 3 (Size)

Family 6 (Volume)

Family 7 (Concentration)

Family 8 (Concentration)

Family 9 (Diameter)

best to minimize the number of separate structural dimensions being postulated.

The treatment of *transitivity* in the present analysis is a further example of this conservatism. Transitivity is the greater tendency for persons *a* and *c* to share a particular type of relationship such as a friendship, communication, etc., with one another if such a relationship also exists between *a* and *b* and between *b* and *c*. Though transitivity seems intuitively to be a more complex theoretical continuum than is *magnitude*, it has been associated with that dimension in the literature. In fact, indices of *balance*—a close relative of transitivity—have occasionally been used to measure network *volume*

(Luce, 1953). Consistent with this literature, transitivity is here treated as a part of the *volume* subdimension. However, results reported here will be shown in the final section to raise doubts about the propriety of this grouping, and to suggest the possibility in the future of examining transitivity as a dimension in its own right.

Construction of Families of Hypothetical Networks

Nine sets, or *families*, of hypothetical networks were constructed to serve as empirical standards representing each of the four subdimensions. In each of these families, a target subdimension was systematically varied from a minimum to a maximum value while the remaining three subdimensions were stabilized at known values. Two examples of each family appear in Figure 1.[3]

The first six families were designed as empirical standards for the *magnitude* dimension, three families for the *size* subdimension, and three families for the *volume* subdimension. In recognition of the intimate relationship between *size* and *volume*, *volume* was stabilized at a different (i.e., *high, medium*, or *low*) value in each of the *size* families, and vice versa for the three *volume* families (in which *size* assumed values of 6, 10, and 14 nodes, respectively). In all six of these families, *concentration* was minimized by assigning an equal number of links to all nodes in a particular network, and *diameter* was minimized through the use of circumscribed configurations rather than open-ended branches (Harary, 1959).

Families 7, 8, and 9 were designed as empirical standards for the *disparity dimension*. Two distinctly different types of *concentration* were used in families 7 and 8. The seventh family was designed to assess the sensitivity of an index to *the positioning of a single link* within the network. For this purpose, a "core" network of ten nodes having 8, 7, 6, 5, 5, 4, 4, 3, 2, and 0 links was created. To the tenth node was attached one end of the movable link. Nine networks were generated by successively attaching the other end of this link to each of the other nodes in the order that they are listed above. Because the indices gave identical readings for the networks in which the receiving nodes originally had the same number of links, one network for each of these two pairs was deleted, leaving a total of seven networks in this family. Throughout this family, *size* was held constant at 10 nodes, and *volume* at 23 links. *Diameter*, though not held totally constant, varied by only one link (from *diameter* = 2 to *diameter* = 3 links), a much smaller variation than exists in the *diameter* family itself.

The eighth family was created to assess the sensitivity of the various indices to *the degree of inequality in the distribution of links* within the network, measured as the variance of the frequency distribution of links received per node. All frequency distributions were symmetric about a midpoint of five links per node. The variances found in this family are: 0.0, 1.0, 2.0, 3.0, 4.0, 5.0, and 6.1. *Size* was held constant at 10 nodes, and *volume*, at 25 links. Control of the *diameter* subdimension was more difficult, owing to its intimate relationship with the *concentration* of links in the network. This relationship is best shown by example. A network in which one node is directly linked to all others (i.e., one in which relationships are *concentrated* upon a particular node) will have a *diameter* of only 2, even if no other links exist in the network. In a network of the same *size* and *volume* which lacks such a coordinating node, however, *diameter* could be considerably larger than 2. In the present case, the effects of *diameter* were minimized through the use of a special procedure for link assignment which connected nodes having relatively few links to those having relatively many. The success of this procedure in minimizing the variation of *diameter* is demonstrated by the fact that *diameters* in this family only varied by one link (from *diameter* = 2 to *diameter* = 3).

Finally, Family 9 represented the *diameter* subdimension. In order to maximize variation in *diameter*, the networks in this family (unlike previous families) were all composed of open branches. The first network in the family (with *diameter* = 2) resembles a bicycle wheel. Subsequent networks were created by removing one spoke at a time and attaching it to the open end of another already centrally connected spoke until, in the final network, the links were stretched out end-to-end. *Size* was held constant at 10 nodes and *volume* at 9 links per network. The close relationship between *diameter* and *concentration* precluded exercising total control over the *concentration* subdimension. The variances of the link frequency distributions for these networks are 8.0, 6.6, 6.4, 4.6, 4.0, 3.6, and 3.4, a range of 4.6. While this range is relatively similar to the range of variances in the second *concentration* family (which was 6.1), it was hoped that it was small enough that the indices would behave differently for the two families. As will be discussed subsequently, this expectation was fulfilled.

Index Selection

A set of indices which showed promise as measures of communication structure was desired. Owing to the assumed bidirectionality of the communication relationship (Guimaraes, 1970), and the necessity to limit the scope of the study, only indices capable of distinguishing among strongly connected networks (i.e., networks in which all members are at least indirectly connected to one another) consisting of bidirectional relationships were considered. In order to assure their comparability, only indices calculated from interactional data were used (thus excluding the *size* subdimension). With these constraints, indices were chosen to represent all three of the remaining subdimensions of structure: *volume, concentration,* and *diameter.* Several indices were chosen from the same subdimension where its importance to network analysis or its popularity in prior research dictated that course.

Those chosen to represent the *volume* subdimension were: *density* (Niemeijer, 1973); *coefficient A* (Davis' 1967 measure of *clusterability*), and *3-balance* (Cartwright & Harary, 1956), each of which combines the *size* and *volume* subdimensions of the *magnitude* dimension.

Those selected for the *concentration* subdimension were: Bavelas' (1950) *global centrality*; Zeisel's (1968) *monopolization*; Coleman's (1964) h_1 measure of hierarchization; Monge's (1971) *relative information*; and Findley's (1966) *group assimilation index.* Finally, those selected for the *diameter* subdimension were: Sabidussi's (1966) *trivial centrality*, Mitchell's (1969) *compactness*; and Harary's (1959) *global status.* The computation formulae for all eleven of these indices are given in the *appendix.*

Evaluation of Index Validity

Index validity was defined above as the monotonic covariation of an index with a target subdimension. Owing to the possibility of unequal intervals between successive networks in the families, *Spearman's rank order correlation* was used to measure this monotonicity. An index which gave the same reading for all networks in a family was termed an *invalid measure* of the target subdimension; an index with a coefficient of +1.0 or −1.0 was *valid*; and an index with a coefficient between 0

and ±1.0 was said to have *moderate validity* for that subdimension.

Since indices with only moderate validity would seem relatively useless, either in measuring the subdimension represented in the family or in avoiding its confounding influence when it was desired to measure other subdimensions, only those indices with perfect correlations were evaluated for their relative sensitivity to a particular subdimension. Index sensitivities were compared in terms of: (1) the overall *shape* of the index-subdimension relationship for a particular family, and (2) the magnitude of the index's *discrimination* between the first and last networks in the family.

With unequal intervals between successive networks in a family, even a maximally sensitive index would not have a linear relationship with a family of networks. For this reason, *shape* was evaluated in terms of both linear and quadratic components. Each network was assigned a numerical value equal to its ordinal position in its family, and these ranks were used in a *polynomial regression*. *Shape* was measured as the percentage of variance in the ordinal ranks which was accounted for by the combined linear and quadratic functions of the index. These percentages were then rank-ordered within each family.

For the *discrimination* measure, each index's values were converted to z-scores, based on its mean and standard deviation for each family considered separately. The discrimination measure was the absolute difference between the z-scores for the first and last networks in the family. These differences were then rank-ordered within each family.

Shape and *discrimination* are both desired properties, but they do not covary perfectly. Thus, a separate coefficient was devised which adjusts the index's ranks on *shape* and *discrimination* for the discrepancy between those ranks. It is calculated as:

$$RS = (Rank_S - Rank_D) + (Rank_S)(Rank_D),$$

where *S* stands for *shape*, and *D* stands for *discrimination.*

RESULTS

As noted above, each index could be judged as

TABLE 1
The Validities and Relative Sensitivities of Each
Index for Each Subdimension

	Index	MAGNITUDE DIMENSION								DISPARITY DIMENSION			
		Size				Volume				Concentration			Diameter
		low vol.	mod. vol.	high vol.	comb.	n=6	n=10	n=14	comb.	1	2	comb.	
MAGNITUDE: Volume	1. Density	4[a]	I[b]	I	M[c]	2	2	2	3	I	I	I	I
	2. Cluster-ability	I	7	I	M	I	M	M	M	2	M	M	I
	3. 3-balance	M	5	I	M	M	M	M	M[A]	2	M	M	4
DISPARITY: Concentration	4. Bavelas	2	2	2	2	I	I	I	I	M	3	M	M
	5. Monopolization	I	4	2	3	I	I	I	I	4	I	2	6
	6. Hierarchization	— · — · — undefined[d] — · — · —								3	und.	und.	und.
	7. Information Theoretic	I	I	I	I	I	I	I	I	I	4	2	3
	8. Group Assimilation	I	I	I	I	I	I	I	I	2	2	I[B]	5
Diameter	9. Sabidussi	6	6	4	5	2	2	I	2	M	M	M	2
	10. Compactness	3	I	I	I	M	M	M	M	M	M	M	3
	11. Harary	5	3	3	4	I	I	2	I	2	M	M	I[C]

[a]Numerical entries are relative sensitivity ranks for valid indices (i.e., those having perfect correlations) for a particular subdimension.
[b]"I" designates invalidity for the target subdimension.
[c]"M" designates moderate validity for the target subdimension.
[d]"undefined" or "undef." indicates the index was not calculable throughout the family.

either *valid* (with rank order correlation of ±1.0), *invalid* (with rank order correlation of 0); or *moderately valid* (with rank order correlation between validity and invalidity). All results are summarized in Table 1.

Numerical entries are relative sensitivity ranks (calculated only for the perfectly valid indices); *M* signifies *moderate validity*; *I* signifies total insensitivity or *invalidity*; and *undef.* indicates that the index could not be calculated for all the networks in the family.

With respect to the *size* subdimension, Indices 4, 5, 9, 10, and 11 appear to be *valid*; Indices 7 and 8 are *invalid*; Index 6 is *undefined*, owing to the low levels at which *concentration* was stabilized; and Indices 1, 2, and 3 behave variably, depending upon the *volume* of links in the network. Of the *valid* indices for this subdimension, Index 10 appears to be the most sensitive, followed in order by Indices 4, 5, 11, and 9.

For the *volume* subdimension, Indices 1, 9, and 11 appear to be *valid*; Indices 4, 5, 7, and 8 are

invalid; Index 6 is *undefined*; and Indices 2, 3, and 10 behave variably, depending on the *size* of the network. Of the *valid* indices, Index 11 is the most sensitive, followed by Index 9 and Index 1.

Since the two types of *concentration* are really quite different, their results are discussed both separately and collectively.

With respect to the relocation of a single link in the network, Indices 2, 3, 5, 6, 7, 8, and 11 are found to be *valid* indices. Of these indices, Index 7 is most sensitive, Indices 1, 2, 8, and 11 are tied for second place, and these are followed in turn by Index 6 and Index 5. Indices 4, 9, and 10 have *moderate validity* for this subdimension, and only Index 1 is found to be *invalid* for it.

For the variance of the frequency distribution of links, Indices 4, 5, 7, and 8 appear to be *valid* indices, Index 5 being the most sensitive, then Index 8, Index 4, and Index 7. Index 1 is *invalid*; Index 6 is *undefined*; and Indices 2, 3, 9, 10, and 11 have *moderate validity*.

When the two families of *concentration* are considered collectively, only Indices 5, 7, and 8 are found *valid* for both types, and only Index 1 is perfectly *invalid* for both. Of these, Index 8 is the most sensitive, followed by Indices 5 and 7.

Finally, with respect to *diameter*, Indices 3, 5, 7, 8, 9, 10, and 11 appear to be *valid* measures, while Indices 1 and 2 are *invalid*, Index 4 is only *moderately valid*, and Index 6 is *undefined*. Of the *valid* indices, Index 11 is the most sensitive, followed in order by Indices 9, 10, 7, 3, 8, and 5.

DISCUSSION

These results may be used in two ways: (1) to compare the validities and sensitivities observed here with those expected from the literature, and (2) to recommend specific uses of particular indices in future research.

For the first purpose, Table 1 was subdivided into *columns*, indicating the subdimensions being operationally defined, and *rows*, indicating the subdimensional affiliations expected for each index, based on the literature. The three partitions for which the column and row headings are the same were labeled A, B, and C. Agreement with the literature was judged in terms of the number of numerical—rather than *M, I,* or *undef.*—entries each partition contained.

An examination of partition A, which pits alleged measures of *volume* against the manipulation of *volume* used here, shows only Index 1 to be valid across all three *volume* families. The fact that neither *clusterability* nor *3-balance* is valid for all three families could be interpreted as evidence that they are simply not very useful indices. However, it seems more reasonable to interpret this as evidence that *volume* and *transitivity* are not as closely related as the literature in the past has suggested. Perhaps these two indices would be perfectly valid for a family manifesting variations in *transitivity* alone, but resolution of this matter awaits further research.

A much better agreement with the literature occurs in partition B. In that partition, all five *concentration* indices are found valid for at least one type of *concentration*, and three of the five are valid for both types. The fact that Bavelas' *centrality* was found valid for the second type of *con-*

centration substantiates Flament's (1963) claim that it is sensitive to the dispersion of links in a network.

Values in partition C are in perfect accord with the classification of these indices as measures of network *diameter*.

In general, there seems to be a close correspondence between the index sensitivities that the literature suggests and those observed in these data. However, the presence of numerical entries in partitions other than A, B, and C shows that many of these indices have multiple sensitivities which are not mentioned in the literature. Since index values on one subdimension may actually be confounded by variation in another (theoretically distinct) subdimension, it is obviously important to keep these multiple sensitivities in mind when selecting or interpreting indices in research. The present multidimensional data seem uniquely well-suited for these activities.

It was noted above that an index with only moderate validity for a particular subdimension seems relatively less useful in either measuring that subdimension or avoiding its confounding influence when measuring other subdimensions. In contrast, the ideal index would be one whose validities are decisive, that is, a mixture of only ±1.0 and 0 correlations. Only three indices satisfied this criterion in the present study. They were *monopolization, relative information,* and *group assimilation.*

The *monopolization index* was found to be a valid measure of *size, concentration,* and *diameter,* but was perfectly insensitive to variations in *volume.* Because these sensitivities cut across the supposedly theoretically distinct dimensions of *magnitude,* and *disparity,* this index might be of little general research value. However, to a researcher interested in measuring all subdimensions *except volume,* this index might be quite useful. If values on this index were implicated in functional relationships with nonstructural variables, a reasonable interpretation would seem to be that whatever structural subdimension was involved in a functional relationship, it was not *volume,* and that it was probably either *size,* or *concentration,* or *diameter,* or some combination of them. These interpretations are stated either negatively or else probabilistically because of the possible existence of additional structural dimensions not yet identified. This issue is addressed in more detail later in this section.

The other two indices, *relative information* and *group assimilation*, were found to be perfectly valid for the two *disparity subdimensions,* and perfectly insensitive to both of the *magnitude subdimensions*. This suggests their possible utility in measuring the *disparity dimension* free from confounding by the *magnitude dimension*. If either of these indices is implicated in a functional relationship with a nonstructural variable, the appropriate interpretation would seem to be that the structural subdimension involved in the observed relationship was neither *size* nor *volume*, and that it was probably either *concentration* or *diameter* or some combination of the two.

Differences in the relative sensitivities of these two indices suggest an even more sophisticated basis for index selection. A researcher wishing his index to be more sensitive to *concentration* than to *diameter* might select *group assimilation* rather than *relative information*. However, the frequently small differences in the *shape* measure and the fact that there were many tied ranks makes this inadviseable on the basis of the present data alone.

Evaluation of the Method

This study has proposed and employed a new method for the validation of structural indices. This method has several important advantages over previous methods. The first advantage is in its use of hypothetical networks rather than actual socionetworks. This allows greater variation in the target subdimensions than would be found in natural settings. Additionally, it enables much greater control over the observational situation. In the natural setting, after all, many subdimensions would vary at once, leaving no possible way of systematically ordering them. A second advantage is that this method provides data-based, rather than merely intuitive, recommendations which have actual, practical utility. One final advantage is its heuristic value. Since its use requires the specification and operational definition of target as well as nontarget subdimensions, it openly encourages the clarification of the structure variable and its most potent dimensions.

While several weaknesses may be noted also, none of them seems inherent in the method itself, as were the shortcomings of most previous methods, but only in its application here. The first of these concerns the inadequate research enumerating theoretically important dimensions of structure. To the degree that the present list is incomplete, and unspecified dimensions are left free to vary, the index sensitivities reported through the use of this method may not be entirely correct. In order to avoid a proliferation of unneeded dimensions, however, a conservative approach seems also needed. This method need not be limited by such conservatism, however. Its results may well suggest additional dimensions needing further study, as was shown in the case of *transitivity*. While clearly a bootstrap operation, this approach seems to have considerable promise.

A second weakness with the current application of this method involves the present choices of stabilizing values for nontarget subdimensions. As Coleman's *hierarchization index* illustrates, index values may be confounded by nontarget subdimensions, even if those subdimensions are held constant. Thus, in the present case, each time *concentration* was minimized, this index was undefined. To minimize a systematic bias of this sort, it is suggested that future researchers select stabilization values at random from a set of logistically possible combinations of them.

A final weakness is the fact that the present application involved variation on only one subdimension at a time. The real world of structure is full of simultaneous variations of various dimensions. To the degree that they are theoretically distinct, the validity of an index for the target subdimension will be lessened, hence potentially reducing the pragmatic utility of the recommendations made from these data. Thus, it is recommended that future applications of this method involve the simultaneous variation of multiple subdimensions.

In addition to making these suggested changes in future applications of this method, it is hoped that future researchers will evaluate more and different indices, and adapt additional methods to the multidimensional validation of structural indices.

Sabidussi's (1966) method seems particularly promising in this regard, since it seems capable of indicating *why* indices measure what they do.

Though the systematic validation of structural indices is currently lacking, it is hoped that its importance will soon be appreciated, and that these and related approaches will be expanded to illuminate the measurement capabilities of many promising indices. Once this is accomplished, theorizing regarding socio-networks generally, and communication networks in particular, will at last be free to advance with well justified self-confidence.

NOTES

1. This research was sponsored by the Organizational Effectiveness Research Program, Office of Naval Research (Code 452), under Contract Number N00014-75-C-0445; Peter R. Monge, principal investigator.
2. This review is available upon request from the authors.
3. While space limitation prevents the inclusion of all 60 networks here, the full set is available on request from the authors.

REFERENCES

ABELSON, R.P. Mathematical models in social psychology. In L. Berkowitz (Ed.) *Advances in experimental psychology*. New York: Academic Press, 1967.

BAVELAS, A. Communication patterns in task-oriented groups. *Journal of the Acoustical Society of America*, 1950, 22, 725-730.

BRIDGMAN, P.W. *Dimensional analysis*. New Haven: Yale University Press, 1922.

CARTWRIGHT, D., & HARARY, F. Structural balance: A generalization of Heider's theory. *Psychological Review*, 1956, 63, 277-293.

COLEMAN, J.S. *Introduction to mathematical sociology*. N.Y.: The Free Press of Glencoe, Collier-MacMillan, 1964.

DAVIS, K. A method of studying communication patterns in organizations. *Personnel Psychology*, 1953, 6, 301-312.

DUBIN, R. *Theory building*. New York: The Free Press, Collier-MacMillan, 1969.

EDWARDS, J.A., & MONGE, P.R. *Descriptive communication structure metrics: A preliminary logical and empirical analysis*. A paper presented at the annual meeting of the International Communication Association, Chicago, April 1975.

EDWARDS, J.A., & MONGE, P.R. *A comparison of methodological approaches to the study of communication networks and structure: Data collection procedures*. Technical Report. Arlington, Va.: Office of Naval Research (Contract No. N00014-73-A-0476-0001), June 1976.

FARACE, R.V., MONGE, P.R., & RUSSEL, H.M. *Communicating and organizing*. Reading, Mass.: Addison-Wesley, in press.

FINDLEY, W.G. Group vs. individual sociometric relations. *International Journal of Sociometry and Sociatry*, 1966, 5, 60-66.

FLAMENT, C. *Applications of graph theory to group structure*. Englewood Cliffs, N.J.: Prentice-Hall, 1963.

GUIMARAES, L.L. *Network analysis: An approach to the study of communication systems*. Unpublished paper, Michigan State University, Department of Communication, 1970.

HARARY, F. Status and contrastatus. *Sociometry*, 1959, 22, 23-43.

HARARY, F., NORMAN, R.Z., & CARTWRIGHT, D. *Structural models: An introduction to the theory of directed graphs*. N.Y.: Wiley, 1965.

JAMES, L.R. Criterion models and construct validity for criteria. *Psychological Bulletin*, 1973, 80, 75-83.

LUCE, R.D. Networks satisfying minimality conditions. *American Journal of Mathematics*, 1953, 75, 825-838.

MITCHELL, J.C. (Ed.) *Social networks in urban situations: Analyses of personal relationships in Central Africa towns*. Manchester, England: University of Manchester Press, 1969.

MONGE, P.R. *The evolution of communication structure*. Unpublished manuscript. Michigan State University, Department of Communication, 1971.

NIEMEIJER, R. Some applications of the notion of density to network analysis. In J. Boissevain and J.C. Mitchell (Eds.), *Network analysis studies in human interaction*. The Hague: Mouton, 1973.

NOSANCHUK, T.A. A comparison of several sociometric partitioning techniques. *Sociometry*, 1963, 26, 112-124.

RICHARDS, W.D., JR. *Network analysis in large complex systems: Metrics*. A paper presented at the annual meeting of the International Communication Association, New Orleans, April 1974.

SABIDUSSI, G. The centrality index of a graph. *Psychometrika*, 1966, 31, 581-603.

WOELFEL, J. *Metric measurement of cultural processes*. A paper presented to the annual meeting of the Speech Communication Association, Chicago, Illinois, December 1974.

ZEISEL, H. *Say it with figures*, 5th ed. revised. N.Y.: Harper and Row, 1968.

Computational Formulae for the Eleven Indices

For each of the indices, the following equivalences hold:

n = the number of nodes in the network

$\displaystyle\sum_{j=1}^{k} X_{j(adj)}$ = the row sum for node i in the adjacency matrix

$\displaystyle\sum_{j=1}^{k} X_{j(dist)}$ = the row sum for node i in the distance matrix

$\displaystyle\sum_{i=1}^{n}\sum_{j=1}^{k} X_{ij(adj)}$ = the total of all rows in the adjacency matrix

$\displaystyle\sum_{i=1}^{n}\sum_{j=1}^{k} X_{ij(dist)}$ = the total of all rows in the distance matrix

N_i = the number of 3-cycles having i positive links

Index	Source	Formula
1. Density	Niemeijer, 1973	$\dfrac{\displaystyle\sum_{i=1}^{n}\sum_{j=1}^{k} X_{ij(adj)}}{n(n-1)}$
2. Cluster-ability	Abelson, 1967	$\dfrac{3N_1N_3 - N_2{}^2}{3N_1N_3 + N_2{}^2}$
3. 3-balance	Cartwright & Harary, 1956	$\dfrac{N_1 + N_3}{N_0 + N_1 + N_2 + N_3}$
4. Global centrality	Bavelas, 1950	$\displaystyle\sum_{i=1}^{n}\left[\dfrac{\displaystyle\sum_{i=1}^{n}\sum_{j=1}^{k} X_{ij(dist)}}{\displaystyle\sum_{j=1}^{k} X_{j(dist)}}\right]$
5. Monopolization	Zeisel, 1968	$\dfrac{\sqrt{\displaystyle\sum_{i=1}^{n}\left[\displaystyle\sum_{j=1}^{k} X_{ij(adj)}\right]^2}}{\displaystyle\sum_{i=1}^{n}\sum_{j=1}^{k} X_{ij(adj)}}$ Exception: When the quantity $\displaystyle\sum_{j=1}^{k} X_{j(adj)}$ equals 1, it appears only in the denominator.
6. "h_1"	Coleman, 1964	$\dfrac{1 - \dfrac{z^*}{\displaystyle\sum_{i=1}^{n}\sum_{j=1}^{k} X_{ij(adj)}}}{}$ where z^* equals: $n\left\{\displaystyle\sum_{i=1}^{n}\left[\dfrac{\displaystyle\sum_{j=1}^{k} X_{j(adj)}}{\displaystyle\sum_{i=1}^{n}\sum_{j=1}^{k} X_{ij(adj)}} - \dfrac{1}{n}\right]^2\right\}$

Index	Source	Formula
7. Relative information	Monge, 1971	$\dfrac{H_{obtained}}{H_{maximum}}$ where: $H_{max} = \log_2 n$ $H_{obt} = -\displaystyle\sum_{i=1}^{n} p_i \log_2 p_i$ $p_i = \dfrac{\displaystyle\sum_{j=1}^{k} X_{j(adj)}}{\displaystyle\sum_{i=1}^{n}\sum_{j=1}^{k} X_{ij(adj)}}$
8. Group Assimilation	Findley, 1966	$100\left(1 - \dfrac{k\sigma^2}{M^2}\right)$, where $\dfrac{k\sigma^2}{M^2}$ equals: $\dfrac{ab^2 - a^2}{(n-1)\left[(n-1) - \dfrac{a}{n}\right]a^2}$, and: $a = \displaystyle\sum_{i=1}^{n}\sum_{j=1}^{k} X_{ij(adj)}$ $b = n\displaystyle\sum_{i=1}^{n}\left(\displaystyle\sum_{j=1}^{k} X_{ij(adj)}\right)$
9. Sabidussi's Trivial Centrality Index	Sabidussi, 1966	$\dfrac{1}{\displaystyle\sum_{j=1}^{k} X_{j(dist)}}$, where $\displaystyle\sum_{j=1}^{k} X_{j(dist)}$ is the smallest row sum in the distance matrix
10. Compactness	Mitchell, 1969	$\dfrac{n(n-1) + \displaystyle\sum_{i=1}^{n}\sum_{j=1}^{k} X_{ij(dist)}}{2nc}$, where c is the maximum cell entry in the distance matrix
11. Harary's Gross Status	Harary, 1959	$\displaystyle\sum_{i=1}^{n}\sum_{j=i}^{k} X_{ij(dist)}$

A COMPARATIVE TEST OF TWO STOCHASTIC PROCESS MODELS OF MESSAGES, MEDIATING VARIABLES, AND BEHAVIORAL EXPECTATIONS

DEAN E. HEWES
University of Wisconsin-Madison

ALAN J. BRAZIL
Arizona State University

DORCAS E. EVANS
University of Wisconsin-Madison

This paper presents an updated version of Hewes' axiomatized, stochastic model of the relationships among messages, mediating variables, and behaviors. Several axioms and theorems of this theory were tested in terms of their predictive accuracy. The theory was also tested against an alternative, and more parsimonious, model. Results of both sets of tests were generally supportive of Hewes' theory with overtime predictions approaching 95% accuracy. Methodological problems and potential extensions of the theory are discussed.

The specification of precise, empirically valid relationships among messages, mediating cognitive variables, and behaviors has become a crucial problem for communication research (Burhans, 1971; Miller, 1967; Seibold, 1975, Simons, 1971), and justifiably so. Unless a precisely determined relationship between messages and behaviors can be identified, much of the utility of persuasion research will be lost. Unless mediating cognitive variables can be linked to behaviors, we will be left with the kind of mind-body dualism which led Descartes to argue that a linkage between cognitions and behavior was beyond the realm of science (1643; T. Mischel, 1969).

Recently one of the authors presented a formalized theory of the message/mediating variable/behavior interrelationship and found indirect support for this theory in a large body of literature (Hewes, 1975b). While this theory is only one of several which attempt to tap these relationships (e.g., Cushman, in press), it does have several advantages which warrant further consideration and testing. First, the theory is formalized mathematically, making its predictions precise enough to be both highly useful and highly falsifiable. As McDermott (1975) notes, "the formulations pro-

posed [by Hewes] are consistent and visual clarity of the phenomenon is increased over most theoretical formulations in the social sciences" (p. 93). Second, the theory is dynamic. It is an attempt to capture the *process* of behavior change in response to messages. Process views of communication are clearly needed in our field (Report on the New Orleans Conference, 1969).

Given these advantages, a test of this theory seems to be in order; this paper attempts to do so. In particular, this paper serves three purposes: (1) it provides an updated description of the theory (see Hewes, in press), (2) the paper reports tests of one assumption and several predictions of the theory, and (3) it compares the predictions of the theory to those generated by a competing and more parsimonious model.

A BRIEF DESCRIPTION OF THE THEORY

The components of the theory and several deductions are presented in this section of the paper. Each component of the theory will be defined conceptually and mathematically. Next, four axioms will be posited, several corollaries to those axioms presented, and a set of theorems deduced.

Components of the Theory

Five components are contained in this theory: (1) *behavioral expectations*, (2) *stability matrices*, (3) *a retention parameter*, (4) *environmental cues*, and (5) *behavior probability distributions*. While each of these variables will be defined and briefly explicated here, a more complete empirical justification for them is provided by Hewes (in press).

Behavioral expectations. The *behavioral expectation* variable is adapted from the conative dimension of attitude, as operationalized by Triandis (1964). A behavioral expectation (B_e) is *a set of probabilities with which one anticipates performing any of a closed set of behaviors*. B_e for any point in time $t+k$ can be rendered mathematically as a row vector of probabilities,

$$B_e(t+k) = (p_1 p_2 p_3 \ldots p_j)$$

where any p_i is the subjectively assessed probability that a person will perform behavior i. By this definition $\sum_i p_i = 1.00$ since the set of behaviors is assumed to be mutually exclusive and exhaustive.

B_e was chosen as a key variable in this theory for two reasons: (1) B_e can "summarize" the effects of a number of other cognitive variables such as beliefs and attitudes in much the same way that *behavioral intentions* serves that purpose for Fishbein (1973), and (2) behavioral expectations have been consistently found to be highly related to behaviors (Fishbein & Ajzen, 1975; W. Mischel, 1968). The first of these reasons helps to simplify the theory, while the second aids in bridging the gap between cognitive variables and observed behaviors.

The stability matrix. Not only do individuals appear to have predispositions to act (usually defined as attitudes) but those predispositions also have measurable stabilities (Belamy & Thompson, 1967; McNemar, 1946; Wiggins, 1973). The stability matrix (S) was created to capture this feature of cognitive change.

S is defined as *the cognitive mechanism which maps the values of B_e at one point in time to those at the next point in time*. S controls both the *amount* and *direction* of stochastic change in B_e by incorporating into the theory the confidence one holds in one's behavioral expectations. Clearly this stability

can be altered by new information. How this is accomplished will be discussed with reference to the next two components of the theory. In the meantime, a mathematical definition of S needs to be provided to help formalize the theory.

S is conceived of as a square matrix with as many levels as are contained in B_e. Formally, S for any time $t+k$ is:

$$S_k = \begin{pmatrix} s_{11} \ s_{22} \ldots \ldots s_{1j} \\ s_{21} \ldots \ldots \ldots s_{2j} \\ s_{j1} \ldots \ldots \ldots s_{jj} \end{pmatrix}$$

where S_k is allowed to change over time in response to perceived cues from the environment and

$$\sum_{k=1}^{j} s_{ik} = 1.00 \text{ for all } i, \ 1 \leq i \leq j.$$

The retention parameter. As noted above, S can be changed by exposure to messages from the environment. According to this theory, perceived messages are integrated into the cognitive structure of the individual by means of a deterministic weighted-averaging process. Part of S is retained, and a part is replaced by input from the environment. Obviously no replacement can take place if there is no message.

The mechanism which facilitates this averaging process is the retention parameter (m). The m parameter is assumed to remain constant over time as long as a message is perceived; otherwise it does not function. The retention parameter is topic-specific and may depend on the traits of the individual. Hewes (in press) provides some suggestions as to the antecedents of m. Until these antecedents can be explored, m simply stands for the process, but does not explain it.

Formally, m is a scalar parameter with the following properties: $m = 0.00$ when no message is received at any time $t+k$, and m = a constant when a message is received; $0 \leq m \leq 1.00$. The m parameter is not to be interpreted as a statement of probability; it is deterministic in nature.[1]

Environmental cues to action. Numerous studies

have indicated that messages received from the environment serve to mediate between intentions and behaviors (Cathcart, 1974, Craig & Cushman, 1975; Fishbein, 1967; McPhee, 1975; Schwartz & Tessler, 1972; Warner & DeFluer, 1969; Wicker, 1971). A communication theory ought, therefore, to include some mechanism for integrating these environmental messages into the cognitive system of the individual. The cues matrix (C) is a necessary first step to this integration. Before a message can be integrated, it must be represented, and represented in such a way as to be conformable with the cognitive system it is supposed to influence. C is this representation.

C is defined as *a representation of perceived cues from the environment. These cues are construed by the individual to support degrees of change or no change from pre-existing behavioral expectations.* Thus C serves the same function as S does in controlling changes in B_e. C is conceived of as representing the strength of the message as it is perceived by the individual. Thus the individual may know that a message is supposed to be very persuasive, but may not see that it is strong in relationship to his or her own position. C is *not* necessarily an objective evaluation of the message.

Mathematically C is a square matrix with the same properties as S. C at time $t+k$ is

$$C_k = \begin{pmatrix} c_{11} \ c_{12} \ldots \ldots \ldots c_{1j} \\ c_{21} \ \ldots \ldots \ldots \ldots c_{2j} \\ c_{j1} \ \ldots \ldots \ldots \ldots c_{jj} \end{pmatrix}$$

where all entries of C are $0 \leq c_{ij} \leq 1.00$, $c(t+k)$ is allowed to change over time, and $\sum\limits_{k=1}^{j} c_{ik} = 1.00$ for all i, $1 \leq i \leq j$. The number of levels of C is the same as the number of states in B_e.

Behavioral probability distribution variable. The behavioral probability distribution variable (B_h) is the output variable of the theory. B_h is highly similar to B_e. Where B_e arrays the subjective expectations that certain behaviors will be performed, B_h *arrays the actual probabilities that a certain behavior will be performed at a particular point in time.*

B_h is a row vector with j entries, each entry corresponding to a behavior included in B_e. B_h for some point in time $t+k$ is

$$B_h (t+k) = (b_1 \ b_2 \ldots \ldots b_j)$$

where any b_i is the actual probability of behavior i at $t+k$. As with B_e, $\sum\limits_{i=1}^{j} b_i = 1.00$; the set of behaviors is assumed to be exhaustive.

Axiomatic Structure

At several points in the preceding definitional section of this paper, mention was made of the relationships among the components of this theory. These relationships are formalized in a set of axioms and corollaries below. However, before we can reach that stage, a word or two must be said about the deductive calculus reflected in those axioms and corollaries.

Quite naturally, the deductive calculus utilized in a theory can influence the deductions made from that theory, as well as the form of the relationships posited between its components. This is also true here.

Probability theory serves as the deductive calculus here and is given the "frequency" interpretation advanced by Reichenbach (1949). This means that the stochastic parameters appearing in this theory must be viewed as having been obtained from a very large number of replications. A replication can mean either the repetition of the response over a large number of similar instances by a single individual or the elicitation of the response in single instances by a number of similar individuals. In other words, all axioms, corrallaries, and deductions of this theory are, and must be, interpreted as representing the *expected distribution* of probabilities that would occur over a large number of replications. Thus, these axioms, etc., are not intended to model what happens in any individual instance but, rather, to model the stochastic process *implicit* in any individual instance but observable only over a large number of instances. This does not mean that the theory cannot be used to increase our ability to predict the behavior of a single individual; however, the prediction is in the form of the *odds* that a given behavior will occur. With this issue clarified, let us move on to the axiomatic structure of the theory.

Axiom 1: Prob(v(t+k)=1 | v(t+k−1)=j,
  v(t+k−2)=m,..., v(t+0)=p) =
  Prob (v(t+k)=i | v(t+k−1)=j)

where v(t+k) is a "state" variable indicating that, at time t+k, an individual would expect to perform behavior i, with the ith probability in the B_e vector, and so on, for v(t+k−1), v(t+k−2), etc. The symbols $i, j, m, . . .$, and p are integers between 1 and n, where n is the number of behaviors in B_e. The symbol k is a positive integer or zero.

Stated verbally, *Axiom 1* implies that the process being described is of the "first order"; that is, predicting a future event is assumed to require no more information than that contained in the immediately prior event and the method of mapping one event onto the other. *Axiom 1* is the same as the order assumption made in Markov chain analysis (Hewes, 1975a).

Since the conventional notation used in this theory is matrix notation, *Axiom 1* will be phrased in that form; $B_e(t+k)=B_e(t+k-1) S_k$.

Corollary 1.1: $B_e(t+k) = B_e(t+0) \prod_{k=1}^{k} S_i$

This corollary can be established by the informal use of mathematical induction. Let us start with the matrix form of *Axiom 1* for *t+1* and restate *Axiom 1* in the same form for *t+2, t+3*, and so on.

$B_e(t+1) = B_e(t+0) S_1$
$B_e(t+2) = B_e(t+1) S_2 = B_e(t+0) S_1 S_2$
$B_e(t+3) = B_e(t+2) S_3 = B_e(t+0) S_1 S_2 S_3$
$\vdots$
$B_e(t+k) = B_e(t+k-1) S_k =$
    $B_e(t+0) S_1 S_2 S_3...S_k$

or, for simplicity

$B_e(t+k)= B_e(t+0) \prod_{i=1}^{k} S_i.$

Axiom 2: $s_{ij}(t+k) =$
    $ms_{ij}(t+k-1) + (1-m)c_{ij} (t+k)$

except when no message is received at t+k

where $s_{ij}(t+k-1)$ is the probability of changing from expectation i, to expectation j, during the period of time from $t+k-1$ to $t+k$, m is the retention parameter, and $c_{ij} (t+k)$ is the perceived change in behavioral expectations being recommended by the environment.

Verbally, *Axiom 2* states that an individual creates a weighted average of his or her cognitive structure for mapping $B_e(t+k-1)$ into $B_e(t+k)$ by combining his or her previous inclinations toward change $[s_{ij}(t+k-1)]$, with another pattern of change recommended by the environment. This averaging is said to occur *only when a message is perceived at t+k*.

In matrix notation *Axiom 2* becomes
  $$S_k=mS_{k-1} + (1-m)C_k$$

Corollary 2.1: $S_k = m^kS_0 + (1-m) \sum_{i=1}^{k} m^{k-i}C$

except when no message is received at some time i, $1 \leqslant i \leqslant k$.

In many practical applications S_0 will be unknown since S_0 maps $B_e (t-1)$ onto $B_e(t+0)$. Since by definition we generally start at t+0, S_0 will not be directly observable from the data, though it can be computed. In the cases where the computation of S_0 is not useful, *Corollary 2.1* can be restated as

$$m^{k-1}S_1 + (1-m) \sum_{i=1}^{k} m^{k-i}C_i) +$$

All symbols are as previously defined.

This corollary can be supported by the informal use of mathematical induction applied to *Axiom 2*. Starting with *Axiom 2* applied to *t+1* and proceeding from there,

$S_1 = mS_0 + (1-m)C_1$
$S_2 = mS_1 + (1-m)C_2 = m(mS_0 + (1-m)C_1) +$
    $(1-m)C_2$
$S_3 = mS_2 + (1-m)C_3 = m(m(mS_0 + (1-m)C_1)$
    $+ (1-m)C_2) + (1-m)C_3$

or

$S_3=m^3S_0+m^2(1-m)C_1+m(1-m)C_2+ (1-m)C_3$

In general,

$$S_k = m^k S_0 + (1-m) \sum_{i=1}^{k} m^{k-i} C_i.$$

Axiom 3: $S_{ij}(t+k) = s_{ij}(t+k-1)$

      when no message is received at $t+k$

where s_{ij} is as before.

Verbally, *Axiom 3* is the logical complement of *Axiom 2*. *Axiom 3* simply states that *if no cues from the environment are received at $t+k$* then the pre-existing cognitive structure for change is retained. In matrix notation $S_k = S_{k-1}$ when no message is received at $t+k$.

Axiom 4: $be_i(t+k) = b_i(t+k)$

where $b_i(t+k) =$ the probability of performing behavior i at $t+k$, $be_i(t+k) =$ the probability of holding behavioral expectation i, at $t+k$, and the i's refer to corresponding behaviors. The symbol be_i is the ith element of vector B_e.

Stated verbally, *Axiom 4* suggests that an individual's expectations are isomorphic (at the stochastic level) to the probabilities of behavioral choice of the point when those behaviors are to be performed. This axiom may be more complex than it appears. For instance, there are different implications to *Axiom 4* when the behavioral choice must be made at a specified time (for example, voting), and when the choice can be made at some free-floating time period. In the latter case, one must know the expectations for behavioral choice, and expectations of time of choice. Alternatively, the time of choice could be incorporated in the expectation. For example, "what is the probability that you will buy a car next week?"

In matrix notation $B_e(t+k) = B(t+k)$ where $B(t+k)$ is a column vector of b_i's with the same number of entries as B_e.

Formal Deductions

The theorems listed below are not a complete set of possible deductions from the four axioms. Without exception, these theorems place no constraints on the values of the variables other than those imposed in the definitions. Obviously when constraints are imposed, a host of special cases of these theorems could be derived.

Theorem 1: $B_e(t+k) = B_e(t+0) \prod_{i=1}^{k} (m^i S_0 +$

$$(1-m) \sum_{j=1}^{i} m^{i-j} C_j)$$

when messages are received for all j, $1 \leq j \leq k$
Theorem 1 can be established directly by substitution of *Corollary 2.1* into *Corollary 1.1*. *Corollary 1.1* defines the mapping of $B_e(t+0)$ onto $B_e(t+k)$. *Corollary 2.1* amplifies on the structure of S_i in *Corollary 1.1* by relating S_i to C_i.

Theorem 1 provides the basis for prediction of values of B_e at any future time $t+k$ knowing only S_0, m and the various values of C which are perceived *at each point in time* from $t+1$ to $t+k$. *Theorem 1* represents the individual as an information processing mechanism which creates a weighted average of previously acquired predispositions toward change and new predisposition suggested by the environment. This averaging takes place each point in time when a message is received. The theory does not dictate whether or not the averaging process is consciously accessible to the individual. The individual is thus seen as being in active adaptation to his or her *perceived* environment. The rate of adaptation is determined by m.

Theorem 2: $B_e(t+k) = B_e(t+0)S_1^k$ when no message is received at $t+i$ where i is any number between 1 and k.

Corollary 1.1 and *Axiom 3* form the basis for *Theorem 2*. *Corollary 1.1* states that $B_e(t+k) =$

$$B_e(t+0) \prod_{i=1}^{k} S_i.$$ According to *Axiom 3*, $S_i = S_{i-1}$

when no message is received at $t+i$. Since no message is received at $i=1$ through k, $S_1 = S_2 = ... = S_k$;

therefore, by substitution, $\prod_{i=1}^{k} S_i = S_1^{k}$.

Theorem 2 provides the same kind of basis for prediction as does *Theorem 1*; however, *Theorem 2* makes prediction much simpler, since there is no need to know m, or the various values of C. Instead, *Theorem 2* describes changes in B_e in terms of a simple first-order Markov chain. The chain is first-order because of *Axiom 1* and stationary because of *Axiom 3*.

Theorem 2 describes the cognitive processing of information by the individual as potentially dynamic *even if no new information is received.* By raising S_1 to successively higher powers, B_e will change across time until it reaches stable equilibrium under most conditions. To be more precise, if S_1 is a "regular" transition matrix, that is, if for some positive integer k, S_1^k has no zero entries, then B_e will achieve stable equilibrium (Kemeny & Snell, 1960). In general, S_1 will be regular. Such changes are entirely in accordance with the empirical evidence mustered in support of the inclusion of S in this theory.

$$\textit{Theorem 3:}\ B_e(t+k) = B_e(t+0) \prod_{j=1}^{k}$$
$$(\delta\ (m^j S_0 + (1-m) \sum_{i=1}^{j} m^{j-i} C_i) +$$

$(1-\delta)S_{j-1})$ where $\delta = 1$ when a message is received at time $t+j$ and $\delta = 0$ otherwise.

In one sense, *Theorem 3* is not a true theorem at all, but rather a combination of the contingencies inherent in *Corollaries 1.1* and *2.1*. Those contingencies involve whether or not a message is received at some point in time. The δ parameter allows for that contingency to be explicitly included in *Theorem 3*, so that the deductions presented in *Theorems 1* and *2* can be combined. *Theorem 3* merely indicates that when a message C_k is received at $t+k$ a weighted average is computed. That average integrates S_{k-1} and C_k into a new cognitive mechanism, S_k. When no message is received at $t+k$, S_k becomes S_{k-1} by default. Thus, *Theorem 3* reduces to *Theorem 1* when δ equals 1 at all points in time. *Theorem 3* reduces to *Theorem 2* when δ equals zero for all points in time.

$$\textit{Theorem 4:}\ B_h(t+k) = B_e(t+0) \prod_{j=1}^{k}$$
$$(\delta\ (m^j S_0 + (1-m) \sum_{i=1}^{j} m^{j-i} C_i) +$$

$(1-\delta)S_{j-1})$ where $\delta=1$ when a message is received at $t+j$ and zero otherwise.

Theorems 5 and *6* are presented together, since they are simple modifications of *Theorem 4* based on *Axiom 4*. *Theorem 5* permits predictions from behavioral distributions to behavior distributions, while *Theorem 6* reverses the direction of prediction presented in *Theorem 4*. The value of *Theorems 5* and *6* is that they demonstrate the flexibility of prediction that can be made by the theory presented here.

Summary

In general, all of the theorems facilitate prediction in ways that are particularly useful to the communication researcher. First, they posit a complex, but precise, linkage between internal mediating variables (B_e and S) and behaviors. The precision of that linkage increases the testability of the theory, while the complexity helps to explain the disconcerting diversity of empirical results found in attitude/behavior studies. Second, *Theorems 1* to *6* explicitly incorporate communication into the process of cognitive and behavioral change; consequently, the theory permits predictions of the cumulative effects of messages. Such considerations are missing from the vast majority of research on the relationships among messages, mediating variables and behaviors. In Seibold's (1975) extensive review of this literature, not a single study was reported employing a multiple message approach to behavioral change.

Both of these advantages will come to nothing if the formalisms presented up until now cannot withstand empirical test. Several such tests are undertaken in the next section of the paper.

TESTS OF THE THEORY

Three aspects of the theory were put to experimental test: an assumption about the retention parameter, the ability of the model to predict behavioral expectations (*Theorems 1 to 3*), and the ability of the theory to predict stability matrices (*Axioms 2 and 3*).

Several aspects of the theory were left untested. In particular *Axioms 1* and *4* as well as *Theorems 4 to 6* were not tested at this time. *Axiom 1* was not tested directly, owing to unsolved technical difficulties, but it was tested indirectly, since it is presumed true in *Theorems 1* to *3*. The tests of *Theorems 4* to *6* and *Axiom 4* were temporarily postponed for the following reasons: (1) gathering over-time behavioral data is extremely difficult, (2) extensive research already supports the relationship between behavioral expectations and behavior (Fishbein & Ajzen, 1975; Mischel, 1968), and (3) the validity of *Axioms 2* and *3*, as well as *Theorems 1 to 3* can be established independently of the other axioms and theorems. In short, the aspects of the theory which were tested appeared to be appropriate points of departure for a more complete validation of the theory.

Hypothesis

Three hypotheses, based on the previous description of theory, were put to two tests. The first hypothesis is derived from the definition of the retention parameter, m. According to that definition the value of m is *not* contingent on the prior expectations held by the individual. Formally,

H_1: Prob $(m=q \mid v=i)$ = Prob $(m=q)$

where m is the retention parameter, q is some particular value of the retention parameter, v is a "state" variable defining which behavioral expectation "state" is held by the individual, and i is the particular state actually held by the individual.

This hypothesis needs to be tested for two reasons. First, in an earlier version of this theory, the intuitive reasonableness of this assumption was specifically questioned (Hewes, 1975b). Second, empirical evidence suggests that evaluations of the plausibility of arguments relates to the perceived strength of those arguments. To the extent that attitudes are crude indications of behavioral expectations, there is just reason to question the validity of Hypothesis 1.

The second hypothesis was derived directly from *Theorem 3*. In particular,

$$H_2: B_e(t+k) = B_e(t+0) \prod_{j=1}^{k} (\delta(m^j S_0 + (1-m)$$
$$\sum_{i=1}^{j} m^{j-i} C_i) + (1-\delta)S_{j-1})$$

where the symbols are defined as they were in the definition and axiomatic structure sections of this paper.[2]

Hypothesis 2 can be tested by checking the predictions of behavioral expectations generated by the theory under two conditions: (1) when messages are being received over several points in time or (2) when no messages are being received. These two conditions correspond to the two possible values of δ; $\delta = 1$ when a message is received at a specified point in time, and $\delta = 0$ when no message is received.

The third hypothesis is somewhat more fundamental than the second, since it is a test of two axioms rather than a theorem which is partially deduced from those axioms. *Axioms 2* and *3* are useful for predicting the expected distribution of the stability matices for various points in time. *Axioms 2* and *3* can be formally integrated into a single hypothesis.

$$H_3: S_k = \delta(mS_{k-1} + (1-m)C_k) + (1-\delta)S_{s-1}$$

where $\delta = 1$ when a message is received at $(t+k-1)$ and zero when no such message is received.[3]

METHOD

Each of these three hypotheses was tested at a number of different times on the same sample of subjects. How this was done is the subject of the following sections.

Procedures

One hundred thirty nonvolunteer subjects (52 females and 78 males) were randomly selected from five undergraduate communication classes. The age range for subjects was 17 to 43, with a median age of 19. The subjects were assigned blinded numbers and pretested for their attitudes toward socialized medicine, employing an undimensional instrument validated for that purpose. This instru-

TABLE 1
Distributions of Expectations for the Test Sample and the Cross-Validation Sample at t + 0

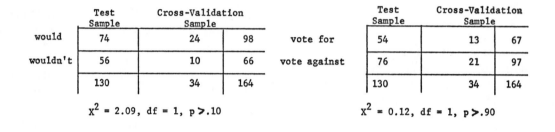

	Test Sample	Cross-Validation Sample				Test Sample	Cross-Validation Sample	
would	74	24	98	vote for	54	13	67
wouldn't	56	10	66	vote against	76	21	97
	130	34	164		130	34	164

$x^2 = 2.09$, df = 1, p > .10 $x^2 = 0.12$, df = 1, p > .90

TABLE 2
Observed S Matrices for Transitions Between Five Points in Time for Two Different Sets of Expectations[a]

TRANSITIONS

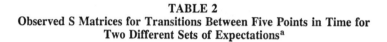

EXPECTATIONS		t + 0 - t + 1		t + 1 - t + 2		t + 2 - t + 3		t + 3 - t + 4	
		would	wouldn't	would	wouldn't	would	wouldn't	would	wouldn't
#1	would	.86	.14	.89	.11	.93	.07	.85	.15
	wouldn't	.55	.45	.38	.62	.50	.50	.29	.71
		for	against	for	against	for	against	for	against
#2	vote for	.08	.92	.78	.22	.53	.47	.92	.08
	vote against	.07	.93	.08	.92	.02	.98	.03	.97

[a]The first expectation is whether or not the subject would take a member of his or her family to a government sponsored medical clinic. The second expectation concerns a choice over voting for or against socialized medicine if given the opportunity.

ment is described in detail by Hewes and Evans-Hewes (1974). The subjects were also asked to provide behavioral expectation data on two behaviors: their expectation that they would or would not take a member of their family to a government-operated medical clinic if given the chance; and their expectation that they would or would not vote for socialized medicine given the opportunity. At approximately three-day intervals following the pretest, the subjects were exposed to a series of three tape-recorded messages from a supposed expert on the subject favoring socialized medicine.[4]

Posttests on the attitude questionnaire alone were obtained immediately after each of these messages, and again three days after the last message. Subjects were debriefed following the completion of the project. They were also interviewed to determine if any of them had talked to others about the topic of the presentation, and whether they had been exposed to any other messages on the topic before the end of the experiment. None had.

Parameter estimation. There were four sets of parameters to be estimated in this study; $B_e(t+k)$,

TABLE 3
Cues Matrices for Three Messages Supporting Socialized Medicine as
Perceived for Two Sets of Expectations[a]

MESSAGES

EXPECTATIONS		Message #1		Message #2		Message #3	
		would	wouldn't	would	wouldn't	would	wouldn't
#1	would	.86	.14	.85	.15	.87	.13
	wouldn't	.22	.78	.34	.76	.46	.54
		for	against	for	against	for	against
#2	vote for	.84	.16	.85	.15	.75	.25
	vote against	.72	.28	.41	.59	.63	.37

[a]The first expectation is whether or not the subject would take a member of his or her family to a government sponsored medical clinic. The second expectation concerns a choice over voting for or against socialized medicine if given the opportunity.

S_k, C, and m. Throughout these estimation procedures, it was assumed that the sample was homogeneous with respect to these parameters. The estimation procedures are discussed below:

First, estimates of $B_e(t+k)$ and S_k were obtained through an indirect procedure. Indirect procedures were necessitated to help minimize the potentially serious effects of pretest *sensation* on this time-series panel study (Glass, Willson, & Gottman, 1975). Instead of asking subjects to provide direct estimates of their behavioral expectations for the last four points in time, two predictive models of their expected choices were generated from data at the pretest $(t+0)$ for both expectations. Discriminant equations were generated using step-up procedures in a stepwise multiple discriminant program (Nie, Hull, Jenkins, Steinbrenner, & Bent, 1975). The criterion for inclusion in each model was a statistically significant ($\alpha=.05$) increase in Rao's V. The attitude questionnaire items served as independent variables. The resultant discriminant equations were then cross-validated on a separate sample of thirty-four subjects drawn from the same population.[5] Behavioral expectations for both the large and small samples were the same, within chance fluctuations for both sets of expectations (See Table 1 for this information).

Cross-validation proved highly successful for both sets of behavioral expectations. In the large sample, the first expectation (taking a member of your family) had a canonical correlation of .55 with the model and an overall classification accuracy of 82.8%. On the smaller, cross-validation sample, the canonical correlation between expected[6] and observed expectations was .483, and overall classification accuracy was 79.9%, with a slightly greater tendency to misclassify those who would *not* take a member of their family to a government-operated medical clinic. The second expectation (voting for or against socialized medicine) yielded even better cross-validations. In the large sample, the canonical correlation was .703, with an overall classification accuracy of 87.1%. In the smaller, cross-validation sample, the canonical correlation was .800, with an overall classification accuracy of 82.7%. In this instance there was slightly greater chance of misclassification of those who opposed socialized medicine.

The cross-validated, discriminant equations were used to generate behavioral expectations (B_e) for each point in time, *including t +0*. Even though we had behavioral expectation data for $t +0$, combining that observed distribution with *expected* distributions would result in unnecessarily biased estimates of the S_k's. The stability matrices (S_k) were estimated by performing crossbreaks on the behavioral expectations for each adjacent point in time $(t +0$ with $t +1$, $t +1$ with $t +2$, etc.). (See Table 2 for the S matrices.)

Second, estimates of the C_k's were obtained directly from a questionnaire devised for that purpose. The 34 subjects used in cross-validating the discriminant equations were used to estimate C_k for each of the three messages in this experiment. The subjects heard one taped message each week for three weeks. Before each message, they provided their behavioral expectations for each of the two issues utilized in this study. After the message, they judged the strength of each message, by giving their perception of the degree of change being recommended by the message on a 0–100 scale. These cues were then averaged and divided by 100, to provide an aggregated cues matrix for each of three messages[7] (See Table 3 for the cues matrices).

Third, the m parameter was estimated indirectly by an optimizing procedure described by Hewes (1976). In general, the approach uses data from three points in time to provide estimates of S_1, S_2 and C_2. *Axiom 2* is then presumed true, and an algebraic estimate is provided for m, subject to the following constraints: (1) the solution must be a positive number and (2) the number must fall between zero and one. When these conditions are not met, the initial algebraic estimate of m is adjusted until it meets these criteria, and yet is the minimum distance from the original solution. This procedure provides for two estimates of m for each expectation, since the matrices for both sets of behavioral expectations are each two by two. This "over identified" solution for m allows a check of Hypothesis 1.[8]

Data processing. Once the initial estimates of each of the parameters were obtained, those estimates were used to generate expected values for the variables appearing in the hypotheses. For instance, in Hypothesis 2, B_e's for $t +3$ and $t +4$ were esti-

mated by the theory and compared to actual values of B_e for those time periods.

The fit of the predictions of the theory to the data were assessed by means of X^2 goodness-of-fit tests described in Suppes and Atkinson (1960).

One note of caution must be made in interpreting these results. The statistical procedures associated with stochastic model testing utilize the predictions of the theory as the *null hypothesis*. This is the reverse of traditional tests of verbal theories where the theory's predictions are associated with largely unquantified *alternative hypotheses*. This difference makes it crucial that the power of each of the tests be reported. The probability that a true alternative hypothesis will be rejected (1-power) must be low for the theory to be rejected.

RESULTS

Hypothesis 1

Employing estimation procedures described elsewhere (Hewes, 1976), the authors found values of m for two expectations; the expectation that an individual would take a member of his or her family to a socialized medical clinic, given the opportunity, and the expectation that the individual would vote for socialized medicine. B_e had two "states" in each case.

For the first expectation (treatment of a relative), the hypothesis of noncontingency proved incorrect. The retention parameter for those willing to have a member of their family receive treatment was 1.00, while for those who were unwilling $m = .736$. These two estimates of m were significantly different at the .01 level.[9] Substantial improvement in prediction was obtained when m was treated as being contingent on the expectations of the individual.

For the second expectation (voting), an even more pronounced difference was found in the values of m contingent on expectation ($p < .01$). For those who expected to vote for socialized medicine, $m = 1.00$. For those who opposed socialized medicine, $m = .09$. In other words, those who supported socialized medicine were unchanged by the messages, while those opposed were extremely susceptible to persuasion.

Clearly, the results obtained in this study suggest a revision in the difinition of m such that it is taken to be *the probability of retaining a given cognitive structure (S) in the face of input from the environment (C) contingent upon the expectations held by the individual prior to receipt of the message.*

Reformulated in this manner, m must be recast as a matrix M with the contingent probabilities of m in the main diagonal and zeroes elsewhere.[10] For instance, M for the voting expectation would appear as

$$M = \begin{pmatrix} 1.00 & 0.00 \\ 0.00 & 0.09 \end{pmatrix}.$$

Throughout the rest of this paper, this matrix interpretation of the retention parameter is utilized in computations.

Hypothesis 2

The second prediction is derived directly from *Theorem 3* as revised to take into account the results of the test of Hypothesis 1. In particular,

$$B_e(t+k) = B_e(t+0) \prod_{j=1}^{k} (\delta(M^j S_0 + (I-M) \sum_{i=1}^{j} M^{j-i}C_i) + (1-\delta)S_{j-1}).$$

As noted above, subjects were exposed to three messages. C's for those messages were obtained from a separate sample. Behavioral expectations were obtained from the audience through a direct measurement at $t + 0$, and a validated indirect technique for measurement at $t + 2$ through $t + 4$. Since some of the data in $t + 2$ were needed to estimate M, predictions of B_e were made for $t + 3$ and $t + 4$.

For $t+3$, the predicted distribution for expectations of taking a family member to a socialized clinic was:

	Would	Wouldn't
$B_e(t+3) = ($	.79	.21)

The actual distribution for that same point in time was:

	Would	Wouldn't
$B_e(t+3) = ($	.85	.15).

A goodness-of-fit test was not significant ($X^2 = 3.315$, df $= 1$, p $> .075$), indicating that the theory accurately predicted the distribution of B_e within the limits of chance. The probability of rejecting a false null hypothesis (the power of this statistic) was approximately .96, for an effects parameter of .10 and .75 for an effects parameter of .05 (Cohen, 1969).[11] In general, the odds of rejecting an incorrect theory were quite good.

A similar prediction of B_e was made for $t+4$. No message was received by the subjects immediately prior to $t+4$, so that $\delta = 0$ in the hypothesis (*Theorem 3*).

The predicted distribution for expectations at $t+4$, of taking a family member to a socialized clinic, was

	Would	Wouldn't
$B_e(t+4) = ($	.77	.23).

The actual distribution for that same point in time was:

	Would	Wouldn't
$B_e(t+4) = ($	.75	.25).

A goodness-of-fit test failed to achieve significance ($X^2 = .409$, df $= 1$, p $> .85$) indicating that, within the limits of chance, the theory accurately predicted the distribution of $B_e(t+4)$. The power of this test was approximately the same as the last test described.

Having tested the ability of the model to predict one set of expectations, it became important to replicate the findings on a different type of expectation. To that end, expectations concerning the subjects' willingness to vote for or against socialized medicine were assessed, using the same procedures over the same time periods.

The predicted distribution of expectations for t+3 was:

	For	Against
$B_e(t+3) = ($	.152	.848).

The actual distribution was:

	For	Against
$B_e(t+3) = ($	.103	.897).

The goodness-of-fit test was not significant at the .05 level ($X^2 = 2.007$, df = 1, p > .15).

For $t+4$ the distribution predicted by the theory was:

$$\begin{array}{ccc} & For & Against \\ B_e(t+4) = (& .173 & .827 \quad), \end{array}$$

while the actual distribution of voting expectations was:

$$\begin{array}{ccc} & For & Against \\ B_e(t+4) = (& .125 & .875 \quad). \end{array}$$

Again, the goodness-of-fit test failed to achieve statistical significance ($X^2 = 1.807$; df = 1; p > .15). The predictions of the theory for both $t+3$ and $t+4$ were well within the limits of chance. Further, as in the previous set of hypotheses, the odds of detecting a violation of the predictions of the theory are relatively high.

The predictions of *Theorem 3* are tentatively supported by these results. At the very least, there is reason to proceed with more detailed and powerful tests of the aspect of the theory investigated in this study.

Hypothesis 3

The third prediction made by the theory is somewhat more basic than the last, since it is a test of two of the axioms. *Axioms 2* and *3* predict the actual values of the stability matrix.[12] Formally:

$S_k = MS_{k-1} + (I-M)C_k$ for *Axiom 2*
and
$S_k = S_{k-1}$ for *Axiom 3*.

The values of S_2 through S_4, for both sets of expectations, were taken from the same sample employed in the other hypotheses. S_1 was excluded because it was taken as a "given" in the test procedures developed by Hewes (1976).

For expectations about taking a member of one's family to a socialized clinic, the cumulative lack of fit for S_2 through S_4 was statistically significant ($X^2 = 9.972$; df = 3; p < .05). For expectations about voting, the cumulative lack of fit was also significant ($X^2 = 12.195$; df = 3; p < .05).

In both of these tests, the statistical significance of the goodness-to-fit tests indicates that *Axioms 1* and *3* do not adequately capture the generative mechanisms for the S matrices. On the other hand, care must be taken not to over-emphasize the importance of the significance tests. For instance, the percentage of people misclassified in the S matrices for the first set of expectations was very small: 3.8% for S_2, 5.8% for S_3 and 4.7% for S_4. For the second set of expectations, the percentages of people misclassified were 0.9%, 7.7% and 5.4% respectively. In other words, the actual errors in estimating S were not large, even though they were statistically significant. This point is supported by the accuracy in predicting B_e, even given the errors in the stability matrices.

CONCLUSIONS

The results of these experiments proved generally supportive of the theory. Clearly the weakest evidence was garnered for the assumption that m is a scalar (Hypothesis 1), and the strongest evidence supported the predictiveness of the theory (Hypothesis 2). While *Axioms 2* and *3* (Hypothesis 3) were not solidly supported, very little practical significance was observed in the deviations from the theory.

To what might these deviations be attributed? There are at least three possibilities. First, it may be that *Axioms 2* and *3* are incorrect. The possibility was already suggested in the description of the retention parameter, and in the discussion of *Axiom 3*. Of course, other potential reformulations of both axioms could be created, and they might prove more predictive.

A second possibility is that the estimation procedures for M, described by Hewes (1976), and implemented here, might have introduced unnecessary unreliability in the estimation of S_3 and S_4. That could well have happened in two ways: (1) the procedures described by Hewes (1976) are admittedly far more optimal, and (2) the sample used to estimate M (34 subjects) may have been too small to yield reliable values. Future research should address these two problems, so that a clear decision can be made concerning the validity of *Axioms 2* and *3*.

The third explanation for the problems with

Axioms 2 and *3* concerns the *ad hoc* assumption introduced by the methodology. In order to test this theory, it was necessary to assume that the population sampled was homogeneous with respect to the *S* matrices, *M* and the *C*'s. This is a large, but not uncommon, methodological assumption. It may be incorrect. Unfortunately several methodological innovations may be necessary before this hypothetical heterogeneity can be accurately detected. Once detected, heterogeneity can easily be introduced into the theory.

Regardless of which, if any, of these explanations is correct, the theory has fared quite well. Direct empirical tests of the theory forced some modifications (of *m*) which were easily incorporated into its structure. The predictions of behavioral expectations were extremely good. The *worst* prediction only misclassified 6.6% of the people! While support for *Axioms* 2 and *3* was weak, more sophisticated estimation procedures, and greater care in sampling, may well prove to be better solutions to the problem of lack of fit than would be a modification of the theory.

COMPARISON OF THE THEORY TO AN ALTERNATIVE

Testing of formalized theories often differs in practice from the testing of conventional verbal theories. As Diesing (1971) so clearly points out, a formal theory cannot be tested in a vacuum. It must be tested in comparison to some viable alternative.

The reason for this is straightforward. More than one formal mechanism can, in any given data set, generate the same prediction. Thus, confirmation of the predictions of a formal theory does not guarantee that the theory is necessarily ''correct'' or even close to it. King (1973) observes that the same is true in verbal theories. He further notes that such contrastive analysis is seldom, if ever, done with such theories. In practice contrastive analysis is carried out much more often in tests of formal theories (Diesing 1971). At any rate, the only way to gain increased confidence in the validity of a formal theory is to contrast it with an alternative which is *just different enough* so that a contrast can be made. Obviously, selecting an alternative ''just different enough'' involves some artistic judgment,

since no precise criteria exist for making the choice.

For our purpose the choice is somewhat simpler than in most cases. Hewes (1975b) has identified the most likely alternative to the present theory. That alternative is the simple, first-order Markov chain. It differs from the present formulation in one important aspect: it does not take into account cues from the environment, *C* matrices, in changing the stability matrices. In other words, a Markov chain is a closed system.

In the following discussion, the Markov chain will be presented briefly, and its assumptions compared with the theory presented here. Subsequently, the Markov chain model will be fitted to the data, its assumptions tested, and its predictions compared to those of the theory presented earlier.

The Markov Chain Model

The Markov chain model has been widely used for examining behavior and attitude change (Anderson, 1954; Bartholomew, 1973; Massy, Montgomery, & Morrison, 1970); consequently, it is reasonable to apply it to the problem of predicting behavioral expectations and behaviors.

The model is simplicity itself. It has three major assumptions (Hewes, 1975a): (1) it is generally assumed to be a first-order process—the same assumption that is made in *Axiom 1;* (2) the transition matrix (S) is assumed to be stationary; this is equivalent to the assumption contained in *Axiom 3* when no messages are received; and (3) the transition matrix is assumed to be homogenous across the population sampled—the same methodological assumption that is made to test the theory presented earlier.

The difference between the Markov chain and the theory centers primarily on *Axiom 2,* which allows for input from the environment to chain the probabilities contained in S (the transition matrix). The components of the theory (m and C_k) which make this possible are not part of the Markov model.

Testing the assumptions. The first step in contrasting the Markov chain model with the theory is to check the assumptions of the Markov chain model. If it cannot meet its own assumptions, then it is unlikely to fare well in a comparison with the theory presented here.

To test the three major assumptions of the Markov chain, the data gathered earlier were re-analyzed. Approximate statistical tests for each of the three assumptions are available in Suppes and Atkinson (1960) and Hewes (1975c). The procedures for data manipulation needed for these tests are described in depth in Hewes and Evans-Hewes (1974).

Generally speaking, the results of these tests of assumptions were not encouraging. The test of the order assumption did conform to the assumptions. The null hypothesis was that the process being observed was a first-order process. This hypothesis was not rejected at the .05 level for either the first set of expectations ($X^2 = 7.0695$; df = 6; p > .30), or for the second set ($x^2 = 4.552$; df = 6; p > .60).[13]

The second hypothesis was that the process was stationary. This hypothesis stands in contradiction to the theory which allows for, but does not require, nonstationary S matrices. For the first set of expectations (taking a relative to a federally controlled clinic), the transition matrices from $t+0$ to $t+1$, from $t+1$ to $t+2$, and from $t+2$ to $t+3$, did not significantly deviate from the null hypothesis of stationarity (X^2's respectively .726, .478 and .981). However, the X^2 for the transition from $t+3$ to $t+4$ did indicate nonstationarity ($X^2 = 5.649$; df = 1; p < .02). It should be noted that a change in the communication environment took place between $t+3$ and $t+4$, in that no message was received.

The second set of expectations (voting for socialized medicine) revealed a stronger pattern of nonstationarity. From $t+0$ to $t+1$, the S matrix was nonstationary ($X^2 = 11.448$; df = 1; p < .001); from $t+1$ to $t+2$ and from $t+2$ and $t+3$ there was no significant deviation from stationarity (X^2's of 3.511 and 1.765 respectively); from $t+3$ to $t+4$ nonstationarity was detected ($X^2 = 7.154$; df = 1; p < .01). Again this last time period differed from the others in that no message was received.

The final assumption of the Markov chain to be tested was the assumption of homogeneity. Since we did not have an a priori reason for choosing exogenous variables that might produce heterogeneity, we employed an indirect test which can be used to diagnose the occurrence of a viola-

tion of this assumption.

Singer and Spilerman (1974), as well as Coleman (1973), indicate that the major diagonal in the Markov transition matrix tends to contain smaller probabilities than those actually observed as the matrix is raised to greater and greater powers when hetrogeneity is present.[14] In other words, the expected transition probabilities from $t+0$ to $t+2$, for a Markov chain model of the first order, are S^2, where S is a stationary transition matrix.[15] If a cross-tabulation were taken of the individuals who actually did make the transition between those points in time, the observed probabilities in the major diagonal would tend to exceed those generated by the Markov model if the homogeneity assumption is violated.

We employed this technique for both expectations for values of S to the second, third and fourth powers. For the first expectation, the second powers of the transition matrices yielded deficient diagonals ($X^2 = 36.108$, df = 3, p < .001); for the cubed matrices, the diagonals did not differ from the expected values ($X^2 = 4.320$; df = 2; p > .05); for the fourth power matrix the deficiency appeared again ($X^2 = 15.142$; df = 1; p < .001). A more severe problem appeared with the data for the second set of expectations. In all instances, the diagonals were deficient, indicating heterogeneity ($X^2 = 96.915$; df = 3; p < .001 / $X^2 = 13.814$; df = 2; p < .01 / $X^2 = 6.991$; df = 1; p < .01).

Some care must be exercised in interpreting these results. While the support for the first-order assumption is apparent, the rejection of the stationarity assumption is by no means clearly mandated, nor can the diagnostic test for heterogeneity be unambiguously interpreted.

The tests of stationarity did not, in general, lead to a rejection of that assumption; however, an interesting pattern revealed itself. In those instances where there was a change in the communication environment, there were also violations in stationarity. This finding is consistent with observations made in marketing research (Massy, Montgomery, & Morrison, 1970). It was anticipated by Hewes (1975b) and used as a possible justification for the use of nonstationary models in communication research. This pattern of nonstationary is the focus of further analysis in a later section of this paper.

On the other hand, the results of tests of homogeneity are not subject to further investigation. The reason is simple. Tests for homogeneity usually presume stationarity (Anderson & Goodman, 1957). This is certainly true of the diagnostic test used here, since nonstationarity also could have produced the variation in the diagonal detected (Henry, 1971). Therefore, the failure to support the stationarily assumption makes the interpretation of the tests for homogeneity ambiguous. The possibility of homogeneity still exists, but it cannot be confirmed by these data.

Predictions of the Markov model. Even with these potential violations of the Markov chain model, it is still highly useful to examine its predictions. As it turns out, the Markov chain is highly robust to violations of assumptions (Bartholomew, 1973; Hewes & Evans-Hewes, 1974). As a consequence, we examined those predictions so that they could be compared to the predictions of the theory presented earlier.

Two sets of predictions were generated: (1) the behavioral expectations (B_e) for $t+3$ and $t+4$ were generated by the Markov chain and compared to the true values; and (2) the transition matrices for $t+0$ to $t+1$, for both expectations, were used to predict later transition matrices. This last test was performed to test the actual predictive ability of the Markov model.

Results of the attempts to predict B_e $(t+3)$ and B_e $(t+4)$ were generally supportive of the Markov chain model. For the first set of expectations, the predicted distribution of B_e $(t+3)$ was:

	Would	Wouldn't
$B_e(t+3) = ($	.79	.21 $)$

while the actual distribution was:

	Would	Wouldn't
$B_e(t+3) = ($	.85	.15 $)$.

For $B_e(t+4)$ the predicted distribution generated by the Markov chain was:

	Would	Wouldn't
$B_e(t+4) = ($	.80	.20 $)$

while the actual distribution was:

	Would	Wouldn't
$B_e(t+4) = ($	.75	.25 $)$.

Neither of those predicted distributions differed from the actual distributions at greater than chance levels (for expectation #1, $X^2 = 2.471$; df $= 1$; p $> .15$; for expectation #2, $X^2 = 2.294$; df $= 1$; p $> .15$).[16]

The second set of expectations were also well matched by the data. For $B_e(t+3)$ the predicted distribution was:

	For	Against
$B_e(t+3) = ($	.071	.929 $)$.

The actual distribution was:

	For	Against
$B_e(t+3) = ($	.103	.897 $)$.

For the $B_e(t+4)$ the predictions generated by the model were:

	For	Against
$B_e(t+4) = ($	.071	.929 $)$.

The observed distribution was:

	For	Against
$B_e(t+4) = ($	.125	.875 $)$.

In this case, the fit of the Markov chain was not quite as good. While the distributions at $t+3$ were equivalent within chance ($X^2 = 1.637$; df $= 1$; p $> .20$), the predictions at $t+4$ were not as good. The actual distribution differed significantly from the predicted distribution at the .05 level ($X^2 = 4.956$; df $= 1$; p $< .03$).

Thus, while the predictiveness of the Markov chain model is quite good, not all predictions fared as well as the nonstationary theory tested earlier. That theory faced its greatest difficulty in predicting the S matrices across time. In order to see if the Markov chain model suffered from the same problem, it too was tested in terms of its ability to predict the S matrices. Since the Markov chain assumes stationarity (constant values of S), it was hypothesized that the S_1 would directly predict the values of the S matrices at later points in time.

These tests were not supportive of the Markov chain. The transition matrices for the first set of expectations deviated significantly from the assumption that S_1 would predict S_2, S_3 and S_4 (X^2 = 13.865; df = 3; p < .01). The same was true to an even greater extent for the second set of expectations (X^2 = 227.621; df = 3; p < .0001). In short, the Markov chain model is very poor in its ability to predict stability matrices.

A Comparison of Prediction

How well do the theory and the Markov chain do comparatively? The answer must be provided in terms of three different sets of predictions: (1) predictions of behavioral expectations, (2) predictions of the stability matrices, and (3) the patterns of error in the predictions of the stability matrices.

Behavioral expectations. For the behavioral expectations, both the theory and the Markov chain predicted admirably. The cumulative fit of the theory over $t+3$ and $t+4$ for the first set of expectations was not significantly different from chance, with an X^2 of 3.814 (df = 2; p > .15). This test has a power of approximately .92, given α = .05, and a .05 effects size, which Cohen (1969) describes as "small," i.e., the departure from fit of the model which can be detected by this test is "small."[17] The success of the fit is highlighted by the fact that, overall, the theory misclassified only 4.5% of the sample.

By comparison, the Markov chain also fits quite well. The cumulative fit for the Markov chain over $t+3$ and $t+4$ comes close to, but does not exceed, chance deviations from fit. The cumulative X^2 was 4.765 (df = 2; p > .07), which is better than twice the X^2 obtained in the theory, though not statistically significant. In general, the present theory seems better able to predict these data; however, that conclusion must be made tentatively, since it is not backed by statistical evidence.

The cumulative fit of B_e, for the second set of expectations, yields more firm support for the theory. For the theory, the X^2 for $t+3$ and $t+4$ was 3.814 (df = 2; p > .15), which does not indicate a departure in fit of the theory to the data.

The Markov chain did not do as well. The cumulative X^2 for $t+3$ and $t+4$ was 6.593 (df = 2; p < .03), which is statistically significant at the .05 level. Clearly the Markov chain does not fit as well

as the nonstationary theory overall. This result is particularly important, since it is the second set of expectations to which the messages in the study were specifically directed.

Stability matrices. Neither the Markov chain nor the theory presented here did well in predicting the S matrices; however, the theory did better. For the first set of expectations, the X^2 for the theory was 9.972 (df = 3; p < .03), while the X^2 for the Markov chain was 13.865 (df = 3; p < .01). The fit is better for the theory, but not significantly so.

For the second set of expectations, the results, again, are much more clearly in support of the theory. The X^2 for the theory is 12.195 (df = 2; p < .01), but for the Markov chain the X^2 was 227.621 (df = 3; p < .0001). The theory has a significantly better fit than does the model at reasonable levels of significance (F = 18.665; df = 3/3; p < .02).

The pattern of errors in predicting S. A simple examination of the predictions of two alternative models does not fully describe their relative merits. It may be informative to examine the patterns of errors in fit to see if they indicate anything about the nature of the mechanism which generates the change in behavioral expectations.

Figures 1 and 2 indicate the pattern of errors in estimating the S matrices for both sets of expectations. Plotted on each figure are the violations in the predictions of S for the Markov chain model for each of the S matrices. The errors in fit for the nonstationary theory are graphed on the same figure.

The figures emphasize a point made previously: the most serious violations in the Markovian predictions of the S matrices occur during that period of time when there is the major change in the communication environment. By contrast the nonstationary model seems to *improve* in its predictions under those same circumstances; precisely as it should for it to be a good communication theory. Further, the errors of Markov chain prediction show a marked tendency to increase linearly and steeply as a function of time. The errors for the nonstationary theory do not increase as rapidly, primarily owing to the improved prediction under the changing communication environment. In general the patterns of errors suggest both the necessity

FIGURE 1
Comparison of Errors of Prediction of S Matrices for Theory and
Markov Model: Data for Expectation #1

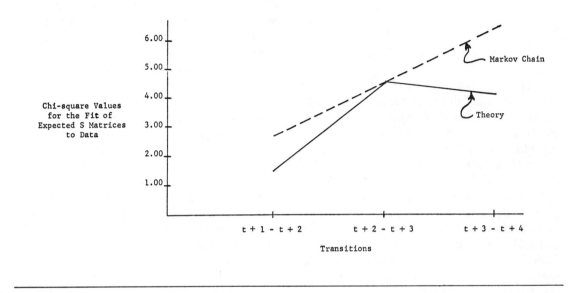

FIGURE 2
Comparison of Errors of Prediction of S Matrices for Theory and
Markov Model: Data for Expectation #2

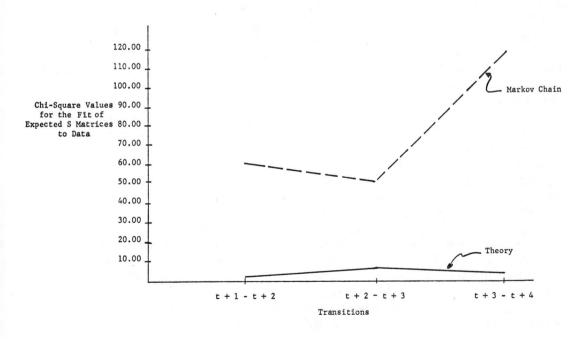

of improving the theory and the superiority of the theory to the Markov chain model.

SUMMARY AND CONCLUSIONS

In the introduction to this paper, we noted that the problem of formulating precise relationshps among messages, as well as mediating cognitive variables and behaviors, was a crucial one of the field of communication. At least one potential solution to that problem was to be found in a theory developed by Hewes (1975b, in press).

The theory is both logically rigorous and supported by the literature in the area. To those recommendations can be added the fact that the theory has also held up well under empirical test. The *worst* prediction of behavioral expectations failed to accurately predict only 6.6% of the subjects, while the best misclassified only 2.4%.

Not only were the predictions of the theory generally accurate in the absolute sense, but they proved to be relatively better than the competing model which is both widely used and more parsimonious. While the comparison did not show the theory to be superior in all instances, it must be remembered that many of the tests took place under conditions which Hewes and Evans-Hewes (1974) described as close to ideal for the Markov chain model. Thus the superiority which did emerge was attained under conditions biased in favor of the competing model.

Of course the test of the theory was not without problems. Direct tests of *Axioms 2* and *3* were equivocal; however, the departure in fit was not large and might be explained by correctable estimation problems. Nevertheless, alternative formulations of *Axiom 2*, in particular, should be investigated and compared to the present version.

The results of the three hypotheses and comparative analysis, taken together, suggest the theory presented here is more likely to require a "tune-up" than an "overhaul." Assuming this assertion is correct, where do we go from here? There are several directions for development and testing of the theory which appear to be particularly important.

First, the theory needs to be tested in a competitive communication environment. The strongest test of this theory, or any theory of communication effects, is one which simulates the contradictory and competing flux of messages which pervades our daily lives. The series of three, one-sided messages used in this experiment did not simulate such an environment. Future studies should attempt to test the theory with a more realistic condition of contradictory messages.

Second, the nature of *retention* (M) must be explored in greater depth. While the estimation procedures described in Hewes (1976), and employed in this study, allow for a relatively precise value to be placed on the elements of retention, there still remains the problem of *predicting M* a priori in terms of its antecedents, and/or possibly *changing M* on the basis of its explanation. Certainly, a message strategy which could selectively alter the size of the elements of M, and then increase the probabilities of change through C, would be much more effective than a message strategy which had to rely solely on the effects of C. At minimum, more background on the elements of retention would improve prediction. At maximum, it would improve control.

In the same vein, the effects of C need to be disaggregated into components which improve our understanding and control of messages. For example, one of the truly valuable aspects of Woelfel's theory of cognitive space (Woelfel, in press) is its ability to aid a communicator in constructing messages. By disaggregating the cues matrices into manipulable components, a similar advantage could be gained for this theory. Once the antecedents of C were understood, messages could be constructed which would have known impact on behavioral expectations. Future theorizing should be focused on this problem.

In summary, we have every reason to be optimistic about a resolution to the message/mediating variable/behavior problem. A precise, dynamic theory has been posited, and the data tend to support it. The theory is far from confirmed, but so is it far from being falsified. We believe this theory, at the very least, points toward a future when communication theories are truly process-oriented, unambiguous, and predictive.

NOTES

1. There is another interpretation of m which leads to a wholly different picture of human cognition. Instead of making m a deterministic parameter, we could say that m is stochastic, that m is the probability that a given internalized S_{k-1} will be retained rather than replaced by C_k. A stochastic m describes a choice process wherein the individual must consciously or subconsciously choose between S_{k-1} or C_k at each point in time $t+k$, given that a message is received at that point in time. This interpretation would substantially alter *Axiom 2, Corollary 2.1* and most of the theorems to follow. I want to thank Robert McPhee of the University of Illinois for making this point clear to me.

2. Hypothesis 1 is rejected, Hypothesis 2 must be revised so that contingent values of m can be included in the model.

3. If Hypothesis 1 is rejected, Hypothesis 3 must be revised to take into account the contingent values of m.

4. Each of these messages was two-and-a-half minutes long, contained the same number of pieces of factual evidence, was delivered by the same source (a professor of medical administration at Boston University), and presented in the same format (as part of a series of radio presentations on the subject). The three messages dealt with the efficiency of a centralized medical care system, the advantages of a national medical data bank, and the necessity of federally sponsored preventive medicine.

5. See Coley and Lohnes (1971) for a discussion of the procedures to be used in cross-validation. We employed their multiple classification analysis with non-Bayesian estimation procedures, since Bayesian procedures would have required us to have prior knowledge of the distribution of behavioral expectations—something we cannot know in this dynamic theory without presuming the theory to be correct.

6. The expected distribution was generated by using the discriminant equation generated on the larger sample.

7. It was assumed that the sample and its associated population was homogeneous with respect to their perceptions of the C_k's. This assumption seemed justified, since the standard errors of the means were quite small.

8. The values for m in the first expectation were estimated using S_2, S_3 and C_3, since the number of individuals who expected to be in one state of C_2 proved too small for a stable estimate.

9. A Z-test for independent samples of the hypothesis that the m's were equal was performed. This test is only approximate, since there is considerable reason to question the distributional properties of m parameters which are estimated indirectly and in a less than optimal way. Nevertheless, the test gives an *indication* that Hypothesis 1 is incorrect.

10. Obviously, redefining m in this manner cannot be done with impunity. Several changes must be made in the axioms and theorems to reflect this change. In Axiom 2, m is replaced by m_i where i indicates the expectation held by the individual prior to receipt of the message. The matrix version of *Axiom 2* can be rephased to incorporate this change in the following manner:

$$S_k = MS_{k-1} + (I-M)C_k$$

where all symbols are defined as before and I is the identity matrix.

   With this change, the alteration of the subsequent theorems flows naturally. For example, Theorem 1 becomes

$$B_e(t+k) = B_e(t+0) \prod_{j=1}^{k}$$

$$(M^i S_0 + (I-M) \sum_{i=1}^{k} M^{j-1}C_i).$$

Other theorems can be changed in a similar fashion.

11. Approximately the same power values apply throughout the rest of the results on this hypothesis.

12. *Axiom 2* is reformulated to take into account the results of Hypothesis 1, which suggests that the retention parameter must be recast as a matrix. See footnote 10 for a complete discussion.

13. An approximate test of the order assumption was applied to three sets of data, each taken over three time periods ($t+0$, $t+1$, and $t+2$; $t+1$, $t+2$ and $t+3$; $t+2$, $t+3$ and $t+4$). The X^2's reported above are the result of summing the X^2's for each of the three sets of data. In no instance did any individual set of data achieve statistical significance.

14. There are other explanations for this "diagonal deficiency" (Coleman, 1973), which is why this test is being billed as "indirect" and "diagnostic." More on this later.

15. The transition matrices for both sets of expectations from $t+0$ to $t+1$ were used in the computations. The violation of the stationarity assumption at various points in time precludes pooling of the transition matrices across time since this would, in effect, "average out" the violations.

16. The power associated with these tests is equivalent to that for the previous tests of the predictions of the theory.

17. These power estimates hold throughout the cumulative predictions of B_e in the remainder of this paper.

REFERENCES

ANDERSON, T.W. Probability models for analyzing time changes in attitudes. In P. Lazarsfeld (Ed.), *Mathematical thinking in the social sciences*. Glencoe, IL: Free Press, 1954, 14-54.

ANDERSON, T.W., & GOODMAN, L.A. Statistical inferences about Markov chains. *Annals of the Mathematical Statistical Association*; 1957, 28, 89-110.

BARTHOLEMEW, D. *Stochastic models for social procsses*. New York: Wiley, 1973.

BELLAMY, M., & THOMPSON, W. Stability of attitude as a predeterminer of experimental results. *Speech Monographs*, 1967, 34, 180-184.

BURHANS, D. The attitude-behavior discrepancy problem: Revisited. *Quarterly Journal of Speech*. 1971, 57(4), 418-428.

CATHCART, E. The importance of situational factors: An examination and extension of the Fishbein models. Unpublished doctoral dissertation, University of North Carolina, 1974.

COOLEY, W.W., & LOHNES, P.R. *Multivariate data analysis*. New York: Wiley, 1971.

COHEN, J. *Statistical power analysis for the behavioral sciences*. New York: Academic Press, 1969.

COLEMAN, J.S. *The mathematics of collective action*. Chicago: Aldine, 1973.

CRAIG, R., & CUSHMAN, D.P. An experimental test of certain attitude change implications of Fishbein's model of attitudes. Paper presented at the annual meeting of the International Communication Association, Chicago, 1975.

CUSHMAN, D.P., (Ed.) *Explorations in the message, attitude, behavioral relationship*. East Lansing: Michigan State University Press, in press.

DESCARTES, R. Letter to Princess Elizabeth, June 28, 1643. In E. Anscombe and P.T. Geach (Eds.), *Descartes: Philosophical writings*. Edinburgh: Nelson, 1954.

DIESING, P. *Patterns of discovery in the social sciences*. Chicago: Aldine-Atherton, 1971.

FISHBEIN, M. Attitudes and the prediction of behavior. In M. Fishbein (Ed.), *Readings in attitude theory and measurement*. New York: Wiley, 1967, 477-492.

FISHBEIN, M. The prediction of behaviors from attitudinal variables. In C.D. Mortensen and K. Sereno (Eds.), *Advances in communication research*. New York: Harper & Row, 1973, 3-31.

FISHBEIN, M., & AJZEN, I. *Belief, attitude, intention and behavior*. Reading, Mass.: Addison-Wesley, 1975.

GLASS, G.V., WILLSON, V.L., & GOTTMAN, J.M. *Design and analysis of time-series experiments*. Boulder, Colo.: Colorado Associate University press, 1975.

HENRY, N.W. The retention model: A Markov chain with variable transition probabilities. *Journal of the American Statistical Association*, 1971, 66, 264-267.

HEWES, D.E. Finite stochastic modeling of communication processes: An introduction and some basic readings. *Human Communication Research*, 1975a, 1 (3), 271-283.

HEWES, D.E. A stochastic model of the relationship between attitudes and behaviors. Paper presented at the annual meeting of the International Communication Association, Chicago, 1975b.

HEWES, D.E. Markov chains and sequential, cross-sectional sampling. Paper presented at the annual meeting of the Speech Communication Association Convention, 1975c, Houston, Texas.

HEWES, D.E. Procedures for estimating "m" and "S$_o$" in a message mediating variable-behavior model. Unpublished paper, Arizona State University, 1976.

HEWES. D.E. An axiomatized stochastic process theory of the relationships among messages, mediating variables and behaviors. In D.P. Cushman (Ed.), *Explorations in the message, attitude, behavior relationship*. East Lansing: Michigan State University Press, in press.

HEWES, D., & EVANS-HEWES, D. Toward a Markov chain model of attitude change. Paper presented at the annual meeting of the Speech Communication Association, Chicago, 1974.

KEMENY, J., & SNELL, J. *Finite Markov chains*. New York: Van Nostrand, 1960.

KING, S.W. Theory testing: An analysis and extension. *Western Speech*, 1973, 37(1), 13-22.

MASSY, W.F., MONTGOMERY, D.B., & MORRISON, D.G. *Stochastic models of buying behavior*. Cambridge, Mass.: MIT Press, 1970.

McDERMOTT, V. The literature on classical theory construction. *Human Communication Research*. 1975, 2(1), 83-102.

McNEMAR, Q. Opinion-attitude methodology. *Psychological Bulletin*, 1946, 4,43.

McPHEE, R. Derivation and test of a new model of message-attitude-behavior relationship. Paper presented at the annual meeting of the International Communication Association, Chicago, 1975.

MILLER, G.R. A crucial problem in attitude research. *Quarterly Journal of Speech*, 1967, 53, 235-240.

MISCHEL, T. Scientific and philosophical psychology: A historical introduction. In T. Mischel (Ed.), *Human Action*. New York: Academic Press, 1969, 1-40.

MISCHEL, W. *Personality and assessment*. New York: Wiley, 1968.

NIE, N.H., HULL, C.H., JENKINS, J.G., STEINBRENNER, K., & BENT, D. *Statistical package for the social sciences*, 2nd ed. New York: McGraw-Hill, 1975.

REICHENBACH, H. *The theory of probability*. Berkeley, Cal.: University of California Press, 1949.

Report of the New Orleans Conference on Research and Instructional Development. In R.J. Kibler and L.L. Barker (Eds.), *Conceptual frontiers in speech-communications*. New York: Speech Communication Association, 1969.

SCHWARTZ, S., & TESSLER, R. A test of a model reducing measured attitude-behavior discrepancies. *Journal of Personality and Social Psychology*, 1972, 24, 225-236.

SEIBOLD, D.R. Communication research and the attitude-verbal report-overt behavior relationship: A critique and theoretical reformulation. *Human Communication Research*, 1975, 2(1), 3-32.

SIMONS, H.W. Psychological theories of persuasion: An auditor's report. *Quarterly Journal of Speech*. 1971, 57(4), 383-392.

SINGER, B., & SPILERMAN, S. Social mobility models for heterogeneous populations. In H. Costner (Ed.), *Sociological methodology 1973-74*. San Francisco: Jossey-Bass, 1974, 356-402.

SUPPES, P., & ATKINSON, R. *Markov learning models of multiperson interactions*. Stanford, Calif.: Stanford University Press, 1960.

TRIANDIS, H. Exploratory factor analysis of behavioral components of social attitudes. *Journal of Abnormal and Social Psychology*. 1964, 68, 420-430.

WARNER, L., & DEFLUER, M. Attitude as an interaction concept: Social constraint and social distance as intervening variables between attitudes and action. *American Sociological Review*, 1969, 34, 153-169.

WICKER, A. An examination of the other variables' explanation of attitude-behavior inconsistency. *Journal of Personality and Social Psychology*, 1971, 19(1), 18-30.

WIGGINS, L. *Panel analysis: Latent probability models for attitude and behavioral processes*. San Francisco: Jossey-Bass, 1973.

WOELFEL, J. Foundations of Cognitive Theory. In D.P. Cushman (Ed.), *Explorations in the message, attitude, behavior relationship*. East Lansing: Michigan State University Press, in press.

INTERPERSONAL COMMUNICATION
Theory and Research: An Overview
Selected Studies

INTERPERSONAL COMMUNICATION THEORY AND RESEARCH: AN OVERVIEW

CHARLES R. BERGER
Northwestern University

Had this overview been written 10 years ago, the characterization of the area of interpersonal communication undoubtedly would have been quite different from the present one. During the 1950s and 1960s the predominant orientation of researchers in the field was attitude change and persuasion. Research in small groups and group discussion was reported, but studies in such areas as source credibility, fear appeals, and counterattitudinal advocacy, were by far the most frequently reported ones in the literature. Some researchers identified themselves with Hovland's Yale group and later with Festinger's (1957, 1964) work in *dissonance theory*. Others utilized such frameworks as *inoculation theory* (McGuire, 1964) and *social judgment theory* (Sherif, Sherif, & Nebergall, 1965) to do communication research.

Immediately following World War II, social psychologists interested in persuasion (e.g., Hovland, Lumsdaine, & Sheffield, 1949) conceived of their research in terms of mass communication situations. While the Hovland research program was experimental, the stimulus presentations were frequently in the form of bogus radio programs or newspaper stories. Curiously, in spite of Hovland's mass communication orientation to persuasion, researchers in interpersonal communication continued to employ his basic model of persuasion in their research instead of studying social influence in more "interpersonal-like" settings.

There has been an apparent decline of traditional persuasion research since the late 1960s and early 1970s in both social psychology and interpersonal communication. The reasons for this decrease are unclear. Perhaps the decline was partly the result of the rise of the humanistic psychology movement, and the apparently antimanipulative value system associated with it. Another factor may have been

dissatisfaction with the public address model of persuasion underlying much of the research. Finally, the seeming decrease in the number of traditional persuasion studies may also be a function of increased interest in interpersonal communication research activity in areas other than attitude change.

Whatever the reason or reasons, relatively few traditional persuasion studies appear on convention programs or in communication journals today. Replacing such research are studies which focus more frequently upon negotiation and cooperation in interpersonal communication, rather than upon face-to-face communication events where persuasion and social influence take place.

THEORIES AND THEORETICAL ISSUES

On Defining Interpersonal Communication

While no attempt will be made here to define *interpersonal communication*, it should be stressed that this definitional problem remains unresolved. As Miller and Steinberg (1975) have noted, many definitions employ the *number of persons* interacting as a criterion for distinguishing interpersonal from noninterpersonal communication. Miller and Steinberg propose that the number of persons involved in a particular transaction ought not be regarded as the critical determinant of whether communication is interpersonal. Instead, they argue, interpersonal communication occurs when information exchanged by participants in an encounter is primarily psychological in nature, as opposed to sociological or cultural. Psychological level information enables the information receiver to distinguish the information giver from cultural or social groups of which the giver is a member. In the view of Miller and Steinberg, communication that primarily involves the enactment of social roles is likely to be noninterpersonal in nature. They further argue that the purpose of communication in general is to increase predictability of the environment (including other people) so that the environment can be controlled and rewards achieved.

In contrast to this view, Pearce (1976a) argues that communication is best conceived as the "coordinated management of meaning." He asserts that for such coordination to take place, persons enacting episodes must: (1) achieve agreement about constitutive rules of the relationships, e.g., decide whether they are friends or neighbors; and (2) regulate the sequence of episodes, i.e., decide what to do or say after the other has stopped speaking. This framework allows for highly predictable role-role interactions to be subsumed under the general rubric of "interpersonal communication." Moreover, Pearce's model of man differs considerably from Miller and Steinberg's. Pearce seems to assume that persons prefer rule consensus and agreement. Miller and Steinberg allow for the possibility that a given actor might well break rules and impose a definition of the situation upon the other interactant in order to gain rewards, even though these rewards may be short-term ones.

The above attempts at defining interpersonal communication highlight the kinds of problems associated with achieving a consensual definition. Theories and methodologies spawned from different models of man may lead to different predictions about human behavior. And the kinds of explanations for behavior which are offered by divergent theories are apt to differ considerably. Theories which stress man's abilities and limitations as an information processor offer explanations for his interpersonal communication behavior which are quite different from those offered by theories which stress the instrumental value of interpersonal communication for obtaining rewards.

An additional problem is that methodologies which are appropriate for studying interpersonal communication from one perspective may not be as useful from another. Theories which emphasize the growth and decay of interpersonal communication systems are likely to demand longitudinal studies and time-series techniques for their testing. By contrast, theories which advance the view that much of

man's behavior is controlled by norms and rules may be best evaluated by methodologies which enable researchers to identify the norms and rules being enacted in various interpersonal situations. These methodologies may be nonquantitative and observational.

Theoretical Positions

The tradition of the interpersonal communication area, as well as the communication discipline as a whole, has been to draw heavily upon theoretical orientations from such disciplines as social psychology, psychology, sociology, political science, and linguistics. Increasingly, however, researchers interested in interpersonal communication are themselves becoming active in the area of theory building and testing. While relatively few theories have been presented in a formal manner, with systematic linkage of hierarchically organized propositions, systematic attempts to build theory are under way. The conceptual framework of Miller and Steinberg (1975) is one such attempt. Working from a reinforcement-oriented framework, they argue that persons attempt to make the behavior of others predictable so as to gain some measure of control in their relationships and gain rewards from them. Their position is steeped in the tradition of the social psychological theories of Adams (1965), Altman and Taylor (1973), Homans (1961), and Thibaut and Kelley (1959), all of which attempt to explain the development of interpersonal relationships in terms of reward and cost constructs.

Reward/cost and related covering law explanations of communication have been contrasted with a "rule governed" perspective (Cushman & Whiting, 1972, Cushman, 1975, Pearce, 1976a, Pearce, 1976b). Essentially, the rule governed position argues that instead of viewing social behavior as causally determined, a more satisfactory explanation can better be achieved by asserting that a given individual's behavior is governed by *rules*. Some rules, it is suggested, are shared widely by members of a particular social group, while other rules may be unique to individual relationships. In such a view, the task of the social scientist is to identify exactly what rules govern interaction in particular social situations. Observing the response to breaking rules is one method (Garfinkel, 1967). The rule governed position has numerous theoretical and methodological implications, and has been dealt with in detail by Harré and Secord (1972), Harré (1974), and Toulmin (1974), to name just a few. The applicability of this approach to interpersonal communication has been explicated at some length by Cushman and Whiting (1972), Cushman (1975), and Pearce (1976a, 1976b). And, although considerable research in the rules tradition exists (see Sudnow, 1972) in sociolinguistics, Nofsinger (1976) has authored one of the few papers to appear in a communication journal which present data reflecting this approach.

Few attempts have been made to develop and test deductive and/or axiomatic theories. Berger and Calabrese (1975) have presented a set of axioms and derived theorems which seek to explain certain communication phenomena occurring during the initial stages of interaction between strangers. The central explanatory construct of their theory is uncertainty. Some studies have attempted to test derivations from the theory as well as the mediational explanation of uncertainty as measured by the uncertainty scale labeled CLUES (Berger & Clatterbuck, 1976; Berger, Munley, & Clatterbuck, 1976; Clatterbuck, 1976; Gardner, 1976; Schulman, 1976). While the findings have not been fully consistent with the theory, certain propositions have received support, including the predicted relationships between similarity and uncertainty, and between uncertainty and liking. From this limited amount of research, it seems evident that some aspects of the theory require extension and possible reformulation. Although Berger and Calabrese (1975) initially intended that their theory only be relevant to initial interaction situations, they wished eventually to add additional constructs in order to account also for the development and disintegration of relationships. An attempt to explain the growth and decline of relationships has been presented by Cappella (1974). In this model, Cappella casts *coorientation theory* (Chaffe & McLeod, 1973) into a systems framework and tests several propositions generated by this analysis.

Another example of systematic theory building is Parks's (1975) axiomatic theory of relational communication, which attempts to bring together a number of diverse constructs and relationships under the umbrella of a single theoretical statement. Burgoon and Jones (1976) have also attempted to summarize and systematically order proxemics research into a single coherent theoretical statement.

Dance and Larson (1976) have begun to develop a functional theory of human communication. They identify three main functions served by communication at the three levels. These functions—each of which is suggested to have consequences for interpersonal communication—are: (1) the linking function, (2) the development of higher mental processes, and (3) the regulation of human behavior or relating self to environment and to others' behavior.

An example of theory recasting is provided by the work of Seibold (1975a). In this paper, seibold explicates the various *attribution theory* positions of Heider (1958), Jones and Davis (1965), and Kelley (1967, 1973), and attempts to define constructs and order propositions in such a way that the theory is clarified and becomes more susceptible to test. He also draws several hypotheses relevant to communication from the reformulated theory.

RESEARCH DIRECTIONS

The following review groups interpersonal communication research into the two broad categories of individual focus and transactional focus. Within each of these categories a general overview of current research trends and interest areas is provided.

Individual Focus

Most research in interpersonal communication has been individually oriented. This orientation focuses on the effects that one actor produces or may produce in another, and de-emphasizes the reciprocal nature of interpersonal communication. In this perspective, interpersonal communication is essentially characterized as a miniature version of persuasion or public address where one person is the "speaker" and the other the "audience."

Communicator style. The general thrust of research on communicator style is to isolate various facets of self-presentation which influence such factors as attractiveness and effectiveness in interaction. Feldman (1973) found that persons scoring high on verbal dogmatism were more attracted to sources who themselves manifested a highly verbally dogmatic communication style. Verbal dogmatism was defined by three components: opinionation, aggressiveness, and authoritativeness. This study also revealed that self-reports of verbal dogmatism correlated highly (in excess of .80) with judges' ratings of verbal dogmatism. Verbal intensity, a variable closely related to verbal dogmatism, has been studied by Mortensen and Arntson (1974), who found a high correlation between self-reports and judges' ratings. Moreover, these results indicated that highly tense persons tended to feel more understood than *moderates* or *lows*. However, Hewes, Haight, and Szalay (1976) have raised some questions concerning the stability of predispositions such as verbal intensity across various social situations.

Norton (1976) and his colleagues (Norton & Miller, 1975; Norton & Pettegrew, 1976; Norton, Schroeder, & Webb, 1975; Norton & Warnick, 1976) have systematically sought to explicate the communicator style construct and to relate it to other variables. These studies, summarized by Norton (1976), indicate nine variables which at least partially comprise this construct: dominance, dramatic, animated, open, contentious, relaxed, friendly, attention, and impression leaving. Norton and his colleagues have also attempted to link these dimensions with such dependent variables as attractiveness and group problem solving. For example, Norton and Pettegrew (1976) found that a dominant, open communication style was judged to be significantly more attractive than dominant and nonopen, nondominant and relaxed, and nondominant and nonrelaxed styles.

An area related to communication style is that of communication apprehension. McCroskey (1970) and his colleagues (Daly, McCroskey, & Richmond, 1974; McCroskey, Daly, Richmond, & Cox, 1975; McCroskey, Hamilton, & Weiner, 1974; Quiggens, 1972), following the work by Phillips (1968), have reported that persons with high levels of communication apprehension are less attractive to both themselves and to others than are less reticent persons. However, the relationship between communication apprehension and attractiveness may not be a simple monotonic function. The possible deleterious effects of "excessive" communication behavior on attraction should be considered. The previously cited Feldman (1973) study found that highly dogmatic verbal styles were consistently rated less attractive than their low dogmatic counterparts. Moreover, in terms of the Norton (1976) research, persons who are prone to communication excesses in terms of amount and/or intensity might be perceived as more dominant and ultimately domineering. Thus, it seems reasonable to expect inverted parabolic relationships between at least some communication style variables and communicator attractiveness when the ranges of communication style variables are set at extreme values.

In research closely related to that subsumed under communicator style, Giles (1976) and his associates have performed numerous studies concerned with the influence of speech style on social evaluation. The influence of dialect, accent, and speech rate differences on evaluations of the speech user have been investigated in a number of cultural contexts. Giles's research, as well as related studies in sociolinguistics, are summarized in Giles and Powesland (1975). In addition, this volume presents rudiments of a theory designed to explain variations in speech style. This framework attempts to explicate the conditions under which speech styles of interactants will converge and those under which divergence will occur. The approach to communicator style represented by Giles and Powesland (1975) also attempts to relate variations in speech behavior to variations in attributions made about the speech user.

Communicative competence.   Recently, a number of researchers in interpersonal communication (Bochner & Kelly, 1974; Delia & O'Keefe, 1975; Hart, Eadie, and Carlson, 1975; Pearce, 1976a; Wiemann, 1976) have begun to draw on the literature of developmental psychology, cognitive psychology, and sociolinguistics as sources of constructs and hypotheses concerning the development of communicative competence. Although no attempt will be made to review the extensive work in these areas, both Delia and O'Keefe (1974) and

Parks (1976) have presented selective reviews of relevant literature.

In general, advocates of the communicative competence position argue that in order for persons to be "effective" communicators, they must learn to enact behavioral routines which are deemed appropriate to the particular individuals and social situations where they are interacting. Hymes (1970) asserts that communicative competence is the way in which a "child perceives and categorizes the social situations of his world and differentiates his way of speaking accordingly" (p. 14). Communicative competence refers to the extent to which one has mastery of an underlying set of rules, determined by culture and situation, which affects language choices in interpersonal communication situations, as well as other potentially communicative behavior. Persons may or may not be aware of the rules they employ in a given situation; they may not be able to articulate the rules until they are violated.

Empathy or *reciprocal role-taking abilities* (Flavell, 1967) are viewed as crucial to gaining an understanding of the relationship between *self, other,* and the particular *social context.* Once such an understanding has been achieved, the communicator engages in behaviors which maximize the probabilities of goal achievement. Of course, the chosen communication strategy may be inappropriate, and thus considered ineffective. Communicatively competent individuals presumably are able to discriminate their lack of success and be flexible enough to change their strategies in order to achieve their goals.

Wiemann (1976), drawing on such writers as Argyle (1969, 1972), Bochner and Kelly (1974), Goffman (1959, 1961), and Weinstein (1966, 1969), provides a bridge between communicative competence and the communicator style research discussed earlier. He argues that there are several dimensions to communicative competence: affiliation/support, social relaxation, empathy, behavioral flexibility, and interaction management skills. In this study, persons watched video tapes of individuals who displayed varying amounts of the five classes of behaviors alleged to comprise communicative competence. They then rated the various tapes to assess the impact of the variations on perceived communicative competence. Thus the Wiemann study dealt with judgments of communicative competence as a consequence of variations in communication style for such dimensions as social support, relaxation, empathy, and behavioral flexibility which can certainly be thought of as communicator style variables.

His results indicated that the dimensions were perceived as interdependent components of communicative competency—the greater the display of behavior indicative of the dimensions of competency, the more competent the communicator was judged to be. Wiemann defined communicative competence as:

> the ability of an interactant to choose among available communicative behaviors in order that he may successfully accomplish his own interpersonal goals during an encounter while maintaining the face and line of his fellow interactants within the constraints of the situation. (p. 7)

The latter section dealing with the maintenance of face and line raises questions concerning the possible manipulation and/or imposition of a face on others. Wiemann's definition does not deal with the possibility that high machiavellians or persons with a high need for power (Veroff, 1958; Veroff & Veroff, 1972) could be competent communicators. Such an assumption seems unwarranted in view of the following conclusions drawn about high machiavellians by Christie and Geis (1970):

> Initially our image of the high Mach was a negative one, associated with shadowy and unsavory manipulations. However, after watching subjects in laboratory experiments, we found ourselves having a perverse admiration for the high Mach's ability to outdo others in experimental situations. *Their greater willingness to admit socially undesirable traits compared to low Mach's hinted at a possibly greater insight into and honesty about themselves* . . . This does not mean that our admiration was unqualified; it might be better described as selective. (p. 339; italics added)

While it may be ethically desirable for face and line to be maintained in social interactions, competent communicators may conceivably violate rules, intimidate, and make others uncomfortable in the course of reaching their goals if they regard the task at hand as more important than the enduring social relationship of the interactants.

Social influence processes. While research in traditional areas of persuasion and attitude change has shown a downturn within the past several years, research interest still continues in these areas. For example, M. Burgoon and King (1974) continue to investigate the induction of resistance to persuasion. Also M. Burgoon, Jones, and Stewart (1975) have formulated the beginnings of a message-centered theory of persuasion. Finally, J. Burgoon (1975) has examined the relationship between the learning of message content and attitude change, an issue which remains unresolved.

Another continuing area of research interest related to social influence processes concerns the relationship between attitudes and behavior and attitude formation processes. Recently, Seibold (1975) has provided a review of the attitude-verbal report-overt behavior problem and attempted to formulate a model for testing these relationships more rigorously. Moreover, Saltiel and Woelfel (1975) have presented both a model and data which show the relationship between accumulated information about an attitude-object and the stability of the attitude.

There is also evidence of continued interest in specific variables traditionally related to persuasion. For example, source credibility continues to be: (1) scrutinized for its "dimensionality" (Cody, Marlier, & Woelfel, 1976), (2) researched in terms of its antecedents (Housel & McDermott, 1976), and (3) studied in terms of the individual's proneness to it (Baxter, 1976). In addition to this continued interest in source credibility, there appears to be a renewed interest in *distraction theory* as an explanatory framework for persuasion outcomes (Brandt, 1976).

In briefly considering communicative competency, the issue of social-influence ability as a legitimate dimension of competence was raised. This notion is not new. Rodnick and Wood (1973) have already examined the extent to which children employ various communication strategies in attempts to persuade their parents. In a similar vein, Marwell and Schmitt (1967) have attempted to determine the conditions under which various compliance-gaining strategies are employed in interaction contexts. Miller, Boster, Roloff, and Seibold (1976) have significantly extended the Marwell and Schmitt research by examining the ways that the various compliance-gaining message strategies cluster across various situations, and the extent to which they are likely to be used in interpersonal and noninterpersonal communication situations with both long- and short-term consequences. Employing the four types of situations follows directly from the Miller and Steinberg (1975) work in the area of theoretical positions.

Nonverbal communication. Despite the fact that communication scholars have authored books in the area of nonverbal communication (e.g., J. Burgoon & Saine, in press; Harrison, 1974; Knapp, 1972), relatively little empirical research has appeared in this area since an initial flurry of interest. Following on the work of Ekman & Friesen (1969), Knapp, Hart, & Dennis (1974), as well as Hocking, Bauchner, Kaminski, and Miller (1976), have examined both verbal and nonverbal communication cues associated with deception in interpersonal communication contexts. These studies reveal that there are reliable indicators of deception in face-to-face communication situations. Reduced eye contact, speaking rates, word variety, and increases in leg movements, and nervous gestures were found to be associated with deception.

As mentioned earlier, J. Burgoon and Jones (1976) have developed a set of propositions summarizing research in the area of proxemics. Heston (1974) and Heston and Garner (1972) have presented empirical research in the area of proxemics, while Jones (1971) has done comparative studies of proxemics in various subcultures of New York City children. In closely related research, McCroskey and Sheahan (1976) have examined the relationship between seating position and group participation.

Keiser and Altman (1976) have sought to isolate those nonverbal behaviors associated with different levels of relationship (good friend versus casual acquaintance) and the topic under discussion (intimate versus nonintimate). Their research generally reveals that good friends were significantly more relaxed than casual acquaintances when discussing an intimate topic, with the two other conditions falling between these extremes on the relaxation-tension continuum. This study represents one of the first attempts to relate nonverbal communication patterns to the more general issue of the development of interpersonal relationships.

Self-disclosure. Self-disclosure is another area that has received relatively little attention from communication researchers. Two recent reviews of the self-disclosure literature (Cozby, 1973; Pearce and Sharp, 1973) point to several possible avenues for communication research in this area. Gilbert and Horenstein (1975) have reported that valence of disclosure (positive versus negative) is a more important determinant of attractiveness than intimacy level. Gilbert and Whiteneck (1976) have suggested that *self-disclosure* is best conceived as a multidimensional construct which differentiates valence of disclosure from intimacy of disclosure. Wheeless (1976) has reported evidence suggesting a possible connection between self-disclosure and interpersonal solidarity (Brown, 1965). Pearce, Wright, Sharp and Slama (1974) found that variables related to type of friendship accounted for more self-disclosure variance than did an index of general "affection."

A study by Jones and Gordon (1972) indicated that timing of disclosure, as well as the level of responsibility involved in the information disclosed, made a significant difference in the attractiveness of the discloser. This research, along with earlier work (e.g., Worthy, Gary, & Kahn, 1969) indicates that the relationship between self-disclosure and attractiveness is not a simple increasing monotonic function.

In addition to the relationship between self-disclosure and interpersonal attraction, Delia (1974) has studied the relationship between self-disclosure and cognitive complexity. Delia found positive relationships between levels of motivational explanation, degree of differentiation, and level of organization and self-disclosure as indexed by Jourard's Self-Disclosure Questionnaire (JSDQ).

Transactional Focus

Studies utilizing a transactional approach emphasize the reciprocal nature of interpersonal communication and embody the notion in a theoretical and/or methodological sense. Relatively few studies clearly represent this perspective. A technique such as analysis of sequential interact rather than individual acts, is one interacts methodological device which attempts to capture the transactive notion.

Relational communication. Considerable energy has been spent developing methods for measuring communication between dyads at the relationship level, as opposed to the content or referential level. The original development of a coding system reported by Mark (1971) has been extended by Rogers and Farace (1975). In analyses of relational communication, the concern is with control patterns manifested in the relationship and changes in these patterns through time. Rogers and Farace (1975) point out that the study of relational communication captures the process aspect of ongoing interaction. Rather than analyzing individual messages, relational coding systems analyze exchanges of messages to determine whether the relationship defined by the exchange is symmetrical, complementary, or transitional. Symmetric relationships are characterized by similarity in the exchange of control messages, while complementary relationships are characterized by exchanges of maximally dissimilar control messages. Changes in the relative power or level of control in the relationship can be charted through time, and control patterns of various groups can be contrasted.

Research employing the relational approach revealed that marital dyads with high levels of role discrepancy tended to manifest higher levels of competitive symmetry in their communication (Rogers, 1972). Millar (1973) found that married couples with more rigid patterns of relational communication reported more agreement and understanding about their marital satisfaction. Parks, Farace, Rogers, Albrecht, and Abbott (1976) have performed Markov process analyses of relational communication in marital dyads. Folger & Puck (1976) have presented an alternative system for coding relational communication, using what they call a "question approach."

Finally, Parks (1975) reviewed the theory and research relevant to the relational communication area, and he has developed several axioms and theorems specifying relationships between various relational variables. However, Parks points out that the relational communication literature is quite diffuse and sometimes unfocused.

Process oriented studies. Of late, finite stochastic modeling is being used more extensively to capture the process nature of communication. Ellis and Fisher (1975), Hawes and Foley (1973), Hewes and Evans-Hewes (1974), Scheidel (1974), and Parks, Farace, Rogers, Albrecht, and Abbott (1976), have employed Markov analyses of interaction data. Hewes (1974) has presented a short overview of such techniques, and in closely related research, Stech (1975) has examined the sequential structure of interaction both in terms of distribution and sequential predictability. While not employing finite stochastic modeling, Mabry (1975a, 1975b) has studied the sequential development of interaction in encounter groups and task-oriented groups respectively. Some of these studies support the notion of various types of phases in group development. Although it is useful to know that groups or communication systems go through various phases or states, why this is the case remains to be explained.

There is growing theoretical concern for these developmental processes. The previously cited work of Delia and O'Keefe (1974) on the development of communicative competence is solidly grounded in cognitive and developmental theory. Altman and Taylor's (1973) social penetration work attempts to explain relationship development and disintegration through a reward/cost approach, while Berger and Calabrese (1975) employ uncertainty as an explanatory construct.

METATHEORETICAL ISSUES

Reference was made previously to contrasting views regarding the most useful way to approach the explanation of communication behavior. For example, some researchers (e.g., Monge, 1973, 1975) have pointed out that the covering-law approach to explanation employed in the physical sciences is inappropriate for the explanation of communication phenomena. Among the weaknesses of the covering-law approach to explanation pointed out by Monge are: (1) the impossibility of finding universal laws of behavior, (2) the sole

reliance on deductive logic, and (3) the inability of the approach to deal with partial explanations. Monge argues that these kinds of problems are remedied through application of the systems approach, although some of the shortcomings of the covering-law approach alleged by Monge have been questioned by Berger (1975).

A second attack on the covering-law approach emanates from those who argue that social behavior is considerably different from "thing" behavior, because persons are conscious of their actions. This line of argument leads to the rejection of explanatory systems of social behavior which emphasize causality and view man as the victim of forces beyond his control (e.g., reinforcement theory). As an alternative, it is proposed that human action is best explained by recourse to rules which guide human conduct (Cushman & Whiting, 1972; Harré & Secord 1972; Harré, 1974). However, Toulmin (1974) has pointed out that both causal and rule-oriented explanations of human behavior are necessary, depending upon what one wishes to explain. In his analysis, Toulmin distinguishes among several types of behavior, ranging from simple reflexes to complex problem-solving, and argues that modes of explanation differ according to the level of behavior to be explained. Cushman (1975) has made much the same point with regard to communication behavior. Even staunch advocates of the rule governed approach (Harré & Secord, 1972) explicitly assert that:

> Though the concept of rule can be used to explain how an actor comes to know what to do, it still leaves open the question as to why he chose that rule to guide his conduct, nor does it explain why he actually acts on the rule, rather than doing nothing. In explaining action by reference to rule it is necessary to add some further accounts of wants, needs, or expectations of others, the awareness of which would prompt a man to action in accordance with the rule. Thus instancing the rule answers the question, "How did he know what to do?" but not the question, "Why did he do this thing then and there?" (pp. 181-182)

At least two crucial points might be made with regard to the above statement. First, the statement seems to clearly invite causal explanation to answer the "why" question. Second, the statement also seems to imply that persons may follow rules in order to obtain various kinds of rewards. These issues are explored in some depth in a series of papers on covering law, rules, and systems approaches to explanation (Berger, 1975; Cushman, 1975; Monge, 1975).

Rather than suggest that any one of the three approaches to explanation is the best for theory construction in interpersonal communication, efforts might profitably be made to clarify the range of interpersonal communication phenomena which can best explain each of the approaches. For example, Giles (1976) has noted that sociolinguists generally explain modifications of speech behavior by recourse to rules. In Giles's view, this approach casts man in the role of social automaton. He argues that there are plausible alternative explanations for modifications of speech behavior which can be found in attraction, attribution, and equity theories. Giles urges sociolinguists to consider these alternatives. Suggestions such as those made by Giles seem important to delineation of the boundaries of a particular approach. A rule-governed perspective may be useful in explaining ritualized communication routines; however, once persons begin to form stabilized attributions about each other, attribution and equity theories may become more useful perspectives from which to explain behavior.

CONCLUSION

One hopes this overview has provided a reasonably accurate and useful picture of the past and current status of theory and research in interpersonal communication. Because of space limitations, the extensive literature relevant to interpersonal communication in such areas as social psychology, developmental psychology, psycholinguistics, sociolinguistics, sociology, and anthropology could not be reviewed here. Thus, for example, the nonverbal communication research by Ekman (1971), Exline (1971), and Mehrabian (1971) was not included. The issues raised throughout this paper are important to communication and one hopes they will be useful, as well, in other behavioral science disciplines.

REFERENCES

ADAMS, J.S. Inequity in social exchange. *Advances in Experimental Social Psychology*, 1965, 2, 267-299.

ALTMAN, I., & TAYLOR, D.A. *Social penetration: The development of interpersonal relationships.* New York: Holt, Rinehart & Winston, 1973.

ARGYLE, M. *Social interaction.* Chicago: Aldine-Atherton, 1969.

ARGYLE, M. *The psychology of interpersonal behavior* (2nd ed.). Baltimore: Penguin, 1972.

BAXTER, L. Credibility proneness: A reconceptualization. Paper presented at the annual meeting of the International Communication Association, Portland, April 1976.

BERGER, C.R. The covering law model in communication inquiry. Paper presented at the annual meeting of the Speech Communication Association, Houston, December 1975.

BERGER, C.R., & CALABRESE, R.J. Some explorations in initial interaction and beyond: Toward a developmental theory of interpersonal communication. *Human Communication Research*, 1975, 1, 99-112.

BERGER, C.R., & CLATTERBUCK, G.W. Attitude similarity and attributional information as determinants of uncertainty reduction and interpersonal attraction. Paper presented at the annual meeting of the International Communication Association, Portland, Oregon, April 1976.

BERGER, C.R., MUNLEY, M.E., & CLATTERBUCK, G.W. Uncertainty, similarity and attraction: When is to know him to love him? Paper to be presented at the annual meeting of the Speech Communication Association, San Francisco, December 1976.

BOCHNER, A.P., & KELLY, C.W. Interpersonal competence: Rationale, philosophy, and implementation of a conceptual framework. *Speech Teacher*, 1974, 23, 279-301.

BRANDT, D. R. Listener propensity to counterargue, distraction, and resistance to persuasion. Paper presented at the annual meeting of the International Communication Association, Portland, Oregon, April 1976.

BROWN, R. *Social psychology.* New York: Free Press, 1965.

BURGOON, J.K. Conflicting information, attitude, and message variables as predictors of learning and persuasion. *Human Communication Research*, 1975, 1, 133-144.

BURGOON, J.K., & JONES, S.B. Toward a theory of personal space expectations and their violations. *Human Communication Research*, 1976, 2, 131-146.

BURGOON, J.K., & SAINE, T.J. *The unspoken dialogue.* Boston: Houghton-Mifflin, in press.

BURGOON, M., JONES. S.B., & STEWART, D. Toward a message centered theory of persuasion: Three empirical investigations of language intensity. *Human Communication Research*, 1975, 1, 240-256.

BURGOON, M., & KING, L.B. The mediation of resistance to persuasion strategies by language variables and active-passive participation. *Human Communication Research*. 1974, 1, 30-41.

CAPELLA, J.N. A derivation and test of a cybernetic coorientational model of interpersonal communication. Paper presented at the annual meeting of the International Communication Association, New Orleans, April 1974.

CHAFFEE, S.H., & McLEOD, J.M. (Eds.) Interpersonal perception and communication. *American Behavioral Scientist*, 1973, 16, entire issue.

CHRISTIE, R., & GEIS, F.L. *Studies in machiavellianism.* New York: Academic Press, 1970.

CLATTERBUCK, G.W. Attributional confidence, uncertainty reduction and attraction in initial interaction. Unpublished dissertation, Department of Communication Studies, Northwestern University, 1976.

CODY, M.J., MARLIER, J., & WOELFEL, J. An application of the multiple attribute measurement model: Measurement and manipulation of source credibility. Paper presented at the annual meeting of the International Communication Association, Portland, April 1976.

COZBY, P.C. Self-disclosure: A literature review. *Psychological Bulletin*, 1973, 79, 73-91.

CUSHMAN, D.P. Alternative theoretical bases for the study of human communication: The rules perspective. Paper presented at the annual meeting of the Speech Communication Association, Houston, December 1975.

CUSHMAN, D., & WHITING, G.C. An approach to communication theory: Toward consensus on rules. *Journal of Communication*, 1972, 22, 217-238.

DALY, J.A., McCROSKEY, J. C., & RICHMOND, V. P. The relationship between vocal activity and perception of communicators in small group interaction. Paper presented at the annual meeting of the Speech Communication Association, Chicago, December 1974.

DANCE, F.E.X., & LARSON, C.E. *The functions of human communication: A theoretical approach.* New York: Holt, Rinehart and Winston, 1976.

DELIA, J.G. Attitude toward the disclosure of self-attributions and the complexity of interpersonal constructs. *Speech Monographs*, 1974, 41, 119-126.

DELIA, J.G., & O'KEEFE, B.J. The development of interpersonal constructs, perspective taking, and communication skills: Theoretical integration and proposed research. Unpublished paper, Department of Speech Communication, University of Illinois at Champaign-Urbana, 1974.

DELIA, J.G., & O'KEEFE, B.J. Social construal processes in the development of communicative competence. Paper presented at the annual meeting of the Speech Communication Association, Houston, December 1975.

EKMAN, P. Universals and cultural differences in facial expressions of emotion. In J. Cole (Ed.) *Nebraska Symposium on Motivation*, Lincoln: University of Nebraska Press, 1971.

EKMAN, P., & FRIESEN, W.V. Nonverbal leakage and clues to deception. *Psychiatry*, 1969, 32, 88-106.

ELLIS, D.G., & FISHER, B.A. Phases of conflict in small group development: A Markov analysis. *Human Communication Research*, 1975, 1, 195-212.

EXLINE, R. Visual interaction: The glances of power and preference. In J. Cole (Ed.) *Nebraska Symposium on Motivation*, Lincoln: University of Nebraska Press, 1971.

FELDMAN, M.L. The relative effects of verbal dogmatism and attitudinal similarity on interpersonal attraction. Unpublished dissertation, Department of Communication Studies, Northwestern University, 1973.

FESTINGER, L. *A theory of cognitive dissonance.* Stanford: Stanford University Press, 1957.

FESTINGER, L. *Conflict, decision and dissonance.* Stanford: Stanford University Press, 1964.

FLAVELL, J.H. Role taking and communication skills in children. In W.W. Hartup and N.L. Smothergill (Eds.), *The young child: Reviews of research.* Washington, D.C. N.A.E.Y.C., 1967.

FOLGER, J., & PUCK, S. Coding relational communication: A question approach. Paper presented at the annual meeting of the International Communication Association, Portland, April 1976.

GARDNER, R.R. Information sequencing, background information and reciprocity in initial interactions. Unpublished dissertation, Department of Communication Studies, Northwestern University, 1976.

GARFINKEL, H. *Studies in ethnomethodology.* Englewood Cliffs: Prentice-Hall, 1967.

GILBERT, S.J., & HORENSTEIN, D. The communication of self-disclosure: Level versus valence. *Human Communication Research*, 1975, 1, 316-322.

GILBERT, S.J., & WHITENECK, G.G. Toward a multidimensional approach to the study of self-disclosure. Paper presented at the annual meeting of the International Communication Association, Portland, April 1976.

GILES, H. The social context of speech: A social psychological perspective. Paper presented in the Symposium on Language and the Social Sciences at Perspectives on Language: An Interdisciplinary Conference, Louisville, Kentucky, May 1976.

GILES, H., & POWESLAND, P.F. *Speech style and social evaluation.* London: Academic Press, 1975.

GOFFMAN, E. *The presentation of self in everyday life.* Garden City, New York: Doubleday Anchor, 1959.

GOFFMAN, E. *Encounters.* Indianapolis: Bobbs-Merril. 1961.

HARRÉ, R. Some remarks on rules as a scientific concept. In T. Mischel (Ed.) *Understanding other persons.* Oxford: Blackwell, 1974, 143-184.

HARRÉ, R., & SECORD, P.F. *The explanation of social behavior.* Oxford: Blackwell, 1972.

HARRISON, R.P. *Beyond words: An introduction to nonverbal communication.* Englewood Cliffs: Prentice Hall, 1974.

HART, R.P., EADIE, W.F., & CARLSON, R.E. Rhetorical sensitivity and communicative competence. Paper presented at the annual meeting of the Speech Communication Association, Houston, December 1975.

HAWES, L., & FOLEY, J. A Markov analysis of interview communication. *Speech Monographs*, 1973, 40, 208-219.

HEIDER, F. *The psychology of interpersonal relations.* New York: Wiley, 1958.

HESTON, J.K. Effects of anomie and personal space invasion on nonperson orientation, anxiety and source credibility. *Central States Speech Journal*, 1974, 25, 19-27.

HESTON, J.K., & GARNER, P. A study of personal spacing and desk arrangement in a learning environment. Paper presented at the annual meeting of the International Communication Association, Atlanta, April 1972.

HEWES, D.E. Finite stochastic modeling of communication processes: An introduction and some basic reading. *Human Communication Research*, 1975, 1, 271-283.

HEWES, D., & EVANS-HEWES, D. Toward a Markov chain model of attitude change. Paper presented at the annual meeting of the Speech Communication Association, Chicago, December 1974.

HEWES, D., HAIGHT, L., & SZALAY, S.M. The utility and cross-situational consistency of measures of verbal output: An exploratory study. Paper presented at the annual meeting of the International Communication Association, Portland, April 1976.

HOCKING, J.E., BAUCHNER, J., KAMINSKY, E., & MILLER, G.R. Detecting deceptive communication from verbal, visual and paralinguistic cues. Paper presented at the annual meeting of the International Communication Association, Portland, April 1976.

HOMANS, G.C. *Social behavior: Its elementary forms.* New

York: Harcourt, Brace, 1961.

HOUSEL, T.J., & McDERMOTT, P.J. The perceived credibility of a message source as affected by initial credibility, style of language and sex of source. Paper presented at the annual meeting of the International Communication Association, Portland, April 1976.

HOVLAND, C.I., LUMSDAINE, A.A., & SHEFFIELD, F.D. *Experiments on mass communication*. Princeton: Princeton University Press, 1949.

HYMES, D. *On communication competence*. Philadelphia: University of Pennsylvania Press, 1970.

JONES, E.E., & DAVIS, K. From acts to dispositions: The attribution process in person perception. *Advances in Experimental Social Psychology* (1965) 2, 220-266.

JONES, E.E., & GORDON, E.M. Timing of self-disclosure and its effects on personal attraction. *Journal of Personality and Social Psychology*, 1972, 24, 358-365.

JONES, S. A comparative proxemics analysis of dyadic interaction in selected subcultures of New York City. *Journal of Personality and Social Psychology*, 1971, 84, 35-44.

KEISER, G.J., & ALTMAN, I. Relationship of nonverbal behavior to the social penetration process. *Human Communication Research*, 1976, 2, 147-161.

KELLEY, H.H. The processes of causal attribution. *American Psychologist*, 1973, 28, 107-128.

KELLEY, H.H. Attribution theory in social psychology. In D. Levine (Ed.) *Nebraska symposium on motivation*. Lincoln: University of Nebraska Press, 1967, 192-240.

KNAPP, M.L. *Nonverbal communication in human interaction*. New York: Holt, Rinehart and Winston, 1972.

KNAPP, M.L., HART, R.P., & DENNIS, H.S. An exploration of deception as a communication construct. *Human Communication Research*, 1974, 1, 15-29.

MABRY, E.A. Sequential structure of interaction in encounter groups. *Human Communication Research*, 1975(a), 1, 302-307.

MABRY, E.A. Exploratory analysis of a developmental model for task-oriented small groups. *Human Communication Research*, 1975(b), 1, 66-74.

MARK, R.A. Coding communication at the relational level. *Journal of Communication*. 1971, 21, 221-232.

MARWELL, G., & SCHMITT, D.R. Dimensions of compliance-gaining behavior: An empirical analysis. *Sociometry*, 1967, 30, 350-364.

McCROSKEY, J.C. Measures of communication-bound anxiety. *Speech Monographs*, 1970, 37, 269-277.

McCROSKEY, J.C., DALY, J.A., RICHMOND, V.P., & COX, B.G. The effects of communication apprehension on interpersonal attraction. *Human Communication Research*, 1975, 2, 51-65.

McCROSKEY, J.C., HAMILTON, P.R., & WEINER, A.N. The effect of interaction behavior on source credibility, homophily and interpersonal attraction. *Human Communication Research*, 1974, 1, 42-52.

McCROSKEY, J.C., & SHEAHAN, M.E. Seating position and participation: An alternative interpretation. Paper presented at the annual meeting of the International Communication Association, Portland, April 1976.

McGUIRE, W.J. Inducing resistance to persuasion: Some contemporary approaches. *Advances in Experimental Social Psychology*, 1965, 1, 191-229.

MEHRABIAN, A. Nonverbal communication. In J. Cole (Ed.) *Nebraska symposium on motivation*. Lincoln: University of

Nebraska Press, 1971.

MILLAR, F.E. A transactional analysis of marital communication patterns: An exploratory study. Unpublished dissertation, Department of Communication, Michigan State University, 1973.

MILLER, G.R., BOSTER, F., ROLOFF, M., & SEIBOLD, D.R. Compliance gaining strategies: A typology and some findings concerning effects of situational differences. Paper presented at the annual meeting of the International Communication Association, Portland, April 1976.

MILLER, G.R., & STEINBERG, M. *Between people: A new analysis of interpersonal communication*. Chicago: Science Research Associates, 1975.

MONGE, P.R. Theory construction in the study of communication: The systems paradigm. *Journal of Communication*, 1973, 23, 5-16.

MONGE, P.R. Alternative theoretical bases for the study of human communication: The systems perspective. Paper presented at the annual meeting of the Speech Communication Association, Houston, December 1975.

MORTENSEN, C.D., & ARNTSON, P.H. The effects of predispositions toward verbal behavior on interaction patterns in dyads. *Quarterly Journal of Speech*, 1974, 61, 421-430.

NOFSINGER, R.E. On answering questions indirectly: Some rules in the grammar of doing conversation. *Human Communication Research*, 1976, 2, 172-181.

NORTON, R.W. Foundation of a communicator style construct. Unpublished paper, Department of Speech Communication, University of Michigan, 1976.

NORTON, R.W., & MILLER, L. Dyadic perception of communicator style. *Communication Research*, 1975, 2, 50-67.

NORTON, R.W., & PETTEGREW, L. Communicator style as an effect determinant of attraction. Paper presented at the annual meeting of the International Communication Association, Portland, April 1976.

NORTON, R.W., SCHROEDER, A., & WEBB, J. Communicator style as a function of effectiveness and attraction in triads. Unpublished paper, Department of Speech Communication, University of Michigan, 1975.

NORTON, R.W., & WARNICK, B. Evaluation of assertiveness as a communication construct. Paper presented at the annual meeting of the International Communication Association, Portland, April 1976.

PARKS, M.R. Toward an axiomatic theory of relational communication. Paper presented at the annual meeting of the International Communication Association, Chicago, 1975.

PARKS, M.R. Communication competency. Unpublished paper, Department of Communication, Michigan State University, East Lansing, Michigan, 1976.

PARKS, M.R., FARACE, R.V., ROGERS, L.E., ALBRECHT, T., & ABBOTT, R. Markov process analysis of relational communication in marital dyads. Paper presented at the annual meeting of the International Communication Association, Portland, April 1976.

PEARCE, W.B. An overview of communication and interpersonal relationships. In Appelbaum, R.L. and Hart, R.P. (Eds.) *Modcom: Modules in speech communication*. Chicago: Science Research Associates, 1976a.

PEARCE, W.B. The coordinated management of meaning: A rules based theory of interpersonal communication. In G.R. Miller (Ed.) *Explorations in interpersonal communication*. Beverly Hills: Sage Publications, 176b.

PEARCE, W.B., & SHARP, S.M. Self-disclosing communication. *Journal of Communication*, 1973, 23, 409-425.

PEARCE, W.B., WRIGHT, P.H., SHARP, S.M., & SLAMA, K.M. Affection and reciprocity in self-disclosing communication. *Human Communication Research*, 1974, 1, 5-14.

PHILLIPS, G.M. Reticence: Pathology of the normal speaker. *Speech Monographs*, 1968, 35, 39-49.

QUIGGENS, J.G. The effects of high and low communication apprehension on small group member credibility, interpersonal attraction, and interaction. Paper presented at the annual meeting of the Speech Communication Association, Chicago 1972.

RODNICK, R., & WOOD, B. The communication strategies of children. *Speech Teacher*, 1973, 22, 114-124.

ROGERS, L.E. Dyadic systems and transactional communication in a family context. Unpublished dissertation, Department of Communication, Michigan State University, 1972.

ROGERS, L.E., & FARACE, R.V. Analysis of relational communication in dyads: New measurement procedures. *Human Communication Research*, 1975, 1, 222-239.

SALTIEL, J., & WOELFEL, J. Inertia in cognitive processes: The role of accumulated information in attitude change. *Human Communication Research*, 1975, 1, 333-344.

SCHEIDEL, T. A systems analysis of two-person conversations. Paper presented at the SCA Doctoral Honors Seminar on modern systems theory in human communication. University of Utah, Salt Lake City, 1974.

SCHULMAN, L.S. Compliments, reciprocity and background information in initial interaction. Unpublished dissertation, Department of Communication Studies, Northwestern University, 1976.

SEIBOLD, D.R. A formalization of attribution theory: Critique and implications for communication. Paper presented at the annual meeting of the Central States Speech Association, Kansas City, April 1975a.

SEIBOLD, D.R. Communication research and the attitude-verbal report-overt behavior relationship: A critique and

theoretic reformulation. *Human Communication Research*, 1975b, 2, 3-32.

SHERIF, C.W., SHERIF, M., & NEBERGALL, R.E. *Attitude and attitude change*. Philadelphia: Saunders, 1965.

STECH, E.L. Sequential structure in human social communication. *Human Communication Research*, 1975, 1, 168-179.

SUDNOW, D. (Ed.) *Studies in social interaction*. New York: Free Press, 1972.

THIBAUT, J.W., & KELLEY, H.H. *The social psychology of groups*. New York: Wiley, 1959.

TOULMIN, S.E. Rules and their relevance for understanding human behavior. In T. Mischel (Ed.) *Understanding other persons*. Oxford: Blackwell, 1974, 185-215.

VEROFF, J. A scoring manual for the power motive. in J.W. Atkinson (Ed.) *Motives in fantasy action and society*. Princeton: Van Nostrand, 1958.

VEROFF, J., & VEROFF, J.B. Reconsideration of a measure of power motivation. *Psychological Bulletin*, 1972, 78, 279-291.

WEINSTEIN, E.A. Toward a theory of interpersonal tactics. In C.W. Backman and P.F. Secord (Eds.), *Problems in social psychology*. New York: McGraw-Hill, 1966.

WEINSTEIN, E.A. The development of interpersonal competence. In D.A. Goslin (Ed.), *Handbook of socialization theory and research*. Chicago: Rand McNally, 1969.

WHEELESS, L.R. Self-disclosure and interpersonal solidarity: Measurement, validation and relationships. Paper presented at the annual meeting of the International Communication Association, Portland, April 1976.

WIEMANN, J.M. An experimental investigation of communicative competence in initial interactions. Paper presented at the annual meeting of the International Communication Association, Portland, April 1976.

WORTHY, M., GARY A.L., & KAHN, G.M. Self-disclosure as an exchange process. *Journal of Personality and Social Psychology*, 1969, 13, 59-64.

THE TRUTH/DECEPTION ATTRIBUTION: EFFECTS OF VARYING LEVELS OF INFORMATION AVAILABILITY[1]

JOYCE E. BAUCHNER, DAVID R. BRANDT, and GERALD R. MILLER
Michigan State University

This study examines the relationship between untrained observers' accuracy in detecting deception on the part of strangers, and available total and nonverbal information as a function of transmission channel. Twelve subjects were put through a deception inducing manipulation procedure almost identical to the one used by Exline et al. (1970) and Shulman (1973). This procedure yielded six subjects lying and six subjects telling the truth in a postprocedure interview. Eighty observers viewed these subjects either live through a one-way mirror, saw them on a videotape, heard them on an audiotape, or read a transcript of the interview, Observers reported whether they thought each subject was lying or telling the truth. Trained coders provided ratio-scaled estimates of how much total and nonverbal information was available when viewing each subject through each channel. The results indicate no significant relationship between amounts of available nonverbal and/or total information and the accuracy with which untrained observers detected deception on the part of strangers.

Stated somewhat precisely, human communication involves an attempt at meaningful information exchange through purposive and systematic manipulation of a symbolic code by its users. Among other things, such a conceptualization implies that in a "true" communication system, the participants proceed from a consensual basis when assigning significance to symbols and behaviors (Cushman & Whiting, 1972; Cushman & Craig, 1976). On the other hand, persons frequently attribute significance to the behavior of others on an idiosyncratic basis (Jones & Nisbett, 1971). This process of attribution becomes particularly interesting, in terms of its potential impact on social interactions, in the absence of communicative intent on the part of the actor whose behavior is in question. Studies of source credibility (Anderson & Clevenger, 1963) and person perception (Tagiuri, 1969) seem to suggest as much.

Assuming that to be able and willing to believe others is fundamental in the development of interpersonal communication relations, one can easily conceive of the negative impact attributions of dishonesty will have on relational development. Yet, despite its potential negative impact, and despite moral admonitions against it, persons have and will likely continue to engage in deception. Social patterns of duplicity are abundant, and humans tend to acquire the meaning of misrepresentation at an early stage of social development (Wile, 1942). Perhaps this prevalence accounts for the increased empirical attention which deception and its detection have received recently (Knapp, Hart, & Dennis, 1974; Motley, 1974; McClintock & Hunt, 1975; Geizer, Rarick, & Soldow, 1975; Hocking et al, 1976).

The present paper examines the ability of untrained observers to make the truth/deception attribution accurately when the availability of verbal and nonverbal information, as a function of the communication channel, is varied. Building particularly on the work of Maier & Thurber (1968) and Hocking et al. (1976), we address the general question: Does accuracy in deception detection vary among individuals when they (1) witness a communicator in a "live" setting, (2) view him or her on videotape, (3) hear him or her on audiotape, or (4) read a transcript of his or her verbal communication?

BEHAVIORAL CORRELATES OF DECEPTION

Two lines of inquiry have characterized prior research in the area of deception. Using content analytic procedures, numerous studies have examined the verbal and nonverbal behaviors of *deceivers* versus *nondeceivers* (Exline et al., 1970; Mattarazzo et al., 1970; Mehrabian, 1971; Ekman &

Friesen, 1972; Ekman & Friesen, 1974; Knapp, Hart, & Dennis, 1974; McClintock & Hunt, 1975). Typical findings indicate that certain behavioral patterns in eye contact, facial affect, body movements, and verbal rate and fluency are correlated with deception. However, as Hocking (1976) has observed, "research on visual, paralinguistic, and verbal correlates of lying and truthful behavior offers little in terms of identifying specific cues on which accurate judgments of deception may be based" (p. 29). One might add that the value of attempts to identify such cues may itself be questionable since, according to Maier and Janzen (1967), judgments of deception seem to be based on impressionistic and intuitive grounds, rather than on specific behaviors. In fact, it seems unlikely that verbal and nonverbal behavioral cues function independently in signaling or "leaking" clues to deception (Ekman & Friesen, 1969); rather, the two probably function conjunctively. If so, what is needed is a methodology which treats these behaviors holistically, perhaps in terms of the *amount of information* they provide for observers who attempt to make a truth-deception attribution. The present study, in part, explores this possibility.

THE DETECTION OF DECEPTION

A second line of research has examined the extent to which untrained observers can accurately detect deception (Fay & Middleton, 1941; Hildreth, 1953; Maier & Thurber, 1968; Shulman, 1973; Ekman & Friesen, 1974; Geizer, Rarick, & Soldow, 1975; Hocking et al., 1976). Results suggest that the detection of deception is not easy under these conditions, with accuracy rates generally ranging between 40 percent and 60 percent. This is not a trivial finding. Given that the majority of our communicative transactions are *noninterpersonal* (Miller & Steinberg, 1975), as in the case of initial interactions, business interviews, etc., a great deal of deception may be going on which remains undetected.

On the other hand, individual differences in "competency" as a deceiver (Fay & Middleton, 1941; Hocking et al., 1976) and variations in the medium or channel through which the deceptive communication is presented (Maier & Thurber,

1968; Hocking et al., 1976) have been shown to affect differences in judgmental accuracy. As in the case of the behavioral correlates of deception previously mentioned, it may be that the differences relate to the amount and quality of the sensory data (potential information) which various channels provide. As Weiner and Mehrabian (1968) have noted, "It is hardly debatable that the greater the quantity and quality of sensory channels available in a communication link, the greater the information put in, through, and out of the system" (p. 82).

RESEARCH QUESTIONS

But what of these differences in the amount of information "put in, through, and out of the system?" How is such information utilized by individuals in making attributions of veracity? Do increases in available sensory data facilitate or inhibit accurate detection of deception? The literature offers very little in the way of theory or hypothetical development with respect to these questions. However, at least three possible explanations can be proposed.

Knowledge Utilization Hypothesis

Let us refer to the first as the *information utilization* hypothesis, which suggests that as the amount and quality of verbal and nonverbal information available to an observer increases, so should his or her accuracy in making attributions of truthfulness or deception. The rationale underlying this explanation suggests that, to the extent that the "richness" of available cues is directly related to increased perceptual acuity on the part of a participant in a deceptive transaction, he should be better able to detect signals of deceit, and thus more accurately judge the veracity of a communicator. This rationale has been offered by researchers involved with the study of teleconferencing (Ryan, 1976), and is at least implied by Ekman and Friesen (1969a, 1974) in their discussions of nonverbal leakage and clues to deception. Ekman and Friesen suggest that if a receiver not only observes behaviors originating in areas of the body having a relatively high sending capacity[2] (e.g., the face and voice), but also cues generated from areas having lower sending capacity (e.g., hands, legs, and feet), the additional information provided by the latter should facilitate detection of deception by increasing signals of its occurrence. However, Ekman and Friesen (1974) only compared the accuracy of judgments of observers who viewed the deceiver's head only with those who viewed the body only, thus not directly testing the information utilization hypothesis.

Hocking et al. (1976) compared accuracy scores over a wider range of conditions, with observers viewing both factual and emotional testimony. Observers who viewed factual testimony had lower accuracy scores (49.7%) when viewing the body only than those viewing factual testimony in the head only condition (57.3%) and the head and body conditions (54.5%). When observers heard testimony concerning the emotional state of the subjects, those in the body-only condition had higher accuracy scores (52%) than observers in either the head & body (49.7%) or the body-only (47.5%) conditions. Disregarding the not highly generalizable body-only condition, the between-camera shot findings of Hocking et al. (1976) seem to support the knowledge-utilization hypothesis. However, the Hocking et al. (1976) findings of the highest testimony in the audio-only (61.8%) and transcript (62.5%) condition contradicts the hypothesis and points to a need for more careful examination of the process surrounding the truth/deception attribution.

Distraction Hypothesis

A second possible explanation, the *distraction* hypothesis, stems from research investigating the effects of distractive stimuli on persuasion and source credibility ratings. It has been argued (and in some cases found) that distraction may facilitate persuasion and perceptions of credibility by dividing the persuadee's attention, reducing his or her ability to scrutinize carefully the oncoming communication, thus increasing his or her susceptibility to influence (Breitrose, 1966; Dorris, 1967; Osterhouse & Brock, 1970; Keating & Brock, 1974; Brandt, 1976).

The previous rationale may be appropriated to explain some experimental findings regarding deception (Maier & Thurber, 1968; Hocking et al.,

1976). Given that a deceiver attempts to "convince" others in the interaction that his or her deceptive performance represents "normal" communicative behavior, persuasive and deceptive settings are analogous. Increasing the number of available verbal and nonverbal cues places greater demands on receiver attention, perhaps reducing the ability to scrutinize any specific behavior or set of behaviors. If so, then behavioral cues which are extraneous to—do not signal the occurrence of—deception may distract attention from cues which are potential indicators of its occurence, resulting in reduced accuracy in deception detection. The authors of at least one study of deceptive communication (Maier & Thurber, 1968) have suggested a distraction effect as a possible explanation for their findings, and at this exploratory stage of research, the distraction hypothesis seems worthy of consideration.

Information Overload Hypothesis

An alternative to the distraction hypothesis is referred to here as the *information overload* hypothesis. The information overload hypothesis predicts results similar to those predicted by the distraction hypothesis, but with a key difference. The distraction hypothesis suggests that since a receiver must attend to increasing amounts of informational stimuli, his accuracy in detecting deception is reduced because he is utilizing extraneous as well as relevant cues. The result is inhibition of the ability to scrutinize relevant cues. The information overload hypothesis, on the other hand, suggests that receivers are *blocking-out* important cues. Danowski (1974) explains that when individuals receive more information than they can process simultaneously, they experience confusion, which results in higher output of error. With respect to deceptive interactions, as visual and paralinguistic cues increase, the total amount of informational stimuli with which receivers must contend increases. It is conceivable that some may reach an information processing threshold where additional data results in overload. *Filtering* and *chunking* (Danowski, 1974) are two processing strategies by which receivers can adapt to overload. Both strategies involve the use of stereotypic cognitive referents to avoid having to process all of the available data in a setting. It may be that stereotypes of deceivers are utilized by receivers in attempting to make attributions of veracity. If such stereotypes are inaccurate, as some research suggests they are (Exline et al., 1970), inaccurate attributions of truth, or its opposite, could be expected. Thus, the information overload hypothesis would predict that the greater the overload on an individual receiver, as a function of increased available data from a broad spectrum sensory channel, the stronger the influence of inaccurate (not highly generalizable) stereotypes on the truth/deception attribution process, and presumably, the lower the accuracy of such attributions.

The Present Study

It is difficult to determine, a priori, which of these hypotheses is most accurate, and under what conditions. However, by varying the channel through which observers view truthful and deceitful communicators, obtaining estimates of the amount of verbal and nonverbal information afforded by each channel, and examining judgment accuracy in relation to this information, some insight may be gained. The present study, in part, attempts to explore such an approach.

Earlier in the paper, it was noted that at least two studies have examined the ability of individuals to detect deception when the channel of communication is varied. Maier and Thurber (1968) examined deception detection under live, audio-only, and transcript conditions. Hocking et al. (1976) compared the accuracy of judgment of observers in video-tape, audio-only, and transcript conditions. It remains to be seen how live, video, audio, and transcript conditions compare in terms of their effects on the ability to attribute accurately truth or dishonesty to communicators, when examined simultaneously. Accordingly, the present research also attempts to address this issue.

METHOD

Subjects

Subjects were six male and six female undergraduate students enrolled at Michigan State Uni-

versity who volunteered to participate in a study of "group problem-solving." Half the subjects were randomly assigned to a deception condition and half to a truthful condition. Each subject worked in a dyad with an experimenter's confederate, whose status was not revealed until after the experiment was completed.

Deception-Inducing Procedure

The "group problem-solving" deception-inducing procedure was essentially identical to that used by Exline et al. (1970) and Shulman (1973). Subjects were told that four-, three-, and two-person groups, as well as individuals, were being asked to engage in the same task—estimating the number of dots on a series of cards—in order to examine how group problem-solving strategies related to group size. They were told that since the government had provided funds for the project, and in order to create more interest in the task, the group in each size category which performed the best would receive $50 to divide among its members. All subjects were informed that they had been randomly assigned to the dyad group and matched with a student from another class (actually the experimenter's confederate).

Prior to the subject's arrival in the experimental waiting room, the conferate randomly assigned subjects to either the truthful or deception condition. The cheating implication procedure was only used for those subjects assigned to the deception condition. The assignment procedure used controlled for sex, so that an equal number of males and females appeared in both the truthful and lying conditions. This was done because past research indicates that significant differences in the ability to use nonverbal information and detect deception occur as the result of varying the sex of both the source and receiver in deceptive interactions. Likewise, the sex of observers was also controlled so that in the final experiment there were equal numbers of male-male, male-female, female-female, and female-male source/receivers dyads in each condition (Fay & Middleton, 1941; Maier, 1965; Mehrabian, 1969, 1971; Shulman, 1973). Since Shulman (1973) found no effects from changing the sex of the confederate in this procedure, the same female confederate was used throughout the experiment. The experimenter remained blind to the experimental condition to avoid differential treatment of subjects based on this knowledge.

The task required the dyad jointly to estimate the number of dots on a series of nine cards, which the experimenter flashed in front of them for 15 seconds. After viewing each card, they were told to confer as long as necessary to come up with one estimate for the number of dots.

A practice sample was presented. Then, before starting, the experimenter mentioned that after each series of three cards she would give the group feedback as to its progress, by informing them of the correct answers for the completed cards. After the third card the confederate always requested this feedback, which the experimenter delayed giving for "a couple of more trials, since you are taking so much time to decide." Between the fourth and sixth card, a second experimenter, who had been listening to the interaction from an observation room, interrupted the experimental session to inform the first experimenter that she had an "important telephone call from the director of the research project." The first experimenter left the room to take the alleged call.

If the subject was in the *truthful* condition, the confederate just engaged him or her in normal conversation during the experimenter's absence. However, if the subject was in the *deception* condition, the confederate went through a procedure to implicate him or her in the act of cheating.

The confederate observed the folder which the experimenter had left on her chair and wondered aloud if it contained the correct answers. She complained that the experimenter had "failed to supply the promised feedback" and that "she could really use the $50." Next, the confederate suggested looking in the folder and, regardless of the subject's reaction, got up and began to leaf through it. Many subjects helped the confederate, but regardless of their reaction, she read the correct answers aloud, identifying them as such, and jotted them down on a piece of scratch paper provided by the experimenter.

Since it was important that the first experimenter not know if the subject was assigned to a lying or truthful procedure and not return early to catch the confederate and subject cheating, a means had to be developed to monitor the whole procedure. A second experimenter listened from the observation room to the conversation of the confederate and subject. After the confederate had implicated the subject in the act of cheating, the second experimenter told the first experimenter she could return from the alleged phone call. The duration of the first experimenter's absence was held constant for all subjects, regardless of condition. This procedure was intended to minimize the chances of cueing the experimenter as to the condition to which a subject had been assigned. The timing also served to protect the confederate's cover in that the subject had little time to question the confederate before the first experimenter returned. The task was then completed, with the confederate always using the dishonestly obtained scores to make accurate estimates. In this way, unless the subject reported the confederate to the experimenter, he or she was implicated in the act of cheating.

Interviewing for Stimuli

After the task was completed, the experimenter took the dyad into another room to interview them concerning the strategies used to arrive at answers to the task. The experimenter always began by interviewing the subject first under the pretense that the confederate would next be asked the same questions. The questions were as follows:

1. Please state your name.
2. Year in school?
3. What are you majoring in?
4. Have you ever been in any research before?
5. How many communication courses have you had?
6. Could you describe the strategy your group used to get their answers?
7. Could you be a little more specific? You did really well, especially toward the end.
8. If you had to describe to the next group what they should do to do as well as you did, what would you tell them, in two short sentences?
9. If you could choose what size group you could do the task over again in, what size would you choose, 4, 3, 2, or alone?

FIGURE 1
Counterbalancing of Observers in Latin Square Design

Subject

	1 2 3	4 5 6	7 8 9	10 11 12
A	LIVE	VIDEO	AUDIO	TRANSCRIPT
B	TRANSCRIPT	LIVE	VIDEO	AUDIO
C	AUDIO	TRANSCRIPT	LIVE	VIDEO
D	VIDEO	AUDIO	TRANSCRIPT	LIVE

A = 20 Observers (5 randomly assigned to each cell)
B = 20 Observers (5 randomly assigned to each cell)
C = 20 Observers (5 randomly assigned to each cell)
D = 20 Observers (5 randomly assigned to each cell)

---

10. Why?
11. Is there anything else you could add about the strategy you used?

The first four questions provided observers with a sample of the subjects' truthful behavior as well as providing demographic information for future examination. If the subject was in the implication procedure, the remainder of his or her answers were untruthful, since no subject had mentioned that either she or he or the confederate had cheated.

During this interview, observers viewed the subjects through a one-way mirror. In addition, videotapes, audiotapes, and transcripts were constructed from a videotape shot from the same angle as the live observation and through the same one-way mirror. Besides controlling for sex of subject/ observer dyads, as previously mentioned, it was made certain that subjects and observers were strangers. All subjects were individually debriefed and given detailed explanations of the procedure upon completion.

Observers

Eighty undergraduate students enrolled at Michigan State University (none of whom knew any of the subjects) participated as observers from whom judgements of veracity were obtained. Because the present study included a "live" condition, a rather serious procedural problem had to be overcome. The time required for briefing, participation, and debriefing of each subject amounted to about one hour. Given 12 subjects, this would have required observers in the "live" condition to attend a twelve hour session—which, because of fatigue and its potential contaminating effects on the experimental results, was deemed impractical. On the other hand, the time actually needed to observe and judge the veracity of subjects was only approximately 10 to 15 minutes. Thus, in the video, audio, and transcript conditions, observers would only need 10 to 15 minutes per person. In order to minimize the time required of each observer and still ensure that he or she judged all twelve subjects, observers were counterbalanced across conditions and subjects using a simple Latin square design (Lindquist, 1953). Thus, all observers were required to observe three subjects in each of the four conditions. Figure 1 illustrates the resulting design, which produced a total of 240 judgments of veracity, 60 in each condition.

After the experimenter explained the implication procedure to all observers, they saw, heard, or read the interview of three subjects in the appropriate condition to which they had been assigned, and made a judgement as to whether or not the subject was lying or telling the truth. Observers in the live condition viewed the interviewing through a one-way mirror; during the task and implication procedure, these observers remained in a separate conference room with no visual or audio access to the subjects. Other observers saw, heard, or read stimuli prepared from a videotape of the live interview.

Development of Information Measures and Coder Training

Eight trained coders provided a holistic estimate of nonverbal and total information available, with estimates based on the following definitions:

> Nonverbal information refers to the amount of information available from nonverbal behaviors such as facial expression, eye contact, nodding, hand and body movement, posture, pausing, the "ums" and "ahs" people say—anything beyond the actual words. Nonverbal information refers to how people say things, not what they say.
>
> Total information is a holistic estimate of all available information provided by a stimulus. It is the kind of judgement you would make if I asked you which of two books provided you with the most information.

Coders were cautioned that total information is not necessarily the sum of verbal and nonverbal information. Redundancy in nonverbal and verbal information may produce a figure for total information lower than the sum of verbal and nonverbal information (Wiener & Mehrabian, 1968). For this reason, it was emphasized that the estimates should be made independently of one another, even though the variables are not theoretically independent. Reliabilities for coder estimates were computed for nonverbal information, total information, the ratio of nonverbal to total information, and the log transformation data of estimates of nonverbal and total information using Cronbach's alphas (Cronbach, 1951). Log transformation reliability is reported, since certain analyses were done on transformed data. The coefficients for reliability were .98, .96, .99, .99, and .98, respectively ($p < .05$).

All information measures were made by coders trained by means of ratio-scaled direct-interval estimation:

> The standard for direct interval estimation consists of two stimuli possessing different amounts of the attribute being rated. Each is assigned a number of points, e.g., 100 and 200. The one with the smallest amount of the attribute is assigned the lowest number of points. The point assignments to the two stimuli should be approximately equal to the ratio of the amounts of the attributes they possess. (Silverman & Johnston, 1975, p. 464)

This standard interval then serves as a psychological "ruler" upon which estimates are based.

Two samples from the Hocking et al. (1976) study were used as the standard interval for coder estimation. These samples were chosen from the original sixteen subjects in the Hocking et al. stimulus, based on reported pretest values obtained from 15 undergraduates concerning available nonverbal, verbal, and total information for each segment. Two segments were chosen from the pretest of the Hocking et al. stimulus, so that the first segment of the standard interval had half as much available nonverbal and total information as the second segment of the standard interval. Accordingly, the first segment was assigned points of 100 units of nonverbal information and 150 units of total information, while the second segment was assigned points of 200 units nonverbal information and 300 units of total information. Coders were trained for four hours a week for six weeks, using these stimuli and values as a standard. Coders then provided estimates of amount of total and nonverbal information available for all subjects via all four transmissions channels.

FIGURE 2
A Model of the Relation Between Accuracy,
Available Information, and Channel

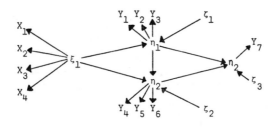

Where:

ξ_1 = Communication Channel (True Variable)

η_1 = Available Nonverbal Information (True Variable)

η_2 = Available Total Information (True Variable)

η_3 = Ability to Attribute Truth or Deception (True Variable)

ζ_1 = Disturbance Term for η_1

ζ_2 = Disturbance Term for η_2

ζ_3 = Disturbance Term for η_3

X_1 = Live Condition (Indicator of ξ_1)

X_2 = Video Condition (Indicator of ξ_1)

X_3 = Audio Condition (Indicator of ξ_1)

X_4 = Transcript Condition (Indicator of ξ_1)

Y_1 = First Coder's Estimate of η_1

Y_2 = Second Coder's Estimate of η_1

Y_3 = Third Coder's Estimate of η_1

Y_4 = First Coder's Estimate of η_2

Y_5 = Second Coder's Estimate of η_2

Y_6 = Third Coder's Estimate of η_2

Y_7 = Observer Judgmental Accuracy

RESULTS

Before discussing the results of the present study, we should briefly describe the analytical tools employed and the rationale for their use.

Earlier it was suggested that the availability of information, particularly nonverbal information, as a function of variations in the communication channel, may affect differences in the accuracy of attributions of veracity made by observers. Thus, a model in which judgment accuracy is the dependent variable, perceived total and nonverbal available information are intermediate endogenous variables, and the various channels are exogenous variables, is suggested.[3] A diagram of the basic model appears in Figure 2.

Accordingly, the above model was estimated utilizing a two-stage least-squares (2SLS) procedure Namboodiri, Carter, & Blalock, 1975).[4]

In addition, *analysis of variance* of judgmental accuracy by experimental condition, as well as *a posteriori* comparison of cell means utilizing the

TABLE 1
First Stage, First Equation of Two-Stage Least-Squares Model

Dummy Variable Structural Model*	F	$p<.05$	Multiple R	R^2
$Y_1 = a + b_o U + b_1 X_1 + b_2 X_2 + b_3 X_3 + b_{K-1} X_{K-1} + E$	27956.6	yes	.998	.997
$Y_1 = -1.30 + 3.66 X_1 + 3.72 X_2 + 3.46 X_3$				

Variable	b	df	F	$p<.05$
X_1 = Live	3.66	3/236	57241.2	yes
X_2 = Video	3.72	3/236	58880.2	yes
X_3 = Audio	3.46	3/236	51165.0	yes
Y_1 = Perceived Available Nonverbal Information				

* See Namboodiri, Carter & Blalock (1975), pp. 138-39, for a discussion of dummy variable regression analysis.

Newman-Keuls procedure, were conducted. This enabled us to examine experimental main effects, as well as facilitating simplicity of presentation. All data were analyzed via SPSS and LISREL programs[5] using a CDC 6500 computer.

Channel Variation and Perceived Information Availability

The first stage of the 2SLS procedure consists of ordinary *least-square regression.* In this case, two separate equations had to be estimated; the first to determine the path coefficients between perceived nonverbal information and the exogenous variables, and the second to determine the paths between perceived available total information and the exogenous, as well as nonverbal information variables.

Table 1 illustrates the results obtained from estimation of the first stage, first equation. It was assumed earlier that variations in the communication channel would result in covariations in coders' perceptions of the amount of available nonverbal in-

formation. The results strongly support this assumption, with variations in the channel accounting for .997 percent of the variance in perceived available nonverbal information. These results also serve as an indirect check of the success of the experimental procedure for manipulating available information (i.e., in terms of communication channel).

It was also assumed that channel variations, as well as perceived available nonverbal information, would result in variations in coders' perceptions of available total information. Table 2 illustrates the results pertaining to this assumption. Again, the results are overwhelmingly supportive ($R^2=.969$), and also serve as an indirect check of the experimental procedure for controlling the availability of information, a crucial variable in the present study.

Information Availability and Judgmental Accuracy

The results pertaining to channel variation and perceived information availability are fairly

TABLE 2
First Stage, Second Equation of Two-Stage Least-Squares Regression
Model

Dummy Variable Structural Model	F	$p<.05$	Multiple R	R^2
$Y_2 = a + b_o U + b_1 X_1 + b_2 X_2 + b_3 X_3 + b_4 Y_1 + b_{K-1} X_{K-1} + E$	1883.92	yes	.984	.969
$Y_2 = 3.22 - 2.64 X_1 - 2.65 X_2 - 2.58 X_3 + 8.24 Y_1$				

Variable	b	df	F	$p<.05$
X_1 = Live	-.264	4/235	873.07	yes
X_2 = Video	-.265	4/235	857.18	yes
X_3 = Audio	-.258	4/235	936.21	yes
Y_1 = Perceived Available Nonverbal Information	.824	4/235	1147.47	yes
Y_2 = Perceived Available Total Information				

TABLE 3
Second Stage, Third Equation of Two-Stage Least-Squares Regression
Model

Structural Model	F	$p<.05$	Multiple R	R^2
$Y_3 = a + b_1 \hat{Y}_1 + b_2 \hat{Y}_2 + E$	.481	no	.064	.004
$Y_3 = -.428 - .004 \hat{Y}_1 + .389 \hat{Y}_2$				

Variables	b	df	F	$p<.05$
$\hat{Y}_1$ = predicted perceived available nonverbal information	-.004	2/237	.825	no
$\hat{Y}_2$ = predicted perceived available total information	-.389	2/237	.956	no
Y_3 = observer judgment accuracy				

TABLE 4
Analysis of Variance of Accuracy by Condition

Source	Sum of Squares	df	MS	F	p
Total	59.496	239	---	---	---
Between	1.913	3	.638	2.613	.05
Within	57.583	236	.244	---	---

straightforward and not particularly surprising. Of greater importance are the results pertaining to information availability as a predictor of the ability to make accurate attributions of veracity. By using the two-stage least-squares procedure, the endogenous variable in the structural model could be "purified" in such a way that their correlations with disturbance terms were eliminated. Thus, given that we had little measurement or sampling error, we should get a fairly accurate estimate of the relation between information availability and observer accuracy.

Table 3 illustrates the results obtained from this procedure. Examination of these results suggests that variations in availability of informational cues, as a function of communication channel, do not predict judgemental accuracy very well. The multiple R was only .064, accounting for less than one percent of the variance in accuracy scores.

Channel Variation and Judgmental Accuracy

One of the major aims of the present research was to examine the ability to make accurate attributions of veracity under "live," video, audio, and transcript conditions. While the results of the two-stage least-squares regression obviously take such variations in communication channel into account, it is not so obvious how each affects judgmental accuracy, based on examination of those results alone. To shed further light on this issue, an analysis of variance of accuracy scores was conducted. The results, summarized in Table 4, were significant at the .05 level of confidence.

A posteriori comparisons of cell means, utilizing the Newman-Keuls procedure (Winer, 1971), indicated that observers in the live condition were significantly more accurate in attributing truthfulness or deception than observers in the audio-only (p < .05). No other individual comparisons were significant (see Table 5).

DISCUSSION

The results of the present study do not appear to support any of the suggested hypotheses—information utilization, information overload, or distraction. In fact the multiple R of .064 indicates that available total information accounts for less than one percent of the variance in accuracy scores. In addition, the mean accuracy scores in each condition indicate that none of the hypotheses can even predict the rise and fall of accuracy scores. The high accuracy score in the transcript condition (46.7%) rules out any linear relationship between available nonverbal and/or total information and the ability of untrained observers to detect deception on the part of strangers. The comparatively high mean accuracy observed in the transcript condition suggests that an attribute of that channel, distinct from type and amount of information, may provide an explanation. Amount of time an observer has to examine the stimulus and the ability of the observer to reexamine the stimulus may be two such attributes of transcripts of interest in future research. Both these sets of findings are supported by past research: (1) the low accuracy scores found by Maier and Thurber (1968), 58.3%, and Hocking et al. (1976), 58.5%, in the conditions where information was most abundant; (2) the conclusion of Maier and Janzen (1967) that judgments of accuracy "seemed to be based upon impressions rather than logic" (p. 105); and (3) the high accuracy scores

TABLE 5
Individual Comparisons of Treatment Means*

Treatment	s.d.	Mean
Live	.499	.567$_a$
Video	.503	.467$_b$
Audio	.470	.316$_a$
Transcript	.503	.467$_c$

*Means having same subscript differ significantly at the
.05 level of confidence. The higher the mean, the greater
the judgment accuracy.

found by Maier and Thurber (1968) and Hocking et al. (1976) in transcript conditions.

Considering the low accuracy scores reported in all conditions—56.7% for the live, 46.7% for the videotape and transcript, and 31.6% for the audiotape—it is highly questionable whether untrained observers can accurately detect deception on the part of strangers. None of the mean accuracy scores differed significantly from the 50 percent criteria researchers have defined as chance accuracy in these studies. It should be noted that this criterion is arbitrary in the sense that all people may not expect sources to by lying 50 percent of the time. However, in the present study subjects were lying half the time and telling the truth half the time.

A few studies have obtained accuracy scores significantly above the 50 percent criteria. Specifically these were in Maier and Thurber's (1968) audio-only and transcript conditions, Ekman and Friesen's (1974) body-only condition, and Hocking's et al. (1976) audio-only and transcript conditions. However, the two types of deception-inducing procedures used in these studies can be criticized for problems which inflate accuracy scores. Maier and Thurber (1968) had students role-play deceivers. When role-playing, lying behavior is not inconsistent with the matters of known fact to the subject; he or she acts as he believes someone who is lying acts. When playing the part of a liar, the tendency is to emphasize lying behavior. The subject has no real motivation to look honest, as in the normal lying situation; rather he or she wants to look like a liar in order to do an effective job. If an individual role-playing a liar looked honest, would anyone think they were playing the role well? Such a technique, at worst, inflates the accuracy scores of observers, while at best it has been seriously questioned as a research technique, since no one seems to know whether role-players "know" how real life liars behave (Freedman, 1969). In both Ekman and Friesen (1974) and Hocking et al. (1976) individuals always lied while observing a very unpleasant stimulus, and told the truth while viewing a pleasant stimulus; this systematically increased the cues of discomfort and arousal coming from the group of liars. These cues of arousal would be attributed by observers to lying, rather than any extraneous stimulus, since that was the explanation offered by the social context in which observers made their attributions, i.e., a detecting deception experiment (Schacter & Singer, 1962). The arousal cues stemming from the unpleasant stimulus, thus, would have made it easier for observers to identify liars.

SUMMARY

The deception-inducing procedure used in this study was chosen to overcome some of the criticism of past deception-inducing techniques. The authors realized that a more generalizable deception-inducing technique might logically produce lower accuracy scores than role-playing or the technique involving the viewing of an unpleasant stimulus; the resultant accuracy scores (56.7%, 46.7%, 46.7%, 31.6%) were lower than, but we believe more generalizable than, past scores. Given the criticism of past deception-inducing techniques, the generally low scores found under these past techniques, and the low scores found in the present study, the claim that untrained observers can accurately detect deception on the part of strangers is highly questionable.

ADDITIONAL RESEARCH

Given these findings, three areas of future research may prove fruitful. All research in the area of detection of deception thus far has examined the process in terms of stranger dyads. Perhaps we should investigate deception detection in established relational settings. Miller and Steinberg (1975) suggest that when an individual engages in interpersonal communication, the accuracy of predictions about others goes up. This is because interpersonal communication involves knowledge on the part of the observer, concerning the idiocyncrasies of the other, and prediction dominated by "stimulus discrimination" based on this knowledge, rather than "stimulus generalization" based on stereotypes (Miller & Steinberg, 1975). Miller and Steinberg's conception of interpersonal communication would predict higher accuracy on the part of observers who communicate interpersonally with the source, owing to the increased knowledge those observers have concerning the source's lying and truth-telling behavior. Examination of accuracy in detection of deception between source and receivers who have interpersonal relationships may prove fruitful in terms of the work of Miller and Steinberg. Hocking (1976) also suggests that lying behavior may not be the same across individuals, but rather is distinguishable from truth-telling behavior only within individuals, based on differences between each individual's own lying and truth-telling behavior. In that case, detailed knowledge available to individuals in an interpersonal relationship as to the truth-telling behaviors of the source would be necessary in order to notice deviations.

The second and third lines of possible research call for careful *cue analysis* of videotapes of the samples of the same individual's lying and truth-telling behavior. Hocking's (1976) hypothesis that lying behavior is a deviation from the individual's idiocyncratic truth-telling behavior could be examined by comparing the cue analysis of lying and truth-telling segments of each subject, rather than across subjects. Finally, knowledge as to the stereotypes people have of liars could be obtained by comparing the cue analyses of segments observers judged as lying with segments observers judged as telling the truth.

NOTES

1. This research was supported by grant #APR75-15815 from the National Science Foundation, Gerald R. Miller, Principal Investigator. The authors would like to acknowledge the helpful advice and assistance of Katrina W. Simmons and Edward L. Fink in completing this research.
2. The sending capacity of a part of the body can be measured by three indices: average transmission time, number of discriminable stimulus patterns which can be emitted, and visibility (Ekman & Friesen, 1969, p. 93).
3. The data were subjected to logarithmic transformation prior to analysis in order to minimize multicollinearity between the two informational variables (nonverbal and total). To the extent that multicollinearity between exogenous variables results in a multiplicative effect on the dependent or predicted variable, such an effect should be minimized by log transformation, since the multiplicative relationship is changed to an additive one (Namboodiri, Carter, & Blaclock, 1975, p. 489). The remainder of the effect of multicollinear variables should have been accounted for by the path from nonverbal to total information.
4. Originally, the authors attempted to analyze the models using *LISREL: A General Computer Program for Estimating a Linear Structural Equation System Involving Multiple Indicators of Unmeasured Variables*, by Joreskog and van Thillo (1972). However, we could not obtain an exact maximum likelihood solution. Instead, the program, during the minimization procedure, estimated a matrix which was not positive definite and aborted. The program indicated that this could be due to the fact that "insufficient arithmetic precision is used" (p. 33). All approximate solutions, however, indicated that the models would likely have been rejected. Similar problems have arisen when other researchers have attempted to subject communication data to the maximum likelihood procedure.
5. Norman H. Nie, C. Hadlai Hull, Jean G. Jenkins, Karin Steinbrenner, and Dale H. Bent, *Statistical Package for the Social Sciences;* New York: McGraw-Hill, 1970. Karl Joreskog and Marielle van Thillo (1972), *LISREL: A General Computer Program for Estimating a Linear Structural Equation System Involving Multiple Indicators of Unmeasured Variables;* New Jersey: Educational Testing Service.

REFERENCES

ANDERSON, K., & CLEVENGER, T. A summary of experimental research in ethos. *Speech Monographs*, 1963, 30, 59-78.

BARRIEN, F., & HUNTINGTON, G. An exploratory study of pupillary responses during deception. *Journal of Experimental Psychology*, 1943, 32, 443-449.

BRANDT, D. Listener propensity to counterargue, distraction, and resistance to persuasion. Paper presented at the annual meeting of the International Communication Association, Portland, Oregon, April 1976.

BREITROSE, H. The effect of distraction in attenuating counterarguments. Unpublished doctoral dissertation, Stanford University, 1966.

CHAMPNESS, B. The scope for person-to-person telecommunication systems in government and business. Communication Studies Group, London, England, 1973.

CRONBACH, L. Coefficient alpha and the internal structure of tests. *Psychometrika*, 1951, 16, 297-334.

CUSHMAN, D., & WHITING, G. An approach to communication theory: Toward consensus on rules. *The Journal of Communication*, 1972, 22, 217-238.

CUSHMAN, D., & CRAIG, R. Communication systems: Interpersonal implications. In G. Miller (Ed.), *Interpersonal communication*, New York: Russell Sage, 1976.

CUTROW, R., PARKS, A., LUSCAS, N., & THOMAS, K. The objective use of multiple physiological indices in the detection of deception. *Psychophysiology*, 1972, 9, 578-588.

DANOWSKI, J. Organizing and communicating. In J. Shubert (Ed.), *Human communication: Concepts, principles and skills*, Michigan: Department of Communication, Michigan State University, 1974, H1-H39.

DAVIDSON, P. Validity of the guilty-knowledge technique: The effects of motivation. *Journal of Applied Psychology*, 1968, 52, 62-65.

DEARMAN, H., & SMITH, B. Unconscious motivation and the polygraph test. *American Journal of Psychiatry*, 1963, 119, 1017-1020.

DORRIS, J. Persuasion as a function of distraction and counterarguing. Unpublished manuscript. University of California, Los Angeles, 1967. Cited in P.G. Zimbardo, M. Snyder, J. Thomas, A. Gold, and S. Gurwitz, Modifying the impact of persuasive communication with external distraction. *Journal of Personality and Social Psychology*, 1970, 16, 669-680.

EISENBERG, A., & SMITH, R. *Nonverbal communication*. New York: Bobbs-Merrill, 1971.

EKMAN, P., & FRIESEN, W. Nonverbal leakage and clues to deception. *Psychiatry*, 1969, 63, 88-106, a.

EKMAN, P., & FRIESEN, W. The repertoire of nonverbal behavior: Categories, origins, usage, and coding. *Semiotica*, 1969, 1, 49-68, b.

EKMAN, P., & FRIESEN, W. Hand movements. *Journal of Communication*, 1972, 22, 353-374.

EKMAN, P., & FRIESEN, W. Detecting deception from the body and face. *Journal of Personality and Social Psychology*, 1974, 29, 288-298.

ENGLISH, H. Reaction-time symptoms of deception. *American Journal of Psychology*, 1926, 37, 428-429.

EXLINE, R., THIBAUT, J., HICKEY, G., & GUMPERT, P. Visual interaction in relation to machiavellianism and an unethical act. In R. Christie and F. Geis (Eds.), *Studies in machiavellianism*, New York: Academic Press, 1970, 53-75.

FAY, P., & MIDDLETON, W. The ability to judge truthtelling, or lying, from the voice as transmitted over a public address system. *Journal of General Psychology*, 1941, 24, 211-215.

FREEDMAN, J. Role playing: Psychology by consensus. *Journal of Personality and Social Psychology*, 1969, 13, 107-114.

GEIZER, R., RARICK, D., & SOLDOW, G. Deception in judgment accuracy: A study in person perception. Unpublished manuscript. University of Minnesota, 1975.

GOLDSTEIN, E. Reaction times and the consciousness of deception. *American Journal of Psychology*, 1923, 34, 562-581.

GUSTAFSON, L., & ORNE, M. Effects of heightened motivation of the detection of deception. *Journal of Applied Psychology*, 1963, 47, 408-411.

GUSTAFSON, L., & ORNE, M. The effects of task and method of stimulus presentation on the detection of deception. *Journal of Applied Psychology*, 1946, 48, 383-387.

GUSTAFSON, L., & ORNE, M. Effects of perceived role and role success on the detection of deception. *Journal of Applied Psychology*, 1965, 49, 412-417.

HILDRETH, R. An experimental study of audiences' ability to distinguish between sincere and insincere speeches. Unpublished doctoral dissertation, University of Southern California, 1953.

HOCKING, J. Detecting deceptive communication from verbal, visual, and paralinguistic cues: An exploratory experiment. Unpublished doctoral dissertation, Michigan State University, 1976.

HOCKING, J., BAUCHNER, J., MILLER, G., & KAMINSKI, E. Detecting deceptive communication from verbal, visual, and paralinguistic cues. Unpublished manuscript. Michigan State University, 1976.

HORVATH, F. Verbal and nonverbal clues to truth and deception during polygraph examinations. *Journal of Police Science and Administration*, 1973, 1, 138-152.

JONES, E., & DAVIS, K. From acts to dispositions: The attribution process in person perception. In L. Berkowitz (Ed.), *Advances in experimental social psychology*, New York: Academic Press, 1965, 2, 219-266.

JONES, E., KANCUS, D., KEELEY, H., NISBET, R., VALENS, S., & WEINER, B. (Eds.). *Attribution*. New Jersey: General Learning Press, 1972.

JORESKOG, K., & VAN THILLO, M. *Lisrel: A general computer program for estimating a linear structural equation system involving multiple indicators of unmeasured variables*. Princeton, N.J.: Educational Testing Service, 1972.

KEATING, J., & BROCK, T. Acceptance of persuasion and the inhibition to counterargumentation under various distraction tasks, *Journal of Experimental Social Psychology*, 1974, 10, 301-309.

KNAPP, M. *Nonverbal communication in human interaction*. New York: Holt, Rinehart and Winston, 1972.

KNAPP, M., HART, R., & DENNIS, H. An exploration of deception as a communication construct. *Human Communication Research*, 1974, 1, 15-29.

LINQUIST, E. *Design and analysis of experiments in psychology and education*. Boston: Houghton, Mifflin, 1953.

MAIER, N., & THURBER, J. Accuracy of judgments of deception when an interview is watched, heard, and read. *Personal Psychology*, 1968, 21, 23-30.

MAIER, N. Sensitivity to attempts at deception in an interview situation. *Personnel Psychology*, 1965, 19, 55-65.

MAIER, N., & JANZEN, J. The reliability of persons used in making judgments of honesty and dishonesty. *Perceptual and Motor Skills*, 1967, 25, 141-151.

MATARAZZO, J., WIENS, A., JACKSON, R., & JANAUGH, T. Interviewer speech behavior under conditions of endogenously present and exogenously-induced motivational states. *Journal of Clinical Psychology*, 1970, 26, 141-148.

MARSTON, W. Reaction-time symptoms of deception. *Journal of Experimental Psychology*, 1920, 3, 72-87.

McCLINTOCK, C., & HUNT, R. Nonverbal indicators of affect and deception in an interview setting. *Journal of Applied Social Psychology*, 1975, 5, 54-67.

McGARTH, J., & ALTMAN, I. *Small group research.* New York: Holt, Rinehart and Winston, 1966.

MEHRABIAN, A. Nonverbal betrayal of feelings. *Journal of Experimental Research in Personality*, 1971, 5, 64-75.

MEHRABIAN, A. Some referents and measures of nonverbal behavior. *Behavior Research Methods and Instrumentation*, 1969, 1, 203-207.

MILLER, G., & BURGOON, M. *New techniques of persuasion.* New York: Harper and Row, 1973.

MILLER, G., & STEINBERG, M. *Between people: A new analysis of interpersonal communication.* Chicago: Science Research Associates, 1975.

MOTLEY, M. Acoustic correlates of lies. *Western Speech*, 1974, 37, 81-87.

NAMBOODIRI, N., CARTER, L., & BLALOCK, H. *Applied multivariate analysis and experimental designs.* New York: McGraw-Hill, 1975.

NIE, N., HULL, C., JENKINS, J., STEINBRENNER, K., & BENT, D. *Statistical package for the social sciences.* New York: McGraw-Hill, 1970.

NISBETT, R., CAPUTO, C., LEGANT, P., & MARECHEK, J. Behavior as seen by the actor and as seen by the observer. *Journal of Personality and Social Psychology*, 1973, 27, 154-164.

OSTERHOUSE, R., & BROCK, T. Distraction increases yielding to propaganda by inhibiting counterarguing. *Journal of Personality and Social Psychology*, 1970, 15, 344-358.

RYAN, M. The influence of teleconferencing medium and status on participants' perception of the aestheticism, evaluation, privacy, potency, and activity of the medium. *Human Communication Research*, 1976, 2:3, 255-261.

SILVERMAN, F., & JOHNSTON, R. Direct interval-estimation: A ratio scaling method. *Perceptual and Motor Skills*, 1975, 41, 464-466.

SHULMAN, G. An experimental study of the effects of receiver sex, communicator sex, and warning on the ability of receivers to detect deceptive communicators. Unpublished masters' thesis, Department of Speech Communication, Purdue University, 1973.

STORMS, M. Videotape and the attribution process. *Journal of Personality and Social Psychology*, 1973, 27, 165-175.

TAGIURI, R. Person perception. In G. Lindzey and E. Aronson (Eds.), *The handbook of social psychology*, Vol. 3. Reading Mass.: Addison-Wesley, 1969, 395-449.

THACKRAY, R., & ORNE, M. A comparison of physiological indices in detection of deception. *Psychophysiology*, 1968, 4, 329-339, a.

THACKRAY, R., & ORNE, M. Effects of the type of stimulus employed and the level of subject awareness on the detection of deception. *Journal of Applied Psychology*, 1968, 52, 234-239, b.

TROVILLO, P. A history of lie detection. *Journal of Criminal Law and Criminology*, 1939, 29, 848-881.

TURNBULL, A., STRICKLAND, L., & SHAVER, K. Medium of communication, differential power, and phasing concessions: Negotiating success and attributions to the opponent. *Human Communication Research*, 1976, 2:3, 262-270.

WESTON, J., & KRISTEN, C. Teleconferencing: A comparison of attitudes, uncertainty and interpersonal atmospheres in mediated and face-to-face group interaction. Prepared for the Department of Communications, Ottawa, Canada, 1973.

WIENER, M., & MEHRABIAN, A. *Language within language: Immediacy, a channel in verbal communication.* New York: Appleton-Century-Crofts, 1968.

WINER, B. *Statistical principles in experimental design.* New York: McGraw-Hill, 1962.

WILE, I. Lying as a biological and social phenomenon. *The Nervous Child*, 1942, 1, 293-313.

WOLK, R., & HENLEY, A. *The right to lie.* New York: Wyden, 1970.

INTERPERSONAL RELATIONSHIP LEVELS
AND INTERPERSONAL ATTRACTION[1]

CHARLES R. BERGER, MARYLIN D. WEBER,
MARY ELLEN MUNLEY, and JAMES T. DIXON
Northwestern University

The present studies were designed to explore the factorial composition of sources of attraction and to see how the various dimensions of attractiveness varied across the relationship levels of formal role, acquaintance, friend, close friend, and lover. In the first phase of the study, persons indicated those attributes they found attractive in specific persons. In the second phase, persons indicated the extent to which persons with whom they had different types of relationships possessed the various attributes suggested by the first phase respondents. Three attractiveness dimensions emerged from the analyses: *sociability, character,* and *supportiveness. Supportiveness* discriminated best among the five relationship categories. These findings were discussed in terms of current theory and research in interpersonal communication and interpersonal attraction.

> Ah, then I love you, not with passion wild,
> But as father loves a trusted child.
> I know you better now, and here confess
> I love you more, though I esteem you less.
> "How can that be?" You say. Your ways, my dear
> Make love more ardent but less kind, I fear.
>
> Gaius Catullus, 60 B.C.
> (quoted in Hunt, 1959, p. 59)

The above quotation from the Roman poet Catullus tells us that over 2,000 years ago observers of human behavior viewed love and attraction as highly complex and multifaceted phenomena. Modern behavioral researchers concerned with the study of interpersonal attraction have seemingly lost the spirit of this complexity in their research. Asking persons how much they would like to work with someone on a task and how much they think they would like a person, after reading some statements he has made, does not seem to do justice to the potential complexity of the interpersonal attraction construct. There are many attributes which can attract persons to each other. Byrne (1971), Heider (1958), and Newcomb (1961) emphasize the role that perceived similarities in attitudes and background play in the generation of attraction. Exchange-oriented theorists (Altman & Taylor, 1973; Homans, 1961; Thibaut & Kelley, 1959)

highlight the role that rewards and costs play in the development of interpersonal attraction. However, Huston (1974) has noted that these theorists tend to ignore the complexity of the interpersonal attraction construct itself, and by doing so they potentially limit the predictive and explanatory power of the theories they have developed. The purpose of the present study was to examine the attraction construct in some detail and to determine the factorial nature of attraction in various kinds of interpersonal relationships.

Interpersonal attraction is a critical construct in the study of interpersonal communication. A number of communication researchers have reported studies which link such communication antecedents as communicator style (Norton, 1976; Norton & Pettegrew, 1976), communication apprehension (McCroskey, Daly, Richmond, & Cox, 1975), speech style (Giles & Powesland, 1975), reciprocity of self-disclosure (Erlich & Greaven, 1971; Sermat & Smyth, 1973) to interpersonal attraction. In addition, interpersonal attraction has been examined as an antecedent to communication behavior (Lott & Lott, 1961; Moran, 1966). Shaw (1971) concludes, in his review of relevant research, that increases in group cohesion are associated with increases in the amount of communication within the group. Finally, Berger and Calabrese's (1975) uncertainty theory stipulates a causal relationship between *uncertainty* and *attraction,* such that decreases in uncertainty are associated with increases in attraction, up to a point. They stress that when a relationship becomes too predictable, the development of boredom may lower mutual attraction. While the above mentioned theory and research offer interesting insights into the relationships between various communication behaviors and interpersonal attraction, they also generally fail to capture the potential complexity of the attraction construct itself.

In one of the few studies designed to explore the factorial nature of the attraction construct, McCroskey and McCain (1974) developed a set of 30 items dealing with physical, social, and task components of attraction. In their initial study, 215 undergraduate students were asked to think of a classmate with whom they were acquainted and to rate the classmate on the 30 scales. Their factor analysis of these data revealed three independent attraction dimensions: *physical, social,* and *task.* Other research reported by McCroskey and McCain supports the reliability of the three attraction dimensions.

There are at least two limitations inherent in the McCroskey and McCain study. First, while the authors relied, in part, upon previous factor analytic work (Kiesler & Goldberg, 1968) to generate their tripartite model of attraction, it would seem to be desirable to generate items for such an analysis by asking large numbers of persons what they find attractive and unattractive in others. Relying upon previous factor analytic work may act to confound initial inadequate sampling of content. This is not to say that the McCroskey and McCain factors are not "correct" or "real"; it is to say, however, that there may be more to the interpersonal attraction construct than these three dimensions. A second

limitation to the McCroskey and McCain approach is that the authors had their respondents fill out their items for "a classmate who is an acquaintance." While this is one possible level of interpersonal relationship, there are several others which can be delineated (e.g., role relationship, friend, close friend, and intimate or lover). It seems reasonable to suppose that the factorial nature of interpersonal attraction varies considerably across such a relationship spectrum.

In the present study, the potential limitations of the McCroskey-McCain research cited above were remedied in the following ways. In the first phase of the present study, persons were asked to think of persons they liked within the relationship categories of formal, acquaintance, friend, close friend and lover. Prior research indicated that these categories form a useful progression, both in terms of intimacy and commitment to a relationship (Munley, 1976). While thinking of a person in each category, respondents were asked to list the attributes which they found attractive in the other. Also, persons were asked to list the attributes of persons they disliked intensely. From these lists of attributes, a final list was developed and employed in the main study. It was felt that this approach would increase the probability of obtaining a representative sample of attributes for different kinds of relationships. In the second phase of the present study, persons were asked to think of an individual they liked to an extreme degree in each of the five relationship categories. They were then given the task of determining the extent to which each of the persons possessed each of 36 attributes culled from the first phase of the study.

By using the approach described above, we hoped to elicit the attributes that persons employ in making judgments of the attractiveness of another. Moreover, we felt that by employing different types of relationships, we might be able to determine the extent to which attributes of attractiveness vary in importance or weight across different types of relationships. In addition, we were interested in determining the extent to which the various attributes clustered together across and within relationships. Because of the approach we employed, we made no a priori assumptions about general dimensions of attractiveness or the possible variations in dimensions owing to differences in relationship type.

METHODS AND PROCEDURES

Phase I

Respondents. Participants in the Phase I study were 85 undergraduate students enrolled in various communication courses. These 85 persons were randomly allocated into five different rating conditions: *Formal relationships, acquaintances, friends, close friends,* and *lovers.*

Questionnaire. On the front of the questionnaire were general instructions which indicated that the study was concerned with finding out what respondents found attractive in other persons. Also a scale ranging from *formal relationships* to *lovers* was included on the first page with the five relationship categories in the order listed above. The category to be considered by the respondent was circled.

On the next page, respondents were asked to think of a person whom they liked very much in the particular relationship category to which they were assigned. In addition, they were given a description of the relationship category. For example, those who received a *formal relationship* questionnaire were asked to think of a person whom they liked very much; whom they dealt with exclusively on the formal level and not on the level of friendship. Role categories such as student, teacher, doctor, salesperson, and gas station attendant were given as examples of possible formal relationships. Respondents were cautioned to think of a person whom they liked in this category, but whom they did not consider a friend.

Respondents were then asked to list as many reasons as they could for their high level of liking for the person. On the following page, respondents were asked to think of a second person in the same category of relationship as the first for whom they had an *intense dislike*. Respondents were then asked to list as many reasons as they could for their intense dislike of the person. On the third page of the questionnaire, respondents were asked to indicate what kinds of *changes* the disliked person considered on the previous page would have to display before the respondent would begin to like the person. Finally, respondents were asked for some demographic information.

The five versions of the questionnaire all followed the same progression as that outlined above. At each relationship level, care was taken to instruct the respondent to think of a person who was appropriate to that level and not to any of the other levels; for example, those who received a *friends* questionnaire were instructed to think of a person whom they considered a friend, but not a close friend or just an acquaintance. It was felt that the scale provided on the front page with the particular relationship category circled helped the respondents to locate appropriate persons for rating.

Procedures. The questionnaires were administered during class time. Respondents did not place their names on the questionnaires.

Phase II

Respondents. Participants in Phase II of the present study were 142 undergraduate students enrolled in various communication studies courses.

Questionnaire. The questionnaire employed in Phase II was based upon the responses given in the Phase I study. Two coders analyzed the attribute lists given in the 85 Phase I questionnaires. It was generally found that the attributes listed for the liked persons were the direct opposite of those listed for the disliked person. In addition, while there were slight wording differences, many of the attributes listed for liked and disliked persons were quite similar across respondents. Thus, 36 attributes were culled from the Phase I data. These attributes were then cast into items which asked, "To what extent is the person _____," or "To what extent does the person _____," and so on. In the Phase II questionnaire, respondents indicated the extent to which the persons they were thinking of possessed the attribute in question on the following scale: *Extremely, very, somewhat, slightly,* and *not at all.* In addition, persons were given a sixth response alternative of "don't know" (whether or not the person possessed the attribute).

In the Phase II questionnaire, all respondents were asked to rate a liked person in each of the five relationship categories. Thus, each respondent did

TABLE 1
Percentage of Know and Don't Know Responses for 36 Items Across Five Relationship Types

Item	Response	FR	A	F	CF	L	Q-Value	p	N**
1. To what extent is the person physically attractive ("beautiful or handsome") and neat or "good looking?"	Know D.K.	100% 0	99% 1	99% 1	99% 1	100% 0	4.00	.40	124
2. To what extent is the person good at various activities such as sports, bridge, playing an instrument, etc.?	Know D.K.	41% 59	70% 30	93% 7	92% 8	97% 3	185.80	.001	123
3. To what extent does the person help you to reach your personal goals or help you out generally?	Know D.K.	94% 6	91% 9	98% 2	99% 1	100% 0	19.35	.001	122
4. To what extent does the person do his or her job well? How well does the person perform in their role relationship to you?	Know D.K.	99% 1	89% 11	96% 4	100% 0	100% 0	33.19	.001	121
5. To what extent are the attitudes and opinions of the person similar to yours?	Know D.K.	72% 28	80% 20	93% 7	100% 0	98% 2	75.44	.001	123
6. To what extent is the person's background (family, hometown, education and age) similar to yours?	Know D.K.	56% 44	79% 21	91% 9	99% 1	99% 1	128.07	.001	124
7. To what extent are you interested in the same kinds of things?	Know D.K.	72% 28	80% 20	98% 2	100% 0	99% 1	92.18	.001	123
8. To what extent is the person intelligent, knowledgeable, smart, etc.?	Know D.K.	100% 0	97% 3	100% 0	100% 0	100% 0	12.00	.01	124
9. How self-confident is the person?	Know D.K.	94% 6	90% 10	97% 3	99% 1	98% 2	19.22	.001	123
10. How sophisticated is the person? How "with it" is the person?	Know D.K.	90% 10	93% 7	98% 2	99% 1	99% 1	28.65	.001	123
11. How approachable is the person? How accessible is the person to others?	Know D.K.	97% 3	98% 2	99% 1	100% 0	100% 0	8.25	.08	123
12. How outgoing is the person?	Know D.K.	93% 7	98% 2	100% 0	100% 0	99% 1	21.33	.001	124
13. To what extent is the person good at making conversation? To what extent is the person a good listener?	Know D.K.	94% 6	98% 2	100% 0	100% 0	100% 0	20.00	.001	124
14. To what extent does the person handle him/herself well in social situations?	Know D.K.	71% 29	93% 7	98% 2	99% 1	100% 0	103.51	.001	123
15. To what extent is the person easy going, relaxed and spontaneous?	Know D.K.	99% 1	98% 2	100% 0	100% 0	100% 0	5.33	.26	124
16. How kind, generous and considerate is this person?	Know D.K.	89% 11	92% 8	98% 2	100% 0	100% 0	32.17	.001	122
17. To what extent is this person interested in your welfare? How concerned is he/she about you?	Know D.K.	91% 9	83% 17	97% 3	100% 0	99% 1	44.88	.001	124
18. To what extent does the person like you?	Know D.K.	78% 22	85% 15	94% 6	100% 0	100% 0	61.67	.001	123
19. How receptive is this person to others' ideas? How open is the person?	Know D.K.	88% 12	84% 16	93% 7	100% 0	100% 0	44.96	.001	122
20. To what extent is this person realistic in terms of knowing his own as well as others' limitations?	Know D.K.	74% 26	63% 37	84% 16	99% 1	96% 4	84.57	.001	122
21. To what extent does this person understand you as an individual?	Know D.K.	81% 19	78% 22	89% 11	100% 0	99% 1	59.68	.001	123
22. To what extent does this person do things which make you feel good about yourself? To what extent does he/she reinforce you?	Know D.K.	97% 3	90% 10	98% 2	100% 0	100% 0	27.56	.001	124
23. To what extent does the person respect you as an individual and not make unreasonable demands upon you?	Know D.K.	88% 12	87% 13	98% 2	100% 0	100% 0	44.53	.001	121
24. To what extent does this person have good rapport with you?	Know D.K.	97% 3	97% 3	100% 0	100% 0	100% 0	9.81	.04	122
25. To what extent does this person have a good sense of humor?	Know D.K.	97% 3	98% 2	100% 0	100% 0	100% 0	10.67	.03	124
26. How sincere is this person?	Know D.K.	90% 10	90% 10	98% 2	100% 0	100% 0	32.00	.001	124
27. How dependable is the person?	Know D.K.	90% 10	78% 22	96% 4	100% 0	100% 0	62.29	.001	124
28. How energetic and enthusiastic is the person?	Know D.K.	98% 2	99% 1	100% 0	100% 0	100% 0	6.18	.18	124
29. To what extent does this person possess high ethical principles?	Know D.K.	60% 40	67% 33	85% 15	97% 3	98% 2	109.57	.001	123
30. To what extent is the person humble and not conceited?	Know D.K.	85% 15	92% 8	100% 0	100% 0	98% 2	46.69	.001	123
31. How loyal is the person to you?	Know D.K.	67% 33	66% 34	89% 11	99% 1	99% 1	109.41	.001	123
32. How friendly and pleasant is this person's personality?	Know D.K.	100% 0	100% 0	100% 0	100% 0	100% 0			
33. How popular is this person with others?	Know D.K.	82% 18	93% 7	98% 2	100% 0	99% 1	53.23	.001	122
34. How romantic is this person?	Know D.K.	22% 78	44% 56	57% 43	88% 12	97% 1	218.68	.001	123
35. How serious is this person?	Know D.K.	87% 13	86% 14	93% 7	100% 0	100% 0	39.53	.001	123
36. To what extent do you trust this person?	Know D.K.	98% 2	92% 8	100% 0	100% 0	100% 0	28.48	.001	124

*FR=Formal Relationship, A=Acquaintance, F=Friend, CF=Close Friend, L=Lover.

**N for each item varies because of varying number of blanks per item. If a respondent had a blank for an item in one relationship, all of his data were excluded for that item across relationships.

five sets of ratings. In order to avoid fatigue and order effects, the five relationship categories were *systematically rotated among questionnaires*. Since there were 120 possible orders for the five relationship categories, there was one complete rotation, plus 22 repeat orders, in the present sample.

Procedures. Questionnaires were administered during regular class time. Students were instructed not to put their names on their booklets.

RESULTS

Specific results for Phase I will not be discussed, since the Phase I data only served to generate the items used in Phase II.

It should also be kept in mind that since respondents were given the option of indicating that they did not know whether or not the person being rated possessed a particular attribute, these "don't know" responses could not be meaningfully placed on the metric represented by the response categories of *extremely, very, somewhat, slightly,* and *not at all*. For example, not knowing whether a person is loyal is not the same as indicating that the person does not possess the attribute of loyalty. Because the don't know responses could not be meaningfully recoded onto the ordered scale, they had to be excluded from certain analyses.

In addition, certain persons left certain items blank. In some cases, for example, respondents could not think of a person to rate in a particular relationship category. In these cases, all 36 items were left blank. When a particular item set was left blank, the person giving the blank response was excluded from the analysis for that particular relationship. Also, at times, a given individual might leave a particular item blank. In these cases, the person was excluded from any analysis of that particular item or from indices which employed that item.

Extent of Knowledge

In an effort to determine the extent to which persons felt able to assess the degree to which persons in the five relationship categories possessed the 36 attributes, an analysis of each of the 36 items

within each of the five relationship categories was performed. In this analysis, the frequency of "don't know" responses was compared with the combined frequency of responses in the other five response categories for each of the 36 items across the five relationship types. These data are displayed in Table 1.

Because the same 142 persons made ratings across the five relationship categories, a series of 36 *Cochran Q tests* (Siegel, 1956) was computed, comparing the frequency of "don't know" and "know" responses for each item across the five relationship types.

Several trends are revealed by the data of Table 1. First, the frequency of don't know responses is generally disproportionately high within the *formal role* and *acquaintance* categories. In 16 of the 36 items, the highest percentage of don't know responses was found in the *formal role* category. In an additional 16 items, the highest percentage of don't know responses was observed in the *acquaintance* category. Two items showed identical don't know percentages in the two relationship categories. Thus, in 34 of the 36 items, the greatest percentage of don't know responses was found in either the *formal role* or *acquaintance* categories. This general trend did not hold for Items 1 and 32, which dealt with physical attractiveness and perceived friendliness of personality. Apparently, these are judgments which are made with some confidence on the basis of relatively little interaction with another person.

Second, in addition to physical attractiveness and perceived friendliness, there appear to be other attributes which persons are willing to make judgments about, regardless of relationship category. Items 8, 11, 15, 24, 25, and 28 showed relatively slight *don't know* rates among relationship categories (even though some of them produced statistically significant differences). From the pattern of data indicated on these items, persons seem to be able to make judgments about such qualities as physical attractiveness, friendliness, intelligence, accessibility, spontaneiety, rapport, sense of humor, and enthusiasm of persons they like, regardless of the relationship they have with those persons. By contrast, several items reflect differences in knowledge as a function of relationship level.

TABLE 2
Extent of Attribution of 36 Characteristics Across Five Relationship Types

Item	Response*	FR	A	F	CF	L	Q-Value	p	N**
1. To what extent is the person physically attractive (beautiful or handsome) and neat or good looking?	4-5 / 1-3	29% / 71	53% / 47	47% / 53	66% / 34	81% / 19	80.49	.001	123
2. To what extent is the person good at various activities such as sports, bridge, playing an instrument, etc.?	4-5 / 1-3	60% / 40	44% / 56	63% / 37	50% / 50	58% / 42	3.70	.45	38
3. To what extent does the person help you to reach your personal goals or help you out generally?	4-5 / 1-3	48% / 52	9% / 91	23% / 77	76% / 24	73% / 27	145.87	.001	101
4. To what extent does the person do his or her job well? How well does the person perform in their role relationship to you?	4-5 / 1-3	82% / 18	66% / 34	57% / 43	89% / 11	82% / 18	41.41	.001	103
5. To what extent are the attitudes and opinions of the person similar to yours?	5 / 1-4	4% / 96	3% / 97	8% / 92	38% / 62	20% / 80	53.48	.001	71
6. To what extent is the person's background (family, hometown, education and age) similar to yours?	4-5 / 1-3	14% / 86	19% / 81	37% / 63	65% / 35	40% / 60	41.88	.001	58
7. To what extent are you interested in the same kinds of things?	4-5 / 1-3	20% / 80	23% / 77	38% / 62	82% / 18	60% / 40	77.80	.001	73
8. To what extent is the person intelligent, knowledgeable, smart, etc?	4-5 / 1-3	85% / 15	73% / 27	74% / 26	87% / 13	87% / 13	16.83	.002	119
9. How self-confident is the person?	5 / 1-4	27% / 73	14% / 86	15% / 85	29% / 71	30% / 70	15.87	.003	105
10. How sophisticated is the person? How "with it" is the person?	4-5 / 1-3	61% / 39	54% / 46	52% / 48	71% / 29	67% / 33	12.48	.01	105
11. How approachable is the person? How accessible is the person to others?	4-5 / 1-3	69% / 31	65% / 35	66% / 34	70% / 30	74% / 26	3.18	.53	115
12. How outgoing is the person?	4-5 / 1-3	60% / 40	58% / 42	54% / 46	60% / 40	64% / 36	3.10	.54	114
13. To what extent is the person good at making conversation? To what extent is the person a good listener?	4-5 / 1-3	71% / 29	66% / 34	60% / 40	85% / 15	90% / 10	41.17	.001	115
14. To what extent does the person handle him/herself well in social situations?	5 / 1-4	25% / 75	27% / 73	18% / 82	30% / 70	29% / 71	4.67	.32	82
15. To what extent is the person easy going, relaxed and spontaneous?	5 / 1-4	25% / 75	18% / 82	17% / 83	37% / 63	38% / 62	27.34	.001	121
16. How kind, generous and considerate is this person?	4-5 / 1-3	67% / 33	60% / 40	55% / 45	80% / 20	77% / 23	25.81	.001	101
17. To what extent is this person interested in your welfare? How concerned is he/she about you?	4-5 / 1-3	41% / 59	18% / 82	33% / 67	87% / 13	87% / 13	152.17	.001	93
18. To what extent does the person like you?	4-5 / 1-3	57% / 43	41% / 59	57% / 43	96% / 4	98% / 2	107.11	.001	83
19. How receptive is this person to other's ideas? How open is the person?	5 / 1-4	16% / 84	7% / 93	8% / 92	24% / 76	23% / 77	21.32	.001	90
20. To what extent is this person realistic in terms of knowing his own as well as other's limitations?	4-5 / 1-3	74% / 26	55% / 45	54% / 46	76% / 24	64% / 36	12.41	.02	59
21. To what extent does this person understand you as an individual?	4-5 / 1-3	20% / 80	10% / 90	26% / 74	91% / 9	70% / 30	172.75	.001	80
22. To what extent does this person do things which make you feel good about yourself? To what extent does he/she reinforce you?	4-5 / 1-3	37% / 63	26% / 74	34% / 66	84% / 16	74% / 26	124.48	.001	106
23. To what extent does the person respect you as an individual and not make unreasonable demands on you?	4-5 / 1-3	61% / 39	60% / 40	73% / 27	88% / 12	74% / 26	29.17	.001	94
24. To what extent does this person have good rapport with you?	4-5 / 1-3	60% / 40	57% / 43	64% / 36	99% / 1	91% / 9	99.06	.001	117
25. To what extent does this person have a good sense of humor?	5 / 1-4	23% / 77	18% / 82	18% / 82	47% / 53	44% / 56	59.55	.001	118
26. How sincere is this person?	5 / 1-4	28% / 72	16% / 84	20% / 80	55% / 45	56% / 44	78.89	.001	101
27. How dependable is the person?	5 / 1-4	28% / 72	22% / 78	22% / 78	48% / 52	47% / 53	31.56	.001	86
28. How energetic and enthusiastic is the person?	5 / 1-4	35% / 65	23% / 77	23% / 77	32% / 68	39% / 61	14.61	.006	119
29. To what extent does this person possess high ethical principles?	5 / 1-4	34% / 66	15% / 85	15% / 85	35% / 65	36% / 64	17.52	.002	53
30. To what extent is the person humble and not conceited?	4-5 / 1-3	37% / 63	47% / 53	49% / 51	65% / 35	56% / 44	20.00	.001	99
31. How loyal is the person to you?	4-5 / 1-3	31% / 69	25% / 75	41% / 59	92% / 8	79% / 21	92.22	.001	61
32. How friendly and pleasant is this person's personality?	4-5 / 1-3	74% / 26	79% / 21	73% / 27	91% / 9	90% / 10	25.91	.001	122
33. How popular is this person with others?	4-5 / 1-3	71% / 29	68% / 32	67% / 33	77% / 23	86% / 16	11.97	.02	97
34. How romantic is this person?	4-5 / 1-3	45% / 55	45% / 55	45% / 55	45% / 55	95% / 5	8.9	.06	20
35. How serious is this person?	4-5 / 1-3	52% / 48	33% / 67	54% / 46	61% / 39	63% / 37	30.28	.001	94
36. To what extent do you trust this person?	4-5 / 1-3	24% / 76	13% / 87	19% / 81	71% / 29	67% / 33	158.30	.001	112

*Based upon median split of attribution scale for each item; where: 1=Not at all, 2=Slightly, 3=Somewhat, 4=Very, and 5=Extremely.

**In this analysis, all persons who answered "Don't know" or who left the item blank were eliminated from the analysis of that item.

Items 2, 5, 6, 7, 14, 18, 20, 21, 27, 29, 31, and 34 each show wide variations in the percentage of *don't know* responses, depending upon the particular relationship category. In all of these cases, the largest proportions of *don't know* responses were either in the *formal role* or *acquaintance* categories. Item 34 has the largest between-category discrepancy. In this case, 78 percent of those responding to the item were unable to rate the person being thought of in the *formal relationship* category, whereas, only 1 percent of the same respondents were unable to rate the person in the *lover* category. Since Item 34 dealt with the extent to which the person being thought of was "romantic," this is a quite understandable result. However, it is curious that 1 percent of the respondents were unable to rate their lover on the romantic dimension!

Since the similarity-attraction relationship is one of the best documented ones in the behavioral sciences, it is instructive to pay particular attention to Items 5, 6, and 7—which dealt with similarity. Of these three items, it appears that Item 6—which was concerned with the extent of background similarity—showed the largest between-category discrepancy. Apparently, similarity of opinions (Item 5) and interests (Item 7) are more apparent in *formal role* relationships than are similarities in background. This result is somewhat difficult to understand, since a number of theorists have suggested that demographic and background information are most likely to be exchanged during initial interactions (Altman & Taylor, 1973; Berger, 1973; Berger & Larimer, 1974; Berger & Calabrese, 1975). It is possible, of course, that within the context of formal role relationships, such biographic and demographic information is not exchanged because of the task-oriented nature of interactions at this level. This interpretation is supported by a comparison of the three similarity items within the *acquaintance* category. Within this category, there are virtually no differences in the percentage of don't know responses among the three similarity items. Moreover, in all of the similarity items the percentage of don't know responses decreases as relationship intensity—as represented by the relationship levels—increases. These trends provide general support for the theoretical positions cited above.

In conclusion, most items reveal a trend for an increasing ability to make judgments about various attributes as the relationship becomes more intense. However, for such attributes as physical attractiveness, friendliness, intelligence, accessibility, spontaneity, rapport, sense of humor, and enthusiasm, persons seem to be able to make judgments no matter what kind of relationship they have with the person being rated, so long as they like the person. These kinds of attributes might be characterized as "surface" attributes, whereas those which showed large differences among and between relationship levels could be conceived of as "core" attributes. Similarities of opinions, background, and interests—as well as abilities, social competence, limitations, ethical principles, and romantic inclinations—are examples of "core" attributes.

Extent of Attribution

More central to our present concern is the extent to which respondents attributed the 36 attributes to the persons representing the five relationship levels. Here we are asking the question of whether there are differences in the degree to which a particular characteristic is attributed across relationship types. Obviously, in this analysis, persons answering "don't know" are excluded. An additional caution is in order. Because Cochran's Q requires *complete* data for each respondent across the five response categories on any particular item, persons who answered "Don't know" for a given attribute within even one of the five categories had to be excluded from the analysis. Thus, even if a person gave responses other than *don't know* on the physical attraction item in the *lover, close friend, friend,* and *acquaintance* categories, if the respondent answered "don't know" in the *formal role* category, all of his data would have to be excluded from the analysis of the physical attractiveness item. This situation is especially troublesome in the case of Item 34, in which 78 percent of the respondents chose don't know in the *formal role* category.

In order to perform *Cochran Q tests,* the response scale was split at the median for each item, based upon the total distribution of responses. Employing median splits on each item does throw away information; however, the use of the Q statistic requires a dichotomous response distribution. Table 2 contains the response distributions across the five relationship types, as well as the Q values and associated probabilities. There are several interesting facets to the data contained in Table 2. First, there are a number of items which fail to discriminate among the five relationship categories, Items 2, 11, 12, 14, and 34. However, in the case of Items 2 and 34, the lack of discrimination may be due to the large sample attrition caused by the large number of *don't know* responses in some categories. Interestingly, Items 11, 12, and 14, all of which deal with gregariousness and social competence, fail to discriminate among the five categories. Since persons were asked to think of a liked person in each category, apparently perceptions of gregariousness do not determine the particular *type of relationship* which will develop; they only determine whether a person will be liked in general.

A second aspect of these data is significant. This facet concerns the items which showed large differences among categories. Items 1, 3, 5, 7, 17, 18, 21, 22, 24, 25, 26, 31, and 36 fall into this category. It is *extremely* important to note that, while these items showed large differences among categories, relatively few showed a linear increasing trend of attribution across the five relationship levels. For example, Item 1, which dealt with the extent of physical attractiveness of the target person, showed a substantial increase in attribution from the *formal role* to the *acquaintance* categories. However, there is little difference between the *acquaintance* and *friend* categories, but a rather large jump from *friend* to *close friend,* and *close friend* to *lover*. While this trend approximates something like a linear one, the plateau between *acquaintance* and *friend* nullifies the simple linear possibility. Item 3 also reveals a complex relationship. In this case, about half of the respondents felt that the person in the *formal role* category helped them to achieve their personal goals either very much or to an extreme degree. However, only 9 percent of the respondents felt that an acquaintance they like helped them to achieve their personal goals to the same extent.

A fascinating trend is revealed in both Items 21 and 22. Item 21 dealt with how much the person understands the respondent as an individual, while Item 22 asked the respondent to attribute the extent to which the target person reinforced him and made him feel good about himself. In both cases, these qualities were more intensely attributed to *close friends* than to *lovers*. In the case of the *understanding* item (Item 21), there is a 21 percent difference between *close friends* and *lovers*. The trend for *close friends* to be attributed more of a characteristic than *lovers* also is evident on Items 5, 6, 7, 20, 23, 30, and 31. Taken as a whole, these data suggest that *close friends* are seen as more similar in opinions, background, and interests, as well as realistic in knowing limitations, understanding, reinforcing, humble, loyal, and less unreasonable in terms of making demands, than are *lovers*.

A final point concerns the *formal role* category. In several cases—for example, Items 4, 8, 9, 10, 13, as well as several others—the person rated in the *formal role* category received as much or more attribution as those persons rated in the *acquaintance* and *friend* categories.

Factor Analyses

In order to achieve a higher level of parsimony than that evidenced in the previous analyses, and to determine whether or not the dimensions of attractiveness would be similar across relationship types, a series of factor analyses were performed on the data. In all of these analyses, principal factor solutions with iterations were obtained using squared multiple correlations as initial communality estimates. These analyses were followed by Varimax rotation procedures employing Kaiser normalization.

Because persons were allowed to respond "don't know" to any particular item, and because these responses could not be meaningfully recoded onto the attribution metric, a pairwise deletion procedure was employed to retain as much data as possible. In this procedure, all 710 sets were included; however, if on a *given item* a specific individual had a blank or a "don't know," his data for that item only were excluded from the analysis.[2]

This analysis yielded four factors, after iterations which accounted for 69, 16, 10, and 5 percent of the common variance, respectively. Table 3 presents

TABLE 3
Factor Loadings for 23 Selected Characteristics

Item	Factor 1	Factor 2	Factor 3
1. To what extent does this person understand you as an individual?	.82	.23	.11
2. To what extent does this person like you	.78	.23	.19
3. To what extent is the person interested in your welfare? How concerned is he/she about you?	.77	.35	.12
4. How loyal is the person to you?	.75	.37	.06
5. To what extent does this person do things which make you feel good about yourself? To what extent does he/she reinforce you?	.72	.32	.18
6. To what extent does this person have good rapport with you?	.69	.30	.23
7. To what extent does the person help you to reach your personal goals or help you out generally?	.67	.28	.17
8. To what extent are you interested in the same kinds of things?	.63	.09	.20
9. To what extent are the attitudes and opinions of the person similar to yours?	.57	.11	.21
10. How sincere is this person?	.33	.71	.19
11. How dependable is the person?	.25	.69	.12
12. To what extent does this person possess high ethical principles?	.11	.64	.11
13. How kind, generous and considerate is this person?	.27	.60	.33
14. To what extent is this person realistic in terms of knowing his own as well as others' limitations?	.15	.53	.15
15. How outgoing is the person?	.06	-.09	.69
16. How popular is this person with others?	.12	.11	.68
17. To what extent does this person handle him/herself well in social situations?	.05	.21	.66
18. How friendly and pleasant is this person's personality?	.30	.38	.62
19. How approachable is the person? How accessible to others is the person?	.11	.22	.58
20. To what extent is the person easy going, relaxed and spontaneous?	.16	.23	.57
21. To what extent is the person good at making conversation? To what extent is the person a good listener?	.25	.25	.56
22. How energetic and enthusiastic is the person?	.12	.28	.53
23. How sophisticated is the person? How "with it" is the person?	.18	.06	.51

the results of the Varimax rotation analysis, excluding the fourth factor because of its small size. Only items with primary loadings of approximately .50 or more and secondary loadings of no more than .38 are presented in the table.

The interpretation of the factor loadings presented in Table 3 is quite straightforward. First, Factor 1 items generally refer to the kinds of things that the target persons can give to the respondents, e.g., understanding, liking, concern, loyalty, reinforcement, rapport, and help. The two similarity items which load on Factor 1 may be indicative of

support provided by the target person. By contrast, Factors 2 and 3 deal with attributes which are essentially independent of the respondent's relationship to the target. The judgments represented on Factors 2 and 3 could be made about an individual without having a relationship with that individual. Factor 1 judgments *require* interaction for their generation.

On an individual basis, the factors seem to be tapping the following general dimensions. Factor 1 generally refers to the extent to which the target person provides various kinds of *support* for the respondent. For the sake of convenience, we will

TABLE 4
Cronbach Alpha Coefficients for Three
Attractiveness Scales Across Five Relationship Types*

Scale	Relationship Type				
	Formal Role	Acquaint- ance	Friend	Close Friend	Lover
Supportiveness (Factor 1)	.91 (n=47)	.81 (n=58)	.86 (n=109)	.85 (n=139)	.86 (n=124)
Character (Factor 2)	.79 (n=70)	.80 (n=66)	.84 (n=109)	.75 (n=135)	.79 (n=122)
Sociability (Factor 3)	.85 (n=78)	.86 (n=104)	.87 (n=132)	.86 (n=138)	.82 (n=125)

> * N's for each cell vary because of differing numbers of "don't know" responses eliminated from the analysis. In order for a given individual to be included in the analysis, he or she had to have no "don't know" responses on any of the items making up the scale.

call this factor *"supportiveness."* Factor 2 clearly refers to a kind of *character or ethical dimension.* Factor 2 is very similar to the safety, trustworthiness or character factors found in studies of source credibility (Berlo, Lemert, & Mertz, 1969; McCroskey, 1966). Factor 3 refers to a kind of *sociability dimension* similar to the weak factor extracted by Berlo, Lemert, & Mertz (1969) in their source credibility research. Moreover, this factor contains several items which Wiemann (1976) found to be a part of a general construct of communicative competence. For ease of discussion, we have chosen to label Factors 2 and 3 *character* and *sociability,* respectively.

The nine items making up Factors 1 and 3, and the five items comprising Factor 2, were analyzed for their internal consistency by computing *Cronbach's Coefficient Alpha* for each scale. The *supportiveness scale* was found to have a high degree of internal consistency, Alpha = .92. The *character scale* had close to an acceptable level of internal consistency with Alpha = .81. The *sociability scale* was found to have an Alpha of .86. These coefficients are generally acceptable. One possible reason for the lower reliability of the *character scale* (Factor 2) is simply that the scale contained only five items, while the other two scales consisted of nine items each.

Reliabilities Across Relationship Levels

Before comparing the means for the three attractiveness scales across the five types of relationships, it was deemed necessary to determine whether or not the scales remained internally consistent across the five relationship levels. If they did not, it would be inappropriate to make such comparisons. Thus, for each relationship level, Cronbach's Alpha was computed for each of the three scales. The results of these analyses are presented in Table 4.

The data presented in Table 4 strongly suggest that the *sociability scale* showed very little variation in internal consistency across the five relationship levels. However, in the case of the *supportiveness* and *character* dimensions, there is a moderate amount of variation. There is a considerable drop in reliability in the *supportiveness scale* between the *formal role* and *acquaintance* relationships. There is also a moderate discrepancy between the *friend* and *close friend* levels for the *character scale.* However, most of the coefficients presented in Table 4 are close to or above acceptable internal consistency levels. In addition, there seems to be no pattern of variation in the reliability coefficients across relationship levels for any of the three scales.

TABLE 5
Interscale Correlations Within Relationship Levels*

Correlation	Relationship Level				
	Formal Role	Acquain- tance	Friend	Close Friend	Lover
Supportiveness with Character	.39 (n=37)	.30 (n=47)	.59 (n=97)	.60 (n=134)	.68 (n=119)
Supportiveness with Sociability	.36 (n=40)	-.05 (n=55)	.39 (n=108)	.40 (n=137)	.46 (n=121)
Character with Sociability	.57 (n=54)	.09 (n=61)	.28 (n=105)	.41 (n=132)	.41 (n=119)

* N's vary between relationship levels because of differing numbers of "don't know" responses.

Scale Independence Across Relationship Levels

Before comparing means for the three scales among the relationship levels, it also was felt necessary to determine the extent to which the three scales remained independent of each other across the various relationship levels. We have seen that each of the three scales displayed a fairly uniform and acceptable level of internal consistency across relationship levels; however, this does not necessarily mean that the three scales are independent of each other across all relationship types. In order to assess possible correlations among scales, the three scales were intercorrelated within each relationship level. The results of this analysis are presented in Table 5.

The correlations contained in Table 5 reveal several important trends. First, for all three measures the *acquaintance* category produced the lowest correlations between the scales. There is virtually no correlation between *supportiveness* and *sociability,* and *character* and *sociability,* within the *acquaintance* category. Second, as relationship levels increase from *acquaintance* through *friend* and *close friend* to *lover,* the correlations between scales become larger—although, in the case of the correlation between *character* and *sociability,* there is no difference between the *close friend* and *lover* categories. Third, the correlations between the pairs of scales within the *formal role* category are always greater than those in the *acquaintance* category.

Furthermore, in the case of the *character-sociability* correlations, the highest correlation was observed within the *formal role* category.

A note of caution should be injected at this juncture. As Table 5 reveals, the correlations between the scales are generally based upon differing sample sizes because of the elimination of persons who answered "don't know" to one or more of the items making up the scales. Since the frequency of "don't know" responses was generally higher in the *formal role* category, the three correlations in that category are based upon the smallest sample sizes. Thus, these correlations are most subject to the highest rates of sampling error. Also, there is a general trend for sample sizes to increase as relationship levels become more intimate, with the exception of the *lover* category, which consistently has a smaller number of respondents than the *close friend* category. The general trend of increasing sample size from *acquaintance* to *close friend* matches the trend for increasing correlations between scales across these categories. Thus, it is possible that the increases in correlations between scales across relationship levels are due to differential respondent attrition or self-selection. However, the fact that in two cases the correlations for the *lover* category are greater than the corresponding two correlations for the *close friend* category, *even though the sample sizes are smaller in the lover category,* is evidence which casts doubt upon a self-selection interpretation of the changes in corre-

TABLE 6
Means, Standard Deviations, and
F-Values for Three Attractiveness Scales Across
Five Relationship Levels

SCALE*

Relationship Level	Supportiveness (n=28)		Character (n=36)		Sociability (n=62)	
	Mean	S.D.	Mean	S.D.	Mean	S.D.
Formal Role	29.57	6.88	20.08	3.26	35.87	5.11
Acquaintance	27.89	5.12	18.39	3.70	34.33	5.07
Friend	31.93	4.96	18.19	4.11	33.54	5.78
Close Friend	39.00	4.36	21.11	2.77	36.58	5.26
Lover	37.57	5.43	20.31	3.48	37.27	5.28

F = 29.35 F = 6.30 F = 6.90
df = 4/108** df = 4/140** df = 4/244**
p < .001 p < .0C1 p < .001

* The Supportiveness and Sociability scales both had possible score ranges of from 9 to 45 where 9 represented the lowest levels of supportiveness and sociability on each scale respectively. The possible range of the Character scale was from 5 to 25 with 5 representing the lowest level of character.

** Error degrees of freedom are based upon <u>repeated measures</u> over the same respondents within each analysis.

lations. Moreover, the highest correlation between *character* and *sociability* was found in the *formal role* level, the level which has the fewest respondents in it.

Given the above caution, it seems reasonable to assert that, with the exception of the *formal role* category, the more intimate relationships become, the more likely it is that the judgments made about the various facets of attractiveness will co-vary together. It is tempting to interpret the data of Table 5 as an indication of a manifestation of a halo effect; that is, as liking for a person increases, there is a tendency to lump together various characteristics and to make fewer finer discriminations. However, it is difficult to interpret the data unambiguously in this way, since respondents were instructed to think of a person whom they liked very much in each of the relationship categories. We have no way of knowing exactly how much each respondent liked

the individuals he or she thought of as target persons. However, if we can assume that liking is generally reciprocated (Gergen, 1969), then Item 18 of Table 2 may provide some insight into the interpretative problem outlined above. This item asked the respondent to indicate the extent to which the person being thought of in the category liked him. The data of Table 2 strongly suggest that perceived liking by the target person increases as relationship levels increase from *acquaintance* to *lover and* the level of perceived liking in the *formal role* category is as high as that manifested in the *friend* category. Since the distribution of perceived liking responses in large measure parallels the increasing tendency for the scales to correlate over relationships, it does seem possible that a kind of halo effect may explain why the three attractiveness dimensions tend to collapse as relationships become more intense.

Attractiveness Scale Differences Across Relationships

Three one-way repeated-measures analyses of variance (ANOVA) were performed using the five relationship levels as the independent variable and the three attractiveness scales as dependent variables. Only respondents who had complete data (no blanks or "don't know" responses) on each of the items which made up the scales and complete data on each scale across all five relationships could be included in these analyses. As a result of the application of these criteria, considerable respondent attrition occurred. However, as Table 6 reveals, some reasonable trends emerged from these analyses.

All of the analyses revealed significant differences among categories. In order to trace down the specific pairwise differences between relationship levels, a series of *Newman-Keuls tests* was performed. The Newman-Keuls procedure detected no significant differences ($p < .05$) on the *supportiveness scale* between the *formal role* and acquaintance or the *close friend* and *lover* categories. Furthermore, for the *supportiveness* scale, no significant difference was found between the *formal role* and *friend* categories. All remaining pairwise comparisons produced statistically significant differences. Thus, there is an increase in *supportiveness* from the *acquaintance* to the *close friend* categories; however, *supportiveness* does not increase when one moves from a *close friend* to a *lover* relationship. Furthermore, the data reveal also that the persons in the *formal role* relationships provide as much *supportiveness* as those in *friend* relationships. Here again, the general pattern of the means suggests no simple linear increasing relationship between relationship level and perceived supportiveness.

The *Newman-Keuls* procedure was also employed to examine the pairwise differences between relationship levels on the *character scale*. These comparisons revealed that both the *acquaintance* and *friend* categories were significantly lower on the character scale than the other three relationship categories. Moreover, no significant differences were found among the *formal role, close friend* and *lover* categories or between the *acquaintance* and

friend categories' means. These outcomes indicate that target persons in the *acquaintance* and *friend* categories were rated significantly lower on the *character scale* than the targets in each of the other three relationship categories. Significantly, there was no difference between the *close friend* and *lover* categories, and the *formal role* category was as high on the *character scale* as the *close friend* and *lover* categories. Again, these outcomes provide little support for any simple linear differentiation on the *character scale* among the five relationship levels.

Newman-Keuls analysis of the five *sociability scale* means revealed that the mean for the *friend* level was significantly smaller than the means for the *formal role, close friend,* and *lover* categories respectively. The mean for the *acquaintance* category was significantly smaller than the means of the *close friend* and *lover* categories. No other pairwise comparisons produced significant differences. This pattern of differences supports a kind of U-curve relationship between the *sociability scale* and the levels of relationship, with the nadir of the U-curve occurring in the *acquaintance* and *friend* categories. However, it should be noted that the range of means for the *sociability scale* was not great; that is, the theoretically possible range was from 9 to 45, whereas the actual range was only about four scale units. The same may be said for the *character scale,* where the theoretical range was 20 points and the actual range only about 3 scale units. The *supportiveness scale* showed the greatest range between extreme means: 12 scale units of a possible 38 units. Moreover, the *supportiveness scale* produced the largest number of pairwise differences between relationship levels. These comparisons suggest that the *supportiveness scale* does the best job of discriminating among relationship levels; although it does not do so in a linear fashion.

DISCUSSION

There are several overall conclusions, theoretical implications, and methodological issues which arise from the present study. First, the data support the general conclusion that relationships do not necessarily develop in an orderly progression along several dimensions. The consistent lack of linear effects across relationship levels in both the analyses of individual items and the analyses of the attractiveness scales lend support to this conclusion. Hence, it is not possible to simply assert, for example, that the more sociable a given individual is perceived to be, the more likely it is that the perceiver will develop an intimate relationship with the person. Apparently, persons who are in formal role relationships, and who are liked, are judged to be as sociable as close friends or lovers. Analyses of the *character* and *supportiveness scales* gave indications that lovers may be perceived as less ethical and supportive than close friends. Although the differences on these two scales did not reach statistical significance in comparisons between the *close friend* and *lover* categories, the lack of statistical significance may have been due to large amounts of sample attrition because of the elimination of "don't know" responses. This interpretation is supported by the analyses of individual items, which clearly showed that *lovers* were judged to be significantly less understanding and reinforcing than were close friends.

A second general conclusion which can be drawn from the present study is that as relationships grow more intense, there is a tendency for judgments about the other to become less differentiated. This conclusion is supported by the tendency for correlations among attractiveness dimensions to increase with the degree to which the person felt liked by the target person. Thus, the present study alerts us to the necessity of considering the intensity of the relationship before we can meaningfully speak of "dimensions of interpersonal attraction." Apparently, when a relationship becomes highly intense, there is a tendency for "dimensions" to disappear and to congeal into a more global evaluative dimension.

Another general conclusion which emerges from the present study is that perceptions of supportiveness may be more important than perceptions of character or sociability in determining the extent to which a relationship will escalate in terms of intimacy. However, here again it must be remembered that even the *supportiveness scale* was unable to discriminate between *formal role* and *acquaintance* relationships, and *close friend* and *lover* relationships, to any great extent. However, several indi-

vidual item analyses, which were based on considerably more respondents than the analyses of the three scales, did show statistically significant and socially significant differences between and among relationship levels on the *supportiveness scale* items. Again, the small number of respondents in the analyses of the three scales, especially *supportiveness,* probably reduced the magnitude of the differences obtained among the five relationship levels.

Although the present study was exploratory in nature, there are a number of theoretical implications which flow from it. First, it appears that any theory which is purported to explain relationship development or the development of interpersonal attraction will have to deal with the problem of differential antecedents to attraction depending upon the kind of relationship being studied. For example, the present data support the notion that the relationship between lovers is *not necessarily* a close friendship plus a sexual relationship. To put it another way, lovers may not be close friends or even friends. One very persuasive demonstration of this possibility is the large number of marriages which end in divorce. A given couple may develop an intense relationship with each other primarily based upon positive perceptions of sociability. However, as time goes on, they may come to realize that neither one of them provides *support* to the other. Thus, attraction based upon the extent of the other's outgoing, friendly, and "competent" communication style gives way to a realization that very little of that "competent" communication style is devoted to the giving of reinforcement, understanding, or other kinds of support.

Consistent with this view is that of Giles and Powesland (1975). These authors argue that, under certain conditions, persons will accommodate their speech behavior to each other in order to enhance perceived similarity and increase attraction. Their notion of convergence of speech style and the more abstract concept of accommodation fit with the supportiveness dimension found in the present study. Specifically, persons who show speech style convergence or accommodation should be perceived as having more rapport, understanding, etc., by the person receiving the converging messages. In terms of the present study, moves toward convergence should produce larger increments in the supportiveness dimension than in the other two dimensions.

Another theoretical issue raised by the present study concerns the *perspective* from which attraction judgments are made. Specifically, the *character* and *sociability scales* represent judgmental dimensions which can be employed by an unobtrusive, noninteractive, or third party observer. Judgments of sociability and—to a lesser extent—character, may be formed in the absence of direct interaction with the person being judged. However, it is impossible to determine how much an individual understands you or reinforces you, etc., without actually engaging in interaction with that person. In a sense, we can question whether judgments of *sociability* and *character* really represent facets of *interpersonal* attraction, since they may be made in the absence of direct interaction with a target. It may be necessary, for the sake of theoretical clarity, to distinguish between these loci of attraction. Perhaps the noninteractive judgments of attraction determine whether or not interaction will be initiated, whereas interactive judgments of attraction may override the noninteractive ones in importance, once the interaction has begun. Clearly, it is one thing to *admire* a public figure before interacting with him, and another matter to judge this level of attractiveness after talking with him for a considerable period of time.

Opinions, Background, and Interests

The findings concerning the role of perceived similarities of opinions, background, and interests in attraction deserve further comment because of the long tradition of similarity-attraction research in social psychology (Byrne, 1971). The findings of the present study suggest that variables other than perceived similarity may be more crucial to relationship development. Granted, in the work of Byrne and his colleagues perceived opinion similarity has been only a convenient operationalization for *extent of reinforcement*. That is, perceived similarities are conceived of as reinforcements; the more similarities that exist in a relationship, especially if they are on important issues, the greater the attraction. However, our factor analytic results suggest that perceived similarities may be only a subset of things which can be *given* in a relationship. In exchange terms, perhaps understanding, loyalty, rapport, and liking are more valued commodities in a relationship than are perceived similarities of various types. Persons may hold similar attitudes on important issues but may not be highly attracted to each other because of perceived lack of support in other areas, e.g., perceived lack of loyalty.

Perhaps the overreliance on perceived similarities of various kinds, as an operational definition of reinforcement, has blinded researchers to other possible sources of attraction revealed by the present study. While a reinforcement-oriented theorist could claim that attributes having to do with supportiveness, character and sociability are all reinforcers, it is evident from the present data that these attributes do not have the same value across different types of relationships. Asserting that perceived similarity, understanding, loyalty, etc., are all instances of "reinforcers" does little in the way of indicating how these various perceptions and judgments interact to propel a relationship to a certain level or to retard relational growth. As we have already noted, more of a particular positive attribute perceived in another does not necessarily increase the other's attractiveness. Given the present data, it is difficult to conceive of relationship growth in terms analogous to the typical cumulative response curve which a rat or pigeon produces under a 100 percent reinforcement schedule in a Skinner box.

The findings of the present study also provide support for the Berger and Calabrese (1975) model of interaction development. In this model, it is posited that reductions in uncertainty or increases in understanding tend to produce increases in liking. It is also suggested that similarity is one antecedent to uncertainty reduction. In the present study, the correlation between judged extent of opinion similarity and extent of felt understanding was .54, and the correlation between felt understanding and the estimated extent to which the target liked the respondent was .69. These findings cannot be taken as direct support for the *causal* relationships posited by *uncertainty theory;* however; they are in line with the predictions of uncertainty theory, and they also fit with the positive relationships among similarity, uncertainty, and attraction reported by Berger and Clatterbuck (1976).

There are a number of limitations to the present study which should be noted. First, a more representative sample of persons must be studied in order to be confident that the factors obtained in the present study, as well as the patterns of differences among relationships, are likely to hold in more heterogeneous groups. Second, it was noted at several places that sample sizes were reduced considerably because of the necessity of eliminating "don't know" responses. It might be worthwhile to have respondents in a future study complete the items of the present study for a close friend without the opportunity of expressing a "don't know" response.

A third limitation to the present study is that only positive attributes were used for rating purposes. An extension study should be done to determine the degree to which negative characteristics are attributed to liked persons in the relationship categories. Not only should negative characteristics be included in such lists, but persons also should be asked to rate target persons in each of the categories whom they *dislike*. Until these follow-up studies are performed, we must view the "dimensions" found in the present study in a tentative way.

CONCLUSION

Attraction and love are complex and multifaceted constructs. Because of their ephemeral nature, they are difficult to explicate and operationalize in a way which captures their complexity. The present study has provided a small glimpse of the structure of this complexity and has attempted to increase our understanding of how attraction varies across relationship levels.

NOTES

1. This paper was selected as one of the outstanding reports prepared for the annual meetings of the International Communication Association, Berlin, 1977.
2. Two overall factor analyses were performed which excluded the "don't know" responses in different ways. Since the 142 respondents each filled out five sets of 36 items, there were a total possible number of 710 rating sets. However, because of blanks and "don't know" responses, there were a total of 327 complete sets; that is, sets in which there were *no blanks or "don't knows" on any of the 36 items*. In the first analysis, these 327 sets were factored. Under the first procedure, the correlations are all based on the same number of responses

(N=327). Under the pairwise deletion procedure, the correlations are based upon varying numbers of responses (and hence varying persons). Pairwise deletion preserves more data; however, it does invite self-selection biases and variations in the stability of correlations, both of which may influence factor coefficients. The sample sizes in the pairwise deletion procedure ranged from 485 to 684. Since the smallest sample size was 485, differential sampling error is probably of little consequence. However, the self-selection bias possibility still remains.

The two factor analyses were computed ignoring relationship categories. A careful comparison of the results revealed virtually no differences between pairwise procedure and the more conservative elimination procedure in terms of the factors obtained and the magnitude of their loadings. Thus, the results for the pairwise procedure are presented here because that analysis utilized more of the data.

REFERENCES

ALTMAN, I., & TAYLOR, D.A. *Social penetration: The development of interpersonal relationships*. New York: Holt, Rinehart and Winston, 1973.

BERGER, C.R. The acquaintance process revisited: Explorations in initial interaction. Paper presented at the annual meeting of the Speech Communication Association, New York, November 1973.

BERGER, C.R., & CALABRESE, R.J. Some explorations in initial interaction and beyond: Toward a developmental theory of interpersonal communication. *Human Communication Research*, 1975, 1, 99-112.

BERGER, C.R., & CLATTERBUCK, G.W. Attitude similarity and attributional information as determinants of uncertainty reduction and interpersonal attraction. Paper presented at the annual meeting of the International Communication Association, Portland, April 1976.

BERGER, C.R., & LARIMER, M.W. When beauty is only skin deep: The effects of physical attractiveness, sex and time on initial interaction. Paper presented at the annual meeting of the International Communication Association, New Orleans, April 1974.

BERLO, D.K., LEMERT, J.B., & MERTZ, R.J. Dimensions for evaluating the acceptability of message sources. *Public Opinion Quarterly*, 1969, 33, 563-576.

BYRNE, D. *The attraction paradigm*. New York: Academic Press, 1971.

ERLICH, H.J., & GRAEVEN, D.B. Reciprocal self-disclosure in a dyad. *Journal of Experimental Social Psychology*, 1971, 7, 389-400.

GERGEN, K.J. *The psychology of behavior exchange*. Reading, Mass.: Addison-Wesley, 1969.

GILES, H., & POWESLAND, P.F. *Speech style and social evaluation*. London: Academic Press, 1975.

HEIDER, F. *The psychology of interpersonal relations*. New York: Wiley, 1958.

HOMANS, G.C. *Social behavior: Its elementary forms*. New York: Harcourt, Brace and World, 1961.

HUNT, M. *The natural history of loving*. New York: Knopf, 1959.

HUSTON, T.L. A perspective on interpersonal attraction. In T.L. Huston (Ed.), *Foundations of interpersonal Attraction*. New York: Academic Press, 1974 3-28.

KIESLER, C.A., & GOLDBERG, G.N. Multidimensional approach to the experimental study of interpersonal attraction: Effect of a blunder on the attractiveness of a competent other. *Psychological Reports,* 1968, 22, 693-705.

LOTT, A.J., & LOTT, B.E. Group cohesiveness, communication level, and conformity. *Journal of Abnormal and Social Psychology,* 1961, 62, 408-412.

McCROSKEY, J.C. Scales for the measurement of ethos. *Speech Monographs,* 1966, 33, 65-72.

McCROSKEY, J.C., DALY, J.A., RICHMOND, V.P., & COX, B.G. The effects of communication apprehension on interpersonal attraction. *Human Communication Research,* 1975, 2, 51-65.

McCROSKEY, J.C., & McCAIN, T.A. The measurement of interpersonal attraction. *Speech Monographs,* 1974, 41, 261-266.

MORAN, G. Dyadic interaction and orientational consensus. *Journal of Personality and Social Psychology,* 1966, 4, 94-99.

MUNLEY, M.E. Toward a taxonomy of relationships: A qualitative approach. Unpublished paper, Department of Communication Studies, Northwestern University, June 1976.

NEWCOMB, T. *The acquaintance process.* New York: Holt, Rinehart and Winston, 1961.

NORTON, R.W. Foundation of a communicator style construct. Unpublished paper, Department of Speech Communication, University of Michigan, 1976.

NORTON, R.W., & PETTEGREW, L. Communicator style as an effect determinant of attraction. Paper presented at the annual meeting of the International Communication Association, Portland, April 1976.

SERMAT, V., & SMYTH, M. Content analysis of verbal communication in the development of a relationship: Conditions influencing self-disclosure. *Journal of Personality and Social Psychology,* 1973, 26, 332-346.

SHAW, M.E. *Group dynamics: The psychology of small group behavior.* New York: McGraw-Hill, 1971.

SIEGEL, S. *Nonparametric statistics for the behavioral sciences.* New York: McGraw-Hill, 1956.

THIBAUT, J.W., & KELLEY, H.H. *The social psychology of groups.* New York: Wiley, 1959.

WIEMANN, J.M. An experimental investigation of communicative competence in initial interactions. Paper presented at the annual convention of the International Communication Association, Portland, April 1976.

A TYPOLOGICAL APPROACH TO COMMUNICATION IN RELATIONSHIPS

MARY ANNE FITZPATRICK
University of Wisconsin-Milwaukee

Two studies were conducted to examine the proposed research questions. The first study developed an eight-factor scale, the Relational Dimensions Instrument (RDI), capable of reliably measuring some salient aspects of relational life. The second study derived an empirical typology of relationships based on couples' responses to the RDI. This study also examined the connection between relationship types and perceived communication styles in ongoing relationships. This paper reports the results of the second study and discusses the implications of relationship typologies for communication research.

At the present time, the study of communication within the context of enduring relationships lacks order, synthesis, and conceptual clarity. Indeed, scholars in the field face not only a surplus of essentially unconnected and atheoretical findings, but also very few precise conceptualizations upon which to base their research. Given these circumstances, it is very difficult to make use of what we do know about communication and relationships.

One possible way to organize the field, and to map out a useful program of research, is to classify individuals according to their beliefs and standards on significant issues and dimensions of relational life—in other words, to create a typology of relationships. An empirically-derived relational typology should yield valuable information about how individuals and couples define their relationships. This research assumes that it is possible to find a few recurring, discrete patterns of ongoing relationships (types) within any heterogeneous sample of couples. Furthermore, it assumes that, in a valid typology, membership within a single discrete class is associated with a more or less extensive cluster of other characteristics (Hempel, 1965). The characteristics of particular interest in this research are the communication behaviors of different relational types.

The main purpose of this research is to develop a reliable, empirically derived classification of relational types. This classification is based on dimensions defined a priori as important aspects of rela-

tional life. A secondary purpose of the research is to examine the empirical connections between various types of relationships and particular kinds of communication. The latter is taken as an initial step in the formulation of a predictive model that will specify the connection between relational types and communication behavior.

REVIEW OF THE LITERATURE

Numerous attempts have been made to establish relationship typologies. Most of these attempts have been made either by observers working in clinical settings (Lederer & Jackson, 1968; Shostrum & Kavanaugh, 1971), investigators reflecting on data collected for other purposes (Goodrich, 1968; Ryder, 1970; Reiss, 1971), or theoreticians working with the benefit of little or no empirical support (Burgess & Wallin, 1953; Cuber & Harroff, 1965; Adams, 1971; Bernard, 1972).

There are two problems with the existing systems. First, most of the typologies lack comprehensiveness, for they focus on a limited number of relational dimensions as ways to categorize couples (Farber, 1949; Burgess & Wallin, 1953; Reiss, 1971). Second, there have been no attempts to develop relational typologies through reliance on empirical observations *in conjunction with* both inference and theory. Previously, the category schemes that have emerged have been developed either through post hoc data examination or theoretical speculation. In both cases, only those who have developed the schema have been able to utilize it. Thus, current relational typologies are of little use to the communication scholar.

A recent development in relational typologies is the work of Kantor and Lehr (1975). These authors adopt a cybernetic model which views the information processed by the couple as distance-regulation information. Within this model, couples evolve particular patterns of interactional activity through the various ways in which they utilize *access* and *target* dimensions. The access dimensions—*space, time,* and *energy*—describe and include the physical aspects of a couple's "quest for experience." The target dimensions—*affect, power,* and *meaning*—describe and include the conceptual aspects of the couple's experience, as well as their specific life goals. Based on the access dimensions utilized by given couples to gain particular targets that they value, Kantor and Lehr (1975) proposed three types of relationships in their model: *the open, the closed,* and *the random.*

Although the names for these dimensions often differ, the *access* and *target* dimensions identified by Kantor and Lehr (1975) have been repeatedly acknowledged by other authors as the most important aspects of relational life (Hess & Handel, 1959; Haley, 1963; Henry, 1965; Rapoport & Rapoport, 1971). Given the pervasiveness of these factors emerging in both theory and research on relational life, it seems reasonable to assume that relational partners make decisions about how to organize *access* to particular *targets*. Thus, these decisions constitute a significant characteristic of relationship definition (types).

Kantor and Lehr's (1975) delineation of access and target dimensions seems reasonable and accurate. *Energy, space, time, affect, power,* and *meaning* are salient dimensions of relational life, but they may not be the only ones, nor are they necessarily of equal importance in all relationships. We do not assume, as do Kantor and Lehr (1975), that these six dimensions yield only three discrete types of relationships. It is rather an empirical question, a hypothesis that awaits empirical verification.

The number of unique relationship types is an empirical unknown. It is possible, for example, that these *access* and *target* dimensions define nine types of couples. The first three are equivalent to Kantor and Lehr's *open, closed,* and *random relationships,* while the last six are comprised of couples that have every possible *access* and *target* combination.

The number and characteristics of relational types should thus emerge from an empirical examination of the importance that couples assign to these six dimensions. The present typological approach will be the first to allow an interaction between the proposed theoretical dimensions of relationship and the empirical identification of types. We believe that the types should emerge from a specific empirical clustering of cases on reliably measured factors that reflect the ways in which couples define their relationship.

Paradoxically, none of the previous typologies have developed a reliable measure for placing couples into types. In many cases, only the investigator-clinician seems capable of having the insight to decide which couples are *vitals, gruesome-twosomes,* or *masters and servants* (Cuber & Harroff, 1965; Lederer & Jackson, 1968; Shostrum & Kavanaugh, 1971).

On the basis of the above reasoning, the following research question is proposed:

> How many discrete types of interpersonal relationships emerge from an empirical examination of the major dimensions by which couples define their relationships?

COMMUNICATION AND RELATIONSHIPS: TWO VIEWS

Communication is universally acknowledged as vital not only to more satisfying marital interaction, but also to the continued growth and development of the individuals involved in the relationship (Lederer & Jackson, 1968; Bach & Wyden, 1969; Clinebell & Clinebell, 1970; Sherwood & Scherer, 1974; Mace & Mace, 1974; Schauble & Hill, 1976). There are, however, two very different views about what characteristics of communication transactions are enhancing to prolonged interpersonal relationships. These two views are the *instrumental* and the *expressive.*

The *expressivist* school of human communication has been derived from the work of such humanistic psychologists as Maslow, Rogers, May, and Jourard, who suggested during the 1960s that the open disclosure of spontaneously experienced feelings, thoughts, and wishes to at least one "significant other" was necessary for the development of a healthy personality. The viewpoint has been translated by advocates of expressivism into the suggestion that complete sharing of feeling and perceptions with one's partner promotes successful relationships (Bernard, 1972; Giffin & Patton, 1974; Rossiter & Pearce, 1975; Stewart & D'Angelo, 1975). Consequently, marital counseling programs throughout the country, to take but one example, have been teaching couples to express feelings openly and to react spontaneously to partners (Clarke, 1970; Miller, Nunnally, & Wackman, 1975; Travis & Travis, 1975).

The instrumental view of human communication has most recently reemerged under the rubric of rhetorical sensitivity (Hart & Burks, 1972; Hart, Eadie, & Carlson, 1975; Phillips & Metzger, 1976). Instrumentalists favor purposively monitoring relationships rather than spontaneously reacting and experiencing them (Phillips & Metzger, 1976). According to the foremost proponents of this viewpoint, Hart and Burks (1972), a rhetorically sensitive person continually adapts to the changing communication situation in order to accomplish predetermined goals. The rhetorically sensitive person therefore communicates primarily to solve problems and to accomplish tasks.

Although there are several very significant differences between expressivism and instrumentalism, both share the premise that it is possible to prescribe one particular communication style for all prolonged relationships. Each assumes that the best way to develop a satisfying interpersonal relationship is by consistently applying a particular philosophy of communication.

In this research it is assumed not only that different individuals and couples define their relationships differently, but also that individuals involved in distinctly different types of relationships will experience different perceptions about the styles of communication that dominate that relationship. For example, if the Joneses define their relationship as an "institutional" one, they will view communication in a manner unlike the Smiths, who define their relationship as a "compasionate" one.

These considerations lead to the following propositions:

Proposition 1: Measures of expressive communication will significantly discriminate among relational types.

Proposition 2: Measures of instrumental communication will significantly discriminate among relational types.

STUDY 1: INSTRUMENT DEVELOPMENT

The first step in the research was to produce a measuring instrument that could reliably assess some of the significant aspects of relational life described in an earlier part of this paper. An initial pool of more than 200 items was drawn from a careful analysis of the work of Kantor and Lehr (1975). Each item corresponded either to an *access (energy, space, time)* or a *target (affect, power, meaning)* dimension. Additionally, 25 of the initial items were specifically designed to assess a person's stand on the importance of *autonomy* and *interdependence* in a relationship (Henry, 1965; Lederer & Jackson, 1968; O'Neill & O'Neill, 1972).

The initial set of items was examined for clarity and consistency by a small number of couples, as well as by several persons who were familiar with Kantor and Lehr's (1975) model. When the redundant and the unclear items were eliminated, 184 remained. The final pilot instrument consisted of approximately 25 items associated with each of the six dimensions, as well as with the *autonomy/interdependence* issue.

Over 900 subjects were interviewed in the first study. The sampling strategy was to gather a large sample of married individuals who would complete the lengthy, self-administered questionnaire in their homes. The large and heterogeneous sample provided a sufficient opportunity to isolate the major patterns in the data and thereby develop a sound measuring instrument. Therefore, a nonpurposive probability sampling technique was used to locate the respondents. Although random probability sampling is preferrable, Zetterburg (1963) has indicated that randomness or sample representativeness is not vital when the problem concerns the relationship among the variables.

In an effort to avoid any response set which might exist in a population of sophisticated test-takers, the majority of the respondents were contacted outside the university community. Questionnaires were distributed to political and social groups, in hospitals, schools, factories, offices, and apartment buildings predominately in the Philadelphia standard metropolitan statistical area. Every attempt was made to have both members of the couple complete a questionnaire.

Through factor and item analysis, the original 184-item scale was reduced to a 64-item, eight-factor instrument. A complete description of the sample, procedures, statistical analysis and results of the development of the *Relational Dimensions Instrument* (RDI) may be obtained in Fitzpatrick (1976).

The first factor reflects all six of the dimensions stipulated by Kantor and Lehr (1975). Of the 23 items loading on this factor, 10 are concerned with affect, while the remaining 13 spanned the other five dimensions. The affect pattern typified by this factor indicates that a continual and mutual exchange of thoughts exists between the relational partners. A high score on this factor would suggest an open sharing of love and caring and the tendency to communicate a wide range and intensity of feelings. There is a sharing of both tasks and leisure time activities, as well as a considerable degree of mutual empathy. Finally, these relational partners not only visit with friends, but also seek new friends and experiences. Given the high frequency of interaction between this couple, as well as between the couple and the outside world, this factor is called *sharing*.

Factor two contains five of the original six dimensions of Kantor and Lehr (1975). Of the eleven items that define this factor, seven were originally conceived as meaning items. These items suggest a strong commitment to tradition, and to conventional values and institutions. Traditional customs are stressed, such as: a woman should take her husband's name when she marries, infidelity is always inexcusable, and the wedding ceremony, per se, is important. Those who score highly on this factor exhibit a certainty about the meaning and the purpose of life, in general, as well as the rules that should govern child-rearing and family behavior.

The lifestyle of these relational partners is a traditional one, and is consistent with Bott's (1957) finding that the more traditional the couple, the more likely their networks are closed. In other words, almost all of this couple's friends know one another. This factor is labeled the *ideology of traditionalism*.

The six items that correlate with the third factor also predominately reflect the meaning dimension. In contrast to the second factor, however, this pattern emphasizes an openness to uncertainty. Indeed, the ideal relationship, from this point of view, is one marked by the novel, the spontaneous, or the humorous. The individuals who score highly on this factor seem open to change. They believe that each should develop his or her own potential, and that relationships should not constrain an individual in any way. For these reasons, this factor is considered the *ideology of uncertainty and change*.

Factor four contains six items that were originally constructed to reflect the power dimension of a relationship. Four of these items tap an *interpersonal persuasion, inducement,* or *combativeness* aspect of a relationship. However, the other two items are concerned with the separate cooking and eating of meals and open arguing before friends or in public, and hence, broaden the factor to one of *assertiveness* toward the relational partner. Thus, the best name for this factor is *assertiveness*.

Factor five consists of three items that are clearly associated with the time dimension. These items suggest a strict scheduling of household events. For this reason, the factor is called *temporal regularity*.

The four items that load on the sixth factor reflect the affect dimension. These items suggest the avoidance of arguments and disputes between the relational partners, as well as the importance of sharing good rather than bad feelings. This analysis suggests that *conflict avoidance* is an appropriate name for this factor. Support for this factor label comes from the work of Raush and his associates (1974) who discovered two distinct patterns of conflict management in the couples they observed. One of those behavioral patterns was conflict avoidance. This factor probably taps the self-report component of that behavioral pattern.

The five items that correlate with factor seven were originally conceived of as spatial items. These items seem to indicate that few constraints are placed on territorial boundaries. The relational partners feel free to open each other's personal mail, to interrupt one another when concentrating, and to share many of their personal belongings with impunity. Respondents with high scores on this factor believe that guests should feel free to enter any room in their homes. They also believe that guests may be brought home without asking the other's permission. The spatial freedom of those who score highly on this factor comes at the expense of privacy. Given this openness between the partners, as well as their openness to guests, this factor is called *undifferentiated space*.

Factor eight consists of six items that are predominately concerned with *space*. In contrast to the spatial fusion of the seventh factor, however, these six items signify a spatial fission. Both spouses take separate vacations, and each has his or her own private space. Private space is highly valued by those who agree with these items. Finally, the fact that such couples can go for long periods of time without spending much time together suggests that this factor can be named *autonomy*.

Having decided on the content of each of the eight subscales of the *Relational Dimensions Instrument* produced by the factor analysis and the item analysis, it was necessary to examine their reliability. Nunnally (1967) maintains that the most sophisticated way to determine the reliability of a scale is to compute coefficient alpha. The overall alpha for the RDI is .71. This is the reliability of each scale divided by the number of items per scale.

STUDY 2: THE RELATIONAL TYPOLOGY

Sixty-eight couples participated in Study 2 (total N=136). The median age of the subjects fell between 30 and 39; on the average, each couple had been living together between six and nine years. Sixty-one of the couples were married, but only 18 individuals had been married more than once. Thirty percent of the sample reported that they had no children. Of those who had children living at home, the median number of children was two. A complete description of this sample can be found in Fitzpatrick (1976).

The use of factor analysis and the reliability esti-

mates in the first study yielded valuable insight into the structure of the scale. A somewhat different approach was required, however, for the analysis of relationship definition among individuals. The method employed in Study 2 to find the typological structure of prolonged relationships was *linear typal analysis* (Overall & Klett, 1972).

Linear typal analysis is a method for studying relationships of observed individuals to underlying pure types. From a theoretical point of view, this method assumes that underlying any heterogenous group of individuals there are a relatively few pure types or classes of persons. Any one individual can be a mixture of several types, although he is likely to resemble most closely only one particular type (Overall & Klett, 1972).

Research Design

The independent variable for Study 2 was *relational type,* that is, the number of relational types resulting from the typal analysis described above. There were four dependent variable measures of perceived communication. Two of these were measures of *expressive communication,* while the other two were measures of *instrumental communication.*

The measures of expressive communication were developed from the self-report instrument of Swenson and Gilner (1973), called the *scale of feelings* and the *behavior of love.* Over 18 factor analyses have been performed on this instrument (Swenson, 1961; Swenson & Gilner, 1964). Seven factors have repeatedly appeared in these analyses. The two factors that were chosen as measures of expressive communication were the *verbal expression of feelings subscale* and the *self-disclosure subscale.* Each of these subscales contains 20 items. Gilner (1967) reports test-retest reliabilities of .89 and .93 for these subscales. In previous research, the alpha reliabilities for these same subscales were .91 and .82 (Swenson, 1968). Each respondent was asked to judge how often his or her mate communicated a particular feeling to them, and how often they communicated the same sentiments to their mate.

In Study 2, subjects were also asked to estimate how often they experienced a particular emotion and yet did *not* communicate it to their mates *(unex-*

pressed feelings subscale). This scale was considered a measure of instrumental communication. Swenson (1968) reports an alpha reliability for this scale of .72 and a test-retest reliability of .77.

The second measure of instrumental communication was the *Rhetsen scale* developed by Hart, Eadie, and Carlson (1975). In a previous report these writers claimed that the scale possessed both convergent and discriminant validity. Although no alpha reliabilities have been reported, the test-retest reliability has been assessed at .83.

Factor Analysis of the Dependent Variables

As described in the previous section, the measurement of instrumental communication was accomplished through the administration of the *Rhetsen scale* (Hart, Eadie, & Carlson, 1975) and the *unexpressed feelings scale* (Swenson & Gilner, 1973). *Expressive communication* was examined by the *self-disclosure* and *verbal expression of feeling scales* (Swenson & Gilner, 1973). To insure that these were unidimensional measures, it was necessary to examine their structure within the context of this study.

The scores for each of the 136 respondents on each of the four dependent variables was submitted to a principal components analysis with unities inserted in the diagonal. *Cattell's Scree test* (1966) was applied to the resultant eigenvalues to determine the number of factors to be rotated. In the cases where only one factor was suggested, the items on the scale were summed for each respondent. When the plot of the eigenvalues indicated that the scale was multidimensional, the intercorrelation matrix of the scale was submitted to a principal axis factor analysis with squared multiple correlations as the estimate of the communalities. Factors were then orthogonally rotated in the *Kaiser varimax case*. To be considered significantly associated with a factor, an item's primary loading was required to be at least .35. Additionally, the secondary loading could not be more than 50% of the primary loading.

The *verbal expression of feelings* and the *unexpressed feelings scales* retained their unidimensionality when factor analyzed. The *Rhetsen scale* and the *self-disclosure scale* were found to be multi-

dimensional. Each consisted of two factors.

The first factor defined on the *Rhetsen scale* indicates that under all circumstances people should "tell it like it is." This factor is thus called *militant frankness*. The second factor on this scale is one that supports following all the social rules of conversation and avoid hurting the feelings of others. This factor is called *social restraint*.

The first factor on the *self-disclosure scale* reflects the disclosure of personal information by the respondent to his mate. Since most of the items, however, concern the discussion of worries or anxieties, this factor is called *self-vulnerability*. The second factor also concerns the communication of worries or annoyances. The direction of the disclosure, however, is from the mate to the respondent. Thus, it is called *mate vulnerability*.

On the basis of the information gained from the factor analyses of the dependent variables, certain items were summed within a scale to create a score for each respondent on each communication variable. Since this study was designed to examine a couple's perceptions of communication within the relationship, rather than merely an individual perception, it was necessary to generate couple communication scores. For this reason, the communication data on each dependent measure for a couple was summed and divided by two.

RESULTS: TYPOLOGICAL ANALYSIS

All one hundred and thirty-six (136) subjects completed the revised sixty-four (64) item relationship dimensions scale that was generated in Study 1. The input for the typal analysis consisted of each subject's total scores (arithmetic sums) for each of the eight scales on the relational dimensions instrument. Each subject, therefore, was assigned eight scores. Using the criteria established previously, a variety of different solutions for the number of types that would provide the best fit for these data were examined. Of the six that were attempted, the linear typal analysis suggested that the three cluster solution provided the clearest explanation of the data.[2] Each of the 136 subjects was therefore assigned a weighted loading based on the degree to which his or her profile corresponded to each of the three pure types.

TABLE 1
Observed Means and Scheffé Results for the Summed
Scale Scores on Relational Dimensions by Type 3

	Type 1	Type 2	Type 3
Sharing FACTOR 1	71.33*	85.35*	55.00*
Idealogy of Traditionalism FACTOR 2	39.20*	26.35*	24.72*
Idealogy Un-certainty and change FACTOR 3	17.67*	18.55*	27.53*
Assertiveness FACTOR 4	33.38**	35.80	35.00
Temporal Regularity FACTOR 5	13.71**	7.25	7.97
Conflict Avoidance FACTOR 6	17.44	11.38***	18.39
Undifferentiated Space FACTOR 7	17.02	20.89***	16.19
Autonomy FACTOR 8	22.71*	32.09*	33.36*

*All significantly different from one another Scheffé (p < .10)
**1 differs significantly from 2 and 3 (p < .10)
***2 differs significantly from 1 and 3 (p < .10)

The rectangular matrix of typal loadings was examined to see the goodness of fit of the three-type solution, and to assign subjects to a type. Goodness of fit was based on the assumption that each group must not only be relatively homogeneous with respect to the eight factors, but also that each individual should clearly resemble one, and only one, type. The criteria used to assign the subjects to types was that the individual's primary loading on a type be above .30, and his or her secondary loading be at least .10 smaller than the primary loading.

Only 10 of the original subjects, or about eight percent (8%), failed to meet these criteria. For the 126 subjects who had relatively pure loadings, 43 were assigned to Type 1, 48 were assigned to Type 2, and 35 were assigned to Type 3.

To test the acceptability of these assignments,

and to aid in the interpretation of the three types, a discriminant function analysis was calculated. This analysis produces mathematical equations for separating these three types, using only the eight scores on the relationship dimensions instrument.[3]

The first discriminant function (Chi Square = 267.88; d.f. = 16; p < .0001; Wilks Lambda = .13), and the second discriminant function (Chi Square = 122.66; d.f. = 7; p < .0001; Wilks Lambda = .39), were significant, indicating that the three types can best be discriminated on two independent dimensions. Table 1 presents the observed means on each of the eight subscales for each relational type.

For the first discriminant function, the best discriminators among the three groups in a positive direction are *conflict avoidance* (.84), the *ideology of uncertainty and change* (.38), and *temporal regularity* (.35), while the highest negatively loaded variables on the same discriminant function are *sharing* (−.69), *autonomy* (−.58), and *undifferentiated space* (−.45).[4]

An examination of the group centroids reveals that group two has the clearest profile on this function. According to the Scheffé (1953) test, Type 2 is significantly lower than Type 1 and Type 3 on *conflict avoidance* (p < .10).[5] Type 2 scored significantly lower than Type 3 on *ideology of uncertainty and change,* but significantly higher than Type 1 on this same dimension. Type 2 is also significantly lower than Type 1 on *temporal regularity.* Type 2 scored significantly higher than types 1 and 3 on both the *sharing* and the *undifferentiated space* factors. Finally, although Type 2 scored significantly higher than Type 1 on *autonomy,* it scored significantly lower than Type 3 on the same factor (p < .10).

In order to interpret the findings on the first discriminant function for group 2, it is necessary to note that the *lower* the score, the more agreement a subject has shown with the statements that comprise a dimension (factor). In other words, *Type 2 is significantly more likely to try to avoid conflicts than the other two types.* Although Type 2 showed significantly more agreement with the *ideology of uncertainty and change* than Type 3, Type 2 showed significantly less agreement with these statements than Type 1. Type 2 exhibited as much *temporal regularity* as Type 3, but significantly more than Type 1.

Typal Differences

The results reveal that Type 2 was marked by significantly less *sharing* and significantly less *undifferentiated space* than the other relational types. Although there was no difference between Type 2 and Type 3 on *autonomy,* Type 2 was significantly less autonomous than Type 1.

On the second discriminant function, the scales for the *ideology of traditionalism* (.50) and *temporal regularity* (.36) form a cluster of positive loadings. An examination of the group centroids reveals that Type 3 has the purest profile on this function. The Scheffé (1953) test indicates that

Type 3 is significantly lower than the other two types on the *ideology of traditionalism.* Although there is no significant difference between Types 2 and 3 on *temporal regularity,* there is a significant difference between Types 3 and 1 on this factor.

The other cluster on this function indicates that the *ideology of uncertainty and change* (−.73) and *autonomy* (−.69) are also discriminating among the groups on this function. According to the Scheffé test, Type 3 scored significantly higher than either Type 1 or Type 2 on both the *ideology of uncertainty and change* factor and on *autonomy.*

Since the lower the score, the more agreement with the factor, we find that *Type 3 showed significantly more agreement with the ideology of traditionalism than the other two types.* Type 3 individuals regulate their daily time schedules significantly more than those in Type 1 relationships. Type 3 was also significantly lower than both 2 and 1 on the *ideology of uncertainty and change,* and on the *autonomy* factor.

The centroids indicate that in order to explain Type 1, both functions must be examined. On the first discriminant function, the Scheffé test suggested that Type 1 scored significantly higher than Type 2, but about the same as Type 3, on *conflict avoidance.* Type 1 also scored significantly higher than the other types on *temporal regularity* and the *ideology of traditionalism,* and significantly lower than the other two types on *autonomy* and the *ideology of uncertainty and change.* While significantly lower than Type 2 on *differentiated space,* Type 1 was about the same as Type 3 on this factor. Finally, Type 1 scored significantly lower than Type 2, but higher than Type 3 on *sharing.*

Since lower scores signify more agreement, Type 1 was less likely than Type 2 to avoid conflict. Type 1 couples exhibited less regularity in their daily time schedules than the other types, and adhered less strongly to a traditional ideology than Types 2 and 3. *Type 1 is the most autonomous relational type as well as the one most committed to an ideology of uncertainty and change.* While significantly higher than Type 2 on the use of *undifferentiated space,* Type 1 was about the same as Type 3 on this factor. Finally, Type 1 couples had a moderate amount of *sharing* in their relationship, lower than Type 3 but higher than Type 2.

Relational Types

Relationship Type 1 seems to be the one most committed to an ideology of uncertainty and change. This type exhibits less temporal regularity in its daily schedule than the others and is opposed to a belief system that stresses traditional values. Although this is the most autonomous type, it is nonetheless defined by a moderate amount of sharing between these partners and not much conflict avoidance. Within the relational context of sharing, this couple also experiences autonomy. Apparently, it is a negotiated autonomy. Given this balance of autonomy and interdependence, Type 1 is labeled the *independents*.

Relational Type 2 is primarily defined by greater conflict avoidance, more differentiated space, and less sharing. This type keeps a fairly regular daily time schedule, but despite their separated space, Type 2 persons do not feel particularly autonomous. This relational type lacks a strong commitment or aversion to either the ideology of traditionalism or the ideology of uncertainty and change. For these reasons, and because the type seems separated, yet neither autonomous nor interdependent, they are referred to as *separates*.

Relationship Type 3 subscribes to a fairly traditional belief system. These individuals prefer a high degree of temporal regularity, as well as very little autonomy. Very few boundaries are stipulated in their use of physical and emotional space. This type is marked by a high degree of sharing and a corresponding tendency to engage rather than avoid each other when conflict arises. Finally, Relational Type 3 is opposed to an ideology that values uncertainty and change. Since this relationship is marked by a high degree of interdependence and very little autonomy within the framework of a traditional value system, couples in this type are called *traditionals*.

To verify the classification of individuals to types, the two significant discriminant functions were used to assign individuals to types. This independent classification was then compared to that produced by the linear typal analysis. An examination of the results of this analysis indicates that 97% of the cases were assigned to the identical group by both procedures (Chi Square=248.53; p < .0001). Only four subjects were incorrectly classified,

suggesting that the three cluster solution was appropriate.

RESULTS: RELATIONAL TYPE BY COMMUNICATION STYLE

In addition to the scores that were calculated for each subject on the eight relational dimensions, six dependent variable scores were also tabulated for each subject. *Expressive communication* was measured by the *militant frankness scale,* the *verbal expression of feelings scale,* and the two *vulnerability* scales. *Instrumental communication,* on the other hand, was measured by the *social restraint* and the *unexpressed feelings scales.*

As mentioned earlier, only those couples who were assigned to the same relational category were considered in this analysis. Of the 68 couples who participated in this phase of the research, slightly over 60% agreed on a relational definition. Of these, 16 couples were classified as *independents,* 17 as *separates,* and 10 as *traditionals.*

Since it was considered necessary to examine the communication of particular relational types, communication scores on the six dependent variables were summed and divided by two. Of course, this was done only for those couples who agreed on a relational definition.

A multivariate analysis of variance was computed, with *couple type* as the independent variable, and the six communication variables as the dependent variables. The overall F test for the equality of the mean vectors, using the *Wilks Lambda criterion,* was significant (F=4.63; d.f.=12.70; p < .0001). Table 2 lists the observed means for each dependent variable.

Since the multivariate test for the equality of the mean vectors was significant, the differences between the groups (types) needed to be probed. This was accomplished through the discriminant analysis. In this case, the standardized discriminant function coefficients represent the linear combination of the variables most sensitive to the departure from the hypothesis that there are no differences between the groups (Bock & Haggard, 1968).

The number of statistically significant discriminant functions was examined first, since this gives the number of dimensions on which there is a size-

TABLE 2
Observed Means and the Newman-Kuels Results for the Summed Scale
Scores[6] on Instrumental and Expressive Communication by Type 6

	Independents	Separates	Traditionals
Militant Frankness	17.88	16.44	20.30*
Social Restraint	20.78**	16.12	16.65
Verbal Expression of Feelings	37.91	37.18***	43.45
Self Vulnerability	21.00	18.59****	22.55
Mate Vulnerability	15.44	14.06	17.60*
Unexpressed Feelings	26.41	32.50****	26.45

*3 significantly different from 1 and 2 Newman-Kuels (p < .05)
**1 significantly different from 2 and 3 (p < .05)
***2 significantly different from 3 (p < .05)
****2 significantly different from 1 and 3 (p < .05)

able separation of the groups (Stevens, 1972). *Bartlett's* (1950) *Chi-Square test* for the significance of the eigenvalues was computed. This determines the number of significant dimensions of variation. The standardized discriminant function coefficients were then examined, because they take into account the fractional contribution of each of the original variables to the spread along the significant discriminant functions.

Bartlett's Chi-Square test indicated that both the first (Chi Square = 43.82; d.f. = 12; p < .0001), and second discriminant function (Chi Square = 16.27; d.f. = 5; p < .006) were significant. Therefore, both the first and the second standardized discriminant function coefficients were utilized to interpret the results of the multivariate analysis of variance.

An examination of the first discriminant function coefficients reveals that the best discriminators among the relational types were *militant frankness* (−.89) and *mate vulnerability* (−.92). An examination of the group centroids shows Group 3, the *traditionals,* were the highest on this function. Since a high score on the *militant frankness scale* indicates disagreement with the scale's items, *tradi-*

tionals are, according to the *Newman-Kuels test,* significantly less likely to be militantly frank.[7] The *traditionals,* however, believed that their mates were more likely than the mates of the *separates* to communicate vulnerability, particularly to the respondents.

The coefficients for the second discriminant function indicated that the best separators of the groups on this function were *social restraint* (.98) and *verbal expressiveness* (−.62). An examination of the observed means and the centroids reveals that the *independents* were the lowest on this function. A high score on the *social restraint scale* reflects a low degree of social restraint; therefore, according to the Newman-Kuels procedure, the *independents* scored significantly lower than the *traditionals* or the *separates* on *social restraint* (p < .05). Although the *traditionals* have the highest score on the *verbal expression of feelings scale,* there are no significant differences among the relational types.

Further examination of the observed means and the group centroids for function one showed that the *separates* (Group 2) scored slightly, but not significantly, higher on *militant frankness* than the *traditionals.* The *separates* also received fewer messages of vulnerability from their mates than the *traditionals*.

The results of this analysis indicate that the *traditionals* are separated on the first function from the *independents* and the *separates* by *militant frankness* and *perceived mate vulnerability*. *Traditionals* are less militantly frank, yet receive more vulnerability communications from their mates than do the *independents* or the *separates*. The second discriminant function differentiates the *independents* from the *traditionals* and the *separates,* because the former are significantly less socially restrained than either the *traditionals* or the *separates*.

SUMMARY

Three discrete types of relationships emerged in this study. The first type, *independents,* are the most committed to an ideology of uncertainty and change. They are opposed to a belief system that stresses traditional values and exhibit a high degree of autonomy in their relationship. Couples in this type engage in a moderate amount of sharing, have few boundaries on their emotional and physical space, and do not necessarily avoid conflict in their relationship. *Independents* rate themselves as significantly less socially restrained in their communication than either *traditionals* or *separates*.

The second type, *separates,* are defined by very little sharing and a high degree of conflict avoidance. Although this type maintains a pattern of differentiated space, they do not feel autonomous. *Separates* perceive significantly more militantly frank communication in their relationships than *traditionals,* while they also perceive themselves as more socially restrained than the *independents*.

The third type, *traditionals,* prefer a high degree of temporal regularity in their lives and follow a fairly traditional belief system. These individuals draw very few boundaries on their use of space, and are not very autonomous. *Traditionals* are marked by a high degree of sharing and prefer to engage in, rather than avoid, conflict with their mates. *Traditionals* also report significantly less militant frankness than *separates,* and significantly more social restraint than the *independents*. Although the differences are not significant, *traditionals* do report

substantially more verbal expression of feelings than the other two groups. *Traditionals* also perceive that their relationship is marked by a high level of mutual disclosure of vulnerability between mates.

The findings of these two studies are encouraging. Although it would be premature to claim that the three relational types isolated in this study constitute the *only* possible relational types, or even the most significant ones, these types are expected to occur in future research with other samples.

The typological method is a fruitful one for the study of communication in relationships. Communication scholars and practitioners who view relationships through a typal framework are more likely to examine the goals and functions of a relationship, and give less attention to styles of interaction that seem pathological or bizarre merely because they are different.

The heuristic potential of the typological method is its greatest strength. A number of hypotheses concerning communication and relationships that are not intuitively obvious are suggested by the typological data. Future research will focus on the autonomy/interdependence issue, dyadic adjustment, and the sex-role orientations of the types, as well as their communication behaviors. The data from these studies, utilizing the relational typology, should produce the necessary information to validate this conceptual framework.

The typological method offers a framework for understanding communication within enduring relationships. A typology only reaches the status of a theory, however, when it proposes empirically testable statements associating the relationship types to a variety of underlying concepts. The present research is considered an initial step in that direction.

NOTES

1. This research, supported through a Biomedical Research Grant awarded by the Graduate School at Temple University, is part of the author's doctoral dissertation completed under the direction of Professor Arthur Bochner. Acknowledgment is given to Professor Bochner and Professor Herbert W. Simons for their valuable assistance throughout this project.
2. The data were examined with eight types, seven types, six types, five types, four types, three types, and two types as the limit to the number of clusters that the program could define. The three-type solution was clearly the best, in that it provided

the most unambiguous assignment of subjects to types.

3. For all factors, the lower the score, the more agreement with the factor.

4. Loadings are not to be confused with valence that is positive or negative in value. Instead, variables that load in the same direction are interpreted as belonging to a unified cluster and are independent from, or at the opposite pole from, those variables holding an opposite sign.

5. The significance level for the multiple comparisons computed by the Scheffé test is .10, as suggested by Scheffé (1953).

6. For militant frankness and social restraint, the *lower* the score, the more agreement with the scale.

7. All post hoc tests in the section were computed with the Newman-Kuels procedure, p < .05.

REFERENCES

ADAMS, B.N. *The American family: A sociological interpretation.* Chicago: Markham, 1971.

BACH, G., & WYDEN, P. *The intimate enemy: How to fight fair in love and marriage.* New York: William Morrow, 1969.

BARTLETT, N.S. Tests of significants in factor analysis. *The British Journal of Psychology,* 1950, 3, 77-81.

BERNARD, J. *The future of marriage.* New York: Bantam, 1972.

BOCK, R.D., & HAGGARD, E.A. The use of multivariate analysis of variance in behavioral research. In D.K. Whitla (Ed.), *Handbook of measurement and assessment in the behavioral sciences.* Reading, Massachusetts: Addison-Wesley, 1968.

BOTT, E. *Family and social network: Roles, norms, and external relationships in ordinary urban families.* London: Tavistock, 1957.

BURGESS, E.W., & WALLIN, P. *Courtship, engagement and marriage.* Philadelphia: Lippincott, 1953.

CATTELL, R.B. The Scrce test for the number of factors. Multivariate Behavioral Research, 1966, 1, 245-249.

CLARKE, C. Group procedures for increasing positive feedback between married partners. *Family Coordinator,* 1970, 19, 324-328.

CLINEBELL, H.J., & CLINEBELL, C.H. *The intimate marriage.* New York: Harper and Row, 1970.

CUBER, J.F., & HARROFF, P.B. *Sex and the significant Americans.* Baltimore: Penguin, 1965.

FARBER, B. A study of dependence and decision-making in marriage. Chicago: University of Chicago Libraries, Unpublished M.A. thesis, 1949.

FITZPATRICK, M.A. A typological approach to communication in relationships. Unpublished Ph.D. dissertation, Temple University, 1976.

GIFFIN, K., & PATTON, B. *Personal communication in human relations.* Columbus, Ohio: 1974.

GILNER, F. Self-report analysis of love relationships in three age groups. Unpublished Ph.D. dissertation, Purdue University, 1967.

GOODRICH, W. Toward a taxonomy of marriage. In J. Marman (Ed.), *Modern psychoanalysis: New directions and perspectives.* New York: Basic Books, 1968.

HALEY, J. *Strategies of psychotherapy.* New York: Grune & Stratton, 1963.

HART, R., & BURKS, D. Rhetorical sensitivity and social interaction. *Speech Monographs,* 1972, 39, 75-91.

HART, R., EADIE, W., & CARLSON, R. Rhetorical sensitivity and communication competence. Paper presented at the annual meeting of the Speech Communication Association, December 1975.

HEMPEL, C.G. *Aspects of scientific explanation.* New York: Free Press, 1965.

HENRY, J. *Pathways to madness.* New York: Vintage Books, 1965.

HESS, R.D., & HANDEL, G. *Family worlds: A psychological approach to family life.* Chicago: University of Chicago Press, 1959.

KANTOR, D., & LEHR, W. *Inside the family: Toward a theory of family process.* San Francisco: Jossey-Bass, 1975.

LEDERER, W.J., & JACKSON, D.D. *The mirages of marriage.* New York: Norton, 1968.

MACE, D., & MACE, V. *We can have better marriages if we want them.* Nashville, Tennessee: Abingdon, 1974.

MILLER, S., NUNNALLY, E.W., & WACKMAN, D.B. The Minnesota couples communication program. *Small Group Behavior,* 1975, 6, 57-71.

NUNNALLY, J. *Psychometric theory.* New York: McGraw-Hill, 1967.

O'NEILL, N., & O'NEILL, G. *Open marriage.* New York: Evans, 1972.

OVERALL, J.E., & KLETT, C.J. *Applied multivariate analysis.* New York: McGraw-Hill, 1972.

PHILLIPS, G.M., & METZGER, N.J. *Intimate communication.* Boston: Allyn and Bacon, 1976.

RAPOPORT, R., & RAPOPORT, R. *Dual-career families.* Baltimore: Penguin, 1971.

RAUSH, H.L., BARRY, W.A., HERTEL, R.K., & SWAIN, M.A. *Communication, conflict and marriage.* San Francisco: Jossey-Bass, 1974.

REISS, D. Varieties of consensual experience, I: A theory for relating family interaction to individual thinking. *Family Process,* 1971, 10, 1-27.

ROSSITER, C.M., & PEARCE, W.B. *Communicating personally.* Indianapolis: Bobbs-Merrill, 1975.

RYDER, R.G. A topography of early marriage. *Family Process,* 1970, 9, 385-402.

SCHAUBLE, P., & HILL, C. A laboratory approach to treatment in marriage counseling: Training in communication skills. *Family Coordinator,* 1976, 25, 277-284.

SCHEFFÉ, H. A method for judging all contrasts in the analysis of variance. *Biometrika,* 1953, 40, 87-104.

SHERWOOD, J.J., & SCHERER, J.J. A model for couples: How two can grow together. *Small Group Behavior,* 1975, 6, 11-29.

SHOSTROM, E., & KAVANAUGH, J. *Between men and women.* Los Angeles: Nash, 1971.

STEVENS, J.P. Four methods of analyzing between variation for the K-group MANOVA problem. *Multivariate Behavioral Research,* 1972, 7, 499-522.

STEWART, J., & D'ANGELO, G. *Together: Communicating interpersonally.* Reading, Massachusetts: Addison, Wesley, 1975.

SWENSON, C.H. Love: A self-report analysis with college students. *Journal of Individual Psychology,* 1961, 17, 167-171.

SWENSON, C.H. Manual and test booklet for the Love Scale. Unpublished manuscript, Purdue University, 1968.

SWENSON, C.H., & GILNER, F. Factor analysis of self-report statements of love relationships. *Journal of Individual Psychology,* 1964, 20, 186-188.

SWENSON, C.H., & GILNER, F. Scale of the feelings and the behaviors of love. Unpublished manuscript, Purdue University, 1973.

TRAVIS, R.P., & TRAVIS, P.Y. The pairing enrichment program: Actualizing the marriage. *The Family Coordinator,* 1975, 24, 161-170.

ZETTERBURG, H. *On theory and verification in sociology.* Totowa, N.J.: Bedminster Press, 1963.

MASS COMMUNICATION
Theory and Research: An Overview
Selected Studies

MASS COMMUNICATION THEORY AND RESEARCH: AN OVERVIEW[1]

JAMES A. ANDERSON
University of Utah

The study of mass communication is initially defined by the media themselves. It is further defined by the areas of interest which have surfaced in scholarly activity and publication. And finally, it can be described by looking at its output in the form of the journals which service the field. In our description of the field, we will briefly expand on each element in this three-dimensional classification scheme.

THE MEDIA

Our first dimension leads us to the fundamental question—What is a mass medium? This is a question which the field has yet to answer satisfactorily. A traditional definition would state: A *mass medium* is one which provides for the simultaneous delivery of the same message to a large, heterogeneous audience (Head 1972, p. 105). This definition has its greatest utility in those countries where the state controls both the content and the operation of the media. In these circumstances, the media can provide the semblance of direct transmission lines, and even trivial messages have the potential of total dominance. The definition has its least utility in those countries where the media are primarily competitive and commercial. In this circumstance, the media take on a reticulated nature characterized by proliferating media outlets and fractionalized audiences. Messages, even those of some impact, flow much as a river through its delta; in some main branches the flow is direct and rapid to some audience elements, but the flow through the entire coverage area may take considerable time and is subject to considerable modification. It takes little insight to state that mass communication is profoundly different in countries with a monolithic media structure than in countries with polymorphic media structures.

Not only do the media change in character from locale to locale, but their availability varies also. Television, which could lead the list in the United States with 98 percent penetration, might not even be ranked in a country like Albania, where there is an estimated one TV receiver per 1000 population.

In considering media, we shall adopt the simple expedient of an alphabetical listing of each vehicle which demonstrates the potential for mass participation, along with a summary of some current research directions and representative sourcebooks.

Broadband Communication

This medium is commonly called "cable TV" in its present configuration, but *broadband communication* actually refers to the domestic availability of a massive communication spectrum, regardless of method of delivery. Broadband represents a technological innovation potential far exceeding our present media. Consequently, it has been both hailed and condemned in a still continuing outpour of position papers. Smith's (1972) revision of his earlier overview is a convenient starting place in this area. The Rand Corporation[2] has prepared a number of reports dealing with studies of economic impact, feasibility, and government policy. The substance of these reports is also available in a four-volume series (Baer, 1974; Baer et al., 1974; Rivkin, 1974; Carpenter et al., 1974).

U.S. government policy and regulation concerning broadband remains in a state of flux. Policy recommendations flow with regularity from citizens groups (CED, 1975; Cabinet Committee on Cable Communications, 1974). Le Duc (1973) has provided an excellent text outlining the chaos of broadband regulation and summarizing the literature in the area prior to 1973. While the specifics discussed are somewhat dated, the principal arguments remain. Systematic studies of the social impact of this communication potential have been limited to the present rather narrow applications. The NSF publication *Social Services and Cable TV* (1976) presents an overview.

Film

It is not altogether a trivial comment that film is the second oldest mass medium, being only several hundred years younger than print. As the senior of the new media, the study of film has retained much of the literary traditions. The literature of film is more critical than quantitative, more theoretical than empirical. Film criticism has its roots in the likes of the poet Lindsay (1922). Film theory springs in part from the dialectics of Eisenstein (1949). The empirical approach, which so strongly permeates the study of television, has little representation in the earlier literature of film with, at least, the obvious exception of Arnheim (1958).

Recent developments in theory and criticism can be usefully described as a split between the semiologists and those with a more phenomenological perspective. *Semiology*, or the study of signs, traces its general beginnings to the work of Saussure (1915), a linguist. Semiology in film received substantial impetus from the work of Wollen (1972) and has been further advanced in the work of Metz (1974a, 1974b).

While semiology argues for a systematic analysis of film, the phenomenological approach observes film in its own state. The nature of this approach, perhaps, precludes a definitive statement, but Linden's *Reflections on The Screen* (1970) is representative.

Historical scholars generally note Knight's *The Liveliest Art* (1957) as a significant milepost in the nine-decade history of film. A more recent effort, Casty's interpretive history (1973) goes beyond chronology to show the interrelationship among events and developments. Barnouw's work on documentary film (1974), while not of the same value as his three-volume history of American broadcasting, has been seen as a work of good utility. Jowett's *Film: The Democratic Art* (1976) is so new that

its place in scholarship has not yet been defined. It appears, however, to be a substantial contribution to the study of film within the American cultural milieu. In addition to criticism, theory and history—three main branches in the study of film—production, technology, genre film, and artists are among the other focal areas for film study.

Newspapers and Periodicals

Newspaper publishing is undergoing rapid change; the role of the newspaper is in evolution, and the scholarly activity in newspaper journalism reflects these diversifying forces. Areas of current academic interest include mass communication law, explorations of the agenda-setting functions of newspapers and other media, and study of co-orientation and accuracy in reporting. Nelson and Teeter (1973) have provided a broad-based look at the control functions of law vis-à-vis print and broadcast information. Agenda setting and co-orientation, popular topics in journals, have yet to be given the fuller treatment that a text allows. Meyer (1973) and McCombs, Shaw, and Grey (1976) in separate works have reviewed issues relating to accuracy in reporting.

Two works of some controversy have recently appeared. Argyris (1974) in a participant-observer study of a newspaper offers insights into journalists as individuals influencing and in turn influenced by the dynamics of the group organization of which they are a part. Weber (1974) provides a review and commentary on the new journalistic approaches to a literate style.

Relevant to newspapers and the media in general, the work of Blumler and Katz (1974) suggest a reconceptualization of mass communication effects research in terms of the uses and gratifications media serve for members of their audiences. The uses and gratifications approach, however, has been decreasing in scholarly popularity.

The mass circulation, general-interest magazine has all but disappeared to be replaced by moderate circulation magazine of more directed interest and innumerable speciality sheets. Scholarly activity in magazine journalism is difficult to identify. It would appear that the systematic study of the magazine as a media force or as to its role in society is in, at least, temporary repose.

Radio

Radio as a medium has three distinct classes of interest: (1) the domestic, commercial, or state-operated service for the general public, (2) international shortwave service, and (3) personal radio particularly as expressed in citizens band radio in the United States.

The study of domestic radio mirrors the relative popular importance attached to the electronic media. Radio in the developed countries is a medium whose time in the sun of social importance has come and gone. Much of the current scholarship surrounding this medium is of an historical nature.

Culbert's (1976) study of news and foreign affairs of the thirties is a good example. The studies of American radio's political impact conducted during the forties (Lazarsfeld et al., 1948) was the last major research program of a socio-psychological nature. The introduction of all-news radio and other all-talk formats may renew a more widespread interest in the social impact of radio, however. Interest in the medium itself, of course, continues, to which Hilliard's (1974) introductory work attests.

Studies relating to international radio broadcasting have been primarily limited to those investigating the effectiveness of official cross-national broadcasts. These studies have declined as the appropriateness of the international service has come into dispute. The United States Information Agency (USIA) appears to be the only national agency to carry on a regular schedule of studies.

Personal Radio—the electronic extension of interpersonal communication—presents a truly unmapped territory. In personal communique, U.S. Federal Communications Commission's desire for research in this area, has been clearly indicated.

Recordings

Visual and aural recordings have also generated a substantial industry. Scholarly response to these media has been notable in its absence. There are, of course, "how-to-do-it" texts such as Weiner

(1973) for video, and Burstein (1974) for audio. Denisoff (1975) has provided an overview of the popular record industry.

Television

Television is the youngest of the major mass media and the literature in the field has a markedly different character. There are at least two reasons for that difference. First, television as a technology developed in the same time frame as two occurrences in the academic scene: the increased access of quantitative methodologies through computer applications and the rapid expansion of the Western university following World War II. The first of these made available a variety of methodological approaches which could be learned within a few weeks of intensive study. The expansion of the Western university, particularly the American university, greatly increased the number of researchers and accelerated the entry of many new content areas into the college catalogue. The consequence on the literature of television has been a heavy dependence on experimental empiricism and, due to the competitive forces for funding and on the practitioners themselves, a proliferation of short-term—less than five year—studies.

Secondly, deriving perhaps from the appeal of television for young viewers, a strong focus of study has been on television and the child. While there are any number of questions of equal scientific impact, society's concern over television's role in socialization of the child directed nearly all major funding, and thus determined research priorities for the field. Beginning with two independent studies on television and the child (Himmelweit et al., 1958, and Schramm et al., 1961), the study of television has been dominated by audience effects studies, with the audience of greatest concern being the child. Studies investigating the effects of television on the behavior of child and adult audiences have been reviewed by Comstock and others in a three-volume effort (Comstock & Fisher, 1975; Comstock et al., 1975; Comstock & Lindsey, 1975). The series also provides an interpretation of findings, methodologies, and suggests future directions.

One of the better known series of effects studies

has been concerned with violent content. Howitt and Cumberbatch (1975) have studied this literature and have concluded that the mass media have little or no effect on the level of violence in society. Cater and Strickland (1975) present other comments and criticism of this effects area. Anderson and Meyer (1974) have conceptualized a theoretical model which provides a logical reconciliation of the diverse effects findings.

Extensive studies of the television audience have been provided by Bowers (1973) for the American audience, and Goodhart et al. (1975) for Great Britain. Unfortunately, both of these works are based on data now more than five years old.

In a further attempt to deal with television and children, Anderson and Ploghoft (1975) have devised a *critical viewing skills* curriculum for children in the middle elementary and junior high grades. The curriculum is designed to heighten the pro-social effects of television and provide conceptual interventions for the negative effects.

Another study of the media and audience outcomes focused on the 1972 U.S. presidential campaign. Patterson and McClure (1976) conclude that television's supposed potential for changing voting behavior is mythical, which suggests that the wrong questions are being asked concerning television campaigns. For example, one function of such campaigns may be to prevent change—to insulate a voter from contrary interpersonal or media pressure.

Audience research, albeit prolific, is but one part of the television scene. One of the more recent developments has been the appearance of a system of formal, rather than social, aesthetics in Newcomb's work (1974). Zettl's applied aesthetic (1973) is also a fertile source of hypotheses for the study of the television presentation. And vocational interests in production techniques continue. A major source has been Millerson (1972), whose latest effort covers lighting. This text, with his other works (Millerson, 1968, 1973) provide a good introduction to the area. Westmoreland's (1974) approach to shortcuts is also useful.

The study of management, economics, and corporate structures in the electronic media also has gained considerable momentum. Quaal and Brown (1976), for example, have applied systematic management principles to the operation of radio and television stations. Owen et al. (1974) have investigated the programming impact of economic structure and management decisions. The processes and techniques of advertising in the U.S. and Europe have been surveyed in two separate works, one by Heighton and Cunningham (1976) and another by the Independent Broadcasting Authority (1974). Paulu (1974) has described the structures of broadcasting in Eastern Europe and Namurois (1973) has examined the structure and organization of broadcasting in over 30 countries. Academic concerns regarding American public television have also begun to be evidenced. As public television continues to evolve as a media force, scholarly work is beginning. Nyhan's (1976) collection considers its future; Katzman (1976) reviews the current forces affecting program decisions; and Anderson (1973) has investigated the funding needs to meet costs of projected operations.

AREAS OF STUDY

Two levels of analysis are required for the systematic investigation of mass communication. First of all, the study of a medium is affected by the different organizational characteristics that the medium can take. These characteristics, in turn, are governed by the scope of the intended audience for the content, and the source of income or purpose of the organization. The preceding sections have reviewed media which present content to personal, local, regional, national and international audiences. And the review listed media organized to gain income from: private sources only, as in wholly commercial forms; tax sources, as in state organized media; combinations of private and tax sources, as in U.S. "public" media; and private and tax sources administered through educational institutions, as in instructional media. These categories of intended audiences and source of income can, of course, be combined to provide additional subcategories.

Secondly, a number of interest areas or disciplines transcend particular media. A list of these disciplines—each of which maintain their own approaches and tools of study—would include: (1) advertising and marketing; (2) criticism; (3) effects;

(4) history; (5) institutional and/or corporate structure; (6) international studies; (7) management and economics; (8) operations and practices within media institutions; (9) policy and regulation; (10) social responsibility; (11) technique and technology; and (12) theory.

Each of these areas has its own body of literature which can again be further described by the medium of specific interest and by the categories of organization for that medium. Thus, the study of management for commercial television stations will produce elements which generalize to the management of, say, a state-run newspaper and elements which are unique. While this statement may appear patently obvious, the notion is often lost in the rush to develop general, covering descriptions or laws applicable to an entire medium or several media.

While each of these areas is an appropriate topic for a thorough review, five selected areas—criticism, effects, international studies, history, and theory—will be summarized by individual scholars who operate in that area.

Criticism

The most active area of criticism[3] within the study of the print and electronic mass media has been within content analysis (Holsti, 1969), where machine-like events are coded and counted, and values are discussed in terms of significant increases or decreases. That content analysis is the primary activity in the criticism of the domestic mass media is not at all surprising, if one considers the role of the critic. The critic is one who first strives to experience fully, then evaluates, synthesizes, illuminates, and assigns values. He is in many ways a catalyst, speeding the reaction between an audience and the work of art. Yet, he also speaks to the artists and producers, encouraging them toward the significant and away from the banal.

Early media criticism was largely centered about the *popular culture* versus *high art* controversy. Social and cultural critics—such as Van den Haag, Arendt, and McDonald—feared that by pandering to the mass audience, the media would induce an aesthetic *Gresham's Law*, resulting in the diminishment of high art, fostering instead the production of a cultural wasteland inhabited by passive "videots." The debate is unresolved, of course, but with the passing of time and the spread of the electronic media, the issues have become quiescent.

It is possible that the seeds have been planted for a flowering of television criticism. In the first place, the interest in the video product is emerging, and we are seeing national and international competition arising. Secondly, Newcomb's work (1974, 1976) is supplying impetus for further activity.

The garden of television criticism is a scrub desert in comparison to the flourishing of film criticism. A brief glimpse at some current directions in film criticism (Tudor, 1974) suggests some paths television criticism might follow.

Perhaps less a theory than a methodology, the *auteur theory* establishes the director as the author of a film. This determination may be a simplification, and not always accurate, but it presumably has corrected an historic injustice produced by the anonymous Hollywood studio system which relegated directors to mere technician status. A primary advantage attributed to the auteur method is that it identifies a single author whose canon can be analyzed with the same sort of thematic analysis long practiced by literary scholars.

Recent developments have introduced more scientific approaches to film criticism: Growing from the *myth analysis* of anthropologist Levi-Strauss, structuralism attempts a systematized analysis of motifs and plot structures. Believing that the work is a function of the forms our consciousness gives it, cinestructuralists dig for the deeper structures underlying films. *Semiology* draws on modern linguistic theory in viewing film as a communication of signs which can be analyzed, classified and coded.

Where might television criticism go in the future? Anything like a television aesthetic is yet to be developed. Even in more practical areas, film criticism would seem to be far ahead. Consider the debate, now decades old, comparing the formalist montage technique as advocated by Eisenstein (1949) and Arnheim (1958) and the realist deep-focus and long-take method championed by Bazin (1967, 1971) and others. There's a wealth of material on both sides of this issue and discussions of a television aesthetic have seemed simplistic by comparison.

Television criticism may well utilize structural analysis to identify those veiled meanings contained in the culture unique to television content. Some auteur analysis may also be useful, for example, looking at the motifs of television producer auteurs such as Norman Lear.

In the structuralist tradition, television critics may want to meld analysis of content with an examination of the cultural effects of such content. Research currently underway at Ohio University has been designed to determine, through projective techniques, just how viewers experience television and perceive the value, role, and behavior models they view on the medium. Such a blend of the humanistic and scientific approaches may prove to be a major contribution to television criticism. A purely scientific approach may miss the aesthetic value, while a purely artistic criticism may produce only the proliferating dissections typical of literary dissertations—increasingly esoteric and often without means of real world external validation. Thus, television's future contributions may well lie in that combination of the artistic critic's insights and the social scientist's validation of those judgments.

Mass Communication Effects

Mass communication effects studies tend to be largely conducted in the domain of television, and are a product primarily of American empiricism and European sociology. American empiricism has been criticized for trivializing serious questions in a welter of statistical methodologies. European sociology has been criticized for statements whose political motivation seem to take precedence over science.

There do appear to be fruitful research territories other than the current content and effects debate in the U.S. and the continuing class and content debate in Europe. Perhaps the clearest of these is the development of a library of case studies which examine human communication behavior in relation to the mass media. Nowhere in our literature can the research scientist turn to find adequate descriptions of the ordinary behaviors that do occur when individuals watch television or read a newspaper. Adequate descriptions might also use more refined measures than the demographic categories of sex, age, and education level which have shown little utility. Adequate descriptions might further distinguish among reception behaviors. Differences in intensity of interest and/or attention would be accounted for. In a similar vein, such research would need to thoroughly describe the conditions of reception, and to identify the extent to which differing environments have differing effects on communication behaviors. Finally, such a description might well include a listing of the content attended to with the concomitant perceived and observed behavioral consequences.

History

Historical studies[4] of broadcasting in the United States (Lichty & Topping, 1975) have barely covered major developmental eras. In areas such as technology, regulation, corporate and program development, definitive histories have yet to be written.

There has been great interest in early technical history for some time, yet scholarly endeavor has often been limited to working through old technical magazines. There is certainly value in updating and expanding Fielding's work (1967), and Shiers' bibliography (1972) would be a significant aid in the task. The technical history of television constitutes a particular need. A simple chronology in both broadband communication and video recording would be useful, and studies of the interrelationships between technology and regulation and technology and creative development might bring a better balance into our understanding of the field.

General legal histories in the major Western countries are sufficient from most standpoints (Gillmore & Barron, 1974). What is lacking, however, are the histories of agency interaction, for example, in the United States, of the cross relationships and procedures among the Federal Trade Commission, the Federal Communications Commission, and the Office of Telecommunications Policy. The historical development of particular precedents and their application over time, showing changes in legal philosophy, has been pursued with some success and would still appear to be profitable.

The growth, development, and present configuration of corporate structures in broadcast, film, and the recording industries, both nationally and internationally, represent major focal points (Baker, 1970). There are methodological difficulties in these areas, however, for companies often have restrictive policies regarding internal files. Finally, the historical development of content in any of the media would seem to remain a domain for exploration. Comparisons between radio programming and television programming are few, although many similarities appear to exist between "golden age radio" (Buxton & Owen, 1972) and contemporary television.

The present direction of film history has been to catalogue the role and place of individual directors and stars (Finch, 1973). With Knight's work (1957) now dated by 20 years, Barnouw's limited in scope (1974) and Casty's primarily an interpretive approach (1973), there is still, it would seem, a need for a multivolume general history of the field.

International Studies

International and multinational studies have progressed to the point where major structural and methodological difficulties have been identified. Mass communication studies bound by common geographical area (e.g. West Africa) search for communalities among countries with varying languages, political organization, and economic needs, with mixed results. Cultural differences within and between countries pose a continuing question about measurement instruments. Languages can form a formidable barrier not only to the mass media but also to the study of communication processes in general. The simple distribution of documents out of a country has become a strain on the budgets of communications agencies. Access is on an individual basis and generally when contacts break the scholar is left without alternative sources for needed data.[5]

Suggestions for study still abound, however. Country-by-country reviews leading to a series of handbooks overviewing mass media in various countries could be an important contribution, if done with resident expertise.

Another approach would be to narrow the scope to a particular media-related problem and to identify the solutions or attempts at solutions by various national media organizations. Berrigan's study of media access in Europe (1974) is a good example.

Theory

Mass communication theory[6] is in an embryonic state. There are many excellent reasons for this condition. For one thing, there is great difficulty advancing a single theoretical framework which is applicable to all mass media, or even a mass medium in its many potential configurations. A second reason is the limited knowledge of the process of communication and how that process is affected by content and media of presentation.

Aside from standard introductory texts dealing heavily with theory, such as Berlo (1960) or the more recent and advanced volume by Mortensen (1972), there are a number of readings and anthologies of considerable use in deriving a general theory of communication into which mass communication theory would fit. The monumental, in scope at least, but already dated Pool and Schramm (1973) provides a 31 chapter overview of the entire field, including perhaps one-third devoted specifically to media, and dealing heavily with theoretical concepts and writing. A *Scientific American* book, *Communication* (1972), deals with animal, cellular, verbal, and mass communication in a useful, illustrated, and clearly explained introductory format. A basic introductory reader is provided by Mortensen (1973), who coedited the earlier, more advanced, Sereno and Mortensen text (1970). Slightly different perspectives are seen in four other recently edited collections on communication theory. McGarry and Burrell (1973) provide a self-instructional introduction and guide to theoretical aspects of communication. Taking a reference and review approach are Blake and Haroldsen (1975), who provide one or two pages of highly digested definitional discussion heavily stressing mass media. A considerably more complicated and advanced work than either of these two is Olson (1974) which concentrates on the role of media in the educational process. Clarke's (1973) collection focuses more specifically on mass communication. The volume offers a review of literature and suggest new directions and models for research in community issues and public affairs knowledge, decision making in mass communication, childrens' information processing in television advertising, marketing communication, and the hierarchy of effects, coorientational states and interpersonal communication, instrumental utilities and information seeking, a conceptual model of information seeking, avoiding, and processing, and information processing and persuasion.

Five fairly recent titles—three from the United States and one each from Britain and Belgium—provide approaches to mass communication. All present heavily sociological introductions to mass media systems and audiences. Chaney (1972) reviews the subjective and objective reality of mass communications. The accent is British, as are most of the examples. A heavily used basic text in undergraduate courses is Schramm (1973), in which the prolific writer and researcher assesses the development of both media and media research, and provides a theoretical construct from which to view changes and project future needs. Updating a classic is Wright (1975), who focuses on the nature and function of mass communication, the media as social institutions, the sociology of the communicator and the audience, cultural content of the American media, and social effects of mass communication. Another recent volume is De Fleur and Ball-Rokeach's *Theories of Mass Communication* (1975). They deal only partially with *theory* in the full sense of the word, for the first hundred pages deal with media systems, history, and context. Bits and pieces of theory are presented and then are pooled together in a final chapter entitled "Toward an Integrated Theory of Mass Media Effects." Finally, in this general category, is Fauconnier (1975), who presents a highly organized outline of primarily European research findings and theory emphasizing a functional approach. The volume is important for both its heavy reliance on theory as an organizing and explanatory device and its European perspective opening a wealth of non-English studies and thinking.

No discussion of volumes on media theory is complete without reference to McLuhan and his ancestors and followers. *Understanding Media* (McLuhan, 1964) is probably the best single statement of McLuhan's own and other theories. Writing about McLuhan is Theall (1971), who details the man, his many books, his changing view of the media, and the effects his writings appear to have had. McLuhan's chief mentor was the late Canadian economist Innis, whose own two works have been reissued (Innis, 1951, 1972). Probably the most recent statement of McLuhan's media theory is provided by Schwartz (1973), who deals specifically with mediated sound and its effects in all walks of everyday life.

Finally, in discussing works on mass communication theory, one must mention the entertainment function of the media. Perhaps, the classic media critique has been the collection edited by Jacobs (1961) in which societal and literary critics attack the media for the bias toward entertainment to the near exclusion of the more serious material. The first serious defense of the media came in Mendelsohn's (1966) lengthy essay reviewing the sociological and psychological functions of media entertainment values. Mendelsohn argues that entertainment is not necessarily bad for either individual or society at large and that the respite granted by media is every bit as important as the didactic role sometimes assumed. Stephenson's (1967) work follows a similar line of argument. And finally Gans (1975) deals with the media as elements of mass culture and their relation with elite culture.

Journals of the Field

There is probably no better exercise to demonstrate the breadth of the field than to survey the academic and professional journals which service the various sections of mass communication. One can identify more than 700 periodicals relevant to the area, all of which could be of legitimate concern to mass communication scholars. In order to organize this collection, individuals from several discipline in mass communication were asked to indicate those journals which had greatest utility for them. The results of this informal survey were broken down by interest area or medium. The list is neither exhaustive nor exclusive.

General Interest

AV Communication Review
Communication Research
ERIC Report
Film Comment
Journal of Applied Communication Research
Journal of Broadcasting
Journal of Communication
Journalism Quarterly
Public Opinion Quarterly
Topicator
Variety*

Advertising and Marketing

Advertising Age*
Journal of Advertising Research
Journal of Marketing
Journal of Marketing Research

Criticism

Art Forum
Film Quarterly
Journal of Popular Culture
Neiman Reports
Television Quarterly

Effects

Child Development
Journal of Personality and Social Psychology
Journal of Social Psychology
Journal of Social Issues
Sociological Abstracts

Education Applications

Audio Visual Communications
Media (France)
Media and Methods

Management and Economics

Bell Journal of Economics
Broadcast Management/Engineering
Printing Management

Print

Editor and Publisher*
Columbia Journalism Review
Journalism Educator
Journalism Monographs
Mass Comm. Review

Technology

American Cinematographer
Broadcast Engineering
Film and Television Technician (GB)

Filmmakers Newsletter
Smpte

Electronic Media

Access
Broadcasting*
Cablevision News (GB)
CATV Newsweekly Magazine*
Journal of the Centre for Advanced Television
   Studies (GB)
Public Television Review
Radio Communication (GB)
QST

Film

Cinema Journal
Film and History
Film Journal
Sight and Sound (GB)
Take One
University Film Association Journal

International

Asian Mass Communication and Information
   Center (Singapore)
BBC Handbook (GB)
Broadcasting in the Netherlands (Netherlands)
Communications (France)
European Broadcasting Union Review (Swiss)
Internationale Zeitschrift fur Medienpsychologie
   und Medienproxis (W. Germany)
The JESCOMEA Newsletter
Media Asia (Malaysia)
Przekozy i Opinie (Poland)

Law, Policy and Regulations

Federal Communications Bar Journal
The Georgetown Law Review
Law and Contemporary Problems
Pike and Fisher

   *Trade journal

   Unless otherwise indicated, journals are
   published in the United States

CONCLUSION

The study of mass communication is as diverse
and pervasive as the media themselves. To chart
this watershed completely is undoubtedly an impossible task. Clearly, the field is embryonic; its
structures are as yet undefined. No one of us can
point with certainty to the direction or approaches

we should take. And, most importantly, none of us knows whether a contribution made shall be of lasting importance.

NOTES

1. This chapter was authored by James A. Anderson, with contributions from Joseph H. Berman, William C. Miller, and Christopher H. Sterling; and comments from Charles Clift, Drew O. McDaniel, George S. Semsel, and Guido Stempel.
2. Information on this extensive list can be obtained from the Rand Corporation, 1700 Main Street, Santa Monica, California 90406.
3. The senior author of this section is William C. Miller, Ph.D.
4. The senior author of this section is Joseph H. Berman, Ph.D.
5. Drew McDaniel, Ph.D. has begun an informal clearinghouse service within the International studies area. Information can be obtained from Dr. Drew O. McDaniel, School of Radio-Television, Ohio University, Athens, Ohio 45701.
6. The senior author of this section is Christopher H. Sterling, Ph.D.

REFERENCES

ANDERSON, J.A. *Operations and costs: A study of educational public television stations*, Washington, D.C.: NAEB, 1973.
ANDERSON, J.A., & MEYER, T.P. *Man and communication*. Washington, D.C.: College and University Press, 1974.
ANDERSON, J.A., & PLOGHOFT, M.E. *Television and you*. Athens, Ohio: Social Science Cooperative Center, 1975.
ARGYRIS, C. *Behind the front page: Organizational self renewal in a metropolitan newspaper*. San Francisco: Jossey-Bass, 1974.
ARNHEIM, R. *Film as art*. Berkeley: University of California Press, 1958.
BAER, W.S. *Cable television: A handbook for decision-making*. New York: Crane Russak, 1974.
BAER, W.S., et al. *Cable television: Franchising considerations*. New York: Crane Russak, 1974.
BAKER, W.J. *A history of the Marconi company*. London: Methuen, 1970.
BARNOUW, E. *Documentary: A history of the non-fiction film*. New York: Oxford University Press, 1974.
BAZIN, A. *What is cinema Vol. I*. Berkeley, California: University of California Press, 1967.
BAZIN, A. *What is cinema Vol. II*. Berkeley, California: University of California Press, 1971.
BERLO, D. *The process of communication*. New York: Holt, Rinehart and Winston, 1960.
BERRIGEN, F. *Access and the media—New models in Europe*. London: Middlesex Polytechnic, 1974.
BLAKE, R., & HAROLDSEN, E. (Eds) *A taxonomy of concepts in communication*. New York: Hastings House, 1975.
BLUMLER, J.G., & KATZ, E. (Eds.) *The uses of mass communications: Gratifications research*. Beverly Hills, California: Sage, 1974.
BOWERS, R.T. *Television and the public*. New York: Holt, Rinehart and Winston, 1973.
BURSTEIN, H. *Questions and answers about tape recording*. Blue Ridge Summit, Pennsylvania: TAB Books, 1974.

BUXTON, F., & OWEN, B. *The big broadcast, 1920-1950*. New York: Viking, 1972.
Cabinet Committee on Cable Communications. *Cable*. Washington, D.C.: USGPO, 1974.
CARPENTER, D., KLETTER, R.C., & YIN, R.K. *Cable television: Developing community services*, New York: Crane Russak, 1974.
CASTY, A. *Development of the film, An interpretive history*. New York: Harcourt, Brace, Janovich, 1973.
CATER, D., & STRICKLAND, S. *TV violence and the child*. New York: Russell Sage Foundation, 1975.
CED. *Broadcasting and cable television*. New York: CED, 1975.
CHANEY, D. *Process of mass communication*. Herder and Herder/McGraw-Hill, 1972.
CLARKE, D. (Ed.) *New models for mass communication research*. Beverly Hills, California: Sage, 1973.
COMSTOCK, G., & FISHER, M. *Television and human behavior: A guide to the pertinent scientific literature*. Santa Monica, California: The Rand Corp., 1975.
COMSTOCK, G. et al. *Television and human behavior: The key studies*. Santa Monica, California: The Rand Corp., 1975.
COMSTOCK, G., & LINDSEY, G. *Television and human behavior: The research Horizon, future and present*. Santa Monica, California: The Rand Corp., 1975.
CULBERT, D.H. *News for everyman: Radio and foreign Affairs in thirties America*. Westport, Conn.: Greenwood Press, 1976.
DEFLEUR, M., & BALL-ROKEACH, S. *Theories of mass communication*. New York: McKay, 1975.
DENISOFF, R.S. *Solid gold: The popular record industry*. New Brunswick, N.J.: Transaction, 1975.
EISENSTEIN, S.M. *Film form, essays in film theory*. Ed. and tr. by Jay Leyda. New York: Harcourt Brace, 1949.
FAUCONNIER, G. *Mass Media and society*. Leuven, Belgium: Leuven University Press, 1975.
FIELDING, R. *A technological history of motion picture and television*. Berkeley, California: University of California Press, 1967.
FINCH, D. *The art of Walt Disney: From Mickey Mouse to the magic kingdoms*. New York: Harry N. Abrams, 1973.
GANS, H. *Popular culture and high culture: An analysis and evaluation of taste*. New York: Basic Books, 1975.
GILLMOR, D.M., & BARRON, J.H. *Mass communication law: Cases and comment*. St. Paul, Minnesota: West Publishing Co., 1974.
GOODHART, G.J., EHRENBERG, A.C., & COLLINS, M.A. *The television audience: Patterns of viewing*. Lexington, Mass.: Lexington, 1975.
HEAD, S.W. *Broadcasting in America*. 2nd Edition. Boston: Houghton Mifflin, 1972.
HEIGHTON, E.J., & CUNNINGHAM, D.R. *Advertising in the broadcast media*. Belmont, Calif.: Wadsworth, 1976.
HILLIARD, R.L. *Radio broadcasting: An introduction to the sound medium*. New York: Hastings House, 1974.
HIMMELWEIT, H., OPPENHEIM, N., & VINCE, P. *Television and the child*. London: Oxford, 1958.
HOLSTI, O.R. *Content for the social sciences and humanities*. Reading, Mass.: Addison-Wesley, 1969.
HOWITT, D., & CUMBERBATCH, G. *Mass media, violence and society*. New York: John Wiley/Halstead Press, 1975.
IBA. *Broadcast advertising in Europe*. Independent Television Publications, 1974.

INNIS, H. *The bias of communication*. Toronto: University of Toronto Press, 1951.

INNIS, H. *Empire and communications*. Toronto: University of Toronto Press, 1972.

JACOBS, N. *Culture for the millions? Mass media in modern society*. Boston: Beacon Press, 1961.

JOWETT, G. *Film: The democratic art*. Boston: Little, Brown, 1976.

KATZMAN, N. *Program decisions in public television*. Washington, D.C.: NAEB, 1976.

KNIGHT, A. *The liveliest art*. New York: MacMillan, 1957.

LAZARFELD, P.F., BERELSON, B., & GAUDET, H. *The people's choice*. 2nd Edition. New York: Columbia University Press, 1948.

LE DUC, D.R. *Cable television and the FCC*. Philadelphia: Temple University Press, 1973.

LICHTY, L.W., & TOPPING, M.C. *American broadcasting: A sourcebook on the history of radio and television*. New York: Hastings House, 1975.

LINDEN, G.W. *Reflections on the screen*. Belmont, Calif.: Wadsworth, 1970.

LINDSAY, N.W. *The art of the moving picture*. New York: MacMillan, 1922.

McCOMBS, M.E., SHAW, D.L., & GREY, J. *Handbook of reporting methods*. Atlanta: Houghton-Mifflin, 1976.

McGARRY, K., & BURRELL, P. (Eds.) *Communication studies: A programmed guide*. Hamden, Conn.: Linnet Books, 1973.

McLUHAN, M. *Understanding media: The extensions of man*. New York: McGraw Hill, 1964.

MENDELSOHN, H. *Mass entertainment*. New Haven, Conn.: College and University press, 1966.

METZ, C. *Language and cinema*. The Hague: Mouton, 1974a.

METZ, C. *Film language: A semiotics of the cinema*. New York: Oxford University Press, 1974b.

MEYER, P. *Precision journalism*. Bloomington, Ind.: Indiana University Press, 1973.

MILLERSON, G. *Technique of television production*. New York: Hastings House, 1968.

MILLERSON, G. *The technique of lighting for television and motion pictures*. New York: Hastings House, 1972.

MILLERSON, G. *TV camera operation*. New York: Hastings House, 1973.

MORTENSEN, C.D. *Communication: The study of human interaction*. New York: McGraw Hill, 1972.

MORTENSEN, C.D. (Ed.) *Basic readings in communication theory*. New York: Harper and Row, 1973.

NAMUROIS, A. *Structures and organization of broadcasting in the framework of radio communications*. Geneva: EBU, 1973.

NELSON, H.L., & TEETER, D.L. *Law of mass communications: Freedom and control of print and broadcast media*. New York: Foundation Press, 1973.

NEWCOMB, H. *TV: The most popular art*. Garden City, N.Y.: Anchor books, 1974.

NEWCOMB, H. (Ed.) *Television: The critical view*. New York: Oxford University Press, 1976.

NSF; CTIC. *Social services and cable TV*. Washington, D.C.: USGPO, 1976.

NYHAN, M.J. (Ed.) *The future of public broadcasting*. New York: Praeger Special Studies, 1976.

OLSON, D. (Ed.) *Media and symbols: The forms of expression, communication, and education*. Chicago: University of Chicago Press, 1974.

OWEN, B.M., BEEBE, J.W., & MANNING, JR., W.G. *Television economics*, Lexington, Mass.: Lexington Books, 1974.

PATTERSON, T.E., & McCLURE, R.D. *The unseeing eye*. New York: G.E. Putnam's Sons, 1976.

PAULU, B. *Radio and television broadcasting in Eastern Europe*. Minneapolis, Minn.: University of Minnesota Press, 1974.

POOL, I., & SCHRAMM, W. (Eds.) *Handbook of communication*. Chicago: Rand McNally, 1973.

QUAAL, W.L., & BROWN, J.A. *Broadcast management in radio and television*. New York: Hastings House, 1976.

RIVKIN, S.R. *Cable television: A guide to federal regulations*. New York: Crane, Russak, 1974.

SAUSSURE, de F. *Course in general linguistics*. London: Peter Owen, 1974.

SCHRAMM, W., LYLE, J., & PARKER, E.D. *Television in the lives of our children*. Stanford University Press, 1961.

SCHRAMM, W. *Men, messages and media: A look at human communication*. New York: Harper and Row, 1973.

SCHWARTZ, T. *The responsive chord*. New York: Doubleday, 1973.

Scientific American. Communication. New York: W.H. Freeman, 1972.

SERENO, K., & MORTENSEN, C.D. (Eds) *Foundations of communication theory*. New York: Harper and Row, 1970.

SHIERS, G. *Bibliography of the history of electronics*. Metuchen, N.J.: Scarecrow Press, 1972.

SMITH, R.L. *The wired nation: Cable TV, The electronic communication highway*. New York: Harper and Row, 1972.

STEPHENSON, W. *The play theory of mass communication*. Chicago: University of Chicago Press, 1967.

THEALL, D. *The medium is the rear-view mirror*. Montreal: McGill-Queen's University Press, 1971.

TUDOR, A. *Theories of film*. London: Secker and Warburg, 1974.

WEBER, R. *The reporter as artist: A look at the new journalism controversy*. New York: Hastings House, 1974.

WEINER, P. *Making the media revolution: A handbook for videotape production*. New York: McMillan, 1973.

WESTMORELAND, R. *Teleproduction shortcuts: A manual for low budget television production in a small studio*. Norman, Okla.: University of Oklahoma Press, 1974.

WOLLEN, P. *Signs and meaning in the cinema*. Bloomington: Indiana University Press, 1972.

WRIGHT, C. *Mass communication: A sociological perspective*. New York: Random House, 1975.

ZETTL, H. *Sight sound motion: Applied media aesthetics*. Belmont, Calif.: Wadsworth, 1973.

THE MEDIATING EFFECT OF THE INTERVENTION POTENTIAL OF COMMUNICATIONS ON DISPLACED AGGRESSIVENESS AND RETALIATORY BEHAVIOR[1]

JENNINGS BRYANT
University of Massachusetts

DOLF ZILLMANN
Indiana University

Subjects were provoked, exposed to one of six pretested communications (audio-visual messages) differing in cognitive intervention potential, and given opportunities to aggress. The six messages represented a four-level differentiation in cognitive intervention potential: minimal, low, moderate, and high. At the moderate level, a humorous message was included with a nonhumorous one, in order to determine the effect of exposure to a message which could potentially evoke an emotional state incompatible with anger. Similarly, at the high intervention level, an aggressive message was included with a nonaggressive one to test predictions relating to the anger reiteration potential of messages with aggressive contents. Measured were: (1) changes in sympathetic excitation, (2) displaced aggressiveness, and (3) retaliatory behavior. It was found that, for nonaggressive communications, the higher the intervention potential, the greater the decrease of annoyance-produced excitation. In contrast, highly involving aggressive messages reduced excitation only to a degree comparable to that of minimally involving messages. Both displaced aggressiveness and retaliatory behavior were found to be a simple function of level of excitation. The highly involving nonaggressive communication lowered aggressive and hostile activities significantly below the level associated with exposure to either the noninvolving and nonaggressive communication or the highly involving but aggressive communication. The aggression-modifying effect of the humorous communication was as predicted from the consideration of this communication's intervention potential alone.

The bulk of the evidence relevant to the effect of aggression-depicting communications or messages on the behavior of initially provoked viewers has been interpreted as accumulating support for the notion that such exposure future aggressively predisposes the viewer, thereby facilitating aggressive behavior (Berkowitz, 1965; Goranson, 1970). For those investigators who have employed theoretical models that are mainly based on the consideration of cognitive processes and stimulus control, communication exposure has generally been interpreted as functioning primarily to provide aggressive cues which in some manner increase the likelihood that the respondent will select an aggressive or hostile option from his response repertoire (Berkowitz, 1965, 1970, 1974). On the other hand, investigators who have relied more heavily on the function of sympathetic activity in their theoretical models have generally considered the primary role of communication exposure to be the evocation of suffi-

cient excitation to intensify any aggressive or hostile response which the individual is predisposed to make (Tannebaum & Zillmann, 1975). A recent investigation by Zillmann and Johnson (1973), however, has challenged the adequacy of experimental designs which have been employed to provide support for *either* of these explanatory models, and has contributed evidence which calls the generalizability of the entire aggression-enhancement interpretation into question.

Zillmann and Johnson proposed that, since all relevant research which reported instigational effects had employed factorial variations of low vs. high provocation and exposure to neutral vs. aggressive communication, it must have been assumed that the so-called *neutral* communication had *no effect* on subsequent aggressive behavior. In other words, it was assumed that the neutral communication produced a quasi-zero impact—as a no-treatment control would. If such an assumption were not made, there would be no grounds for interpreting the relatively higher level of aggressiveness, which has been observed after exposure to aggressive communications, as a facilitation of aggression. In order to test the validity of this no-impact assumption for nonaggressive fare, Zillmann and Johnson involved a no-communication control in their investigation. This inclusion provided an anchor point from which to interpret the direction of any differences that occurred between communication conditions. It was found that under conditions of extreme provocation, relative to the no-exposure condition, the neutral messages significantly reduced subsequent aggression, whereas the aggressive communication reduced it to an insignificant degree only; that is, it perpetuated aggressiveness. It was proposed that, whereas exposure to "neutral" messages acts to divert the individual's attention from provoking circumstances and thoughts of retaliation, thereby allowing provocation-produced sympathetic activity to dissipate, messages involving contents which relate to the individual's acute emotional state potentially reiterate arousal-maintaining cognitions. Thus, aggression-depicting messages are conceived of as reminding the individual of the instigating confrontation with his annoyer. This reiteration of cognitions relating to a noxious state is seen to maintain (rather than to increase) sympathetic excitation in the individual. The perpetuated high intense feelings of anger, and, ultimately, as main-intense feelings of anger, and, ultimately, as maintaining the motivation to retaliate.

If the proposed mechanism of excitation-maintenance through the reiteration of provocation-related cognitions is indeed operative, exposure to messages with aggressive contents primarily functions to extend the provoked individual's status quo. Although this evidence certainly does not offer an acquittal to the mass media for contributing to hostile and aggressive actions, it does suggest that exposure to aggressive media fare does not make the situation any worse for the person who is already angry and upset. It also suggests that nonaggressive ("neutral") messages merit careful theoretical and empirical consideration in their own right. Neutral messages apparently do have all but a quasi-zero effect on motivated aggressive behavior.

Exposure to such communication has to be viewed as a potentially highly effective aggression-modifying treatment.

ENTERTAINMENT

The use of entertaining communication to furnish stimuli for relaxation or diversion of attention is rather well documented (Berelson, 1949; Weiss, 1969; Greenberg, 1974). However, although some normative data have been gathered on what type of content people expose themselves to in order to relax and "unwind" (Waples, Berelson, & Bradshaw, 1949; Steiner, 1963; Mendelsohn, 1964; Greenberg, 1974), no research appears to have been done on the actual psychological mechanisms operative in this diversion process. More specifically, the properties of *entertaining* content which functions in the mitigation of noxious emotional states has been left entirely unexplored. The present investigation addresses this void.

In order to examine properties of messages which may optimally serve to reduce anger or other acute noxious states, it is necessary to make some assumptions about cognitive processes associated with such states. It may be assumed that, subsequent to a hostile encounter in which direct and immediate retaliation is not feasible, the provoked individual engages in some sort of "secondary appraisal" process (Lazarus, 1966) in which he ponders the circumstances of the encounter, evaluates alternative adaptive behavior or coping strategies, rehearses ways to "get back at" or "put down" his annoyer, or simply berates himself for being so dumb as to be victimized. If so, the ameliorative function of entertaining communication may be the diversion of the individual's attention from appraisal-specific cognitions. More colloquially, in order for a provoked person to relax, the entertaining communication must "take his mind off of his problems." In order to function effectively in this capacity, the communication must induce cognitive processes which overpower and supersede the provocation-related ones. Consequently, the communication must be involving in its own right. It would appear that *the more a message can interrupt the rehearsal of anger-inducing and anger-maintaining cognitions, the more complete will be the dissipation of anger.* A message's *cognitive intervention potential*, that is, the degree to which a message attracts an emotionally aroused viewer's attention and involves him cognitively, should thus be considered a critical determining factor in providing relief from a vexing emotional state.

Although the notion of cognitive intervention potential obviously features cognitive processes, excitatory aspects of the response to communication are also being considered. The function of the cognitive intervention mechanism is seen to be the interruption of the rehearsal of provocation-related cognitions. However, these cognitions, in turn, are seen to be the direct source of the maintenance of sympathetic activity. The more thoroughly the aggressively motivated person becomes immersed in communication-induced cognitions which do not relate to experiences of annoyance, the more effectively his attention should be turned away from the vexing incident, and the more completely his excitation should subside. Therefore, incorporating the tenets of *two-factor theory* (Schachter, 1964, 1971) and *excitation-transfer theory* (Zillmann, 1971, 1972), which treat the intensity of aggressive responses after exposure to communication as a direct function of the excitation that the provoked person can attribute to his state of anger, an inverse relationship between the cognitive intervention potential of a message and the level of hostile and aggressive activities should be expected for the post-exposure behavior of a provoked person.

This investigation constitutes a first test of the effect on motivated aggressiveness of exposure to messages associated with various levels of cognitive intervention potential. It employed the conventional experimental paradigm used to study the consequences of media aggression (i.e., provocation, communication exposure, retaliation), with exposure to various nonaggressive and nonhumorous messages, chosen and pretested to provide a variation in intervention potential. However, by additionally incorporating an aggression-depicting communication with measured cognitive intervention potential, elimination of confoundings between alternative theoretical models is attempted. This addition, for all practical purposes, also provides a replication of Zillmann and Johnson's (1973) study. However, whereas that investigation utilized a no-

communication control condition, the present experiment employs a communication with minimal intervention potential.

THE STUDY

The inclusion of the aggression-depicting communication permits the evaluation of various predictive rationales. First, Berkowitz' reasoning (1965, 1969, 1970) leads to the expectation that the aggressively instigated individual will display more aggressiveness toward his tormenter after seeing an aggressive communication than after seeing a neutral one. Berkowitz has stressed the aggression-triggering function of aggressive cues in media fare. In his proposal of a completion tendency for motivated aggression, he also emphasized the provoked individual's persistence in trying to get back at his annoyer. It should be expected, then, that the individual, no matter to what degree he has been temporarily districted by a message, when provided with an opportunity to retaliate will execute the aggressive responses which were "put into motion" (Berkowitz, 1965, p. 324) earlier. Differentially involving communications should thus not differentially affect subsequent aggressive behavior, but exposure to aggressive contents should produce aggressiveness at levels above that evoked by exposure to nonaggressive materials.

Second, Bandura's (1965) reasoning on attentional shift may be used to develop contrasting expectations. He has proposed that a provoked person may experience a reduction of noxious arousal during exposure to communication, even those depicting aggressive activity. He suggested that exposure to communication serves to divert the individual's attention from an instigational experience. As the provoked person becomes engrossed in cognitions that supersede his preoccupation with aggravation, anger and aggression should be reduced. In Bandura's scheme, the criterion for effectively reducing aggressiveness is the degree to which the communication involves or absorbs the viewer. The magnitude of aggression-reduction is thus considered to be directly proportional to the capacity of the message to affect attentional shifts. Differences in content, such as aggressive vs. nonaggressive, appear to be insignificant. Bandura's model, then, leads to the expectation that the higher the cognitive intervention potential of communication, the greater the decline in postexposure aggression, regardless of the presence or absence of aggressive cues.

Finally, the reasoning on cognitive intervention potential provides a basis for unique predictions. This reasoning is similar to Bandura's (1965) in that it also proposes that a provoked individual's anger and readiness to aggress diminish through exposure to involving messages. However, departing here from Bandura's reasoning, and in line with Zillmann and Johnson's (1973) reasoning on motivation reiteration, it is proposed that communication content directly associated with the individual's acute emotional state potentially reiterate arousal-maintaining cognitions. Specifically, a message depicting provocation and aggressive reprisals is expected to reinstate the annoyance and aggressive predispositions associated with the initial instigational experience. In other words, although it is anticipated that involving messages generally take the severely provoked person's mind off disturbing incidents, aggressive content fails to do so. The intervention potential of aggressive content may be quite high for unprovoked persons. But, according to this reasoning, it should be disproportionally low for provoked persons. The aggression-reducing effect of exposure to communication, then, is seen to be a *joint function* of a message's intervention potential and the degree of its relatedness to the experiential state in which it intervenes. In general, *the aggression-reducing effect of exposure to communication should be more pronounced, the greater the message's intervention potential, and the lower the degree of relatedness between prior and featured states.* This proposal leads to the expectation that the effect of the nonaggressive communications on subsequent aggressiveness will be inversely proportional to the messages' measured intervention potential, but that the effect of the aggressive communication will be decisively above the level which would be expected from the consideration of its general intervention potential alone.

Two additional considerations are treated in the present investigation. First, it has been suggested that nonhostile humorous stimuli have aggression-inhibiting properties. Baron and Ball (1974) found aggressiveness to be lower after exposure to humorous communications than after exposure to neutral stimuli, and they proposed that the humorous materials elicited emotional states incompatible with anger or overt aggression. However, Tannenbaum (Tannenbaum & Zillmann, 1975) has produced contradictory evidence. He observed arousing humorous materials to have a facilitatory effect on aggression. This finding casts doubt on the interpretation that humor constitutes a reaction incompatible with anger, which necessarily inhibits aggressive behavior. An alternative explanation would be that the humorous stimuli were more cognitively involving than the neutral stimuli (i.e., pictures of scenery, furniture, and abstract paintings), and therefore, the reduction in displayed aggressiveness may have been due to the differential cognitive intervention potential of the two sets of stimuli. To examine this possibility, a humorous, nonaggressive communication with measured cognitive intervention potential was included in the design of the present experiment. The comparison of the effect of this humorous communication with that of the nonhumorous communications with measured intervention potential will determine whether the aggression-inhibiting impact of humorous stimuli can be accounted for by their intervention potential, or whether other mechanisms need be invoked. The possible more effective reduction in aggressive behavior produced by exposure to the humorous communication, relative to the nonhumorous controls, would have to be attributed to special aggression-modifying properties of humorous materials.

As a second additional consideration, the present study examines the relationship between direct hostility and displaced aggression under the same conditions of provocation and communication exposure. *Direct hostility* is defined as nonphysical harm which is directed toward the proper target (the annoyer), whereas *displaced aggression* is defined as physical injury or pain directed toward an improper target (a person not responsible for an annoyance suffered). To determine this relationship, two dependent measures were employed. The first opportunity to behave aggressively was presented within the context of a competitive game in which the provoked subject was allowed to aggress against a peer who had done him no harm (displaced aggression). Afterwards, the subject was given an opportunity to retaliate against the experimenter who had treated him in a demeaning, rude manner (direct hostility). Additionally, physiological measures were taken immediately prior to obtaining both dependent measures in order to determine the effect of sympathetic activity on hostile and aggressive behavior.

METHOD

Selection of Experimental Materials

Pretest design. In order to select appropriate materials for the main experiment, six videotaped segments were pretested. Three measures of cognitive intervention potential were obtained: (1) subjects' ability to recall facts presented prior to communication exposure, (2) subjects' performance on a signal-detection test during communication exposure, and (3) subjects' ratings of the message on several indices of cognitive intervention potential.

Materials. The videotaped segments were selected on intuitive grounds to meet stimulus requirements regarding differentiation in intervention potential. All messages tested were in color and were 10 minutes long.

In order to obtain a minimally involving stimulus, a silent film showing a blue foreground superimposed over a barely perceptible, slow moving wave pattern was created. Another especially created communication, designed to be low in intervention potential, was composed of scenes of swimming fish, and was presented with commentary in Korean. Four additional segments were selected and edited from broadcast entertainment programs, and contained the actual video and audio of the broadcast shows. There were two *nonhumorous, nonaggressive* segments; one *humorous, nonaggressive segment; and one nonhumorous, aggressive* segment. The two *nonhumorous, nonaggressive* communications examined were edited segments from the daytime quiz show "Jackpot" and from a nonaggressive sport event, a figure-skating exhibition. The *humorous, nonag-*

gressive communication was an edited segment of three comedians: Johnny Carson, Rodney Dangerfield, and Jonathan Winters. The *nonhumorous, aggressive* communication was an edited segment from an aggressive sport event, a professional ice-hockey match. The segment presented "aggressive" ice-hockey and a fist fight involving various players.

Subjects. Forty-eight male undergraduates at Indiana University, all enrolled in an introductory communication course, served as subjects in the pretest. They participated in order to fulfill a class requirement.

Procedure. Subjects participated two at a time. The paired subjects, seated in booths to prevent their interaction, were randomly assigned to one of the six communication conditions. The pretest was introduced as an experiment designed to measure an individual's ability to assess the personality of a communicator from being exposed to excerpts of his messages received through one or more sensory modalities, and to determine the relationship between impressions of the communicators and the appreciation of various types of communication presented under varying conditions of mild physical distraction. The subjects were then familiarized with the distracting activity, which was actually a signal-detection task. Each subject was given a small box containing a penny-sized disc and a small push-button. They were instructed to place the distal pad of the index finger of their left hand on the disc. It was explained that, at random intervals, they would feel various patterns of pulses from the button. The subjects were told to be concerned with only one pattern, five pulses in rapid succession, and to report this signal by immediately pressing the pushbutton with the index finger of their right hand. The experimenter then demonstrated the task. Subjects were then exposed to a first communication, an auditory-only, fairly monotonous 5-minute speech. While listening to the speech, they performed the signal-detection task. The experimenter then administered a bogus questionnaire which assessed the subjects' perceptions of the personality of the speaker. The procedure up to this point served to familiarize the subject with his task and to provide a plausible cover story for the experiment. The subjects then heard a 3-minute, auditory-only speech which provided the material for the later surprise recall test. This speech was a description of papermaking. Immediately after the speech, the bogus questionnaire was again administered. The subjects were next exposed to one of the six experimental communications and, during exposure, engaged in the signal-detection task. The recall test about papermaking was administered thereafter. Finally, subjects evaluated the experimental communication on several scales. After they had completed these ratings, they were dismissed. All subjects were debriefed after the study had been completed.

Recall test. Based on the rationale that the retention of materials greatly suffers as recall-facilitating rehearsal processes are impaired and disrupted (Norman, 1969; Peterson & Peterson, 1959; Waugh & Norman, 1968), the relative capacity of messages to intervene in such rehearsal processes, as measured by its negative effect on recall, was taken to index cognitive intervention potential. Eighteen facts about papermaking constituted the items of the recall test. Responses were coded by a judge who was naive about experimental conditions.

Signal-detection test. Based on the rationale that the attention-demanding performance of a signal-detection task is impaired as a competing task requires attention and absorbs the respondent (Broadbent & Gregory, 1961; Mackworth, 1969; Jerison, 1970), the messages' intervention potential were measured in the frequency of errors made in the test. Subject monitored the tactile stimuli (i.e., barely noticeable bobs of a button) as they were exposed to communication. Per minute, one "correct" and four "incorrect" randomly placed stimuli were presented in random order. The "correct" stimulus was defined as 5 pulses in rapid succession; the "incorrect" stimuli were defined as 3, 4, or 6 pulses in rapid succession. Omission errors, that is, failures to report the occurrence of "correct" signals, constituted the primary measure of intervention potential. Commission errors, that is, reports of "correct" signals when they did not occur, served as a secondary index.

Rated cognitive intervention potential. Seven rating scales, all assumed to reflect cognitive intervention potential, were included in a questionnaire administered immediately after the recall test. All rating scales ranged from 0 to 100, were marked and numbered at intervals of 10, and were labeled at both ends. The following questions were asked: (1) "How *absorbing* was the program segment?" (2) "How *eventful* was the program segment?" (3) "To what degree was it necessary to *concentrate* to follow the program segment?" (4) "How *boring* was the program segment?" (5) "How *cognitively involving* was the program segment?" (6) "How *interesting* was the program segment?" (7) "To what degree did your *mind wander* while watching the program segment?" The label associated with 0 was "Not at all . . ." and that associated with 100 was "Extremely. . . ."

Results. As can be seen from Table 1, a four-level differentiation in cognitive intervention potential (minimal, low, moderate, high) was obtained with considerable consistency. The *monotonous stimulus* (i.e., blue screen) yielded very low scores on all measures of intervention potential. It was consequently considered to have *minimal* intervention potential. The *nature film* (i.e., underwater scenes) yielded similarly low, yet generally higher scores. It was considered to have a low potential. As can be seen, the *nonaggressive sport event* and the *comedy show* were associated with relatively *moderate* intervention potentials. The *quiz show* and *aggressive sport event*, in turn, were associated with *high* intervention potentials.

It should be noted that the two messages at each of the two higher levels of intervention potential yielded highly similar means on the various indices. This circumstance provides ideal conditions for the evaluation of effects unique to humor or depicted aggression.

The statistical evaluations of the differentiations of means reported in Table 1 is as follows: The analysis of variance performed on the recall data yielded a highly significant effect ($F = 23.32$; $p < .001$; df = 5,42). Analyses of subjects' performance scores on the signal-detection test also yielded significant effects: For omission errors, $F = 9.78$, $p < .001$, df = 5,42 and for commission errors,

TABLE 1
Differentiation of Means of Various Indices of Cognitive Intervention
Potential According to Pretest

Dependent Measure	Communication					
	Monotonous stimulus	Nature film	Comedy show	Nonaggressive sport	Quiz show	Aggressive sport
Recall test:	12^d	9^c	6^b	6^b	4^a	4^a
Signal detection task:						
Omission errors	1^a	2^{ab}	3^{bc}	3^{bc}	4^{cd}	5^d
Commission errors	0^a	0^a	1^{ab}	1^{ab}	2^b	2^b
Ratings:						
Absorbing	4^a	29^b	60^c	58^c	76^d	79^d
Eventful	12^a	36^b	51^c	54^c	75^d	76^d
Demanding	11^a	22^b	54^c	57^c	55^c	51^c
Boring	81^a	61^b	29^c	33^c	20^c	12^c
Involving	6^a	30^b	49^c	42^{bc}	72^d	69^d
Interesting	14^a	34^b	54^c	61^{cd}	72^{cd}	79^d
Mind wander	87^a	72^a	34^b	38^b	20^b	19^b

Note. High scores on the "boring" and "mind wander" scales indicate low cognitive intervention potential; high scores on all other scales indicate high cognitive intervention potential.
Means having no letter in their superscripts in common differ significantly at $p<.05$ by Newman-Keuls' test.

$F=5.78$, $p<.01$, df$=5.42$. Analyses of variance performed on all questionnaire rating scales again yielded highly significant effects: *absorbing*, $F=55.31$; *eventful*, $F=28.02$; *demanding*, $F=27.23$; *boring*, $F=15.62$; *involving*, $F=28.40$; *interesting*, $F=16.23$; *mind wander*, $F=24.82$. All F ratios are associated with $df=5,42$ and $p<.001$.

Main Experiment

Design. Subjects were provoked by a rude experimenter while performing a frustrating task. After instigation, they were exposed to one of the six pretested communications differentiated in cognitive intervention potential. The subjects played a competitive game in which they were given an opportunity to displace aggressiveness by delivering noxious noise to an innocent opponent. Finally, confidential evaluations of the rude experimenter,

which purportedly were to have real consequences for his academic future, served to assess the subjects' retaliatory behavior. Measures of excitation were taken at critical times to determine the arousal-mediating effect of exposure to communication.

Subjects. Sixty male undergraduates at Indiana University, all of whom were enrolled in introductory communications courses, served as subjects. They received either a monetary incentive for participating or credit toward class requirements.

Procedure. The subject was met by a pleasant experimenter who directed him into the experimental room, seated him behind a table, and played an instruction tape which explained that the experimental session had been divided into three separate 10-minute sections, with each part focusing on different commonly used communication skills. It was explained that the primary research interest was in the interrelations of these communication processes. The experimenter explained to the subject that physiological measures would be taken at various times prior to and after communication exposure. He then attached a cuff for the measurement of blood pressure and electrodes for the measurement of heart rate. After the subject had relaxed, base-level measures were taken.

The experimenter then announced that they would begin the first portion of the experiment, the strategy game. The instructions for this part of the session were also taped. Although the competitive game would not actually be played until much later, it was necessary that the subject master the relatively complicated procedure prior to the time of instigation. Otherwise, the complexity of the instructions could have provided a potentially powerful cognitive intervention treatment, interrupting provocation-induced rehearsal. This section was described as serving as an investigation into game strategy, particularly into the interdependencies between different strategies of attack which are known to be effective, and misleading, deceptive feedback used as a means of defense and counterattack. The procedure is detailed elsewhere (Zillmann & Bryant, 1974). In brief, the subject was informed that the experiment involved two subjects, himself and his opponent. He was then informed that he had been chosen, by a prior random procedure, to defend or counterattack against his attacking opponent in a game of strategy. His opponent, it was explained, who was working in the adjacent room with another experimenter, was being taught a superior strategy of attack, which he, the subject, was to defend against by using deceptive feedback. The game was described as a simplified one-way "battleship game," in which the subject would choose a position for his ship on a board, and the opponent would try to locate the ship. A successful "hit" would mark the end of the game. Each miss, on the other hand, would call for deceptive feedback from the subject to his attacker, to be followed by another trial, until a successful hit was achieved. The subject was informed that the critical feedback could be either positive or negative, both to different degrees. Negative feedback consisted of the delivery

of noxious noise to the opponent, ranging from very low to very intense. Positive feedback consisted of the removal of a moderately intense noxious noise to which the opponent would continuously be exposed. Various intensities of negative and positive feedback were demonstrated stereophonically to the subject. He was told, however, that his opponent would receive the feedback through a headphone, that is, dichotically, with negative feedback to one ear and positive feedback to the other. After the subject had familiarized himself with the apparatus and was given an opportunity to ask clarifying questions, the experimenter addressed the other experimenter in the adjacent room over an intercom to determine if the opponent was ready to play the game. The other experimenter explained that the subject's opponent was not ready and that he still needed to spend some time learning strategy. Both experimenters then decided to utilize the time and have the subject now perform one of the tasks scheduled for later. The other experimenter was to conduct this part of the investigation. Since he was to apply the provocation treatment, he will from here on be referred to as the "hostile experimenter."

As the polite experimenter left, the hostile experimenter arrived and presented tape-recorded instructions. He was uninformed about the experimental condition the subject would be placed in. It was explained that the upcoming task was an auditory acuity test. The subject would, through headphones, be hearing a message composed of music and a speech. The subject was informed that he was to press a button whenever he heard any extraneous animal noises that had been added at various places. Examples of the different types of noises were included in the instructions. It was explained that the noises to be heard varied in intensity from quite loud to quite faint. After turning off the tape recorder, the experimenter, not allowing any questions for clarification, told the subject to put on his headphones. The experimenter's manner of interacting with the subject was curt and very harsh throughout the experimental session. The hostile experimenter then administered the acuity test. The tape which the subjects heard contained five loud and seven very faint extraneous noises. After playing the tape, the experimenter looked down at the event recorder and, regardless of the subject's performance, stated rather contemptuously that the subject had missed a great majority of the noises on the tape. He then said, "Let's try it again, and try to pay attention this time." Any comments or protests from the subject were ignored by the experimenter. The hostile experimenter then played the tape a second time. After the second time, he again examined the event recorder, this time tearing the results from the second trial off the paper roll and throwing them in the waste basket. He muttered, "Oh, boy," shook his head in disbelief and walked out of the room and called the polite experimenter.

Upon entering the room, the polite experimenter informed the subject that his opponent was still going over the instructions, so it would be necessary to change the schedule once more and now show the televised communication and monitor his physiological responses to it. The polite experimenter then explained that another base-level reading was necessary, and obtained a set of physiological measures which actually assessed the subject's reactions to the provocation treatment. He then positioned the subject in front of a television monitor and played one of the six experimental communications. Heart rate was continuously recorded during exposure. After exposure, blood pressure readings were again obtained.

The polite experimenter then addressed the hostile experimenter over the intercom, inquiring if the opponent was ready to play the game. Upon receiving an affirmative reply, the subject began the game. The subject chose a location for his battleship. Ostensibly his opponent, but actually the hostile experimenter, administered a fixed set of trials and final hits. Informed about the ship's location, the confederate placed hits in predetermined proximities to the target. The subject administered feedback after every miss. After 25 misses, the confederate hit the target, terminating the game.

The polite experimenter then took final physiological readings and informed the subject that he had completed the main part of the experiment, but that there were still some forms to fill out. He requested that the subject evaluate the two experimenters. He explained that this evaluation was part of a new procedure that had been devised for the protection of human subjects. The procedure is detailed elsewhere (Zillmann, Bryant, Cantor, & Day, 1975). In short, it was explained that the Committee on Research Subjects (a fictitious label) requires every subject to complete a standard form for every experiment in which the subject takes part. The polite experimenter elaborated that the top half of the form related to the experiment itself and would be used by the committee as an administrative check on the experiment. The bottom half was said to deal with the experimenter who ran a study or a part of a study. The ratings made on this half of the form were purportedly to be forwarded to the experimenter's major department, and they were to be used in deciding on the coming year's financial aid to research assistants. The subject was assured that the evaluation was strictly anonymous. The forms and envelopes used in the evaluation were stamped with an official-looking rubber stamp reading "Committee on Research Subjects, 309 Bryan Hall" (this was an arbitrarily chosen room in the Research and Advanced Studies section of the Administration Building). The experimenter handed the subject two forms with the experimenters' names already written in. He also supplied envelopes. He left the room while the subject completed the evaluation forms, enclosed them in the envelopes, and placed the sealed envelopes in a ballot-type box stamped with the "Committee on Research Subjects" label. The polite experimenter finally returned to the room and dismissed the subject. All subjects were debriefed in class after the experiment had been completed.

Displaced aggressiveness. Frequency and accumulated intensity of punishing noxious noise, as negative feedback ostensibly administered to the opponent in thwarting the successful completion of the task, served as the primary measures of displaced aggressiveness. It should be noted that the opponent had in no way provoked the subject, so that any aggressiveness displayed toward him was aggressiveness toward an "inappropriate" target.

Retaliatory behavior. The subjects' evaluations of the hostile experimenter, that is, of their annoyer, constituted the measures of hostility directed against the appropriate target. Since it was explicitly stated that the evaluation of the experimenter would be used in determining his future academic and financial support as a graduate student, decisively unfavorable ratings of the hostile experimenter have to be considered attempts to produce adverse consequences for him. The subjects thus could retaliate for their having been mistreated, by bringing harm to their annoyer.

The experimenter-evaluation form contained six rating scales. The upper three dealt with the experiment as such (e.g., whether demands made were excessive in any way). Responses were to be forwarded to the Committee on Research Subjects. A dotted cutting-line separated the upper and the lower part of the form. Below the line, the evaluations concerned the experimenter himself, and it was indicated that the Committee would forward the bottom half of the form to the experimenter's major department "to aid the departments in determining stipends for research assistantships." The experimenter's name was hand-written into both the upper and lower part of the form. The first question on the bottom half read "How well did the above-named graduate student perform in his role as an experimenter?" It was answered on a bipolar scale ranging from *poorly* (−100) to *excellently* (100). The second question read "How would you rate his manner of interacting with others?" The associated scale ranged from *extremely unpleasant and discourteous* (−100) to *extremely pleasant and courteous* (100). The third and final question, which was considered to provide a most direct avenue of retaliation, read "In your opinion, should this student be reappointed as a research assistant?" The associated scale ranged from *definitely not* (−100) to *definitely yes* (100).

Sympathetic excitation. Systolic and diastolic blood pressures and heart rate were employed as the primary measures of excitation. Measures of blood pressure were taken at four times: (1) prior to instigation; (2) after instigation, and prior to communication exposure; (3) after communication exposure, and prior to the measurement of displaced aggression; and (4) prior to the measurement of retaliation. Heart rate was continuously recorded. A composite measure of sympathetic activation (Zillmann, 1971) was computed on the basis of all direct measures for all indices of excitation. Measures of ex-

citatory change were computed as the difference between a subject's base level of excitation and excitation at all other times. Additionally, change scores in the continuously recorded heart rate were determined for every minute of exposure to communication.

Apparatus. The experimental messages were presented via a Sony VO-1600 videocassette recorder on an RCA 21″ color television monitor. An especially constructed apparatus generated the buttom pulses for the signal detection test employed in the pretest. The signal patterns and the subjects' responses were recorded on a Gerbands G3360 event recorder. Blood pressure was recorded on a Sears sphygmomanometergraph. Heart rate was assessed on a Hewlett-Packard 7754A recorder. An Esterline-Angus multichannel event recorder was used to record the negative and positive feedback administered by the subject.

RESULTS

Excitatory Reactions

Excitation after provocation. The instigational treatment markedly elevated *level of excitation.* Systolic blood pressure increased by 7.3 mm of mercury, the change being associated with $F = 5.70$, $p < .025$, df $= 1,54$. Similarly, heart rate increased by 8.2 beats per minute, the change being associated with $F = 4.05$, $p < .05$, df $= 1,54$. On diastolic blood pressure, however, the effect was trivial ($F < 1$). In fact, measures of diastolic blood pressure failed to yield any reliable effects throughout the experiment (all $F < 1$), and these measures will consequently be excluded from further discussion. Results for sympathetic activation are reported in Table 2.

Excitation prior to displaced aggressiveness. Whereas differences in *excitation* between communication conditions were trivial both for base-level measures and for measures after provocation ($F < 1$ on all indices), exposure to communication resulted in pronouncedly different excitatory changes. Changes were highly consistent across the various indices of *excitation.* Only the composite

TABLE 2
Mean Difference Scores of Sympathetic Activation at Various
Critical Times

Communication	Time of measurement		
	After provocation	Before displaced aggressiveness	Before retaliation
Monotonous stimulus	$1214^{a,C}$	$624^{d,B}$	$309^{c,A}$
Nature film	$1294^{a,B}$	$267^{c,A}$	$183^{bc,A}$
Comedy show	$1299^{a,B}$	$-291^{ab,A}$	$-56^{ab,A}$
Nonaggressive sport	$1225^{a,B}$	$-167^{b,A}$	$-70^{a,A}$
Quiz show	$1218^{a,C}$	$-462^{a,A}$	$-200^{a,B}$
Aggressive sport	$1269^{a,C}$	$531^{d,B}$	$253^{c,A}$

Note. The simple main effect immediately after instigation was nonsignificant ($F<1$). Prior to the measurement of displaced aggression, the effect yielded $F(5,54)=20.79$, $p<.001$. Prior to the measurement of retaliation, it yielded $F(5,54)=4.29$, $p<.005$. Vertical comparisons are reported in lower-case superscripts. Means having no letter in their superscripts in common differ significantly at $p<.05$ by Cochran's method. Horizontal comparisons are reported in upper-case superscripts. Means having different superscripts differ significantly at $p<.05$ by Newman-Keuls' test.

measure of *sympathetic activation* will therefore be reported. As can be seen from Table 2, the effect of exposure to messages which differed in intervention potential was substantial. First, it should be noted that *sympathetic activation*, which had been elevated by the earlier instigation experience, *declined* during the 10-minute exposure period *in all communication conditions*. The impact of the monotonous stimulus was the least pronounced. Exposure to the aggressive sports event, in spite of the message's high intervention potential, produced a very similar effect. The nature film reduced *excitation* to a greater extent. However, exposure to either one of these messages tended to perpetuate *excitation*, maintaining *sympathetic activation* above base level. In contrast, exposure to the highly absorbing quiz show brought about a substantial decrement in *sympathetic activation,* ultimately yielding levels that were markedly below the basal measures. Also yielding mean scores of *sympathetic activation* below base levels, but somewhat higher than those associated with the quiz show, were the nonaggressive sport event and the comedy show. In spite of the dramatic difference in content (serious vs. humorous), these similarly involving messages yielded similar effects.

The analysis of the minute-by-minute changes in heart rate during communication exposure revealed that decay was approximately linear in all conditions. In the first minute of exposure, heart rate dropped somewhat more sharply than at all later times, but the more pronounced drop during the quiz show, the comedy show, and the nonaggressive sport event were already in evidence.

As can be seen from Tables 1 and 2, the relationship between a messages intervention potential and its mediating effect on the decay of prevailing *excitation*, in general, is proportional: The higher the intervention potential, the more rapid and effective the decay of *sympathetic excitation* deriving from pre-exposure experiences. The exception to this rule is evident in the aggressive-sport condition. The message featuring the aggressive sport event had proved highly absorbing, yet exposure to it failed to reduce excitation accordingly. Its intervention effect is comparable to that of the minimally involving, monotonous stimulus. This deviant effect is, of course, as anticipated from the reiteration rationale (Zillmann & Johnson, 1973) which projects the failure of effective intervention when message contents are closely related to the pre-exposure experiential state.

Excitation prior to retaliation. As can be seen from Table 2, the performance of aggressive activities directed toward the opponent who had done the subject no harm did not entirely eradicate the differentiation in *sympathetic excitation* observed after exposure to communication. Although most conditions show a regression toward the baseline, *excitation* is still significantly differentiated as a function of exposure to communication. Prior to *retaliation*, *level of excitation* in the quiz-show, non-aggressive-sport, and comedy-show conditions was still markedly below that in the aggressive-sport, monotonous-stimulus, and nature-film conditions.

Displaced Aggressiveness

Exposure to communication produced significant effects on *displaced aggression.* The analysis of the frequency of negative feedback—that is, the administration of noxious noise—yielded a significant differentiation ($F=2.59$; $p<.05$; df=5,54). The distribution of means is displayed in Table 3. As can be seen, *displaced aggressiveness* after exposure to the nature film and the aggressive sport event, in spite of the latter communication's high general intervention potential, was at comparable levels. After exposure to the nature film, the comedy show, and the nonaggressive sport event, it was slightly but not reliably lower. After exposure to the highly absorbing quiz show, however, *displaced aggressiveness* was significantly below the levels associated with the minimally involving, monotonous stimulus and the aggressive sport event.

The communication effect on the accumulated intensity of *negative feedback* ($F=2.68$; $p<.05$; df=5,54) was highly redundant with that on the frequency of its use. The analysis of the accumulated intensity of *positive feedback* produced the inverse pattern of means. The differentiation was

again quite redundant, but it was not entirely reliable ($F=2.38$; $p<.10$; df=5,54).

The comparison of *level of excitation* prior to the performance of aggressive activities with level of *displaced aggressiveness* shows a close correspondence. To determine the extent to which the variation in *level of excitation* can account for the variation in *displaced aggressiveness,* an analysis of covariance with *excitation* as the covariate and *aggressiveness* as the criterion was performed in order to control for the differences in excitation. All analyses yielded $F<1$, attesting to the aggression-mediating function of excitation.

Retaliatory Behavior

On the most direct measure of *retaliation,* the subject's recommendation of the hostile experimenter's reappointment, that is, his verdict concerning merit or lack thereof of the experimenter's renewed support as a research assistant (the final question on the evaluation form), a highly significant effect was obtained ($F=3.93$; $p<.005$; df=5,54). The distribution of means is shown in Table 3. As can be seen, the pattern is the same as that of *displaced aggressiveness* detailed earlier. The evaluation of the experimenter's courtesy or lack thereof produced totally redundant results ($F=3.25$; $p<.025$; df=5,54; differentiation of means exactly as reported in Table 3 for recommended reappointment). The evaluation of the experimenter's general performance, while also redundant, only approached significance, however ($F=2.31$; $p<.10$; df=5,54).

Analogous to the treatment of the measures of *displaced aggressiveness,* the measures of *retaliatory behavior* were subjected to the analysis of covariance with *level of excitation* prior to the performance of retaliatory acts as a covariate. Thus controlling for differences in level of excitation, all effects significant in the analysis of variance were again removed. This again attests to the mediating function of *excitation* in hostile behaviors.

It is conceivable that the subjects' engagement in the competitive game, by providing them with an opportunity to "act out" their annoyance, partly as a function of exposure to communication, intro-

TABLE 3
Differentiation of Mean Scores Indexing Displaced Aggressiveness and
Retaliatory Behavior

Response	Communication					
	Monotonous stimulus	Nature film	Comedy show	Nonaggressive sport	Quiz show	Aggressive sport
Displaced aggressiveness	14^b	13^{ab}	11^{ab}	10^{ab}	8^a	14^b
Retaliatory behavior	-12^b	14^{ab}	37^{ab}	35^{ab}	61^a	-10^b

Note. The frequency of noxious noise ostensibly administered to an opponent who had brought no harm to the annoyed subject is the reported measure of displaced aggressiveness. The recommendation of a hostile experimenter's reappointment as a research assistant is the reported measure of retaliatory behavior. Means having no letter in their superscripts in common differ at $p < .05$ by Newman-Keuls' test.

duced a bias in their inclination to retaliate against their annoyer. To guard against such possible bias, *displaced aggressiveness* was controlled by covariation. Analyses of covariance were performed on the reappointment measure of *retaliation*, with frequency of *negative feedback* and the accumulated intensity of *negative* and of *positive feedback* as covariates. In these analyses, the impact of exposure to communication appeared somewhat weaker. Statistically speaking, however, effects were not altered (all F ratios were associated with $p < .025$). The pattern of means also remained essentially the same.

DISCUSSION

Exposure to Communication and
Excitatory Reactions

The findings show quite unequivocally that the reduction of the aggressively instigated individual's sympathetic activity is determined by the degree to which subsequent exposure to communication proves involving and absorbing. More specifically, the acutely annoyed and angry person will experience a more complete alleviation from his state of arousal, (1) the higher the general intervention potential of communication, and (2) the less its contents relate to the experience of annoyance and anger. As predicted from the intervention rationale developed earlier, postexposure *levels of excitation* were found to vary inversely with the intervention potential of communication which did not entail the provocation-retaliation motif. Also as predicted from the intervention rationale, exposure to hostile and aggressive fare failed to reduce *level of excitation* as would be expected on the basis of the message's general intervention potential alone. The findings thus lend strong support to this rationale.

As long as the deviant effect of the message featuring aggressive events is disregarded, Bandura's (1965) suggestions concerning attentional shifts are also borne out by the excitatory changes observed. It is the fact that the aggression-depicting communication proved highly involving under different motivational circumstances, but failed to promote the decay of *excitation* in the annoyed subjects, presumably because it reinstated their annoyance, which makes these suggestions untenable and demands the qualification expressed in the intervention rationale.

Displaced Aggressiveness

The findings demonstrate that the annoyed individual's exposure to communication can affect his inclination to act out his annoyance in aggressing against a target other than his annoyer. It should be noted that, in the present investigation, the inappropriate target was in no way affiliated with the annoyer, but that their working together (i.e., the hostile experimenter's efforts at teaching the opponent a superior offensive strategy) may have established an association which favored the displacement of aggressiveness. It is thus conceivable that the reported displacement effects are restricted to conditions under which such or similar associations between the appropriate and the inappropriate target exist.

The data show that relatively uninvolving messages (presumably because they fail to disrupt the individual's brooding over a mistreatment) and generally involving messages which feature aggression, (presumably because they reinstate aspects of the mistreatment), tend to perpetuate the annoyance-induced *level of excitation,* which in turn fosters more intense aggressive reactions. The data also show that highly absorbing messages which do not entail aggressive actions tend to alleviate the individual from the pre-exposure experience of annoyance, presumably because they effectively intervene in and disrupt the cognitive preoccupation with the annoyance, and consequently reduce the intensity of aggressive activities. The results show displaced aggressiveness to be a simple function of the apparently cognitively mediated level of *sympathetic excitation* after exposure to communication. Sympathetic arousal can thus be viewed as simply having "energized" the *displaced aggressive* reactions performed (cf. Tannenbaum & Zillmann, 1975).

Retaliatory Behavior

The findings also demonstrate that the provoked individual's exposure to communication can substantially alter his *retaliatory behavior.* The mediational process is exactly the same as described above. Differential levels of retaliatory action result from the differential reduction of annoyance-produced *excitation,* with involving and nonaggressive communications effecting a greater alleviation than noninvolving and/or aggressive communications. A distinct difference in reasoning concerns the appropriateness of the target for hostile action. Unlike in the displacement of aggressive activities, the subject's postcommunication reconfrontation with his annoyer reinstates the experience of anger which is attributed to the annoyer, making him not only the appropriate, but also a deserving target for compensatory action (Zillmann, 1971).

It is likely that communication-specific effects on *retaliation* would have been more pronounced in the present investigation if the subject would have been provided with an opportunity to retaliate immediately after exposure to communication. At this time, *sympathetic excitation* was more strongly differentiated than later at the time of *retaliation.* Interestingly, the subject's performance of *displaced aggressive* acts failed to entirely eradicate the differentiation. Given the observed differences in *displaced aggressiveness*, this means that, in the acutely annoyed subjects, the displacement of aggression removed neither the state of elevated *excitation* nor the inclination to retaliate.

Facilitation vs. Reduction of Hostility and Aggression

If data from only some conditions of the present experiment are selected, the often-reported "aggression-facilitating" effect of exposure to aggressive content may be considered to have been replicated. As discussed earlier, the typical media-aggression experiment has involved a "neutral" vs. an aggressive communication. The so-called neutral stimuli have often been "travelogues" or clips from educational or documentary films. Although empirical verification is lacking, these films have probably been somewhat more involving than the extensively edited nature film used in the present investigation. Employing the terminology of this study, the neutral films probably were associated with moderate intervention potential. If the conditions involving moderately to highly absorbing communications are compared to the condition involving aggressive events, it would appear that exposure to aggressive fare facilitated hostile and aggressive behavior. This finding could be interpreted as supporting Berkowitz' (1965) reasoning on aggression-eliciting cues. However, by including in this comparison the effect obtained in the monotonous-stimulus condition—a condition which can be considered to approximate a truly "neutral" stimulus more closely—it becomes apparent that the impact of exposure to communication is not one of facilitation of hostile and aggressive behavior, but rather one of a differential reduction. Additionally, it should be noted that exposure to all messages employed effected an alleviation of arousal, and that hostile and aggressive behavior probably would have been more intense, had it been enacted immediately after provocation. These findings essentially replicate those reported by Zillmann and Johnson (1973).

The Effect of Humorous Communication

The results of the present investigation fail to support Baron and Ball's (1974) proposition that humorous stimuli, by eliciting an emotional state incompatible with anger, inhibit aggressive behavior. The comedy show employed was rated as significantly more humorous than the nonaggressive sport event. Yet on no measure of *displaced aggressiveness* or *retaliation* did the humorous communication produce less aggressiveness or less hostility than the nonhumorous but equally absorbing communication. Apparently, humorous messages have no unique aggression-reducing properties. Their effect is adequately accounted for by considering their intervention potential. It is, however, quite possible

that humorous materials are generally effective in reducing aggressiveness and hostility. The data on hand suggest that, if this is indeed the case, it may be so because humorous materials are generally very absorbing.

Evidence for Salutary Communication Effects

The findings of the present investigation offer support for the notion that involving messages can effect a decisive reduction of hostile and aggressive behavior which serves retaliation, or which is displaced onto alternative targets. The aggression-reducing effect of any particular message is, of course, relative to that of other messages. It is largely unclear how activities other than exposure to communication would affect the behavior in question. It may well be that sitting quietly, washing the dishes, playing cards, etc., have a more beneficial effect than watching a television program for the same period of time. The present investigation did not include such "no-communication" controls. This means that generalizations from the present investigation are restricted to the relative effects of communications with certain intervention potentials. Within these limits, however, it is apparent that involving and absorbing, but nonaggressive, communications have a more beneficial effect than boring or aggressive ones.

By suggesting salutary effects of exposure to communication, the present investigation points up a new direction for future research on the effect of aggressive communication. It appears that investigators have been preoccupied with the demonstration of negative effects of media exposure. They have made every effort to delineate what could further hostility and aggressiveness. The present investigation's concern with communication intervention potential reverses this emphasis, making it equally important to delineate those properties of communications which create involvement, which absorb the viewer (or the listener and the reader), which disrupt the individual's rumination in the aggravations and annoyances he has suffered through the day, and which ultimately alleviate his tensions and his hostile and aggressive inclinations. One hopes such a new orientation will help to uncover the elements of entertainment which can produce beneficial effects, and one hopes it will promote a view of media effects less one-sided than that which seems to dominate at this time.

NOTE

1. This research was supported by Grants GSOC-7205471 and SOC75-13431 from the National Science Foundation.

REFERENCES

BANDURA, A. Vicarious processes: A case of no-trial learning. In L. Berkowitz (Ed.), *Advances in experimental social psychology*. Vol. 2. New York: Academic Press, 1965.

BARON, R.A., & BALL, R.L. The aggression-inhibiting influence of nonhostile humor. *Journal of Experimental Social Psychology*, 1974, 10, 23-33.

BERELSON, B. What missing the newspaper means. In P. Lazarfeld and F. Stanton (Eds.), *Communications Research, 1948-1949*. New York: Harper, 1949.

BERKOWITZ, L. The concept of aggressive drive: Some additional considerations. In L. Berkowitz (Ed.), *Advances in experimental social psychology*. Vol. 2. New York: Academic Press, 1965.

BERKOWITZ, L. The frustration-aggression hypothesis revisited. In L. Berkowitz (Ed.), *Roots of aggression: A reexamination of the frustration-aggression hypothesis*. New York: Atherton, 1969.

BERKOWITZ, L. The contagion of violence: An S-R mediational analysis of some effects of observed aggression. In W.J. Arnold and M.M. Page (Eds.), *Nebraska symposium on motivation*. Lincoln, Nebraska: University of Nebraska Press, 1970.

BERKOWITZ, L. Some determinants of impulsive aggression: Role of mediated associations with reinforcements for aggression. *Psychological Review*, 1974, 81, 165-176.

BROADBENT, D.E., & GREGORY, M. On the recall of stimuli presented alternatively to two sense-organs. *Quarterly Journal of Experimental Psychology*, 1961, 13, 103-109.

GORANSON, R.E. Media violence and aggressive behavior: A review of experimental research. In L. Berkowitz (Ed.), *Advances in experimental social psychology*. Vol. 5. New York: Academic Press, 1970.

GREENBERG, B.S. Gratifications of television viewing and their correlates for British children. In J.G. Blumler and E. Katz (Eds.) *The uses of mass communications: Current perspectives on gratifications research*. Beverly Hills: Sage, 1974.

LAZARUS, R.S. *Psychological stress and the coping process*. New York: McGraw-Hill, 1966.

JERISON, H.J. Vigilance, discrimination, and attention. In D.A. Mostotsky (Ed.), *Attention: Contemporary theory and analysis*. New York: Appleton-Century-Crofts, 1970.

MACKWORTH, J.F. *Vigilance and habituation*. Baltimore: Penguin, 1969.

MENDELSOHN, H. Listening to radio. In L.A. Dexter and D.M. White (Eds.), *People, Society and Mass Communications*. New York: Free Press, 1964.

NORMAN, D.A. *Memory and attention*. New York: Wiley, 1969.

PETERSON, L.R., & PETERSON, M.J. Short-term retention of individual verbal items. *Journal of Experimental Psychology*, 1959, 58, 193-198.

SCHACHTER, S. The interaction of cognitive and physiological determinants of emotional state. In L. Berkowitz (Ed.), *Advances in experimental social psychology*, Vol. 1, New York: Academic Press, 1964.

SCHACHTER, S. *Emotion, Obesity, and Crime*. New York: Academic Press, 1971.

STEINER, G. *The people look at television*. New York: Alfred Knopf, 1963.

TANNENBAUM, P.H., & ZILLMANN, D. Emotional arousal in the facilitation of aggression through communication. In L. Berkowitz (Ed.), *Advances in experimental social psychology*. Vol. 8. New York: Academic Press, 1975.

WAPLES, D., BERELSON, B., & BRADSHAW, F.R. What reading does to people. Chicago: University of Chicago Press, 1940.

WAUGH, N.C., & NORMAN, D.A. The measure of interference in primary memory. *Journal of Verbal Learning and Verbal Behavior*, 1968, 7, 617-626.

WEISS, W. Effects of the mass media of communication. In G. Lindsey and E. Aronson (Eds.), *Handbook of social psychology*. Vol. 5. Reading, Massachusetts: Addison-Wesley, 1969.

ZILLMANN, D. Excitation transfer in communication-mediated aggressive behavior. *Journal of Experimental Social Psychology*, 1971, 7, 419-434.

ZILLMANN, D. The role of excitation in aggressive behavior. In *Proceedings of the Seventeenth International Congress of Applied Psychology, 1971*. Brussels: Editest, 1972.

ZILLMANN, D., & BRYANT, J. The effect of residual excitation on the emotional response to provocation and delayed aggressive behavior. *Journal of Personality and Social Psychology*, 1974, 30, 782-791.

ZILLMANN, D., BRYANT, J., CANTOR, J.R., & DAY, K.D. Irrelevance of mitigating circumstances in retaliatory behavior at high levels of excitation, *Journal of Research in Personality*, 1975, 9, 282-293.

ZILLMANN, D., & JOHNSON, R.C. Motivated aggressiveness perpetuated by exposure to aggressive films and reduced by exposure to nonaggressive films. *Journal of Experimental Research in Personality*, 1973, 7, 261-276.

A CORRELATION ANALYSIS OF INTERNATIONAL NEWSPAPER COVERAGE AND INTERNATIONAL ECONOMIC, COMMUNICATION, AND DEMOGRAPHIC RELATIONSHIPS

ANDRÉ J. DE VERNEIL
Ohio University

This study attempts to develop a general theory about the relationship between the extent of international news coverage and the level of international economic and communication relations in various countries. The study further attempts to apply this model to individual nations by correlating their patterns of international news reporting with their patterns of international economic, communication, and demographic relationships. Results do not indicate a correlation between amounts of international news coverage and the trade and communication variables. Findings indicate that, on the global level, international news reporting is not uniformly related to other international activities. The reasons for this are traced to four contrasting interaction patterns operating within individual nations.

Studies of international news diffusion have either been descriptive of news flow or have analyzed flow in terms of the *gatekeeper* concept, which basically involved intrapersonal variables. The present study views international communications as part of a larger system of international relations. Communications systems are part of a larger system of interactions. Indeed, all social interactions could be looked upon as communication.

The study explores patterns of economic, demographic, and communication relations between countries. It seeks to test the theory that these patterns of relations are significantly correlated with the patterns of news coverage among these countries. This interaction approach benefits from its attempt to integrate international communications into a larger system of international relations. And in integrating the two, a more parsimonious description is achieved.

The study examined international news coverage on two levels. The first level attempted to develop a general theory about the overall relationship between the extent of countries' international news coverage and the extent of their other international relations.

The second level of this study fulfilled two objectives. First, it attempted to confirm the general theory by testing its applicability to 15 countries tested separately. Second, patterns of relationships among the variables which were manifested by various countries were investigated.

Economic Variables Used to Predict International Information Flow

Hester (1973) suggested the utilization of economic, political, cultural, and historical variables to predict international information flows. Of these, only the economic variable, international trade, was readily quantifiable and had appropriate data available.

Only one study actually tried to predict international news coverage from other variables. Dupree (1971) sought to predict the number of articles appearing in the newsmagazine *Atlas* by using a stepwise multiple regression analysis involving 11 independent variables. The findings of his study can be summarized by giving the resulting ranking of the 11 variables: (1) foreign stock residing in the United States, (2) gross national product per capita, (3) population, (4) language "translatability," (5) literacy rate, (6) newspapers available, (7) import/export volume, (8) distance from United States, (9) gross national product,

(10) population density per square kilometer, and (11) continent.

Communication Variables Used to Predict International Information Flow

While making a distinction between *organization media* and *information media,* Cherry (1971) implicitly presented a model relating the two by way of their mutual relation to economic development. By *organization media,* Cherry meant telegraph, telephone, and telex. The *information media* are radio, newspapers, television, and cinema.

In the present study, *organization media* development preceeds industrial development, which in turn preceeds *information media* development. Cherry's (1971) model supported this study's use of an economic trade variable and *organization media* variables in trying to study one of the international *information medium's* flows—international news coverage.

Demographic Variables Used to Predict International Information Flow

Four articles supported the applicability of a demographic variable in predicting international news flow. MacLean and Pinna (1958) found a significant correlation between *physical distance* and *news interest.* Rosengren (1970) pointed out that the more distant an event, the less important it seemed. And, Liu and Gunaratne (1972) found neighboring countries accounted for most of the international news coverage. Zipf (1953), using population and distance data, found that the demographic energy ratio, P_1P_2/d, determined the circulation of information between two points.

HYPOTHESES

Based on the foregoing, the following hypotheses were advanced.

H_{1a}: A significant positive correlation exists between the relative importance of international news in countries' newspapers and the relative importance of import trade in their economies.

H_{1b}: A significant positive correlation exists between the relative importance of international news in countries' newspapers and the relative importance of foreign mail in their mail traffic.

H_{1c}: A significant positive correlation exists between the relative importance of international news in countries' newspapers and the relative importance of foreign telegrams in their telegram traffic.

H_{1d}: A significant positive correlation exists between the relative importance of international news in countries' newspapers and the relative importance of foreign telephone calls in their telephone traffic.

H_{2a}: A significant positive correlation exists between the proportion a country's newspaper "news hole" devoted to other countries and the proportion of its import trade which is with these other countries.

H_{2b}: A significant positive correlation exists between the proportion a country's newspaper "news hole" devoted to other countries and the proportion of its total number of leased full-time foreign INTELSAT half-circuits which are to these other countries.

H_{2c}: A significant positive correlation exists between the proportion a country's newspaper "news hole" devoted to other countries and the demographic energy ratios between this country and the other countries.

Table 1 presents an outline of the dependent and independent variables and statistical analyses for the study's two levels of hypotheses.

METHODOLOGY

Operational Definitions

1. *The relative importance of international news in countries' newspapers* was measured as the proportion of sampled newspapers' "news holes" which were devoted to international news. This variable is referred to as *international news interest.*

TABLE 1
Schema of the Hypotheses and Their Analysis

Linear, Quadratic, and Cubic Correlations--

35 Countries Combined

Hypotheses	Dependent Variable	Independent Variable
H_{1a}	International News Interest	Importance of Imports
H_{1b}	International News Interest	Importance of International Mail
H_{1c}	International News Interest	Importance of International Telegrams
H_{1d}	International News Interest	Importance of International Telephone Calls

Linear Correlation and Stepwise Multiple Correlation--

15 Countries on a Country-by-Country Basis

Hypotheses	Dependent Variable	Independent Variable
H_{2a}	News Interest in Other Countries	Trading Interest in Other Countries
H_{2b}	News Interest in Other Countries	INTELSAT Circuits with Other Countries
H_{2c}	News Interest in Other Countries	Demographic Energy

2. *The relative importance of import trade in their economies* was measured as the proportion of a country's gross domestic product which was spent on foreign commodity imports. This variable is referred to as the *importance of imports* for various countries.

3. *The relative importance of foreign mail in their mail traffic* was measured as the proportion of the total number of mail items handled by a country's postal system, inclusive of domestic mail, foreign mail received, and mail sent overseas, which was accounted for by the number of foreign mail items received. This variable is shortened to the *importance of international mail.*

4. To understand *the relative importance of foreign*

telegrams in their telegram traffic, a short preface must first be given. Data on countries' foreign telegrams received were lacking, but statistics reporting foreign telegrams sent were recorded. Assuming that countries' incoming and outgoing communication flows are closely balanced, the data reporting the number of foreign telegrams sent can also be used as an estimate of the number of foreign telegrams received.[1]

Thus, *the relative importance of foreign telegrams in their telegram traffic* was measured as the proportion of a country's total number of telegrams which were accounted for by the number of foreign telegrams sent. A country's total number of telegrams was estimated by adding the number of domestic telegrams and twice the number of foreign telegrams sent. This variable is referred to as the *importance of international telegrams* for various countries.

5. Because data on foreign telephone calls received were lacking, it was assumed that the number of foreign telephone calls originated closely approximated the number of foreign telephone calls received. Thus, *the relative importance of foreign telephone calls in their telephone traffic* was measured as the proportion of a country's total number of telephone calls. This was indicated by the number of all domestic telephone calls plus twice the number of foreign telephone calls originated by that country. This variable is called the *importance of international telephone calls* for various countries.

6. *The proportion a country's newspaper international "news holes" devoted to other countries* was measured as the proportion of a country's newspapers, international news coverage which was accounted for by news from each of 37 countries. These 37 countries were the same 35 countries whose newspapers were measured, plus New Zealand and Colombia. This variable is called the country's *news interest* in other countries.

the country's *news interest* in other countries.

7. *The proportion of its import trade which is with other countries* was measured as the proportion of a country's import trade which was accounted for by the value of its import trade with each of 37 countries. This variable is called one country's *trading interest* in other countries.

8. *The proportion of its total number of leased full-time foreign INTELSAT half-circuits which are to other countries* was measured as the proportion of a country's number of full-time foreign INTELSAT half-circuits which was accounted for by the number of foreign INTELSAT half-circuits which each of 37 countries. This variable is shortened to *INTELSAT circuits* with other countries.

9. *The demographic energy ratios between this country and other countries* means the 36 separate ratios of the cross product of the populations of the original country, and each of the 36 other countries, to the distance between the cities of

publication of the newspapers representing these countries, i.e., P_1P_2 / d.

NEWSPAPER SELECTION

The first step in the selection of newspapers for this study was to determine which newspapers would best represent their respective countries. This was done by first checking Merrill's (1968, p. 45) list of elite newspapers. From this search, the following 17 newspapers were selected: Primary elite—*ABC* (Madrid, Spain), *Le Monde* (Paris, France), *Neue Zurcher Zeitung* (Zurich, Switzerland), the *New York Times* (New York, United States), the *Times* (London, United Kingdom); Secondary elite—*Corriere della Sera* (Milan, Italy), *O Estado de Sao Paulo* (Sao Paulo, Brazil), *Excelsior* (Mexico City, Mexico), *Frankfurter Allgemeine* (Frankfurt, West Germany), the *Globe and Mail* (Toronto, Canada), *La Prensa* (Bueno Aires, Argentina); Tertiary elite—the *Hindu* (Madras, India), *Le Soir* (Brussels, Belgium); Near elite—*Cape Times* (Cape Town, South Africa), *El Comercio* (Lima, Peru), *Manila Times* (Manila, Philippines), *El Mercurio* (Santiago, Chile).

Because a larger sample size was desirable to improve the sensitivity of the statistical tests, a second phase of the newspaper selection chose 18 more newspapers published in countries not previously selected. These newspapers were selected from Merrill, Bryan, and Alisky's (1970) *The Foreign Press*, choosing newspapers which they highly regarded: *Bangkok Post* (Bangkok, Thailand), the *Daily Gleaner* (Kingston, Jamaica), *Daily Times* (Lagos, Nigeria), *Dawn* (Karachi, Pakistan), *East African Standard* (Nairobi, Kenya), *Egyptian Gazette* (Cairo, Egypt), *La Estrella de Panama* (Panama City, Panama), *Guardian* (Rangoon, Burma), *Indonesian Observer* (Djakarta, Indonesia), *Irish Times* (Dublin, Ireland), *Japan Times* (Tokyo, Japan), *Jerusalem Post* (Jerusalem, Israel), *Korea Times* (Seoul, Korea), *La Prensa* (Managua, Nicaragua), *La Prensa Libre* (San Jose, Costa Rica), *O Seculo* (Lisbon, Portugal), *South China Morning Post* (Hong Kong), *Sydney Morning Herald* (Sydney, Australia).

The second aspect of the newspaper selection was to determine the number of issues to be sampled and the specific days to be studied. Based on work by Stempel (1952), it was determined that 12 issues of each of the 35 newspapers would provide an adequate sample size.

The year 1972 was chosen as the sample year because it was the most recent year for which widely comparable data were available. It was decided to construct two composite weeks to represent 1972, using a table of random numbers to select months and dates.

The days selected were as follows: Monday—April 1 and May 8; Tuesday—February 29 and July 4; Wednesday—May 3 and August 2; Thursday—April 6 and July 27; Friday—May 5 and November 3; Saturday—July 1 and July 22.

Newspaper Measurement

According to the given definitions, the types of news which were measured fell generally into the category of *hard news,* i.e., politics, economics, social welfare, science, and major events.

With few exceptions, the country of origin of a newspaper article was determined by the article's dateline. Some articles had datelines from international centers and were not about the country where the articles were filed. Examples would be the OPEC Ministers' meeting in Vienna or Paris, or the SALT talks in Geneva. Such articles were classified as *international.* International news entered into the calculations of the proportions used in the hypotheses, but was not attributed to a particular country. In addition, this *international* category contained news from countries not included in the review of news from 37 specific countries. The hypotheses also required that all domestic news be recorded. In summary, each newspaper article was placed in one of 37 country categories, the *international* category, or the domestic category.

Content was measured in column-inches. The column-inch totals for each of the categories were converted to the proportions appropriate to the hypotheses. It was necessary to use proportionate measures owing to the variable lengths of newspapers and to the variable page dimensions. A raw score of column-inches would be biased in favor of the larger newspapers. In effect, raw score measures would measure, in part, the size of the newspa-

pers rather than the comparative importance newspapers placed on various sources of news.

Measures for the Independent Variables

The hypotheses required that the data for the independent variables also be expressed in proportions. The raw scores would be measuring economic development or communication development. In order to eliminate national development as a factor, proportions were utilized. Additionally, the hypotheses were formulated in terms of the relative importance countries placed upon dealings with other countries. It was thought relative importance was better measured by proportions than by raw data.

Sources

The materials needed to accomplish this study were basically the sources of data for each of the dependent and independent variables. The newspapers from which the newspaper data were derived were available either from Ohio University's library, or from the Center for Research Libraries' collection. The needed foreign trade statistics were available in the *United Nations Yearbook of International Trade Statistics 1974* and the *United Nations Yearbook of National Accounts Statistics 1974, Volume III.*

Needed statistics concerning international mail traffic were available in the *United Nations Statistical Yearbook 1974.* Data on international telegram and international telephone traffic were published in *Telecommunication Statistics.* The number of INTELSAT full-time half-circuits each member country leased was available in the monthly INTELSAT publication *System Status Report*[2]. Data on countries' populations were also recorded in *Telecommunication Statistics.* The air distances between cities were available in the publication *Air Tariff*[3] and in *The Odyssey World Atlas.*

Statistical Analyses

To a large extent, the shape of this study's statistical analyses was determined by the research goals embodied in the hypotheses' two levels, and by the available data. For each of the first level hypotheses, linear, second degree curvilinear, and third degree curvilinear correlation analyses were conducted to see which best fitted the situation. The computer subprogram REGRESSION, contained in the *Statistical Package for the Social Sciences,* was used to calculate the statistical tests called for in the first set of hypotheses.

Only linear correlations were used in testing the three hypotheses at the second level. Because it tried to analyze countries' situations in greater detail, this second set of hypotheses was tested by simultaneously calculating the linear correlations among the dependent and the three independent variables for each country, thereby producing a 4-by-4 intercorrelation matrix for each country. This procedure showed how strongly the independent variables correlated with the dependent variable and among themselves. To further determine the relative importance of the independent variables' importance, a stepwise multiple-correlation was computed for each of the 15 countries in this second hypothesis set.

Because the separate testing of all of the 35 countries included in the first set of hypotheses was thought to be a repetitive and time-consuming task of marginal usefulness, it was decided to select 15 countries on the basis of the range of their economic development and geographic locations. The 15 countries selected to test the second set of hypotheses were: Argentina, Australia, Brazil, Canada, Egypt, India, Israel, Japan, Kenya, Mexico, Nigeria, Thailand, United Kingdom, United States, and West Germany.

The Statistical Package for the Social Sciences' subprogram PEARSON CORR was used to calculate the matrices of *Pearson product-moment r* intercorrelations; the subprogram REGRESSION was used to compute the stepwise multiple correlations.

RESULTS OF THE STUDY

Hypothesis 1a

The *r* coefficient derived from the Pearson product-moment correlation analysis was 0.1932, which was not significant at the .05 level. The second degree polynomial addition to the correlation analysis afforded an improvement of only $F=0.0420$. Likewise, the addition of this second power did not make the overall quadratic correlation significant, producing an F-value of only 0.6422. At this stage, the addition of the third degree polynomial only added an F-value of 0.0400 to the previous step. And the overall F-value of the cubic correlation fell to 0.4197. The phenomenon of a decreasing F-value of overall significance, even though more variance was accounted for by each step, was due to the fact that the subprogram REGRESSION charged a degree of freedom for each step of the analysis. In all three degrees, the first hypothesis of the first set was not supported.

Hypothesis 1b

The linear correlation analysis yielded an *r* coefficient of only 0.1207, which was not significant at the .05 level. The amount of additional variance accounted for by the use of the second degree polynomial was an F-value of only 0.4038, which was not significant. The addition of the third degree polynomial accounted for a much larger amount of variance than did the previous two degrees, but it still did not produce a significant improvement over the previous two degrees. Its addition improved the third degree correlation's accounting for variance by an F-value of 2.2300. But this step still left the third degree polynomial not significant, with an overall F-value of 1.0235.

Hypothesis 1c

The *r* coefficient calculated by the Pearson product-moment correlation analysis was 0.0227, nowhere near significance at the .05 level. Nor did the quadratic correlation produce a significant overall result. The F-test for overall significance resulted in an F-value of 0.7166. And the quadratic correlation was not a significant improvement over the linear correlation, as measured by an F-value of 1.4170. The further calculation of the cubic correlation likewise did not produce significant results. The overall F-value for this step was 0.4951, which meant an improvement of $F=0.0950$ over the quadratic correlation.

Hypothesis 1d

The first step in testing this hypothesis resulted in a Pearson *r* coefficient of 0.1150, which was not significant at the .05 level. The second step in testing this hypothesis was to calculate a second degree polynomial correlation. This procedure produced an improvement over the simple *r* coefficient of F 0.5900, which was not significant. The F-test of overall significance of this second step resulted in an F-value of 0.4266, also not significant. The third degree polynomial correlation produced an improvement over the second degree of F=1.5080, which was not significant. The F-test of the overall significance of this third step produced an F-value of 0.7947, again not significant.

By way of summarizing the results of testing the first set of hypotheses, one can say that none of the hypothesized relationships attained statistical significance. Indeed, none even approached significance at any of the three degrees tested.

Second Set of Hypotheses–Summary

The test results for the second set of hypotheses would indicate that *trading interest,* with 14 countries reporting significant *r* coefficients for hypothesis II-1, was the most consistently significant variable correlating with *news interest* in other countries. The second most consistent variable was *INTELSAT circuits,* with 13 countries reporting significant *r* coefficients for hypothesis II-2. Lastly, *demographic energy* significantly correlated with *news interest* nine times, which, of course, was still a majority of the time.

But in addition to knowing which variables most *consistently* correlated with *news interest* in other countries, this study sought to discover which variables most *strongly* and consistently correlated with *news interest* in other countries. This led to an examination of the order of the independent variables' entries into the stepwise multiple correlation analyses.

Although *trading interest* was the independent variable with the highest overall frequency of being significantly correlated with *news interest, INTELSAT circuits* was the best correlate because it consis-

tently had the highest frequency of first entries into the stepwise multiple correlations, and because it had the highest frequency of contributing significant improvements to the stepwise multiple correlations.

Second Set of Hypotheses–Country-by-Country Test Results

This presentation of the statistical test results for the second set of hypotheses on a country-by-country basis was influenced to a degree by an interpretation of the results. Rather than presenting the results for each of the countries in alphabetical order, this presentation organizes the 15 countries' test results according to four patterns which emerged from the stepwise multiple correlation analyses.

"Model" group. This first group of countries was called "model" because the order in which the independent variables entered into the stepwise multiple correlation exactly corresponded to the overall results obtained in testing the second set of hypotheses. This "model" group of countries— Egypt, Israel, Japan, and United Kingdom— consistently had *INTELSAT circuits* as the best correlate with *news interest.* Their second best correlate was *trading interest,* followed by *demographic energy.*

"Alternate" group. This second category contained the largest single group of countries. Its pattern of independent variables slightly differed from the "model" pattern, reversing the order of the "model's" first two independent variables. For this group, *trading interest* was the best correlate with *news interest; INTELSAT circuits* was the second best, with *demographic energy* remaining in third position. Since there could be some debate over whether *INTELSAT circuits* or *trading interest* was the best overall correlate with *news interest,* it was thought that a reversing of order between these two strong variables was not a major distortion of the "model." The countries included in this group were Australia, Canada, India, Mexico, Nigeria, and West Germany.

"Variant" group. The third group of countries manifested a pattern designated "variant," so-called because the order in which the variables entered into the stepwise multiple correlation differed from the "model" by dropping a strong overall variable, *trading interest,* to third place, while it moved the weakest overall variable, *demographic energy,* up to the second position. This was considered to be a rather drastic change in order, more so than in the "alternate" pattern. The "variant" group included Argentina, Brazil, Thailand, and the United States.

"Divergent" group. Kenya was the sole "divergent" country. While not exactly the opposite of the "model", it came close to being so. *Trading interest,* which was the second best correlate in the "model" group, was the best correlate in the "divergent" category. Likewise, the third best correlate with *news interest* in the "model" group, *demographic energy,* moved up to become the second best in this category. The sharpest difference between the "model" and "divergent" categories was the dramatic drop of *INTELSAT circuits* from a significant first rank in the "model" group to third place in the "divergent" pattern.

DISCUSSION

First Set of Hypotheses

The first set of hypotheses proposed that countries' levels of international news coverage would be significantly correlated with their levels of international trade and communication relations. These hypotheses clearly are not supported by the statistical test results. Looking at the consistent, extremely low *r* and multiple *r* coefficients for all four hypotheses, one could safely say there is no unequivocal relationship between a country's international news interest and its other international interests. Based on the results of the analyses of the first hypotheses, one might conclude that, as likely as not, a country heavily reporting international news would import relatively little trade.

Implicit in this study's use of the second and third degree curvilinear correlation analyses is the expectation that there would be various stages of growth

manifested in the independent variables' correlations with international news coverage. Quite obviously, this expectation was not fulfilled. No pattern of significant relationships were manifested, much less stages of development. Since nations are unique, their growth patterns are also unique.

Second Set of Hypotheses: Hypothesis-by-Hypothesis Discussion

In considering the second set of hypotheses, the simplest interpretation is to total the number of times each hypothesis' independent variable significantly correlated with *news interest.* This first level of analysis indicates that *trading interest* is the best correlate with *news interest,* followed by *INTELSAT circuits* and *demographic energy.*

But as a consequence of the stepwise multiple correlation findings, it was decided that overall *INTELSAT circuits* is the best correlate with *news interest,* and *trading interest* a close second, while *demographic energy* is unquestionably third.

The analyses testing the second set of hypotheses indicate that countries have patterned relations with other countries. But there is no single pattern which applies to all countries. Nevertheless, an unexpected finding of this study is that the independent variables entered into the stepwise multiple correlations in only four orders.

Four Patterns

To help in interpreting the results of this study, data were gathered concerning the subsample of 15 countries' economies, newspapers, and INTELSAT usage. These supplementary data are used to help explain the characteristics of each of this study's four patterns.

In essence, this approach implies that what the countries have in common is already determined by their membership in the group. The focus of this discussion of the findings is to see how these countries, as groups, differ from other groups by examining their supplementary data characteristics.

"Model" group. The "model" countries could be characterized as being open to the world. An integral part of their openness is the importance of

communications with the world. They publish newspapers heavily reporting international events from a relatively large number of countries. In turn, these four countries are news centers for other countries. The importance of international news for these countries is congruent with the fact that *INTELSAT circuits,* a communication variable, ranked first for this group.

The supplementary data appear to indicate that "model" countries' economies are strongly influenced by import trade. This interpretation is borne out by the strong second ranking *trading interest* had in their test results. In short, the test results and the supplementary data concur in characterizing these countries as internationally active. All four of the group's countries are newsmakers. Also, all four countries are heavily dependent on the outside world for their well-being. These countries share the quality of simultaneously being important to other countries and dependent on other countries.

"Alternate" group. The "alternate" group's supplementary data exhibit a pattern nearly the opposite of the "model" group's pattern. If one could characterize the "model" newspapers as internationally involved, the "alternate" newspapers could be characterized as domestically oriented. The economic statistics continue to be the reverse of the "model" pattern.

If the "model" countries were accurately characterized as "open to the world," then the "alternate" countries could be characterized as "closed to the world." In this "closed" situation, the communication variable, *INTELSAT circuits,* dropped in importance, and the *import trade* variable assumed primary importance. This double circumstance would seem to further indicate that *INTELSAT circuits* is the best overall correlate with *international newspaper coverage,* because it is the most important variable for those countries whose newspapers heavily report international affairs, and it drops in importance for countries whose newspapers are domestically oriented.

"Variant" group. Generally speaking, the "variant" supplementary newspaper data closely follow the "model" supplementary newspaper data. The "variant" countries present a pattern of supplementary economic data similar to the "alternate" group's pattern.

These countries publish newspapers with an international outlook, but they have economies which are not heavily dependent on imports. This evaluation is congruent with this group's placing *INTELSAT circuits,* a communication variable, as its most important independent variable, and its putting *trading interest* in last place.

"Divergent" group. Kenya, the only member of the "divergent" category, manifests once again a mix of patterns in its supplementary data. The supplementary newspaper data closely exhibit the "alternate" pattern, while the supplementary economic data manifest the "model" pattern.

Kenya publishes a domestically-oriented newspaper, but its economy is internationally dependent. These conditions probably explain why *trading interest* is its first-ranking independent variable, and why *INTELSAT circuits* is its least important independent variable.

SUMMARY

This study attempted to test the notion that nations' international relations are systematically reflected in their news coverage. It sought to explain newspapers' differing amounts of international news coverage by relating these differences to economic and communication conditions in these countries.

This study's first level of analysis attempted to develop a general theory about the overall relationship between the extent of countries' international news coverage and the extent of their other international relations. One would expect countries to maintain uniform degrees of involvement across all their international dealings. The second level attempted to apply this model to individual nations by correlating their patterns of international news reporting with their patterns of other international dealings.

The first level statistically correlated 35 countries' 1972 international news coverage quantities with their 1972 amounts of international import trade, incoming mail, telegram, and telephone traffic. This analysis used linear, quadratic, and cubic correlations to study each of the hypothesized relations.

The second level separately correlated 15 countries' coverage of 37 countries with their imports from, the number of INTELSAT circuits with, and demographic energy ratios (the cross product of their populations divided by their distance apart) with these countries. This analysis used Pearson product-moment and stepwise multiple correlation procedures to rank the importance of these three variables' correlations with *news interest* in other countries.

The newspaper measures and the *demographic energy ratios* were generated by this researcher. INTELSAT data were obtained from INTELSAT publications, while the other measures came from United Nations statistical publications. Additionally, supplementary data concerning these 15 countries' newspapers, INTELSAT usage, and economic conditions were collected to aid in interpreting the statistical results.

The first level results leave totally unsupported any form of correlation between amounts of international news coverage and the trade and communications variables. Contrary to expectations, these results seem to indicate that, on the global level, international news reporting is not uniformly related to other international activities. The reason discovered for this phenomenon is that, at the second level, four contrasting interaction patterns are operative.

Based on the order of entry of independent variables into the stepwise multiple correlations, the second level results produced four patterns. Taking the 15 countries' results as a whole, the summary ranking indicates the order of overall importance of variables. This category is called the "model" pattern: *INTELSAT circuits, trading interest,* and *demographic energy.* International communications are a better correlate with international news coverage than trade or demographic relations. Nevertheless, trade is a strong second-ranking correlate. Four countries with internationally oriented newspapers and internationally dependent economies exhibited this pattern. Seven countries manifested the "alternate" pattern: *trading interest, INTELSAT circuits,* and *demographic energy.* These countries have domestically oriented newspapers and

economies. For internationally inactive nations, trade is a better correlate with news coverage than are communications. The "variant" pattern orders the variables *INTELSAT circuits, demographic energy,* and *trading interests.* This group's four countries publish internationally oriented newspapers but have domestically oriented economies. The "divergent" pattern has only one country and orders the variables *trading interest, demographic energy,* and *INTELSAT circuits.* This country's newspaper is domestically oriented but the nation has an economy dependent on imports. These results indicate that four interaction patterns, existing on a country-by-country basis, affect international news coverage.

Contrary to conventional wisdom, no single pattern of international relationships exists. Rather, there are, in the world, sets of patterns within which the relationships are amazingly strong. Further, in thinking about international communications, one ought to consider the conditions of economics and institutional communications as *defining* the nature of the relationships which emerge.

NOTES

1. The assumption that international communication flows are balanced was tested by performing a Pearson product-moment analysis on 1972 data reporting incoming and outgoing foreign mail for 115 countries. The result of this test was that the two directions of foreign mail traffic correlated 0.9651. The mean difference between the two mail flows was 5% of each of these flows for the 115 countries, and 2% for this study's sample of 37 countries. These results were interpreted to mean that international communication flows' directions were closely balanced.
2. INTELSAT. *System status report.* Washington, D.C., 1972.
3. International Air Transport Association. *Air tariff.* New York: Swift, 1975.

REFERENCES

CHERRY, C. *World communication: Threat or promise?* New York: Wiley, 1971.
DUPREE, J.D. International communication: View from "a window on the world." *Gazette,* 1971, 17, 224-235.
HESTER, A. Theoretical considerations in predicting volume and direction of international information flow. *Gazette,* 1973, 19, 239-247.
International Telecommunications Union. *Telecommunication Statistics.* Geneva, 1972.
KERLINGER, F.N. *Foundations of behavioral research* (2nd ed.). New York: Holt, Rinehart and Winston, 1973.
LIU, H.C., & GUNARATNE, S.A. Foreign news in two Asian dailies. *Gazette,* 1972, 18, 17-41.

MacLEAN, M.S., JR., & PINNA, L. Distance and news interest: Scarperia, Italy. *Journalism Quarterly,* 1958, 35, 36-48.

MERRILL, J.C. *The elite press.* New York: Pitman, 1968.

MERRILL, J.C., BRYAN, C.B., & ALISKY, M. *The foreign press.* Baton Rouge, Louisiana: Louisiana State University Press, 1970.

Odyssey World Atlas. New York: Odyssey, 1966.

ROSENGREN, K.E. International news: Time and type of report. In H.D. Fischer and J.C. Merrill (Ed.), *International communication: media, channels, functions.* New York: Hastings House, 1970.

STEMPEL, G.H., III. Sample size for classifying subject matter in dailies. *Journalism Quarterly,* 1952, 29, 333-334.

United Nations Statistical Yearbook, 1974. New York: United Nations, 1975.

United Nations Yearbook of International Trade Statistics, 1974. New York: United Nations, 1975.

United Nations Yearbook of National Accounts Statistics, *Volume III, 1974.* New York: United Nations, 1975.

ZIPT, G. Some determinants of the circulation of information. *American Journal of Psychology,* 1953, 59, 401-421.

EFFECTS OF PRO- AND ANTISOCIAL TELEVISION CONTENT ON CHILDREN WITH VARYING DEGREES OF SELF-ESTEEM AND DIFFERENT TELEVISION CHARACTER PREFERENCES

TIMOTHY P. MEYER
University of Texas at Austin

STANLEY J. BARAN
Cleveland State University

The study sought to identify the effects of observing a television program containing both pro- and antisocial content on 64 eight-year-olds who were divided on the basis of self-esteem (high vs. low) and sex. Also incorporated as a major variable was an index of favorite TV characters elicited from the children (scored from non-antisocial to regularly antisocial). The results showed that self-esteem was a significant personality variable which clearly affected what was learned from observing the two kinds of TV content. Low self-esteem males, and females of high and low self-esteem, tended to imitate the prosocial content, while high self-esteem males chose to imitate the antisocial content. Moreover, preference for antisocial TV characters also predicted imitative antisocial behavior for males. Because of the nearly total absence of prosocial TV models, character preferences did not predict imitative prosocial behavior.

Research investigating the effects of film and television violence on viewer aggression has centered primarily on the variables of content portrayals (e.g., justified vs. unjustified violence), characteristics of the film's aggressor and/or victim, or viewer type—demographically grouped by sex, age, race, etc. Despite the accumulation of findings, however, Liebert and Baron (1972) have emphasized that "not all children will become more aggressive, even temporarily, as a function of observing aggressive programs" (p. 192).

This study examines a personality variable of the child viewer, *self-esteem*, and the preference patterns of children's favorite television characters as they related to their modeling of pro- and antisocial television content. Rather than selecting viewer variables through traditional demographic groupings, it was the purpose of this experiment to assess the different effects of pro- and antisocial TV content on children who differed in self-esteem.

PREVIOUS RESEARCH

The personality variable of *self-esteem* appears to be an important determinant affecting a great deal of an individual's behavior. Rosenberg (1965) has referred to self-esteem as the major single "anchorage point" to which new experiences or stimuli are assimilated into the individual's existing frame of reference. Moreover, past research evidence suggests that a low level of self-esteem would indeed be related to greater amounts of modeling from television. First, low self-esteem individuals are field-dependent, using concrete environmental cues, including those provided by ever-present television models, to evaluate new information; they tend to passively accept and conform to the influence of prevailing environments (Ziller, Hagey, & Smith, 1969). Second, low self-esteem individuals are likely to be more susceptible to both normative and informational social influences in making judgments than high self-esteem individuals (Deutsch & Gerard, 1955). Television models can and do provide such sources of social influence (Bandura, 1973). Finally, it has been demonstrated that the low self-esteem individual, because of an apparent heightened responsiveness to external reinforcement, will engage in continuing attempts to be the same as, or similar to other people, in order to receive that reinforcement (Lesser & Abelson, 1959). Behavior transmitted via television's models may also be used by low self-esteem persons in much the same way as information transmitted directly from those individuals in the environment.

It is also important to note the significance of sex differences as they relate to behavior modeling, since they have a direct bearing on the hypotheses tested in this experiment. While not dealing with the self-esteem variable, several researchers have reported that in modeling aggression, males exhibit greater amounts of such behavior; but, in modeling non-aggressive behaviors, sex differences disappear (Bandura, 1973; Hicks, 1965). The finding of sex differences for only certain kinds of behavior—i.e., antisocial behavior—is apparently a function of sex role expectations via cultural conditioning and past reinforcement histories (Bandura, 1973).

Previous research findings indicate that television can effectively impart modes of both pro- and antisocial behavior; independent of these results is the body of research pointing to the importance of self-esteem as a determinant of behavior. The relationships between television viewing preferences, pro- and antisocial television content, and the corresponding degrees of viewer self-esteem provided the key variables for this experiment; their interactive effects on the display of pro- and antisocial behavior were observed and measured.

HYPOTHESES

Based on previous research, the following four hypotheses were tested:

H_1: Children with low levels of self-esteem will display a significantly greater amount of imitative prosocial behavior after seeing a television program containing both pro- and antisocial modeled behaviors than will high self-esteem children.

H_2: Because antisocial behaviors typically promise less positive reinforcement or punishment, low self-esteem children will display significantly greater amounts of imitative prosocial behavior than antisocial; high self-esteem males, however, will be more likely to model antisocial behavior than their low self-esteem peers.

H_3: Males will prefer significantly more violent TV characters as their favorites, compared with females; high self-esteem males will prefer significantly more violent TV characters than low self-esteem males.

H_4: Self-esteem and anti/non-antisocial TV character preferences will be significant predictors of antisocial behavior for males under conditions of exposure to a pro- and antisocial TV program; since prosocial models are so infrequently a part of TV content, only self-esteem should be a significant predictor of a prosocial behavior modeling.

METHOD

Self-esteem Inventory

A total of 20 items from the elementary form of Gordon's (1968) "How I See Myself" rating scale was administered to 120 second and third grade children aged 7-9 at a public, big city school in the Northeast. These items represented the *Interpersonal Adequacy* and the *Physical Appearance Factors* of Gordon's scale. The "How I See Myself" scale was designed as a group-administered self-rating inventory. Ellis (1946), however, has objected to such impersonally administered self-rating inventories on the grounds that subjects often attempt to "put their best foot forward" or often do not completely understand the individual scales. To guard against such possibilities, each child was interviewed individually, face-to-face, with the experimenter reading each statement on the inventory and recording the subject's subsequent responses. Coopersmith (1959) and Mann (1959) have both demonstrated the validity of such a procedure in obtaining a relatively accurate assessment of the individual's level of self-esteem.

Subjects

Sixty-four subjects were used in the experiment; 16 male and 16 female low self-esteem subjects were assigned at random to the television exposure group (TV) and to the No Model Exposure Group (No-TV). Likewise, the 16 male and 16 female high self-esteem subjects were randomly assigned to the TV or No-TV condition.

Experimental and Control Conditions

The 32 subjects in the TV condition viewed a 10-minute videotaped segment depicting two adult male models engaging in both pro- and antisocial behaviors. Each subject was escorted individually from his or her classroom to a small room which included a videotape replay unit, two tables, and several chairs. The experimenter explained that as payment for helping his project (answering the initial self-esteem inventory questions), he had arranged an "extra recess" for the child. Informing him that there was already someone else "at recess," the experimenter asked the child to sit and watch television while he or she waited his turn. The experimenter then busied himself with some paperwork, and the child was left to watch television.

At the conclusion of the videotaped segment, the experimenter explained to the child that he had put "all kinds of toys" in the recess room. He informed the child that he would be free to play with any or all of the toys for 20 minutes, after which a woman would come to get him and return him to his classroom. He was further told that to keep people from interrupting him, the window to the room had been covered by a large mirror (actually a one-way mirror through which the child could be observed and rated). At the end of 20 minutes, the subject was returned to his classroom.

The same procedure was followed with children in the control condition. The only difference between the two conditions was that subjects in the No-TV group watched an 11-minute model-less film entitled "Introduction to Feedback" in lieu of the experimental videotape.

Experimental Videotape

The videotaped stimulus shown to the 32 experimental subjects was a 10-minute program clearly identified with a beginning and ending. As the segment opens, both adult male models are seated at a table, one playing with a deck of large cards and the other playing with modeling clay. Then they move to the blackboard and begin to scribble furiously; next they try jumping rope with a hula hoop. After repeated failures, they throw away these toys and dump a wastepaper basket, throw cups of water around the room, throw balls and toys at each other, punch and kick the bobo doll and beat on it furiously with the hula hoop, jump rope, and a plastic baseball bat, and kick around all the toys within reach. Then, after examining the mess they made, one of the models erases the blackboard, wipes up the spilled water, picks up the paper and puts it in the wastepaper basket, puts all the toys in their proper places, and returns to his seat. Soon, a third person enters the room, asking them to leave. The nonprosocial model becomes irate and only leaves reluctantly; the prosocial model who cleaned up the room arranges his toys neatly on the table and leaves quietly.

Response Categories

The experimental room contained a variety of objects and toys, most of which were present in the television segment. Two general response categories were established to test the hypotheses:

Imitative prosocial behavior. Any of the peaceful or prosocial, helping behaviors that were exhibited in the segment and modeled by the subjects were included in this category. Such behaviors as picking up the toys and returning them to their proper places, wiping up spilled water, cleaning the blackboard, etc., were classified as prosocial behaviors.

Imitative antisocial behavior. Any of the destructive or aggressive behaviors that were exhibited by the TV models and subsequently displayed by the children were classified as imitative antisocial behavior. These behaviors included: spilling the water, throwing the wastepaper basket, scribbling on the blackboard, kicking or punching the bobo doll, throwing toys around the room, etc. Thus, these two classes of behavior constituted the key dependent measures of interest in this study.

Each subject spent 20 minutes in the test room while his behavior was rated in terms of the predetermined response categories by a specially trained, naive (to the experiment's conditions) adult

TABLE 1
Imitative Antisocial and Prosocial Mean Scores*

			Antisocial Group Means				
TV-LowSE-Males	TV-HiSE-Females	TV-LowSE-F	NoTV-HiSE-F	NoTV-LowSE-F	NoTV-HiSE-M	NoTV-LowSE-M	TV-HiSE-M
4.06a	4.35a	4.53a	5.17a	5.93a	6.05a	7.31b	9.74b

Prosocial Group Means

	TV	NoTV
High Self-Esteem	12.22a	13.78b
Low Self-Esteem	14.54b	13.44b

*Means with uncommon subscripts are significantly different at the .05 level via Tukey's HSD.

judge who observed the child through a one-way mirror in an adjoining observation room. The 20-minute session was divided into 5-second intervals by means of a tape recorded message designed to indicate each interval. In order to eliminate the possibility of variations in behavior owing to the placement of the toys and objects, the same set arrangement of these materials was used for all subjects.

One rater scored the test sessions for all 64 children. In order to provide an estimate of interobserver reliability, the responses of six children were scored independently by a second observer. Neither of the raters had knowledge of the treatment conditions to which the children were assigned. Since the raters simply recorded the frequency of occurrence of clearly defined responses, interrater reliabilities were very high, with all coefficients being above .90; this procedure was the same as used by Bandura, Ross, and Ross (1963).

TV Character Preferences

Each child who participated in the study was interviewed individually by the experimenter to determine the general viewing habits and choices of favorite TV shows and favorite TV characters. All children were able to identify at least three best-liked TV characters; these choices were then used for scoring in subsequent data analyses.

RESULTS

To analyze the results, a *factorial analysis of variance* was performed using the three factors of sex, level of esteem (high vs. low), and condition (TV vs. No-TV). Three measures were analyzed: *imitative prosocial behavior, imitative antisocial behavior,* and *antisocial TV character preference scores.* When *F values* were significant at the .05 level of confidence, *Tukey's HSD* (honest significant difference) *test* was used to make comparisons among the individual means to identify significant differences. The .05 level of significance was again used.

Prior to the analysis of variance, an *F max test* for homogeneity of variances indicated that the data violated the homogeneity assumption. To deal with this situation, the scores were transformed to achieve homogeneity via the transformation $Y = \sqrt{X}$ (where Y is the transformed score and X the original raw score). *F max tests* then revealed that,

TABLE 2
Group Means for Violent TV Character Scores*

Males	Females
2.51a	1.47b

High Self-Esteem	Low Self-Esteem
2.54a	1.44b

*Means with uncommon subscripts are significantly different at the .05 level via Tukey's HSD.

TABLE 3
Group Means: High Self-esteem Males*

	Saw TV Show	NoTV Show
Violent TV Character Scores:	3.50a	2.89a
Imitative Antisocial Behavior:	9.74a	6.05b
Imitative Prosocial Behavior:	11.43a	13.45b

*Row means with different subscripts are significantly different at the .05 level via Tukey's HSD.

with the transformed scores, homogeneity of variance had been achieved.

Imitative Antisocial Behavior

The analysis of variance for imitative antisocial behavior revealed a significant second order interaction effect among the three variables of self-esteem, sex, and condition ($F = 5.47$; $p < .025$). *Tukey's HSD test* indicated (see Table 1) that high self-esteem males who viewed the TV segment displayed significantly more imitative antisocial be-

havior than any of the other groups; no other differences were significant.

Imitative Prosocial Behavior

Results of the three factor analysis of variance of imitative prosocial behavior revealed a first order interaction for the self-esteem and TV/No-TV variables ($F = 13.52$; $P < .001$). *Tukey's HSD test* showed (see Table 1) that high self-esteem children seeing the TV program were significantly less prosocial than the low self-esteem group seeing the program and the high and low self-esteem No-TV groups. A significant main effect for self-esteem was also in evidence (F = 7.51; p < .025), indicating that low self-esteem children displayed significantly more prosocial behavior than high self-esteem children. Since the self-esteem variable interacted with the TV/No-TV variable, however, the main effects required qualification, as noted previously in this section.

Violent TV Character Preferences

Each of the three television characters mentioned by the children were classified according to their frequency of participation in violent or antisocial behavior. A panel of three judges familiar with the characters and programs independently rated each of the characters as *nonviolent* (scored 0), *occasionally violent* (scored 1), or *regularly violent* (scored 2). Of the 87 different characters mentioned, the classifications of 15 were not unanimous. All but one of these 15 situations centered on the two categories of occasionally versus regularly violent; the other case involved a split between occasionally violent and nonviolent. The cases were resolved by classifying the 14 former cases as occasionally violent and the one latter case as nonviolent. Each child thus showed a score ranging from 0 to 6 on the violent character index.

Results of the three factor analyses of variance for the violent television character scores are shown in Table 2. The findings indicated a significant main effect for self-esteem (F = 10.57; p < .01), in that high self-esteem children preferred significantly more violent characters than low self-esteem children. A significant main effect for sex of child was also observed (F = 9.40; p < .01), with males preferring significantly more violent characters than females.

Correlation Analysis

Given the violent TV character scores, pro- and antisocial behavior scores for each child, correlation analyses were used to describe the overall relationships among the variables for the various dependent measures, testing the predictions presented in the fourth research hypothesis.

Using males' violent TV character scores and self-esteem ratings as predictors of antisocial behavior displayed by the children during the 20-minute play period, the following correlations resulted: antisocial behavior and self-esteem, .75; antisocial behavior and violent TV character preferences, .62; between the predictors of self-esteem and character preferences, .50. All three of these correlations were significant beyond the .05 level. The multiple correlation coefficient of the two predictors with the criterion of antisocial behavior was .802, which was significant beyond the .01 level (F = 7.89).

With the same two predictors of prosocial behavior displayed by the children during the play period, correlations were not as substantial as they were with antisocial behavior. The correlations were: prosocial behavior and self-esteem, .67 (p < .05); prosocial behavior and TV character preferences, −.24 (not significant); between predictors, .50 (p < .05). The multiple correlation between prosocial behavior and the two predictors was also not significant.

The correlation results indicated that self-esteem was a reliable predictor of both pro- and antisocial imitative behavior. Violent TV character preferences, however, were only reliable predictors of antisocial behavior and were not related to prosocial behavior.

Additional Results

For the two groups of males with high self-esteem, there was no significant difference on the violent TV character index, but these two groups generally did prefer significantly more violent TV characters than all the other groups. Given the fact that the groups were identical in terms of sex, self-esteem, and preference for violent TV characters, it is important to note how the two groups behaved when one saw the TV segment containing both pro- and antisocial behavior while the other saw no program; Table 3 summarizes the results. The difference between these two groups on the pro- and antisocial measures is most enlightening. High self-esteem males seeing the TV program displayed significantly more imitative antisocial behavior and significantly less imitative prosocial behavior than the group seeing no TV program. These results clearly indicate that high self-esteem males, who prefer violent TV characters, can be influenced to behave more antisocially than prosocially when exposed to a program containing both pro- and antisocial elements. Given the choice of pro- and antisocial behavior, the high self-esteem male will apparently choose antisocial behavior to imitate, while rejecting prosocial behavior.

DISCUSSION

The first hypothesis predicted that low self-esteem children would display a significantly greater amount of imitative prosocial behavior than high self-esteem children after both groups had viewed a TV program with both pro- and antisocial content. The results confirmed the prediction, with a significant main effect for self-esteem; a significant interaction with the TV/no-TV variable qualified the main effect, in that less prosocial behavior was displayed by the high self-esteem group than the other three groups. With the low self-esteem child's field dependence on positive reinforcement conditions in the environment, and the negative reinforcement usually associated with antisocial behavior, the findings appear consistent with the implications of previous research and speculation. Seeking recognition for "good behavior," the low self-esteem child apparently can use TV content to selectively influence his or her behavior.

A related prediction stated in hypothesis 2 contended that, while low self-esteem children would display significantly less antisocial behavior than prosocial behavior, high self-esteem males would display significantly more antisocial behavior than low self-esteem males. This hypothesis was supported. When given the opportunity to choose pro- or antisocial behavior, high self-esteem males select antisocial behavior, while low self-esteem males select prosocial behavior. The high self-esteem male would seem to be more susceptible to antisocial TV content's influence, perhaps because antisocial behavior has been more effective in that he has been able to exert his power and influence over his peers to gain objectives and maintain leadership. Even though antisocial behavior may seem to offer the rewards of excitement, success, or

"fun" to the low self-esteem child, the uncertainty and desire for recognition may deter him, as opposed to the high self-esteem male who is much less field dependent and more assertive as an individual.

The third hypothesis predicted that males will prefer significantly more violent TV characters as their favorites, as compared with females; the results confirmed this prediction. This finding is wholly consistent with previous research (Meyer, 1973; Greenberg & Gordon, 1972; McIntyre & Treevan, 1972). It was also predicted that high self-esteem males would prefer significantly more violent TV characters than low self-esteem males; this prediction was confirmed. One reasonable explanation for this finding is that high self-esteem males, being more independent in their judgments than low self-esteem males, may identify more readily with characters who are rewarded and admired for their antisocial behavior. Again, low self-esteem males may be impressed by the success of antisocial characters, but it may be easier for them to admire non-antisocial TV characters who are sometimes rewarded for other more acceptable behaviors. Examining the kinds of characters named by both groups lends credibility to this interpretation. High self-esteem males frequently mentioned characters like Steve McGarrett of "Hawaii Five-O" and Joe Mannix or Kojak—people whose roles are based on power and authority in dealing with others. Low self-esteem males, however, made more frequent mention of characters like Samantha of "Bewitched" and Letterman of the "Electric Company"—TV people who are popular characters because they are funny and/or helpful, or, as is perhaps the case with Samantha, characters who control their environments with unrealistic, fantasy-oriented techniques. Since low self-esteem males' reinforcement histories may include direct or vicarious experiences which showed antisocial behavior being punished while other behaviors were either rewarded or not punished, the preference for more non-antisocial characters seems to be a sensible result.

The fourth hypothesis tested was that self-esteem and TV character preferences would be significant predictors of antisocial behavior, but that only self-esteem would be a significant predictor of prosocial behavior. *Regression analysis* confirmed these predictions. Given the preponderance of both antisocial and non-antisocial TV characters in comparison to prosocial characters, the findings point to one of the potentially undesirable consequences resulting from the present imbalance of current television programming which markedly favors antisocial characters over prosocial characters. The consistent presence of antisocial and non-prosocial TV models can apparently contribute to the conditions under which some children will acquire and display antisocial behavior.

Taken in total, this study clearly identified the importance of viewer self-esteem as a determinant of the types and amounts of behavior which will be imitated or acquired from exposure to antisocial and prosocial TV content. The results also establish TV character preferences as being related to the imitation of antisocial behavior and interacting with the level of self-esteem of the child viewer. Thus, the combination of conditions which will produce the most imitative antisocial behavior indicates the following: High self-esteem males, preferring favorite TV characters who behave antisocially, reliably display the most imitative antisocial behavior when exposed to a TV program with pro- and antisocial content. In the absence of prosocial TV characters, TV viewing behavior is not related to prosocial behavior modeling.

The principal conclusion warranted by the findings of this experiment is that increasing prosocial models on television will increase the prosocial behavior of viewers, especially those children who are low in self-esteem; low self-esteem children show a willingness to model prosocial behaviors and indicate ready identification with the few prosocial TV characters that are available. Assuming that suitable rewards would be available and forthcoming in their environment, the increased display of prosocial behaviors by low self-esteem children may be an effective way of increasing self-esteem and building the confidence of these children to be more assertive in dealing with others.

Regarding high self-esteem children, the need to increase the amount and types of prosocial models on television seems to be as great as it is for low self-esteem children. This study has demonstrated that, when given the choice, high self-esteem males will choose to imitate antisocial behavior over pro-

social behavior. For those who are not given the choice, however, it seems likely that if only prosocial behavior is presented, this will be the behavior that is modeled. Support for this notion is derived from the findings of Friedrich and Stein (1972) in their long-term study of the effects of pro- and antisocial television content on the pro- and antisocial behavior of preschool children. Friedrich and Stein (1972) argue that children will be affected by the nature of the content that is viewed; that is, aggressive children will behave antisocially if exposed to a regular dose of TV violence, or prosocially if exposed to a regular diet of prosocial programming. Their results, in fact, indicate that those children who displayed the most prosocial behavior were those children who were exposed to the prosocial TV programs *and* were high in aggressive behavior prior to exposure to the shows. One suspects that these high aggressive children also were high in self-esteem; at least it is an interesting hypothesis. If this is the case, however, it seems that children who are high in self-esteem and past aggressiveness will also be likely to profit the most from a steady diet of prosocial programs and models. Their rate of modeling would be higher. In short, those who most need prosocial models would be affected most by them. Future research not only needs to explore personality variables other than self-esteem as they relate to modeling from television, but also the other variables that are related to varying states of self-esteem—those patterns of variables that interact to affect the amount and type of modeling from television.

REFERENCES

BANDURA, A. *Aggression: A social learning analysis.* Englewood Cliffs, N.J.: Prentice-Hall, 1973.
BANDURA, A., ROSS, D., & ROSS, A. Imitation of film-mediated aggressive models. *Journal of Abnormal and Social Psychology*, 1963, 66, 3-11.
COOPERSMITH, S. A method for determining types of self-esteem. *Journal of Abnormal and Social Psychology*, 1959, 59, 87-94.
DEUTSCH, M., & GERARD, H. A study of normative and informational social influences upon individual judgment. *Journal of Abnormal and Social Psychology*, 1955, 51, 629-636.
DOMINICK, J., & GREENBERG, B. Attitudes toward violence: The interaction of television exposure, family attitudes, and social class. In G. Comstock and E. Rubenstein (Eds.), *Television and Social Behavior, Vol. III: Television*

and Adolescent Aggressiveness. Washington, D.C.: U.S. Government Printing Office, 1972.

ELLIS, A. The validity of personality questionnaires. *Psychological Bulletin*, 1946, 43, 385-440.

GORDON, I. *How I see myself: A self rating scale for students.* Gainesville, Fla: Institute for Development of Human Resources, University of Florida, 1968.

HICKS, D. Imitation and Retention of film-mediated aggressive peer and adult models. *Journal of Personality and Social Psychology*, 1965, 2, 97-100.

LESSER, G., & ABELSON, R. Personality correlates of persuasibility in children. In C. Hovland and I. Janis (Eds.), *Personality and persuasibility.* New Haven: Yale University Press, 1959.

LIEBERT, R., & BARON, R. Short-term effects of televised aggression on children's aggressive behavior. In J. Murray, E. Rubenstein, and G. Comstock (Eds.), *Television and Social Behavior, Vol. II: Television and Social Learning.* Washington, D.C.: U.S. Government Printing Office, 1972.

MANN, R. A Review of the relationships between personality and performance in small groups. *Psychological Bulletin*, 1959, 56, 241-270.

McINTYRE, J., & TREEVAN, J. Television violence and deviant behavior. In G. Comstock and E. Rubenstein (Eds.), *Television and Social Behavior, Vol. III: Television and Adolescent Aggressiveness.* Washington, D.C.: U.S. Government Printing Office, 1972.

MEYER, T. Children's perceptions of favorite television characters as behavioral models. *Educational Broadcasting Review*, 1973, 7, 25-33.

STEIN, A., & FRIEDRICH, L. Television content and young children's behavior. In J. Murray, E. Rubenstein, and G. Comstock (Eds.), *Television and Social Behavior, Vol. II: Television and Social Learning.*

ZILLER, R., HAGEY, J., & SMITH. Self-esteem: A self-social construct. *Journal of Consulting and Clinical Psychology*, 1969, 33, 84-95.

ORGANIZATIONAL COMMUNICATION
Theory and Research: An Overview
Selected Studies

ORGANIZATIONAL COMMUNICATION
THEORY AND RESEARCH: AN OVERVIEW

GARY M. RICHETTO
The Williams Companies

Organizational Communication is a discipline in search of a domain.
—*Bernstein, 1976*

Bernstein's comment reflects the critical issue confronting our field today. On one hand, it suggests that perhaps a new discipline has indeed begun to emerge from diverse organizational theory and research being pursued by a large number of behavioral and social scientists. (For an appreciation of the diversity of this theory and research, see *Organizational Communication Abstracts, 1974* and *1975,* edited by Falcione and Greenbaum [1975, 1976].)

On the other hand, Bernstein's observation suggests that perhaps we have been so intent on integrating methodologies from these various sources that we have failed to articulate theoretical parameters within which to employ our tools.

Thus, when one views organizational communication in 1976-77, one finds, not surprisingly, far more research than theory. In less academic terms, organizational communication, like the teary-eyed little girl in party dress, appears to be "all dressed up with no place to go."

And yet, there has been an undeniable acceleration of interest and activity in this emerging field by both academics (Downs & Larimer, 1973) and practitioners (Bernstein, 1976). Researchers and practioners alike seem to suggest that, despite the enormous difficulties in forging coherent, integrated theory and methods for studying communication processes in on-going organizations, the goal should be pursued nonetheless. And, that task becomes increasingly more difficult with the passage of time. Our organizations will never be smaller, less complex, more "manageable" than they are today. Even the giants among them—big business, big government, big university—if temporarily dismantled will likely spawn offspring which, one day, will dwarf even the most overwhelming organ-izations of 1976. Drucker (1974) provides evidence for this likelihood from the not-too-distant past:

> The octopus which so frightened the grandparents of today's Americans, Rockefeller's giant Standard Oil Trust, was split into fourteen parts by the U.S. Supreme Court in 1911. Thirty years later, on the eve of America's entry into World War II, every single one of these fourteen Standard Oil daughters had become at least four times as large as the octopus when the Supreme Court divided it—in employment, in capital, in sales, and in every other aspect. (p. 4)

The need for systemic study of organizational communication processes, then, is not unlike the need for studies aimed at projecting the future in a world of unprecedented change. And, as Bennis (1968) has said of the latter undertaking, ". . . (it) is as absurd as it is necessary."

HISTORICAL HIGHLIGHTS: THE ROOTS OF ORGANIZATIONAL COMMUNICATION

Since this overview is the first in a series of annual assessments of the field, it seems appropriate to lay at least a brief historical foundation for the study of organizational communication. This treatment will, of necessity, be merely a sketch of some fifty years of communication research in on-going organizations. For more comprehensive historical reviews of the literature, see Redding (1966, 1972), Tompkins (1967), and Pietri (1974).

The 1920s

> We trained hard, but it seemed that every time we were beginning to form up into teams we would be reorganized. I was to learn later in life that we tend to meet any new situation by reorganizing; and a wonderful method it can be for creating the illusion of

progress while producing confusion, inefficiency and demoralization. (Petronius Arbiter, 210 B.C.)

This 2,000-year-old echo from an embittered legionnaire suggests that starting this historical sketch of organizational communication research with the 1920s is a bit arbitrary. Nonetheless, in terms of stimulating research aimed specifically at learning more about communication behavior in formal organizations, the 1920s provide the clearest point of departure.

First, there was the undeniable influence during the 1920s of Dale Carnegie's ideas on the thinking of American administrators, particularly those in private enterprise. While most scholars in communication may shudder at the notion of thousands of managers flocking to courses providing insights to "winning friends and influencing people," Carnegie nonetheless linked "communication skills" and "managerial effectiveness" in the minds of countless organizational leaders (Sanborn, 1967).

Secondly, organizational research at Western Electric's Hawthorne facility in 1927 "accidentally" stimulated the "first scientific attack upon the problems of employee communication" (Sanborn, 1967). Assigned initially to investigate the effects of working conditions on productivity, Mayo and others from Harvard's Graduate School of Business Administration gained considerable, unexpected insight into the importance of employees' communication behavior (Roethlisberger & Dickson, 1943).

Tompkins (1965) traces the impact of the Hawthorne studies on communication scholars even further. He notes that Irving Lee's interest in communication in organizations which began with his review of this research, led to his visiting the Harvard group, and culminated in Lee's influencing his colleagues in the field of speech to become more interested in organizational communication.

The 1930s

The most widely-recognized influence on the field of organizational communication during the 1930s was the thinking of Chester Barnard. Influenced by the organizational theories of Mary Parker Follett (1941), Barnard saw communication as the "heart" of executive functioning. While president of The New Jersey Bell Telephone Company, he stated that the "first function" of the executive was "to develop and maintain a system of communication" (Barnard, 1938).

Barnard was also sensitive to the psychological qualities of that "system of communication." He contended that such a system must be "receiver-oriented," in that "authority" of the source (management) alone would not guarantee employee acceptance of the message. Rather, the conditions of (1) understanding, (2) consistency with organizational purpose or objectives, (3) consistency with personal goals or objectives, and (4) mental and physical capacity to comply, must also be satisfied (p. 226).

Drucker (1974) credits both Follett and Barnard with likely being the first to study the role of communication in decision-making, and in developing theories to illuminate relationships between the *formal* and *informal* organizations (p. 26).

The 1940s

During the decade which Dover (1959) has described as the *Era of Information* in terms of organizational communication activity, early signs of the initial "human relations movement" began to appear in organizations, particularly within the business community.

An economy spurred by the war effort and the general notion that "informed employees are productive employees" led to increased employee publications, with significant changes in message content. In contrast to pre-war content dealing with essentially superficial information (the *Era of Entertainment*, Dover, 1959), organizational communication systems of the 1940s carried information on company growth, share of market, and various financial data aimed at explaining the virtues of the free enterprise system.

In keeping with the general drift toward human relations in management, the 1940s saw two important contributions to organizational communication as a "two-way" process. Heron (1942) focused on superior-subordinate reciprocity in communication, articulating the need for both upward- and downward-initiated messages within the organization. And, at the end of the decade, Pigors (1949) provided a thread of continuity for this concept of reciprocity between hierarchical levels, stressing that communication was, what he called, a *joint process.*

Reciprocity and upward-initiated communication flow in organizations received further attention by Given (1949) in a text which suggested that effective management worked from the "bottom up," rather than relying solely upon downward-directed communication systems.

Message studies within organizational contexts were conducted during this decade as well. Paterson and Jenkins (1948) employed Flesch readability formulae in content analyzing industrial relations and personnel policy statements. A series of studies focused on downward-directed written communications in both management and union organizations (Baker, 1948; Baker, Ballantine, & True, 1949).

Classic research on the effects of employee involvement in decision-making on organizational change was conducted late in the decade by Coch and French (1948). Still influencing work in the field of *organization development* (OD), their studies were perhaps the first to indicate that there is a need for sharing both information and influence with organization members to be directly affected by organizational changes.

Finally, important research on mass media and interpersonal communication interfaces was conducted by Lazarsfeld, Berelson, and Gaudet (1948). Essentially, their work identified the "gatekeeping" role in the flow of information from the mass media to central members of subgroups in the audience and, subsequently, to others within their sphere(s) of influence—the so-called *two-step-flow* of communication. Their studies evidenced the importance of focusing on receivers of information as members of *networks,* linked together by persons functioning as communication liaisons. Katz (1957) was later to reinforce this network notion during a decade within which studies on the diffusion of information in rural communities was to corroborate the same phenomenon (Rogers, 1962).

The 1950s

While business and other organizations were providing information to their members—within what Dover (1959) termed the *Era of Interpretation and Persuasion*—academic institutions were involved in launching both laboratory and field research with a fervor unmatched to that time.

Bavelas and Barrett (1951), replicating experiments by Leavitt (1951), studied the effects of simulated organizational communication networks on information flow. Identifying indices of *dispersion* for organizational patterns, and calculating gradient indices of *centrality* and *peripherality* for network members, their work formed the theoretical basis for present-day research in network analysis in ongoing organizations (e.g., Danowski, 1976; Monge et al., 1976; Richards, 1976). The highly significant role of network analysis in current research, discussed later in this overview, attests to the prophetic quality of Bavelas and Barrett's predictions:

> Clearly, these experiments are only the beginning of a long story. The findings, although they promise much, settle nothing; but they do suggest that an experimental approach to certain aspects of organizational communication is possible and that, in all probability, it would be practically rewarding. As the characteristics of communication nets and their effects upon human performance *as they occur in the laboratory* become better understood, the need will grow for systematic studies of actual operating organizations. The job of mapping an existing net of communications even in a relatively small company is a complicated and difficult one, but it is not impossible . . . (p. 371)

The last statement from Bavelas and Barrett is particularly interesting, considering that, within twenty-odd years, not only is the mapping of communication networks within ongoing organizations possible, but researchers can presently analyze networks in organizations as large as 5,000 members and 50,000 communication links (Richards, 1971).

Also during this decade, Leavitt and Mueller (1951) conducted their classic research on the effects of feedback on task performance. Their laboratory studies on controlled feedback and its operational effects provided the theoretical basis for current research, such as that on project managers' abilities to accurately project completion dates (Adams & Swanson, 1976), and the effects of feedback on job satisfaction (Steers, 1976).

Climate studies in organizational communication began to appear in greater number in the early 1950s, sponsored chiefly by Lull, and later Redding and associates at Purdue University. This research was characterized by its applicability within ongoing organizations and by its focus upon perceptual and attitudinal data. During its first decade of activity, the Purdue group investigated alternative communication modes and their effects (Dahle, 1953), attitudes of corporate managers toward correlates of communication and productivity (Funk, 1956), perceptions of communication "breakdown" in organizations (Ross, 1954), the role of organizational communication practices among first-line supervisors (Piersol, 1955), information flow within the banking industry (Level, 1959), and other communication variables operating within formal organizations.

Research similar to that being conducted at Purdue was appearing during the 1950s at Northwestern (Nielsen, 1953) and Ohio State University (Freshley, 1955; Dee, 1959).

Problems specific to upward-initiated communication began to appear during the 1950s, focusing attention on the tendency for lower-level persons to "filter" or otherwise distort their upward-directed messages (Maier, Read, & Hooven, 1959; Planty & Machaver, 1952; Jackson, 1953) and on the effects of perceived "upward influence" of one's supervisor on the subsequent initiation of upward communication (Pelz, 1952).

Building upon the work of Jacobson and Seashore (1951), Davis (1953) employed a new organizational communication research technique he termed "ECCO" (Episodic Communication Channels in Organizations) analysis, tracking the flow of information through networks within the employee grapevine. The ECCO analysis approach to organizational communication research has recently been appraised by Rudolph (1972).

Also in 1954, Odiorne was first to use the term *communication audit* to describe the process by which he assessed the accuracy with which higher level management could predict lower levels' perceptions of information flow. After nearly 20 years,

the term *communication audit*—albeit describing a far more comprehensive procedure for analyzing organizational communication—was to reappear at the 1971 International Communication Association Convention in Phoenix, and later to become a new approach to organizational communication research of interest to some 150 communication researchers and practitioners from five countries (Goldhaber, 1976).

In terms of methodological developments, the 1950s saw attempts to devise new techniques for studying communication in organizations per se, such as those by Funk and Becker (1952) for measuring downward communication effectiveness, Browne and Neitzel (1952) for assessing communication discrepancies between hierarchical levels, and Flanagan (1954), whose "critical incidents" technique is often used in current organizational communication research.

Finally, the 1950s spawned the formal beginnings of general systems theory, reflected in the works of von Bertalanffy (1950, 1956), Boulding (1956), Hall & Fagen (1956), Ashby (1958), and Bakke (1959). The general system theory model, focusing on systemic qualities of components, attributes, relationships, and levels of discourse (Toronto, 1975), is in evidence in some of the communication theory-building efforts of this decade (Deutsch, 1952; March & Simon, 1958; Haire, 1959). The systems perspective on communication in organizations was to gain important momentum during the following decade (Katz & Kahn, 1966), leading to contemporary theory-building in the field. Recent work by Miller (1975) in *living systems theory*—a subset of general systems theory—promises to have significant impact on future theory development in organizational communication. Miller's work and its implications are discussed later in this overview.

The 1960s

Summarizing theory and research relevant to organizational communication during the 1960s is even more difficult than in earlier decades. Many of the trends begun in the 1950s were very much in evidence during this decade as well. Among these was the acceleration of so-called climate studies, generated predominately by the Purdue group (Pace, 1960; Sanborn, 1961; Simons, 1961; Tompkins, 1962; Miraglia, 1963; Smith, 1967; Zima, 1967; Minter, 1969; Richetto, 1969) which focused chiefly on organization members' perceptions of communication phenomena.

These and similar studies provided insights into communication variables in ongoing organizations. During this decade, various attempts were made to develop taxonomies within which to organize and describe the various findings such studies had generated.

Field researchers of the 1960s often employed directional information-flow taxonomies within which to attack organizational communication problems (Redding, 1964; 1972). Frequently, the terms *upward, downward,* and *horizontal* were utilized in descriptions of research methods and findings during this period. While such taxonomies undoubtedly aided researchers in isolating variables and reporting results, a negative by-product was probably an increased retardation of broad, integrated theory-building. As Redding (1972) notes:

> . . . the conventional analysis of organizational communication in terms of up, down, and horizontal is perhaps not the most appropriate for yielding valuable insights. (p. 489)

To focus on one aspect (e.g., *downward-directed communication*) of organizational communication, was, by definition, to deemphasize the impact of other equally important aspects (Richetto, 1975). While gaining information about the nature of individual, directional subsystems, communication research in organizations often neglected to investigate the relationships *among* subsystems and *between* systems and their environments. The result was a decade of field research with few attempts to integrate findings into holistic frameworks.

A second influence on organizational communication research and theory during the 1960s was increased sophistication in network analysis. Building upon the earlier works of Lazarsfeld (1948), Bavelas and Barrett (1951), and Rogers (1962), and aided by progressively more effective graph and computational techniques, network researchers began to investigate more complex networks and organizations. During this decade, the work done at

Michigan State University (e.g., Farace and MacDonald, 1971) and MIT (e.g., Allen, 1966a, 1966b, 1970) especially influenced organizational communication research in field settings.

The movement from the laboratory to natural organizational settings (Walton, 1962; Allen, 1966; Allen & Cohen, 1966; Wickesberg, 1967; Schwartz, 1968) was of particular importance to current network research and theory-building. Farace and MacDonald (1971) comment on the significance of this increased intervention into ongoing organizations:

> It (laboratory research) is the line of research that is most often cited when organizational writers discuss communication . . . While these authors typically make quite clear that they are on shaky grounds in generalizing such findings to large, on-going organizations, they nevertheless find themselves relying heavily on the experimental network studies. (p. 10)

One of the first attempts at this shift from laboratory to ongoing organization was that of Walton (1962). Studying information flow in a government laboratory, Walton devised a *magnetic theory of communication* based upon his discovery of *centrals* (liaisons) in networks who (1) sent more *action messages,* (2) had greater access to information outside their work units, and (3) felt they had more influence in organizational affairs than did their more *peripheral* counterparts. He concluded that such centrals served as human "magnets," drawing information and then diffusing it throughout the system.

According to Farace and MacDonald (1971), research at the end of the decade by Schwartz (1968) and MacDonald (1970) was of particular significance to network analysis in that it utilized network-sociometric techniques to analyze liaison communication structures in organizations. These techniques had not been used since earlier work by Jacobson and Seashore (1951).

During this same period, there were several notable attempts to devise broad, integrated theory. Thayer's (1967) framework for viewing organizational communication within human and organizational *levels* of analysis remains as one of the most cogent treatments of theory-building in the field.

Guetzkow (1965) also contributed significantly

to theory-building in organizational communication during this decade. Integrating research findings on message flows, networks and their differentiations, message contents, information accuracy, rumor transmission, and task (problem-solving) variables, Guetzkow provided a theoretical perspective on organizational communication considerably broader in scope than most earlier attempts.

It is important to note that neither Thayer nor Guetzkow felt they had done more than scratch the surface in developing organizational communication theory. As Thayer (1967) noted:

> We have just begun to develop some first glimmerings of the tremendous significance of communication systems, within which organisms and organizations are in-formed, but I know of no studies that purport to specify the conditions or the consequences for the individual(s) or the organizations involved when two (or more) of these in-forming communication systems interpenetrate each other in certain ways.
>
> I should think that such studies will have to come— if we are to fully comprehend the issues, the elements, and the dynamic relationships involved in communication within organizations. (p. 98)

And from Guetzkow (1965):

> It may not be accidental that research in communication has lagged behind studies concerning other features of organizational life, such as authority, division of work, and status . . . For example, vertical flows of communication depend upon size of organization, but lateral flows seem to be independent of size. Such contingency is found also in the way the very reward system embodied in a communication system makes the use of reward channels punishing. As a final example, remember that the adequacy of a net for task performance could be completely reversed, when a change in problem-solving technique was permitted. Do we find in communications in organizations an area of study in which there is special richness in contingent, interactive effects? Or is it merely that a clarifying perspective—which would make the pieces fall more simply in the whole—remains hidden? (p. 569)

The Early 1970s

Influences on organizational communication theory and research of the 1970s are only now beginning to emerge. A few themes appear likely to extend through the decade.

First, it would appear that the three major streams of organizational communication research— climate studies, information flow studies, and message content studies—will continue on a growth curve at least as steep as that of the 1960s. Research highlighted so far, and that to be reviewed later in this overview, attest to the viability and complementarity of all three research perspectives.

Second, within each of these research streams there will likely be continued attempts at integrating and synthesizing findings. (See, for example, Redding's [1972] integration and synthesis of climate research.)

Third, more effort is likely to be directed toward synthesizing and integrating theory *across* these three major research perspectives, resulting in broader, more comprehensive frameworks for viewing communication phenomena in ongoing organizations. (See, for example, the works of Greenbaum, 1971, 1972a, 1972b.)

Finally, more emphasis is likely to be given to the role of organizational *structure* in studies of communication and information flow within formal organizations. Rogers and Rogers (1976) contend, in fact, that *the* distinctive aspect of organizational communication is that it occurs in a highly structured environment. While others may disagree with this structural emphasis, there is little doubt that we have yet to adequately integrate organizational communication theory with the broader theories of organization (Roberts et al., 1973; Bernstein, 1976).

CURRENT ORGANIZATIONAL COMMUNICATION RESEARCH

A review of organizational communication research of the past year or so reveals divergent, yet complementary, trends. It would appear that traditional research areas in organizational communication, such as dyadic, interpersonal, man-machine and information networks are receiving continued investigation. Additionally, communication behaviors of females and minorities are being studied specifically.

Communication relationships between organization members are, likewise, receiving more focused investigation. For example, in studying supervisor-subordinate dyads, there appears to be a trend toward examining relational consequences such as trust, credibility, or satisfaction in terms of specific, antecedent conditions, as with studies of the effects of *homophily* on perceived trust or credibility or the effects of perceived *openness* in communication on overall supervisor satisfaction.

Feedback processes have also received attention among organizational communication researchers, particularly in field research. Communication training and its impact on individual and organizational performance has also become the subject of renewed interest, as reflected by quasi-experimental attempts to measure the effects of Transactional Analysis and other training on communication behavior.

There appears also to be growing interest and research activity in the interdependence of larger systems that points to the development of *interorganizational* communication theory. And, finally, one cannot help but see new opportunities for organizational communication research within broader contexts such as organization development (OD) or quality of working life (QWL).

Refined Organizational Groupings

Not surprisingly, current organizational communication research reflects concern for contemporary social issues. And perhaps the most significant social issue for modern organizations is the changing role of the female. The re-examination of traditional sexual roles in ongoing organizations represents a new arena for applied communication research, and considerable research has been undertaken with this focus.

Hagen and Kahn (1975) suggest that highly competent females may have greater difficulty in being assimilated into organizations than less competent females. They found: (1) males preferred to view competent females "from afar," rather than interacting with them directly; (2) less competent females and males preferred working with incompetent females as much as with competent females; (3) competent females were more likely to be excluded from their groups than were their less-competent counterparts; and, generally, (4) in on-

going organizations, a female's perceived competence may provide her with prestige and status, but at the same time may limit her acceptance by males and less competent females.

Best (1975) investigated attitudes toward women as managers, perceptions of barriers the female manager might encounter, and managerial traits. Managers studied indicated that cultural and biological characteristics of women are impediments to functioning effectively in a management role. Analysis indicated also that *formal education* (i.e., Masters Degree or higher), and *former work experience with females,* were positively correlated with more favorable views toward women as potential managers.

Patterson (1975) investigated potential sex bias in performance ratings and promotability ratings. His findings suggested a bias against women in general in performance ratings, and a significantly greater bias against married as opposed to single women in the areas of promotion ratings and perceived promotability.

Chapman (1975), in a study of male and female leadership styles, found no differences between male and female postures, with the exception that females tended to become more task-oriented as the number of males they supervised increased.

Investigating differences in male and female views of the formal and informal organization, Reif, Newstrom, and Monczka (1975) found more similarity than dissimilarity between the sexes. They measured attitudes toward features of the *formal* organization—authority, job descriptions, performance appraisals, chain of command, policies, controls, organizational objectives, supervision, and aspects of *informal* organization—voluntary teamwork, cliques, personal influence, co-worker evaluations, social intervention, group cohesion, social group membership, grapevine. Their findings suggest:

1. Male and female views were generally similar, though females held more positive views toward the formal organization in its ability to satisfy interpersonal needs.
2. Females tended to see the organization more holistically than did males; females viewed the *task* elements of organizations and the *human*

elements of organizations as complementary; males tended to see distinctions and discrepancies between the two.

3. Preparation of females for entrance into organizations in managerial capacities may be less necessary than efforts preparing male counterparts for likely differences in perception.

In related research, Brief and Wallace (1976) reported that *job* stereotypes, rather than *sex* stereotypes, may account for resistance against female occupancy of certain vocational positions.

A second organizational area which has been a research focal point is racial groups. In studying differences in self-concept between blacks and whites that have pertinence to organizational communication, Watson and Barone (1976) found no differences on measures of *self-acceptance, ideal self,* or *divergence* (*ideal self* minus *self-concept*). Further, blacks and whites did not differ significantly in value orientation; both races valued "pragmatism" first and "moralism" second. In terms of *achievement, power,* and *affiliation* needs, no differences were reported, with the exception that whites were reported to have greater needs for power.

Jedel and Kujawa (1976) investigated black/white attitudes toward organizational practices and policies. Their data indicated differences in perceptions of: (1) ease in obtaining jobs, (2) establishment of racial quotas, (3) hiring and promotability, (4) Affirmative Action and Equal Employment Opportunity (EEO) activities, and (5) qualifications and job criteria.

Kraut (1976) reported results of a longitudinal study of black and white management trainees. He found that blacks had few problems in becoming assimilated into organizations. Members of both races reported that problems of adaptation they had expected did not emerge.

Communication Relationships in Organizations

Research over the past year or so reflects more specific treatments of interpersonal relationships in organizations, particularly within supervisor-subordinate dyads.

The *homophily-heterophily* construct (McCros-key, Richmond, & Daly, 1975) in supervisor-subordinate communication relationships appears to be gaining interest and broader application among organizational communication researchers.

Daly, McCroskey, and Falcione (1976) measured the effects of five dimensions of supervisor-subordinate similarity—attitude, background, values, appearance, and job—on subordinates' satisfaction with supervisors. They found both attitude-homophily and values-homophily to be significant predictors of subordinate satisfaction with supervisors.

Hellweg (1976) investigated relationships between externally-generated *conflict, homophily,* and *perceived credibility* within a military organization. She found no significant relationships between variables investigated.

Openness in supervisor-subordinate dyadic communication has received increasing attention in recent research. Stull (1975) studied perceived rewards associated with communication openness and found: (1) significant agreement among superior-subordinate as to the desirability of *acceptance* as a supervisory behavior, (2) significant agreement on *reciprocal openness* as a desirable communication behavior, (3) a preference for *acceptance,* as opposed to *reciprocity* among supervisors, and (4) at lower organizational levels, a tendency for dyads to disagree on frequency of supervisors' acceptance and reciprocity in actual day-to-day interaction with subordinates.

In similar research, Hawkins (1975) investigated the relationship between supervisor-subordinate communication behavior and the satisfaction of interpersonal needs. Findings indicated that needs for affection and dominance accounted for significant variance in frequency and duration of messages. Needs for certainty, however, were not significantly related to either message frequency or duration.

Krivonos (1975) investigated relationships between supervisor-subordinate communication, *intrinsic* and *extrinsic motivation,* and *perceived communication climate.* Results indicated that intrinsically-motivated subordinates perceived the communication climate as more ideal and supportive than extrinsically-motivated subordinates.

Several other recent studies have dealt with communication apprehension within organizational contexts. Daly and McCroskey (1975) found *communication apprehension* a good predictor of *occupational choice* and *desirability*. McCroskey and Lepard (1975) found inverse relationships between *communication apprehension* and selection of occupations requiring high levels of interpersonal interaction.

Research by Daly and Leth (1976) focused on *communication apprehension* in personnel selection. Their work fused two apparently contradictory research lines. Earlier evidence suggested that applicants who are perceived as similar to interviewers would receive more favorable ratings, while conflicting evidence from apprehension research suggested that high apprehension applicants would receive negative ratings, regardless of similarity between the two. Among the Daly and Leth findings were:

1. *High* apprehensive applicants received favorable ratings when applying for positions of low communication demand. Conversely, *low apprehensives* were rated highly when considered for positions of high communication demand.
2. Subjects perceived significant "fit" (as measured by recommendation for organizational position) between *apprehension* and *occupational communication demand*.
3. Subjects perceived significant "fit" between *apprehension, occupational position,* and subsequent "job success."
4. Subjects perceived significant "fit" between apprehension, occupational position, and subsequent "job satisfaction."

In discussing the implications of their research for applied organizational communication studies, Daly and Leth suggest that:

> . . . the conception of communication demands needs greater attention when job descriptions are formulated. Certainly instruments such as the often-mentioned "communication audit" cannot fail to consider . . . the communication requirements of various positions within an organization. (p 16)

Communication apprehension in the written mode was also investigated recently. Daly and Miller (1975), building upon the earlier work of Burgoon and Miller (1971), found that subjects who reported *high* communication apprehension in writing behavior tended to choose less intense words when selecting adjectives to be incorporated in written messages.

Effects of Communication Training in Organizations

Several recent studies have sought to measure the effects of various types of communication training on interpersonal and organizational performance.

Latham, Wexley, and Pursell (1975) trained managers to make more objective decisions in employee selection. The researchers attempted to teach subjects to avoid halo effects stemming from "similar-to-me" *(homophily)* and "contrast" *(heterophily)* cues exhibited by applicants during personnel selection interviews. The experimental "workshop" training group revealed significant improvements among managers, while the "discussion" training group and control group did not.

There also appears to be considerable interest in testing the effects of one specific interpersonal theory—Transactional Analysis (Berne, 1961)—on individual and organizational behavior. Transactional Analysis (TA) has enjoyed accelerated application in ongoing organizations over the past several years (Goldhaber, 1974, 1976; Jongeward, 1973). The Organizational Communication Division of the Academy of Management devoted a program to TA applications and effects at its 1976 Convention (Dutton, 1976; Lesikar, 1976; Urban, 1976; Vroman, 1976).

Empirical research on TA in organizations appears minimal at this point, though increasing research is likely (Goldhaber, Baker, & Richetto, 1976). Two studies investigating the effects of TA training have recently been reported. McCann and McCann (1975) investigated the impact of an eight-week program in TA, in terms of the group's responses in areas of self-actualization, cooperation, communicativeness in problem solving, and creativity. The experimental group's scores indicated significant differences from the control group's scores in all areas but creativity.

Williams (1975) correlated scores on a commercial managerial style instrument with judges' perceptions of TA ego states. He found no significant correlations, whereas, hypothetically, behaviors operating from the "parent" ego state ought to reflect "authoritarian" or "task-related" management styles.

Feedback in Organizational Communication Systems

As noted previously, the concept of *feedback* is increasingly of interest in organizational communication research. In one study Steers (1976) found that feedback provided for employees on *goal-setting, goal-difficulty,* and *goal-specificity* was positively correlated with both *job involvement* and *job satisfaction*. Adams and Swanson (1976) determined that the accuracy with which project managers predicted completion of projects was largely dependent on their voluntary, self-initiated attempts to solicit feedback from others within the organization.

Interorganizational Communication

There appears to be increasing interest and research in *interorganizational communication*—communication between larger systems. A systems perspective (Miller, 1965, 1975) appears to have significant value to communication research regarding ongoing organizations (Wigand, 1976).

A recent catalyst for interorganizational research is the work of Miller (1975). Miller describes the systems-relationships of *space* (physical and conceptual), *time* (particular instant and duration), *mass, matter,* and *energy* (ability to do work). His model distinguishes between *information* and *communication,* the latter described as the process by which systems adjust to their environments and the suprasystem—the next higher system in which the system being analyzed is a component or subsystem.

Researchers have built upon such systems concepts, exploring information flow between large, often competing, organizations. Czepiel (1975) indicates the value of studying information diffusion as a systemic process. Czepiel contends that one cannot understand intraorganizational dynamics without first taking into account the flow of interorganizational information.

Adkinbode and Clark (1976) have advanced a conceptual framework for viewing interorganizational relationships which they contend extends earlier social or psychological models. Their data indicate that cooperation between organizations is correlated with democratic leadership styles within organizations. Conversely, they conclude that competition between organizations is spurred by centralized administrative practices and/or sudden changes in within-organization leadership styles.

Metcalfe (1976) describes *communicative integration* as a key variable in interorganizational relationships. Again working with government agencies, Metcalfe differentiates between *responsive* organization-environment relationships (those modifying the organization) and *effective* organization-environment relationships (those modifying the environment), stressing the need for third-party communication linkages between organizations.

Schermerhorn (1976) investigated interorganizational communication patterns between hospital administrators. Using a relationship taxonomy of (1) organizational interdependence, (2) component interdependence, (3) cooperation, (4) exchange, and (5) concerted decision making, Schermerhorn found:

1. Openness to interorganizational communication was enhanced when an administrator perceived his own hospital as a high performing institution.
2. Professional identification and state identification of administrators were positively correlated with openness to interorganizational communication.
3. Administrators having higher levels of boundary activity (essentially central or liaison behaviors) were more favorably disposed to, and more active in, interorganizational communication.

Schermerhorn sees important implications from his research for within-organization communication, namely, the need for administrators to expand decision making to include additional agents in the hospital authority structure.

Communication and Organization Development

The interests of organizational communication researchers and organization development (OD) theorists and practitioners appear to overlap more and more as these two fields mature (Richetto, 1975; Hain & Tubbs, 1974; Hain & Widgery, 1973).

Communication and information flow variables are implicit, for example, in recent research by Franklin (1975) who studied the influence process from higher to lower organizational levels in one company. He concluded that group dynamics at higher organizational levels established the organizational climate for lower levels and subsequent organizational change.

Nielsen and Kimberly (1976) describe a communication intervention strategy that can be used during the stage of transition from one leadership style to another. A two- to three-day session is held for employees and both the outgoing and incoming manager. The meeting itself consists of (1) clarifying goals and objectives, (2) clarifying the status of current projects and assignments, (3) clarifying likely changes in managerial style, and (4) acknowledging previously-collected data on concerns about forthcoming change(s). Finally, the incoming manager and the work group move through a third phase, during which they (1) plan the transition processes, (2) define new roles where necessary, (3) set new goals and objectives, and (4) establish mechanisms for evaluation and follow-up.

Finally, there appears to be potential contribution for both organizational and interorganizational communication research within sociotechnical experiments being conducted in various organizations on the "quality of working life." According to the National Quality of Work Center (1975), "restructured communications information flow" is among the specific issues which joint management and union task forces are confronting in several "project sites" across the nation.

SUMMARY

A review of current research in organizational communication reveals, not surprisingly, the best and the worst reflections of its past. From one vantage point, one sees healthy diversification—an emerging field, broad in scope and potential. From another vantage point, however, one sees disarray approaching anomie—a kaleidoscopic view of communication behavior and organizational theory appearing in blurred, disjointed images that defy attempts to bring them into focus.

Despite methodological and theoretical advancement, components of the field have yet to be linked into comprehensive theory of communication processes in ongoing organizations. Research summarized in this overview fails generally to overcome the methodological and, particularly, theoretical problems in the field identified by numerous writers (Redding, 1972; Price, 1972; Porter & Roberts, 1972; Roberts & O'Reilly, 1974; Goldhaber, 1974; Porter, 1976; Piersol, 1976).

Among the shortcomings of organizational communication research most frequently citied are:

"Single instrument" approaches. For the most part, communication research in ongoing organizations has relied on one methodology for gathering data. Given the tremendous complexities involved in organizational communication systems, multimeasurement approaches appear far more appropriate (Yates et al., 1976).

Situational variables. Redding (1972) has described problems of generalizing from one organizational context to another. Parochial approaches to studying communication in organizations have made cross-organization comparisons nearly impossible.

Small, perhaps unrepresentative, samples. Porter and Roberts (1972) contend that our "knowledge base" of human communication behavior in organizations consists of fewer than 1500 persons. While some may question this figure, and while others may comment on the difficulty of capturing larger samples in ongoing organizations, the size and nature of our collective data base is questionable.

Lack of normative data. Only recently has there appeared the potential for establishing organizational communication norms across a large sampling of organizations. Until the International

Communication Association Audit, no substantial data bank has been available to organizational communication researchers. Even now, only the mechanism for establishing this base exists; the base itself must yet be built.

Limited examples of actual communication behavior. In reflecting upon historical and contemporary research in organizational communication, one finds measures of attitudes, measures of information flow, and measures of message content. In none of these approaches is the observation of actual communication behavior evident. In very few instances (e.g., Piersol's use of the "shadow technique," 1954) do we find systematic "clinical" approaches to observing actual communication behavior.

Static, rather than dynamic measures. The importance of time as a variable has been reported in organizational research (Likert, 1967; Hain, 1970). With few exceptions (Burns, 1954; Kelly, 1962; Sutton & Porter, 1968), time-series analyses have not been conducted in organizational communication research. Roberts and O'Reilly (1974) suggest the need for such measures in organizational communication research.

Uncertain predictive validity. There has been a paucity of research aimed at determining the role of communication in organizational performance. Most researchers, like most managers and administrators, have implicitly assumed the marriage of "effective communication" and "effective organization." While this assumption may be accurate, it is based more upon faith or common sense than upon empirical evidence.

Conclusions

A "Future" Direction: The International Communication Association Communication Audit

Recent research has been undertaken within the International Communication Association which attempts to minimize some of the shortcomings of earlier organizational communication research.

Since 1971, some 100 scholars and pratitioners have contributed to the development of the *ICA Communication Audit*—a comprehensive, multiphased procedure for the collection, storage, analysis, and feedback of data on communication behavior and information flow in ongoing organizations. Description of this procedure, its rationale, development history, and data analysis techniques have been provided in-depth elsewhere (Yates, et al. 1976; Goldhaber, 1976). Essentially, the *Audit* employs the data-gathering and analysis techniques of survey-feedback, network analysis, critical incidents, and interview within the research perspectives of communication climate, information flow, and message content.

Chief among the *Audit's* potential contributions to organizational communication research is its capacity to integrate these four data-gathering techniques and three research perspectives into a comprehensive model of the organization as a total communication system. Additionally, the *Audit* provides a means by which findings gleaned from these data and research orientations may be compared with one another. For example, the *Audit* can use network analysis to identify liaisons among existing networks in an organization, and then compare survey data obtained from these individuals with those from other organization members to detect differences in perceptions of the organization's communication climate. Or, in a similar vein, it is possible to gather critical incidents of "effective" or "ineffective" communication behavior among liaisons, gaining insights into differences in perception between them and less influential organization members. Also, using the *Audit's* integrative capability, researchers can contrast message type, frequency, and duration in organizations whose survey results suggest a *supportive* communication climate, with those whose survey results suggest a *defensive* communication climate.

Specifically (and in light of the shortcomings of organizational communication research cited earlier) the *ICA Communication Audit* would appear to offer these research and theory-building strengths:

1. *Multiple data-gathering instruments*, compensating for earlier single instrument approaches for measuring communication processes in the highly complex environment of

formal organizations.

2. *Standardized data-gathering and analysis procedures* from one study to another, thus attempting to better account for *situational* variables and afford greater generalizability of findings.

3. *Development and maintenance of a large, normative data bank* against which to compare present research; at this writing, the *Audit* data bank contains measurements from over 5,000 subjects in a variety of on-going organizations.

4. *Development of a critical incidents taxonomy* of "effective" and "ineffective" communication behaviors; while not based upon researchers' direct observations, this subject-generated taxonomy approaches the identification of *actual* face-to-face communication behavior in on-going organizations.

5. *Establishment of baseline data* for conducting *time-series analyses,* thus identifying trends or patterns in communication behaviors within a given organization over time.

6. *Increasing predictive validity of instruments* used to investigate relationships between organizational communication processes and overall organizational performance; this potential improvement in predictive validity can result when host organizations provide researchers access to such performance criteria as absenteeism, turnover, grievances, productivity, quality, "customer satisfaction," etc., with which to correlate their findings.

Drucker (1974) relates a "parable" of sorts which I find timely in closing this overview of the field:

An old story tells of three stonecutters who were asked what they were doing. The first replied, "I'm making a living." The second kept on hammering while he said, "I am doing the best job of stonecutting in the entire country." The third one looked up with a visionary gleam in his eyes and said, "I am building a cathedral." (p 431)

Reflecting on the state-of-the-art of organizational communication, it appears that some important stonecutting in theory and research has been done—perhaps even some of the best stonecutting that could have been done—but the building of a cathedral is only just beginning.

REFERENCES

ADAMS, J., & SWANSON, L. Information process behavior and estimating accuracy in operations management. *Academy of Management Journal,* 1976, 19, 1.

AKINBODE, I., & CLARK, R. A framework for analyzing inter-organizational relationships. *Human Relations,* 1976, 29, 2, 111-114.

ALLEN, T. Performance information channels in the transfer of technology. *Industrial Management Review,* 1966, 8, 87-98.

ALLEN, T., & COHEN, S. Information flow in an R and D laboratory. Monograph, MIT, 1966.

ALLEN, T. Communication networks in R and D laboratories. *R and D Management,* 1970, 1, 1, 14-21.

ASHBY, W. General systems as a new discipline. *General Systems,* 1958, 3, 1-6.

BAKER, H. Company-wide understanding of industrial relations policies: A study in communication. Monograph, Princeton University, 1948.

BAKER H., BALLANTINE, J., & TRUE, J. Transmitting information through management and union channels. Monograph, Princeton University, 1949.

BAKKE, E. Concept of the social organization. *General Systems,* 1959, 4, 95-122.

BARNARD, C. *The functions of the executive.* Cambridge: Harvard University Press, 1938.

BAVELAS, A., & BARRETT, D. An experimental approach to organizational communication. *Personnel,* 1951, 27, 366-371.

BENNIS, W., & SLATER, P. The temporary society. New York: Harper and Row, 1968.

BERNE, E. *Transactional analysis in psychotherapy.* New York: Grove Press, 1961.

BERNSTEIN, B. Organizational communication: Theories, issues, analysis. Paper presented at the annual meeting of the International Communication Association, Portland, Oregon, 1976.

BERTALANFFY, L. VON. The theory of open systems in physics and biology. *Science,* 1950, 3, 23-29.

BERTALANFFY, L. General systems theory. *Yearbook of Society for General Systems Research,* 1956, 1, 3.

BEST, L. An assessment of the attitudes of a corporation's male managers toward women in business. Unpublished doctoral dissertation, University of Toledo, 1975.

BOULDING, K. General system theory: The skeleton of science. *Management Science,* 1956, 2, 197-208.

BOULDING, K. The unity of the social sciences. *Human Organization,* 1975, 4, 332.

BRIEF, A., & WALLACE, M. The imact of employee sex and performance on the allocation of organizational rewards. *Journal of Psychology,* 1976, 92, 25-34.

BROWNE, C., & NEITZEL, B. Communication, supervision, and morale. *Journal of Applied Psychology,* 1952, 36, 86-91.

BURGOON, M., & MILLER, G. Prior attitude and language intensity as predictors of message style and attitude change following counter-attitudinal advocacy. *Journal of Personality and Social Psychology,* 1971, 20, 246-253.

BURNS, T. The directions of activities and communication in a departmental executive group. *Human Relations,* 1954, 7, 73-97.

CHAPMAN, J. Comparison of male and female leadership styles. *Academy of Management Journal,* 1975, 18, 3, 645-650.

COCH, L., & FRENCH, J. Overcoming resistance to change. *Human Relations*, 1948, 1, 512-532.

CZEPIEL, J. Patterns of inter-organizational communication and the diffusion of a major technological innovation in a competitive industrial community. *Academy of Management Journal*, 1975, 18, 1, 6-23.

DAHLE, T. An objective and comparative study of five methods of transmitting information to business and industrial employees. Unpublished doctoral dissertation, Purdue University, 1953.

DALY, J., & LETH, S. Communication apprehension and the personnel selection decision. Paper presented at the annual meeting of the International Communication Association, Portland, Oregon, 1976.

DALY, J., & McCROSKEY, JR. Occupational choice and desirability as a function of communication apprehension. *Journal of Counseling Psychology*, 1975, 22, 309-313.

DALY, J., McCROSKEY, J., & FALCIONE, R. Homophily-heterophily and the prediction of supervisor satisfaction.

DALY, J., & MILLER, M. Apprehension of writing as a predictor of message intensity. *Journal of Psychology*, 1975, 89, 175-177.

DANOWSKI, J. Environmental uncertainty and communication network complexity: A cross-system, cross-cultural test. Paper presented at the annual meeting of the International Communication Association, Portland, Oregon, 1976.

DAVIS, K. Management communication and the grapevine. *Harvard Business Review*, 1953, 31, 43-49.

DEE, J. An analysis of the formal channels of communication in an industrial union local. Unpublished doctoral dissertation, Purdue University, 1959.

DEUTSCH, K. On communication models in the social sciences. *Public Opinion Quarterly*, 1952, 16, 356-380.

DOVER, C. The three eras of management communication. *Journal of Communication*, 1959, 9, 168-172.

DOWNS, C., & LARIMER, M. The status of organizational communication in speech departments. Unpublished manuscript, 1973.

DRUCKER, P. *Management: tasks, responsibilities, practices*. New York: Harper and Row, 1974.

DUTTON, R. TA: Is it a four letter word? Unpublished paper, Paper presented at the annual meeting, *Academy of Management*, Kansas City, 1976.

FALCIONE, R., & GREENBAUM, H. (Eds.) *Organizational communication abstracts, 1974 and 1975*. Urbana, Illinois: American Business Communication Association, 1975, 1976.

FARACE, V., & MacDONALD, D. New directions in the study of organizational communication. Unpublished manuscript, 1971.

FLANAGAN, J. The critical incident technique. *Psychological Bulletin*, 1954, 51, 327-358.

FOLLETT, M. in *Dynamic administration: the collected papers of Mary Parker Follett* (Metcalf, G. and Urwick, L., Eds.), New York: Harpers, 1941.

FRANKLIN, J. Down the organization: Influence processes across levels of hierarchy. *Administrative Science Quarterly*, 1975, 20, 2, 153-163.

FRESHLEY, D. A study of the attitudes of industrial management personnel toward communication. Unpublished doctoral dissertation, The Ohio State University, 1955.

FRIEDLANDER, F. OD reaches adolescence: An exploration of its underlying values. *Journal of Applied Behavioral Science*, 1976, 12, 1,

FUNK, H., & BECKER, R. Measuring the effectiveness of industrial communications. *Personnel*, 1952, 29, 237-240.

FUNK, F. Communication attitudes of industrial foremen as related to their productivity. Unpublished doctoral dissertation, Purdue University, 1956.

GIVEN, W. *Bottom-up management*. New York: Harper, 1949.

GOLDHABER, G., BAKER, E., & RICHETTO, G. TA and OD: Research needs. In *Transactional analysis*, G. Goldhaber and M. Goldhaber (Eds.), Boston: Allyn and Bacon, 1976.

GOLDHABER, G. *Organizational communication*. Dubuque: Wm. C. Brown, 1974.

GOLDHABER, G. The ICA communication audit: Rationale and development. Paper presented at the annual meeting of the *Academy of Management*, Kansas City, 1976.

GREENBAUM, H. Organizational communication systems: Identification and appraisal. Paper presented at the annual meeting of the International Communication Association, Phoenix, 1971.

GREENBAUM, H. The appraisal of organizational communication systems. Paper presented at the annual meeting of the International Communication Association, Atlanta, 1972.

GREENBAUM, H. Management's role in organizational communication analysis. *Journal of business Communication*, 1972, 39-52.

GUETZKOW, H. Communication in organizations. In *Handbook of organizations*. J. March (Ed.) Chicago: Rand McNally, 1965, 534-573.

HAGEN, R., & KAHN, A. Discrimination against women. *Journal of Applied Social Psychology*, 1975, 5, 4, 362-376.

HAIN, T. *Organizational change patterns*. Monograph, General Motors Institute, 1972.

HAIN, T., & WIDGERY, R. Organizational development: The role of communication in diagnosis, change and evaluation. Paper presented at the annual meeting of the International Communication Association, Montreal, 1973.

HAIN, T., & TUBBS, S. Organizational diagnosis: The significant role of communication. Paper presented at the annual meeting of the International Communication Association, New Orleans, 1974.

HAIRE, M. (Ed.) *Modern organization theory*. New York: John Wiley and Sons, 1959.

HALL, A., & FAGEN, R. In *Modern systems research for the behavioral scientist*. W. Buckley (Ed.), Chicago: Aldine, 1968.

HAWKINS, B. Supervisor-subordinate communication as related to interpersonal need confirmation. Unpublished doctoral dissertation, Purdue University, 1975.

HELLWEG, S. Perceived immediate superior credibility and homophily as a function of external conflict within a military organization. Paper presented at the annual meeting of the International Communication Association, Portland, Oregon, 1976.

HERON, A. *Sharing information with employees*. Stanford University Press, 1942.

JACKSON, J. Analysis of interpersonal relations in a formal organization. Unpublished doctoral dissertation, University of Michigan, 1953.

JACOBSON, E., & SEASHORE, S. Communication practices in complex organizations. *Journal of social issues*, 1951, 7, 28-40.

JEDEL, M., & KUJAWA, D. Racial dichotomies in employment perceptions: An empirical study of workers in selected Atlanta-based firms. *Academy of Management Journal*,

1976, 2, 19.

JONGEWARD, D. *Everybody wins: Transactional analysis applied to organizations.* Reading, Massachusetts: Addison-Wesley, 1973.

KATZ, D., & KAHN, R. *The social psychology of organizations.* New York: Wiley, 1966.

KATZ, E. The two-step flow of communication: An up-to-date report on an hypothesis. *Public Opinion Quarterly,* 1957, 21, 61-78.

KELLY, C. Actual listening behavior of industrial supervisors as related to listening ability, general mental ability, selected personality factors and supervisory effectiveness. Unpublished doctoral dissertation, Purdue University, 1962.

KRAUT, A. The entrance of black employees into traditionally white jobs. *Academy of Management Journal,* 197 , 3, 18.

KRIVONOS, P. Subordinate-superior communication as related to instrinsic and extrinsic motivation: An experimental field study. Unpublished doctoral dissertation, Purdue University, 1975.

LATHAM, G., WEXLEY, E., & PURSELL, E. Training managers to minimize rating errors in the observation of behavior. *Journal of Applied Psychology,* 1975, 60, 5, 550-555.

LAZARSFELD, P., BERELSON, B., & GAUDET, H. *The people's choice.* New York: Columbia University Press, 1948.

LEAVITT, H., & MUELLER, R. Some effects of feedback on communications. *Human Relations,* 1951, 4, 401-410.

LEAVITT, H. Some effects of certain communication patterns on group performance. *Journal of Abnormal and Social Psychology,* 1951, 46, 38-50.

LESIKAR, R. TA: Are all the facts in? Paper presented at the annual meeting, *Academy of Management,* Kansas City, 1976.

LEVEL, D. A case study of human communications in an urban bank. Unpublished doctoral dissertation. Purdue University, 1959.

LIKERT, R. *The Human Organization.* New York: McGraw-Hill, 1967.

LULL, P., FUNK, F., & PIERSOL, D. Business and industrial communication from the viewpoint of the corporation president. Monograph, Purdue University, 1954.

MAIER, N., READ, W., & HOOVEN. J. Breakdown in boss-subordinate communication. In *Communication in organizations: Some new research findings.* Monograph, Foundation for Research on Human Behavior, University of Michigan, 1959.

MARCH, J., & SIMON, H. *Organizations.* New York: John Wiley and Sons, 1958.

McCANN, F., & McCANN, M. An experimental study of transactional analysis as a vehicle of organizational development. Unpublished doctoral dissertation, United States International University, 1975.

McCROSKEY, J., & LEPARD, T. The effects of communication apprehension on nonverbal behavior. Paper presented at the annual meeting of the Eastern Speech Association, New York, 1975.

McCROSKEY, J., RICHMOND, V., & DALY, J. The development of a measure of perceived homophily in interpersonal communication. *Human Communication Research,* 1975, 1, 323-332.

MacDONALD, D. Communication roles and communication content in a bureaucratic setting. Unpublished doctoral dissertation, Michigan State University, 1970.

METCALFE, J. Organizational strategies and inter-organizational networks. *Human Relations,* 1976, 29, 4, 327-343.

MILLER, J. *Living systems: Basic concepts. Behavioral Science,* 1965, 10, 193-237.

MILLER, J. The nature of living systems. Living systems: The society. *Behavioral Science,* 1975, 20, 6, 343-366.

MINTER, R. A comparative analysis of managerial communication in two divisions of a large manufacturing company. Unpublished doctoral dissertation, Purdue University, 1969.

MIRAGLIA, J. An experimental study of the effects of communication training upon perceived job performance of nursing supervisors in two urban hospitals. Unpublished doctoral dissertation, Purdue University, 1963.

MONGE, P., BOISMIER, J., COOKE, A., DAY, P., EDWARDS, J., & KIRST, K. Determinants of communication structure in large organizations. Paper presented at the annual meeting of the International Communication Association, Portland, Oregon, 1976.

National Quality of Work Center. The quality of work program: The first eighteen months. Monograph, 1975, NQWC, Washington, D.C.

NIELSEN, T. The communication survey: A study of communication problems in three office and factory units. Unpublished doctoral dissertation, Northwestern University, 1953.

NIELSEN, W., & KIMBERLY, J. Smoothing the way for organizational changes. *Advanced Management Journal,* 1976, 41, 2, 4-16.

PACE, W. An analysis of selected oral communication attributes of direct-selling representatives as related to their sales effectiveness. Unpublished doctoral dissertation, Purdue University, 1960.

PATTERSON, R. Women in management: An empirical study of the effects of sex and marital status on job performance ratings, promotion ratings, and promotion decisions. Unpublished doctoral dissertation, University of Minnesota, 1975.

PATERSON, D., & JENKINS, J. Communication between management and workers. *Journal of Applied Psychology,* 1948, 32, 71-80.

PELZ, D. Influence: A key to effective leadership in the first-line supervisor. *Personnel,* 1952, 29, 209-217.

PIGORS, P. *Effective communication in industry.* New York: National Association of Manufacturers, 1949.

PIERSOL, D. Panel forum: Evolution and future of organizational communication—perspectives from management scholars. Unpublished remarks presented to the International Communication Association, Portland, Oregon, 1976.

PIERSOL, D. A case study of oral communication practices of foremen in a mid-western corporation. Unpublished doctoral dissertation, Purdue University, 1955.

PIETRI, P., et al. Organizational communication: An historical survey. *Journal of Business Communication,* 1974, 12, 3-25.

PLANTY, E., & MACHAVER, W. Upward communications: A project in executive development using the syndicate method. *Personnel,* 1952, 28, 304-318.

PORTER, L. Panel forum: Evolution and future or organizational communication—perspectives from management scholars. Unpublished remarks, International Communication Association annual convention, Portland, Oregon, 1976.

PORTER, L., & ROBERTS, K. Communication in organizations, Technical Report #12. Contract #N00014-69-A-0200-9001, NR151-315, Washington, D.C., Office of Naval Research, July 1972.

PRICE, J. *Handbook of organizational measurement.* Lexington, Massachusetts: D. C. Heath and Co., 1972.

REDDING, W., & SANBORN, G. *Business and industrial communication.* New York: Harper and Row, 1964.

REDDING, W. The empirical study of human communication in business and industry. In *Frontiers in experimental speech communication research,* Reid, P. (ed.) Syracuse University Press, 1966.

REDDING, W. *Communication within the organization.* New York: Industrial Communication Council; Lafayette, Indiana: Purdue Research Foundation, 1972.

REIF, W., NEWSTROM, J., & MONCZKA, R. Exploding some myths about women managers. *California Management Journal,* 1975, 17, 4, 72-79.

RICHARDS, W. A conceptually based method for the analysis of communication networks in large complex organizations. Paper presented at the annual meeting of the International Communication Association, Phoenix, 1971.

RICHARDS, W. A coherent systems approach for the study of large complex systems. Paper presented at the annual meeting of the International Communication Association, Portland, Oregon, 1976.

RICHETTO, G. Source credibility and personal influence in three contexts: A study of dyadic communication in a complex aerospace organization. Unpublished doctoral dissertation, Purdue University, 1969.

RICHETTO, G. Organizational communication: An "unconventional" perspective. In R. Applbaum, O. Jenson and R. Carroll (Eds.), *Speech communication: a basic anthology.* New York: Macmillan, 1975.

ROBERTS, K., & O'REILLY, C., Measuring organizational communication. *Journal of Applied Psychology,* 1974, 59, 321-326.

ROBERTS, K. O'REILLY, C., BRETTON, G., & PORTER, L. *Organizational theory and organizational communication: A communication failure?* Technical report #2, Contract #NOOO314-69-A-0222, Washington, D.C., Office of Naval Research, 1973.

ROETHLISBERGER, F., & DICKSON, W. *Management and the worker.* Cambridge: Harvard University Press, 1943.

ROGERS, E. *Diffusion of innovations.* New York: Free Press, 1962.

ROGERS, E., & AGARWALA–ROGERS. *Communication in organizations.* New York: Free Press, 1976.

ROSS, R. A case study of communication breakdowns in the general telephone company of Indiana. Unpublished doctoral dissertation, Purdue University, 1954.

RUDOLPH, E. An evaluation of ECCO analysis as a communication audit methodology. Paper presented at the annual meeting of the International Communication Association, Atlanta, 1972.

SANBORN, G. A case study of human communication in a nationwide retail sales organization. Unpublished doctoral dissertation, Purdue University, 1961.

SANBORN, G. Communication in business: An overview. In Redding, W. and Sanborn, G. (Eds.), *Business and industrial communication.* New York: Harper and Row, 1967.

SCHERMERHORN, J. Openness to inter-organizational cooperation: A study of hospital administrators. *Academy of Management Journal,* 1976, 19, 2, 225-236.

SCHWARTZ, D. Liaison-communication roles in a formal organization. Monograph, North Dakota State University, 1968.

SIMONS, H. A comparison of communication attributes and

rated job performance of supervisors in a large commercial enterprise. Unpublished doctoral dissertation, Purdue University, 1961.

SMITH, R. Communication correlates of interpersonal sensitivity among industrial supervisors. Unpublished doctoral dissertation, Purdue University, 1967.

STEERS, R. Factors affecting job attitudes in a goal-setting environment. *Academy of Management Journal,* 1976, 19, 1, 6-16.

STULL, J. Openness in supervisor-subordinate communication: A quasi-experimental field study. Unpublished doctoral dissertation, Purdue University, 1975.

SUTTON, H., & PORTER, L. A study of the grapevine in a governmental organization. *Personnel Psychology,* 1968, 21, 223-230.

TAYLOR, J., & BOWERS, D. Survey of organizations. Ann Arbor, Institute for Social Research, 1972.

THAYER, L. Communication and organization theory. In Dance, F. (Ed.), *Human communication theory.* New York: Holt, Rinehart, and Winston, 1967.

TOMPKINS, P. An analysis of communication between headquarters and selected units of a national labor union. Unpublished doctoral dissertation, Purdue University, 1962.

TOMPKINS, P. General semantics and human relations. *Central States Speech Journal,* 1965, 285-289.

TOMPKINS, P. Organizational communication: A state-of-the-art review. In *Proceedings: conference on organizational communication,* NASA, 1967.

TORONTO, R. A general systems model for the analysis of organizational change. *Behavioral Science,* 1975, 20, 3, 145-156.

URBAN, T. TA: Panacea or placebo? Paper presented at the annual meeting, *Academy of Management,* Kansas City, 1976.

VROMAN, W. TA: The adult as the effective executive. Paper presented at the annual meeting, *Academy of Management,* Kansas City, 1976.

WALTON, E. A magnetic theory of organizational communication. Monograph, US Naval Ordnance Test Station, China Lake, California, 1962.

WATSON, G., & BARONE, S. The self-concept, personal values and motivational orientations of black and white managers. *Academy of Management Journal,* 1976, 19, 1, 36-48.

WICKESBERG, A. Communications networks in the business organization structure. *Academy of Management Journal,* 1967, September, 253-262.

WIGAND, R. Communication and inter-organizational relationships among complex organizations in social service settings. Paper presented at the annual meeting of the International Communication Association, Portland, Oregon, 1976.

WILLIAMS, D. An analysis of the relationship of selected ego state frequency patterns to selected task and social leadership styles of participants in problem-solving groups. Unpublished doctoral dissertation, University of Texas at Austin, 1975.

YATES, M., PORTER, T., GOLDHABER, G., DENNIS, H., & RICHETTO, G. The ICA communication audit system: Results of six studies. Paper presented at the annual meeting of the International Communication Association, Portland, Oregon, 1976.

ZIMA, J. The counseling communication of supervisors in a large manufacturing company. Unpublished doctoral dissertation, Purdue University, 1967.

INTERVIEWER AND CLIENT BEHAVIORS
IN SUPPORTIVE AND DEFENSIVE INTERVIEWS[1]

JEAN M. CIVIKLY, R. WAYNE PACE, and RICHARD M. KRAUSE
University of New Mexico

At the core of the process by which social services are delivered is the interview between providers and low-income clients. These interviews, while crucial to the continuation of the interviewer-interviewee relationship, are inhibited by forces such as the apparent defensive nature of the communication environment. Gibb's (1961) supportive-defensive paradigm was used as the conceptual basis for an investigation of the pattern of verbal and nonverbal behaviors manifest in such interviews. Communicative behaviors were examined to identify situations rated as defensive, supportive, or intermediate.

Interview behaviors were analyzed using videotape in the field settings, and interview climates were characterized. The results suggest the validity of the supportive-defensive paradigm and further indicate that individual behaviors may be less important in identifying interview climate than are behavioral repertoires.

Each year large numbers of individuals apply to local, state, and federal agencies for assistance and services to improve their personal circumstances. Delivery of assistance through such programs as employment security, legal aid, food stamps, and medical care invariably include some form of interpersonal contact between the client and a representative of the service agency. As Meyer, Borgatta, and Fanshel (1964, p. 253) assert, "casework, whatever else it may include, has the direct face-to-face interaction of caseworker and client in the interview situation as the primary component." The interaction between client and agency worker provides the information necessary to diagnose and to establish level of need, but it also has potential for establishing the client's perception of the agency, or determining the client's willingness to reveal the extent of the problem. Handled well, this interaction has the potential to serve as the vehicle for problem-solving influence. Handled poorly, the result may be the failure to provide the necessary assistance and a bitterness on the part of the client.

The ability to recognize what kinds of behavior affect others, positively and negatively, demands a sensitivity to patterns of interaction not often recognized by many agency employees, especially when an employee is struggling to cope with the specific problems of clients from a different socioeconomic class. In a comparison of the styles of communication of lower and middle socioeconomic-class individuals, Schatzman and Strauss (1955) discovered "striking" differences in the perspectives evidenced in communicating, in the ability to take the listener's role, in the handling of classifications, and in the frameworks and stylistic devices which order and implement communication. From the perspective of the lower-class person, Schatzman and Strauss (1955) report:

> The interviewer is of higher social class than the respondent, so that the interview (is) a conversation between the classes . . . It is entirely probable that more effort and ability are demanded by a cross-class conversation of this sort than between middle-class respondent and middle-class interviewer. (p. 337)

Schatzman and Strauss (1955) concluded that it was not surprising that the interviewer was often baffled and that the respondent frequently misunderstood what the interviewer wanted.

A similar disparity in perspectives of client and social worker was also noted by Stark (1959), in a study of 20 intake interviews at a family service agency. The analysis indicated that clients could be helped if the social worker was able to understand the framework within which the clients viewed their problems. Indicative of disparate frameworks was the agency's misconception that all clients have some knowledge of the agency functions. Too often in interviews the social worker gave an intellectualized explanation of the purposes of the service agency, instead of a description in language understandable to the client. These differences in orientation may account for the difficulties experienced by social workers which Stark (1959) noted: (1) identifying the client's characteristically defense responses, (2) obtaining a full and clear statement of the request, and (3) responding in an unstereotyped fashion to the requests.

In a British study, John Mayer and Noel Timms (1969) hypothesized that the casework process would increase in efficiency as more attention was given to the outlook of the client. Their study, based upon semistructured research interviews with psychotherapy clients, sought information on the events which drew the client to the agency. They concluded that working class clients came to the interview with a method of problem solving that precipitated difficulty in interaction with social caseworkers. The caseworkers tended to assume that the clients' views were essentially the same as theirs, although they were decidedly different. Mayer and Timms (1969) conclude, "It is our impression that the social workers were unaware that the clients entered the treatment situation with a different mode of problem solving and that the client's behavior (discontinuance) was in part traceable to that fact" (p. 37).

Gibb (1961) has suggested that one of the sources of distortion and misunderstanding between interactants is a defensive attitude. "As a person becomes more and more defensive," Gibb (1961) comments, "he becomes less and less able to perceive accurately the motives, the values, and the emotions of the sender" (p. 148). Where behaviors perceived as threatening and punishing are predominant in a relationship, the climate is called *defensive*. Where behaviors perceived as positive and rewarding are predominant in a relationship, the climate is called *supportive*. Gibb defined six behavior pairs characteristic of defensive and supportive climates in small groups: *evaluation* versus *description*, control versus *problem orientation, strategy* versus *spontaneity*, neutrality versus *empathy, superiority* verses *equality*, and *certainty* versus *provisionalism*. Gibb (1961) concluded that

"arousing defensiveness interferes with communication and thus makes it difficult—and sometimes impossible—for anyone to convey ideas clearly and to move effectively toward the solution of therapeutic, educational, or managerial problems" (p. 142).

Ostensibly, however, there is little research on the influence of supportive and defensive climates as discussed by Gibb (1961) in interviews. Yet, studies in various disciplines (notably counseling and psychotherapy) have used a variety of labels to describe similar behaviors.

The most common equivalent term for supportiveness appears to be *empathy*. Rollo May (1967) cites this variable as the "key to the counseling process" (p. 75). Greif and Hogan (1973) factor analyzed an empathy scale and found three subordinate factors to be of importance: *sociability, tolerance,* and *humanism*. Rogers (1962) discussed three behaviors to consider in the counselor-client relationship: *congruence (genuineness), empathy,* and *positive regard*. He also noted that the interviewer should not only strive for these behaviors, but must also *communicate* them to the client in such a way that the client does not misconstrue empathy for the lack of involvement, or warmth for threatening closeness. Although information about these feelings may be communicated verbally, evidence indicates that nonverbal aspects may be at least as important, if not more so (Haase and Tepper, 1972). Other terms which relate closely to *supportiveness* and which have been researched include *facilitative behaviors, warmth, acceptance, understanding, friendliness, rapport, patience, respect, honesty, sincerity, interest,* and *recognition*.

Defensive behaviors exhibited in the interview setting are also referred to by many different labels. Some terms used are *ego threat, repression, hostility, withdrawal, inhibitors, evasion, duplicity, authoritarianism, maneuvers, control,* and *anxiety*.

There are frequent discussions of defensive behaviors in the literature of psychology, but it appears that the studies focus more on extreme psychological defense mechanisms, rather than Gibb's (1961) categories, which are only mild manifestations of serious disorders. Nevertheless, the effects of defensive behaviors are relevant to two-person interviews in nonclinical settings. Doster and Strickland (1971) found that topics with a high-risk expectation resulted in less self-disclosure and more defensiveness, as measured by lengthy silences. They also found that subjects assessed as high in need for social approval characteristically engaged in socially desirable behaviors, avoided actions that were likely to result in social disapproval, and tended to be guarded and defensive.

Considering the interview as a special instance of interaction, Garfield and Affleck (1961) noted that therapists reacted to defensiveness in clients with extremely negative feelings, thus producing a spiraling cycle of defensiveness. Additional research suggests that client defensiveness predisposes the client to terminate counseling sessions prematurely (Hiler, 1959; McNair, Lorr, & Callahan, 1963; Taulbee, 1958). Overall and Aronson (1963) suggest that the effectiveness of initial interviews with individuals of low income may be a significant determinant of whether they return or drop out of a program. In other words, the way in which applicants for services are treated and communicated with may critically influence whether they continue to seek services.

THE PRESENT RESEARCH

Underlying the present study is the assumption that a situation in which low-income clients must come to a government agency to apply for services, has, for the interviewee, the potential of being more threatening and punishing—hence more defensive than supportive. On the other hand, one would expect caseworkers with certain interpersonal communication skills to be able to foster patterns of strong supportiveness, thus acting as a deterrent to defensiveness. Therefore, one might find interviews in service agencies that appear: (1) highly supportive; (2) highly defensive; and (3) highly traditional—with alternating periods of defensiveness and supportiveness. From an analysis of interviews with *directional* climates—essentially supportive or defensive—and those with *nondirectional* climates—essentially balanced amounts of both defensive and supportive interaction—it may be possible to identify behaviors that characterize supportive and defensive climates in inter-

views between low-income clients and agency personnel.

RESEARCH QUESTIONS

The specific research questions that were investigated in this study focused on verbal and nonverbal behavior in two-person interviews. Three questions were asked:

1. What pattern of verbal and nonverbal behaviors seem to characterize the interaction in interviews involving a person of low income and a caseworker, counselor, or interviewer?
2. What kinds of verbal and nonverbal behaviors seem to characterize interviews whose climates are rated as primarily supportive?
3. What kinds of verbal and nonverbal behaviors seem to characterize interviews whose climates are rated as primarily defensive?

Methods and Procedures

To answer these questions, an intricate methodology was developed. As is the case with many studies in field or naturalistic settings, a large percentage of the total effort was devoted to obtaining appropriate access to the agency settings where interviews could be observed. The review of relevant literature suggested that most data about the effectiveness of delivery of services in agencies was self-reported. Such data are limited in their ability to answer the research questions raised in this study. Thus, the core of the methodology of this study was the gathering of videotape recordings of interviews in the normal work setting. Videotapes were most suitable for repeated viewing of the interviews and for the multiple analyses to which the interaction was subjected (verbal, vocal, nonverbal). This advantage, nevertheless, was accompanied by serious concern on the part of the research team for maintaining the dignity and privacy of the regular interview. Videotaping of the interviews required, therefore, the formulation of a policy to govern data-collection procedures:

1. Taping was made obvious to all potential participants. The equipment was visible but set far

enough away so as to not be obtrusive.

2. Informed consent was obtained from participants prior to taping. It was made clear that a client's decision not to participate in a taped interview would not influence the purpose for which the client came to the agency.

3. Client participants who gave initial agreement to record their interviews were encouraged to view the completed recording immediately after the interview. At that time, if they so decided, the tape was erased. Effectively, then, the participants had multiple opportunities to withdraw from the project.

4. Only the research team had access to the videotapes. Once the recordings were analyzed, all tapes were completely erased.

With this policy formulated,[2] access to locations in the Albuquerque, New Mexico area was secured through responsible parties. Approval was obtained from the Bernalillo County Mental Health Center, Albuquerque Legal Aid Society, Bernalillo County Social Service Agency, Bernalillo County Public Assistance Agency, and the North Valley Manpower Service Center (Employment Security Commission).

Videotapes were made of interviews in these agencies between interviewers/caseworkers/counselors and clients who came seeking services because they were of low income. The tapes allowed for the full reconstruction of the interview, or for a separate focus upon the interviewer or client alone. The nonverbal analysis was conducted by using only the visual portion of the tapes. Likewise, the verbal and vocal analyses were accomplished by using only the audio portion of the tapes. In addition to gathering tape-recorded data in the field, both interviewers and clients were asked to respond to questionnaires concerning their perception of the interview based upon the *supportive-defensive* paradigm.

A total of 47 taped interviews were collected from the five participating agencies.

Climate Analysis

Observers. Six observers (the three authors—2 male, 1 female, and three graduate research assistants—1 male, 2 female) viewed the tapes in teams of three. To preclude a possible inter-rater bias and a halo effect, each coder was assigned to a team on a rotating basis, resulting in a total of 16 combinations of team coders. The tapes were rank-ordered according to length, and distributed to each team in such a way that an individual coded approximately 350 minutes (in rotating teams).

Training. Prior to actual coding, each researcher received a *Climate Analysis Training Manual* and participated in a training session designed to teach distinctions between supportive and defensive climates.

Criteria for the six categories of supportive and defensive climates listed by Gibb, (1961) were presented, and examples for each were provided. In addition to Gibb's distinctions, which focus on the *sender* of supportive and defensive messages, models of supportive and defensive *responses,* both *verbal* and *nonverbal* dimensions, were listed. These responses were similar to those discussed by Haigh (1949).

Climate coding. Using the Climate Analysis Coding Form, coders rated the interaction during each 30-second tape segment in one of the following categories: *high supportive, low supportive, undecided, low defensive,* and *high defensive.* The criterion for inter-rater reliability was .66, i.e., agreement by two of the three judges on the categorization. This criterion was achieved in 94% of the total number of tape segments. Tapes with a .66 or higher ratio of supportive or defensive tallies were labeled accordingly. Tapes with a ratio less than .66 (generally ± .05 around .50) were labeled *nondirectional.*

Analysis of these three tape types served two functions. First, analysis of the supportive and defensive tapes provided a catalog of verbal and nonverbal behaviors which characterize these two climates. Second, analysis of nondirectional tapes provided a catalog of verbal and nonverbal behaviors which tended to generate or produce a shift toward either a supportive or defensive climate.

Coding interaction type. Procedures for analyzing 20 tapes, representing each of the types of interactions (*supportive, defensive, nondirectional*), were developed in a manner similar to the climate analysis.

Categories for the verbal and vocal analyses of the interviewer and client's behavior were selected on the basis of research in interviewing behaviors (Adams, 1958; Caplow, 1956; Fenlason et al., 1962; Gorden, 1969; Maier, 1958; Matarazzo & Wiens, 1972). The categories for the nonverbal analysis were based on an earlier nonverbal system devised for classroom settings (Civikly, 1973). Appendix I lists the behaviors for the verbal, vocal, and nonverbal analyses.

As was true in the *Climate Analysis,* the coding forms for the verbal and nonverbal behaviors were in 30-second intervals. An additional *Verbal Overall Coding Form* was developed to record general impressions of the syntactic, phonological, and miscellaneous behaviors exhibited by the interviewer or client.

Verbal-vocal coding procedure. Prior to coding the verbal and vocal behaviors of the interviewer and client, raters memorized the category numbers assigned to each behavior and completed a practice worksheet appearing in the training manual.

To facilitate accurate coding of the categories, posters indicating the category and appropriate number were situated above the monitor on which the tape was to be rated, and all coders attended a training session at which time the categories were clarified and a tape was analyzed. The criterion set for inter-rater reliability was 100% agreement by two coders rating the tape.[3]

For the verbal-vocal coding, only the audio portion of the interview was used. Each coder classified the verbal and vocal behaviors of the interviewer or client by recording a category number for each statement or question occurring in each 30-second segment. Also coded at this time was the category number for the vocal quality of the question or statement, such as loud, slow, etc.

Prior to coding the nonverbal behaviors of the interviewer or client, each researcher reviewed the training manual developed for this purpose. The manual described the procedure for coding and defined the categories to be coded. Coders also attended a training session, at which time the categories were clarified and a tape was analyzed. It was determined during this session that difficulties and inaccuracies in coding would result if both viewers watched the tape *and* coded (due to looking down at the coding form and missing potentially significant nonverbal behaviors). Several procedures to improve on this were tested, the most accurate being for one rater to view the tape and call out the behavior observed, while the second rater recorded the appropriate category number. With practice, and depending on the activity in each tape, it was also possible for the recorder to verify the observer's statements of behaviors.

During the nonverbal coding of the tape, the teams viewed the interaction without the audio portion, thus basing their ratings solely on visual cues. The procedure for coding provided for the raters to first view the tape and acquire a familiarity with the situation and to begin coding following this "orientation" period.

Statistical analyses. After coding the verbal, vocal, and nonverbal behaviors of each interview, the research team worked in pairs and transcribed each behavior onto computer coding sheets. From these sheets, computer cards were punched, indicating the number of times a particular behavior occurred in each 30-second segment. Each computer card represented one 30-second segment, with each column representing one of the *verbal, vocal,* or *nonverbal* behavior variables. In addition to the code number of each behavior, each card also indicated the *tape number, agency, tape length, sex, approximate age of the interviewer, sex of the client, segment number, segment description, analysis type,* and *profile type.*

Having cards punched with this information allowed for sorting the data to determine the specific verbal, vocal, and nonverbal behaviors occurring in the four profiles, and in each tri-cluster of 30-second segments *(directional supportive, directional defensive, nondirectional supportive, nondirectional defensive).*

A cross-tabulation program from *Statistical Programs for the Social Sciences* (Nie, Bent, & Hull, 1970) for analyzing nominal data was chosen. Data were grouped into two categories indicating the number of segments in which a given behavior did *not* occur. The significance of differences between the two independent groups of frequencies was determined by applying the *chi square* statistical test.

TABLE 1
Comparison of Significant Interviewer Verbal, Vocal, and Nonverbal
Behaviors in Supportive and Defensive Climates

Interviewer	
Supportive	Defensive
Verbal gives directions (42.9) gives short info. response (50.0) agrees with opinion (73.3) gives opinion (44.7)	Verbal off topic tangents (60.3) *asks for client's opinion (100)
Vocal pauses, hesitates (46.2) uhs, ums, etc. (45.7)	Vocal speaks loudly (43.9) speaks quickly (50.0)
Nonverbal smiles (51.2) extended eye gaze (53.8) thinking gestures (54.0) sits back (63.6) arms at sides (100) nods head (45.5) *smokes (100) leans forward (46.9) #frowns (41.6) #small hand gestures (33.3)	Nonverbal frowns (48.1) small hand gestures (37.6) raises brows (54.6) serious (74.4) looks away (50.5) looks down (60.9) writes (44.6) fiddles with objects (62.3) #leans forward (38.5)

*small frequency
#similar %

Behaviors that were distributed with a statistical significance at the .05 level of confidence, or beyond, were accepted as having a significant occurrence in the specified climates.

The cross-tabulations which were performed indicate how frequently each behavior variable occurred in each of nine categorizations:

1. Tape number (1-53) by variables.
2. Agency (5 agencies) by variables.
3. Tape length (0-3 minutes) by variables.
4. Interviewer sex and age (older, same age, younger) by variables.
5. Client sex by variables.
6. Segment number (0-30) by variables.
7. Segment description (SSS, DUS, SDS, etc.) by variables.

8. Analysis type (interviewer verbal, interviewer nonverbal, client verbal, client nonverbal) by variables.
9. Profile analysis (supportive, defensive, nondirectional supportive, nondirectional defensive) by variables.

The cross-tabulations discussed in depth in this report are those of item 9, Profile Analysis by Variables.

RESULTS AND DISCUSSION

Table 1 contrasts *interviewer verbal, vocal,* and *nonverbal* behaviors in *supportive* and *defensive* climates. Table 2 contrasts *client verbal, vocal,* and *nonverbal* behaviors in *supportive* and *defensive*

TABLE 2
Comparison of Significant Client Verbal, Vocal, and Nonverbal
Behaviors in Supportive and Defensive Climates

Client	
Supportive	Defensive
Verbal agrees with opinion (66.7) *disagrees with opinion (85.7) provides explanation (45.3) gives opinion (62.8)	Verbal
Vocal pauses, hesitates (39.2) uhs, ums, etc. (50.9)	Vocal #pauses, hesitates (33.0) *generally good (100) monotone (59.2) speaks loudly (95.5) *laughs (92.3)
Nonverbal smiles (48.4) raises brows (52.5) serious (55.2) extended eye gaze (46.7) small hand gesture (36.8) clasps hands (50.0) *taps fingers (71.4) folds arms across chest (54.9) shrugs shoulders (57.1) #nods head (41.9) #shakes head (40.8) tilts head (44.8) scratches (35.1)	Nonverbal #extended eye gaze (42.1) #small hand gesture (33.0) nods head (44.8) shakes head (41.3) looks away (45.9) looks down (56.0) thinking gestures (34.7) sits back (62.5) arms at sides (83.3) fiddles with objects (45.3)

*small frequency
#close %

climates. to illustrate the interactional nature of the interviews, interviewer, and client information compared according to climate is provided in Tables 3 and 4.

Interviewer Behaviors

Interviewer verbal behaviors rated as *supportive* might be explained by the fulfillment of the client's expectations of agency representatives to provide information, suggestions, and service in an efficient manner.

This expectation or predisposition toward service-providing might also explain the defensive categorization of the interviewers who exhibited off-topic discussions, and of, in a somewhat vague way, interviewers asking for the client's opinion. This latter behavior might create a *defensive* climate if clients feel that the interviewer is incompetent or unable to provide them with the "right" answer, or to correct their problem.

It might also be that Rogers' (1962) nondirective approach to counseling lacks validity in the service-provider environment. This is an important

TABLE 3
Comparison of Significant Interviewer and Client Verbal, Vocal,
and Nonverbal Behaviors in the Supportive Climate

Supportive	
Interviewer	Client

Verbal

Interviewer	Client
gives directions (42.9) gives short info. response (50.0) agrees with opinion (73.3) gives opinion (44.7)	agrees with opinion (66.7) disagrees with opinion (85.7) provides explanation (45.3) gives opinion (62.8)

Vocal

Interviewer	Client
pauses, hesitates (46.2) uhs, ums (45.7)	pauses, hesitates (39.2) uhs, ums, etc. (50.9)

Nonverbal

Interviewer	Client
smiles (51.2) extended eye gaze (53.8) thinking gesture (54.0) sits back (63.6) arms at sides (100) nods head (45.5) *smokes (100) leans forward (46.9) #frowns (41.6) #small hand gestures (33.3)	smiles (48.4) raises brows (52.5) serious (55.2) extended eye gaze (46.7) small hand gestures (36.8) clasps hands (50.0) *taps fingers (71.4) folds arms across chest (54.9) shrugs shoulders (57.1) #nods head (41.9) #shakes head (40.7) tilts head (44.8) scratches (35.1)

*low frequency
#close %

consideration, and a concept which should be studied in a variety of environments with different participant expectations.

Comparison of the interviewer *vocal* behaviors in the *supportive* and *defensive climates* shows clear distinctions. Interviewer behaviors in the *supportive climate* are characterized by *nonfluences*: unfilled pauses, hesitations, and filled pauses (uhs, ums, etc.). The interviewer behaviors in the *defensive climate* suggest an abrupt manner characterized by speaking loudly and quickly, perhaps communicating an impersonal concern, and mechanical handling of the client's request.

Although the vocal behaviors in the *supportive climate* may seem negative, research in *hesitation behavior* (Goldman-Eisler, 1968) concludes that spontaneous speech is actually highly fragmented, and that fluency is an aural "illusion." This research would, therefore, predict that some pauses and hesitations would be perceived as "normal."

For the most part, the interviewer's *nonverbal* behaviors in the *supportive* and *defensive* profiles adhere to previous research in the nonverbal communication of attitudes (Knapp, 1972; Mehrabian, 1969, 1972). Such interviewer behaviors as *smiles, extended eye gaze, thinking gestures, sits back,*

TABLE 4
Comparison of Significant Interviewer and Client Verbal, Vocal,
and Nonverbal Behaviors in the Defensive Climate

Defensive	
Interviewer	Client
Verbal	
off topic tangents (60.3) asks for client's opinion (100)	
Vocal	
speaks loudly (73.9) speaks quickly (50.0)	pauses, hesitates (33.0) speaks loudly (95.5) monotone (59.2) laughs (92.3)
Nonverbal	
frowns (48.1) small hand gestures (37.6) raises brows (54.6) serious (74.4) looks away (50.5) looks down (60.9) writes (44.6) fiddles with objects (62.3) leans forward (38.5)	extended eye gaze (42.1) small hand gestures (33.0) nods head (44.8) shaes head (41.3) looks away (45.9) looks down (56.0) thinking gestures (34.7) sits back (62.5) arms at sides (83.3) fiddles with objects (45.3)

nods head, smokes, and *leans forward* communicate a comfortable setting and an active interest in the client. One behavior, *arms at sides,* lacks explanation in the nonverbal research to date. It may be the case that interviewers with arms at their sides communicate their openness and receptivity to the client's request. Two interviewer nonverbal behaviors which occurred at a high rate in the *supportive climate* (but lower than in the *defensive climate*) were *frowns,* and *small hand gestures.* While the latter is a rather neutral behavior, the former generally implies a negative evaluation. That this behavior should appear in the *supportive climate* (41.6% of the segments) is puzzling. It may be that the interviewer's face was set in an expression indicating to the client that he or she (the interviewer) was empathizing with the client's problem or was trying to come up with a solution to the problem. It may also be the case that the interviewer was frown-

ing to indicate his or her personal disapproval of the unfortunate circumstances afflicting the client. However, the present data do not provide sufficient information to confirm any of these explanations.

Client Behaviors

Examination of Table 2 indicates no preponderance of client *verbal* behaviors in the *defensive climate.* In the *supportive climate,* four client verbal behaviors predominated: *agrees with opnion* (66.7%); *disagrees with opinion* (85.7%); *provides explanation* (45.3%); and *gives opinion* (62.8%). That *agrees with* (Interviewer's) *opinion* is a common client behavior in the *supportive climate* seems reasonable, based on theories of reinforcement, balance, and attraction. The basic premise of each of these theories is that individuals tend to like

APPENDIX

Behavior Coding Categories
Numbered According to
Computer Coding Column

INTERVIEWER

VERBAL CATEGORIES

20. gives information, explains
21. gives directions, commands, orders
22. gives short information response
23. agrees with opinion
24. disagrees with opinion
25. off-topic tangents
26. asks for information
27. asks for C's opinion
28. asks for clarification
    (paraphrases)
29. closed question:
    asks for information
30. open question:
    asks for information
31. closed question:
    asks for opinion
32. open question:
    asks for opinion
33. closed question:
    asks for clarification
34. open question:
    asks for clarification
35. clarifies C
36. gives opinion
37. other:
38. continuing

VOCAL CATEGORIES

50. generally good, varied
51. speaks in monotone
52. speaks in low tone
53. speaks loudly
54. speaks slowly
55. speaks quickly
56. pauses, hesitates
57. uses uh, um, hmmm, oh, O.K.
    etc.
58. laughs
59. coughs
60. sighs
61. clears throat
62. speaks abruptly
63. mumbles
64. other:

---

and be attracted to other individuals who have similar attitudes or opinions. If agreeing behavior is reciprocated by the interviewer, then the giving of opinions is encouraged—a process which would explain the occurrence of *gives opinions. Provides explanation* is generally considered a neutral behavior, and *disagrees with opinion* a defensive behavior. However, the interviewer cannot make decisions or suggestions unless the client provides information about the particular circumstances. Clients who provide explanations may be facilitating the interviewer's job, and are likely to be perceived as cooperative, thus creating a *supportive* atmosphere.

According to reinforcement and attraction theories, clients who disagree with the interviewer's opinion would be perceived in a negative manner, yet this is not always the case. This behavior was observed in only 14 segments, and may have been perceived by the interviewer as an open and honest statement of feeling, thereby fostering a *supportive climate*. These findings on *disagreeing* behaviors emphasize the need for further research on this form of communication, how it is perceived

APPENDIX (cont.)

CLIENT

VERBAL CATEGORIES	VOCAL CATEGORIES
20. gives short information responses	50. generally good, varied
21. agrees with opinion	51. speaks in montone
22. disagrees with opinion	52. speaks in low tone
23. off-topic tangents	53. speaks loudly
24. provides an introductory summary of request	54. speaks slowly
	55. speaks quickly
25. asks for information	56. pauses, hesitates
26. asks for I's opinions	
27. asks for clarification	57. uses uh,um,hmmm,oh,O.K., etc.
28. provides explanation	58. laughs
29. gives opinions	59. coughs
30. clarifies I	60. sighs
31. other:	61. clears throat
32. continuing	62. speaks abruptly
	63. mumbles
	64. other

by different individuals, and its effect on the overall communicative environment in interviews.

For the most part, client *vocal* behaviors are differentiated into *supportive* and *defensive* climates, as might be expected. Tapes in which the clients paused or hesitated or used *uhs* and *ums* were more often judged to be *supportive* than *defensive*, as was true for the interviewer.

Comparison of *hesitations* in *supportive* and *defensive climates* does indicate a substantial number in each, suggesting that although this is a significant behavior, it is distributed across the two climates. Other client behaviors characterizing the *defensive climate* involve *speaking in a monotone, speaking loudly,* and *laughing.* It is true that laughing is generally perceived as evidence of a happy and satisfied individual, but there might also be a nervous laughter, or a laugh to fill tense periods of silence. Overall, client laughter occurred infrequently (in only 13 segments), but 12 of these segments were in tapes judged to be *defensive.* The explanation of why this behavior was distributed in such a manner is not readily apparent. To better determine the reason, a specification of laughter types specific to the situation or context is necessary.

As seen in Table 2, client *nonverbal* behaviors appearing in the *supportive* and *defensive climates* were extensive. In the tapes rated as *supportive,* clients behaved in a number of ways: they *smiled, looked serious, used extended eye gaze, clasped their hands, used small hand gestures, shrugged their shoulders, raised their eyebrows, folded their arms across their chests,* and *scratched.*

The overall impression is one of activity, yet several of these behaviors require further explanation. One of the possible explanations is couched in the expectations of the interviewer. Interviewers are likely to respond favorably to clients who act serious and communicate their concern for service. These messages could very well be communicated by serious facial expression, extended eye gaze, clasped hands, head movements, and small hand gestures. Raised brows and shrugged shoulders, on the other hand, are usually perceived as skeptical feedback. But the entire context of the situation would need to be examined to determine the specific connotation of these nonverbal behaviors.

APPENDIX (cont.)

Nonverbal Categories

Facial Expression

20. smiles, laughs

21. frowns

22. wrinkles eyebrows

23. raises eyebrows

24. purses lips, mouth

25. other

26. serious (not frowning)

27. continuing

Eye Expression

28. maintains eye contract

29. uses extended eye gaze

30. squints, peers, rolls eyes

31. looks away (at notes, desk, cameras, out window, etc.)

32. looks down

33. other:

34. continuing

Hand Gestures

35. uses small hand gestures

36. clasps hands together

37. uses "thinking gestures":
   a. hand on face
   b. hand across forehead
   c. hand over mouth

38. taps fingers on desk

39. shakes hand

40. writes

41. points

42. other:

43. continuing

Posture-Position

44. sits back in chair

45. leans forward in chair

46. orients body toward C, I

47. folds arms across chest

48. puts hands on his head, behind neck

49. keeps arms down at sides

50. sits cross-legged

51. orients body away from C, I

52. shifts, squirms, fidgets

53. lifts, shrugs shoulders

54. hand(s) on hip(s)

55. other:

56. continuing

Head Behavior

57. nods head

58. shakes head

59. tilts head to one side

60. other:

51. continuing

Personal Acts

62. adjusts clothes

63. adjusts glasses

64. jingles coins in pockets

65. plays with jewelry

66. fiddles with an object, pen, doodles

67. preens: pushes hair back, smooths moustache, etc.

68. scratches

69. chews gum, tobacco, pencil

70. smokes

71. other:

72. continuing

Defensive client nonverbal behaviors overlap somewhat with *supportive* ones, and suggest that the same behaviors may be interpreted differently, depending on their duration and on the contextual factors surrounding them.

Behaviors appearing to a large extent in both *supportive* and *defensive climates* were *extended eye gaze, small hand gestures, nods head,* and *shakes head.*

It is feasible that, if eye gaze is extended beyond a set time, the interviewer might sense a subtle confrontation. Shaking one's head as a sign of disagreement or dissatisfaction with the situation is also expected, but it occurs at an almost equal frequency in the *supportive climate.* Nodding one's head, however, cannot be explained so readily; again, this behavior is frequent in the *supportive climate,* as would be expected. It may be that head movements are common means by which clients indicate to the interviewer that they understand what the interviewer is saying, and additional cues would indicate whether the client agrees or not.

The remaining client nonverbal behaviors found in *defensive climates* include *looking away, looking down, thinking gestures, sitting back, arms at sides,* and *fiddling with objects*—most of which are fairly static behaviors.

Research in eye behavior suggests that individuals look at persons or objects about which they have a positive feeling. There would be less eye contact if the persons did not like each other—for example, if the client expected he or she was not getting the anticipated service. Eye contact is also related to the topic of discussion and to the status relationship between the participants. If the topic is embarrassing, the individual generally maintains less eye contact. If the person being addressed is perceived as having higher status, eye contact is moderate (Hearn, 1957). From observing the tapes, it was also apparent that clients would look away when explaining situations, which is consistent with research by Kendon (1967), or when the interviewer was writing, completing forms, calculating figures, or talking on the telephone.

Behaviors That Characterize a
Supportive Climate

A cross-tabulation of *verbal, vocal,* and *nonverbal* behaviors of *interviewers* and *clients* with climate type provided answers to the second and third research questions. For interviewers, the behaviors appearing most often in the supportive climate suggest that the interviewer serves a guidance function. The interviewer *gave directions, responded with information, expressed his or her opinion,* and *agreed with the client's opinions.* Nonverbally, the interviewer in the *supportive climate smiled, used extended eye contact, nodded his or her head,* and *leaned forward;* these appear to be behaviors that communicate a personal interest in the client's situation.

For the client, the significant behaviors suggest an active participant who *provides information* and *gives his or her opinion* and who *smiles, looks serious,* and *uses head motions* and *small hand gestures.* These behaviors indicate an involvement in the interview, and a concern that the client is eager for assistance.

Behaviors That Characterize a Defensive Climate

Analysis of defensive interviews indicated several distinctive interviewer and client behaviors. For the interviewer, the verbal behaviors included a tendency to get off the topic and to ask for client opinions. Nonverbally, the interviewer used many facial expressions which apparently communicated a very serious countenance; the *defensive* climate included behaviors such as *frowning, raising brows, looking serious, looking away,* and *looking down.* With the exception of small hand gestures, the interviewer in the defensive climate used the face and eyes extensively in a serious manner.

No client *verbal* behaviors emerged as significantly related to a *defensive* climate. It appears that client indicators of a defensive climate come from vocal and nonverbal behaviors. Client *vocal* behaviors in a defensive climate suggested somewhat guarded reactions: *speaking in a monotone, pausing,* or *speaking loudly.* Client nonverbal behaviors may be interpreted as generally static: *arms at sides, sits back, looks down, looks away, fiddles with objects, nods and shakes head, uses thinking gestures.*

CONCLUSIONS

Results of this study suggest that the *supportive-defensive paradigm* is valid. Nevertheless, the lack of specificity suggests that the twelve subcategories of behaviors that comprise the climates should be studied to determine which of the subcategories represent the most valid discriminators of the general climates. In analyzing interview interactions, for example, it was noted that while several of Gibb's (1961) subcategories repeatedly appeared as examples of supportive or defensive climates, other categories occurred infrequently or not at all. In order to relate specific interview behaviors from studies such as this one to Gibb's overall system, more information about behaviors that comprise the subcategories must be made available.

It is also evident that individual behaviors are not always the key to identifying interview climate, and that behavior combinations or repertoires might be the determining factor in clearly distinguishing supportive and defensive climates.

Coding of verbal, vocal, and nonverbal behaviors in interactions produce comprehensive profiles of interviews. While the coding system was found to be both valid and reliable, it was, nevertheless, time consuming and subject to errors. Advanced technology, such as the computerized system for storing and retrieving usual information developed by Ekman and Friesen (1967), could certainly improve the quality and analytical accuracy of ongoing interaction studies and provide researchers with a wide variety of behavioral repertoires for related research.

Results of this study suggest that the behavior coding produced data about behaviors in initial screening interviews for individuals seeking services from an agency; however, the results also suggest that the circumstances of those types of interviews may be sufficiently unique so as to preclude generalizations to other interview situations. Thus, an intensive analysis of selected interviews in a wide variety of discretely different interview settings ought to be completed. Sales, teacher-student, complaint and reprimand, information-seeking and information-getting, merit rating and appraisal, and journalistic interviews may all have different behavioral emphases that contribute to significantly different perceptions of climate and the way in which climate affects the effectiveness of the interview. It would seem profitable to develop and validate the analytical system used in this study so as to make it readily available for research in other situations.

NOTES

1. This research was supported by a grant with the Office of Economic Opportunity, Contract No. OEO-60349-D-74-01.
2. More detailed information about issues of informed consent confidentiality can be found in the final report.
3. Since the time for analyzing the verbal and nonverbal behaviors of the Interviewer and Client was at least four times that of the actual tape length, three intact teams of two coders, composed of one senior researcher and one graduate research assistant, were created.

REFERENCES

ADAMS, J. S. *Interviewing procedures: A manual for survey interviews*. Chapel Hill: University of North Carolina Press, 1958.
CAPLOW, D. The dynamics of information interviewing. *American Journal of Sociology*, 1956, 62, 165-171.
CIVIKLY, J. M. A descriptive and experimental analysis of teacher nonverbal communication in the college classroom. Unpublished doctoral dissertation, Florida State University, 1973.
DOSTER, J. A., & STRICKLAND, B. R. Disclosing of verbal material as a function of information requested, information about the interviewer, and interviewee. *Journal of Consulting and Clinical Psychology*, 1971, 37, 187-194.
EKMAN, P., FRIESEN, V. W., & TAUSSIG, T. J. VID-R and SCAN: Tool and methods for the automated analysis of visual records. Paper presented at the National Conference on Content Analysis. The Annenberg School of Communications, University of Pennsylvania, Philadelphia, November 1967.
FENLASON, A., BEALS, G., & ABRAHAMSON, A. *Essentials in interviewing*. New York: Harper and Row, 1962.
GARFIELD, S. L., & AFFLECK, D. C. Therapists judgments concerning patients considered for psychotherapy. *Journal of Consulting Psychology*, 1961, 25, 505-509.
GIBB, J. R. Defensive communication. *The Journal of Communication*, 1961, 11, 141-148.
GOLDMAN-EISLER, F. *Psycholinguistics: Experiments in spontaneous speech*. New York: Academic, 1968.
GORDEN, R. L. *Interviewing: Strategy, techniques, and tactics*. Homewood, Illinois: Dorsey, 1969.
GREIF, E. B., & HOGAN, R. The theory and measurement of empathy. *Journal of Counseling Psychology*, 1973, 20, 280-284.
HAASE, R. F., & TEPPER, D. T. Nonverbal components of empathic communication. *Journal of Counseling Psychology*, 1972, 19, 417-424.
HAIGH, G. Defensive behavior in client-centered therapy. *Journal of Consulting Psychology*, 1949, 13, 181-189.
HEARN, G. Leadership and the Spatial Factor in Small Groups. *Journal of Abnormal and Social Psychology*, 1957, 104, 269-72.
HILER, E. W. The sentence completion test as a predictor of continuation in psychotherapy. *Journal of Consulting Psychology*, 1959, 23, 544-549.
KENDON, A. Some Functions of Gaze-Direction in Social Interaction. *Acta Psychologica*, 1967, 26, 22-63.
KNAPP, M. L. *Nonverbal communication in human interaction*. New York: Holt, Rinehart and Winston, 1972.
MAIER, N. R. F. *The appraisal interview: Objectives, methods and skills*. New York: Wiley, 1958.
MATARAZZO, J. D., & WIENS, A. N. *The interview: Research on its anatomy and structure*. Chicago: Aldine-Atherton, 1972.
MAY, R. *The art of counseling*. New York: Abingdon, 1967.
MAYER, J. E., & TIMMS, N. Clash in perspective between worker and client. *Social Casework*, 1969, 50, 32-40.
McNAIR, D. M., LORR, M., & CALLAHAN, D. M. Patient and therapist influences in quitting psychotherapy. *Journal of Consulting Psychology*, 1963, 27, 10-18.
MEHRABIAN, A. "Significance of posture and position in the communication of attitude and status relationships," *Psychological Bulletin*, 1969, 71, 359-72.
MEHRABIAN, A. *Nonverbal communication*. Chicago: Aldine, 1972.
MEYER, H. J., BORGATTA, E. F., & FANSHEL, D. A study of the interview process: The caseworker-client relationship. *Genetic Psychology Monographs*, 1964, 69 (2), 247-295.
NIE, N., BENT, D. H., & HULL, C. H. *Statistical package for the social sciences*. New York: McGraw Hill, 1970.

OVERALL, B., & ARONSON, H. Expectations of psychotherapy in patients of lower socioeconomic class. *American Journal of Orthopsychiatry,* 1963, 33, 421-430.

ROGERS, C. R. The interpersonal relationship: The core of guidance. *Harvard Educational Review,* 1962, 32, 416-429.

SCHATZMAN, L., & STRAUSS, A. Social class and modes of communication. *The American Journal of Sociology,* 1955, 60, 329-338.

STARK, F. B. Some Barriers to Client Worker Communication at Intake. *Social Casework,* 1959.

TAULBEE, E. S. Relation between certain personality variables and continuation in psychotherapy. *Journal of Consulting Psychology,* 1958, 22, 83-89.

JOB SATISFACTION AS A FUNCTION OF EMPLOYEES' COMMUNICATION APPREHENSION, SELF-ESTEEM, AND PERCEPTIONS OF THEIR IMMEDIATE SUPERVISORS

RAYMOND L. FALCIONE
University of Maryland

JAMES C. McCROSKEY
West Virginia University

JOHN A. DALY
Purdue University

The study indicated that subordinate satisfaction with immediate supervision is closely associated with perceptions of supervisor communication behavior, credibility, attractiveness, and attitude homophily, and to a lesser extent with oral communication apprehension and self-esteem. It was further suggested that while these variables are good predictors of satisfaction with immediate supervision, they may have little or no effect on other dimensions of job satisfaction.

While the assumption that "a happy employee is a productive employee" is an overgeneralization of the relationship between job satisfaction and employee productivity, the assumption is more likely true than false in many instances. While the primary goal of management is the enhancement of productivity—getting the job done—it has long been recognized that an important mediator of that goal may be the satisfaction level of the employees in the organization. Beyond the possible link between satisfaction and productivity, there has been considerable interest in employee satisfaction as a variable in and of itself (Korman, 1971). In fact, Locke (1976) estimates more than 3,300 studies on the subject of job satisfaction have been published to date.

The research program described in this paper sought to determine the role of a wide variety of variables on job satisfaction. Self-descriptions of *esteem* and *communication propensity,* as well as subordinate perceptions of supervisor *credibility, homophily, attraction,* and *communication behavior,* were related to five dimensions of job satisfaction. The overall intent was to explain a large percentage of the variation in job satisfaction as a function of these variables.

REVIEW OF RELATED LITERATURE

The Nature of Job Satisfaction

An individual's satisfaction with his or her job has been defined and operationalized in a number of different ways. For example, some have viewed satisfaction as a derivative of need or value fulfillment (Hackman & Lawler, 1971; Locke, 1969; Lofquist & Dawis, 1969; Maslow, 1954; McGregor, 1960; Pelz & Andrews, 1966; Porter, 1962). Others, operating within an equity framework (Adams, 1965), have viewed satisfaction as a consequence of a comparison between perceived inputs and outputs (Pritchard, Dunnette, & Jorgensen, 1972). Similarly, expectancy-instrumentality-valence models have conceptualized satisfaction as a function of the individual's expectations of rewards owing to his behaviors on the job (Jorgensen, Dunnette, & Pritchard, 1973; Graen, 1969; Pritchard & DeLeo, 1973; Vroom, 1964). The approaches described so far tend to emphasize a highly cognitive approach to job satisfaction. The individual is assumed to be a rational, highly input-output oriented being who engages in logical comparisons, rankings, and orderings.

Alternatively, a number of other theorists have seen organizational satisfaction as being much more affective in nature. That is, the individual's level of satisfaction is essentially viewed as a reaction to a variety of salient likes and dislikes that may be specified along content dimensions. It is reasonable to assume that perceived job satisfaction is comprised of multiple dimensions (Locke, 1976; Quinn, 1974; Vroom, 1964). These dimensions constitute one's affect responses to various facets of the work environment. For example, these may include one's perceptions of his or her supervision, pay, promotion, co-workers, and the work itself. Considerable support exists for the viability of these as the primary dimensions of job satisfaction (Smith, Kendall, & Hulin, 1969).

While the dimensions of job satisfaction appear fairly clear, the causal agents of satisfaction are far less so. Certainly, variables such as opportunity to participate in decision making (Daly, McCroskey, & Falcione, 1976a; Falcione, 1974a; Falcione, 1974c; Vroom, 1964), job enlargement (Argyris, 1964; 1965), job enrichment (Herzberg, 1966), working conditions (Barnowe et al., 1972), and the individual's perceptions of his or her success and the internal-external feedback one receives from his or her performance (Hackman & Lawler, 1971; Herzberg, 1966; Locke, 1965), all have some effect. In addition, three other variables may play crucial roles in job satisfaction. These are the individual's self-esteem, his perceptions of his immediate superior, and his orientations toward communication.

The present study examined the above three correlates of job satisfactions from the vantage point of the employee. Our purpose was to generate a predictive model for employee satisfaction that would generalize across organizational types and provide information suggestive of intervention procedures which might be implemented within organizations and lead to increased employee satisfaction.

Communication Apprehension

Communication apprehension is a broad-based fear or anxiety associated with either real or anticipated communication with another person or persons. High levels of communication apprehension

have been found to result in withdrawal from and avoidance of communication with others (McCroskey, 1976). Two dimensions of communication apprehension have been isolated and found related to the work environment: oral (McCroskey, 1970, 1976) and written (Daly & Miller, 1975). The impact of communication apprehension on choice of employment (Daly & McCroskey, 1975; Daly & Shamo, 1976) and application for employment (Daly & Leth, 1976; Richmond, 1976) have been clearly established. In addition, employees with low levels of communication apprehension have been found to be retained in an organization almost 50 percent longer (with age held constant) than employees with high levels of apprehension (Scott, McCroskey, & Sheahan, 1976). The data relating to retention is particularly suggestive of a relationship between communication apprehension and employee satisfaction, hence the inclusion of apprehension in our model.

Self-esteem

Self-esteem has been referred to as *self-concept, self-evaluation, self-image, self-satisfaction,* and *self-acceptance.* As Wylie (1961) has noted, these terms "all refer to approximately the same variable." Whatever label is employed, the construct refers to the ways a person perceives her or himself and the evaluations the individual develops as a result of those perceptions. The self-esteem of individuals has often been found to be related to their perceptions of their environments and their behaviors (Wylie, 1961).

Within organizations, the individual's view of himself is bound to impact on job attitudes and perceptions. People with high self-esteem, for example, have been found to engage in more self-disclosure than those with lower self-esteem (McCroskey & Richmond, 1975). Korman (1968) argues that *high* self-esteem employees enjoy task success more than *low* self-esteem employees. Locke (1976) has predicted ways in which *high* self-esteem people would react in the work environment: (1) they would value challenging tasks; (2) pleasure derived from achievement would be more intense and enduring; (3) they would be more likely to want promotions for reasons of justice rather than prestige and status; (4) they would not rely highly on prestige, approval, and verbal recognition as sources of self-assurance; (5) they would be less emotionally affected by criticism than low self-esteem persons; (6) they would experience fewer conflicts and feelings of anxiety in the work environment; and (7) they would be less defensive and would employ fewer defense mechanisms. Finally, Weiner et al. (1971) and Lewin (1963) found that *low* self-esteem people tend to disassociate themselves from failure by projecting it into others, often leading to dissatisfaction with the target person. In the work environment, this may often be his or her immediate supervisor. Because it was believed that a person's self-esteem would have an impact on the way he or she reacts to the environment, it was felt important that the construct be included in our model.

Perceived Supervisor Credibility

Source credibility has long been viewed by communication scholars as an extremely important variable in human interaction. However, little empirical investigation of the effect of credibility in organizational settings has been conducted. Research in a large medical research organization suggests that if a supervisor is not trusted by subordinates, or vice versa, the resulting communication between the parties will tend to be evasive or compliant. Such responses may lead to unwarranted or overestimated degrees of agreement being assumed (Mellinger, 1956). Read (1962) obtained similar findings in an industrial organization. Levels of distrust also appear to be compounded in organizations because of the inherent hierarchical status relationships in organizations (Porter & Roberts, 1976).

Perceived credibility does appear to affect satisfaction in organizations. Falcione (1973, 1974c, 1975) found a significant relationship between subordinate satisfaction and subordinate perceptions of their supervisors' credibility, particularly as it related to the character-sociability (safety) dimension. Because credibility is viewed as a particularly important component of source valence, particularly in an organizational environment, the construct was added to our model.

Perceived Supervisor Attractiveness

Employees in organizations are often attracted to their supervisors for different reasons. These relationships are called *functional* and *entity relations* (Locke, 1976). Functional relationships between supervisor and subordinate are based on what services can be provided for each other. An employee may be attracted to his or her supervisor to the degree that he or she views the supervisor providing or helping to attain salient job values (Locke, 1970a, 1970b). These values are normally task-related, or are related to the rewards the employee can accrue for task performance.

The entity relationships of subordinates and supervisors are based on the bond between the persons rather than the services obtainable from the relationship. This attraction is a function of the social exchanges between the subordinate and supervisor (Rosen, 1969; Tosi, Chesser, & Carroll, 1972).

Because *interpersonal attraction* has been found also to be highly predictive of the amount of communication in which people engage (Berscheid & Walster, 1969), this was added to our model. The assumption underlying our inclusion of employees' perceptions of supervisor attractiveness in our model was that attraction facilitates communication, which, in turn, may facilitate satisfaction.

Perceived Supervisor Homophily

Perceptions of fundamental similarity in attitudes, background, and values have been shown to profoundly affect relationships (Byrne, 1969; Daly, McCroskey, & Falcione, 1976b). The degree of *interpersonal homophily* has also been found in extensive previous research to be predictive of both amount and effectiveness of communication between people (Rogers & Shoemaker, 1971). Our inclusion of *homophily* in our model was based on the assumption that more—as well as more effective—communication between the subordinate and supervisor would lead to greater satisfaction.

Perceived Listening, Understandingness, and Communication Quality

These three variables were included in our model in an attempt to tap the role of the employee's perception of his or her communicative relationship with supervision. Our assumption was that an employee would be more satisfied if a positive communicative relationship with the supervisor was perceived (Locke, Cartledge, & Koeppel, 1968). While these three variables have been examined previously (Daly, 1975; Daly & Lashbrook, 1976), they have not been extensively studied in the organizational environment. However, similar constructs under a variety of labels such as *consideration* (Fleishman, 1957a, 1957b; Halin & Winer, 1975; Halin, 1957; Seeman, 1957), *maintenance* (Fiedler, 1966; Hunt, 1967; Hill, 1969), and *receptivity* (Daly, McCroskey, & Falcione, 1976a; Falcione, 1974a; Redding, 1970) dot the literature. Previous research has, for the most part, failed to clearly differentiate the various aspects of the supervisor-subordinate communicative relationship. Consequently, the three variables of *perceived listening, understandingness,* and *communication quality* were included in our model.

ELEMENTS OF THE PROPOSED MODEL

Based on the above literature review, the model which we generated for this research included 22 variables: two dimensions of *employee communication apprehension,* five dimensions of *employee self-esteem,* five dimensions of *perceived supervisor credibility,* three dimensions of *perceived supervisor attractiveness,* four dimensions of *perceived homophily,* plus *perceived quality of the supervisor's listening, understandingness,* and *communication.*

Research Questions

Our primary concern in this study was the development and testing of a predictive model of employee satisfaction. This led us to address three research questions: (1) To what extent is each variable in the model associated with employee satisfaction? (2) To what extent can we predict employee satisfaction by employing all of the variables in the model? (3) What is the most parsimonious combination of variables from our model for predicting employee satisfaction?

In order to obtain data relevant to these questions, information was collected from two highly divergent subject populations.

METHOD

Data Collection

The measures of *communication apprehension, self-esteem, supervisor credibility, attractiveness, homophily, listening ability, understandingness,* and *communication quality* noted above, were administered to 211 employees of a large federal research establishment and 189 elementary and secondary teachers from a variety of schools in three states. The age range in both samples was from 22 to 64. The majority of the federal employees were male; the majority of teachers were female.

Measurement

The following instruments were used to measure the variables in our model:

Job satisfaction: In order to measure job satisfaction on a variety of dimensions, the *Job Descriptive Index* (JDI) developed by Smith, Kendall, and Hulin (1969) was administered. The JDI includes five scales pertaining to work, pay, promotions, co-workers, and supervision. These scales have been described by Vroom (1964) as the most carefully developed to date. They have been found to be reliable and have had factoral stability in previous studies (Smith, Kendall, & Hulin, 1969).

Communication apprehension: The measures of communication apprehension employed for this study were the *Personal Report of Communication Apprehension* (PRCA; McCroskey, 1970) for the oral dimension and the *Writing Apprehension Test* (WAT; Daly & Miller, 1975) for the written dimension. Both of these measures have been found to have satisfactory reliability and validity in previous research.

Self-esteem: The measure of self-esteem employed in this study was the *McCroskey/Richmond Self-Esteem Index* (MRSEI; McCroskey & Richmond, 1975). The measure has been found to be highly reliable across a variety of subject populations, and to have concurrent validity with other measures of this construct (McCroskey, Richmond, Daly, & Falcione, 1976). The five dimensions of *self-esteem* measured by the MRSEI have been labeled *competence, character, sociability, composure,* and *extroversion.*

Perceived supervisor credibility: As noted earlier, previous research has found a relationship between the perceived credibility of the supervisor and employee satisfaction (Falcione, 1973, 1974c, 1975). Inclusion of the dimensions of *supervisor credibility* in our model permitted replication of that research and the testing of the strength of *credibility* as a predictive variable in comparison with other *employee perceptions of supervisors.*

The measure of supervisor credibility was a five-dimensional instrument drawn from the work of Falcione (1974b) and McCroskey, Jensen, and Valencia (1973). The five dimensions measured were *competence, character, sociability, composure,* and *extroversion.* Each dimension was measured by 4 seven-point bipolar scales. Previous research has indicated that the reliability of measurement for each dimension was satisfactory (above .80).

Perceived supervisor attractiveness: The measure of attractiveness was multidimensional (McCroskey & McCain 1974). The dimensions of *task, social,* and *physical attraction* were each measured by five *Likert-type* scales. The reliability of measurement for each dimension has been found to be satisfactory (above .80) in several previous studies.

Perceived supervisor homophily: The measure of *homophily* was that developed by McCroskey, Richmond, and Daly (1975). This instrument measures four dimensions of *homophily*—*attitude, background, appearance,* and *morality.* Each dimension is measured by seven-point bipolar scales. Four scales were employed for each dimension except *morality.* Two scales were employed for the *morality* dimension.

Perceived listening, understandingness, and communication quality: Seven-point bipolar scales were used to measure these variables. The scales employed for *perceived listening ability* were *bored-alert, listens-doesn't listen, attentive-inattentive,* and *uninterested-interested.* The scales for *perceived understandingness* were *sensitive-insensitive, responsive-unresponsive, cold-warm, empathic-unempathic,* and *not understanding-understanding.* To measure the *perceived quality of the supervisor's communication,* the following scales were employed: *high quality-low quality, poor-excellent, correct-incorrect, worthless-worthwhile,* and *satisfactory-unsatisfactory.*

Data Analyses

The data from the two subject samples were analyzed separately. Preliminary analyses were concerned with the factoral stability and reliability of each of the measures, since some of the measures had not previously been employed with similar subject samples. Items for each measure or group of measures were subjected to factor analysis with oblique rotation (since several dimensions were known from previous research to be correlated), and internal (split-half) reliability estimates were computed. The results of these analyses (detailed results will not be reported here because of their volume) indicated that the dimensionality of each instrument was the same as was expected on the basis of previous research. Internal reliability for the variables ranged from a low of .84 (JDI pay dimension, *federal sample*) to a high of .95 (WAT, *teacher sample*). On the basis of these preliminary analyses, it was concluded that the data obtained from the various instruments were satisfactory for the purposes of the main analyses.

In order to provide information relevant to the first two research questions, two major analyses were performed. The first analysis assumed an underlying construct of *job satisfaction* as a linear combination of the five dimensions of the JDI. In this analysis a *canonical correlation* was computed between all of our predictor variables and the five dimension scores from the JDI. The results of this

TABLE 1
Correlations of Predictor and Criterion Variables
with Canonical Variable

	Federal Sample	Teacher Sample
Predictor Variables		
Communication Apprehension		
PRCA	-.24	-.28
WAT	-.12	-.07
Self-Esteem		
Sociability	.32	.01
Composure	.24	.16
Competence	.26	.10
Extroversion	.20	.21
Character	.26	.11
Supervisor Perceptions		
Sociability	.80	.76
Composure	.58	.60
Competence	.78	.76
Extroversion	.38	.49
Character	.79	.75
Attitude Homophily	.70	.70
Background Homophily	.17	.11
Morality Homophily	.42	.50
Appearance Homophily	.11	.01
Social Attraction	.71	.72
Physical Attraction	.48	.46
Task Attraction	.73	.81
Listening	.84	.84
Understandingness	.87	.85
Communication Quality	.87	.84
Criterion Variables		
Supervisor	.99	.99
Work	.43	.07
Pay	.03	.14
Promotions	.34	.20
Co-workers	.44	.11

Correlations   .14 are significant at alpha .05.

analysis provided one overall canonical correlation between the two groups of variables and an indication of the degree to which each variable was correlated to the canonical variable generated by the analysis.

The second analysis assumed that the dimensions of the JDI were relatively independent. Thus, this analysis did not focus on an overall construct of *job satisfaction;* rather, the focus was on the five sub-

parts of that construct. In this analysis, simple correlations were computed between each predictor variable and each JDI dimension. Additionally, *multiple regression* analyses employing all of the predictor variables were performed on the scores for each JDI dimension.

In order to answer our third research question, stepwise multiple regression analyses were performed on the scores on each JDI dimension employing all of our predictor variables. The backward stepwise procedure was employed. Two criteria were employed in selecting the best model: (1) all predictor variables in the model were required to be significant at the .10 alpha level, and (2) a model with fewer predictors was selected over other models if the reduction in explained variance was less than one percent.

The criterion for statistical significance was set at alpha = .05 for all tests except those for beta weights of predictor variables noted above.

RESULTS

Canonical Analyses

The canonical correlation analyses for the data from the two samples yielded significant canonical correlations for the first variable generated in both data sets (*federal sample* rc = .89; chi-square = 433.15; p < .0001; *teacher sample* rc = .88; chi-square = 351.24; p < .0001). An examination of the correlations between the satisfaction variables and the canonical variable (see Table 1), indicates that supervisor satisfaction was the dominant contributor to the generated variable in both samples. Satisfaction with promotions was also significantly associated with the generated variable in both samples. Satisfaction with work and co-workers were associated with the canonical variable for the *federal sample* but not for the *teacher sample*. Satisfaction with pay was not correlated with the generated variable in either analysis.

Among the predictor variables, only WAT and *appearance homophily* failed to be significantly correlated with the canonical variables in both analyses. All other predictors were significantly correlated with the canonical variable in the *federal sample*. In the data from the *teacher sample*, *background homophily* and the *sociability, competence,* and *character dimensions* of *self-esteem* were not correlated significantly with the canonical variable.

While these results suggest some support for our assumption that overall satisfaction can be conceived of as a linear combination of the five JDI dimensions, that support is not strong. A predictive model based on the canonical correlation results would be primarily oriented toward supervisor sat-

isfaction and would not be particularly helpful in predicting the other satisfaction elements. Thus, the results of our other analyses will form the basis for the conclusions we will draw relating to our three research questions.

Correlation Analyses

The results of the correlational analyses for both samples are reported in Table 2. These results indicate that while the PRCA was a significant predictor of *supervisor satisfaction* in both samples, and of satisfaction with work in the *federal sample*, the WAT was not significantly correlated with any dimension of satisfaction in either sample.

The results relating to *self-esteem* also present a mixed picture. *Sociability* was a significant predictor of *satisfaction with work* for both samples, and of *satisfaction with supervisor, promotions,* and *co-workers* for the *federal sample*. *Composure* was significantly correlated with *supervisor satisfaction* for both samples, and with *work* and *co-workers* for the *federal sample*. While *competence* was not significantly correlated with any dimension of satisfaction for the *teacher sample*, it was correlated with *supervisor, work,* and *co-worker satisfaction* for the *federal sample*. *Extroversion* was significantly correlated with *supervisor* and *work satisfaction* for both samples, and with *co-worker satisfaction* for the *federal sample*. *Character* was significantly correlated with *supervisor* and *co-worker satisfaction* for the *federal sample*, but not correlated significantly with any satisfaction variable for the *teacher sample*.

Taken together, these results suggest a moderate relationship between *self-oriented perceptions* (*communication apprehension, self-esteem,* and *employee satisfaction*). In general, the relationship appears stronger for the *federal sample* than for the *teacher sample*, and to be most associated with *supervisor, work,* and *co-worker dimensions of satisfaction*.

The data concerning supervisor perceptions provide a somewhat clearer picture. While all of these perceptions, with the exceptions of *background* and *appearance homophily*, formed strong positive relationships with *supervisor satisfaction* for both samples, they all had low or nonsignificant relation-

TABLE 2
Correlations Between Predictor Variables
and Dimensions of Job Satisfaction

Predictor Variable	Supervisor		Work		Pay		Promotions		Co-workers	
	Federal Sample	Teacher Sample	Federal Sample	Teacher Sample	Federal Sample	Teacher Sample	Federal Sample	Teacher Sample	Federal Sample	Teacher Sample
Communication Apprehension										
PRCA	-.19	-.23	-.29	-.08	.10	-.01	-.11	-.14	-.13	-.02
WAT	-.09	-.05	-.14	-.03	.03	.04	-.08	-.09	-.04	.01
Self-Esteem										
Sociability	.28	.00	.17	.23	-.14	-.08	.17	-.03	.27	.01
Composure	.21	.15	.16	.08	-.04	.03	.14	.11	.20	.13
Competence	.19	.09	.29	.12	.01	.01	.00	-.12	.35	.10
Extroversion	.16	.16	.25	.20	-.11	-.01	.13	.11	.22	-.05
Character	.21	.12	.12	.11	.14	.11	-.02	-.12	.29	.14
Supervisor Perceptions										
Sociability	.70	.67	.32	.11	-.05	.12	.18	.04	.27	.11
Composure	.51	.53	.23	-.03	.00	-.01	.18	.08	.20	.13
Competence	.68	.67	.37	-.01	-.04	.13	.32	.14	.35	.14
Extroversion	.33	.43	.22	.03	-.01	.10	.27	.17	.22	.06
Character	.70	.66	.27	.05	.03	.12	.19	.08	.29	.10
Attitude Homophily	.63	.60	.21	.00	-.01	.12	.25	.14	.20	-.03
Background Homophily	.16	.09	.02	.08	.07	.06	.10	-.02	.13	-.03
Morality Homophily	.37	.44	.21	.11	.05	.02	.13	.01	.13	.06
Appearance Homophily	.11	.00	-.02	.00	-.08	.02	-.03	.06	.03	-.12
Social Attraction	.62	.62	.27	.15	-.01	.13	.18	.06	.23	-.04
Physical Attraction	.43	.39	.14	.09	-.05	.01	.07	.20	.14	-.01
Task Attraction	.65	.70	.24	.02	-.02	.10	.28	.10	.25	.06
Listening	.75	.73	.32	.05	.02	.06	.30	.16	.31	.10
Understandingness	.78	.74	.22	.08	-.01	.10	.28	.15	.32	.09
Communication Quality	.78	.74	.32	.04	.05	.09	.30	.19	.30	.11

Correlations > ± .14 are significant at alpha .05.

TABLE 3
Results of Multiple Regression Analyses

Criterion Variable	F-Ratio	Probability	R^2
Supervisor			
Federal Sample	29.37	<.0001	.77
Teacher Sample	24.27	<.0001	.76
Work			
Federal Sample	3.54	<.0001	.29
Teacher Sample	1.15	.30	.13
Pay			
Federal Sample	1.36	.14	.14
Teacher Sample	1.04	.41	.12
Promotions			
Federal Sample	2.02	<.01	.19
Teacher Sample	1.40	.12	.16
Co-workers			
Federal Sample	2.04	<.01	.19
Teacher Sample	.89	.61	.11

ships with the remaining dimensions for the *teacher sample*. A few moderate relationships between these perceptions and *work, promotion,* and *co-worker satisfaction* appeared for the *federal sample*.

Multiple Regression Analyses

The results of the multiple regression analyses are summarized in Table 3. For the *federal sample,* significant models were generated for all dimensions of satisfaction except *pay*. The only significant model generated for the *teacher sample* was that for *satisfaction with supervision*.

The models for *satisfaction with supervisor* for the two samples accounted for very similar (and high) percentages of variance (*federal* =77%; *teachers* = 76%). Thus, it is clear that our model is capable of substantial prediction of at least one

dimension of satisfaction. Results on the other four dimensions, however, present a picture that is less encouraging, as well as less clear. On the *work dimension* of satisfaction, a significant and moderately powerful model was generated for the *federal sample* (R^2 = .29), but the model for the *teacher sample* was not significant and, had it been, would have accounted for much less variance (R^2 = .13). Differences in variance accounted for from the models of the two samples on the other three dimensions were much smaller, but large enough to cross the border of significance for the *federal sample* on the *promotion* and *co-worker dimensions*.

Caution should be exercised in drawing any conclusions from these results, however. Because of the large number of predictor variables employed and the redundancy of these variables (as evidenced by their substantial intercorrelations), the regression analyses provide an extremely conservative

TABLE 4
Models Generated by Stepwise Regression Procedures

Criterion Variable	Federal Models Predictor	Beta	Teacher Models Predictor	Beta
Supervisor	PRCA*	-.09	PRCA*	-.15
	MRSEI-Competence	.09	WAT	-.07
	MRSEI-Extroversion	-.09	MRSEI-Sociability	-.10
	Composure	.10	Sociability	.30
	Competence*	.24	Competence*	.18
	Extroversion	-.10	Communication Quality*	.12
	Character	.17	Social Attraction	.09
	Understandingness	.27	Task Attraction	.21
	Communication Quality*	.28	Attitude Homophily	.11
	Morality Homophily*	-.08	Morality Homophily*	.09
	Physical Attraction	.11	Appearance Homophily	-.07
	(F_2 = 59.61, p <.0001, R^2 = .77)		(F_2 = 50.13, p <.0001, R^2 = .76)	
Work	PRCA	-.21	MRSEI-Sociability	.18
	MRSEI-Competence	.18	MRSEI-Extroversion	.13
	Sociability	.29	Social Attraction	.22
	Composure	.13	Attitude Homophily	-.14
	Competence	.21	(F_2 - 5.21, p <.001, R^2 = .10)	
	Understandingness	-.25		
	(F_2= 12.08, p <.0001, R^2 = .26)			
Pay	MRSEI-Sociability*	-.27	MRSEI-Sociability*	-.19
	MRSEI-Extroversion	-.11	MRSEI-Character*	.20
	MRSEI-Character*	.24	Extroversion	.12
	Communication Quality	.13	(F_2 = 3.20, p <.05, R^2 = .05)	
	Appearance Homophily	-.15		
	(F_2 = 4.79, p <.001, R^2 = .10)			
Promotions	MRSEI-Character	-.11	WAT	-.15
	Competence	.19	MRSEI-Competence	-.15
	Extroversion	.14	Sociability	-.20
	Understandingness	.14	Communication Quality	.24
	(F_2 = 8.26, p <.0001, R^2 = .14)		Social Attraction	.19
			(F_2 = 4.40, p <.05, R^2 = .11)	
Co-workers	Competence*	.24	Competence*	.13
	Understandingness	.18	MRSEI-Character	.13
	(F_2 = 17.32, p <.0001, R^2 = .14)		(F_2 - 3.57, p <.05, R^2 = .04)	

*Predictor for both samples on same dimension.

statistical estimate of the ability of our general model's predictive power. As noted below, the stepwise regression procedure produced statistically significant models for all five satisfaction dimensions for both samples. Because the stepwise regression procedure excludes redundant predictor variables, the models generated are typically more powerful and better estimators of variance accountable than the multiple regression procedure reported here.

Stepwise Regression Analyses

Table 4 summarizes the models generated by the stepwise regression procedures, including the predictors retained, their standardized *beta weights,* the statistical test of each model, and the variance predictable (R^2) by each model. As noted in Table 4, statistically significant models were generated for both samples on all five dimensions of satisfaction. The number of predictor variables retained from the original 22 ranged from a high of 11 for both samples, for *supervisor satisfaction,* to a low of 2 for both samples, for *co-worker satisfaction.*

An examination of the models reported in Table 4 yields two important observations. First, there is little similarity among the models across the different dimensions of *employee satisfaction* or across the two samples on the same dimension. For example, although the models for *supervisor satisfaction* for both samples included 11 predictors, only 4 predictors appeared in both models (PRCA, *competence, communication quality,* and *morality homophily*); In addition, only the *composure dimension* of *self-esteem, listening,* and *background homophily* failed to appear in any model for either sample. Second, although the amount of variance predictable for the generated models for *supervisor* and *promotion satisfaction* were very similar for both samples, predictable variance on the other dimensions of satisfaction varied substantially across the two samples.

DISCUSSION

As noted early in this paper, our primary purpose was to generate a predictive model for employee satisfaction that would generalize across diverse types of organizations and provide information suggestive of intervention procedures which might lead to improved employee satisfaction. That purpose was not fully accomplished. It is clear that our original model which included 22 predictor variables cannot be reduced to a small number that can be expected to be predictive of all five satisfaction dimensions across diverse subject populations. Rather, different subsets of the predictor variables are needed to obtain maximum predictive power for the various dimensions of satisfaction both within and across subject populations.

Although our primary goal was found to be unachievable, the present research yielded data of considerable value for understanding and predicting subordinate satisfaction in organizations. It is clear that both subordinate perceptions of their supervisors and the subordinate's own orientations and self-concepts are related to satisfaction.

Supervisor satisfaction appears to be most closely associated with *perceived communication behavior (perceived listening, understandingness, quality), credibility, attractiveness,* and *attitude homophily,* and to a lesser extent with *oral communication apprehension* and *self-esteem.* Thus, the supervisor's behaviors, particularly communication behaviors, might be expected to enhance or detract from subordinate satisfaction. However, it is also clear that certain employees—those with high oral communication apprehension and/or low self-esteem—are less likely to be satisfied with supervision regardless of the supervisor's behavior. These results suggest three possible alternatives for intervention that might be expected to enhance the level of subordinate satisfaction in any organization: (1) provide training in effective communication for supervisors, (2) provide programs designed to overcome high oral communication apprehension and/or low self-esteem of subordinates, and (3) reevaluate or avoid hiring individuals with high oral communication apprehension and/or low self-esteem.

Clearly, each of these alternatives has advantages and limitations, depending on the nature of the organization and financial limitations. Of particular significance, however, is that, based on the data from this study, we should expect that implementation of any of these intervention strategies should be expected to have either positive impact or no impact on other dimensions of satisfaction beyond the supervision dimension. In no case would we expect that enhancement of one dimension of satisfaction would lead to less satisfaction on another dimension.

REFERENCES

ADAMS, J.S. Inequity in social exchange. In L. Berkowitz (Ed.), *Advances in experimental social psychology,* Vol. 2. New York: Academic Press, 1965, 267-299.

ARGYRIS, C. *Integrating the individual and the organization.* New York: Wiley, 1964.

ARVEY, R.D. Task performance as a function of perceived effort-performance and performance-reward contingencies. *Organizational Behavior and Human Performance,* 1972, 8, 423-433.

BARNOWE, J.T. et al. The relative importance of job facets as indicated by an empirically derived model of job satisfaction. Unpublished report, Survey Research Center, University of Michigan, Ann Arbor, 1972.

BERSCHEID, E., & WALSTER, E.H. *Interpersonal Attraction.* Massachusetts: Addison-Wesley, 1969.

BYRNE, D. Attitude and attraction. In L. Berkowitz (Ed.), *Advances in experimental social psychology,* Vol. 4. New York: Academic Press, 1969, 36-89.

DALY, J.A. Listening and interpersonal evaluations. Paper presented at the annual meeting of the Central States Speech Association, Kansas City, 1975.

DALY, J.A., & LASHBROOK, W.B. Time pressure, vocal activity and interpersonal evaluations. Paper presented at the annual meeting of the Central States Speech Association, Chicago, 1976.

DALY, J.A., & LETH, S. Communication apprehension and the personnel selection decision. Paper presented at the annual meeting of the International Communication Association, Portland, Oregon, 1976.

DALY, J.A., & McCROSKEY, J.C. Occupational desirability and choice as a function of communication apprehension. *Journal of Counseling Psychology,* 1975, 22, 309-313.

DALY, J.A., McCROSKEY, J.C., & FALCIONE, R.L. Communication apprehension, supervisor communication receptivity and satisfaction with superiors. Paper presented at the annual meeting of the Eastern Communication Association, Philadelphia, 1976 (a).

DALY, J.A., McCROSKEY, J.C., & FALCIONE, R.L. Homophily-Heterophily and the prediction of supervisor satisfaction. Paper presented at the annual meeting of the International Communication Association, Portland, Oregon, 1976 (b).

DALY, J.A., & MILLER, M.D. The empirical development of an instrument to measure writing apprehension. *Research in the Teaching of English,* 1975, 9, 242-249.

DALY, J.A., & SHAMO, W. Writing apprehension and occupational choice. *Journal of Occupational Psychology,* 1976 (in press).

FALCIONE, R.L. The relationship of supervisor credibility to subordinate satisfaction. *Personnel Journal,* 1973, 52, 800-803.

FALCIONE, R.L. Communication climate and satisfaction with immediate supervision. *Journal of Applied Communication Research,* 1974, 2, 13-20 (a).

FALCIONE, R.L. The factor structure of source credibility scales for immediate superiors in the organizational context. *Central States Speech Journal* 1974, 25, 63-66 (b).

FALCIONE, R.L. Credibility: Qualifier of subordinate participation. *Journal of Business Communication,* 1974, 11, 43-54 (c).

FALCIONE, R.L. Subordinate satisfaction as a function of perceived supervisor credibility. Paper presented at the annual meeting of the International Communication Association, Chicago, 1975.

FIEDLER, F.E. *A theory of leadership effectiveness.* New York: McGraw-Hill, 1967.

FLEISHMAN, E.A. A leader behavior description for industry. In R.M. Stogdill and A.E. Coons (Eds.), *Leader behavior: Its description and measurement.* Columbus: Ohio State University, Bureau of Business Research, Research Monograph No. 88, 1957, 103-119 (a).

FLEISHMAN, E.A. The leadership opinion questionnaire. In R.M. Stogdill and A.E. Coons (Eds.), *Leader behavior: Its description and measurement.* Columbus: Ohio State University, Bureau of Business Research, Research Monograph No. 88, 1957, 120-133 (b).

GRAEN, G. Instrumentality theory of work motivation: Some experimental results and suggested modifications. *Journal of Applied Psychology Monograph,* 1969, 53, 1-25.

HACKMAN, J.R., & LAWLER, E.E. Employee reactions to job characteristics. (Monograph) *Journal of Applied Psychology,* 1971, 55, 259-286.

HALPIN, A.W. The leader behavior and effectiveness of aircraft commanders. In R.M. Stogdill and A.E. Coons (Eds.), *Leader behavior: Its description and measurement.* Columbus: Ohio State University, Bureau of Business Research, Research Monograph No. 88, 1957, 52-64.

HALPIN, A.W., & WINER, B.J. A factorial study of the leader behavior descriptions. In R.M. Stogdill and A.E. Coons (Eds.), *Leader behavior: Its description and measurement.* Columbus: Ohio State University Bureau of Business Research, Research Monograph No. 88, 1957, 39-51.

HERZBERG, F. *Work and the nature of man.* Cleveland: World, 1966.

HILL, W. The validation and extension of Fiedler's theory of leadership effectiveness. *Academy of Management Journal,* 1969, 33-47.

HUNT, J.G. A test of the leadership contingency model in three organizations. *Organizational Behavior and Human Performance,* 1967, 2, 290-308.

JORGENSEN, D.O., DUNNETTE, M.D., & PRITCHARD, R.D. Effects of the manipulation of a performance-reward contingency on behavior in a simulated work setting. *Journal of Applied Psychology,* 1973, 57, 271-280.

KORMAN, A.K. Task success, task popularity, and self-esteem as influences on task liking. *Journal of Applied Psychology,* 1968, 52, 484-490.

KORMAN, A.K. *Industrial and organizational psychology.* Englewood Cliffs: Prentice-Hall, 1971.

LOCKE, E.A. The relationship of task success to task liking and satisfaction. *Journal of Applied Psychology,* 1965, 49, 379-385.

LOCKE, E.A., CARTLEDGE, N., & KOEPPEL, J. Motivational effects of knowledge of results: A goal-setting phenomenon? *Psychological Bulletin,* 1968, 70, 474-485.

LOCKE, E.A. What is job satisfaction? *Organizational Behavior and Human Performance,* 1969, 4, 309-336.

LOCKE, E.A. The supervisor as "motivator": His influence on employee performance and satisfaction. In B.M. Bass, R. Cooper, and J.A. Hass (Eds.), *Managing for accomplishment.* Lexington: 1970, 57-67 (a).

LOCKE, E.A. Job satisfaction and job performance: A theoretical analysis. *Organizational Behavior and Human Performance,* 1970, 5, 484-500 (b).

LOCKE, E.A. Nature and causes of job satisfaction. In M.D. Dunnette (Ed.), *Handbook of Industrial and Organizational Psychology.* Chicago: Rand McNally, 1976, 1297-1349.

LOFQUIST, L.H., & DAWIS, R.V. *Adjustment to work.* New York: Appleton-Century-Crofts, 1969.

MASLOW, A.H. *Motivation and personality.* New York: Harper and Row, 1954 (2d ed., 1970).

McCROSKEY, J.C. Measures of communication-bound anxiety. *Speech Monographs,* 1970, 37, 269-277.

McCROSKEY, J.C. Validity of the PRCA as an index of oral communication apprehension. Paper presented at the annual meeting of the Speech Communication Association, Houston, 1975.

McCROSKEY, J.C., JENSEN, L., & VALENCIA, C. Measurement of the credibility of peers and spouses. Paper presented at the annual meeting of the International Communication Association, Montreal, 1973.

McCROSKEY, J.C., & McCAIN, T.A. The measurement of interpersonal attraction. *Speech Monographs,* 1974, 41, 261-266.

McCROSKEY, J.C., & RICHMOND, V.P. Self credibility as an index of self-esteem. Paper presented at the annual meeting of the Speech Communication Association, Houston, 1975.

McCROSKEY, J.C., & RICHMOND, V.P. Communication apprehension as a predictor of self-disclosure. *Communication Quarterly,* 1976 (in press).

McCROSKEY, J.C., RICHMOND, V.P., & DALY, J.A. The development of a measure of perceived homophily in interpersonal communication. *Human Communication Research,* 1975, 1, 323-332.

McCROSKEY, J.C., DALY, J.A., RICHMOND, V.P., & FALCIONE, R.L. Studies of the relationship between communication apprehension and self-esteem. *Human Communication Research* (in press).

McGREGOR, D. *Human side of enterprise.* New York: McGraw-Hill, 1960.

MELLINGER, G. Interpersonal trust as a factor in communication. *Journal of Abnormal and Social Psychology,* 1956, 52, 304-309.

PELZ, D.C., & ANDREWS, F.M. *Scientists in organizations.* New York: Wiley, 1966.

PORTER, L.W. Job attitudes in management: I. Perceived deficiencies in need fulfillment as a function of job level. *Journal of Applied Psychology,* 1962, 46, 375-384.

PORTER, L.W., & ROBERT, K.H. Communication in organizations. In M.D. Dunnette (Ed.), *Handbook of Industrial and Organizational Psychology.* Chicago: Rand McNally, 1976, 1553-1589.

PRITCHARD, R.D., & DeLEO, P.J. Experimental test of the valence-instrumentality relationship in job performance. *Journal of Applied Psychology,* 1973, 57, 264-270.

PRITCHARD, R.D., DUNNETTE, M.D., & JORGENSEN, D.O. Effects of perceptions of equity and inequity on worker performance and satisfaction. *Journal of Applied Psychology,* 1972, 56, Monograph No. 1, 75-94.

QUINN, R. et al. Job satisfaction: Is there a trend? *Manpower Research Monograph* No. 30, U.S. Government Printing Office, Washington, D.C., 1974.

READ, W. Upward communication in industrial hierarchies. *Human Relations,* 1962, 15, 3-16.

REDDING, W.C. Human communication behavior in complex organizations: Some fallacies revisited. In C.E. Larson and F.E.X. Dance (Eds.), *Perspectives on Communication.* Shorewood, Wis.: Helix Press, 99-112.

RICHMOND, V.P. Communication apprehension and success in the job applicant screening process. Unpublished paper, University of Nebraska, Lincoln, 1976.

ROGERS, E.M., & SHOEMAKER, F.F. *Communication of innovations.* New York: Free Press, 1971.

ROSEN, N.A. *Leadership change and work-group dynamics.* Ithaca, N.Y.: Cornell University Press, 1969.

SCOTT, M.D., McCROSKEY, J.C., & SHEAHAN, M.E. The development of a self-report measure of communication apprehension in organizational settings. Paper presented at the annual meeting of the International Communication Association, Portland, 1976.

SEEMAN, M.A. A comparison of general and specific leader behavior descriptions. In R.M. Stogdill and A.E. Coons (Eds.), *Leader behavior: Its description and measurement.* Columbus: Ohio State University, Bureau of Business Research, Research Monograph No. 88, 1957, 86-102.

SMITH, P.C., KENDALL, L.M., & HULIN, C.L. *The measurement of satisfaction in work and retirement.* Chicago: Rand McNally, 1969.

TOSI, H.L., CHESSER, R.J., & CARROL, S.J. A dynamic model of certain aspects of the superior-subordinate relationship. Paper presented at the annual meeting of the Eastern Academy of Management, 1972.

VROOM, V.H. *Work and motivation.* New York: Wiley, 1964.

WEINER, B. et al. *Perceiving the causes of success and failure.* New York: General Learning Press, 1971.

WYLIE, R. *The self-concept: A critical survey of pertinent research literature.* Lincoln, Neb.: University of Nebraska Press, 1961.

THE DEVELOPMENT OF A MEASURE OF PERCEIVED ORGANIZATIONAL INNOVATIVENESS

H. THOMAS HURT and C. WARD TEIGEN
West Virginia University

This paper presents the results of the development of a self-report measure of perceived organizational innovativeness (PORGI). The 25-item instrument was found to have excellent reliability, and construct and predictive validity. PORGI was found to be a significant predictor of four measures of employee job satisfaction. Employees' satisfaction with their own work was best predicted by individual innovativeness. In addition, both PORGI and individual innovativeness were found to be significant predictors of employee participation at each stage of the organizational innovation-decision process.

Research in organizational behavior has focused for some time on the innovativeness of organizations (Ginzburg & Reilly, 1957; Bennis, 1966; Burns & Stalker, 1966; Becker, 1967; Knight, 1967; Lawrence & Lorsch, 1967; Beckhord, 1969; Jones, 1969; Miller, 1971; Utterback, 1971; Zaltman, Duncan, & Holbek, 1973). Only recently, however, have scholars specifically concerned with organizational communication begun to examine the impact of organizational innovativeness on selected system variables (Rogers & Rogers, 1976). The results of this research suggest that organizational innovativeness, or adaptability, is related to such communication variables as vertical and horizontal information and feedback flow, restriction of information flow, informal communication roles, and communication interaction. In addition, Hage and Aiken (1970) have posited that these communication variables, together with organizational innovativeness, are positively related to job satisfaction. Thus, the results of the analysis of data generated by both empirical and nonempirical investigations, coupled with the sheer bulk of information, justify continued and increasing focus on the effects of organizational innovativeness on job behavior.

THE MEASUREMENT OF ORGANIZATIONAL INNOVATIVENESS

In the past, the measurement of organizational innovativeness has relied heavily on observing and recording certain physical characteristics of the organizational structure (Zaltman, Duncan, & Holbek, 1973), the innovative behavior of executives (Forehand, 1963), or employee attitudes about organizational changes (Patchen, 1965). There are, however, certain measurement problems associated with these techniques. Rogers and Rogers (1976, p. 173) point out:

> There is a logical difficulty in this use of retrospective data about innovativeness in an analysis including independent variables that are measured cross-sectionally: in essence, one is correlating yesterday's innovativeness with today's independent variables. Often the problem is worse; the correlations are between today's variables and the cognitive dissonance-reducing perception of yesterday's innovativeness. Success is more likely to be remembered than failure; the organization's files may even be purged of records of unsuccessful innovations. The past constantly tends to be reinterpreted in terms of the present or the anticipated future.

Consequently, it is difficult to assess the validity of such measures, let alone the degree of congruency between these measures and the extent to which employees perceive the organization for which they work to be innovative. This is a critical measurement failure, for without a direct measure of employees' perceptions, the relationships between organizational innovativeness and selected employee-related variables remain locked in the domain of indirect investigator judgments. Thus, the first purpose of this paper was to develop a direct measure of perceived organizational innovativeness which would not be bound by the measurement problems discussed above.

The needs for such a measurement device in organizational communication research are many. First, we believe that employees' perceptions of organizational innovativeness have the potential to be more closely related to employee attitudes about work than other less direct measures of organizational innovativeness. Second, measuring organizational innovativeness through the assessment of employee perceptions follows a long research tradition of investigating other internal employee variables such as motivation, attitudes, and morale (Lodahl & Kejner, 1965). Finally, self-report measures of employee perceptions of organizational innovativeness make possible more powerful and complex statistical analyses, unlike past research which has been primarily dependent upon descriptive and nonparametric types of analyses.

Recently, Hurt and Joseph (1976) reported the development of a scale designed to measure self-reports of individual innovativeness, or willingness-to-change. The results of their work relating to the distribution of perceptions of individual innovativeness have been particularly useful in helping us to develop the construct *perceived organizational innovativeness*. Although some organizations (like individuals) would obviously be perceived as being more or less innovative, most organizations (again, like individuals) would most probably be perceived as being not particularly innovative or non-innovative. Thus, we began our research with the assumption that perceptions of organizational innovativeness would be *normally* distributed. This was a particularly useful assumption, since its confirmation makes possible statistical tests of predictions relating organizational innovativeness to other variables.

Hurt and Joseph (1976) also demonstrated that individual innovativeness was a unidimensional construct measured by an underlying continuum of willingness-to-change. We also assumed that organizational innovativeness could best be described as a unidimensional construct, with an underlying continuum of perceived organizational willingness-to-change.

THIS STUDY

In order to assess the utility of a measure of perceived organizational innovativeness for communication research, we posited two hypotheses relating to perceptions of organizational innovativeness and organizational behavior.

The first of these hypotheses was based upon the work of Rogers and Rogers (1976) who identified four stages in the organizational innovation-decision process. The first of these stages involves matching an organizational problem with a new solution. The second involves checking the accuracy with which the new solution has been matched to a problem. The last two stages are concerned with connecting the new way to doing things to the ongoing structure and activities of the organization, and making the new way of doing things a routine part of the organization.

Congruent with the work of Zaltman, Duncan, and Holbek (1973), who argued that the more innovative the organization the greater the amount of employee participation in the decision making process, we concluded that more innovative organizations would be more likely to seek out innovative employees to participate in each stage of the innovation-decision process. Thus, we hypothesized that:

H_1: Perceived organizational innovativeness and individual innovativeness will be significant predictors of employee participation in all stages of the innovation-decision process (relationship: positive, linear).

Hage and Aiken (1970) reported that the lower the rate of organizational change, the higher the feelings of dissatisfaction and "malaise" among employees. Hage and Aiken further concluded that there was a significant relationship between organizational innovativeness and job satisfaction.

We expanded Hage and Aiken's 1970 proposition to include individual innovativeness. We reasoned that, regardless of the extent of organizational rigidity, innovative employees would still be more satisfied with their own work, since they would be more likely to find unusual and interesting ways of doing it. On the other hand, organizational innovativeness would primarily impact employees' satisfaction with the *total system* aspects of their work which could not be divorced from the organizational structure. Consequently, our second hypothesis stated that:

H_{2a}: Perceived organizational innovativeness will be significantly related to employees' satisfaction with their supervisor, co-workers, opportunities for promotion, and pay (relationship: positive, linear).

H_{2b}: Individual innovativeness will be significantly related to employees' satisfaction with their own work (relationship: positive, linear).

METHODS

Subjects

Subjects were 401 public school teachers and administrators representing 22 school districts and 5 states. All were voluntarily enrolled in a graduate workshop dealing with communication in the classroom.

Measurement of the Independent Variables

Development of the Perceived Organizational Innovativeness Scale (PORGI). An initial pool of 37 items was generated. Fourteen of these items were written on the basis of the characteristics of innovative organizations discussed by Rogers and Rogers (1976); Zaltman, Duncan, and Holbek (1973); and Hage and Aiken (1970). Twenty items were adapted and modified to fit organizational contexts from the original innovativeness scale developed by Hurt and Joseph (1976). The final three items were original.

Since we have taken the position that perceived organizational innovativeness is a normally distributed construct, the 37 items were administered in a 7-choice Likert-type response format to the 401 subjects in order to produce a range of continuous scores. Subjects were asked to indicate the extent of

was related to the organization (school district) by which they were employed. Responses were scored so that higher scores indicated higher levels of perceived organizational innovativeness. The results of the analyses are reported below.

The Measurement of Individual Innovativeness (IS). The innovativeness or willingness-to-change of the subjects was measured using the 20-item *Innovativeness scale* (Hurt & Joseph, 1976). In this study, the split-half corrected reliability of the *Innovativeness Scale (IS)* was found to be .86.

Measurement of the Dependent Variables

Job Satisfaction. Scales developed by Smith, Kendall, and Hulin (1969) and factor analyzed by McCroskey, Daly, and Falcione (1977), using public school employees as subjects, were employed to measure types of job satisfaction with subjects' *own work*, their *supervisors*, their *pay*, their chances for *promotion*, and their *co-workers*. In order to reduce subjects' fatigue and hostility, four 7-choice Likert-type items with the highest loadings on each dimension analyzed by McCroskey, Daly, and Falcione (1977), were selected for use in this study.[1] Use of Nunnally's (1967) techniques yielded the following reliabilities for each of the 5 dimensions of job satisfaction: *own work* = .81; *supervisor* = .80; *co-workers* = .93; and *promotion* = .82.

Participation in the Organizational Decision Process. Participation in the decision-making process of the organizations by which subjects were employed was measured using four items, each of which represented a stage in the organizational innovation-decision process described by Rogers and Rogers (1976). Subjects were asked to indicate the extent of their agreement or disagreement, using a 7-choice Likert-type response format, to four statements indicating that they participated *a great deal* at the various stages of the organizational decision-making process.[2]

RESULTS

Analyses of the Perceived Organizational Innovativeness Scale

The responses of the 401 subjects were submitted to principal components factor analysis and varimax rotation. In addition, the scree procedure was used to determine the number of factors present. An item was considered loaded on a factor if it had a prime loading $\geq$ .60 and no secondary loadings greater than the variance accounted for by the prime loadings.

Although we believed that perceived organizational innovativeness was a unidimensional construct, the original factor analysis did not call for a specific number of factors to be extracted. When the eigenvalues obtained in the analysis were plotted, the Scree procedure clearly indicated the presence of a two-factor solution. Consequently, a second analysis requesting a two-factor solution was obtained. The results of this second analysis indicated that the two factors were artificially created as a result of the directionality of the wording of the items (positive or negative), and not their content. Thus, the single factor extracted from the unrotated correlation matrix was used. From this analysis, 25 items whose loadings on the first factor were $\geq$ .60 were selected for use as the *PORGI* scale. All 25 of these items discriminated (determined by *t*-tests) between the upper and lower 27 percent of the *PORGI* distribution. A Chi-square test for goodness-of-fit revealed that the distribution of these responses did not differ significantly from normality (X^2 = 2.59; df = 2). Since the factor loadings of each of the selected items were relatively homogenous, a total *PORGI* score was created by summing responses across each of the 25 items. The obtained scores ranged from 25 to 160 (theoretical range; 25-175), with a mean of 98 (theoretical mean; 100), and a standard deviation of 28. The corrected split-half (odd-even) reliability estimate of the 25-item *PORGI* scale was .96. The 25-item *PORGI* scale is shown in Table 1.

The Construct Validity of the PORGI Scale

Determining the validity of any self-report measure is difficult, and the *PORGI* scale is no excep-

tion. Of course, the items shown in Table 1 are suggestive of face validity. Fortunately, however, the distribution of *PORGI* responses provided crude, but also suggestive, implications for assessing the construct validity of the instrument.

We have defined *PORGI* as a normally distributed construct. In the analysis discussed above, the obtained distribution did not differ significantly from normality. Following a recommendation by Rogers and Shoemaker (1971) for defining degrees of individual innovativeness, we identified organization adopter categories within the distribution of *PORGI* responses by segmenting the distribution into five categories defined by the obtained standard deviation. Theoretically, those organizations perceived as most innovative should comprise 2.5 percent of the population (in our sample, n = 10.03); early adopting organizations, 13.5 percent (n = 54.13); early majority organizations, 34 percent (n = 136.34); late majority organizations, 34 percent (n = 136.34); and laggard organizations, 16 percent (n = 64.16). In our obtained data, innovative organizations comprised 2 percent (n = 8); early adopting organizations, 15.2 percent (n = 61); early majority organizations, 31.4 percent (n = 126); late majority organizations, 33.9 percent (n = 136); and laggard organizations, 17.4 percent (n = 70). Consequently our data did not differ significantly (as the Chi-square test suggested) from the frequencies which would be theoretically expected in an ideal distribution of *PORGI* responses. Further, we defined *PORGI* as an unidimensional construct, and this factor structure provided the best solution in our analysis of the scales.

Other evidence for the construct validity of the scales was provided by the correlation between individual innovativeness and *PORGI*. Although both constructs have certain superficial similarities (e.g., both are normally distributed), the perception of one's *own* innovativeness, and an employee's perception of the innovativeness of the organization for which he or she works, should be substantially unrelated (Rogers & Rogers, 1976). In order to test this assumption, *PORGI* responses were correlated with the *IS* responses. The resulting correlation (r = .073; N = 401; p > .05) was highly encouraging. Both constructs maintained their independence in spite of the fact that 20 of the 37 items on the *PORGI*

TABLE 1
Factor Loadings of the PORGI Scales: Unrotated Matrix

PORGI Item	Factor Loading
The Organization I Work For (is):	
** 1. cautious about accepting new ideas	.67
* 2. a leader among other organizations	-.74
** 3. suspicious of new ways of thinking	.72
* 4. very inventive	-.76
* 5. often consulted by other organizations for advice and information	-.65
** 6. skeptical of new ideas	.70
7. frequently improvises methods for solving problems when a traditional answer is not suitable	-.57
8. very complex in its structure and number of specialized jobs	-.19
9. challenged by unanswered questions	-.46
10. frequently allows employees to change the manner in which they do their job without approval of higher authority	-.37
*11. creative in its method of operation	-.74
**12. usually one of the last of its kind to change to a new method of operation	.73
*13. considered one of the leaders of its type	-.74
*14. receptive to new ideas	-.80
*15. challenged by unsolved problems	-.60
**16. follows the belief that "the old way of doing things is the best"	.73
*17. very original in its operational procedures	.73
18. maintains frequent communication with similar type organizations	-.49
19. often assigns employees additional responsibilities without additional rewards	.36
20. expects employees to strongly conform to its rules	.46
**21. does not respond quickly enough to necessary changes	.75
**22. reluctant to adopt new ways of doing things until other organizations have used them successfully	.71
*23. frequently initiates new methods of operation	-.70
**24. slow to change	.83
**25. rarely involves employees in the decision making process	.66
*26. maintains good communication between supervisors and employees	-.65
27. has a high level of power concentrated in a few people	.36
28. emphasizes the quality rather than the quantity of the work I do	-.54
29. does not offer good opportunities for promotions	.39
*30. influential with other organizations	-.60
31. has very formalized rules and procedures for controlling job performance	.16
32. rarely enforces rules governing job performance	.14
*33. seeks out new ways to do things	-.79
**34. rarely trusts new ideas and ways of functioning	.74
**35. never satisfactorily explains to employees the reasons for procedural changes	.62
*36. frequently tries out new ideas	-.77
*37. willing and ready to accept outside help when necessary	-.66

* All items preceded by at least one asterisk comprise the 25 item PORGI Scale. Suggested scoring procedure: 112 + sum of ** items minus sum of * items; only to be used when Strongly Agree = 1, Strongly Disagree = 7.

scale were adapted from the *IS* scale. Thus, responses to items measuring perceived organizational innovativeness were apparently elicited by an independent and distinct class of stimuli, as opposed to those used to elicit responses measuring individual innovativeness. Given the descriptive attributes of the *PORGI* construct as we have defined it, it would appear then that our instrument was consistent with all of them.

The Predictive Validity of the PORGI Scale

Our best estimate of the predictive validity of the *PORGI* scale was derived from the tests of the two hypotheses.

Test of Hypotheses 1. Hypothesis 1 stated that *both* individual innovativeness and *PORGI* would best predict subjects, participation at each stage of the organizational-decision process. Since responses to each stage of the process were significantly intercorrelated, these data were analyzed using a canonical correlation procedure, with *IS* and *PORGI* as the predictor variables, and the four questions relating to innovation-decision participation as the dependent variables. The results of this analysis are shown in Table 2.

The results of the canonical analysis produced a single significant canonical correlation (canonical r = .46; Chi-square = 93.98; df = 8, p < .0001). Both *IS* and *PORGI* were highly and positively correlated on the first vector associated with the predictor variables, and all four of the questions relating to participation in the innovation-decision process were highly and positively correlated with the first vector associated with the dependent variables. As can be seen in Table 2, the variable accounting for the most variance on the canonical vector associated with the predictor variables was *PORGI*. Individual innovativeness was also highly associated with that vector, but accounted for substantially less variance. Thus, it would appear that as both organizational and individual innovativeness increased, employee participation in each stage of the innovation-decision process increased. These results provided confirmation of our first hypothesis.

Test of Hypothesis 2. Hypothesis 2 stated that *PORGI* would be significantly and positively related to *employees' satisfaction with their supervisor*, their *opportunity for promotion*, their *pay*, and their *co-workers*, while *IS* would be significantly related to employees' satisfaction with their own work. Since none of the job satisfaction measures were intercorrelated, a series of Pearson product-moment correlations were computed between each of the predictor variables and their associated dependent variables. The results of these analyses are shown in Table 3.

As can be seen in Table 3, our second hypothesis was also confirmed. *PORGI* was significantly, positively correlated with *employees' satisfaction measures of their supervisors, chances for promotion, co-workers* and *pay*, and unrelated to *employees' reported satisfaction with their own work*. *IS* was significantly, positively correlated only with *employees' satisfaction with their own work*. It should be noted that the relatively small, but significant, correlation between *PORGI* and pay satisfaction probably stemmed from the fact that salaries for public school employees are both notoriously low and usually under the control of state legislatures, *not* school districts. Thus, pay increments remain relatively fixed and stable across school organizations. Nonetheless, this lower correlation, together with confirmation of our two hypotheses, provided strong evidence for the predictive validity of the *PORGI* scales.

Supplementary Analyses

In order to determine whether or not levels of participation in the organizational innovation-decision process were related to job satisfaction, we summed across the four correlated measures of decision participation to obtain a gross measure of employee involvement. A series of partial-correlations, with *IS* and *PORGI* removed, were then computed between the employee involvement measure and the various measures of job satisfaction. These results are shown in Table 4.

Clearly, these results demonstrated that *employee involvement* was positively related to all measures of *job satisfaction*, with the exception of *pay*.

TABLE 2
Canonical Correlation Between IS and PORGI and PARTICIPATION in the Four Stages of the Innovation-Decision Process

canonical variable	canonical correlation	Chi-square	df	$p=x^2$
1	.454	93.99	8	.0001

Correlation Coefficients between Canonical Variables

canonical variable	IS	PORGI		
1	.55	.83		

canonical variable	Stage I	Stage II	Stage III	Stage IV
1	.86	.89	.82	.90

TABLE 3
Correlations Between IS and PORGI with Job Satisfaction Measures

Independent Variable	Dependent Variable				
	Supervisor	Promotion	Own Work	Co-Workers	Pay
PORGI	.77*	.62*	.05	.58*	.16*
	(.59)**	(.38)		(.34)	(.02)
IS	.01	.02	.78	.02	.01
			(.61)		

* p < .05
** variance accounted for.

DISCUSSION

The results of our initial attempt to develop a measure of perceived organizational innovativeness have been very positive. The scale has exceptional reliability and equally acceptable construct and predictive validity. In addition, its implications for heuristic research and applications in organizational settings are excellent.

First, the scales are easy and inexpensive to administer, both in terms of time and money, thus making rapid scoring and analysis of data possible. This is particularly important when a researcher is concerned with applying and communicating the results of an organizational study to concerned individuals within the organization.

Second, the ability of the scales to correctly predict satisfaction with certain aspects of employment, and the degree of employee participation in the organizational-decision process, raises an interesting issue about differences between *perceived* and *actual* organizational innovativeness. Our data provide no information about the relationship between these two variables. Nevertheless, the variance accounted for by the correlations between *PORGI* and the various measures of job satisfaction tend to reconfirm our belief that employees' perceptions of organizational innovativeness may be at least as important as predictors of job satisfaction as the *actual* innovative behavior of organizations. Thus, a change in organizational structure to facilitate adaptability to needed innovations may not

TABLE 4
Partial Correlation Coefficients Between Total Employee Involvement and Types of Job Satisfaction (IS and PORGI Removed)

Independent Variable	Dependent Variables				
	Supervisor	Promotion	Own Work	Co-Workers	Pay
Employee Involvement	.25* (.06)**	.17* (.03)	.14* (.02)	.16* (.03)	.03

* p < .05
** variance accounted for.

FIGURE 1
A Preliminary Path Model Predicting Various Measures of Job Satisfaction

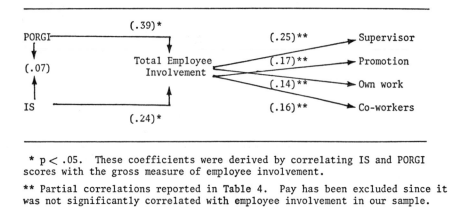

* p < .05. These coefficients were derived by correlating IS and PORGI scores with the gross measure of employee involvement.

** Partial correlations reported in Table 4. Pay has been excluded since it was not significantly correlated with employee involvement in our sample.

result in increased job satisfaction unless there is a concomitant attempt to change employees' perceptions. The results of the tests of our hypotheses imply that the former does not necessarily result in the latter.

Third, the use of the *PORGI* scales makes possible investigations exploring the impact of perceptual discrepancies of organizational innovativeness between employees and management personnel on the acceptance and continued use of an innovation by the "adoption unit" (employees). This discrepancy is a particularly important variable for organizational communication researchers. Gardner

(1965, pp. 78-79) indirectly referred to these discrepancies as the "filtered experience," the phenomenon whereby the picture of reality held by persons at the top of the organizational hierarchy is "often a dangerous mismatch with the real world" (Rogers & Shoemaker, 1971, p. 314). It may well be the case that a quantitatively derived difference in perceptions of organizational innovativeness between management and employees is a variable which will account for substantial variance in employee attitudes about changes in organizational performance.

Finally, the results of our canonical correlation

analysis, coupled with the results of our supplementary analyses, provided the groundwork for the development of a preliminary path-analytic model predicting job satisfaction. This model is shown in Figure 1. In short, we would argue that organizations which are perceived as being more innovative are most likely to select innovative employees to participate in the decision-making process. As this level of participation increases, a substantial increase in job satisfaction should result.

NOTES

1. The scales used to measure the dimensions of job satisfaction were: *My immediate supervisor or department head is*—hard to please, tactful, annoying, intelligent; *My work*—is fascinating, is not very useful, is challenging, does not give me a sense of accomplishment; *My pay*—is adequate to meet normal expenses, is barely enough to live on, is very good, makes me underpaid; *The place where I work*—provides good opportunity for advancement, provides for regular promotion, does not promote people on ability, provides limited chance for promotion; *My co-workers are*—boring, slow, responsible, hard workers.
2. The scales used to measure employee involvement in each stage of the organizational innovation-decision process were *within the organization I work for, I am often involved in helping to:* match an organizational problem with a new solution, check the accuracy of a solution which has been matched to a problem, connect the new way of doing things to the ongoing structure and activities of the organization, make a new way of doing things a routine part of the organization.

REFERENCES

BECKER, S., & WHISLER, T. The innovative organization: A selective view of current theory and research. *Journal of Business*, 1967, 4, 462-469.

BECKHARD, R. *Organizational development: Strategies and models*. Reading, Mass.: Addison-Wesley, 1969.

BENNIS, W. *Changing organizations*. New York: McGraw-Hill, 1966.

BURNS, T., & STALKER, G. *The management of innovation*. London: Tavistok Publications, 1961.

FALCIONE, R., McCROSKEY, J.C., & DALY, J. Job satisfaction as a function of employees' communication apprehension, self-esteem, and perceptions of their immediate supervisor. In B. Ruben (Ed.), *Communication Yearbook 1*, New Brunswick, N.J., Transaction-International Communication Association, 1977.

FOREHAND, G. Assessments of innovative behavior: Partial criteria for the assessment of executive performance. *Journal of Applied Psychology*. 1963, 47, 206-213.

GARDNER, J.W. *Self renewal*. New York: Harper & Row, 1965.

GINZBURG, E., & REILLY, E. *Effective change in large organizations*. New York: Columbia University Press, 1957.

HAGE, J., & AIKEN, M. *Social change in complex organizations*. New York: Random House, 1970.

HURT, H.T., & JOSEPH, K. Scales for the measurement of innovativeness. Presented at the annual meeting of the International Communication Association, Portland, 1976 tion Association, Portland, 1976.

JONES, G. *Planned organizational change*. New York: Frederick Praeger, 1969.

KNIGHT, K. A descriptive model of the intra-firm innovation process. *Journal of Business*, 1967, 40, 478-496.

LAWRENCE, P., & LORSCH, J. Differentiation and integration in complex organizations, *Administrative Science Quarterly*, 1967.

LODAHL, T., & KEJNER, M. The definition and measurement of job involvement. *Journal of Applied Psychology*, 1965, 49, 24-33.

MILLER, R. *Innovation, organization, and environment*. Sherbrooke: Institute De Recherche et Perfectionment en Administration, Université de Sherbrooke, 1971.

NUNNALLY, J.C. *Psychometric theory*, New York: McGraw-Hill, 1967.

PATCHEN, M. *Some questionnaire measures of employee motivation*. Ann Arbor, Mich., University of Michigan, 1965.

ROGERS, E., & ROGERS, R.A. *Communication in organizations*. New York: Free Press, 1976.

ROGERS, E., & SHOEMAKER, F. *Communication of innovations: A Cross cultural approach*. New York: Free Press, 1971.

UTTERBACK, J. The process of technological innovation within the firm. *Academy of Management Journal*, 1971, 14, 75-88.

ZALTMAN, G., DUNCAN, R., & HOLBECK, J. *Innovations and organizations*. New York: Wiley, 1973.

INTERCULTURAL COMMUNICATION
Theory and Research: An Overview
Selected Studies

INTERCULTURAL COMMUNICATION
THEORY AND RESEARCH: AN OVERVIEW

TULSI B. SARAL
Governors State University

The field of intercultural communication is relatively young, and its boundaries are not yet clearly identified. The newness of the field has attracted scholars from varying disciplines who, while enriching and broadening the area, have also rendered the field so diverse and discursive that it defies definition. Conceptualizations of intercultural communication range from those which regard intercultural communication as a subsystem of human communication to those that consider it as an independent and respectable area of study that cuts across various disciplines, including communication.

In the inaugural session of the Intercultural Communication Division of the International Communication Association, Sitaram (1970) defined intercultural communication as the art of understanding and being understood by the audience of another culture. Samovar and Porter (1972) maintain that *intercultural communication* obtains whenever the parties to a communication act bring with them different experiential backgrounds that reflect a long-standing deposit of group experience, knowledge, and values. By the way of distinction, Rich (1974) contends that communication is intercultural when occuring between peoples of different cultures. Stewart (1974) defines intercultural communication as communication which occurs under conditions of cultural difference—*language, values, customs,* and *habits*. Similarly, Sitaram and Cogdell (1976) describe intercultural communication as interaction between members of differing cultures.

CULTURE AND COMMUNICATION

A common feature of all these definitions is the mention of the concepts *culture* and *communication,* neither of which have widely agreed-upon definitions. Sitaram (1970), for example, defines *culture* as the sum total of the learned behaviors of a group of people that are generally considered to be the tradition of that people and that are transmitted from generation to generation. According to Porter (1972), *culture* refers to the cumulative deposit of knowledge, experience, meanings, beliefs, values, attitudes, religions, concepts of self, the universe and self-universe relationships, hierarchies of status, role expectations, spatial relations, and time concepts acquired by a large group of people in the course of generations through individual and group striving. In anthropology, *culture* is an omnibus term designating both the distinctly human forms of adaptation and the distinctive ways in which the different human populations organize their lives on earth (Levine, 1973). Levine broadly employs the term *culture* to mean an organized body of rules concerning the ways in which individuals in a population should communicate with one another, the manner in which they think about themselves and their environments. These rules need not be universally or constantly obeyed, but they are recognized by all, and they ordinarily operate to limit the range of variation in patterns of communication, belief, value, and social behavior in that population.

According to Deutsch (1966), culture is based on the community of communication. In this view, *culture* consists of socially stereotyped patterns of behavior, including habits of language and thought, and is transmitted through various forms of social learning, particularly through methods of early child-rearing standardized in that culture. Alfred Smith (1966) regards *culture* as a code which we learn and share. Learning and sharing require communication, and communication requires coding and symbols, which must be learned and shared. Smith, therefore, considers communication and culture inseparable.

Definitions of *communication* are even more diverse and varied in nature and scope. Psychologist Stevens (1950), for example, defines *communication* as the discriminatory response of an organism to a stimulus. The definition implies that communication occurs when some environmental disturbance (the stimulus) impinges upon an organism, to which the organism reacts (makes a discriminatory response). In such a view, if the stimulus is ignored by the organism, there has been no communication.

Colin Cherry (1957), on the other hand, points out that *communication* is not the response itself but is essentially the *relationship* set up by the transmission of stimuli and the evocation of responses. Approaching communication from a psychiatric perspective, Ruesch and Bateson (1949) maintain that communication does not refer to verbal, explicit and intentional transmission of message alone. Rather, they argue, the concept of *communication* includes all those processes by which people influence one another. One implication of this definition is that all actions and events perceived by a human being have communicative implications. This definition further assumes that perception transforms the information an individual possesses, and that transformation influences the perceiver.

Gerbner (1958) defines *communication* as social interaction through messages—messages that can be formally coded, symbolic or representational events of some shared aspect of a culture. Berelson and Steiner (1964) emphasize the transmission of information, ideas, emotions, skills, etc., by use of symbols. According to them, it is the *act* or *process* of transmission that is usually called *communication*.

For Shannon and Weaver (1949), *communication* references all of the procedures by which one mind may affect another. They present a mathematical model of communication which involves a *source* selecting a message that is *encoded* into *signals* by a *transmitter*, and a *receiver* decoding those signals so that the *destination* can recover the original message. This is a linear process; it has a beginning and an end—a source and a destination. Exploring various perspectives from which to approach communication, John Parry (1967) contends that it is appropriate to regard the communicative act as a special instance of the interplay of an organism in relation with its environment, or we can reverse the order and see perception, the basic link between man and his external world, as the prototype of communication.

Given the multiplicity of conceptualizations of *communication* and *culture*, the definitions of intercultural communication provided earlier are of limited value in explaining or clarifying the nature and scope of intercultural communication. Each can be interpreted in a variety of ways, depending upon which definition of the concepts "culture" and "communication" one selects. This does not discount or invalidate the insights provided by the scholars in this field. It is difficult, if not impossible, to specify a definition which completely delineates the meaning of the concept unless that definitional map is so complex and detailed as to be essentially the equivalent of the territory it is intended to chart (Newman, 1960). As an alternative, Newman advocates the use of a pragmatic definition which ". . . should be a calculus that is validly derived; it may, and perhaps should, remain 'in process.' "

CONTEXTUAL ENVIRONMENT

One such approach that has the potential to serve as calculus, and at the same time to preserve the "in process" nature of intercultural communication, is to define the phenomenon in terms of its *contextual environment*. As Smith (1966) pointed out, no one aspect of human communication is really understandable apart from all the other codes of human interaction. Things only have meaning in their relation to other things . . . Our facts become meaningful by being related to each other. Levine (1973) seems to be suggesting a similar view when he states that, for the individual, the sociocultural environment is made up of situations, roles, and institutions that represent normative pressure on him for correct performance, while also offering opportunities for personal expression and satisfaction. Barnlund (1968) reminds us that the subtle and unsensed influences of the physical and humanly created environment are among the most overlooked factors in communication study.

The importance of the contextual environment in

communication is underlined in Gerbner's (1958) general model of communication, which considers situation and context as integral elements of communication process, both at the encoding and the decoding levels. Hall (1976) notes that context and communication are intimately interrelated. In some cultures, he contends, messages are explicit—the words carry most of the information. In other cultures, such as China, Japan, or the Arab cultures, less information is contained in the verbal part of a message, since more is contained in the context. Commenting upon Hall's work on proxemics, Jones (1976) states that the picture of cultural proxemic differences which emerges is more complex than that originally painted by Hall, and indicates that cultural differences seem to be more apparent in some contexts than in others.

Approaching culture from a cognitive orientation, Cole et al., (1971) arrive at a similar conclusion. They argue that what seem to be cultural differences in cognition are better accounted for by situational differences than by cultural variation in cognitive processing. In a similar vein, Cole and Scribner (1974) emphasize that there are variations in the situations within which people manifest particular cognitive processes. They indicate what they believe to be an urgent need to develop a *theory of situations,* and they suggest that no such theory is likely without the close participation of cultural anthropologists.

Increasingly, scholars and students of communication have begun to identify the role played by contextual and situational variables in intercultural communication. Cartier (1976), for example, remarks that much of what has been written on intercultural communication misses the mark because of a failure to consider the purposes that two people have in communicating the situation in which communication occurs. These purposes (and situations) nearly always, he contends, involve factors which have nothing to do with communicating, per se, but which are the primary variables of the interaction. Cissna (1976), shares a similar concern with the conceptualization of intercultural communication and, as such, with the domain which that definition circumscribes. He believes that we should be studying those *situations* in which com-

munication occurs between people of different cultures.

Stewart (1974) cautions against cultism that could result from considering intercultural communication as a separate field. He considers it safer to speak of human communication as a field with specific applications to the intercultural context, arguing that intercultural communication always occurs in a particular setting—never in a vacuum.

Unhappy with the wrangling over definitions which has characterized conferences and publications about intercultural communication for some years, Badami (1976) attempts to redefine *intercultural communication* as a variable of participants or of setting—that is, a context for communication rather than as a separate phase or level of communication. She takes issue with Brooks (1974), who specifies the "levels of speech communication" as *intrapersonal, interpersonal, public,* and *cross-cultural.* According to Badami, *cross-cultural communication* is not defined by number of interactants, degree of mediation, potential for privacy, or clarity of distinction between sender and receiver roles. Rather, she indicates, intercultural communication is best defined as a variable of setting or communicator characteristics which applies to any of the levels of communication described above.

A valuable feature of the contextual-environmental approach to the study of intercultural communication is its potential as a means of accounting for a steadily growing list of variants and subvariants of intercultural communication. Sitaram (1970), for example, perceives *intercultural communication* as distinctly different from *international communication.* He defines international communication as interaction between political structures or nations, often carried on by representatives of those nations. *Intracultural communication,* suggest Sitaram (1970), takes place among individuals of the same culture and not between individuals of different cultures. Communication between the people of a minority subculture and those of the majority dominant culture, Sitaram terms *minority communication.* Rich (1974), however, feels that the terms "minority" and "majority" are relative, and are usually based upon personalized and subjective systems of classification.

She prefers to use the terms *interracial communication* (representing communication between members of different racial groups), *interethnic communication* (referring to communication between members of differing ethnic groups), and *contracultural communication* (covering communication between members of two strange but relatively equal cultures in a colonial relationship where one culture is forced to submit to the power of the other).

Arthur Smith (1971) introduces the concept of *transracial communication,* which he uses to refer to the understanding that persons from different ethnic or racial backgrounds can achieve in a situation of verbal interaction. Positing the definition so that it includes both racial and ethnic dimensions, he seeks to differentiate transracial communication from the much-used term *interracial,* which usually denotes differences in race only.

Prosser (1973) uses the term *intercommunication* to describe communication that crosses national or cultural boundaries. Jain and Schlow (1974) define *international communication* as that interaction which occurs between communicators of different nations. Their definition deals primarily with face-to-face interaction between persons from different nations and directs focus to the processes and problems of international communication at the interpersonal level.

None of the foregoing definitions suggest any fundamental differences in the nature and process of intercultural communication; they are merely pointing out the variations in the contextual environments within which various communications take place. Krippendorff (1976) seems to be focusing on this very feature when he remarks that intercultural communication pertains to several levels of cultural phenomena, starting perhaps with explanation of communication processes in terms of different family culture (the conventions that develop in separate families) and ending up with explaining communication in terms of different national cultures (e.g. Samoan, North American).

CULTURE AND LANGUAGE

Inquiries into the nature of intercultural communication have mostly concerned themselves with definitions of the term with construction of models to demonstrate how intercultural communication operates in a variety of situations, and with cataloging and describing a number of cultural variables such as language, values, norms, role-behaviors, time and space concepts, that affect communication. We are told, for example, how culture exerts influence over our use of language, and how it determines what our language is and how we use it. What comes to be symbolized and what symbols represent are very much functions of culture. Similarly, how we use our symbols is also a function of culture. Kluckhohn (1949) maintains that every language is also a special way of looking at the world and interpreting experience. The Sapir-Whorf hypothesis (Whorf, 1956) maintains that language functions not simply as a device for reporting experience, but also, and more significantly, as a way of defining experience for its speakers. It is indeed difficult to sort out whether it is the language that determines how members of a particular culture define social reality, or whether it is the culture that determines the expressive features of a language. Niyekawa (1968), for example, observes that the Japanese language has an "adversative passive" grammatical form, which implies "am not responsible for it." It is generally used when referring to some unpleasant event. She concludes that the Japanese culture provides experiences that are likely to lead to the attribution of responsibility to others, but these tendencies are enhanced by linguistic factors. However, as Triandis (1972) points out, one could also argue that Japanese culture is so sensitive to the attribution of responsibility for unpleasant events that it has developed particular linguistic forms which make it easier to avoid blame.

As in the case of language, literature on intercultural communication abounds in theoretical propositions and empirical findings about the effect of values, norms, role-expectations, perceptions, etc., on intercultural communication. Most of this work is descriptive, which is perhaps natural in any newly-evolving discipline. The act of describing an event, an experience, or a phenomenon tends to segment both knowledge and human identity into fragments. As there are some limitations merely in approaching human beings as aggregates of skills, behaviors, roles, fragmented faculties, or segments of processes, so viewing cultures solely as aggregates of values, norms, role expectations etc., of its members yields a limiting definition.

Transactional System

Intercultural communication has been described as communication among members of two or more different cultures. *Culture* may be conceived as a dynamic process; it develops and lives as a continuum, defined by a constant flow of exchanges among its members and their environments, all of which are in a process of continuous change. Individuals and their environment are inextricably meshed and involved within a transactional process which fundamentally prevents knowing either one unless they are viewed as a part of a whole system.

It may, perhaps, be that we have been so heavily preoccupied with the listings and the cataloguings of the categories and the components of intercultural communication experience that, in the process, we have forgotten about the experience itself. It may also be that the time has come when it becomes appropriate to ask an entirely different set of questions than have been asked thus far. Rather than focusing attention on what seems to be the surface structure of cultural features such as *attitudes, norms, values, role-perceptions,* and *language* it is useful to begin to center upon the deep structure of cultural experience characterized by the *reception, organization,* and *utilization* of information gained through contact with environment.

One approach to the study of the deep structure of cultural experience, suggested by Saral (1976) focuses upon the *reception, organization,* and *utilization* of information gained through contact with the environment. In this perspective, the process of intercultural communication is viewed as analogous to the process of communication among various states of human consciousness. Each state of consciousness is a unique psychological configuration which enables the individual to sense the external and internal environment, and to select, abstract, and process sensory input that is ''important'' or ''relevant'' by personal and cultural (consensus reality) standards. The perspective is based on the view that there is no absolute reality, nor universally valid (or invalid) way of perceiving or thinking, and that each state of consciousness and each culture has a unique logic, a unique set of rules that govern the manipulation of information, and unique assumptions about time and space. Intercultural communication, according to Saral, requires a person to learn to suspend the rules, logic, and the assumptions that usually govern his own state of consciousness.

Commenting upon the scope and method of cross-cultural research, Frijda and Jahoda (1966) observe that we can compare only when we have dimensional identity. That is, only when two behaviors fall on a single dimension, is it legitimate to relate one to the other for comparative purposes. Otherwise, one descends to the proverbial comparison of apples and oranges. The same would seem to hold true for communication among various cultures. Cultures vary along many dimensions. To bring about any meaningful communication among these varying cultures, it is necessary to identify the various dimensions involved and the varying location of various cultures on each of these dimensions. Intercultural communication is possible only to the extent that there are some common dimensions involved, albeit with varying locations. In situations where no such commonality exists, no communication will be possible until, and unless, one of the communicants is willing to suspend his or her mode of sensing, perceiving and/or attending to the reality.

INTERCULTURAL COMMUNICATION RESEARCH

How one defines and conceptualizes intercultural communication, has a great bearing on how he approaches research in the area. Many of the ambiguities of definition discussed previously are reflected, in kind, in intercultural communication research. On the one hand, one cannot but feel overwhelmed by a huge number of studies dealing with the variables that, in one fashion or another, affect the process of intercultural communication. On the other hand, one is struck by the lack of specific focus or direction in such studies.

Most of the studies described, discussed, and/or cited in intercultural communication literature refer to research carried out by anthropologists, linguists, psychologists, sociologists, and scholars from other disciplines interested in the study of culture, and its effect on human behavior, examined typically from the perspective of the particular discipline involved. There are no criteria clearly spelled out for distinguishing such studies from "intercultural communication research" if indeed there is such a distinction, or for including certain studies under the umbrella of intercultural communication and excluding others. It is probably this state of affairs that leads communication scholars like Ellingsworth (1976) to raise serious questions as to whether intercultural communication is—or ought to be—spoken of as a field, and whether there is any point in seeking or claiming any uniqueness of intercultural communication research. Others share a similar concern but prefer to follow Becker's (1969) advice to do the best they can, recognizing the breadth and complexity of intercultural communication and intercultural communication research.

Becker (1969), draws an important distinction between "research on the communication process *within* various cultures (the sort of work many linguists, cultural anthropologists, and diffusion scholars are doing) and research on communication process across various cultures." Porter and Samovar (1973) emphasize that our research must focus on intercultural rather than cross-cultural situations, and that we must investigate communication situations where interpersonal relations occur between members of different cultures. Ellingsworth (1976) would like to see included under intercultural communication research only such studies where "the design makes possible the statement that the variance in the outcome can be assigned to cultural differences between participants, *and to no other factor.*"

The bulk of the research in the field of intercultural communication concerns itself with what Becker terms the communication process within cultures. This is perhaps unavoidable, for some basic understanding of the processes of intracultural communication is a necessary prerequisite to developing, testing, and refining any exploratory hypotheses about various intercultural communication processes. The frustration that seems to be shared, and occasionally voiced, by students and scholars of intercultural communication alike is that not enough tangible progress has been made in the direction of isolating those numerous variables that affect the nature and process of communication interaction among members with varying cultural orientations.

Maruyama (1961) suggests that the principle of unidirectional causual relationships has been deeply internalized in the thinking of the natural, as well as human, scientists. It may be difficult, almost impossible, he argues for a researcher, entrenched in a *cause-effect paradigm,* to recognize the continually ongoing interplay among personal, cultural, and environmental contexts, which is a distinguishing feature of any intercultural communication interaction.

On somewhat similar lines, Daniel (1973) raises the issue of the compatability of research methodologies to the primary assumptions of the cultures involved. Elaborating upon this point, Daniels writes:

> One of the fundamental differences between the academic stream of thought and Black communication might entail one's understanding of cause and effect. By its emphasis on objectivity, quantification, empirical verification, etc., the academic stream of thought might lead one to believe that the world of causation is quite "visible," and therefore, is capable of empirical verification. However, one of the primary assumptions of the African world view is that the invisible world constitutes the world of causation and the visible world merely constitutes the world of effects. With this fundamental difference in primary assumptions, an intercultural, methodological question is raised. How does one develop research methodologies that are in keeping with the primary assumption that the invisible subjective world is the world of causation, and the objective, visible, empirical world is the world of effect?

Culture is not a static concept. It is dynamic, continually evolving, and changing. A person belonging to a particular culture does not lose his or her individual uniqueness and does not fully assume a fixed "cultural identity." Furthermore, each member of a culture is also subject to the continuous process of growth, evolution, and change experienced by different members at different speeds and in different directions. And, in addition to the highly intricate interaction among inumerable personal and cultural characteristics of the communicants any adequate research design must also take into account that continual and seemingly unpredictable change occurs at varying speeds among various cultures and their members.

These issues are conceptual in nature, methodological and pragmatic in implication. At this stage of the growth and development of the field of intercultural communication, research focus is primarily upon framing the appropriate questions in a fashion reflective of the complexity of the phenomena under investigation.

REFERENCES

BADAMI, M.K. *Outcomes of interpersonal communication under cooperative and competitive sets in an intercultural simulation game*. Doctoral Dissertation Proposal, Northwestern University, 1976.

BARUND, D.C. Nonverbal interaction: Introduction in Barlund, D.C. (Ed.) *Interpersonal communication: Survey and studies*. Boston: Houghton Mifflin, 1968.

BECKER, S.L. Directions for intercultural communication research. *Central States Speech Journal*, Vol. 20, Spring, 1969.

BERELSON, B., & STEINER, G.A. *Human behavior*. New York: Harcourt, Brace and World, 1964.

BROOKS, W.D. *Speech communication*. Dubuque, Iowa, Wm. C. Brown, 1974.

CARTIER, F.A. Personal communication, April 10, 1976.

CISSNA, K.N. Personal communication, 1976.

CHERRY, C. *On human communication*. Cambridge, Mass.: The M.I.T. Press, 1957.

COLE, M., GAY, J., & SHARP, D. *The cultural context of learning and thinking*. New York: Basic Books, 1971.

COLE, M., & SCRIBNER, S. *Culture and thought: A psychological introduction*. New York: Wiley, 1974.

DANIEL, J.L. Black communication research: A problem in intercultural communication. In David S. Hoopes (Ed.), *Readings in intercultural communication*, Vol. III, Pittsburgh, Pa.: Regional Council for International Education, 1973.

DEUTSCH, K.W. *Nationalism and social communication*. Cambridge, Mass.: The M.I.T. Press, 1966.

ELLINGSWORTH, H.W. Personal communication, August 31, 1976.

FRIJDA, N., & JAHODA, G. On the scope and methods of cross-cultural research. *International Journal of Psychology*, 1966, I, 102-27.

GERBNER, G. Content analysis and critical research in mass communication. *AV Communication Review*, 6, 3, 1958, 85-108.

HALL, E.T. How cultures collide. (As interviewed by Elizabeth Hall) *Psychology Today*, Vol. 10, No. 2, July, 1976.

JAIN, N.C., & SCHLOW, M. Definition and process observation of intercultural communication: International emphasis. In N.C. Jain, M.H. Prosser, and M.H. Miller (Eds.), *Intercultural Communication: Proceedings of the Speech Communication Association Summer Conference*. New York: Speech Communication Association, 1974.

JONES, S. Integrating emic and etic approaches in the study of intercultural communication, paper presented at the annual meeting of the International Communication Association. Portland, Oregon, April 1976.

KLUCKHOHN, C. *Mirror for man*. New York: McGraw Hill, 1949.

KRIPPENDORFF, K. Personal communication, May 12, 1976.

LEVINE, R.A. *Culture, behavior, and personality*. Chicago: Aldine, 1973.

MARUYAMA, M. The multilateral mutual casual relationships among the modes of communication, sociometric pattern and the intellectual orientation in the Danish culture. *Phylon*, 1961, 22, 41-5.

NEWMAN, J.B. A rationale for a definition of communication. *Journal of Communication*, 1960, 10: 115-124.

NIYEKAWA, A.M. *A study of second language learning*. Final Report to Department of Health, Education and Welfare, 1968.

RICH, A.L. *Interracial communication*. New York: Harper and Row, 1974.

PARRY, J. *The Psychology of human communication*. London: University of London Press, 1967.

PORTER, R.E. An overview of intercultural communication. In Samovar, L.A. and Porter, R.E. (Eds.), *Intercultural communication: A reader*. Belmont, Calif.: Wadsworth, 1972.

PORTER, R.E., & SAMOVAR, L.A. Intercultural communication research: Where do we go from here? In D.S. Hoopes (Ed.), *Readings in intercultural communication*, Vol. III, Pittsburgh, Pa.: Regional Council for International Education, 1973.

PROSSER, M.H. Communication, communications and intercommunication. In Prosser, M.H. (Ed.), *Intercommunication among nations and peoples*. New York: Harper and Row, 1973.

RUESCH, J., & BATESON, G. Structure and process in social relations. *Psychiatry*, 1949, 12: 105-124.

SAMOVAR, L.A., & PORTER, R.E. Intercultural communication: An introduction. In L.A. Samovar, and R.E. Porter, (Eds.), *Intercultural communication: a reader*. Belmont, Calif.: Wadsworth, 1972.

SARAL, T.B. Consciousness theory of intercultural communication. Paper presented at the annual meeting of the International Communication Association, Portland, Oregon, 1976.

SHANNON, C.E., & WEAVER, W. *The mathematical theory of communication*. Urbana, Illinois: University of Illinois Press, 1949.

SITARAM, K.S. Intercultural communication: the what and why of it. Paper presented at the annual meeting of the International Communication Association, Minneapolis, 1970.

SITARAM, K.S., & COGDELL, R.C. *Foundations of intercultural communication*. Columbus, Ohio: Charles E. Merril, 1976.

SMITH, A. Introduction: Communication and culture. In A.G. Smith, (Ed.), *Communication and culture*. New York: Holt, Rinehart and Winston, 1966.

SMITH, A.L. Interpersonal communication within transracial contexts. In L.L. Barker and R.J. Kibler (Eds.), *Speech communication behavior*. Englewood Cliffs, N.J.: Prentice-Hall, 1971.

STEVENS, S.S. Introduction: A definition of communication (In Proceedings of the Speech Communication Conference at M.I.T.), *Journal of the Acoustical Society of America*, 22:6, November, 1950.

STEWART, E.C. Definition and process observation of intercultural communication. In N.C. Jain, M.H. Prosser, and
M.H. Miller (Eds.), *Intercultural communication: Proceedings of Speech Communication Association Summer
Conference X*. New York: Speech Communication Association, 1974.

TRIANDIS, H.C. Theoretical framework. In H.C. Triandis and
Associates (Eds.), *The analysis of subjective culture*. New
York: John Wiley, 1972.

WHORF, B.L. *Language, thought and reality:* Selected writings of Benjamin Lee Whorf. J.B. Carroll (Ed.). New York:
Wiley, 1956.

LINGUISTIC RELATIVITY:
THE ROLE OF THE BILINGUAL[1]

GEORGE A. BARNETT
Rensselaer Polytechnic Institute

The role of linguistic relativity was examined through the use of multidimensional scaling (MDS). Direct pair comparisons of the similarity among a set of translated equivalent lexical items dealing with the mass media were made by subjects monolingual in English or French, or bilingual, using either of the languages. Using MDS as a measure of semantic structure, the following results are reported. The semantic structure of Anglophones and Francophones are significantly different, despite apparent similarities in terms of dimensionality and the general arrangement of the items. The semantic structure of bilinguals using French, and others using English, were significantly different from each other, and from both monolingual groups. While the results are not unequivocal, they suggest that the difference between the bilinguals' semantic structure and those of the monolinguals is less than the difference between the two monolingual groups. These results are interpreted to suggest that these patterns are not inherent in the specific languages, but rather result from the communication patterns of the individual.

One of the central concerns of intercultural research is how the relative differences between cultures affect the communication process among members of different societies. While a plethora of variables may be identified as affecting the fidelity of information exchange, communication scientists are usually interested in a narrower range of variables that deal with the actual perception of linguistic or nonverbal messages which cross cultural boundaries. Indeed, the *Journal of Cross-Cultural Psychology* is filled with examples of psychological differences between members of different cultures. Although a good number of the reported findings have implications for intercultural communication by limiting the parameters of the cultures, thus defining the "cultural experience," they do not deal directly with the transfer of information among cultures. This paper will deal with an intercultural communication phenomenon: the notion of linguistic relativity. It will also examine the role of the bilingual individual, the linking agent between two cultures, in this process. The paper will center around these general questions: (1) *How do members of different cultures organize their semantic structures?* (2) *How does the semantic system of individuals, bilingual in two different languages,*

compare? It is hoped that the research reported here will better describe the semantic aspects of linguistic relativity and add to our general understanding of the intercultural communication process.

On the basis of his investigation of Native American languages (Eskimo, Aztec, Navaho, & Hopi) Whorf (1956) concluded that speakers of these languages organize their experiences differently than speakers of English. This has become known as the notion of *linguistic relativity.* It has been discussed in depth by Chapman and Kowieski (1975). Because of cultural differences, a word in one language may have a different set of associations than its translated equivalent (Barnett, 1976). A lexical item in one language may cover a different domain than its translated counterpart, and therefore both symbols will have a different set of relationships with the other words in both languages. Thus, the semantic structures will be different.

Rosenzweig (1957) compared the associational responses of groups of American and French students. He noted that the French group gave more diversified responses than the American group, and that the two groups had equivalent responses in only half of the cases. In a later study, Rosenzweig (1959) used free association tests to compare word associations between English and French speaking populations. He found the degree of overlap (the relative frequency of associative equivalence of French and English words with a given stimulus term) to be high. He concluded that "associative habits tend to be held in common among different language communities" (1959, p. 347). These results were substantiated in a later study (Rosenzweig, 1961) with French, Italian, German, and American subjects.

Similar conclusions are reported by Osgood (1974), based on data from 27 countires with the semantic differential. He reports that three dimensions—*evaluative*, *activity* and *potency*—can be found in varying degrees in the affective semantic spaces of all languages. The loadings on these dimensions were in the .8 to .9 range on the *evaluative dimension*, .4 to .7 for the *potency factor*, and .3 to .7 for the *activity dimension*. From these results, Osgood concluded, "This is rather convincing evidence for the universality of the affective meaning system" (1974, pp. 33-34).

Thus, while the individual responses may vary by degree between different cultures, the process by which language is organized is identical despite cultural differences. This is not surprising for we are all people, and we all have the same physiological makeup. As a result, the process of communication is not likely to work in a totally discrepant manner, despite cultural variation. Additionally, in this discussion the medium of communication has been limited to language, which invariably requires the same sensory-motor mechanisms to operate in order for the exchange of ideas to be completed. What may be considered unique to each language is the cultural context in which associations between the label and referent are formed, although similarity may be taken to be the primary principle of organization of semantic information in all societies. Thus, while the linguistic process by which information is communicated, and meaning attributed, to objects and relations can be considered identical across language boundaries, culture produces individual variations in the semantic structure of a language to render it significantly different from any other.

This discussion suggests the following theoretical hypotheses:

H$_1$: The semantic structure generated by symbols from one language will be significantly different from the structure generated from its translated equivalents, for monolingual subjects.

H$_2$: The semantic structure generated by symbols from one language will be described by the same number of underlying dimensions as the semantic structure generated by its translated equivalents.

There is some support for these two hypotheses. Barnett and Wigand (1975), using multidimensional scaling (MDS), found little difference between two English-language societies (United States and South Africa), and greater discrepancy between the English and Spanish (Mexico) speaking cultures. However, in all cases, four dimensions provided the best description of the data.

The bilingual individual has the ability to receive information from two different language groups. This suggests that he or she forms associations in a manner that takes into account both languages, resulting in a semantic structure significantly different from both, but not nearly as different as the two are from each other. Lambert and Moore (1966), using free association, found that bilinguals living in the same environment have intermediate degrees of response similarity, between French and English monolinguals.

> In communication, the two monolingual groups could easily miss the full significance of one another's messages because such associational discordances color the meaning and shunt the line of associations off on quite different routes. In this example, the bilinguals would likely transmit the discrepancy with fidelity from one monolingual group to another, switching from one associational network to another as they change languages. (Lambert & Moore, 1966, p. 319)

The notion that the bilinguals' semantic structure will be significantly different from both the groups from which they obtain their language is perhaps a linguistic manifestation of Durkheim's (1951) notion of *anomie*. Bilinguals may in fact be incapable of internalizing the semantic rules of either language, owing to their use of both.

It should be pointed out that bilinguals can communicate successfully in either of their two languages. This suggests that they have the ability to switch codes, or at least to use one language's semantic rules when speaking that language. Thus, the bilingual's semantic structure while using one language would be more similar to that language's monolinguals than to people who use the other language.

Based upon the above discussion, the following hypotheses seem justified.

H₃: The semantic structure generated by symbols from one of a bilingual's languages will be significantly different from the semantic structure generated by symbols from the other language.

H₄: The degree of discrepancy between the semantic structure produced by a group of bilinguals (in either of their two languages) and a group of monolinguals in one of the bilingual's languages will be less than the discrepancy between the two monolingual groups.

H₅: The degree of discrepancy between semantic structures of equivalent terms will be ordered in the following manner: monolingual language A, bilingual in A, bilingual in B, and monolingual in B.

METHODS

The semantic structure of an individual may be measured through the use of metric multidimensional scaling (Barnett, 1976). An in-depth discussion of the theoretical significance for the measurement of meaning, and the advantages of this method, are presented by Barnett (1976). The method takes a matrix of dissimilarities (or distances) and converts the data to a series of loadings on a limited number of dimensions. Mathematically, the process is analogous to converting a matrix of city-to-city mileages to a graphic representation such as a map. In that special case an $N \times N$ matrix of cities (N = the number of cities) would be reduced to a two-dimensional configuration with little loss of information.

Barnett (1972) and Danes and Woelfel (1975) report reliability coefficients for the method of between .85 and .90 with as few as 50 cases, and discuss ways of increasing the overtime reliability. The predictive validity of time-series metric multidimensional scales has been demonstrated by Mar-

lier (1974) in a test of *social judgment theory*, and by Barnett, Serota, and Taylor (1976), who demonstrated that the outcome of a political campaign could be accurately predicted with this method.

Non-metric multidimensional scaling has been used extensively to study human information processing (Schroder, Driver, & Streufert, 1967; Rips, Shoben & Smith, 1973; Rumelhart & Abrahamson, 1973) and to measure semantic structure (Miller, 1969; Henley, 1969; Szalzy & Bryson, 1974).

Multidimensional scaling has been used successfully with subjects from non-English speaking cultures. The languages in which the research has been conducted were: Japanese (Kuno & Suga, 1966), Dutch (Van Der Kamp & Pols, 1971), Swedish (Ekman, 1955; Hanson, 1963), Finnish (Nordenstreng, 1968) and Spanish (D'Andrade, et al., 1972; Barnett & Wigand, 1975). Heider and Olivier (1972) used the scaling technique for cross-cultural comparisons to test the *Whorfian hypothesis* concerning the relation between cognitive and linguistic structure. Subjects from the United States and the Dani culture of New Guinea were asked to perform two tasks. One involved scaling color names, and the other Munsell color chips. Multidimensional scales on the four data sets yielded structures that were more similar under the cognitive conditions than the naming condition. In neither culture were distinct colors confused in memory more than across name boundaries. Thus, retention of color images appears to be unaffected by cultural differences in the semantic reference of color words.

Hypothesis Operationalized

Theoretical hypothesis one may be operationalized as follows:

H₁: A space generated by symbols from one language will be significantly different from a space generated from its translated equivalents, for monolingual subjects.

It can be tested in the following manner: Generate spaces in two different languages from a series of translated equivalents. Next, through a series of translations and rotations, place the two spaces to a least-square best fit.² Then, through the use of *t-tests*, using concepts as the unit of analysis, see if the differences between the spaces differ significantly from zero. The null hypothesis would be that the two spaces are not significantly different.[3]

H$_2$: The space generated by symbols from one language will be described by the same number of underlying dimensions as a space generated by its translated equivalents.

Hypothesis two can be tested through the use of the *scree test* (Tatsuoka, 1971). It operates as follows: Plot the absolute values of the eigenroots for each dimension of each space.[4] Then connect these values. The number of underlying dimensions is determined where there is a drastic change in the slope of the line, an "elbow" in the graph. This quantity is the number of dimensions which lie off the line connecting the smallest root to this point (Tatsuoka, 1971).

Theoretical hypothesis three then becomes:

H$_3$: The space generated by symbols from one of a bilingual's languages will be significantly different from the space generated by symbols from the other language.

Hypothesis three can be tested in the same manner as hypothesis one.

Theoretical hypothesis four becomes:

H$_4$: The degree of discrepancy between a space produced by a group of bilinguals (in either of their two languages) and a group of monolinguals in one of the bilingual's languages will be less than the discrepancy between the two monolingual groups.

H$_4$ can be tested as follows: Rotate all three spaces to a least-squared best fit, with the bilingual space placed between the monolingual spaces. Then perform a *t-test* to see if the degree of discrepancy between the bilingual space and one of the monolingual spaces is significantly less than the discrepancy between the two monolingual spaces. Again, the unit of analysis is *concepts,* rather than *subjects.*

H$_5$: The order of discrepancy between spaces of equivalent terms will increase in the following manner: monolingual language A, bilingual in language A, bilingual in B, and monolingual in language B.

H$_5$ can be tested through the use of *trend analysis*. The hypothesis, as stated, only indicates a monotonic relationship between the discrepancies and their rank orders. As such, a linear function may provide the best estimate of the relation. Thus, *linear trend analysis* will be the method of choice. It is discussed in depth by Hays (1973, pp. 691-694). Linear trend analysis operates in the same manner as any comparison among means. However, since analysis of variance in the linear case agrees exactly with linear regression, the latter method may be used. The significance test will be performed on the correlation between the predicted rank order and the discrepancy scores among the spaces.

Instrumentation

The instrument used to test the above hypotheses was composed of 45 direct-pair comparisons based on ten different concepts, using the criterion standard of red and white as 100 units or "galileos" apart. The questions were asked in the following form: "If Red and White are 100 galileos apart, how far apart are Books and Magazines?" This process was repeated for all 45 pairs. In this way a 10-by-10 *dissimilarity matrix* was generated. These were then converted into a multidimensional space to examine the perception of the words. The concepts were:

1. Books (Des Livres)
2. Magazines (Des Revues)
3. Newspapers (Des Journaux)
4. Music (La Musique)
5. Radio (La Radio)
6. Television (La Télévision)
7. Sports (Le Sport)
8. Movies (Le Cinéma)
9. Information (L'information)
10. Entertainment (Le Divertissement)

These concepts were chosen for a number of reasons. First, since this study was part of a larger one which attempted to relate media exposure to semantic structure, among the logical domain of concepts which would be affected by the variable

FIGURE 1
Media Function and Content Classification

| | Domain 1
Media Names | | Domain 2
Media Functions and Content | |
	Male	Female	Male	Female
Hi $\geq 100/10^6$	Newspapers Books			Music
Med 50-100/10^6	Movies Magazines	Television	Information	
Low $\leq 50/10^6$		Radio	Sports	Entertainment

use of the mass media would be the perception of that institution itself. Thus, six different media were chosen, two functions of the media—*entertainment* and *information*—and two terms which dealt with the content of the media, *sports* and *music*. Terms which dealt with the perception of the media were used by Barnett and Wigand (1975), with success in three different countries. Additional data concerned with the perception of the media are being gathered in five additional countries, including Micronesia, Israel, Great Britain, Australia, and Nigeria. This has been planned so that Canadian data will be comparable to this multinational study.

The second reason for the choice of these terms dealt with the gender of the concepts in French and their frequency of use in English. Additionally, it was felt that frequency of use may affect a symbol's degree of association with related terms. The specific concepts were generated in the following manner: Using Thorndike and Lorge (1944), and Carroll, Davies, and Richman (1971), a pool of potential terms was divided into *high* frequency of use (more than 100 times per million), moderate use (50-100 times per million), and *low* frequency of use (less than 50 times per million). Next, the gender of each word in French was determined in order to control for the potential acoustic relatedness of the items. The cells of the matrix presented in Figure 1 were filled such that concepts from both domains (media names and media functions or content) were present, and at least one male or female

term at each level of use. The concepts were then placed in random order in the form presented on the questionnaire so as to minimize the effects of order on the scale values. Finally, the concepts were translated into French following the back-translation procedure.[5]

The setting. The setting for the test of the above hypotheses was Canada's capital, Ottawa, and its sister city, Hull. This metropolis rests on the border between Quebec, with its Francophone culture, and the English-language culture of Ontario. Here both cultures meet and their languages mix. According to the Royal Commission of Bilingualism and Biculturalism (1969, p. 35), 30.8 percent consider English to be their mother tongue, and 37.7 percent French; 55.8 percent are Anglophones and 13.2 percent are Francophones, while the remaining 30.8 percent are bilingual (RCBB, 1969, p. 35). Of the bilinguals, fewer than 15 percent of the English ethnics speak both languages, while almost 85 percent of the French are bilingual. Thus, French and English will be the languages used to test the hypotheses.

Mass Media. The mass media also reflect this unequal distribution. There is more English language content available than French. Certain content may be available only in English. This is probably the case with television. Programs from the United States are only available in English. The same is true of movies, because of the importance of Hollywood productions. At the time of the study, there were 14 television stations broadcasting on cable in Ottawa. Three were in French, 11 in English. Of these 11, four emanated from the United States, and seven from Canada. There are a total of 21 movie theatres in Ottawa-Hull, 18 featuring English-language pictures and three French. Radio was balanced. There are 12 stations which can be received, 6 AM and 6 FM. On the AM band, there are two French and four English stations, and on the FM frequencies, four French and two English. Three daily newspapers are published in Ottawa: the *Ottawa Journal* and *The Citizen* in English, and *Le Droit* in French. In addition, newspapers from both Toronto and Montreal are available.[6] Thus, although there is an unequal distribution of the media in each language, both French and English material are readily available.

Design

The design for the study included four groups.

1. English monolinguals
2. French monolinguals
3. Bilinguals with an English instrument
4. Bilinguals with a French instrument

The bilinguals (groups three and four) emerged out of the presentation of the questionnaire in either language to large groups of subjects. This was made possible because of the large numbers of bilinguals and their high degree of integration in the Ottawa area. The English-language instrument was administered to a large group of English-speaking subjects, some of whom are monolingual and others bilingual. Likewise, the French-language instrument was given to a sample of French speakers, some of whom were Francophones and others bilingual. On the top of a page of the questionnaire was a set of instructions which read: "If you speak both French and English, please complete this page. If not, go on to the next page. Thank you." In this way bilinguals were sorted out from the Anglophones and Francophones. While this may seem a poor method to separate bilinguals from monolinguals, it should be noted that in Canada, generally, and specifically in Ottawa, there are strong social norms

connected with bilingualism. Thus, it is not likely that subjects would take lightly a series of questions concerning their use of the second language.

An additional design manipulation check was performed. The author examined all the bilinguals' completed questionnaires and then noted if the respondent made *any* use of the second language. If the reporting of mass media usage and interpersonal communication was *all* in a single language, then that potential bilingual was reclassified as a monolingual. This was a very minimal criterion for a bilingual, because most monolinguals make at least some use of the second language.

Administration and subjects. On February 10, 11, and 12, 1975, questionnaires were administered to a series of large university classes in Ottawa. The administration took 30 minutes. The institutions were Carleton University, where the language of instruction is English, and the University of Ottawa and St. Paul's University, where French was used in the classrooms in which data were gathered.[7] The present author administered the questionnaires at Carleton, and a bilingual professor performed this function at Ottawa and St. Paul's after being briefed.[8] Because the subjects for this study were all students at Canadian universities in Ottawa, there are obvious limits to generalizability.

The total sample consisted of 324 subjects, 232 students at Carleton, and 92 at Ottawa and St. Paul's. Of the 232 students at Carleton who participated in the study, 150 (64 percent) were monolingual in English and 82 (36 percent) were bilingual. Of the 92 students at Ottawa and St. Paul's who served as subjects, 15 (16 percent) were Francophones, and 77 (84 percent) were bilinguals. This is in line with what Lieberson (1970) describes as the language usage patterns for Ottawa. More of the English-background subjects are bilingual than one might expect from the general population. This is probably due to the fact that the subjects are college students, who typically are required to learn French as a second language.

The overall sample was disproportionately male (57.7 percent male to 42.3 percent female), and almost entirely white, (95.3 percent). The average subject had completed 14.27 years of school. On these variables, the Anglophones, Francophones,

TABLE 1
Spatial Coordinates for Monolingual English

	1	2	3	4	5	6	7	8	9	10
1. Books	−78.65	3.15	−30.65	−10.62	−10.37	.01	−9.42	3.39	−17.91	−37.49
2. Magazines	−32.88	−23.24	.83	−23.74	26.17	−.08	1.17	−16.57	−4.45	1.47
3. Newspapers	−15.65	−66.82	2.89	−11.41	−2.77	−.22	13.91	22.42	−.42	9.21
4. Music	−10.32	84.65	23.71	−6.95	4.86	.27	5.66	10.26	29.36	−23.30
5. Radio	2.41	10.83	53.55	−5.63	−12.65	.01	.34	−9.87	−36.60	10.87
6. Television	39.57	.26	2.88	37.46	14.69	.00	−9.78	15.44	−23.34	−1.45
7. Sports	111.01	−28.36	−9.67	−13.58	−5.80	−.09	−.85	−7.99	11.48	−35.71
8. Movies	4.86	36.31	−40.02	26.26	−3.57	.12	14.63	−11.72	−12.49	14.84
9. Information	−42.07	−40.91	15.61	33.46	−6.13	−.13	−5.06	−10.28	41.39	6.41
10. Entertainment	21.68	24.18	−19.12	−25.26	−4.43	.08	−10.59	4.85	13.00	55.17

Eigenvalues (roots) of eigenvector matrix--

	23776.95	16680.98	6691.95	4921.40	1302.97	.17	−764.03	−1559.18	−5257.75	−6735.97

Percentage of distance accounted for by individual vector--

	44.55	31.25	12.54	9.22	2.44	.00	−1.43	−2.92	−9.85	−12.62

Cumulative percentages of real distance accounted for--

	44.55	75.80	88.34	97.56	100.00	100.00	98.57	95.65	85.80	73.18

Cumulative percentages of total (real and imaginary) distance accounted for--

	60.88	103.59	120.72	133.32	136.66	136.66	134.70	130.71	117.25	100.00

Trace 39057.50

and bilinguals did not differ significantly. Comparing the three groups, the French-language subjects tended to be younger than the other groups. Also, they differed significantly by religion and socioeconomic status. While the total sample had a mean age of 20.8 years, the English average was 21.6, the bilinguals, 20.2, and the French 19.8 years. This difference is significant at the .05 level. However, it is not clear what effect, if any, this difference should have on the results of this study. As expected, the Francophones were all Catholic, while the bilinguals were 59.2 percent Catholic, 17.2 percent Protestant, 5.1 percent Jewish, and 17.2 percent atheists or other. The Anglophones were 25.3 percent Catholic, 47.3 percent Protestant, 2.0 percent Jewish, and 25.3 percent atheists or other. The fathers of the English-language sample had significantly more years of education ($p \leq$ .05) than the bilinguals and the Francophones. The Anglophones' fathers had significantly higher oc-

cupational status ($p \leq$ .05) and income ($p \leq$ .05) than the French group, but did not differ from the bilinguals on these variables. However, the bilinguals had significantly higher social status than the Francophones on these two variables ($p \leq$ .05 on both). Following Lieberson (1970), these relationships were expected.

RESULTS

Hypothesis One

H_1: A space generated by symbols from one language (English) will be significantly different from a space generated from its translated equivalents (in French) for monolingual subjects.

During the February data collection, 150 Anglophones at Carleton and 15 Francophones at Ottawa and St. Paul's completed the questionnaires

TABLE 2
Spatial Coordinates for Monolingual French

	1	2	3	4	5	6	7	8	9	10
1. Des Livres	3.09	59.65	3.88	-7.97	-19.61	-1.71	.01	-2.77	-8.49	-15.49
2. Des Revues	11.53	27.01	6.75	-12.69	19.99	-9.65	.02	12.16	6.00	-7.56
3. Des Journaux	46.65	12.21	6.51	-6.53	1.69	16.04	.01	3.06	9.23	15.13
4. La Musique	-45.95	1.63	-34.03	-12.26	10.37	7.41	-.07	-1.15	-19.54	1.25
5. La Radio	11.73	-27.77	-40.75	-11.35	-5.69	-3.35	-.09	-6.14	22.15	-13.32
6. La Télévision	1.35	-27.83	-5.51	31.32	-8.38	1.52	-.01	16.85	-6.44	-12.30
7. Le Sport	-5.94	-44.90	44.39	-19.37	.45	1.63	.10	-5.44	-6.04	-17.70
8. Le Cinéma	-33.24	19.86	14.51	34.36	8.53	1.87	.03	-11.11	14.16	-3.26
9. L'Information	49.16	-11.38	-6.42	13.73	3.54	-8.10	-.01	-10.16	-18.41	17.02
10. Le Divertisse-ment	-38.39	-8.49	10.68	-9.25	-10.88	-5.65	.02	4.69	7.37	36.23

Eigenvalues (roots of eigenvector matrix--

	9600.42	8596.51	5288.84	3357.30	1201.19	525.69	.03	-765.70	-1737.59	-2782.56

Percentage of distance accounted for by individual vector-

	33.60	30.09	18.51	11.75	4.20	1.84	.00	-2.68	-6.08	-9.74

Cumulative percentages of real distance accounted for--

	33.60	63.69	82.20	93.96	98.16	100.00	100.00	97.32	91.24	81.50

Cumulative percentages of total (real and imaginary) distance accounted for--

	41.23	78.15	100.87	115.29	120.44	122.70	122.70	119.41	111.95	100.00

Trace   23284.12

in their respective languages. The results are presented as the *spatial coordinate matrices* (Tables 1 and 2). These sets of data were first aggregated, in that each cell represented the mean distance estimate between any pair of concepts. A scree test on both sets of data determined that a two-dimensional solution, made up of the two largest positive roots, was appropriate for the English and French languages spaces. In the case of the English space, these two dimensions explained 71.24 percent of the variance. The first two dimensions accounted for 63.69 percent of the variance for the Francophones. The graphic representation of the English spatial manifold is presented in Figure 2 and and French space in Figure 3. The first dimension may be labeled *evaluative*—it separated print media from electronic media—and the second, *entertainment-information*.

The French space was then rotated to a least-square congruence upon the English space, using all ten factors. The distances between the two samples for each concept are given in Table 3. The mean difference was 35.59 units. Under the assumption that, if these two spaces were the same (the null hypothesis) the distances between the concepts would be zero, a *t-test* was performed to determine if these distances differed significantly from zero; t equalled 10.41. This is significant beyond the .001 level, (df = 18). Thus, the null hypothesis of no difference between the two spaces can be rejected.

Hypothesis Two

H_2: The space generated by symbols from one language (English) will be described by the same number of underlying dimensions as a space generated by its translated equivalents (French).

TABLE 3
Differences Between the French and English Monolinguals' Spaces After Least-Square Rotation on All 10 Dimensions

Concept	Differences in Spatial Position
Books	39.08 Units
Magazines	40.26 Units
Newspapers	37.43 Units
Music	41.67 Units
Radio	25.48 Units
Television	27.83 Units
Sports	59.28 Units
Movies	27.13 Units
Information	35.59 Units
Entertainment	22.12 Units
Mean Difference	35.59 Units

FIGURE 2
Graphic Representation of English Monolingual Space (N=1.50)

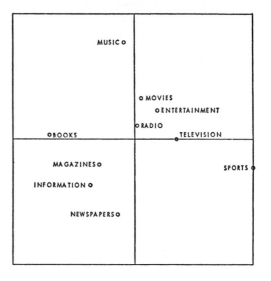

FIGURE 3
Graphic Representation of French Monolingual Space (N=15)

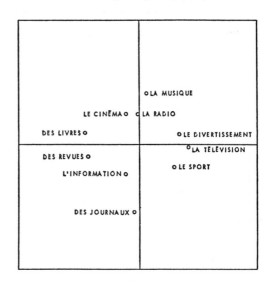

Based on the *scree tests* from the English-language sample, the French-speaking subjects, and both sets of bilinguals in either of their two languages, it was determined that there were two underlying dimensions. In all cases, the dimensions selected were the two largest positive dimensions. They may be labelled *evaluative (print media-electronic media)* and *entertainment-information.* For the English monolinguals, these two dimensions accounted for 71.24 percent of the variance in the space. For the French monolinguals, it accounted for 63.69 percent; for bilinguals in English, 75.80 percent; and for the bilinguals in French, 72.50 percent. Thus, this hypothesis seems to be supported by the data.

Although no significance test was applied to these values, confidence may be placed in them owing to the consistency of these scores. The range in the proportion of explained variance is only 12.11 percent, and the greatest deviation from the mean percentage (70.80) of variance explained by these two factors is only 7.97 percent. Additionally, both dimensions can be easily identified, and the same label can be applied equally well to the corresponding dimensions in each space. In summary, hypothesis 2 can be confirmed with a high degree of confidence.

TABLE 4
Spatial Coordinates for Bilinguals in English

	1	2	3	4	5	6	7	8	9	10
1. Books	-29.43	-70.94	-29.50	-2.68	-13.97	-.06	-4.56	23.13	6.66	-28.82
2. Magazines	-47.56	-32.73	16.40	-28.11	24.74	-.10	-2.69	-17.84	-10.33	-16.48
3. Newspapers	-74.93	18.94	14.03	10.19	-5.12	-.15	22.55	.64	17.69	13.70
4. Music	81.70	-25.26	28.15	-11.56	1.79	.17	1.61	-2.78	39.62	3.41
5. Radio	20.18	15.54	54.37	4.31	-19.03	.04	-.44	-2.82	-29.73	-22.36
6. Television	25.69	42.76	-2.19	21.93	22.82	.05	1.38	30.81	-6.91	-13.15
7. Sports	-11.06	87.32	-30.89	-20.54	-8.22	-.02	-10.14	-10.14	14.50	-15.61
8. Movies	45.03	-20.13	-45.42	25.32	.60	.09	10.23	-27.23	-13.77	-5.37
9. Information	-30.69	-12.08	11.02	33.80	.16	-.06	-20.76	-6.87	5.30	34.98
10. Entertainment	21.08	-3.42	-15.96	-32.65	-3.77	.04	2.84	13.11	-23.03	49.69

Eigenvalues (roots) of eigenvector matrix--

20020.10	17357.24	8483.35	4805.07	1801.89	-.09	-1187.78	-2882.07	-3924.08	-5939.70

Percentage of distance accounted for by individual vector--

38.16	33.08	16.17	9.16	3.43	-.00	-2.26	-5.49	-7.48	-11.32

Cumulative percentages of real distance accounted for--

38.16	71.24	87.41	96.57	100.00	100.00	97.74	92.24	84.76	73.44

Cumulative percentages of total (real and imaginary) distance accounted for--

51.95	97.00	119.01	131.48	136.16	136.16	133.08	125.60	115.41	100.00

Trace   38533.95

FIGURE 4
Graphic Representation of English Bilingual Space
(N=82)

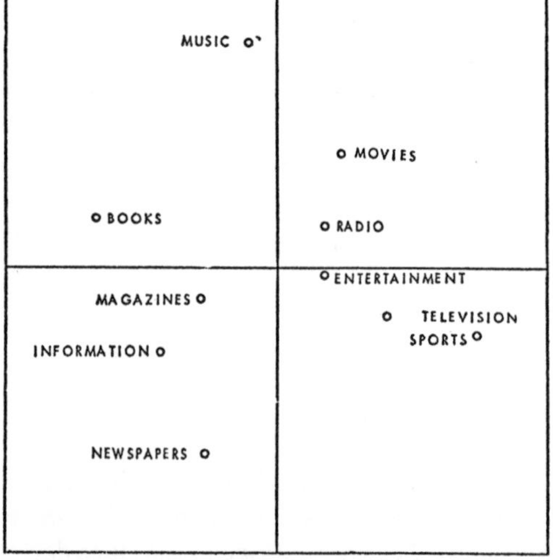

Hypothesis Three

H$_3$: The space generated by symbols from one of a bilingual's languages (English) will be significantly different from the space generated by symbols from the other language (French).

During the February data collection, 82 bilinguals completed the English-language version of the questionnaire at Carleton, and 77 bilinguals completed the French version at Ottawa and St. Paul's. The results of the aggregated sets of data are presented as the spatial coordinate matrices (Tables 4 and 5). A scree test on both sets of data determined that a two-dimensional solution made up of the two largest vectors was appropriate for both spaces. In the case of the English bilinguals, these two factors explained 75.80 percent of the variance. The first two dimensions accounted for 72.50 percent of the variance for the French bilinguals. The graphic representations of the English bilingual space is

TABLE 5
Spatial Coordinates for Bilinguals in French

	1	2	3	4	5	6	7	8	9	10
1. Books	86.46	−50.05	16.98	2.29	−6.28	.27	−6.22	−7.79	6.55	−34.41
2. Magazines	41.85	9.63	21.80	−22.08	28.50	.13	6.66	5.95	−15.72	−3.33
3. Des Journaux	48.23	42.05	−1.42	−3.43	−24.16	.15	10.99	2.32	12.42	10.39
4. La Musique	−57.00	−48.70	−18.91	−30.40	4.74	−.18	2.08	−.78	33.44	1.95
5. Radio	−22.58	16.82	−39.04	−27.86	−12.40	−.07	−5.21	3.51	−30.58	−19.35
6. La Télévision	−34.00	10.47	−25.53	30.50	8.84	−.11	6.30	−18.27	−7.64	−17.87
7. Sports	−56.27	62.19	43.52	7.54	.26	−.18	−5.58	4.50	14.32	−26.23
8. Le Cinéma	−21.37	−54.07	−2.55	35.35	−3.14	−.07	2.08	19.10	−8.30	1.51
9. L'Information	44.15	34.57	−35.22	13.37	11.69	.14	−8.85	1.85	12.84	38.16
10. Entertainment	−29.45	−22.90	40.39	−5.28	−8.05	−.09	−2.24	−10.39	−17.32	49.18

Eigenvalues (roots) of eigenvector matrix--

	1	2	3	4	5	6	7	8	9	10
	22908.24	15638.88	8070.85	4648.21	1900.96	.23	−393.89	−944.48	−3294.59	−6564.87

Percentage of distance accounted for by individual factor--

	1	2	3	4	5	6	7	8	9	10
	43.09	29.41	15.18	8.74	3.57	.00	−.74	−1.78	−6.20	−12.35

Cumulative percentages of real distance accounted for--

	1	2	3	4	5	6	7	8	9	10
	43.09	72.50	87.68	96.42	100.00	100.00	99.26	97.48	91.29	78.94

Cumulative percentages of total (real and imaginary) distance accounted for--

	1	2	3	4	5	6	7	8	9	10
	54.58	91.85	111.09	122.15	126.68	126.68	125.74	123.49	115.64	100.00

Trace   41968.53

presented in Figure 4, and the French bilingual in Figure 5. As in all the other cases, the first dimensions may be labelled *evaluative* (*print media-electronic media*) and the second, *entertainment-information.*

The French bilingual space was then rotated to a least-square best fit upon the English bilingual space. The mean discrepancy between the individual concepts was 21.84 units. The distance between the concepts is given in Table 6. A test was performed to see if these two spaces were significantly different: *t* equalled 7.96, which was significant beyond the .001 level (df = 18). Thus, the null hypothesis of no difference between the spaces can be rejected.

Hypothesis Four

H₄: The degree of discrepancy between a space produced by a group of bilinguals (in either French of English) and a group of monolinguals in one of the bilingual's languages will be less than the discrepancy between the two monolingual groups.

The test of hypothesis 4 was performed in the following manner. The bilingual spaces both in English and French (Tables 4 and 5) were rotated to a least-square best fit upon the Anglophone space (Table 1) and the Francophones' coordinate system (Table 2). These operations produced a mean discrepancy of 19.28 units between the monolinguals and the bilinguals in English, a mean difference of 21.92 between the English monolingual and the bilinguals' French space, a difference of 29.10 units between the bilinguals' French space and its monolingual counterpart, and a mean distance of 28.95 between the Francophones' spatial manifold and the bilinguals in English. The vectors of dis-

FIGURE 5
Graphic Representation of French Bilingual Space
(N=77)

o DES LIVRES

LE CINÉMA
o   o LA MUSIQUE

o LE DIVERTISSEMENT

DES REVUES o   o LA TÉLÉVISION
o
LA RADIO

DES JOURNAUX o
o
L'INFORMATION

o LE SPORT

crepancy are given in Tables 7 to 10. These degrees of discrepancy are all smaller than the 35.59 units between the two monolingual spaces. Thus, all the relations were in the predicted direction.

Next, a series of *t-tests* (differences of means) were performed to determine whether the differences between the bilingual spaces and ones produced by monolinguals were significantly less than the degree of discrepancy between the two monolingual spaces. The *t-test* found that the degree of difference between the English monolingual and its bilingual space was significant at the .025 level ($t = 2.48$, df $= 18$). The other differences were not significant. The English and the bilinguals in French difference was not significantly smaller than the discrepancy between the two monolingual spaces ($t = 1.62$). This is significant between the .10 and .05 levels. While it is in the predicted direction, it does not meet the probability level traditionally required to reject the null hypothesis.

FIGURE 6
Graphic Representation of Combined Spaces of All Groups. The English monolingual space is closest to the label, followed by the English bilingual, French bilingual, and finally, the French monolingual at the end of the connecting line

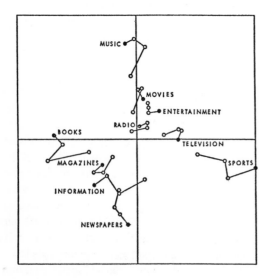

TABLE 6
Differences Between the Bilinguals' English and French Spaces After Least-Square Rotation on All 10 Dimensions

Concept	Differences in Spatial Position
Books	31.99 Units
Magazines	18.07 Units
Newspapers	22.97 Units
Music	17.95 Units
Radio	8.96 Units
Television	14.97 Units
Sports	35.23 Units
Movies	19.69 Units
Information	32.51 Units
Entertainment	16.10 Units
Mean Difference	21.84 Units

TABLE 7
Differences Between the English Monolingual and the Bilinguals' English Spaces After Least-Square Rotation on All 10 Dimensions

Concept	Differences in Spatial Position
Books	19.44 Units
Magazines	20.02 Units
Newspapers	22.72 Units
Music	12.53 Units
Radio	10.34 Units
Television	16.07 Units
Sports	29.22 Units
Movies	20.92 Units
Information	23.38 Units
Entertainment	18.15 Units
Mean Difference	19.28 Units

TABLE 8
Differences Between the English Monolingual and the Bilinguals' French Spaces After Least-Square Rotation on All 10 Dimensions

Concept	Differences in Spatial Position
Books	30.13 Units
Magazines	18.33 Units
Newspapers	23.05 Units
Music	25.57 Units
Radio	13.75 Units
Television	21.68 Units
Sports	15.99 Units
Movies	22.20 Units
Information	30.85 Units
Entertainment	17.66 Units
Mean Difference	21.92 Units

The differences between the French and bilingual in English, and French and French bilingual, were also not significant: $t = .87$ for the former groups and $t = .91$ for the later. These results are summarized in Table 11.

In summary, while all four comparisons are in the predicted direction, only one of the four is significant beyond the .05 level. One reached a probability level of .1, and the other two failed to reach even this degree of confidence. Thus, while the null hypothesis for hypothesis 4 cannot be rejected, there seems to be a certain level of support for the notion that the degree of discrepancy between the bilingual and one monolingual will be less than the difference between the two monolingual spaces.

Hypothesis Five

H$_5$: The degree of discrepancy between spaces of equivalent terms will increase in the following manner: monolingual language A (English),

bilingual in language A, bilingual in B (French) and monolingual in language B.

In order to test hypothesis 5, all spaces were rotated upon all the others' coordinate systems. A graphic representation of all four spaces together is presented in Figure 6 for explanatory purposes. The discrepancies between them produced the matrix of mean differences presented in Table 12. With the exception of the difference between the Francophones' space and the one produced by the French-bilinguals, the results are in the predicted order. The means were then entered into a linear trend analysis. That is, the means were correlated with their predicted rank order of discrepancy from the monolingual spaces. In other words, the English monolingual system was assigned a position of zero. The discrepancy from the English monolingual space was *one* for the English bilingual space, *two* for the French bilingual manifold, and *three* for the Francophones. Likewise, the discrepancy between the English bilingual space and the Francophone system was assigned a value of *two* and the

TABLE 9 Differences Between the French Monolingual and the Bilinguals' English Spaces After Least-Square Rotation on All 10 Dimensions	
Concept	Differences in Spatial Position
Books	34.15 Units
Magazines	20.96 Units
Newspapers	23.35 Units
Music	36.05 Units
Radio	16.81 Units
Television	23.57 Units
Sports	54.29 Units
Movies	17.20 Units
Information	39.06 Units
Entertainment	24.02 Units
Mean Difference	28.95 Units

TABLE 10 Differences Between the French Monolingual and the Bilinguals' French Spaces After Least-Square Rotation on All 10 Dimensions	
Concept	Differences in Spatial Position
des livres	46.71 Units
des revues	29.83 Units
des journaux	21.65 Units
la musique	35.35 Units
la radio	21.04 Units
la télévision	17.38 Units
le sport	35.55 Units
le cinéma	26.90 Units
l'information	32.52 Units
le divertissement	24.09 Units
Mean Difference	29.10 Units

French bilingual Francophone discrepancy a *one*. These values produced a correlation of .6548. A significance test was then performed on this ceofficient, which failed to reject the null hypothesis at the .05 level (F=6.00, df=1.5). Thus, although the means are in the predicted order, their placements are not significant, and therefore, the null hypothesis of hypothesis 6 cannot be rejected.

DISCUSSION

The results from the research reported above for hypothesis 1 and 3 suggest that there are significant differences between cultural groups with regard to the semantic component of language. While the arrangement of the semantic structures of these groups are statistically different, all groups, monolingual and bilingual, used the same number of dimensions to describe the symbols—hypothesis 2—and a similar arrangement of the words occurred in all spaces (see Figure five). This is in line with the results Osgood (1974) reported. The differences that do exist may be a function of cultural differ-

ences produced by the communication patterns of each group. Indeed, as J. Woelfel, J. Woelfel, Gillham, and McPhail (1974) and Barnett and McPhail (1975) report, the communication patterns of Francophones and Anglophones are significantly different with regard to the mass media and interpersonal relations. Clearly, the communication distribution among the groups are restricted by language, and perhaps social structural variables. Thus, shared past experiences of the members of the groups with references to the particular set of scaled concepts may be very limited, despite the fact that both groups live in approximately the same social environment.

The semantic structure of bilinguals may be considered to be moderate between the structures of the two monolingual groups from which their languages are taken. Hypothesis 4 was only partially supported. Although all the coefficients were in the predicted direction, only one of the four values was significant at the .05 level. While all the effects hypothesized were observed in this sample, in only one were the results strong enough to warrant generalization to a larger population with great confidence. Support for this conclusion may also be gained by an examination of Figure 6. This may be taken to indicate that the meaning system of bilinguals contains elements from both cultures. Bilinguals can share common experiences with either monolingual group, owing to their ability to communicate with both linguistic systems. However, rather than suggesting that the cause for this relation is inherent in the language, as the *Sapir-Whorf hypothesis* suggests, the author feels that the sociolinguistic notion of a *speech community* should be applied (Fishman, 1968). Thus, the language groups should be described as separate cul-

TABLE 11
t-tests Performed to Test Hypothesis 5

Group	t	Significance (p)
English Monolingual- Bilingual in English	2.48	$\leq$.025
English Monolingual- Bilingual in French	1.62	$\leq$.10
French Monolingual- Bilingual in English	.91	>.10
French Monolingual- Bilingual in French	.87	>.10

TABLE 12
Matrix of Discrepancies Between All Spaces

	English Monolingual	English Bilingual	French Bilingual	French Monolingual
English-Monolingual	0.0			
Bilingual-English	19.28	0.0		
Bilingual-French	21.92	21.84	0.0	
French-Monolingual	35.59	28.95	29.10	0.0
N	150	72	77	15

tural entities with a different language. This would make more sense when considering that the semantic system may be independent of a specific language. The individuals' semantic systems are contingent upon their past experiences. A common language makes shared experiences possible to a far greater degree. The meaning of linguistic symbols must be defined in terms of the language user's perception of the relationship between lexical items. The users of English are the Anglophones and the bilinguals. The bilinguals also use French, as do the Francophones. This would seem to imply that the semantic system of bilinguals should be described by some balance between the consensual

structure of each language. This seems to be the case, because the bilingual can integrate into either the French or the English speech community.

Finally, some limitations of this study should be pointed out. First, there were only fifteen francophone subjects. This may limit the confidence of the internal validity of the results, although with 45 pair comparisons, this is not likely. Second, the subjects were all college students. This may limit the external validity of the results. Given insufficient funding, they provide a better alternative than not researching the phenomenon at all. Third, only ten concepts dealing with a very limited topic, the mass media, were scaled. This may be too few to produce generalizable results which would lend support for an adequate description of the problem of linguistic relativity and the role the bilingual individual plays in the process of intercultural communication. Sociolinguists report that bilinguals often use one of their languages in one functional context and the other in some different setting. Fishman (1969) and Cooper (1969) report that Spanish-English bilinguals living in the United States used English in formal settings and Spanish in informal. Rubin (1968) reports similar results with Native American-Spanish bilinguals. Thus, future research should be carried out with symbols from a variety of contexts, both formal and informal.

A final possible criticism of the external validity might be the sample of languages used. Only two languages were involved in the study, French and English. Both are Indo-European languages, and they share many lexical items. In this sample of concepts, the translated equivalents of radio, television, sport, and information are identical, except for phonological variation. Perhaps a better sample of languages might have been to use a Native American or Sino-Tibetan language with English. However, despite these possible limitations, the author feels confident in concluding that, despite the similarities between Canadian English and French, the semantic structures of both monolinguals and bilinguals when using each separate language are significantly different, and that the differences between the bilinguals' semantic structure and those of the monolinguals is less than the differences between the two monolingual groups.

NOTES

1. The author would like to thank Thomas McPhail, Joseph Woelfel, Edward L. Fink, and Communication Research Services, Inc., East Lansing, Michigan, without whom this paper would not have been possible.
2. A computer program (Galileo) which accomplishes the calculations necessary to rotate two or more spaces to a least-square congruence is available at Communication Research Services, East Lansing, Michigan. For an in-depth discussion of the procedures, see Serota (1974). A number of rotational algorithms exist which provide variable quality of solution. At present, the least-squares best-fit seems to provide an optimum result compared with other rotations. Inherent in this procedure is the problem of overestimating some changes

while underestimating others. The author is currently involved in the testing of a new procedure in which a theoretically defined set of concepts is held constant (this subset is rotated to a least-squares best-fit) and the remaining concepts are positioned accordingly. It is identical to the heliocentric notion for calculating the motions of celestial bodies. For an in-depth discussion of this topic, see Woelfel et al. (1975). While the least-squares rotation is appropriate for the comparisons of static samples like these, the overtime analysis of changes requires the alternative procedures suggested by Woelfel et al. (1975).

3. The use of significance tests and inferential statistics of any sort runs against the spirit of the method. Metric MDS is a series of continuous ratio scaled distance estimates. It assumes the height of absurdity to reduce these estimates to a dichotomous decision of an acceptance or rejection of the null hypotheses. These data can and should be used as a description of the structure of the semantic space of individuals or groups. Thus, one could say they describe a certain relationship without attempting to infer beyond the sample of subjects or concepts. Additionally, these data are based on a large number of independent observations of the relationship between a particular pair of concepts. This notion is not taken into account by this significance test, where the unit of analysis is the number of concepts or spaces and thus the degrees of freedom are some small numbers rather than the number of independent observations.

   At the present time, there does not exist an adequate significance test for the differences between multidimensional spaces or, for that matter, factor structures. Although there have been a number of notable attempts (among them Lawley and Maxwell, 1963), these have been inadequate. The Lawley and Maxwell solution takes the natural log of the determinant of one matrix (factor structure) and subtracts it from the log of the other. The resultant value may be then tested for significance by the use of the chi square distribution. This solution is inappropriate, because the structure of the MDS produces a singular matrix. It is of rank N-1. It has one column of zeros, making the determinant zero by definition and the test inapplicable. The test presented in the text will serve in this dissertation, but the author's reservations concerning the use of any test of statistical inference should be noted.

4. The reason why the absolute values of the eigenroots are used is because metric scaling inherently results in a nonpositive semi-definite matrix. The multidimensional space is non-Euclidean. When this matrix is orthogonally decomposed, negative roots result. These imaginary roots are reliable, and meaning can be attributed to them (Danes & Woelfel, 1975). As a result, their absolute value, rather than signed-value, should be used in the scree test.

5. The author would like to thank Timothy Mabee and Elizabeth Ekdahl for their help in the translation of the instrument into French.

6. Data on the availability of the media were gathered by the author in a number of ways: through newspaper advertisements and listings, the listings in the Ottawa-Hull telephone book, and direct participation with the media.

7. The author would like to thank Dr. Thomas McPhail, School of Journalism, Carleton University, Ottawa, Canada, for making all the necessary arrangements at Carleton, the University of Ottawa, and St. Paul's University. Without Dr. McPhail this research would only be a dream. The author also would like to thank Dr. Roger Byrd and Dr. Peter Johansen,

Carleton University; Dr. Ross Hastings, University of Ottawa; and Dr. Andrew Ruszkowski, St. Paul's University for the use of their classes.
8. Dr. Hastings administered the questionnaire at the University of Ottawa, as did Dr. Ruszkowski at St. Paul's University.

REFERENCES

BARNETT, G. Reliability and metric multidimensional scaling. Unpublished research report, Department of Communication, Michigan State University, 1972.

BARNETT, G. Bilingual information processing: The effects of communication on semantic structure. Unpublished doctoral dissertation, Department of Communication, Michigan State University, 1976.

BARNETT, G., & McPHAIL, T. A comparison of mass media usage patterns in monolinguals and bilinguals. Paper presented at the annual meeting of the Association for Education in Journalism, Ottawa, Canada, August 1975.

BARNETT, G., SEROTA, K., & TAYLOR, J. Political attitude change: A multidimensional analysis. *Human Communication Research*, 1976, 2, 227-244.

BARNETT, G., & WIGAND, R. Measuring the national development process: An improved method through multidimensional scaling. Paper presented at the annual meeting of the International Communication Association, Chicago, April 1975.

CARROLL, J., DAVIES, P., & RICHMAN, B. *The word frequency book*. New York: American Heritage, 1971.

CHAPMAN, G., & KOWIESKI, R. Toward an empirical validation of the theory of linguistic relativity through an analysis of clustering in free recall. Paper presented at the annual meeting of the International Communication Association, Chicago, April 1975.

COOPER, R. Contextualized measures of degree of bilingualism. *Modern Language Journal*, 1969, 53, 172-178.

D'ANDRADE, R., QUINN, N., NERLOVE, S., & ROMNEY, A. Disease categories in American-English and Mexican-Spanish. In R. Shepard, A. Romney, and S. Nerlove, (Eds.), *Multidimensional scaling: Theory and applications in the behavioral sciences, Vol. 11*. New York: Seminar, 1972.

DANES, J., & WOELFEL, J. An alternative to the "traditional" scaling paradigm in mass communication research: Multidimensional reduction of ratio judgements of separation. Paper presented at the annual meeting of the International Communication Association, Chicago, April 1975.

DURKHEIM, E. *Suicide: A study in sociology*. G. Simpson (trans.), Glencoe, Illinois: Free Press, 1951.

EKMAN, G. Dimensions of emotions. *Acta Psychologica*, 1955, 11, 279-288.

FISHMAN, J. Sociolinguistic perspective on the study of bilingualism. *Linguistics*, 1968, 39, 21-49.

FISHMAN, J. The measurement and description of widespread and relatively stable bilingualism. *Modern Language Journal*, 1969, 53, 152-156.

HANSON, G. A factorial investigation of speech sounds perception. *Scandinavian Journal of Psychology*, 1963, 4, 123-128.

HAYS, W. *Statistics for the social sciences*. New York: Holt, Rinehart and Winston, 1973.

HEIDER, E., & OLIVIER, D. The structure of the color space in naming and meaning for two languages. *Cognitive Psychology*, 1972, 3, 337-354.

HENLEY, N. Psychological study of the semantics of animal terms. *Journal of Verbal Learning and Verbal Behavior*, 1969, 8, 176-184.

KUNO, U., & SUGA, Y. Multidimensional scaling mapping of piano pieces. *Japanese Psychological Research*, 1966, 8, 119-124.

LAMBERT, W., & MOORE, N. Word association responses: A comparison of American and French monolinguals and bilinguals. *Journal of Personality and Social Psychology*, 1966, 3, 313-320.

LAWLEY, D., & MAXWELL, A. *Factor analysis as a statistical method*. London: Butterworth, 1963.

LIEBERSON, S. *Language and ethnic relations in Canada*, New York: Wiley, 1970.

MARLIER, J. Procedures for a precise test of social judgement predictions of assimilation and contrast. Paper presented at the annual meeting of the Speech Communication Association, Chicago, December 1975.

MILLER, G. A psychological method to investigate verbal concepts. *Journal of Mathematical Psychology*, 1969, 6, 169-191.

NORDENSTRENG, K. Comparison between the semantic differential and similarity analysis in the measurement of musical experience. *Scandinavian Journal of Psychology*, 1968, 9, 89-96.

OSGOOD, C. Probing subjective culture—Part 1: Cross-linguistic tool making. *Journal of Communication*, 1974, 24, 21-35.

RIPS, L., SHOBEN, E., & SMITH, E. Semantic distance and the verification of semantic relations. *Journal of Verbal Learning and Verbal Behavior*, 1973, 12, 1-20.

ROSENZWEIG, M. Etudes sur l'association des mots. *L'Annee Psychologique*, 1957, 57, 23-32.

ROSENZWEIG, M. Comparisons between French and English word association norms. *American Psychologist*, 1959, 14, 363.

ROSENSWEIG, M. Comparison among word association responses on English, French, German and Italian. *American Journal of Psychology*, 1961, 74, 347-360.

Royal Commission on Bilingualism and Biculturalism Report. Ottawa: Queen's Printer, 1969.

RUBIN, J. Bilingual usage in Paraguay. In J. Fishman, (Ed.), *Readings in the sociology of language*. The Hague: Mouton, 1968.

RUMELHART, D., & ABRAHAMSON, A. A model of analogical reasoning. *Cognitive Psychology*, 1973, 5, 1-28.

SCHRODER, H., DRIVER, M., & STREUFERT, S. *Human information processing*. New York: Holt, Rinehart and Winston, 1967.

SEROTA, K. Metric multidimensional scaling and communication: Theory and implementation. Unpublished masters thesis. East Lansing, Michigan State University, 1974.

SZALAY, L., & BRYSON, J. Psychological meaning: Comparative analyses and theoretical implications. *Journal of Personality and Social Psychology*, 1974, 30, 860-870.

TANAKA, Y., OYAMA, T., & OSGOOD, C. A cross-cultural and cross-concept study of the generality of semantic spaces. *Journal of Verbal Learning and Verbal Behavior*, 1963, 2, 392-405.

TATSUOKA, M. *Multivariate analysis techniques for education and psychological research*. New York: Wiley, 1971.

THORNDIKE, E., & LORGE, I. *The teacher's word book of 30,000 Words*. New York: Columbia University, 1944.

VAN DER KAMP, L., & POLS, L. Perceptual analysis from confusion between vowels. *Acta Psychologica*, 1971, 35, 64-77.

WHORF, B. *Language, thought and reality: Selected writings of Benjamin Lee Whorf*. J. Carroll, (Ed.). New York: Wiley, 1956.

WOELFEL, J., SALTIEL, J., McPHEE, R., DANES, J., CODY, M., BARNETT, G., & SEROTA, K. Orthogonal Rotation to a theoretical criterion: A comparison of multidimensional spaces. Paper presented at the annual meeting of the American Psychological Association, Mathematical Division, West Lafayette, Indiana, August 1975.

WOELFEL, J., WOELFEL, J., GILLHAM, J., & McPHAIL, T. Political radicalization as a communication process. *Communication Research*, 1974, 1, 243-263.

DETERMINANTS OF THE SOJOURNER'S ATTITUDINAL SATISFACTION: A PATH MODEL[1]

WILLIAM B. GUDYKUNST, RICHARD L. WISEMAN, and MITCHELL HAMMER
University of Minnesota

This paper develops a sequential model that specifies the interrelationships among six major variables which determine a sojourner's attitudinal satisfaction with living in another culture. Attitude theory and previous findings on sojourner's adjustment provided the theoretical foundation for the model. The paper argues that a sojourner's general *cross-cultural attitude* can be separated into its three components: (1) the affective component—the perspective the sojourner uses to evaluate intercultural interactions; (2) the cognitive component—the stereotypes the sojourner has of host nationals; and (3) the conative component—the behavioral tendencies that the sojourner has toward interacting with host nationals. It is theorized that these three components interact together to influence the amount and type of interaction that the sojourner has with host nationals. Further, the nature of this interaction influences the sojourner's attitudinal satisfaction with her or his stay in the host culture. Finally, the paper suggests, this process can be positively affected by participation in cross-cultural training. Six hypotheses were generated. The hypotheses and the adequacy of the model were empirically tested utilizing path analysis.

Previous works by Cleveland, Mangone, and Adams (1960), Gullahorn and Gullahorn (1963), Jacobson (1963), Kelman (1965), Brein and David (1971), Spaulding and Flack (1976), Brislin and Pedersen (1976), and Gudykunst, Hammer, and Wiseman (1976) have discussed various aspects of adjustment and sojourning. These studies have used the term *sojourner* to refer to many types of travelers, including military personnel, tourists, businesspersons, students, missionaries, and others who have lived and worked in a foreign culture. This research has mainly concentrated on foreign nationals who have traveled to the United States. However, in recent years there has been an increase in the research done on U.S. nationals who have traveled to other cultures. These studies have focused primarily on students and educational advisers (Brein & David, 1971). The emphasis of all of the studies mentioned above has been upon specific aspects of life styles and social relationships or problems the sojourner faces in the host culture.

It is apparent from reviewing the research findings on the adjustment of sojourners that there is very little theoretical consistency among the studies. According to Brein and David:

The approaches of various investigators have been so divergent that it is difficult to either inter-relate their findings or to develop any consistencies among the factors deemed relevant to intercultural adjustment. Moreover, even when the investigators apparently study the same or similar factors, the results usually fail to show any consistent patterns. Several of the more common approaches to describing and explaining the sojourner's adjustment include the following: curves of adjustment, culture shock, personality typologies and traits, background and situational factors, and social interactions. (1971, p. 216)

Furthermore, Spaulding and Flack (1976) found, in their review of 42 empirical studies which focused on foreign students' attitudes and problems of social adjustment, that only two attempted interdisciplinary theory or model building.

The current paper is concerned with one specific aspect of adjustment—the sojourners' attitudinal satisfaction with living and working in another culture. For simplicity's sake, this will be referred to as *tour satisfaction* in this work. This research develops a theoretical model which specifies the interrelationships among major variables which determine a sojourner's tour satisfaction. Attitude theory and the results of previous studies on sojourner's adjustment provide the foundation from which our model was developed. The adequacy of the model was tested empirically utilizing path analysis.

A MODEL OF SOJOURNERS' ATTITUDINAL SATISFACTION

Research findings on the adjustment of sojourners have not, to date, been related to the theory and research on attitudes. It is the contention of the current writers that the literature on attitude theory is a fruitful place to begin to develop an explanatory model of the sojourner's attitudinal satisfaction with her or his stay in a foreign culture.

It has long been recognized that an attitude consists of three components: *cognitive, affective* and *conative* (Campbell, 1947; Krech & Crutchfield, 1948; Newcomb, Turner, & Converse, 1964; McGuire, 1969). Research indicates that these three components of attitudes are highly intercorrelated (Campbell, 1947; Kahn, 1951). The *cognitive component* of an attitude—also referred to as the perceptual or stereotypic component—refers to how the person perceives the attitude object. In other words, it is the *stereotype* the person has of the attitude object. The *affective component*—also called the emotional or feeling component—deals with the person's feelings of like or dislike toward the attitude object. As the purely evaluative component of an attitude, many theorists have argued that the affective component is the "core" of a person's attitude. The *conative component*—also referred to as the action or behavioral component—refers to an individual's gross behavioral tendencies toward an attitude object.

One approach to explaining the sojourner's attitudinal satisfaction with living in another culture is to begin by examining what could be considered a general *cross-cultural attitude*. Consistent with the above, this *cross-cultural attitude* is composed of three parts: *affective, cognitive*, and *conative*. The *affective component* of the cross-cultural attitude is the psychological perspective that the sojourner uses in evaluating intercultural encounters. The *cognitive component* is composed of the *stereotypes* that the sojourner has of the host culture and people. The behavioral tendencies the sojourner has toward interacting with the host nationals comprises the

conative component of the cross-cultural attitude.

The psychological perspective is used by the sojourner for evaluating the host culture, its people, and intercultural interactions in general. Ideally this perspective includes a psychological framework which aids the sojourner in better understanding the unfamiliar situations encountered in a foreign culture. This ideal psychological viewpoint is neither from the sojourner's own culture nor from the host culture. Rather, it is a frame of reference for understanding intercultural interactions in general. This "third-culture" perspective acts as a psychological link between the sojourner's own cultural perspective (i.e., assumptions, values, learned behaviors, etc.) and the perspective of another culture (Gudykunst, Hammer, & Wiseman, 1976).[2] Since this *affective component* is the core of the *cross-cultural attitude*, it is hypothesized that the perspective held will: (1) affect the other two components of the attitude, (2) facilitate interactions with host nationals, and (3) increase attitudinal satisfaction with living in another culture. Lundstedt (1963), Gardner (1962), and Brein and David (1971), support the importance of the sojourner's perspective in influencing their interactions and adjustment in a foreign culture.

The stereotypic tendencies that the sojourner has toward the host culture and its people can be seen as the *cognitive component* of the cross-cultural attitude. These stereotypes will be affected by the perspective that the sojourner has. Further, the stereotypes held will affect the type of interaction that the sojourner has with host nationals.

The behavioral tendencies that the sojourner has toward interacting in the host culture can be seen as representing the *conative component* of the cross-cultural attitude. These behavioral tendencies could include, for example, learning the host language and learning how to use local transportation systems, as well as other "skills" which would help the sojourner to meet and effectively interact with host nationals. As with the stereotypes, the behavioral tendencies will be effected by the perspective held. These behavioral tendencies will, in turn, affect the type and amount of interaction that the sojourner has with host nationals.

It is theorized that the three components of the cross-cultural attitude interact to influence the

FIGURE 1
A Path Diagram of Sojourners' Attitudinal Satisfaction

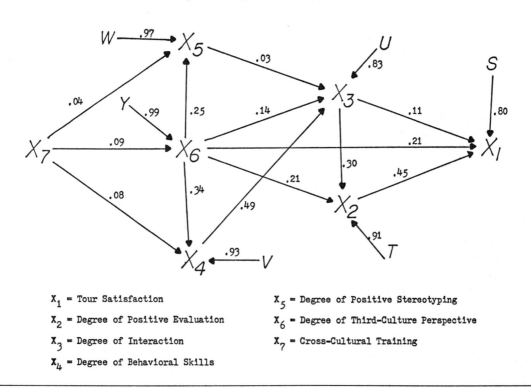

X_1 = Tour Satisfaction

X_2 = Degree of Positive Evaluation

X_3 = Degree of Interaction

X_4 = Degree of Behavioral Skills

X_5 = Degree of Positive Stereotyping

X_6 = Degree of Third-Culture Perspective

X_7 = Cross-Cultural Training

amount and type of interaction that the sojourner has with host nationals. Support for this contention is provided by Morris (1960), Kelman (1962), and Selltiz, Christ, Havel, and Cook (1963). It is further hypothesized that the cross-cultural attitude, in conjunction with host culture interactions, determines the sojourner's relative attitudinal satisfaction with his or her stay in the host culture. In order to better understand this relationship, we need to briefly look at the literature on intergroup contact.

Intergroup Contact

There have been several reviews on the effect of intergroup contact on intergroup attitudes (Allport, 1954; Cook, 1962; Amir, 1969). The major assumption of these studies has been that intergroup contact tends to produce better intergroup relations. At the present time there is conflicting evidence on the exact nature of the impact of contact on intergroup attitudes. Because of the divergent nature of

the findings Sherif and Sherif (1953) have argued that "In any discussion on the effects of contact on intergroup attitudes, we must specify: What kind of contact? Contact in what capacity?" (p. 221). Cook (1957) presents three dimensions for evaluating the contact situation and its potential for positive attitude change: (1) the opportunity that the contact situation offers for personal interaction, (2) the relative status levels of the participants, and (3) the nature of the social norms toward interracial contact. Intergroup contact has a positive impact on intergroup relations when: (1) personal interaction occurs, (2) participants have equal status, and (3) the social norms favor contact. Previous research by Morris (1960) and Sewell and Davidson (1961) has also found that there is a positive relationship between a sojourner's interaction with host nationals and satisfaction with the sojourn. Thus we would expect that sojourners who have positive interactions—interaction that met the three conditions listed above—with people in the host culture will have a higher degree of attitudinal satisfaction with their stay than those who don't interact with the host nationals.

At this point it should be noted that the cross-cultural attitude discussed earlier can be modified or affected by participation in a cross-cultural training program. It is the current writers' contention that one of the objectives of cross-cultural training is, in fact, attitude change. In addition, the aims of cross-cultural training should include: (1) helping the sojourner develop a third-culture perspective for evaluating intercultural interactions, (2) helping the sojourner assess his or her intercultural communication (interaction) behavior, and (3) teaching the sojourner the behavioral skills that will help them more effectively function in the host culture. (For an outline of a training program designed to meet these objectives, see Gudykunst, Hammer, and Wiseman, 1976.)

In summary, we have argued that the three components of the sojourner's cross-cultural attitude interact to affect the amount and type of interaction they have with host nationals. Further, the nature of this interaction influences the sojourner's attitudinal satisfaction with his or her stay in the host culture. Finally, this process can be positively influenced by participation in a cross-cultural training program. A diagram illustrating the variables discussed and their interrelationships is presented in Figure 1. The model outlined yields six hypotheses:

H_1: The sojourners' tour satisfaction will depend upon their interactions with host nationals, their evaluation of these interactions, and their degree of third-culture perspective.

H_2: The sojourners' evaluation of their interactions with host nationals will depend upon their actual interactions and their degree of third-culture perspective.

H_3: The interaction that sojourners have with host nationals will depend upon the degree of behavioral skills they possess, their stereotypes of host nationals, and their degree of third-culture perspective.

H_4: The degree of behavioral skills necessary to interact effectively with host nationals possessed by the sojourners will depend upon their degree of third-culture perspective and participation in cross-cultural training.

H_5: The stereotypes the sojourners have about the host nationals will depend upon their degree of third-culture perspective and their participation in cross-cultural training.

H_6: The degree of third-culture perspective that the sojourner develops can be increased by participation in cross-cultural training.

PROCEDURES

Questionnaire

The questionnaire was originally designed to help ascertain the effectiveness of the United States Navy's Intercultural Relations (ICR) program in Japan in increasing the tour satisfaction of personnel who attended an ICR seminar. This was accomplished by conducting a pre- and post-test of participants in an ICR seminar and in a control group who had not attended. The questionnaire was designed to examine how much an individual used the Japanese language, how much they used the public transportation system in Japan, the amount of interaction they had with Japanese people, and whether or not the individual was satisfied with being stationed in Japan. In addition, there were questions on stereotypes held and how people felt about certain conditions in Japan (i.e., food, sanitation, crowds, etc.).

Sample

The questionnaire was administered to a random sample of 450 naval personnel stationed on or around Yokosuka Naval Base. The questionnaire was also administered to 80 people just prior to beginning an ICR seminar. Six months later, the survey was mailed out to each individual who had participated before.[3]

The Variables

X_1: *The dependent variable—Tour Satisfaction (TS).* This variable was measured by a single *Likert-type* item that asked how satisfied the respondent was with his or her stay in Japan. This item was asked after the subject had responded to several items about the Japanese culture and people.

X_2: *Degree of Positive Evaluation of Interactions (DPE)*. After the respondent was asked to rate the degree to which he or she participated in several forms of possible interactions with Japanese people, the respondent then reported how much he or she enjoyed the interactions in a single *Likert-type* item.

X_3: *Degree of Interaction (DI)*. A list of eight possible forms of interaction was developed for this variable (e.g., dining with a Japanese, having a Japanese friend). The respondent was asked to specify the number of times he or she had engaged in each of the activities in the past month. These data were then subjected to Guttman scaling—a scaling technique designed to test the unidimensionality and hierarchical structure of the scale items (Guttman, 1944). The *coefficient of reproducibility*—an indication of "the percent accuracy with which responses to the various statements can be reproduced from the total scores" (Edwards, 1957, p. 183)—was .83. This was substantially higher than what might be expected from a chance ordering of the responses based upon the marginals (minimum marginal reproducibility = .36). From this we can infer that there are varying levels of difficulty in interacting with people from the host culture. Furthermore, these levels are hierarchically ordered (i.e., if you are able to pass the more difficult items, then you should pass the easier items). The construct *degree of interaction* was calculated for each respondent on the basis of the following formula:

$$DI = \sum_{i=1}^{8} S_i R_i$$

where DI equals the degree of interaction, S_i equals the Guttman scale value for item i, and R equals the respondent's answer to item i. Basically, the algorithm would place greater weight on the more difficult items. The effect of using a multiplication model would be to magnify the differences between respondents on the basis of their ease of interacting in a foreign culture (see Anderson, 1969, for a discussion of multiplicative models).

X_4: *Degree of Behavioral Skills (DBS)*. This variable corresponds to the *conative component* of an attitude. It measures the degree to which an individual is motivated to learn behaviors which would facilitate interaction with a member of the host culture (e.g., learning phrases of the host language). A list of six items was developed to measure this variable. The responses of the six items were subjected to a *Guttman scalogram analysis*. The coefficient of reproducibility (.82) favorably compared to the minimum marginal reproducibility (.38). As discussed above, the value of this variable was calculated by summing the products of the Guttman scale value for each item and the respondent's corresponding answer. This facilitated the distinguishability of respondents with a greater predisposition for learning behaviors conducive to interaction from those with lesser predispositions.

X_5: *Degree of Positive Stereotyping (DPS)*. This variable corresponds to the *cognitive component* of an attitude. Since we were interested in which stereotypes were conducive to positive attributions of the Japanese people, the values of the eleven Likert-type items were scaled such that, the larger the scale value, the greater the positive stereotype. These scale items were then subjected to *Guttman scalogram analysis*. Again the coefficient of reproducibility (.85) was substantially greater than the minimum marginal reproducibility (.43). The multiplicative model was then applied, and values for this variable were derived, such that respondents with greater values would have more beliefs facilatative to positive attributes of the Japanese people.

X_6: *Degree of Third-Culture Perspective (DT-CP)*. This variable is the evaluative core of the sojourner's cross-cultural attitude. Respondents were asked to rate each of twelve conditions on the basis of how much that condition bothered the respondent (e.g., sanitation conditions, being stared at, Japanese table manners). These twelve Likert-type items were subjected to *Guttman scalogram analysis*. The coefficient of reproducibility was a .79, a considerable improvement over the minimum marginal reproducibility of .35. The operationalization of the third-culture perspective was the sum of

TABLE 1
Intercorrelations of the Variables

	X_7	X_6	X_5	X_4	X_3	X_2	X_1
X_7 (CCT)	1.0						
X_6 (DT-CP)	.09	1.0					
X_5 (DPS)	.06	.25	1.0				
X_4 (DBS)	.11	.35	.07	1.0			
X_3 (DI)	.09	.32	.10	.54	1.0		
X_2 (DPE)	.09	.31	.07	.27	.37	1.0	
X_1 (TS)	.12	.38	.21	.24	.34	.55	1.0

the products of the Guttman scale values for each item and the respondent's answer to that item. A large value for this variable would indicate that the respondent was, for example, less ethnocentric and more open-minded.

X₇: Cross-Cultural Training (CCT). This variable was operationalized by whether or not the respondent had participated in the three day intercultural relations seminar.

Statistical Technique

The hypothesized interrelationships between the preceding variables were assessed via *path analysis*—a statistical "method of measuring the direct influence along each separate path in a system and thus of finding the degree to which variation of a given effect is determined by each particular cause" (Wright, 1921, p. 557). The path model was derived from the hypothesized relationships. From the path model, a set of structural equations was developed and then solved by path estimation equations which utilized correlation coefficients to discern the path coefficients. The six hypothesized relationships are depicted by the following equations:

$$Z_1 = P_{12} Z_2 + P_{13} Z_3 + P_{16} Z_6 + P_{1S} S$$
$$Z_2 = P_{23} Z_3 + P_{26} Z_6 + P_{2T} T$$
$$Z_3 = P_{34} Z_4 + P_{35} Z_5 + P_{36} Z_6 + P_{3U} U$$
$$Z_4 = P_{46} Z_6 + P_{47} Z_7 + P_{4V} V$$
$$Z_5 = P_{56} Z_6 + P_{57} Z_7 + P_{5W} W$$
$$Z_6 = P_{67} Z_7 + P_{6Y} Y$$

where Z_i is variable i in standard unit form; P_u is the path coefficient between dependent variable i and determining variable j. S is the residual variable of Z_1; T is the residual variable of Z_2, etc.

RESULTS

The zero order correlations among the variables are presented in Table 1. Consistent with the theory, tour satisfaction significantly correlated with the positive *evaluation of interactions* ($r_{12} = .55$), *degree of third-culture perspective* ($r_{16} = .38$), and *degree of interaction* ($r_{13} = .34$). There are, however, substantial positive correlations between *tour satisfaction* and *degree of behavioral skills* ($r_{14} = .24$) and between *tour satisfaction* and *degree of positive stereotyping* ($r_{15} = .21$). According to the theory, these two correlations should be mediated by the *degree of interaction* and the *positive evalua-*

TABLE 2
Standardized Path Coefficents with Their Corresponding t-values

Dependent Variables

Independent Variables	z_1 (TS)		z_2 (DPE)		z_3 (DI)		z_4 (DBS)		z_5 (DPS)		z_6 (DT-CP)	
	p	t	p	t	p	t	p	t	p	t	p	t
z_2 (DPE)	.45	191.7*	-	-	-	-	-	-	-	-	-	-
z_3 (DI)	.11	11.7*	-	-	-	-	-	-	-	-	-	-
z_4 (DBS)	-	-	-	-	.49	15.0*	-	-	-	-	-	-
z_5 (DPS)	-	-	-	-	.03	.45	-	-	-	-	-	-
z_6 (DT-CP)	.21	40.4*	.21	6.13*	.14	18.1*	.34	96.8*	.25	6.8*	-	-
z_7 (CCT)	-	-	-	-	-	-	.08	2.37*	.04	1.2	.09	2.51*

*t = 1.9 at .05 level; and 2.5 at .01 level.

---

tion of these interactions. If, indeed, the theory is correct, then r_{14} and r_{15} would be explained by r_{12} and r_{13}, and thus r_{14} and r_{15} would be spurious. With the path analysis, we can determine whether such relationships are spurious or whether the path model is structurally incomplete (e.g., missing necessary causal links).

One method of testing the structure of the model would be to compare the amount of variance explained by the path (restricted) model to the amount of variance explained by the general model where we predict the dependent variable with all the temporally prior variables. Land (1973) provides a formula for making such a test:

$$L = N \sum_{i=1}^{n-1} \log \frac{(1 - R^2_{ri})/dri}{(1 - R^2_{fi})/dfi}$$

where the numerator is the variance explained by the *restricted model*, the denominator is the variance explained by the *general model*, and L is a statistic with the same distribution as chi-square (x^2). The derived model, as depicted in Figure 1 and

Table 2, yielded a nonsignificant L (4.8). From this we can infer that there would be no significant improvement by adding new paths to the model. Next, the individual paths were tested by examining whether or not the paths explain the zero order correlations. Only two test equations proved troublesome: $r_{12} = P_{12}$ (.10 difference), and $r_{13} = P_{13} + r_{23} P_{12}$ (.06 difference). The two plausible explanations for these mismatches are: (1) intercorrelations among the residuals, or (2) misordering of the temporal sequence of DI and DPE.

The intercorrelations between the residuals are presented in Table 3. With three exceptions, the path model has met one of path analysis' more stringent assumptions—uncorrelated error residuals. The correlation between T and U (r = .158) could, in part, explain why the two test equations above were slightly off. If the residuals are correlated, then there could exist a third variable which is causally related to both DI and DPE (Cappella, 1975). Also, since there is a correlation between S and Y (r = .26), there may be a third variable causally related to TS and DT-CP. The third correlation, that between W and S (r = .182), helps

TABLE 3
Intercorrelations of the Residuals

	S	T	U	V	W	Y
S (TS)	1.0					
T (DPE)	-.091	1.0				
U (DI)	-.019	.158	1.0			
V (DBS)	.06	.053	-.009	1.0		
W (DPS)	.182	.033	.000	.061	1.0	
Y (DT-CP)	.26	.000	.000	.007	-.004	1.0

answer a question posed earlier: Is the zero order correlation between DBS and TS spurious or causal? It would appear that an unmeasured third variable is covarying with both DBS and TS, thus inflating the zero order correlation. Even with these three possible exceptions, it is safe to say that the path model depicted in Figure 1 and Table 2 provides a fairly good fit with the data.

Hypothesis 1

The derived path model shows support for the first hypothesis: The *sojourner's tour satisfaction* is significantly influenced by the *degree of interaction* ($P_{13} = .11$), the *positive evaluation of these interactions* ($P_{12} = .45$), and the *degree of third-culture perspective* held ($P_{16} = .21$). *Positively evaluating interactions* that the sojourner has with host nationals greatly enhance *tour satisfaction*. Although the path between TS and DI may be slightly inflated, owing to intercorrelations of their residuals, the path coefficient is still significant, even after partialling out the correlated portion of the residual from the zero order correlation. The adjusted path coefficient was then substituted into the test equation to ascertain whether a fit had been achieved. Although the fit was closer, there still existed a discrepancy, suggesting that there may exist some

feedback from DPE to DI. Lastly, a *third-culture perspective* seems to facilitate the sojourners' *tour satisfaction,* but this may be due to a third unmeasured variable which is causally related to both (see above).

Hypothesis 2

There is also support for the second hypothesis: The positive *evaluation of interactions* is significantly influenced by the *degree of third-culture perspective* ($P_{26} = .21$) and the *degree of interaction* ($P_{23} = .30$). As discussed above, this last relationship might be better depicted as interdependent rather than unidirectional. Also, the *degree of third-culture perspective* seems to facilitate one's positive *evaluation of interactions* in the host culture.

Hypothesis 3

There is partial support for the third hypothesis: The degree of interaction is strongly influenced by the degree of *behavioral skills* ($P_{34} = .49$), relatively independent of degree of *positive stereotyping* ($P_{35} = .03$), and directly influenced by the degree of *third-culture perspective* ($P_{36} = .14$). Consistent with the theory, having interactions in the host culture is dependent on possessing the *behavioral skills* necessary for interaction and having a *third-culture perspective*. The degree of *positive stereotyping* has virtually no influence on one's *degree of interaction*.

Hypothesis 4

There is also support for hypothesis four: The degree of *behavioral skills* is strongly influenced by the degree of *third-culture perspective* (P_{46} = .34) and slightly influenced by *cross-cultural training* (P_{47} = .08). In essence, possessing a *third-culture perspective* induces one to learn skills necessary to interact in the host culture. Although statistically significant (p = .052), the *cross-cultural training* exhibited only a weak influence on the degree of *behavioral skills* possessed.

Hypothesis 5

The model provides partial support for hypothesis five: The degree of *positive stereotyping* is moderately influenced by the degree of *third-culture perspective* (P_{56} = .25) and relatively independent of *cross-cultural training* (P_{57} = .04). Having a *third-culture perspective* seems to elicit positive stereotyping of the host nationals. Further, *cross-cultural training* had little influence on the degree of *positive stereotyping*.

Hypothesis 6

Lastly, the model supports hypothesis six: The degree of *third-culture perspective* is influenced by one's participation in *cross-cultural training*. Although the path is weak (P_{67} = .09), it was significant at the .01 level. On the basis of the above, we can conclude that *cross-cultural training* would have the most impact on the system via its influence on the sojourner's *third-culture perspective*, which, as we have seen, has a pervasive influence throughout the system.

DISCUSSION OF THE RESULTS

The path model presented, in general, supports the theoretical model discussed in this paper. It has

been found that the sojourner's *third-culture perspective* is the core of the *cross-cultural attitude*. Further, the model demonstrates that this *third-culture perspective* pervasively influences all the other variables tested. Based upon these results, five conclusions appear warranted: (1) The higher degree of *third-culture* perspective that the sojourner has, the higher will be the degree of his or her *positive stereotyping* and *behavioral skills*. (2) The degree of interaction that the sojourner has with host nationals is influenced significantly by *third-culture perspective* and *behavioral skills,* and to a lesser extent, by the *stereotypes* held of host nationals. (3) The higher the degree of the sojourner's *third-culture perspective* and *interactions with host nations,* the more likely will the sojourner positively evaluate these interactions. (4) The higher the degree of the sojourner's *third-culture perspective, interactions with host nationals,* and the positive evaluation of these interactions, the higher will be *tour satisfaction.* (5) *Cross-cultural training* is most effective in influencing the sojourner's *third-culture perspective* and *behavioral skills,* and not effective in influencing *stereotypes of host nationals.*

In the presentation of the results, it was stated that there could be another variable intervening to cause intercorrelation of the residuals between: (1) TS and DBS, (2) TS and DT-CP, and (3) DI and DPE. One plausible explanation for the first two intercorrelations listed above is based on the assumption that an attitude is greater than the sum of its parts. If this is true, then it's possible that the residual of the *cross-cultural attitude* that was lost when it was broken down into its three components could be acting as another variable, which is intervening to cause intercorrelations between TS and DBS and TS and DT-CP. The intercorrelation between the residuals of DI and DPE is more complicated. This intercorrelation could be due to either an intervening third variable or misordering of the temporal sequence. Since we are in basic agreement with Bem's (1967) contention that when people see themselves engaged in certain behaviors they feel they must like them, we feel that the temporal order of DI and DPE is correct and there must be another variable intervening. As with the other two intercorrelations, we hypothesize that part of the *cross-*

cultural attitude not accounted for when it was broken into its three parts is also intervening between DI and DPE to cause intercorrelation among the residuals.

The path analysis presented supports the effectiveness of *cross-cultural training* in influencing the development of a *third-culture perspective* and, to a certain extent, learning *behavioral skills* necessary for *effective interaction*. The analysis did not support the influence of *cross-cultural training* on the degree of *positive stereotyping*. Intuitively this makes sense, in that the training program studied was only three days long and we can't expect to change stereotypes in that short of a period. Further, the path model did not find any effect of *positive stereotyping* on the degree of *interaction with host nationals*. Post hoc speculation yields two possible explanations for this. First, it's possible that the stereotypes that a sojourner has of host nationals does not actually affect the interactions they have with host nationals. Second, it's possible that the eleven scale items used to construct DPS may not have tapped the salient stereotypes that affect interaction.

SUMMARY

The results of the path analysis clearly indicate that the degree of *third-culture perspective* held by the sojourner pervasively influences all other aspects of the model. This is consistent with the theoretical position that the *third-culture perspective*— the affective component of the *cross-cultural attitude*—is the core of the attitude which should influence the other two components and the rest of the model. This *third-culture perspective* is a frame of reference for evaluating the unfamiliar situations found in a foreign culture. If the sojourner has developed this perspective, then he or she will be better able to understand what happens to him or her while in a foreign culture, and thus be able to more effectively function in that culture. One major implication of this finding relates to the objectives of cross-cultural training. Given the effect of the *third-culture perspective*, both direct and indirect, on increasing the sojourner's *tour satisfaction*, and given that the perspective can be influenced by cross-cultural training, it would follow that one of

the major objectives of any cross-cultural training program should be to help the sojourner develop this perspective.

In conclusion, the model presented in this paper has attempted to overcome one of the major inadequacies of previous studies—isolating single dependent and independent variables and testing only their bivariate relationships without investigating interrelationships with other influential variables. Six major variables that effect the sojourner's attitudinal satisfaction with living in another culture were discussed and the interrelationships among these variables were specified. The theoretical model presented was empirically tested via path analysis and found to be adequate.

NOTES

1. Support for the collection of the data discussed in this paper was given by the U.S. Navy's Human Resource Management Detachment, Yokosuka, Japan. The data were collected by the senior author while he was assigned as an Intercultural Relations Specialist with the U.S. Navy in Japan. The opinions expressed in this paper are those of the authors and in no way represent the opinions of the U.S. Navy.

2. To further explain this *third-culture perspective*, we can say that people who have highly developed this perspective can be characterized as follows: (1) they are open-minded toward new ideas and experiences; (2) they are empathic toward people from other cultures; (3) they accurately perceive differences and similarities between the host culture and their own; (4) they tend to describe behavior they don't understand rather than evaluating unfamiliar behavior as bad, nonsensical, or meaningless; (5) they are relatively astute noncritical observers of their own behavior and that of others; (6) they are better able to establish meaningful relationships with people from the host culture; and (7) they are less ethnocentric (i.e., they try to first understand and then evaluate the behavior of host nationals based upon the standards of the culture they are living in).

3. The number of respondents were as follows: control group, time one = 428; control group, time two = 200; ICR group, time one = 80; and ICR group, time two = 37.

REFERENCES

ALLPORT, G.W. *The nature of prejudice*. Cambridge: Addison-Wesley, 1954.

AMIR, Y. Contact hypothesis in ethnic relations. *Psychological Bulletin*, 1969, 71, 319-342.

ANDERSON, N. Cognitive algebra: Integration theory applied to social attribution. In L. Burkowitz (Ed.), *Advances in experimental social psychology*, Vol. 7. New York: Academic Press, 1969.

BEM, D.J. Self-perception: An alternative interpretation of cognitive dissonance phenomena. *Psychological review*, 1967, 74, 183-200.

BREIN, M., & DAVID, K.H. Intercultural communication and the adjustment of the sojourner. *Psychological bulletin*, 1971, 76, 215-230.

BRISLIN, R.W., & PEDERSEN, P. *Cross-cultural orientation programs*. New York: Gardner Press, 1976.

CAMPBELL, D.T. The generality of social attitudes. Ph.D. thesis, University of California, Berkeley, 1947.

CAPPELLA, J. An introduction to the literature on causal modeling. *Human communication research*, 1975, 1, 362-377.

CLEVELAND, H., MANGONE, G.J., & ADAMS, J.C. *The overseas Americans*. New York: McGraw Hill, 1960.

COOK, S.W. Desegregation: A psychological analysis. *The American psychologist*, 1957, 12, 1-13.

COOK, S.W. The systematic analysis of socially significant events: A strategy for social research. *Journal of social issues*, 1962, 18, 66-84.

EDWARDS, A. *Techniques for attitude scale construction*. New York: Appleton, Century, Crofts, 1957.

GARDNER, G.H. Cross-cultural communication. *Journal of social psychology*, 1962, 58, 241-256.

GUDYKUNST, W.B., HAMMER, M., & WISEMAN, R. Cross-cultural training: Current status and suggested future directions: A paper presented at the annual meeting of the Intercultural Communication Division of the Speech-Communication Association, December 1976.

GULLAHORN, J.T., & GULLAHORN, J.E. An extension of the U-curve hypothesis. *Journal of social issues*, 1963, 19, 33-47.

GUTTMAN, L. A basis for scaling qualitative data. *American sociological review*, 1944, 9, 139-150.

JACOBSON, E.H. Sojourn research: A definition of the field. *Journal of social issues*, 1963, 19, 123-129.

KAHN, L.A. The organization of attitudes toward the Negro as a function of education. *Psychological monographs*, 1951, 65, No. 13.

KELMAN, H.C. Changing attitudes through international activities. *Journal of social issues*, 1962, 18, 68-87.

KELMAN, H.C. (ed.). *International behavior*. New York: Holt, Rinehart and Winston, 1965.

KRECH, D., & CRUTCHFIELD, R.S. *Theory and problems in social psychology*. New York: McGraw-Hill, 1948.

LAND, K. Identification, parameter estimation, and hypothesis testing in recursive sociological models. In A. Goldberger and O. Duncan (Eds.) *Structural equations models in the social sciences*. New York: Seminar Press, 1973.

LUNDSTEDT, S. An introduction to some evolving problems in cross-cultural research. *Journal of social issues*, 1963, 19, 1-9.

McGUIRE, W.J. The nature of attitudes and attitude change. In G. Lindzey and A. Aronson (Eds.) *The handbook of social psychology*, Vol. III, second edition. Reading, Pa.: Addison-Wesley.

MORRIS, R.T. *The two-way mirror: National status in foreign students' adjustment*. Minneapolis: University of Minnesota Press, 1960.

NEWCOMB, T.M., TURNER, R.H., & CONVERSE, P.E. *Social psychology*. New York: Holt, Rinehart and Winston, 1964.

SELLTIZ, C., CHRIST, J.R., HAVEL, J., & COOK, S.W. *Attitudes and social relations of foreign students in the United States*. Minneapolis: University of Minnesota Press, 1963.

SEWELL, W.H., & DAVIDSON, O. *Scandinavian students on an American campus*. Minneapolis: University of Minnesota Press, 1961.

SHERIF, M., & SHERIF, C.W. *Groups in harmony and tension: An integration of studies in intergroup relations*. New York: Harper, 1953.

SPAULDING, S., & FLACK, M.J. *The world's students in the United States: A review and evaluation of research on foreign students*. New York: Praeger, 1976.

WRIGHT, S. Correlation and causation. *Journal of agricultural research*, 1921, 20, 557-585.

POLITICAL AND SOCIAL IMPLICATIONS OF COMMUNICATIONS SATELLITE APPLICATIONS IN DEVELOPED AND DEVELOPING COUNTRIES[1]

HAMID MOWLANA
American University

Communication technology has a direct role in national and international political systems, and therefore is not politically neutral. Communication satellites, for instance, affect power distributions and social control, and revise traditional views about national sovereignty which should be conceptualized in informational as well as spatial terms. Sovereignty can be assured only when nations control the channels via which messages are sent as well as the expertise to program messages for distribution. There is presently a struggle to prevent a single country's monopoly of these capabilities. The next decade will therefore be an extraordinarily active political period for satellite communications, and the political problems of regulating and coordinating international communications urgently require international cooperation and international solutions. A model of the communication technology cycle has been presented to show some aspects of this dependency.

That technology is, in fact, politically neutral is a myth. The assumption in this article is that technology plays a political role in contemporary society, a role intimately related to the distribution of power and the exercise of political, social, and economic controls. Thus, technological development—including the development of communications satellite technology—is essentially a political process.

This article seeks to assess some political and social implications of communications satellite applications. The theoretical underpinnings of this analysis can be outlined in the following manner. First, it is assumed that politics can be defined as a particular type of information exchange, and that information is a resource convertible to political power. Thus, in this process, there is a direct linkage between information and politics. Second, international and national systems are going through profound change as a result of the current technical revolution in information exchange and communications. Indeed these technical innovations appear to be creating the conditions which may lead to a "perceptual" revolution—a type of revolution from which political and social institutions will not be immune.

COMMUNICATIONS TECHNOLOGY CYCLE

There is a need for a shift in emphasis in the analysis of communication systems—especially mass communication—from an exclusive concern with the *source* and *content* of messages to analysis of the message *distribution* process (Mowlana, 1975a, 1976a). Control of the distribution process is the most important index of the way in which power is distributed in a communication system, which may be the global community, a country, or some smaller political unit. The dissemination of information in the international system, when the above distinction is made, may then be represented in rudimentary terms suggested in Figure 1.

The growth of communication technology, the expanding national and international market, and the creation of institutional policies and regulations all have made the distribution stage the most important sequence in the chains of communication systems. Emphasis upon the distribution stage affords an immediate advantage in analyzing the message-sending activities of national actors. Unless a nation has control over the entire distribution process, its messages may be ineffectual. Certainly, the most

FIGURE 1
Distribution of Information in the International System

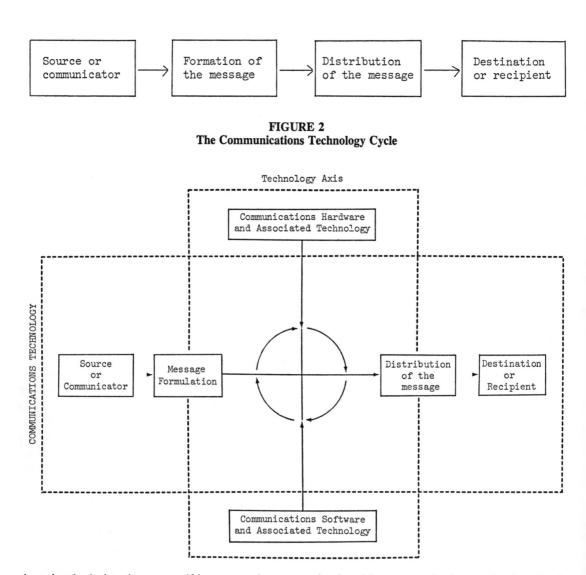

FIGURE 2
The Communications Technology Cycle

ingeniously designed message, if it goes nowhere, will have no effect.

A further elaboration of the process of information distribution in the international system shown in Figure 1 is provided in Figure 2, wherein a technology axis is added to the communications axis.

Figure 2, representing the communications technology cycle, now properly depicts the pivotal role played by communications technology in the international communications process. Between the formation and distribution of messages stands the *means of distribution*—communication technology—itself divisible into two components. This is the communications hardware, the actual physical carriers of messages (i.e., satellites, broadcasting and receiving equipment, microwave relay station), and the communications software, which is in the broadest sense the know-how and means to utilize the hardware (i.e., program production, manpower skills, education, etc.)

In the case of communication by satellite especially, the paramount concern, when considering political implications, is in determining who controls the means of distribution. The central focus of an inquiry into the political impacts of satellite communication must, therefore, be upon ownership, transfer, access and control of the hardware and software of communications technology.

The distinction between the two components of communications technology—hardware and software—to which the above diagram draws attention, is an important one, but one which frequently is ignored. Even when the importance of control over the technology is recognized, it is often assumed that ownership of the actual physical components of the system is sufficient to confer control over it. But just as the ability to form messages by itself affords no guarantee that those messages will be disseminated, neither is control only of communications hardware sufficient to assure the distribution of one's own intended message. Absolute sovereignty in the formation and distribution of messages is assured only when a nation controls both the hardware channels via which the messages are sent and the necessary know-how to program its messages for effective distribution.

Recent analysis of the transfer of communications technology from the industrialized to developing countries (Mowlana, 1975b), and of the cultural dependency which is being attributed to this transfer (Schiller, 1971, 1973; Wells, 1972), illustrates the importance of the distinction between hardware and software.

Aspects of Dependency

During the last decade, a significant number of developing countries have become the willing "beneficiaries" of an assortment of communications hardware from the industrialized countries. This transfer of technology has not been entirely without a software component. There has been, for example, an accompanying transfer of the knowledge and skills necessary for the operation and maintenance of the new communications equip-

ment. What has infrequently been transferred, however, is either the hardware or software relating to the formation of messages—the means, in terms of both knowledge and technical know-how to utilize the communications system for one's own ends.

This point may be illustrated by examining the communications technology cycle, represented in Figure 2, in terms of the quadrants created by the communications technology axes. The type of communications technology that has been most frequently transferred from industrial to nonindustrial countries falls in the upper right-hand quadrant—technological hardware for the distribution of communication messages, (i.e., television programs, international news). In comparison, transfer of the types of technology represented by the other three quadrants—hardware for message formation, and software for both the formation and distribution of messages—has played a much less prominent role.

The implications of this pattern of technology transfer become clear when the diagram is seen as representing the components of control in a communication system, absolute control over which accrues only with the possession of all four components. Effective control of a system, however, will fall to the possessor of certain of the components. For example, in the instance at hand, a country may have the most sophisticated television broadcasting apparatus imaginable and the technical know-how to disseminate messages through it. But unless this country is also producing its own messages, its control over the total communications process is lost to the outsider, and hence its dependency on the outsider system increases (see lower right portion of communications technology cycle as shown in the diagram).

The "Americanization" of world culture, so often commented on and criticized, might be understood as the interaction of such a message producing and distributing system vis-à-vis the hardware and software components of technology. If American pop culture is successful around the world—and it is—it is by this circular process. The software aspect of communication technology, in the form of programs, shows, film, enters into a national system seeking to reflect some popular culture tastes;

the product in turn feeds back into the system and reinforces that which has already been found popular.

Cultural Identity

The phenomenon of cultural identity, referred to earlier, is very much to the point here. Certain critics of patterns of American communication penetration into the culture of developing countries have described at length the unfolding of the above pattern of control. Interpretations as to the significance and effects of satellite communication have shown as many facets as there are theories and philosophies underpinning the role, function, and effect of communication upon individuals and societies. Whatever the theoretical position selected, anxieties and fears expressed regarding the possibility of unwanted television broadcasts via satellites do in fact illustrate the importance of both technology, in the form of the medium, and communication, in the form of messages, being produced and distributed.

One of the main capabilities of the communications satellite is its capacity to provide instantaneous and universally available information in forms of news or educational materials. However the problems related to the social and political aspects of such a technology is not one of availability, but of control and selectivity. The real question is by whom, how, for what purpose and with what consequences are these controls exercised? In fact, "radio pollution," "television pollution," and "mail pollution" are becoming key concepts in describing the indiscriminate use of electronics and other communications appliances. This interference and the result of such disturbances has popularized concerns relative to "cultural imperialism," "cultural integrity," and "cultural identity."

The debate. The defenders of the "free flow of information" argue that there are built-in economic and political controls. They explain that direct broadcast satellites will not become operative in the foreseeable future, owing to the high costs and many practical problems of reaching the intended distribution targets. They indicate further that most

satellite broadcasting projects envisioned for operational service in the near future are actually based upon distributional ground stations, and thus require the cooperation of the receiving country. It is also suggested that a country wishing to disseminate direct television to others today would have an extremely small audience limited to those with special receivers. Professor Ithiel de Sola Pool (1975) of the Massachusetts Institute of Technology takes the view that "whatever one's value position, the fact is that in the modern world, there is international cultural intrusion." In arguing that this foreign influence is but a special case of the disruptive impact of intellectual and cultural media in general, he writes:

> In general, culture does not need protection. People are already attached to culture. If the culture is satisfactory, if it is not already in process of decomposition, and if local media are doing their job of providing products which fit the culture, the audience will not look abroad. (1975, p. 53)

The direct broadcast satellite, however, is only a very small part of this controversy. Global electronic networks, including systems for economic mail transmission, teletype data-pocket networks, and information-bank retrieval systems—some of which are already in operation—will pose real questions about information flow and cultural intrusion. The willingness of some 100 countries in the United Nations in 1972 to support the resolution reciting both the potential benefits of satellite broadcasting and the need to respect the sovereignty of states in its use, was both a political and nationalistic move in the direction of control of information distributed by satellite. At that time, the United States cast the only vote against this resolution.

Concurrently, the United Nations Educational, Scientific and Cultural Organization (UNESCO) issued a "Declaration of Guiding Principles and the Use of Satellite Broadcasting for the Free Flow of Information, the Spread of Education, and Greater Cultural Exchange," affirming at the same time the principles of sovereignty and international cooperation, the free flow of information and "the rights of audiences," "contact between peoples," and the "preservation of cultures." For example,

Article IV (2) of this declaration provided that:

> . . . each country has the right to decide on the context of the educational programmes broadcast by satellite to its people and, in cases where such programmes are produced in cooperation with other countries, to take part in their planning and production, on a free and equal footing.

Interestingly, while Article VII of the declaration contained the following statement:

> . . . the objective of satellite broadcasting for the promotion of cultural exchange is to foster greater contact and mutual understanding between peoples by permitting audiences to enjoy, on an unprecedented scale, programmes on each other's social and cultural life including artistic performances and sporting and other events. . . .

it contained the following clause in regard to cultural identity:

> Cultural programmes, while promoting the enrichment of all cultures, should respect the distinctive character, the value and the dignity of each, and the right of all countries and peoples to preserve their cultures as part of the common heritage of mankind.

The defenders of the preservation of national cultures argue that the imported, commercially-oriented mass media material not only undermines family-centered traditional culture, but also that it is simply "cheap" and "junk." For example, in rejecting the American position on the uninhibited free flow broadcasting as an international expression of freedom of speech, a group of Canadian scholars (Gotlieb, Dalfen, & Katz, 1974) have written:

> It is questionable, however, how far the American Government would be prepared to defend this principle, if American viewers were being subjected to programs transmitted from other countries, the content of which seriously offended basic American morals and political values. (1974, p. 239)

The one-way flow of television programs, (Varis, 1973), documented by such studies as the University of Tampere's "International Inventory of Television Programme Structure and the Flow of TV Programmes Between Nations" in Finland (Varis, 1973), and the uneven distribution of news and journalists around the world (Mowlana, 1975c), can be cited to illustrate the cultural and political imbalances existing in the communications/technology cycle. These studies describe a process wherein a country "buys in" to the flow of international telecommunications by purchasing hardware from the West. Most commonly, such initiatives are taken by the country's political and economic leaders, who, as a number of critics have noted, are more likely to share the value and cultural preferences of their Western counterparts than those of their native countrymen.

Most of the studies dealing with the United States dominance in international communications address the processing and distribution of such messages, rather than the effects of such programs upon the national culture. Yet it is the influence and probable effects of this type of communications that have made most Communist and developing countries view the development of unrestricted satellite communications, and the extension of any external communications technology to their territories, as a political threat.

This controversy over cultural identity can also be analyzed in the context of a larger pattern of major power or neocolonial domination. For example, the French position on the use of space broadcasting for the free flow of information—as expressed at UNESCO's twenty-fifth anniversary—seems to have been affected in part by their relationship with the French-speaking states of Africa and elsewhere. Similarly, the Soviet Union's position was determined, in part, by a concern not to permit the American lead in space communications activities to give the United States a stronger position to influence the Soviet's cultural and political relations with its socialistic countries.

Issues of cultural identity include, among others, computer-related, extraterritorial, decision-making processes. Such issues are becoming increasingly important as the result of communications satellite technology. It has been argued that the new mechanized data-control systems have led to the loss of political power, and that "the extranational exercise of power forces acceptance of the cultural norms, which the use of that power will reflect." According to Gotlieb, Dalfen, and Katz (1974), the results of a Delphi technique survey presented at the National Conference of the American Federation of

Information Processing Societies in June 1973, supports the hypothesis that "discounting differences in process, transborder use of computers will contribute to homogenization of cultural tastes and attitudes" (1974, p. 247).

National Integration

More and more countries are turning to satellites for communications within their own borders, for national political integration, and reduction of disparities between the geographic power centers and their peripheries. Perhaps the leaders of these countries realize that an information infrastructure that caters only to an information elite—and serves to widen the gap between the rich and poor, urban and rural, educated and uneducated—may have short-run advantages to elites already in power. Such gaps can lead to national disintegration and may not only limit the scope of economic growth, but also risk political upheaval.

Today, countries such as Algeria, Australia, Brazil, Canada, Colombia, India, Indonesia, Iran, Malaysia, Nigeria, Norway, Philippines, Sudan, Saudi Arabia, Spain, the United States, and Zaire are using—or planning to use—satellites for domestic communications. Realizing the above factors, and in an attempt to integrate planning for social, economic, and political problems, the Iranian government has launched a major campaign for national development in which telecommunication plays a considerable role. At the heart of Iran's new system is the Integrated National Telecommunication System (INTS), which will eventually link some 90 cities in every part of the country. This new communication system is being followed by the installation of a domestic satellite system and the creation of a communication research center for training. Given the region's strategic, military and economic importance, such national communication policies may eventually be followed in other Middle Eastern countries (Mowlana, 1976b).

The rising interest in national communications policies in recent years is largely due to the increased importance of communication as a factor in social struggles with political and economic consequences. For example, in the recent history of Canada, the dominant arena of social struggle has been the effort to preserve national unity in the face of severe geographical, cultural, and linguistic forces tending toward disintegration. The Canadian government has been in the forefront of communication policy research and the development of a satellite communications system. This can be explained by the perceived importance of mass communication as a means of countering influences of cultural diversity, geographical separation, and proximity to the United States. The prime motivating factor behind these policies has been the perceived need to disseminate Canadian national symbols to counter the forces of disintegration. The new Telesat Canada system is meant to facilitate linkage of geographically isolated regions, to bolster Canadian expertise in communication technology, and to ensure Canadian sovereignty over its distributional system for the future.

National Sovereignty

Recent discussions in the communication literature of international communication flow, and the issue of *cultural dependency*, illustrate the growing realization of the profound consequences of the revolution in communication technology, one of which is a transformation in the concept of national sovereignty. Debate over issues such as direct broadcasting from satellites is, in one sense, only the most recent chapter in the historic process in which governments have attempted to balance conflicting values for sovereignty on the one hand, and the free flow of information and ideas on the other. The resolution of this conflict in an earlier day, and with a more primitive technology, is exemplified by the configuration of the European telegraphic system a hundred years ago. Messages were telegraphed to every territorial outpost of one state, and then physically carried across the border for retransmission at the sovereign discretion of the other state. But in another sense, the new technologies have fundamentally altered the terms of this debate. The traditional notions of sovereignty, which have been expressed in *geographic or spatial* terms, are being redefined in terms of concerns about informational sovereignty or integrity.

The case of Canada—which was one of the first

countries to formulate a formal national communication policy highlighting the issues of sovereignty and similar concerns—is illustrative (Department of Communications, 1973). The new communication and computer technologies have served as powerful stimuli in the development of these national communications policies in Canada. Canada has assumed the task of tying together East and West, as well as several diverse cultures, while resisting the powerful economic and cultural pulls from its southern neighbor. Today, Canada feels the impact of the communication satellite, modern microwave, and the computer, which make possible ever more rapid transmission of even larger quantities of information across national borders, as well as more efficient distribution of foreign-developed information within its borders.

Activities facilitated by the new technology include the transborder transmission of television programs, the communication by satellite of information about the environment and natural resources, and the transfer via satellite, cable, or microwave of data from computers, data banks, or other sources in one country to a counterpart facility in another. Such developments raise new issues of property, economics, security, and human rights.

Canada has already acted in response to issues arising out of the first of these activities. Transborder television communication policy was most certainly a response to the growing cultural and economic domination of Canadian broadcasting by United States interests. (Department of Communications, 1973).

Another area related to the question of sovereignty is the operation of remote earth-sensing satellites—the so-called "spy in the sky" satellites—that have been operated by military authority in the United States and the Soviet Union for several years. Although there is no principle or rule of international law that makes it explicitly unlawful for one country to freely observe everything in another country, so long as it carries out its mission from beyond the limits of national sovereignty, obtaining information about another country from outer space may be interpreted as an act of conflict. Such operations, direct or indirect, might be designed to impede the exercise of the sovereignty of any state over its resources. Two U.S. NASA pro-

grams—Earth Resource Technology Satellites (ERTS) and Land Satellite (Landsat)—will undoubtedly raise serious questions in this regard.

The development of high power direct-broadcast communications satellites will also undoubtedly play a primary role in transforming perceptions of the nature of sovereignty.

Individual and Human Rights

Communication by satellite about man's environment and resources, and the capacity to obtain vital information in any area of the globe, involve questions of human rights, property, and the individual freedom. As a consequence of those developments, the relationships between the individual and information, and society and the individual, are rapidly changing.

Satellite remote-sensing, and the storage of data across national borders, may involve transmitting information which individuals might consider private. There has been considerable acknowledgment in Canadian publications of the increasing fears of Canadians about the establishment and abuse of data banks in the U.S. in which information about Canadians would be located. Whether such fears of abuse are well-founded or not, it is clear that great volumes of information about individuals, such as financial status and medical history, are being transferred across the Canadian border, usually as a result of corporate relationships or corporate mergers. Besides the fear about invasion of individual privacy, this southward flow of data is seen as further erosion of Canadian sovereignty and an aggravation of the imbalance of economic control between the United States and Canada.

Such are the issues being created and the incentives provided for a redefinition of the concept of national sovereignty. These same issues give rise to the debate over the value of sovereignty, on one hand, and the free flow of information on the other. The vastly increased capacities to transfer information over great distances, and the demonstrated cultural and economic powers that accrue to such a capacity, are shattering once-sacred beliefs about the free flow of information. A new balance seems desirable through bilateral or multilateral agreement, which will allow a state to regulate the flow of information into or out of its boundaries. This will also raise the important issue of how each country will perceive and define guidelines to protect the "best interests" of its citizens, either in a liberal or conservative sense. While some countries have traditionally supported the sanctity of the idea of unhindered flow of information, the evidence of the far-reaching impact of modern communications and computer technology on individual, as well as social and cultural, values dictates a serious reconsideration of that stance.

Political and Commercial Propaganda

The development of the capability of satellite communications in innumerable areas has also raised concern about political and commercial propaganda. In the past, aerial broadcasting has been used to violate national boundaries against the wishes of other governments. With the modern proliferation of satellite communication, this concern is even greater. Where the general population of a country cannot utilize printed media owing to illiteracy or economic factors—or is limited to censored information of its government—there is an increased capacity for using broadcasting for either maintaining political stability or fermenting revolution.

Many other countries are not so much concerned about political and psychological warfare propaganda as the possibility that a national culture and policy will be submerged by commercial and advertising messages. Implicit in this is the notion that commercial messages and consumer-oriented programs will lead to displacement of local products and industries, thus creating unfair economic competition. Further, this type of propaganda will generate a demand for consumer goods among the population, which may run contrary to national plans for social and economic development.

Although Resolution 428A of the Radio Regulations of the International Telecommunication Union (ITU) places limits on the transmission of satellite signals into countries that do not want them, it does not prohibit "unavoidable" messages, through so-called "spillover" transmission. Spillover describes the straying signals from one country's satellite beyond their designated geo-graphical target or intended frequency, to permit reception by the citizens of another nation (Thomas, 1970). A satellite signal intended for India may easily stray into Pakistan, Bangladesh, or Sri Lanka.

Although the ITU is concerned with the technical question of resolving the problems of interference and system coordination, there is often no clear line between what a country considers as technical interference and what it sees as international, political or cultural intrusion. Regulation of propaganda and spillover requires that the interests of the sending and receiving nations be balanced. Usually, the transmitter will seek fewer broadcasting restrictions and the receiver will want more, if the recipient country perceives unwanted signals as a national threat. In such an event, the nations must decide whether they believe there is a self-imposed legal right for international broadcasting, and if the effects of such broadcasting upon viewers differ sufficiently from other mass media sources, to justify specific regulations.

Where bargaining between sending and receiving countries is impossible or unlikely, regulation of community receivers for these satellite transmissions can serve as a means of controlling spillover as agents of the concerned government. There are negative aspects to this, however: (1) the expense of controlling reception to avoid unwanted signals is placed upon the entire population; (2) government control here may well sacrifice freedom of information to information considered "safe" from a national defense view; (3) progress in the evolution of other forms of information distribution may be impeded.

In India, where there is a lack of electricity, a need is seen for low-cost and maintenance-free battery-powered mobile receivers. Receivers of such a design would be less susceptible to government control, however. Hence, there would be a deterrent to their manufacture by governments of some developing countries, and the population will accordingly suffer from the loss of information.

There is little likelihood that propaganda will be regulated by international agreement. Although there are many justifications for such a conclusion, a primary reason is that an adequate definition of propaganda does not exist. Historically, international proposals to control propaganda have made little headway. The less powerful states have been the ones pressing for strong propaganda controls in order to avoid being victimized by the more powerful ones. Many weaker authoritarian states are willing to buy security at the cost of freedom of information and civil liberty, whereas many stronger democratic powers are prepared to risk some insecurity and political violence in order to maintain freedom of information and civil liberty. The pattern generally applies to stronger authoritarian states and weaker democratic states as well.

To overcome the propaganda problems of communications satellite, several possibilities for control have been suggested (Thomas, 1970):

1. *Mutual technical-administrative control.* One example would be dual polarization of the satellite signal and use of opposing polarization in the earth stations of adjacent countries. This would require voluntary accord between the affected countries, which may well be an unlikely occurance in the propaganda context.

2. *Technological control.* The government might cut off reception of unwanted signals at its receiving stations or allow only home or community receivers capable of receiving approved messages or channels to be imported or manufactured locally. Further, conventional jamming could also be employed.

3. *Legal control.* Examples of such controls might include: (a) prior consent by the countries whose boundaries are within the radius of the signal; (b) a code of conduct or a ban on certain types of propaganda; and/or (c) a conduct or a contextual approach—wherein policy guidelines are established for various situational factors in which propaganda occurs.

Propaganda can have a positive side. It has been argued that certain forms of persuasion can be a permissable means of influencing foreign events, especially in the context of diplomacy. Indeed, propaganda can sometimes be a logical extension of diplomacy by peaceful means.

Effects on Decision-making Process

One of the most important implications of com-

munications satellite technology is that once it is linked to computers and computerized data banks, it can alter the locale in which information is kept. Thus the gap between the center and the periphery of communications network is closed, and information can be accessible to individuals hundreds or thousands of miles away. This process permits instantaneous, regional computer-data traffic and serves to eliminate the need for national autonomous data repositories. Since data accumulation and storage are part of the process of decision making, the physical location and diffusion of data would both be important factors in regulating access to information and, therefore, in affecting the decision-making ability of an institution or a country.

The issue of control of information and the impact on national sovereignty arises from concerns about national decision making and cultural identity, as well as national security and the circumstances under which social policies are formulated. Canadian perceptions about the storage of Canadian data in the United States contain these elements, as expressed by a group of Canadian communications experts (Gotlieb, Dalfen, & Katz, 1974):

> The transfer of Canadian data to American data banks means that potentially, at least, Americans will have the means to make decisions about Canadians that depend on that data. Conversely, to the extent that Canadians lack data about themselves—whether because they lack the computer capacity needed to effectively use the data or because important parts of the data are withheld by another state—they will be unable to make important decisions affecting their future. (p. 247)

Education and Social Planning

The possible use of broadcast satellite technology for education and family planning is being explored today by scientists in both developed and developing countries. The satellite experiments that are being conducted—and those which are being planned for the future—may produce a new concept of education. Combined with growing cable systems and other technology, satellite technology may be the heart of a new revolution in education.

The type and amount of information that can be

provided from greater distances by such a system could well require the rethinking of the form that the educational system itself should take. For example, the Indian site experiment with the ATS-F communications satellite may provide the answers to many of the questions that communication experts, educators, engineers and others have asked about the operational feasibility of using satellites in developed and less developed countries. Consequently, the value of the experiment extends beyond the dollar investment for immediate results, because the knowledge gained can provide guidelines for policy, design of hardware and software, and the economics of system development, implementation, and operation.

One of the early reports of viewers' response to programs presented under the satellite instructional television experiment (SITE) of India, dispels several myths about the awareness and interests of the people in the countryside. The growing volume of mail received from the viewers at Akashawani Bhavan area, for example, underscoies the quest for detail relevant to the day-to-day life of these people. The authorities believe that the suggestions and feedback received by the viewers are extremely helpful in giving a new direction to the "teacher in the sky," as well as to their efforts to persuade the villagers to send their children to school, plan their families, keep their surroundings clean, and learn how to use fertilizer and pesticides.

Interestingly, according to one report, not many of the SITE viewers desire to see exclusively entertainment program, such as feature films. In fact, not a single one of the scores of letters received during the first six months had asked for showing of a feature film. Instead the requests were for a repeat of a classroom educational explanation ranging from the use of pesticide to instruction in cricket playing (Times of India, 1975).

CONCLUSIONS

Some key political and social implications of communications satellite applications have been outlined in this paper. It has been shown that communications satellite technology plays a direct role in national and international political systems, a role intimately related to the distribution of power and the exercise of social control.

The implications of the new communications technology in terms of international relations are immense. A vast new capacity to communicate will be available through communications satellites, but its potential may not be realized unless the nations of the world are somehow able to cooperate in an effort to write rules or procedures which avoid technological and political conflict and permit the new innovation to develop in an orderly way. The growth of communications satellites has required a certain amount of international cooperation, but it represents only a fraction of that which will be necessary to encourage and protect the growth of worldwide space communications in the future.

Problems of dependency, cultural identity, national integration, political and sociological propaganda, individual privacy, human rights, national sovereignty, the decision-making process, and social policy are among the matters of broad international concern. Because of this development, international and national political systems are going through a profound change. For example, it has been demonstrated that the influence of communications satellite technology is transforming the traditional views about sovereignty, which has always been expressed in spatial terms, to a new kind of perception which may be called *informational sovereignty*.

The analytical framework of a communications technology cycle is a useful means of showing the relation between control of information distribution and national sovereignty. Absolute sovereignty in the formation and distribution of messages is assured only when a nation controls both the hardware channels via which the messages are sent and the necessary know-how to effectively program its messages for distribution.

There is, thus, a series of interlocking demands resulting from the advent of satellite communications which are emerging at national, regional, and global levels. They include problems of sharing the overcrowded radio frequencies in geosynchronous orbit, space policy, and long-term investment decisions in communications software and hardware. The immediate effect is the struggle now developing to prevent a single country's monopoly of these developments. The development and implementation of communications satellite technology, in a sense, reflects these struggles and gives rise to a wide variety of concerns on the part of great powers, industrialized countries, and developing countries.

Until now, international communications have been regulated with remarkable smoothness through organizations such as the International Telecommunications Union, the Universal Postal Union, INTELSAT, and others. Even during the coldest episodes of cold war, it remained possible to agree, for example, on postage rates and frequency allocations for radio and television. But the growth of the communications satellite is beginning to generate enormous administrative and political pressures, and the old machinery is already creaking under the strain.

In the development of communications satellites, competition for geo-stationary orbital locations has been increasing. The United States, the undisputed leader in the field for the past decade, is now facing the challenge, and sometimes criticism, of not only the Soviet Union and the socialist countries, but also the industrialized and developing countries. The Soviet Union, having the *Molniya* system in operation for many years, is now establishing several STATSIONAR satellites in geosynchronous orbit for global distribution, and plans call for a total of 10 to be launched by 1980. The next few years will decide what will be the relationship between the Soviet Union and INTELSAT.

With this substantial beginning, it is interesting to speculate on what the next 10 years will bring. A number of nations are planning their own communications satellites for domestic purposes. An even larger number of countries are beginning national satellite communications systems by building their own earth stations and leasing transponders from INTELSAT. Two new satellite services— aeronautical and maritime—will soon receive decisive tests of economic viability. Broadcast satellites, not only in the field of television, but also radio, can also be anticipated. Finally, the present trend of rapid expansion in domestic and international use of telephone and data can be expected to continue through larger and more powerful communications satellites.

In summary, then, the next decade will be an extraordinarily active political period for satellite communications. It is clear that, as with other kinds of technology, our understanding of, and planning for, the impact of communications satellites has lagged far behind the technical capabilities. Political problems relating to international signals crossing national boundaries, rewriting of copyright conventions to make them applicable to an entirely new technology, drafting an international convention which can guarantee equal access to the new facilities, centralizing or regionalizing authority with responsibility for policy planning and coordination, and establishing an international or global center for developmental television for educational purposes, are among the areas urgently requiring international cooperation and solution.

NOTE

This paper was selected as one of the outstanding reports prepared for the annual meeting of the International Communication Association, Berlin, 1977.

REFERENCES

Department of Communications. Proposals for a communications policy for Canada—A position paper for the Government of Canada. Unpublished report, Ottawa, Ontario, Canada, 1973.

GOTLEIB, A., DALFEN, C., & KATZ, K. The transborder transfer of information by communications and computer systems: Issues and approaches to guiding principles. *The American Journal of International Law*, 1974, 68.

MOWLANA, H. A paradigm for source analysis in events data research: Mass media and the problems of validity. *International Interaction*, 1975, 2.

MOWLANA, H. The multinational corporation and the diffusion of technology. In A. A. Said and L. R. Simons (Eds.), The new sovereigns: Multinational corporations as world powers, Englewood Cliffs, N.J.: Prentice-Hall, 1975a.

MOWLANA, H. Who covers America? *Journal of Communication*, 1975a, 25, pp. 86-91.

MOWLANA, H. A paradigm for comparative mass media analysis. In H.D. Fischer and J.C. Merrill (Eds.), International and intercultural communication, New York: Hastings, 1976a.

MOWLANA, H. Trends in Middle Eastern societies. In G. Gerbner (Ed.), *Mass communications policies in changing cultures.* New York: Wiley, 1976b.

POOL, I.S. Direct-broadcast satellite and cultural integrity. *Society*, 1975, 12.

SCHILLER, H.I. *Mass communications and American empire.* Boston: Beacon, 1971.

SCHILLER, H.I. *The mind managers.* Boston: Beacon, 1973.

THOMAS, G.L. Approaches to controlling propaganda and spillover from direct broadcast satellites. *Stanford Journal of International Studies*, 1970, 5.

The Times of India. Growing volume of mail from viewers of SITE. Ahmedabad edition, December 17, 1975.

VARIS, T. International inventory of television programme structure and the flow of TV programmes between nations. Tampere, Finland: Center of Mass Communications, Tampere University, 1973.

WELLS, A. *Picture-tube Imperialism?* New York: Orbis, 1975.

POLITICAL COMMUNICATION
Theory and Research: An Overview
Selected Studies

POLITICAL COMMUNICATION THEORY AND RESEARCH: AN OVERVIEW

DAN NIMMO
University of Tennessee, Knoxville

Scholars have been interested in relating communication and politics at least since Aristotle's analyses of deliberative, forensic, and epideictic modes of public discourse. Gordon (1971, p. 54) dates the concern earlier, to overtones in the first recorded instance of persuasion, i.e., Eve's offer of the apple to her husband in *Genesis*, 3, 6. Be that as it may, a focus upon communication in generating and regulating social conflict—and in achieving social order and/or disorder—is relatively recent. The purpose of this overview is to describe political communication as a field of inquiry which focuses the research and theory-building energies of scholars from many disciplines, chiefly from mass communication, speech communication, and political science, but including sociologists, social psychologists, and others as well. Brevity requires that the discussion be general and taxonomic rather than detailed and evaluative. Instead of selecting a small number of studies of political communication and reporting the research questions and findings with respect to them, the overview illustrates the diversity of topic areas that engage students in this evolving and dynamic field. References cited are but a suggestive sampling of the burgeoning literature.

EMERGENCE OF A FIELD

In their classic work on inquiry, Dewey and Bentley distinguish three subject matters of science—physical, physiological, and behavioral (1949, p. 64ff.). As inquiry proceeds, scientists develop techniques of investigation, specifications of interesting phenomena, and distinctive names for their efforts; these activities partition general subject matters into scholarly disciplines. But as Swanson notes (1976) these disciplinary commitments may confine rather than facilitate understanding. If the urge for mutual collaboration is stronger than

disciplinary chauvinism, scholars forge a multidisciplinary effort. Such is the defining attribute of political communication. The field, notes Swanson, is not a discipline distinguished by manner of explanation but a study guided by the phenomena it explains. It is a field exceedingly diverse in theoretic formulations, research questions, and methods of inquiry that transcend the boundaries of the separate disciplines from which it draws.

A variety of research traditions contribute to the emergence of political communication as a field. Four are noteworthy. The first consists of emphases scholars in the era surrounding two World Wars placed upon propaganda in forming public opinion. What appeared as striking, and frightening, rhetorical successes of Lenin in Russia, Hitler in Germany, and Mussolini in Italy provoked detailed analyses of political persuasion. Scholarly monographs and articles in the tradition of propaganda research appeared (Doob, 1950). Texts in public opinion published after World War II devoted major sections to propaganda (Doob, 1948). And, content analysis was a prominent research tool (Lasswell & Leites, 1949).

Political communication also borrowed from the study of voting. Scholars were impressed by survey research undertaken by the Bureau of Applied Social Research at Columbia University (Lazarsfeld, Berelson, & Gaudet, 1944; Berelson, Lazarsfeld, & McPhee, 1954) and the Survey Research Center/Center for Political Studies of the University of Michigan (Campbell, Gurin, & Miller, 1954; Campbell, Converse, Miller, & Stokes, 1960, 1966). The bulk of "the voting studies" raised serious doubts regarding the notion that campaign communication influences citizens' voting decisions.

A related and third research antecedent for political communication was the study of the effects of mass communication. Inquiries produced evidence of minimal consequences of communication on political behavior. Selectivity in exposure, perception, and recall of mass communication made for reinforcement or certainly no more than minor change of political predispositions. Conversion was unlikely (Klapper, 1961; Weiss, 1969). Many media effect studies relied upon experimental techniques used by social psychologists to examine attitude change. Although minimizing the impact of communication upon attitude change, persuasion studies nonetheless provided documentation for how best to "influence people." Texts and monographs summarized the relative effects of presentation of issues, ordering of arguments, social groups, audience characteristics, persuader credibility, etc. upon attitude change (Abelson, 1959).

The fourth major tradition of inquiry underlying the emergence of the field of political communication derived from the long-standing interest of scholars in exploring the interplay between the press, government, and public opinion. Lippmann (1922) typified the early concerns, but not the totality of viewpoints, of both journalists and political scientists. As noted later, this tradition contributes various research foci regarding the political effects of the news media.

Recent research has spawned revisionist points of view regarding the conclusions drawn from the four principal research traditions of political communication. In some instances these revisions arise from within the tradition itself, as, for instance, contemporary voting studies stressing the active rather than passive responses of voters to campaigns (Mendelsohn & O'Keefe, 1976), and recent descriptions of political effects of the media (Seymour-Ure, 1974). In other cases, as noted in later portions of this overview, revisions of conventional wisdom derive from asking questions in different ways and/or examining different types of data than traditional studies (Stephenson, 1967). In still other instances, a scholar approaches a point of earlier concern, from a perspective different from that emphasized in traditional studies. For example, Ellul's (1964) analysis of the role of propaganda in a technological society derives more from the classic tradition of sociology reminiscent of Marx and Durkheim (combined with a point of view in Christian ethics), than from previous propaganda analyses.

In characterizing the stream of political communication research that flows from traditional tributaries, several organizing frameworks are available. Chaffee (1975), for example, has used a systems model of politics formulated in the writings of political scientist David Easton (1965) to explain patterns in the diffusion of political information. Fagan (1966) opts for the structural-functional model derived by Gabriel Almond (Almond & Coleman, 1960, pp. 3-64) for cross-national study of communication networks, patterns of media use, and the distribution and flow of political images. One could adapt either Deutsch's early efforts in studying nationalism and social communication (1953), or his cybernetic model (1963) that examines all of politics as communication rather than focusing upon political communication as but one function of a political system. Other frameworks abound (Bauer, Pool, & Dexter, 1963; Davison, 1965; Doob, 1961).

A FRAMEWORK

This overview, however, adapts Lasswell's (1948; pp. 37-51) deceptively simple, yet serviceable, approach. Taking Lasswell's formulation that a "convenient way" to think of communication is to ask the question "Who Says What in Which Channel to Whom With What Effects?" the study of political communication examines (1) political communicators; (2) the use of languages, symbols, and techniques; (3) the media of political communication; (4) audiences of political actors; and (5) the effects of communication in politics.

CHARACTERIZING POLITICAL COMMUNICATORS

The research concentrating upon identifying key political communicators and describing their attributes, beliefs, values, and motives draws much from the tradition of propaganda analysis. Writing in the 1930s, Lasswell, for instance, distinguished between (1) the propagandist, a communication specialist skilled in techniques of social control, (2) the principal, who finances the propagandist's appeals, and (3) the laymen, whose impulses are beset by cross-purposes so as to enhance the propagandist's "rational" pursuit of aims "thoughtfully defined in advance" (1935, pp. 188, 190-93). Borrowing from the works of political scientists, social psychologists, and communication scholars it is possible to extend the typology of political communicators beyond Lasswell's specialists, principals, and laymen. Contemporary research typically examines actors in one or more of three categories of key political communicators—*as politicians, professional communicators, or activists.*

Katz (1973) contrasts two types of politician: (1) the partisan representative of a group and (2) the ideologist, or policy formulator. The former seeks prestige, privilege, or power for the advance of a group's cause, the latter appeals to people's values in the pursuit of reforms or revolutionary change. Communication is an essential element of the performance of both the representative and ideologist role, be the actors elected, appointed, or career public servants; be they executive, legislative, or judicial officials. Studies of the communication plans, styles, and motives of politicians in the representative role extend both to office-holders—including, for example, the president of the United States (Minow, Martin, & Mitchell, 1973). Congress (Blanchard, 1974), policy administrators (Chittick, 1970), and judicial officers (Wasby, 1970)—and to candidates for office (see Kaid, Sanders, & Hirsch, 1974, for a comprehensive and annotated bibliography). The emphasis in studies of ideologists has been upon personality-based origins of communication style, rhetoric, or motives. Thus, Wolfenstein (1971) explores the personality and styles of Lenin, Trotsky, and Gandhi; Barber (1972) relates presidential style to presidential character; and Duncan (1962, pp. 225-249) describes the motives underlying Adolph Hitler's appeals.

The revolution in communication technology stimulated the emergence of the professional communicator as a distinctive social role (Carey, 1969). Professional communicators mediate between sources and audiences (e.g., officials and citizens, candidates and voters) by manipulating symbols to "translate the language, values, interests, ideas and purposes of one group into an idiom acceptable to a

differentiated speech community" (Carey, 1969, pp. 27-28). The politician's vocation is politics, and communication is an essential tool; for the professional communicator politics is but one setting for plying the vocation of communicator. Researchers have examined two principal sets of professional communicators in politics: (1) the journalist informing, explaining, and prescribing happenings of a political nature and (2) the promoter (government public information officer, press secretary, public relations person, political campaign consultant, etc.) advancing the cause of a political group, party, personality, or interest. Studies of political journalists include Rosten's seminal (1937) work on the Washington press corps and updatings (Nimmo, 1964; Rivers, 1964); Tunstall (1970, 1971) provides insights into the political role of specialist correspondents in British politics. The promoter has been extensively examined in many settings: as an adjunct to government public information functions (Schiller, 1973), as specialists in election campaigns (Kaid et al., 1974), and as propagandists promoting leaders and policies (Doob, 1950).

The third category of political communicators includes all other political activists. First, spokespersons for private and public interest groups, e.g., the president of the AFL-CIO, chairman of the Democratic National Committee, John Gardner of Common Cause, Ralph Nader, etc. Comparatively few studies emphasize the communication aspects of such leadership. These include Rosenau's (1963) examination of the social backgrounds, perceptions, evaluations, and communication channels of national opinion-makers; a view of congressional lobbying as a communication process (Milbrath, 1963); a study of communication patterns within political parties (Eldersveld, 1964); and various community power and elite studies (see Harley & Svara, 1972, for a bibliography). Second, there are *opinion leaders,* including trusted persons to whom friends, co-workers, colleagues, and others turn for political advice in the *two-step flow of information* (Katz & Lazarsfeld, 1955). Although estimated to be a minority of the adult population, opinion leaders influence voting, attitude and opinion formation (Lazarsfeld et al., 1944), and the diffusion of political knowledge (Chaffee, 1975).

Many studies of politicians, professionals, and

activists as political communicators echo the common theme that communication skills, capacities, opportunities, etc. are important to political leadership. Implicitly or explicitly, research regarding political communicators reflects a distinction between *task* and *emotional* leadership (Stogdill, 1974). Researchers distinguish between leaders who communicate, on the one hand, to achieve material, tangible ends—the "all too executive" leader (Jennings's, 1960, pp. 19-31)—or Klapp's (1964) "organizational leader," and, on the other hand, "symbolic leaders" (Klapp, 1964) who communicate to achieve status, prestige, and reputation, or to fulfill the function of a condensation symbol (Sapir, 1930, p. 493).

Research examining political organizational leaders in formal positions of authority, such as public officeholders, emphasizes social backgrounds and recruitment patterns associated with communicator roles. A point of focus is the elitist-pluralist controversy: Is American political leadership an interlocking, self-perpetuating elite (Dye, 1976) or a complex of competing special interest groups, each dominant in a policy sphere (Dahl & Lindblom, 1953)? That controversy, however, has not been confined solely to charting the social characteristics of officeholders; recent studies raise questions about the elitist character of the communication establishment (Seiden, 1974). Although elitist and pluralist interpretations also enter into the study of recruitment patterns, that literature centers primarily upon the factors associated with the activation, nomination, and selection of leaders. The general thesis is that there is a social bias to leadership recruitment, at least in the United States, with upper middle-class ranks favored (Czudnowski, 1975).

Studies of symbolic leaders emphasize popular perceptions of political officeholders and office-seekers. A number of these studies, for example, identify forces contributing to the rise and fall of the popularity of the U.S. president, such as presidential appeals to patriotism during national crises, economic downswings, the general tenor of news as good and bad, or simply time (Mueller, 1973; Brody & Page, 1975; Stimson, 1976). Research concerned with citizens' perceptions of office-seekers tries to clarify the conceptual, methodolog-ical, and substantive issues surrounding discussions of the images of political candidates. Studies in the United States, Great Britain, and other electoral systems raise such questions as whether images are most appropriately conceived as stimuli—qualities projected by candidates—or are perceiver determined and sourced in voters' preconceptions. Also considered are questions as to whether such images are relatively permanent or shift during campaigns, whether they emphasize personal or nonpersonal attributes, and whether they are products of contemporary campaign technology (Nimmo & Savage, 1976).

SYMBOLS, LANGUAGES, AND PERSUASION

If students of political communication explore the "Who?" of Lasswell's formulation by concentrating upon political communicators in leadership roles, they examine the "Says What?" through two lines of inquiry: political linguistics and political persuasion.

Studies in political linguistics (Graber, 1976) are relatively recent. They derive from propaganda analysis, the concern with symbols represented in symbolic interactionist (Mead, 1934) and dramatistic perspectives (Burke, 1966) and both psycholinguistics (Miller & McNeill, 1969) and sociolinguistics (Robinson, 1972). Students of political linguistics identify the functions, types, and styles of political discourse. Three general functions emerge: (1) the use of political symbols by ruling elites to achieve mass quiescence and/or arousal to advance elitist interests (Edelman, 1964); (2) employment of symbols on behalf of status enhancement, as in Gusfield's (1963) description of the prohibition movement as a symbolic crusade; and (3) the use of symbols as an expressive outlet for frustrations and anxieties or to display self-images, patriotism, loyalties, chauvinism, etc. (Himmelstrand, 1960).

Sociologist Claus Mueller (1973) and political scientist David V. J. Bell (1975) identify forms of language unique to politics. Mueller notes how governments restrict full public discussion by distorting communication through: (1) directed communication in government policies, to structure language (as when a policy of "detente" is relabeled "peace through strength"); (2) arrested communication arising from the restricted speech codes of deprived populations; and (3) constrained communication using language to serve selfish interests of private and governing elites. Bell classifies power, influence, and authority talk as distinctive types of political language and describes the permeation of these forms throughout all phases of everyday activity. Political styles, including alternative ways to say things as opposed to what is said, also interest students of political communication. Edelman (1964) has been influential in demonstrating how hortatory, legal, administrative, and bargaining styles structure mass responses to leaders and thereby contribute to arousal or quiescence among mass audiences.

Research emphases in political persuasion emerge from all of the leading traditions in the study of political communication. Propaganda analysis stresses purposes and techniques of persuasion. Voting and media effect studies address questions of the effectiveness of political persuasion. And studies of government-press relations raise questions about how government and news media influence public opinion. In their seminal model, Westley and MacLean (1957) contrast purposive and nonpurposive messages, as well as affective and cognitive meanings of symbols. The bulk of research in political persuasion accepts these distinctions. Persuasion research examines whether purposive messages achieve affective changes in attitudes. Scholars designate nonpurposive messages resulting in cognitive change as "information" rather than "persuasive" effects (Becker, McCombs, & McLeod, 1975). Stephenson (1967) draws parallel distinctions between *communication*—which deals with the transfer, formation, and change of self-referent opinions—and *information*, the supply, storage, and retrieval of facts.

Although some paradigms view persuasion and information as aspects of a single, indivisible process (McGuire, 1973), the typical posture regards the intent of persuasion as attitude change (Sears & Whitney, 1973). Studies explore three modes of political persuasion—propaganda, mass advertising, and rhetoric. Contemporary students (Ellul, 1964; Stephenson, 1967) emphasize the organized character of propaganda. Propaganda appeals to persons as members of structured groups—political parties, institutions, communities, etc. Although sharing with mass advertising the characteristic of being one-to-many communication, propaganda reaches the individual as a specific group member. Advertising, in contrast, speaks to the person as an anonymous unit in the larger mass. Both differ from rhetoric, the one-to-one, reciprocal process of identifying speaker and audience in communion (Burke, 1969). The party rally, political spot commercial, and televised chat of a candidate with constituents are propaganda, advertising, and rhetoric respectively. The first is a technique of organized social control, the second of convergent selectivity (Stephenson, 1967), and the third a negotiated "para-social" relationship between communicator and audience (Rosengren & Windahl, 1972). The tricotomy of persuasive techniques parallels the principal media of political communication—organizational, mass, and interpersonal.

THE MEDIA OF POLITICAL COMMUNICATION

Although often examined in isolation, students of political communication consider interpersonal, organization, and mass media together. Studies of face-to-face communication in politics probe the character of opinion leadership, interpersonal discussion in electoral campaigns, the two-step flow of communication, and information diffusion. Graber (1976), for example, explores the interpersonal give-and-take of political actors in public assemblies and small bargaining groups, while Edelstein (1973) investigates the role of interpersonal communication in decision-making. As yet, however, relatively few studies capitalize fully upon insights derived by applying such notions as coorientation, the game-like aspects of political conversation, the homophily principle, and self-disclosure.

Public organizations, especially of a bureaucratic character, offer opportunities for generating and testing propositions regarding both internal and external organization communication. Downs (1967, pp. 112-31) provides a propositional inventory describing communication networks—formal, sub-formal, and interpersonal—in governmental bureaus. Yet, as Etzioni (1961, p. 137) remarks, much of current thinking about internal communication in government structures is a mixture of theoretical speculation and direct observation rather than a distillation of replicated empirical findings. Studies of communication between public organizations and their surroundings focus chiefly on the functions of external communication—consultation with legislative bodies, positioning for budgetary and operating purposes, inter-agency bargaining, the use of publicity as an enforcement device, exposure of internal disputes for wider resolution, enhancement of an agency head's prestige, etc. Katz and Danet (1973, p. 669), looking at a single aspect of organizations' external communication—official-client contact—develop useful typologies of the interrelations between organization and interpersonal communication.

Students of political communication emphasize the political implications of the mass media far more than those of either interpersonal or organization channels. The two principal research foci have been the role of mass media in political campaigns and the relationship between governments and the news media. In addition to a growing number of studies of media effects, discussed later, the campaign focus has been upon technique: planning televised campaigns, alternative media modes of political advertising, and techniques of projection (See Kaid et al., 1974 for a bibliography). Although most studies successfully identify the techniques employed in contemporary elections, few answer the relatively simple question of what works *generally* in campaigning. Recent research suggests breakthroughs (Woelfel, Holmes, Fink, Cody, & Taylor, 1976); however, considerable testing remains. Some studies are campaign-specific and treat each election as so unique that generalizations about effects across campaigns is difficult (Kessel, 1968). Others are technique-specific and explore the impact of but one of a variety of ways of influencing voters—direct mail, canvassing, telephone contact, newspaper editorials, television commercials, etc. And, studies that transcend single campaigns and techniques unfortunately are too impressionistic for reliable generalizations

about campaign persuasion (Wyckoff, 1968; Napolitan, 1972).

Scholars probing government-news media relations indicate a wide variety of research interests (summarized in the typology provided by Rivers, Miller & Gandy, 1975). Illustrative of the range of studies are those of relations between public officials and journalists (Sigal, 1973); the scope of governmental publicity and secrecy in a democracy (Rourke, 1961); political implications of newsmaking (Roshco, 1975); partisan and legal problems of the press (Krieghbaum, 1972); the interplay of politics and economics in the development of the press (Hoyer, Hadenius, & Weibull, 1975); the burgeoning concern with the political consequences of television news (Patterson & McClure, 1976); organizational factors influencing the reporting of news (Epstein, 1973); perspectives on the world reinforced and repeated by the process of gathering news material (Halloran, Elliott, & Murdock, 1970); and implications for the flow of information between and among nations inherent in the growth of international television broadcasting (Varis, 1974). Reviewing and classifying numerous studies, Rivers et al. (1975) specify the major failings: too much focus on individual attitudes and individual characteristics; attention to attitudes instead of actual behavior; reliance on interviews, questionnaires, or other subject-supplied information; and taking-for-granted of theories about governmental operations.

AUDIENCES OF POLITICAL COMMUNICATION

As with any field of scientific inquiry, political communication has alternative theories, methods, and findings. Conflicting theoretical postures and conclusions are drawn from studies of political communicators, messages, and media. But the major controversies in the contemporary study of political communication revolve about types of political audiences, what they are like, and effects of political messages upon them.

Turn-of-the-century research in political communication generally dealt with audiences of a "public" variety. There was a tendency to regard the politician, professional communicator, or political activist as speaking to "the public." The focus was "public opinion" (Bryce, 1900). With the advent of opinion polls and survey research, there was an inclination to equate the definition of *public* with the audience polls sample (Nisbet, 1975). Gradually conceptual distinctions emerged, three of which emphasize different facets of public opinion: (1) *popular* opinion, or the aggregate of individual opinions expressed on specific issues, or the public opinion measured in polls and surveys; (2) *mass* opinion, the sometimes measured and sometimes intuited consensus regarding political beliefs, institutions, procedures, and policies—as, for example, the liberal democratic, Lockean political culture of the United States measured by Devine (1972), or the traditionalistic, moralistic, and individualistic political cultures identified by Elazar (1966); and (3) *publics* opinion, or the opinions of organized and unorganized political interests.

There are also competing schools of thought about the behavior of political audiences. The first—the dependent voter model (Pomper, 1975), the mechanistic model (Swanson, 1976), or model of the passive citizen (Campbell, 1962)—posits that people react to political stimuli in fixed, stable, almost conditioned ways on the basis of enduring predispositions. Voting and media effect studies published through the mid-1960s revealed a curious relationship between such audiences and political communication. Persons most likely to be interested and involved in politics and, hence, to pay attention to political messages, were least likely to be influenced by those messages (except, perhaps, insofar as appeals reinforced partisan predispositions and preferences). Alternately, those most "persuadable" through political communication—weakly identified partisans or independents with no identifications at all—were least likely to attend to political media and messages (Converse, 1962). In either case, the stable political attitudes of audience members, not political communication, shaped behavior.

Contemporary research offers an alternative characterization of political audiences—i.e., the responsible electorate (Key, 1966), the responsive voter (Pomper, 1975), or the active perceiver

(Swanson, 1976). Vaguely akin to earlier symbolic interactionist perspectives (Blumer, 1959), the viewpoint is of a citizen who actively takes account of political messages, creates meanings through a process of imagery and interpretation, and constructs a line of meaningful conduct in response. Assuming that "human perception is not a passive registering process but an active organizing and structuring process" (Carey & Kreiling, 1974, p. 227), it is a small step to argue that audiences heed messages that gratify perceived needs, a hallmark of the "uses and gratifications" approach (Katz, Blumler, & Gurevitch, 1974, pp. 19-32).

THE EFFECTS OF POLITICAL COMMUNICATION

Differing assumptions about the nature of audiences contribute to contrasting assessments of the effects of communication in politics. An emphasis on passive audience orientations parallels what Blumer (1959, p. 197) termed the "variable analysis" approach to the study of media effects. Given such a posture, one strives to identify the categories of variables, both attitudinal (partisanship ideology, class consciousness, personality, etc.) and ascriptive/achievement (sex, race, age, education level, occupation, income, etc.) that are associated with particular responses or nonresponses to political communicators, messages, and media. In the absence of any concern with active interpretation by audience members, scholars assume that political behavior is a direct product of predispositions or social forces. *What do the media do to people?* (Katz, 1959) is the key question, and the answer depends upon the relatively fixed qualities of political audiences. As Katz notes, however, the view of an active audience suggests a different question, or at least an added one. *What do people do with the media?* People—and not their attitudes, traits, or sociodemographic characteristics—are independent variables in more recent efforts to pinpoint media effects.

Students of political communication, whether conducting variable analysis (as in the voting studies) or needs and gratifications research (as in recent investigations, such as Blumler & McQuail,

1969, and Mendelsohn & O'Keefe, 1976), have investigated the effect of communication upon political socialization, participation and voting, agenda-building, and policy-making. Political socialization studies are extensive in number and volume (Dennis, 1973) and deny brief summary. One can generally assert, however, that interpersonal communication within the family, school, and peer group plays an important role in a child's acquisition of emotional attachments to abstract political figures and institutions, especially to such authority figures as the president, and affective identification with political parties (Easton & Dennis, 1969). Mass media are a major source of political information for young people and have vital cognitive effects, but they are less influential than interpersonal communication in developing affective orientations or producing overt political activity (Atkin, 1975). Organizational communication—in school, political parties, labor unions, etc.—influences socialization, but it is uncertain how much. Hess and Torney (1967) attribute influence to the school in socializing preadults to a variety of political orientations; Jennings and Niemi (1974), however, doubt the impact of certain types of school experience, especially the civics curriculum.

The literature on political participation is also extensive and growing. Recent research centers upon a dual question: What ways do citizens participate in political life and what is the effect of participation upon how governments respond to citizens? Exploring the first question, Verba and Nie (1972) factor analyzed survey data and derived four principal modes of participation among Americans: campaign activity, communal activity—for example, working on local problems—voting, and contacting public officials. Their research confirms the hypothesis that citizens of higher social and economic status participate more in politics, a finding established many times in many nations. From this, Verba and Nie (1972) fashion a relatively simple model in which socioeconomic standing shapes civic attitudes and attitudes shape participation levels. Insofar as participation is associated with influence, those in the upper strata are more likely to influence officials. Thus, there is a class bias in access to and influence on policy-making.

Participation studies also test the effects of communication on promoting political activity. Many of the early ones (Hyman & Sheatsley, 1947) were pessimistic on this point, but Mendelsohn (1973) recently has provided a more optimistic view.

Research pertaining to the complex interplay between political communication and specific forms of participation, such as voting, suggests the following proposition: Communication makes voters aware of candidates and informs them about those candidates (cognitive effects), is less influential in directly changing how people feel about candidates and issues but may enhance positive or negative responses for some persons (affective orientations), and is but one of many factors persuading people how to vote (conative effects). McClure and Patterson (1974) found that political commercials change people's beliefs about candidates; exposure to television news, however, had no direct, independent effect. Other studies indicate that political commercials do not alter popular feelings about candidates (although changing their beliefs), because voters distort the contents of advertising to agree with their predispositions (Donohue, 1973-74). And, tests of the claim that exposure to the media is a major source of ticket-splitting in the 1970s specify different influences for each medium (Atwood & Sanders, 1975).

An increasing number of researchers have identified "the ability of the media to structure our world for us" (Becker, McCombs, & McLeod, 1975, p. 38) as one of the most important effects of modern mass communication. Research on the *agenda-setting* function of political communication dates back at least to Lippmann (1922), but more recently offers a variety of promising inquiries related to policy-making processes. (For a brief yet comprehensive review of the major studies and themes of agenda-setting research, see McCombs, 1976; see also Cobb & Elder, 1972, for the policy implications of agenda-setting.) Aside from agenda-setting, the policy-making functions of political communication explored by scholars center upon linkages between public opinion and policy-making, the second aspect of the dual question of research into participation mentioned above. The linkage question takes a number of forms, but two are illustrative. First, some scholars are interested in the means leaders and followers use to communicate with one another. Luttbeg (1968) offers a variety of linkage models: (1) a rational-activist model maximizing citizen participation; (2) the political parties model emphasizing electoral institutions in political communication; (3) the pressure groups model that public opinion consists of the views of organized opinion publics; (4) the sharing model which says that officials hold the same basic beliefs, values, and expectations as citizens and express them through policies; and (5) the role-playing model linking citizen and official through the development of mutual expectations of one another's sentiments, wants, and demands. Second, some scholars endeavor to specify the function of public opinion in policy-making. Graber (1968), for example, formulates a model of the flow of opinion in making foreign policies. She concludes that perhaps the greatest public opinion influence on governmental decision-making is "the sharing of a common political culture by the people and those whom they freely elect to public office" (Graber, 1968, p. 363). Graber's study thus offers support for Luttbeg's *sharing model;* however, *role-playing* and other models are also useful ways of conceptualizing the opinion-policy process (Bauer, et al., 1963).

METHODS IN THE STUDY OF POLITICAL COMMUNICATION

As it has evolved into a distinctive field, political communication has been influenced by the methods and techniques associated with the various traditions of inquiry underlying its origins. (The reader should consult Rothschild, 1975, for a brief inventory of current practices.) From the tradition of propaganda studies, early political communication research relied to a considerable degree upon content analysis. Although no longer the leading means of inquiry, content analysis remains a major technique in contemporary studies of the content of political editorials, campaign speeches, inauguration addresses, and presidential State of the Union messages (Kessel, 1974). From its traditional basis in the voting studies, political communication drew upon survey research. Large-sample surveys (both single studies and panel studies) provide the data for

employing a variety of sophisticated analytical tools—factor analysis, cluster analysis, causal modeling, multidimensional scaling, etc. (Barnett, Serota, & Taylor, 1976). From media effect studies comes the controlled laboratory experiment examining the range of theories pertaining to changes in cognition, affect, and conation. And, out of government-press relations research emerge techniques of participant observation and the use of small-sample designs for exploring the characteristics and attitudes of policy officials, information personnel, reporters, and group leaders (see Chittick, 1970, as one example).

As the study of political communication develops, it is apparent that researchers will continue to use such methods. In addition other techniques will be adopted. Techniques for intensive analysis offer promise of advancing understanding of how people construct responses to political symbols and formulate their images of politics. Among these are Q-methodology (Nimmo & Savage, 1976) and repertory grid approaches (Fransella & Bannister, 1967). Moreover, as researchers examine communication in real-life political settings, field experiments will be used more (Miller & Robyn, 1975).

CONCLUSION

In an ambitious effort to integrate theoretical perspectives extracted from classical sociological literature and current approaches to media effects, including the uses and gratifications approach, Ball-Rokeach and DeFleur (1976) describe a "dependency" model of media effects suggestive for future research into the consequences of political communication. In their formulation, the range of potential media effects increases when media systems serve many unique and central information functions, that is, when people depend upon media, and when society is characterized by structural instability, conflict, and change. Under such conditions there is a broad range of effects: cognitive (creation and resolution of ambiguity, attitude formation, agenda-setting, expansion of belief systems, and value clarification), affective (changes in anxiety levels, shifts in morale and alienation), and behavioral (activation and deactivation of people, issue formation or issue resolution, and formulation of action strategies). A key notion in the formulation is that not only are audience cognitions, affects, and behavior altered by the media, but that in turn these changes alter both society and the media, thus performing precisely the function of regulating social conflict and conditions generally attributed to politics. In sum, the inference is that *communication is political* by virtue of its consequences for the social order. Such a proposition might well serve as a guideline for the continuing development of political communication as a unique field of inquiry.

REFERENCES

ABELSON, H.I. *Persuasion*. New York: Springer, 1959.

ALMOND, G., & COLEMAN, J. *The politics of the developing areas*. Princeton: Princeton University Press, 1960.

American Institute for Political Communication. *The federal government-daily press relationship*. Washington, D.C.: AIPC, 1967.

ATKIN, C. Communication and political socialization. *Political Communication Review*, 1975, 1, 2-6.

ATWOOD, E.L., & SANDERS, K.R. Perception of information sources and likelihood of split ticket voting. *Journalism Quarterly*. 1975, 52, 421-428.

BALL-ROKEACH, S.J., & DEFLEUR, M.L. A dependency model of mass-media effects. *Communication Research*, 1976, 3, 3-21.

BARBER, J.D. *The presidential character*. Englewood Cliffs, N.J.: Prentice-Hall, 1972.

BARNETT, G.A., SEROTA, K.B., & TAYLOR, J.A. Campaign communication and attitude change: A multidimensional analysis. *Human Communication Research*, 1976, 2, 227-244.

BAUER, R.A., POOL, I., & DEXTER, L.A. *American business and public policy*. New York: Atherton Press, 1963.

BECKER, L.B., McCOMBS, M.E., & McLEOD, J.M. The development of political cognitions. In S. Chaffee, (Ed.), *Political Communication*. Beverly Hills: Sage Publications, 1975.

BELL, D.V.J. *Power, influence, and authority*. New York: Oxford University Press, 1975.

BERELSON, B.R., LAZARSFELD, P.F., & McPHEE, W.N. *Voting*. Chicago: University of Chicago Press, 1954.

BLANCHARD, R.O. (Ed.) *Congress and the news media*. New York: Hastings House, 1974.

BLUMER, H. Suggestions for the study of mass media effects. In E. Burdick and A.J. Brodbeck (Eds.), *American voting behavior*, Glencoe, Ill.: The Free Press, 1959.

BLUMLER, J.G., & McQUAIL, D. *Television in politics*. Chicago: University of Chicago Press, 1969.

BRODY, R.A., & PAGE, B.I. The impact of events on presidential popularity. In A. Wildavsky (Ed.), *Perspectives on the presidency*. Boston: Little, Brown, 1975.

BRYCE, J. *The American commonwealth*. New York: Macmillan, 1960.

BURKE, K. *Language as symbolic action*. Berkeley: University of California Press, 1969.

BURKE, K. *A rhetoric of motives*. Berkeley: University of California Press, 1969.

CAMPBELL, A. The passive citizen. *Acta Sociologica*, 1962, 6, 9-21.

CAMPBELL, A., CONVERSE, P., MILLER, W., & STOKES, D. *The American voter*. New York: John Wiley & Sons, 1960.

CAMPBELL, A., CONVERSE, P., MILLER, W., & STOKES, D. *Elections and the political order*. New York: John Wiley & Sons, 1966.

CAMPBELL, A., GUREN, G., & MILLER, W. *The voter decides*. Chicago: University of Chicago Press, 1954.

CAREY, J.W. The communications revolution and the professional communicator. In P. Halmos (Ed.), *The sociology of mass media communications*. Keele, Staffordshire: University of Keele, 1969.

CAREY, J.W., & KREILING, A.L. Popular culture and uses and gratifications: Notes toward an accommodation. In J.G. Blumler and E. Katz (Eds.), *The uses of mass communications*. Beverly Hills: Sage Publication, 1974.

CHAFFEE, S. The diffusion of political information. In S. Chaffee, (Ed.), *Political communication*. Beverly Hills: Sage Publications, 1975.

CHITTICK, W.O. *State department, press and pressure groups*. New York: Wiley, 1970.

COBB, R.W., & ELDER, C.D. *Participation in American politics*. Boston: Allyn and Bacon, 1972.

CONVERSE, P.E. Information flow and the stability of partisan attitudes. *Public Opinion Quarterly*, 1962, 26, 577-599.

CZUDNOWSKI, M.M. Political recruitment. In F.I. Greenstein and N.W. Polsby (Eds.), *Handbook of political science* (Vol. 2), Reading, Mass.: Addison-Wesley, 1975.

DAHL, R.A., & LINDBLOM, C.E. *Politics, economics and welfare*. New York: Harper & Row, 1953.

DAVISON, W.P. *International political communication*. New York: Praeger, 1965.

DENNIS, J. *Political socialization research: A bibliography*. Beverly Hills: Sage Publications, 1973.

DEUTSCH, K.W. *Nationalism and social communication*. Cambridge, Mass.: The M.I.T. Press, 1953.

DEUTSCH, K.W. *The nerves of government*. New York: The Free Press, 1963.

DEVINE, D.J. *The political culture of the United States*. Boston: Little, Brown, 1972.

DEWEY, J., & BENTLEY, A.F. *Knowing and the known*. Boston: Beacon Press, 1949.

DONOHUE, T.R. Impact of voter predispositions on political TV commercials. *Journal of Broadcasting*, 1973-74, 18, 3-15.

DOOB, L.W. *Communication in Africa*. New Haven: Yale University Press, 1961.

DOOB, L.W. Goebbels' principles of propaganda. *Public Opinion Quarterly*, 1950, 14, 419-42.

DOOB, L.W. *Public opinion and propaganda*. New York: Holt, Rinehart and Winston, 1948.

DOWNS, A. *Inside bureaucracy*. Boston: Little Brown, 1967.

DUNCAN, H.D. *Communication and social order*. New York: Oxford University Press, 1962.

DYE, T.R. *Who's running America?* Englewood Cliffs, N.J.: Prentice-Hall, 1976.

EASTON, D. *A systems analysis of political life.* New York: Wiley, 1965.

EASTON, D., & DENNIS, J. *Children in the political system.* New York: McGraw-Hill, 1969.

EDELMAN, M. *The symbolic uses of politics.* Urbana: University of Illinois Press, 1964.

EDELSTEIN, A.S. Decision-making and mass communication. In Clarke, P. (Ed.), *New models for mass communication research.* Beverly Hills: Sage Publications, 1973.

ELAZAR, D.J. *American federalism.* New York: Thomas Y. Crowell, 1966.

ELDERSVELD, S.J. *Political parties.* Chicago: Rand McNally, 1964.

ELLUL, J. *Propaganda.* New York: Random House, 1965.

EPSTEIN, E.J. *News from nowhere.* New York: Random House, 1973.

ETZONI, A. *A comparative analysis of complex organizations.* New York: Free Press, 1961.

FAGEN, R.R. *Politics and communication.* Boston: Little, Brown, 1966.

FRANSELLA, F., & BANNISTER, D. A validation of repertory grid techniques as a measure of political construing. *Acta Psychologica,* 1967, 26, 97-106.

GORDON, G. *Persuasion.* New York: Hastings House, 1971.

GRABER, D.A. *Public opinion, the president, and foreign policy.* New York: Holt, Rinehart and Winston, 1968.

GRABER, D.A. *Verbal behavior and politics.* Urbana: University of Illinois Press, 1976.

GUSFIELD, J.R. *Symbolic crusade.* Urbana: University of Illinois Press, 1976.

HAWLEY, W.D., & SVARA, J.H. *The study of community power.* Santa Barbara, Calif.: ABC-CLIO, 1972.

HESS, R.D., & TORNEY, J.V. *The development of political attitudes in children.* Chicago: Aldine, 1967.

HIMMELSTRAND, J. *Social pressures, attitudes and democratic processes.* Stockholm: Almquist and Wicksell, 1960.

HOLLORAN, J.D., ELLIOTT, P., & MURDOCK, G. *Communication and demonstration: A case study.* Middlesex, England; Penguin, 1970.

HOYER, S., HADENIUS, S., & WEIBULL, L. *The politics and economics of the press.* Beverly Hills: Sage Publications, 1975.

HYMAN, H., & SHEATSLEY, P.B. Some reasons why information campaigns fail. *Public Opinion Quarterly,* 1947, 11, 412-423.

JENNINGS, M.K., & NIEMI, R.G. *The political character of adolescence.* Princeton: Princeton University Press, 1974.

KAID, L.L., SANDERS, K.R., & HIRSCH, R.O. *Political campaign communication.* Metuchen, N.J.: The Scarecrow Press, 1974.

KATZ, E. Mass communications research and the study of popular culture. *Studies in Public Communication,* 1959, 2, 1-6.

KATZ, E., BLUMLER, J., & GUREVITCH, M. Utilization of mass communication by the individual. In J.G. Blumler and E. Katz, *The uses of mass communications.* Beverly Hills: Sage Publications, 1974.

KATZ, E., & DANET, B. Communication between bureaucracy and the public. In Pool, I., and Schramm, W. (Eds.), *Handbook of communication.* Chicago: Rand McNally, 1973.

KATZ, E., & LAZARSFELD, P.F. *Personal influence.* New York: The Free Press, 1955.

KESSEL, J.H. *The Goldwater coalition.* New York: Bobbs-Merrill, 1968.

KESSEL, J.H. The parameters of presidential politics. *Social Science Quarterly,* 1975, 55, 8-24.

KEY, V.O., JR. *The responsible electorate.* Cambridge: Belknap Press, 1966.

KLAPP, O.E. *Symbolic leaders.* Chicago: Minerva Press, 1964.

KLAPPER, J.T. *The effects of mass communication.* Glencoe: The Free Press, 1960.

KRIEGHBAUM, H. *Pressures on the press.* New York: Thomas Y. Crowell, 1972.

LASSWELL, H.D. The structure and function of communication in society. In Bryson, L. (Ed.), *The communication of ideas.* New York: Harper & Row, 1948.

LASSWELL, H.D., & LEITES, N. *Language of politics.* Cambridge: The M.I.T. Press, 1949.

LAZARSFELD, P., BERELSON, B., & GAUDET, H. *The people's choice.* New York: Duell, Sloan and Pearce, 1944.

LIPPMANN, W. *Public opinion.* New York: Macmillan, 1922.

LUTTBEG, N.R. *Public opinion and public policy.* Homewood, Ill.: Dorsey Press, 1968.

McCLURE, R.D., & PATTERSON, T.E. Television news and political advertising. *Communication Research,* 1974, 1, 3-31.

McCOMBS, M. Agenda-setting research: a bibliographic essay. *Political Communication Review,* 1976, 1, 1-7.

McGUIRE, W.J. Persuasion, resistance, and attitude change. In I. Pool & W. Schramm (Eds.), *Handbook of communication.* Chicago: Rand McNally, 1973.

MEAD, G.H. *Mind, self, and society.* Chicago: University of Chicago Press, 1934.

MENDELSOHN, H. Some reasons why information campaigns can succeed. *Public Opinion Quarterly,* 1973, 37, 50-61.

MENDELSOHN, H., & O'KEEFE, G.J. *The people choose a president.* New York: Praeger, 1976.

MILBRATH, L.W. *The Washington lobbyists.* Chicago, Rand McNally, 1963.

MILLER, G.A., & McNEILL, D. *Psycholinguistics.* In G. Lindzey and E. Aronson (Eds.), *Handbook of social psychology* (Vol. III) Reading, Mass.: Addison-Wesley, 1969.

MINOW, N.W., MARTIN, J.B., & MITCHELL, L.M. *Presidential television.* New York: Basic Books, 1973.

MUELLER, C. *The politics of communication.* New York: Oxford University Press, 1973.

MUELLER, J.E. *War, presidents, and public opinion.* New York: Wiley, 1973.

NAPOLITAN, J. *The election game.* Garden City: Doubleday, 1972.

NIMMO, D. *Newsgathering in Washington.* New York: Atherton Press, 1964.

NIMMO, D., & SAVAGE, R.L. *Candidates and their images.* Pacific Palisades: Goodyear, 1976.

NISBET, R. Public opinion versus popular opinion. *The Public Interest,* 1975, 41, 166-192.

PATTERSON, T.E., & McCLURE, R.D. *The unseeing eye: the myth of television power in national politics.* New York: G.P. Putnam, 1976.

POMPER, G. *Voters' choice.* New York: Dodd, Mead, 1975.

RIVERS, W. *The opinionmakers*. Boston: Beacon Press, 1965.

RIVERS, W., MILLER, S., & GANDY, O. Government and the media. In S. Chaffee (Ed.), *Political Communication*. Beverly Hills: Sage Publications, 1975.

ROBINSON, W.P. *Language and social behavior*. Middlesex, England: Penguin, 1972.

ROSENAU, J.N. *National leadership and foreign policy*. Princeton: Princeton University Press, 1969.

ROSENGREN, K.E., & WINDAHL, S. Mass media consumption as a functional alternative. In D. McQuail (Ed.), *Sociology of mass communications*. Middlesex, England: Penguin, 1972.

ROSHCO, B. *Newsmaking*. Chicago: University of Chicago Press, 1975.

ROSTEN, L.C. *The Washington correspondents*. New York: Harcourt, Brace, 1937.

ROTHSCHILD, M.L. On the use of multiple methods and multiple situations in political communications research. In S. Chaffee (Ed.), *Political communication*. Beverly Hills: Sage Publication, 1975.

ROURKE, F.E. *Secrecy and publicity*. Baltimore: The Johns Hopkins Press, 1961.

SAPIR, E. Symbolism. In *Encyclopedia of the social sciences*. New York: Macmillan, 1930.

SCHILLER, H.I. *The mind managers*. Boston: Beacon Press, 1973.

SEARS, D.O., & WHITNEY, R.E. *Political persuasion*. Morristown, N.J.: General Learning Press, 1973.

SEIDEN, M.H. *Who controls the mass media?* New York: Basic Books, 1974.

SEYMOUR-URE, C. *The political impact of the mass media*. Beverly Hills: Sage Publications, 1974.

SIGAL, L.V. *Reporters and officials*. Lexington, Mass.: D.C. Heath, 1973.

STEPHENSON, W. *The play theory of mass communication*. Chicago: University of Chicago Press, 1967.

STIMSON, J.A. Public support for American presidents: A cyclical model. *Public Opinion Quarterly*, 1976, 40, 1-21.

STOGDILL, R.M. *Handbook of Leadership*. New York: The Free Press, 1974.

SWANSON, D.L. Some theoretic approaches to the emerging study of political communication: A critical assessment. Paper presented at the annual meeting of the International Communication Association, Portland, Oregon, April 1976.

TUNSTALL, J. *Journalists at work*. Beverly Hills: Sage Publications, 1971.

VARIS, T. Global traffic in television. *Journal of Communication*, 1974, 24, 102-109.

VERBA, S., & NIE, N. *Participation in America*. New York: Harper & Row, 1972.

WASBY, S.L. *The impact of the United States Supreme Court*. Homewood, Ill.: Dorsey Press, 1970.

WEISS, W. Effects of the mass media of communication. In G. Lindzey and E. Aronson (Eds.), *The handbook of social psychology*, Vol. 5, Reading, Mass.: Addison-Wesley, 1969, 77-195.

WESTLEY, B.H., & MACLEAN, M.S., Jr. A conceptual model for communications research, *Journalism Quarterly*, 1957, 34, 31-38.

WOELFEL, J., HOLMES, R., FINK, E., CODY, M., & TAYLOR, J. A mathematical procedure for optimizing political campaign strategy. Paper presented at the annual meeting of the International Communication Association, Portland, Oregon, April 1976.

WOLFENSTEIN, E.V. *The revolutionary personality*. Princeton: Princeton University Press, 1971.

WYCKOFF, G. *The image candidates*. New York: Macmillan, 1968.

INSTANT ANALYSIS OF TELEVISED POLITICAL ADDRESSES: THE SPEAKER VERSUS THE COMMENTATOR

LYNDA LEE KAID
University of Oklahoma, Norman

DONALD L. SINGLETON
North Texas State University, Denton

DWIGHT DAVIS
University of Oklahoma, Norman

This study explored the importance of "instant analysis" of televised political addresses by exposing four groups of respondents to a 30-minute political speech by Ronald Reagan followed by a neutral, a positive, a negative, and no commentary by a newscaster. Evaluations of the speaker were not affected by type of commentary, and the speaker was evaluated higher than the commentator in all treatment groups. The presence of a commentary in most cases resulted in higher recall of issues stressed by the speaker than did the speech alone. Supplementary factor analyses revealed great diversity in the dimensions in which both speaker and commentator were perceived by respondents.

The term "instant analysis" of televised speeches was popularized by former Vice-President Spiro T. Agnew (1969) in his well-known attacks on the media. Agnew criticized television networks for allowing news commentators to provide several minutes of criticism, commentary, and interpretation immediately following nationwide television addresses of the president. Agnew's remarks stimulated considerable controversy over this network policy, and at one point in 1973 CBS prohibited its commentators from engaging in such analysis until several hours after a speech was aired.

The furor over instant analysis of speeches assumes that negative commentary by a newscaster actually affects viewer perceptions of the speaker and the speech. Although no empirical evidence exists to support this assumption, several factors suggest that it might be so. For one thing, television itself is a highly credible medium in America. Large majorities of the public rely on television news, and thus commentators, for information about political affairs (Roper Organization, 1975). Increasingly, television is also viewed as an unbiased medium (Hickey, 1972; Roper Organization, 1975). These perceptions suggest that the viewer might consider the television commentator a fairer, more objective source than a president or politician advocating a particular, self-interested point of view. Con-

sequently, it does not seem unreasonable that observers such as Herschensohn (1976) maintain that commentators can be very damaging to political figures.

On the other hand, some characteristics of a nationwide address favor the speaker, rather than the commentator. Referring to presidential use of television, Minow, Martin, and Mitchell (1973) declare that the formal address is a powerful communication tool because the president has complete control over content, format, and presentation. In addition, they say, broadcasters are hesitant to treat the president roughly on the air. The view that the president may come out on top despite negative commentaries by newsmen is indirectly supported by the fact that presidential speeches are generally followed by increases in his opinion poll ratings (Gilbert, 1972; Minow, Martin, & Mitchell, 1973).

The popular interest in the policy question of whether newscasters should be allowed to engage in instant analysis has overshadowed the equally interesting theoretical questions involved in such a communication situation. For instance, what are the effects of competing sources and competing messages on audience perceptions of both sources?

The application of previous research and theory to this situation provides only limited and sometimes contradictory predictions of the relative impact of the speaker and the commentator. Although a highly credible source generally results in more opinion change than a source with low credibility (Hovland, Janis, & Kelley, 1953), both a president (or other national political figure) and a news commentator are usually highly credible sources so other factors must come into play. One factor favorable to the commentator is the general finding that a source is more persuasive if he is perceived as disinterested and objective, although circumstances may alter this common-sense hypothesis (McGuire, 1968; 1973). Alternatively, the research on the primacy-recency effect would give the edge to the speaker, since both learning theory and perceptual theory assumptions indicate an advantage for the speaker in this situation on the basis of primacy (McGuire, 1968).

Although many of the communication variables at issue here—source credibility, order of presentation, and other related concepts—are among the most heavily researched in the field, this multitude of research has yet to describe the impact of many of these variables in complex real-life communication contexts. Much of the research has been experimental and conducted in very isolated environments where extreme control over message and source was possible. The study reported here was designed to explore these variables in a somewhat more natural setting, a nationwide television address by a major political figure followed immediately by neutral, positive, negative, and no commentary by a newscaster. The study focus, however, was on the theoretical relationships among communication variables, rather than on modeling a natural mass communication process.

The following specific hypotheses were tested:

H_1: A negative commentary following an address will result in significantly lower evaluation of the speaker than will a positive, neutral, or no commentary.

H_2: A positive commentary will result in significantly higher evaluation of the speaker than will a negative, neutral, or no commentary.

H_3: The commentator will be evaluated significantly higher than the speaker.

H_4: With a negative commentary, high evaluation of the speaker will result in significantly lower evaluation of the commentator than will low evaluation of the speaker.

H_5: With a positive commentary, high evaluation of the speaker will result in significantly higher evaluation of the commentator than will low evaluation of the speaker.

H_6: Commentaries of all types will result in significantly higher recall of the speech content than will no commentary.

METHOD

The speech selected for the study was the 30-minute nationwide television address by Ronald Reagan on July 6, 1976. An experienced, local news commentator who was not currently appearing in the market area was selected to do the commentaries. Neutral, positive, and negative commentaries were written, videotaped and edited onto the end of three copies of the 30-minute Reagan speech. All three commentaries were as identical as possible in terms of points stressed, issues raised, wording, etc. However, in the neutral version only descriptive comments were made, in the positive version the commentator indicated approval or agreement with various points made by the speaker, and in the negative version the commentator indicated disapproval or disagreement with the speaker.

This resulted in four treatment groups—the speech plus a neutral commentary, the speech plus a positive commentary, the speech plus a negative commentary, and the speech with no commentary. Four groups of undergraduate students (N=99) were randomly assigned to these treatment groups, and they viewed the tapes on television monitors in classrooms during the last week of July 1976.

Immediately following the viewing, questionnaires were distributed with the following measurement items:

1. A 7-point semantic differential with 12 bipolar adjective scales[1] on the speaker, Reagan.
2. The same semantic differential on the commentator (except, of course, in the no-commentary group).
3. An open-ended question asking students to list things they recalled Reagan stressing in the speech.

TABLE 1
Effect of Commentary on Source Evaluation and Recall: Comparison of
Mean Scores

	Neutral (N=18)	Positive (N=29)	Negative (N=28)	No Commentary (N=24)
Reagan	5.11	4.83	4.79	5.06
Commentator	4.42[a]	4.39[a]	4.11[a]	
Recall	4.06	4.66	4.39	3.63[b,c]

a significantly different from Reagan mean in same group
b significantly different from recall in positive group
c significantly different from recall in negative group

4. Demographic data on age, sex, and partisan affiliation of the respondents.

The alpha level required for significance throughout the results and analysis was .05.

RESULTS

Evaluation of the Speaker

Respondent evaluations of the speaker, Reagan, were measured by the 12-item semantic differential. A mean of the 12 items was calculated for each respondent, and then for each group. These means, displayed in Table 1, indicate that the negative commentary did result in a slightly lower overall evaluation of the speaker. However, the results of t-tests among the groups show no significant difference between the negative commentary mean and the means of the neutral, positive, or no commentary groups. Thus, Hypothesis 1 (that a negative commentary would result in significantly lower evaluation of the speaker) was rejected.

Hypothesis 2 suffers the same fate. In fact, in terms of absolute mean scores, the group viewing the positive commentary evaluated Reagan lower than the neutral or no commentary groups, and only slightly higher than the negative group. Indeed, Reagan scored his highest absolute rating in the neutral commentary treatment. But again, none of

the differences between groups were significant, using t-tests. Since a positive commentary was not responsible for a higher evaluation of the speaker, Hypothesis 2 was also rejected.

Evaluation of the Commentator

Evaluation of the commentator was measured in exactly the same manner as was evaluation of the speaker, and Table 1 also displays the mean scores of the commentator by groups. The commentator received his highest ratings in the *neutral treatment* and his lowest in the *negative commentary treatment,* although, as in the case of the speaker, t-tests did not reveal any statistically significant difference among treatment groups.

Hypothesis 3 predicted that the commentator would be rated significantly higher than the speaker. Table 1 shows that this was not true in any of the three commentary treatments. In fact, the opposite appears to be true. In each group, the commentator received a lower rating than did Reagan, and in each case the difference between the commentator mean and the Reagan mean was significant at .05.

H_4 and H_5 also concerned the evaluation of the commentator in relation to the speaker, using only the positive and negative cells, where clear distinctions could be expected. For the purpose of comparison, those with high evaluation of the speaker were considered to be those whose mean rating of the speaker exceeded the overall mean of the entire group in that treatment, and those with low evaluation were those whose means were lower than the mean of that group. In the negative cell, those who ranked the speaker high (above 4.79; N=14) rated the commentator considerable lower (3.89 versus 4.33) than did those whose speaker rating was low (below 4.79; N=14). Although this difference is not quite significant (t= -1.41;df=26; p < .09) and Hypothesis 4 was not confirmed. The difference is clearly in the predicted direction and does indicate that those who regarded Reagan highly tended to derogate the source of a negative message about him.

The tendency to evaluate the commentator based on regard for the speaker is more clear in examination of Hypothesis 5, where it was predicted that in the positive commentary treatment, those with high evaluation of Reagan (above 4.83; N=14), would rate the commentator significantly higher than would those with low evaluation of Reagan (below 4.83; N=15). This was, in fact, the case. Those with high evaluation of speaker gave the commentator a mean rating of 4.78, compared with the 4.02 rating given the commentator by those who evaluated Reagan low, and this difference in the predicted direction was significant (t= 3.05; df=27; p < .01).

Commentary Effect on Recall

Hypothesis 6 was based on the supposition that the commentaries would act as repetition of at least some message elements within the speech and that, consequently, the commentaries would stimulate greater recall than the speech alone. This hypothesis was tested by measuring the mean number of items the respondents recalled in answer to the open-ended question: *List the things you recall Reagan stressing in his speech.* For the entire sample, the number of items per person ranged from 1 to 9, with a mean of 4.22.

Examination of the items recalled by commentary group resulted in confirmation of the hypothesis for two of the three groups: positive and negative commentary. The group which viewed the speech alone with no commentary recalled a mean

of only 3.63 items compared with 4.06 for the neutral commentary group, 4.66 for the positive, and 4.39 for the negative. The 3.63 mean for the no commentary group was significantly lower than the positive mean (t=2.02; df=51; p < .03); and the negative commentary mean (t= 1.68; df=50; p < .05); but not significantly different from the neutral commentary mean (t= .80; df=40; p < .21).

ANALYSIS AND DISCUSSION

The results indicate that, for this speech with this audience, the effect of "instant analysis" by a newscaster is minimal. While the speaker received slightly higher ratings with a neutral or no commentary, the existence of a negative commentary, while lowering ratings somewhat, is not damaging to any significant degree.

In considering these results, it seemed possible that the use of the overall mean score from the semantic differential might have obscured some differences between groups in ratings of the speaker on particular scales. Consequently, Table 2 displays the mean score for each group on each of the 12 scales in the semantic differential. While there are some interesting differences in absolute scores, few of the ratings are significantly different from cell to cell. Those viewing the neutral commentary saw the speaker as somewhat more honest, more qualified, and more sincere than did other groups, while those viewing the speech without any commentary found the speaker slightly more successful.

Perhaps the most interesting aspect of the findings is the relationship between evaluations of the two scores—speaker and commentator. The commentator received a higher evaluation when presenting a neutral commentary, perhaps indicating that viewers perceive objectivity and neutrality as a desirable stance for a commentator and view him less positively when he takes on an advocacy (either positive or negative) role. The fact that in all cases the speaker was rated significantly higher than the commentator may be a reflection of Reagan's superior ability to communicate via the television medium. Alternatively, this might be a result of the lack of familiarity with the commentator. The use of

TABLE 2
Speaker Evaluation: Individual Scale Means

	Neutral	Positive	Negative	No Commentary
Qualified	5.17	4.90	4.50	5.04
Sophisticated	5.33	5.10	5.18	5.25
Honest	5.17	4.55	4.50	4.71
Serious	4.83	4.55[a]	5.11	5.42
Sincere	5.67	5.03	4.75[b]	5.17
Modern	4.11	4.07	3.39	4.21
Successful	5.50	5.34[a]	5.39	5.96
Handsome	4.28	4.28	4.18	4.46
Friendly	5.39	5.28	5.14	5.50
Conservative	5.61	5.52	5.46	5.17
Calm	5.06	4.52[c]	5.32	4.67
Saver	5.22	4.86	4.57	5.13

a   significantly different from no commentary group
b   significantly different from neutral commentary group
c   significantly different from negative commentary group

a major nationally-known commentator might have changed the results, and replication of the study with this modification could prove fruitful.

An additional way of analyzing the effect of the varying commentary treatments was considered by factor analyzing the semantic differentials used to measure the evaluation of both speaker and commentator. The use of factor analysis of semantic differentials to isolate dimensions of respondent perceptions of political figures is a common technique (Nimmo & Savage, 1976). The *rotated factor matrices*[2] for both the speaker and the commentator, in all treatment groups, appear in Tables 3 and 4. The most striking characteristic of these factor solutions for both sources is the great diversity and complexity of factor structures present among the treatment groups. For instance, in the neutral group for the speaker, Factor 1, accounting for the most variance (17.8%) is characterized by scales representing a *political philosophy* dimension (liberal-conservative; modern-outdated) while the factor accounting for the most variance in the negative commentary group represents a *character* dimension (honest-dishonest; serious-not serious; sincere-insincere). The factor accounting for the most variance in the no commentary group (Factor 1 = 15.4% of total variance) is not clearly dominated by any one dimension and seems to be composed of a combination of *competence* (successful-unsuccessful), *political philosophy* (modern-outdated), and *personal image* (calm-excitable) scales. Analysis of the positive commentary group indicated two very weak factors—the entire solution accounted for only 25.1% of total variance.

TABLE 3
Rotated Factor Matrices for Speaker

Neutral	Factor 1	2	3	4	Com.
Factor 1					
Honest	.683	-.206	.052	.037	.513
Modern	.779	.088	.057	-.266	.689
Conservative	-.883	-.324	.097	-.193	.931
Factor 2					
Friendly	.142	.777	-.016	.161	.649
Sophisticated	.254	-.676	.158	-.050	.549
Saver	.223	.667	.222	-.337	.658
Factor 3					
Calm	-.085	-.142	.793	.051	.659
Serious	.160	-.042	.561	-.059	.346
Qualified	-.070	.146	.557	.275	.413
Factor 4					
Successful	-.151	-.065	.088	.640	.444
Handsome	-.264	.023	-.182	-.490	.344
Sincere	-.120	.461	-.260	.743	.847
Total Variance					
per factor	.1777	.1601	.1211	.1280	.5868
cumulative	.1777	.3378	.4589	.5868	
Com. Variance					
per factor	.3028	.2728	.2063	.2180	1.000
cumulative	.3028	.5756	.7820	1.0000	
Positive					
Factor 1					
Calm	.754	.002			.569
Successful	.630	-.112			.409
Handsome	-.271	-.097			.083
Sincere	.213	-.122			.060
Friendly	.507	.332			.367
Qualified	.518	.374			.408
Factor 2					
Serious	.005	.216			.047
Sophisticated	-.004	-.028			.001
Saver	.131	.686			.487
Modern	.055	-.160			.029
Honest	-.225	.545			.347
Conservative	.303	-.344			.210
Total variance					
per factor	.1477	.1037			.2514
cumulative	.1477	.2514			
Com. Variance					
per factor	.5875	.4125			1.0000
cumulative	.5875	1.0000			

TABLE 3 (cont.)

		Factor			
	1	2	3	4	Com.
Negative					
Factor 1					
Serious	-.794	-.122	.121		.659
Successful	-.545	.199	-.120		.351
Sophisticated	.635	-.178	.208		.478
Sincere	.653	.221	-.194		.517
Honest	.436	.132	-.251		.271
Factor 2					
Qualified	-.084	-.447	-.017		.207
Calm	.127	.814	-.196		.717
Friendly	-.070	.680	.277		.544
Conservative	-.191	.430	-.320		.324
Factor 3					
Handsome	-.050	.030	.502		.256
Modern	.133	-.000	.746		.574
Saver	-.215	-.050	.529		.329
Total Variance					
per factor	.1731	.1388	.1233		.4352
cumulative	.1731	.3119	.4352		
Com. Variance					
per factor	.3977	.3190	.2833		1.0000
cumulative	.3977	.7167	1.0000		
No Commentary					
Factor 1					
Successful	.791	.139	-.056		.647
Modern	-.612	.131	.170		.420
Calm	.729	-.060	.268		.607
Factor 2					
Saver	.077	.466	.112		.236
Serious	-.037	.706	.225		.550
Conservative	-.096	.527	-.216		.334
Honest	.195	.526	-.172		.344
Handsome	.177	-.496	.184		.311
Factor 3					
Friendly	-.041	-.105	.433		.200
Sincere	-.034	.114	.350		.137
Qualified	.111	-.265	.833		.777
Sophisticated	.464	-.084	.617		.603
Total Variance					
per factor	.1539	.1380	.1386		.4305
cumulative	.1539	.2919	.4305		
Com. Variance					
per factor	.3575	.3206	.3219		1.0000
cumulative	.3575	.6781	1.0000		

TABLE 4
Rotated Factor Matrices for Commentator

	Factor				
Neutral	1	2	3	4	Com.
Factor 1					
Serious	.190	-.070	.108	.175	.876
Saver	.929	-.018	.157	-.249	.951
Conservative	.621	.158	-.262	.038	.480
Handsome	.601	-.334	-.554	-.006	.780
Factor 2					
Honest	.127	.586	-.080	.081	.373
Friendly	-.152	.662	.168	-.073	.495
Modern	.001	-.454	.090	.258	.281
Sophisticated	.342	-.676	.315	-.107	.684
Sincere	.114	.600	.273	.401	.609
Factor 3					
Qualified	.098	-.156	.800	.068	.678
Successful	-.170	.103	.648	-.482	.692
Factor 4					
Calm	-.041	.061	.089	.789	.636
Total Variance					
per factor	.2207	.1655	.1413	.1004	.6280
cumulative	.2207	.3862	.5275	.6280	
Com. Variance					
per factor	.3514	.2636	.2251	.1599	1.0000
cumulative	.3514	.6150	.8401	1.0000	

	Factor				
Positive	1	2	3		Com.
Factor 1					
Calm	-.782	-.005	-.053		.614
Honest	.696	-.055	-.020		.487
Saver	.420	.049	.083		.186
Serious	.522	.440	.024		.466
Factor 2					
Modern	-.084	.353	.038		.133
Handsome	.128	.676	-.178		.505
Qualified	.338	.416	-.203		.369
Sophisticated	-.049	.547	.495		.547
Factor 3					
Successful	-.078	-.019	-.252		.070
Conservative	.104	-.201	.562		.367
Friendly	-.416	.035	.511		.435
Sincere	-.462	-.040	.485		.450
Total Variance					
per factor	.1740	.1114	.1005		.3858
cumulative	.1740	.2854	.3858		
Com. Variance					
per factor	.4509	.2887	.2604		1.0000
cumulative	.4509	.7396	1.0000		

TABLE 4 (cont.)

	Factor 1	2	3	4	Com.
Negative					
Factor 1					
Handsome	.636	-.009			.405
Friendly	-.845	.153			.737
Sincere	.618	.117			.395
Conservative	.462	-.107			.225
Sophisticated	.438	-.177			.223
Saver	.143	.059			.024
Modern	-.596	-.395			.511
Factor 2					
Honest	-.003	.482			.233
Calm	-.073	-.418			.180
Serious	-.202	.852			.766
Qualified	.148	.540			.313
Successful	-.408	.651			.591
Total Variance					
per factor	.2097	.1739			.3836
cumulative	.2097	.3836			
Com. Variance					
per factor	.5466	.4534			1.0000
cumulative	.5466	1.0000			

Apparently, then, differing commentary treatments resulted in differing dimensions of speaker evaluation. The extent of these differences was confirmed by the performance of correlational analyses between the factor structures of each group. Using a program (SIMFAC) designed to compare the similarity of factor structures (Harman, 1960; Van Tubergen, 1971), it is clear from Table 5 that no factor grouping was similar to any other. A common criterion for evaluating factor similarity in this situation is that any factors which correlate at .80 or better could be considered similar. The highest correlation present in Table 5 is the +.61 correlation between Factor 3 of the neutral group and Factor 1 of the positive group.

As was the case for the speaker, the factor structures for the commentator from group to group are quite dissimilar. However, as Table 4 indicates, the commentator was often evaluated in terms of *appearance* and *demeanor*—scales related to this dimension (handsome-ugly; friendly-unfriendly;

calm-excitable; serious-not serious) emerge with high loadings in the factors accounting for the most variance across all three groups. In the neutral and negative commentary groups, there also appears to be a *competency* dimension (qualified-unqualified; successful-unsuccessful). However, despite these surface similarities, the factor structures as a whole are so diverse that the correlations displayed in Table 6 again indicate no correlations among any factors from the various groups which exceed .80.

Not only were the factor structures different for the speaker among groups and for the commentator among groups, but also for the speaker and commentator within each group. Table 7 contains the correlations among the factors for the speaker in each treatment group with the factors for the commentator in the same treatment group. None of these correlations approach .80, although some similarity (+.67) is apparent in the positive treatment group between Factor 2 for the speaker and Factor 1 for the commentator. This lack of substan-

TABLE 5
Comparison of Factor Structures: Speaker by Treatment Groups

REAGAN	Positive Factor		Negative Factor			No Commentary Factor		
	1	2	1	2	3	1	2	3
Neutral								
Factor 1	-.22	.43	.27	-.20	.48	-.19	.16	.17
2	.25	.13	-.15	.20	.35	-.27	-.01	.20
3	.61	.38	-.31	.18	-.00	.44	.29	.49
4	.50	-.13	.13	.16	-.52	.35	.01	.22
Positive								
Factor 1			-.19	.57	-.12	.51	.07	.49
2			-.05	-.40	.09	.15	.36	.12
Negative								
Factor 1						-.02	-.28	.19
2						.33	.14	-.03
3						-.30	-.12	.34

tial correlation between factor structures indicates that subjects in all groups viewed the speaker in quite different dimensions than they viewed the commentator.

Without some additional and more complex analyses, these findings are difficult to interpret further. Future research in this area, however, might isolate more clearly the meaning of these differences. Although the speaker and the commentator were the same in each treatment group, and therefore one might expect to attribute differences to the varying treatment stimuli, this is probably a premature conclusion. Although time constraints precluded the inclusion of a pretest in this study, pretest semantic differentials on both the speaker and commentator would provide more basis for analysis and interpretation.

In regard to the *learning/recall* hypothesis, it is apparent that in most cases respondents' recall was increased and stimulated by the presence of a commentary. Broadcast professionals can point to this as an educational/informative function of such commentaries. In fact, every item recalled by subjects in all groups was a specific issue position. Of interest for future research is the question of whether or not the content of the commentator's remarks determines and structures the respondents' recall. If respondents tend to recall only issues or items mentioned by the commentator, then the power and influence of the commentator through selection and omission may be great.

In this particular study, the political figure enjoyed a significant advantage over the commentator. This provides some support for the Minow, Martin, and Mitchell (1973) view that control of the event by the speaker results in considerable

TABLE 6
Comparison of Factor Structures: Commentator by Treatment Groups

COMMENTATOR	Neutral Factor	Positive Factor			Negative Factor	
Neutral		1	2	3	1	2
Factor 1		.50	.08	.26	.41	.30
2		-.12	-.53	.27	-.18	.31
3		.02	.13	.01	-.24	.51
4		-.43	-.04	.15	.12	-.31
Positive						
Factor 1					.14	.56
2					.26	-.23
3					.17	-.19

advantage for him—an advantage which could be expected to be even greater in the context of a presidential address. Whether this would hold true for *all* speakers, and whether it is due to a primacy effect, cannot be determined without further study with a more complex design.

SUMMARY AND CONCLUSION

This study explored the importance of "instant analysis" of televised political addresses by exposing four groups of respondents to a 30-minute political speech by Ronald Reagan followed by a neutral, a positive, a negative, and no commentary. Evaluations of the speaker were not affected by type of commentary, and the speaker was evaluated higher than the commentator in all treatment groups. The presence of a commentary in most cases resulted in higher recall of issues stressed by the speaker than did the speech alone. Supplementary factor analyses revealed great diversity in the dimensions in which both speaker and commentator were perceived by respondents.

NOTES

1. The 12 scales used appear in Table 2. The semantic differential used in this study has been the result of extensive testing and research since 1968. Originally, 45 scales were derived from laboratory experimentation on candidate image at Southern Illinois University. After factor analysis, the 29 scales with the highest loadings were administered to a statewide sample in Texas. Again factor analysis was used, and the final list of 12 scales with the highest loadings was obtained. This specific semantic differential, with slight variations, has been successfully used to tap dimensions of respondent perceptions of political figures in numerous studies including Sanders, Pace, McNeil, and Dybvig (1971), Russell (1971), and Kaid and Hirsch (1973).

2. The factor analysis was a principal components solution with varimax (orthogonal) rotation. Minimum eigenvalue was set at 1.0.

REFERENCES

AGNEW, S. T. Speech in Des Moines, Iowa, November 13, 1969. In M. C. Emery and T. C. Smythe (Eds.), *Readings in mass communication: Concepts and issues in the mass media*, 2nd. ed., Dubuque, Iowa: Brown, 1974, 497-506.

GILBERT, R. E. *Television and presidential politics*. North Quincy, Mass.: Christopher Publishing House, 1972.

TABLE 7
Comparisons of Factor Structures: Speaker Versus Commentator

SPEAKER	COMMENTATOR								
	Neutral Factor				Positive Factor			Negative Factor	
Neutral	1	2	3	4	1	2	3	1	2
Factor 1	-.08	-.09	.19	.07					
2	.04	.50	.18	-.03					
3	.36	-.16	.37	.43					
4	-.41	.51	.67	.03					
Positive									
Factor 1					-.46	.01	.20		
2					.67	.01	-.35		
Negative									
Factor 1								.38	-.49
2								-.24	-.20
3								-.22	-.16

HARMAN, H. H. *Modern factor analysis*. Chicago: University of Chicago Press, 1960.

HERSCHENSOHN, B. *The gods of antenna*. New Rochelle, N.Y.: Arlington House, 1976.

HICKEY, N. The TV Guide poll: Final results. *TV Guide*, December 20, 1972, 20, A1-A3.

HOVLAND, C. I., JANIS, I. L., & KELLEY, H. H. *Communication and persuasion*. New Haven: Yale University Press, 1953.

KAID, L. L., & HIRSCH, R. O. Selective exposure and candidate image: A field study over time. *Central States Speech Journal*, 1973, 24, 48-51.

McGUIRE, W. J. The nature of attitudes and attitude change. In G. Lindzey and E. Aronson (Eds.), *The handbook of social psychology*, Vol. 3. Reading, Mass.: Addison-Wesley, 1968, 136-314.

McGUIRE, W. J. Persuasion, resistance and attitude change. In I. de Sola Pool, et al. (Eds.), *The handbook of communication*. Chicago: Rand McNally, 1973, 216-252.

MINOW, N. N., MARTIN, J. B., & MITCHELL, L. M. *Presidential television*. New York: Basic Books, Inc., 1973.

NIMMO, D., & SAVAGE, R. *Candidates and their images*. Pacific Palisades, Ca: Goodyear, 1976.

Roper Organization. *Trends in public attitudes toward television and other mass media, 1959-1974*. New York: Television Information Office, 1975.

RUSSELL, C. A multi-variate descriptive field study of media and non-media influences on voting behavior in the 1970 Texas gubernatorial election. Unpublished doctoral dissertation, Department of Speech, Southern Illinois University-Carbondale, 1971.

SANDERS, K. R., PACE, T., McNEIL, K., & DYBVIG, E. The impact of communication media on candidate image. Center for Communication Research Report #9, Southern Illinois University-Carbondale, 1971.

VAN TUBERGEN, N. Coefficient of factor similarity (SIMFAC). Information Processing Center, Southern Illinois University-Carbondale, 1971.

THE INFLUENCE OF SPEECH COMMUNICATION ON THE IMAGE OF A POLITICAL CANDIDATE: "LIMITED EFFECTS" REVISITED [1]

KEITH R. SANDERS and THOMAS J. PACE
Southern Illinois University

Drawing on the selective exposure hypothesis and related literature, this paper presents the results of a "natural experiment" designed to test hypotheses regarding the demographic composition and partisan affiliations of the audiences attracted to political campaign speeches. The immediate effects on candidate image of the speeches were also measured. Seventeen audiences of a Republican gubernatorial candidate completed a nine-scale semantic differential before he spoke and immediately afterward. Data analysis revealed that, although a majority of those in the candidate's audiences were Republican, partisan composition shifted significantly from one audience situation to another. In addition, the candidate's speeches produced significant positive shifts in image across all audience situations. Finding the "limited effects" perspective uninspiring as an explanation for these outcomes, the authors invoke, tentatively, a "uses and gratifications" rationale.

It is widely assumed that, in the age of television, political oratory is an anachronism about which little of value remains to be learned. Heavily influenced by a "limited effects" communication model, most scholars who hold an opinion on the matter appear to believe that they know, at least in general terms, who comes to hear the speeches of a political candidate and what effect, if any, these speeches have (Scammon & Wattenberg, 1968; Lamb & Smith, 1968; Swanson, 1972). The immediate audiences of political candidates are thought to be relatively homogeneous, highly partisan, and rather resistant to change. It is reasoned that those who attend political meetings are so firmly committed to their opinions and to their candidate; that there is little room for further conversion and little likelihood of a reduction in their commitment. At best, it is thought that political rallies serve to reinforce pre-existing attitudes (MacNeil, 1968; Kelley, 1960).

Those who hold this point of view could, until recently, find a great deal of support for their position in the literature of selective exposure. Through the mid-1960s no psychological principle was more widely accepted than the assertion that individuals are motivated to seek information which supports their opinions and to avoid information which contradicts them. Festinger (1957) made selective ex-posure one of the two basic precepts of his highly heuristic theory of cognitive dissonance. Berelson and Steiner (1964) presented it as a basic principle of human behavior. The Behavioral Sciences Subpanel (1962, p. 57) of the President's Science Advisory Committee asserted flatly, ". . . individuals engage in selective exposure . . .", and Richard Hofstadter (1966) included selective exposure in his description of the "paranoid style" in American politics.

Indeed, such conclusions as the foregoing seemed, at the time, irrefutable, when one considered the dearth of studies which supported the notion of selectivity. For example, after their classic study of the 1940 presidential election campaigns, Lazarsfeld, Berelson, and Gaudet (1948) concluded that "voters turn to propaganda which affirms that validity and wisdom of their original decision" (p. 90). In studying exposure patterns resulting from an information campaign favorable to the United Nations, Star and Hughes (1950) found exposure was considerably higher among persons who were already favorable to the United Nations. Schramm and Carter (1959) found that a larger percentage of Republicans than Democrats had watched a telethon given by the Republican candidate. It was evidence of this sort, and more, which led to universal acceptance of the doctrine of selectivity and the implication that political messages, especially during campaigns, produce little attitude change (Blumler & McLeod, 1974; Sanders in press).

However, Freedman and Sears (1975) published a review of the experimental studies which had tested the selective exposure hypothesis and concluded that "experimental evidence does not demonstrate that there is a general psychological tendency to avoid nonsupportive and to seek out supportive information" (1965, p. 94). Not convinced by the Freedman and Sears analysis, Mills (1968) reviewed the same set of studies, plus some which were done after the Freedman-Sears review, and decided the evidence warrants the conclusion that people tend to seek out supporting information and avoid discrepant information. Katz (196⌃ has also called for a less than total rejection of the hypothesis, based upon field research in mass communications. Sanders and Newman (1971) found in a limited test of Hofstadter's description of the paranoid political style that political "paranoids" do not actively avoid discrepant information. In fact, they found some evidence that such persons actively seek discrepant information, distort it, and use it as data in support of their world view.

Motivated Versus De Facto Selectivity

The major issue in the controversy has to do with the "voluntary" or "motivated" nature of selectivity and not with the selective exposure per se. All disputants agree that de facto selectivity has been well documented. Persons are exposed more to communication with which they agree, than to communication with which they disagree. However, this does not demonstrate the presence of a general psychological predisposition in favor of supportive information. Selectivity could be due to a variety of other factors, such as the availability of more supportive information in the individual's natural environment (Sears, 1968), the greater perceived utility of some information over other information, or a combination of reasons. A conservative Republican may read the *Wall Street Journal* because it includes supportive information, is in the offices and homes of all of his colleagues, and/or

because it contains much useful information about day-to-day trends in the business and industrial community. The position one takes when explaining selectivity, de facto or motivated, dictates, to a large extent, the inference he will draw about the probability that partisan political messages will change the attitudes of those who attend partisan political rallies.

If one is a "limited effects" theorist, holding the view that political messages in campaigns exert few influence partly because of selective exposure, then one must hold that political oratory will have few if any additional effects on its immediate audience. Unlike the more or less passive selectivity involved in deciding to watch one television program over another, the taking of oneself to a political rally requires effort. In fact, it is difficult to imagine a more overt act of selective exposure. Sears and Whitney (1973, p. 259) contend that: "Face-to-face political meetings may elicit more de facto selectivity than communications in newspapers, magazines, TV and radio because they attract fewer people and hence probably only the most involved partisans." If Sears and Whitney are correct, political meetings constitute a propitious setting in which to test the hypothesis that partisan messages have little impact on partisan audiences. Unfortunately, few empirical studies have been conducted in this setting.

Although speech-communication scholars have given a great deal of attention to political public speaking, it has, as Swanson (1972) rightly contended, come almost exclusively from those who hold a nonempirical orientation. In this literature there is much speculation regarding the composition of audiences and the impact of speeches on immediate audiences. In fact, a review (Trent, 1975) of the most pertinent literature reveals only two field studies on the direct effects of political oratory.

Brooks (1967) studied the influence on attitudes toward the candidates of speeches given at political rallies in Pittsburgh during the Goldwater-Johnson campaign. He found that Goldwater was successful in changing audience attitudes toward himself on two of the five scales used in the study. Johnson, however, failed to produce a significant change on any of the five scales.

Kaid and Hirsch (1973) found that a 1972 campaign speech by Edmund Muskie produced a positive shift in mean image score as measured by twelve semantic differential scales, but no change in the overall image structure as indicated by factor analysis of pretest and posttest scores. A follow-up study conducted two to three weeks after the Muskie rally indicated that, while the changes in mean image scores held, image structure had changed. The researchers concluded that "A single appearance by a political candidate can result in a favorable shift in image, and that shift can persist over time."

Both the Brooks (1967) and Kaid and Hirsch (1973) studies call in to question inferences drawn from the much embattled "limited effects" model (Becker, McCombs, & McLeod, 1975) that political partisans are the exclusive audience of political oratory and that such oratory has little impact. As a further test of the implications of this model, this study was designed to test the following hypotheses:

H_1: At least a majority (51%) of those who come to hear a political candidate speak will be members of his political party.

H_2: Sex, age, and political party affiliation will not vary significantly from one audience situation to another during a political campaign.

H_3: The speeches of a political candidate will have no significant influence on his image as perceived by his immediate audiences.

PROCEDURES

Subjects

The subjects from whom data were gathered for this study were selected from 17 different audiences who came to hear a political speech by Paul Eggers during the final six weeks of his 1968 campaign as Republican candidate for governor of Texas. The 17 audiences were chosen in an attempt to include in the study a representative sample of the immediate audiences to whom the candidate spoke.

In about the proper proportions they represented the three different types of audiences to whom the candidate spoke during the period under study: civic and fraternal organizations, university-related

groups, and political rallies. At least two, but not more than three, audiences were chosen from each of the last six weeks of the campaign during which the largest number of speeches were given. Audiences were selected from a variety of geographical areas within the state.

The selection of subjects within the 17 audiences was less complicated. In audiences of thirty or fewer, largely civic and fraternal organizations, the entire audience served as subjects. In larger groups, such as political rallies, subjects were selected as they entered the meeting by randomly handing them a questionnaire or by moving through an already assembled audience and passing out questionnaires. Subjects were not chosen from any particular place in the meeting room or from those arriving early or late. Questionnaires were in the hands of subjects before the candidate was introduced.

A total of 763 questionnaires were distributed. Of this number, 553 (or about 80%) were retrieved. Complete and usable data were obtained from 491, or 64%, of the total: 127 from civic and fraternal groups, 189 from university related groups, and 175 from political rallies.

Design

The pretest—posttest design pattern was used across all audiences. All data were gathered by the researchers. Before the candidate began speaking, subjects were given a three page questionnaire calling for information regarding their sex, age, political party affiliation, and presidential preference. It also asked whether they had seen the candidate on television or on billboards; whether they had heard him on radio, or read about him in newspapers; and whether they had heard him speak in person earlier in the campaign. The individual introducing the candidate was asked to tell the audience that a study was being conducted and to call for their cooperation.

The questionnaire also contained two nine-scale semantic differentials and instructions for completion. Subjects were asked to complete one set of scales before the candidate was introduced and an identical set after the speech and the question and answer period.

Measuring Instrument

The nine scales used in the semantic differential were derived especially for this study. Sixty-seven graduate and undergraduate students on the campus of Southern Illinois University at Carbondale listened to an audio tape of Paul Eggers giving a speech and being interviewed. As they listened, they were asked to write down adjectives describing Eggers as they came to mind. From these adjectives 35 recurring scales were selected and converted to bipolar semantic differential form. These 35 scales plus an additional 10 which had been used to assess the image of participants in the 1960 Kennedy-Nixon debates comprised a 45-item semantic differential which was administered to another group of 153 undergraduate and graduate students after they had viewed a video tape of Eggers giving a speech and/or being interviewed.

Factor analysis of the data obtained from this experiment produced 10 scales with high loadings on an evaluative factor, a dynamism factor, and a weakly defined "ideological" factor. These 10 scales were tested on the campus of the University of Texas in mid-September just prior to the period under study. Seventy-one subjects who had heard of the candidate and were Texans of voting age completed the semantic differential on the concept "Paul Eggers." These data were factor analyzed and produced a factor structure basically similar to the one obtained in Illinois, suggesting that the candidate's image was being defined in basically three dimensions of meaning. Thus, eight of the original 10 scales were used in the study reported here. Two were added to give strength to what appeared to be a stable, but heretofore weakly defined, "ideological" factor.

RESULTS

Hypothesis 1

The data summarized in Table 1 clearly indicate that hypothesis 1 is confirmed. More than a majority of those who came to hear the candidate speak were members of his party. Sixty percent of those who came were Republicans while 21% were Democrats, and 18% were either American Independents or designated their affiliation as "other." A comparison of 297 with the hypothesized value of 250 (51%) produced a z of 3.16 which was significant beyond .05. Thus, when one looks at the total sample, there were clearly more representatives of the candidate's party than of all other parties combined.

However, a somewhat different picture emerges when one tests the stability of party affiliation across audience situations. Civic, fraternal, and university audiences were split almost in half between Republicans and non-Republicans while 81% of those who attended rallies were Republican and 19% non-Republican. Testing the number of Republicans who attended speeches in civic/fraternal contexts against those who attended in university contexts produced a nonsignificant z of .20 (p>.05). However, the same statistic revealed significant differences when the number of Republicans at civic/fraternal speaking events and the number at university related events were compared with the number of Republicans at political rallies. These scores were, respectively: z=6.60, (p<.05), and z=6.40, (p<.05). A political speaker can, therefore, expect a highly partisan audience at a rally but not in the other two contexts studied here. Political party affiliation does vary from one audience situation to another.

Hypothesis 2

A review of the data in Table 1 on the sexual composition of political audiences indicates that in all three audience situations males tended to predominate. Overall, 67% of those present were male and 33% were female. There was some variation across audience types. Although comparison of the number of males in the civic/fraternal setting with the number of males in university setting failed to produce a significant difference (z=1.00, p>.05) as did a comparison of males in civic/fraternal audiences with males who attended political rallies (z=1.75, p>.05), the number of males in university audiences did differ from the number at political rallies (z=3.19, p<.05). Thus, the sexual composition of political audiences can vary across audience situations.

The same general pattern holds true for the age

TABLE 1
Frequency Distribution and Percentages on Sex, Party Affiliation, and
Age of Subjects in Civic/Fraternal, University, and Political Rally
Audience Situations

| | Audience Situations | | | |
Variable	Civic-Frat.	Univ.	Pol. Rally	Total
Sex				
Male	87(69%)	140(74%)	103(59%)	330(67%)
Female	40(31%)	49(26%)	72(41%)	161(33%)
Totals	127	189	175	491
Party				
Republican	64(50%)	92(49%)	141(81%)	297(60%)
Democrat	35(28%)	62(33%)	5(3%)	102(21%)
Amer. Ind.	10(8%)	10(5%)	7(4%)	27(5%)
Other	18(14%)	25(13%)	22(13%)	65(13%)
Totals	127	189	175	491
Age				
0 - 20	13(10%)	75(40%)	21(12%)	109(22%)
21 - 30	39(31%)	108(51%)	45(26%)	192(39%)
31 - 40	44(35%)	5(3%)	59(34%)	108(22%)
41 - 50	17(13%)	1(1%)	35(20%)	53(11%)
51 - 60	10(8%)		9(5%)	19(4%)
61 plus	4(3%)		6(3%)	10(2%)
Totals	127	189	175	491
Mean Age	33.9	22.2	32.3	28.8

variable. As Table 1 reveals, there was a considerable difference in the range and variation around the mean from one audience type to another. The t-test for differences between means of independent samples indicates that the mean age of the civic/fraternal audiences differed significantly from the mean age of the university audiences ($t=84.35$, $p<.05$), that the mean age of civic/fraternal audiences differed significantly from the mean age of the political rally audiences ($t=215.92$, $p<.05$), and that the mean age of university audiences differed significantly from the mean age of political rally audiences ($t=156.68$, $p<.05$). Thus, hypothesis 2 must be rejected. Sex, age, and political party affiliation all tend to vary from one audience type to another.

Hypothesis 3

Table 2 summarizes the data collected in the testing of hypothesis 3. It indicates overwhelmingly that hypothesis 3 must be rejected. The speeches of the candidate under study had a significant influence on his image in all three audience situations. The scores which served as raw data for the means

TABLE 2
Means, Standard Deviations, and F. Ratio for Pretest and Posttest
Scores on the Semantic Differential

Aud. Sit.	N	Pretest	S.D.	Posttest	S.D.	F-Ratio[1]
Civic/Frat.	127	34.12	6.03	37.41	5.21	75.47
University	189	34.05	5.15	38.86	5.15	132.48
Rally	175	36.82	6.09	39.58	5.06	173.50
Over-All	491	35.05	5.88	37.97	5.09	413.74

[1] All F-Ratios were significant beyond the .001 level

TABLE 3
Factor Loadings Yielded by Varimax Analysis of Pretest and Posttest
Data Gathered from Civic/Fraternal Audiences

Pretest			
Factor 1 (.58)[1]		Factor 2 (.42)	
Unresponsive-Responsive	.74	Talker-Doer	.71
Bad-Good	.74	Old Ideas-New Ideas	.71
Unfair-Fair	.69	Weak-Strong	.55
Dishonest-Honest	.68		
Liberal-Conservative	.66		
Spender-Saver	.31		

Posttest			
Factor 1 (.62)		Factor 2 (.38)	
Unresponsive-Responsive	.69	Bad-Good	.60
Old Ideas-New Ideas	.65	Weak-Strong	.55
Unfair-Fair	.61	Liberal-Conservative	.51
Dishonest-Honest	.58	Spender-Saver	.37
Talker-Doer	.56		

[1] Percent of common variance

TABLE 4
**Factor Loadings Yielded by Varimax Analysis of Pretest and Posttest
Data Gathered from University Audiences**

Pretest			
Factor 1 (.85)[1]		Factor 2 (.15)	
Bad-Good	.79	Spender-Saver	.45
Dishonest-Honest	.74	Liberal-Conservative	.31
Unfair-Fair	.70		
Unresponsive-Responsive	.70		
Weak-Strong	.66		
Old Ideas-New Ideas	.59		
Talker-Doer	.46		

Posttest			
Factor 1 (.86)		Factor 2 (.14)	
Unfair-Fair	.80	Spender-Saver	.49
Bad-Good	.75	Liberal-Conservative	.30
Weak-Strong	.72		
Unresponsive-Responsive	.72		
Dishonest-Honest	.65		
Old Ideas-New Ideas	.54		
Talker-Doer	.52		

[1] Percent of common variance

reported in Table 2 ranged from a low of 9 to a high of 45 for each subject. In other words, the lowest score any subject could give was one on each of the nine scales, for a total of 9, and the highest score was 45 or a 5 on each of the nine scales. The means reported in Table 2 revealed a positive shift in the candidate's image.

As a supplement to the *analysis of variance,* we performed a *varimax orthogonally-rotated factor analysis* on the pretest and posttest data gathered in each of the three audience situations. With the eigenvalue set at 1.00, the first run yielded a one factor solution on all six sets of data (three pretests and three posttests). However, it did appear that there might be a second related factor. Tables 3, 4, and 5 contain the scales and loadings extracted during a second analysis wherein a two factor solution was requested.

At first glance, Table 3 might lead one to conclude that there was a substantial change in audi-

ence perceptions of the candidate between the pretesting and posttesting of the civic/fraternal audiences. For example, posttest factor 2 retained only one of the three scales it held in the pretest, dropped two scales, and added three. However, the results from an application of program SIMFAC do not support this conclusion. SIMFAC compares factor structures and provides a coefficient which is indicative of the extent to which the factors are related. Pretest factor 1 correlates highly with posttest factor 2 ($r=.90$, $R^2=.81$), and pretest factor 2 correlates highly with posttest factor 1 ($4=.96$, $R^2=.92$). It can, therefore, be concluded that those who came to hear the candidate on civic/fraternal occasions did not restructure their image of the candidate after hearing him speak.

Table 4 illustrates a similar result for those who heard the candidate in university settings. There is obviously great similarity between pretest factor 1 and posttest factor 1, and between pretest factor 2

TABLE 5
Factor Loadings Yielded by Varimax Analysis of Pretest and Posttest
Data Gathered from Political Rally Audiences

Pretest			
Factor 1 (.68)[1]		Factor 2 (.32)	
Dishonest-Honest	.86	Talker-Doer	.65
Unfair-Fair	.82	Spender-Saver	.63
Unresponsive-Responsive	.76	Old Ideas-New Ideas	.61
Bad-Good	.76		
Weak-Strong	.70		
Liberal-Conservative	.50		

Posttest			
Factor 1 (.65)		Factor 2 (.35)	
Bad-Good	.82	Talker-Doer	.69
Unfair-Fair	.80	Old Ideas-New Ideas	.65
Weak-Strong	.72	Spender-Saver	.54
Dishonest-Honest	.70		
Unresponsive-Responsive	.47		
Liberal-Conservative	.18		

[1] Percent of common variance

and posttest factor 2. The loadings for each factor are similar, as is the amount of variance accounted for by each factor. SIMFAC compared pretest factor 1 with posttest factor 1 and yielded a similarity coefficient of .99 ($R^2 = .98$). A similar comparison of pretest factor 2 and posttest factor 2 produced a r value of .93 ($R^2 = .88$). Thus, although the analysis of variance results reported in Table 2 indicate that there was a significant shift in candidate image, this shift was not accompanied by a restructuring of the candidate's image.

The data reported in Table 5 on political rallies follows a general pattern almost identical to the one evident in Table 4. Pretest factor 1 and posttest factor 1 correlate highly ($r = .97$, $R^2 = .95$), and pretest factor 2 correlates highly with posttest factor 2 ($r = .99$, $R^2 = .98$). Again, analysis of variance results show a shift in image, but this shift does not include any significant restructuring.

DISCUSSION

This study, which has elsewhere been called a "natural experiment" (Sanders & Pace, 1969), suffered from the problem of the nonrespondent, as do many nonlaboratory studies. And in this study nonrespondents were not systematically examined. However, a cursory analysis of the incomplete data produced by some subjects and brief interviews with a few nonrespondents suggest that some did not understand the instructions and that others were less friendly to the candidate than were respondents. Thus, it is possible that the image pretest is somewhat inflated and, perhaps, the posttests as well. This does not, in our judgment, compromise the worth of the study, because each subject served as his own control. Whether viewed on an audience-by-audience, or a scale-by-scale basis, as we did in a preliminary analysis of variance, or in a more collective audience-situation-by-audience-situation context, as we have done in this report, the shift in image is substantial.

More importantly, however, this study raises new questions regarding the adequacies of the "limited effects" perspective as an explanation for political information-seeking behavior and communication outcomes. The partisan diversity of the audiences which came to hear Paul Eggers, as well as their demographic heterogeneity, suggest that many persons came for reasons other than to have their partisan dispositions reinforced. Party affiliation as an indicator of audience composition or audience response may be losing its strength. There is much evidence from other sources that identification with the major parties is decreasing and that the power of party affiliation as a predictor of voting behavior is diminishing (Dreyer, 1971-1972). As voters become less interested in party cues and more attentive to the characteristics of individual candidates, which recent data (DeVries & Tarrance, 1972; Atwood & Sanders, 1975) suggest, the reasons for attending a political meeting may become more complicated.

In fact, so inadequate is the "limited effects" perspective, one is tempted to abandon it as a heuristic stimulus and as an explanatory tool, in spite of its profound influence on the planning and conduct of this study. In its place, one is inclined to substitute the recently reemergent *uses and gratifications* model (Blumler & McQuail, 1969; Blumler & Katz, 1974) which offers several possible explanations for the motivations behind political information-seeking of the kind studied here. This approach would suggest that when members of the electorate make the effort necessary to attend a political meeting, they may be exhibiting evidence of a variety of needs, including the need to learn more about the issues, the need to be seen in proper political company, the general need to "feel better" about the political process, or the explicit need to have their attitudes toward the candidate changed in a positive direction. There are data from a recent study of voter behavior in Ohio (O'Keefe, 1976) indicating that those who were most influenced by mass communication over the course of the campaign were those who most expected to be influenced. This suggests, however tentatively, that there may be a strong relationship between audience needs and expectations and the immediate, and, perhaps, long-term effects of political messages, and that this relationship may be much more complicated than the selective exposure hypothesis implies.

At any rate, we do not believe that changes in candidate image of the magnitude found in this study can be explained satisfactorily as mere reinforcement of pre-existing attitudes toward the candidate. Even if such changes could be explained in that fashion, we doubt that such an explanation would hold the long-term heuristic value of the yet embryonic *uses and gratifications* rationale which we have offered, ex post facto. There is an indication in this study, and in others, that the insistence by many speech communication theorists and rhetorical critics that oral communication behavior is inherently an independent variable should be abandoned. To paraphrase, members of a political audience may do more with a political speech in terms of satisfying their needs than the speech may do to them. (Katz, Blumler, & Gurevitch, 1974). Political speeches should be viewed as dependent variables as well as independent variables. Wide ranging, diverse, and complex audience needs may, in the long-run, be more predictive of communication outcomes than either source or message variables, the traditional concerns of speech communication process and criticism. The time has come to investigate this possibility.

NOTE

1. The authors wish to express their appreciation to Professor Douglas Bock of the University of Florida and to Professor Joe Stearns of Western Kentucky University for their help in gathering data; to Paul Eggers, the 1968 Republican Candidate for governor of Texas, for allowing unrestrained access to his campaign appearances; and to the Office of Research and Projects, SIU-C, for its monetary support.

REFERENCES

ATWOOD, E., & SANDERS, K. Perception of information sources and likelihood of split ticket voting. *Journalism Quarterly*, 1975, 52, 3, 421-428.

BECKER, L.B., McCOMBS, M.E., & McLEOD, J.M. The development of political cognitions. In S.H. Chaffee (Ed.), *Political communication*. Beverly Hills: California, 1975.

BERELSON, B.R., & STEINER, G.A. *Human behavior*. New York: Harcourt Brace, 1964.

BLUMLER, J.G., & McQUAIL, D. *Television in politics: Its uses and influence*. Chicago, Illinois: University of Chicago Press, 1969.

BLUMLER, J.G., & KATZ, E. (Eds.), *The uses of mass communications*. Beverly Hills, California: Sage, 1974.

BLUMLER, J.G., & McLEOD, J.M. Communication and voter turnout in Britain. In T. Leggart (Ed.), *Sociological theory and survey research*. Beverly Hills, California: Sage, 1974.

BROOKS, W.D. A field study of the Johnson and Goldwater campaign speeches in Pittsburgh. *The Southern Speech Journal*, 1967, 32, 273-281.

DeVRIES, W., & TARRANCE, V.L. *The ticket-splitter*. Grand Rapids, Michigan: Eardmans, 1972.

DREYER, E.C. Media use and electoral choices: Some political consequences of information exposure. *Public Opinion Quarterly*, 1971-72, 35, 3, 545-553.

FESTINGER, L. *A theory of cognitive dissonance*. Stanford, California: Stanford University Press, 1957.

FREEDMAN, J.L., & SEARS, D.O. Selective exposure. In Leonard Berkowitz (Ed.), *Advances in experimental social psychology*, Vol. 2. New York: Academic Press, 1965.

HOFSTADTER, R. *The paranoid style in American politics, and other essays*. New York: Knopf, 1966.

KAID, L.L., & HIRSCH, R.O., Selective exposure and candidate image: A field study over time. *Central States Speech Journal*, 1973, 24, 48-51.

KATZ, E. On reopening the question of selectivity in exposure to mass communications. In Robert P. Abelson, et al., (Eds.), *Theories of cognitive consistency*. Chicago, Illinois: Rand McNally, 1968, 788-796.

KATZ, E., BLUMLER, J.G., & GUREVITCH, M. Utilization of mass communication by the individual. In J.G. Blumler and E. Katz (Eds.), *The uses of mass communication*. Beverly Hills, California, Sage, 1974.

KELLEY, S., JR. *Political campaigning*. Washington, D.C.: The Brookings Institute, 1960.

LAMB, K.A., & SMITH, P.A. *Campaign decision-making: The presidential election of 1964*. Belmont, California: Wadsworth, 1968.

LASARSFELD, P.F., BERELSON, B., & GAUDET, H. *The people's choice*. New York: Duell, Sloan and Pearce, 1948.

MacNEIL, R. *The people machine*. New York: Harper & Row, 1968.

MILLS, J. Interest in supporting and discrepant information. In Robert P. Abelson, et al., (Eds.), *Theories of cognitive consistency*. Chicago, Illinois: Rand McNally and Company, 1968, 771-776.

O'KEEFE, G. The uses and gratifications approach and political communication research. *Political Communication Review*, 1976, 1, 3, 8-11.

Report of behavioral sciences subpanel. President's Science Advisory Committee. Washington, D.C.: Government Printing Office, 1962.

SANDERS, K.R. A critique of contemporary approaches to the study of political communication. In R. Davis (Ed.), *Proceedings of the speech communication association summer conference, 1975*. Falls Church, Virginia: Speech Communication Association (in press).

SANDERS, K.R., & NEWMAN, R.P. John A. Stormer and the Hofstadter hypothesis. *Central States Speech Journal*, 22, 1971, 218-227.

SANDERS, K.R., & PACE, T.J. The natural experiment as a research methodology in speech communication. In James E. Roever (Ed.), *Proceedings of the Speech Association of America summer conference on research and action*. New York: Speech Association of America, 1969, 80-87.

SCAMMON, R.M., & WATTENBERG, B.J. *The real majority*. New York: Coward-McCann, 1970.

SCHRAMM, W., & CARTER, F. Effectiveness of a political telethon. *Public Opinion Quarterly*, 1959, 23, 188-190.

SEARS, D.O. The paradox of de facto selective exposure without preferences for supportive information. In Robert P. Abelson, et al., (Eds.), *Theories of cognitive consistency*. Chicago, Illinois: Rand McNally, 1968.

SEARS, D.O., & WHITNEY, R.E. Political persuasion. In I. de Sola Pool, et al., (Eds.), *Handbook of communication*. Chicago, Illinois: Rand McNally, 1973.

STAR, S.A., & HUGHES, H.M. Report of an educational campaign: The Cincinnati plan for the United Nations. *American Journal of Sociology*, 1950, 55, 389-400.

SWANSON, D.L. The new politics meets the old rhetoric: New directions in campaign communications research. *Quarterly Journal of Speech*, 1972, 53, 31-40.

TRENT, J.S. A synthesis of methodologies used in studying political communication. *Central States Speech Journal*, 1975, 26, 287-297.

PRECISE PROCEDURES FOR OPTIMIZING CAMPAIGN COMMUNICATION

KIM B. SEROTA
Product and Consumer Evaluations, Inc.

MICHAEL J. CODY
Michigan State University

GEORGE A. BARNETT
Rensselaer Polytechnic Institute

JAMES A. TAYLOR
Michigan State University

Multidimensional scaling has been used in political campaigns because it offers several advantages over the use of unidimensional scaling procedures. Specifically, multidimensional scaling allows the researcher to simultaneously observe change and rates of change with the public's attitudes toward the candidates and issues in the election campaign. Further, multidimensional scaling reveals the dimensions voters use to differentiate the candidates and their stands on issues. The goal of this paper is to describe two innovations which will enhance the utility of multidimensional scaling in campaign research: (1) a new least-squares procedure for rotating multidimensional configurations over time, and (2) a precise mathematical procedure for optimizing message strategies and for assessing the effectiveness of implemented message strategies. Reanalysis of campaign research data, over three points in time from a local Congressional election, indicates that the mathematical procedures provide a significant contribution to devising message strategies and in assessing the effectiveness of such strategies.

Recent years have seen an accelerating trend toward sophisticated mathematical theories and models, along with precise quantitative research techniques among human communication scientists. Among these, a simple "inertial" theory (Saltiel & Woelfel, 1975; Danes, Hunter, & Woelfel, 1976), and a combination of ratio-scaled dissimilarities estimates (Danes & Woelfel, 1975), and metric multidimensional scaling (Torgerson, 1958), have found particularly promising applications to questions of cultural belief, public opinion, and other macro-communication topics.

Following the procedures defined by Woelfel (1973, 1974), Barnett, Serota, and Taylor (1974) and Taylor, Barnett, and Serota (1975) asked randomly selected voters in a Michigan congressional district to estimate the dissimilarities among all nonredundant pairs of a set of 10 empirically derived issues in a congressional election campaign in ratio-level scales. Based on metric multidimensional scaling analyses of these data, Barnett et al. (1974), advised one of the candidates about the most effective campaign strategies. Subsequently repeated measurements showed substantial evidence of the effectiveness of the strategy, and the candidate was elected by a large margin.

The present paper addresses two central developments in applied multidimensional scaling (MDS), and provides a significant reanalysis of the Barnett, Serota, and Taylor (1976) congressional campaign study. The first of these developments is the establishment of a theoretical reference frame against which to observe, systematically, the consequent effects of campaign communication strategies (Woelfel et al., 1975). The second development is a technique for the identification of optimized message strategy, and subsequent comparison of optimal strategies, actual campaign communications, and resultant attitude change (Woelfel et al., 1976). In the original analysis of the 1974 Congressional data, neither procedure was available to the researchers. Reanalysis yields new and surprising results which significantly support the trend toward mathematical optimizing in political communication and formation of persuasive communication strategy.

THE MULTIDIMENSIONAL SCALING
TECHNIQUE

The significance of a multidimensional technique is its power for representing various influences in the projection of structure, simultaneously. Unlike unidimensional scaling, in which error is often better attributed to multiple influences upon judgment (Thurstone, 1927), multidimensional scaling accounts for all of the influences inherent and necessary in a *specific* set of judgments. According to Torgerson:

> . . . the notion of a single unidimensional, underlying continuum is replaced by the notion of an underlying multidimensional space. Instead of considering the stimuli to be represented by points along a single dimension, the stimuli are represented by points in a space of several dimensions. Instead of assigning a single number (scale value) to represent the position of the point along the dimension, as many numbers are assigned to each stimulus as there are independent dimensions in the relevant multidimensional space. Each number corresponds to the projections (scale value) of the points on one of the axes (dimensions) of the space. (1958, p. 248)

By repeating the spatial representation through several points in time, it becomes possible to observe simultaneous changes, and to use the trajectories of motion (across time changes in position) to make mathematically descriptive statements about those changes. It also becomes possible to examine change in light of the causal influences of communicative behavior.

The procedures for generating a metric MDS analysis, which are described in detail by Woelfel and Barnett (1974) and Barnett, Serota, and Taylor (1976), are presented here, briefly.

Subjects are given a complete ($n[n-1]/2$) list of pair comparisons for a set of concepts being scaled. They are asked to make ratio judgments of the dissimilarity between concepts using the form:

> If x and y are u units apart, how far apart are concept a and concept b?

Such a procedure requests a distance judgment from a respondent (". . . how far apart are a and b?") for all [$n(n-1)/2$] pairs of concepts. Specifically, it requests that this judgment be made as a proportion of a standard distance provided by the researcher ("if x and y are u units apart . . ."). This format allows the respondent to report any positive value; the scale is thus unbounded at the high end, continuous, and grounded with a true zero (meaning identity—two concepts are perceived to be the same).

Since the goal of public opinion research is to measure shared *social* or *cultural* conceptions or the attitudes toward a series of issues held by a defined population, one may use aggregation techniques to improve the measurements. By invoking the *Central Limits Theorem* and *Law of Large Numbers* one finds that the arithmetic average of all responses, for any cell in the matrix, will converge on the true mean for the population as the sample grows large. Thus, the first step in the analysis of the distance estimates is to determine the mean estimate for all possible pairs of n concepts (each cell in the n x n matrix). To the extent that the sample size is large, that cell estimate will be reliable.

The *mean-distance matrix* is then converted into a *scalar-products matrix*, which has been transformed (Torgerson, 1958) to establish an origin at the centroid of the distribution. This matrix is subsequently factored (using an unstandardized direct iterative or diagonalization procedure), to achieve a *coordinate matrix* whose columns are orthogonal axes, and whose rows are the projections of the concept location on each of the axes. This space has the property of representing the average distance judgments for all possible pairs simultaneously. Since the multidimensional space is constructed from the *unstandardized* distance vectors between all possible pairs, variance in the sample population is thus completely accounted for by the multidimensional space.

Finally, this procedure is repeated at each point in time, and the spaces are rotated about the centroid to congruence, to obtain approximations of the concept motions over time. From these resultant cross-time coordinate matrices, one can fit curves (trajectories) of motion which describe the relational changes from the set. Further, the cross-time loadings allow one to make predictions of consequent attitude change.

This scaling procedure has been extensively tested, and aggregate test-retest reliability coefficients of .90 and above have been reported by

Barnett (1972) with as few as 50 cases, and by Gillham and Woelfel (1976) with 29 cases. Simultaneous but separate random samples of approximately 100 have produced intergroup correlations ranging from .93 to .97 in repeated tests (Gordon, 1976). These coefficients, of course, are dependent upon the scaled concepts and the homogeneity of the population.

In the earlier analysis by Barnett, Serota, and Taylor (1976) the general utility of this procedure in the examination of political attitude formation was demonstrated. These data, which provided clear evidence for the validity of longitudinal application of metric multidimensional scaling, are reconsidered here in light of the new methodological developments. A brief review of the previous analysis provides a context for this reanalysis.

REVIEW OF THE EXISTING ANALYSIS AND CONGRESSIONAL STUDY

Data collection procedures are described in Barnett, Serota, and Taylor (1976). Separate random samples were employed in place of a single panel to insure against sensitization and subject mortality. Personal interviews were conducted by trained, professional interviewers using the following question format to generate ratio distance judgments for all possible pairs of concepts at three points in time:

> If John F. Kennedy and Dwight D. Eisenhower are 10 political inches apart, how far apart are:
> —Crime Prevention and the Republican Party
> —Crime Prevention and Inflation

This analysis utilized concepts selected either for reasons related to partisan political theory (party labels, candidate names, and self) or because they were identified in a pretest as being issues which the population under study was going to use to decide whom to vote for. The concepts scaled were:

1. Crime prevention
2. Integrity and honesty in government
3. The Republican party
4. Inflation
5. The Democratic party
6. Democratic candidate (actual name)
7. Campaign reform
8. Busing
9. Me (representing the "self" concept)
10. Republican candidate (actual name)

The district selected for this project is located in north-suburban Detroit. The racial composition is 99% white, with a median age of 39.9 years and a median education for registered voters of 12.4 years (Barone, Ujifusa, & Matthews, 1974).

This district has been traditionally Democratic. In 1968, Nixon received 35% of the vote, Wallace 10%, and Humphrey 54%. However, in 1972, Nixon captured 63%. The incumbent Republican Congressman received 53% of the vote in 1972 (Barone et al., 1974).

The incumbent was clearly recognized as conservative, and strongly identified with limited government spending and opposition to bussing to achieve racial integration. He had close ties with corporate business interests, and was a publicly ardent supporter of former President Nixon. The Democratic challenger (now Congressman) was a former assistant state attorney general. The 1974 campaign was his first attempt at elected office. Virtually unknown six months before the election, he won a hotly contested primary against three other candidates, with 34% of the vote.

The results of the three data collections are summarized in Barnett, Serota, and Taylor (1976). Figure 1 represents the changes in concept positions over time. Based upon the data structure at time one, which showed certain concepts clustering together, or located in the same general region of the spatial representation, the Democratic candidate was advised that campaign messages should stress identification with the Democratic party, and simultaneously emphasize his association with crime prevention. The vector representing the combination of these two messages appeared, upon inspection of the spatial representation, to most closely resemble the vector from the candidate to the self concept, *Me*. Previous political campaign research using multidimensional scaling (Barnett, Serota, & Taylor, 1974), suggested that this association, rather than the traditional association with an ideal candidate, would produce the desired effect for the campaign.

As a consulting strategy, it would appear to be conventional wisdom to have a candidate stress his or her party affiliation as well as personal associations with popular stances on the issues (Butler & Stokes, 1969). However, the salience and issue interrelationships present among a set of issues during a given political campaign may be misleading. For example, while the busing issue had high salience during the 1972 campaign in this district, it was neither an important issue nor an issue which was favorably located relative to the other issues and concepts. While the candidate had intended to take a strong stand on busing, it was advised that the issue be treated as unimportant to this race.

It was emphasized to the challenger that he should work to associate himself with desired concepts rather than attacking his opponent. Since the challenger was relatively unknown, his information history was much less than the incumbent and therefore much less resistant to change (Saltiel & Woelfel, 1975; Danes, Hunter, & Woelfel, 1976). The ramifications of this strategy include the possibility that the public may actually have agenda-setting powers commonly thought to have been usurped by the media and politicians, and that political advantage may belong to those candidates who orient themselves to entering the political process consonant with dominant public opinion.

Between the first and second data collection, the Democratic challenger distributed 145,000 leaflets, 100,000 of which went to areas of lowest awareness. This message dealt with his experience as an assistant attorney general and his position in law enforcement. It also clearly identified him as a candidate of the Democratic party. During this period the candidate also received major media coverage stressing the same basic concept associations.

Using a simple least-squares orthogonal rotation, the following analysis of motion between time 1 and time 2 was made. Concepts which appeared to move more than average were *crime prevention* (11.71), the *Republican party* (15.15), the *Democratic candidate* (12.90) and *Me* (10.81). These motions could be explained in terms of significant news events and the campaign of the Democratic challenger. The *Republican party* may have moved

because the reaction to the pardoning of Richard Nixon had subsided and the people were moving back toward their traditional party affiliations. The *Democratic candidate's* motion appeared to be a function of his campaigning, which had somewhat stabilized his position in the space. His net movement was toward *Me,* the *Democratic party,* and *crime prevention,* which reflected his campaign and messages stressing the fact that he was a crime fighter and a Democrat. The Republican incumbent was the most stable concept in the space, moving only 3.81 units. At this point, a prediction was made that if rates of change remained constant with those of late September, the Democratic challenger would be the new Congressman.

Based on the above discussion, the following strategies were recommended to the Democratic candidate. First, reference should be made to the opponent as a Republican, reinforcing his deviation from the Democratic plurality. Second, messages which would move the Republican away from *integrity and honesty in government* and *campaign reform* would also facilitate his movement away from the self concept, *Me.*

In general, these second-stage recommendations were not implemented and the earlier campaign strategy was sustained, however in less intensive form. During this later phase of the campaign, the incumbent employed most of his campaign messages, with little effect. The combined result of ineffective campaigning by the Republican candidate and low activity by the Democratic candidate, and the increased inertial mass of the concepts or issues, was less *relative* change during the month prior to the election. The Democratic candidate, however, continued to move toward the concept of *Me* in the space. The exact nature of this motion will be discussed in the section of this paper entitled *Computation of Message Effectiveness.*

Using the simple least-squares rotation the average motion in the space between t_2 and t_3 was 3.95 units; this was considerably less than between the first and second points in time. This indicates that by the second measurement the concepts had stablized in the space. Those concepts with movement greater than the mean were the *Republican party,* the *Democratic party,* the *Democratic candidate,* and *Me.* Again, the Republican

FIGURE 1
Trajectories of Motion for the Political Concepts Prior to the 1974 Congressional Election. Note That Changes Between Times Two and Three are Considerably Less Than Changes Between Times One and Two (Concepts Identifed in the Text)

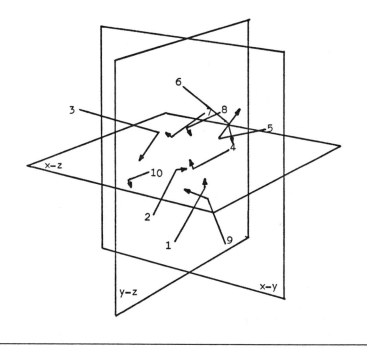

incumbent was the most stable concept in space. If one examines Figure 1, it becomes apparent that *Me* had changed direction and was approaching the position of the *Republican candidate;* further, the little movement of the incumbent is in the direction of *Me*. Three hypotheses were confirmed, which further demonstrate the validity of the technique.

First, the candidates converged with those issues with which they were publicly associated. The Democrat came out in favor of crime prevention between the first and second points in time. At time one, the mean distance between the candidate and *crime prevention* was 32.42 units. At time two the distance, or discrepancy, had dropped to 8.85 units, a change of 23.57 units. The average motion of all concepts in the space was 9.23 units, and both concepts showed great movement toward each other in excess of the mean.

Between the second and third points in time, the campaign stagnated. This is reflected in the stable relationship between the candidate and *crime prevention*. On *busing* and *inflation* the challenger had made no public statements. His distance relative to these concepts, accordingly, remained stable throughout the campaign.

Second, the candidate clustering most closely to the issue positions that the respondents identified as central to themselves (*Me*) did converge with the average self position. At time one *crime prevention* was the issue located closest to the collective self concept, *Me; busing* was the furthest concept from *Me*. The *Democrat* would have to move in the direction of *crime prevention* and away from *busing*. If one examines the plot (see Figure 1) this can be seen in the trajectories of the three concepts; the Democratic candidate moved past *busing,* in the direction of *crime prevention*.

Third, the candidate whose distance from the position of the respondents (represented by *Me*), was minimized at the time of the election was the candidate chosen by the population. At time three, the distance between *Me* and *Democrat* was 8.6 units while *Me* was 10.8 from the Republican. If one sums the magnitudes of these vectors, then divides each individual distance by this total, and finally, subtracts this proportion from one, the result is the predicted vote. In the above case, the predicted percentage of the vote was 55.7% for the Democratic candidate and 44.3% for the Republican. The actual vote total for the area of study was 57.7% for the Democrat, 41.3% for the Republican and 1.09% for the independent candidates.

REVISED ROTATION AND OPTIMIZATION PROCEDURES

While the 1974 Congressional Study (Barnett et al., 1976) represents a significant innovation in polling methods, it is not without faults. Most important among the problems raised by this approach are the rotation of subsequent measurements into a congruence for "correct" interpretation of concept movements, and the precise optimization of campaign strategies.

In the earlier analysis, the static representations were rotated to congruence with an ordinary least-squares rotation (Cliff, 1966) of the configurations. That is, the squared discrepancies between the corresponding concepts at successive points in time were minimized. First, a translation with a common origin for all three spaces was applied. The operation superimposes the centroid of one distribution (time two) upon the centroid of the other (time one), and successive distributions upon the previous one. Then, the axes were rotated pairwise so that the distance between all concepts, on all possible pairs of axes, were minimized to a Gaussian least-squares best fit. This is given by the formula:

$$\text{Min} \quad \sum_{i=1}^{n} \sum_{j=1}^{m} \sum_{k=1}^{m-1} [\Theta_{ijk(t)} - \Theta_{ijk(t-1)}]^2 \quad (j<k), \quad (1)$$

where i is the subscript for concepts in the set of n concepts, j and k are the dimensions being paired for comparison, m is the rank or dimensionality of the space, and t and $t-1$ designate the two sets of data to be rotated (Serota, 1974).

In a recent article, Woelfel and associates (1975)

critized the use of the rotation of spaces to a least-squares best fit (cf. Cliff, 1966; Schönemann, 1966). The reason they suggest is that

> . . . such a solution uniformly attributes resistance to motion to all the data points regardless of position in the space. This method is disadvantageous because it renders highly complex the apparent change in situations where relatively simple laws could describe the "actual" change, given a more insightful rotation. (p. 4)

The least-square rotation has the effect of overestimating some changes, while underestimating others. This may lead to erroneous conclusions, such as the interpretation that the public's attitude toward a series of issues has changed when in fact only their attitude toward the candidates has been altered.

As an alternative to the least-squares procedure, Woelfel et al. (1975), propose a method which makes use of theoretical or "extra" information to provide a rotation yielding far simpler apparent motion. This information concerns the interrelationships of the concepts in the space, and is independent of their coordinate values. The information variable may be such things as the amount of coverage an issue has received in the mass media, a political candidate's use or lack of a campaign issue, some sociological invariants such as the perception of certain aspects of the occupational prestige structure, or an attitude theoretic construct such as Woelfel's inertial mass (Saltiel & Woelfel, 1975). Since this information is independent of the coordinate values, its value may be treated as invariant under rotation and the translation of the coordinates.

Two procedures for rotation to theoretical criteria have been developed by Woelfel, et al (1975). The first of these assumes a simple dichotomy between stable and motion concept sets; the concepts may be either components of a spatial reference system or elements of the set being quantified against the reference frame. The second assumes a more complex system of weights proportional to the stability of each of the elements in the concept set. This analysis will employ the first of these procedures.

Given m stable concepts out of n concepts represented as points in an r dimensional space $(m>r)$, the rotation procedure suggested here consists of two primary operations: (1) the establishment of a common origin for the t_n and the t_{n+1} spaces, and (2) the rotation of the t_{n+1} space to the t_n space so that the separation of any one of the m *stable* concepts from itself is a minimum.

Establishing a common origin consists of a straightforward translation of coordinate axes such that the centroid (of each axis) for both spaces is at the midpoint of the distribution for the hypothesized stable concepts. It is important to emphasize that these concepts are hypothesized to be stable *relative to each other;* against this stable reference constellation, location changes by the more volatile concepts will be calibrated.

Given the following coordinate matrices:

X = the matrix of coordinates at t_n, and
Y = the matrix of coordinates at t_{n+1}

the first task is to find:

A = the matrix X on the common reference system, and
B = the matrix Y on the common reference system.

Finding the centroid of a space which is to be used as the origin for a common reference system is accomplished by first determining the average of the coordinate loadings of the m stable concepts for each of the r dimensions; that is:

$$c_{kk} = \sum_{j=1}^{m} x_{jk}/m \qquad (k = 1,2,\ldots,r) \qquad (2)$$

$$h_{kk} = \sum_{j=1}^{m} y_{jk}/m \qquad (k = 1,2,\ldots,r) \qquad (3)$$

where, m = the number of stable concepts, and x_{jk} and y_{jk} are the projections of the jth stable concept on kth dimensions in X and Y respectively. The translation of the coordinate matrices from the old origin to the new "stable centroid" origin is given by:

$$a_{ik} = x_{ik} - c_{kk} \qquad (4)$$

$$b_{ik} = y_{ik} - h_{kk} \qquad (5)$$

where i refers to each of the concepts in the matrix, and c_{kk} and h_{kk} are the elements of the diagonal matrices C and H.

With both A and B coordinate matrices now lo-

cated at a common origin, the next task is to rotate the B coordinates so that the distance for any stable concept j from itself is minimized; this amounts to the following minimizing function:

$$\text{Min } \sum_{j=1}^{m} s_{jj}^2 = \sum_{j=1}^{m} \sum_{k=1}^{r} (a_{jk} - b^\circ_{jk})^2 \qquad (6)$$

where b°_{jk} are the stable projections in the rotated B matrix (denoted B°), and s_{jj} is the distance of concept j in matrix A to concept j in matrix B°. The value $\sum s_{jj}^2$ is a minimum because, while the equation is computed by the method of least squares, it is unlikely that either the distribution of points in A or B will be a straight line. Hence, the sum of squares is not likely to equal the absolute value of zero. The purpose of this minimization is to find, among several alternatives, that set of elements, b°_{jk}, which most closely fit the elements of matrix A.

In order to find the elements of B°, b°_{jk}, it is necessary to perform a series of transformations on the set of all possible axis pairs. The transformation series, designated T_{pq} $(p<q)$, is defined as the two-space orthogonal transformation series commonly used in classical mechanics:

$$T_{pq} = \begin{bmatrix} \cos\Theta_{pq} & -\sin\Theta_{pq} \\ \sin\Theta_{pq} & \cos\Theta_{pq} \end{bmatrix} \qquad (7)$$

where,

Θ_{pq} = the angles needed to minimize the distance of the m stable concepts in matrix A from those in matrix B.

The angles of rotation Θ_{pq} are determined by first noting that the projections of the stable concepts j on the p and q coordinates in the matrix B° are given by:

$$b^\circ_{jp} = b_{jp} \cos \Theta_{pq} + b_{jq} \sin \Theta_{pq} \qquad (8)$$

$$b^\circ_{jq} = -b_{jp} \sin \Theta_{pq} + b_{jq} \cos \Theta_{pq} \qquad (9)$$

The angle Θ_{pq} which minimizes the j concepts at two points in time in a pq plane is determined by:

$$S_{\Theta_{pq}} = \sum_{j=1}^{m} (a_{jp} - b^\circ_{jp})^2 +$$

$$\sum_{j=1}^{m} (a_{jq} - b^\circ_{jq})^2 = \text{MIN} \qquad (10)$$

By substituting 8 and 9, in 10 and expanding, yields:

$$S_{\Theta_{pq}} = \Sigma a^2_{jp} + \Sigma a^2_{jq} + \Sigma b^2_{jp} + \Sigma b^2_{jq} -$$

$$2 \cos \Theta \ (\Sigma a_{jp}b_{jp} + \Sigma a_{jp}b_{jp}) -$$

$$2 \sin \Theta \ (\Sigma a_{jp}b_{jq} - \Sigma a_{jq}b_{jp}) \qquad (11)$$

Taking the first derivative of $S_{\Theta_{pq}}$ with respect to the angle Θ_{pq} and setting it to zero gives:

$$\frac{dS_{\Theta_{pq}}}{d_{\Theta_{pq}}} = \sin \Theta_{pq} \ (\Sigma a_{jp}b_{jp} - \Sigma a_{jq}b_{jq}) -$$

$$\cos \Theta_{pq} \ (\Sigma a_{jp}b_{jq} +$$

$$\Sigma a_{jq}b_{jp}) = 0 \qquad (12)$$

which leads to the following solutions for the angle Θ_{pq}:

$$\mathrm{Tan}_{\Theta_{pq}} = \frac{\Sigma a_{jp}b_{jq} + \Sigma a_{jq}b_{jp}}{\Sigma a_{jp}b_{jp} - \Sigma a_{jq}b_{jq}} \qquad (13)$$

The arc-tangent of the expression in the right side of equation 13 will yield Θ_{pq}. The second derivative of equation 12 will indicate whether Θ_{pq} is a minimum or maximum for the transformation. If the second derivative is negative, then it is necessary to add 180° to angle Θ_{pq}.

Following each transformation, Tpq, the new values of $b°$ for vectors p and q are substituted into matrix $B°$. The subsequent transformation may then be performed.

Utilizing the above rotation procedure, stable and free-moving concepts can be differentiated and accommodated in the observation of concept motions. Accordingly, a more theoretically precise reference frame is generated, and the systematic nature of concept motions as a result of information influence is more readily evident.

A BRIEF SUMMARY OF MESSAGE OPTIMIZING PROCEDURES

After respondents have made distance estimates between all non-redundant pairs of concepts used in the pair comparison questionnaire, responses are averaged across respondents, yielding an aggregate matrix $\overline{S}$ (a matrix of arithmetic means). This matrix is then orthogonally decomposed to yield a mul-

tidimensional spatial coordinate system R in which candidates, issues, and a target concept are arrayed. The purpose of the optimizing procedure is to provide information about which subset of concepts in this array can be combined and included in a message that would move a candidate toward the target concept. The exact mathematical algorithm by which this subset of concepts can be selected utilizes the following procedure.

First, we center the coordinate system R on the concept representing the candidate for whom the strategy is to be devised, by the translation of coordinates

$$R^i_j = R^{i'}_u - R^{c'}_j \qquad (14)$$
$$j = 1, 2, \ldots, k$$

where, $R^i = $ the position vector of the ith concept after recentering,

$R^{i'} = $ the original position vector of the ith concept, and

$R^{c'} = $ the original position vector of the candidate.

(R can be any coordinate system, in a series of data collections, at the point in time the researcher wishes to devise the message strategy.) Due to this recentering, the candidate's position vector R^c is now the null vector $|R^c| = 0$, and the position vector R^m, representing the location of the target concept, also represents the vector path along which the conception of the candidate is intended to move.

Further, R^i is the vector originating at the candidate's location and extending to each of the i concepts. It is assumed that any assertion which associates the candidate with concept i will move that candidate along the vector R^i. Similarly, R^i is further generalized to any combination of concepts by a vector addition procedure. R^i will be called the predicted vector.

Based on the above assumption, determination of a single optimal issue may be simply accomplished: first, the angle α_{im} between any predicted vector (R^i) and the target vector can be conveniently calculated from the scalar product

$$\alpha_{im} = \cos^{-1} \frac{(\ \cdot \ R^iR^m \ )}{|R^i| \ \ |R^m|} \qquad (15)$$

$$i = i, 2, \ldots, k{-}1.$$

That concept whose position vector forms the smallest angle with the target vector will represent the concept that will draw the candidate most nearly in the *direction* of the target concept. The *amount of change* advocated by this message strategy is given straightforwardly by the length of the predicted vector $|R^i|$, which is given by

$$|R^i| = (\sum_{j=1}^{r} (R_j^i)^2)^{1/2} \qquad (16)$$

where r is the dimensionality of R. The above equations are more fully elaborated in Woelfel, Fink, Holmes, Cody, and Taylor (1976). The computer subroutine computes the distance of R^m, distance of R^i, angles between R^m and R^i, the ratio of R^i and R^m, and the correlation between R^i and R^m.

R^i in these equations is used in a general sense. The optimal message strategy (R^i) may be any single concept vector solution (Candidate A is Y), two-pair message solution (Candidate A is X and Y), three-pair message solution, or four-pair message solution. What is important to show, is that the manipulated candidate moves along the *predicted vector*. Procedures for such an analysis are given by Woelfel, et al. (1976) as follows.

Evaluation of the success or failure of such predictions is given straightforwardly by the cosines (correlations) of the angles between the predicted vector R^i and the vector observed, $R^c(t_2)$, across the time interval of the message Δt. Given measures at two points in time t and $t + \Delta t$, we define the predicted vector across t as

$$R^i(t_2) - R^i(t_1) = R^i(\Delta t) \qquad (17)$$
where $R^i(t_2)$ = the coordinates of R^i at $t + \Delta t$
$R^i(t_1)$ = the coordinates of R^i at t

Similarly, the observed vector across Δt is given by

$$R^c(t_2) - R^c(t_1) = R^c(\Delta t) \qquad (18)$$
where $R^c(t_2)$ = the coordinates of R^c at $t + \Delta t$
$R^c(t_1)$ = the coordinates of R_c at t

But, due to the centering operation, $R^c(t_1) = 0$, so $R_c(\Delta t) = R^c(t_2)$. Since we make no prediction about the magnitude of either $R^i(\Delta t)$ or $R^c(\Delta t)$, then it is sufficient to confirm the prediction that cos $\alpha \simeq 1.00$, $\alpha \simeq 0.00$.

In practice, however, it is difficult to hold the center of the coordinate system precisely on the spot where the candidate concept was at t for $t + \Delta t$, and so, frequently, a third origin may be chosen, generally at the centroid of the issues and concepts considered stable or least likely to move across the interval based on some criterion (see Woelfel et al., 1975). In this event the components of R_c at t_1 cannot be neglected, and we require

$$\frac{R^i(\Delta t) \cdot R^c(\Delta t)}{|R^i(\Delta t)| \quad |R^c(\Delta t)|} = \cos \alpha \qquad (19)$$

Functionally, these procedures translate any sequential pair of configurations to a centroid which is the candidate's time-one null vector (the first two steps of the procedure to obtain the message, but performed on both sets of data after a least-squares rotation of theoretically stable concepts). The difference between the candidate's time-two location and time-one location represent the candidate's motion vector $[R^c(\Delta t)]$. This motion vector is correlated with the time-one predicted motion vector (R^i).

Woelfel et al, (1976), generalize these equations to account for the non-Euclidean characteristics of the multidimensional spaces.

CALCULATION OF MESSAGE STRATEGIES

The message optimizing procedure was used with the time-one data in order to construct message strategies that would move the candidate directly towards the target concept. This procedure produced five, single-concept solutions, and a large number of two-pair, three-pair, and four-pair message solutions. Recall that the solution (or a set of message solutions) in which the angle between R^i and the target vector is (or are) minimal provide the best message strategy(ies). In this section of the paper we shall describe a number of "fair" and "good" message strategies.

Before discussing these solutions, let us first briefly describe the interrelations between concepts when employing the new rotation (Figure 2). The concepts, and concept identification labels, are referenced previously. The number represents the location of the concept at time one, and the dots along

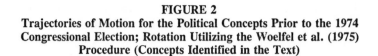

FIGURE 2
Trajectories of Motion for the Political Concepts Prior to the 1974
Congressional Election; Rotation Utilizing the Woelfel et al. (1975)
Procedure (Concepts Identified in the Text)

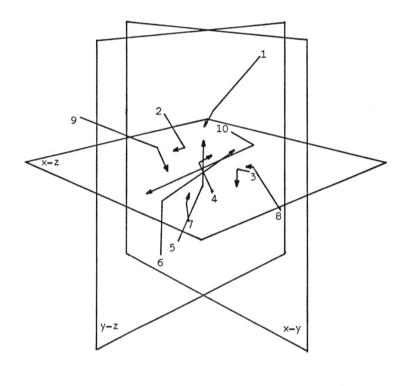

the lines report the concept's location at subsequent points in time. Note that Figure 2 is rotated at a different angle for representation—this rotation does not affect the location of the concepts in relation to each other, but does influence the ability to interpret the three dimensional representation. Some of the concepts appear to be in different quadrants of the space, and the reader should keep in mind that these quadrants are arbitrary. What is important is the relative motion between concepts.

The *Democratic candidate,* the *Democratic party,* the *Republican candidate,* and the target concept *Me* move more than the other concepts in the space. Even when employing the rotation with the least-squares rotation for the stable concepts, the *Democratic candidate* (concept 6), the *Democratic party* (5) and *crime prevention* (1) converge. Also, the aggregate *Me* (9) similarly converges to-

ward these concepts—except less so between time two and time three. The *Republican candidate* (10) appears first to move towards the *Republican party* (3) and *Busing* (8) between time one and time two (although this movement appears to be small in magnitude), and then moves toward *campaign reform* (7) and *inflation* (4) between time two and time three.

By simply assessing the graphic illustration of the concepts in the first three dimensions, it would appear that the Democratic candidate's best time-one message strategy would be to use the issue of *integrity and honesty in government* (2) than any other single concept message strategy. Between time two and three, it would appear that the two-pair message strategy using *integrity and honesty in government* (2) and *crime prevention* (1) would move the candidate more closely toward the target

FIGURE 3
A Possible Message Strategy Based on Time One Data

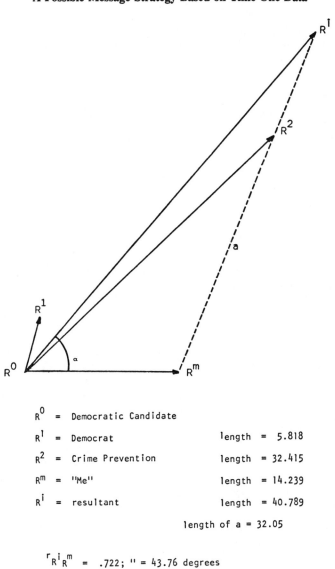

R^0	=	Democratic Candidate	
R^1	=	Democrat	length = 5.818
R^2	=	Crime Prevention	length = 32.415
R^m	=	"Me"	length = 14.239
R^i	=	resultant	length = 40.789

length of a = 32.05

$r_{R^iR^m}$ = .722; " = 43.76 degrees

Me than the message strategy of *crime prevention* and *Democratic party* (5).

Note that the major differences between Figure 1 and Figure 2 is that the candidate's movements are attenuated when they are included as concepts in which the least-squares rotation procedure is implemented. In Figure 2, the candidates move more, and even among the theoretically stable concepts,

the movement of the concepts which do exhibit true change (*Democratic party, Me,* and *crime prevention*) is not overly attenuated by the rotation.

Mathematical Message Optimizing Procedures

There is a serious qualification in using an eyeball approach to devising message strategies, as we briefly have done above for the Figure 2 configuration. Specifically, these configurations only represent three of the dimensions in the multidimensional configuration, and there exists considerable information in the remaining dimensions. Secondly, it is difficult to interpret depth in these three-dimensional configurations. Therefore, we shall now turn to the results of employing the mathematical message optimizing procedure.

Figure 3 presents the message strategy implemented during the campaign. This solution indicates that if the candidate were to move along the resultant vector for the concepts *Democrat* and *crime prevention,* he would move at an angle of 43.76 degrees from the target vector (a correlation of .722). It also reveals that if full effects of the message strategy were obtained, the candidate would move to a point 32.05 units away from the target—of course, we only expect the candidate to exhibit a certain percentage of distance moved along the R^1 vector. The following section will report the correlation between observed motion and predicted motion.

While a correlation of .722 may appear to be reasonably high, this solution should be considered a "fair" one. Since there will be potential variability in the motion of the candidate once a message strategy is implemented, one should attempt to reduce the angle between the message strategy (resultant vector) and the target vector. In the solution presented in Figure 3, this angle is 43.76 degrees. Once the message strategy is implemented, there will be some angle (small to moderate in magnitude) between the candidate's observed motion and the message strategy. Therefore, the angle between the candidate's observed motion and the target vector may be, in some cases, larger than 43.76 degrees. Thus, it is very important to select a message strategy in which the angle between the resultant and target vector is as small as possible.

While the message strategy illustrated in Figure 3 is a "fair" solution, it is one of the best two-pair message solutions. There are only a few message strategies generated by our procedures which are better than this strategy for time-one data. A good single concept solution would be one that utilizes *integrity and honesty in government*—the vector of which correlates .867 with the target vector (an

angle of 29.92 degrees). Another good single concept solution would be *crime prevention*—the vector of which correlates .823 with the target vector (an angle of 34.63 degrees). Besides the message strategy illustrated in Figure 3, the only other good two-pair message strategy is utilization of *inflation* and *Democratic party*—a resultant vector which correlates .921 with the target vector (an angle of 22.93 degrees).

Let us now turn to a post hoc analysis of time-two message strategies. Unfortunately, when the time-two data were used in the message optimizing procedure, the solution actually implemented in the campaign did not even appear as a solution. We hypothesize that the reason for this is that at time two, the candidate was located at some point which was approximately between the locations of *Democratic party* and *crime prevention* and that adding these vectors would provide a "bad" solution. (The message optimizing procedure is written such that any "solution" with an angle greater than 90 degrees is not printed. This is to keep the computer program from providing an excess of "solutions" which would be inappropriate. Any resultant vector whose angle with the target vector is more than 90 degrees would move the candidate either at a right angle to the target or away from the target. Obviously, such solutions are not worthy of consideration.)

Figure 4 presents one of the best time-two message strategies. The resultant vector includes the concepts *integrity and honesty in government* and *crime prevention* correlates .995 with the target vector (an angle of 5.74 degrees). If full effects of such a message strategy were obtained, the candidate would move to a location only 4.23 units from the target. The small angle between this resultant vector and the target vector indicates that if such a message strategy had been employed, the candidate would move directly toward the target.

In terms of single concept solutions, there are three worth mentioning. *Crime prevention* used by itself provides a vector which correlates .979 with the target vector (an angle of 11.90 degrees). *Inflation* used by itself also provides a good strategy—the vector of which correlates .889 with the target vector (an angle of 27.22 degrees). Further, *campaign reform* was also a good single concept solution. The vector representing *crime prevention* cor-

FIGURE 4
A Possible Message Strategy Based on Time Two Data

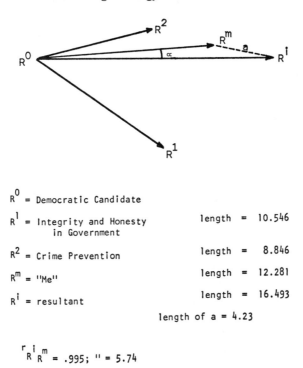

R^0 = Democratic Candidate

R^1 = Integrity and Honesty   length = 10.546
        in Government

R^2 = Crime Prevention   length =   8.846

R^m = "Me"   length = 12.281

R^i = resultant   length = 16.493

length of a = 4.23

$r_{R^i R^m}$ = .995; " = 5.74

---

relates .932 with the target solution (an angle of 21.16 degrees).

Overall, there were more "fair" to "good" solutions obtained at time two than at time one. We shall discuss one other "good," usable solution. Utilizing *integrity and honesty in government* and *Democratic party,* provides a resultant vector which correlates .976 with the target vector (an angle of 12.65 degrees). The length of this resultant vector is 12.726 units and if full effects were obtained, the candidate would move to within 2.79 units of the target. What is important about his solution (as with the other "good" time two, two-pair message solution described above), is that it would move the candidate in a fairly direct path towards the target.

Figure 5 illustrates a solution that suggests the qualifications that should be placed on the use of the mathematical procedure—the use of sound reasoning in selecting a message strategy. The four-pair message strategy which utilizes *integrity and honesty in government, crime prevention, Republican party,* and *inflation* is a "good" solution—but only mathematically speaking. Obviously, no Democratic candidate would use such a strategy, despite the fact that the solution correlates .981 with the target vector (an angle of 11.13 degrees). The existence of such solutions does not necessarily indicate a fault with these mathematical procedures. Rather, they suggest that the use of sound reasoning be conjunctionally employed, since a potentially effective message may frequently be culturally taboo. While the "solution" in Figure 5 is a gross example of what may happen during the vector addition procedure, all solutions need to be carefully assessed for both pragmatic implications and ethical considerations.

The message strategy optimizing procedures generated a number of solutions. It is obvious, given the solutions presented briefly in this section of the paper, that a number of better strategies could have been designed for the Barnett, Serota, and Taylor (1976) study.

FIGURE 5
Potential Message Strategy Based on Time Two Data

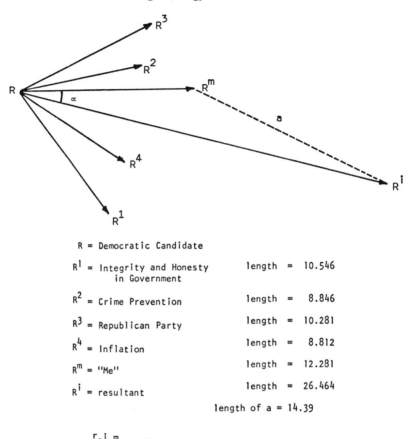

R = Democratic Candidate

R^1 = Integrity and Honesty   length = 10.546
       in Government

R^2 = Crime Prevention   length = 8.846

R^3 = Republican Party   length = 10.281

R^4 = Inflation   length = 8.812

R^m = "Me"   length = 12.281

R^i = resultant   length = 26.464

length of a = 14.39

$r_{R^i R^m}$ = .981; " = 11.13 degrees

In the next section, the extent to which the candidate moved as predicted will be discussed.

CALCULATION OF MESSAGE EFFECTIVENESS

To obtain a measure of message effectiveness, it is necessary to calculate a correlation between the observed candidate motion and predicted motion. To do this, the time-two configuration is rotated to the time-one configuration, utilizing a least-squares orthogonal rotation. Within this procedure those concepts which are theoretically stable (not predicted to move) are specified as stable and included in the minimizing procedures of the rotation. Those concepts which have been manipulated or are ex-

pected to vary then appear to move freely in the otherwise stable configuration (see Woelfel et al., 1975). The candidate's time-one coordinates are then subtracted from all time-two coordinates, to center the time-two space on the candidate's time-one position. Functionally, these two steps (rotation and subtraction) locate the two configurations at a common centroid for the purpose of the stable concepts rotation, and then disjoins the two concept structures to produce a candidate motion vector among the time-one concept position vectors. Vectors for the candidate's time-two location (the motion vector) and the predicted motion can then be compared and correlated.

Table 1 presents the results of the message effectiveness computations. Between time one and time

TABLE 1
Results of Message Effectiveness

	Time One- Time Two	Time Two- Time Three
Correlation between R^i and observed motion vector:	.865	.875
Angle between R^i and observed motion vector:	30.12°	28.90°
Length of Resultant Vector (R^i):	40.789	21.830

Distance between candidate and target:

Time One	Time Two	Time Three
14.239	12.512	8.577

two, the correlation between the predicted motion—that the candidate would move along the *Democrat* and *crime prevention* resultant vector at time one—and the observed motion of the candidate between time one and time two is .865. This is an angle of 30.12 degrees. The distance between the candidate's location, and the target concept's location, decreased by 1.727 units. The correlation between the predicted motion and observed motion, between time two and time three, is equally high, .875. This is an angle of 28.90 degrees. The distance between the candidate's location and the target concept's location decreased by 3.935 units. Note that the resultant vector's length also decreases over time. This provides support for the notion that the candidate is converging toward these concepts—adding the vectors *crime prevention* and *Democrat* at time one resulted in a length of 40.789 units; at time two, this length decreased to a distance of 23.66 units.

Utilization of the message effectiveness procedure, then, indicates that the campaign strategy was successful—the candidate moved along the predicted vector. The candidate continued to move along the resultant vector between time two and

time three, when the campaign faltered, because of a time-lag in which campaign information permeated the congressional district. Therefore, the candidate moved closely along a resultant vector which was a fair solution at time one, but only a "poor" solution at time two.

There are two possible explanations for the candidate's continued motion along the resultant vector. The first concerns the diffusion of campaign information. It takes considerable time for the information about a congressional candidate's position on the issues to diffuse throughout his district. One reason for this is that campaign information is primarily spread through interpersonal channels rather than by the mass media. This is especially the case in large urban areas, where the media must simultaneously cover a number of congressional campaigns. Also, in these media markets, the cost of advertising is high and candidates would tend to use their scarce resources in a more effective manner. Added to these factors, was the fact that in 1974, there were no national offices at stake, thus limiting the coverage of campaign rhetoric. While, the candidate may have stopped campaigning on these issues, his stand on them may have continued to diffuse through the contituency's interpersonal networks to the people he did not reach directly.

The second possible explanation derives from the work of Saltiel and Woelfel (1975), who suggest that the *rate* of change of an attitude, rather than the *amount* of change, is proportional to the force to which it is exposed and inversely related to its inertial mass. Rather than assuming that attitude change is instantaneous, they argue that discrepant information initiates a process of change which takes place over time, and continues until an equilibrum point is reached. (These notions seem compatible with more informal notions of the "momentum" of a political campaign.) There is no set time limit by which the process is completed (Cody, Marlier, & Woelfel, 1976). In the example in this paper, there is no reason to expect that the process would not continue after the second measurement. This would clearly be the case if, as indicated above, an alternative campaign strategy were not implemented.

SUMMARY AND IMPLICATIONS

While the procedures discussed above have not yet been utilized throughout the life of a campaign, it is not difficult to see the extent to which these developments will aid researchers and campaign strategists in future political work. At time one, the candidate wished to campaign on the issue of *busing*. However, *busing* never appears to be an issue that would facilitate movement towards the target concept *Me*. Further, at time one, the candidate wished to campaign on *inflation*. This, however, was not a good single concept solution, but would have been a good message strategy if implemented in conjunction with the concept of *Democratic party*. The resultant vector of these two concepts correlated .921 with the target vector.

While the strategy that was implemented (*Democratic party* and *crime prevention*) was a "fair" strategy (r=.722), our reanalysis indicates that for the time one-time two period of the campaign, the use of *crime prevention* alone would have been a good campaign strategy (a correlation of .823 with the target vector). Unfortunately, between time two and time three, the candidate continued to move along the resultant vector that was no longer as good

a solution as it was at time one, nor as good as a number of possible time two solutions. Specifically, the candidate could have campaigned on the issues of *integrity and honesty in government* and *crime prevention*.

The data reanalyzed in the present paper is based on an aggregation of all respondents. It is entirely possible, indeed preferable, for large sets of data to subdivide various respondents on the basis of the usual demographics, partisanship, or even behavioral ticket-splitters (DeVries & Tarrence, 1972), and to devise a set of message strategies for each subgroup or combination thereof. In deed, one may wish to use a message strategy that is a "good" strategy across particular target audiences.

Given time-one data, and an implementation of a campaign strategy on the part of an opponent, it is conceivable to estimate the potential effects of the opponent's campaign, and adjust one's campaign accordingly. Such adjustments are made all the time in a high activity campaign, and these procedures provide a precise means for estimating effects and adjustments.

Finally, we would like to stress several qualifications of these procedures. First, the vector addition procedure that serves as the basis for generating messages is oblivious to what concepts it adds together to form resultant vectors. Therefore, some solutions will be mathematically very good, but totally impractical to use. It is up to the researcher/ campaign strategists to select a message that is both credible and ethically suitable to a candidate's philosophy.

In addition, it would also be extremely judicious to examine how *both* the target concept and the candidate move. The analyses presented in the present paper have sought to answer the question: *Does the candidate move along the resultant vector?* However, between any two points in time, the implementation of the message strategy (and other causes in the environment) may influence the location of the target concept *Me* in the space, particularly early in the campaign before the political domain crystalizes in the minds of the electorate. Thus it would be important to calculate motion vector correlations between the two moving objects. Such an analysis would address the following question: *Do the two concepts both move and con-*

verge towards each other over time? These analyses, while straightforward, were not yet available within the operational software existing at the time of this writing, and will be the subject of further analysis.

REFERENCES

BARNETT, G. Reliability and metric multidimensional scaling. Unpublished research report, Department of Communication, Michigan State University, 1972.

BARNETT, G., SEROTA, K., & TAYLOR, J. A method for political communication research. Paper presented at the annual meeting of the Association for Education in Journalism, San Diego, 1974.

BARNETT, G., SEROTA, K., & TAYLOR, J. Campaign communication and attitude change. *Human Communication Research,* 2, 3, 1976, 227-244.

BARONE, M., UJIFUSA, G., & MATTHEWS, D. *Almanac of American politics.* Boston: Gambit, 1974.

BUTLER, D., & STOKES, D. *Political change in Britain.* New York: St. Martin's Press, 1969.

CLIFF, N. Orthogonal rotation to congruence. *Psychometrika,* 1966, 31, 32-42.

CODY, M., MARLIER, J., & WOELFEL, J. An application of the multiple attribute measurement model: Measurement and manipulation of source credibility. Paper presented at International Communication Association, Portland, Oregon, April, 1976.

DANES, J., & WOELFEL, J. An alternative to the traditional scaling paradigm in mass communication research: Multidimensional reduction of ratio judgments of separation. Paper presented at the annual meeting of the International Communication Association, Chicago, Illinois, April 1975.

DANES, J., HUNTER, J., & WOELFEL, J. Belief change as a function of accumulated information. Unpublished manuscript, Department of Communication, Michigan State University, East Lansing, Michigan, 1976.

DeVRIES, W., & TARRENCE, V.L. JR. *The ticket splitter: A new force in American politics.* Grand Rapids, Michigan: William B. Eerdmans, 1972.

GILLHAM, J., & WOELFEL, J. The Galileo system of measurement: Preliminary evidence for precision, stability, and equivalence to traditional measures. *Human Communication Research,* in press.

GORDON, T. Subject abilities to use metric multidimensional scaling: Effects of varying the criterion pair. Paper presented at the annual meeting of the International Communication Association convention, Portland, Oregon, April 1976.

SALTIEL, J., & WOELFEL J. Accumulated information and attitude change. *Human Communication Research,* 1, 4, 1975, 333-344.

SCHONEMANN, P. A generalized solution on the orthogonal Procrustes problem. *Psychometrika,* 31, 1, 1966, 1-10.

SEROTA, K. Metric multidimensional scaling and communication: Theory and implementation. Unpublished M.A. thesis, Michigan State Univesity, 1974.

TAYLOR, J., BARNETT, G., & SEROTA, K. A multidimensional examination of political attitude change. Paper presented at the annual meeting of the International Communication Association, Chicago, April 1975.

TORGERSON, S. *Theory and methods of scaling.* New York: Wiley, 1958.

THURSTONE, L. A law of comparative judgment. *Psychological Review* 34, 1927, 273-286.

WOELFEL, J. Procedures for the precise measurement of cultural processes. Unpublished manuscript, Michigan State University, East Lansing, Michigan, 1973.

WOELFEL, J. Metric measurement of cultural processes. Paper presented to the annual meeting of the Speech Communication Association, Chicago, Illinois, December 1974.

WOELFEL, J., & BARNETT, G. A paradigm for mass communication research. Paper presented at the annual meeting of the International Communication Association, New Orleans, April 1974.

WOELFEL, J., SALTIEL, J., McPHEE, R., DANES, J., CODY, M., BARNETT, G., & SEROTA, K. Orthogonal rotation to theoretical criteria: Comparison of multidimensional spaces. Paper presented at the annual Mathematical Psychology Meetings, Purdue, Indiana, 1975.

WOELFEL, J., FINK, E., HOLMES, R., CODY, M., & TAYLOR, J. A mathematical procedure for optimizing political campaign strategy. Paper presented at the annual meeting of the International Communication Association, Portland, Oregon, April 1976.

INSTRUCTIONAL COMMUNICATION
Theory and Research: An Overview
Selected Studies

INSTRUCTIONAL COMMUNICATION THEORY AND RESEARCH: AN OVERVIEW

MICHAEL D. SCOTT and LAWRENCE R. WHEELESS
West Virginia University

The richness of the term *instructional communication*, as well as the ill-defined parameters for theory and research in the area, make this overview difficult to write. There are too many interpretations of the field, too many potential theory bases to consider, and too many investigations which could legitimately be labeled instructional communication research. There is, of course, a long history of research on instruction and learning, as well as a substantial body of literature in learning theory. Likewise, a sizable amount of research exists in communication.

Since the initial examination of the interdependencies between communication and learning in Berlo's *Process of Communication* (1960), communication scholars have become increasingly active in exploring this relationship. This activity was spurred by the 1972 International Communication Association convention on communication and learning, developed by the late Malcolm MacLean, and by the formation of the Instructional Communication Division of ICA during the same year.

BASIC DEFINITIONS

For the purposes of this overview, *learning* has been defined as a process involving the acquisition or modification of cognitive, affective, and/or behavioral capabilities. *Communication* is viewed as the process of eliciting cognitive, affective, and/or behavioral communalities through verbal and nonverbal messages. The obvious linkage between the two concepts has been frequently noted since Berlo's (1960) discussion. The overview endeavors to provide a survey of current instructional communication research as applied to the classroom. Excluded from consideration are cultural and social learning, as well as unintended learning, such as from the mass media.

CONCERNS OF INSTRUCTIONAL COMMUNICATION RESEARCH

A perusal of much of the instructional communication research published in the past ten years might prompt the uninitiated reader to conclude that instructional communication research is simply another way of saying "communication education." As evidenced by both experimental and theoretical/philosophical contributions to the literature (Bochner & Kelley, 1974; Cheatham & Erickson, 1975; Haynes, 1975; Richmond, Groeshner, Paterline, & Springhorn, 1975; Baxter, 1976; DeWine, 1976; Fieweger & Yerby, 1976; Friedman, 1976; Frost, 1976; Rushing, 1976; Wilmot, 1976), efforts at finding ways to facilitate the acquisition of communication skills among students is and no doubt will continue to be a major concern in the field.

In addition to the pedagogical concerns, however, there are increasing efforts to integrate traditional notions of learning and instructional methodology with human communication. Since 1970, for example, attempts have been made to integrate human communication phenomena with theories of learning (Hsia, 1974; V. Lashbrook, 1976); to identify the relevancy of human communication phenomena to extant models of instructional design (Bassett & Kibler, 1972; Cegala & Kibler, 1972; Smyth, Kibler, & Hutchins, 1972; Spell, Parks, & Kibler, 1972; Rosenfield, Kurnit, Rosenberg, & Sussis, 1973; Sproule, 1974; Civikly, 1975; Merrill, 1976); and to specify the impact of human communication phenomena on various measures of cognitive growth (Andersen, 1973; Guthrie, 1972; Wheeless, 1972; J. Burgoon, 1975).

The past seven years also have witnessed a remarkable growth in research on communicator pathologies and their effects on learning. Considerable research has sought to identify anxieties associated with oral messages (Friedrich, 1970; McCroskey, 1970; Behnke & Carlile, 1971; Porter & Burns, 1973; Porter, 1974); written messages (Miller & Daly, 1975; Daly & Miller, 1975a; 1975b); and the receiving function of communication (Wheeless, 1975; Williams, 1976; Wheeless & Scott, 1976). Similarly, energies have been expended to explore the relationship between pathologies of the communicator and traditional concerns of the educational psychologist like criterion-referenced measures of achievement (Daly & Miller, 1975b; McCroskey & Andersen, in press; Scott & Wheeless, in press); preferred instructional settings and strategies (Scott, Yates, & Wheeless, 1975; Scott & Wheeless, in press; McCroskey, 1976); and sociometric choice in the school environment (McCroskey & Sheahan, 1976; Hurt, Preiss, & Davis, 1976).

Other instructional communication researchers are concerned with human information processing (Genova, Cole, & Gee, 1976; McCain & Ross, 1976; Sproule & Sproule, 1976), and instructional strategies outside the confines of academia (Pryor, 1976; Taylor, 1976; Strawn, 1976).

Thus, it should be clear at this point that instructional communication encompasses more than research focusing on communication education. The present, much less future concerns of instructional communication research, include the interdependencies between human learning and human communication as well as the science of teaching. Moreover, assuming this trend continues we can expect the focus of instructional communication research to become even more diffused.

INSTRUCTIONAL COMMUNICATION RESEARCH

While volumes of research focusing on questions of *learning* and *instruction* have been compiled in this century, communication seldom has been explicitly emphasized as part of the conceptual and methodological underpinnings of this research.

Data-based research in instructional communication is relatively new. For convenience, categories similar to the Source-Message-Channel-Receiver model (Berlo, 1960) are used for grouping research in this overview.

Teachers as Sources and Receivers

Few variables in communication research have captivated as much attention and research energy as the "source," and, within the traditional instructional environment, the dominant source is the classroom teacher. Considerable analysis has focused on the impact of source variables (Andersen & Clevenger, 1963; Lashbrook, 1971).

At least two studies found that perceptions of how admirable and authoritative the communicator was significantly influenced learner comprehension and understanding (Nichols, 1948; Livingston, 1961). With more sophisticated methodologies and more precise measures of receiver perceptions, a host of studies have extended these findings. More recent studies have found, for example, that receiver perceptions of a source's credibility—particularly on the dimensions of competence, character, and sociability—are related to learning outcomes such as recognition and recall of acquired information (Zagona & Harter, 1966; Seiler & Cheatham, 1971; Andersen, 1972; Guthrie, 1972; Wheeless, 1972; 1974a; Wheeless & Willis, 1975).

In addition to the effects of perceived source credibility on learning outcomes, researchers have also demonstrated that perceived interpersonal attraction and perceived homophily are related to learning. For example, data reported by Berscheid and Walster (1969), McLaughlin (1971), Rogers and Shoemaker (1971), and Wheeless (1975) indicate that in addition to the competence and character dimensions of perceived source credibility, perceptions of attitudinal homophily, as well as social and task attraction, are related to perceptual accuracy and the immediate recall of information within an instructional setting. Evidently, positive perceptions of a communication source and perceived similarities between source and receiver have much the same influence inside the classroom as they do in any other social context. In this instance, however, the influence of receiver perceptions is manifest in his or her abilities to process information rather than in changed attitudes.

Research concerning selectivity processes and

information acquisition supports this conclusion. Research internal and external to the classroom suggests that the predispositions of the receiver toward the source, as well as attitudes toward concepts associated with the source, appear to be related to the receiver's initial receptivity to information and subsequent information-seeking behavior. While a majority of this research has been concerned with selectivity in the public arena (Lashbrook, Hamilton, & Todd, 1972), there is evidence which indicates that selectivity in exposure, attention, etc., operate fully in the instructional environment as well. Some of the important variables in these selectivity processes have been isolated through exploratory investigations. In one study (Wheeless, 1974b), receptivity to library sources of information (exposure preference) was explored. In brief, the study indicated that perceived competence of the source of information, general attitudinal homophily, and involvement on the issue or subject were the dominant predictors of receptivity to information.

Apparently, then, the classroom is perceived like any other social setting in which positive perceptions of the communicator facilitate informational learning. Whether these effects obtain over time or for learning outcomes other than perceptual accuracy, recall, and selectivity options remains in question. Teacher biases and teacher expectancies probably mediate these effects over time, as student perceptions of the instructor, grades, and other forms of reinforcement become reciprocally related.

Although communication researchers are just now beginning to systematically investigate the classroom impact of variables like teacher credibility, a wealth of data has been collected in concern with the impact of teacher perceptions of students. Largely instigated by the publication of Rosenthal and Jacobson's *Pygmalion in the Classroom* (1968), this body of data has evolved from research focusing on two questions: (1) does information a teacher receives about students from sources external to the classroom, such as from cumulative records and other teachers, bias the teacher toward students; and (2) do teacher expectancies based upon a student's classroom behavior appear related to student performance?

While there is evidence in support of the notion that information available to a teacher will bias responses to the students, findings are mixed with respect to the actual influence of this bias on academic performance. At least three studies have demonstrated that the direction, positively or negatively, in which teachers are biased toward their students, will manifest itself in student achievement (Rosenthal & Jacobson, 1968; Meichenbaum, Bowers, & Ross, 1969; Rosenthal, Baratz, & Hall, 1974). In these three instances, data supported the hypothesis that students would demonstrate an increase in achievement when working with teachers who had been led to believe the student's achievement scores would increase. By way of contrast, a majority of the studies investigating teacher bias have not found it to be a significant predictor of learning or the preceding kind of "blooming effect" (Carter, 1969; Jose & Cody, 1971; Dusek & O'Connell, 1973; Mendels & Flanders, 1973; O'Connell, Dusek, & Wheeler, 1974).

Although the learning effects of teacher bias are unclear, there is abundant evidence in support of the notion that teacher expectancies are meaningfully related to student achievement. A number of studies have found a high degree of correspondence between a teacher's expectations of a student's academic capabilities and the student's actual performance (Brophy & Good, 1974; Rist, 1970; Dusek & O'Connell, 1973; O'Connell et al., 1974). At issue here is the question of whether or not self-generated teacher expectancies are based on sound criteria (Dusek, 1975).

In terms of instructional communication research, the most intriguing findings of the preceding two strains of research concern teacher-student interactions. Teacher bias research clearly indicates that what a teacher is told about a student will influence the way in which the teacher communicates with the student. Specifically, teachers led to believe they are working with "gifted" children expose them to more information, praise them more often, and interact with them differently than teachers led to believe they are working with students of a lesser caliber. Research focusing on teacher expectancies, moreover, indicates that teachers who assume they are working with bright students engage in many more behaviors designed to motivate their students than teachers who assume their students are of average intelligence. Finally, there is evidence from both strains of research indicating that preceding effects are confounded by a student's race (Finn, 1972; Long & Henderson, 1974), a teacher's previous contact with a student's siblings (Seaver, 1971), and stereotypes based on a student's name (Harari & McDavid, 1973).

Researchers have yet to discern the major origins of teacher bias and teacher expectancies, and to fully delineate the effects of communication behaviors on learning and student perceptions.

Students as Sources and Receivers

In addition to research focusing on the teacher, a number of variables related to the student as source and receiver also have been explored. Of those, three seem to have rather significant implications for questions regarding the role of communication instruction, and warrant primary consideration here: oral communication apprehension, receiver apprehension, and writing apprehension.

Oral communication apprehension. Numerous researchers have contributed to the conceptualization and measurement of communication apprehension, speech anxiety, and similar constructs (Gilkinson, 1942; Clevenger, 1959; Paul, 1966; Phillips, 1968; Friedrich, 1970; McCroskey, 1970; Behnke & Carlisle, 1971; Porter & Burns, 1973; Porter, 1974; Lustig, 1974). *Oral communication apprehension* is conceptualized as a broadly based fear or anxiety associated with oral communication across a wide variety of settings, and may be identified through self-reports, a number of physiological indices, and repeated observations of behavior.

The deleterious effects of oral communication in classrooms directed at improving the oral communication behaviors of students have been extensively researched and are well documented. Well over 200 articles, papers, and research studies exploring this area have been reported (Daly, 1974; McCroskey, 1970, 1975).

More recently, though, oral communication apprehension has been linked to academic achievement and learning in courses covering a wide array of topics and employing different instructional strategies. Recent summaries of research focusing on the linkages between oral communication apprehension, academic achievement, and learning have also been conducted (McCroskey, in press; McCroskey & Andersen, 1976; McCroskey & Daly, 1976). In brief, this body of literature indicates that *high communication apprehensives* have the following learning/achievement characteristics: (1) they learn less through elementary and secondary education levels as indicated by standardized achievement tests; (2) they have significantly lower grade-point averages at the college level; (3) they receive lower scores on objective tests; (4) they receive lower grades on instructor evaluated written projects; (5) they are expected by teachers to do worse in a number of subject areas, especially at the elementary level; and (6) they generally achieve less, although they are as intelligent as moderate and low communication apprehensives. In one direct test of achievement in a specific college course (Scott & Wheeless, in press), high versus low communication apprehension levels were found to account for 13 percent of the variance in scores for objective, criterion-references tests, as well as behaviorally specified applications involving oral and written communication.

These results, however, appear at this point to be due partially to teacher bias, self-generated teacher expectancies, and graded evaluations in regard to oral participation in the classroom. These results also appear to be a consequence of the student's socialization, apprehension level, and expectancies about *self*. A series of federally funded research projects (directed by Raymond S. Ross of Wayne State University in the 1960s) indicated that marked increases in communication apprehension begin to appear between the third and fifth grades, as socialization and self-expectancies develop (Wheeless, 1971). Likewise, Hurt, Preiss, and Davis (1976) have found more recently in sociometric research that there is a substantial correlation between communication apprehension and less favorable attitudes toward school in general among middle-school children. Similar results have been found among college students (McCroskey & Sheahan, 1976). In summary, oral communication apprehension has been demonstrated clearly to be a serious problem affecting student learning and perhaps the evaluation of that learning.

Perhaps the most commonly employed methods of coping with communication apprehension involve adaptation of instructional strategies. One technique provides situations, rewards, and incentives which attempt to motivate the reticent student to "achieve success" rather than "avoid failure," (Giffin & Gilham, 1971). However, recent research (Wheeless & Scott, 1975) found motivation to achieve success and motivation to avoid failure to be highly correlated. Focusing upon success motivation serves to raise the motivation to prevent failure also. Although students who are predominantly success motivated have lower communication apprehension, focusing upon success motivation does not appear to be desirable for the communication apprehensive. In fact, stressing learning goals and strategies other than success or failure appear at this point to be more desirable. Within alternative systems of instruction, such as self-paced instruction, where face-to-face communication may be avoided, high communication apprehensives have been found to achieve normally (Scott, Wheeless, Yates, & Randolph, 1977).

In the small classroom environment where face-to-face communication often is mandatory (Scott & Wheeless, in press), oral communication apprehensives have been found to have less favorable attitudes and lower levels of satisfaction with oral assignments and in-class discussions. Consistent with these results is the finding that oral communication apprehensives prefer nonmediated mass lectures to small classes where interaction is more likely (McCroskey & Andersen, 1976). While some adaptation of instructional strategies to the special needs of the communication apprehensive appears to be possible, research indicates the most effective strategy continues to be some form of direct treatment which alleviates or reduces apprehension levels. Examples include systematic desensitization (McCroskey, Ralph, & Barrick, 1970), behavior and reality therapy (Phillips, 1968), and cognitive restructuring (Fremouw & Harmatz, 1975).

Receiver apprehension. Receiver apprehension—generalized anxiety associated with receiving and processing communication—has been concep-

tualized and measured as a fear of misinterpreting, inadequately processing, and/or not being able to adjust psychologically to messages received from others (Wheeless, 1975b). As such, it is associated with decoding rather than with encoding, as is the case with oral communication apprehension. The construct is also differentiated from *generalized anxiety* (which applies beyond communication) and *test anxiety* (which applies to a specific type of communication apprehension).

Drawing upon this conceptualization, recent research has tested the impact of receiver apprehension on learning. In one study (Wheeless & Scott, 1976), high receiver apprehensives displayed significantly lower achievement across a number of criterion-referenced indices of achievement. In fact, one to two letter grade differences between high and low receiver apprehensives were discovered. Subsequent research on learning in a specific course revealed similar effects (Scott & Wheeless, 1976). Examination and project averages again were found to be significantly lower (13%) for high receiver apprehensives than for low receiver apprehensives. In this study, results were compared with those of oral communication apprehension and were found to be comparable, even though previous research (Wheeless, 1975b; Wheeless & Scott, 1976) demonstrated the two constructs were orthogonally distinct. Similar research has investigated student attitudes and levels of satisfaction with differing instructional strategies as a function of receiver apprehension (Scott & Wheeless, in press). High receiver apprehensives displayed significantly less favorable attitudes and satisfaction for (1) course lectures, (2) oral assignments, and (3) in-class discussions. Very few of the subjects (fewer than 4%) were *both* receiver *and* oral communication apprehensives. Again, while these results are suggestive of adaptation of instructional strategies, treatment programs have not been developed.

Writing apprehension. Comparable research exists in reference to *writing apprehension,* where the focus is upon the individual's anxiety relative to effectively encoding written messages (Daly & Miller, 1975b). Like oral and receiver apprehension, writing apprehension may be adequately measured via self-report. However, the instrument currently available (Daly & Miller, 1975b) appears to assess predispositions toward writing activities as well as anxiety and/or fears associated with such tasks. Research using this instrument found writing apprehension to be associated with lower achievement in English writing classes and with lower levels of language intensity encoded (Daly & Miller, 1975a).

In subsequent research, Daly and Miller (1975c) investigated the relationships among writing apprehension, SAT scores, and success expectations in writing courses. While causality could not be inferred in each instance, students who reported low levels of writing apprehension scored significantly higher on the verbal dimension of SAT than students who reported high levels of writing apprehension. Moreover, students reporting high levels of writing apprehension expected to be less successful in their writing endeavors than students reporting low levels. No achievement differences were discovered in a course in interpersonal communication where writing ability was not directly evaluated (Scott & Wheeless, in press). However, in a similar course, *high writing apprehensives* displayed more negative attitudes and lower levels of satisfaction for written assignments in class, out-of-class assignments requiring writing, and in-class discussions (Scott & Wheeless, in press).

In summary, it should be noted that researchers have yet to investigate the learning effects of any of the three types of apprehension in an experimental setting. Moreover, while programs are available for the treatment of oral apprehension, the task of devising treatment programs for the receiver and writing apprehensive has yet to be realized. Beyond these directions for future research, there is also the question of the origins of the communication apprehension.

Message Variables

Message strategies designed to maximize the probability of the student displaying and internalizing behaviors associated with learning goals are essential to most instructional strategies. Unfortunately, research focusing on the properties of verbal messages largely has been concerned with the effects of messages on attitude formation and change,

and upon behavior change. As a result, findings related to the linkages between message properties, attitudes, and behavior have limited generalizability. Except for research focusing on visual grammars and visual literacy, studies concerned with the nonverbal properties of messages also have only indirect bearing on instructional communication research. The following discussion is restricted to a very general consideration of that message-centered research which appears to directly relate to learning processes and outcomes.

Most relevant research has considered verbal and nonverbal messages as general stimuli within a stimulus-response model. Furthermore, most studies have focused upon a single message characteristic as it relates to the recognition or recall of information (Petrie, 1963) with only modest concern for perceptual accuracy (Beighley, 1954). Educational and experimental psychologists, however, have long noted a number of properties of stimuli which influence attention, perception, and subsequent retention (Woodworth, 1918, 1938). Among these properties are intensity, size, concreteness, complexity, contrast, repetition, and movement of stimuli/messages (or units of messages) against the background or setting in which they occur. To the extent that verbal and nonverbal instructional materials display these characteristics, then greater attention is focused upon relevant rather than marginal stimuli. Consequently, retention and recall are facilitated. Also, messages which make use of tendencies toward grouping (laws of proximity and similarity) closure, and continuation (Koffka, 1935) may further facilitate learning.

Verbal messages. Studies of specific messages variables which make use of these properties and principles tend to confirm their efficacy. A modest sampling of research examples follow. Grouping of larger message units appears to have a modest impact on learning (Darnell, 1963; Thompson, 1967; Frase, 1969; Johnson, 1970; Schutz & DiVesta, 1972; Perlmutter & Royer, 1973; Spicer & Bassett, 1976). Likewise, syntax within the smaller sentence unit may have impact (Mazza, Jordan, & Carpenter, 1972), particularly when redundancy is enhanced. Redundancy and repetition of larger message units as well as repeated reading also appear to increase recall (Jersild, 1928; Ehrensberger, 1945; Idstein & Jenkins, 1972; Winne, Hauk, & Moore, 1975). Whether this generalization may be applied to both verbal and nonverbal stimuli may need additional testing. It appears, however, that repetitive verbal transitions and proactive emphasis appear to increase comprehension.

Researchers have also investigated the effects of message concreteness and specificity, intense metaphors and analogical contrast, the juxtapositioning of arguments in two-sided messages, conclusion drawing, message complexity, difficulty, and readability. While this research has been conducted outside the instructional environment, the findings of this body of data have obvious implications for instructional communication research.

For example, when compared to abstractness, ambiguity, or vagueness, message concreteness and specificity appear to facilitate both accurate perceptions and information recall (Zimbardo, 1960; MacKay & Bever, 1967; Yuille & Paivio, 1969; Shamo & Bittner, 1971; Goss, 1972). In addition, the remainder of the above message characteristics generally have been found to influence message comprehension (Flesch, 1948; Chall & Dial, 1948; Chall, 1958; Allen, 1952; Harwood, 1955; Beighley, 1954; Goldhaber & Weaver, 1968; Sticht & Glasnapp, 1972). Of course, whether these stimulus-response linkages generalize to instructional settings, where mediating variables like grades or predispositions toward the instructor come into play, is a question which awaits attention.

Nonverbal messages. Within the realm of nonverbal communication, a number of studies indicate differential learning consequences which may be due to certain properties of nonverbal messages. For a number of years, researchers have been studying the effects of rate of speech on listener comprehension. Time-compressed speech—a technique of shortening speech by deleting a large number of minute elements at regular intervals—has been extensively studied as an outgrowth of research efforts to aid the deaf in acquiring information. While comprehension decreases if the rate of normal speaking becomes excessive, controlled

time-compressed speech can be comprehended and retained at a rate of nearly 300 words per minute with only minimal training (Orr, Friedman, & Williams, 1965). *The Journal of Communication* devoted an entire issue to oral word rate, learning, reading and the like in 1968.

Aside from vocalic concerns, a number of studies have been reported in regard to the issue of *proxemics,* specifically classroom arrangement and the grouping of students. Generally, these studies have examined proxemic effects on interaction and zones of interaction, feedback, and related factors. While unequivocal findings in this regard are beginning to emerge, all that can be said about proxemic variables presently is that they do appear to affect the conditions under which learning takes place (Sommer, 1969; Adams & Biddle, 1970; Hurt, Preiss, & Davis, 1976; McCroskey & Sheahan, 1976).

In other instructional studies, manipulation of nonverbal variables designed to enhance the apparent intensity of verbal messages has been demonstrated to increase cognitive learning. For example, underlining key phrases or words in written material appears to increase the acquisition and retention of relevant information (Cashen & Lieght, 1970; Crouse & Idstein, 1972; Idstein & Jenkins, 1972; Rickards & August, 1975). Similarly, visible movement on the part of a speaker which "underlines" aspects of the verbal message appears to facilitate comprehension and retention (Jersild, 1928; Loder, 1937; Ehrensberger, 1945; Kramer & Lewis, 1955; Gauger, 1951). Apparently, the movement itself, as well as the "underlining" of verbal information by the movement, mediates this learning outcome.

Learning Strategies

As used here, the term learning strategy encompasses the traditional elements of the communication process, and includes such methods of instruction as lecturing, discussion groups, and role playing. As might be expected, there are numerous approaches to instruction which may be viewed as learning strategies. These strategies are based on a variety of philosophies of instruction.

Although debates concerning the efficacy of one learning strategy over another are not uncommon among theorists, researchers, and teachers, these debates appear to be based on passions rather than sound empirical evidence. For example, after experimentally pitting several conventional strategies against each other, Wallen and Travers (1963) concluded the learning strategy a teacher selects has little bearing on student achievement. Within the past decade, moreover, this conclusion has been reaffirmed by Dubin and Taveggia (1968) who, after reviewing 50 years of past research, proclaimed that differential learning strategies fail to produce differential learning outcomes.

While there is little evidence in support of one learning strategy over the other, research has indicated that some of the components or devices within these larger strategies may influence outcomes.

Learning objectives. Regardless of the overall learning strategy, teachers seem well aware of the need to state learning goals in objectifiable manners. By far, a majority of the research focusing on the efficacy of stating learning goals in an objectifiable manner has been concerned with the use of behavioral objectives. Ausubel (1967) contends behavioral objectives serve as advance organizers for learning. Others (Davies, 1973; Byers, Bassett, & Kibler, 1976) suggest objectives increase the correspondence between a teacher's requests and a learner's behaviors, as well as reduce any uncertainty the learner may experience as a function of the instructional setting. In a very real sense, then, behavioral objectives reflect long-established principles of communication theory.

Although behavioral objectives have sound conceptual roots (Bloom, 1956; Krathwohl, Bloom, & Masia, 1964; Kibler, Barker, & Miles, 1970), research findings are mixed with respect to their effectiveness as a learning device. As recently pointed out by Byers, Bassett, and Kibler (1976), well over 150 experimental studies have focused on the nature, use, and effectiveness of behavioral objectives. While these studies suggest behavioral objectives may "cue" learners to important information (Frase, 1968; Morse & Tillman, 1972), there is little evidence which would suggest this *cueing* effect enhances learner outcomes. Following their in-depth review of the literature, Byers et al. (1976) conclude: (1) student use of behavioral objectives

appear to have no appreciable impact on learning; (2) the ways in which behavioral objectives are stated appear to have no appreciable impact on student learning; (3) teacher use of behavioral objectives may be of little consequence to student learning; and (4) behavioral objectives do not appear to increase learner efficiency (p.8).

However, Byers et al., strongly criticize the methodology of the studies they examined and offer a number of suggestions. Specifically, they argue the need for experimental research under conditions in which: (1) students and teachers have been trained in the use of objectives; (2) objectives are operationalized in a generalizable manner; (3) levels of behavior and the domains of learning toward which the objective is targeted are specified; (4) incentives have been provided for the teacher; and (5) the span of time and length of instructional units are incorporated with the experimental design. They contend that until such recommendations are implemented, conclusions about the effectiveness of behavioral objectives are unwarranted.

Note-taking. A second learning device, note-taking, is intended to assist the learner in organizing messages in a manner which is consistent with his cognitive structure (V. Lashbrook, 1976b).

As early as 1925, Crawford (1925a, 1925b) reported: (1) a positive relationship between the number of ideas appearing in notes and the number recalled in quizzes; (2) clear notes facilitated quiz performance when compared to sketchy notes; (3) accurate note-taking facilitated quiz performance; (4) note-taking facilitated both immediate and delayed quiz performance; (5) note-taking did not facilitate performance on true-false tests.

Recent studies have demonstrated that note-taking and rehearsal facilitate immediate recall (DiVesta & Gray, 1972); the reviewing of one's own notes is superior to reviewing the notes of others in terms of recall (Fisher & Harris, 1973); information density, rate of presentation, and note-taking are related to delayed recall (Aiken, Thomas, & Shennum, 1975); and the effects of note-taking are mediated by the presence or absence of reviews, timing, and retention intervals (Carter & Van Matre, 1975).

With the exception of the research of Aiken et al.

(1975), however, most of the research on note-taking has been only indirectly concerned with communication variables which may mediate note-taking behaviors. For example, learner perceptions of information sources (Wheeless, 1974b), message variables like language compatibility (Boyd, 1973), and receiver apprehension (Wheeless & Scott, 1976) should influence both learner receptivity toward information and learner abilities to restructure messages to correspond to extant cognitive structures.

Media

Research concerning the use of mediated instructional devices warrant two rather broad generalizations: (1) students can, in fact, learn from mediated materials, and (2) the effectiveness of mediated materials as learning devices depends on their appropriateness to specified learning objectives and the nature of the learning task. For the most part, these two generalizations are predicated on research which has focused on the effectiveness of audio materials, simple visual aids, films, and television. Generally, research concerning audio materials alone, or in comparison with some other mode of presentation, has failed to reveal significant differences or has found audio materials inferior (Musterberg, 1894; Day & Beach, 1950; Pophman, 1962; Hinz, 1969; Menne, Hannum, Klingensmith, & Nord, 1969).

While simple visual aids such as line drawings, pictures, photographs etc., appear to enhance learning outcomes (Gropper, 1966), some appear to be more effective than others. Simple line drawings, for example, appear best suited to learning tasks involving visual discriminations, concept attainment, and three-dimensional models (Black, 1962; Dwyer, 1967). Pictures are effective only to the extent they are rich in relevant cues and vacuous of irrelevant cues, and detailed photographs appear to be the least effective of any of the simple visual aids in use (Vernon, 1953; Dwyer, 1967).

Most of the recent research focusing on mediated instruction has been concerned with television and film. Of this research, that which has probably received the most attention has concerned the relative effectiveness of televised and standard lecture formats (Carpenter & Greenhill, 1958; Gropper, 1966; Taylor, Lipscomb, & Rosemier, 1969). Research in this regard has produced two findings of interest: (1) televised lectures (live and video-taped) with only one-way communication capacities are not significantly different from the standard lecture format, and (2) students prefer televised lectures with the capacity for two-way communication to televised lectures where feedback is not possible (Carpenter & Greenhill, 1958).

Research concerning film as an instructional device has garnered similar results which are detailed in an exhaustive survey by Hoban (1960). In brief, the research suggests film is as good, but not better than other conventional instructional devices. Film does, however, seem to be the most effective medium of instruction for objectives which involve psychomotor skills (Sheffield, Margolius, & Hoehn, 1961; Wendt & Butts, 1962).

Feedback and Reinforcement

Feedback, both as a corrective device and as an agent of reinforcement, is present in a majority of learning strategies. Whether feedback is used to its fullest potential in these strategies, of course, is open to question. While much of the research focusing on the various effects of feedback have been conducted outside the instructional environment, a few studies have examined feedback within the confines of the classroom. Moreover, feedback research both internal and external to the classroom has been critically reviewed by Ayres (1971) and Gardiner (1971).

Within the instructional environment, feedback serves a number of important functions. Frequently, for example, feedback regulates the communication behaviors of teachers. Specifically, audience feedback influences the confidence and verbal delivery of the communicator (Leavitt & Mueller 1951; Miller, Zavas, Vlandis, & Rosenbaum, 1961; Stolz & Tannenbaum, 1963; Miller, 1964; Sereno, 1965), the content of the communicator's message (Karns, 1969), and the communicator's attitudes toward *self* (Insko, 1965). Furthermore, research concerned with intra-audience feedback suggests receivers are sensitive to each other's verbal and nonverbal cues, and this may influence the communicator (Sawyer, 1955; Hylton, 1968).

Additionally, feedback increases the perceptual accuracy of the source's judgments concerning receivers (Jecker, Maccoby, Brietose, & Rose, 1964; Dickens & Krueger, 1969; Ayres, 1970) and, in general, increases the accuracy with which information is transmitted. Furthermore, the presence of positive feedback reduces hostility, defensiveness, and the potential for conflict (Leavitt & Mueller, 1951; Gibb, Smith, & Roberts, 1955; McCroskey & Wheeless, 1976).

It is clear that a great deal more research needs to be conducted in concern with the nature, use, and effects of feedback as it relates to the instructional environment. Questions concerning the most effective ways to use feedback as a regulator of classroom interaction, as a clarifying device, and as an agent of reinforcement have yet to be answered.

AVAILABLE THEORY BASES

While communication is most frequently not an overt concern in the psychological literature on learning and instruction, one would be hard-pressed to find an extant theory of learning or model of instruction in which communication is not an inherent factor. There are a number of conceptual bases in psychological literature on learning and instruction which lend themselves to instructional communication research and practice. These bases not only are concerned with psychological development and learning (Piaget, 1952, 1954, 1957; Erickson, 1950, 1968; Sears, 1957), but also with the conditions under which psychological development and learning will most likely occur (Dewey, 1938; Bruner, 1961, 1966, 1971; Skinner, 1953, 1968). Moreover, they reflect a full range of epistomologies and appear amendable to varying units of analysis. Two major conceptual and operational bases pertaining to learning and instruction have dominated the thinking of theorists, researchers, and practitioners in the last three decades: Cognitive-Field Theory and S-R Associationism.

Cognitive-Field Theory

Currently, the leading proponent of Cognitive Field Theory is Bruner. Influenced by the early

Gestaltists (Koffka, 1937; Kohler, 1945), Bruner and other proponents of this approach argue that psychological research should focus on cognitive processes as well as overt behavior. Rather than attempt to tightly control the learner's environment and the contingencies of reinforcement within the environment, field theorists attempt to facilitate individual learning as a function of the way in which the environment is arranged. Like Dewey, cognitive theorists are concerned with establishing a pattern of learning which will enhance creativity, and emphasis is placed on the learner acquiring principles or concepts via experience and insight.

While Cognitive Field Theory has not been the focus of a great deal of research, it has given rise to receiver-centered learning strategies like gaming and simulation (Tansey & Unwin, 1969) where the learner is expected to "discover" as a function of purposeful introspection and experience. Bruner (1966) suggests that those who employ the discovery approach should pattern behaviors along lines similar to the following: (1) *emphasis of contrast* (e.g., dyadic communication as contracted to small group communication); (2) *inviting informed guessing* (e.g., hypotheses about the relationship between attitude similarity and interpersonal attraction); (3) *inviting participation* (e.g., employing acquaintance games); and (4) *encouraging awareness* (e.g., analyzing one's own communication behaviors during or after interpersonal encounters). Advocates of the discovery approach contend that such methods can increase comprehension and long-term memory, encourage transfer and symbolic thought, and foster independence as well as facilitating the acquisition of favorable attitudes toward the subject matter being taught.

These assertions have not gone unnoticed. The discovery approach as well as popularized methodologies which reflect its orientation (e.g., Postman & Weingartner, 1969), are represented quite well in textbooks on communication (e.g., Johnson, 1972; Krupar, 1973; Meyers & Meyers, 1973; Johnson, Senatore, Liebig, & Minor, 1974; Ruben & Budd, 1975). Furthermore, such receiver-centered approaches have been conceptually and operationally explained as they relate to the teaching of communication theory (Maclean & Talbott, 1969; Ruben, 1969, 1973, 1974).

At issue here, however, is the fact that instructional communication researchers interested in receiver-centered approaches to learning have yet to engage in experimental research along these lines. Considering the claims made for receiver-centered strategies like the discovery approach are far from unequivocal, instructional communication researchers might want to assess their effectiveness experimentally. In order to do so, though, researchers should not divorce their investigations from the conceptual base of such approaches — *cognitive field theory.*

S-R Associationism

In contrast to Cognitive-Field Theorists, Stimulus-Response psychologists are concerned only with observable behavior. Influenced by the early behaviorists (Watson, 1925; Thorndike, 1932), Skinner and others have generalized the results of animal experimentation to the classroom. The argument between field and S-R psychologists has been explicated elsewhere (Combs & Snygg, 1959; Skinner, 1968, 1972). Briefly the S-R model suggests that the potential for learning can be maximized where: (1) the desired terminal or goal behavior are stated in objective terms; (2) the child's behavioral repertory relevant to the task is assessed; (3) the stimulus material or behavioral criteria for reinforcement are arranged in sequence; (4) the child is started on that unit in the sequence to which he can respond correctly about 90 percent of the time; (5) the contingencies of reinforcement are managed with the aid of teaching machines and other devices to strengthen successive approximations to the terminal behavior and to build conditioned reinforcers that are intrinsic to the task; and (6) records of the child's responses are kept as a basis for modifying the materials and teaching procedures (Bijou, 1970, p. 404).

Unlike the discovery approach, the preceding strategy argues for a highly controlled learning environment in which the contingencies of reinforcement are managed. Depending on individual orientations, instructional communication researchers might use this type of strategy along with its parent theory base (Skinner, 1938, 1953, 1968) as a conceptual and operational framework from which to deduce hypotheses and research questions focusing on human communication pedagogy.

SUMMARY

Regardless of their conceptual origins, learning strategies of the preceding kind are intended to maximize the *fidelity of communication* within a particular instructional system, through the negotiation of meaning. They employ message strategies which will facilitate the acquisition of cognitive, affective, and behavioral skills among students. It seems reasonable to assume, therefore, that some of the traditional concerns of the communication scientist are an inherent, but as of yet unarticulated, feature of these strategies and the conceptual bases from which they evolved.

There is little to be gained from instructional communication researchers turning their backs to extant psychological interpretations of learning and instruction. At a minimum, instructional communication researchers may be able to refine human communication pedagogy as a function of attending to the interpretations of theorists already referenced, as well as the interpretations of taxonomists like Bandura (1965, 1969, 1971), Ausubel (1963, 1963b, 1968), Bloom (1956), and Gagne (1965). Aside from improving instruction, instructional communication researchers may be able to give meaning to the term *instructional communication theory* by reinterpretations from a communication perspective.

REFERENCES

ADAMS, R. S., & BIDDLE, B. *Realities of teaching: Explorations with video tape.* New York: Holt, Rinehart & Winston, 1970.

AIKEN, E. G., THOMAS G. S., & SHENNUM, W. A. Memory for a lecture: Effects of notes, lecture rate, and information density. *Journal of Educational Psychology,* 1975, 67, 439-444.

ALLEN, W. H. Readability of instructional film commentary. *Journal of Applied Psychology,* 1952, 36, 164-168.

ANDERSEN, P. A. Credibility and learning. Paper presented at the annual meeting of the Speech Communication Association, New York, 1973.

ANDERSEN, K., & CLEVENGER, T., JR. A summary of experimental research in ethos. *Speech Monographs,* 1963, 20, 59-78.

ATKIN, C. Television advertising and children's observational modeling. Paper presented at the annual meeting of the International Communication Association, Portland, 1976.

AUSUBEL, D. P. Cognitive structure and the facilitation of meaningful verbal learning. *Journal of Teacher Education*, 1963a, 14, 217-230.

AUSUBEL, D. P. *The psychology of meaningful and verbal learning*. New York: Greene and Stratton, 1963b.

AUSUBEL, D. P. A cognitive-structure theory of learning. In L. Siegel, (Ed.), *Instruction: Some contemporary viewpoints*. San Francisco, California: Chandler, 1967.

AUSUBEL, D. P. *Educational psychology: A cognitive view*. New York: Holt, Rinehart & Winston, 1968.

AYRES, H. J. A baseline study of nonverbal feedback: Observer's judgments of audience member's attitudes. Unpublished doctoral dissertation, University of Utah, 1970.

AYRES, H. J. An overview of theory and research in feedback. Paper presented at the annual meeting of the International Communication Association, Phoenix, 1971.

BANDURA, A. Behavioral modifications through modeling procedures. In K. Knasner and L.P. Ullman (Eds.), *Research in behavior modification*. New York: Holt, Rinehart & Winston, 1965.

BANDURA, A. *Principles of behavior modification*. New York: Holt, Rinehart & Winston, 1969.

BANDURA, A. *Psychological modeling: Conflicting theories*. Chicago: Aldine. Atherton, 1971.

BASSETT, R. E., & KIBLER, R. J. A critical analysis of research on behavioral objectives with implications for needed research in communication instruction. Paper presented at the annual meeting of the International Communication Association, Atlanta, 1972.

BAXTER, L. Contemporary measurement devices: Applications to change in conflict relationships. Paper presented at the annual meeting of the International Communication Association, Portland, 1976.

BEHNKE, R. R., & CARLISLE, L. W. Heart rate as an index of speech anxiety. *Speech Monographs*, 1971, 38, 65-69.

BEIGHLEY, K. C. An experimental study of the effect of three speech variables on listener comprehension. *Speech Monographs*, 1954, 21, 248-253.

BERLO, D. K. *The Process of Communication*. New York: Holt, Rinehart & Winston, Inc., 1960.

BERGER, C. Interpersonal communication theory and research: An overview. In B. Ruben (Ed.), *Communication Yearbook I:* New Brunswick, N.J.: Transaction-International Communication Association, 1977.

BERSCHEID, E., & WALSTER, E. *Interpersonal attraction*. Reading, Mass.: Addison-Wesley, 1969.

BIJOU, S. W. What psychology has to offer education now. In P. B. Dews (Ed.), *Festschrift for B. F. Skinner*. New York: Appleton, Century, Crofts, 1970, 401-407.

BLACK, H. B. *Improving the programming of complex pictorial materials: Discrimination learning as affected by prior exposure to and relevance of the figural discriminanda*. Bloomington, Indiana: University of Indiana School of Education Memorandum, 1962, 111-112.

BLOOM, B. A. (Ed.) *Taxonomy of educational objectives* (Handbook I: Cognitive Domain). New York: David McKay, 1956.

BOCHNER, A. P., & KELLEY, C. W. Interpersonal competence: Rationale, philosophy, and implementation of a conceptual framework. *The Speech Teacher*, 1974, 23, 279-301.

BOWERS, J. W., & OSBORN, M. Attitudinal effects of selected types of concluding metaphors in persuasive speeches. *Speech Monographs*, 1966, 33, 147-155.

BOYD, J. A. Language compatibility and course grade in the basic communication course. Paper presented to the annual meeting of the International Communication Association, Montreal, 1973.

BROPHY, J. E., & GOOD, T. L. *Teacher-student relationships: Causes and consequences*. New York: Holt, Rinehart & Winston, 1974.

BRUNER, J. S. *The Process of education*. Cambridge, Mass.: Harvard Press, 1961.

BRUNER, J.S. *Toward a theory of instruction*. New York: Norton, 1966.

BRUNER, J.S. *The relevance of education*. New York: Norton, 1971.

BURGOON, J. Predictors of learning and persuasion. *Human Communication Research*, 1975, 1, 133-144.

BYERS, J. P., BASSETT, R. E., & KIBLER, R. J. Behavioral objectives and communication education. Paper presented at the annual meeting of the International Communication Association, Portland, 1976.

CARPENTER, C. R., & GREENHILL, L. P. An investigation of closed-circuit television for teaching university courses. In *Instructional Television Research Project No. 2.*, University Park: Pennsylvania State University, 1958.

CARTER, R. M. Locus of control and teacher expectancy as related to achievement in young school children. Unpublished doctoral dissertation, Indiana University, 1969.

CARTER, J. F., & VAN MATRE, N. H. Notetaking versus note having. *Journal of Educational Psychology*, 1975, 67, 900-904.

CASHEN, V. M., & LIEGHT, K. L. Role of the isolation effect in a formal educational setting. *Journal of Educational Psychology*, 1970, 61, 484-486.

CEGALA, D. J., & KIBLER, R. J. Development of a modified mastery learning system for an introductory communication course. Paper presented at the annual meeting of the International Communication Association, Atlanta, 1972.

CHALL, J. S., & DIAL, H. E. Predicting listener understanding and interest in newscasts. Educational Research Bulletin, 1948, 27, 141-153, 168.

CHALL, J. S. *Readability*. Columbus: The Ohio State University Press, 1958.

CHEATHAM, T. R., & ERICKSON, K. V. A survey of the use of communication games in speech communication. Paper presented at the annual meeting of the International Communication Association, Chicago, 1975.

CIVIKLY, J. The effect of varying degrees of specificity of objectives on student cognitive and affective performance in a unit of instruction in speech communication. Paper presented at the annual meeting of the International Communication Association, Chicago, 1975.

CLEVENGER, T., JR. A synthesis of experimental research in stage fright. *Quarterly Journal of Speech*, 1959, 45, 134-145.

COMBS, A. W., & SNYGG, D. *Individual behavior* (rev. ed.), New York: Harper, 1959.

CRAWFORD, C. C. The correlation between college lecture notes and quiz papers. *Journal of Educational Research*, 1925a, 12, 282-291.

CRAWFORD, C. C. Some experimental studies of the results of college notetaking. *Journal of Educational Research*, 1925b, 12, 379-386.

CROUSE, J. H., & IDSTEIN, P. Effects of encoding cues on prose learning. *Journal of Educational Psychology*, 63, 1972, 309-313.

DALY, J. A. Communication apprehension: A preliminary bibliography of research. Unpublished report, Purdue University, 1974.

DALY J. A., & MILLER, M. D. Apprehension of writing as a predictor of message intensity. *The Journal of Psychology*, 1975a, 89, 175-177.

DALY, J. A., & MILLER, M. D. The empirical development of an instrument to measure writing apprehension. *Research in the Teaching of English*, 1975b, 9, 242-249.

DALY, J. A., & MILLER, M. D. Further studies on writing apprehension: SAT scores, success expectations, willingness to take advanced courses, and sex differences. *Research in the Teaching of English*, 1975c, 9, 250-256.

DARNELL, D. K. The relation between sentence-order and comprehension. *Speech Monographs*, 1963, 30, 97-100.

DAVIES, I. K. *Competency based learning: Technology, management, and design*. New York: McGraw-Hill Book Company, 1973.

DAY, W. F., & BEACH, B. R. *A survey of the research literature comparing visual and auditory presentation of information*. U.S. Air Force Technical Report No. 5921, 1950.

DeWINE, S. The communication journal: A new tool for building interpersonal relationships in the communication classroom. Paper presented at the annual meeting of the International Communication Association, Portland, 1976.

DEWEY, J. *Experience and education*. New York: MacMillan, 1938.

DICKENS, M., & KRUEGER, D. H. Speaker's accuracy in identifying immediate audience responses during a speech. *Speech Teacher*, 1969, 18, 303-307.

DiVESTA, F. J., & GRAY, G. S. Listening and notetaking. *Journal of Educational Psychology*, 1972, 63, 8-14.

DUBIN, R., & TRAVEGGIA, T. C. *The teaching-learning paradox: A comparative analysis of college teaching*. Eugene, Oregon: University of Oregon, Center for Advanced Study of Educational Administration, 1968.

DUSEK, J. B. Do teachers bias student learning. *Review of Educational Research*, 1975, 15, 661-684.

DUSEK, J. B., & O'CONNELL, E. J. Teacher expectancy effects on the achievement test performance of elementary school children. *Journal of Educational Psychology*, 1973, 65, 371-377.

DWYER, F. M. Adapting visual illustrations for effective learning. *Harvard Educational Review*, 1967, 37, 250-263.

EHRENSBERGER, R. An experimental study of the relative effectiveness of certain forms of emphasis in public speaking. *Speech Monographs*, 1945, 12, 94-111.

ERICKSON, E.H. *Childhood and society*. New York: Norton, 1950 (2nd rev. ed., 1963).

ERICKSON, E.H. *Identity: Youth and crisis*. New York: Norton, 1968.

FERSTER, C. B., & SKINNER, B. F. *Schedules of reinforcement*. New York: Appleton, Century, Crofts, 1957.

FIEWEGER, M., & YERBY, J. Values and behavior skills as variables in interpersonal communication instruction. Paper presented at the annual meeting of the International Communication Association, Portland, 1976.

FINN, J. D. Expectations and the educational environment. *Review of Educational Research*, 1972, 42, 387-410.

FISHER, J. L., & HARRIS, M. B. Effect of notetaking and review on recall. *Journal of Educational Psychology*, 1973, 65, 321-325.

FLESCH, R. A new readability yardstick. *Journal of Applied Psychology*, 1948, 32, 221-233.

FOULKE, E. Listening comprehension as a function of word rate. *Journal of Communication*, 1968, 18, 198-206.

FRASE, L. T. Questions as aids to reading: Some research and theory. *American Educational Research Journal*, 1968, 5, 319-322.

FRASE, L. T. Paragraph organization of written materials: The influence of conceptual clustering upon the level and organization of recall. *Journal of Educational Psychology*, 1969, 60, 394-401.

FREMOUW, W. J., & HARMATZ, M. G. A helper model for behavioral treatment of speech anxiety. *Journal of Consulting and Clinical Psychology*, 1975, 43, 652-660.

FRIEDMAN, P. G. Flexibility training: Developing communicative freedom. Paper presented at the annual meeting of the International Communication Association, Portland, 1976.

FRIEDRICH, G. W. An empirical explication of a concept of self-reported speech anxiety. *Speech Monographs*, 1970, 37, 67-72.

FROST, J. L. Issue analysis and goal negotiation: A group training approach. Paper presented at the annual meeting of the International Communication Association, Portland, 1976.

GAGNE, R. M. *The conditions of learning*. New York: Holt, Rinehart & Winston, 1965.

GARDINER, J. A. A synthesis of experimental studies in feedback. *Journal of Communication*, 1971, 21, 17-35.

GAUGER, P. W. The effect of gesture and the presence or absence of the speaker on the listening comprehension of eleventh and twelfth grade high school pupils. Unpublished doctoral dissertation, University of Wisconsin, 1951.

GENOVA, B. L. K., COLE, E., & GEE, G. Differential patterns of information acquisition from the media. Paper presented at the annual meeting of the International Communication Association, Portland, 1976.

GIBB, J. R., SMITH, E. E., & ROBERTS, A. H. Effects of positive and negative feedback upon defensive behavior in small problem-solving groups. *American Psychologists*. 1955, 10, 335.

GIFFIN, K., & GILHAM, S. M. Relationships between speech anxiety and motivation. *Speech Monographs*, 1971, 38, 70-73.

GILKINSON, H. Social fears as reported by students in college speech classes. *Speech Monographs*, 1942, 9, 141-160.

GOLDHABER, G. M., & WEAVER, C. H. Listener comprehension of compressed speech when the difficulty, rate of presentation, and sex of listener are varied. *Speech Monographs*, 1968, 35, 20-25.

GOSS, B. The effect of sentence context on associations to ambiguous, vague, and clear nouns. *Speech Monographs*, 1972, 39, 286-289.

GREENBERG, B. S., HEALD, G., REEVES, B., & WAKSHOLAG, J. TV character attributes and children's modeling tendencies. Paper presented at the annual meeting of the International Communication Association, Portland, 1976.

GROPPER, G. L. Learning from visuals: Some behavioral considerations, *AV Communication Review*, 1966, 14, 75-85.

GUTHRIE, E. *The psychology of learning*. New York: Harper & Brothers, 1952.

GUTHRIE, M. L. Effects of credibility, metaphor and intensity on comprehension, credibility, and attitude change. Unpublished master's thesis, Illinois State University, 1972.

HARARI, H., & McDAVID, J. W. Name stereotypes and

teacher expectancies. *Journal of Educational Psychology,* 1973, 65, 222-225.

HARWOOD, K. A. Listenability and readability. *Speech Monographs,* 1955, 22, 49-53.

HAYNES, J. L. Implementing mastery learning in a high school speech classroom. Paper presented to the annual meeting of the International Communication Association, Chicago, 1975.

HINZ, M. Effect of response mode on learning efficiency. *AV Communication Review,* 1969, 17, 77-83.

HOBAN, C. F. The usable residue of educational film research. *Teaching aids for the American classroom.* Stanford, Calif.: Institute for Communication Research, 1960.

HOVLAND, C. I., & MANDELL, W. An experimental comparison of conclusion-drawing by the communicator and by the audience. *Journal of Abnormal and Social Psychology.* 1952, 45, 175-182.

HSIA, H. J. Learning as a communication process. Paper presented at the annual meeting of the International Communication Association, New Orleans, 1974.

HULL, C. *Essentials of behavior.* New Haven: Yale University Press, 1951.

HURT, T., PREISS, R., & DAVIS, B. The effects of communication apprehension of middle-school children on sociometric choice, affective and cognitive learning. Paper presented at the annual meeting of the International Communication Association, Portland, 1976.

HYLTON, C. G. The effects of observable audience response on attitude change and source credibility. Unpublished doctoral dissertation, Michigan State University, 1968.

IDSTEIN, P., & JENKINS, J. R. Underlining versus repetitive reading. *Journal of Education Research,* 1972, 65, 321-323.

INSKO, C. A. Verbal reinforcement of attitude. *Journal of Personality and Social Psychology,* 1965, 2, 621-623.

JECKER, J., MACCOBY, N., BRIETROSE, H., & ROSE, E. Teacher accuracy in assessing cognitive visual feedback from students. *Journal of Applied Psychology,* 1964, 48, 393-397.

JERSILD, A. T. Modes of emphasis in public speaking. *Journal of Applied Psychology,* 1928, 12, 611-620.

JOHNSON, A. A preliminary investigation of the relationship between message organization and listener comprehension. *Central States Speech Journal,* 1970, 21, 104-107.

JOHNSON, D. W. *Reaching out.* Englewood Cliffs, N.J.: Prentice-Hall, 1972.

JOHNSON, K. G., SENATORE, J. J., LIEBIG, M. C., & MINOR, G. *Nothing never happens.* Beverly Hills, California: Glencoe, 1974.

JOSE, J., & CODY, J. Teacher pupil interaction as it relates to attempted changes in teacher expectancy of academic ability and achievement. *American Educational Research Journal,* 1971, 8, 39-49.

KARNS, C. F. Speaker behavior to nonverbal aversive stimuli from the audience. *Speech Monographs,* 1969, 36, 126-130.

KIBLER, R. J., BARKER, L. L., & MILES, D. T. *Behavioral objectives and instruction.* Boston: Allyn and Bacon, 1970.

KOFFKA, K. *Principles of gestalt psychology.* New York: Harcourt, Brace, 1935.

KOHLER, W. *Gestalt psychology.* New York: Liverright, 1947.

KRAMER, E. J. J., & LEWIS, T. R. Comparison of visual and non-visual listening. *Journal of Communication,* 1955, 1, 16-20.

KRATHWOHL, D. R., BLOOM, B. S., & MASIA, B. B. *Taxonomy of educational objectives* (Handbook II: Affective

Domain). New York: McKay, 1964.

KRUPER, K. *Communication games.* New York: Free Press, 1973.

LASHBROOK, V. J. Source credibility: A summary of experimental research. Paper presented at the annual meeting of the Speech Communication Association, San Francisco, 1971.

LASHBROOK, V. The application of learning theories to communication instruction. Paper presented at the annual meeting of the International Communication Association, Portland, 1976a.

LASHBROOK, V. Facilitative behaviors for the processing of oral messages. Unpublished doctoral dissertation, West Virginia University, 1976b.

LASHBROOK, W. B., HAMILTON, P. R., & TODD, W. A theoretical consideration of the assessment of source credibility as a function of information seeking behavior. Paper presented at the annual meeting of the Western Speech Communication Association, Honolulu, November, 1972.

LEAVITT, H. J., & MUELLER, R. A. Some effects of feedback on communication. *Human Relations,* 1951, 4, 401-410.

LEWIN, K. *Field theory in social sciences: Selected theoretical papers.* New York: Harper & Brothers, 1951.

LIVINGSTON, H. M. An experimental study of effects of interest and authority upon understanding of broadcast information. Unpublished doctoral dissertation, University of Southern California, 1961.

LODER, J. E. A study of aural learning with and without the speaker present. *Journal of Experimental Education,* 1937, 6, 46-60.

LONG, B. H., & HENDERSON, E. H. Certain determinants of academic performance expectancies among southern and non-southern teachers. *American Educational Research Journal,* 1974, 11, 137-147.

LUSTIG, M. W. Verbal reticence: A reconceptualization and preliminary scale development. Paper presented at the annual meeting of the Speech Communication Association Convention, Chicago, 1974.

MACCOBY, N., & MARKLE, D. G. Communication in learning. In I. S. Pool, W. Schramm, F. W. Frey, N. Maccoby, and E. G. Parker (Eds.), *The handbook of communication.* Chicago: Rand McNally College Publishing Company, 1973.

MacKAY, D. J., & BEVER, T. In search of ambiguity. *Perception and Psychophysics,* 1967, 2, 193-200.

MacLEAN, M. S., & TALBOTT, A. D. An approach to communication theory through simulation. Paper presented at the annual meeting of the International Communication Association, New York, 1969.

MAZZA, I., JORDAN, W., & CARPENTER, R. The comparative effectiveness of stylistic sources of redundancy. *Central States Speech Journal,* 1972, 23, 241-245.

McCAIN, T., & ROSS, M. G. Cognitive switching: A behavioral trace of human information processing. Paper presented at the annual meeting of the International Communication Association, Portland, 1976.

McCROSKEY, J. C. Measures of communication bound anxiety. *Speech Monographs,* 1970, 37, 241-245.

McCROSKEY, J. C. The implementation of a large scale program of systematic desensitization for communication apprehension. *Speech Teacher,* 1972, 21, 255-264.

McCROSKEY, J. C. Classroom consequences of communication apprehension. Paper presented at the annual meeting of the Speech Communication Association, Houston, 1975a.

McCROSKEY, J. C. Validity of the PRCA as an index of oral communication apprehension. Paper presented at the annual meeting of the Speech Communication Association, Houston, 1975b.

McCROSKEY, J. C. The problem of communication apprehension in the classroom. Paper presented at the annual meeting of the Pacific Communication Association, Tokyo, 1976.

McCROSKEY, J. C., & ANDERSEN, J. F. The relationship between communication apprehension and academic achievement among college students, *Human Communication Research,* 1976, 3, 73-81.

McCROSKEY, J. C., & COMBS, W. H. The effects of the use of analogy on attitude change and source credibility. *Journal of Communication,* 1969, 19, 333-339.

McCROSKEY, J. C., & DALY, J. A. Teacher's expectations of the communication apprehensive child in the elementary school. *Human Communication Research,* 1976, 3, 67-72.

McCROSKEY, J. C., RALPH, D., & BARRICK, J. E. The effects of systematic desensitization on speech anxiety. *Speech Teacher,* 1970, 19, 32-36.

McCROSKEY, J. C., & SHEAHAN, M. E. Communication apprehension, social preferences, and social behavior. Unpublished paper, West Virginia University, 1976.

McCROSKEY, J. C., & WHEELESS, L. R. *An introduction to human communication.* Boston: Allyn & Bacon, 1976.

McLAUGHLIN, B. Effects of similarity and likableness on attraction and recall. *Journal of Personality and Social Psychology,* 1971, 85, 51-64.

MEICHENBAUM, D., BOWERS, K., & ROSS, R. A. A behavioral analysis of teacher expectancies among southern and non-southern teachers. *Journal of Personality and Social Psychology,* 1969, 13, 306-316.

MENDELS, G. E., & FLANDERS, J. P. Teacher's expectations and pupil performance. *American Educational Research Journal,* 1973, 10, 203-211.

MENNE, J. W., HANNUM, T. E., KLINGENSMITH, J. E., & NORD, D. Use of taped lectures to replace class attendance. *AV Communication Review.* 1969, 17, 42-46.

MERRILL, J. R. The systems approach to instructional design. Paper presented at the annual meeting of the International Communication Association, Portland, 1976.

MEYERS, G. E., & MEYERS, M. T. *The dynamics of human communication: A laboratory approach.* New York: McGraw-Hill, 1973.

MILLER, G. A., GALANTER, E., & PRIBRAM, K. H. *Plans and the structure of behavior.* New York: Holt, 1960.

MILLER, G. R., ZAVAS, H., VLANDIS, J. W., & ROSENBAUM, M. The effect of differential reward on speech patterns. *Speech Monographs,* 1961, 28, 9-15.

MILLER, G. R. Variation in the verbal behavior of a second speaker as a function of varying audience responses. *Speech Monographs,* 1964 31, 109-115.

MILLER, M. D., & DALY J. The development of a measure of writing apprehension. Paper presented at the annual meeting of the International Communication Association, Chicago, 1975.

MORSE, J. A., & TILLMAN. Effects on achievement of possession of behavioral objectives and training concerning their use. Paper presented to the annual meeting of the American Educational Research Association, Chicago, 1972.

MUSTERBERG, H. Studies from the Harvard psychological laboratory. *Psychological Review,* 1894, 1, 34-38.

NICHOLS, R. G. Factors in listening comprehension. *Speech Monographs,* 1948, 15, 154-163.

O'CONNELL, E. J., DUSEK, J. B., & WHEELER, R. A follow-up study of teacher expectancy effects. *Journal of Educational Psychology.* 1974, 66, 325-328.

ORR, D. B., FRIEDMAN, H. L., & WILLIAMS, J. C. Trainability of listening comprehension of speeded discourse. *Journal of Educational Psychology,* 1965, 66, 148-156.

PAUL G. *Insight versus desensitization in psychotherapy.* Stanford: Stanford University Press, 1966.

PAULSON, S. The effects of the prestige of the speaker and acknowledgement of opposing arguments on audience retention and shift of opinion. *Speech Monographs,* 1954, 21, 267-271.

PERLMUTTER, J., & ROYER, J. M. Organization of prose material stimulus, storage, and retrieval. *Canadian Journal of Psychology,* 1973, 27, 201-209.

PETRIE, C. R., JR. Informative speaking: A summary and bibliography of related research. *Speech Monographs,* 1963, 30, 79-91.

PHILLIPS, G. M. Reticence: Pathology of the normal speaker. *Speech Monographs,* 1968, 35, 39-49.

PIAGET, J. *The origin of intelligence in children.* New York: International Universities Press, 1952.

PIAGET, J. *The construction of reality and the child.* New York: Basic Books, 1954.

PIAGET, J. *The child's conception of the world.* London: Routledge & Kegan Paul, 1957.

POPHAM, W. J. Pictorial embellishments in a tape-slide instructional program. *AV Communication Review,* 1969, 17, 29-35.

PORTER, D. T., & BURNS, G. P., JR. A criticism of "heart rate as an index of speech anxiety." *Speech Monographs,* 1973, 40, 156-159.

PORTER, D. T. Self-report scales of communication apprehension and autonomic arousal (heart rate): A test of construct validity. *Speech Monographs,* 1974, 267-276.

POSTMAN, N., & WEINGARTNER, C. *Teaching as a Subversive Activity.* New York: Delacorte, 1969.

PRYOR, A. An experimental investigation of juror comprehension of standardized pattern instructions. Paper presented at the annual meeting of the International Communication Association, Portland, 1976.

RICHMOND, V. P., GROESHNER, J. C., PATERLINE, E. J., & SPRINGHORN, R. G. Computer modeling in the communication classroom: Follow-up and extension. Paper presented to the annual meeting of the International Communication Association, Chicago, 1975.

RICKARDS, J. P., & AUGUST, G. J. Generative underlining strategies in prose recall. *Journal of Educational Psychology,* 1975, 67, 860-865.

RIST, R. G. Student social class and teacher expectations: The self-fulfilling prophecy in ghetto education. *Harvard Educational Review,* 1970, 40, 411-451.

ROGERS, E., & SHOEMAKER, F. F. *Communication of innovations.* New York: Free Press, 1971.

ROSENFIELD, L. W., KURNIT, P., ROSENBERG, D., & SUSSIS, D. Multimedia instruction: The intellect as a design consideration. Paper presented at the annual meeting of the International Communication Association, Montreal, 1973.

ROSENTHAL, R., BARATZ, S. S., & HALL, C. M. Teacher behavior, teacher expectations, and gains in pupil's rated creativity. *The Journal of Genetic Psychology,* 1974, 124, 115-121.

ROSENTHAL, R., & JACOBSON, L. *Pygmalion in the classroom.* New York: Holt, 1968.

RUBEN, B. D., Communication, information and education systems: Some perspectives. Paper presented at the annual meeting of the National Society for the Study of Communication, Cleveland, Ohio, 1969.

RUBEN, B. D., *Interact,* Kennebunkport, Maine: Mercer House, 1973.

RUBEN, B. D., The what and why of gaming: A taxonomy of experiential learning systems. In J. E. Moriarty (Ed.), *Simulation and gaming. Proceedings of the annual symposium of the National Gaming Council and the annual conference of the International Simulation and Gaming Association,* Gaithersburg, Md., National Bureau of Standards, Publication 395, Washington, 1974.

RUBEN, B. D., & BUDD, R. W. *Human communication handbook: Simulations and games.* Rochelle Park, N.J.: Hayden Books, 1975.

RUSHING, J. Training students in the participant observation approach to research: Application for conflict in relationship definitions. Paper presented at the annual meeting of the International Communication Association, Portland, 1976.

SAWYER, T. M. Persuasion and estimate of major attitude. *Speech Monographs,* 1955, 22, 68-78.

SCOTT, M. D., & WHEELESS, L. R. Communication apprehension, student attitudes, and levels of satisfaction. *Western Speech Communication* (in press).

SCOTT, M. D., & WHEELESS, L. R. The relationship of three types of communication apprehension to classroom achievement. *Southern Speech Communication Journal* (in press).

SCOTT, M. D., YATES, M. D., & WHEELESS, L. R. An exploratory investigation of the effects of communication apprehension in alternative systems of instruction. Paper presented at the annual meeting of the International Communication Association, Chicago, 1975.

SCOTT, M. D., WHEELESS, L. R., YATES, M. D., & RANDOLPH, F. The effects of communication apprehension and test anxiety on three indicants of achievement in an alternative system of instruction: A follow-up study. In B.D. Ruben (Ed.), *Communication Yearbook I.* New Brunswick, N.J.: Transaction-International Communication Association, 1977.

SEARS, R. R., MACCOBY, E., & LEVIN, H. *Patterns of child rearing.* New York: Harper & Row, 1957.

SEAVER, W. B. Effects of naturally induced teacher expectancies on the academic performance of pupils in primary grades. Unpublished doctoral dissertation, University of Illinois, 1971.

SEILER, W. J., & CHEATHAM, T. R. The conjunctive influence of source credibility and the use of visual materials on communication effectiveness. Paper presented at the annual meeting of the International Communication Association, Phoenix, 1971.

SERENO, K K Changes in verbal behavior of a speaker during two successive speech performances as a function of the sequence of listener responses. *Speech Monographs,* 1965, 32, 261.

SHAMO, W. G., & BITTNER, J. R. Information recall as a function of language style. Paper presented at the annual convention of the International Communication Association, Phoenix, 1971.

SHEFFIELD, F.D., MARGOLIUS, G.J., & HOEHN, A.J. Experiments on perceptual mediation in the learning of organizable sequences. In A.A. Lumsdaine (Ed.) *Student response in programmed instruction:* A symposium.

Washington, D.C.: National Academy of Sciences-National Research Council, Publication No. 943, 1961.

SHUTZ, C. B., & DiVESTA, F. J. Effects of passage organization and notetaking on the selection of clustering strategies and on recall of textual materials. *Journal of Educational Psychology,* 1972, 63, 244-252.

SKINNER, B. F. *The behavior of organisms.* New York: Appleton, Century, Crofts, 1938.

SKINNER, B. F. *Science and human behavior.* New York: Free Press, 1953.

SKINNER, B. F. *Verbal behavior.* Englewood Cliffs: Prentice Hall, 1957.

SKINNER, B. F. *The technology of teaching.* New York: Appleton, Century, Crofts, 1968.

SKINNER, B. F. *Contingencies of reinforcement: A theoretical analysis.* New York: Appleton, Century, Crofts, 1969.

SKINNER, B. F. *Cumulative record: A selection of papers.* New York: Appleton, Century, Crofts, 1972.

SMYTHE, M. J., KIBLER, R. J., & HUTCHINS, P. W. A comparison of norm referenced and criterion referenced measurement with implications for communication instruction. Paper presented at the annual meeting of the International Communication Association, Atlanta, 1972.

SOMMER, R. *Personal space.* Englewood Cliffs, N.J.: Prentice-Hall, 1969.

SPELL, G. R., PARKS, A. M., & KIBLER, R. J. A comparison of mastery and traditional learning systems with implications for communication instruction. Paper presented at the annual meeting of the International Communication Association, Atlanta, 1972.

SPICER, C., & BASSETT, R. E. The effect of organization on learning from an informative message. *The Southern Speech Communication Journal,* 1976, 41, 290-299.

SPROULE, B. A., & SPROULE, J. M. A system simulation of overload conditions in decision making. Paper presented at the annual meeting of the International Communication Association, Portland, 1976.

SPROULE, J. M. Instructional communication in a new setting. Paper presented at the annual meeting of the International Communication Association, New Orleans, 1974.

STICHT, T. G., & GLASNAPP. Effects of speech rate, selection difficulty, association strength and mental aptitude on learning by listening. *Journal of Communication,* 1972, 22, 174-188.

STOLZ, W. S., & TANNENBAUM, P. H. Effects of feedback on oral encoding behavior. *Language and Speech,* 1963, 6, 218-228.

STRAWN, D. V. A pilot project in instructional communication: A communication course for jurors. Paper presented at the annual meeting of the International Communication Association, Portland, 1976.

TANSEY, P.J. & UNWIN, D. *Simulations and gaming in education.* London: Metheun Education, Ltd., 1969.

TAYLOR, D. R., LIPSCOMB, E., & ROSEMEIR, R. Live versus video-tape student-teacher interaction. *AV Communication Review,* 1969, 17, 47-51.

TAYLOR, K. P. Proposed instructional techniques that may significantly improve juror comprehension and effectiveness. Paper presented at the annual meeting of the International Communication Association, Portland, 1976.

THOMPSON, E. Some effects of message structure on listener's comprehension. *Speech Monographs,* 1967, 34, 51-57.

THORNDIKE, E. *Human learning.* New York: Appleton, Century, Crofts, 1931.

THORNDIKE, E. L. *The fundamentals of learning*. New York: Teachers College, Columbia University, 1932.

VERNON, M. D. The value of pictorial illustration. *British Journal of Educational Psychology*, 1953, 23, 29-37.

WALLEN, N. E., & TRAVERS, R. M. W. Analysis and investigation of teaching method. In N. L. Gage (Ed.), *Handbook of research on teaching*. Chicago: Rand McNally, 1963, 449-505.

WATSON, J. B. *Behaviorism*. New York: Norton, 1925.

WENDT, P.R., & BUTTS, G.K. Audio-visual materials. *Review of Educational Research*, 1962, 32, 141-155.

WHEELESS, L.R. Communication apprehension in the elementary school. *Speech Teacher*, 1971, 10, 297-299.

WHEELESS, L. R. The relationship of attitude and credibility to comprehension. Paper presented at the annual meeting of the Speech Communication Association, Chicago, 1972.

WHEELESS, L. R. The relationship of attitude and credibility to comprehension and selective exposure. *Western Speech*, 1974a, 38, 85-97.

WHEELESS, L. R. The effects of attitude, credibility, and homophily on selective exposure to information. *Speech Monographs*, 1974b, 41, 329-338.

WHEELESS, L. R. Relationship of four elements to immediate recall and student-instructor interaction. *Western Speech Communication*, 1975, 39, 131-140.

WHEELESS, L. R. An investigation of receiver apprehension and social context dimensions of communication apprehension. *Speech Teacher*, 1975b, 261-268.

WHEELESS, L. R., & SCOTT, M. D. Communication apprehension and success motivation: Implications for measurement and treatment. Paper presented at the annual meeting of the Western Speech Communication Association, Seattle, 1975.

WHEELESS, L. R., & SCOTT, M. D. The nature, measurement, and potential effects of receiver apprehension. Paper presented at the annual meeting of the International Communication Association, Portland, 1976.

WHEELESS, L. R., & WILLIS, M. The relationship of attitudes toward course and instructor to learning and student-instructor interaction in instructional assessment. Paper presented at the annual meeting of the Speech Communication Association, Chicago, 1974.

WILLIAMS, B. The development and measurement of the concept of informational anxiety. Unpublished master's thesis, West Virginia University, 1976.

WILMOT, W. The influence of personal conflict styles of teaching on student attitudes toward conflict. Paper presented at the annual meeting of the International Communication Association, Portland, 1976.

WINNE, P. H., HAUK, W. E., & MOORE, J. W. The efficiency of implicit retention and cognitive restructuring. *Journal of Education Psychology*, 1975, 67, 770-775.

WOODWORTH, T. *Dynamic psychology*. New York: Columbia University Press, 1918.

WOODWORTH, R. *Experimental psychology*. New York: Holt, 1938.

YUILLE, J.C., & PAIVIO, A. Abstractness and recall of connected discourse. *Journal of Experimental Psychology*, 1969, 82, 467-471.

ZAGONA, S., & HARTER, R. Credibility of source and recipient attitude: Factors for the perception and retention of information on smoking behavior. *Perceptual Motor Skills*, 1966, 23, 155-168.

ZIMBARDO, P. Verbal ambiguity and judgmental distortion. *Psychological Reports*, 1960, 6, 57-58.

THE EFFECTS OF TALKING APPREHENSION ON STUDENT ACADEMIC ACHIEVEMENT: THREE EMPIRICAL INVESTIGATIONS IN COMMUNICATION-RESTRICTED AND TRADITIONAL LABORATORY CLASSES IN THE LIFE SCIENCES

JOHN P. GARRISON, WILLIAM J. SEILER, and RICHARD K. BOOHAR
The University of Nebraska-Lincoln

This study investigated the relationship of oral communication apprehension and academic achievement in communication-restricted lecture courses and traditional life science laboratory courses. Three studies were conducted to test the effects of talking apprehension on academic achievement. Study One consisted of nonscience majors in the basic course in life science. Study two selected a sample of science majors in the basic course. Study three consisted of upper-division pre-medical, pre-dental, and pre-pharmacy majors. No significant differences were detected. Pedagogical implications for reducing academic achievement problems associated with oral communication apprehension are also discussed.

In recent years a variable that has received considerable attention, under a variety of names, in communication, psychology, and education is *communication apprehension* (CA). Communication apprehension, or more specifically talking apprehension (J. Andersen, P. Andersen, & J. Garrison, 1976), refers to an anxiety syndrome which is associated with either real or anticipated communication (talking) with another person or persons (McCroskey, 1975a). The *low apprehensive* person anticipates communication with another person or persons as a pleasant and rewarding experience, while the highly apprehensive person expects either no reward, or a high degree of punishment, as a result of his or her communicating with others. The purpose of this study was to examine the effects of communication apprehension on student academic achievement, when comparing communication-restricted lecture classes to traditional laboratory classes.

It was originally thought by human communication researchers that communication apprehension was only related to the context of public speaking. Phillips (1968), however, has suggested that communication apprehension is more pervasive than was originally thought, stating that it goes beyond the public speaking context to all situations in which communication can occur. Phillips argues further, that apprehension occurs in any context where an individual perceives that his or her potential gains for participating in communication situations are outweighed by anxiety and the negative effects of such participation. Thus, as a consequence, a highly apprehensive person is likely to withdraw from situations that place him or her in a communicative role.

Oral communication apprehension has been found to accurately predict occupational choice and desirability (Daly & McCroskey, 1975), to lower the amount of interaction within small groups (Phillips & Metzger, 1973; Wells & Lashbrook, 1970), and to predict the selection of positions within groups (McCroskey, 1976b). It has also been found that *high apprehensives* are apt to rate themselves lower in self-esteem and credibility (McCroskey & Wheeless, 1976; Hamilton, 1972; McCroskey, Daly, Richmond, & Falcione, 1977), avoid situations which are competitive (Giffin & Gilham, 1971), and lack trust in others' communicative behaviors (Giffin & Heider, 1967; Low, 1950). All of the above variables may have effects on academic achievement, based on a subject's level of talking apprehension.

It has also been found that persons who have been

perceived by others to be highly apprehensive are consistently rated lower on the dimensions of credibility, attraction, power, leadership, and influence (Daly, McCroskey, & Richmond, 1977). Individuals who are described as apprehensive are also evaluated lower in interpersonal attractiveness (McCroskey, Daly, Richmond, & Cox, 1975) and significantly more negative than low apprehensives in personnel interviews, regardless of the perceived level of need for communication skills, in relation to possible job success (Daly & Leth, 1976). It was also found, in the same study by Daly and Leth that highly apprehensive applicants make significantly less favorable impressions on interviewers in regard to their willingness to interview, recommendations, competency, perceived satisfaction of the job, ability to adjust to co-workers, and their need for further training.

It is interesting to note, also, that Daly and McCroskey (1975), in the occupational desirability study mentioned earlier, found that science areas are perceived as a low communication field; this finding was also replicated by McCroskey and Richmond (1976). If this finding is valid, then science majors should show higher overall levels of communication apprehension.

RATIONALE FOR HYPOTHESES

The capability of a student to succeed in today's learning environment is partially determined by his or her ability to effectively communicate. Scott, Yates, and Wheeless (1975) found that the effects of communication apprehension in a modularized, criterion-based, system of instruction significantly affected the efficiency of the learner. However, their results did not show significant effects for levels of satisfaction within the learning environment, when highly apprehensive persons rated the course method or course content. McCroskey and Daly (1976) found that elementary and secondary school teachers evaluated children who were described as highly apprehensive lower in performance in all areas of the school environment, including science, when compared to children who were described as not apprehensive.

Bashore (1971), studying high school seniors, found a slight negative relationship between *communication apprehension* and *intelligence*, but did not account for a significant portion of the variance. Bashore also failed to find a significant correlation between *communication apprehension* and grade-point average in the same study. McCroskey, Daly, and Sorensen (1976) have recently reported a nonsignificant negative ($-.18$) relationship between talking apprehension and intelligence among college students, similar to Bashore's observation.

McCroskey and J. Andersen (1976), studying the relationship between CA and academic achievement among college students, found that high communication apprehensives preferred mass lecture classes over small classes, while moderate and low communication apprehensives reversed this preference. It was also found that highly apprehensive college students performed better in lecture classes than when they were enrolled in "communication intensified" small classes. Moreover, McCroskey and J. Andersen (1976) observed that there were significant differences between a students level of CA and their natural science score on the American College Test. Highly apprehensive students had lower scores.

According to McCroskey and J. Andersen (1976), there are two barriers to sufficient teacher-student interaction. The first barrier is due to the large number of students in class—the greater the number of students, the less potential there is for effective student-teacher interaction. Thus, it could be argued that a larger classroom of students creates some effects detrimental to learning.

The second barrier, according to McCroskey and J. Andersen, is communication apprehension which has its effects primarily in small classes. While smaller classes generally allow for more potential student-teacher interaction, McCroskey and J. Andersen (1976) suggest that some students, because of their communication apprehension, are not able to function adequately in this environment either. Their apprehension is so great, they state, that their inability to communicate with their teachers and fellow students inhibits or effectively reduces their success. The highly apprehensive student, placed in a small class situation where he or she is expected to participate more, may be less effective and thereby achieve less academically, than those students who are low or moderate apprehensives. To substantiate this point, McCroskey (1977) reports the startling fact that between 15 and 20 percent of American college students suffer from the debilitating effects of CA.

These research findings generated our rationale and led to the examination of the following hypotheses.

H_1: High and low oral communication apprehensive students will not differ in academic achievement in a communication-restricted lecture class.

H_2: High oral communication apprehensive students will have significantly lower academic achievement in a traditional laboratory class than will low apprehensive students.

METHOD

Three studies were conducted to test our hypotheses. In each study subjects completed McCroskey's (1970) *Personal Report of Communication Apprehension, College Form* (PRCA). The PRCA was chosen because it has consistently been found to be a reliable and valid measure of oral (talking) communication apprehension (McCroskey, 1975). Oral (talking) communication apprehension served as the independent variable for all three studies, and subsequently provided for the testing of the experimental hypotheses.

Sample and Procedures for Study One

Subjects in this study were 164 undergraduate students enrolled in the basic life science course at University of Nebraska-Lincoln during the spring semester of 1976. More than half of the sample were freshmen; approximately half of the sample were female, half were male.

The lecture portion of this course was taught by a single lecturer in a large and rather impersonal lecture hall. Opportunity was always available for students to ask questions, but none of them were actively sought out by the lecturer to promote further discussion.

The laboratory portion of the basic course consisted of multiple sections of 24 students each, but each section was divided into two groups of approx-

imately 12 students who attended at different times. In each of these sections, students had to interact with their instructor as he or she examined their laboratory notebooks. The students were also under some pressure to talk with other students around them, as well. Thus, communication with the instructor was required; communication with other students was encouraged, but was not required.

Sample and Procedures for Study Two

Subjects in Study Two were 86 undergraduate life science majors at the same midwestern university. This sample was primarily male, and was drawn from a course similar to the basic course sampled for Study One, but was designed more as a higher-level course for students planning to become professional scientists.

The lecture portion of this course was team-taught, with three lecturers teaching portions of the course for a minimum of four or five lectures each, and usually more. The format was that of a traditional communication-restricted lecture course with some opportunity for students to ask questions, but no requirement that they do so.

The laboratory sections were limited to 16 students each, with students working in small groups of four members each. In addition to having close contact with others, encouraged by this type of small group interaction, each group completed a joint laboratory report, which required each person to work directly on the writing of the report. It was possible for students to avoid communicating with their fellow students, but they would have been quite noticeable if they did.

Sample and Procedures for Study Three

Subjects in the third study were 62 junior and senior pre-medical, pre-dental, and pre-pharmacy majors enrolled in a vertebrate physiology course at the same university during the same semester. The lecture portion of this course was also a traditional communication-restricted lecture course using a single lecturer, with liberal use of overhead visual aids and movies, and with time allotted for questions from class members.

TABLE 1
Statistical Analysis System—
Factor Analysis of PRCA

Unrotated Factor Matrix

	1	2	3	4	5
PRCA1	0.58947	-0.34170	0.13938	0.00429	-0.31833
PRCA2	0.55906	0.39697	0.04806	0.22974	-0.29436
PRCA3	0.56610	-0.20675	-0.12355	0.01983	-0.40672
PRCA4	0.60763	-0.14325	-0.46002	-0.06546	0.05976
PRCA5	0.69646	-0.34837	-0.19934	-0.06537	-0.04785
PRCA6	0.65408	0.37229	-0.17151	-0.01654	0.04522
PRCA7	0.40385	0.38975	-0.11153	-0.50651	0.17537
PRCA8	0.48116	-0.22456	0.43073	-0.20339	-0.19447
PRCA9	0.64301	-0.35644	0.16661	-0.12617	-0.06690
PRCA10	0.70241	0.14085	0.19990	0.05877	0.00239
PRCA11	0.55347	-0.33485	-0.21280	0.25548	-0.12193
PRCA12	0.46073	0.14002	0.37332	-0.35676	0.15320
PRCA13	0.71384	0.17804	-0.00693	-0.08406	0.06355
PRCA14	0.53172	0.07034	-0.20814	-0.00752	-0.26228
PRCA15	0.67038	0.09872	0.14244	0.07509	0.03102
PRCA16	0.67750	0.06723	0.34587	-0.02232	-0.08921
PRCA17	0.57500	-0.19135	-0.37259	-0.29605	0.24009
PRCA18	0.53127	0.29663	-0.08983	-0.03498	-0.25605
PRCA19	0.41635	-0.23046	0.30905	0.43540	0.37324
PRCA20	0.52043	-0.06449	0.12898	-0.20583	0.29895
PRCA21	0.62845	0.03846	0.12539	-0.07377	-0.03822
PRCA22	0.57905	-0.07067	0.11539	0.31064	0.28304
PRCA23	0.60032	0.40725	-0.12683	0.27744	0.08016
PRCA24	0.45866	-0.53374	-0.19607	0.00966	0.27551
PRCA25	0.60437	0.34288	-0.16565	0.26159	0.11076

- CONTINUED -

The laboratory sections of the physiology course were taught by graduate and undergraduate teaching assistants under supervision of the course lecturer. The laboratory sessions were based on exercises from the course laboratory manual. Teams of students worked together to complete the exercises, which required considerable communication and cooperation to complete accurately. The student who was an ineffective communicator could have had difficulty in this type of classroom environment.

Independent Variable

Oral (talking) communication apprehension was the independent variable for all three studies. Thus, measurement on the 25 *Likert-type scales* of McCroskey's PRCA served as the operationalization of the independent variable.

Selection of scales after factor analysis. The PRCA was submitted to two factor analyses, prior to the testing of the experimental hypotheses, revealing a unidimensional factor solution in each data analysis. Since the PRCA is known to be a reliable and valid multi-generational research instrument, we expected a single factor with primary loadings of at least .55. The first factor analysis was checked for the possible existence of multiple factors. McCroskey and Young's (1975) criteria for factor analysis in communication research were then used in the second analysis of loadings on the single PRCA factor. In addition to the factor analytic programs of the Statistical Analysis System (Barr & Goodnight, 1972), the Biomedical Computer Program P–4M (Dixon, 1975) was used as an additional check on the factor structure of the PRCA. Kaiser's (1970) second generation *Little Jiffy* program was included in these data analyses, because a measure

TABLE 1 (cont.)
Statistical Analysis System

Rotated Factor Matrix

PRCA1	0.15893	-0.68139	-0.00472	-0.28395	0.12167
PRCA2	0.70626	-0.23153	0.04336	0.05362	0.09914
PRCA3	0.31316	-0.54428	-0.10783	-0.36565	-0.06820
PRCA4	0.33967	-0.10705	0.09497	-0.68782	0.01574
PRCA5	0.21987	-0.42039	0.09934	-0.63241	0.13355
PRCA6	0.67065	-0.06111	0.29298	-0.23831	0.04485
PRCA7	0.33940	0.06127	0.64768	-0.17109	-0.21685
PRCA8	0.02114	-0.66749	0.28622	-0.02931	0.13374
PRCA9	0.08795	-0.58828	0.22612	-0.36570	0.22357
PRCA10	0.49641	-0.36931	0.28596	-0.10347	0.28522
PRCA11	0.25960	-0.34721	-0.21347	-0.50810	0.22846
PRCA12	0.15328	-0.29051	0.62866	0.03532	0.13278
PRCA13	0.51645	-0.24212	0.36791	-0.26481	0.14699
PRCA14	0.46124	-0.29189	0.01471	-0.29948	-0.10952
PRCA15	0.46075	-0.32443	0.24812	-0.15304	0.28898
PRCA16	0.39205	-0.52050	0.31936	-0.02304	0.25391
PRCA17	0.16277	-0.06872	0.34701	-0.70647	0.02494
PRCA18	0.57793	-0.25573	0.13342	-0.10800	-0.12738
PRCA19	0.09905	-0.16202	0.02403	-0.10488	0.77667
PRCA20	0.12477	-0.18069	0.47696	-0.27064	0.27282
PRCA21	0.36454	-0.37968	0.28920	-0.18439	0.15612
PRCA22	0.32438	-0.15497	0.10982	-0.23139	0.57912
PRCA23	0.73780	0.01332	0.10182	-0.12924	0.23264
PRCA24	-0.08642	-0.17587	0.06676	-0.66866	0.34601
PRCA25	0.69464	0.02050	0.09964	-0.19887	0.24195

Cumulative Percentage of Eigenvalues					
	0.34027	0.41571	0.46857	0.51470	0.55621
Eigenvalues					
	8.50668	1.88608	1.32145	1.15336	1.03761

of sampling adequacy (MSA) for factor analysis is included as part of the Biomed package (Kaiser & Hunka, 1973).

Kaiser (1970) reports that his "MSA is a function of four 'main effects': (1) MSA improves as the number of variables (P) increases; (2) MSA improves as the (effective) number of factors (q) decreases; (3) MSA improves as the number of subjects (N) increases; and (4) MSA improves as the general level of correlation (r) increases" (p. 405). Kaiser and Hunka (1973) interpret the strength of their measures of sampling adequacy for factor analysis by arguing that "good factor analytic data doesn't exist until MSA gets to be at least .80, and 'really excellent' data doesn't occur until MSA

reaches the .90's" (p. 102).

The factor analyses of both orthogonal and oblique solutions revealed the existence of five factors with eigenvalues greater than 1.0, but several of the a priori criteria indicated the existence of fewer factors were actually valid for subsequent data analyses. Table 1 combines factor loadings for the orthogonal and oblique solutions for these factors and *Kaiser's* MSA (1970).

Table 2 revealed 17 *Likert-type scales*[2] meeting the a priori loading criteria. The MSA for the second factor analysis was .95.

Based upon a survey of over 20 studies that have used the PRCA, McCroskey (1975) concluded that researchers "can employ the PRCA as an index of

TABLE 2
Factor Analysis of 25 Likert-type PRCA Scales

PRCA1	0.58947*
PRCA2	0.55906*
PRCA3	0.56610*
PRCA4	0.60763*
PRCA5	0.69646*
PRCA6	0.65408*
PRCA7	0.40385
PRCA8	0,48116
PRCA9	0.64301*
PRCA10	0.70241*
PRCA11	0.55347*
PRCA12	0.46073
PRCA13	0.71384*
PRCA14	0.53172
PRCA15	0.67038*
PRCA16	0.67750*
PRCA17	0.57500*
PRCA18	0.53127
PRCA19	0.41635
PRCA20	0.52043
PRCA21	0.62845*
PRCA22	0.57905*
PRCA23	0.60032*
PRCA24	0.45866
PRCA25	0.60437*

Eigenvalue 8.50668

Overall reliability (Nunnally) of 17 PRCA scales = .93

Measure of sampling adequacy = .95

*Indicates primary loading

oral (talking) communication apprehension with confidence in both its reliability and validity." Study One of this report revealed a split-half reliability of .93 and an estimate of .94, using *Nunnally's reliability formula 6-18* (cf. Nunnally, 1967; Davis & Garrison, 1976). Study Two showed a reliability of .92 using the split-half method, and .94 using Nunnally's formula. Study Three showed similar reliability estimates of .92 using the split-half method, and .94 using Nunnally's formula. Thus, the PRCA had substantial reliability[3] for the measurement of the independent variable in all three studies.

Construct validity. Scales developed through fac-

tor analysis have factorial validity (Cronbach, 1949), which provided evidence for the overall construct validity of the PRCA instrument. The exact replication of the talking apprehension measurement instrument, on highly dissimilar student populations, offers considerable support for the talking apprehension construct and the PRCA instrument in this series of investigations.

Dependent Variables

The two dependent variables measured in each study were *academic achievement in a communication-restricted lecture environment* and *academic achievement in a traditional laboratory*

TABLE 3
Number of Oral (Talking) Communication Apprehensives in Studies One, Two, and Three

Study 1: Non-Life Science Majors	N	Per cent
High Apprehension Level	22	13.4%
Moderate Apprehension Level	120	73.2%
Low Apprehension Level	22	13.4%
Total	164	100.0%
Study 2: Life Science Majors	N	Per cent
High Apprehension Level	14	16.3%
Moderate Apprehension Level	56	65.1%
Low Apprehension Level	16	18.6%
Total	86	100.0%
Study 3: Pre-Medical, Pre-Dental, and Pre-Pharmacy Majors	N	Per cent
High Apprehension Level	13	21.0%
Moderate Apprehension Level	42	67.7%
Low Apprehension Level	7	11.3%
Total	62	100.0%
Overall: Combined Samples of Studies One, Two, and Three	N	Per cent
High Apprehension Level	49	15.7%
Moderate Apprehension Level	218	69.9%
Low Apprehension Level	45	14.4%
Total	312	100.0%

environment. In no case were the dependent variables significantly correlated ($r = .08 - .10$).

Lecture. Academic achievement of university science students in a communication-restricted learning environment was operationalized as the summed score of three multiple choice examinations (average $r = .80$) in mass lecture portions of the courses in life sciences.

Laboratory. Academic achievement in a traditional laboratory environment was operationalized in terms of the summed scores from several exercises in the laboratory portions of the courses in life

TABLE 4
Mean Scores of Student Learning Variables in Three Samples of College
Science Students

LEVEL OF COMMUNICATION APPREHENSION	(1) Non-Majors		(2) Majors		(3) Upper Division	
	Lecture	Lab	Lecture	Lab	Lecture	Lab
Mean Scores						
High	77.23	77.14	64.64	80.43	77.85	80.38
Moderate	73.58	76.33	68.45	80.61	72.29	77.86
Low	77.55	76.77	71.00	84.69	77.43	82.71

sciences. No reliability estimates were available for these laboratory exercises. Achievement data for both the lecture and laboratory sections were obtained from individual section instructors and from university grade reports, after the semester had ended. The confidentiality of an individual's student records were maintained by using coded student numbers, and neither the students nor their instructors were aware that they were part of an experiment.

Statistical Analyses

Subjects in all three studies were classified as *high, moderate,* or *low apprehensives* based on their scores on the PRCA. The mean PRCA score for all three studies was 49.03, standard deviation 12.88, with the lowest possible score being 17 and the highest being 85 (cf. Note 2). The PRCA scores in these studies ranged from 17 to 74. Subjects scoring more than one standard deviation above the mean were classified as *high apprehensives.* Subjects scoring one deviation either side of the mean were classified as *moderate apprehensives.* Those subjects scoring more than one devia-

tion below the PRCA mean were classified as *low apprehensives.* The percentage of students categorized in each classification are reported in Table 3.

The lecture and laboratory academic achievement dependent variables were submitted independently to a single classifcation the *analysis of variance* model, employing scores on the PRCA instrument as the classification system. The *alpha level* for testing the experimental hypotheses was .05.

RESULTS

Study One

A single classification analysis of variance did not support either hypothesis. Table 4 indicates that talking apprehension did not have a significant effect on the lecture grades of nonlife science majors ($F = 2.47$; df = 2.161; $p > .05$) or on their laboratory grades ($F < 1$) in the overall one-way analysis of variance model. Statistical power ($1 - \beta$) was calculated at $> .85$ (cf. Cohen, 1969), for detecting an effect size of .15, for both hypotheses in Study One.

TABLE 5
PRCA Instrument Used in Studies One, Two, and Three

DIRECTIONS: This instrument is composed of 25 statements concerning feelings about communicating with other people. Please indicate the degree to which each statement applies to you by marking whether you (1) Strongly Agree, (2) Agree, (3) are Undecided , (4) Disagree, or (5) Strongly Disagree with each statement. There are no right or wrong answers. Work quickly; just record your first impression.

		SA	A	UN	D	SD
*1.	While participating in a conversation with a new acquaintance I feel very nervous.	1	2	3	4	5
*2.	I have no fear of facing an audience.	1	2	3	4	5
*3.	I talk less because I'm shy.	1	2	3	4	5
*4.	I look forward to expressing my opinions at meetings.	1	2	3	4	5
*5.	I am afraid to express myself in a group.	1	2	3	4	5
*6.	I look forward to an opportunity to speak in public.	1	2	3	4	5
7.	I find the prospect of speaking mildly pleasant.	1	2	3	4	5
8.	When communicating, my posture feels strained and unnatural.	1	2	3	4	5
*9.	I am tense and nervous while participating in group discussions.	1	2	3	4	5
*10.	Although I talk fluently with friends I am at a loss for words on the platform.	1	2	3	4	5
*11.	I have no fear about expressing myself in a group.	1	2	3	4	5
12.	My hands tremble when I try to handle objects on the platform.	1	2	3	4	5
*13.	I always avoid speaking in public if possible.	1	2	3	4	5
14.	I feel that I am more fluent when talking to people than most other people are.	1	2	3	4	5
*15.	I am fearful and tense all the while I am speaking before a group of people.	1	2	3	4	5
*16.	My thoughts become confused and jumbled when I speak before an audience.	1	2	3	4	5
*17.	I like to get involved in group discussions.	1	2	3	4	5
*18.	Although I am nervous just before getting up, I soon forget my fears and enjoy the experience.	1	2	3	4	5
19.	Conversing with people who hold positions of authority causes me to be fearful and tense.	1	2	3	4	5
20.	I dislike to use my body and voice expressively.	1	2	3	4	5
*21.	I feel relaxed and comfortable while speaking.	1	2	3	4	5
*22.	I feel self-conscious when I am called upon to answer a question or give an opinion in class.	1	2	3	4	5
*23.	I face the prospect of making a speech with complete confidence.	1	2	3	4	5
24.	I'm afraid to speak up in conversations.	1	2	3	4	5
*25.	I would enjoy presenting a speech on a local television show.	1	2	3	4	5

* Indicates primary factor loading

(See Table 2 for summary of factor loadings)

Study Two

Data from Study Two did not confirm either hypothesis. Table 4 reveals that *talking apprehension*, consistent with the results of study one, did not show significant differences on mean *lecture grades* ($F = < 1$; $df = 2, 83$), or on the mean laboratory grades ($F = 1.15$; $df = 2, 83$; $p > .05$) of life science majors in the analysis of variance model. Statistical power $(1 — \beta)$ was $> .56$ (Cohen, 1969), for detecting an effect size of .15, for both hypotheses in Study Two.

Study Three

Results of the third study, a sample of junior and senior pre-medicine, pre-dental, and pre-pharmacy majors, indicated that neither of the hypotheses were confirmed. Table 4 reports that *talking ap-prehension* did not show significant differences on *lecture grades* ($F = 1.79$; $df = 2, 59$; $p > .05$), or on *laboratory grades* ($F < 1$). Statistical power ($1 - \beta$) was $> .41$ (Cohen, 1969), for detecting an effect size of .15, for both hypotheses in study three.

DISCUSSION

The rationale that generated our hypotheses indicated consistent results from previous empirical research suggesting that some students are more likely to seek communication with others, while some actively avoid it. Since research and personal testimony of high communication apprehensives reveals that their apprehension interferes with performance, it is important that some techniques be discovered that allow students to accurately demonstrate their academic achievement (Burgoon, 1975). It was hypothesized that undergraduate students suffering from the debilitating effects of talking apprehension would manifest detrimental effects, in academic achievement, in both communication-restricted and traditional laboratory environments. The overall results of the three studies failed to support the experimental hypotheses.

Interpretation of Results

Previous empirical research by McCroskey and J. Andersen (1976) indicated that "there may be some *very* small relationship between *oral (talking) communication apprehension* and *achievement in a communication-restricted instructional system*." Study One, however, did not detect a significant relationship for either hypothesis. Thus, our results indicated that academic achievement of highly apprehensive students was not significantly affected when they are placed in communication-restricted learning environments.

Results from Study Two, the sample of life science majors, prevent us from giving full support to either hypothesis.

The results of Study Three, the sample of pre-medicine, pre-dental, and pre-pharmacy majors, had the highest overall apprehension level (see

Table 1) among all of the subjects we sampled. We would have expected the effects of communication apprehension on academic achievement to be the most significant in this sample. We can only conclude that oral (talking) communication apprehension did not have a detrimental effect on academic achievement in either lecture or laboratory learning environments. However, one possible explanation may be that students who become professionally committed to a specific subject area are, in a sense, forced to learn to cope with their communication apprehension. Another possible explanation is that as students become older and reach their junior or senior year, they eventually learn to control and cope with their communication apprehension (K. Garrison & J. Garrison, 1977). Finally, statistical power was low in studies two and three, thereby minimizing the chance of detecting real differences had they *truly* existed.

Methods for Coping with Communication Apprehension

A number of different techniques have been utilized by psychologists and communication scientists to treat oral (talking) communication apprehension, ranging from sensitivity training to hypnosis (Burgoon, 1975). The most successful has appeared to be *systematic desensitization* (SD) (McCroskey, 1972; McCroskey & Wheeless, 1976). A number of communication apprehension treatment laboratories and research centers using SD are scattered across the country, including the universities of Florida, Oklahoma, Nebraska, and West Virginia, and Illinois State and Iowa State Universities. *Systematic desensitization* is a counter-conditioning technique that teaches students to relax, thereby allowing students to overcome their high levels of apprehension in approximately five or six hours.

Burgoon (1975) reports results of a recent study that tested the relationship of anxiety to student preferences for various tasks and evaluation procedures. Her results clearly indicated that highly apprehensive students have a preference for activities and evaluation procedures that minimize their need to communicate orally. The students preferred: (1) to do assignments in written form rather than orally; (2) to have more lectures than class discussion; (3)

to be tested in written form rather than orally; (4) to be graded on test performance rather than class participation; and (5) to be graded on the quality of written work rather than the quality of oral presentations.

Pedagogical implications. While the subjects we observed in this series of studies were enrolled in both communication-restricted and traditional courses concurrently, and in some cases did group work rather than individual, one manner of coping with communication apprehension may be to lessen the perceived anxiety-producing environment by providing special course sections for highly apprehensive students. The results of our studies provide implications not only for the college teacher of science, but for all educators in higher education, particularly for teachers of human communication. First, instructors should utilize therapy approaches, when they are available at their college or university. Second, instructors in all areas of higher education should counsel their highly apprehensive students regarding the optimal evaluation procedures for them. Finally, college and university instructors can alter their teaching strategies to avoid increasing the likelihood of detrimental effects of talking apprehension occurring in their classrooms. This report, therefore, offers evidence that talking apprehension is important in areas of the university environment other than just communication, and is deserving of continued empirical investigation.

NOTES

1. Only 17 of the 25 Likert-type PRCA scales that had primary loadings of .55 or higher were included in the studies (see Table 6). The decision model we utilized assessed the factor structure of the measurement instrument for the whole population sampled, and thus mandated the use of only those scale items that met each of our a priori measurement criteria. Even though McCroskey (1975b) has indicated that his widely-used Personal Report of Communication Apprehension measures only *oral, verbal (talking) communication apprehension* in a reliable and valid manner, we decided to assess whether that observation held for each of our studies as well. Based on the judgments of several human communication researchers, this is a practice that should become more common in our field. Researchers have often failed to indicate which scales of a measurement instrument they actually used, which had significant primary factor loadings, or which indices actually possessed adequate overall reliability. Reporting the reliability of seminal measurement studies, the reliabilities observed by others, or test-retest reliabilities of past research should not be

taken as an argument for reliability of measurement in a current research study. Empirical investigations should compute reliability coefficients each time a measurement instrument is used. The possibility of literal or operational replications (Lykken, 1968), therefore, has been reduced far more often than it should be in future human communication research.

2. Coefficients of internal reliability were computed using the *Spearman-Brown prophecy formula* for split-half reliability (Wood, 1960), and *Nunnally's* (1967) *formula 6-18*. Nunnally's formula

$$(r_{kk} = \frac{kr_{ij}}{1 + (k - 1) r_{ij}})$$

is computed by taking the average correlation among all items in a measure multiplied by the number of items in the measure, divided by 1 plus the number of items minus one, times the average correlation. *Pearson product-moment correlations* are transformed to Z scores before summing in the averaging step, and the average Z score is then transformed back to the equivalent average Pearson product-moment correlation before use in Nunnally's formula (Nunnally, 1967, pp. 193-194) and Davis and Garrison's (1976) computer program. These high reliability coefficients—even based on a reduced number of PRCA items, computed using two different methods across three diverse populations—provided substantial evidence for the internal reliability of the talking apprehension measurement instrument in each of our studies.

REFERENCES

ANDERSEN, J.F., ANDERSEN, P.A., & GARRISON, J.P. Singing apprehension and talking apprehension: The development of two constructs. Paper presented at the meeting of the Western Speech Communication Association, San Francisco, November 1976.

BARR, A.J., & GOODNIGHT, J.H. *A user's guide to the statistical analysis system.* Raleigh: North Carolina State University Press, 1972.

BASHORE, D.N. Relationships among speech anxiety, IQ, and high school achievement. Unpublished Masters Thesis, Illinois State University, 1971.

BURGOON, J.K. Teacher strategies for coping with communication apprehension. Paper presented at the annual meeting of the Speech Communication Association, Houston, December 1975.

COHEN, J. *Statistical power analysis for the behavioral sciences.* New York: Academic Press, 1969.

CRONBACH, L.J. *Essentials of psychological testing.* New York: Harper, 1949.

DALY, J.A., & LETH, S. Communication apprehension and the personnel selection decision. Paper presented at the annual meeting of the International Communication Association, Portland, April 1976.

DALY, J.A., & McCROSKEY, J.C. Occupational desirability and choice as a function of communication apprehension. *Journal of Counseling Psychology*, 1975, 22, 309-313.

DALY, J.A., McCROSKEY, J.C., & RICHMOND, V.P. The relationships between vocal activity and perceptions of communication in small group interaction. *Western Speech Communication*, 1977, 41, in press.

DAVIS, B.F., & GARRISON, J.P. NUNREL: A Statistical Analysis System (SAS) program to compute Nunnally's reliability formula 6-18. Unpublished computer program, 1976 (available from Department of Speech Communication, West Virginia University, Morgantown).

DIXON, W.J. (Ed.) *BMDP: Biomedical computer programs.* Berkeley: University of California Press, 1975.

GARRISON, K.R., & GARRISON, J.P. Measurement of communication apprehension among children. Paper presented at the annual meeting of the International Communication Association, Berlin, Germany, May 1977.

GIFFIN, K., & GILHAM, S.M. Relationships between speech anxiety and motivation. *Speech Monographs*, 1971, 38, 70-73.

GIFFIN, K., & HEIDER, M. The relationship between speech anxiety and the suppression of communication in childhood. *The Psychiatric Quarterly Supplement*, Part 2, 1967.

HAMILTON, P.R. The effects of risk proneness on small group interaction, communication apprehension, and self disclosure. Unpublished Masters Thesis, Illinois State University, 1972.

KAISER, H.F. A second generation Little Jiffy. *Psychometrika*, 1970, 35, 401-415.

KAISER, H.F., & HUNKA, S. Some empirical results with Guttman's stronger lower bound for the number of common factors. *Educational and Psychological Measurement*, 1973, 33, 99-102.

LOW, G.M. The relation of psychometric factors to stage fright. Unpublished Masters Thesis, University of Utah, 1950.

LYKKEN, D.T. Statistical significance in psychological research. *Psychological Bulletin*, 1968, 70, 151-159.

McCROSKEY, J.C. Measures of communication-bound anxiety. *Speech Monographs*, 1970, 37, 267-277.

McCROSKEY, J.C. The implementation of a large-scale program of systematic desensitization for communication apprehension. *Speech Teacher*, 1972, 21, 255-264.

McCROSKEY, J.C. Classroom consequences of communication apprehension. Paper presented at the annual meeting of the Speech Communication Association, Houston, December 1975a.

McCROSKEY, J.C. The validity of the PRCA as an index of oral communication apprehension. Paper presented at the annual meeting of the Speech Communication Association, Houston, December 1975b.

McCROSKEY, J.C. The effects of communication apprehension on nonverbal behavior. *Communication Quarterly*, 1976, 24, 39-44.

McCROSKEY, J.C. Oral communication apprehension: A summary of recent theory and research. Paper presented at the annual meeting of the International Communication Association, Berlin, Germany, May 1977.

McCROSKEY, J.C., & ANDERSEN, J.F. The relationship between communication apprehension and academic achievement among college students. *Human Communication Research*, 1976, 3, 73-81.

McCROSKEY, J.C., & DALY, J.A. Teachers' expectations of the communication apprehensive child in the elementary school. *Human Communication Research*, 1976, 3, 67-72.

McCROSKEY, J.C., DALY, J.A., RICHMOND, V.P., & COX, B.G. Communication apprehension and interpersonal attraction. *Human Communication Research*, 1975, 2, 51-65.

McCROSKEY, J.C., DALY, J.A., RICHMOND, V.P., & FALCIONE, R.C. Studies of the relationship between communication apprehension and self-esteem. *Human Communication Research*, 1977, 3, in press.

McCROSKEY, J.C., DALY, J.A., & SORENSEN, G.A. Personality correlates of communication apprehension: A research note. *Human Communication Research*, 1976, 2, 376-380.

McCROSKEY, J.C., & RICHMOND, V.P. The effects of communication apprehension on the perception of peers. *Western Speech Communication*, 1976, 40, 14-21.

McCROSKEY, J.C., & WHEELESS, L.R. *Introduction to human communication.* Boston: Allyn and Bacon, 1976.

McCROSKEY, J.C., & YOUNG, T.J. The use and abuse of factor analysis in communication research. Paper presented at the annual meeting of the International Communication Association, Chicago, April 1975.

NUNNALLY, J.C., JR. *Psychometric theory.* New York: McGraw-Hill, 1967.

PHILLIPS, G.M. Reticence: Pathology of the normal speaker. *Speech Monographs*, 1968, 35, 39-49.

PHILLIPS, G.M., & METZGER, N.J. The reticent syndrome: Some theoretical considerations about etiology and treatment. *Speech Monographs*, 1973, 40, 220-230.

SCOTT, M.D., YATES, M.P., & WHEELESS, L.R. An exploratory investigation of the effects of communication apprehension in alternative systems of instruction. Paper presented at the annual meeting of the International Communication Association, Chicago, April 1975.

WELLS, J., & LASHBROOK, W.B. A study of the effects of systematic desensitization on the communication anxiety of individuals in small groups. Paper presented at the annual meeting of the Speech Communication Association, New Orleans, December 1970.

WOOD, D.A. *Test construction.* Columbus: Merrill, 1960.

TEACHER EFFECTIVENESS AS A FUNCTION OF COMMUNICATOR STYLE

ROBERT W. NORTON
University of Michigan

This report provides strong evidence that perceived teacher effectiveness is related to perceived communicator style—that is, the way one is perceived to communicate. A communicator style construct, consisting of eleven independent variables (*precise, contentious, relaxed, impression leaving, voice, dominant, dramatic, open, attentive, animated,* and *friendly*) and one dependent variable (*communicator image*) provides the framework with which teacher effectiveness is analyzed. Sixty-five professors evaluated themselves on the variables, and an average of 9.2 (596) students per teacher rated the teachers on the variables.

The communicative act entails two components: (1) what is said and (2) the way it is said. Reusch and Bateson (1951) label the respective components the *report* and the *command* aspects of communication:

> The report aspect of a message conveys information and is, therefore, synonymous in human communication with the *content* of the message. It may be about anything that is communicable regardless of whether the particular information is true or false, valid, invalid, or undecidable. The command aspect, on the other hand, refers to what sort of a message it is to be taken as, and, therefore, ultimately to the *relationship* between the communicants. (pp. 51-52)

Obviously, the classroom is one of the most interesting exemplars of a communicative process in our society. Consequently, it is natural to ask how the communicative act is related to effective teaching. This research focuses upon the *command* aspect of communication to examine teacher effectiveness. This is not to deny the importance of the *report* aspect, but the emphasis does recognize its limitations, especially in light of the awesome and confounding intricacies of the problem. Specifically, this research investigates teacher effectiveness as a function of the way one communicates—that is, one's communicator style.

Excellent reviews of the literature regarding the general problem of evaluating teacher effectiveness are available, including Roberson (1971), Null and Walter (1972), Rodin and Rodin (1972), Gage (1972), Gessner (1973), Kauffman, Hallahan, Payne, and Ball (1973), Plant (1974), Coppernoll and Davies (1974), Centra (1974), Hind, Dornbusch, and Scott (1974), Scriven (1974), and Rippey (1975). None of the researchers study communicator style as it relates to teacher effectiveness, although many researchers (Costin, Greenough, & Menges, 1971; Rico, 1971; Feather, 1972; Greenwood, Bridges, Ware, & McLean, 1973; Frey, 1973; Finkbeiner, Lathrop, & Schuerger, 1973; Meredith, 1975) periodically allude to dimensions, components, or characteristics which entail stylistic aspects.

Flanders (1973), for example, presents a comprehensive model for analyzing listening. This component falls into the *attentiveness domain* in the communicator style construct. Breed, Christiansen, and Larson (1972) examine the effect of a lecturer's gaze direction upon teaching effectiveness. This component falls into the *animated domain* of the communicator style construct. Costin, Greenough, and Menges (1971) investigated items such as, "A professor who tells good jokes will get a good rating," as a function of teaching effectiveness. This component falls into the *dramatic domain* of the communicator style construct. The examples of stylistic aspects in approaches to evaluate teacher effectiveness are abundant. Nevertheless, no researcher uses a communicator style construct as the primary framework to investigate teacher effectiveness.

THIS STUDY: AN OVERVIEW

This study specifically examines the self evaluations of the university professor on 12 components of a communicator style construct and an overall assessment of teaching effectiveness. These evaluations are compared with student ratings of the professor on the same 12 components of communicator style and an overall assessment of teaching effectiveness. From this data base, four areas are explored.

First, within the context of a teaching situation, how do the communicator style variables behave structurally? The expectation is that if the teaching effectiveness variable is strongly associated with the way one communicates, then it should be centrally located in the communicator style variable set. *Factor analysis* and *smallest space analysis* (Lingoes, 1973) support the analysis. *Teacher effectiveness is shown to be intrinsically related to the way one communicates.*

Second, the behaviors manifested by the teacher should be apparent to both teacher and students in relatively the same way. One of the assumptions is that structural relationships of the variables for the teachers and for the students rating the teachers will be similar. Configurational comparisons show this to be the case.

Third, communicator style variables should predict teacher effectiveness. A set of regression analyses provides the evidence. In general, the effective teacher tends to be an *attentive* and *impression leaving* communicator, according to teachers rating themselves. According to students rating the teachers, the effective teacher not only is an *attentive* and *impression leaving* communicator, but also *relaxed, not dominant, friendly,* and *precise.* In short, seven of the style variables, including an overall rating of *communicator image*, were useful in predicting teacher effectiveness.

Fourth, the degree to which teachers manifest different style behaviors should depend upon whether the teachers sensitively and frankly assess their own styles of communicating, and whether the students perceive these behaviors in a relatively homogeneous fashion. It may be, for example, that the student who displays a *dramatic communicator style* tends to be appreciative of and sensitive to the dramatic style of others. This study found that the teachers saw themselves as more *attentive, impression leaving, relaxed,* and *friendly* than the students did. Also, the teachers saw themselves as better communicators and more effective teachers than the students did.

Finally, the limitations of this study should be identified. First, the data set was generated on a volunteer basis. It may be that ineffective teachers wanted nothing to do with this kind of study. Second, the data set was self-report evaluation from the teachers. A person may not know the stylistic characteristics of his or her communication. Third, no attempt was made to account for class sizes, content, or level of difficulty. A seminar should create a more intimate and informal setting than a large lecture course. A theoretical math class may be less influenced by style components than a theatre course studying motivation of acting.

METHOD

Subjects

Nine hundred professors at the University of Michigan were asked by letter whether they would participate in a communication study relating to teacher effectiveness. Eighty-eight professors initially indicated that they would participate. Sixty-five professors completed the study.

Each professor was asked to randomly select at least ten of his or her students to evaluate him or her for the study. An average of 9.2 (N=596) students per teacher responded. The teachers were asked not to influence the student responses and to encourage the students to be frank.

Procedure

The professors were sent a packet of 13 questionnaires. One questionnaire was designated for the teacher to use in evaluating himself or herself, and twelve questionnaires were designated for the students to use to evaluate the teacher.

To assure anonymity, the teachers were asked to write a random four-digit number on the packet when returning the questionnaires. When the study was completed, summary sheets for the pertinent

FIGURE 1
Smallest Space Analysis of Students Rating Teachers

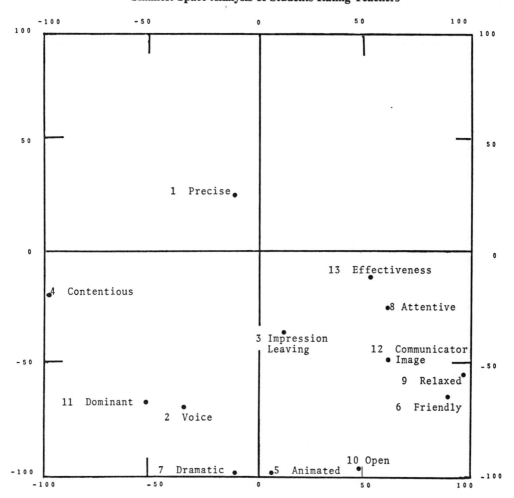

variables were sent to the professors. They could acquire feedback by identifying their random number. The procedure was adopted to help obtain some frank assessments. The teachers participated in the study during the third to last week of the semester so that the students would have some sense of the teacher's communicator style.

MEASURES

Two constructs were built into the questionnaires. First, a measure of *communicator style* was included. Second, a measure of *teacher effectiveness* was used.

Communicator Style Measure

Communicator style is broadly conceived to mean "the way one verbally and paraverbally interacts to signal how literal meaning should be taken, interpreted, filtered, or understood." Eleven independent variables (*dominant, dramatic, animated, open, contentious, relaxed, friendly, attentive, impression leaving, precise*, and *voice*) and one dependent variable (*communicator image*) operationally define the construct. Figures 1 and 2 show the relationships among the variables.

Each subconstruct is defined as a function of four items, using a four-point scale. The exact wording

FIGURE 2
Smallest Space Analysis of Teachers Rating Themselves

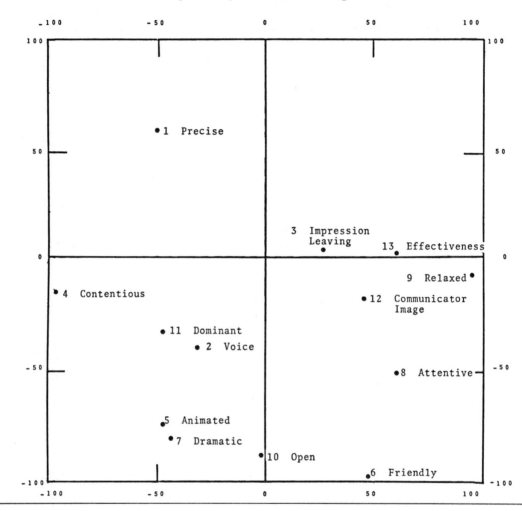

of the items for seven of the constructs (*communicator image, attentive, impression leaving, relaxed, dominant, friendly,* and *precise*) is reported subsequently. The *contentious subconstruct*, made up of the following items, is illustrative:

— When this person disagrees with someone he/she is very quick to challenge him or her.

— This person is very argumentative.

— Once this person gets wound up in a heated discussion he or she has a hard time stopping himself/herself.

— It bothers this person to drop an argument that is not resolved.

Briefly, the communicator style components include these variables:

Dominant. The dominant communicator talks frequently, takes charge in a social situation, comes on strong, and controls informal conversations.

Dramatic. The dramatic communicator manipulates exaggerations, fantasies, stories, metaphors, rhythm, voice, and other stylistic devices to highlight or understate content.

Contentious. The contentious communicator is argumentative.

Animated. The animated communicator provides frequent and sustained eye contact, uses many facial expressions, and gestures often.

Impression leaving. The impression leaving communicator tends to be remembered because of the stimuli which are projected. What is said and the way it is said is emphasized.

Relaxed. The relaxed communicator is calm and collected, not nervous under pressure, and does not show nervous mannerisms.

Attentive. The attentive communicator really likes to listen to the other, shows interest in what the other is saying, and deliberately reacts in such a way that the other knows he or she is being listened to.

Open. The open communicator readily reveals personal things about the self, easily expressed feelings and emotions, and tends to be unsecretive, unreserved, and somewhat frank.

Friendly. The friendly communicator is encouraging to people, acknowledges other's contributions, openly expresses admiration and tends to be tactful.

Precise. The precise communicator tries to be strictly accurate when arguing, prefers well-defined arguments, and likes proof or documentation when arguing.

Voice. Voice is a style component which focuses upon how recognizable a person sounds in terms of loudness.

Communicator image. A person with a good communicator image finds it easy to talk with strangers, to small groups of people, and with members of the opposite sex.

Teacher Effectiveness

Teacher effectiveness was operationalized as a function of six items. The first four items used a nine-point scale ranging from "less than 30% of them" to "all of them." The scale was incremented in units of 10%. The items included:

— Out of the total number of class periods this person teaches in a semester, he or she is effective in. . . .

— Out of the total number of class periods this person teaches in a semester, he or she is *extremely effective* in. . . .

— Out of the total number of students this person teaches in a semester, he or she is effective in motivating. . . .

— Out of the total number of students this person teaches in a semester, he or she is *extremely effective* in motivating. . . .

The fifth item used an 11-point scale ranging from "top 5%" to "less than top 50%." The scale was incremented in units of 5%. First, the person was asked to name the most effective teacher in his or her college career. Then, the person was asked to compare the teacher to the named teacher:

> In terms of effective teaching, indicate on the scale where you would place your present teacher in relation to the "most effective teacher in your college career."

The sixth item used a six-point scale ranging from "none of them" to "all of them." The scale was incremented in units of one. The item read:

> Out of a random group of six teachers in his/her discipline, including the present teacher, he or she is probably a better overall teacher than . . .

These six items were standardized, summed, and averaged to create a total effectiveness score, which was used as a dependent variable in regression analyses.

RESULTS

Four analyses are used to examine the relationship between *communicator style variables* and *teacher effectiveness*. First, clustering techniques identify how variables group for the teachers and students. A *principal axis factor analysis with orthogonal rotation* shows a general breakdown of the variable groups. *Smallest space analysis* (Lingoes, 1973) provides graphic representation of the variable groups for both samples. Second, the configurations are compared to see whether they differ significantly. CS-I (configurational similarity-I), a subroutine in smallest space analysis, is used. If the configurations are not different, a straightforward interpretation is indicated. If the configurations are different, a more complex explanation is mandated because the teachers and students probably treated the *communicator style construct* in unique ways. Third, regression techniques identify the best predictors of *teacher effectiveness*. Both traditional and stepwise regression analyses are presented. Fourth, mean differences are analyzed for each style variable and for teacher effectiveness in both samples.

TABLE 1
Factor Analysis with Varimax Rotation:
Communicator Style and Effectiveness Variables

Factor I 24%		Factor II 20%		Factor III 10%	
Variable	Loading	Variable	Loading	Variable	Loading
Communicator Image	.78	Dramatic	.77	Precise	.69
Attentive	.75	Animated	.69	Contentious	.57
Effective Teacher	.69	Voice	.62		
Friendly	.69	Dominant	.59		
Relaxed	.54	Open	.57		
Impression Leaving	.52				

Note.—The percentages under the factor headings are percent of explained variance.

Variable Clusters

The variables group together as they did in previous studies. The items for each subconstruct were standardized, summed, and averaged to obtain a total subconstruct score. The 12 *communicator style variables* and the *effectiveness variable* were factor analyzed.

Table 1 reports a three-factor solution. Factor one accounts for 24% of the explained variance. In this factor, *effectiveness*, the dependent variable, is associated with *communicator image, attentive*, and *friendly*. The grouping suggests that an effective teacher finds it easy to communicate with people, provides them with obvious and intended feedback, and readily gives strokes. *Effectiveness* is related to a weaker degree to *impression leaving* and *relaxed*. The association indicates that an *effective teacher* tends to be remembered and manifests a calm and collected image. Factor two accounts for 20% of the explained variance. Highly visible, active, and energy expending behaviors load on this factor. The *dramatic communicator* often tells jokes, anecdotes, and stories, physically and vocally acts out what is to be communicated, and exaggerates often to emphasize a point. The *animated communicator* has expressive eyes, facial cues, and gestures. The *open communicator* reveals personal things about the self and freely expresses feelings and emotions. Similarly, the *voice* variable reflects a highly noticeable component in terms of loudness and distinctness. Finally, the *dominant* variable is associated with this factor. It may be that having a loud, distinct voice, being dramatic, animated, and open are vehicles which allow a person to come on strong socially, speak frequently, and take charge of things.

Factor three accounts for 10% of the explained variance. *Precise* and *contentious* constitute the factor. The *precise communicator* insists upon accuracy, clear definitions in arguments, and documentation or proof in arguments. Similarly, but with a more negative orientation, the *contentious communicator* is challenging, is argumentative, and has

TABLE 2
Correlation Coefficients for Students Rating Teachers
and Teachers Rating Themselves

	1	2	3	4	5	6	7	8	9	10	11	12	13
1 Precise		29	38	34	17	06	14	44	13	08	24	25	35
2 Voice	04		46	30	44	14	51	22	12	29	55	27	21
3 Impression Leav.	-02	36		13	43	33	39	44	35	32	41	50	56
4 Contentious	36	42	-18		17	-27	28	-10	-17	-04	42	-13	06
5 Animated	06	45	26	31		29	63	27	13	52	32	40	31
6 Friendly	-20	23	16	-36	19		25	62	36	48	04	58	44
7 Dramatic	02	45	-02	30	63	35		19	17	48	42	33	26
8 Attentive	09	22	29	-22	20	46	20		35	34	13	59	52
9 Relaxed	-02	16	23	-06	-07	15	-10	25		35	18	57	39
10 Open	-06	34	34	-01	59	39	44	20	12		34	52	32
11 Dominant	02	59	31	48	45	05	41	12	19	36		27	11
12 Com. Image	04	25	51	-15	12	30	10	49	32	36	27		58
13 Effective	05	05	41	28	06	25	05	50	35	08	07	56	

Note.--The upper triangular matrix is made up of correlation coefficients from students rating teachers. The lower triangular matrix is made up of correlation coefficients from teachers rating themselves.

Note.--For the upper triangular matrix, N=372 with r(.05)=.10 and r(.01)=.13. For the lower triangular matrix, N=53 with r(.05)=.27 and r(.01)=.35.

Note.—Decimals are omitted in the table.

a reluctance to leave an argument unfinished or unanswered.

A smallest space analysis was done for each sample. Table 2 reports the correlation coefficients for the students rating the teachers and the teachers rating themselves. Correlations were used as the distances in the smallest space solutions. Table 3 lists the coordinates for a two-dimensional solution for each sample. It also reports the *phi* contributions of each variable for the respective solutions. The

phi-coefficients indicate how much each variable individually contributes to the *coefficient of alienation*. The *coefficient of alienation* with semistrong monotonicity for the teachers rating themselves is .18; the *coefficient of alienation* for the students rating the teachers is .13. Figures 1 and 2 show the relationships in graphic form. The variables which are closest to each other in the space are the variables most related to each other.

Table 4 lists the original correlations and the

TABLE 3
Coordinates and Phi Contributions for Two Dimensional Solution

Variable	Teachers Rating Themselves			Students Rating Teachers		
	Dimensions		Phi	Dimensions		Phi
	I	II		I	II	
1 Precise	-51	57	.0010	-10	27	.0003
2 Voice	-33	-40	.0003	-31	-64	.0002
3 Impression Leaving	26	2	.0012	16	-31	.0003
4 Contentious	-100	-15	.0008	-100	-22	.0004
5 Animated	-46	-73	.0004	13	-100	.0003
6 Friendly	48	-100	.0003	93	-64	.0002
7 Dramatic	-44	-81	.0002	-8	-97	.0001
8 Attentive	61	-53	.0003	65	-10	.0005
9 Relaxed	100	-7	.0012	100	-29	.0002
10 Open	-3	-89	.0006	49	-93	.0002
11 Dominant	-48	-34	.0001	-50	-61	.0002
12 Communicator Image	-45	-17	.0004	63	-48	.0001
13 Effectiveness	-63	1	.0004	49	-7	.0002

TABLE 4
Original and Derived Distances Associated with Effectiveness

Variable	Teachers Rating Themselves		Students Rating Teachers	
	Original Distances	Derived Distances	Original Distances	Derived Distances
Communicator Image	.56	25	.58	43
Attentive	.50	54	.52	16
Impression Leaving	.41	36	.56	41
Relaxed	.35	111	.39	55

TABLE 5
Coordinates for Configuration Comparison

Variables	Target Configuration — Teachers Rating Themselves — Dimensions I	II	Fitted Configuration — Students Rating Teachers — Dimensions I	II
1 Precise	20	36	5	32
2 Voice	13	-2	22	-3
3 Impression Leaving	-10	14	0	6
4 Contentious	39	8	46	21
5 Animated	18	-15	7	-21
6 Friendly	-18	-25	-28	-14
7 Dramatic	18	-18	15	-18
8 Attentive	-23	-7	-22	10
9 Relaxed	-38	11	-34	0
10 Open	2	-21	-8	-22
11 Dominant	19	0	29	0
12 Communicator Image	-17	7	-18	-5
13 Effective	-24	14	-16	13

derived distances associated with the dependent variable, *effectiveness*. In the teachers rating themselves sample, the overall evaluation, *communicator image*, and the subconstruct of *attentiveness* are closest to *effectiveness*. *Impression leaving* is the third strongest variable associated with *effectiveness*. *Relaxed* is the fourth strongest. In the students rating the teachers sample, the associations with *effectiveness* are ordered identically for the same variables.

With the addition of *friendly*, all variables from factor one are included. This means that the best predictor of *effectiveness* should emerge from factor one. The next best predictors should come from other factors or factor one depending upon the degree that the factor one variables explain each other.

Configuration Comparisons

It seems obvious from inspection that the configurations in Figures 1 and 2 are the same. A subroutine in smallest space analysis based upon the *Schöenemann-Carroll (1970) algorithm* provides a statistical test. With CS-I, one configuration is stipulated as the target—in this case, the teachers rating themselves was so designated. The second configuration is optimally fitted in the same space; that is, the students rating the teachers configuration is fitted.

Two basic operations are used to fit the configurations. First, the configurations can be rotated such that each variable is moved optimally close to its corresponding variable in the space. Second, the

FIGURE 3
Configuration Comparisons

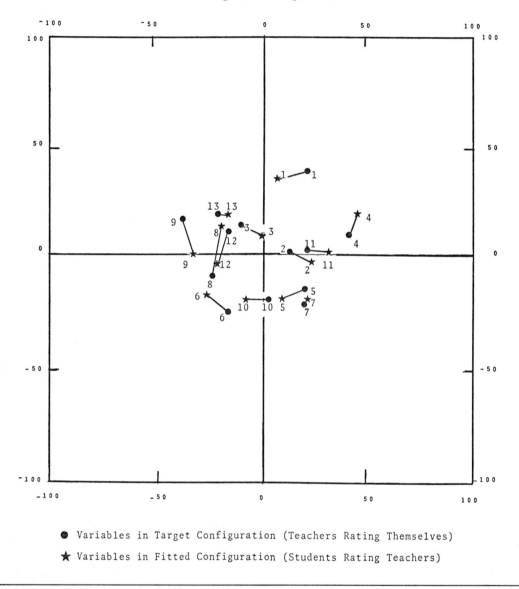

● Variables in Target Configuration (Teachers Rating Themselves)

★ Variables in Fitted Configuration (Students Rating Teachers)

variables can be stretched such that they are moved optimally close to the corresponding variables. The operations can be used together or separately.

Table 5 lists the coordinates for the target configuration and the fitted configuration. Figure 3 shows the graphic representation. The lines connecting the respective variables were added to show closeness of fit. Table 6 reports how well the configurations

fit. The percent of variance explained by one configuration predicting the other is shown. Dimension one of the target configuration correlates .93 with dimension one of the fitted configuration. Dimension two of the target configuration correlates .86 with the fitted configuration. Clearly, the dimensions of the configurations are highly related. In fact, the configurations are so similar that the stretching and rotating procedures add little to the explained variance. The conclusion is that the underlying structure of the *communicator style construct* is being treated similarly by the teachers rating themselves and the students rating the teachers.

Best Predictors

Teacher effectiveness is strongly related to the *communicator style construct*. Four regression analyses provide support for the conclusion. First, a least squares regression with *effectiveness* as the dependent variable shows the overall relationship to *communicator style variables*. Second, a least squares regression with *communicator image* as the

TABLE 6
Percent of Variance Explained Using Different Fitting Procedures

Fitting Procedure	Percent of Explained Variance
Without rotating or stretching	82%
Rotated, but not stretched	82%
Stretched, but not rotated	88%
Stretched and rotated	88%

TABLE 7
Regression on Effectiveness

Predictor Variable	β	t-test	Sig. Level
3 Impression Leaving	.33	7.05	.00
12 Communicator Image	.27	5.03	.00
11 Dominant	-.14	-2.93	.00
1 Precise	.13	2.89	.00
8 Attentive	.12	2.45	.01
7 Dramatic	.08	1.69	.09
9 Relaxed	.07	1.59	.11
6 Friendly	.06	1.24	.21
2 Voice	.06	-1.24	.22
4 Contentious	.03	-.62	.54
10 Open	.03	-.62	.54
5 Animated	.01	.18	.86

Note.--There were 426 complete questionnaires out of a possible 659. The regression analysis explains 50% of the variance.

TABLE 8
Regression on Communicator Image

Predictor Variable	β	t-test	Sig. Level
9 Relaxed	.28	8.17	.00
8 Attentive	.27	6.25	.00
6 Friendly	.16	3.83	.00
3 Impression Leaving	.14	3.65	.00
10 Open	.14	3.42	.00
4 Contentious	-.09	-2.14	.03
11 Dominant	.08	1.97	.05
5 Animated	.04	1.01	.31
2 Voice	-.04	-.98	.33
1 Precise	.03	.92	.36
7 Dramatic	.03	.75	.46

Note.--With effectiveness exclude, there were 469 complete questionnaires out of a possible 659. The regression analysis explains 59% of the variance.

dependent variable shows the relationship of the style variables to an overall assessment of communicator ability. Third, a stepwise regression across the two samples with *effectiveness* as the dependent variable indicates whether the teachers rating themselves have a different set of predictor variables from the students rating the teachers. Fourth, a stepwise regression across the two samples with the same dependent variable, but omitting *communicator image*, shows the direct impact of the style variables in the respective sets of predictor variables.

With effectiveness as the dependent variable, five style variables get into the equation ($F[12,413]=34.3$; p<.001). Table 7 reports the statistics. *Communicator image* and *impression leaving* are the two strongest predictors of effectiveness. An effective teacher is a good communicator and leaves an impression. Furthermore,

an effective teacher is *precise, attentive,* and *not dominant.*

Since *communicator image* is usually treated as a dependent variable in its own right in the *communicator style construct*, a regression analysis was done to show its major predictors. Seven out of eleven independent style variables make it into the equation ($F[11,457]=60.9$; p<.001). Table 8 reports the statistics. A person who perceives oneself as a good communicator in all kinds of situations also sees himself or herself as a *relaxed, attentive, friendly, impression leaving, open, not dominant,* and *not contentious.*

Table 9 reports the regression analyses across the two samples. The first set of analyses includes communicator image in the independent variable set; the second set of analyses excludes it. For the teachers rating themselves, *communicator image* and *attentive* are the best predictors of effectiveness

TABLE 9
Stepwise Regression on Effectiveness Across Conditions:
With and Without the Communicator Image Variable

Sample		Predictor Variable	β	R²	Sig. Level
Teachers Rating	12	Communicator Image	.31	.32	.00
Themselves	8	Attentive	.29	.38	.02
Students Rating	12	Communicator Image	.37	.34	.00
Teachers	3	Impression Leaving	.33	.43	.00
	8	Attentive	.17	.46	.00
	11	Dominant	-.18	.48	.00
	1	Precise	.11	.49	.02
Teachers Rating	8	Attentive	.41	.25	.00
Themselves:	3	Impression Leaving	.25	.33	.02
Communicator Image					
Variable Omitted					
Students Rating	3	Impression Leaving	.36	.30	.00
Teachers:	8	Attentive	.21	.41	.00
Communicator Image	9	Relaxed	.14	.43	.00
Variable Omitted	11	Dominant	-.16	.45	.00
	6	Friendly	.18	.46	.02
	1	Precise	.14	.47	.01

($F[2,50]=15.5$; p<.001). For the same sample, omitting *communicator image, attentive* and *impression leaving* are the best predictors ($F[2,50]=12.2$; p<.001). Teachers see themselves as effective if they leave an *impression* and are *attentive*.

For the students rating the teachers, the same variables get into the equation, plus *impression leaving, dominant* and *precise* ($F[5,366]=69.8$; p<.001). For the same sample, omitting *communicator image*, the previous variables make it into the equation, plus *friendly* and *relaxed*

($F[6,374]=54.7$; p<.001). In short, the students have more predictor variables in the model to predict an effective teacher.

Mean Differences

Finally, mean differences between the teachers rating themselves and the students rating the teachers were examined. Table 10 lists the statistics and Figure 4 shows the graphed means of the differences.

The teachers rated themselves as more *attentive*,

TABLE 10
Means for Teachers and Students Across
Style and Effectiveness Variables

| Variable | Teacher Sample | | | Student Sample | | | ANOVA Stat. | |
	Mean	N	Stand. Dev.	Mean	N	Stand. Dev.	Error	F-stat.
Attentive	.49	63	.60	-.06	551	.73	.52	31.9**
Com. Image	.38	64	.79	-.05	496	.77	.60	17.6**
Imp. Leav.	.29	64	.70	-.03	572	.80	.63	9.6**
Effective	.25	60	.58	.02	499	.81	.62	6.3**
Relaxed	.18	64	.66	.03	573	.82	.65	3.7*
Friendly	.19	64	.68	-.02	560	.78	.60	4.3*
Dominant	.16	62	.71	-.01	485	.76	.57	2.8
Precise	.11	65	.65	-.05	566	.75	.55	1.8
Animated	.10	61	.46	-.03	512	.68	.46	2.0
Dramatic	.04	65	.74	-.02	566	.71	.51	.4
Contentious	-.04	65	.75	.01	527	.69	.48	.3
Open	-.02	64	.76	.02	556	.67	.46	.2
Voice	-.02	63	.75	-.01	556	.75	.56	.0

Note.--The means are expressed as standardized scores.

Note.--The varying sizes in the cells are because of missing data.

**p<.01   p<.05

---

better communicators, more impression leaving, better teachers, more relaxed, and *more friendly* than the students did. The largest difference, of the significant effect, concerned *friendly.* In fact, only the variables in factor I (Table 1) resulted in differences between the samples.

DISCUSSION

Evaluating effective teachers as a function of any variable set is always a difficult task. The variables are, in a sense, fragile. That is, slight semantic shifts can result in dramatically different conclusions. To examine teacher effectiveness as a function of a communicator style construct is especially complex because the variable set is composed of complicated concepts involving a process between at least two individuals. The process is ongoing (operates over time), complex (often centering about multidimensional effects), and interrelated (behaviors are mutually dependent).

Four questions guided this research: (1) What is the structure of the variable set of teacher effectiveness within the domain of communicator style? (2) Do teachers and students treat the communicator style construct similarly? (3) Which communicator style variables best predict teacher effectiveness? (4) Are there differences between the way teachers rate themselves and the way students rate the teachers regarding communicator style variables and teacher effectiveness?

FIGURE 4
Means of Style and Effectiveness Variables

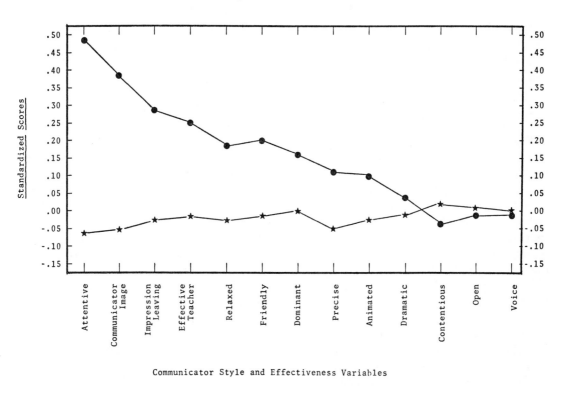

Communicator Style and Effectiveness Variables

The first question provides the perspective for the research. *Teacher effectiveness* was embedded in the *communicator style construct*. Its structural location, as expected, indicated that effectiveness related to *communicator image, attentive, impression leaving, relaxed,* and *friendly.*

The second question is often ignored in comparisons between samples, but is important. If the teachers and students treated the construct differently in terms of underlying structure, then significant effects could be explained by idiosyncratic orientations to the variables. In this project, however, the results show that both samples treat the construct similarly.

The third question is the primary reason for this research. The first conclusion has the impact of a truism. *The effective teacher has a good communicator image.* The effective teacher rated high on each of the following items:

— This person is a *very* good communicator.

— This person always finds it *very easy* to communicate on a one-to-one basis with strangers.

— In a small group of strangers this person is a *very good* communicator.

— This person finds it extremely easy to maintain a conversation with a member of the opposite sex whom he/she has just met.

Both the students and teachers agree that *attentive* and *impression leaving* are good predictors of *teacher effectiveness.* For the *attentive style variable*, the *effective* teacher rated high on these items:

— This person can always repeat back to someone else *exactly* what was meant.

— Usually, this person *deliberately reacts* in such a way that people know that he/she is listening to them.

— This person really *likes* to listen *very carefully* to people.

— This person is an *extremely attentive* communicator.

For the *impression leaving style variable*, the *effective* teacher rated high on these items:

— *What* this person says *usually* leaves an impression on people.

— This person leaves people with an impression which they definitely tend to remember.

— The *way* this person says something *usually* leaves an impression on people.

— This person leaves a *definite* impression on people.

These results suggest that, to understand teacher effectiveness better, it is worthwhile to examine the theoretical and pragmatic phenomena associated with *attentive* and *impression leaving*. The attentive style of communication seems to directly signal verbally and paraverbally that interest (concern, enthusiasm, notice) is being shown and that the person is being listened to. The impact can range from the deeply therapeutic (Shave, 1974) to the trivially pragmatic. The style indirectly suggests that: (1) the person is empathetic (accurate, warm, genuine; (2) the person is tolerant; (3) the person is caring; and (4) the person is *other-oriented*.

The *impression leaving* style of communication seems to be closely related to the content of the speaker. It centers around what is said and the way it is said. What the teacher chooses to present from a body of knowledge undoubtedly influences the students' interest. The "what" can be designed to have a punch, be exotic, be whimsical, be paradoxical, or be disturbing. The choice of the "what" may determine the levels of perceived teacher effectiveness. Also, the way the teacher presents the material causes the students to remember the content or the teacher. The same material presented with a different communicator style should have a different impact. The material Johnny Carson uses would not be the same without the Carson style of delivery.

The students included four other style variables to explain teacher effectivemess—*relaxed, dominant, friendly,* and *precise*. The *effective* teacher tended to be *relaxed*. He or she scored high on these items:

— This person has no nervous mannerisms in his/her speech.

— This person is a very relaxed communicator.

— The rhythm or flow of this person's speech is not affected by nervousness.

— Under pressure this person comes across as a relaxed speaker.

The relaxed style variable is particularly rich and complex. Sullivan (1950) defined psychiatry as the study of interpersonal relations in terms of anxiety. He saw the *anxious-not-anxious, relaxed-not-relaxed,* and *tense-not-tense* dimensions as a key to personality. There are many causes or correlates of the relaxed component that can be explored in the teaching context. The effective teacher may be relaxed because he or she is confident about the body of material being presented, is comfortable with the student-teacher role, or is self assured. On the other hand, some negative aspects may influence this style variable. The teacher could be relaxed because he or she is entrenched in the position or because he or she does not care anymore.

The students see the effective teacher as one who is not dominant. The following items characterize the assessment:

— In most social situations this person (does not) generally speak very frequently.

— This person is (not) dominant in social situations.

— This person (does not) try to take charge of things when he/she is with other people.

— In most social situations this person (does not) tend to come on strong.

This does not mean that the students prefer the teacher to be passive; it does suggest that they prefer the teacher not to come on too strong. The finding could reflect the preference for a non-authoritarian classroom environment. The next style component supports such a hypothesis.

The *effective* teacher, according to the students, has a *friendly style of communication*. He or she scores high on the following items:

— This person readily expresses admiration for others.

— To be friendly, this person habitually acknowledges verbally other's contributions.

— This person is always an *extremely* friendly communicator.

— Whenever this person communicates, he/she tends to be very encouraging to people.

The style variable taps behaviors and feelings which could range from simply being unhostile to deep intimacy. A friendly style tends to confirm the other. In the teaching context, the overt message of being friendly is "I care about your worth; I want to encourage you." It is a style of communication in keeping with a deeply interpersonal approach to teaching.

Finally, the effective teacher tends to be *precise*. The following items reflect the style:

— This person is a very precise communicator.

— In an argument this person insists upon very precise definitions.

— This person likes to be strictly accurate when he/she communicates.

— Very often this person insists that other people document or present some kind of proof for what they are arguing.

To the extent that precision eliminates ambiguity in a subject matter, it should be valued by the student. Also, the effective teacher should eliminate confusion about the way grades are given, the work expected, and personal biases.

Each of the style predictors of teacher effectiveness need further examination incorporating a variety of empirical methods. For example, it would be instructive to videotape the teacher in the classroom, have the students rate the teacher, and then let the teacher rate himself or herself *after viewing the tape*. The objective feedback should help the teacher to become more sensitive to his or her style of communicating. Problem areas could be identified, and methods for improvement could be suggested.

Finally, the fourth question—Are there differences in the way teachers see themselves and the way students see the teachers?—points to any disparity between students and instructors. If the style variable generally does not pertain to the teaching process, there should be no differences between teachers' and students' ratings. For example, it probably does not make a difference in teacher effectiveness whether the person is open. The converse is not true, however. If there are no differences between samples, it does not mean that the variable does not pertain to the teaching process. It could simply mean that the teachers and students

agree on the level of intensity for that variable.

On the other hand, for the pertinent variables, as identified by the regression equations, there are two reasons why there might be a discrepancy between the samples. First, the teachers may inflate their scores on particular variables because it is socially desirable. For instance, it is good to be *attentive* rather than *not attentive*. Second, the average rating by the students reflects not only those in the sample who see the teacher as the teacher sees himself or herself, but also includes the bored, distracted, insensitive, or unperceptive student. An obvious hypothesis is suggested: The more effective teacher can evaluate his or her communicator style *as others see it* better than the less effective teacher. The assumption is that the poorer teacher is less aware of how others see him or her.

In summary, this research provides strong evidence that perceived effectiveness in teaching is inextricably related to one's style of communication. If this is true, the quality of teaching can be improved by improving specific communicative behaviors relating to attentive, impression leaving, relaxed, dominant, friendly, and precise style components.

REFERENCES

BREED, G., CHRISTIANSEN, E., & LARSON, D. Effect of a lecturer's gaze direction upon teaching effectiveness. *Catalog of Selected Documents in Psychology*, 1972, 2, 115.

CENTRA, J. Effectiveness of student feedback in modifying college instruction. *Journal of Educational Psychology*, 1973, 65, 395-401.

COPPERNOLL, P., & DAVIES, D. Goal-oriented evaluation of teaching methods by medical students and faculty. *Journal of Medical Education*, 1974, 49, 424-430.

COSTON, F., GREENOUGH, W., & MENGES, T. Student ratings of college teaching: Reliability, validity, and usefulness. *Review of Educational Research*. 1971. 41, 511-535.

FEATHER, N. Dimensions of teaching effectiveness and course evaluation based upon judgments of psychology students. *Australian Psychologist*, 1972, 7, 180-189.

FINKBEINDER, C., LATHROP, J., & SCHUERGER, J. Course and instructor evaluation: Some dimensions of a questionnaire. *Journal of Educational Psychology*, 1973, 64, 159-163.

FLANDERS, N. Basic teaching skills derived from a model of speaking and listening. *Journal of Teacher Education*, 1973, 24, 24-37.

FREY, P. Student ratings of teaching: Validity of several rating factors. *Science*, 1973, 182, 83-85.

GAGE, N. Teacher effectiveness and teacher education: *The search for a scientific basis*. Palo Alto, California: Pacific Books, 1972.

GESSNER, P. Evaluation of instruction. *Science*, 1973, 180, 566-570.

GREENWOOD, G., BRIDGES, C., WARE, W., & McLEAN, J. Student evaluation of college teaching behaviors instrument: A factor analysis. *Journal of Higher Education*, 1973, 44, 596-604.

HIND, R., DORNBUSCH, S., & SCOTT, W. A theory of evaluation applied to a university faculty. *Sociology of Education*, 1974, 47, 114-128.

KAUFFMAN, J., HALLAHAN, D., PAYNE, J., & BALL, D. Teaching/learning: Quantitative and functional analysis of educational performance. *Journal of Special Education*, 1973, 7, 261-268.

LINGOES, J. *The Guttman-Lingoes Nonmetric Program Series*. Ann Arbor, Michigan: Mathesis Press, 1973.

MEREDITH, G. Structure of student-based evaluation ratings. *Journal of Psychology*, 1975, 91, 3-9.

NULL, E., & WALTER, J. Values of students and their ratings of a university professor. *College Student Journal*, 1972, 6, 46-51.

RUESCH, J., & BATESON, G. *Communication: The Social Matrix of Psychiatry*. New York: Norton, 1951.

RICO, G. College students' perception of teacher effectiveness along five postulated dimensions. *St. Louis University Research Journal*, 1971, 2, 363-438.

RIPPEY, R. Student evaluations of professors: Are they of value? *Journal of Medical Education*, 1975, 50, 951-954.

ROBERSON, E. Teacher self-appraisal: A way to improve instruction. *Journal of Teacher Education*, 1971, 22, 469-473.

RODIN, M., & RODIN, B. Student evaluations of teachers. *Science*, 1972, 177, 1164-1166.

SCHÖNEMANN, P., & CARROLL, R. Fitting one matrix to another under choice of a central dilation and a rigid motion. *Psychometrika*, 1970, 35, 245-255.

SCRIVEN, M. The evaluation of teachers and teaching. *California Journal of Educational Research*, 1974, 25, 109-115.

SHAVE, D. *The Therapeutic Listener*. Huntington, New York: Robert Krieger, 1974.

WATZLAWICK, P., BEAVIN, J., & JACKSON, D. *Pragmatics of human communication: A study of interactional patterns, pathologies, and paradoxes*. New York: W. W. Norton, 1967.

THE EFFECTS OF COMMUNICATION APPREHENSION AND TEST ANXIETY ON THREE INDICANTS OF ACHIEVEMENT IN AN ALTERNATIVE SYSTEM OF INSTRUCTION: A FOLLOW-UP STUDY

MICHAEL D. SCOTT
West Virginia University

LAWRENCE R. WHEELESS
West Virginia University

MICHAEL P. YATES
The State University of New York-Buffalo

FRED L. RANDOLPH
West Virginia University

On the basis of the findings and weaknesses of an earlier exploratory study, this investigation assessed the effects of communication apprehension and test anxiety on three indices of achievement in an alternative system of instruction. An hypothesized relationship predicting a significant correlation between a linear combination of communication apprehension and test anxiety, and a linear combination of the three indices of achievement, was confirmed. In addition, exploration of a research question surfaced findings somewhat contrary to those reported in previous research focusing on the relationship between communication apprehension and student achievement.

The past seven years have borne witness to a remarkable growth in research focusing on a broadly-based fear or anxiety known as communication apprehension. While much of this research has been concerned with the conceptualization and measurement of communication apprehension (Friedrich, 1970; McCroskey, 1970; Behnke & Carlisle, 1971; Porter & Burns, 1973; Porter, 1974; Lustig, 1974), a number of recent studies have been concerned with its consequent effects on learning in the classroom. In the past two years alone, instructional communication researchers have studied communication apprehension as it relates to standardized measures of achievement and grade-point averages (McCroskey & Andersen, 1976), student achievement in small, discussion-oriented classrooms (Scott & Wheeless, in press), classroom seating (McCroskey & Sheahan, 1976), preferred instructional strategies and settings (McCroskey & Andersen, 1976; Scott & Wheeless, in press), teacher expectancies (McCroskey & Daly, in press), and student attitudes toward school (Hurt, Preiss, & Davis, 1976).

Although communication apprehension and intelligence do not appear to be correlated (McCroskey, Daly, & Sorensen, 1976), the preceding studies suggest a high degree of communication apprehension can be a serious learning disability. Among other things, students classified as high communication apprehensives have been found to: (1) score significantly lower on standardized measures of achievement than their counterparts (McCroskey & Andersen, 1976); (2) achieve less as evidenced by their grade point averages and examination scores (McCroskey & Andersen, 1976; Scott & Wheeless, in press); (3) avoid classroom seating areas which research suggests are zones of high interaction (McCroskey & Sheahan, 1976); (4) favor instructional strategies and settings which do not emphasize oral communication (McCroskey & Andersen, 1976; Scott & Wheeless, in press); (5) elicit negative teacher expectancies (McCroskey & Daly, in press); and (6) exhibit unfavorable attitudes toward school in general (Hurt, Preiss, & Davis, 1976). Since these findings cannot be attributed to differential levels of intelligence between *high* and *low communication apprehensives,* there is some question as to their causes.

CAUSES OF CLASSROOM EFFECTS

Whereas it appears clear from the research that high communication apprehension negatively impacts learning outcomes within conventional classrooms, researchers are just now beginning to speculate about the possible causes of the negative effects they have observed. Of the possibilities which have been mentioned to date, three in particular seem to be worth discussing: (1) communication avoidance, (2) teacher expectancies, and (3) student attitudes.

Communication Avoidance

In conventional classrooms where the lecture-discussion strategy is the primary means of disseminating and clarifying content, teachers commonly place a high premium on a student's ability to ask intelligent questions, probe topical issues, and defend his or her ideas. It is not uncommon for teachers who employ this type of instructional strategy to make qualitative judgments about a student's intellectual worth as a function of the quality of the student's oral communication behaviors while in class. In the extreme, moreover, it is not uncommon to learn from the syllabi of such courses that the quality of a student's oral contributions to the class will weigh significantly in his or her final grade. Classes where oral communication is both encouraged and reinforced may or may not work in favor of the academic progress of a student who views communication as a highly rewarding activity—that is, the low communication apprehensive. For the student who is extremely apprehensive about communicating, however, taking advantage of a teacher's favorable predispositions toward oral communication would be out of the question.

Based upon the available evidence, communication avoidance appears to be a customary way of behaving among high communication apprehensives (Daly & McCroskey, 1975; McCroskey & Sheahan, 1976; Scott, McCroskey, & Sheahan, in press). While the evidence in support of this conclusion largely has been conducted outside the learning environment (e.g., organizations and living arrangements), there is little reason to believe that high communication apprehensives abandon their customary communication behaviors once inside the classroom. The finding that high communication apprehensives fail to achieve at a level comparable to their low apprehensive counterparts, consequently, may be a result of their inability to take

advantage of classroom rewards which only can be obtained through oral communication behaviors.

Of course, not all teachers gauge a student's abilities on the basis of the student's communication behaviors or take such behaviors into account when assigning grades. Be that as it may, much of what is learned in traditional courses frequently is the result of student-teacher interactions—for example, question-asking. Research concerning patterns of interaction within traditionally situated classrooms indicates there are certain seats in these classrooms which are characterized by high levels of interaction between individual students, as well as between students and the teacher (Sommer, 1969). Furthermore, as McCroskey (1976) points out:

> Recent research indicates that while low communication apprehensives are twice as likely to sit in this high interaction area (20 percent of the total seats) as they are to sit anywhere else (80 percent of the total seats), high communication apprehensives are four times as likely to sit outside this interaction area as sit in it. (p. 8)

Thus, the discrepancies between the achievement scores of high and low communication apprehensives also may be a function of highly apprehensive students avoiding this zone of interaction, and low apprehensive students occupying it. In doing so, students who are high in communication apprehension may effectively cut themselves off from information which might clarify issues about which they are confused, or reinforce points which they may overlook, as a result of their oral pacificity.

Teacher Expectancies

A wealth of data concerning the nature and effects of teacher expectancies about students has been collected since the publication of Rosenthal and Jacobson's *Pygmalion in the Classroom* (1968). Rosenthal and Jacobson reported research which suggested that what a teacher is led to expect about a student's academic performance actually will influence the student's performance. While the validity of this conclusion is far from settled, research subsequent to that reported by Rosenthal and Jacobson generally supports the notion that teacher expectancies and student performance are meaningfully related (Dusek & O'Connell, 1973; O'Connell, Dusek, & Wheeler, 1974). To date, however, there is only one example of instructional communication research in which the relationship between teacher expectancies and communication apprehension has been assessed. In this single example, McCroskey and Daly (in press) provided elementary and secondary teachers with descriptions of two students. While the two descriptions differed in the sense that one of the students was depicted as *quiet* and the other was depicted as *verbal,* the descriptions were otherwise identical. Although the two descriptions were otherwise identical, elementary and secondary school teachers expected the quiet student to achieve significantly less in a majority of subject matters than the student who was described as verbal. Obviously, this single study does not warrant a conclusion concerning teacher expectancies as an underlying cause for differential levels of achievement among high and low communication apprehensive students. At a minimum, though, it does suggest that, within the conventional classroom, teacher expectancies based on the amount of oral communication in which a student engages may be a potential cause for what has become a rather consistent finding in communication apprehension research.

Student Attitudes

As McCroskey (1976) has pointed out, the relationship between student attitudes and communication apprehension is analogous to that of the chicken and the egg. Although research clearly demonstrates high degrees of communication apprehension and negative attitudes toward school are associated with one another (Hurt, Preiss, & Davis, 1976; McCroskey & Sheahan, 1976), it is not clear whether a student's high communication apprehension or negative attitudes toward education most affect his or her level of achievement. Does communication apprehension, for example, give rise to negative attitudes which affect achievement? Or, are these negative attitudes the result of the student failing to achieve as a function of avoiding learning activities which require oral communication? Because of potential reciprocal causality, answers to the preceding two questions will have to come from

future instructional communication research.

Conclusions

Given the preceding framework, it is clear that instructional communication researchers have yet to develop a unified and coherent explanation for the finding of differential levels of achievement among high and low communication apprehensive students. While this finding may be a result of communication avoidance, teacher expectancies, and negative student attitudes, it also may be a result of the learning environment in which the majority of studies have been conducted, or communication apprehension being confounded by other variables relevant to the instructional process. For example, a close examination of the studies previously cited will reveal that each has been conducted within the confines of the traditional classroom, and each has been only marginally concerned with variables which have been demonstrated to negatively impact learning outcomes. Whether or not the effects observed in these studies would generalize to studies conducted in unconventional learning environments is open to question. Furthermore, the question of whether or not these effects would hold up when other important variables, such as *test anxiety,* are considered needs to be investigated.

Finally, it should be pointed out that conclusions about the relationship between communication apprehension and achievement have been based largely on comparisons of high and low communication apprehensives. To the best of our knowledge, only one study has included moderate levels of communication apprehension within the analysis (McCroskey & Andersen, 1976). While significant differences in achievement were found on a number of relevant indices in this study, the pattern of means indicated that the largest differences in achievement in some cases were between *moderate* and *low communication apprehensives,* not between *moderate* and *high communication apprehensives.* Since these differences were not compared statistically, conclusions about their meaning are not warranted. Taking into account the fact that the preceding study focused on a mass lecture course where oral communication was restricted, however, the pattern of means observed raises an issue which needs to be investigated. Put simply, the possibility exists that in learning environments where oral communication is restricted or can be avoided without negative consequences, high communication apprehensives may achieve at a level which is comparable to those who display what might be called "normal" levels of communication apprehension.

RATIONALE

In light of the preceding issues, the present study was designed to assess the impact of communication apprehension as well as test anxiety (Mandler & Sarason, 1952), on achievement in an individualized, criterion-referenced, system of instruction adhering to the principle of mastery learning. Contrary to much of the previous research, the study also was concerned with the impact of these two variables on students exhibiting moderate levels of apprehension or anxiety about communicating and test-taking, as well as students exhibiting high or low levels of communication apprehension and test anxiety.

Communication Apprehension

As intimated earlier, most studies focusing on the relationship between communication apprehension and achievement have been conducted in relationship to conventional learning environments—small classes where the lecture-discussion strategy is the primary means by which content is disseminated and clarified. While not all of these classes make specific communication demands on the student, at least one researcher has implied that the more a student communicates in these classes, the more likely it is the student will elicit positive perceptions from the teacher, acquire favorable attitudes toward the course content and methods, and achieve at a level which corresponds to his or her ability (McCroskey, 1976). Also, research concerning teacher expectancies (McCroskey & Daly, in press), student attitudes toward course content and methods (Scott & Wheeless, in press), and achievement among highly apprehensive students (Scott & Wheeless, in press) supports this conclu-

sion. If this is the case, the differential levels of achievement which have been observed among high and low communication apprehensive students may be more a result of the communication demands inherent to conventional classrooms than the inabilities of the highly apprehensive student to learn. The question becomes, therefore, whether the achievement effects, noted in previous research, are generalizable to an environment void of the kind of communicative demands present in conventional classrooms; for example, a learning environment where highly apprehensive students could learn on their own, and could conceivably achieve at a level which corresponds to their abilities without ever engaging the instructor in sustained periods of face-to-face communication. Unfortunately, only one study has addressed this question (Scott, Yates, & Wheeless, 1975). While this study reported findings suggesting the achievement effects observed in other studies appeared to hold for an unconventional instructional setting, the study was exploratory and methodologically flawed. As a result, it seems safe to assume that the preceding question is still in need of an answer.

Test Anxiety

In addition to the above issue, there is some question concerning the amount of variability in the achievement scores of high, moderate, and low communication apprehensives which is attributable to test anxiety. Aside from the fact that test anxiety has been found to be inversely correlated with test performance on both aptitude and achievement tests (Berkley & Sproule, 1973), test anxiety and communication apprehension have been found to be significantly and positively correlated (McCroskey, 1970). Since conclusions drawn about the discrepancies between the achievement scores of high and low communication apprehensives have been based in part on individual test scores such as ACT scores, one would think the potentially mediating effects of test anxiety would have been controlled or covaried in prior research. This has not been the case. Apparently, instructional communication researchers have overlooked the degree to which test anxiety and communication apprehension are associated with one another and the similarities between their own results and those appearing in the literature on test anxiety.

RESEARCH HYPOTHESIS

The preceding discussion suggests the generalizability of research focusing on the relationship between communication apprehension and achievement has been limited as a result of researchers conducting their inquiries within the confines of conventional classrooms, failing to concern themselves adequately with the normal population of communication apprehensives and the potentially mediating effects of test anxiety. Thus, this study initially was concerned with assessing the impact of communication apprehension and test anxiety on achievement within an individualized, criterion-referenced, mastery-learning course in educational psychology. Briefly, this course employed the following educational procedures:

1. Students learned individually using a course workbook and through interacting with teaching machines.
2. Students were required to master (90% criterion) a given instructional unit prior to moving to the next unit and were required to master all units in order to receive a grade of "A".
3. Students were allowed to make three attempts at mastery of a given instructional unit prior to being *required* to seek tutorial assistance from course personnel.
4. Students could attempt mastery by way of an objective test between 8 a.m. and 9 p.m., seven days a week.
5. Students were required to attend once-a-week group sessions (20-30 people) which had no bearing whatsoever on their progression through the instructional sequence.

While tutorial assistance was available to students at all times, the nature of the course was such that a student could avoid sustained interaction with course personnel altogether, as long as the student mastered each unit within three attempts. Moreover, the course also was structured in such a way that failure to communicate with course personnel had no bearing on a student's final grade, unless the student failed to seek tutorial assistance

after failing in three attempts to master a unit of instruction. It was quite conceivable, then, that a student could complete the course without ever engaging in sustained periods of interaction with course personnel or other students enrolled in the course. Finally, there were three indicants of student achievement in the course since it stressed *mastery learning:* (1) the number of instructional units the student completed, (2) the number of trials a student engaged in the attempt to master a unit, and (3) the number of times students needed tutorial assistance. At the time this study was conducted, the maximum number of units which could have been completed was ten. Thus, achievement would be highest and most efficient for those students who completed ten instructional units, in ten trials, and with zero tutorials.

On appearances alone, the almost nonexistent emphasis on oral communication and the heavy reliance on testing in the course might lead one to speculate that high communication apprehensive students would be less affected by the course than students who are highly anxious about test-taking. By the same token, the absence of communication demands which are inherent to more conventional courses might lead one to speculate the probability of differential achievement among high and low communication apprehensive students would be lessened within this particular type of course. While either of these two lines of speculation may be intuitively compelling, the significant and positive correlation between communication apprehension and test anxiety as well as previous research, suggested directional predictions along these lines were not warranted. As a result, the present study was designed to test the following research hypothesis:

H: A linear combination of communication apprehension and test anxiety will be significantly correlated with a linear combination of total units, trials, and tutorials.

Given what we know from previous research, we tentatively would expect communication apprehension to be most associated with the number of tutorials in which students of varying levels of apprehension engage. Similarly, we tentatively would expect test anxiety to be most associated with the number of trials required for mastery which, in turn, would influence both the number of tutorials in which the student engaged and the number of instructional units actually completed.

Research Question

In addition to being concerned with the impact of communication apprehension and test anxiety on achievement in an unconventional course, the present study also was concerned with the achievement of students exhibiting *moderate* levels of communication apprehension or test anxiety. As pointed out earlier, much of the previous research focusing on the relationship between achievement and communication apprehension has been restricted to the study of high and low communication apprehensives. To some extent, the same can be said for test anxiety research (Mandler & Sarason, 1952; Paul & Ericksen, 1965).

This practice not only has given rise to the notion that achievement decreases as communication apprehension increases, but also has given rise to the notion that high communication apprehensives are deficient learners. While there is reason to believe both notions, at least two other possibilities need to be explored. First, the possibility exists that the relationship between communication apprehension and achievement is not the linear relationship suggested by the research to date. Second, the possibility exists that the differential levels of achievement which have been reported among high and low communication apprehensives, are attributable to the tendency of low communication apprehensives to excel in conventional courses rather than high communication apprehensives being deficient. Since this line of thought is contrary to what one would be led to believe on the basis of previous research, there was no justification for a specific hypothesis which reflected it. Consequently, the following research question, which included all three levels of communication apprehension and test anxiety, also was explored in the present study:

Q: What is the nature of the relationship among communication apprehension, test anxiety, the number of units of instruction completed, the number of trials required for mastery, and the number of tutorials in which students engage?

METHOD

Procedures and Sampling

To test the preceding hypothesis and examine the research question, 300 students enrolled in an educational psychology course employing the aforementioned instructional practices were administered measures of oral communication apprehension and test anxiety on the first day of class. During the fifteenth week of class, records concerning the number of instructional units completed, the number of examination trials required for mastery, and the number of tutorials in which students engaged were tabulated. Since the course was self-paced, this meant the maximum number of instructional units completed at the time this information was compiled was ten. The three data sets were merged. The *n* for each of the measures varied somewhat as a function of student absences during the initial data collection period, and failure to match data sets because of errors in student identification numbers reported on IBM answer sheets.

Measurement

Oral communication apprehension was measured via the 25-item version of the *Personal Report of Communication Apprehension* (McCroskey & Wheeless, 1976). The *Personal Report of Communication Apprehension* (PRCA) is a Likert-type, self-report measure designed to ascertain feelings of apprehensiveness in a full range of social contexts. In the present study, PRCA displayed the following descriptive characteristics: split-half reliability = .90, mean = 72.16, standard deviation = 13.79.

Anxiety about test-taking was measured via a 30-item version of the *Test Anxiety Inventory* (Emery & Krumboltz, 1967). The *Test Anxiety Inventory* (TAI) is also a Likert-type, self-report measure. In the present study, TAI displayed the following descriptive characteristics: split-half reliability = .86, mean = 87.59, standard deviation = 16.37.

Given an absolute 0 point, achievement was operationalized in terms of the total number of instructional units completed, the total number of examination trials (i.e., equivalent form examinations) required for mastery, and the total number of tutorials in which students engaged.

Statistical Analysis

In order to test the research hypothesis, *canonical correlation* was utilized. PRCA and TAI scores were correlated with total examination trials, total units completed, and total tutorials. The .05 level of statistical significance was required in this hypothesized test. In order to examine the research question, *Pearson Product-Moment* correlations among all variables were employed. As a consequence of this exploration, *analyses of covariance* also were used to further examine the research question. The independent variables, PRCA and TAI, were categorized into high, moderate, and low levels based upon the standard deviation criterion. Those subjects scoring *beyond* a standard deviation *above* the mean were classified as high; those *within* a standard deviation *above* or *below* the mean, as moderate; and those *beyond* a standard deviation *below* the mean, as low. Based upon previous research (McCroskey, 1970) and a preliminary analysis in this study indicating a significant correlation ($r = .32$) between PRCA and TAI, TAI served as the covariate in ANACOVA's concerned with the impact of communication apprehension (PRCA). Likewise, PRCA served as the covariate in ANACOVA's concerned with the impact of test anxiety (TAI). Dependent variables were again total units of instruction completed, total trials, and total number of tutorials. Differences among adjusted means were tested with Scheffe's procedure. Following the advice of Scheffè, and recognizing his procedure to be conservative, the alpha level was set at .10.

Test of Hypothesis

A significant canonical correlation was observed when PRCA and TAI were correlated with total units, total trials, and total tutorials ($r = .37$; $X^2 = 24.19$; d.f. $= 6$). Thus, the hypothesis was supported, with 14 percent shared variance between the anxiety measures and the indices of achievement. Considering that 14 percent shared variance represents a considerable impact on achievement, and that for a large percentage (approximately 68 percent) of persons who have normal levels of anxiety we would expect a minimum relationship with achievement, the magnitude of this relationship appears to be quite substantial. Moreover, the nature of the multivariate relationships were also reflected in the analysis. The anxiety measures were correlated with the canonical variable representing them at the following levels: PRCA: $r = -.40$ and TAI: $r = .75$. The achievement measures were correlated with the canonical variable representing them at the following levels: *total units* ($r = -.12$), *total trials* ($r = .80$), and *total tutorials* ($r = .78$). Thus, predominantly test anxiety, and to a lesser extent communication apprehension, were associated primarily with total trials and tutorials. PRCA tended to be associated positively with total units and negatively with total trials and tutorials. However, TAI tended to be associated negatively with total units and positively with total trials and tutorials. Apparently, the greater the communication apprehension, the greater the tendency to test over units successfully in order to avoid interaction involved in attempting more trials and tutorials. Likewise, the greater the test anxiety, the greater the apparent tendency to have more examination trials and tutorials in order to test successfully on fewer units. While these tendencies appear to be present in this multivariate analysis, the strength of individual relationships are examined below.

Tests of Research Question

As a preliminary measure, Pearson Product-Moment correlations were computed between the variables under consideration (see Table 1 for resulting r's). As reported, PRCA and TAI were significantly correlated. Whereas TAI also was significantly correlated with the total number of units completed, the total number of trials, and the total number of tutorials, PRCA was significantly correlated only with TAI. Finally, total units completed, total trials, and total tutorials were significantly correlated with one another. The preceding findings deserve some comment. First, the fact that PRCA and TAI were significantly correlated suggests both communication apprehension and test anxiety are associated with some broader form of anxiety. Second, the finding that TAI, units completed, trials, and tutorials were significantly correlated with one another was not altogether unexpected because of

TABLE 1
Correlations Among Variables Considered

	Units	Trials	Tutorials	PRCA	TAI
Units	1.00*	.45*	.15*	.02	.04
Trials	.45*	1.00*	.82*	-.11	.16*
Tutorials	.15*	.82*	1.00*	-.10	.17*
PRCA	.02	-.11	-.10	1.00*	.32*
TAI	-.04	.12*	.16*	.32*	1.00*

TABLE 2
Unadjusted and Adjusted Posttest Means for Total Trials and Tutorials

	TRIALS		TUTORIALS	
PRCA LEVEL	Unadjusted	Adjusted	Unadjusted	Adjusted
Low	18.58	19.41	4.03	4.49
Moderate	15.75	15.61	2.41	2.33
High	16.50	16.05	2.68	2.43

the nature of the course investigated. How many attempts a subject made in the attempt to master a unit, for example, largely determined the number of tutorials in which the subject engaged, as well as the number of units the subject actually completed. Since the number of trials needed for mastery most likely is a function of the level of test anxiety the subject experiences, the fact that TAI was found to be positively correlated with trials and tutorials but negatively correlated with the number of units completed is wholly understandable.

Since the nature and magnitude of the relationships among the independent and dependent variables were revealed in the multivariate test of the research hypothesis, univariate analyses were used in the exploration of the research question.

Communication Apprehension

In order to assess the impact of low, moderate, and high levels of communication apprehension on each of the dependent measures, three separate analyses of covariance were computed, with TAI scores serving as the covariate. While communication apprehension did not significantly affect the total number of instructional units completed, significant effects were revealed for total trials ($F = 3.58$; d.f. $= 2/162$; $p < .05$) and the total number of tutorials in which subjects engaged ($F = 4.12$; d.f. $= 2/162$; $p < .05$). Differences among the adjusted means resulting from the preceding two tests (see Table 2 for adjusted means) were probed with Scheffè's procedure. In terms of the number of

TABLE 3
Unadjusted and Adjusted Posttest Means for Total Trials and Tutorials

	TRIALS		TUTORIALS	
TAI LEVEL	Unadjusted	Adjusted	Unadjusted	Adjusted
Low	14.93	14.28	1.62	1.28
Moderate	16.08	16.17	2.67	2.71
High	19.65	20.01	4.54	4.73

trials needed for mastery, no significant differences were found between high and moderate apprehensives (critical K .10 = 3.19, $\overline{X}_d$ = .44) or between high and low apprehensives (critical K .10 = 3.85, $\overline{X}_d$ = 3.36). Somewhat contrary to what typically would be expected from most previous research, however, low communication apprehensive subjects engaged in significantly more trials than moderately apprehensive subjects (critical K .10 = 3.00, $\overline{X}_d$ = 3.80).

In terms of the total number of tutorials in which subjects engaged, no significant differences were found between moderate and high communication apprehensives (critical K .10 = 1.69, $\overline{X}_d$ = .10). As intimated in our discussion on the test of the research hypothesis, though, low communication apprehensive subjects engaged in significantly more tutorials than either moderate (critical K .10 = 1.61, $\overline{X}_d$ = 2.16) or high (critical K .10 = 2.05, $\overline{X}_d$ = 2.06) communication apprehensives.

On the whole, the preceding findings suggest that, within an unconventional learning environment, highly apprehensive students achieve no differently than a majority of students. This conclusion is based on the fact that highly and moderately apprehensive subjects did not differ on a single dependent measure under consideration. What is surprising, however, is the finding that low apprehensive students appeared to achieve less efficiently than their counterparts in such learning environments. While the opportunity to avoid communication may be a source of motivation for the highly apprehensive student, therefore, the absence of communication-based rewards may minimize

any advantage the verbal student might have in a more conventional course.

Test Anxiety

In the effort to assess the impact of low, moderate, and high levels of test anxiety on each of the dependent variables, three separate analyses of covariance initially were computed, with PRCA scores serving as the covariate. Although no significant effects were observed for the number of instructional units completed when PRCA scores were used as the covariate, significant effects were observed for total trials (F = 4.55; d.f. = 2/162; p < .05) and the total number of tutorials in which subjects engaged (F = 5.44; d.f. = 2/162; p < .05). Again, differences among the adjusted means resulting from these analyses (see Table 3 for adjusted means) were probed with Scheffè's procedure. No significant difference was found for the total number of test trials in which low and moderately test-anxious subjects engaged (critical K .10 = 3.16, $\overline{X}_d$ = 1.89). In contrast, it was found that highly anxious subjects engaged in significantly more test trials than both moderately (critical K .10 = 3.30, $\overline{X}_d$ = 3.84) and low anxious subjects (critical K .10 = 4.09, $\overline{X}_d$ = 5.73).

In terms of the total number of tutorials in which subjects engaged, an identical pattern of differences was observed. While low and moderately test anxious subjects failed to significantly differ (critical K .10 = 1.69, $\overline{X}_d$ = 1.43), high test anxious subjects required significantly more tutorials than moderately (critical K .10 = 1.78, $\overline{X}_d$ = 2.02) and low test

TABLE 4
Unadjusted and Adjusted Posttest Means for Total Units

TAI LEVEL	Unadjusted	Adjusted
Low	8.31	8.43
Moderate	7.61	7.70
High	7.73	7.38

anxious subjects (critical K .10 = 2.18, $\bar{X}_d$ = 3.45).

Unlike some of the findings concerning the achievement effects of communication apprehension, the preceding findings appear to be wholly compatible with previous research on test anxiety. While significant differences between low and moderately test anxious subjects were not observed, the pattern of adjusted means in both analyses suggest the relationship between test anxiety and learner efficiency in an unconventional learning system is a linear one. As test anxiety increases, learner efficiency decreases.

Post Hoc Analysis

Since the number of trials in which subjects engaged largely determined the number of units subjects actually completed, a post hoc analysis was conducted in the effort to determine the impact of test anxiety on the number of units completed when trials were removed as a source of variance. Specifically, analysis of covariance was computed with the three levels of test anxiety constituting the independent variable, total number of units completed constituting the dependent variable, and trials serving as a covariate.

Using trials as a covariate, test anxiety was found to significantly affect the total number of instructional units completed (F = 3.95; d.f. = 2/162; p < .05). As was the case with all other analyses, differences among the adjusted means (see Table 4) were probed with Scheffé's procedure. Although no significant difference was revealed between moderate and high test anxious subjects (critical K .10 = .64, $\bar{X}_d$ = .32), low anxious subjects completed

significantly more units than moderately (critical K .10 = .64, $\bar{X}_d$ = .73) and high test anxious subjects (critical K .10 = .79, $\bar{X}_d$ = 1.05). Had the course investigated not adhered to the principle of mastery learning, therefore, low test anxious subjects would have had an obvious advantage over their counterparts.

CONCLUSIONS

Previous research concerning the impact of communication apprehension on student achievement not only has found differential levels of achievement among high and low communication apprehensives, but also has given rise to the notion that high communication apprehension is a severe learning disability. The results of this investigation suggest this notion is in need of re-examination and further research. While the generalizability of the findings in this study largely are restricted to a particular type of learning environment, students exhibiting what generally would be considered debilitating levels of communication apprehension achieved as efficiently as students exhibiting normal levels of apprehension about oral communication. Even more surprising, high communication apprehensives achieved more efficiently than low communication apprehensives. The question is why?

Within traditional classrooms, the possibility exists that verbal students achieve at a level above that of students who are either moderately or highly apprehensive about oral communication as a function of the system of rewards within these classrooms. This possibility has been inadequately in-

TABLE 5
Achievement Means for Small, Interactional Classroom

	Communication Apprehension Levels			
Achievement Index	Low	Moderate	High	F-ratio
1. Examination Average	41.63	38.49	38.54	3.64, 2/194 d.f., p < .03
2. Project Average	45.54	42.17	41.03	4.06, 2/194 d.f., p < .02
3. Canonical Mean	0.62	0.57	0.56	2.80, 4/388 d.f., p < .03

vestigated, though, because previous researchers have overlooked potential achievement differences among a full range of communication apprehensives. Assuming the findings in this study concerning achievement between moderate and high communication apprehensives may generalize to more conventional learning environments, this would mean that previous researchers have compared the achievement of high apprehensives with the achievement of students in the interactive classroom who excel—low communication apprehensives. To aid interpretation of this important issue, data collected in a previous study (Scott & Wheeless, in press), concerned with communication apprehension and achievement in small sections of an interpersonal communication course, were re-examined by including moderate levels of communication apprehension (20-25 per section, total n = 197). Since interaction was encouraged in these small sections, the question relevant to interpreting the present study was the following: Were the differential achievement levels found in the original study a function of the debilitative effects of high communication apprehension, or the facilitative effects of low communication apprehension? An examination of the means (see Table 5) revealed that achievement on exams and projects probably was a function of the facilitative nature of low communication apprehension in classrooms where interaction is encouraged. The high communication apprehensives appeared to achieve at levels comparable to the "normal" moderates. This interpretation appears consistent with the one study previously discussed (McCroskey & Andersen, 1976) which examined various indices of achievement in relation to communication apprehension levels.

In light of the preceding, the findings of this study suggest that individualized learning systems such as that investigated in this study may effectively remove any competitive edge which verbal students may have within classrooms characterized by high interaction, or where interaction is encouraged. Had grades in this course been based on the number of trials required for mastery instead of the number of instructional units completed, for example, low communication apprehensives would have appeared to achieve less than moderate and high communication apprehensives. Whereas the opportunity to avoid oral communication may have been a source of motivation for highly apprehensive students in this study, it may have been a source of frustration for low communication apprehensives. Moreover, this frustration may have interfered with low communication apprehensives achieving in an efficient manner. This seems a reasonable conclusion, for previous research (McCroskey & Andersen, 1976; Scott & Wheeless, in press) has found that low communication apprehensives prefer, and are more satisfied with, instructional practices which involve some oral communication and interaction.

Finally, the results of this study suggest the achievement effects reported in previous research may have been mediated by test anxiety (a highly specialized form of communication apprehension). Aside from the fact that test anxiety and communication apprehension were found to be significantly correlated, the multivariate test of the research hypothesis suggested that achievement in this study was most associated with anxieties about test taking. Thus, future research along these lines may improve upon current explanations of the relationship between communication apprehension and achievement.

Regardless of the conclusions drawn from this study, one thing seems certain. It is far too early for instructional communication theorists and researchers to close the book on the relationship between communication apprehension and achievement. The findings of this investigation suggest knowledge claims about this relationship must be bolstered by systematic programs of research where the field of inquiry is neither restricted to conventional learning environments, nor questions concerning the extremes of the communication apprehension distribution, and where the potential mediation of variables such as test anxiety are considered.

REFERENCES

BEHNKE, R. R., & CARLISLE, L. W. Heart rate as an index of speech anxiety. *Speech Monographs,* 38, 1971, 65-69.

BERKLEY, C. S., & SPROULE, C. F. Test anxiety and test-unsophistication: The effects, the cures. *Public Personnel Management,* 2, 1973, 55-59.

DALY, J. A., & McCROSKEY, J. C. Occupational desirability and choice as a function of communication apprehension. *Journal of Counseling Psychology,* 22, 1975, 309-313.

DUSEK, J. B., & O'CONNELL, E. J. Teacher expectancy effects on the achievement test performance of elementary school children. *Journal of Educational Psychology,* 65, 1973, 371-377.

EMERY, J. R., & KRUMBOLTZ, J. D. Standard versus individualized hierarchies in desensitization to reduce test anxiety. *Journal of Counseling Psychology,* 14, 1967, 204-209.

FRIEDRICH, G. W. An empirical explication of a concept of self-reported speech anxiety. *Speech Monographs,* 37, 1970, 67-72.

HURT, T., PREISS, R., & DAVIS, B. The effects of communication apprehension of middle-school children on sociometric choice, affective and cognitive learning. Paper presented at the annual meeting of the International Communication Association, Portland, Oregon, 1976.

LUSTIG, M. W. Verbal reticence: A reconceptualization and preliminary scale development. Paper presented at the annual meeting of the Speech Communication Association, Chicago, 1974.

MANDELER, G., & SARASON, S. B. A study of anxiety and learning. *Journal of Abnormal and Social Psychology,* 47, 1952, 166-173.

McCROSKEY, J. C. Measures of communication bound anxiety. *Speech Monographs,* 37, 1970, 269-277.

McCROSKEY, J. C. Classroom consequences of communication apprehension. Paper presented at the annual meeting of the Speech Communication Association, Houston, 1975.

McCROSKEY, J. C. The problem of communication apprehension in the classroom. Paper presented at the annual meeting of the Pacific Communication Association Convention, Tokyo, 1976.

McCROSKEY, J. C., & ANDERSEN, J. F. The relationship between communication apprehension and academic achievement among college students. *Human Communication Research,* 3, 1976, 73-81.

McCROSKEY, J. C., & DALY, J. A. Teachers expectations of the communication apprehensive child in the elementary school. *Human Communication Research,* 3, 1976, 62-72.

McCROSKEY, J. C., DALY, J. A., & SORENSEN, G. A. Personality correlates of communication apprehension. *Human Communication Research,* 2, 1976, 376-380.

McCROSKEY, J. C., & SHEAHAN, M. E. Seating position and participation: An alternative theoretical explanation. Paper presented at the annual meeting of the International Communication Association, Portland, Oregon, 1976.

McCROSKEY, J. C., & WHEELESS, L. R. *An introduction to human communication.* Boston: Allyn and Bacon, 1976.

O'CONNELL, E. J., DUSEK, J. B., & WHEELER, R. A follow-up study of teacher expectancy effects. *Journal of Educational Psychology,* 66, 1974, 325-328.

PAUL, G. L., & ERIKSEN, C. W. Effects of test anxiety on "real life" examinations. *Journal of Personality,* 1, 1965, 493-496.

PHILLIPS, G. M. Reticence: Pathology of the normal speaker. *Speech Monographs,* 35, 1968, 39-48.

PORTER, D. T., & BURNS, G. P., JR. A criticism of "heart rate as an index of speech anxiety." *Speech Monographs,* 40, 1973, 156-165.

PORTER, D. T. Self-report scales of communication apprehension and autonomic arousal (heart rate): A test of construct validity. *Speech Monographs,* 41, 1974, 267-276.

ROSENTHAL, R., & JACOBSON, L. *Pygmalion in the classroom.* New York: Holt, Rinehart, and Winston, 1968.

SCOTT, M. D., YATES, M. P., & WHEELESS, L. R. An exploratory investigation of the effects of communication apprehension in an alternative system of instruction. Paper presented at the annual meeting of the International Communication Association, Chicago, 1975.

SCOTT, M. D., & WHEELESS, L. R. Communication apprehension, student attitudes, and levels of satisfaction. *Western Speech Communication,* (in press).

SCOTT, M. D., & WHEELESS, L. R. The relationship of three types of communication apprehension to student achievement. *The Southern Speech Communication Journal* (in press).

SCOTT, M. D., McCROSKEY, J. C., & SHEAHAN, M. E. The development of a self-report measure of communication apprehension in organizational settings. *The Journal of Communication,* (in press).

SOMMER, R. *Personal space.* Englewood Cliffs, New Jersey: Prentice Hall, 1969.

HEALTH COMMUNICATION
Theory and Research: An Overview
Selected Studies

HEALTH COMMUNICATION THEORY
AND RESEARCH: AN OVERVIEW

DANIEL E. COSTELLO
Vanderbilt University

What we know about how communication functions within health and medicine has come basically from anthropology, medical psychiatry, psychology, and sociology. A review of the literature points up the importance of understanding the communication phenomenon, but also reveals the lack of a concentrated and cohesive effort in its study. Some recent reviews (Dervin & Harlock, 1976; Rossiter, 1975; Costello, 1972) have included communication templates for looking at specific theoretical and methodological issues. Interest in applying communication Theory and research to the medical domain has been broadening. In response to a growing concern by communication researchers, the International Communication Association (ICA) organized a Division of Health Communication in 1975.

Interest by communication scholars is paralleled in other behavior disciplines. Seventeen years ago, the American Sociological Association (ASA) established a section on Medical Sociology. This section attracts the largest numbers of participants of any within the association (Hollingshead, 1973). Also, since 1960, research in the social and cultural aspects of health care has tripled (Mechanic, 1968; Coe, 1970; Susser & Watson, 1971; Jaco, 1972).

Similar developments have taken place in anthropology and psychology, and together they have formed the nucleus around which behavioral science units have developed within medical education.

HEALTH AND DISEASE

Throughout the history of medicine, health has been seen as a condition of equilibrium, and disease has been viewed as disruption of that balanced state. In this context, *disease* is defined as a form of biological adaptation and an outgrowth of the body's accommodation to internal stress and noxious external conditions. The balanced state was regarded as desireable or "normal," while any deviation from this standard was generally thought to be undesirable or "abnormal." The biological system has traditionally been regarded as the most important aspect of medical science, and the major part of a doctor's training is devoted to biological aspects of bodily functioning and disease.

Rene Dubos (1965) offers a fascinating discussion of some of these issues. He points out that what is an acceptable biological adaptation is often determined by the social context in which it occurs. As Mechanic (1968) notes, dyschromic syirochetosias—a disease characterized by spots of various colors that appear on the skin—was so common in a particular South American tribe that Indians who did not have them were regarded as abnormal and were even excluded from marriage. Also, in some cultures the obese man or woman is an object of envy and desire, while others define obesity as a physical or emotional disease. Sometimes a disease is whatever a doctor is willing to treat. Alcoholism, schizophrenia, obesity, crime, suicide, political deviation, all have the potential of being labeled as a disease under various conceptions. Implicit in disease definitions are assumptions about what states of physical and social being are desirable and undesirable, damaging and benign.

Of course, as has often been noted, the difficulty with gauging departures from the norm is that normalcy itself may take different forms. Even when one defines normalcy as the statistical average, or as an ideal model, disease evaluations implicitly depend upon the value orientations and life situations of the people concerned.

Thus, social values play an essential part in medical determinations and in the provision of medical care. Social judgments are implied, for example, in the definitions and care of the mentally retarded, in family planning and in birth control, and in attitudes toward abortion and sterilization. The criteria of healthiness vary, as do the rights and obligations that form the substance of ones social, familial, and occupational roles.

In trying to resolve this dilemma, many health professionals adopt the definition provided by the World Health Organization which indicates that health is "state of complete physical, mental, and social well-being" (WHO, 1958, p.453). Troubled by the notion that health must be "complete," Merrell and Reed (1949) have suggested that "we could . . . think of a graded scale of health from positive through zero through negative health. On such a scale people would be classified from those who are in top notch condition with abundant energy, through the people who are well, down to the people who are feeling rather poorly, and finally to the definitely ill" (p.106).

Underpinning definitions of this later sort is the view that health and disease are not static entities, but rather are concepts used to characterize the processes of adaptation to the changing demands of life, and the changing meanings given to living.

COMMUNICATION

If *communication* is defined as the process of an individual acquiring and converting event data into meaningful or consumable information, the ends served by communication are those of adaptation (Thayer, 1968). Thus, the link between health and communication is of a fundamental nature.

Communication also affords a useful perspective for examining the doctor-patient relationship. As will be discussed later in this paper, doctor-patient interactions can be comprehended using the traditional $S \rightarrow M \rightarrow C \rightarrow R = E$ communication model. The doctor's communication behaviors are largely molded in his professional training and clinical experience. The patient's communication behaviors are influenced by the need to cope with a particular problem, and by his cultural and social understanding of the nature of the problem.

FUNCTIONS OF COMMUNICATION

Within the American health system, the doctor plays a key role in administering medical care. He functions as a gatekeeper for the entire medical establishment. While the contemporary treatment of illness involves a complex array of facilities and personnel, an individual must present himself to a doctor in order to gain access to this system. (While we shall deal here only with the experience between a doctor and his patient, what is said of this relationship is equally applicable to most encounters with health professionals.) The administration of modern therapeutic agents—from drugs to radiology to admission to the hospital and even referral to medical specialists—is always conditional, to a great or small extent, on the patient's placing himself in the hands of a doctor.

Much of the existing theory on doctor-patient relationship can be traced to the work of Henderson (1935) who viewed the relationship as a social system. The sociological formulations stemming from his work include that by Parsons (1951), Fox (1959), and Bloom (1963). Parsons specifies the key qualities of a doctor and the rights and duties of the patient, based upon the concept of the "sick role." Parsons indicates that the most important attitude of a doctor toward the patient is "affective neutrality." He is to refrain from too much empathy, to be neutral in judgment, and to maintain self-control.

Other interpretations of the doctor-patient relationship date to Freud (1946) and his interest in the nature of the therapeutic process. He emphasized the power of transference, whereby the patient redirects toward the doctor his feelings for his parents or other persons significant to him. Szasz and Hollender (1956) provide another approach to the doctor-patient relationship which involves three interaction models. In the first model—*active/passive*—the doctor takes charge and the patient is passive, as would be the case if a patient were in a coma. In the second model—*guidance/cooperation*—the doctor guides the patient when he is able to follow directions, as in infectious disorders. In the *mutual participation model*, doctor and patient carry out the treatment together, for example, in the management of chronic illness. Implicit in these formulations of the doctor-patient relationship is the premise that a relationship of mutuality exists between the roles that a doctor and a patient assume (Crane, 1975).

Bird (1955) suggests that of all the factors which enhance the doctor's role, none are nearly as valuable as skillful use of the spoken word—the words of the doctor and the words of the patient. He points out that, in addition to healer, the doctor plays a variety of roles such as sympathetic listener, director, and guidance counselor, each of which depends on his capacity to communicate.

FUNCTIONS OF COMMUNICATION

Review of the literature suggests that four basic functions are served by communication between health professionals and patients: *diagnosis, cooperation, counsel,* and *education.*

Diagnosis

The doctor or his assistant must secure data for diagnosis. He takes the patient's history, which requires considerable skill in interviewing. Stevenson (1960) states that if the physician has not acquired comfort and dexterity in his history-taking and interviewing by the time he graduates from medical school, he will practice medicine with incomplete data, for which no other skills can compensate him or his patients. Jason (1970) maintains that the quality of the interview with the patient, defined by the accuracy and completeness of the history, depends on the doctor's capacity to establish an atmosphere of openness and trust.

For the most part, the doctor's cognitive abilities required in data-gathering, data-interpretation, and problem-solving have been regarded as technical skills and have been separated from his ability to conduct the necessary verbal and nonverbal communication with his patients. However, there are two reasons for assigning a more important role to the doctor's interpersonal communication in an evaluation of performance: (1) interpersonal communication contributes, along with technical skills, to diagnosing disease problems, and (2) interpersonal communication is critical in the treatment of nondisease problems.

A study of general practitioners (Brown, Robertson, Kosa, & Alpert, 1971) found, for example, that nonsickness accounted for almost 25 percent of the diagnoses made on over 12,000 patients. Similarly, Mace (1971) estimates that from 25 to 50 percent of all patients who go to doctors are not suffering from any pathological disorder. Thus, the doctor's domain may be a broadly viewed one which includes aspects of preventive, rehabilitative, social, and psychological skills (Donabedian, 1968).

Cooperation

The course of a patient's treatment, and the patient's involvement in his own recovery and health maintenance, seem to largely depend on efforts at communication concerning the nature of his illness and the implication of measures prescribed for his care. Studies which consider this function and examine how interpersonal communication affects health outcomes are almost nonexistent. Most information on this communication function has been derived from studies on patient compliance and, to a lesser degree, from studies on patient satisfaction (Blackwell, 1973; Gillum & Barsky, 1974; Haggerty & Roghmann, 1972; Stimson, 1974).

Several studies (Skipper, Mauksch, & Tagliacozzo, 1963; Korsch, Gozzi, & Francis, 1968; Collins, 1955) indicate that the quality of communication between patient and doctor is adversely affected by the doctor's use of technical language and a failure to educate the patient about his problem. There is an indication also that doctors are often unaware of the patient's level of medical knowledge, and that this adversely affects their communication (Pratt, Seligmann, & Reader, 1957; Golden & Johnson, 1970). A study of doctors' perceptions of patients' comprehension of information (Kane & Deuschle, 1967) found that the patients actually knew more than their doctors had anticipated.

Other researchers (Ley, 1972; Ley, Bradshaw, Eaves, & Walker, 1973) have studied ways of increasing patient recall of information presented by the doctor. The implicit assumption being made is that the recall of medical information is necessary for patient compliance. *Patient compliance* is defined as the degree to which patients follow the medical regimen that the doctor has prescribed. Subjective reports and objective physical measurements have provided the basis for measuring compliance.

Davis (1971) has devised an index of compliance which is composed of patients' perceptions of their compliant behavior, doctors' perceptions of the patients' compliant behavior, and an independent review of patients' medical records. Medical records are used to indicate follow-through involving the use of a hospital. The physical measurement approach, for example, may include an assessment of prescriptions taken and an analysis of urine specimens. Decastro (1972) found that variation in compliance was correlated with the comprehension and recall of diagnostic and treatment information by patients. However, it has also been pointed out that patient understanding of medical information does not in itself insure compliance (Arnold, Adebonojo, Callas, Carte, & Stein, 1970).

Patient negligence or patient resistance to instruction were the most frequent explanations for noncompliance found by Donabedian and Rosenfeld (1964). Only eight percent of the patients mentioned inadequate understanding of instructions as a reason for not following doctor directives. Research by Spelman, Ley, and Jones (1966) suggests similarly that increasing levels of medical knowledge do not increase patient satisfaction. In a review of the compliance studies, Harper (1970) and Marston (1970) conclude that doctors have absolutely no basis for determining patient compliance and, for the most part, doctors are unaware of the level of compliance for all their patients. Harper (1971) found that noncompliance ranged from 30 to 50 percent of all patients studied. Furthermore, doctors reported that their greatest source of dissatisfaction stems from their inability to control their relationships with patients (Ort, Ford, & Liske, 1964).

The crucial factor in whether a patient will comply or not seems to lie in the nature of the medical regimen. The findings suggest that very complex regimens will not be followed as closely as less complex ones (Davis, 1968a; Davis & Eickhorn, 1963; Francis, Korsch, & Morris, 1969). A complex regimen involves the establishment and maintenance of the doctor-patient relationship over a considerable period of time. Harper (1971) states that family stability was positively related to the compliance of patients. Thus, family role responsibilities and expectations may help to explain the anxieties that accompany complex regimens and the importance of the family in tension reduction (Korsch, Gozzi, & Francis, 1968; Freemon, Negrete, Davis, & Korsch, 1971). Furthermore, Davis (1968a, 1968b) concluded that demographic characteristics of patients do not explain variations in their compliance.

There are some difficulties in assessing compliance, and different measures are appropriate for different purposes. Psychiatrists and those concerned with measuring the effects of psychotherapy, for example, assess the social function of the individual. Lubrosky (1962) developed a *Health-Sickness Rating Scale* to record patient improvement. Each patient is rated on seven dimensions: (1) ability to function autonomously, (2) seriousness of symptoms, (3) degree of discomfort, (4) effect upon the environment, (5) utilization of abilities, (6) quality of interpersonal relationships, and (7) breadth and depth of interest.

Rice, Berger, Sewall, and Lemkau (1961) developed a questionnaire to assess patient adjustment to the community before and after treatment in a public psychiatric hospital. The questionnaire evaluates four areas of social adjustment: (1) social and family relations, (2) social productivity (areas such as work and school), (3) self-management (personal care and conduct), and (4) antisocial behavior. In another instance, evaluation of functional capacity includes measures of occupational function (work time loss, work modification, job change, job loss), social function (household and family composition changes, daily activity changes), and personal function (degree of self-care, sleep and rest patterns, personal hygiene habits, recreational activity).

In the area of patient satisfaction, interviewing is a common method used to elicit information. For instance, Gozzi, Morris, and Korsch (1969) and Mindlin and Lobach (1971) have all used some type of structured interview to ask patients and family members to express satisfaction and dissatisfaction with their doctors. These studies do not provide information on the individual doctor's performance, however.

Different writers' conceptions regarding outcomes vary with respect to: (1) emphasis on final end results, as opposed to intermediate consequences of medical intervention, (2) long-run versus short-run orientation, and (3) generality versus specific attention to particular diseases or problems.

Counsel

The difference between professional counseling and the kind that is carried on between people under ordinary circumstances is that in therapeutic situations the intention of one of the participants is clearly directed at bringing about a change in relationships and manner of communication (Watzlawick, Beavin, & Jackson, 1967). Basically, the role of the health professional as therapist is to match the individual with the social systems in which he participates. Lennard and Bernstein (1969) describe a therapist as a professional who interacts with other persons, designated as patients or clients, for the purposes of changing them in some beneficial way. Many health professionals, doctors, psychiatrists, nurses, social workers, etc., are called upon to provide this function.

The therapist's mode of treatment has little resemblance to that of most doctors (Crisp, 1970; Kertesz, 1970; Clyne, 1972). In the treatment of patients, the therapist has to rely on his ability to communicate with his patient to determine the nature of the disorder. In a one-to-one situation the therapist questions his patient, listens to him, probes into his patient's feelings and general background and strives to help the patient develop some communication behavior that will help him function more effectively. The therapist constructs a communication situation that will allow the patient to develop an understanding of his own problems (Rogers, 1951; Ruesch, 1961; Sullivan, 1953).

Through the patient's communication behavior, the therapist analyzes and diagnoses the patient's problems. Unlike the general physician, who deals with a patient's physical symptoms, the therapist must deal with "symbolic" symptoms. A person's behavior, or so called "symptoms," usually arises from a need to influence what is perceived as a troublesome environment. In this sense, symptoms are usually indirect, symbolic attempts to communicate (Ruesch & Bateson, 1951).

One of the features of therapeutic communication is that people set aside a period of time for the purpose of communicating about communication in order to become more aware of their own behavior. The skill is to develop an awareness of the appropriate spacing, timing, and selection of one's own messages in reply to the messages of others (Fuller & Quesada, 1973). Ruesch (1961) states:

> The closer the understanding, acknowledgement, and reply of the therapist match the empirical experience of the patient, the more effective therapy becomes. The working hypothesis is based upon the following observations:
> —That understanding is based upon the mutual appreciation of actions and words.
> —That verbal or action signals, if they are to be mutually understood, have to be coded in ways that are intelligible to all.
> —That a reply amplifies, connects, or alters the initial statement of the patient.
> —That such a reply is effective the more it is phrased in the language of the patient. (p. 36)

Traditionally, the therapy process is directed toward changing the patient rather than changing his environment. The mere fact that the person selects himself or is selected for treatment places the major impetus for change on him. The primary question to which therapists have sought an answer is why some people perceive and react to certain stresses as though they were severe, while others experience them as mild. In the past, therapists seeking this answer focused upon the misery a patient created for himself or his internal system. As more and more people seek the services of therapists, many therapists are questioning the individual-defect model and are looking to the patient's environment and his transaction with it for the causes.

As Costello (1972) points out, the most important environmental stresses are those imposed upon man by other men or by man-created social institutions. In this perspective, the role of the therapist is to help an individual understand the stresses of his environment and, if need be, to find ways of changing not only himself but perhaps also the environment. In the early 1960s, some therapists became concerned with the emotional distresses suffered by large groups of people. Some have even called this movement a "psychiatric revolution" (Dumont, 1969). These therapists are concerned with the broader problems of society, such as crime, alcoholism, the needs of the aged, and care for retarded children. Programs for fostering social change, political involvement, and community planning, as well as efforts aimed toward influencing laws and regulations, are but a few of the directions of this movement (Caplan, 1964; Feinberg, 1968).

As an outgrowth of this orientation, communication is being increasingly regarded as a reciprocal process. The emphasis is not on a single message or a single individual, but on the relation between events or individuals (Costello, 1969). The relation involves the receipt of and response to as well as the emission of messages. Verbal utterances, facial expressions, bodily gestures, and the social and cultural context all become a part of the analysis of communication (Mehrabian, 1970; Kelly, 1973; Ekman, 1967). As Birdwhistell (1959, p.104) noted:

> An individual does not communicate; he engages in or becomes part of communication. He may move, or make noises . . . but he does not communicate. In a parallel fashion, he may see, he may hear, smell, taste, or feel—but he does not communicate. In other words, he does not originate communication; he participates in it. Communication as a system, then, is not to be understood on a simple model of action and reaction, however complexly stated. As a system, it is to be comprehended on the transactional level.

This philosophical shift has had some impact on counseling, but more theory-building and research is needed before this perspective will be integrated into the conceptions of the other three purposes served by communication.

Education

For the most part, doctors have not been known to spend time educating their patients and/or the general public. Other health professionals have tried to educate the public in the sensible use of medical care. They have assumed that extensive information campaigns can modify the cultural and social beliefs of the general public that act as a barrier to optimal health care. In addition, for health education to be most effective, it is critical to avoid the view that members of the audience are what

Polgar (1962, p.159) terms "empty vessels." By way of distinction, he argues that the predispositions current in the population need to be taken fully into account in designing health education programs.

THE NATIONAL OPINION RESEARCH CENTER

Since the early 1940s, National Opinion Research Center has conducted surveys to test the effects of educational programs and campaigns on a fairly regular basis (NORC, 1944-1975). Studies have either been intensive examinations of the behavior of individuals in one or two restricted health-related situations or a less intensive coverage of the wide range of health-related phenomena. In most of the studies correlational techniques have provided the basis of inference, and people's knowledge of health facts and attitudes toward health care have served as the major dependent variable under investigation. The evidence reported in the following pages is a general summary of those findings.

GENERAL FINDINGS

Knowledge is generally greatest for those aspects of health which have received the broadest publicity and have been the focus of long and intensive educational campaigns (Seligmann, McGrath, & Pratt, 1957). The more publicity a disease gets because of, for instance, a famous person's affliction with it, an epidemic, or a dramatic development or discovery in connection with it, the more widespread information about it is likely to be (Horn & Waingrow, 1964). These assertions are supported by a considerable body of evidence that the mass media are the primary source of much of what people know about diseases (Hassinger & Anderson, 1964). One cannot assume, however, that the information campaigns are the chief cause of the increased knowledge. Publicity alone will not decide which illness arouses the most public concern, but volume of publicity is an important factor.

Health information is generally aimed at a mass audience, but not all members of this audience are equally good prospects for the educator (Stephenson, 1972). Survey findings, from a descriptive standpoint, distinguish the groups in the population who are poorly informed from those who are relatively well-informed. Families in which the primary income earner is employed in a low-status or farm occupation are considerably less knowledgeable than others. Similarly, persons in low-income families score well below average on indices of health information. Younger adults are much better informed than older adults. The informational level of men is inferior to that of women. Persons residing in the South and in rural areas score below the average for other parts of the country.

While these findings have been used to identify the appropriate targets for intensified educational efforts, there is, of course, a question as to whether the relationship between these variables and the level of knowledge may be a spurious one. As many have noted (Feldman, 1966; Samora, Saunders, & Larson, 1962) when education is controlled, most of the economic and occupational differences disappear, but when occupation or income is controlled, the educational differences still remain. This does not mean that a person's income and occupation are not important, since both are integral to a person's social position, and one's social position substantially influences the extent to which he learns. Still, one can largely account for variations in health knowledge by factors closely related to an individual's educational attainment.

Age differences may also be spuriously inflated by differences in educational attainment. The findings show that a considerable number or adults who are 65 or older have only a grade school education, while in the youngest age group this is relatively rare. In part, therefore, the upward trend in educational attainment accounts for the higher level of information among younger adults. Yet when allowances are made for these educational differences, moderately large differences in knowledge still remain among the age groups. The reasons for this lower level of information among the aged—whether they are less interested in acquiring health information, have less opportunity to become exposed to it, learn less easily than young people, or simply more readily forget what they have learned—has not been clearly established. But the fact that this segment of the public, which is the least healthy, is also the least informed is a finding of some importance.

Women are substantially better informed than men about matters of health. The fact that women are better informed suggests that the broad area of health and illness may be largely a feminine concern. The findings concerning the sex differentials would seem to make sense primarily in terms of corresponding difference in interest. Thus, one could suppose that the key motive for acquiring health information is its immediate personal relevance. Accordingly, individuals who consider themselves to be in poor health, or who show concern about their health, should be among the most knowledgable. Such an expectation contrasts, however, with data on age indicating that older people, who are by and large considerably less healthy than the rest of the population, tend to be less informed than younger people.

Levels of Information and Concern

Among those who say they have seldom been ill and who also express little concern about their health, the proportion having assimilated very little information seems to be only somewhat higher than does the proportion in the remainder of the population. Thus, while the individual's perception of his health status strongly determines his use of physician's services, it seems to have little to do with his acquisition of health information. Persons who have experienced a great deal of illness, and who expresses considerable concern about their health, are not better informed than persons with average health and minimal concern and are only slightly better informed than persons with very good health and minimal concern (Eichhorn & Anderson, 1962).

At the same time, the absence of a substantial relationship between concern over health and knowledgeability implies that learning about disease does not necessarily increase one's anxiety about his health. Those who are relatively well-informed about illness express no greater concern about their health than those who are relatively uninformed. At least on a manifest level, there is certainly no evidence here to support the widely-held belief that knowledge tends to induce a morbid preoccupation with health. Also, not only are both the respondent's present health status and his concern about his personal health substantially unrelated to the amount of health information he has acquired, but the extent of his contact with ill health in the past also appears to have little influence on him. Those who reported that they have suffered from relatively poor health during childhood were only slightly better informed than those who reported a healthy childhood. In the same vein, those who reported considerable illness among other members of their family during their childhood were only slightly superior in their current level of knowledge.

The fact that knowledge about health correlates with age and sex, and particularly with education, suggests that certain types of persons will be well-informed about many different health questions, while others will be generally uninformed. The young woman with a college education is likely to know not only the symptoms of cancer but many other facts about health and illness as well. The elderly man with only a grade school education who knows no symptoms of cancer is also likely to be uninformed on other health matters.

Media Effects

These findings point up perhaps the most difficult problem faced by persons engaged in health education, or indeed in any form of public education: informational materials generally reach and are assimilated by the better educated and more interested groups in the population over and over again, while they miss the very groups who are in the greatest need of them (Hyman & Sheatsley, 1947; Klapper, 1960; Berelson & Steiner, 1964).

What, then, does account for the lower information levels of the less educated groups? A partial answer is suggested by Hovland, Lumsdaine, and Sheffield (1949): Their intellectual ability is less; they do not have the same reserve of related information into which they can fit new facts; and their techniques of learning and remembering are inferior. Another factor is their less frequent and less intensive exposure to the health information available through the mass media.

In each case, the groups who are best informed

already—women, younger adults, and those with highest level of education—are the ones who most often read the health columns and articles in newspapers and magazines and most often listen to radio and television programs about health.

Media Selection

The overlapping use of the major media may also account for the high levels of health information acquired by particular audience groups. The correlation between newspaper and magazine exposure, for example, is particularly high. Different media constitute overlapping, rather than complementary, sources of information, even among those with only a grade school education.

Persons who are handicapped by underdeveloped reading skills might be thought to compensate for this by avid consumption of radio and television health education materials, but the findings do not confirm this.

Almost all studies of the sources of health information agree that the major function of the mass media is instructing the better educated segments of the population. The more poorly educated, who make much less use of these media, appear to rely more often on personal contacts for their information.

For both men and women, the college educated who do not read health articles are still better informed than the less educated persons who do read them. The mere exposure to information does not insure the gaining of knowledge. Thus, even though the less educated may have some interest in health information, they have less potential to acquire knowledge. In contrast, the college educated who read the papers but skip the health columns are far more likely to read magazines, listen to the radio, and watch television. And though they may not concentrate on health information in these media, their greater exposure leads them to absorb some knowledge about illness in spite of their lack of special interest in the subject.

SUMMARY

What difference does it make that some people know more than others? How much better care of their health is taken by those who are better informed about health and disease than by those who are less informed? Unfortunately, until fairly recently we have know very little about the function of information in regulating health-related behavior (Maccoby & Fasquhar, 1975).

The primary goal of health professionals, as now defined, focuses on what they do *to* and *for* the patient. The patient's role in influencing the outcome is not well defined. As Straus (1972) points out, the patient's characteristics and behavior help determine the response of doctors, nurses, and other health professionals toward him. Each patient has a unique personality and his own way of feeling, thinking, believing, and acting. He has unique life experiences shared with a combination of reference groups, whose beliefs, attitudes, values, and customs have significantly influenced his own behavior. Perhaps most significant of all, he has had prior experiences (or no prior experiences) with illness and hospitalization, and from these he has either preconceived expectations or the anxiety of uncertainty, or both. The patient's expectations are learned in and through his communication relationships.

As Mackay (1961, p.24) has pointed out: "The effect of any information . . . is to determine the form of some aspect of the state of readiness or (conditional) orientation of the receiver—to select one such state from a possible range." This makes possible a definition of the *meaning* of a communication, which seems freer from philosophical objections than some others. Briefly, we can define meaning-to-the-receiver as the *selective function* of the communicator on the range of his states of readiness for goal-directed activity, or in short, its *orienting function*. Without going into more detail, we may note that the definitive notion here is neither the *logical structure* of the message per se, nor its *effect* in the receiver, but the relation (orienting) function of which the effect is the exercise.

Communication research may usefully begin to focus on the dynamics by which the health professional and patient establish, maintain, exploit, and/or alter their relationships. Such research would seek to identify those conditions which: (1) determine whether beneficial and facilitating relationships between health professionals and patients

will or will not be established; (2) determine whether health professionals and patients attempt to exploit and/or alter existing relationships; and (3) determine whether existing relationships evolve into long-range functional or dysfunctional relationships.

Whether the subject of investigation is medical education, the health care delivery system, or doctor-patient interaction, a body of theoretical knowledge about health communication is needed. This would seem to require study of specific health-related activities and health care environments in terms of communication and communication *relationships*.

REFERENCES

ARNOLD, R., ADEBONOJO, F., CALLAS, E., CARTE, E., & STEIN, R. Comprehension and compliance with medical instructions in a suburban pediatric practice. *Clinical Pediatrics*, 1970, 9, 48-51.

BERELSON, B., & STEINER, G.A. *Human behavior: An inventory of scientific findings*. New York, Harcourt, Brace, and World, 1964.

BIRD, B.R. *Talking with patients*. Philadelphia and Montreal: J.B. Lippincott, 1955.

BIRDWHISTELL, R.L. Contributions of linguistic-kinesic studies to the understanding of schizophrenia. In A. Auerback (Ed.), *Schizophrenia: An integrated approach*, New York: Ronald, 1959.

BLACKWELL, B. Patient compliance. *New England Journal of Medicine*, 1973, 289, 249-252.

BLOOM, S.W. The process of becoming a physician. *Annals of the American Academy*, 1963, 346, 77-87.

BROWN, J.W., ROBERTSON, L.S., KOSA, J., & ALPERT, J.J. A study of general practice in Massachusetts. *Journal of the American Medical Association*, 1971, 216, 301-306.

CAPLAN, G. *Principles of preventive psychiatry*. New York: Basic Books, 1964.

CLYNE, M.B. The doctor-patient relationship as a diagnostic tool. *Psychiatry in Medicine*, 1972, 3, 343-355.

COE, R.M. *Sociology of medicine*. New York: McGraw-Hill, 1970.

COLLINS, E. Do we really advise the patient? *Journal of the Florida Medical Association*, 1955, 42, 111-115.

COSTELLO, D.E. Communication patterns in family systems. *Nursing Clinics of North America*, 1969, 4, 4, 721-729.

COSTELLO, D.E. Therapeutic transaction: An approach to human communication. In R. Budd and B. Ruben (Eds.), *Approaches to human communication*, New York: Spartan, 1972, 420-435.

CRANE, D. The social potential of the patient: An alternative to the sick role. *Journal of Communication*, 1975, 25, 3, 131-139.

CRISP, A.H. Therapeutic aspects of the doctor-patient relationship. *Psychotherapy and Psychosomatics* 1970, 18, 12-33.

DAVIS, M. Physiological, psychological, and demographic factors in patient compliance with doctors' orders. *Medical Care*, 1968a, 6, 115-122.

DAVIS, M. Variations in patients' compliance with doctors' advice: An empirical analysis of patterns of communication. *American Journal of Public Health*, 1968b, 58, 274-288.

DAVIS, M., & EICKHORN, R. Compliance with medical regimens: A panel study. *Journal of Health and Human Behavior*, 1963, 4, 240-249.

DAVIS, M. Variation in patients' compliance with doctors' orders: Medical practice and doctor-patient interaction. *Psychiatry in Medicine*, 1971, 2, 31-54.

DECASTRO, F. Doctor-patient communication; exploring the effectiveness of care in a primary care clinic. *Clinical Pediatrics*, 1972, 11, 86-87.

DERVIN, B., & HARLOCK, S. Health communication research: The state of the art. Paper presented at the annual meeting of the International Communication Association, Portland, Oregon, 1976.

DONABEDIAN, A., & ROSENFELD, L. Follow-up study of chronically ill patients discharged from hospital. *Journal of Chronic Disease*, 1964, 17, 847-862.

DONABEDIAN, A. Promoting quality through evaluating the process of patient care, *Medical Care*, 1968, 6, 181-202.

DUBOS, R.J. *Man adapting*, New Haven, Conn.: Yale University Press, 1965.

DUMONT, M. *The absurd healer*. New York: Science House, 1969.

EICKHORN, R.L., & ANDERSON, R.M. Changes in personal adjustment to perceived and medically established heart disease: A panel study. *Journal of Health and Human Behavior*, 1962, 3, 242-249.

EKMAN, P. Nonverbal behavior in psychotherapy research. In J. Shlien (Ed.), *Research on psychotherapy, III*, American Psychological Association, 1967.

FEINBERG, G. *The prometheus project*. Garden City, N.Y.: Doubleday, 1968.

FELDMAN, J.J. *The dissemination of health information*. Chicago: Aldine, 1966.

FOX, R. *Experiment perilous: Physicians and patients facing the unknown*. Glencoe, Illinois: The Free Press, 1959.

FRANCIS, V., KORSCH, B., & MORRIS, M. Gaps in doctor-patient communication: Patients' responses to medical advice. *New England Journal of Medicine*, 1969, 280, 535-540.

FREEMON, B., NEGRETE, V., DAVIS, M., & KORSCH, B. Gaps in doctor-patient communication: Doctor-patient interaction analysis. *Pediatrics Research, 1971*, 5, 298-311.

FREUD, S. The dynamics of the transference. In *Collected papers*, Vol. 2, London: Hogarth Press, 1946, 312-322.

FULLER, D.S., & QUESADA, G.M. Communication in medical therapeutics. *Journal of Communication*, 1973, 23, 3, 361-370.

GILLUM, R.F., & BARSKY, A.J. Diagnosis and management of patient noncompliance. *Journal of the American Medical Association*, 1974, 228, 1563-1567.

GOLDEN, J.S., & JOHNSON, G.D. Problems of distortion in doctor-patient communications. *Psychiatry in Medicine*, 1970, 1, 127-149.

GOZZI, E.K., MORRIS, M.J., & KORSCH, B.M. Gaps in doctor-patient communication. *American Journal of Nursing*, 1969, 69, 529-533.

HAGGERTY, R.J., & ROGHMANN, K.J. Noncompliance and self-medication: Two neglected aspects of pediatric pharmacology. *Pediatric Clinics of North America*, 1972, 19, 101-115.

HARPER, D. Patient follow-up of medical advice. A literature review. *Journal of the Kansas Medical Society*, 1971, 72, 265-271.

HASSINGER, E.W., & ANDERSON, T.M. Information and beliefs about heart disease held by the public in five areas of Missouri. *Series in Rural Health, No. 20*, University of Missouri Agricultural Experiment Station, 1964.

HENDERSON, L.J. Physician and patient as a social system. *New England Journal of Medicine*, 1935, 212, 819-823.

HOLLINGSHEAD, A.B. Medical sociology: A brief review. *Health and Society*, 1973, 51, 4, 531-542.

HORN, D., & WAINGROW, S. What changes are occurring in public opinion toward cancer: National public opinion survey. *American Journal of Public Health*, 1964, 54, 431-440.

HOVLAND, C.J., LUMSDAINE, A.A., & SHEFFIELD, F.D. Studies in social psychology in world war II. Vol. 3. *Experiments on mass communication*. Princeton: Princeton University Press, 1949.

HYMAN, H.H., & SHEATSLEY, P.B. Some reasons why information campaigns fail. *Public Opinion Quarterly*, 1947, 11, 412-423.

JACO, E.G. *Patients, physicians, and illness*. 2nd ed. New York: The Free Press, 1972.

JASON, H. The relevance of medical education to medical practice. *Journal of the American Medical Association*, 1970, 212, 2092-2095.

KANE, R., & DEUSCHLE, K. Problems in patient-doctor communication. *Medical Care*, 1967, 5, 260-271.

KELLY, F.D. Paralinguistic indicators of patient's affect: Attitudinal significance of length of communication. *Psychological Reports*, 1973, 32, 1223-1226.

KERTESZ, R. Research on doctor-patient relationship in a general hospital setting. *Psychotherapy and Psychosomatics*, 1970, 18, 50-55.

KLAPPER, J.T. *The effects of mass communication*. Glencoe: Free Press, 1960.

KORSCH, B.M., GOZZI, E.K., & FRANCIS, V. Gaps in doctor-patient interaction and satisfaction. *Pediatrics*, 1969, 42, 855-871.

LENNARD, H.L., & BERNSTEIN, A. *Patterns in human interaction*. San Francisco: Jossey-Bass, 1969.

LEY, P.L. Primacy, rated importance, and the recall of medical statements. *Journal of Health and Social Behavior*, 1972, 13, 311-317.

LEY, P.L., BRADSHAW, P.W., EAVES, D., & WALKER, C.M. A method of increasing patients' recall of information presented by doctors. *Psychological Medicine*, 1973, 3, 217-220.

LUBORSKY, L. Clinicians' judgments of mental health. *Archives of General Psychiatry*, 1962, 7, 401-417.

MACCOBY, N., & FARQUHAR, J.W. Communication for health: Unselling heart disease. *Journal of Communication*, 1975, 25, 3, 114-126.

MACE, D.R. Communication, interviewing, and the physician-patient relationship. In R.H. Coombs and E.E. Vincent (Eds.), *Psychological aspects of medical training*, Springfield, Illinois: Charles C. Thomas, 1971.

MacKAY, D.M. *The science of communication - A Bridge between disciplines*. Keele: University College of North Staffordshire, 1961.

MARSTON, M. Compliance with medical regimens: A review of the literature. *Nursing Research*, 1970, 19, 312-323.

MECHANIC, D. *Medical sociology: A selective view*. New York: The Free Press, 1968.

MEHRABIAN, A. Semantic space for nonverbal behavior. *Journal of Counseling and Clinical Psychology*, 1970, 35, 248-257.

MERRELL, M., & REED, L.J. The epidemiology of health. In I. Galdstone (Ed.), *Social medicine: Its derivations and objectives*. New York: Commonwealth Fund, 1949, 105-110.

MINDLIN, R., & LOBACH, K.S. Consistency and change in choice of medical care for preschool children. *Pediatrics*, 1971, 48, 426-432.

National Opinion Research Center. *Monographs in social research*, Chicago: NORC, 1944-1975.

ORT, R., FORD, A., & LISKE, R. The doctor-patient relationship as described by physicians and medical students. *Journal of Health and Human Behavior*, 1964, 5, 25-34.

PARSONS, T. *The social system*. Glencoe, Illinois: The Free Press, 1951.

POLGAR, S. Health and human behavior: Areas of interest common to the social and medical sciences. *Current Anthropology*, 1962, 3, 159-205.

PRATT, L., SELIGMANN, A.S., & READER, G. Physicians' views on the level of medical information among patients. *American Journal of Public Health*, 1957, 47, 1277-1283.

RICE, C.E., BERGER, D.G., SEWALL, L.G., & LEMKAU, P.V. Measuring social restoration performance in public psychiatric hospitals. *Public Health Report*, 1961, 76, 437-446.

ROGERS, C.R. *Client-centered therapy: Its current practice, implications, and theory*. Boston: Houghton-Mifflin, 1951.

ROSSITER, C.M. Defining "therapeutic communication." *Journal of Communication*, 1975, 25, 3, 127-130.

RUESCH, J., & BATESON, G. *Communication: The matrix of psychiatry*. New York: Norton, 1951.

RUESCH, J. *Therapeutic communication*, New York: Norton, 1961.

SAMORA, J., SAUNDERS, L., & LARSON, R.F. Knowledge about specific diseases in four selected samples. *Journal of Health and Human Behavior*, 1962, 3, 176-185.

SELIGMANN, A.W., McGRATH, N.E., & PRATT, L. Level of medical information among clinic patients, *Journal of Chronic Disease*, 1957, 6, 497-509.

SKIPPER, J.K., MAUKSCH, H.O., & TAGLIACOZZO, D. Some barriers between patients and hospital functionaries. *Nursing Forum*, 1963, 2, 14-23.

SPELMAN, M.S., LEY, P., & JONES, C. How do we improve doctor-patient communications in our hospitals. *World Hospitals*, 1966, 2, 126-134.

STEPHENSON, W. Vergent report: Communication research unit. Unpublished report, Columbia, Missouri: Missouri Regional Medical Program, 1972.

STEVENSON, I. *Medical history-taking*. New York: Paul B. Hoeber, 1960.

STIMSON, G.V. Obeying doctor's orders: A view from the other side. *Social Science and Medicine*, 1974, 8, 97-104.

STRAUS, R. Hospital organization from the viewpoint of patient-centered goals. In B.S. Georgopoulos (Ed.), *Organization research on health institutions*. Ann Arbor, Michigan: University of Michigan, 1972, 203-222.

SULLIVAN, H.S. *The interpersonal theory of psychiatry*. New York: Norton, 1953.

SUSSER, M.W., & WATSON, W. *Sociology in medicine*. 2nd ed. New York: Oxford University Press, 1971.

SZASZ, T.S., & HOLLENDER, M.H. A contribution to the philosophy of medicine: The basic models of the doctor-patient relationship. *Archives of Internal Medicine*, 1956, 97, 585-592.

THAYER, L. On communication and change: Some provocations. Unpublished talk before the 11th Annual Institute in Technical and Organizational Communication, Colorado State University, June 1968.

WATZLAWICK, P., BEAVIN, J., & JACKSON, D. *Pragmatics of human communication*. New York: Norton, 1967.

World Health Organization. *The first ten years of the world health organization*. Geneva, Switzerland: WHO, 1958.

RURAL HEALTH COMMUNICATION

CURT LATHAM
North Vancouver,
British Columbia

GAIL M. MARTIN
Simon Fraser University

Systems theory provides a model useful for describing the characteristics of healthy functioning in a biological organism and a human community. Communication is central in the process of maintenance and adaptation of the system-environment relationship which occurs between the individual and his community, and between community and the larger world environment. Health communication involves the modulation, direction, and careful introduction of environmental change in such a way as to maximize the ability of the individual and his community to adapt successfully. The conclusion as to the choice of health care workers, use of media, and methods of health communication suggested by the model developed, support the recommendations of experienced health-care workers from various parts of the globe.

The largest proportion of the world's population lives a rural, agrarian life with access to the least amount of resources through the poorest transportation and communications facilities. It is now well recognized in both the East and the West, and in international organizations, that the solution to medical and health needs in rural areas does not lie in the transplanting of high cost, high-technology metropolitan systems with disproportionate and often inappropriate use of medical personnel. Rather, the solution lies in the development of decentralized community health models in which the hierarchy of care and responsibility begins at the level of the individual and his immediate, supportive culture.

In this model, health workers are members of the communities to be served, providing the critical nexus through which the health care system can become an integral part of the indigenous culture instead of an alien imposition. Training programs for these health care workers thus involve not only instruction in preventive measures in sanitation, nutrition, and well-baby care, but also dialogue in order to mutually discover appropriate ways to integrate the new learning into the ongoing way of life of his or her people.

This is the communications challenge involved in the adaptation of any sophisticated system—finding the means to translate it into the daily idiom of a people such that it becomes an organic part of the social, cultural, and economic fabric, changing with and being itself changed by the society of which it becomes a part. This approach—when complemented by a locally-controlled communications system which utilizes simple technology and moves information rather than expensive personnel—could promote the physical and mental health of a community and this is survival in a total sense. It is precisely to such conjoint models that we have been committed since our work began in 1967.

Rural areas, in our formulation, include agrarian, hunting, and fishing communities, not only in developing countries, but also any such community in North America where the culture is clearly distinct from Western industrialized society, as with Eskimos and Indians, for example. The most useful conceptualization in this work for us has come from the ecological models of systems theory, based on the analysis and observation of the behavior of biological systems. Without becoming lost in the philosophical niceties of system theories, we use elements of them as a heuristic model generative of useful, practical insights. From a system perspective, the two elements—*health* and *communication*—become, if not indistinguishable in theory, at least inseparable in practice.

A SYSTEMS MODEL OF HEALTH

We conceptualize the field of health care as a system of hierarchical components. Elements of such a system range from molecular levels of influence centering on the *person* as a focal adjustive point in the system, to higher levels of organization—the family, community, society, nation, or species as a whole. Rules of information exchanges between these levels constitute feedback loops that are both spatially and temporally related. Health is seen as a system of resistances and tolerances within the individual. These feedback loops enable the individual to function internally—as a biosocial organism—and externally—as a social being in relation to his environment (Latham, 1976).

The sum of each of these components—or subsystems—in the person, plus their interactions, constitute the organization of the system and produce the state of harmonious and dynamic equilibrium that characterizes a properly functioning system. This is the state referred to by the concept of *health*. To some extent this must be qualified, in that there is a value judgment being made—an ethical one. We are more or less designating what *health* is in terms of an *ideal* level of balance. We are assuming that each of these component systems, on each level, must be intact and functioning, and all of the feedback loops must be free from distraction and impedance to signal flow. That's a very technical explanation, but a simple example is the effect of alcohol or drugs on the perception of environmental threat. What we are looking at in terms of illness is a perturbation or disturbance of this functioning which tends to disrupt and/or destroy the organism. As René Dubos (1965) has noted:

> The words health and disease are meaningful only when defined in terms of a given person functioning in a given physical and social environment. The nearest approach to health is a physical and mental state fairly free of discomfort and pain, which permits the person concerned to function as effectively and as long as possible in the environment where chance or choice has placed him. (p. 351)

Therapy, therefore, is a point of intervention arbitrarily chosen as a focus to try to readjust or restabilize the system to proper functioning. This puts the traditional views of therapy and health in much more difficult perspective. One realizes, for instance, that in treating a specific illness or a specific condition such as a high risk pregnancy, the treatment itself may produce serious consequences in adjacent parts of the social system. For example, the fact you may deliver high input technology, or you raise expectations of level of care for one patient, has very serious disruptions for another patient who perhaps cannot get that care. Or the level of treatment may impose a population growth factor on the population that is dying of some particular epidemic, and the population may then overgrow its food supply. Conventional ways of looking at problems—from a very narrow perspective in a specific etiology—are not compatible with the systems view of health care and prevention. The old "drug for a bug" mentality will not work.

CHANGE

Man exists on many levels, but the point at which therapy enters is at the level of the individual person. The *person* is important here because he or she is the central point for making decisions. Although man relates to multiple levels of function, from his subcellular chemistry to his role in a social process, he is most adaptive and amenable to change in his role as a free-thinking and perceptive individual. Therapy aimed at controlling the perturbations of the illness within a system, will, therefore, focus on an individual level. Provision of choice of action, with a data base defining illness and its consequences, allows the *person* to take action within the community, reestablishing all its subsystems toward a condition of health. Health communication thereby provides options and information, but the *person* makes a decision in management. This *contractual model* (Veatch, 1972, p. 56) is an ethically-oriented approach, aimed at maximizing the power of individuals to relate outside information, including technical aid, to problems facing a given culture.

Human perceptions are governed by an individual's past and cultural beliefs, some of which are based on fear and ignorance. Only within the historical perspective of his own life, and filtered through his own shadowy experiences, can medical advances and enrichment of biologic survival be made possible. Imposition of change from outside this context, whether of sophisticated health services, revolutionary methods of food production, improved sanitation and water systems or the like, too often fail. They do not involve the individual in a way that is meaningful in terms of his past. To survive under the pressure of change, he breaks with tradition and becomes ruthless and dependent, no longer a decision-maker and master of his lifestyle but a slave to it.

As the systems model makes clear, change in terms of adjustment and growth can be incorporated by the organism, if it is gradual and perceived within an historical perspective—in terms of an individual's lifestyle and personal history, as well as in terms of cultural history and lifestyle of the community as a whole. Change is destructive and disease-generating, however, if it is produced on a rapid, overwhelming basis, as so often happens in primitive communities under the influence of tourism, technological change, massive environmental damage, and population overgrowth. These are all major influences in communities undergoing the rapid transition from peasant, isolated, mystical communities to modern, industrial nations.

Adjustments that are made too rapidly cause tremendous loss of individual levels of adjustment, particularly social interaction. These disturbed social interactions lead to destruction of health at levels below the level of the *person*, such as typical psychosomatic adjustments resulting in apathy, indolence, and lassitude which accompany malnutrition, anemia, and lowered resistances to communicable illness. Witness the Indian, who is rendered sick by living on a reservation:

A very large percentage of illnesses are the expressions of inadequate responses to the environment; they include in varying proportions effects that are directly caused by physiochemical forces and effects that are primarily determined by the highly individual interpretation the person puts on the events of the external world. (Dubos, 1965, p. 268)

HEALTH CARE IN PRIMITIVE CULTURES

If we can somehow control the rate of change, so that the individual has time to perceive the change, its repercussions, and its relevance for him in his community—and has time to make the necessary adaptations, and adjustment—and if we can provide him with intelligent methods of doing so, we have taken a major step toward the health of that individual himself or herself, and in relation to his or her community. We must always remember in assessing effects of change that the individual is not being approached in the traditional, Western allopathic sense of one-to-one medicine. Rather, each individual is, in fact, regarded and is treated as a component of a whole community or whole society.

As we said, a sense of powerlessness, hopelessness, and alienation develops in the face of overwhelming change. We can modulate and regulate change by providing the individual with adequate data. That is, in fact, what the task of the health or communications team will be in the future.

Reaching these people can, of course, be done only through the idiom of their own culture. This may involve interactions with traditional figures, such as tribal leaders, or more likely shamans. The individual must be reached through the kinds of cultural exchanges that he or she is familiar with. As a health worker in Samoa observed (Babbie, 1975):

There's one other problem . . . that anybody designing the program really should be aware of, and that is that Western medicine never goes into an area where there's not already something being done to meet the same problem . . . an effort has been made for years to meet that need and there is a danger to just setting that aside and saying, "we'll do it this way." In many areas two systems of medicine are being practiced every day, side by side . . . The person who designs the system . . . really ought to know what goes on in the minds of the people he's dealing with. (p. 44)

We are not mandating a system; we are, in fact, providing rational choice. We are, further, trying to increase the amount of data and choice and, thereby, increase the individual's involvement in his community at a social level. This, of course, demands that the health interventionist be primarily an educator. He must be able to explain medical choices and procedures in a language that the patient can understand. This is a process of sharpening the levels of prediction and outcome of prognosis, and giving the individual a choice between what happens to him by default and what may happen to him by design.

The British Columbia Program

Training allied health workers who are native Indians to care for expectant Indian mothers and their newborn has produced dramatic results in British Columbia. With such workers as casefinders and health communicators, Indian women are availing themselves of health services in a more total way, including self-assessment, and prevention of high risk complications. The British Columbia Perinatal Programme has designed a comprehensive set of clinical records drawn from questionnaires of sociocultural and nutritional status which are completed by Indian women themselves. Analysis of these records provides continuing feedback for instruction at the level of the village outpost and the native health workers. Since such workers are hired by and responsible to band councils, they serve as intermediaries for change and lobbyists for the health status of the community as a whole.

There are four steps generally recognized in the planning of educational and health services (Fry & Ferndale, 1972): (1) collection and evaluation of data through an epidemiological research and evaluation component; (2) development of a policy and planning unit; (3) establishment of a training organization for all levels of health manpower; and (4) creation of a service organization with total outreach (p. 243).

It is with the service organization of total outreach that we are primarily concerned in this paper. We are talking about paramedical auxiliaries and health personnel who are chosen, in fact, from the community hierarchy. These will be the change agents at the level of primary care, at the level of the actual community. Such persons would presumably operate in local aid stations or dispensaries.

In summary, when planning for health care systems for primitive communities one must take cog-

nizance of the five factors: (1) excessive fertility levels, (2) limited economic resources, (3) a paucity of educational resources and trained manpower, (4) the pattern of disease and malnutrition, and (5) the cultural pattern of traditional societies (Fry & Ferndale, 1972, p. 243).

If we are to act as change agents, we have to understand man holistically in his concept of community, both at the level of a psycho-biological organism, and in terms of the cultural and social levels of organization he has within his environment. We must understand the pressures of diseases, malnutrition, and limited economic resources that affect most vitally the rural communities. We need to apply our concept as change agents in our approach to the *person* by giving him more rational, meaningful choices in the deliberation of his life.

RURAL HEALTH FROM A COMMUNICATION PERSPECTIVE

The problems encountered in rural health communication provoke a reexamination of assumptions and principles concerning the general role of communication in development.

We are dealing here with the problem of the introduction, imposition, and/or communication of a Western system of health care onto a non-Western community or group of people. The Western system of medicine grows out of a societal tradition that includes a constellation of values, expectations in interprofessional relationships, and a host of techniques, traditions and beliefs that are entirely alien to those held by the community where the system of medicine is imposed or introduced.

Health communication presents a subset of the larger set of problems involved in change or modernization when introduced to traditional, largely agrarian patterns of life. The basic perspective from which decisions about development have been made in the past has been primarily *economic*. Education, for example, was viewed as an indispensable means to develop a literate population capable of working in factories, and thus able to raise the gross national product. Traditional agricultural patterns were shifted in the interest of increasing greater output; population control was sold as a step in increasing the statistics on per capita income.

This one-sided economic perspective resulted, as nearly everyone acknowledges now, in short-term changes that brought about large-scale social and cultural disruptions—displaced rural populations, for example, huddled together in urban slums that provide worse living conditions than the people had experienced before. Any intervention that fails in this way to take into account the potential repercussions of change on the entire system always brings forth alterations that are costly in the long run.

We have, in short, transferred the methodologies by which we are destroying our own ecology onto other people's societies and environment. As Bateson (1972) expresses it:

Courses which offered short-term advantage have been adopted, have become rigidly programmed, and have begun to prove disastrous over longer time. This is the paradigm for extinction by way of loss of flexibility. And this paradigm is more surely lethal when the courses of action are chosen in order to maximize single variables [e.g., short-term economic gain]. (p. 501)

The first corollary that follows from this is that no outsider is in any position to assess the possible repercussions of his intervention on a system (a community) that he does not know. He cannot anticipate the possible reverberations of his actions on the structures and patterns of the society because he does not know what they are to begin with, what is related to what, and what other parts of the system the part he intends to alter will affect most closely.

The first task the would-be health interventionist has to perform, therefore, is to find a native communicator—someone who is part of the community—to identify the key structures and patterns with which he will be dealing. These include kinship structures, status and authority patterns, property ownership arrangements, child-rearing patterns, and so on. An investigation into the anthropology of the community is advocated. A systems view of change leads to the unavoidable conclusion that successful health intervention requires, first of all, as thorough an understanding of the functioning of the system as can possibly be obtained. Without this knowledge, one is acting, quite literally, in ignorance of what one is really doing.

One could, for example, launch an advertising campaign as the Nestlé company did in recent years in Africa, extolling the virtues of a powdered milk formula for babies as being superior to mother's milk. The African women, lacking the alternative sources of information and the relatively sophisticated skepticism of North American and European women, took the ad literally. The result: a number of African babies died of malnutrition, and Nestlé faces a common action lawsuit.

Doubtless this example illustrates the validity of the preoccupations of so much of mass media communication research over the past years: Nestlé's advertising managers know how to persuade, change attitudes and behaviors and produce "effective" messages. From a systems point of view, such manipulative use of media to short-term purposive ends can be clearly seen as exploitative and destructive.

It is not so readily apparent, however, that apparently well-meaning communications—such as those involved in health education—can be equally destructive and exploitative if they too are short-term, goal-oriented, and divorced from an understanding of the cultural complex they will affect. Infant care classes for young mothers aimed at improving cleanliness and nutrition for the newborn illustrate the point. In some cultures, for example, infant care is traditionally the prerogative of the grandmother, whose status, authority, and self-worth in the social structure is tied up with being the one who hands on the traditional know-how for baby care.

This not uncommon example illustrates, among other things, how communication could succeed and yet fail. The patterns of nutrition and cleanliness will not change, because the young mother is in no position to change them. Secondly, if she tries, the reverberations sent through the social structure will so disturb the patterns within which the young and the older woman are accustomed to functioning, that one or both of them may be rendered ill or so unsettled that the baby's health will be affected as much or more than by the original sanitation and nutrition problems.

It seems that we have recognized these things in retrospect and belatedly. A variety of projects under various auspices have tried to use native health workers, or to employ folk communications patterns. But these efforts are always seen as adjuncts to the preoccupation with making more effective messages. They are not seen as necessary corollaries of a holistic understanding of the functioning of social systems, and of the integral role communications plays in maintaining healthy functioning.

Systems

From the systems view, it is easy to see that communication is not just one more facet of study—something that behaves and can be studied independently of social, political, and economic structures. As the distinguished biologist C.H. Waddington (1968) put it, life itself is defined nowadays in communication terms: "A system is living if it encodes hereditarily transmittable information, if this information sometimes suffers alterations, and if the altered information is then transmitted" (p. 3).

In a social system, the locus for storing, altering, and transmitting of information is the individual human consciousness or mind. The *person* is the focus of communication. He or she is the user of language, the consciousness that is aware of the values, traditions, and goals that direct the traditional and current life of the people of his or her community. In the mind dwells the remembrance of the personal past and of the community's past, and the anticipations of the future. So it is in communication with the individual human beings that the community is educated, or changed, or made aware of whatever alternatives one may wish to present for the conduct of their lives. We shall be able to influence that individual little, or none at all, if we do not speak his or her language, are not aware of the significant others who influence his attitudes and decisions, or if our intended messages contradict or otherwise conflict with ideas and practices critical to his continued harmonious existence in the milieu that is his environment. Understanding the interdependence of the person and his environment is critical to communication thought.

Diffusion

The classic model of the diffusion of innovation presupposes a discrete, atomistic sort of society in which the only relationships of interest are those assumed to be pertinent to change in behavior. Only later has it occurred to us that adoption of new methods is positively and consistently related to income and educational level, social prestige, and exposure to mass media, which means that responsiveness to change is directly related to an individual's position in the power structure. Advanced communications technology and professionally designed messages will not change the behavior of someone whose position in the social hierarchy makes it impossible for him to change (Beltran, 1975, p. 190).

Mass Media

This brings us to the fallacy of the concept of the "mass" media. Again, from a systems point of view, the idea that has occupied so much work in communication and development becomes an empty concept. There are no mass audiences: there are only individual human consciousnesses receiving what they can of a message in the context of the values, attitudes, and objectives that are theirs *as a function* of their membership in a particular culture at a particular time in a particular place. What the individual can do about a message is also a function of his place in a cultural, political, social, and economic context. There is no way to deal with any entities but individual human beings. The individual human consciousness remains the locus for the storing, alteration and transmission of the information that informs and forms a culture and a social group.

Change Agents

In practical terms, this suggests the value of choosing carefully those people who are best positioned to be effective change agents. This means not simply selecting them for training courses so they can be white-coated Western health workers, but working with them to learn from and with them what techniques and methods will be least disruptive and most effective.

Choosing the appropriate people with which to work involves a constellation of factors that have to be identified in the early anthropological research we spoke of earlier. Among the Indians of the British Columbia coast, for example, one cannot ever assume that the elected chief is the man with real authority in the village. Separating out the *actual* lines of status and power from the *apparent* ones that are identified through Western-style, political elections can be a time-consuming and difficult business. For example, in ex-colonial nations—particularly in rural areas—parliamentary-style political arrangements are often superficial additions that only mask the traditional power structures. Superimposed on those are, of course, the health bureaucracies and the nodes of power which must be included and dealt with sensitively in any health communication program. As a health worker (Babbie, 1973) observed of conditions in American Samoa, Guam, and the Hawaiian outer islands, any team has to work

> through leaders and managers in Health Services rather than through field personnel (health aides, medical officers). Partly because I'm not terribly sure if they (field personnel) will understand what it is you're really after and partly because the managers and leaders will make decisions anyway. (p. 42)

The practical corollary of working within the existing culture calls also for ingenuity in using the communications media that are the local folk art. For example, a child care nutrition program in Tanzania, run by Tanzanian medical personnel, uses as visual aids sculptures by the region's famous Makonde carvers. Three statues depicting three different types of children are used. Each holds an empty bowl. One child is fat, healthy; another is thin; the third is emaciated, with the bloated stomach of the final stages of malnutrition. Into each statue's bowl the health educator places the kind of food that produces the condition, pointing out to the responsible adult the relationship between the food and the sickness or health of the infant. As an educational and communications tool, the system is elegant in its simplicity and proximity to the culture of the individuals concerned. (However elegant the communication, one assumes that health educators have made sure that the foods required for good nutrition are available to the people of the region. Information is hardly usable by people who have no access to the means of acting upon it.)

As Eapen (1976) has commented in giving a critique of India's Satellite Instruction Television Experiment (SITE):

> There is a great need for the research and evaluation of potential folk media roles in bringing about desirable social change. These media are comparatively cheap. They do not have to be imported and therefore involve no foreign exchange. They belong to the community and not to individuals, state or private/public industry. The wiser use of folk media for community development would indirectly encourage local cultures instead of ruining them. They avoid the threats of cultural colonialism and foreign ideological domination. Local talent and localized messages, moreover, have more credibility than those centralized ones now emanating from state capitals. (p. 25)

Change in Rural Environments

Disappointed advocates of rural change have, from time to time, pointed their finger at their hoped-for target populations, labeling them as indolent, recalcitrant, ignorant, or whatever epithet seemed to explain their unwillingness to change, and to excuse the would-be change agent's failure. The description of the community may be, for example, "entrenched conservative peasant culture."

In systems terms, such labeling becomes meaningless. All behavior is essentially conservative. The primary objective of the system is to maintain itself in existence, to preserve its identity. Any change in response to changing environmental conditions is in the interests of maintaining and conserving the stability of the system. The sine qua non for such change in the service of stability is the perception by the organism of the changing environmental conditions, and of the implications for its own adjustment and adaptation to that change. Those who would introduce change into a rural agrarian community are up against the fact that they are dealing with other human beings who will be motivated to change their own and their group's behavior only when they perceive on their own terms, and in the context of their own structures, the need for change—and its relevance for their continued survival as a community and as individuals.

Hence we come full circle, to the original observation on the absolute necessity for close and painstaking attention to the structures and patterns of the community with which we wish to deal.

Without elaborate knowledge of its relationships and codes, we cannot translate desirable change into language that conveys to the people that it is desirable and to their advantage in survival terms.

The communities with which we are concerned are characterized by rather rigid structures, appropriate to the community for its existence within a limited environmental range under relatively unvarying conditions. Then this stable and limited system is assaulted from without by the demands of modernization; it is impinged upon by demands to change its primitive agricultural (or hunting or fishing or husbandry) technologies for more advanced ones, its age-old methods for streamlined ones. In the process, the one-variable proponents of economic progress conceive the entrenched social hierarchy or religious ceremony and belief to be in the way of progress. The village elder, for example, may refuse to countenance the introduction of a tractor into the fields, most of which belong to his family. He does not understand the tractor's usefulness. He is afraid of change. He is intuitively aware, in all probability, that it will destroy the work patterns, and hence roles and status, of his sons, nephews, and brothers. He realizes, again perhaps unconsciously, that the machine places requirements for operation, maintenance, and fueling that are alien to anything he or his group knows how to cope with.

The apostles of development decide that the elder, standing in the way of greater efficiency in feeding the hungry, must be unseated from his position of authority if modernization is to take place. To place a tractor, a social and familial system is unnecessarily destroyed, and the villages' existing level of efficiency is undermined. Undoubtedly, there is a value question here, and the wise solution is not always obvious. But the proponents of intermediate technology recognize that, for many reasons, a plow might be the preferable choice to the tractor. In human and community terms, the lesser nature of the disruption—the possibility of introducing moderate change without radical unsettling of structures and patterns—is intuitively obvious and experientially demonstrable.

Media

Similar principles of intermediate technology apply to the choice of communication media. Mention has already been made of the use of folk media and of the fallacy of thinking in terms of mass media. The conventional media have, however, been recruited in the service of rural education on an alarming scale, and invariably with the same results: in American Samoa they were labeled as cultural genocide; in Niger the children refuse to sing in their native languages and use only French, which their parents cannot understand. As Eapen (1976) comments:

> The cancerous growth of mass media may be an index of development, but it need not be a sign of good health. (p. 25)

Our experience indicates that health communication media in a development setting must have several characteristics, none of which are met by *conventional* television and radio:

1. They must be simple enough to operate and to program that they can be used by the people themselves in their own idiom and for their own purposes.
2. They must permit access to information at the time when the need arises in the community, i.e., interactive, permitting inquiry and immediate response.
3. They must not reinforce the exploitative patterns of center to periphery that have tended to keep rural areas in poverty and backwardness, i.e., they should promote communication among villages of the rural area rather than one-way reception from the urban centers.

The two-way radio sets pioneered for the Australian Flying Doctor Service, and adapted for use in Nigeria, Kenya, and Canada, fulfill the technical requirements. Located in a village in such a way that general access is possible, manned by personnel sensitive to the nature of the health communication task, they can be valuable adjuncts in bringing the benefits of health knowledge and technique to deprived areas.

CONCLUSION

We have concentrated in this paper on the basic level of health care—the individual human being in his family and community relationships. Obviously, sophisticated health care delivery systems operate at the higher levels of district medical care, urban specialization, and even super specialization (Fry & Ferndale, 1972) Communication techniques can be invaluable in bringing these higher levels of expertise to rural settlements, and, as we have pointed out, some of the basic and simple ones can be of great help in this effort.

In the main, however, at present we are concerned with bringing the basic elements of sanitation and health information that will, for example, cut the high incidence of bilharzia among children in Africa. The thrust of the paper was that we abandon the one-variable cause-and-effect models in our practice of medicine, our design of research, and our development of objectives. Instead, we suggest the more difficult task of taking a holistic diagnostic, research, and methodological approach to health. Health exists in the context of a functioning community, responding as best as it can, with its present level of information, to the unavoidable demands of change that are being made upon it. Health is not just concerned with the prevention of disease, but with the promotion and preservation of total community well-being.

The individual human being is the locus of consciousness, and thus of change. Giving him the information he needs to understand what he must do for his own and his community's continued healthy functioning is the central concept. The need for careful anthropological research, attention to language, and choice of media, flow from that premise. Paolo Freire has expressed it this way:

> Information for technification [communication for adoption of innovations] can lead peasants to genuine and emancipatory development only if it is accompanied by information for "conscientization" [communication to foster free and creative awareness of the physical and sociocultural reality and of one's own potentialities to alter it in the direction of overall human enhancement and social justice]. (translated by Beltran, 1975, p. 191)

Our effort has been directed toward elaborating on what is involved in such an objective, and sketching some of the practical ramifications for health communication in attempting to achieve it.

REFERENCES

BABBIE, S. *Medical communication requirements: U.S. Pacific*. Springfield, Va.: National Technical Information Service, U.S. Department of Commerce, 1973.

BATESON, G. *Steps to an ecology of mind*. New York: Ballantyne, 1972.

BELTRAN, L.R. Research ideologies in conflict. *Journal of Communication*, 1975, 15, 187-193.

DUBOS, R. *Man adapting*. New Haven: Yale University Press, 1965.

DUBOS, R. *Man, medicine and environment*. New York: Mentor, 1969.

EAPEN, K.E. SITE: A Critique. *Intermedia*, 1976, 3, 24-25.

FRY, J., & FERNDALE, N.A. (Eds.) *International medical care*. Oxford: Medical and Technical Publishing, 1972.

LATHAM, C. Getting it together: Health care in a rural community. *Canadian Family Physician*, June 1976, 88-93.

MARTIN, G.M. Raven: "Intermediate" communications technology and rural isolation. In D. Theall and G. Robinson (Eds.) *Studies in Canadian communications*. Montreal: McGill, 1975, 163-174.

VEATCH, R.M. *Medical opinion*, 1972, 8, 56.

WADDINGTON, C.H. (Ed.) *Towards a theoretical biology*. Chicago, Aldine: 1968.

THE ROLE OF OPINION LEADERSHIP IN A
CARDIOVASCULAR HEALTH EDUCATION CAMPAIGN[1]

ANTHONY J. MEYER, NATHAN MACCOBY, and JOHN W. FARQUHAR
Stanford University

Opinion leadership was measured as it occurred during a major heart disease prevention field experiment in three California communities, each with a population of about 15,000. It was hypothesized that a risk-reduction intervention strategy which utilized mass media, plus change agent instruction, would generate more extensive opinion leadership than would an intervention solely consisting of mass media. Random samples of subjects were selected from cohorts of subjects participating in the larger field experiment to represent various treatments. These subjects were interviewed to assess their extent of opinion leadership. In addition, the impact of opinion leadership was assessed by interviewing random samples of persons nominated as having been talked with about heart disease. The hypothesis was confirmed. Moreover, the data suggest that opinion leadership played a major role in the diffusion of heart disease information during the larger field experiment.

Premature cardiovascular disease, principally coronary heart disease and stroke, has reached epidemic proportions in industrialized countries. In the United States, for example, diseases of the heart and blood vessels effect more deaths than any other cause; in 1972, over one million people died of such diseases and over 28 million had some type of cardiovascular disease (American Heart Association, 1975). Moreover, many of the precursors of cardiovascular disease are, or implicate, health-related behaviors associated with the affluence of Western industrialized societies. For example, cigarette smoking, elevated plasma cholesterol, and hypertension have been identified as principal risk factors (Intersociety Commission, 1970). Both cholesterol and blood pressure are strongly influenced by relative body weight (Blackburn, 1974) and are responsive to the behavioral factors of diet (Keys, Anderson, & Grande, 1965) and physical activity (Fox & Haskell, 1968) Thus a diet high in saturated fat and cholesterol, cigarette smoking, being overweight, and sedentary living habits severely resistant to change, are well established indicators of the risk of premature cardiovascular disease.

Clearly, community-wide reduction of premature cardiovascular disease through the modification of high risk behavior requires a "counter-epidemic" of information, public opinion, and skills-training of great magnitude. Indeed, if entire communities are to be reached in a cardiovascular health education campaign, networks of opinion leaders in a multistep flow of information and influence are likely to play a critical role. This study examines the role of informal face-to-face communication, specifically of opinion leadership, in one such cardiovascular health campaign conducted by the Stanford Heart Disease Prevention Program (SHDPP).

OPINION LEADERSHIP, MEDIA, AND HEALTH CAMPAIGNS

The role of opinion leadership in conjunction with formal campaign efforts has clearly had importance in other areas of public health and preventive medicine. The *Mtu ni Afya* (Man is Health) and *Chabula ni Uhai* (Food is Life) campaigns in Tanzania have applied the radio listening group strategy, commonly associated with the agricultural extension "Farm Forum" program in Canada and India, to the problems of basic health, sanitation, insect control, and nutrition (Hall & Dodds, 1974; Hall & Zikambona, 1974; Mahai et al., 1975).

Although evaluation of these campaigns is not yet complete, data indicating major achievements have been reported. For example, in *Mtu ni Afya*, between 1.5 and 2 million Tanzanians were enrolled in radio listening groups and hundreds of thousands of latrines were constructed (Hall & Zikambana, 1974). These data imply that a fairly intense informal exchange of information and influence took place during these campaigns, particularly stemming from the activities of the listening groups.

In the United States, there has been similar indirect evidence of the importance of opinion leadership to public health campaigns. Campaigns to fluoridate city water supplies have often been successfully opposed. Crain and Rosenthal (1966) identify the opposition as an organized minority, and conclude that fluoridation can be adopted only by cities in which political support is sufficient "to offset the virulent opposition of a minority of ordinary citizens, and only when it is possible to keep bounds on the level of public discussion so that the argument does not escalate into a confused debate involving large numbers of the general public" (p. 174).

During the Salk polio vaccination campaign, more than half the targeted persons had not been vaccinated 18 months after the initiation of the program. Glasser (1958) reports that this slower-than-hoped-for progress, in an otherwise excellent campaign, was not due to public resistance to the vaccination, but to lack of definite positive influence of the type that comes from neighbors, relatives, and friends. He concludes that "those already vaccinated are the most effective protagonists for further vaccinations," and that informal communication would be the most direct method of accelerating the program (Glasser, 1958, p. 145).

Unfortunately, while the importance of opinion leadership has been suggested and indirectly documented in the evaluation of such campaigns, its exact character and extent has not been clearly identified. Perhaps the most salient example of this is the study of a family planning campaign in Taichung, Taiwan (Freedman & Takeshita, 1969), which in many ways is a precursor of the SHDPP cardiovascular health campaign. Over 2,300 *lins* (small neighborhoods of from 20 to 30 families) in Taichung were randomly assigned to two major

treatment conditions and control. Some *lins* were blanketed through face-to-face, household-to-household persuasion efforts by health auxiliaries with a poster campaign and intermittent use of other mass media. Other *lins* were covered by a direct mail campaign in addition to the poster-media effort. Control *lins* received only the usual government program. Moreover, Taichung was divided into three "density sectors," one sector receiving the most intense treatment in a greater proportion of *lins* than in a second sector, and the second sector in a greater proportion of lins than in the third sector. Freedman and Takeshita (1969) report that the face-to-face plus media treatment achieved better results than did either the direct mail or the usual government program. Less obviously predictable, however, were three other findings: (1) during the entire two years of campaigning, the face-to-face plus media treatment achieved better results in the high density sector than in the other sectors; (2) during the second year of the study, the direct mail and government program conditions experienced a 100 percent increase in acceptance of family planning techniques per 100 married women aged 20-39; and (3) greatest improvement in the direct mail and government program conditions took place in the high density sector (Freedman & Takeshita, 1969, p. 126). These findings are perhaps best understood as the result of the informal exchange of information and influence, taking place most intensely in the sector with the greatest proportion of intensely treated *lins*. Thus the Taichung study clearly demonstrates the importance of opinion leadership in health campaigns, and it indicates that the occurrence and efficacy of opinion leadership depends upon the magnitude of treatment in a given area. The Taichung evaluation, however, did not directly measure the extent of opinion leadership so generated.

Between 1972 and 1975, SHDPP conducted a field experiment in three northern California agricultural communities of approximately 15,000 population in order to study the modification of cardiovascular disease risk factors through community education. In all three communities, a baseline survey and three annual follow-up surveys were conducted among a random sample of individuals between the ages of 35 and 59 to assess

TABLE 1
Mean Risk Score at Baseline (0) and Percent Change
from Baseline at 1, 2, and 3 Follow-up Surveys*

Total Participants

	0	1	2	3
Tracy (n=365)	.081	+ 8.7	+ 6.3	+ 2.3
Gilroy (n=363)	.076	- 3.0	-17.7	- 8.4
Watsonville reconstituted (n=385)	.093	- 5.8	-16.1	-14.8
Watsonville (n=385)	.091	-12.3	-17.9	-16.5

High Risk Participants

	0	1	2	3
Tracy (n=90)	.176	+ 5.7	- 2.3	- 8.0
Gilroy (n=85)	.161	- 8.1	-25.5	-16.1
Watsonville randomized control (n=37)	.199	-11.6	-25.6	-23.1
Watsonville intensive instruction (n=67)	.176	-27.8	-30.1	-29.0

*The groups presented here consist of individuals who attended baseline and all three annual follow-up surveys.

FIGURE 1
Percent Change from Baseline (0) in Risk of Coronary Heart Disease
After 1, 2, and 3 Annual Follow-up Surveys

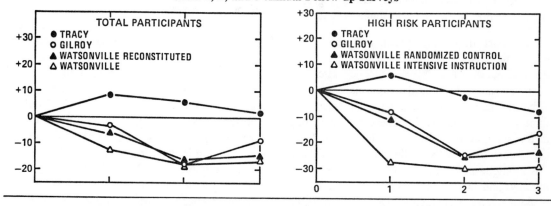

---

the effects of the campaign. In Gilroy and Watsonville, an extensive mass media campaign was conducted for two years, and maintained at a lower level of intensity during a third year. A broad range of media materials was utilized, including over 150 radio and television spots, several hours of radio and television programming, weekly newspaper columns, newspaper advertisements and stories, billboards, bus posters, and printed material sent via direct mail to persons in the random sample selected for the surveys. In Watsonville, this media effort was supplemented with change-agent instruction in risk-reduction. Such instruction was administered to a randomly selected two-thirds of the top quartile at risk in the random survey sample. The change agent instruction took place primarily during the final four months of the first-year campaign effort, and consisted of ten 1-to-3-hour group or home classes related to dietary modification, weight loss, smoking cessation, and increase of physical activity. This type of instruction was maintained at a lower level during the second year of the campaign. In a third community, Tracy, no campaign was conducted. A full discussion of design, methods, and data analysis pertaining to the three-community study are available elsewhere (Meyer & Henderson, 1974; Maccoby & Farquhar, 1975; Farquhar et al., 1976; Meyer et al., 1976).

Table 1 and Figure 1 indicate the major results of this study over three years in terms of percent change for a single summary mean risk factor score for groups studied. The risk factor score represents a multiple logistic function of risk factors, predicting the probability of developing coronary heart disease within 12 years according to a person's age, sex, plasma cholesterol concentration, systolic blood pressure, relative weight, smoking rate, and electrocardiographic findings.[2] The "Watsonville reconstituted" group refers to the Watsonville sample reconstituted after the deletion of intensively instructed subjects from the data, and the substitution of weighted means for the one-third nonintensively instructed high risk subjects in Watsonville. These nonintensively instructed, high-risk subjects were the "Watsonville randomized control" group, also referred to in Table 1 and Figure 1.

The most important findings of the three-community study were that the media intervention itself stimulated notable risk reduction after two years in Gilroy, and that the even more dramatic effect of intensive instruction was maintained after three years in Watsonville. The most interesting data with implications for opinion leadership, however, were the "Watsonville reconstituted" and "Watsonville randomized control" results which initially, and in the long run, indicate the occurrence of greater risk reduction than in Gilroy. While not ruling out the possibility of nonrandom between-town or intervention differences, the opinion leadership data presented below describe a powerful, interpersonal influence operating with particular force on these groups. If, as predicted, the risk-reduction campaign efforts in Watsonville were broadly magnified through opinion leadership, it would then be desirable in future campaigns to deliberately generate opinion leadership as part of an intervention strategy.

THIS RESEARCH

For this study, the extent of opinion leadership, exercised by random samples of subjects drawn from the Gilroy and Watsonville SHDPP survey samples, was measured at the first SHDPP follow-up survey. In addition, 215 persons in Watsonville, randomly selected from the lists of names of persons nominated as having been talked with about heart disease, were interviewed to assess the impact of opinion leadership. It was hypothesized that the media plus change agent intervention, or intensive instruction, would generate more extensive opinion leadership than would the media-only intervention.

METHOD

Gilroy and Watsonville were selected by SHDPP from 33 candidate towns according to criteria considered important for the proper conduct of a behavioral and epidemiologic study involving a lengthy mass media campaign: comparable demographic characteristics; relative absence of potentially "contaminating" health education programs; community newspaper and television service; and reasonable proximity.

Probability samples of households designed to provide approximately 500 persons in each town between the ages of 35 and 59 were drawn from the Polk Directory (an official listing of all addresses). Additional samples of 150 persons in each town were drawn for use as an "after-only" (Hovland, Lumsdaine, & Sheffield, 1949, p. 308 ff.) control for *pretest sensitization*. All individuals in the age group, living in the selected households, were defined as eligible for inclusion in the study.

Based on an initial medical examination, each sample member was assigned a single summary risk score as described above. Subjects in the top quartile were defined as being at *high risk*. A randomly selected two-thirds of the high risk subjects in Watsonville constituted the target audience for media plus change-agent, risk-reduction instruction.

Thus, six groups of subjects, one *high risk* group, one *media-instructed* group, and one *after-only* group in each of the two towns, provided the subject pool for the opinion leadership study reported here. Only English-speaking subjects, and one subject to

TABLE 2
Demographic Characteristics for Each Treatment Group

Characteristic	Treatment					
	WII (n=77)	GHR (n=61)	WMO (n=80)	GMO (n=83)	WAO (n=64)	GAO (n=65)
Male/female ratio	1.17*	1.44*	.56	.52	.69	.92
White ethnic background (%)	90	93	90	92	88	92
High school completed (%)	69	73	69	63	62	57
Annual family income >$10,000 (%)	68	74	55	64	66	70

*Men are more likely than women to be at higher than average risk of premature heart disease.

a household were included. In the main three-community study, it often happened that the sample included households in which more than one person was a subject. In these households, a single subject was randomly selected. The following six groups of subjects resulted from this process:

1. *Watsonville high risk* (WII: n=77). These intensively-instructed subjects received the baseline survey, the media campaign, and change agent instruction before attending the first annual follow-up survey.
2. *Watsonville media only* (WMO: n=80). These subjects received the baseline survey and the media campaign before the first follow-up survey.
3. *Watsonville after-only* (WAO: n=64). These subjects received only the media campaign before the first follow-up survey.
4–5. *Gilroy high risk* (GHR: n=61) and *Gilroy media only* (GMO: n=83). These subjects received the baseline survey and the media campaign before the follow-up survey. They serve as points of comparison with their Watsonville counterparts.
6. *Gilroy after-only* (GAO: n=65). These subjects, like the Watsonville after-only subjects, received only the media campaign before the follow-up survey.

Since the SHDPP campaigns were directed at entire communities, random assignment of individuals to treatment or control condition was not feasi-

ble. Nor was it possible to treat a large number of communities and to assign communities randomly to treatment or control conditions. Thus, a "quasi-experimental" (Cook & Campbell, 1975) research approach was taken in the three-community study and, necessarily, in this study. Roughly comparable communities were selected, and the high risk or after-only groups within Watsonville were designed to be counterparts to similar groups in Gilroy. Table 2 presents demographic characteristics for the six groups described above which reflect this effort.

In addition to these six major groups drawn from participants in the first SHDPP follow-up survey, three groups of Watsonville subjects were randomly selected from among the persons nominated by WII, WMO, and WAO subjects as having been talked with about heart disease. This was done to obtain some estimate of the impact of the opinion leadership relationships suggested by the follow-up survey data. These groups are WII_N (n=99), WMO_N (=70), and WAO_N (n=56); that is, Watsonville residents who were nominated (N) by WII, WMO, and WAO, respectively.

Survey Procedure

Subjects in the six major study groups were interviewed to assess their demographic background and opinion leadership at the first annual follow-up survey of the SHDPP three-community study. The overall Watsonville and Gilroy response rate for completion of the baseline survey was 78%; among those completing the baseline survey, overall Watsonville and Gilroy response rate for completion of the first annual follow-up survey was 87%; the response rate among after-only subjects selected for the follow-up survey was 76%. The survey, which included the collection of knowledge, behavioral, and physiologic data related to heart disease, was conducted at a survey center by interviewers and physicians trained and supervised by SHDPP. The entire SHDPP survey took approximately 1.5 to 2 hours for each subject, and was conducted during two visits to the survey center, one "medical" and one "behavioral."

Subjects in the WII$_N$, WMO$_N$, and WAO$_N$ groups were interviewed in their homes by SHDPP interviewers to assess the impact of opinion leadership. The response rate for this survey of nominees was 78%. The interview required approximately one-half hour for each subject.

Opinion Leadership

There has been virtually complete agreement over the definition of *change agents*. They are professionals, such as salesmen, government agents, or trained community volunteers, who influence innovation decisions in a direction deemed desirable by a change agency (Rogers & Shoemaker, 1971).

Opinion leaders, on the other hand, have been understood in a variety of ways. Lazarsfeld, Berelson, and Gaudet (1944) describe opinion leaders as "certain people who are most concerned about [an] issue as well as most articulate about it. . . . [They] could be best identified and studied by asking people to whom they turn for advice on the issue at hand" (p. 49).

Katz and Lazarsfeld (1955) describe opinion leadership as "leadership at its simplest; it is casually exercised, sometimes unwitting and unbeknown, within the smallest grouping of friends, family members, and neighbors . . . It is the almost invisible, certainly inconspicuous, form of leadership at the person-to-person level of ordinary, intimate, informal, everyday contact" (p. 138). Katz and Lazarsfeld include "general influentials," persons "in whom one has confidence and whose opinions are held in high regard," and "specific influentials," persons who influence a specific opinion change in their conceptualization of an opinion leader (p. 140).

Lionberger (1960), in his review of diffusion research in the rural sociology tradition, describes "key communicators" and "influentials." *Key communicators* "are persons who are more important in the communication of information than others. They are generally defined in terms of high mentions received in response to questions regarding persons as sources of information used for general or specific purposes. They have been called 'opinion leaders,' 'local leaders,' 'adoption leaders,' 'informal leaders,' 'communicators,' or just simply 'leaders' " (p. 56). *Influentials* are "individuals who are alleged to have exercised a determining influence in one or more decisions of other persons" (Lionberger, 1960, p. 59). Since there is a fine line between the transfer of information "used for general or specific purposes" and influence, it is possible to see in the "key communicator" and "influential," taken together, the "opinion leader" type proposed in the communication research tradition, who is both information source and influencer.

Rogers (1962), more recently, has emphasized the influencing dimension of opinion leadership and the stability of the opinion leader role. Following Merton's definition of opinion leaders as "men who exert personal influence upon a certain number of other people in certain situations" (Merton, 1957, p. 410), Rogers describes opinion leaders as "individuals who exert an unequal amount of influence on the decisions of others . . . individuals from whom others seek advice and information" (1962, p. 435). He later redefines opinion leadership as "the degree to which an individual is able to informally influence other individuals' attitudes or overt behavior in a desired way with relative frequency" (Rogers & Shoemaker, 1971, p. 35).

Marketing research has, in general, followed the lead of communication research and rural sociology in defining opinion leadership. According to Robertson (1967), opinion leadership is indicated by "the frequency with which the individual is turned to for advice and information" (p. 330). Opinion leaders have been those individuals crucial to others' awareness of a new product or service (Kelly, 1967) and individuals influencing others to try a new product or service (Arndt, 1968).

Thus, three characteristics are typically present in some combination in the classical definitions of opinion leaders. Opinion leaders are individuals (other than change agents) who: (1) communicate information about something and/or (2) influence another's opinion or decision with regard to something (3) on a regular basis or in at least a single instance (Meyer, 1974). Clearly, opinion leaders are numerous, in all classes, and of both sexes; they change with topics and situations; they are influenced as well as influencing. Indeed, at one time or another, everyone exercises opinion leadership. In defining opinion leadership in so broad a fashion, then, it is construed to be nothing less than one of the basic channels in the human communication process.

Indicators

Four indicators of opinion leadership were used in this study which treat opinion leadership as a continuous variable, more or less manifest in a subject's behavior: (1) the number of persons talked with about matters related to heart disease, (2) the frequency of these conversations, (3) the direction of information flow in these conversations (who gave more information to whom), and (4) the number of specific cardiovascular disease-related topics talked about.

These indicators emphasize sheer volume of information transfer, and leave implicit the extent to which this information transfer implies behavioral influence. This focus was felt to be appropriate in the context of a heart-disease prevention campaign, in which knowledge itself is an important factor, and in which repeated interaction with influences other than opinion leadership contact, such as the mass media, plays an important role.

As a basis for computing the number of persons talked with about things related to heart disease, subjects were asked to indicate by name and approximate address in separate interview items: (1) relatives outside their immediate household, (2) co-workers, and (3) neighbors or friends with whom they could remember talking about things related to

heart disease during the summer preceding the interview. The total number of persons nominated by each subject, the number of households they represented, whether they were relatives, co-workers, neighbors, or friends, and whether they were male or female and local to Watsonville or Gilroy or not, were tabulated.

A score for the frequency of conversations related to heart disease was computed by summing responses to five forced-choice items which inquired about conversations with relatives, co-workers, neighbors and friends, other casually encountered persons not remembered by name, and persons in the respondent's immediate household. Respondents were asked to indicate whether such conversations occur daily (6 points), about twice a week (5 points), once a week (4 points), about twice a month (3 points), once a month (2 points), less than once a month (1 point), or not at all (0).

The direction of information flow in these conversations was assessed by asking: "In these same conversations you have had with people during the past summer—except those in your immediate household—how often would you say you *gave out* more information about heart disease than you received?" Forced-choice responses were scored in the following manner: *almost always* (4 points), *more than half the time* (3 points), *about half the time* (2 points), *less than half the time* (1 point), and *seldom or never* (0).

Two open-ended items requested a brief description of the heart disease-related topics discussed with: (1) relatives and household members, and (2) co-workers, neighbors, and friends. The responses to these two items were combined to obtain a single list of topics.

Opinion Leadership Impact

The impact of opinion leadership among diffusion survey participants was assessed, first of all, with a basic recall item: "Do you remember talking with (*nominator's name*) about things related to heart disease?"

Four other indicators of opinion leadership impact were included in the diffusion survey: (1) the frequency of conversations held with the follow-up survey nominator, (2) the direction of information

TABLE 3
Opinion Leadership Indicators

Indicator	Treatment					
	WII (n=77)	GHR (n=61)	WMO (n=80)	GMO (n=83)	WAO (n=64)	GAO (n=65)
Total nominated persons*	7.9**	1.9	4.6$^+$	2.8	1.9	2.2
Frequency of conversations	13.2**	4.8	7.9$^+$	5.1	4.9	5.3
Gave more information	2.7**	1.1	1.7^{++}	1.3	1.2	.9
Number of topics	3.1***	2.0	2.7^{+++}	2.3	2.0	2.0

*Categories in mean scores.

**Difference with each other treatment is significant:
p<.001, one-tailed.

***Difference with each other treatment except WMO is significant:
p<.001, one-tailed.

$^+$Difference with each other treatment is significant:
p<.01, one-tailed.

$^{++}$Difference with each other treatment is significant:
p<.05, one-tailed.

$^{+++}$Difference with each other treatment except WII and GMO is
significant: p<.05, one-tailed.

flow in these conversations, (3) general influence on behavior attributed to these conversations, and (4) the number of specific behaviors influenced.

Respondents reported the frequency of conversations with their nominator in response to an item similar to the frequency items described above: "How often would you say you talked with (nominator's name) about things related to heart disease during the past summer?" Forced-choice responses were scored as reported above, zero through six. Respondents were then asked: "Do you feel that you gave (nominator's name) more information about heart disease than he gave you, or did he give you more information than you gave him?" Forced-choice responses were scored in the following manner: nominator gave more (2 points); neither gave more/not sure (1 point); respondent gave more (0). General behavioral influence was assessed by asking: "Do you feel that talking with (nominator's name) influenced you to do anything to protect yourself against heart disease?" "Yes" was scored 2 points; "not sure" as 1 point; and

"no" as 0. Respondents were then asked to name the specific behaviors, if any, influenced.

RESULTS

Opinion Leadership

The four opinion leadership indicators were correlated significantly with one another, zero-order correlations ranging from .31 to .69 (p<.001). Table 3 presents mean opinion leadership scores and the results of between-group t-tests for significance. The data confirm the hypothesis that intensive instruction (change agent plus mass media) generates significantly greater opinion leadership than do media campaigns alone. WII frequently receives more than double the mean score of the other groups, and all mean differences between WII and the other groups are statistically significant except for WII with WMO for the number of topics discussed. In more descriptive terms, the 77 intensively instructed subjects talked with 608 persons in

TABLE 4
Nominated Persons and Households

Indicator	Treatment					
	WII (n=77)	GHR (n=61)	WMO (n=80)	GMO (n=83)	WAO (n=64)	GAO (n=65)
Total nominated persons*	7.9	1.9	4.6	2.8	1.9	2.2
Total households	6.4	1.6	3.9	2.4	1.8	1.9
Local persons	5.1	1.2	2.8	1.7	1.4	1.6
Local households	4.3	1.0	2.5	1.5	1.3	1.4
Relatives	3.6	.9	2.2	1.2	.8	1.1
Friends/co-workers	4.2	.9	2.3	1.6	1.1	1.0
Male nominated persons	4.0	.7	1.6	1.1	.6	1.0
Female nominated persons	3.9	1.0	2.9	1.7	1.3	1.2

*Categories in mean number of persons or households.

TABLE 5
Conversation Topics

Topics	Treatment					
	WII (n=77)	GHR (n=61)	WMO (n=80)	GMO (n=83)	WAO (n=64)	GAO (n=65)
Quality of diet*	78	36	70	52	61	32
Weight	22	33	22	20	23	20
Physical activity	46	16	35	22	27	18
Smoking	38	16	22	16	27	15
Tension/blood pressure	17	15	14	16	14	18
Lipids	36	15	11	26	16	15
SHDPP	17	10	6	8	11	8
Death by heart disease/ medicine/physician's advice	0	8	4	6	5	11
Other	18	33	38	34	25	35
None	4	21	11	16	20	28

*Categories in percent making one or more mention.

493 households other than their own, or 86% of the Watsonville inhabitants nominated. As a group, they talked with other persons with great relative frequency about heart disease, reporting regularly giving more information than they received. Compared with other subjects, the topics they discussed more often fell in the category of cardiovascular health related behavior than in more peripheral categories.

Tables 4 and 5 provide a more complete description of the categories of persons and households nominated and of the topics discussed in heart-disease related conversations. It appears that communication was fairly evenly divided between relatives on the one hand, and friends and co-workers on the other, and flowed from household to household, the reported contacts tending to occur with single rather than multiple members of a household (the total persons' score not greatly exceeding the total households' score). Such communication was conducted predominantly within community boundaries (69% with local households), and involved females slightly more than males. Quality of diet, that is, mention of specific foods such as eggs and whole milk, was the overall leading topic discussed (47% of the respondents). Weight and blood pres-

TABLE 6
Percent of Variance Explained by SES, Sex, and
Age for Opinion Leadership Indicators*

Predictor	Treatment					
	WII (n=77)	GHR (n=61)	WMO (n=80)	GMO (n=83)	WAO (n=64)	GAO (n=65)
SES						
Total nominated persons			11		2	
Frequency of conversations			8	1	5	
Gave more information		1	4		5	2
Number of topics	4		6	2	4	
Sex						
Total nominated persons	2	6	13		5	7
Frequency of conversations		7	10		2	4
Gave more information	2	2	8		13	5
Number of topics	3	2	8	4	9	11
Age						
Total nominated persons		2	2			
Frequency of conversations					3	
Gave more information	2				5	2
Number of topics					7	2

*The predictor is reported only when it accounts for at least
one percent of the variance.

sure are mentioned fairly evenly across conditions, whereas quality of diet, physical activity, smoking, and lipids (plasma cholesterol and triglycerides) are emphasized by WII. The SHDPP treatment program itself was a reported topic of conversation for 10% of the respondents. Discussion of death by cardiovascular disease, medicines, and physicians' advice—topics less directly germane to preventive behavior—was notably absent from WII subjects, and only 4% of WII subjects were unable to specify topics discussed.

These opinion leadership data show an unexpected effect in WMO. All but one of the 16 mean opinion leadership score comparisons between WMO and the other treatment groups, except WII, indicate significantly greater opinion leadership in WMO. This finding is apparently not due to pretest sensitization alone, since the effect is not shared by the other two media-only groups which participated in the baseline survey (GHR and GMO). Nor is it

due simply to living in Watsonville and being proximate to the change agent instruction program, since the effect is not shared by WAO. The WMO effect is apparently best explained by the interaction between pretest sensitization and proximity to the change-agent supplemented treatment. Pretest screening procedures demanded substantial time and involvement from participants. Survey participants were given an hour-long behavioral interview, and subsequently experienced blood drawing and other medical measures administered under the direction of prestigious Stanford University physicians. When approximately 20% of these individuals were notified of their higher than average risk, and approximately 30% came into direct contact with the change agent treatment program (high risk subjects plus spouses), it is likely that consciousness of this event spread quickly to the one-third not notified of their higher than average risk or not directly involved in change agent treatment. It is

TABLE 7
Opinion Leadership Impact Indicators

Indicator	Treatment		
	WII_N (n=99)	WMO_N (n=70)	WAO_N (n=46)
Frequency of conversations with nominator*	2.7*	2.0	2.0
Reception of nominator information	1.4**	1.2	1.0
General behavioral influence	.8***	.6	.4
Specific areas influenced	.6	.5	.4

*Categories in mean scores.

**Difference with each other treatment is significant: p<.01, one-tailed.

***Difference with WAO_N is significant: p<.01, one-tailed.

also possible that discovery of nonrisk reduced the threshhold for receiving information about heart disease prevention.

Table 6 presents the percent of variance explained by SES (socioeconomic status), sex, and age in an *analysis of variance* of the four opinion leadership indicators for each treatment group. SES was computed as the sum of unweighted values for education, occupation, and income. In general, the predictive power of these demographic and background variables is not strong. WMO showing the greatest effect. WII, which received the highest opinion leadership scores, shows little effect. It would appear that a sufficiently powerful intervention can counteract much of the relationship typically obtained between opinion leadership and SES and other such life history variables.

Opinion Leadership Impact

Overall, 83% of the 215 diffusion survey subjects remembered the conversations; 4% were uncertain; 13% did not remember. The 13% figure for not remembering is in line with other studies (Katz & Lazarsfeld, 1955; Troldahl & Van Dam, 1965). The four opinion leadership impact indicators were cor-

related significantly with each other, zero-order correlations ranging from .36 to .82 (p<.001). The .82 correlation between the general and specific behavioral influence attributed to the nominator reflects the lack of true independence between these two measures. Table 7 presents the mean scores for the opinion leadership impact indicators, and the results of between-group *t*-tests for significance. These data lend additional support to the hypothesis that the change-agent supplemented treatment would generate significantly greater opinion leadership than the media-only treatment, in that opinion leadership impact is significantly greater among subjects nominated by the intensively instructed subjects (WII_N) than among subjects nominated by the media-only instructed subjects (WMO_N and WAO_N). WII_N subjects claim significantly more nominator conversations, and claim to have received significantly more information than they gave in these conversations than WMO_N or WAO_N subjects. WII_N attributes greater general behavioral influence to WII than WMO_N attributes to WMO and significantly greater general behavioral influence than WAO_N attributes to WAO. Mean differences for the number of behavioral areas influenced are in the same direction.

DISCUSSION

Let us return to the general concern which motivated this study of opinion leadership. What role did the informal flow of information and influence play in supplementing the SHDPP campaign effort in Watsonville? To what extent is it plausible that such opinion leadership had an effect on the Watsonville risk reduction scores reported in Table 1?

It is interesting to recall that the 215 subjects included in the WII$_N$, WMO$_N$, and WAO$_N$ groups are a randomly selected representation of 706 Watsonville residents, nominated by name and address by SHDPP respondents in the first annual follow-up survey. Generalizing from the data of the 215 interviewed nominees, it can be said that these 706 persons talked about heart disease from one to two times a month with their nominators, and that about half of them would report being influenced to behave differently with regard to at least one behavior as a result of these conversations.

Similarly, the 80 subjects included in group WMO, and the 64 subjects included in group WAO, were randomly selected for the opinion leadership study from "media only" and "after-only" groups more than twice their size. If the WMO or WAO opinion leadership mean score for the number of local persons talked with were applied to these larger groups, it can be estimated conservatively that participants in the first annual SHDPP follow-up survey talked about heart disease with 1,020 persons, approximately 10% of the 10,053 Watsonville residents estimated to be over 17 years of age. Half of this number would claim to have been influenced with regard to at least one behavior relevant to heart disease prevention owing to these conversations. When it is considered that this line of reasoning takes into account opinion leadership data for only one period of time in a lengthy campaign, it appears safe to conclude that opinion leadership played an ubiquitous and critical role in the community-wide SHDPP campaign. On the other hand, it must be cautioned that omnipresence does not, in this case, imply omnipotence. The behavioral gains attributable to opinion leadership influence alone are likely to be quite limited and fleeting, requiring many rounds of learning and forgetting per person before significant impact is felt.

NOTES

1. This study was supported by the Stanford Heart Disease Prevention Program through its supporting resource of the Specialized Center of Research in Arteriosclerosis (HL 14174) and the Lipid Research Clinic (NIH NHLI 71-2161-L) at Stanford University.
2. The multiple logistic function of risk factors used in this work is described in Truett, Cornfield, and Kannel (1967) with the modifications noted in Farquhar et al. (1976, pp. 36-37).

REFERENCES

American Heart Association. *1975 heart facts*. New York: American Heart Association, 1975.

ARNDT, J. A test of the two-step flow in the diffusion of a new product. *Journalism Quarterly*, 1968, 45, 457-465.

BLACKBURN, H. Progress in the epidemiology and prevention of coronary heart disease. In P. Yu and J. Goodwin (Eds.), *Progress in Cardiology*. Philadelphia: Lea and Febiger, 1974, 1-36.

COOK, T.D., & CAMPBELL, D.T. The design and conduct of quasi-experiments and true experiments in field settings. In M.D. Dunnette (Ed.), *Handbook of industrial and organizational research*. New York: Rand McNally, 1976, 223-326.

CRAIN, R.L., & ROSENTHAL, D.B. Structure and values in local political systems: The case of fluoridation decisions. *Journal of Politics*, 1966, 28, 169-196.

FARQUHAR, J.W., et al. Community education for cardiovascular health. Submitted for publication, 1976.

FOX, S.M., & HASKELL, W.L. Physical activity and the prevention of coronary heart disease. *Bulletin of New York Academy of Medicine*, 1968, 44, 950-967.

FREEDMAN, R., & TAKESHITA, J.Y. *Family planning in Taiwan: An experiment in social change*. Princeton: Princeton University Press, 1969.

GLASSER, M.A. A study of the public's acceptance of the Salk Vaccine programs. *American Journal of Public Health*, 1958, 48, 141-146.

HALL, B., & DODDS, T. *Voices for development: The Tanzanian National Radio study campaigns*. Cambridge: International Extension College, 1974.

HALL, B., & ZIKAMBANA, C. *An evaluation of the 1973 mass health education campaign in Tanzania*. Dar es Salaam: Institute of Adult Education, 1974.

HOVLAND, C.I., LUMSDAINE, A.A., & SHEFFIELD, F.D. *Experiments on mass communication*, Vol. 3. Princeton: Princeton University Press, 1949.

Intersociety Commission for Heart Disease Resources. Primary prevention of the atherosclerotic diseases. *Circulation*, 1970, 42, A55-A95.

KATZ, E., & LAZARSFELD, P.F. *Personal influence*. New York: Free Press, 1955.

KELLY, R.F. The role of information in the patronage decision: A diffusion phenomenon. *Proceedings of the American Marketing Association*, 1967, 25, 119-129.

KEYS, A., ANDERSON, J.T., & GRANDE, F. Serum cholesterol response to changes in the diet. *Metabolism*, 1965, 14, 747-787.

LAZARSFELD, P.F., BERELSON, B., & GAUDET, H. *The people's choice*. New York: Columbia University Press, 1944.

LIONBERGER, H.F. *Adoption of new ideas and practices.* Ames: Iowa State University Press, 1960.

MACCOBY, N., & FARQUHAR, J.W. Communication for health: Unselling heart disease, *Journal of Communication,* 1975, 25, 114-126.

MAHAI, B.A.P. et al. *The second follow-up formative evaluation report of the "Food is Life" campaign.* Dar es Salaam: Institute of Adult Education, 1975.

MERTON, R.K. *Social theory and social structure.* Glencoe, Ill.: Free Press, 1957.

MEYER, A.J. *Generating unbiased diffusion of preventive health innovations.* Unpublished doctoral dissertation, Department of Communication, Stanford University, 1974.

MEYER, A.J., & HENDERSON, J.B. Multiple risk factor reduction in the prevention of cardiovascular disease. *Journal of Preventive Medicine,* 1974, 3, 225-236.

MEYER, A.J. et al. Maintenance of cardiovascular risk reduction: Results in high risk subjects. Abstract in press, *Circulation,* 1976.

ROBERTSON, T.S. Determinants of innovative behavior. *Proceedings of the American Marketing Association,* 1967, 26, 328-332.

ROGERS, E.M. *Diffusion of innovations.* New York: Free Press, 1962.

ROGERS, E.M., & SHOEMAKER, F.F. *Communication of innovations.* New York: Free Press, 1971.

TROLDAHL, V.C., & VAN DAM, R. Face-to-face communication about major topics in the news. *Public Opinion Quarterly,* 1965, 29, 626-634.

TRUETT, J., CORNFIELD, J., & KANNEL, W. A multivariate analysis of the risk of coronary heart disease in Framingham. *Journal of Chronic Diseases,* 1967, 20, 511-524.

AN INVESTIGATION OF THERAPEUTIC COMMUNICATOR STYLE

LOYD S. PETTEGREW
University of Michigan

The relational aspects of therapeutic communication have been shown to be important determinants of successful therapeutic outcomes. There is still lacking, however, a holistic construct of communicator style which is operable in therapeutic relationships. This research presents the first in a series of investigations which seeks to establish such a construct. A rationale is provided for studying therapeutic communication in relation to a more general construct of communicator style. A definition is presented which integrates the communicator style construct with emergent concepts from the literature on therapeutic communication. Finally, two research hypotheses are tested through a comparative analysis of variable means, profiles, and configurations of general and therapeutic communicator styles. The results confirm the research hypotheses, suggest areas of refinement for the test instrument, and move closer to a complex, holistic theory of communicator style in therapeutic relationships.

Interpersonal communication has served therapeutic functions since humans began to verbally and paraverbally relate to one another; there is evidence that therapeutic communication was a topic which interested the scholars of the classical rhetorical period (Zilboorg, 1941). Although therapeutic communication as a field of study and a vocational practice has made significant progress during the twentieth century, there remain large gaps in our knowledge and understanding of the therapeutic communication process. One area which remains largely uncharted concerns the *structure* and *domain* of stylistic variables which comprise therapeutic interpersonal communication. While there exists a body of research which has identified "central therapeutic ingredients," to date there has been no investigation which has taken a more holistic view of the style-related components of therapeutic interaction.

The present research reports the results of an investigation on therapeutic communicator style. First, a rationale is presented for studying therapeutic communication in relation to a more general construct of interpersonal communicator style. Second, a mapping sentence and definition are provided which integrate the construct of communicator style with emergent concepts from the literature on therapeutic communication. Third, a comparative analysis is performed on the variable means, profiles, and configurations representing a general and a therapeutic communicator style baseline. Fourth, a model of the therapeutic communicator style domain is presented which can be used to generate hypotheses, refine the test instrument further, and move closer to a complex, more holistic theory of therapeutic communicator style.

THERAPY AS A CONTEXT OF INTERPERSONAL COMMUNICATION

Formal therapeutic communication, as it emerged and developed during the first part of this century, was characterized by Freudian psychoanalysis. It was a parochial discipline whose central concern was with the *intrapsychic*. Neither Freud nor his contemporaries placed much emphasis on the relational aspects of their communication—the way in which the therapist communicated with the client (Haley, 1963). This was largely due to their fear of instigating a *countertransference* relationship with the client—bringing the therapist's own emotional attachments into the therapeutic relationships (Freud, 1909).

The therapeutic community remained entrenched in the intrapsychic paradigm for many years, and its influence is still felt today in the form of the *disease model* of personality development (Schofield, 1964; Laing, 1967; Cooper, 1967; Szasz, 1974).

There came, however, a significant break from the psychoanalytic concern with the intrapsychic world of the individual client. During the 1940s the therapeutic paradigm began to shift toward the *relationship* and *interactions* between the therapist and client. This influence was promulgated by the work of Harry Stack Sullivan (1953), Karen Horney (1937), and Erik Erickson (1963). Sullivan (1953) is credited with coining the term *interpersonal* by which this new therapeutic paradigm came to be identified. Bordin (1955, p. 136) has characterized this interpersonal therapeutic paradigm in the following manner:

> Our preferred concept of personality development visualizes the individual's growth as a function of and intimately reflected in his interpersonal relationships. This tells us that the major medium for contribution to his psychological growth will also be interpersonal relationships.

While the field of therapeutic communication (psychiatry, clinical psychology, and psychiatric social work) was just beginning to recognize the fundamental importance of interpersonal communication to the therapeutic process, social psychology had already embraced the interpersonal paradigm. Mead (1934) hypothesized the interdependence between the mind, the self, and the surrounding social nexus. This became known as *symbolic interactionism*. As Meltzer (1972, p. 9) puts it: "It is through language (significant symbols) that the child acquires the meanings and definitions of those around him. By learning the symbols of his groups, he comes to internalize their definitions of events or things, including their definitions of his own conduct." The fundamental feature of both symbolic interactionism and the interpersonal therapeutic paradigm is the notion that the *self-concept arises from and is in part characteristic of the social context in which it is placed.*

At this stage, two fundamental points emerge which are essential to our understanding of the therapeutic communication process. First, the development of the self, be it healthy or dysfunctional, is due largely to the experience an individual has with interpersonal relationships; this is especially the case in relationships with *significant others* (Sullivan, 1953). Second, the therapeutic relationship is most essentially an interpersonal relationship of *mutual* affect.

With these two tenets underscoring the present paradigm of therapeutic communication, it is not surprising to find increasing emphasis being placed on the interpersonal communication aspects of therapeutic relationships. As Strupp (1973, p. 24) has indicated, "the therapeutic relationship consists of transactions between two persons; it is not, as Macalpine asserted, the relationship of an analysand to a therapist." More precisely, "in communication terms, the analytic situation, no matter how passive or anonymous the analyst, is a *real situation, for two persons communicate as any other*" (Jackson, 1968, p. 104, emphasis added). If the therapeutic relationship is most fundamentally a process of interpersonal communication, we are left with a most difficult but important question: *Who engages in therapeutic communication and how might this process be uniquely characterized?*

The Therapeutic Relationship

Formal therapeutic communication, as represented by psychoanalysis and its related disciplines, is largely a product of this century. This in no way assumes that communication which serves essentially therapeutic ends was not practiced before this time. In a cogent historical review, Frank (1961) argues that mankind has practiced therapeutic communication, albeit informally, throughout its history. He states that therapeutic communication can be performed by any helper whose "influence is primarily exercised by words, acts, and rituals in which sufferer, healer, and—if there is one—group, participate jointly" (Frank, 1961, p. 3). From this characterization, it is not difficult to identify a rather large domain of helpers who can and do serve an essentially therapeutic function within our society. Such a domain probably includes religious leaders, lawyers, teachers, parents, politicians, spouses, close peers, etc. What appears to be most characteristic about the role of therapeutic communicators is their helping function as a significant other, and not their professional status. Gurney (1969, pp. 2-3) has stated that therapeutic communication techniques, "while they call for personal qualities not found in everyone, do not by any means call for the very special attributes and training of therapists following a psychoanalytic model.''

A more difficult question than who performs therapeutic communication is that of characterizing the goal of this process. Reviewing the psychoanalytic literature provides no clear answer to this second question. Therapeutic communication has been oriented toward personality integration, symptom relief, behavior change, communication competence, self-actualization, ontological security, relief of emotional discomfort, assertiveness training, rebirth of the self, etc. Raimy's (1950, p. 93) critique of the goal of therapeutic communication appears to be a most accurate characterization: ''. . . an undefined technique applied to unspecified problems with unpredictable outcomes.'' Perhaps a less insouciant description would be that of Abroms and Greenfield (1973, p. 10):

> Psychotherapy would encompass virtually every form of individual and group treatment relationship so long as the primary interchange is verbal or nonverbal communication. Rather than impose precise meanings where none in fact exist, we are content to note that virtually no one conceives of psychotherapy as involving more than a psychological or interpersonal mode of intervention.

Before presenting a definition of therapeutic communication which seeks to organize the many disparate notions of the therapeutic process, a final issue needs to be discussed. This concerns therapeutic outcome.

Therapeutic Outcomes

If we are to gain a more complete knowledge of therapeutic communication, it is essential to consider the *effects,* as well as the goals and the participants, of the interaction. It is reasonable to hypothesize that even if an interaction has a helper and a helpee whose stated or implicit purpose is some form of psychological, behavioral, or emotional assistance, if the results of the interaction do not achieve this goal, then the interaction is not truely therapeutic.

As with all scientific disciplines guided by a paradigmatic foundation (Kuhn, 1970), the field of therapeutic communication has been continually

involved in evaluating its ''state of the art''—the effectiveness of therapeutic outcome. Since the pioneer work of Eysenck (1952), the controversy of therapeutic effectiveness has raged throughout the field. In spite of opposition based on methodological issues, there is growing evidence that most formal therapeutic communication has not adequately achieved its goals (Levitt, 1957; Frank, 1961; Truax & Wargo, 1966; Truax & Carkhuff, 1967; Bergin, 1971). From a comprehensive review of the research on therapeutic outcome, Truax and Carkhuff (1967, pp. 20-21) state that ''the evidence now available suggests that on the average, psychotherapy [formal therapeutic relationships] may be harmful as often as helpful with an average effectiveness comparable to receiving no help.'' The overpowering indictment of this body of research has paved the way for a more complete understanding of therapeutic communication. Researchers are beginning to study therapeutic communication outside of the formal, professional relationship.

Studies include the therapeutic effects of interpersonal relationships with symbionts (Gurney, 1969), the inherently helpful person (Shapiro, Krauss, & Truax, 1969; Shapiro & Voog, 1969; Truax & Mitchell, 1971), spontaneous remission (Endicott & Endicott, 1963; Kringlen, 1965; Paul, 1967; Beiser, 1972; Moss & Borden, 1972), and lay therapy (Berenson, Carkhuff, & Myrus, 1966; Truax & Silber, 1966; Ivey, 1971). This body of research clearly establishes the fact that individuals in nonprofessional capacities *can* and *do* provide effective therapeutic communication. The fact that these nonprofessional therapeutic communicators often provide more effective counsel than professionals is probably due to their role as naturally significant others, and their availability to a broader range of the population.

From the above considerations of the therapeutic process, several conclusions emerge which can be incorporated into a working definition of therapeutic communication. First, therapeutic communication is most essentially an interpersonal communicative relationship. Second, such interaction takes place between at least one helper (professional or nonprofessional) and at least one helpee who suffers from some discomfort regarding his thoughts, feelings, and or actions. Third, therapeutic communication must provide some minimum of help or relief for the helpee for it to be considered truly therapeutic and distinct from more general interpersonal communication. From these conclusions, the following definition of therapeutic communication is advanced:

> Therapeutic communication is the verbal and paraverbal communicative transactions between a helper and a helpee which results in the feeling of psychological (thoughts), emotional (feelings), and or physical (actions) relief by the helpee.

Communicator Style

In a landmark study on the *pragmatic* aspects of human communication, Watzlawick, Beavin, and Jackson (1967) indicate that two distinct components exist in all communication: *content* and *relationship*. A growing body of literature today has established the importance of the relationship aspect of communication in interpersonal affect. Perhaps the most vivid example comes from the 1960 Nixon-Kennedy presidential debates. Kraus (1962) has convincingly demonstrated that it was the *charismatic style* of Kennedy which won him popular support over Nixon's superior communication *content*.

Although there have been several comprehensive studies on communicator style (Leary, 1957; Schutz, 1958; Mann, Gibbard, & Hartman, 1967; Bales, 1970; Lieberman, Yalom, & Miles, 1973), they represent only a fractionalized view of the entire domain of stylistic variables. Norton (1974a, 1974b, 1976) has sought to develop a more holistic and unified framework from which to study the way individual's "verbally and paraverbally interact to signal how literal meaning should be taken, filtered, or understood" (Norton, 1976, p. 1). Toward this end, he has developed and refined a *Communicator Style Measure* (CSM) which has been shown to have both high validity and reliability. A variation of this test instrument, the *Therapeutic Communicator Style Measure* (TCSM) will be employed in the present study.

EXPERIMENT

If we are to contribute to a more holistic theory of therapeutic communication, it is important to gain a comprehensive understanding of the salient stylistic variables which are involved. Strupp (1973, p. 28) has called for research which "may help sort out the various influences impinging on the interpersonal process called psychotherapy, and eventually permit the assignment of relative weights—statistical or practical—to the relevant variables." Although there currently exists a large body of research on therapeutic communicative behavior, there has yet to emerge a unified, holistic construct of such behavior. As Matarazzo (1971, p. 896) has reported, "descriptions of the attributes of the 'ideal' therapist are diverse, poorly defined, and incredibly numerous . . . we are only beginning to define the dimensions of therapeutic behavior."

In the previous section, the importance of studying communicator style in regard to interpersonal affect was established. Since therapeutic communication can be considered to be a specific context of interpersonal communication where the goal is positive affect toward the helpee, it makes good sense to study the stylistic components which uniquely characterize therapeutic communication. As Raush, Barry, Hertel, and Swain (1974) have indicated, "communication styles that enable and foster conjoint learning and a continued evolution of the relationship offer special scope for the future [of therapeutic research]."

Previous Research on Style Variables

There currently exists empirical evidence that specific therapist communicator style variables are related to positive therapeutic outcome. As previously stated, however, there has been no attempt to study these variables holistically—how they function together in the therapeutic encounter.

The greatest amount of empirical research has focused on the Rogerian variables of *warmth, accurate empathy,* and *genuineness*. Summaries of this research (Truax & Carkhuff, 1967; Truax & Mitchell, 1968; Ivey, 1971) conclude that these three variables constitute "essential therapeutic style ingredients."

Bordin (1955) and Lennard and Bernstein (1960) report that successful therapeutic outcome and helpee satisfaction is related to the *ambiguity* of the therapist's communication. Lennard and Bernstein (1960) also found *communicative activity* to be an important component of therapeutic communication. Shapiro, Krauss, and Truax (1969) and Simonson and Bahr (1974) report evidence that amount and kind of *self-disclosure* is directly related to positive therapeutic outcome. Finally, in a comprehensive study on group therapies, Lieberman, Yalom, and Miles (1973) report four basic leadership styles which affect therapeutic outcome: *caring, emotional stimulation, meaning attribution,* and *executive function.* They conclude their research with the observation that therapeutic outcome was related significantly more to the communicator style of the facilitator than to the specific therapeutic technique or school to which the facilitator paid allegiance.

Method

From the review of the literature in the first section of this report, the following research hypotheses were adopted: (1) since therapeutic communication can be validly considered to be a specific context of interpersonal communication, the underlying organic structure of the stylistic variables will not differ significantly, and (2) because of the contextual differences, an identifiable domain of variables will emerge in the therapeutic context which differ significantly in intensity from those in a general interpersonal context. These style variables should be consistent with those found in the therapeutic literature.

In order to test these research hypotheses, two baseline populations were needed for comparison: one representing a general communicator style, and the other representing a therapeutic communicator style. A sample of 1,700 college students from the University of Michigan, Indiana University, and San Diego State University were used for the general communicator style baseline. All subjects voluntarily completed the Communicator Style Measure (CSM).

A student sample of 81 college students (44 females and 37 males) from the University of Michigan voluntarily completed the Therapeutic Communicator Style Measure (TCSM). The TCSM was adapted from the CSM. Both measures contain 51 items on a four-point *Likert type* scale representing eleven independent variables (*dominant, dramatic, animated, open, contentious, relaxed, friendly, attentive, precise, voice,* and *impression leaving*) and one dependent variable (*communicator image*). Each variable is defined as a function of four items which have been shown to possess good content validity and reliability (Norton, 1976).

The therapeutic communicator style construct, as operationalized in the TCSM, can be more clearly represented by the following *mapping sentence:*

The *Therapeutic Communicator Style Measure* (TCSM) is the (a_1 cognitive) assessment by respondent (X) of his or her (b_1 self-perception) of the way a specified helper verbally and paraverbally interacts with him or her to signal how literal meaning should be taken, filtered or understood in the helper's (c_1 therapeutic face-to-face) communication with respect to (d_1 dominant) (d_2 dramatic) (d_3 animated) (d_4 open) (d_5 contentious) (d_6 relaxed) (d_7 friendly) (d_8 attentive) (d_9 voice) (d_{10} precise) (d_{11} impression leaving) (d_{12} communicator image) according to normative criteria for that communicative style behavior ranging from (very strong) to (very weak) manifestations of the representative item.

The use of mapping sentences performs two vital functions in theory building. First, it allows one to graphically portray the elements of the construct under investigation. Second, it reveals specific components of the construct which can be modified in order to expand and enrich the theory (Elizur, 1970; Levy, 1976). For example, facet b_1 can be expanded to include b_2 *(helper's self-perception)* and b_3 *(independent rater's perceptions).* The variables in facet d can be expanded or contracted to represent more completely the full range of stylistic variables which are operable in therapeutic interactions (both independent and dependent variables).

The TCSM requested the subjects to *think of the person whom they desire to communicate with most when they have personal problems, feel distressed or emotionally uncomfortable.* Subjects then entered this person's name on the front of the TCSM and completed the measure in regard to his/her communicator style. The strategy behind this

TABLE 1
Significance Test for Difference Between Means for General
and Therapeutic Communicator Style Variables

Style Variables	General Mean	Therapeutic Mean	t-statistic	significance level
Precise	2.40	2.09	3.44	.001
Voice	2.57	2.35	2.44	.05
Impression-Leaving	2.19	1.77	6.00	.001
Contentious	2.40	2.37	.30	ns
Animated	2.29	2.12	1.70	ns
Friendly	2.17	1.88	3.63	.001
Dramatic	2.49	2.41	.84	ns
Attentive	2.30	1.96	3.78	.001
Relaxed	2.83	2.09	10.57	.001
Open	2.58	2.36	2.24	.05
Dominant	2.68	2.34	3.40	.001
Communicator Image	2.44	1.92	11.11	.001

**Note: df= 1779

operationalization of a therapeutic communicator was that most people do seek out therapeutic communicators. The fact that the target person was someone whom the subjects *first and most consistently sought out* during troubled times would insure that their communication, no matter what their formal role, would be truly therapeutic.

Results

Three statistical analyses were used to compare the *general* and *therapeutic* communicator style baselines. Mean scores for each of the twelve style variables were computed for both test groups. It should be noted that an inverse relationship exists between the mean score and the direction of the variable. For example, a low mean (1.96) on the *attentiveness* variable indicates a positive direction *(very attentive)* for that variable.

The means from both test groups were compared via a two-sample t-test. Table 1 reports variable means and the results of this test for significant differences. Using Kirk's (1968, pp. 82-83) criterion for multiple comparisons, five style

FIGURE 1
Graphed Means for General and Therapeutic
Communicator Style Variables

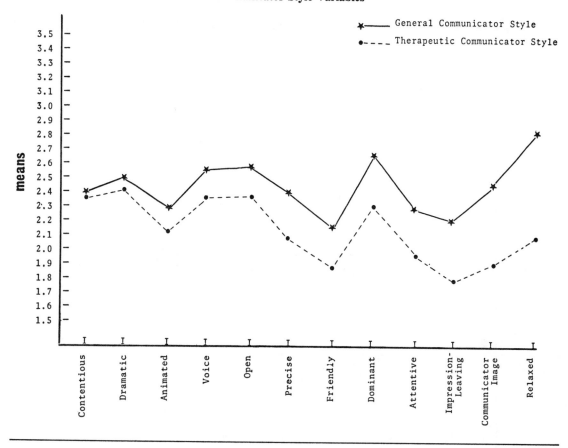

variables—*contentious, animated, dramatic, voice* and *open*—failed to reach significance. All the remaining variables—*precise, impression leaving, friendly, attentive, relaxed, dominant,* and *communicator image*—differed for the two groups at the p > .001 level of significance.

Figure 1 shows the profiles for both general and therapeutic communicator style variables. The results of the profile analysis indicate that the parallelism of the profiles differ significantly (p > .0000; F-statistic 10.64).

In order to determine whether the general and therapeutic communicator style constructs were similar enough to warrant the assumption that therapeutic communicator style differs from general communicator style only on a contextual level, two *Smallest Space Analysis* (SSA-I) solutions were

generated. SSA-I is a non-metric, multidimensional scaling program, the object of which is to map a set of variables or objects into a set of points in metric space (Lingoes, 1973). In so doing, it accurately reflects the underlying organic relationships within a variable set. The closer the variables are mapped together, the stronger their relationship. An overall measure of *goodness of fit* is the output in the SSA-I program. This provides an indication of the minimum number of dimensions in which the variable set can be explained. Figure 2 represents a two-dimensional SSA-I solution of the therapeutic communicator style construct. A goodness of fit measure *(Guttman-Lingoes Coefficient of Alienation)* of .15 was obtained. This indicates that the TCSM construct can be adequately represented in two dimensions.

FIGURE 2
Two Dimensional SSA-I Solution
for Therapeutic Communicator Style Variables

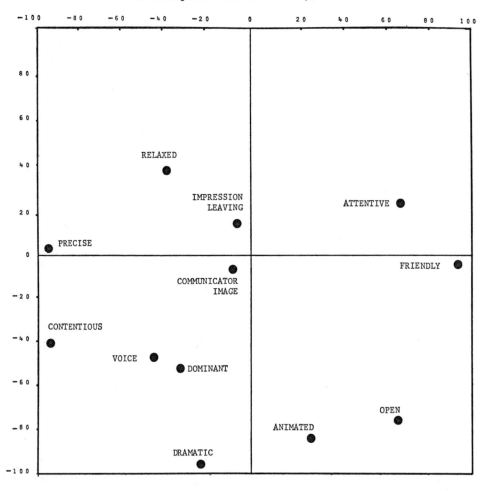

Figure 3 represents a two-dimensional SSA-I solution of the general communicator style construct. A goodness of fit measure of .17 was obtained for this solution, indicating that the CSM construct can be best represented in three dimensions.

Two subroutines of smallest space analysis *(Configural Similarity—CS-I,* and *PINDIS)* were used to test whether the configurations of the therapeutic and general communicator style variables differed significantly. It was hypothesized that since the SSA-I solutions represent the organic structures of both constructs, a comparison of their structures would reveal meaningful similarities or differences. If therapeutic communicator style differs from general communicator style only on a contextual level, there should be no significant differences in their structures.

CS-I tests both the correlation matricies from which the SSA-I solution is derived and the coordinate matrix which is the metric SSA-I solution. The result of CS-I showed that the general and therapeutic communicator style configurations differed from a 0 relationship (r = .85; p > .01 for the correlation matrix and p > .05 for the coordinate matrix). The PINDIS subroutine also compares configurations,

FIGURE 3
Two Dimensional SSA-I Solution for General
Communicator Style Variables

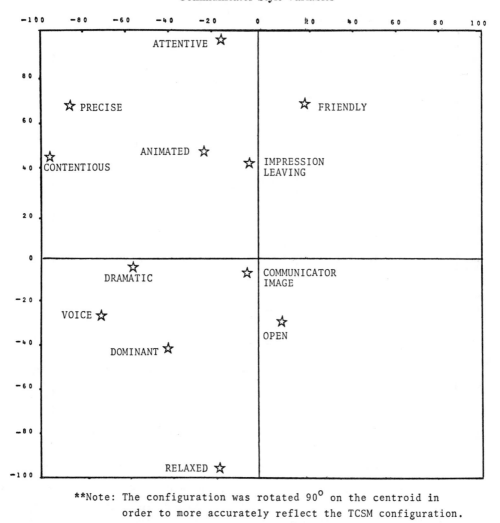

**Note: The configuration was rotated 90° on the centroid in order to more accurately reflect the TCSM configuration.

but unlike CS-I, it expands and contracts the configurations, seeking the best fit possible. It also compares each dimension of the configurations and outputs a correlation coefficient for each. The results of PINDIS showed a very high degree of similarity between the two solutions. The overall correlation between the general and therapeutic communicator style configurations after rotation and contraction was $r = .96$. It should be noted that a three-dimensional solution was used for con-

figural comparisons owing to the inferior two-dimensional fit for the CSM construct. The first dimensions correlated $r = .85$, the second dimensions at $r = .92$, and the third dimensions at $r = .86$. Finally, PINDIS places both configurations in a metric, three-dimensional space. Figure 4 represents the three-dimensional relationship between the therapeutic and general communicator style constructs.

FIGURE 4
**Three Dimensional Solution Showing the Relationship Between General
and Therapeutic Communicator Style Constructs**

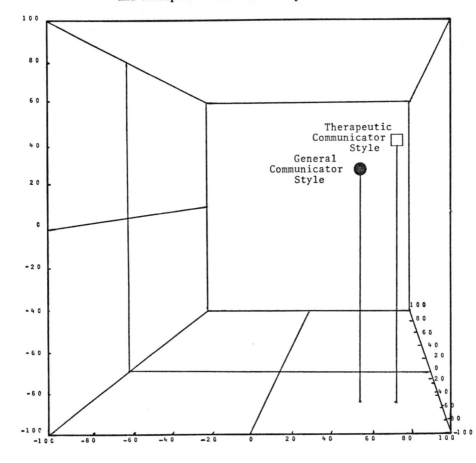

Discussion

The results of this investigation offer tenative support for both research hypotheses. First, the configural comparisons of both constructs suggest that therapeutic communicator style can be accurately reflected in the general communicator style construct. This result is not surprising, since the therapeutic communication literature considers the therapeutic process to be essentially a process of interpersonal communication. The importance of this finding lies in the empirical verification of a previously theoretical hypothesis.

Second, this study suggests specific ways in which therapeutic communicator style differs from a more general stylistic context of communication. The mean differences and tests of significance suggest that a therapeutic communicator (as a function of the therapeutic context) adapts his communicator style in certain salient ways in order to function more successfully in a helping relationship. For example, a therapeutic communicator is significantly more *precise*. This finding is consistent with the work of Bordin (1955) and Lennard and Bernstein (1960), who found that lack of ambiguity was related to successful therapeutic outcome. A therapeutic communicator is also significantly more *friendly* and *attentive* than a general communicator style. This finding is consonant with the Rogerian essential therapeutic ingredients of *warmth* and *accurate empathy*. Further research by the author (Norton & Pettegrew, 1976) has provided further support for this relationship. It is also reasonable to assume that because of the therapeutic communicator's role and the context of the encounter, his *image* as a communicator and the *impression that he leaves* on the helpee will be different than for a more general communicator style. This assumption also received empirical support. The therapeutic communicator is also seen as more *dominant* than a general communicator. As Jackson (1968) and Haley (1963) have indicated, no matter how active or passive the therapeutic technique, the therapeutic communicator exerts a dominating influence in the encounter. The fact that a therapeutic communicator is also perceived to be more *relaxed* makes good intuitive sense. It is doubtful whether a nervous, uptight, tense, or anxious style of communication would be of much therapeutic value to a person who is psychologically, physically, or emotionally uncomfortable.

One final consideration is warranted from the results of the configural comparisons. It is interesting to note that, while the variable structures are closely related for general and therapeutic styles, the therapeutic configuration can be accurately reflected in one less dimension than the general configuration. While it is impossible to provide an empirically defensible explanation for this finding, the following hypothesis is suggested: Since therapeutic communication appears to be a specific context of interpersonal communication, it is possible that a subset of style variables function in such a cohesive manner for this context that they exert less stress when multidimensionally analyzed; hence they can be accurately reflected in fewer dimensions. This would probably entail the subset of variables which differed significantly from a more general style of communication. Less stress could, however, also be a function of the difference in sample sizes.

CONCLUSION

At this juncture, it is important to address the question of where does the researcher go from here. Several directions will be offered by returning to the mapping sentence: (1) if we are to gain a richer understanding of therapeutic communicator style, facet b needs to be expanded to include the self-perception of the helper as well as the perception of the helpee; (2) facet d needs to be expanded to include variables which are relevant to successful therapeutic outcome. These can be used as dependent variables from which a set of predictor style variables might be generated; (3) one can specify more exactly the role of the helper. The strategy in the present research was to allow the respondent to pick his own therapeutic communicator—the one he naturally sought out in troubled times. Future research should be extended to include more specific information on the professional status of the helper, in order to determine any salient differences in communicator style that might be role-related.

In conclusion, the therapeutic communicator style construct promises to provide important information on the salient relational aspects of interpersonal communication which are operable in therapeutic relationships, both formal and informal.

REFERENCES

ABROMS, G. M., & GREENFIELD, N. S. A new mental health profession. *Psychiatry,* 1973, 36, 10-22.

BALES, R. F. *Personality and interpersonal behavior.* New York: Holt, Rinehart and Winston, 1970.

BEISER, M. The lame princess: A study of the remission of psychiatic symptoms without treatment. *American Journal of Psychiatry,* 1972, 129, 33-38.

BERENSON, B. G., CARKHUFF, C. B., & MYRUS, J. The interpersonal functions and training of college students. *Journal of Counseling Psychology,* 1966, 13, 4.

BERGIN, A. E. The evaluation of therapeutic outcomes. In Bergin, A. E. and Garfield, S. L. (Eds.), *Handbook of psychotherapy and behavior change: An empirical analysis.* New York: John Wiley, 1971.

BORDIN, E. S. *Psychological counseling.* New York: Appleton-Century-Crofts, 1955.

COOPER, D. *The death of the family.* New York: Vintage, 1971.

COOPER, D. *Psychiatry and antipsychiatry.* New York: Ballantine, 1967.

ELIZUR, D. *Adapting to innovation.* Jerusalem: Jerusalem Academic Press, 1970.

ENDICOTT, N. A., & ENDICOTT, J. "Improvement" in untreated psychiatric patients. *Archives of General Psychiatry,* 1963, 9, 575-585.

ERICKSON, E. *Childhood and society.* 2nd Rev. New York: Norton, 1963.

EYSENCK, H. J. The effects of psychotherapy: An evaluation. *Journal of Consulting Psychology,* 1952, 16, 319-324.

FRANK, J. *Persuasion and healing.* New York: Schocken, 1961.

FREUD, S. *The dynamics of transference*. Standard edition, Vol. 12. London: Hogarth, 1909.

GURNEY, B. G. *Psychotherapeutic agents: New roles for nonprofessionals, parents, and teachers*. New York: Holt, Rinehart and Winston, 1969.

HALEY, J. *Strategies of psychotherapy*. New York: Grune and Stratton, 1963.

HORNEY, K. *The neurotic personality of our time*. New York: Norton, 1937.

IVEY, A. E. *Microcounseling: Innovations in interviewing training*. Springfield, Illinois: Thomas, 1971.

JACKSON, D. D. Psychoanalytic education in the communication processes. In Jackson, D. D. (Ed.), *Therapy, communication, and change*. Vol. 2. Palo Alto, California: Science and Behavior, 1968.

KIRK, R. E. *Experimental design: Procedures for the behavioral sciences*. Belmont, California: Brooks-Cole, 1968.

KRAUS, S. *The great debates*. Bloomington, Indiana: Indiana University Press, 1962.

KRINGLEN, E. Obsessional neurosis: A long term follow-up. *British Journal of Psychiatry*, 1965, 111, 709.

KUHN, T. S. *The structure of scientific revolutions*. 2nd. ed. Chicago: University of Chicago Press, 1970.

LAING, R. D. *The politics of experience*. New York: Ballantine. 1967.

LEARY, T. *Interpersonal diagnosis of personality: A functional theory and methodology for personality evaluation*. New York: Ronald, 1957.

LENNARD, H. L., & BERNSTEIN, A. *The anatomy of psychotherapy*. New York: Columbia University Press, 1960.

LIEBERMAN, M., YALOM, I., & MILES, M. *Encounter groups: First facts*. New York: Basic, 1973.

LINGOES, J. *The Guttman-Lingoes nonmetric program series*. Ann Arbor, Michigan: Mathesis Press, 1973.

LEVITT, B. E. The results of psychotherapy with children: An evaluation. *Journal of Consulting Psychology*, 1957, 21, 189-196.

LEVY, S. Political involvement and attitude. Publication No. SL/550/E, The Israel Institute of Applied Social Research, Jerusalem, 1975.

MANN, R., GIBBARD, G., & HARTMAN, J. *Interpersonal styles and group development*. New York: Wiley, 1967.

MATARAZZO, R. G. Research on the teaching and learning of psychotherapeutic skills. In A. E. Bergin and S. L. Garfield (Eds.), *Handbook of psychotherapy and behavior change*. New York: Wiley, 1971.

MEAD, G. H. *Mind, self, and society*. Chicago: University of Chicago Press, 1934.

MELTZER, B. N. Mead's social psychology. In J. Manis and B. N. Meltzer (Eds.), *Symbolic interaction*, 2nd. ed. Boston: Allyn and Bacon, 1972.

NORTON, R. W. Foundations of a communicator style construct. Unpublished manuscript, University of Michigan, 1976.

NORTON, R. W. Components of communicator style. Paper presented at the annual meeting of the Speech Communication Association, Chicago, 1974.

NORTON, R. W. Communicator style: Theory and application. Paper presented at the annual meeting of the Speech Communication Association, Chicago, 1974.

NORTON, R. W., & PETTEGREW, L. S. Communicator style as an effect determinant of attraction. Paper presented at the annual meeting of the International Communication Association, Portland, Oregon, 1976.

NORTON, R. W., & PETTEGREW, L. S. Attentiveness as a style of communication. Paper presented at the annual meeting of the International Communication Association, Berlin, 1977.

PAUL, G. L. Insight versus desensitization in psychotherapy two years after termination. *Journal of Consulting Psychology*, 1967, 31, 333-348.

RAIMY, V. (Ed.) *Training in clinical psychology*. Englewood Cliffs, New Jersey: Prentice-Hall, 1950.

RAUSH, H. L., BARRY, W. A., HERTEL, R. K., & SWAIN, M. A. *Communication, conflict, and marriage*. San Francisco: Jossey-Boss, 1974.

SCHOFIELD, W. *Psychotherapy: The purchase of friendship*. Englewood Cliffs, New Jersey: Prentice-Hall, 1964.

SCHUTZ, W. *FIRO: A three dimensional theory of interpersonal behavior*. New York: Holt, Rinehart and Winston, 1958.

SHAPIRO, J. G., KRAUSS, H. H., & TRUAX, C. B. Therapeutic conditions and disclosure beyond the therapeutic encounter. *Journal of Consulting Psychology*, 1969, 16, 290-294.

SHAPIRO, J.G., & VOOG, T. Effect of the inherently helpful person on student academic achievement. *Journal of Consulting Psychology*, 1969, 16, 505-509.

SIMONSON, N. R., & BAHR, S. Self-disclosure by the professional and paraprofessional therapist. *Journal of Counseling and Clinical Psychology*, 1974, 42, 359-363.

STRUPP, H. H. *Psychotherapy: Clinical research and theoretical issues*. New York: Jason Aronson, 1973.

SULLIVAN, H. S. *The interpersonal theory of psychiatry*. New York: Norton, 1953.

SZASZ, T. *The myth of mental illness*. 2nd. ed. New York: Harper and Row, 1974.

TRUAX, C. B., & CARKHUFF, R. R. *Toward effective counseling and psychotherapy*. Chicago: Aldine, 1967.

TRUAX, C. B., & MITCHELL, K. M. The psychotherapeutic and psychonoxious: Human encounters that change behavior. In Feldman, M. (Ed.), *Studies in psychotherapy and behavior change*. Buffalo, New York: State University of New York Press, 1968, 55-92.

TRUAX, C. B., & MITCHELL, K. M. Research on certain therapist interpersonal skills in relation to process and outcome. In Bergin, A. E. and Garfield, S. L. *Handbook of psychotherapy and behavior change*. New York: Wiley, 1971, 299-344.

TRUAX, C. B., SILBER, L. D., & CARKHUFF, R. R. Accurate empathy, non-possessive warmth, genuiness, and therapeutic outcome in lay group counseling. Unpublished manuscript, Arkansas Rehabilitation Research and Training Center, University of Arkansas, 1966.

TRUAX, C. B., & WARGO, D. G. Psychotherapeutic encounters that change behavior for better or worse. *American Journal of Psychotherapy*, 1966, 20, 499-520.

WATZLAWICK, P., BEAVIN, J. H., & JACKSON, D. D. *Pragmatics of human communication*. New York: Norton, 1967.

ZILBOORG, G. *A history of medical psychology*. New York: Norton, 1941.

APPENDIX

APPENDIX

A HISTORY OF THE INTERNATIONAL COMMUNICATION ASSOCIATION

CARL H. WEAVER

This is a story of a learned society, born of necessity and reared with great difficulty.
It is not a history of ideas, but a story of what happened and how it happened.
Everything in the history is quoted or based on fact. Some of it is excerpted from letters. Some of it is belated history, written to help fill the gaps left by missing records. Despite the gaps, the story is there—the hopes, the dreams, the struggles, the frustrations, the satisfactions.

From the Notes of Elwood Murray . . .

(Editor's Note: On January 17, 1973 Elwood Murray, at the University of Denver, recorded the notes in this appendix on the origin of the International Communication Association, originally called the National Society for the Study of Communication.)

In the early 1940s, basic communication courses were mushrooming throughout the country. There was great enthusiasm and interest in integrating reading, writing, speaking, and listening. During this time, while rhetoric was ablaze in the National Association of Teachers of Speech, a monumental program in research was conducted on rhetoric and public speaking, and there was continued controversy over the nature of the speech fundamentals course.

In the Speech Association of America there was a strong commitment to rhetoric. Many members assumed that their teaching of rhetoric was all that was necessary, and that it included communication. Although they had, in their departments, incorporated work in phonetics and speech science, this work was not approached in terms of the more generic communication process. They generally eschewed psychology, personality approaches, and general semantics. Speech pathology and radio-television were being chopped off from the old speech tree and were growing into their own national organizations.

In the summer of 1949, it was learned that a committee of the speech association was going to report that the Speech Association of America should have nothing to do with basic communication. This really activated me, because basic communication was burgeoning all over the country. Having been involved in teaching experimental courses for two or three years, it had become apparent to me that the right kind of basic communication course could provide more speech experiences and speech development than the regular basic speaking courses.

In the autumn of 1949, after discussions with the six members of the speech staff at Denver (I was director of the School of Speech at that time), and in particular with Dr. Keith Case, Dr. Johnnye Akin, Dr. Ray Barner, and Dr. Jasper Garland, I wrote to Dr. James McBurney, then president of the Speech Association of America (SAA), to inquire whether he would assign a room at the Chicago Convention in December for a group of us to start a new organization to be affiliated with the SAA. McBurney was a little fearful of further splittings of the old speech tree, but he graciously agreed to the arrangement desired.

After McBurney gave us permission to meet, I wrote Dr. W.N. Brigance, the famous rhetorician at Wabash College, Dr. Paul Bagwell, and Dr. Charles Redding, about the idea for a new organization, which I suggested would be called the National Society for the Study of Communication.

Their responses were enthusiastic and reinforcing, and they gave me the courage to proceed with the meetings which eventuated in the International Communication Association.

I invited the members of Dr. Wesley Wiksell's committee—the committee which was going to recommend against communication—to join with us. One of the first to respond with enthusiasm and suggestions was Dr. Ralph Nichols, who was pioneering research in listening. Other members of this committee, rather to my surprise, came to our support and we left the convention with a full set of officers and a pro-tem constitution.

There seemed to be no opposition to what we were doing. Dr. Nichols and I were appointed to carry on further work during 1950 for formal adoption of the constitution the next December. This constitution remained very little changed for some 14 years thereafter.

Dr. Paul Bagwell was the first president of the newly formed organization—The National Society for the Study of Communication (NSSC). Dr. Nichols was the second, and I was the third to hold this office.

With the assumption that the process of interpersonal communication carries on in all teaching, in all disciplines and professions, our policy was to have scholars, researchers, and practitioners from the whole realm of human relationships. Our hopes were that the organization would immediately foster research and deep-level study in the human relations, personality, and psychological divisions of communication. But almost all of our people had been trained in the traditional backgrounds, and most of us didn't know enough to move very far. The result was we were very slow in developing the research and also the philosophy of speech and communication. We had not defined our field very well. There was no generally accepted model of the communication process, and our early efforts were devoted to attempting to make progress in these directions.

EARLY DEVELOPMENTS

Wesley Wiksell had been working in communication as long as Murray had, and his history in many ways tells the story of the forces that erupted in the birth of the new society.

In 1939, as head of a new communication division at Stephens College, he attended a session at the Central States Speech Convention where Malcolm MacLean spoke on communication. In 1944, he read a paper on communication at a convention of the Speech Association of America. And, in 1946, the first article on listening, written by Wiksell, appeared in the *Quarterly Journal of Speech*. Wiksell also presented papers that year at the conventions of the Speech Association of America and the National Council of Teachers of English.

According to Wiksell, since so many students found English so easy and painless, there had resulted great numbers of English majors and, in turn, a plethora of teachers. As a result of this, teachers salaries had dropped and so had the quality of teaching.

English composition courses, he said, had become one of the most ineffective courses taught on campuses as a result. Teachers of English were becoming reactionary and administrators were casting about for some solution to the problem. Communication was growing in popularity.

Wiksell urged speech departments to encourage the new trend toward communication, rather than trying to avoid it. He advised them to take the initiative in the move which he saw as inevitable. "If we as smart, progressive, energetic speech teachers will recognize the fact that the lumping of language courses is practically inevitable, and if we then prepare ourselves to take the initiative in a program of this kind, we can then exert a primary influence in this field. We can then insure speech a proper place in a language program taught by men and women who are qualified to teach it," Wiksell wrote in 1946.

At a time when the SAA was having difficulties holding itself together, Bagwell says those wanting change were "looked upon by some members of the SAA as 'mavericks,' possibly as 'radicals' whose primary inter-

est was the promulgation of esoteric and 'far-out' theories of communication within the SAA. "Since the majority of the members of the executive council at that time had done their terminal graduate work in speech (rhetoric), public address, argumentation and debate, or some combination thereof, it was only natural that they would look upon additional interest groups with a 'jaundiced eye,' especially since many of them on the council had won their freedom (departmentally) from the domination of English departments within their own lifetimes," Wiksell continued. "The important thing, I think, for us to remember is that NSSC was formed at a time when radio, television, the computer and techniques for polling public opinion were in their infancy compared with the sophisticated uses being made of them today."

The Beginning

The objectives of the new organization, according to Murray, would be to foster "methodologies, philosophies, courses and curricula in so-called basic communication, speech, journalism, radio and other mass media (including English, etc.) which would implement training more directly for the needs of human relations at all levels. The organization would be especially concerned with this training as an integrating factor in so-called general education. It would also be concerned with the development of unified approaches in the clinical methods for speech-listening, reading, writing, perception, and evaluation at all age levels and all areas of education."

Before Murray wrote to McBurney, then president of the Speech Association of America, he circulated his ideas among several of his colleagues in his own department and at other universities, seeking their views. One of the issues discussed was whether the new organization should be affiliated with SAA or whether it should be separate. Reactions to this issue were mixed. Murray wrote to McBurney, who referred the matter to an SAA Committee on Problems in Communication, chaired by Wiksell.

Murray was not pleased with McBurney's action. "To me this attack on the problem is a wholly negative one and puts the profession in the position of standing in the way of this developmental approach, which we should be supporting in every possible way," Murray wrote to John Keltner at the University of Oklahoma.

When, after a month, Murray still had not heard from Wiksell, he again contacted McBurney. He asked McBurney if he could present a draft of the plan for the new organization to the executive Council of the SAA at the December convention.

But Murray was exploring other avenues of establishing the organization also. He suggested to W. Charles Redding of the University of Southern California that, if the SAA were definitely not interested, he might attempt to get the National Research Council to subsidize a conference at the University of Denver to launch such a society.

McBurney, however, agreed to a meeting with the Executive Council. The special committee which McBurney appointed included Murray, Redding, W. Norwood Brigance of Wabash College, and Paul Bagwell of Michigan State. The committee was also invited to appear before Wiksell's committee.

In the meantime Wiksell was circulating Murray's letter to McBurney among his committee. The reaction of Bagwell, who was also a member of Wiksell's committee, was fairly typical: "I predicted two years ago that the movement in communication would progress to the place where those interested in the program would want to get together for specific study, research, etc., in that area. . . . Accordingly, I would go along with Murray's idea and recommend that if a society for the study of communication is formed that it become an affiliate of the S.A.A. I can be entirely wrong, but in my opinion the number of those interested in the broad area will continue to increase."

Thus, there were two committees involved in the matter. Apparently, the attitude of both committees—perhaps with one or two exceptions—was favorable toward the study of communication and toward the formation of the NSSC. But nearly everyone on both committees wanted the NSSC to be a part of, or closely affiliated with the SAA.

According to the prospectus presented to the SAA executive council, the new society saw the field of communication as including: basic communication (discussion, public address, and oral reading); radio and television broadcasting; theatre arts, motion picture production and appreciation; industrial communication; intercultural communication; civic and governmental communication; communication in education; clinical methods in speech, reading, and listening; and writing and journalism.

Among the several objectives set forth in this prospectus, two stand out as central: "To bring greater unity into the whole field of speech education by showing the interrelations of the basic speech and language communication behavior to the total interpersonal communication"; and "To enlarge the place of speech education in education generally as administrators see speech in its wider context of communication and as speech teachers become able to present their subject accordingly."

Also in the organization's prospectus is a comment on the era of American history during which the new society was being formed. Among the standing committees which were proposed was one to "study the operation of infiltration and propaganda techniques of such ideologies as communism and fascism, and the methods for combatting these influences."

The 1949 Convention. Of major concern during the 1949 SAA convention was the relationship the new group would have with SAA. Sentiment was strong that it should remain loyal. This sentiment even affected the naming of the new society. The name finally decided upon was the National Society for the Study of Communication. "Study" was the key word. It was felt that a study group would not be a competing group with the SAA.

Bagwell was elected the first president of the NSSC, and Clyde Dow, also of Michigan State, was made executive secretary so that the two of them could work closely as the new society tried to build up a membership.

There were 214 original charter members of the new society, the establishment of which was approved by the Executive Council of the SAA at the 1949 convention.

All of the founders of NSSC were academic people, and all were members of the SAA. All had been anxious to remain a part of SAA, and some believed the SAA would see the emerging new field of communication as they did and change its own orientation. Many hoped that within a few years the NSSC might find its interests and objectives to be the same as those of the SAA and it could be absorbed again by the parent organization, having accomplished its objective. That did not happen, although a quarter of a century later SAA did change its name to the Speech Communication Association to reflect its changed orientation.

In 1954-55 the SAA adopted a new constitution, which among other things set up "area groups" and fixed rules for their operation. It authorized 16 area groups, one of which was communication. It prescribed the names (chairman, vice chairman, secretary) of their officers, their terms and methods of election. It named their duties and their relations to officers of SAA. Perhaps most binding for the NSSC was a provision that any plan for assessing dues or otherwise raising funds would have to be approved by the Finance Committee of the SAA, and another that the Executive Committee of the Legislative Assembly must approve "all policies with reference to projects, services, questionnaires and meetings between conventions . . ." Thus, the only way NSSC could remain in the SAA was to become an interest group, and it was not thought possible to follow the guidelines and, at the same time, maintain an identity.

Nevertheless, NSSC remained an affiliated organization. Little by little, as the NSSC grew older and its origins were forgotten by changing officers and national councils, the feeling of kinship weakened, and in 1968 the relationship came to an end.

THE INITIAL STRUCTURE

On January 1, 1950 the Society was born, and the travail, though heavy indeed, was less troublesome than expected. It had a president (Bagwell), two vice presidents (Murray and Wiksell), and a secretary-treasurer (Clyde Dow).

With a set of administrators and a legislature, the Society set forth to justify its creation and continued existence. The procedure envisioned by its creators as most vital was the *study* of communication. In its prospectus and planning, study and research committees were central to this justification. Although the functions of any scholarly association—conventions, getting acquainted with other workers in the field, listening to papers in section meetings—could be rather easily envisioned and executed, the study and research committees, structured to do original research, were regarded as the critical working units. The conventions would inspire and provide opportunity for discussion. Reporting of research could be done there, too, and society publications could also perform this function. If the Society were to fulfill the dreams of its fathers, it would become a national hub of research in communication, not merely a center for dissemination of armchair philosophy.

Bagwell asked Murray to assume the responsibility of organizing and implementing the various committees approved by the Executive Council, and Murray immediately began sending out a snowstorm of letters.

By the end of the year, Murray had staffed nine of 12 committees, and the other three were partly completed. By March, 1951, the list had been expanded to 15, and the committees were almost completely staffed. No form letters were used. Every letter was a personal letter, explaining, asking, hoping. There were hundreds and hundreds of them, all typed by Murray's secretary.

Some of those on the first committees were: Gail Sullivan, executive director of Theatre Owners of America; Wayne Britton, San Francisco State; Donald Blanding, M.S.C.; Bess Sondel, University of Chicago; Waldo Phelps, University of Southern California; W. Charles Redding, USC; Clyde R. Miller, former director of the Institute of Propaganda Analysis; Uni Ollie Backus, University of Alabama Speech Clinic; Solomon Simonson, State Teachers College, Fredonia, N.Y.; Seth Fessendon, University of Denver; Lee Bradford, director, Adult Education Services, Washington, D.C.; Allen W. Read, Columbia University English Department; Wendell Johnson, University of Iowa; Irving Lee, Northwestern University; Bernice Prince, University of Denver; I. Kenneth Hance, Northwestern University; Kenneth Benne, University of Illinois School of Education; Armand Hunter, Temple University; Emmet Betts, Temple University; Ralph Nichols, University of Minnesota; Capt. Kenneth Clark, Air University; Thomas R. Lewis, Florida State University; Betty Bebout, Stephens College; Donald Bo Blanding, Michigan State College; and Bernice Prince, San Francisco State College.

There were nine academic development committees of the NSSC at the 1950 convention: Elementary and Secondary School Programs, College Programs, Clinical Programs, Propaganda, Evaluation Procedures, Listening, Reading, Mass Communications, and Social Relations.

The first issue of the *Journal of Communication* was published in May 1951, by which time 15 committees had

been established, with 7 to 15 members each. These were the first of the NSSC Study and Research Committees. Chairmen of those committees were: James Platt, Primary and Secondary School Programs; Harold Lillywhite, College Communication Programs; Russell Meyers, Clinical Methods in Communication Disorders; Seth Fessenden, General Methodologies; John Keltner, Basic Research and Evaluation; Armand Hunter, Mass Media; Solomon Simonson, Propaganda; John Riebel, Communication in Industry (Charles T. Estes, consulting chairman); S.I. Hayakawa, Intercultural Relations; Kenneth Clark, Military Services and Civilian Morale; D.P. McKelvey, Communication in Government; Lionel Crocker, Communication in the Family; James Brown, Reading Comprehension; Charles Irvin, Listening Comprehension; and E.C. Mabie, Communication Centers.

Three committees which had been planned were never staffed: the Committee on Communication in Public Opinion, Public Relations, and Distribution; the Committee on Communication in Civilian Morale and Mobilization; and the Committee on Communication in Religious Institutions and Programs.

The 15 study and research committees established—but not necessarily operating—in March, 1951, were considered by many for 17 years to be the heart of the society. The committees were designed to do original research. A study committee was to identify a problem, prepare hypotheses, and collect data that would test them. This idea died hard. It was difficult to find committee chairmen who had a keen interest in a problem and who had time to work on it.

There was constant speculation about the reasons why the committees did not do what was expected of them. It was suggested that perhaps the fault was to be found in the manner in which the committees were created in the first place. Ordinarily a problem exists, several people recognize it, and they form a group to solve the problem. The study and research committees were created in reverse order: the groups were organized and then told to find problems.

In 1954 it was suggested that NSSC be reorganized into three divisions: Research or Study, Training and Education, and Application or Methods and Procedures. Each of these divisions would then be responsible for publications in every third issue of the *Journal of Communication*.

There was no alternative but to work within the current structure, however. Another plan was tried which provided each committee with some portion of a giant study designed to occupy the attention of the whole Society and galvanize it into action. The effort met with little success.

It was probably significant that when the committees were abolished in 1967, the furious battles in the National Council and the General Business Meetings over a change in the name of the Society came to an end. The new name—the International Communication Association—was formally accepted in 1969. Why should it be called The National Society for the Study of Communication if there were no longer any study and research committees?

Yet there had been some significant work done by the study committees. Several committees, for example the Committee on Listening, produced carefully selected and complete bibliographies. And many committees reported sound, original research done by the chairman himself, by his graduate students, and by others the chairmen knew. Some of this work found its way into the *Journal of Communication*, or appeared in the form of committee reports, especially during the early years.

An Advisory Committee to Headquarters, AFROTC, was established to review texts and curriculum organization of the problem-solving and communication phases of the new Air Force Reserve Officers Training Corps program.

Local Chapter

During much of this period, the concept of local chapters had been quite important to the officers of NSSC. Presidents wrote letters of encouragement, and the executive secretary kept membership lists, enforced national requirements, and published local chapter reports in the newsletter.

Seven chapters were initiated: two were started in 1952 at Michigan State and Denver; Murray started two in Hawaii in 1953; and three more were formed during the next five years.

The Michigan and Denver chapters did the work in setting up national Summer Conferences of the NSSC. The Portland Chapter developed into a resource group for the entire city, sometimes providing 15 or 20 speakers and discussions each year on communication and, in one case at least, conducting a training course. Their meetings had speakers on such subjects as group dynamics, general semantics, communication disorders, communication in industry, intergroup communication, listening, and communication in elementary education.

The Seattle chapter, started by Clark, was smaller than the Portland Chapter, enrolling at its peak about 30 people. The Michigan chapter, under the initial leadership of Russell Jenkins, had the same kind of programs. The three chapters started by Murray (Denver, Maui, and Honolulu) worked on the same kinds of problems in general semantics as Murray covered in his courses, which had been their inspiration.

Projects

During this period also, several projects were initiated. A consultation program, started in 1951 by Nichols, lasted five years. Teams were formed to go out on request and spend time without pay to help college, high school, or business firms with communication problems. Nichols group apparently was the only team which actively did

any consulting. In 1952, it visited 12 colleges, 13 high schools, and 4 educational associations.

Development of an Information Distribution Center was a dream that never came true. In its long and spotty life, it wore out four directors and never produced the service its sponsors envisioned. The need for it was significant. If it had worked out as it was planned, the Society might have established itself as the center of knowledge in the whole area. The main reason for the failure of the Center was probably the prodigious amount of work involved and the lack of staff.

In December 1961, a speakers' bureau was established with Dover as chairman. He set up a panel of individuals who were willing to speak to groups for expenses only. The honoraria went into the NSSC treasury. On the list were Byers, Cartier, Dance, Dover, Thorrel Fest, Frank Funk, Knower, Lillywhite, Nichols, Darrel Piersol, Harold Weiss, Milton Wiksell, Wesley Wiksell, C. W. Wright, and Zelko.

The speakers' bureau was intended to perform some of the functions of the defunct consultation teams. However, funds from the honoraria were used to finance conferences, rather than for publicity. When Dover set up his own business and became too busy to operate the bureau, it died and was never revived.

FINANCES

The founders of the Society went through a painful process to keep it solvent. Not until its twelfth year did the Society have as much as $5,000, and the annual income reached that level only three times in the first 15 years. Printing and mailing the *Journal of Communication* consumed the major protion of that sum. Invitation and registration forms and information folders designed to attract new members could not even be printed in the early years. They were mimeographed. Even the *Newsletter* was at first mimeographed.

Many times the Executive Secretary had to order the printing of the *Journal of Communication*, at a cost of somewhere between $500 and $1,200, in the devout faith that enough members would renew their memberships to bail him out. They always did.

Membership

In 1953 the cost of an active membership increased from $3.50 to $5.00 and the student membership was established. Neither of these benefited the Society's coffers significantly. The student membership, however, started a long-range trend which probably accounts in some large part for the affluence the Society enjoys today. The membership dues structure remained static until 1964, although nearly every year someone suggested that it be reexamined. Finally, in 1964, student and active memberships were increased $1 but the significant changes, which finally began to produce enough money for the Society to operate, came only after a financial crisis in 1967.

The membership in the Society remained fairly stable through 1962, when it began to climb. The appearance of stability is deceptive. Each year 100 to 150 members stopped paying dues and were replaced by new members. A membership surge began in 1966 and has continued. A determined effort by Pace, and others, produced a membership list of over 900 by the end of 1967. By November 1968, the membership was 1,300. In June 1968, the membership list reached 1,000 at the Annual Conference in New York. By 1971 there were 1,598 members from all 50 states and 43 foreign countries, and that figure has remained relatively constant through 1974. By January 1977, membership exceeded 2,000.

Throughout the organization's history, there has been some conflict between two philosophies of membership. On the one hand, it was believed by some—and still is—that membership should be selective. On the other hand, others believed it was appropriate to extend membership to anyone who was willing to pay the dues. Applications for membership still require a recommendation by an active member.

Revenue from the Journal

During the first five years, the *Journal of Communication* produced virtually no income of its own. It was a service—and by far the most important service—provided by the Society to its members. It was not until 1964 that the income from advertisements became an important part of the Society's income.

The Society turned to a professional advertising salesman in 1964. In 1965 the annual advertising revenues reached $1,500—25 percent of which, however, went to commissions. This was far more than anyone had dreamed of, but it did not continue, partly because of the rather complicated lines of management within the NSSC itself. In 1968 professional ad sales were terminated.

For two years (1968-70) Martin Hunt was advertising manager. In 1970 Gerald Goldhaber was appointed, and though the sales of advertising did not match those of 1964, no commission was paid either.

In 1971, sixteen advertisements brought in $956, an increase of 37 percent over the preceding year. In 1972, sixteen advertisements returned $1,235.

The sales of back issues of the *Journal of Communication* were even more impressive. In the 1950s, sales were negligible. In 1959, combined advertising and back-issue sales were $314. In 1962 back issues netted $293, and the total rose steadily each year after that, until in 1970 the total was $2,345, after which the sum tapered off, presumably because libraries which had been trying in the late 1960s to secure complete sets had been satiated.

Perhaps the biggest change in the financial fortunes of the Society was caused by the steady increase through the sixties in institutional subscription rates and in the number of subscriptions. Subscription rates rose from $2, which held constant throughout the fifties, to $15 in 1969. In addition, the increasing popularity of the *Journal* caused a surge in the number of subscriptions. In 1953 there were 57 institutions subscribing to the *Journal*. In 1960 there were 524; in 1966, 587; in 1970, 1,300; and in 1971, 1,500. The combination of higher rates and increased numbers produced an income of $20,844 in 1970. In 1953 it had been $114.

Financial Crisis

Early financial difficulties recurred in 1967. There were, however, some differences. In 1953, the reason for the crisis was simply an income near the poverty level. After this experience, the Society tightened its belt and carried on its business for six straight years without deficit spending. Accordingly, it was a shock to discover that, with an income of $12,825 in 1967, the Society had overspent by $3,363.

The Society was not in red ink for its ordinary expenditures. The final balance for the year was $686. The problem was the printing of the 1967 Convention Proceedings. Lee Thayer who, as first Vice-President, had coordinated the convention, secured persmission of the National Council to print a Proceedings. Unfortunately, the actual cost of the publication exceeded amounts budgeted by over $4,500. The Society was able to keep its head out of the red ink by a narrow margin. Conditions stabilized in 1969 with the increase in membership dues, along with rapid growth in the size of the membership rolls. The income from that source alone was $1,000 greater than in 1968.

THE JOURNALS

Of all the ventures of the NSSC, the *Journal of Communication* was probably the one that made the Society successful. It is quite likely that what readers saw in the *Journal* they saw in the Society, and, as the *Journal* grew in esteem, the Society grew in numbers.

The Journal of Communication

Not much is known about the problems Tom Lewis, the first editor, faced in getting the new publication started. He designed the format of the *Journal*. He solicited and prepared for publication every word that was printed. His first issue was about two months late, but the other three issues he guided were published on time. He served two years. At the end of that time, Francis Cartier agreed to become editor.

The *Journal* was at first essentially a house organ. This was not the aim of the editors, however. They wanted the *Journal* to become the recognized leader in the publication of scholarly reports of research in communication. It is likely that the house-organ function was performed only because of the difficulty of obtaining satisfactory manuscripts fast enough to keep the *Journal* published.

Comments about the difficulty of getting good articles abound in editor's reports until the early and middle 1960s. By 1967, manuscripts were pouring in to the editor. The rate of submission of manuscripts for publication doubled over that of the preceding year. Out of 223 manuscripts, 30 were accepted for publication.

What was described by Ted Clevenger as a glut of manuscripts created a curious combination of elation and despair in the editorial offices. While it was highly desirable to have a wide range of manuscripts from which to choose, neither the editor nor the staff bargained for a workload of such magnitude.

For the first three years of its publication, the *Journal of Communication* was published twice a year. Efforts were made constantly to expand it to a quarterly. There were two obstacles to this dream. One was the difficulty of securing enough material to fill four issues. The other was lack of money. The small membership and the low membership fee did not generate much money, nor did advertising. Francis Cartier finally found a way to make the *Journal* a quarterly publication in 1954 by reducing the number of pages in each issue.

The most rigorous restraint on the editor was the number of pages he could print. Beyond this the editor was, for some 20 years, given almost a free hand in generating the kind of *Journal* he thought best. It is curious that this should be so. There was much discussion in business meetings of the character the *Journal* should assume, but little agreement.

In spite of the efforts of editors to accommodate different editorial perspectives, inevitably there was criticism. Within the academic membership, the perennial conflict between the scientist and the artist persisted. The aim of almost all the editors was to fill the *Journal* with hard, dependable data. As a result, there was constant, though muted, complaining that the *Journal* was neglecting the humanistic aspect of communication.

There was also a clear division of interest between academic and nonacademic members. Nonacademicians have argued that the *Journal*—even the entire Society—was owned and operated by college professors. Cartier, and probably most of the other editors, tried hard to get articles from nonacademic members, but they were not easy to come by.

In 1961, the editor requested and received permission to print a Tenth Anniversary Issue. It turned out to be an issue and a half. Too many manuscripts were received for a single issue, which aimed at both reporting progress during the first decade of the NSSC and at assessing the 1961 situation in communication theory and practice.

Content of the Journal

A content analysis of the first 22 years of the *Journal* was made by Charles M. Rossiter and John R. Luecke for this article. They categorized "journal items" in two ways—by type and by general content area. Here is their analysis:

The six divisions for the "types" of items, definitions of these devisions, and example of such items were as follows:

Theoretical. Articles which proposed definitions or models of communication. These articles were well-documented and integrated with the scholarly literature; e.g., Krippendorff's "On Generating Data in Communication Research" (20:241-269, 1970).

Empirical. Articles which reported experiments and field studies based on empirical data; e.g., Orr et al. "The Effect of Listening Aids on the Comprehension of Time-Compressed Speech" (17:223-227, 1967).

Summary. Articles which summarized the literature about specific topics; e.g., Beighley, "A Summary of Experimental Studies Dealing with the Effect of Organization and Skill of Speaker on Comprehension" (2:58-65, 1952).

Organization-related. Articles about the association, reports by association committees, statements about where the association has been, was, or should be going; e.g., Lillywhite, "A Progress Report of the Committee on College Programs" (1:51-53, 1951).

Unsubstantiated. Articles that generally offered advice about what to do or how to do it, such as why and how listening should be taught in the basic course. Often these articles were statements about the importance of something like "discussion" or "communication in a democracy." At times they were "quasi-theoretical." Sometimes they looked like theoretical articles by title and general subject area, or offered empirical generalizations.

Miscellaneous. Introductory remarks for symposia, occasional bits of metaphorical whimsy, and all else that failed to fit clearly into any of the other five categories; e.g., Darnell, "On the Art of Herding" (20:227-230, 1970).

In the second major way of classifying the articles, "general content area," nine divisions or areas were identified: interpersonal communication, organizational communication, intercultural communication, information systems, general communication, language, communication education, public communication, and other.

In 1965 Kenneth Frandsen proposed to the National Council that he would prepare a key-word index to the *Journal of Communication*, which had not been indexed since Francis Cartier prepared the Ten Year Index in 1960. The Council approved, and Frandsen, using an indexing program from the computer center at the University of Wisconsin-Milwaukee, prepared a supplement to the *Journal*, which was distributed to members in 1969.

Borden and Frandsen developed a pilot project in 1969 to produce a thesaurus of terms. During the summer of 1971, the thesaurus became operable. It was demonstrated at the SCA convention in December 1971, and at the ICA convention in April 1972. The data index began in 1969 and extended to 1972.

In December 1970, Carl Larson proposed that the *Journal* emphasize basic theoretical formulations more than it had and suggested that a second journal, the *Journal of Communication Research*, be started. Larson also suggested that special issues of the *Journal of Communication* should be devoted to consulting, diagnostic, and assessment procedures, training designs, and training aids for the practitioner.

After discussion among the Board of Directors and the new editor of the *Journal*, a somewhat modified policy statement was formulated in March 1971. It included a call for a *Journal of Applied Communication Theory* as soon as it was financially feasible. The content of the statement was debated at some length.

In 1974, George Gerbner was named editor of the *Journal*, and all rights to its publication were turned over to the Annenberg School of Communication, University of Pennsylvania. Association members continue to receive the *Journal* at a reduced cost, and realize some benefit from all institutional subscriptions. By agreement, the editorial board of the publication is composed of an equal number of members appointed separately by the association and by the Annenberg School. By 1976, the circulation of the *Journal* had more than doubled, and it maintained a very substantial international circulation.

Human Communication Research

In 1973 the ICA Board approved a proposal to commence publication of a second quarterly journal, *Human Communication Research*. Gerald Miller was named first editor. The first issue of the new journal was published and distributed in the Fall of 1974. The goal of the publication was to include quality research and scholarship in human communication and, additionally, features of broad professional and intellectual interest such as book review essays, and, occasionally, dialogue about papers. More specifically, according to Miller, *Human Communication Research* would publish: (1) reports of original research, (2) descriptions of methodological approaches, (3) critical synthesis of research literature, and (4) theoretical papers. Initially, the journal subscribers came almost exclusively for the International Communication Association membership, but by 1976 subscriptions totalled nearly 2,300.

Communication Yearbook

A proposal to begin publication of a preconvention proceedings was approved by the ICA Board in 1975, and

Brent Ruben was asked to develop the publication concept and serve as first editor. According to Ruben, the *Communication Yearbook* series was developed to provide a combination of a preconference proceedings and a disciplinary annual. It would contain papers competitively selected from each division and from the Association as a whole, along with annual reviews of theory and research within the field and its subdivisions. Specifically, the publication will include: (1) generic reviews and commentaries on theoretical and research developments of the field, (2) theory and research overviews in each of the Divisions of ICA, and (3) selected studies from each division and the Association as a whole.

THE NEW ASSOCIATION

Few documents have been changed so much and yet so little as the first constitution of the National Society for the Study of Communication. The first document was revised six times before it was replaced at midnight, December 31, 1967; yet through all those six changes the structure remained essentially the same.

Much more important, however, was the change in its membership. Although from its very first days it had tried to enroll members from all academic disciplines and from all nonacademic vocations, the Society had remained academic and was composed of speech communication people. Its leadership, in spite of its own efforts to avoid it, was academic. President Kenneth Clark, from the Air Force, was enlisted to run for president *because* he was not a college professor. Nonacademic members were pushed in the direction of leadership, but the nonacademic people in the Society did not control the Society. Harwood became president in 1956, Cartier in 1959, and Haney in 1962. All of them were from the Air Force, but all were essentially academic. It was not until Dover became president in 1965 that a really nonacademic member was president of the Society.

Among the academic presidents, members of speech communication faculties predominated. Lillywhite (1953) was in speech therapy. After that, not until 1967 when Lee Thayer became president and 1971 when Malcolm MacLean Jr. was elected, did an academic person from a department other than speech communication reach the highest office.

Divisions

When the old research and study committees were abolished, four divisions were created and members were invited to join one or more of them.

The four divisions met for the first time at the annual convention in New York in April 1968 and elected officers. The divisions were numbered as follows: (1) Information Systems, (2) Interpersonal Communication, (3) Mass Communication, and (4) Organizational Communication. In 1970, Division 5, Intercultural Communication, was formed. In 1973, two new divisions were approved: (6) Political Communication and (7) Instructional Division. Division 8, Health Communication, was approved in 1974.

In 1975, legislation was adopted by the Board of Directors to require each division to maintain a membership equal to 10 percent of the total membership of the Association. The new rule was implemented to provide the Association with a renewal mechanism, and to counter a trend toward excessive splintering through the proliferation of divisions.

The Change of Name

As noted previously, the name, the National Society for the Study of Communication, was chosen for a reason. It was felt that a "study" group would not be a competing group with the Speech Association of America, an important issue at the time. Periodically proposals were made to change the name. None of them really generated much support until 1969, when the Board of Directors unanimously passed a motion proposing to change the name to the International Communication Association. At the time, the organization had more than 150 members from 27 foreign nations.

Presidents Smith and MacLean expended considerable efforts toward the emphasis of the international commitments of the Association. In May of 1977, President Budd presided over the first convention held outside of the North American continent—West Berlin.

Incorporation

In 1970 the ICA was incorporated as a not-for-profit organization, under the laws of the State of Ohio, as I.C.A., Inc. The nonprofit status has affected ICA in two ways, besides relieving it of a heavy tax burden: (1) it must be careful not to make a profit or to become too affluent and (2) it must not engage in activities which might be considered political.

In 1971, the Association was reincorporated in the state of Michigan, and in 1976, still as a nonprofit organization, incorporated in the state of Texas, site of ICA national headquarters.

Activities

During this period a number of projects were initiated. At the August 1967, convention, Ed Safford, president of the National Council on Communication Arts and Sciences, had offered the services of a full-time secretary if the NSSC would implement the beginnings of a communication federation. In October of that year, representatives of four societies met in Chicago and formed the Council of Communication Societies. Invitations to join were sent to 51 societies. The minimum of seven, fixed at

the Chicago meeting, was met in November 1969. They were: American Business Communication Association, American Forensic Association, American Medical Writers Association, International Communication Association, Society for Technical Communication, Society for Federal Linguists, and the Speech Communication Association.

In 1970 the Industrial Communication Council joined, and in 1973 the American Translator's Association became a member. The Council is supported by fees from each association ranging from $100 per year for a society with fewer than 100 members to $1,200 for a society with more than 16,000 members.

The CCS was conceived as an "umbrella organization" to perform functions which, it was believed, could be better done in concert than by each member society alone. The Council's brochure credits Hans Peter Luhn, a president of the American Society for Information Science, with originating the idea.

Projects proposed, and in part performed, by the Council included the publication of a directory of communication societies and research institutes (printed by the National Council on Communication Arts and Sciences), the issuance of a calendar of the major meetings of member societies, and the publication of a directory of speakers on communication.

In 1973 the council began to collect data from 2,800 university department heads, program directors, and center directors which could be used to persuade the United States Government to establish a federal agency dedicated to funding research projects in communication. It also began to collect support for a CCS Communication Center, which would combine research facilities, conference facilities, association offices, and a public exhibition hall.

In 1970 the Board of Directors applied for affiliation with the American Association for the Advancement of Science and was accepted.

Student Conference. In August 1972, the ICA held its first student conference at the General Motors Institute in Flint, Michigan, directed by Stewart Tubbs. Students paid only their travel expenses. ICA published a Proceedings containing papers by keynote speakers and students. ICA has continued the Student Summer Conference. In 1973 two conferences were held, one in Athens, Ohio and one in Eugene, Oregon.

The Placement Service. The NSSC placement service, started initially on a small scale in 1957 under the direction of Hans Gottschalk, died in 1959. Six years later the Society tried again to establish a placement service, with Dean Ellis as its director. It ran into financial difficulties, but in 1971 the service, as it exists today, became operational.

The Communication Audit. The idea of the communica-

TABLE 1
Membership by Year

Year	Regular, Sustaining, Patron, Associate, Honorary	Student	Total
1950	91		91
1951	412		412
1952	410		410
1953	447		447
1954	444	5	449
1955	418	6	424
1956	492	9	501
1957	518	11	529
1958			
1959	308	8	316
1960	386		386
1961	422		422
1962	386		386
1963	452		452
1964	465		465
1965	502	34	536
1966	706	40	746
1967	857	56	913
1968	1009	86	
1969	1943	108	
1970	1154	369	
1971	1340	258	1598
1972	1192	248	1724
1973	1619	507	2126
1974	1266	506	1772
1975	1516	707	2223
1976	1668	570	2238

tion audit of complex organization began during the 1971 convention in Phoenix when Donald Faules conducted a workshop on the subject. Howard Greenbaum and Brent Peterson arranged a continuation of this workshop at the convention in Atlanta in 1972. From these discussions came the appointment by Mark Knapp, Chairman of Division 4, of three Task Groups: (1) a group to design an auditing instrument, (2) a group to generate a list of organizations suitable and available for auditing, and (3) a group to set up research teams all over the country to do the auditing, using the instrument and design prepared by Task Group 1. The most important of these Task Groups was the first, coordinated by Gary Richetto and Gerald Goldhaber.

The research objectives of the project were: (1) to describe an organizational communication system, (2) to establish national norms for comparative purposes, (3) to establish a data bank, (4) to provide research outlets for graduate students and faculty members, and (5) to begin the solid foundations on which to build a theory of organizational communication which has both internal and external validity.

NOTE

1. This edited version of Carl Weaver's complete and highly detailed history of the International Communication Association was prepared especially for inclusion in Volume I of the *Communication Yearbook* by Lee M. Brown. Dr. Weaver's full version of the history of ICA, commissioned by the Board of Directors in 1971, is in the Association archives at its national headquarters, Austin, Texas.

TABLE 2
Locations of NSSC-ICA Annual Conferences

December 1950	New York, Hotel Commodore (with SAA)
December 1951	Chicago, Conrad-Hilton Hotel (with SAA)
December 1952	Cincinnati, Netherland Plaza Hotel (with SAA)
December 1953	Estes Park, Colorado; With SAA in New York
December 1954	Estes Park, Colorado; With SAA in Chicago
December 1955	Michigan State University; With SAA in Los Angeles
December 1956	Aspen, Colorado; With SAA in Chicago
August 1957	Boston (with SAA)
August 1958	Estes Park, Colorado
August 1959	Elkhart Lake, Wisconsin
August 1960	Elkhart Lake, Wisconsin
August 1961	University of Buffalo
August 1962	Purdue University
August 1963	University of Denver (with SAA)
August 1964	State University College, Geneseo, New York
August 1965	Hillsdale College, Michigan
August 1966	University of Maryland
August 1967	Boulder, Colorado
Spring 1968	New York, Waldorf-Astoria
Spring 1969	Cleveland, Ohio; Statler-Hilton Hotel
Spring 1970	Minneapolis, Minnesota; Leamington Hotel
Spring 1971	Phoenix, Arizona; Ramada Inn
Spring 1972	Atlanta, Georgia: Sheraton-Biltmore Hotel; Student Summer Conference at Flint, Michigan
Spring 1973	Montreal, Quebec, Canada; Queen Elizabeth Hotel; Student Summer Conference in Athens, Ohio and in Eugene, Oregon
Spring 1974	New Orleans, Louisiana; Monte Leone Hotel
Spring 1975	Chicago, Illinois; La Salle Hotel
Spring 1976	Portland, Oregon; Portland Hilton
Spring 1977	Berlin, Germany; Kongresshalle

Journals and Publications—Editors

The Journal of Communication

1951-1952	Thomas R. Lewis
1953-1955	Francis A. Cartier
1956-1958	C. Merton Babcock
1959-1961	Wayne N. Thompson
1962-1964	Frank E. X. Dance
1965-1967	Ted Clevenger, Jr.
1968-1970	Sam Duker
1971-1972	Paul D. Holtzman
1973	Paul D. Holtzman and Daniel E. Costello
1974-present	George Gerbner

Human Communication Research

1974-1976	Gerald R. Miller
1977-1979	James C. McCroskey

Communication Yearbook

1976-1978	Brent D. Ruben

ICA Newsletter

1953	Herold Lillywhite
1954	Kenneth B. Clark and Donald E. Bird
1955-1956	Donald E. Bird
1957-1958	Jerome G. Kovalcik
1959	Seth A. Fessenden
1960-1961	Carl H. Weaver
1962-1963	F. Craig Johnson
1964	Edward M. Penson
1965-1968	J. Harold Janis
1969	Martin F. Hunt, Jr.
1970	Michael Z. Sincoff
1971-1973	Roger P. Wilcox
1973-1975	John Bittner
1975-	Robert Cox

APPENDIX (continued)

Officers, 1950–1978

Year	President	1st Vice President	2nd Vice President	Executive Secretary
1950	Paul D. Bagwell	Ralph G. Nichols	Wesley Wiskell	Clyde Dow
1951	Ralph G. Nichols	Elwood Murray	Wesley Wiksell	James I. Brown
1952	Elwood Murray	Herold Lillywhite	Anne McGurk	Joseph H. Baccus
1953	Herold Lillywhite	Kenneth Clark	Wesley Wiskell	Joseph H. Baccus
1954	Kenneth Clark	Burton H. Byers	Joseph H. Baccus	Donald E. Bird
1955	Burton H. Byers	Kenneth H. Harwood	Joseph H. Baccus	Donald E. Bird
1956	Kenneth H. Harwood	Thomas R. Lewis	John Keltner	Donald E. Bird
1957	Thomas R. Lewis	Donald E. Bird	John Keltner	Jerome Kovalcik
1958	Donald E. Bird	Francis A. Cartier	William A. Conboy	Jerome Kovalcik
1959	Francis A. Cartier	Wesley Wiksell	William A. Conboy	Seth A. Fessenden
1960	Wesley Wiksell	Thorrel Fest	William V. Haney	Carl H. Weaver
1961	Thorrel Fest	John B. Haney	William V. Haney	Carl H. Weaver
1962	John B. Haney	W. Charles Redding	Milton J. Wiksell	Roger L. Baumeister
1963	W. Charles Redding	James I. Brown	Milton J. Wiksell	Roger L. Baumeister
1964	James I. Brown	Clarence J. Dover	Charles S. Goetzinger	Roger L. Baumeister
1965	Clarence J. Dover	Harold P. Zelko	Charles S. Goetzinger	R. Wayne Pace
1966	Harold P. Zelko	Frank E. X. Dance	George A. Sanborn	R. Wayne Pace
1967	Frank E. X. Dance	Lee Thayer	George A. Sanborn and R. Wayne Pace	R. Wayne Pace
		President-elect	(office discontinued)	
1967-68	Lee Thayer	Darrell T. Piersol		Ronald Smith
1968-69	Darrell T. Piersol	Robert S. Goyer		Ronald Smith
1969-70	Robert S. Goyer	R. Wayne Pace		Michael Z. Sincoff
1970-71	R. Wayne Pace	Ronald L. Smith		Michael Z. Sincoff
1971-72	Ronald L. Smith	Malcolm S. MacLean, Jr.		Michael Z. Sincoff
1972-73	Malcolm S. Maclean, Jr.	Alfred G. Smith		Michael Z. Sincoff
1973-74	Alfred G. Smith	Nathan Maccoby		Michael Z. Sincoff
19774-75	Nathan Maccoby	Mark Knapp		Robert Cox
1975-76	Mark Knapp	Richard W. Budd		Robert Cox
1976-77	Richard W. Budd	Robert Kibler		Robert Cox
1977-78	Robert Kibler	Frederick Williams		Robert Cox

The Roster at the End of the First Year

1. Paul D. Bagwell
2. Edward C. Mabie
3. Elwood Murray
4. Wesley Wiksell
5. Franklin H. Knower
6. Ralph Nichols
7. Helen Liggett
8. Clyde Dow
9. James Platt
10. Russell Jenkins
11. Ann McGurk
12. Don Blanding
13. Lois Banzet
14. Robert Starring
15. William N. Brigance
16. Harold Crain
17. Frederic L. Darley
18. Hugh F. Seabury
19. M. Blair Hart
20. Lionell Crocker
21. Francis E. Drake
22. Lawrence E. McKune
23. James I. Brown
24. Jack Hall Lamb
25. Kenneth B. Clark
26. Leroy Laase
27. Thomas R. Lewis
28. Thomas D. Pawley
29. Herold Lillywhite
30. David M. Grant
31. A. Craig Baird
32. Joseph H. Baccus
33. Wayne L. Britton
34. Woodson Tyree
35. Charles F. Prickett
36. Harold B. Allen
37. Marjorie H. Thurston
38. Donald Woods
39. Wendell Johnson
40. Lindsey S. Perkins
41. E. S. Brandenburg
42. Lauren L. Brink
43. Alvar B. Sandquist
44. Myfanwy E. Chapman
45. Paul S. Hagen
46. Maude Shapiro
47. Betty Bebout
48. Betty Mitchell
49. John W. Keltner
50. Waldo W. Braden
51. E. W. Ziebarth
52. Elbert W. Harrington
53. Charles W. Philhour
54. Ralph W. Widener, Jr.
55. C. David Cornell
56. Orville A. Hitchcock
57. Raymond R. Jones
58. Gael Sullivan
59. Clyde R. Miller
60. W. Kenneth Christian
61. Waldo W. Phelps
62. Bess Sondel
63. Bernice L. Prince
64. Allen Walker Read
65. Seth Fessenden
66. F. L. Whan
67. John Q. Jennings
68. Laurence B. Goodrich
69. Franklyn S. Haiman
70. John H. Jacobs
71. W. Howard Chase
72. Gerald L. Kinkaid
73. Kenneth D. Benne
74. S. I. Hayakawa
75. D. P. McKelvey
76. A. H. Monroe
77. Nathan A. Miller
78. Ronald Cutler
79. H. P. Constans
80. Meredith R. Taylor
81. Erna P. Triplett
82. Helen E. Righter
83. Clair M. Gurwell
84. Lyman Bryson
85. Armand L. Hunter
86. Murray Deutsch
87. C. Merton Babcock
88. Francis P. Chisholm
89. Herold T. Ross
90. Esther Dominick
91. Halbert E. Gulley

ABOUT THE AUTHORS

James A. Anderson (Ph.D., University of Iowa) is professor of communication at the University of Utah. He is on extended leave from Ohio University where he has been professor of Radio-Television and director of the Broadcast Research Center. He is a theorist and research methodology specialist and has also been active as a management consultant for public and commercial broadcasting.

Stanley J. Baran received his Ph.D. in Mass Communications from the University of Massachusetts, Amherst. His research interests include the social impact of television on children and adolescents and TV as a teaching/learning tool for the mentally retarded. He has recently completed a major study of TV and retarded children funded by the Cleveland Foundation.

George Barnett (B.A., M.A., University of Illinois-Urbana; Ph.D., Michigan State University) is currently assistant professor in the Department of Language, Literature, and Communication, Rensselaer Polytechnic Institute. He has conducted research in political, intercultural, and mass communication and has done extensive developmental work on multidimensional scaling techniques. He is the author of papers in these areas and is currently editing a reader on multidimensional scaling, time-series analysis, and communication.

Joyce E. Bauchner (B.A., Rutgers, M.A., Michigan State) is a Ph.D. candidate in the Department of Communication at Michigan State University. Her research and teaching areas include language behavior, nonverbal and interpersonal communication, communication theory and research design. She has spent the past two years working on a National Science Foundation grant examining the use of videotape in the courtroom. She has coauthored a number of scholarly papers including "Detecting Deceptive Communication from Verbal, Visual, and Paralinguistic Cues," which was selected as a top three paper of the Interpersonal Division of the International Communication Association in 1976.

Charles Berger (Ph.D., Michigan State) is associate professor of Communication Studies and director of the Communication Research Center at Northwestern University. He is author of articles examining the study of communication in initial phases of interpersonal interaction, development and disintegration of interpersonal relationships, and interpersonal epistemology. He is currently chairperson of the International Communication Association, Division of Interpersonal Communication.

David K. Berlo is president of the Center for Communication Analysis in St. Louis, Washington, D.C., and St. Petersburg, Florida. He also serves as chairman of the Research Advisory Council of the Market-Opinion Research Corporation. He has been chairman of the Department of Communication at Michigan State University, and president of Illinois State University. He is a consultant, author, film-maker, and lecturer. His writings include *The Process of Communication* (1960) and *Information and Communication* (1977), both published by Holt, Rinehart, and Winston. His 10 films on management and communication have been produced by BNA Communications,

Washington, D.C. He is listed in *Who's Who in America, Who's Who in Education, Who's Who in Politics*, and *Who's Who in Business and Industry*.

Richard K. Boohar (Ph.D., University of Wisconsin, 1966) is associate professor in the School of Life Sciences, University of Nebraska-Lincoln. He has published primarily in science-related journals, including the *Journal of College Science Teaching*. His present research interests are related to the area of bioethics. He has also presented a number of papers at regional science association meetings.

George Borden has received degrees from the University of Denver (B.A. in Mathematics, 1958, M.A. in Mathematics, 1959, M.A. in Communication Methodology, 1962) and Cornell University (Ph.D. in Speech Behavior). He was at Pennsylvania State University from 1964 through 1975 and in 1975 he accepted the chairmanship at the Department of Communication, University of Delaware. He has authored *Speech Behavior and Human Interaction* (with Gregg and Grove, 1969), *Introduction to Human Communication Theory* (1971), *Human Communication: The Process of Relating* (with Stone, 1976), and has contributed articles to professional journals.

David R. Brandt (B.A., Purdue, M.A., Indiana) is a Ph.D. candidate in the Department of Communication at Michigan State University. At the 1976 ICA Convention in Portland, Oregon, he received a Student Award from the Interpersonal Division for a paper entitled "Listener Propensity to Counterargue, Distraction, and Resistance to Persuasion." Mr. Brandt is presently conducting research on the impacts of video technology on the legal process, and the relationship between communicator style and interpersonal attraction.

Alan J. Brazil received his B.S. in economics and mathematics from Arizona State University in 1977. His areas of specialization are mathematical modeling and research methodology.

Jennings Bryant is an assistant professor in the Department of Communication Studies at the University of Massachusetts, Amherst.

Richard W. Budd is president of the International Communication Association. He received his B.S. from Bowling Green University, and his M.A. and Ph.D. from the University of Iowa. He is chairman of the Department of Human Communication and a Distinguished Professor at Rutgers University. He has served as president-elect and member of the board of directors of ICA. He is associate editor of *Human Communications Research*, and editorial board member of *Journal of Communication* and *Communication Quarterly*. His publications include coauthor-editorship of *Approaches to Human Communication, Human Communication Handbook: Simulations and Games, Content Analysis of Communications, Mass Communication and Mass Communication Institutions*, as well as a number of journal articles and monographs. He has consulted widely with business, government, and education.

Joseph N. Cappella received his M.A. and Ph.D. in Communication at Michigan State University and is currently assistant professor and director of the Center for Communication Research in the Department of Communication Arts at the University of Wisconsin-Madison. His teaching and research interests center on interpersonal interaction, human information processing, and mathematical modeling.

Jean M. Civikly (Ph.D., 1973, Florida State University) is assistant professor in the Department of Speech Communication at the University of New Mexico (Albuquerque). Her primary research interests are nonverbal communication, communication education, and intercultural communication. She is the editor of *Messages: A Reader in Human Interaction* (New York: Random House, 2nd ed., 1977), and coauthor (with Lawrence B. Rosenfeld) of *With Words Unspoken: The Nonverbal Experience* (New York: Holt, Rinehart and Winston, 1976).

Michael Cody (B.A., California State University-Sacramento; M.A., Michigan State University) is currently a Ph.D. candidate in Communication at Michigan State University. He has coauthored several papers on interpersonal communication and the methodology of political communication, and is currently conducting research in the general areas of methodology, person perception, political communication, and interpersonal communication.

Dan Costello (B.S., M.A., Ohio State; Ph.D., Michigan State) is a member of the faculty of the School of Medicine, and is director of the Medical Center's Communication Research Program, where patient and practitioner problems at the interpersonal, organizational, and mediated levels of communication are studied. He is also a research associate at the Vanderbilt Institute for Public Policy Studies, focusing upon communication policy formulation within health care systems. He is author of "Therapeutic Transactions: An Approach to Human Communication," in *Approaches to Human Communication* and other articles on the relationship of communication to health. Currently, he is chairman of the International Communication Association, Division of Health Communication.

D. P. Cushman (M.S., Ph.D., University of Wisconsin) is associate professor in the Department of Communication, Michigan State University. He has published articles in *Human Communication Research, Quarterly Journal of Speech, Journal of Communication, Issues, American Bar Association Journal,* and *Philosophy and Rhetoric.* He is a consultant for the American Advertising Council, Electric Energy Association, Department of Labor, Bell Telephone, and other organizations.

John A. Daly is completing his doctorate in Communication at Purdue University, with concentrations in interpersonal and nonverbal communication and research methods. His publications include articles in *Human Communication Research, Journal of Counseling Psychology, Journal of Occupational Psychology, Research in the Teaching of English,* and the *Journal of Psychology.* He has presented papers at meetings of the Speech Communication Association, Western Speech Association, Central States Speech Association, Eastern Communication Association, and the International Communication Association.

Dwight Davis is assistant professor of Political Science at the University of Oklahoma at Norman. He received his Ph.D. from Florida State University. He has published articles in the area of small group behavior, and his major research interests also include political communication, applications of experimental methodologies in political science, policy analysis, and evaluation of governmental programs.

Paul Dayton is a research scientist with the Cancer Control Bureau, New York State Department of Health. He did his undergraduate work at the State University of New York at Albany. Current research interests include developing a methodology for analysis of time-space clusters.

James Dixon is a graduate student of Communication Studies and research assistant for the Dean of the School of Speech at Northwestern University. He received his B.S. in Communication Studies and Radio, Television and Film at Northwestern. His interests include interpersonal communication in organizations and interpersonal components of mass-communicated attitude change.

Jane A. Edwards obtained B.A. and M.A. degrees in Speech-Communication from San Jose State University. While there, she coauthored several convention papers and technical reports dealing with communication networks. She also obtained an M.A. degree in Psychology. Currently she is at the University of California, Berkeley, working toward a doctorate degree in cognitive psychology with an emphasis in language behavior.

Huber W. Ellingsworth is professor of communication at the University of Hawaii-Manoa, where he served as department chairman from 1972 to 1976. He is a graduate of Pacific University and Washington State and received the Ph.D. from Florida State. His previous appointments have included Connecticut and Michigan State. He has served as director of the Communication Seminars conducted by Michigan State for the Agency for International Development, with subsequent travel and research in Latin America under Ford Foundation Sponsorship. He was a Visiting Colleague at the East-West Center's Communication Institute in 1971-72 and participated in planning for an international training program in population communication. In 1972 he was project leader for a comparative study of the administration of family planning communication programs in the Phillipines and Malaysia.

Dorcas E. Evans received her B.S. in communication and psychology in 1974 from Florida State University and her M.A. in Communication from Arizona State University in 1975. Presently she is a doctoral student in sociology at the University of Wisconsin, Madison, with specialization in social psychology, medical sociology, and research methodology. She is a student board member of the International Communication Association.

Raymond L. Falcione received his Ph.D. from Kent State University. He is currently assistant professor of Speech Communication at the University of Maryland. His research interests include interpersonal and organizational communication. With Howard Greenbaum, he coauthored the International Communication Association/American Business Communication Association *Organizational Communication Abstracts 1974* and *1975*, with publication of the *1976* volume due in June 1977. He has also served as a consultant to numerous private and government organizations.

John W. Farquhar (M.D., University of California School of Medicine, San Francisco) completed training in internal medicine and cardiology. His early research was directed toward the biochemical and physiological basis for diabetes and atherosclerosis and clinical problems of coronary artery disease. He studied epidemiology and statistics and has been active in interdisciplinary studies designed to identify causes of cardiovascular disease and intervention methods. He is presently the director of the Stanford Heart Disease Prevention Program, which pursues research in social, psychological, and medical issues relevant to cardiovascular disease prevention.

Mary Anne Fitzpatrick is assistant professor in the Department of Communication at the University of Wisconsin-Milwaukee. Her current research interests include analyses of relational interaction systems—especially friendship networks and intimate relationships—as well as the application of multivariate techniques to communication research.

John P. Garrison (M.A., West Virginia University, 1975) is an instructor, Department of Speech Communication, University of Nebraska-Lincoln. He is currently completing a Ph.D. in interpersonal communication, research methodologies, and statistics. His recent research has been concerned with communication apprehension, the impact of communication on learning, a definition of nonverbal communication based on neurophysiology and brain sidedness, and the context of dyadic communication systems.

Peter Greenwald is director of the Cancer Control Bureau, New York State Department of Health. He received his M.D. from the State University of New York College of Medicine at Syracuse and a Dr. P.H. from the Harvard University School of Public Health. He has published over 40 articles on cancer epidemiology and cancer control.

William B. Gudykunst received his B.S. and M.A. degrees at Arizona State University. He is a Ph.D. candidate and teaching associate in Speech Communication at the University of Minnesota. His major research interests are intercultural communication and cross-cultural training.

Mitchell R. Hammer received his M.A. degree from Ohio University. He is currently a Ph.D. student in the Department of Speech Communication and a teaching associate in the Department of Rhetoric at the University of Minnesota. His research interests include intercultural communication and intercultural adjustment.

Dean E. Hewes received his B.S. in physics and mathematics from the College of William and Mary in 1969, his M.S. in Speech from Southern Illinois University, Carbondale in 1971 and his Ph.D. in Communication from Florida State University in 1974. He is presently an assistant professor of communication arts at the University of Wisconsin, Madison. His research interests include child language development, personality

theory, social interaction, and the message-attitude-behavior relationship.

H. Thomas Hurt is assistant professor in the Department of Speech Communication, West Virginia University. He received his Masters and Ph.D. degrees from Ohio University in Communication and Psychology. He has published articles in the *Central States Speech Journal, Communication Education, Media Ecology Review,* and has articles in press in *Human Communication Research.* In addition, he is the senior author, with M.D. Scott and J.C. McCroskey, of *Communication in the Classroom: The Difference Between Knowing and Teaching,* published by Addison-Wesley. His research interests include the communication of innovations in social systems and formal organizations, network analysis, and communication and instruction.

Lynda Lee Kaid is assistant professor of Speech Communication at the University of Oklahoma at Norman. She received her Ph.D. from Southern Illinois University-Carbondale. She has published several articles in political communication, and is editor of *Political Communication Review.* She is also a coauthor of *Political Campaign Communication: A Bibliography and Guide to the Literature.*

Richard M. Krause is assistant professor in the Department of Speech Communication at the University of New Mexico. His primary research interest is in the area of the responsiveness of media institutions to public need and the use of videotape methodologies in the research setting.

Klaus Krippendorff received his Ph.D. in Communication from the University of Illinois, Urbana, and is an associate professor of Communication at the University of Pennsylvania, Philadelphia. He is coeditor of *The Analysis of Communication Content* and editor of *Communication and Control in Society.* His primary interests include cybernetics, information theory, and systems theory and the application of models to social communication processes. Published articles include "Values, Modes and Domains of Inquiry into Communiction," "On Generating Data in Communication Research," "A Calculus of Disagreement," "Communication and the Genesis of Structure," "Some Principles of Information Retrieval in Society," "The Systems Approach to Communication," "Information Theory," and "A Spectral Analysis of Relations."

Curt Latham (M.D., University of British Columbia) has been a practicing physician for 12 years. For the last seven years, he has occupied a major role in the British Columbia Perinatal Morbidity and Mortality Programme. He has been involved in planning to develop a Department of Environmental Health at Simon Fraser University, and was project director of a rural environmental health study, *Port Alice: A Communication in Transition,* funded by the Canadian Federal Government.

Nan Lin is a professor of sociology at the State University of New York at Albany. He has conducted communication research projects in Central America, Haiti, the Far East, as well as the United States. In addition to authoring several books, and many book chapters, his work has appeared in *American Journal of*

Sociology, Social Forces, Public Opinion Quarterly, Science, International Social Science Journal, and other professional journals.

Nathan Maccoby received his Ph.D. in Psychology from the University of Michigan, where he served as a study director at the Survey Research Center. He was Newsom professor of opinion research, chairman of research in the School of Public Communication, and chairman of the Psychology Department, Boston University. At Stanford University, he is currently Janet M. Peck professor of international communication, director of the Institute for Communication Research, and co-director of the Stanford Heart Disease Prevention Program. He has published research in learning and persuasion, with emphasis on mass communication.

Gail M. Martin (B.A., College of New Rochelle, New York; M.S. New Mexico Highlands University) is an associate professor in the Department of Communication Studies, and research director of the Telecommunications Research Group at Simon Fraser University. She has been involved in research and development in both urban and rural communications and co-designed the RAVEN project—Radio and Visual Educational Network: a system of two-way radio and bicycled videotape for health and educational needs, that serves more than 100 Indian settlements in British Columbia and Northwest Territories.

James C. McCroskey (D.Ed., Pennsylvania State University) is professor and chairperson of the Department of Speech Communication at West Virginia University. He has served as chairperson of the Interpersonal Communication Division of the International Communication Association. He is editor-designate of *Human Communication Research,* and is author or coauthor of over 75 papers published in various communication-related journals. Included among his nine authored or coauthored books in the communication field are *Introduction to Human Communication, Communication in the Classroom,* and *Introduction to Rhetorical Communication,* 3rd edition.

Klaus Merten studied mathematics, *publicistics,* and sociology at the Universities of Aachen and Muenster (Germany), where he earned his *diplom* in sociology. He then joined the faculty of sociology at the University of Bielefeld as an assistant, teaching statistics, methodology and communication theory. His dissertation (1975) dealt with definitions and process analysis of communication. At present he is a visiting professor in communication research at the University of Mainz.

Anthony J. Meyer received his Ph.D. in Communication Research from Stanford University. He was visiting research fellow at the Institute for Development Studies, University of Nairobi, Kenya, and post-doctoral fellow at Stanford University School of Medicine. At Stanford University, he is research associate at the Institute for Communication Research and a staff member of the Stanford Heart Disease Prevention Program. His research has emphasized the design and evaluation of communication strategies for public health and disease prevention.

Timothy P. Meyer received his Ph.D. in Mass Communication

Research from Ohio University. His principal research interest is the social effects of varying types of television content on children and adolescents. Research articles by him have been published in the *Journal of Broadcasting, Journal of Communication, Journalism Quarterly, Journal of Personality and Social Psychology, Journal of Mental Retardation,* and elsewhere; he is also coauthor (with James A. Anderson) of *Man and Communication.*

Gerald R. Miller, received his B.A. and M.A. in political science and his Ph.D. in psychology and speech from the University of Iowa. Currently, he is professor of Communication at Michigan State University. Prior to his arrival at Michigan State University in 1963, he was a member of the faculties at the University of Iowa and the University of Washington. He has authored seven books and numerous articles for journals of communication, psychology, speech, and law. Presently he is the editor of *Human Communication Research.* He received the Speech Communication Association's Golden Anniversary Award for outstanding scholarly publication in 1967 and again in 1974, the Distinguished Faculty Award and the *Centennial Review* Lectureship from Michigan State University, and a Joint Resolution of Tribute from the Michigan Legislature for his research dealing with the courtroom uses of videotape.

Peter R. Monge obtained a Ph.D. degree in Communication from Michigan State University. and is currently associate professor at San Jose State University. He has published several papers in communication journals in the areas of systems theory and communication networks. He is a coauthor of the recently published book, *Communicating and Organizing.*

Hamid Mowlana is professor and director of the Program in International Communication Studies at the School of International Service, American University, Washington, D.C. He holds the Ph.D. from Northwestern University and has taught in England, Iran, and Argentina. He is an editor of *Journal of Communication,* mass media editor of *Intellect,* and the author of a number of books and monographs on communication and international relations.

Mary Ellen Munley is a second-year doctoral student in the department of Communication Studies at Northwestern University. She received her B.A. from the University of Wisconsin-Milwaukee and M.A. in Communication and Public Address from the same institution. Her research interests include: the development of a relationship taxonomy; differential notions of expectations, satisfaction, and growth in various types of relationships; and the process of development and the organization of self-concept and its subsequent effect on attentional processes in social cognition.

Dan Nimmo (B.A., University of Missouri; M.A., Ph.D., Vanderbilt) is professor of Political Science, University of Tennessee-Knoxville. He has formerly taught at Texas Tech University, University of Houston, and University of Missouri-Columbia. He is author of *The Political Persuaders* (1970), *Popular Images of Politics* (1974), and *Newsgathering in Washington* (1964); coauthor of *Candidates and Their Images* (1976), *American Political Patterns* (1967, 1969, 1973), and *The Texas Political System* (1971); and coeditor of *Political*

Attitudes and Public Opinion (1972). He has published journal articles in the general areas of voting behavior, political perceptions and roles, and methodology, and is currently chairperson of the International Communication Association, Division of Political Communication.

Kaarle Nordenstreng studied at Helsinki where he received his Ph.D. in 1969. His primary research focused on the measurement of meaning. He has served as a journalist at Finnish Broadcasting since 1957, and from 1967-1971 was head of audience research and long-range planning. Since 1971 he has been professor of journalism and mass communication at Tampere University in Finland. He has been a consultant to UNESCO since 1969, a member of several governmental committees in communication and foreign policy, and has authored six books and nearly two hundred reports and articles.

Robert Norton received his Ph.D. from the University of Wisconsin (Madison) in 1973. His dissertation focused on manifestations of ambiguity tolerance in small groups. He teaches interpersonal communication, persuasion theory, communicator style and methodology courses at the University of Michigan.

R. Wayne Pace (Ph.D., 1960, Purdue University) is professor and chairman of the Department of Speech Communication at the University of New Mexico (Albuquerque). His primary research interests are in interpersonal communication, seriality in human communication systems, and instructional development. He is an author or editor of five books: *Communicating Interpersonally* (with B.D. Peterson and T.R. Radcliffe), *The Human Transaction* (with R.R. Boren), *Communication Probes* (with B.D. Peterson and G.M. Goldhaber), *Communication Behavior* (with R.R. Boren and B.D. Peterson), and *Communication Experiments* (with B.D. Peterson and R.R. Boren). He was president of the International Communication Association in 1970-1971.

Thomas J. Pace, Ph.D., University of Denver, has done postdoctoral study in philosophy, psychology, and communication at Northwestern and Duquesne Universities. He is presently professor of speech and director of Graduate Studies in Speech at Southern Illinois University-Carbondale. His interests and publications are in the areas of political communication, general semantics, field methodologies, and phenomenological approaches to the study of communication.

W. Barnett Pearce (M.A., Ph.D., Ohio University) is associate professor in the Department of Communication Studies, University of Massachusetts. He is coauthor of *Communicating Personally*, and author of *An Overview of Communication and Interpersonal Relationships*. He has published articles in the *Journal of Communication, Human Communication Research,* and others.

Loyd Pettegrew is a Ph.D. candidate in the University of Michigan, Department of Speech Communication. He received his B.A. from Brigham Young University and his M.A. from California State University, San Diego. He is a teaching fellow and research assistant, and his primary interests are in the area of interpersonal communication.

Fred L. Randolph received his B.A. in Psychology from West Virginia University (1976) and currently is completing his M.A. in Speech Communication at the same institution.

Gary M. Richetto is manager of Organization Development for The Williams Companies. He is presently vice president and chairperson of the Organizational Communication Division of ICA. He received his Ph.D. in organizational communication from Purdue University in 1969. His former positions include: associate professor of Communication and Organizational Behavior, General Motors Institute; co-director, ICA Communication Audit Project; director, Studies in Organizational Behavior, Combat Developments Command, United States Army; coordinator, Communication Research, Marshall Space Flight Center, NASA. He is presently coauthoring a text entitled *Information-Power and the Management Function.* He has coauthored *Effective Interviewing,* a series of videotapes and accompanying text, and *Fundamentals of Interviewing,* MODCOM series, with J.P. Zima. He has authored or coauthored chapters in *Approaches to Human Communication, Speech Communication: A Basic Anthology,* and *Transactional Analysis.* He has also authored articles in the areas of organization development and organizational change. He is a member of the Academy of Management, The OD Network, The World Future Society, and an advanced member of the International Transactional Analysis Association.

Brent D. Ruben (B.A., M.A., Ph.D., University of Iowa) is assistant chairman of the Department of Human Communication and associate professor of communication at Rutgers University. Since 1971 he has also been director of the Institute for Communication Studies at Rutgers. He is author, coauthor, or coeditor of *General Systems Theory and Human Communication, Mass Communication and Mass Communication Institutions, Human Communication Handbook: Simulations and Games (Volumes I and II), Approaches to Human Communication, Intermedia, Interact,* and articles, book chapters, and scholarly papers on communication theory, communication systems, experiential learning, mass, and cross-cultural communication. He is a contributing editor for *Communication* and manuscript review editor in communication for *Behavioral Science.* He has been vice president of the Northeast Division of the Society for General Systems Research, and serves as a consultant to government, business, and education in interpersonal, group, and intercultural communication.

Keith. Sanders, Ph.D., University of Pittsburgh, is associate professor of speech at Southern Illinois University. He is a former chairperson of the Political Communication Division of the International Communication Association. He is coauthor of *Political Campaign Communication* and author or coauthor of numerous papers, articles, and book reviews in such journals as *Journalism Quarterly, Journal of Broadcasting,* and the *Quarterly Journal of Speech.* His research interests focus on the role of interpersonal and mass communication in political decision making.

Tulsi Saral (M.A., University of Pennsylvania; Ph.D., University of Illinois) is university professor of Communication Science and assistant dean of the College of Human Learning and Development at Governors State University. He is a registered psychologist in the state of Illinois. He is currently vice-chairman of the International Communication Association, Division of Intercultural Communication, and will assume chairmanship of the division for the 1977-1979 term. He is also secretary of the Society of Intercultural Education, Training, and Research.

Michael D. Scott received his Ph.D. from the University of Southern California (1974) and is assistant professor of Speech Communication and Educational Psychology at West Virginia University. He is the coauthor of *Principles of Human Communication, Communication in the Classroom, Interpersonal Communication: A Question of Needs,* and has been a contributor to *Speech Monographs, Communication Education, The Journal of Communication, Western Speech Communication, The Southern Speech Communication Journal,* and *Speech Communication: A Basic Anthology.*

William J. Seiler (Ph.D., Purdue University, 1971) is associate professor of Speech Communication, University of Nebraska-Lincoln. His research interests are in the area of communication education; he has published research in a variety of speech and communication journals including *Speech Monographs, Central States Speech Journal, Speech Teacher, Communication Education,* and *Southern Speech Communication Journal.* He has also presented numerous papers at regional, national, and international meetings.

Kim Serota (B.A., M.A., Michigan State University) is currently project director at PACE, Inc., a national marketing research firm. He is also a Ph.D. candidate in Communication at Michigan State University and has formerly taught at Arizona State University. He has conducted research on communication and political change and has done work in multidimensional scaling analysis. He is the coauthor of papers on multidimensional scaling, political communication, and political change.

Donald L. Singleton is assistant professor of Speech Communication and Drama at North Texas State University at Denton. He received his M.A. from the University of California-Los Angeles. His research interests include political communication, international broadcasting, and mass communication. He is a former program manager of the Oklahoma Educational Television Authority and developed the first National Public Radio system in West Virginia.

Alfred G. Smith is professor and director of the Center for Communication Research, University of Texas at Austin. Previously, he was professor of Anthropology at the University of Oregon. He is the author of numerous publications in anthropology and communication, and has served as a consultant to the United States Government as a specialist in Far Eastern and Pacific area affairs. He is also editor of *Communication and Culture.*

James Taylor (B.A., University of California-Berkeley; M.A., Michigan State University) is currently a Ph.D. candidate in Communication at Michigan State University. He has conducted research in organizational communication and structure. He is coauthor of several papers on organizational, health, and political communication.

C. Ward Teigen is a graduate assistant in the Department of Speech Communication, West Virginia University. He received his A.A. degree from Highline College and his B.A. degree from the University of Washington. His research interests include organizational communication, communication and instruction, and conflict management in interpersonal relationships.

Wayne M. Towers is an acting assistant professor in the Radio-Television-Film sequence of the Speech Communication Department at the University of Oklahoma in Norman, and is completing work on a doctorate in Communication at the S. I. Newhouse School of Public Communication, Syracuse University.

André J. De Verneil is assistant professor in the Broadcast and Cinematic Arts area of Central Michigan University's Speech Department. He received his Ph.D. in Mass Communications from Ohio University in August 1976. His previous education included an A.B. in philosophy from Gonzaga University, and an S.T.M. in theology from the Jesuit School of Theology at Berkeley.

Marylin Daly Weber is a Ph.D. candidate in Communication Studies at Northwestern University. She earned her B.S. degree in Journalism and Communications at the University of Illinois-Urbana and M.A. in Journalism at the University of Iowa. Her present research considers how situational perceptions affect interpersonal communication behavior. Her research interests also include the relationship between mass media usage and interpersonal behavior.

Lawrence R. Wheeless received his Ph.D. from Wayne State University (1970) and is associate professor of Speech Communication at West Virginia University. He is vice-chairperson of the Instructional Communication Division of the International Communication Association. He is the author of *Practical Experiences in Interpersonal Communication* and coauthor of *An Introduction to Human Communication.* He is the author or coauthor of numerous research reports and reviews which appear in *Speech Monographs, The Speech Teacher, The Journal of Communication, Language and Style, The Journal of Broadcasting, Journal of the American Forensic Association, Southern Speech Communication Journal, Communication Yearbook, Western Speech Communication,* and *Human Communication Research.* Also, he is president of the West Virginia Communication Association, vice-chairperson of the Organizational and Interpersonal Communication Division of the Eastern Communication Association, and vice-chairperson of the Instructional Communication Division (VII), International Communication Association.

Richard L. Wiseman, who received his M.A. at the University of Oregon, is currently a doctoral student in the Department of Speech Communication at the University of Minnesota. His research interests include interpersonal and nonverbal communication.

Michael P. Yates received his M.A. in Speech Communication from West Virginia University (1975) and currently is completing his doctoral studies at The State University of New York, Buffalo.

Dolf Zillmann is professor of Communication and director of the Institute for Communication Research at Indiana University.

INDEX

SUBJECTS

AUTHORS

Minor, G. 504, 508
Minow, N. 443, 451, 453, 462, 464
Minter, R. 335, 345
Miraglia, J. 335, 345
Mischel, T. 44, 52, 195, 214
Mischel, W. 196, 214
Mitchell, J.C. 188, 192, 193
Mitchell, K.M. 595, 596, 604
Mitchell, L.M. 443, 451, 453, 462, 464
Monczka, R. 337, 346
Monge, P.R. 163, 168, 170, 183, 184, 185, 192, 193, 224, 225, 227, 333, 345
Montgomery, D.B. 207, 208, 214
Moore, J.W. 501, 511
Moore, N. 398, 413
Moran, G. 246, 261
Moray, N. 176, 181
Morris, C.G. 44, 51
Morris, M.J. 560, 566
Morris, R.T. 417, 425
Morrison, D.G. 207, 208, 214
Morse, J.A. 502, 509
Mortensen, C.D. 220, 227, 285, 289
Motley, M. 229, 243
Mowlana, H. 427, 429, 431, 432, 437
MRSEI 367
Mueller, C. 444, 451
Mueller, J.E. 444, 451
Mueller, R.A. 333, 345, 503, 504, 508
Mulaik, S.A. 38, 47, 52
Munley, M.E. 219, 225, 246, 261
Murdock, G. 446, 451
Musterberg, H. 503, 509
Myers, G.E. 89, 97
Myers, M.T. 89, 97
Myrus, J. 595, 603

Nagel, E. 39, 52
Namboodiri, N. 236, 237, 241, 243
Namurois, A. 282, 289
Napolitan, J. 446, 451
National Quality of Work Center 341, 345
Nebergall, R.E. 37, 38, 53, 217, 228
Negrete, V. 560, 566
Neitzel, B. 334, 343
Nelson, C.E. 6
Nelson, H.L. 280, 289
Nerlove, S. 413
Newcomb, H. 282, 283, 289
Newcomb, T. 124, 131, 245, 261, 416, 425
Newman, J.B. 390, 395
Newman, R.P. 466, 474

Newstrom, J. 337, 346
Nichols, R.G. 83, 88, 496, 509
Nie, N.H. 207, 214, 241, 243, 351, 360, 448, 452
Nielsen, T. 334, 340, 345
Niemeijer, R. 183, 188, 192, 193
Niemi, R.B. 448, 451
Nimmo, D. 443, 444, 449, 451, 457, 464
Nisbet, R. 32, 33, 34, 35, 36, 229, 242, 447, 451
Niyekawa, A.M. 392, 395
Noelle-Neumann, E. 130, 131
Noell, J.J. 41, 51
Nofsinger, R.E. 44, 48, 49, 53, 59, 72, 219, 227
NORC (Natl. Opin Rsch Cen) 562, 567
Nord, D. 503, 509
Nordenstreng, K. 4, 6, 73, 74, 78, 399, 413
Norman, D.A. 296, 306
Norman, R.Z. 41, 51, 185, 192
Norton, R.W. 220, 227, 245, 261, 596, 597
Nosanchuk, T.A. 185, 192
NSF; CTIC 280, 289
Null, E. 525, 542
Nunnally, E.W. 267, 274
Nunnally, J.C. 265, 274, 379, 385, 518, 523, 524
Nunrel, J. 518, 524
Nynan, M.J. 282, 289

O'Connell, E.J. 497, 507, 509, 545, 554
O'Gorman, H.J. 126, 131
O'Keefe, B.J. 220, 224, 226
O'Keefe, D.J. 37, 38, 44, 48, 51, 53
O'Keefe, G.J. 442, 448, 451, 473, 474
Olien, C.N. 56, 64, 71, 72
Olivier, D. 399, 413
Olson, D. 285, 289
O'Neill, G. 265, 274
O'Neill, N. 265, 274
Oppenheim, N. 288
O'Reilly, C. 341, 342, 346
Orne, M. 243
Orr, D.B. 501, 509
Ort, R. 560, 567
Osborn, M. 506
Osgood, C.E. 87, 88, 398, 410, 413
Osterhouse, R. 231, 243
Overall, B. 349, 360
Overall, J.E. 267, 274
Oyama, T. 413
Owen, B.M. 282, 285, 288, 289

Page, B.I. 444, 450
Pace, T.J. 463, 464, 472, 474
Pace, W. 335, 345
Paisley, W.J. 87, 88
Paivio, A. 501, 511
Parker, E.D. 289
Parks, A.M. 495, 510, 242
Parks, M.R. 219, 221, 223, 224, 227
Parry, J. 390, 395
Parsons, T. 150, 167, 170, 558, 567
Patchen, M. 377, 385
Paterline, E.J. 495, 509
Paterson, D. 333, 345
Patterson, R. 337, 345
Patterson, T.E. 282, 289, 446, 448
Patton, B. 265, 274
Paul, G.L. 498, 509, 534, 548, 595, 604
Paulu, B. 282, 289
Paulson, S. 509
Payne, J. 525, 542
Pearce, A. 64, 72
Pearce, W.B. 44, 48, 53, 265, 274, 218, 219, 220, 223, 227, 173, 177, 178, 179, 181, 57, 66, 67, 71, 72
Pedersen, P. 415, 425
Pelz, D.C. 46, 53, 334, 345, 363, 375
Perlmutter, J. 500, 509
Pervin, L.A. 44, 53
Peterson, L.R. 296, 306
Peterson, M.J. 296, 306
Peterson, R.A. 169
Petrie, C.R., Jr. 500, 509
Pettegrew, L.S. 220, 227, 245, 261, 604
Philipsen, G. 49, 53
Phillips, G.M. 220, 228, 267, 274, 498, 499, 509, 513, 524, 554
Phillipson, H. 130
Piaget, J. 170, 504, 509
Piersol, D. 334, 341, 342, 345
Pietri, P. 331, 345
Pigors, P. 333, 345
Pinna, L. 308, 316
Pinto, P.R. 87, 88
Pitts, W. 170
Plant 525, 542
Planty, E. 334, 345
Platt, H. 37, 53
Platt, J. 161, 170
Ploghoft, M.E. 282, 288
Polanyi, M. 38, 53
Polgar, S. 562, 567
Pols, L. 399, 414
Pomper, G. 447, 457
Pool, I.S. 78, 285, 289, 430, 437, 442, 450

Webb, J. 220, 227
Webb, E.J. 35, 36
Weber, R. 280, 289
Weibull, L. 446, 451
Weiner, A.N. 220, 227
Weiner, B. 242, 365, 375
Weiner, P. 281, 289
Weingartner, C. 504, 509
Weinstein, E.A. 221, 228
Weiss, W. 292, 306, 442, 452
Weitz, S. 59, 72
Weizenbaum, J. 18, 27
Wells, A. 429, 437
Wells, J. 513, 524
Wendt, P.R. 503, 511
Westley, B.H. 43, 53, 161, 171, 445, 452
Westmoreland, R. 282, 289
Weston, J. 243
Wexley, E. 339, 345
Wheeler, R. 497, 509, 545, 546, 548, 554
Wheeless, L.R. 223, 228, 495, 496, 497, 498, 499, 500, 503, 504, 509, 510, 511, 513, 514, 522, 524, 543, 546, 553, 554
Whisler, T. 385
White, Eugene 94, 97
White, H.C. 41, 50, 53
White, W.F. 105, 106
Whitehead, A.N. 12, 20, 26, 27
Whiteneck, G.G. 223, 226
Whiting, G.C. 44, 51, 178, 179, 181, 218, 219, 224, 226, 229, 242
Whitney, R.E. 445, 452, 466, 474
Whorf, B. 392, 395, 397, 414
Wiberg, D.M. 50, 53

Wicker, A. 197, 214
Wickesberg, A. 335, 346
Widgery, R. 341, 344
Wiemann, J.M. 58, 59, 67, 72, 220, 221, 228, 254, 261
Wiener, M. 230, 235, 243
Wiener, N. 149, 171
Wiens, A. 229, 243, 351, 360
Wigand, R. 340, 346, 398, 399, 400, 413
Wiggins, L. 196, 214
Wile, I. 229, 243
Wiley, D.E. 46, 50, 53
Wiley, J.A. 46, 53
Williams, B. 496, 509, 511
Williams, D. 340, 346
Williams, J.C. 501
Willis, M. 496, 511
Willson, V.L. 46, 51, 203, 207, 214
Wilmot, W. 495, 511
Windahl, S. 445, 452
Winer, B.J. 239, 243, 366, 374
Winne, P.H. 501, 511
Winograd, T. 41, 42, 50, 53
Wiseman, R. 415, 416, 418, 425
Woelfel, J. 41, 53, 59, 72, 175, 182, 183, 192, 212, 214, 222, 225, 228, 399, 410, 412, 413, 414, 446, 452, 475, 477, 478, 480, 483, 488, 491
Wohl, R.R. 126, 130
Wolf, G. 46, 52, 58, 72
Wolfenstein, E.V. 443, 452
Wolk, R. 243
Wollen, P. 280, 289
Wood, B. 222, 228
Wood, D. 523, 524
Wood, H. 49, 52

Woods, W. 41, 53
Woodworth, R. 511
Woodworth, T. 500, 511
World Health Organization 558, 567
Worthy, M. 223, 228
Wright, C. 286, 289
Wright, P.H. 63, 67, 72, 223, 228
Wright, S. 420, 425
Wyckoff, G. 446, 452
Wyden, P. 264, 274
Wylie, R. 364, 375

Yalom, I. 596, 597
Yates, M.D. 341, 342, 346, 496, 499, 510, 514, 524, 546, 554
Yerby, J. 495, 507
Young, O.R. 171
Young, T. 516, 524
Yuille, J.C. 501, 511

Zadeh, L.A. 86, 88
Zagona, S. 496, 511
Zaltman, G. 377, 378, 379, 385
Zavas, H. 503, 509
Zeisel, H. 188, 192, 193
Zettl, H. 282, 289
Zetterberg, H.L. 40, 53, 265, 274
Zikambana, C. 579, 580, 590
Zilboorg, G. 593, 604
Ziller, R. 319
Zillmann, D. 291, 292, 293, 294, 298, 299, 300, 302, 304, 305, 306
Zima, J. 335, 346
Zimbardo, P. 501, 511
Zipt, G. 308, 317